GIRL FRIENDS

The Complete Collection 1

STORY & ART BY
Milk Morinaga

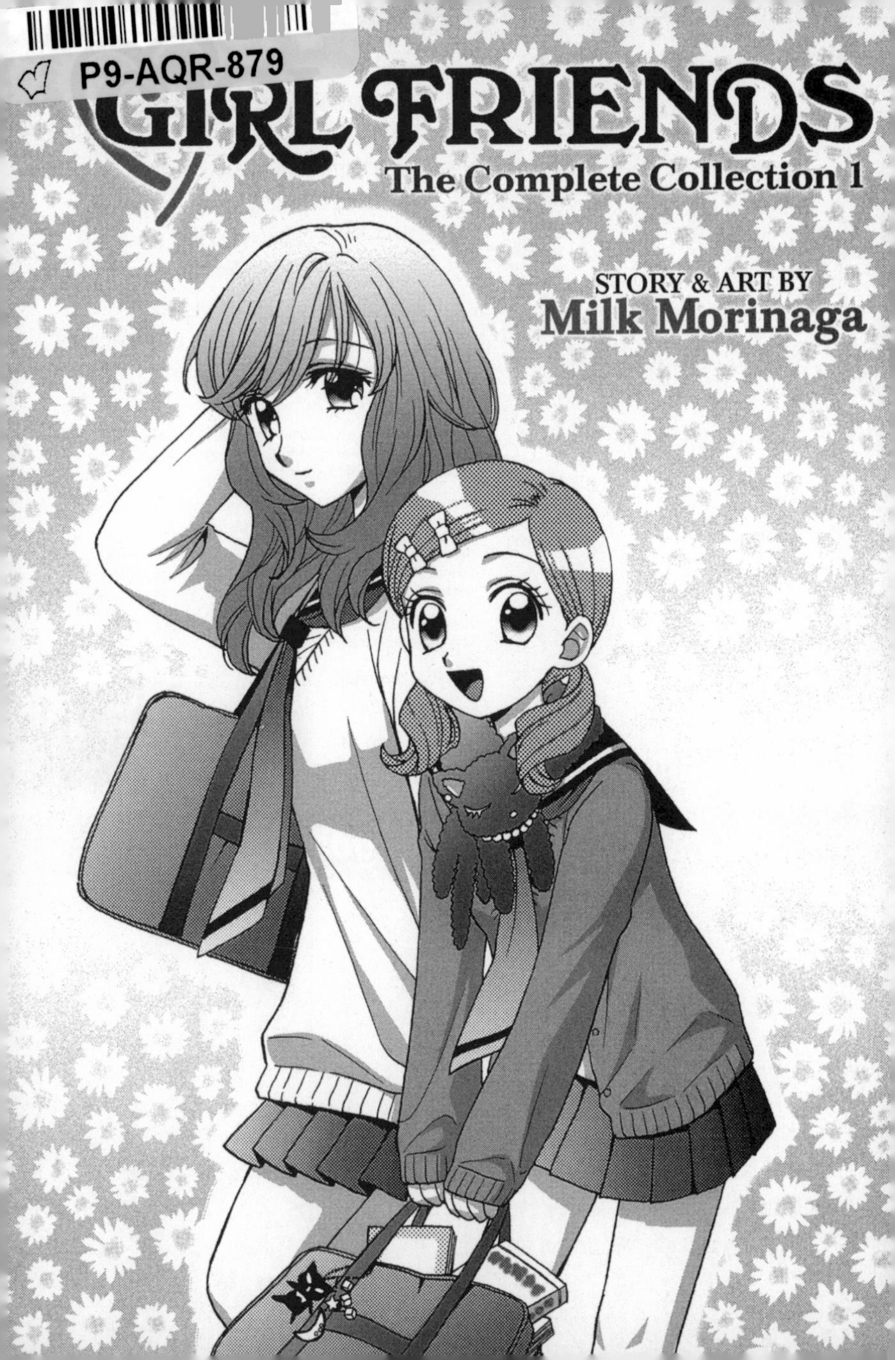

GIRL FRIENDS
The Complete Collection 1

STORY & ART BY
Milk Morinaga

STAFF CREDITS

translation	**Anastasia Moreno**
adaptation	**Shannon Fay**
lettering & retouch	**Jennifer Skarupa**
cover design	**Nicky Lim**
assistant editor	**Katherine Bell**
editor	**Adam Arnold**
publisher	**Jason DeAngelis**
	Seven Seas Entertainment

GIRL FRIENDS: THE COMPLETE COLLECTION 1
© MIRUKU MORINAGA 2006
All rights reserved.
First published in Japan in 2006 by Futabasha Publishers Ltd., Tokyo.
English version published by Seven Seas Entertainment, LLC.
Under license from Futabasha Publishers Ltd.

ISBN: 978-1-935934-89-9

Printed in the USA

First Printing: October 2012

10 9 8 7 6 5 4 3 2 1

FOLLOW US ONLINE: *www.gomanga.com*

READING DIRECTIONS

This book reads from *right to left*, Japanese style.
If this is your first time reading manga, you start
reading from the top right panel on each page and
take it from there. If you get lost, just follow the
numbered diagram here. It may seem backwards
at first, but you'll get the hang of it! Have fun!!

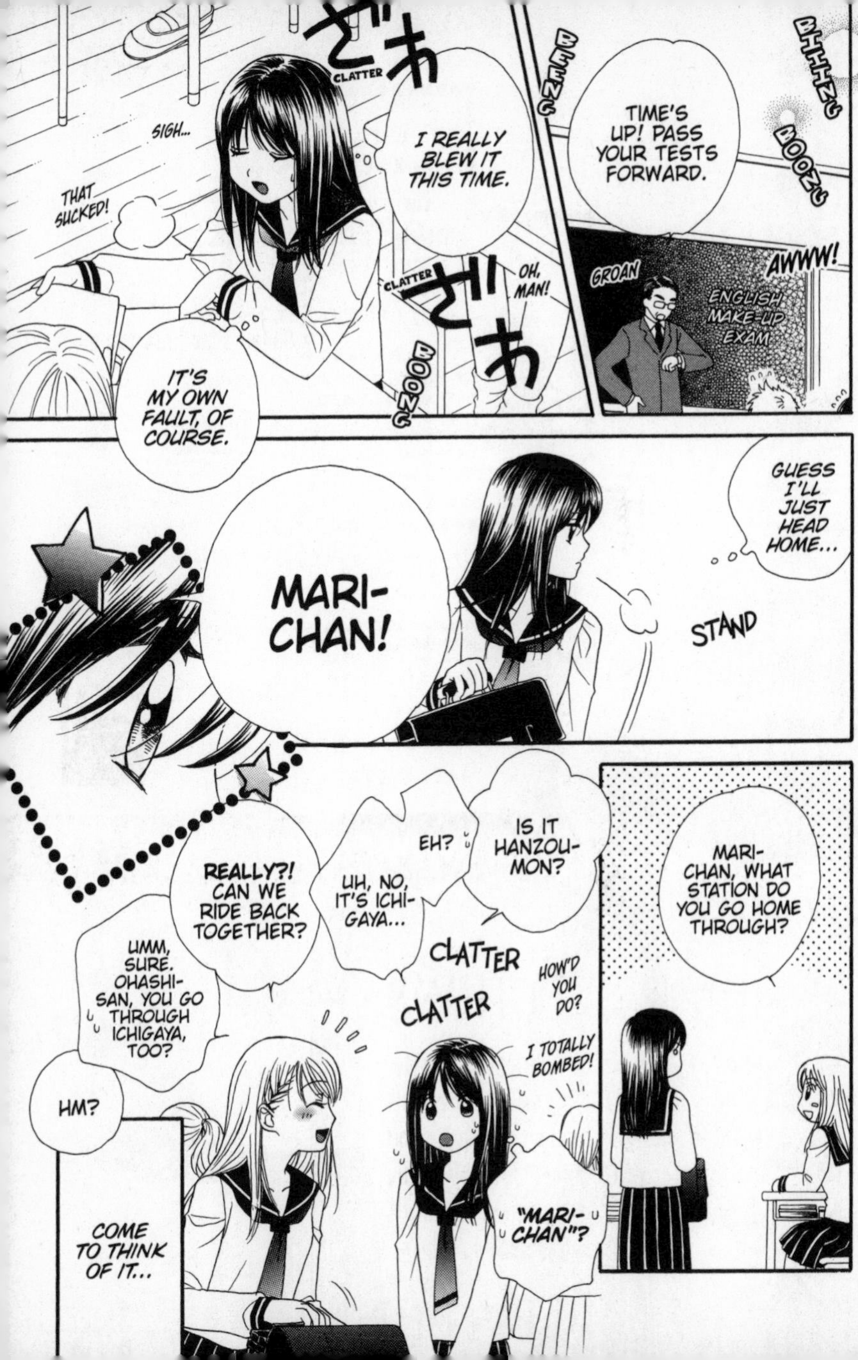
BIIIING
BOOONG
BEEENG
TIME'S UP! PASS YOUR TESTS FORWARD.
AWWW!
GROAN
ENGLISH MAKE-UP EXAM
ざわ
CLATTER
I REALLY BLEW IT THIS TIME.
SIGH...
THAT SUCKED!
OH, MAN!
CLATTER
ざわ
BOOONG
IT'S MY OWN FAULT, OF COURSE.
GUESS I'LL JUST HEAD HOME...
STAND
MARI-CHAN!
MARI-CHAN, WHAT STATION DO YOU GO HOME THROUGH?
IS IT HANZOU-MON?
EH?
UH, NO, IT'S ICHI-GAYA...
REALLY?! CAN WE RIDE BACK TOGETHER?
UMM, SURE. OHASHI-SAN, YOU GO THROUGH ICHIGAYA, TOO?
HM?
CLATTER
CLATTER
HOW'D YOU DO?
I TOTALLY BOMBED!
"MARI-CHAN"?
COME TO THINK OF IT...

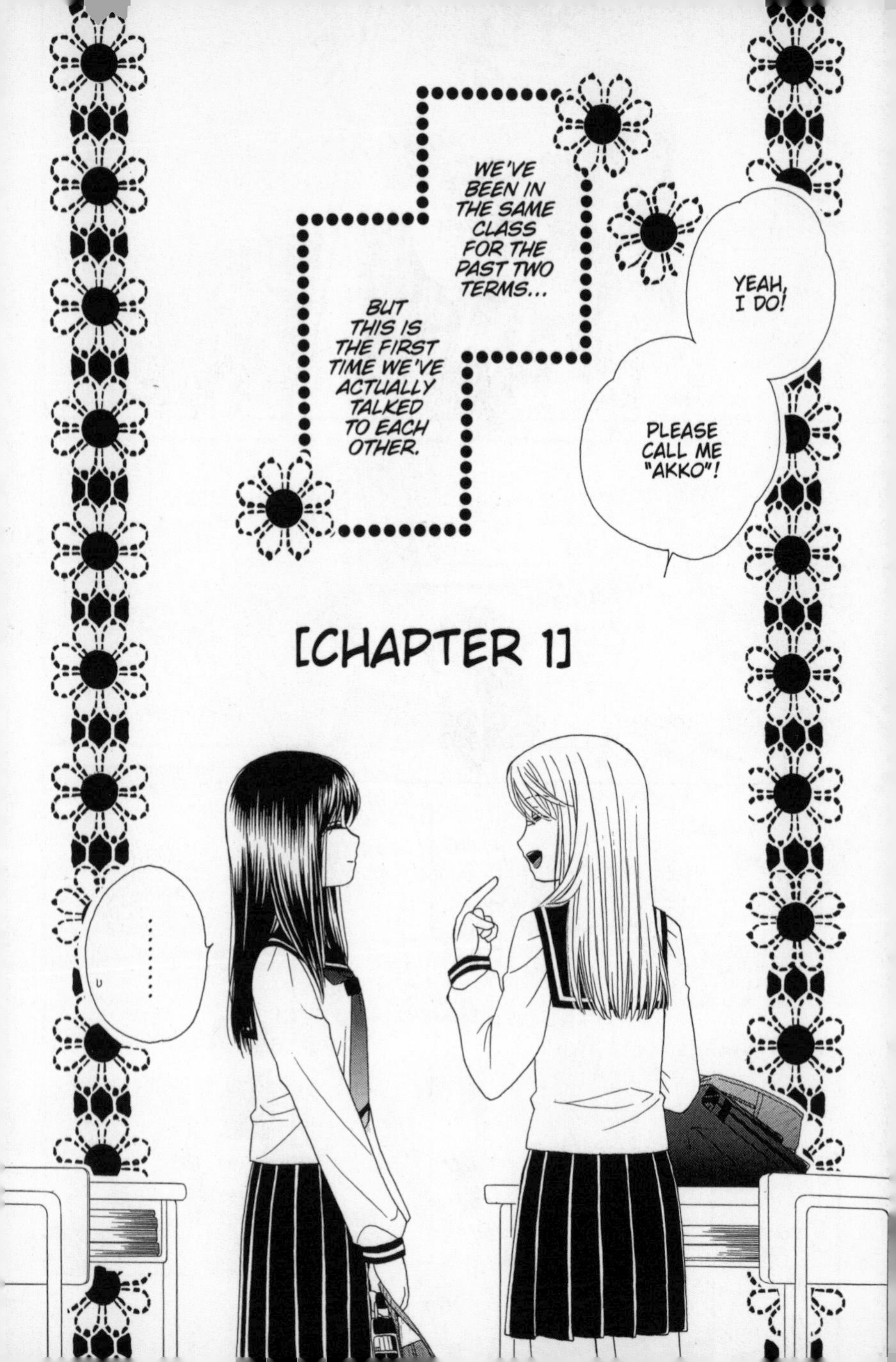
YEAH, I DO!
PLEASE CALL ME "AKKO"!
WE'VE BEEN IN THE SAME CLASS FOR THE PAST TWO TERMS...
BUT THIS IS THE FIRST TIME WE'VE ACTUALLY TALKED TO EACH OTHER.
[CHAPTER 1]
......

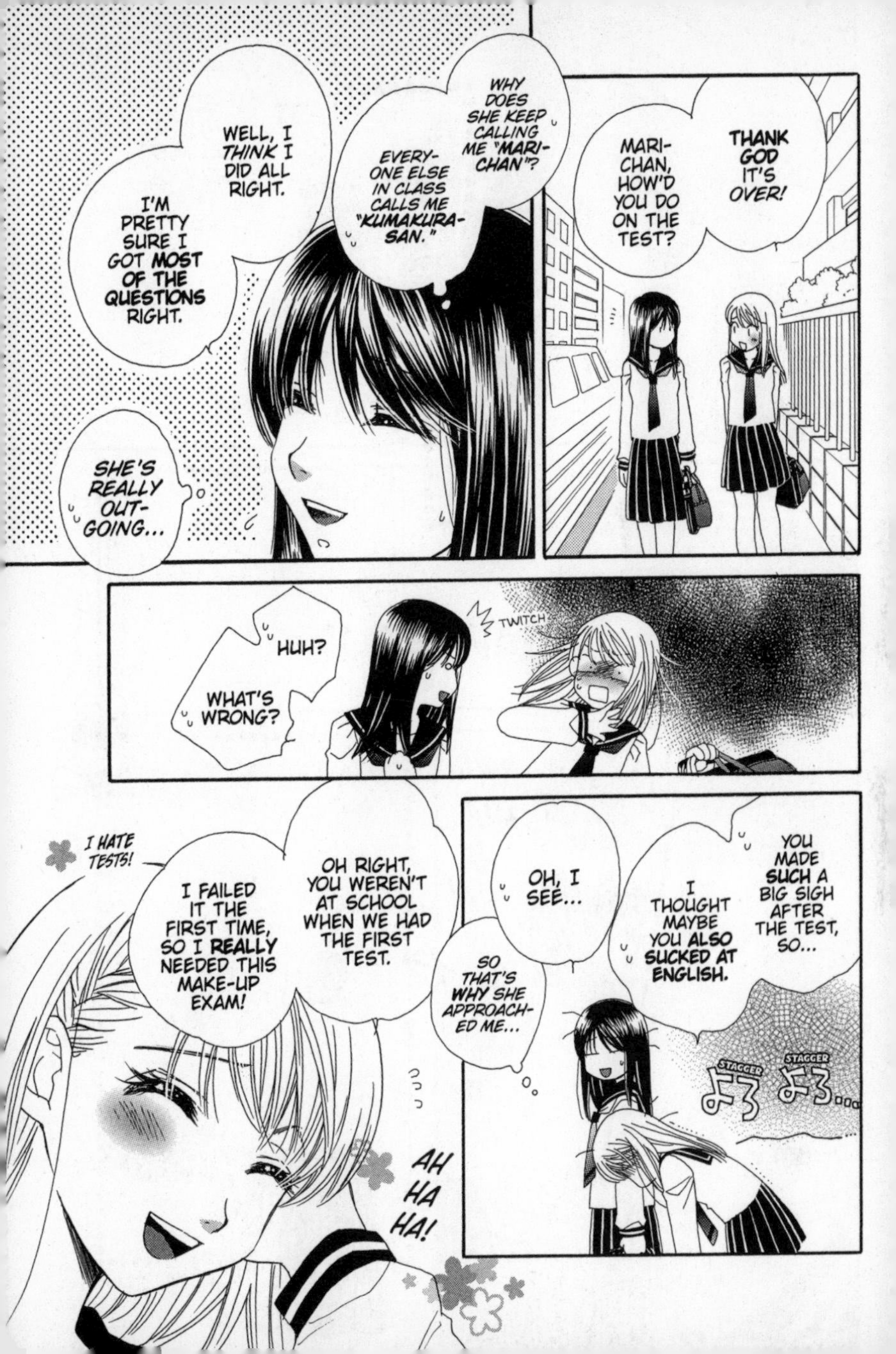
THANK GOD IT'S OVER!
MARI-CHAN, HOW'D YOU DO ON THE TEST?
WHY DOES SHE KEEP CALLING ME "MARI-CHAN"?
EVERY-ONE ELSE IN CLASS CALLS ME "KUMAKURA-SAN."
WELL, I THINK I DID ALL RIGHT.
I'M PRETTY SURE I GOT MOST OF THE QUESTIONS RIGHT.
SHE'S REALLY OUT-GOING...
TWITCH
HUH?
WHAT'S WRONG?
YOU MADE SUCH A BIG SIGH AFTER THE TEST, SO...
I THOUGHT MAYBE YOU ALSO SUCKED AT ENGLISH.
OH, I SEE...
SO THAT'S WHY SHE APPROACHED ME...
STAGGER STAGGER
よろよろ...
OH RIGHT, YOU WEREN'T AT SCHOOL WHEN WE HAD THE FIRST TEST.
I FAILED IT THE FIRST TIME, SO I REALLY NEEDED THIS MAKE-UP EXAM!
I HATE TESTS!
AH HA HA!

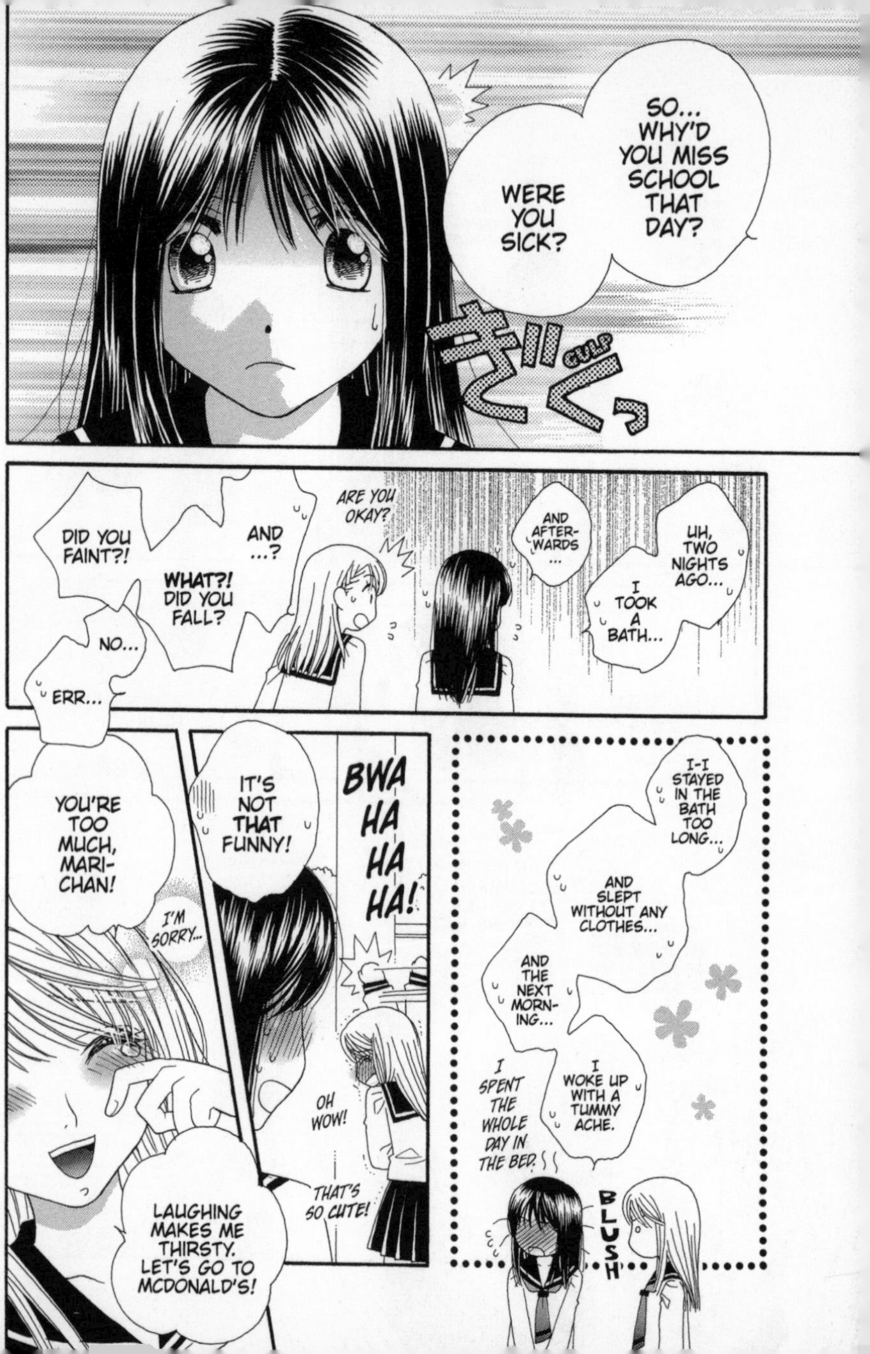
SO... WHY'D YOU MISS SCHOOL THAT DAY?
WERE YOU SICK?
ぎくっ
GULP
UH, TWO NIGHTS AGO... I TOOK A BATH...
AND AFTER-WARDS...
ARE YOU OKAY?
AND ...?
WHAT?! DID YOU FALL?
DID YOU FAINT?!
NO...
ERR...
I-I STAYED IN THE BATH TOO LONG...
AND SLEPT WITHOUT ANY CLOTHES...
AND THE NEXT MORN-ING...
I WOKE UP WITH A TUMMY ACHE.
I SPENT THE WHOLE DAY IN THE BED.
BLUSH
BWA HA HA HA!
IT'S NOT THAT FUNNY!
OH WOW!
THAT'S SO CUTE!
YOU'RE TOO MUCH, MARI-CHAN!
I'M SORRY...
LAUGHING MAKES ME THIRSTY. LET'S GO TO MCDONALD'S!

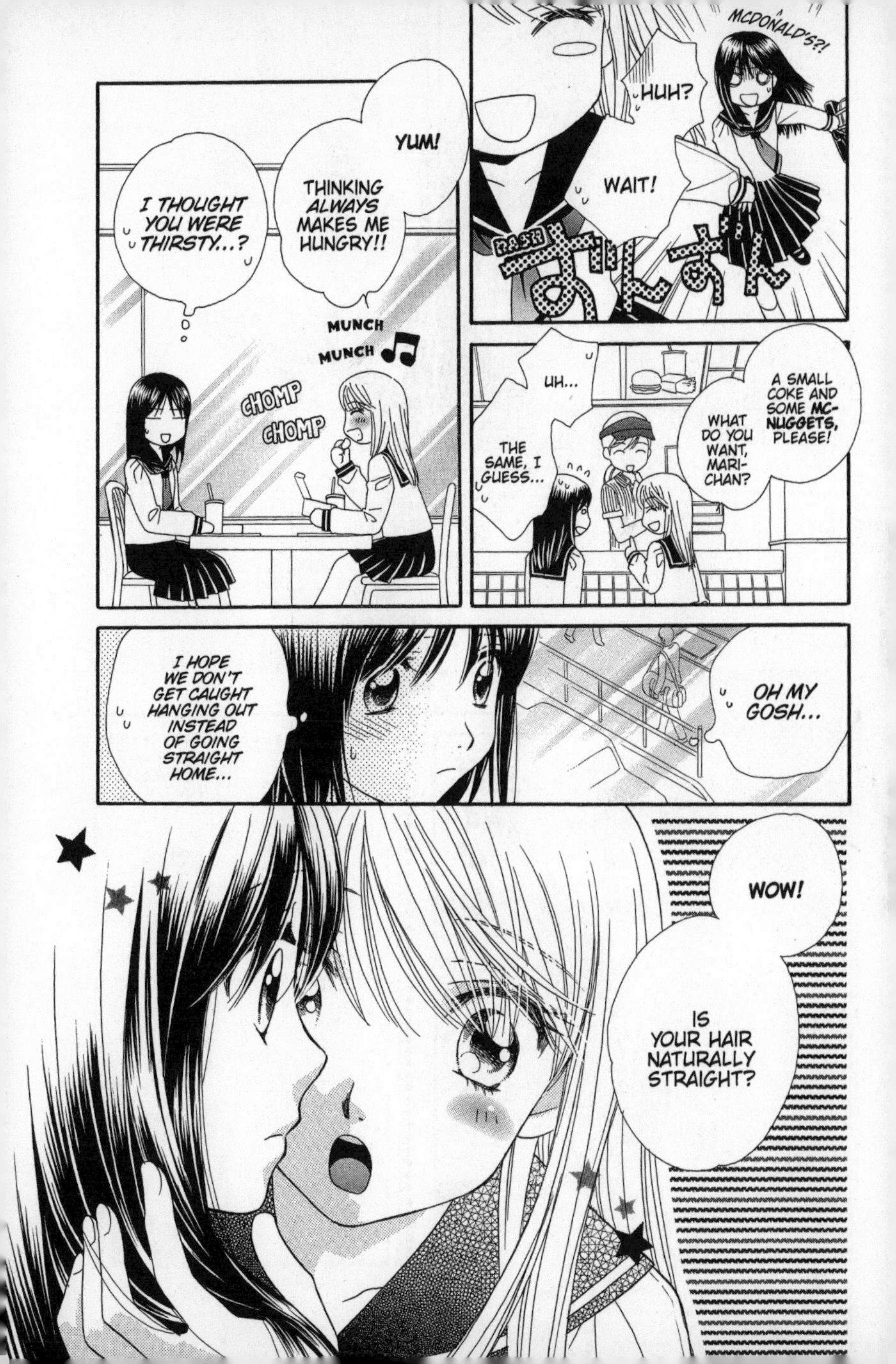
MCDONALD'S?!
HUH?
WAIT!
DASH
A SMALL COKE AND SOME MC-NUGGETS, PLEASE!
WHAT DO YOU WANT, MARI-CHAN?
UH...
THE SAME, I GUESS...
YUM!
THINKING ALWAYS MAKES ME HUNGRY!!
I THOUGHT YOU WERE THIRSTY...?
MUNCH MUNCH
CHOMP CHOMP
OH MY GOSH...
I HOPE WE DON'T GET CAUGHT HANGING OUT INSTEAD OF GOING STRAIGHT HOME...
WOW!
IS YOUR HAIR NATURALLY STRAIGHT?

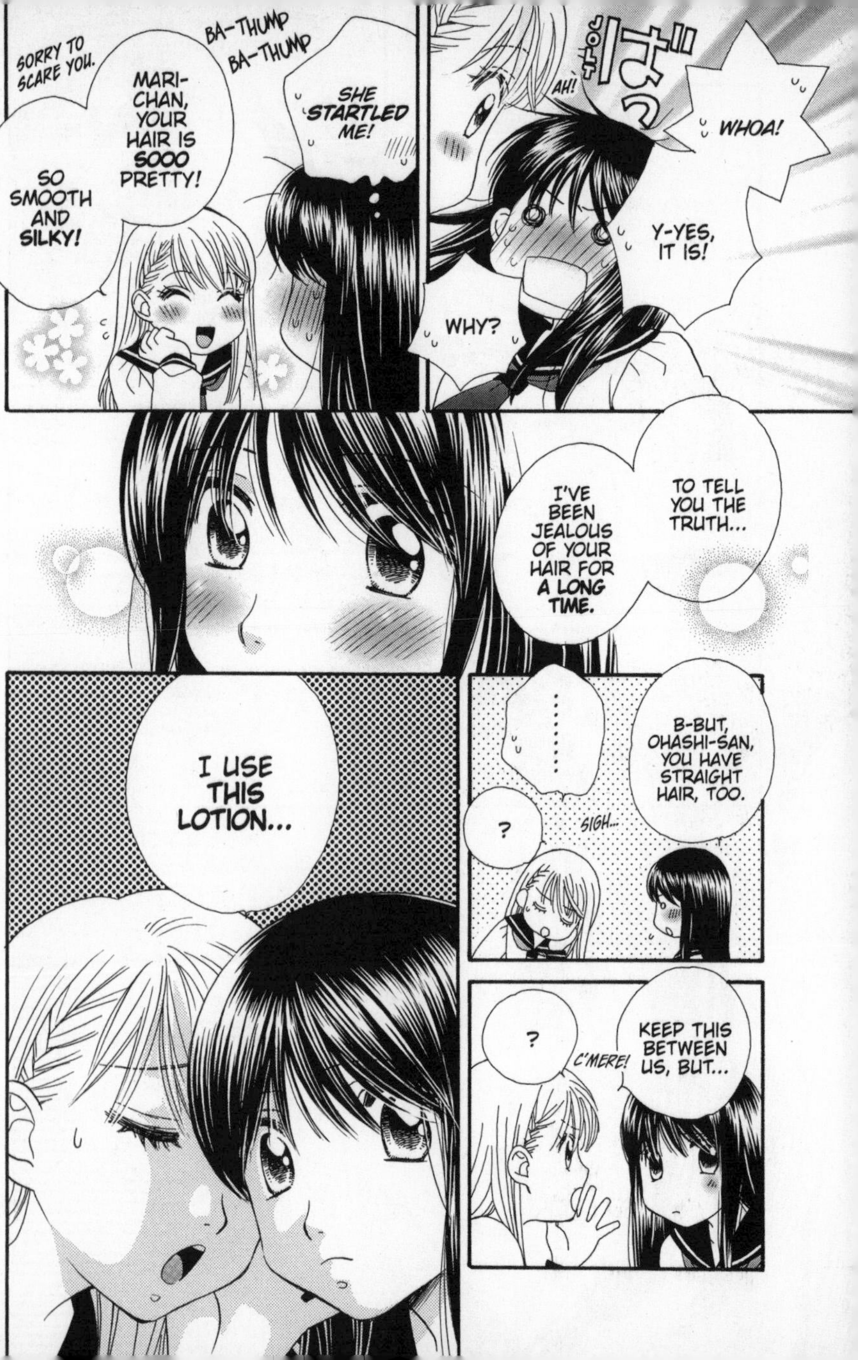
WHOA!
ぱっ
AH!
Y-YES, IT IS!
WHY?
BA-THUMP BA-THUMP
SHE STARTLED ME!
MARI-CHAN, YOUR HAIR IS SOOO PRETTY!
SORRY TO SCARE YOU.
SO SMOOTH AND SILKY!
TO TELL YOU THE TRUTH...
I'VE BEEN JEALOUS OF YOUR HAIR FOR A LONG TIME.
B-BUT, OHASHI-SAN, YOU HAVE STRAIGHT HAIR, TOO.
......
SIGH...
?
KEEP THIS BETWEEN US, BUT...
C'MERE!
?
I USE THIS LOTION...

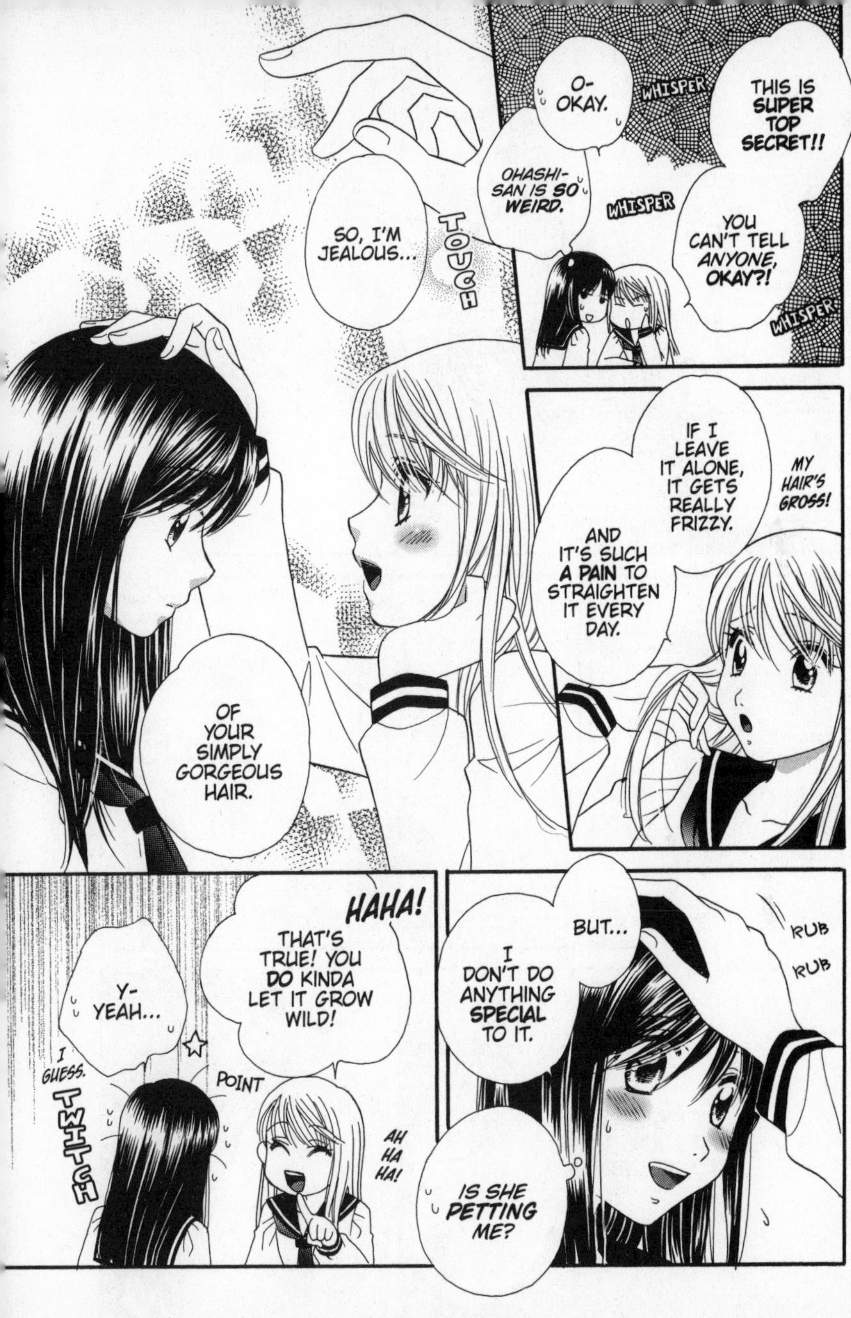
THIS IS SUPER TOP SECRET!!
WHISPER
YOU CAN'T TELL ANYONE, OKAY?!
WHISPER
O-OKAY.
WHISPER
OHASHI-SAN IS SO WEIRD.
MY HAIR'S GROSS!
IF I LEAVE IT ALONE, IT GETS REALLY FRIZZY.
AND IT'S SUCH A PAIN TO STRAIGHTEN IT EVERY DAY.
TOUCH
SO, I'M JEALOUS...
OF YOUR SIMPLY GORGEOUS HAIR.
RUB
RUB
BUT...
I DON'T DO ANYTHING SPECIAL TO IT.
IS SHE PETTING ME?
HAHA!
THAT'S TRUE! YOU DO KINDA LET IT GROW WILD!
POINT
AH HA HA!
Y-YEAH...
I GUESS.
TWITCH

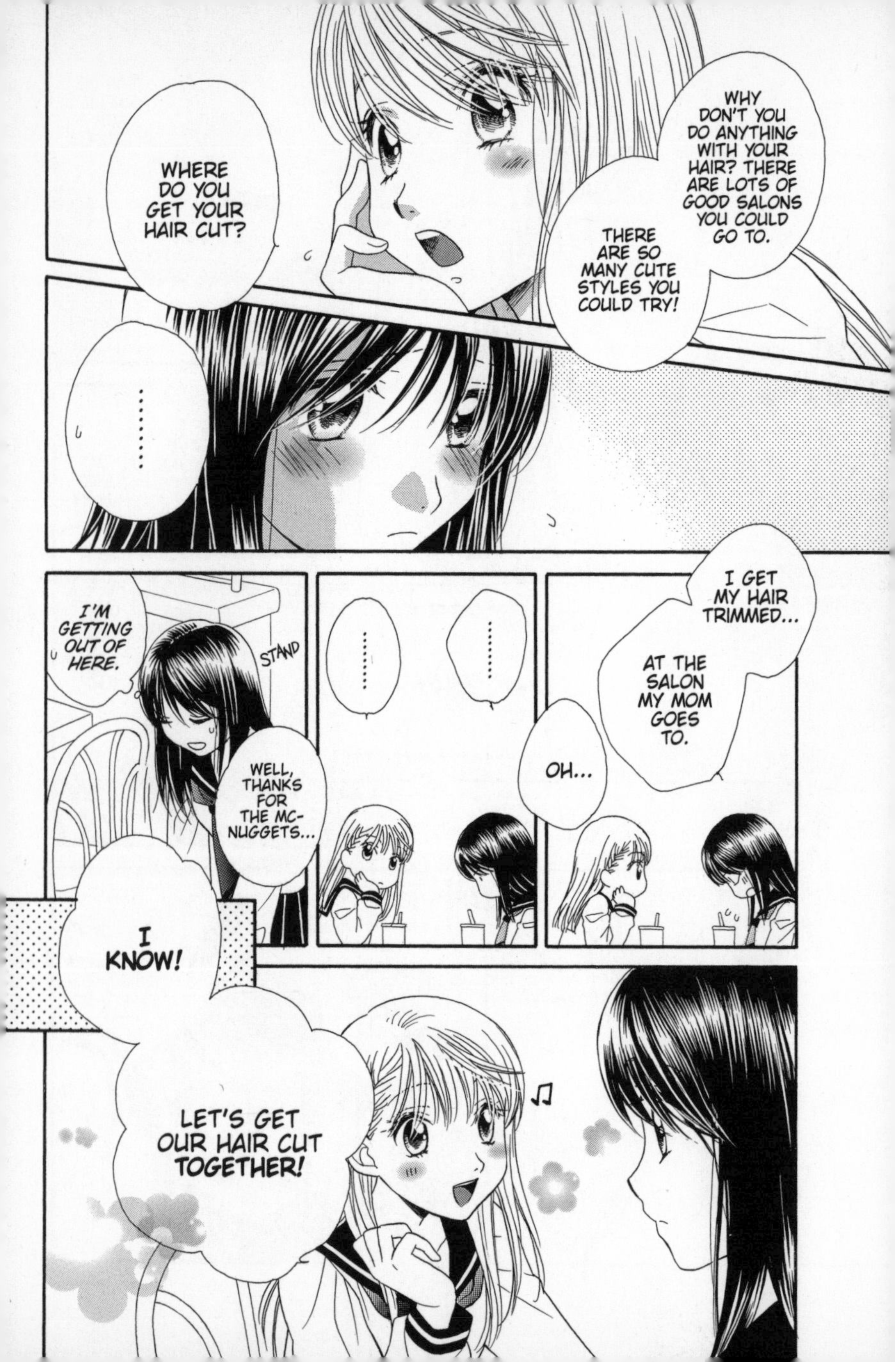

WHY DON'T YOU DO ANYTHING WITH YOUR HAIR? THERE ARE LOTS OF GOOD SALONS YOU COULD GO TO.
THERE ARE SO MANY CUTE STYLES YOU COULD TRY!
WHERE DO YOU GET YOUR HAIR CUT?
......
I GET MY HAIR TRIMMED...
AT THE SALON MY MOM GOES TO.
OH...
......
......
I'M GETTING OUT OF HERE.
STAND
WELL, THANKS FOR THE MC-NUGGETS...
I KNOW!
LET'S GET OUR HAIR CUT TOGETHER!

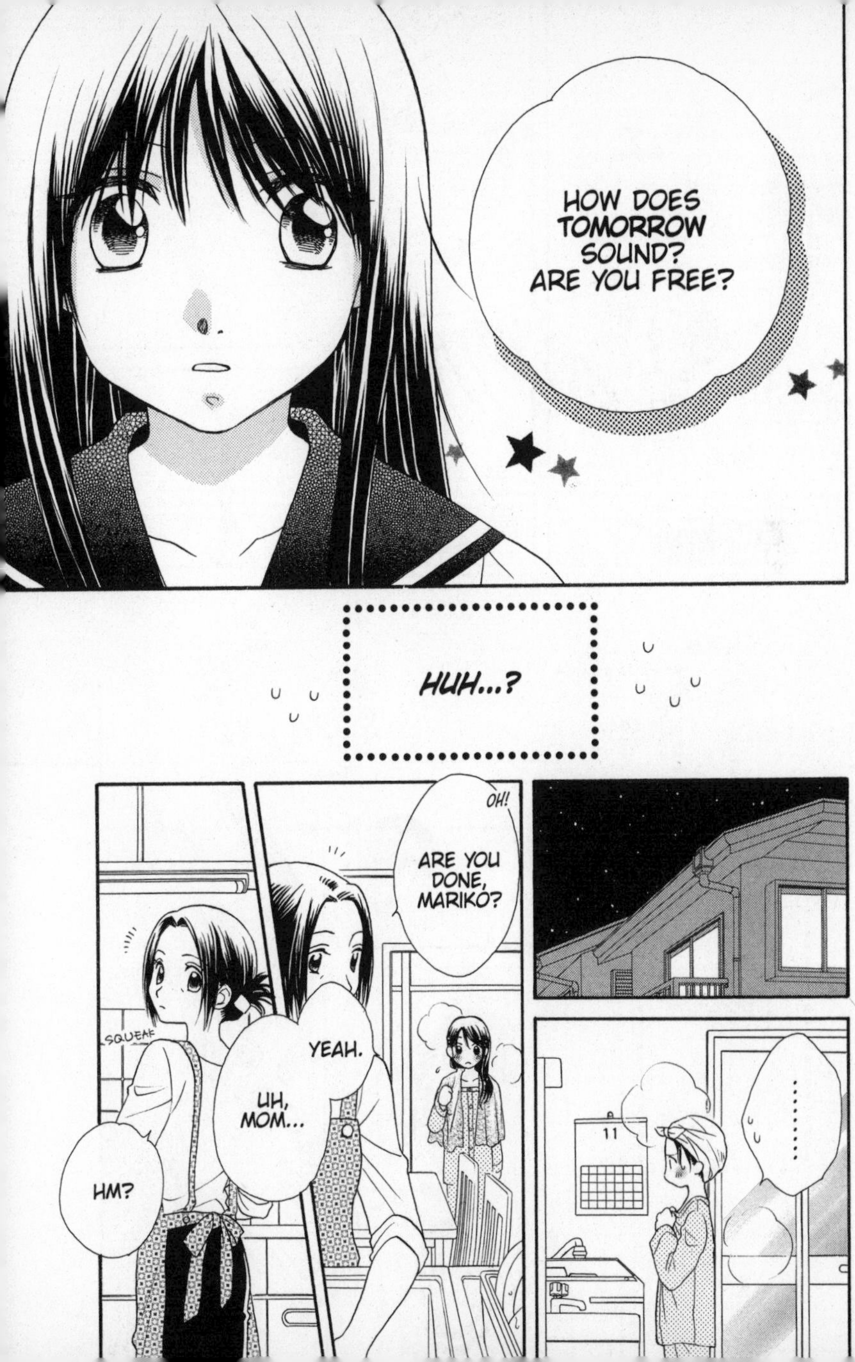
HOW DOES TOMORROW SOUND? ARE YOU FREE?
HUH...?
......
OH!
ARE YOU DONE, MARIKO?
YEAH.
SQUEAK
UH, MOM...
HM?

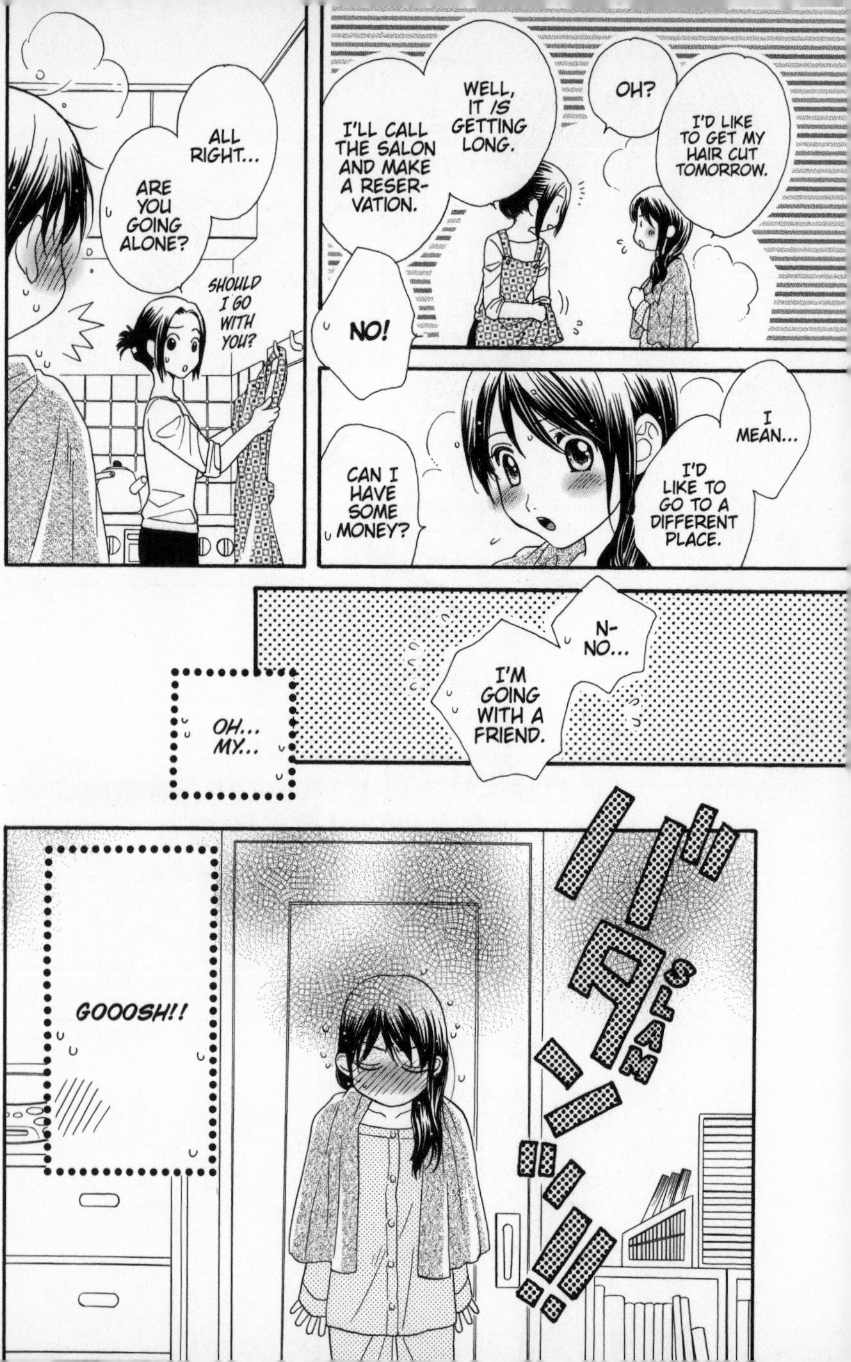
OH?
I'D LIKE TO GET MY HAIR CUT TOMORROW.
WELL, IT *IS* GETTING LONG.
I'LL CALL THE SALON AND MAKE A RESER-VATION.
NO!
I MEAN...
I'D LIKE TO GO TO A DIFFERENT PLACE.
CAN I HAVE SOME MONEY?
ALL RIGHT...
ARE YOU GOING ALONE?
SHOULD I GO WITH YOU?
N-NO...
I'M GOING WITH A FRIEND.
OH... MY...
SLAM
GOOOSH!!

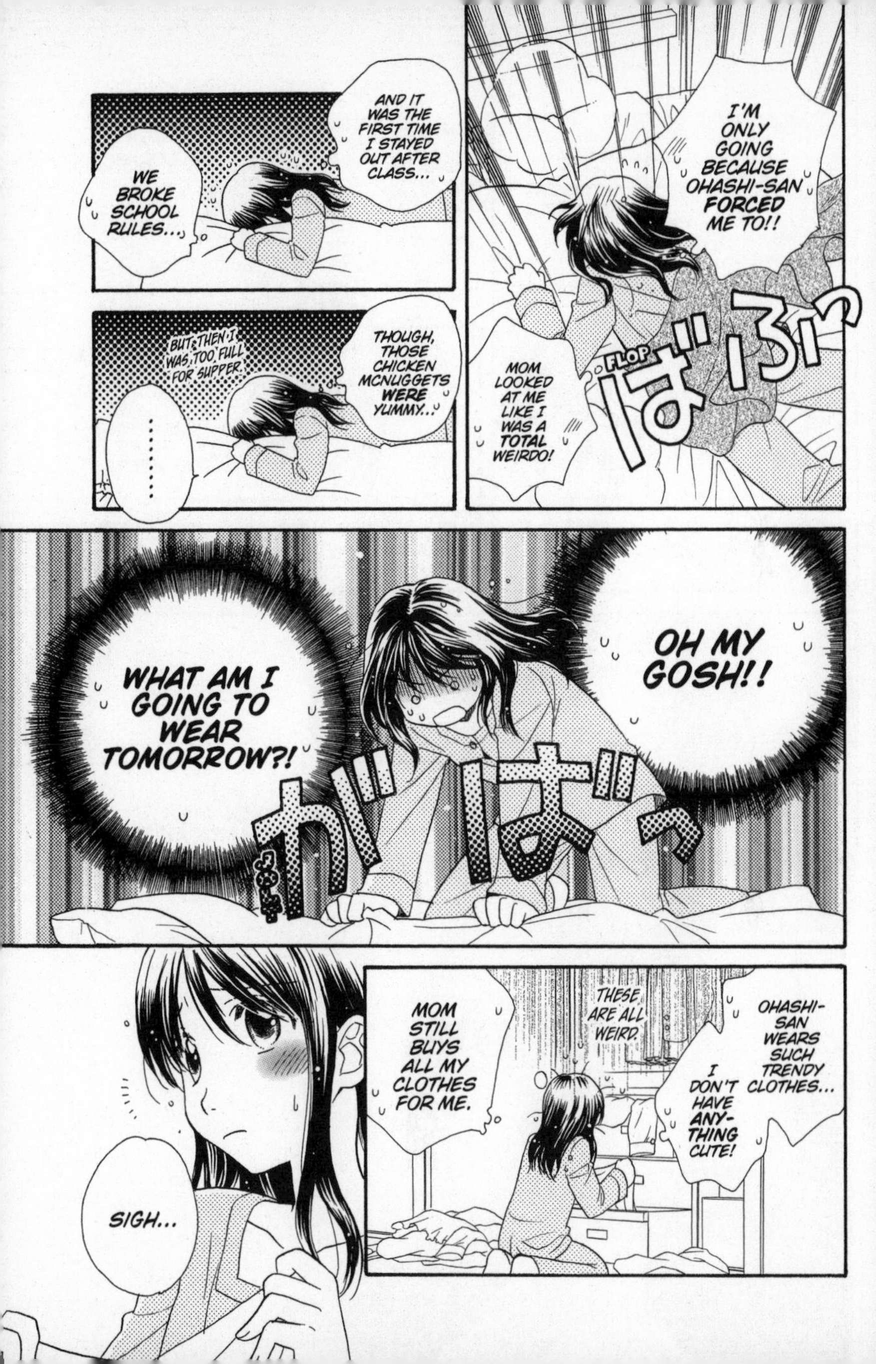

I'M ONLY GOING BECAUSE OHASHI-SAN FORCED ME TO!!
FLOP
ばふっ
MOM LOOKED AT ME LIKE I WAS A TOTAL WEIRDO!
AND IT WAS THE FIRST TIME I STAYED OUT AFTER CLASS...
WE BROKE SCHOOL RULES...
THOUGH, THOSE CHICKEN MCNUGGETS WERE YUMMY...
BUT THEN I WAS TOO FULL FOR SUPPER.
......
OH MY GOSH!!
WHAT AM I GOING TO WEAR TOMORROW?!
がばっ
OHASHI-SAN WEARS SUCH TRENDY CLOTHES...
I DON'T HAVE ANYTHING CUTE!
THESE ARE ALL WEIRD.
MOM STILL BUYS ALL MY CLOTHES FOR ME.
SIGH...

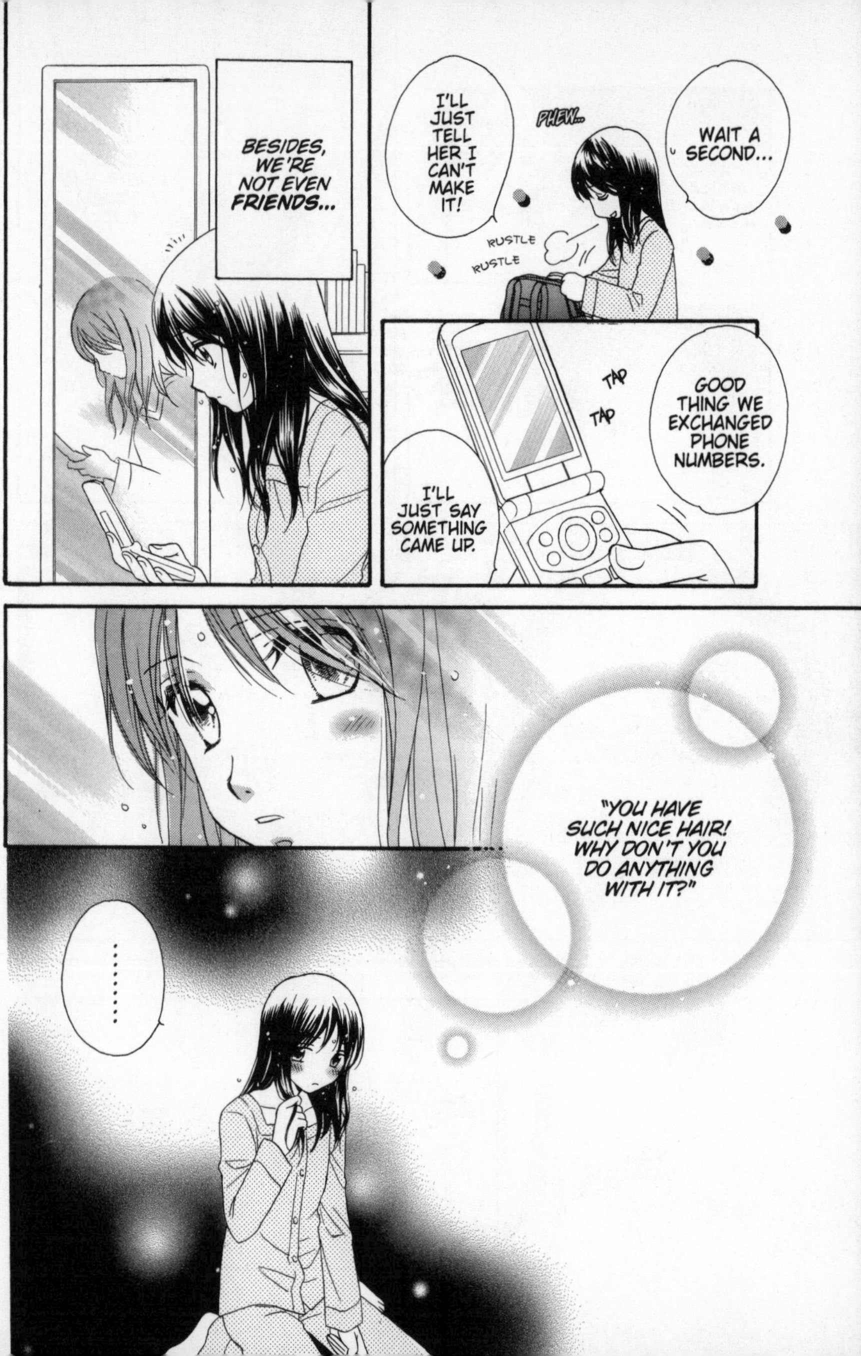
WAIT A SECOND...
PHEW...
I'LL JUST TELL HER I CAN'T MAKE IT!
RUSTLE
RUSTLE
GOOD THING WE EXCHANGED PHONE NUMBERS.
TAP
TAP
I'LL JUST SAY SOMETHING CAME UP.
BESIDES, WE'RE NOT EVEN FRIENDS...
"YOU HAVE SUCH NICE HAIR! WHY DON'T YOU DO ANYTHING WITH IT?"
......

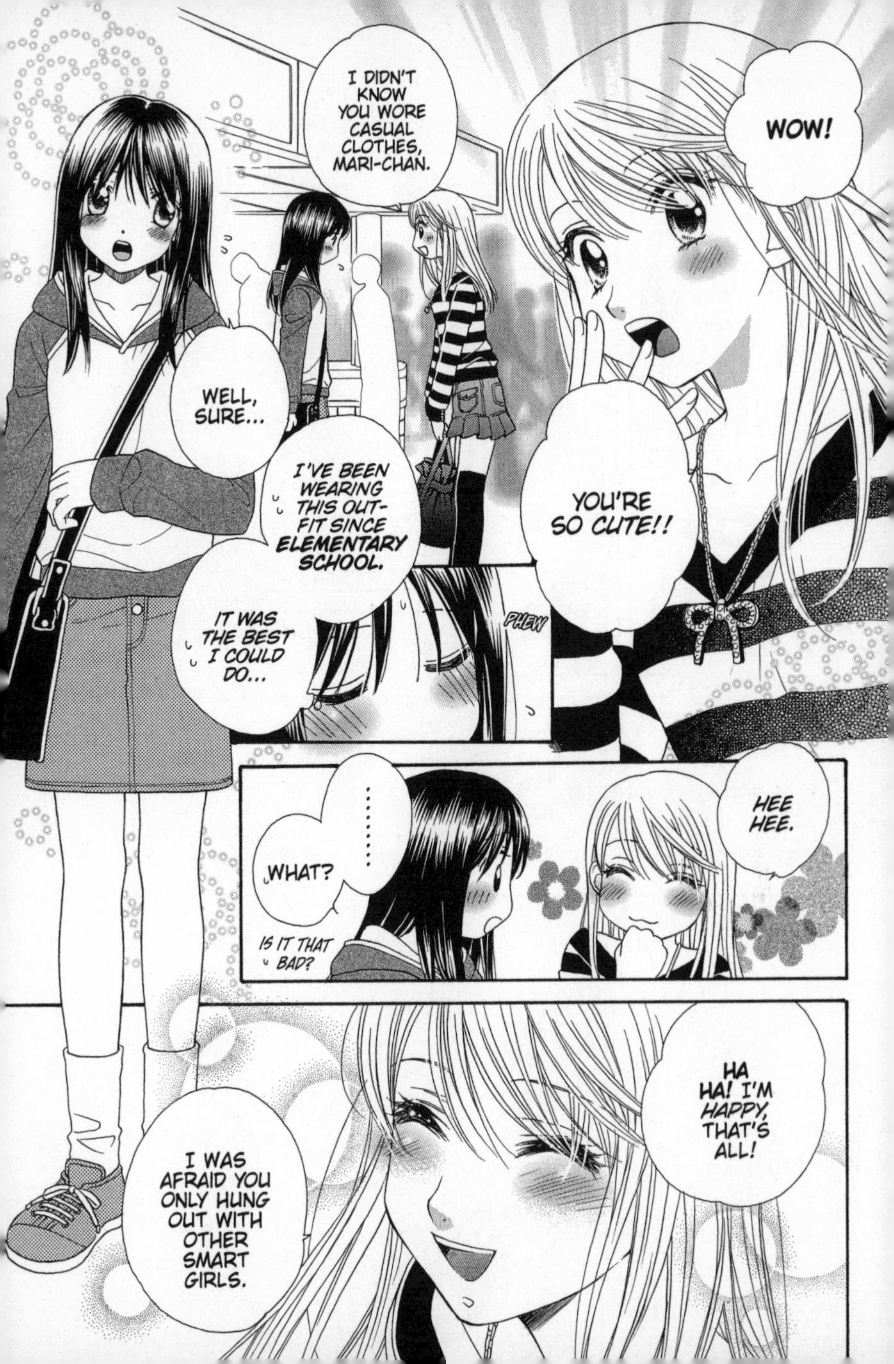

WOW!
I DIDN'T KNOW YOU WORE CASUAL CLOTHES, MARI-CHAN.
YOU'RE SO CUTE!!
WELL, SURE...
I'VE BEEN WEARING THIS OUT-FIT SINCE ELEMENTARY SCHOOL.
PHEW
IT WAS THE BEST I COULD DO...
HEE HEE.
......
WHAT?
IS IT THAT BAD?
HA HA! I'M HAPPY, THAT'S ALL!
I WAS AFRAID YOU ONLY HUNG OUT WITH OTHER SMART GIRLS.

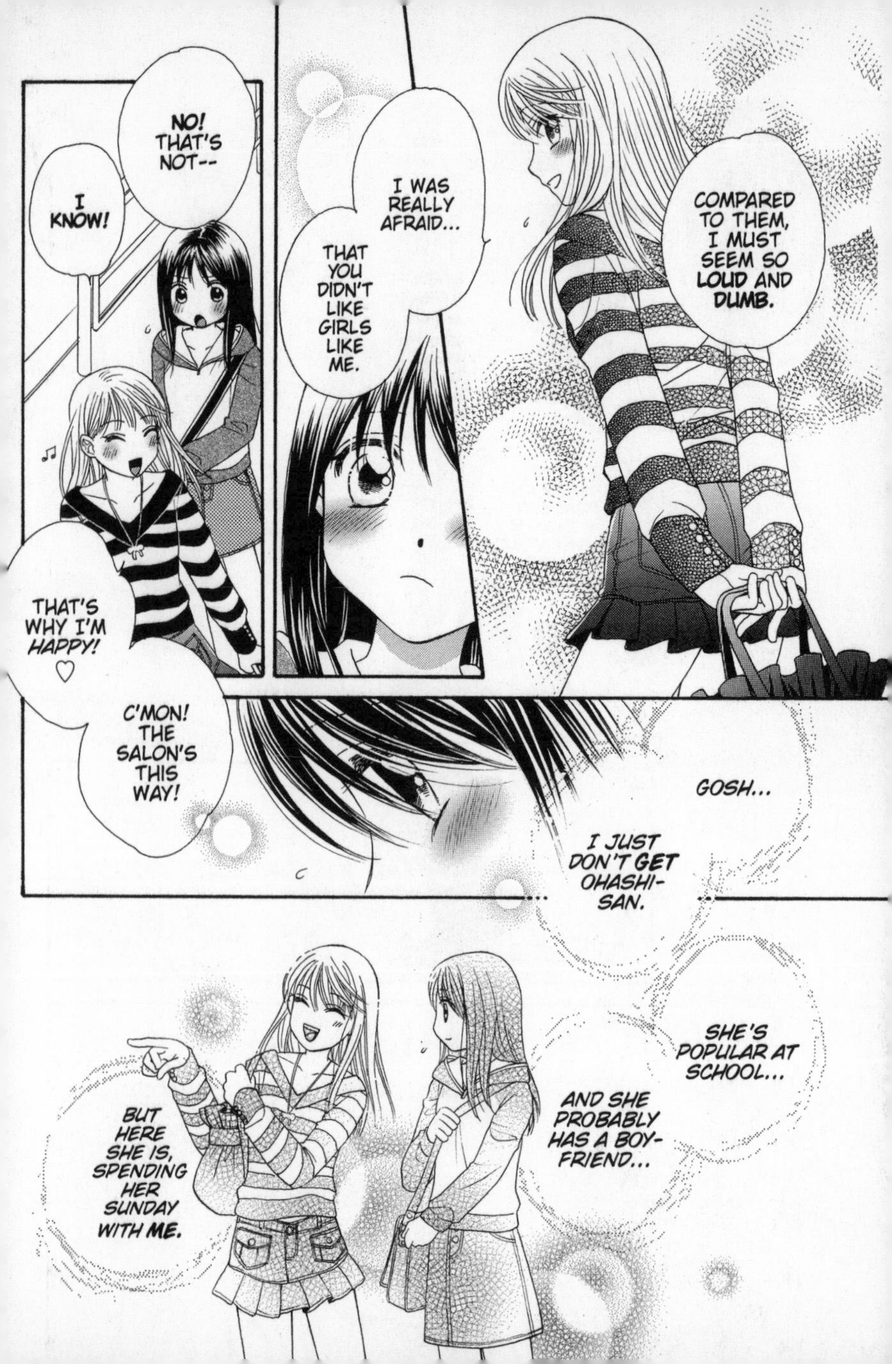
COMPARED TO THEM, I MUST SEEM SO LOUD AND DUMB.
I WAS REALLY AFRAID...
THAT YOU DIDN'T LIKE GIRLS LIKE ME.
NO! THAT'S NOT--
I KNOW!
THAT'S WHY I'M HAPPY! ♡
C'MON! THE SALON'S THIS WAY!
GOSH...
I JUST DON'T GET OHASHI-SAN.
SHE'S POPULAR AT SCHOOL...
AND SHE PROBABLY HAS A BOY-FRIEND...
BUT HERE SHE IS, SPENDING HER SUNDAY WITH ME.

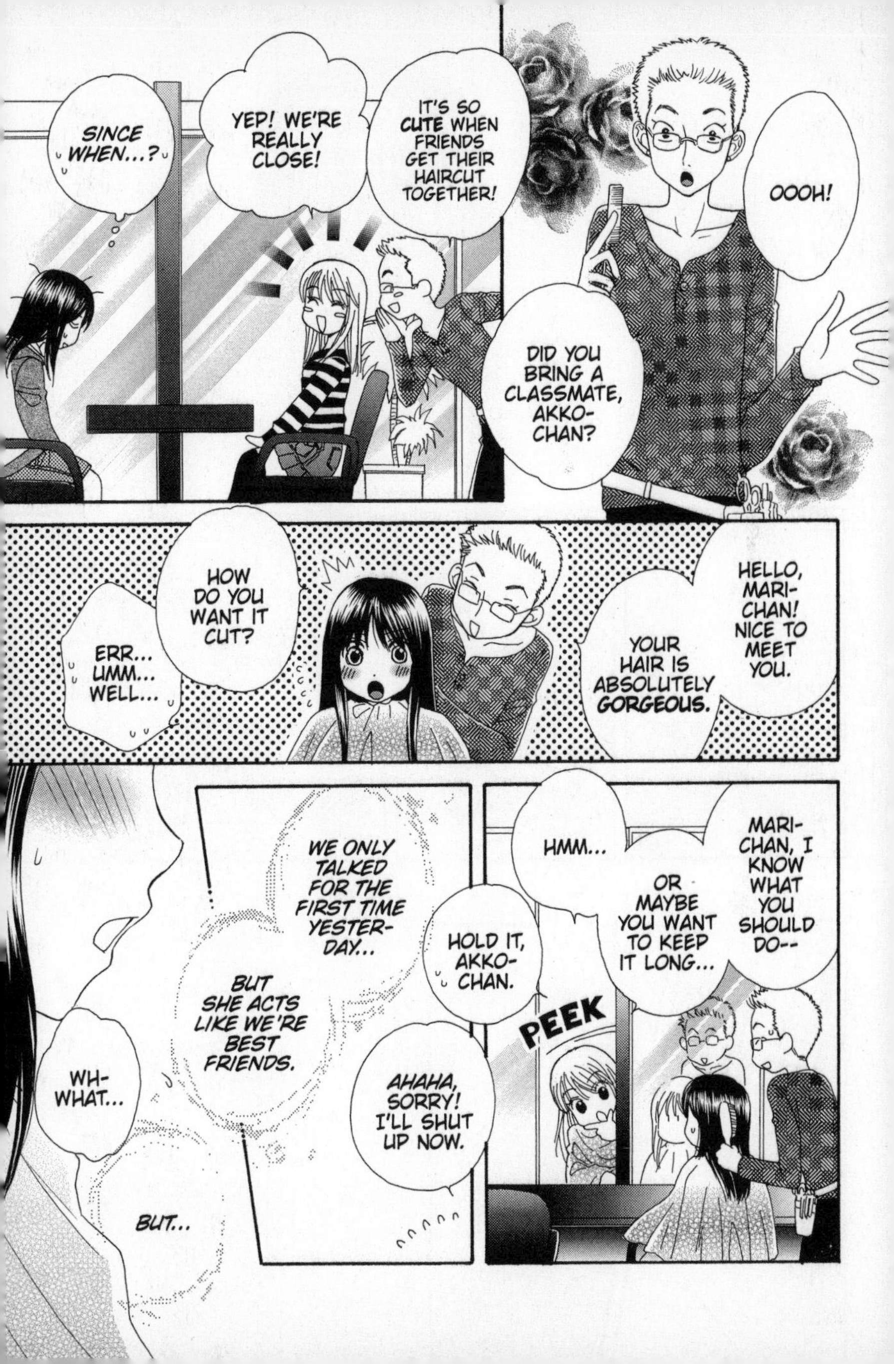
OOOH!
DID YOU BRING A CLASSMATE, AKKO-CHAN?
IT'S SO CUTE WHEN FRIENDS GET THEIR HAIRCUT TOGETHER!
YEP! WE'RE REALLY CLOSE!
SINCE WHEN...?
HELLO, MARI-CHAN! NICE TO MEET YOU.
YOUR HAIR IS ABSOLUTELY GORGEOUS.
HOW DO YOU WANT IT CUT?
ERR... UMM... WELL...
MARI-CHAN, I KNOW WHAT YOU SHOULD DO--
HMM...
OR MAYBE YOU WANT TO KEEP IT LONG...
HOLD IT, AKKO-CHAN.
PEEK
AHAHA, SORRY! I'LL SHUT UP NOW.
WE ONLY TALKED FOR THE FIRST TIME YESTER-DAY...
BUT SHE ACTS LIKE WE'RE BEST FRIENDS.
WH-WHAT...
BUT...

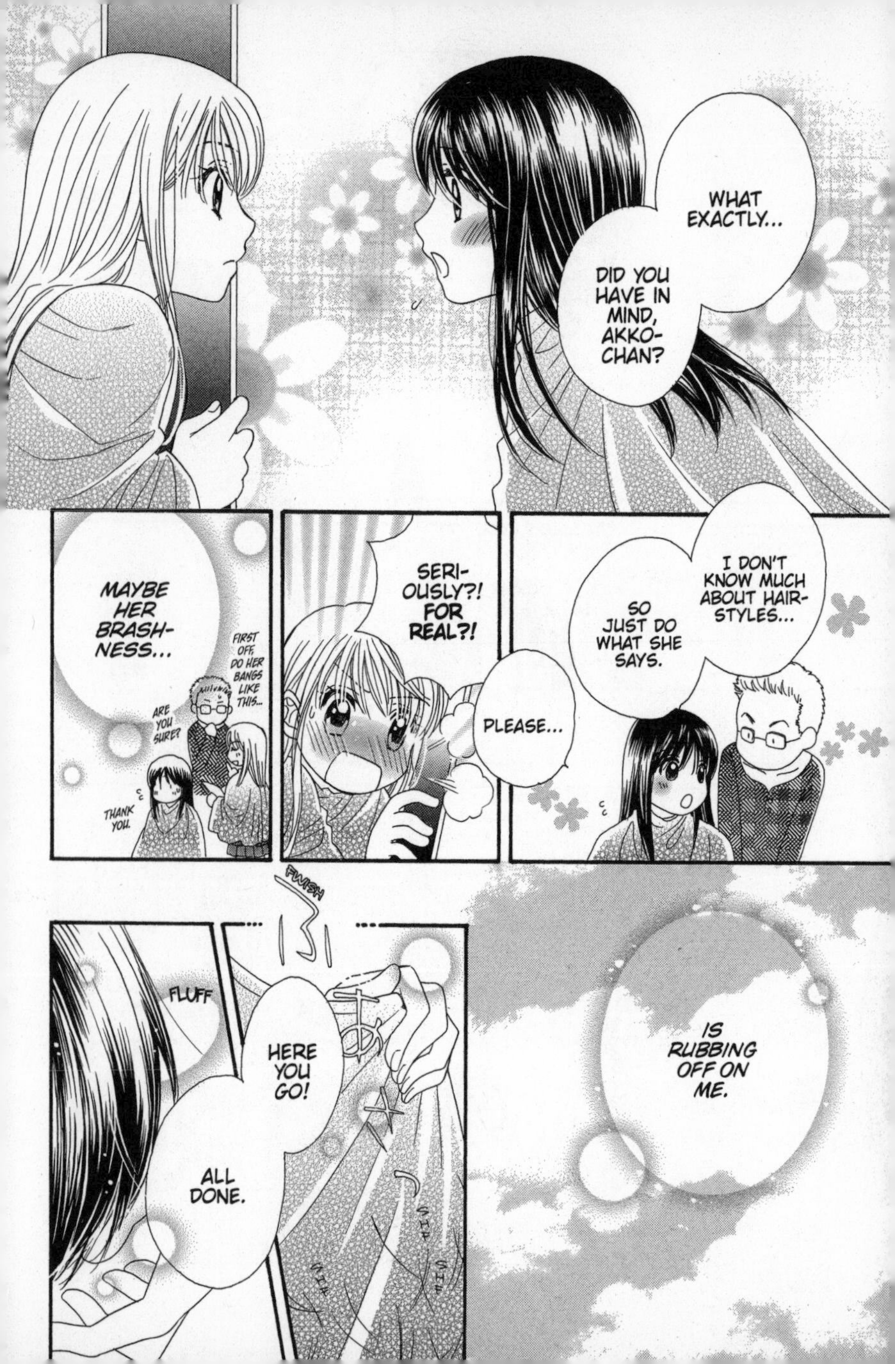
WHAT EXACTLY...
DID YOU HAVE IN MIND, AKKO-CHAN?
I DON'T KNOW MUCH ABOUT HAIR-STYLES...
SO JUST DO WHAT SHE SAYS.
PLEASE...
SERI-OUSLY?! FOR REAL?!
MAYBE HER BRASH-NESS...
FIRST OFF, DO HER BANGS LIKE THIS...
ARE YOU SURE?
THANK YOU.
IS RUBBING OFF ON ME.
FWISH
FLUFF
HERE YOU GO!
ALL DONE.
SHF
SHF

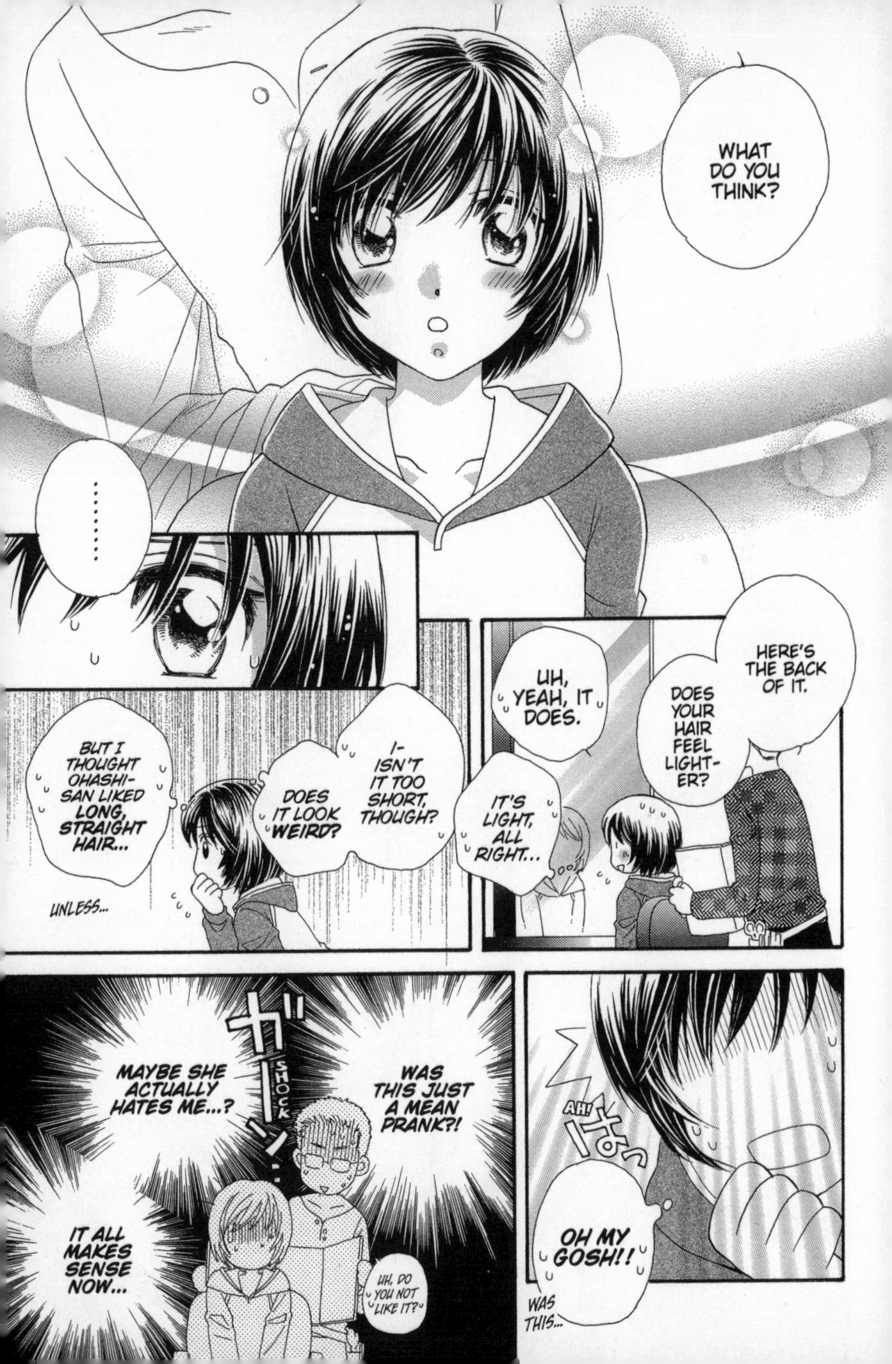
WHAT DO YOU THINK?
......
HERE'S THE BACK OF IT.
DOES YOUR HAIR FEEL LIGHTER?
UH, YEAH, IT DOES.
IT'S LIGHT, ALL RIGHT...
I- ISN'T IT TOO SHORT, THOUGH?
DOES IT LOOK WEIRD?
BUT I THOUGHT OHASHI-SAN LIKED LONG, STRAIGHT HAIR...
UNLESS...
AH!
はっ
OH MY GOSH!!
WAS THIS...
WAS THIS JUST A MEAN PRANK?!
MAYBE SHE ACTUALLY HATES ME...?
ガーン
SHOCK
IT ALL MAKES SENSE NOW...
UH, DO YOU NOT LIKE IT?

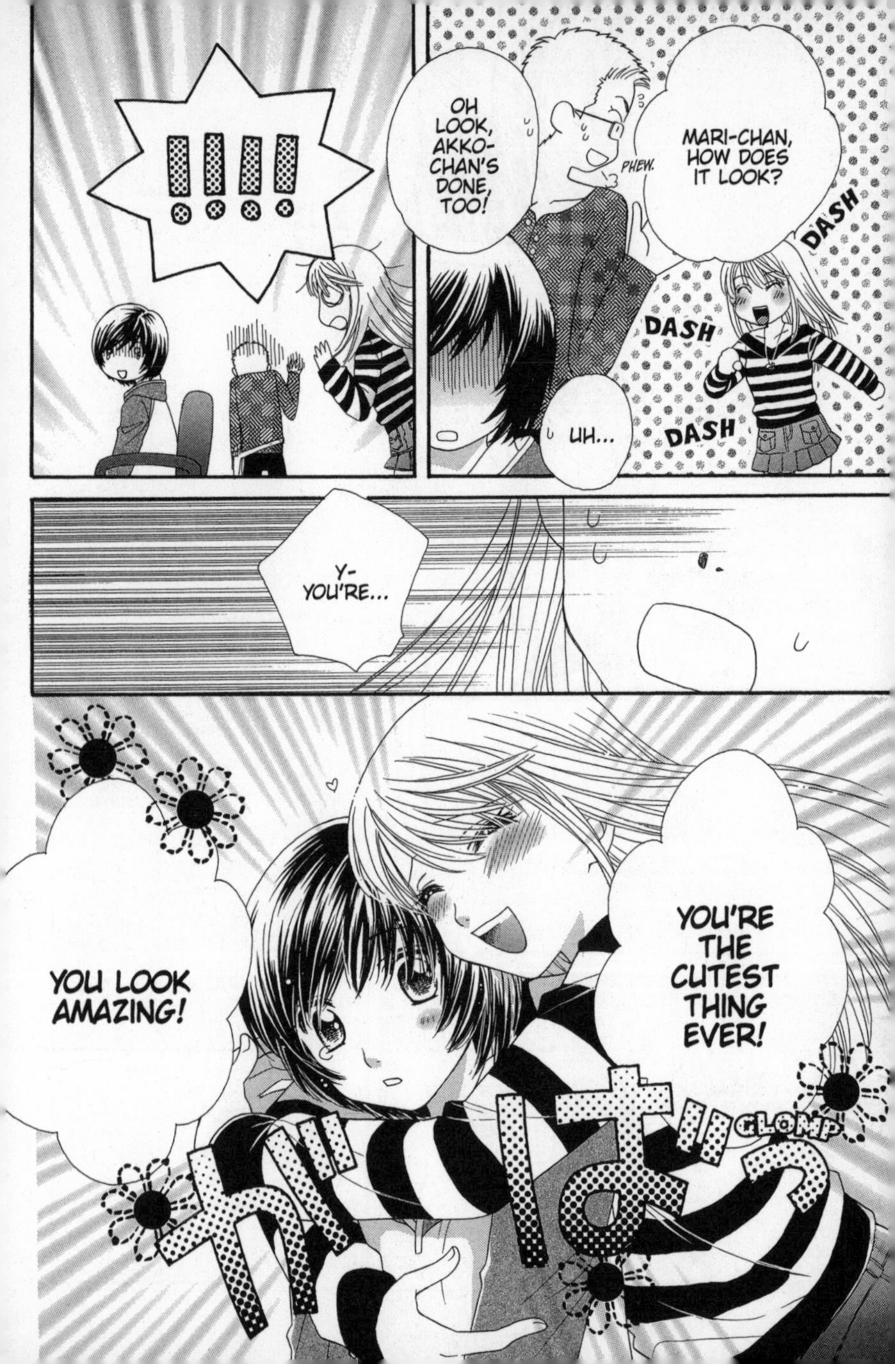

MARI-CHAN, HOW DOES IT LOOK?
DASH
OH LOOK, AKKO-CHAN'S DONE, TOO!
PHEW.
DASH
DASH
UH...
!!!!
Y-YOU'RE...
YOU'RE THE CUTEST THING EVER!
YOU LOOK AMAZING!
GLOMP

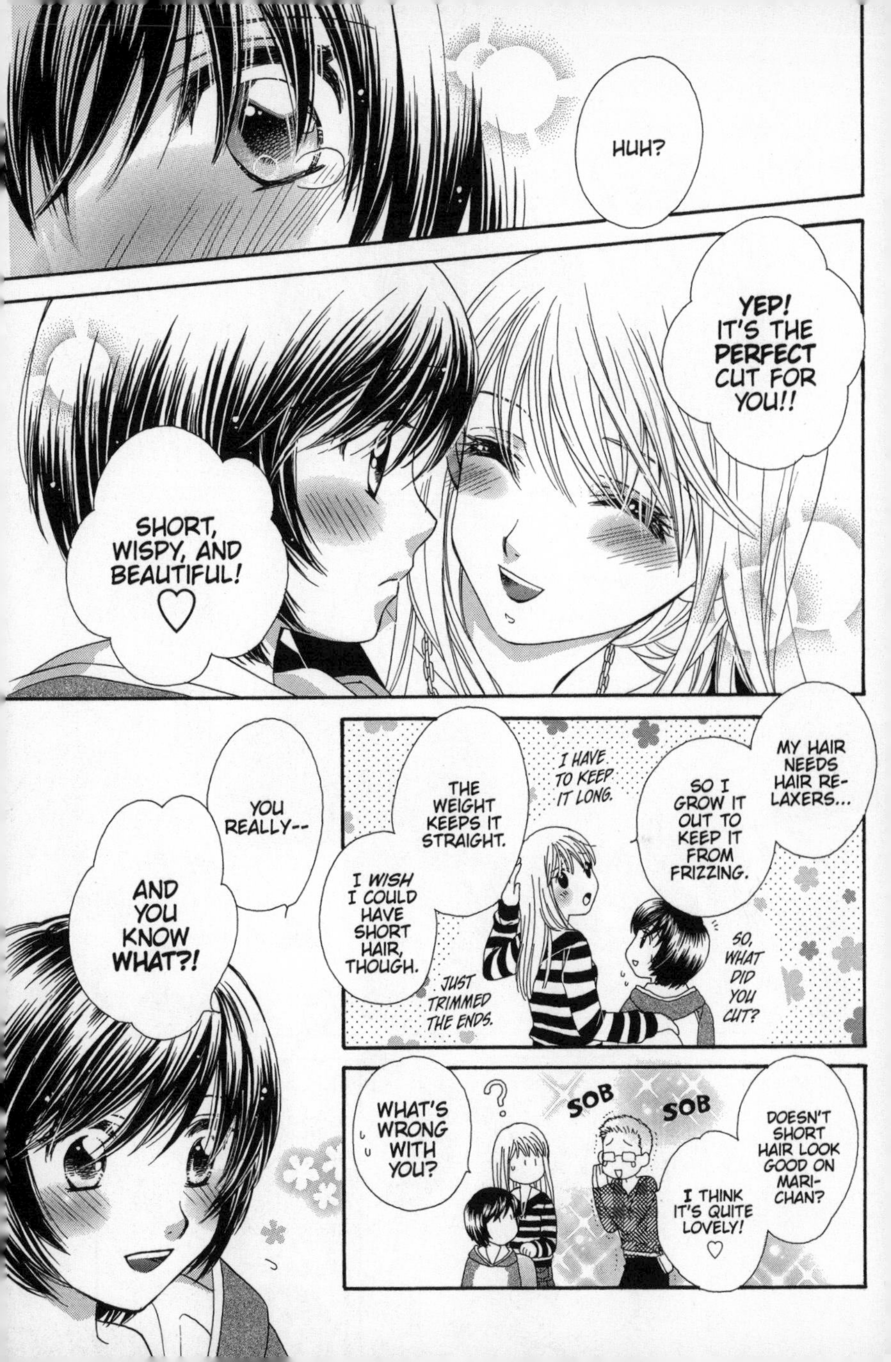

HUH?
YEP! IT'S THE PERFECT CUT FOR YOU!!
SHORT, WISPY, AND BEAUTIFUL! ♡
SO, WHAT DID YOU CUT?
JUST TRIMMED THE ENDS.
MY HAIR NEEDS HAIR RE-LAXERS...
SO I GROW IT OUT TO KEEP IT FROM FRIZZING.
I HAVE TO KEEP IT LONG.
THE WEIGHT KEEPS IT STRAIGHT.
I WISH I COULD HAVE SHORT HAIR, THOUGH.
DOESN'T SHORT HAIR LOOK GOOD ON MARI-CHAN?
I THINK IT'S QUITE LOVELY! ♡
SOB
SOB
WHAT'S WRONG WITH YOU?
YOU REALLY--
AND YOU KNOW WHAT?!

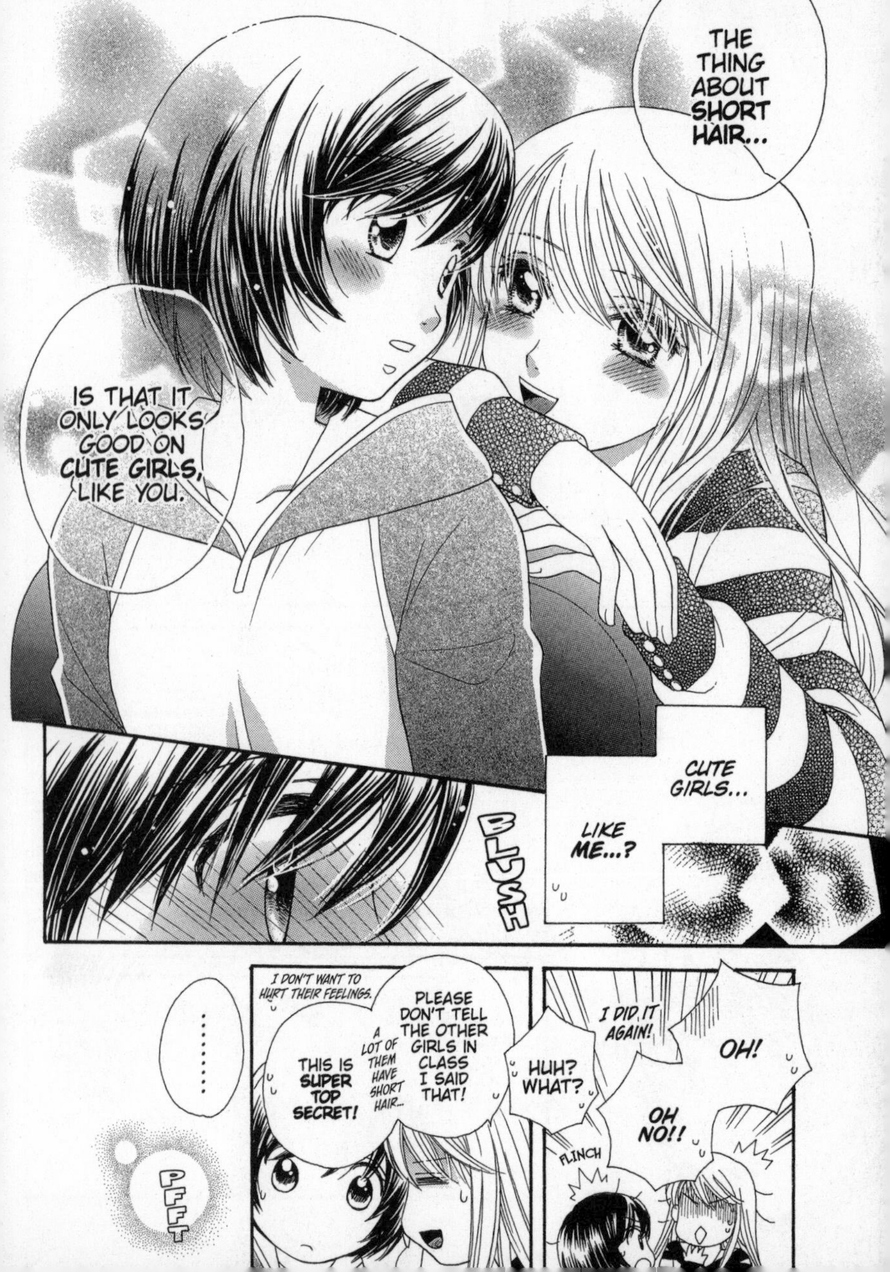
THE THING ABOUT SHORT HAIR...
IS THAT IT ONLY LOOKS GOOD ON CUTE GIRLS, LIKE YOU.
CUTE GIRLS...
LIKE ME...?
BLUSH
OH!
I DID IT AGAIN!
HUH? WHAT?
OH NO!!
FLINCH
I DON'T WANT TO HURT THEIR FEELINGS.
PLEASE DON'T TELL THE OTHER GIRLS IN CLASS I SAID THAT!
A LOT OF THEM HAVE SHORT HAIR...
THIS IS SUPER TOP SECRET!
......
PFFT

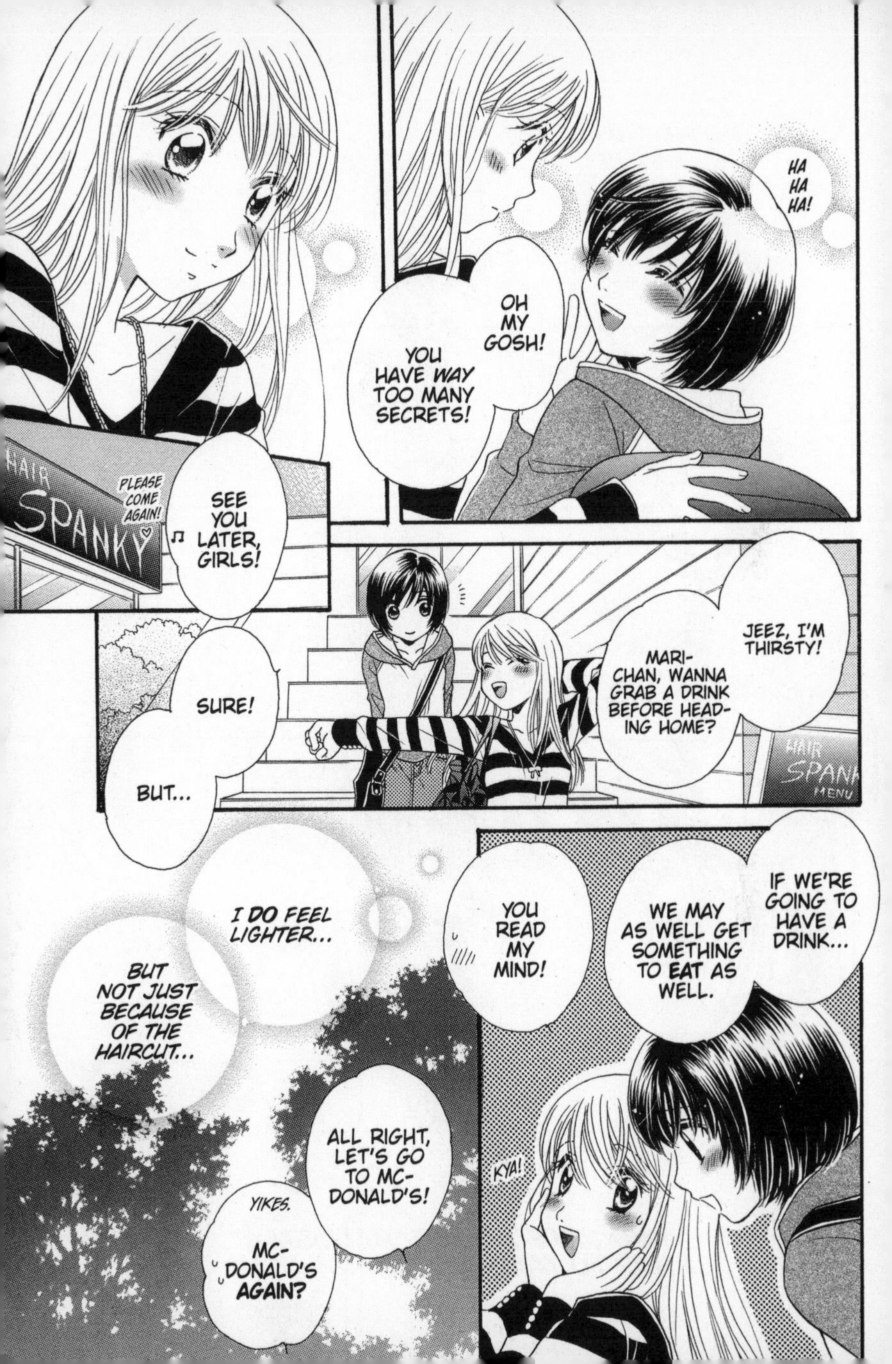
HA HA HA!
OH MY GOSH!
YOU HAVE WAY TOO MANY SECRETS!
HAIR SPANKY
PLEASE COME AGAIN!
SEE YOU LATER, GIRLS!
JEEZ, I'M THIRSTY!
MARI-CHAN, WANNA GRAB A DRINK BEFORE HEAD-ING HOME?
HAIR SPANK MENU
SURE!
BUT...
IF WE'RE GOING TO HAVE A DRINK...
WE MAY AS WELL GET SOMETHING TO EAT AS WELL.
YOU READ MY MIND!
KYA!
I DO FEEL LIGHTER...
BUT NOT JUST BECAUSE OF THE HAIRCUT...
ALL RIGHT, LET'S GO TO MC-DONALD'S!
YIKES.
MC-DONALD'S AGAIN?

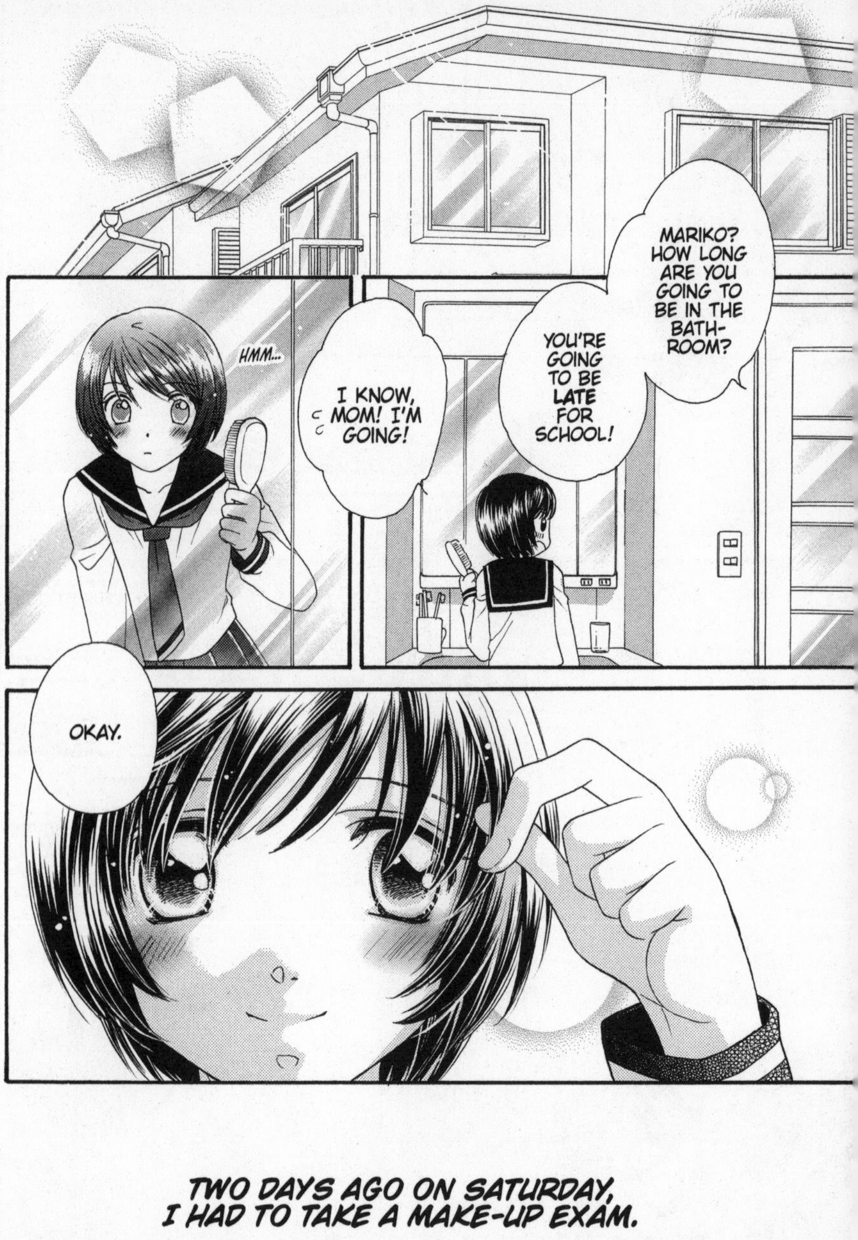
MARIKO? HOW LONG ARE YOU GOING TO BE IN THE BATH-ROOM?
YOU'RE GOING TO BE LATE FOR SCHOOL!
I KNOW, MOM! I'M GOING!
HMM...
OKAY.

*TWO DAYS AGO ON SATURDAY,
I HAD TO TAKE A MAKE-UP EXAM.*

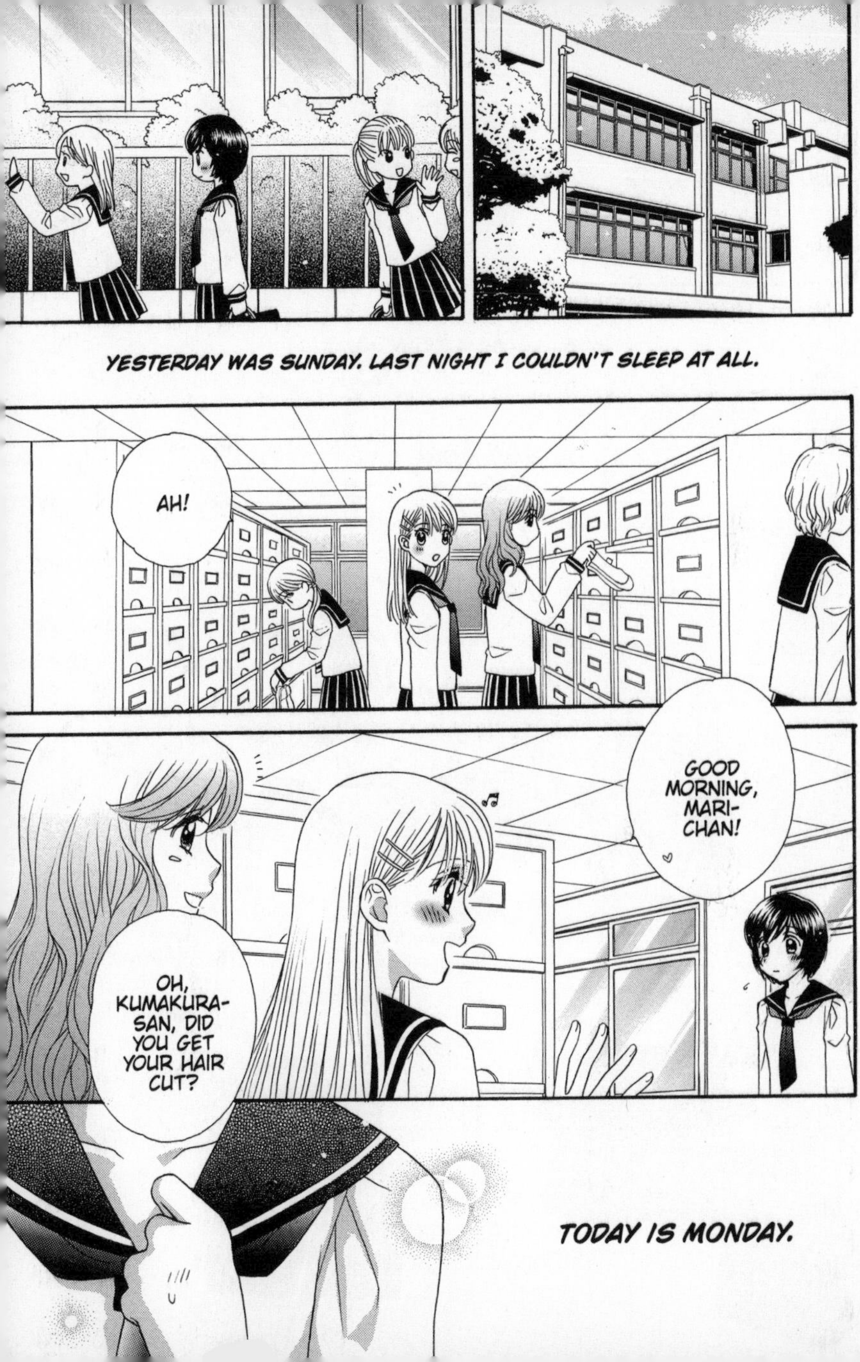
YESTERDAY WAS SUNDAY. LAST NIGHT I COULDN'T SLEEP AT ALL.
AH!
GOOD MORNING, MARI-CHAN!
OH, KUMAKURA-SAN, DID YOU GET YOUR HAIR CUT?
TODAY IS MONDAY.

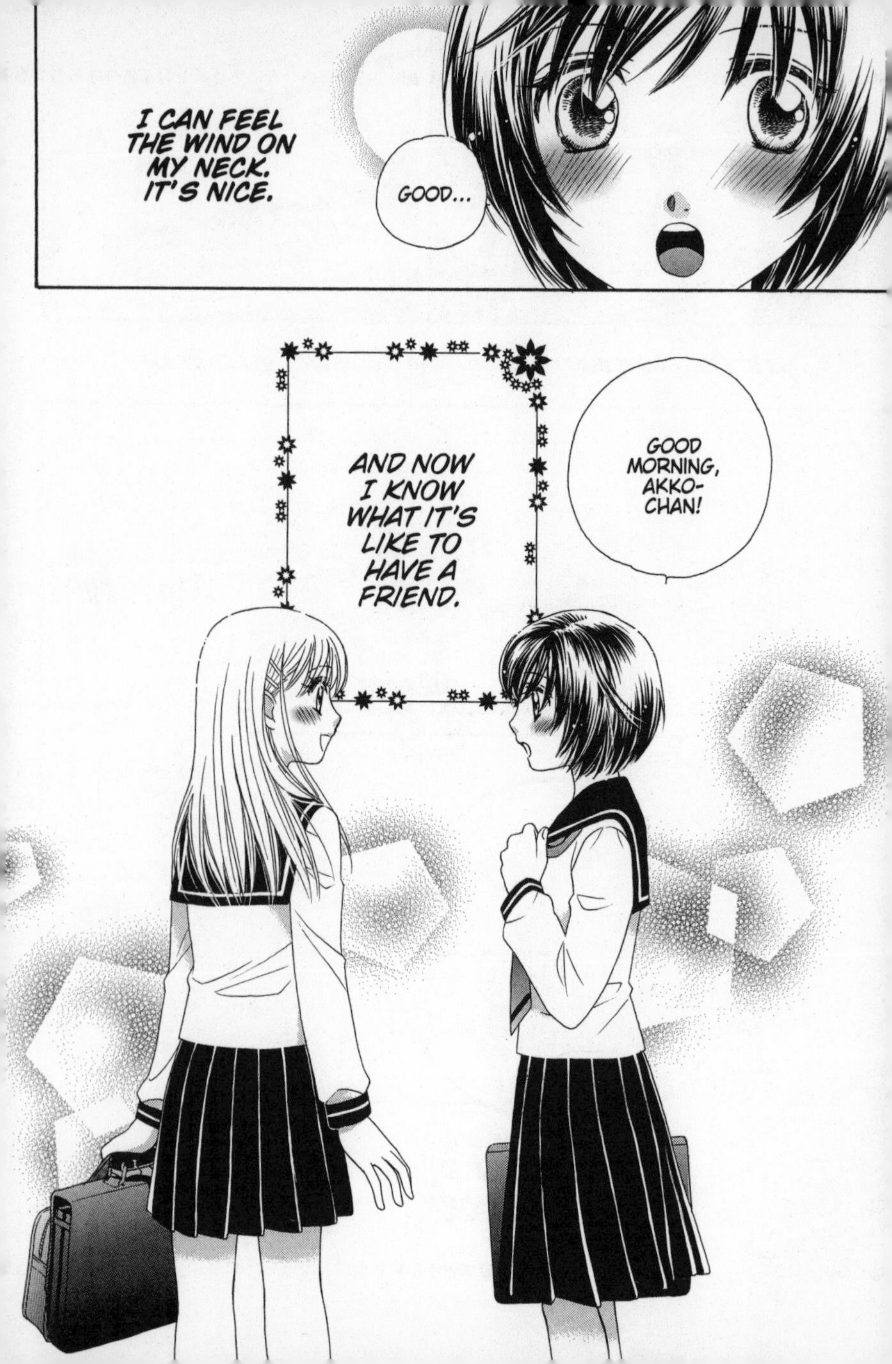
GOOD...
I CAN FEEL THE WIND ON MY NECK. IT'S NICE.
GOOD MORNING, AKKO-CHAN!
AND NOW I KNOW WHAT IT'S LIKE TO HAVE A FRIEND.

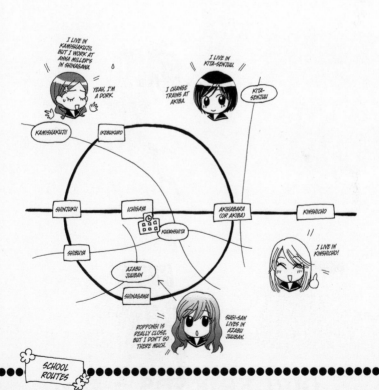

I LIVE IN KAMISHAKUJII, BUT I WORK AT ANNA MILLER'S IN SHINAGAWA.
YEAH, I'M A DORK.
I LIVE IN KITA-SENJUU.
I CHANGE TRAINS AT AKIBA.
KITA-SENJUU
KAMISHAKUJII
IKEBUKURO
SHINJUKU
ICHIGAYA
AKIHABARA (OR AKIBA)
KINSHICHO
KUDANSHITA
SHIBUYA
AZABU JUUBAN
SHINAGAWA
I LIVE IN KINSHICHO!
SUGI-SAN LIVES IN AZABU JUUBAN.
ROPPONGI IS REALLY CLOSE, BUT I DON'T GO THERE MUCH.

SCHOOL ROUTES

GIRL FRIENDS－ガールフレンズ－

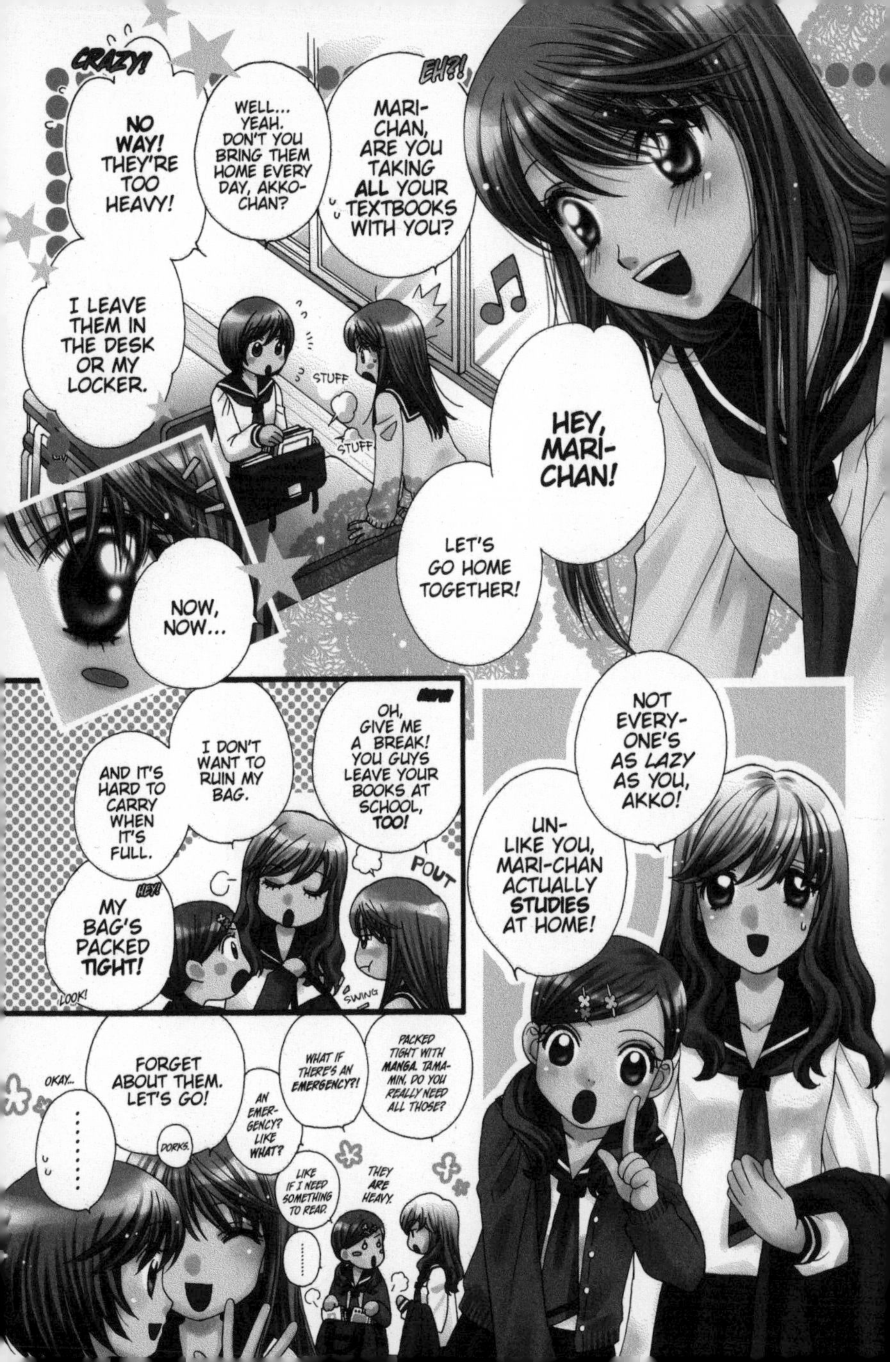
HEY, MARI-CHAN!
LET'S GO HOME TOGETHER!
EH?!
MARI-CHAN, ARE YOU TAKING ALL YOUR TEXTBOOKS WITH YOU?
WELL... YEAH. DON'T YOU BRING THEM HOME EVERY DAY, AKKO-CHAN?
CRAZY!
NO WAY! THEY'RE TOO HEAVY!
I LEAVE THEM IN THE DESK OR MY LOCKER.
STUFF
STUFF
NOW, NOW...
NOT EVERY-ONE'S AS LAZY AS YOU, AKKO!
UN-LIKE YOU, MARI-CHAN ACTUALLY STUDIES AT HOME!
OH, GIVE ME A BREAK! YOU GUYS LEAVE YOUR BOOKS AT SCHOOL, TOO!
I DON'T WANT TO RUIN MY BAG.
AND IT'S HARD TO CARRY WHEN IT'S FULL.
POUT
HEY!
MY BAG'S PACKED TIGHT!
LOOK!
SWING
PACKED TIGHT WITH MANGA. TAMA-MIN, DO YOU REALLY NEED ALL THOSE?
WHAT IF THERE'S AN EMERGENCY?!
AN EMER-GENCY? LIKE WHAT?
LIKE IF I NEED SOMETHING TO READ.
THEY ARE HEAVY.
......
FORGET ABOUT THEM. LET'S GO!
DORKS.
OKAY...
......

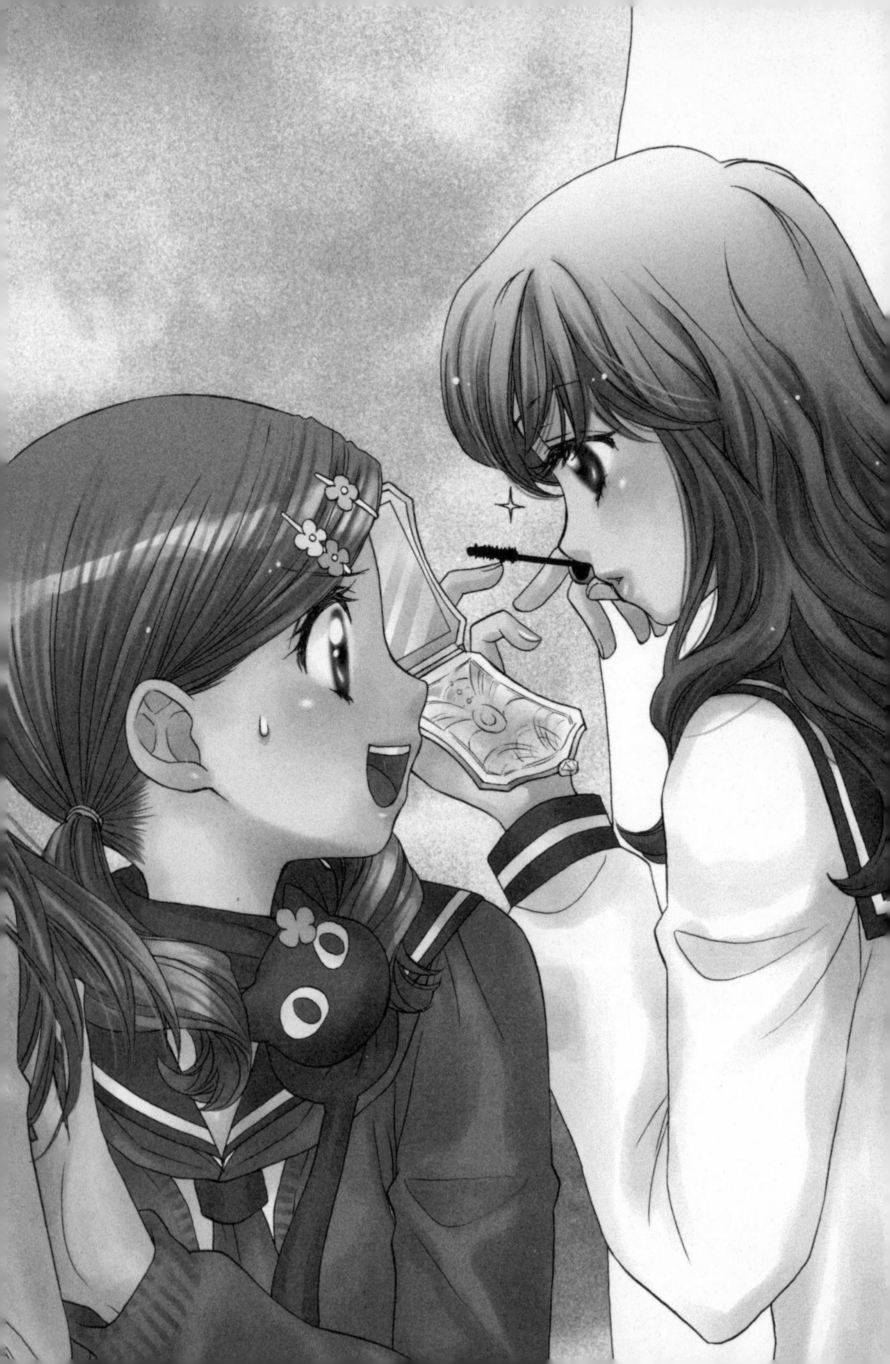

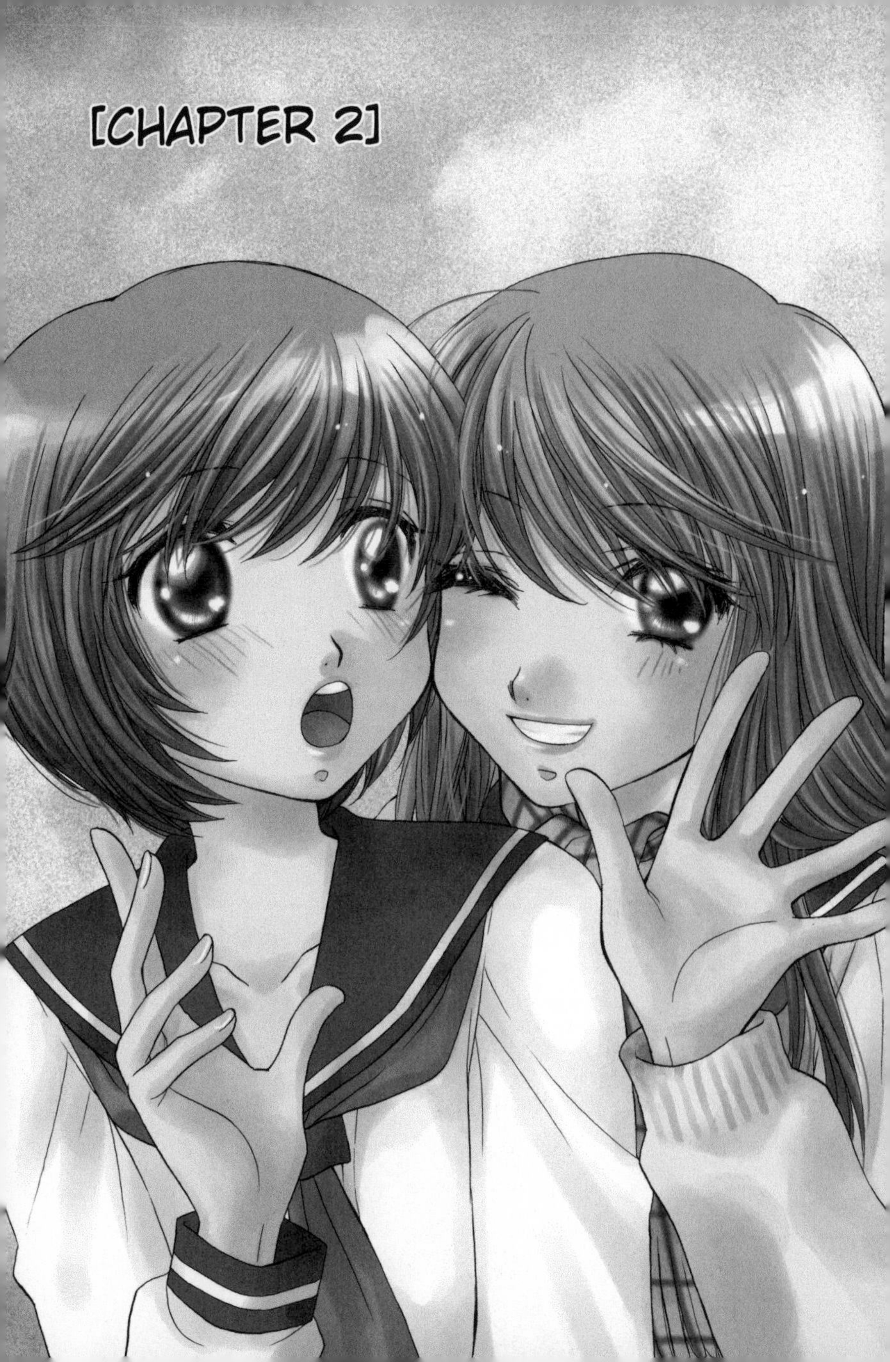
[CHAPTER 2]

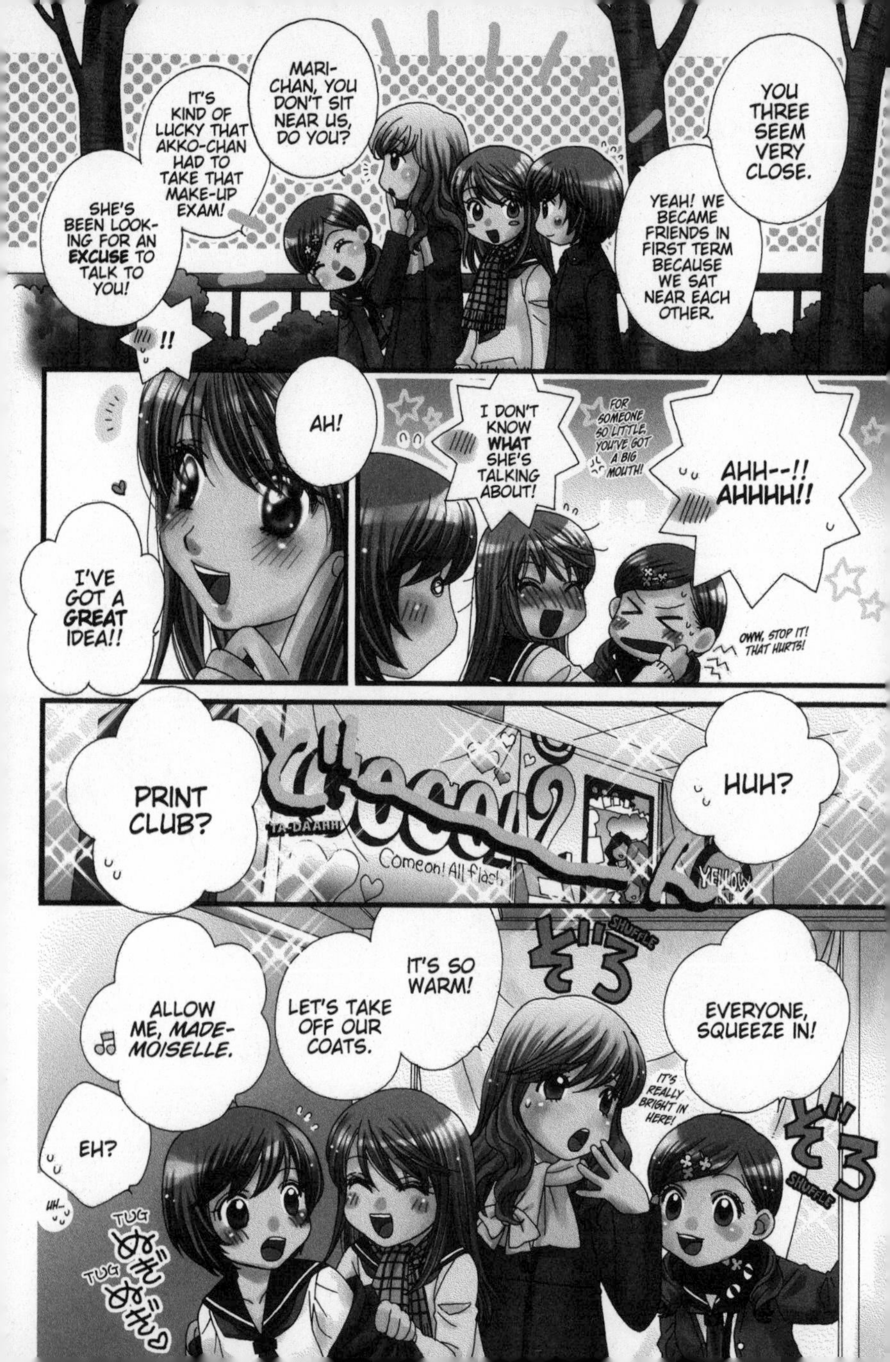

YOU THREE SEEM VERY CLOSE.
YEAH! WE BECAME FRIENDS IN FIRST TERM BECAUSE WE SAT NEAR EACH OTHER.
MARI-CHAN, YOU DON'T SIT NEAR US, DO YOU?
IT'S KIND OF LUCKY THAT AKKO-CHAN HAD TO TAKE THAT MAKE-UP EXAM!
SHE'S BEEN LOOKING FOR AN EXCUSE TO TALK TO YOU!
!!
AHH--!! AHHHH!!
FOR SOMEONE SO LITTLE, YOU'VE GOT A BIG MOUTH!
I DON'T KNOW WHAT SHE'S TALKING ABOUT!
OWW, STOP IT! THAT HURTS!
AH!
I'VE GOT A GREAT IDEA!!
HUH?
YELLOW
Comeon! All flash
TA-DAAHH
PRINT CLUB?
EVERYONE, SQUEEZE IN!
SHUFFLE
IT'S REALLY BRIGHT IN HERE!
SHUFFLE
IT'S SO WARM!
LET'S TAKE OFF OUR COATS.
ALLOW ME, MADE-MOISELLE.
EH?
UH...
TUG TUG

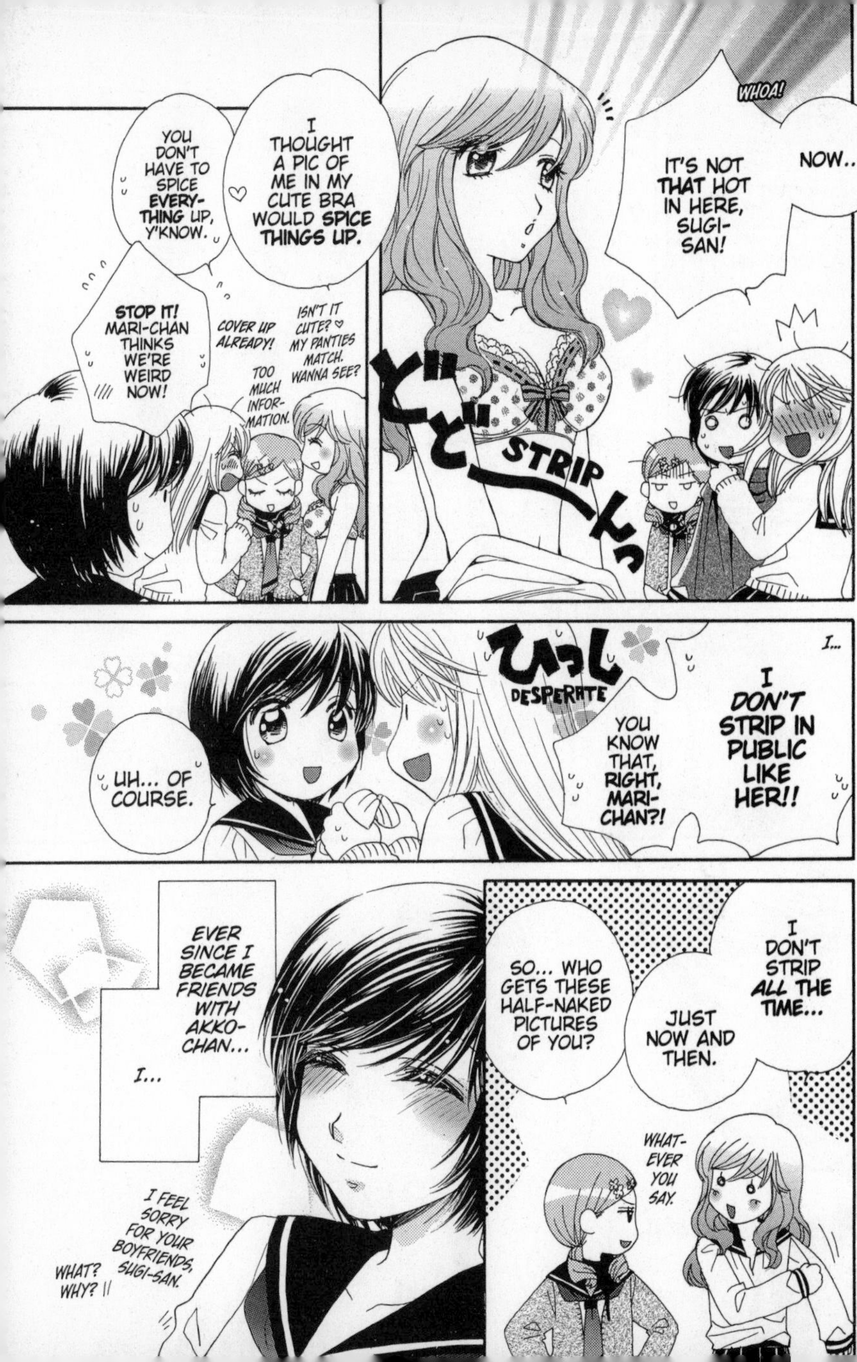
WHOA!
NOW...
IT'S NOT THAT HOT IN HERE, SUGI-SAN!
I THOUGHT A PIC OF ME IN MY CUTE BRA WOULD SPICE THINGS UP.
STRIP
YOU DON'T HAVE TO SPICE EVERYTHING UP, Y'KNOW.
ISN'T IT CUTE? MY PANTIES MATCH. WANNA SEE?
COVER UP ALREADY!
TOO MUCH INFORMATION.
STOP IT! MARI-CHAN THINKS WE'RE WEIRD NOW!
I...
I DON'T STRIP IN PUBLIC LIKE HER!!
YOU KNOW THAT, RIGHT, MARI-CHAN?!
DESPERATE
UH... OF COURSE.
I DON'T STRIP ALL THE TIME...
JUST NOW AND THEN.
SO... WHO GETS THESE HALF-NAKED PICTURES OF YOU?
WHATEVER YOU SAY.
EVER SINCE I BECAME FRIENDS WITH AKKO-CHAN...
I...
I FEEL SORRY FOR YOUR BOYFRIENDS, SUGI-SAN.
WHAT? WHY?

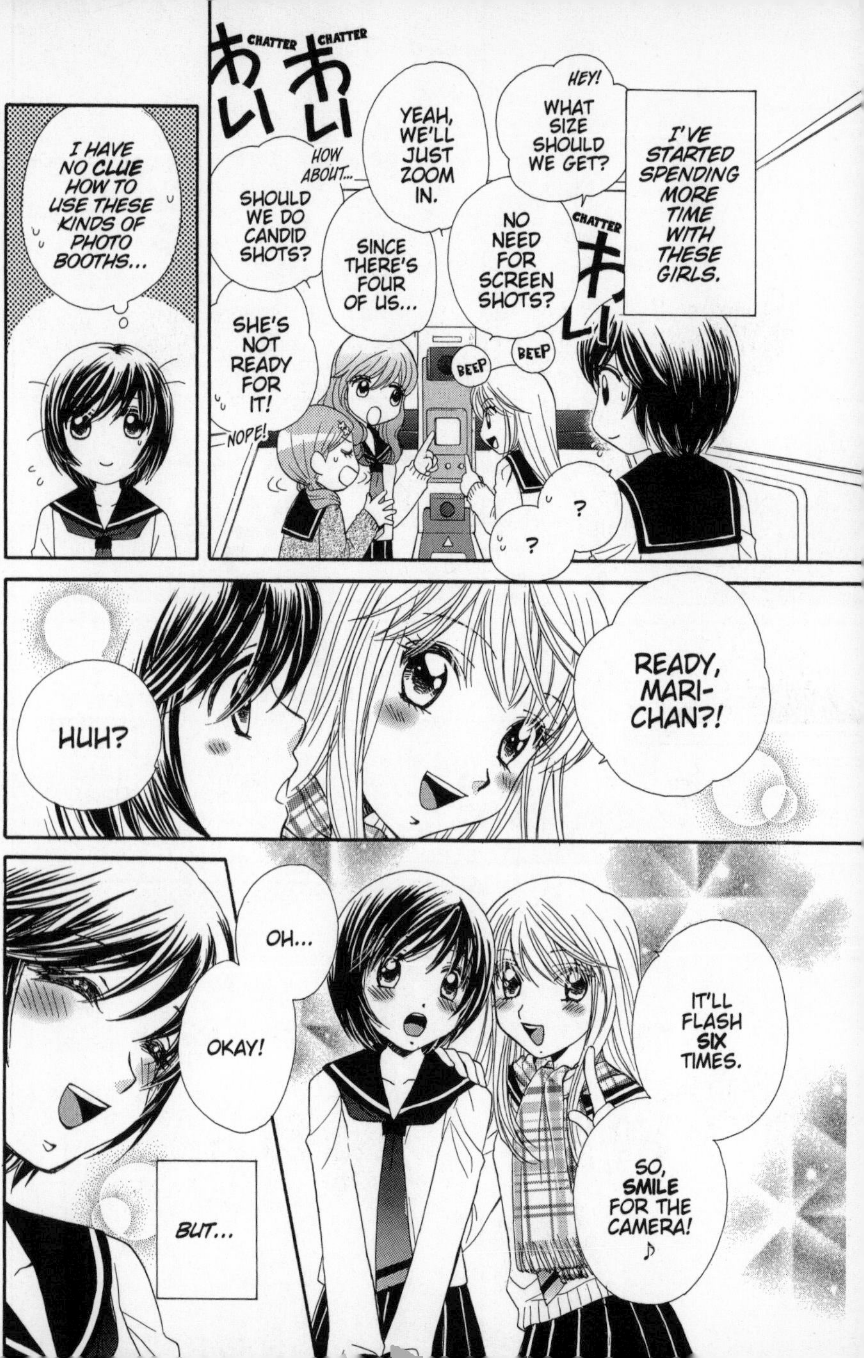
I'VE STARTED SPENDING MORE TIME WITH THESE GIRLS.
HEY!
WHAT SIZE SHOULD WE GET?
CHATTER
おい
NO NEED FOR SCREEN SHOTS?
YEAH, WE'LL JUST ZOOM IN.
CHATTER CHATTER
おいおい
HOW ABOUT...
SHOULD WE DO CANDID SHOTS?
SINCE THERE'S FOUR OF US...
BEEP
BEEP
SHE'S NOT READY FOR IT!
NOPE!
?
?
I HAVE NO CLUE HOW TO USE THESE KINDS OF PHOTO BOOTHS...
READY, MARI-CHAN?!
HUH?
IT'LL FLASH SIX TIMES.
SO, SMILE FOR THE CAMERA! ♪
OH...
OKAY!
BUT...

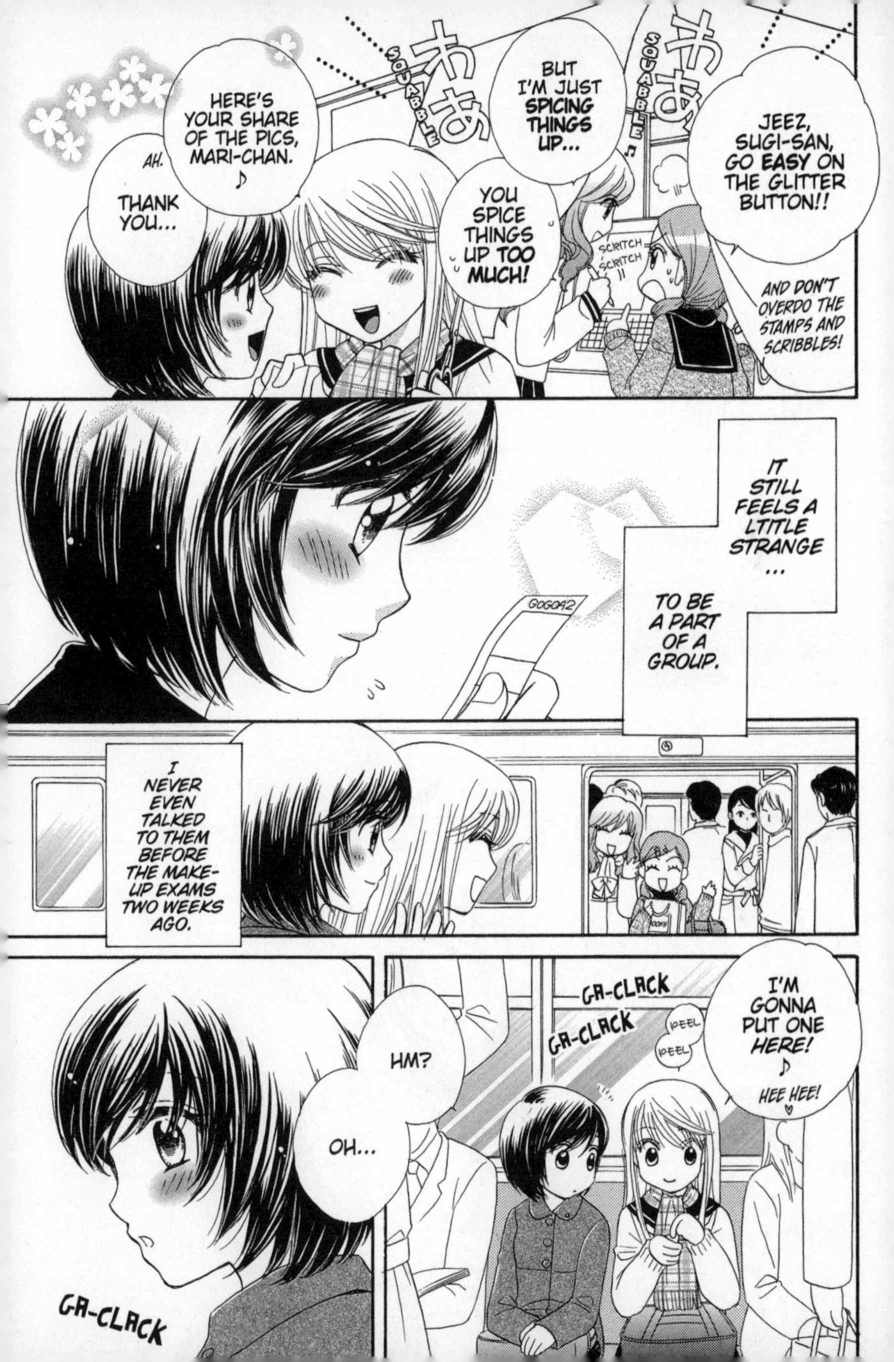
JEEZ, SUGI-SAN, GO EASY ON THE GLITTER BUTTON!!
AND DON'T OVERDO THE STAMPS AND SCRIBBLES!
SQUABBLE
SQUABBLE
BUT I'M JUST SPICING THINGS UP... ♪
YOU SPICE THINGS UP TOO MUCH!
SCRITCH SCRITCH
HERE'S YOUR SHARE OF THE PICS, MARI-CHAN. ♪
AH. THANK YOU...
IT STILL FEELS A LTITLE STRANGE ...
TO BE A PART OF A GROUP.
I NEVER EVEN TALKED TO THEM BEFORE THE MAKE-UP EXAMS TWO WEEKS AGO.
I'M GONNA PUT ONE HERE! ♪
HEE HEE! ♥
PEEL
PEEL
GA-CLACK
GA-CLACK
HM?
OH...
GA-CLACK

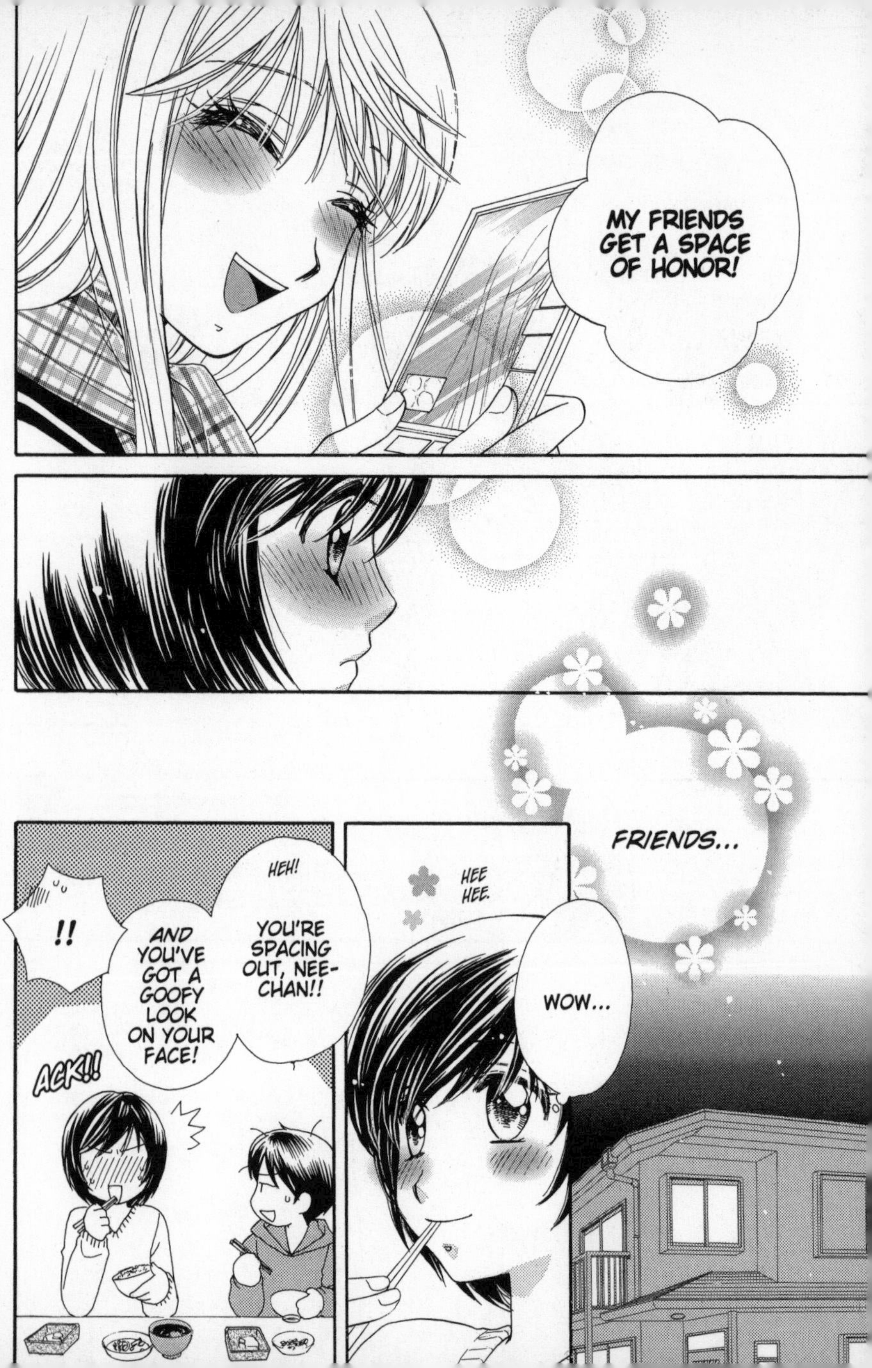
MY FRIENDS GET A SPACE OF HONOR!
FRIENDS...
HEE HEE.
WOW...
HEH!
YOU'RE SPACING OUT, NEE-CHAN!!
AND YOU'VE GOT A GOOFY LOOK ON YOUR FACE!
!!
ACK!!

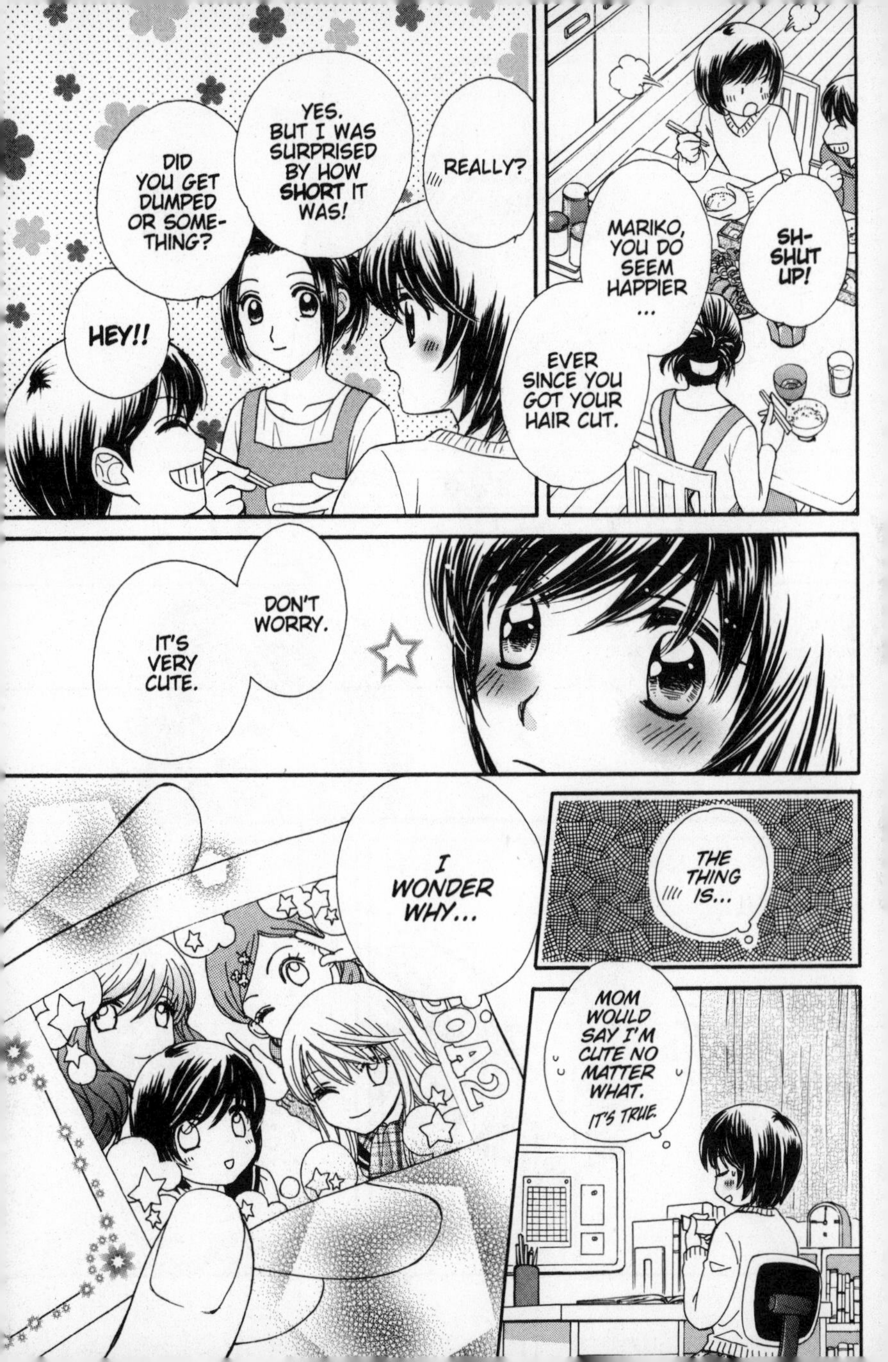
MARIKO, YOU DO SEEM HAPPIER ...
EVER SINCE YOU GOT YOUR HAIR CUT.
SH-SHUT UP!
REALLY?
YES. BUT I WAS SURPRISED BY HOW SHORT IT WAS!
DID YOU GET DUMPED OR SOME-THING?
HEY!!
DON'T WORRY.
IT'S VERY CUTE.
THE THING IS...
MOM WOULD SAY I'M CUTE NO MATTER WHAT.
IT'S TRUE.
I WONDER WHY...

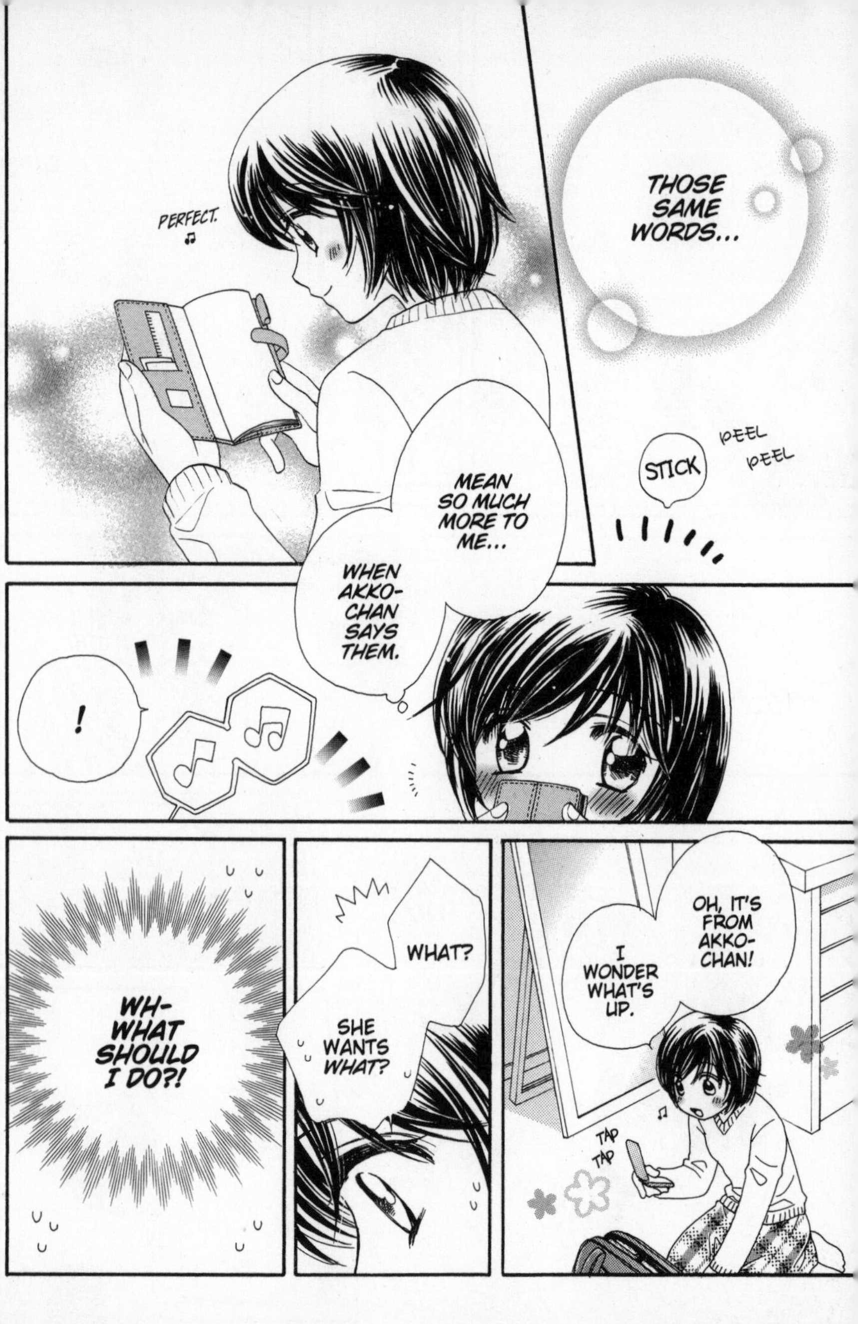
THOSE SAME WORDS...
MEAN SO MUCH MORE TO ME...
WHEN AKKO-CHAN SAYS THEM.
PERFECT. ♫
STICK
PEEL PEEL
!
OH, IT'S FROM AKKO-CHAN!
I WONDER WHAT'S UP.
TAP TAP
WHAT?
SHE WANTS WHAT?
WH-WHAT SHOULD I DO?!

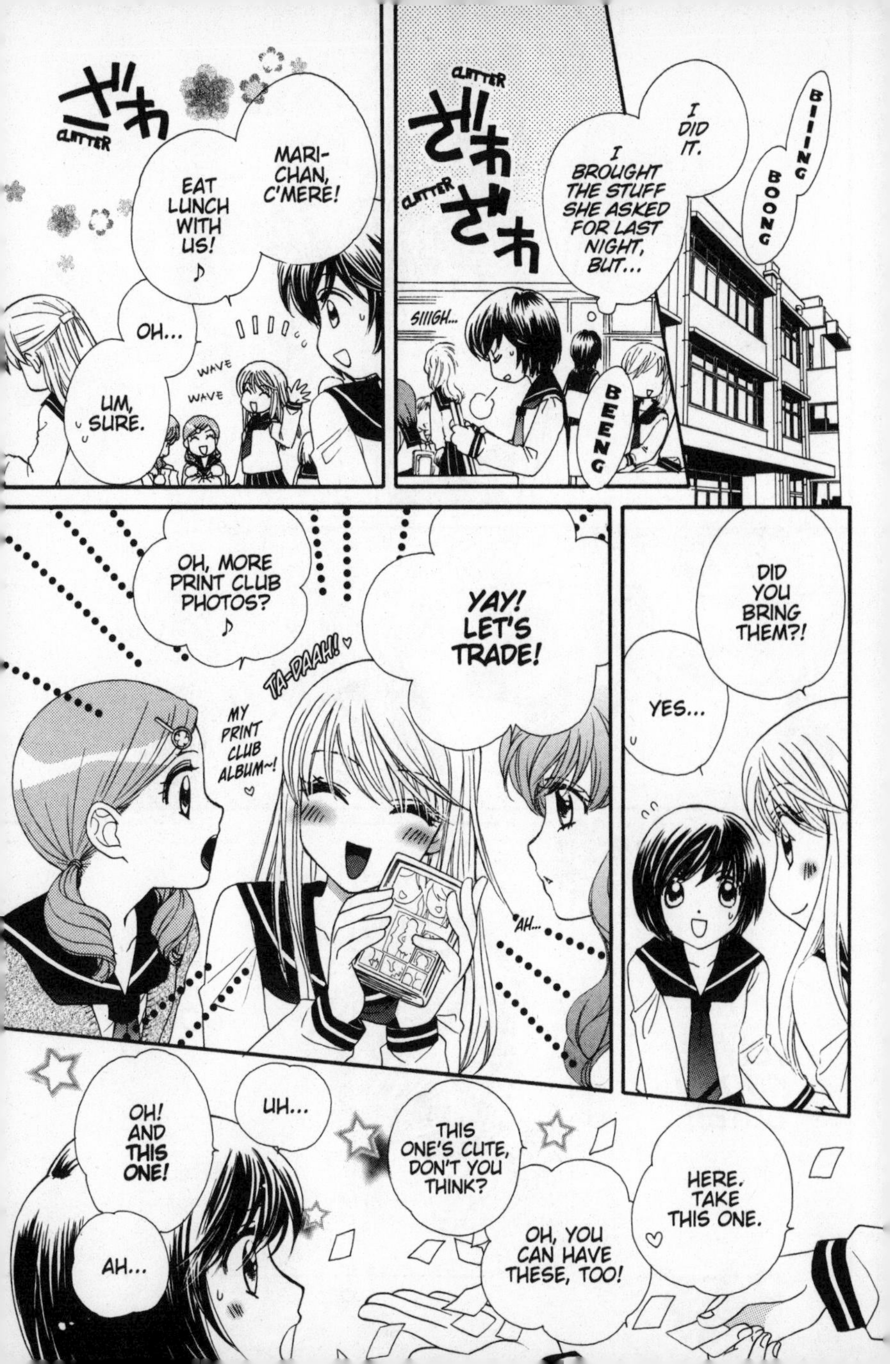
BIIING
BOONG
I DID IT.
I BROUGHT THE STUFF SHE ASKED FOR LAST NIGHT, BUT...
CLITTER
ざわ
CLITTER
ざわ
BEEENG
SIIIGH...
MARI-CHAN, C'MERE!
EAT LUNCH WITH US! ♪
ざわ
CLITTER
OH...
UM, SURE.
WAVE
WAVE
DID YOU BRING THEM?!
YES...
YAY! LET'S TRADE!
OH, MORE PRINT CLUB PHOTOS? ♪
TA-DAAH!
MY PRINT CLUB ALBUM~!
AH...
HERE. TAKE THIS ONE.
THIS ONE'S CUTE, DON'T YOU THINK?
OH, YOU CAN HAVE THESE, TOO!
UH...
OH! AND THIS ONE!
AH...

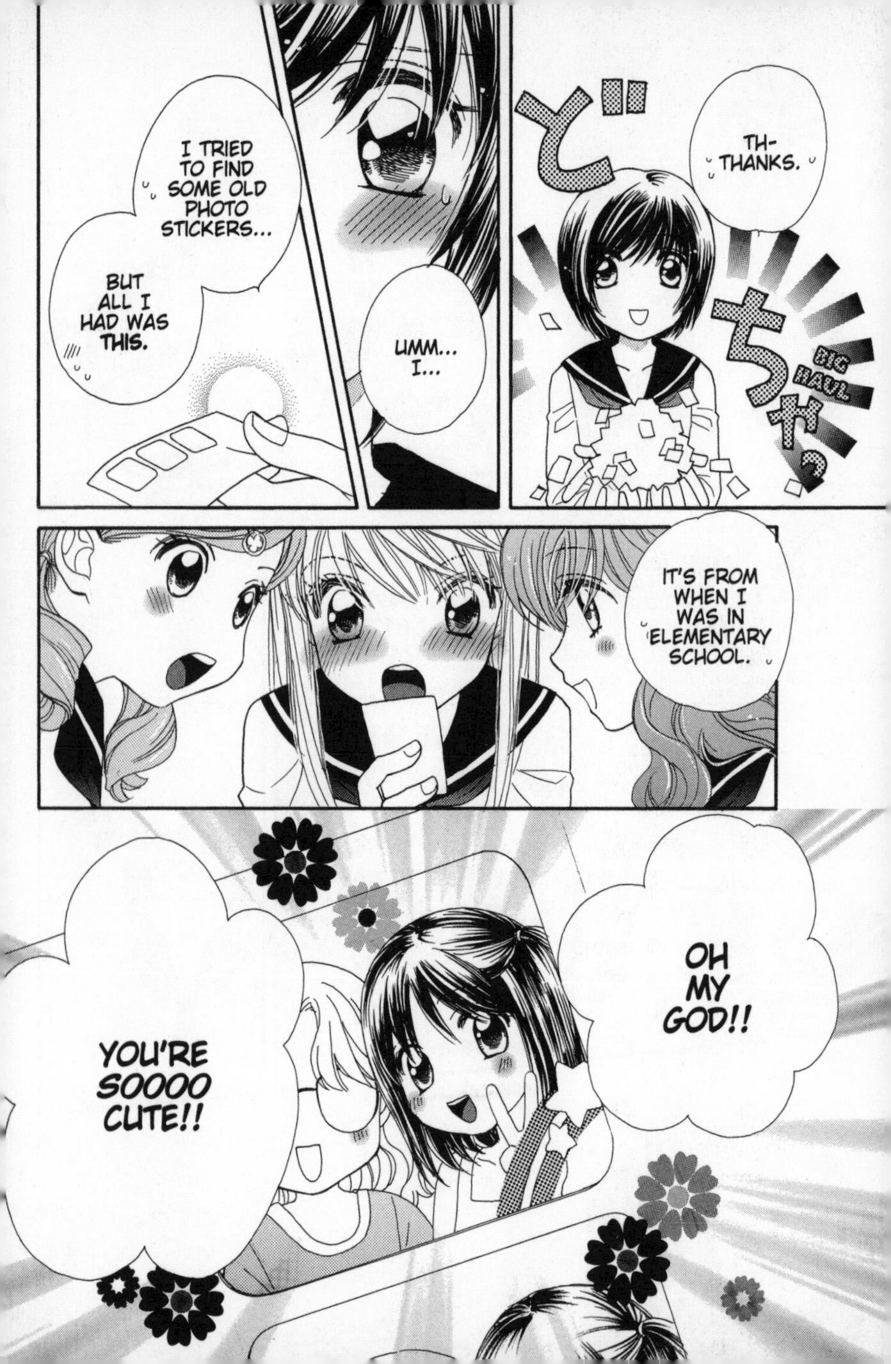
TH-THANKS.
BIG HAUL
UMM... I...
I TRIED TO FIND SOME OLD PHOTO STICKERS...
BUT ALL I HAD WAS THIS.
IT'S FROM WHEN I WAS IN ELEMENTARY SCHOOL.
OH MY GOD!!
YOU'RE SOOOO CUTE!!

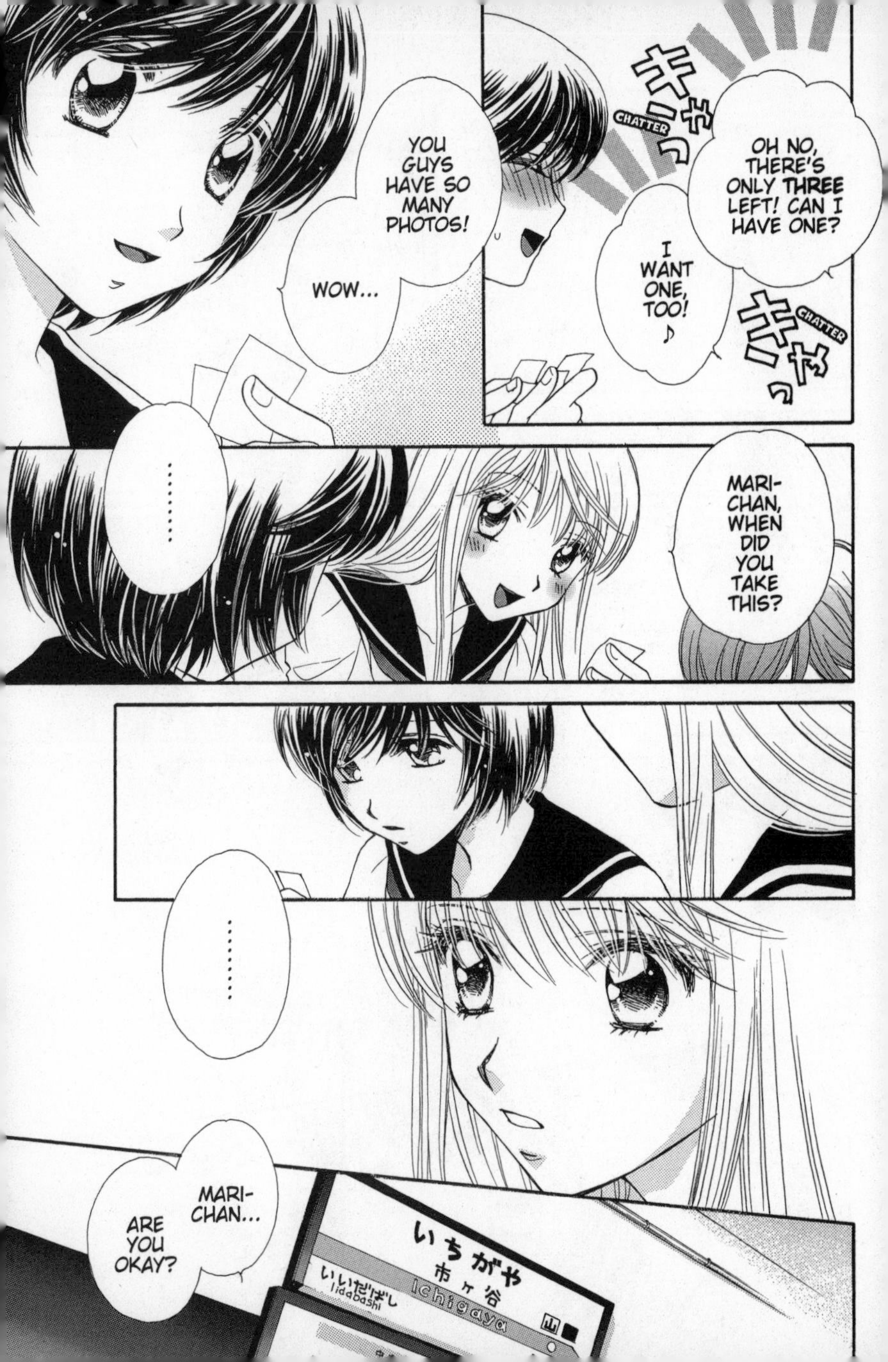
キャッ
CHATTER
OH NO, THERE'S ONLY THREE LEFT! CAN I HAVE ONE?
I WANT ONE, TOO! ♪
キャッ
CHATTER
YOU GUYS HAVE SO MANY PHOTOS!
WOW...
MARI-CHAN, WHEN DID YOU TAKE THIS?
......
......
MARI-CHAN...
ARE YOU OKAY?
いちがや
市ヶ谷
Ichigaya
いいだばし
Iidabashi

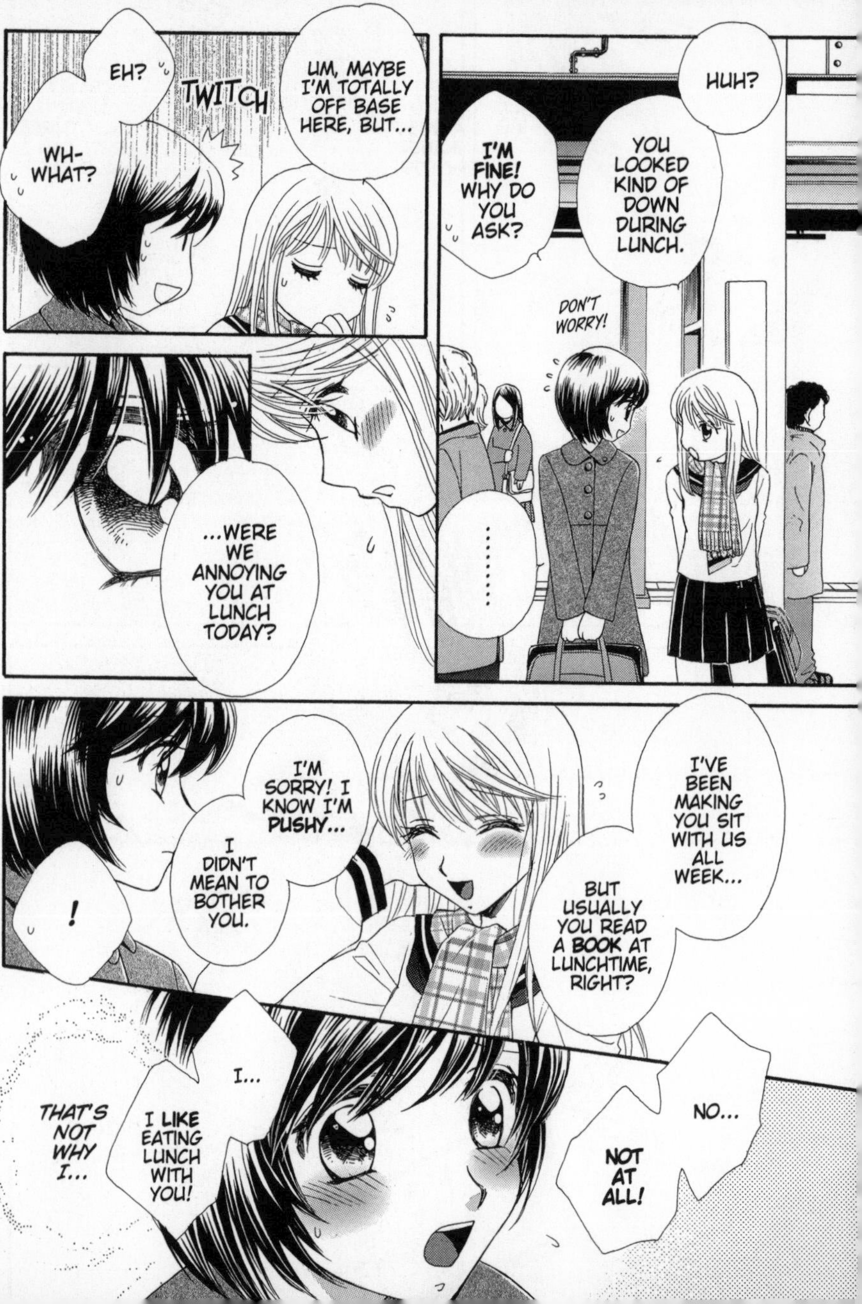
HUH?
YOU LOOKED KIND OF DOWN DURING LUNCH.
I'M FINE! WHY DO YOU ASK?
DON'T WORRY!
......
UM, MAYBE I'M TOTALLY OFF BASE HERE, BUT...
TWITCH
EH?
WH-WHAT?
...WERE WE ANNOYING YOU AT LUNCH TODAY?
I'VE BEEN MAKING YOU SIT WITH US ALL WEEK...
BUT USUALLY YOU READ A BOOK AT LUNCHTIME, RIGHT?
I'M SORRY! I KNOW I'M PUSHY...
I DIDN'T MEAN TO BOTHER YOU.
!
NO...
NOT AT ALL!
I...
I LIKE EATING LUNCH WITH YOU!
THAT'S NOT WHY I...

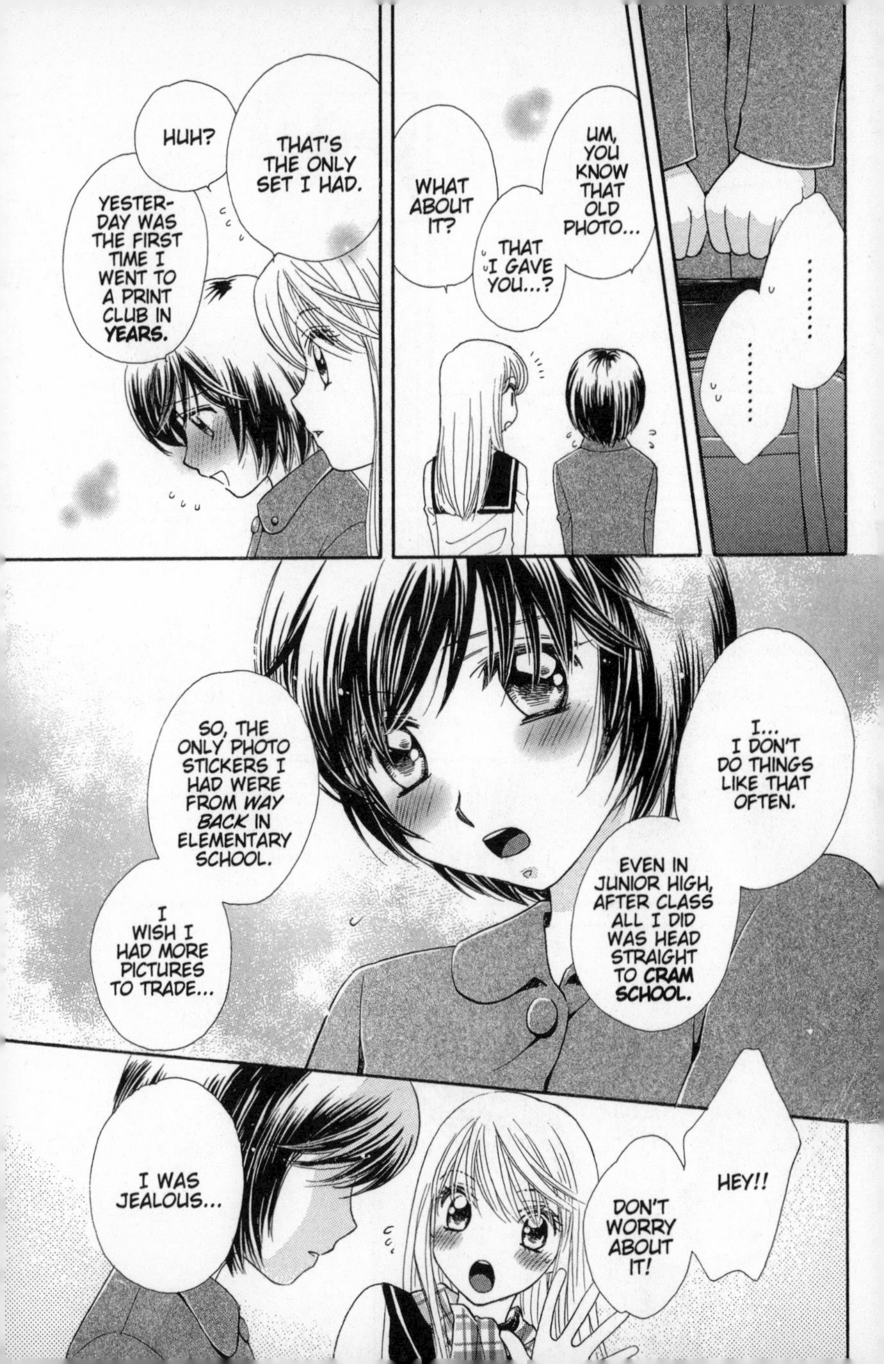
......
......
UM, YOU KNOW THAT OLD PHOTO...
THAT I GAVE YOU...?
WHAT ABOUT IT?
THAT'S THE ONLY SET I HAD.
HUH?
YESTER-DAY WAS THE FIRST TIME I WENT TO A PRINT CLUB IN **YEARS.**
I... I DON'T DO THINGS LIKE THAT OFTEN.
EVEN IN JUNIOR HIGH, AFTER CLASS ALL I DID WAS HEAD STRAIGHT TO **CRAM SCHOOL.**
SO, THE ONLY PHOTO STICKERS I HAD WERE FROM *WAY BACK* IN ELEMENTARY SCHOOL.
I WISH I HAD MORE PICTURES TO TRADE...
HEY!!
DON'T WORRY ABOUT IT!
I WAS JEALOUS...

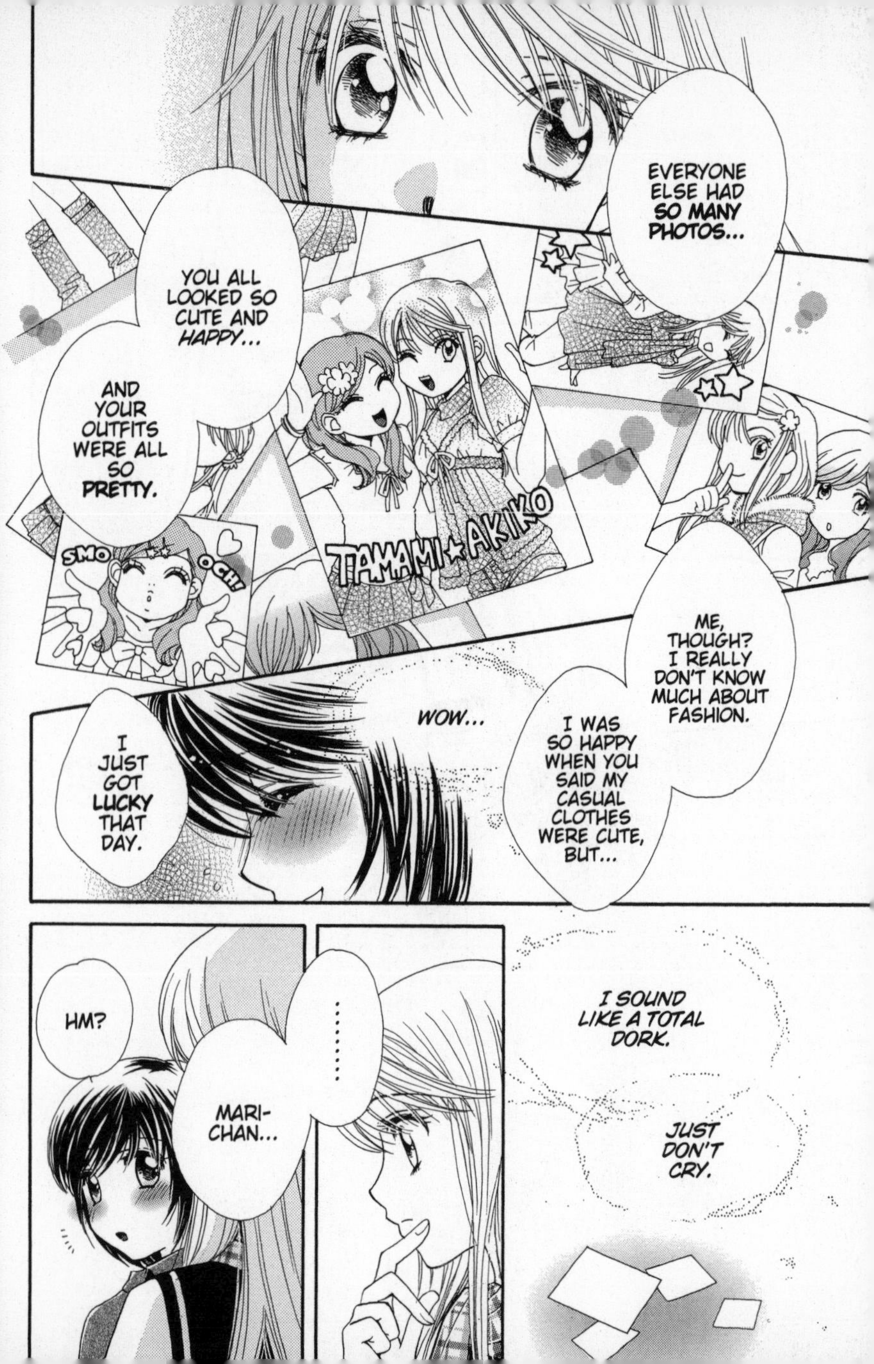
EVERYONE ELSE HAD SO MANY PHOTOS...
YOU ALL LOOKED SO CUTE AND HAPPY...
AND YOUR OUTFITS WERE ALL SO PRETTY.
TAMAMI★AKIKO
SMO OCH!
ME, THOUGH? I REALLY DON'T KNOW MUCH ABOUT FASHION.
I WAS SO HAPPY WHEN YOU SAID MY CASUAL CLOTHES WERE CUTE, BUT...
WOW...
I JUST GOT LUCKY THAT DAY.
I SOUND LIKE A TOTAL DORK.
JUST DON'T CRY.
......
MARI-CHAN...
HM?

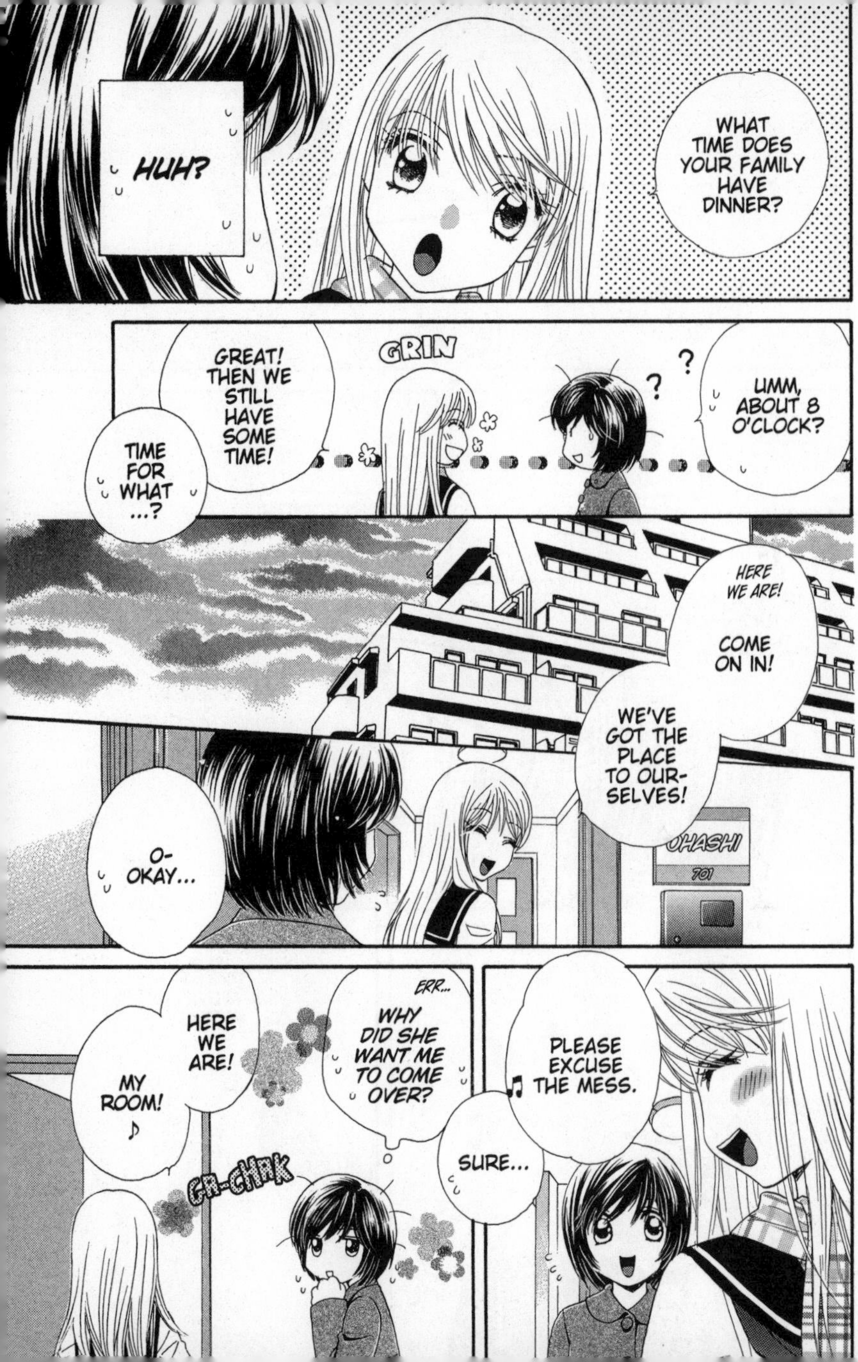
WHAT TIME DOES YOUR FAMILY HAVE DINNER?
HUH?
UMM, ABOUT 8 O'CLOCK?
? ?
GRIN
GREAT! THEN WE STILL HAVE SOME TIME!
TIME FOR WHAT ...?
HERE WE ARE!
COME ON IN!
WE'VE GOT THE PLACE TO OUR-SELVES!
OHASHI
701
O-OKAY...
PLEASE EXCUSE THE MESS. ♫
SURE...
ERR...
WHY DID SHE WANT ME TO COME OVER?
HERE WE ARE!
MY ROOM! ♪
GA-CHAK

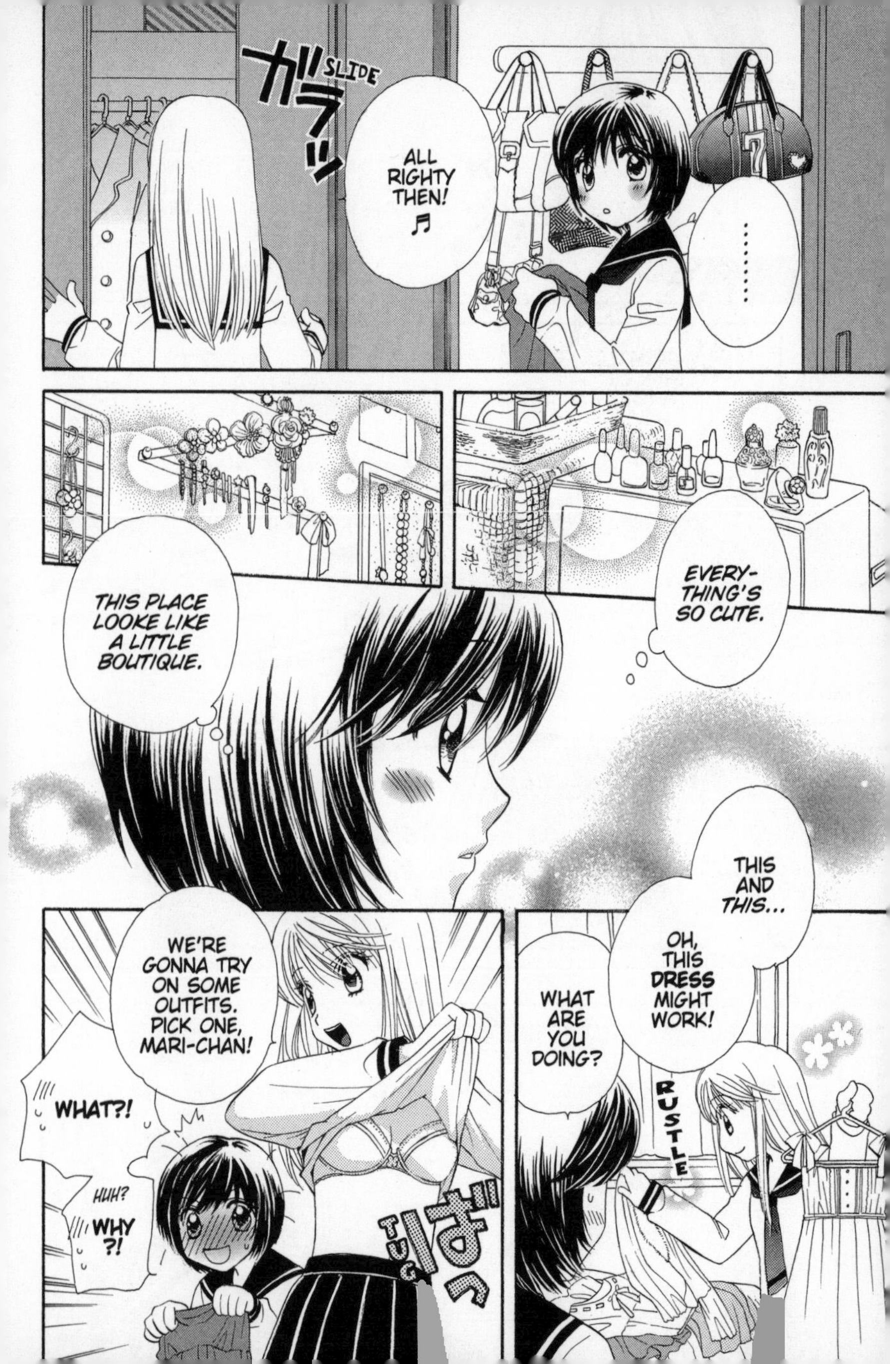

......
ALL RIGHTY THEN! ♪
SLIDE
EVERY-THING'S SO CUTE.
THIS PLACE LOOKE LIKE A LITTLE BOUTIQUE.
THIS AND THIS...
OH, THIS DRESS MIGHT WORK!
RUSTLE
WHAT ARE YOU DOING?
WE'RE GONNA TRY ON SOME OUTFITS. PICK ONE, MARI-CHAN!
WHAT?!
TUG
HUH? WHY?!

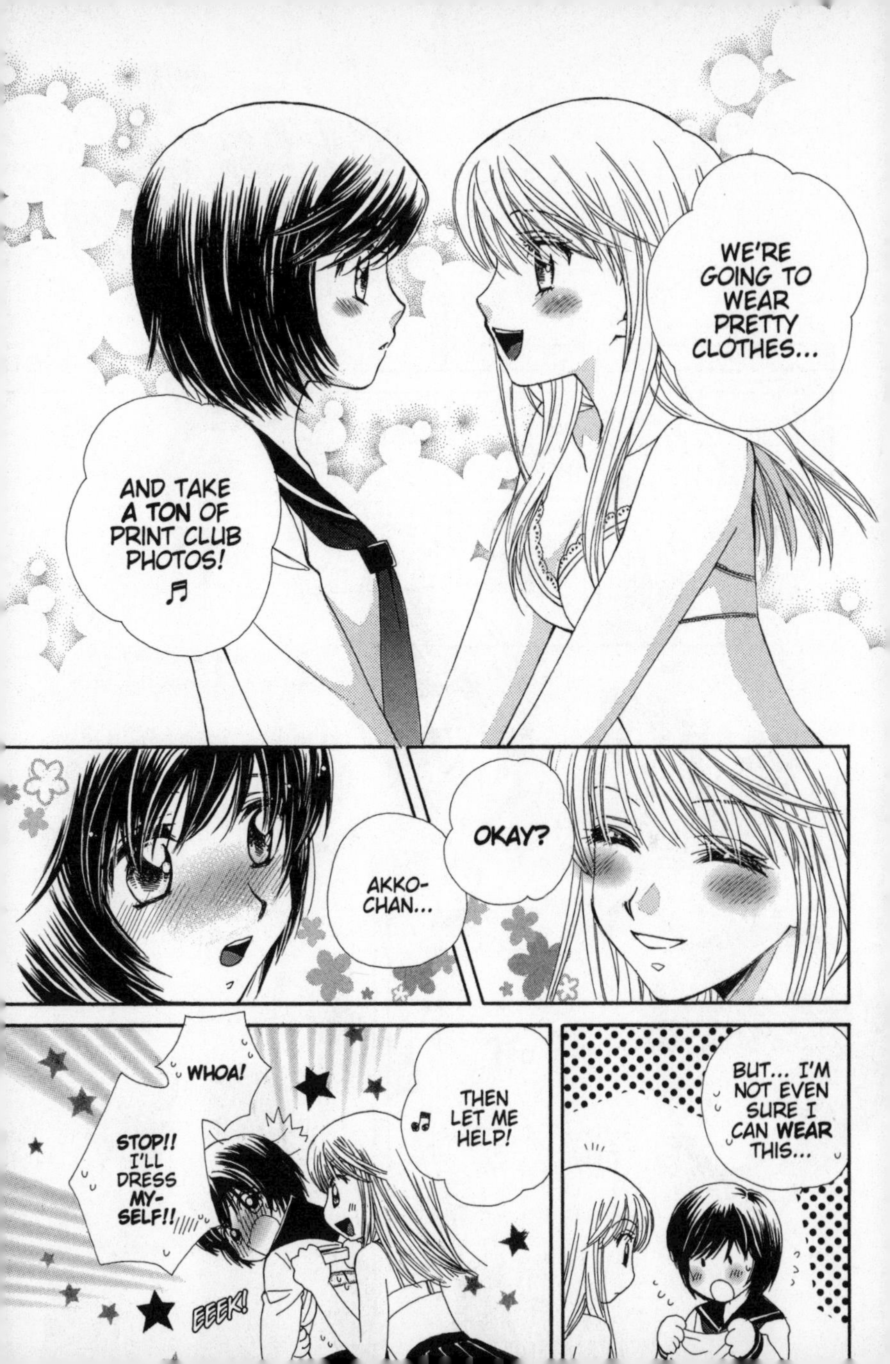
WE'RE GOING TO WEAR PRETTY CLOTHES...
AND TAKE A TON OF PRINT CLUB PHOTOS! ♬
OKAY?
AKKO-CHAN...
BUT... I'M NOT EVEN SURE I CAN WEAR THIS...
THEN LET ME HELP! ♫
WHOA!
STOP!! I'LL DRESS MY-SELF!!
EEEK!

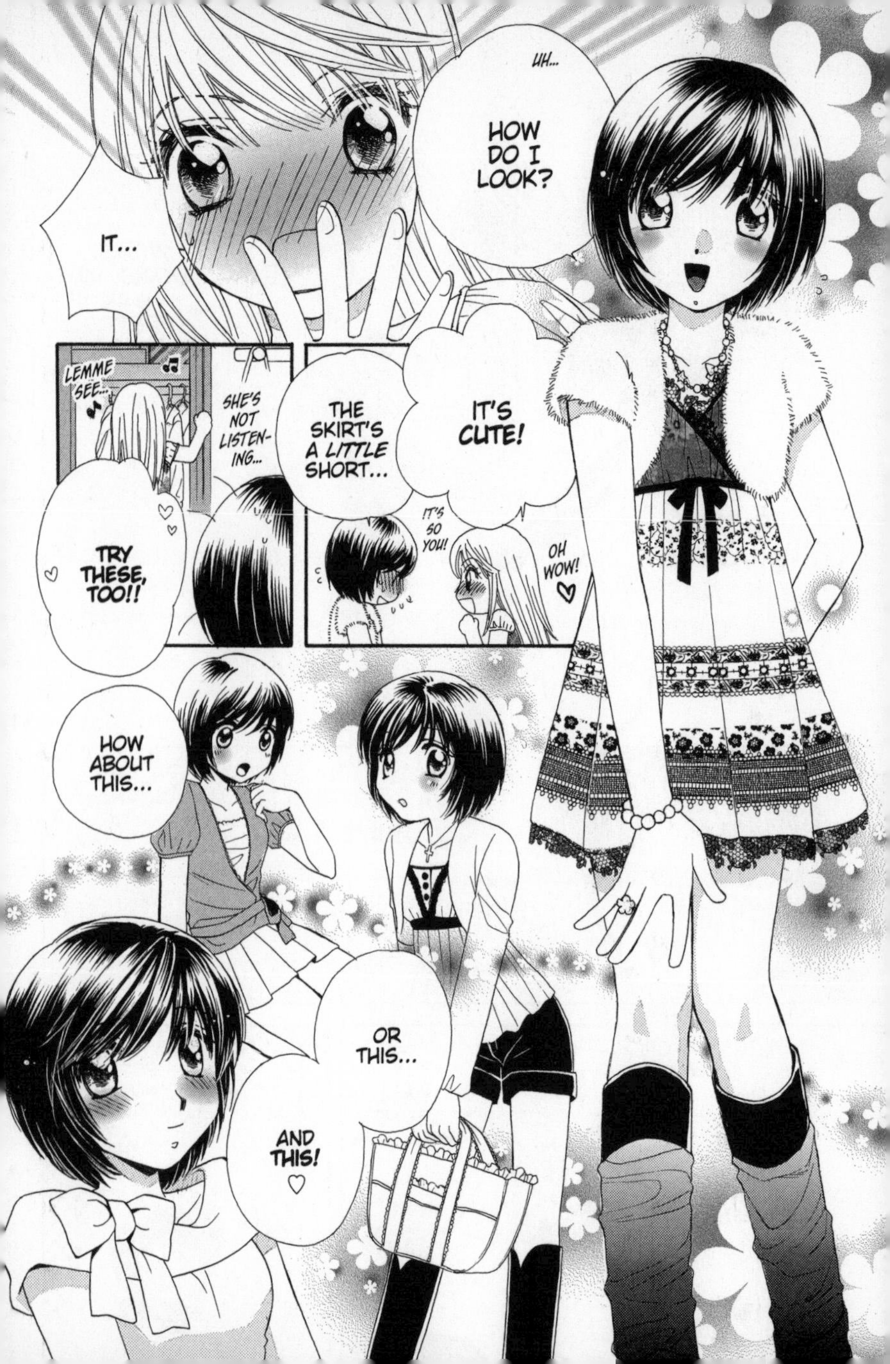
UH...
HOW DO I LOOK?
IT...
IT'S CUTE!
THE SKIRT'S A LITTLE SHORT...
OH WOW!
IT'S SO YOU!
SHE'S NOT LISTENING...
LEMME SEE...
TRY THESE, TOO!!
HOW ABOUT THIS...
OR THIS...
AND THIS!

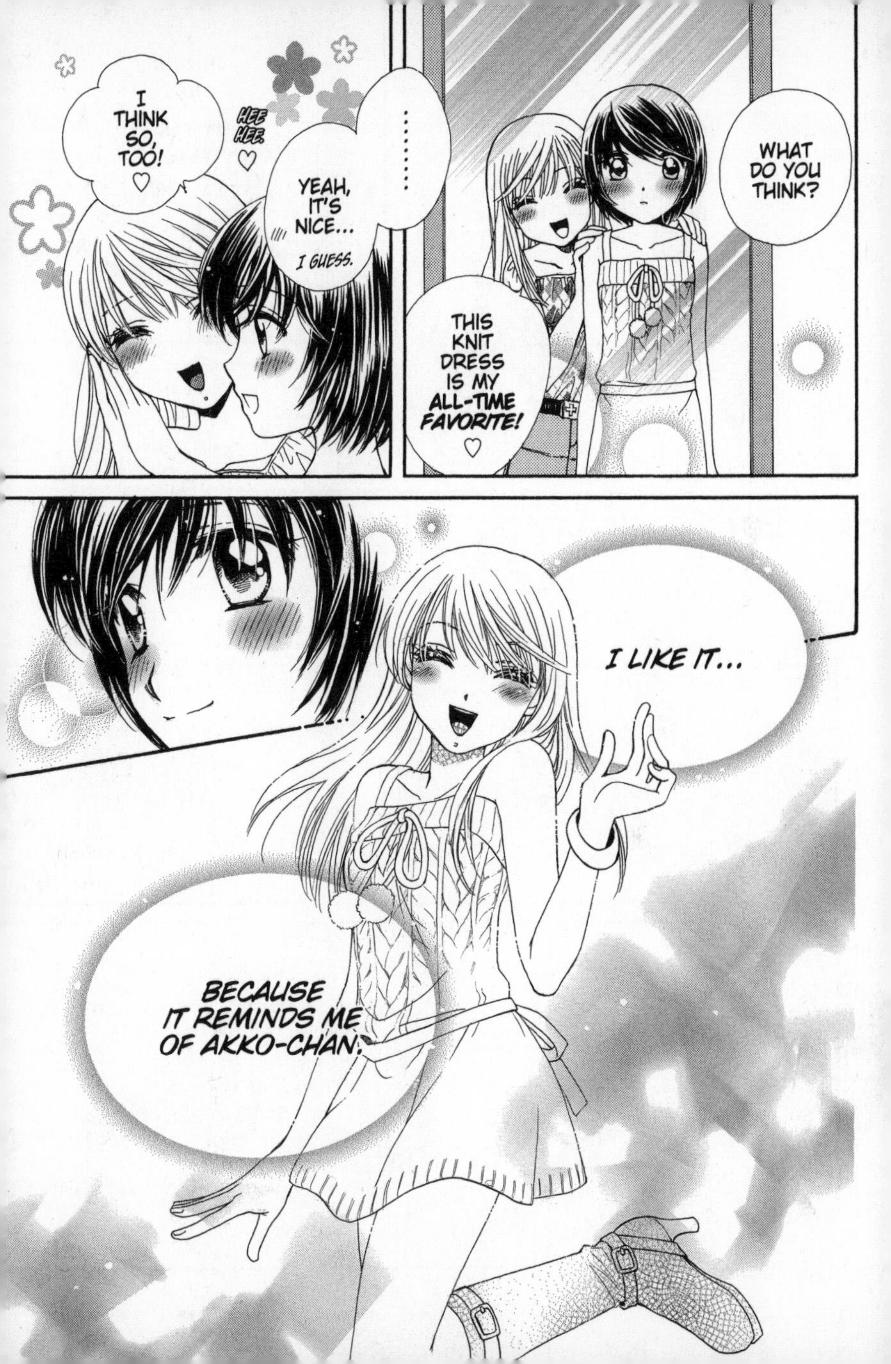
WHAT DO YOU THINK?
THIS KNIT DRESS IS MY ALL-TIME FAVORITE! ♡
......
YEAH, IT'S NICE... I GUESS.
HEE HEE. ♡
I THINK SO, TOO! ♡
I LIKE IT...
BECAUSE IT REMINDS ME OF AKKO-CHAN.

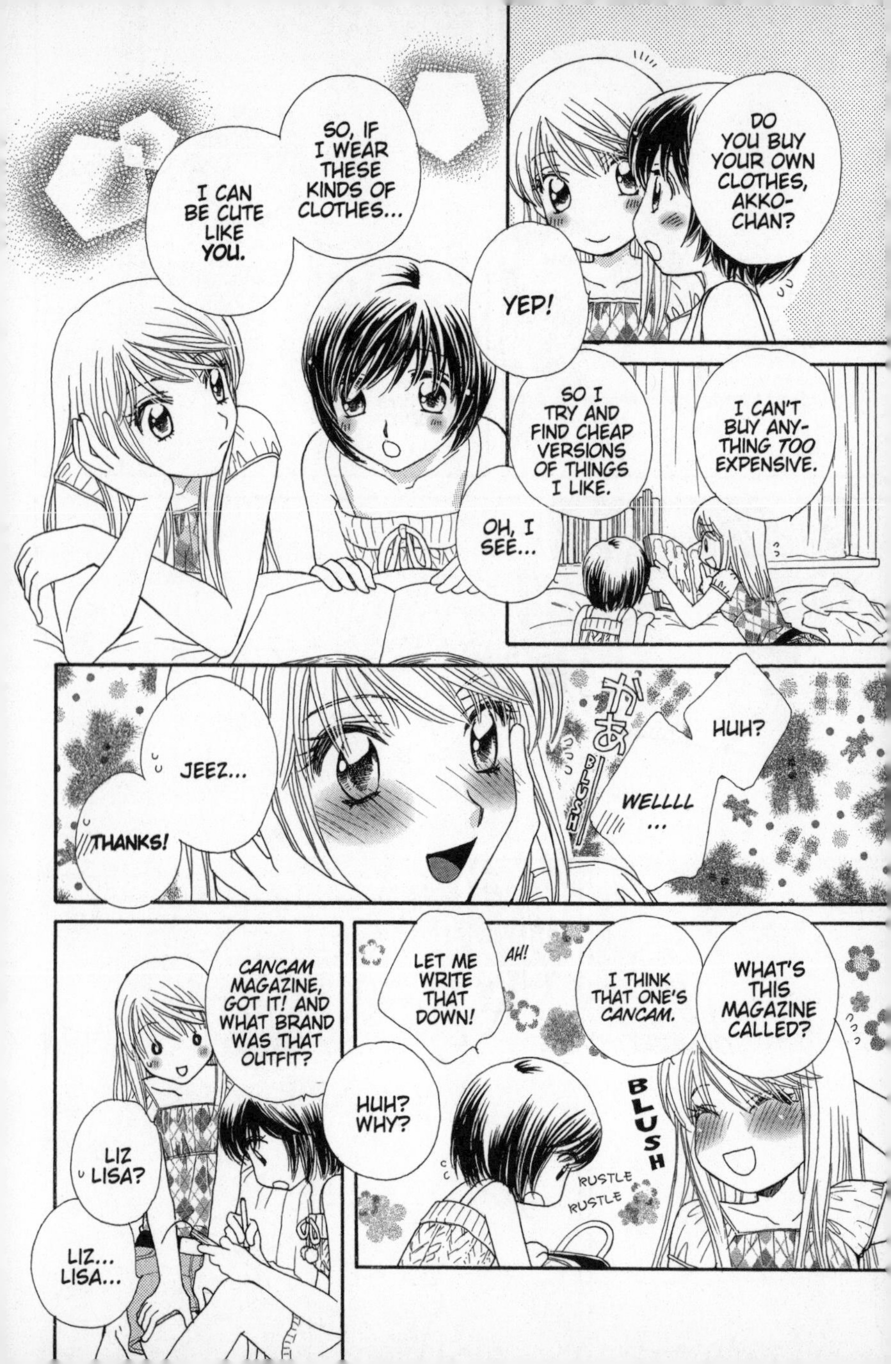
DO YOU BUY YOUR OWN CLOTHES, AKKO-CHAN?
YEP!
I CAN'T BUY ANY-THING TOO EXPENSIVE.
SO I TRY AND FIND CHEAP VERSIONS OF THINGS I LIKE.
OH, I SEE...
SO, IF I WEAR THESE KINDS OF CLOTHES...
I CAN BE CUTE LIKE YOU.
HUH?
WELLLL...
かあ
BLUSH
JEEZ...
THANKS!
WHAT'S THIS MAGAZINE CALLED?
I THINK THAT ONE'S CANCAM.
AH!
LET ME WRITE THAT DOWN!
BLUSH
HUH? WHY?
RUSTLE
RUSTLE
CANCAM MAGAZINE, GOT IT! AND WHAT BRAND WAS THAT OUTFIT?
LIZ LISA?
LIZ... LISA...

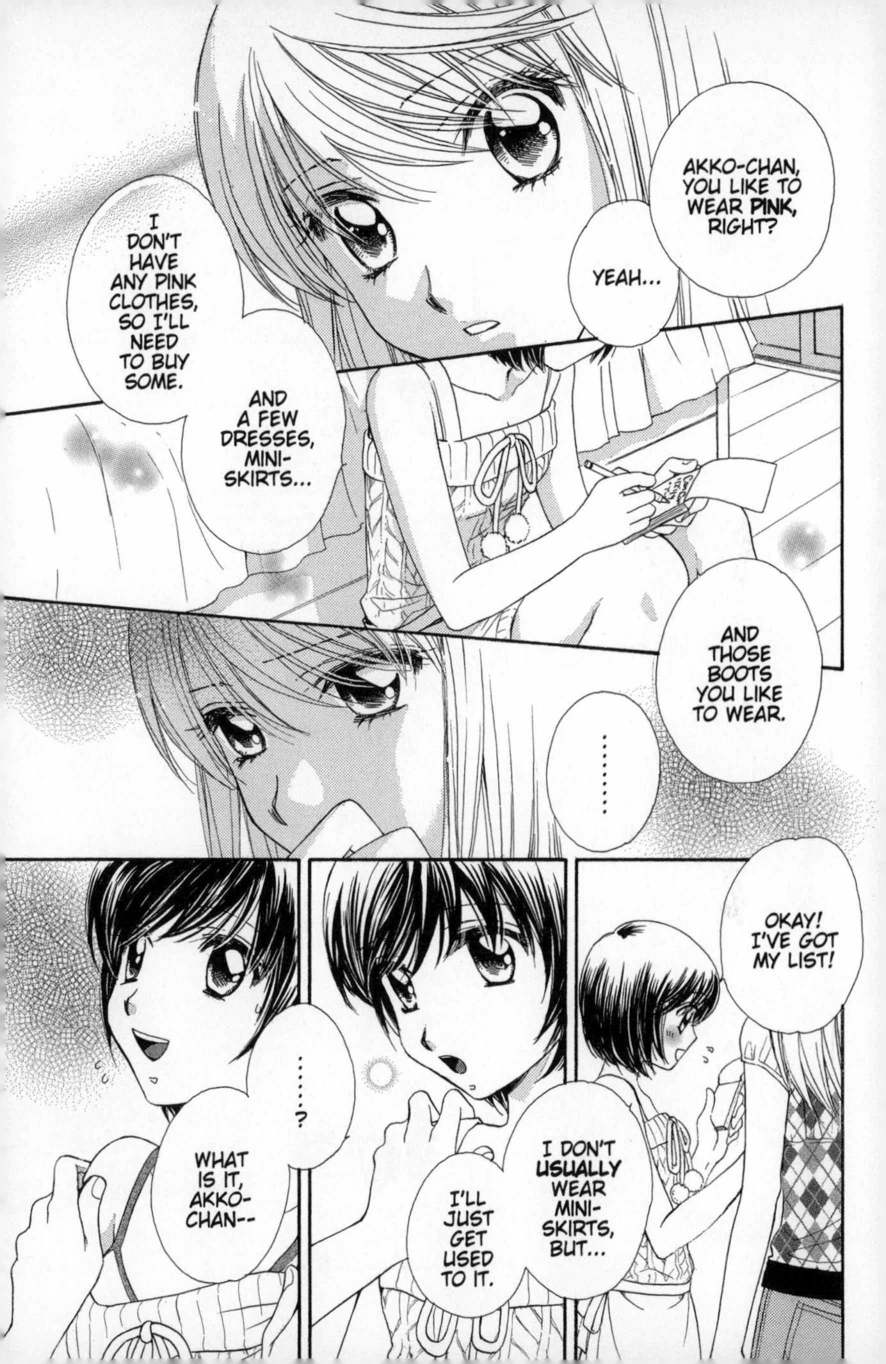
AKKO-CHAN, YOU LIKE TO WEAR **PINK**, RIGHT?
YEAH...
I DON'T HAVE ANY PINK CLOTHES, SO I'LL NEED TO BUY SOME.
AND A FEW DRESSES, MINI-SKIRTS...
AND THOSE BOOTS YOU LIKE TO WEAR.
......
OKAY! I'VE GOT MY LIST!
I DON'T **USUALLY** WEAR MINI-SKIRTS, BUT...
I'LL JUST GET USED TO IT.
......?
WHAT IS IT, AKKO-CHAN--

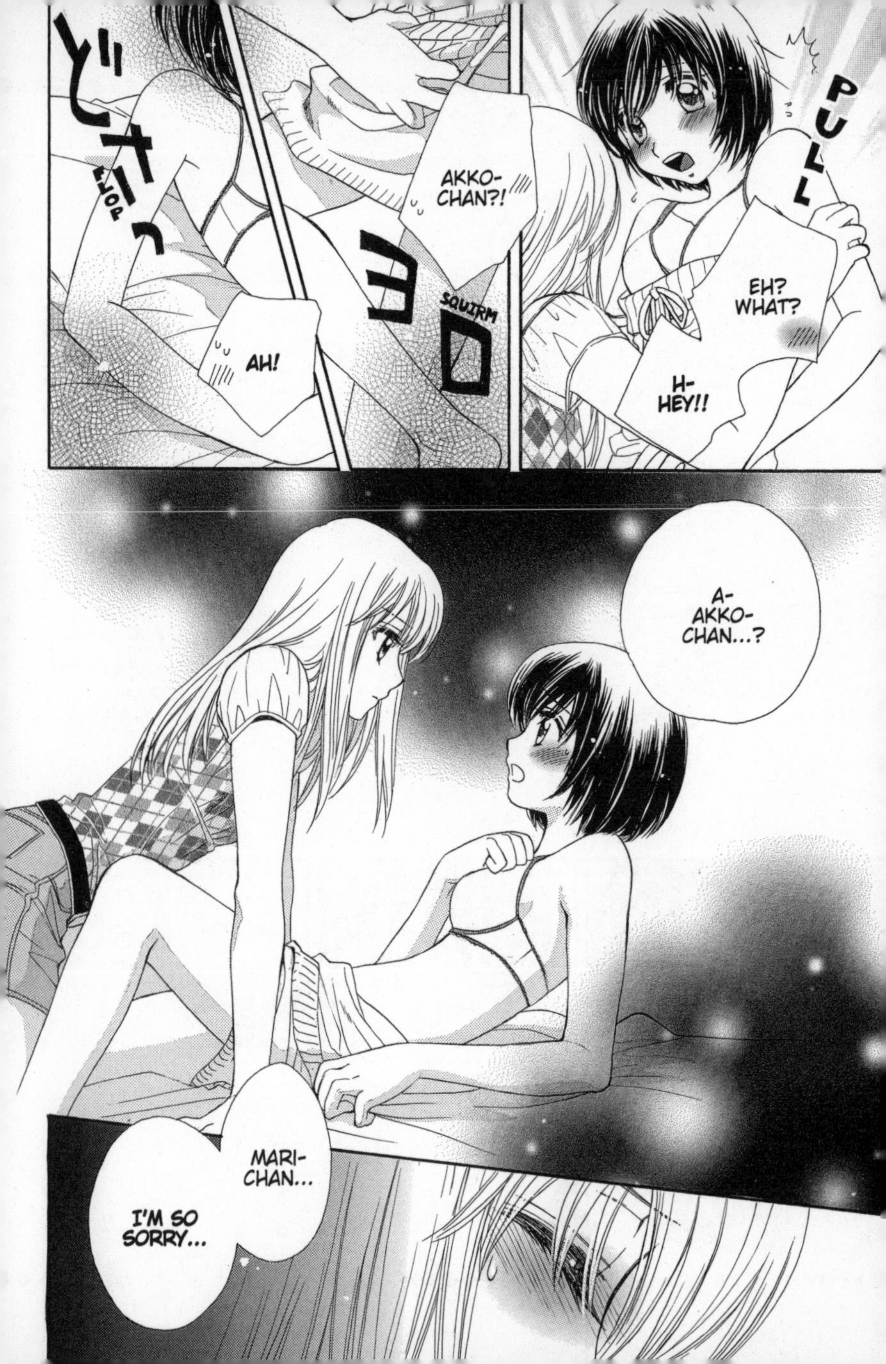
PULL
EH? WHAT?
H-HEY!!
AKKO-CHAN?!
SQUIRM
AH!
FLOP
A-AKKO-CHAN...?
MARI-CHAN...
I'M SO SORRY...

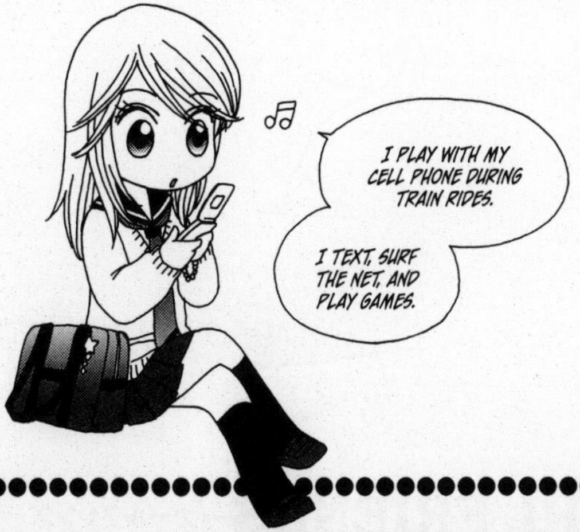
I PLAY WITH MY CELL PHONE DURING TRAIN RIDES.
I TEXT, SURF THE NET, AND PLAY GAMES.

GIRL FRIENDS —ガールフレンズ—

[CHAPTER 3]

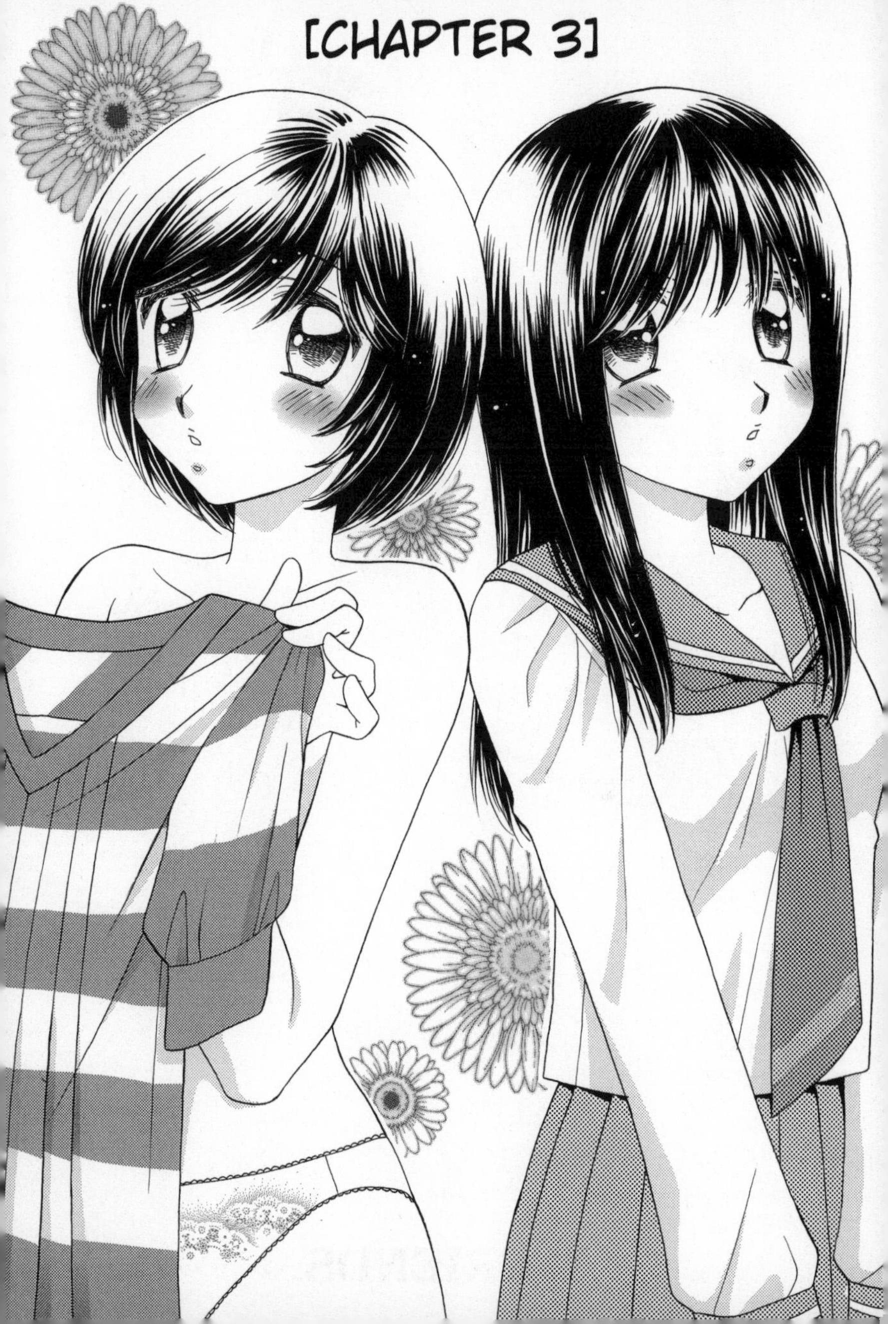

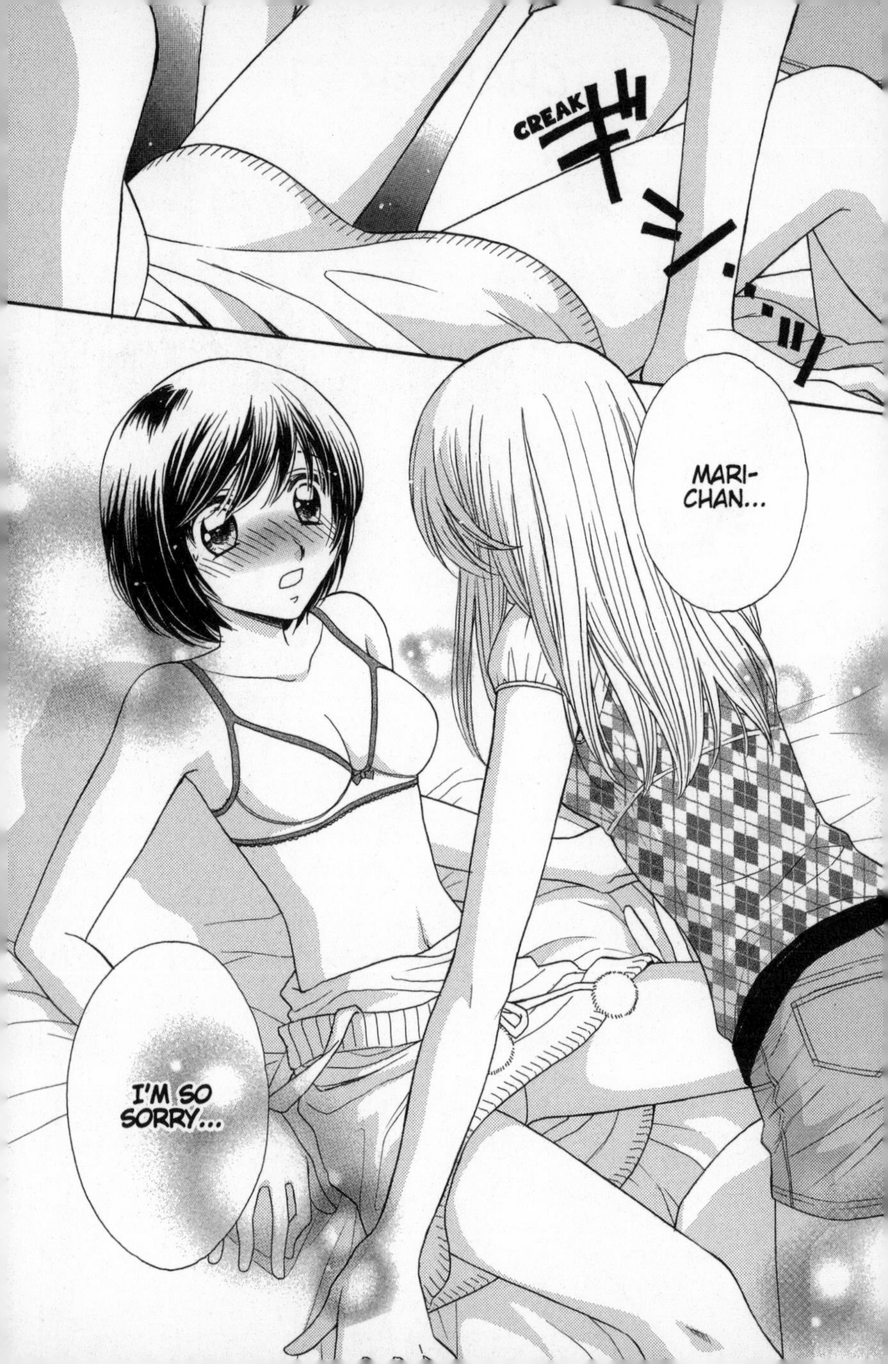
CREAK
MARI-CHAN...
I'M SO SORRY...

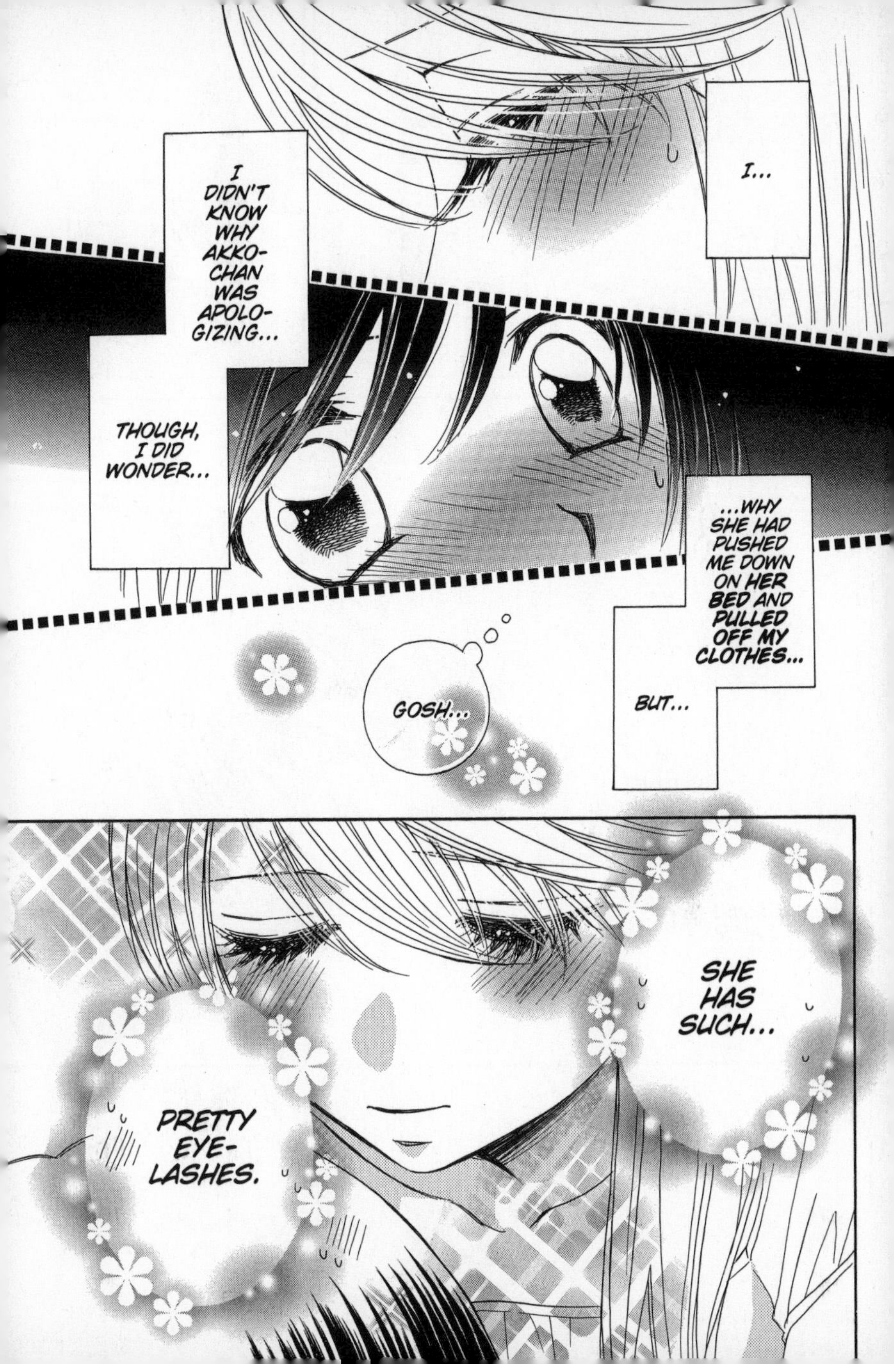

I...
I DIDN'T KNOW WHY AKKO-CHAN WAS APOLOGIZING...
THOUGH, I DID WONDER...
...WHY SHE HAD PUSHED ME DOWN ON HER BED AND PULLED OFF MY CLOTHES...
BUT...
GOSH...
SHE HAS SUCH...
PRETTY EYE-LASHES.

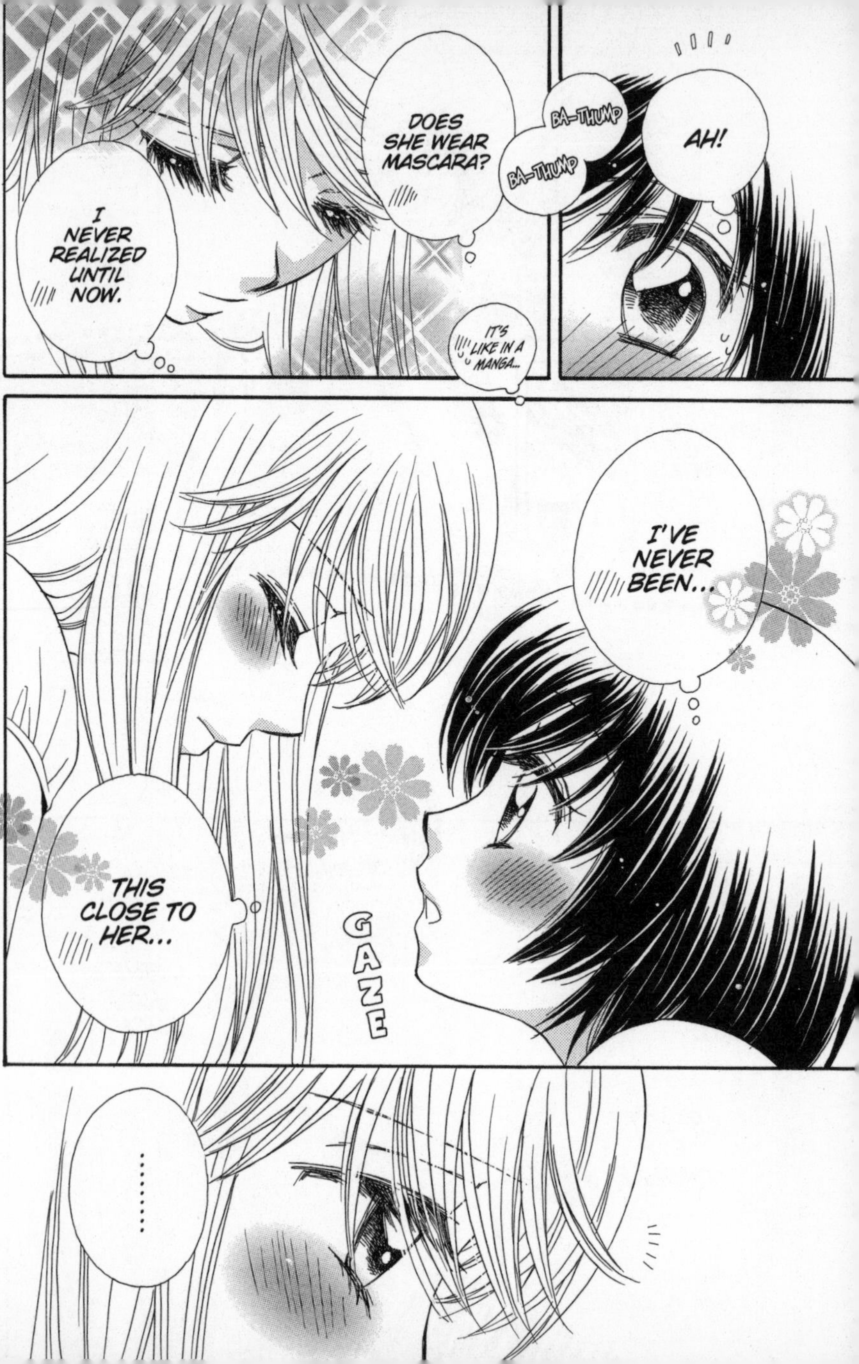
AH!
BA-THUMP
BA-THUMP
DOES SHE WEAR MASCARA?
IT'S LIKE IN A MANGA...
I NEVER REALIZED UNTIL NOW.
I'VE NEVER BEEN...
GAZE
THIS CLOSE TO HER...
......

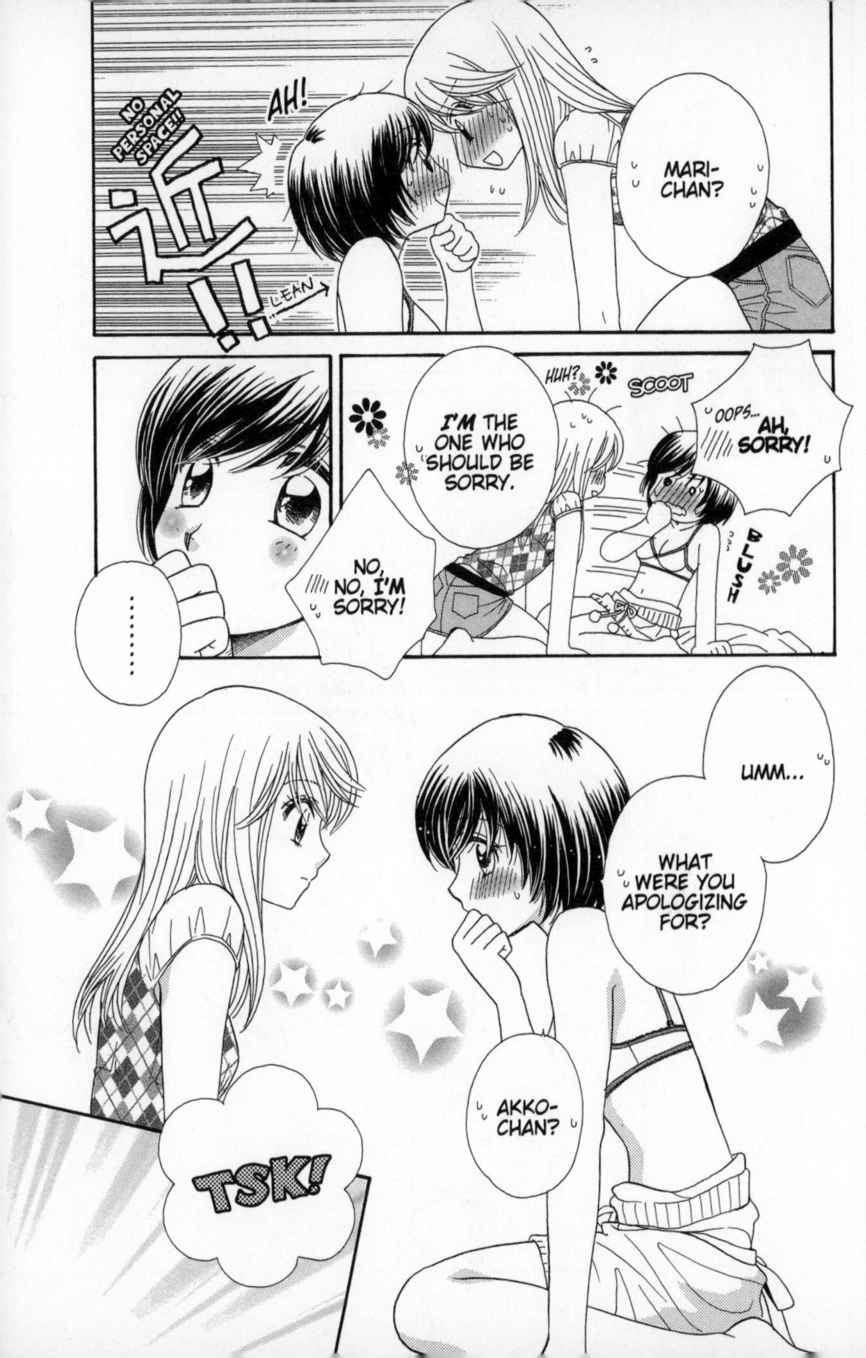
MARI-CHAN?
AH!
NO PERSONAL SPACE!!
LEAN
OOPS... AH, SORRY!
SCOOT
HUH?
I'M THE ONE WHO SHOULD BE SORRY.
BLUSH
NO, NO, I'M SORRY!
......
UMM...
WHAT WERE YOU APOLOGIZING FOR?
AKKO-CHAN?
TSK!

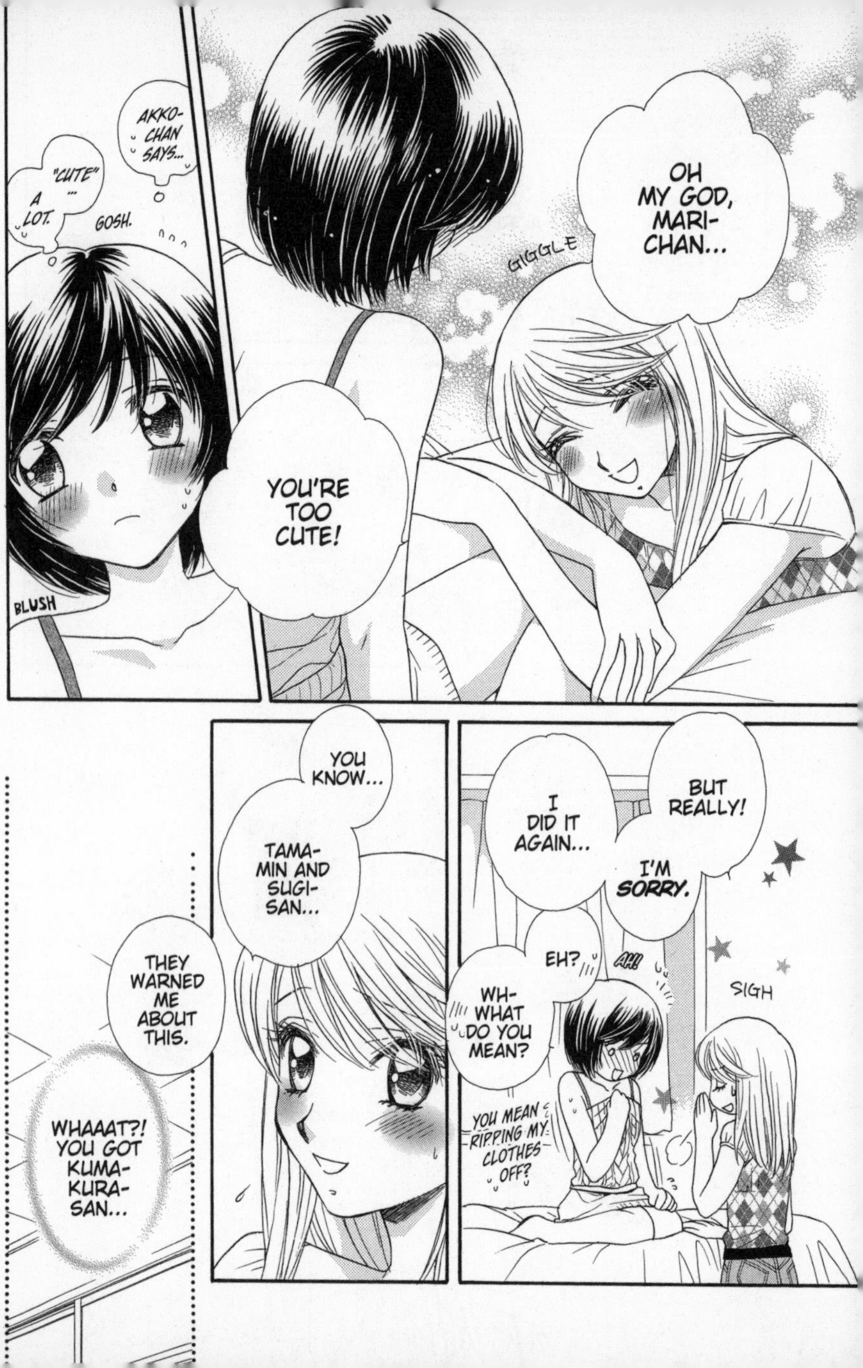
GIGGLE
OH MY GOD, MARI-CHAN...
YOU'RE TOO CUTE!
AKKO-CHAN SAYS...
"CUTE" ... A LOT.
GOSH.
BLUSH
BUT REALLY!
I DID IT AGAIN...
I'M SORRY.
SIGH
EH?
AH!
WH-WHAT DO YOU MEAN?
YOU MEAN RIPPING MY CLOTHES OFF?
YOU KNOW...
TAMA-MIN AND SUGI-SAN...
THEY WARNED ME ABOUT THIS.
WHAAAT?! YOU GOT KUMA-KURA-SAN...

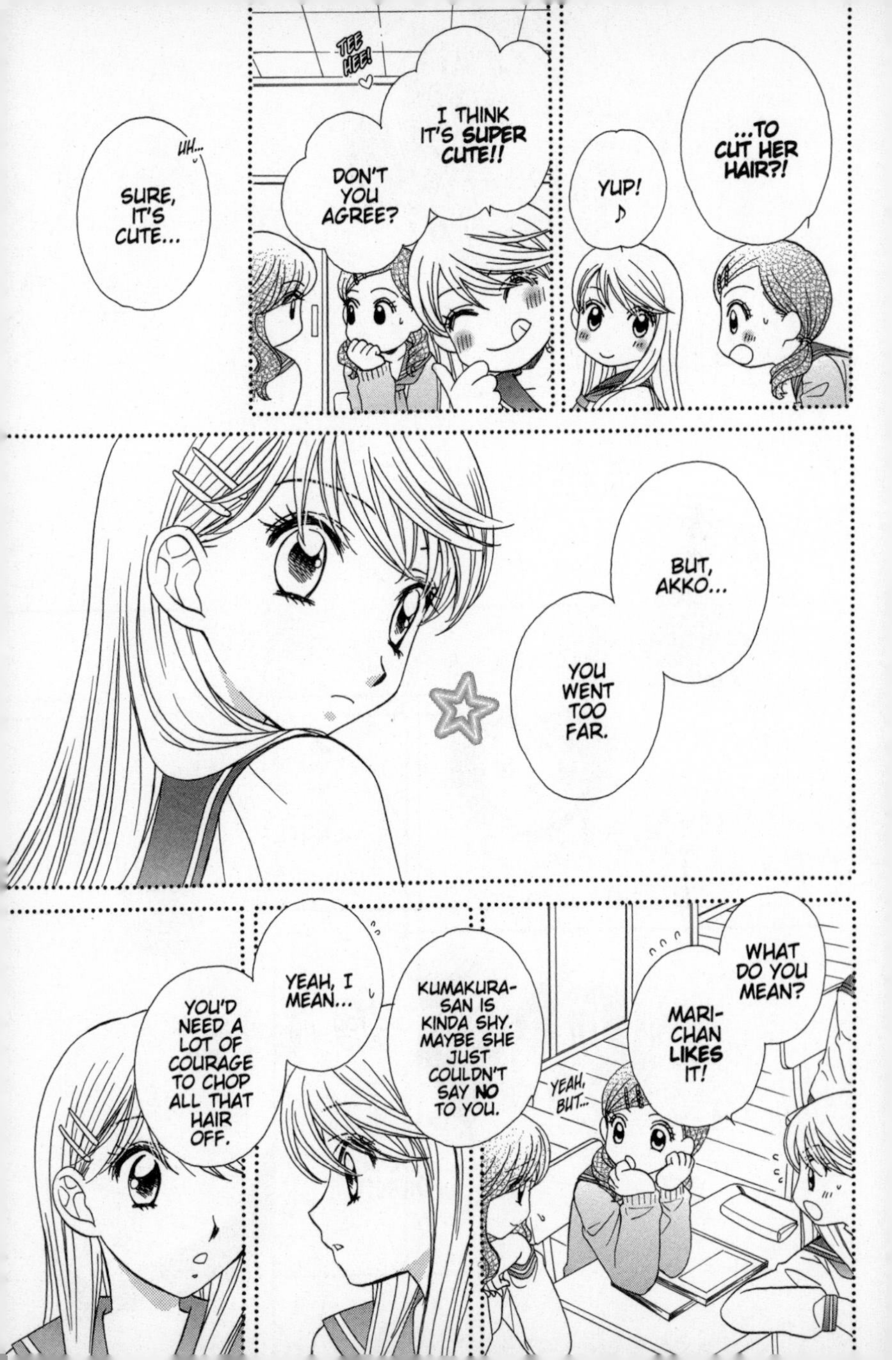
...TO CUT HER HAIR?!
YUP! ♪
TEE HEE! ♡
I THINK IT'S SUPER CUTE!!
DON'T YOU AGREE?
UH...
SURE, IT'S CUTE...
BUT, AKKO...
YOU WENT TOO FAR.
WHAT DO YOU MEAN?
MARI-CHAN LIKES IT!
YEAH, BUT...
KUMAKURA-SAN IS KINDA SHY. MAYBE SHE JUST COULDN'T SAY NO TO YOU.
YEAH, I MEAN...
YOU'D NEED A LOT OF COURAGE TO CHOP ALL THAT HAIR OFF.

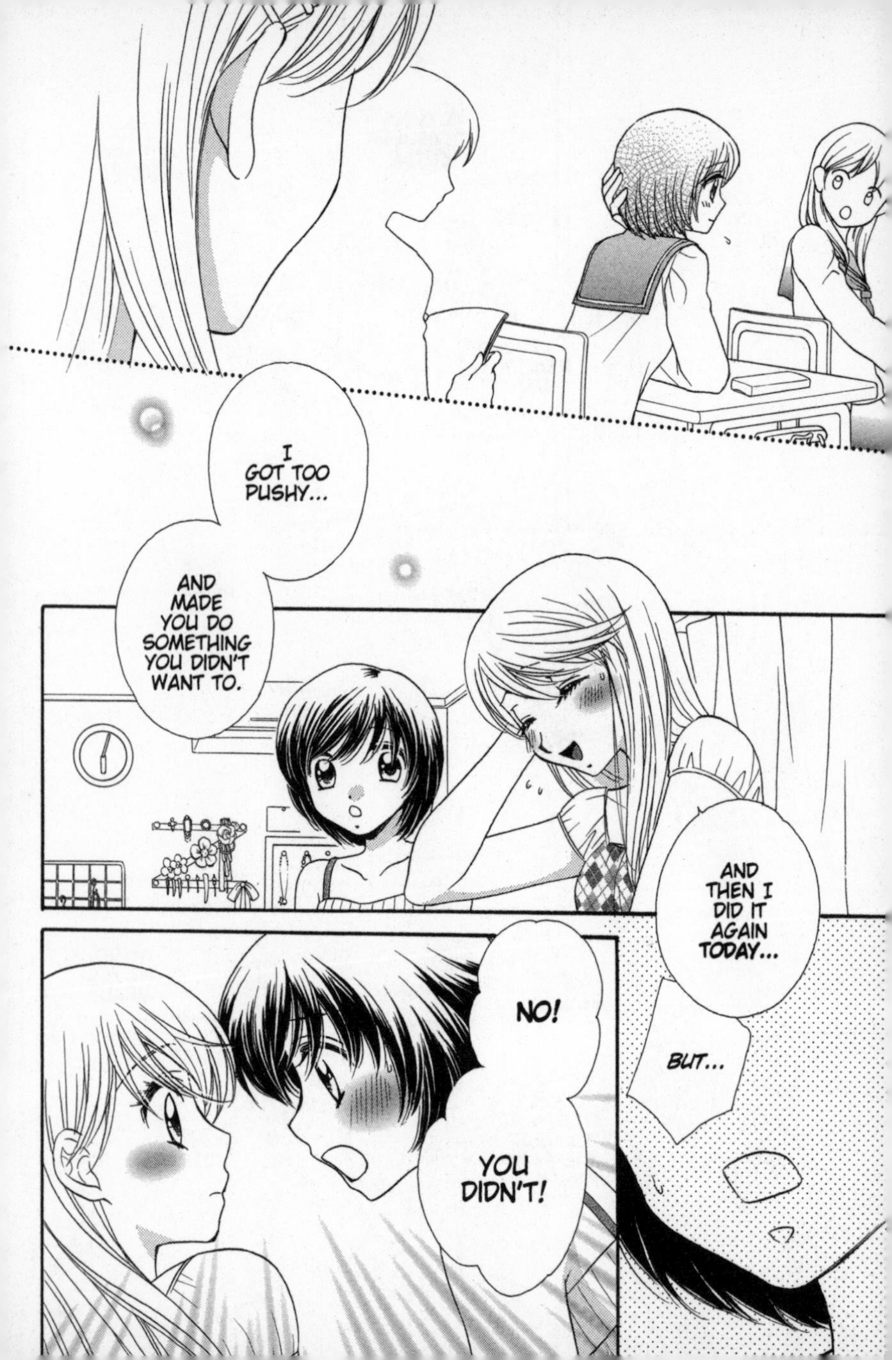

I GOT TOO PUSHY...
AND MADE YOU DO SOMETHING YOU DIDN'T WANT TO.
AND THEN I DID IT AGAIN TODAY...
BUT...
NO!
YOU DIDN'T!

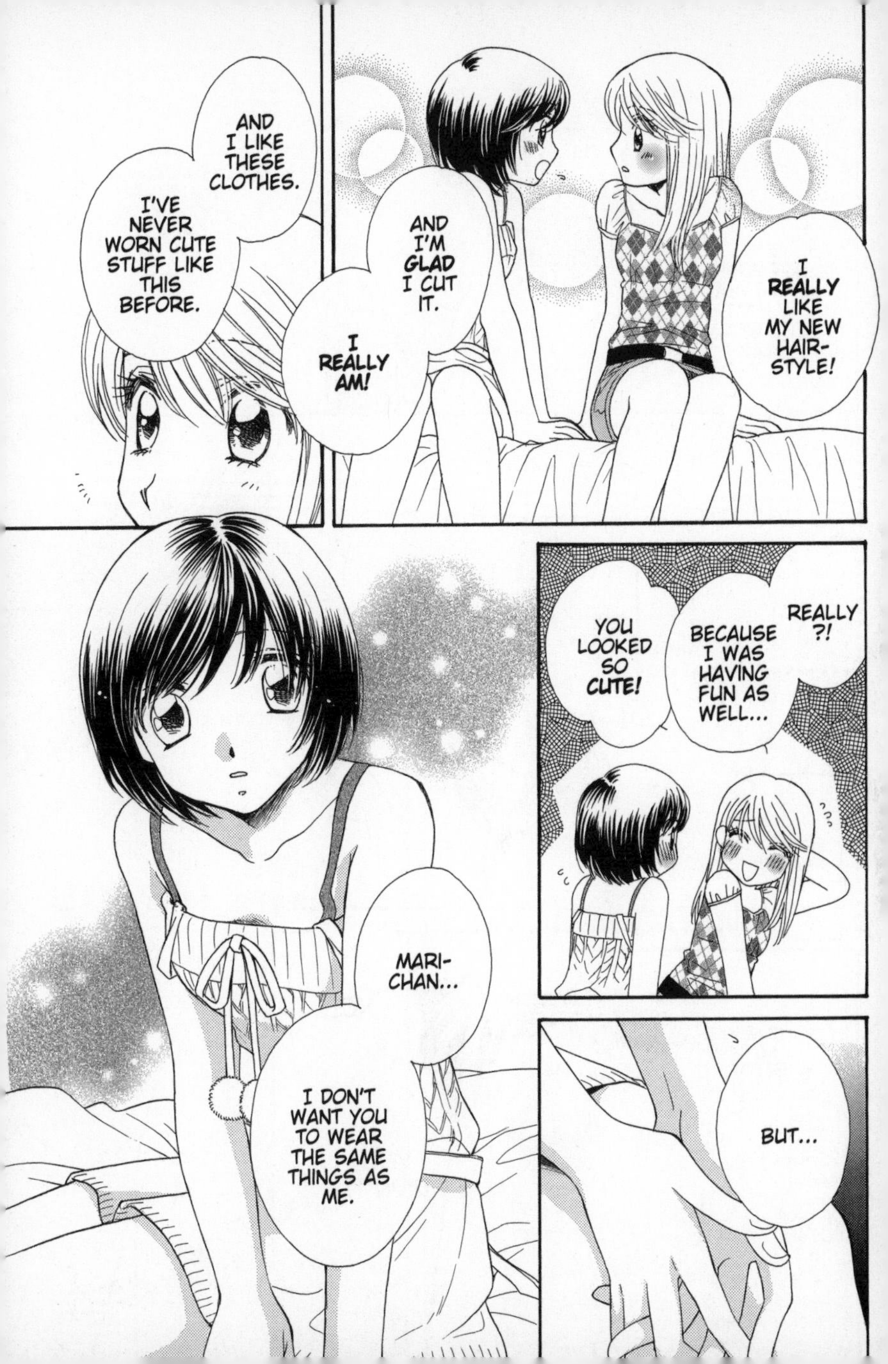
I REALLY LIKE MY NEW HAIR-STYLE!
AND I'M GLAD I CUT IT.
I REALLY AM!
AND I LIKE THESE CLOTHES.
I'VE NEVER WORN CUTE STUFF LIKE THIS BEFORE.
REALLY ?!
BECAUSE I WAS HAVING FUN AS WELL...
YOU LOOKED SO CUTE!
BUT...
MARI-CHAN...
I DON'T WANT YOU TO WEAR THE SAME THINGS AS ME.

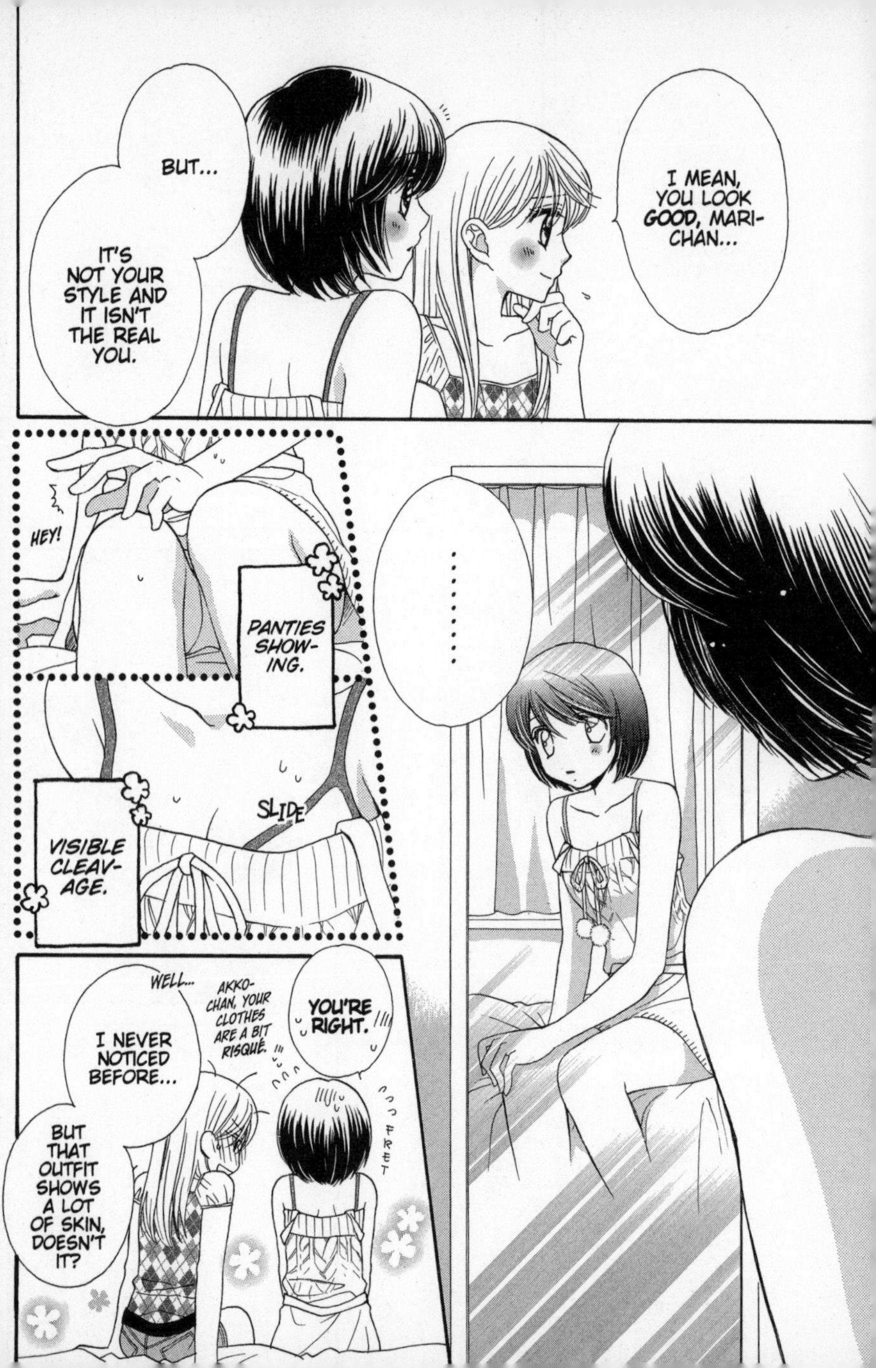

I MEAN, YOU LOOK GOOD, MARI-CHAN...
BUT...
IT'S NOT YOUR STYLE AND IT ISN'T THE REAL YOU.
......
HEY!
PANTIES SHOWING.
SLIDE
VISIBLE CLEAVAGE.
YOU'RE RIGHT.
AKKO-CHAN, YOUR CLOTHES ARE A BIT RISQUÉ.
WELL...
I NEVER NOTICED BEFORE...
BUT THAT OUTFIT SHOWS A LOT OF SKIN, DOESN'T IT?
FRET

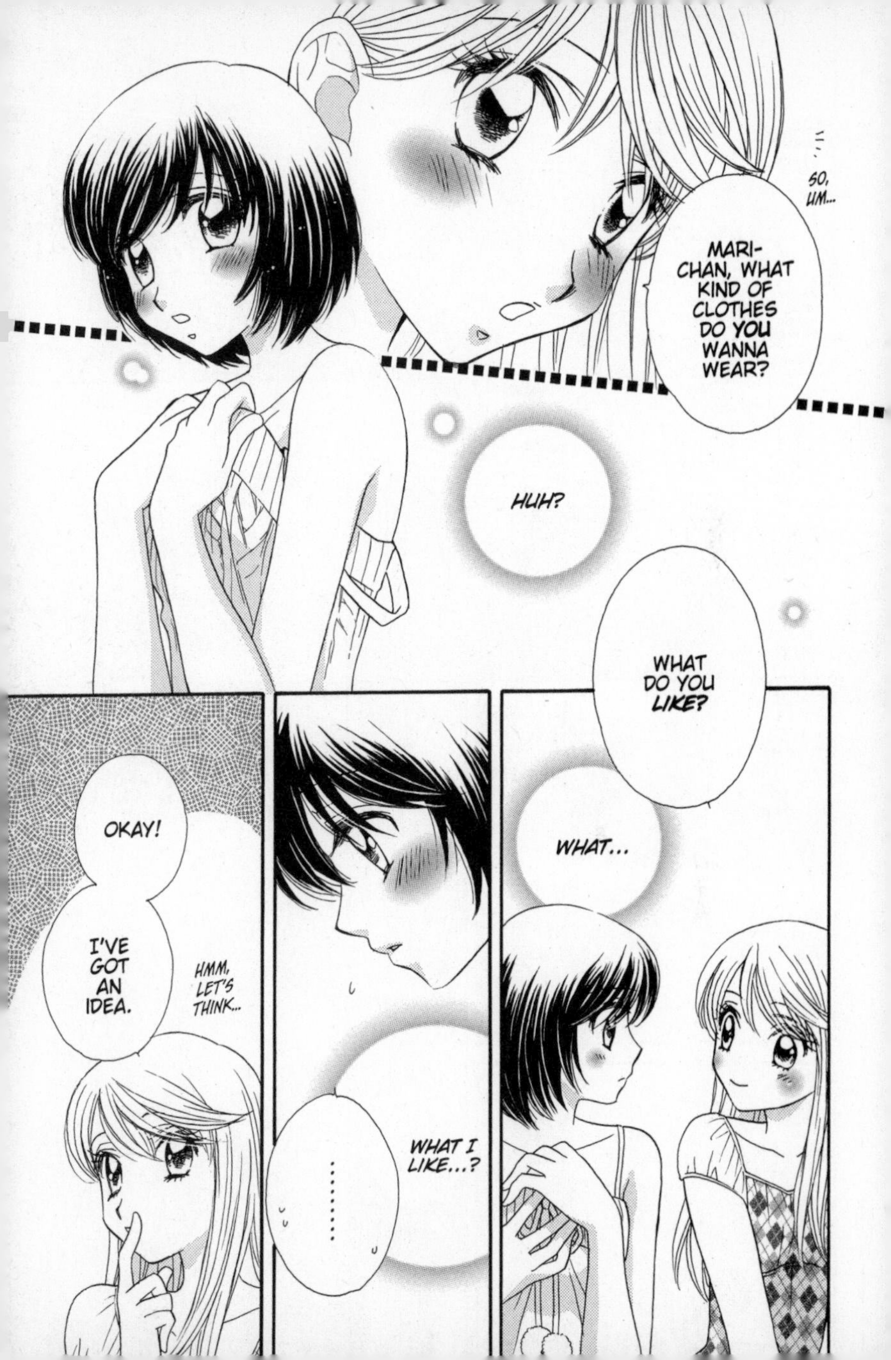
SO, UM...
MARI-CHAN, WHAT KIND OF CLOTHES DO YOU WANNA WEAR?
HUH?
WHAT DO YOU LIKE?
WHAT...
WHAT I LIKE...?
......
OKAY!
I'VE GOT AN IDEA.
HMM, LET'S THINK...

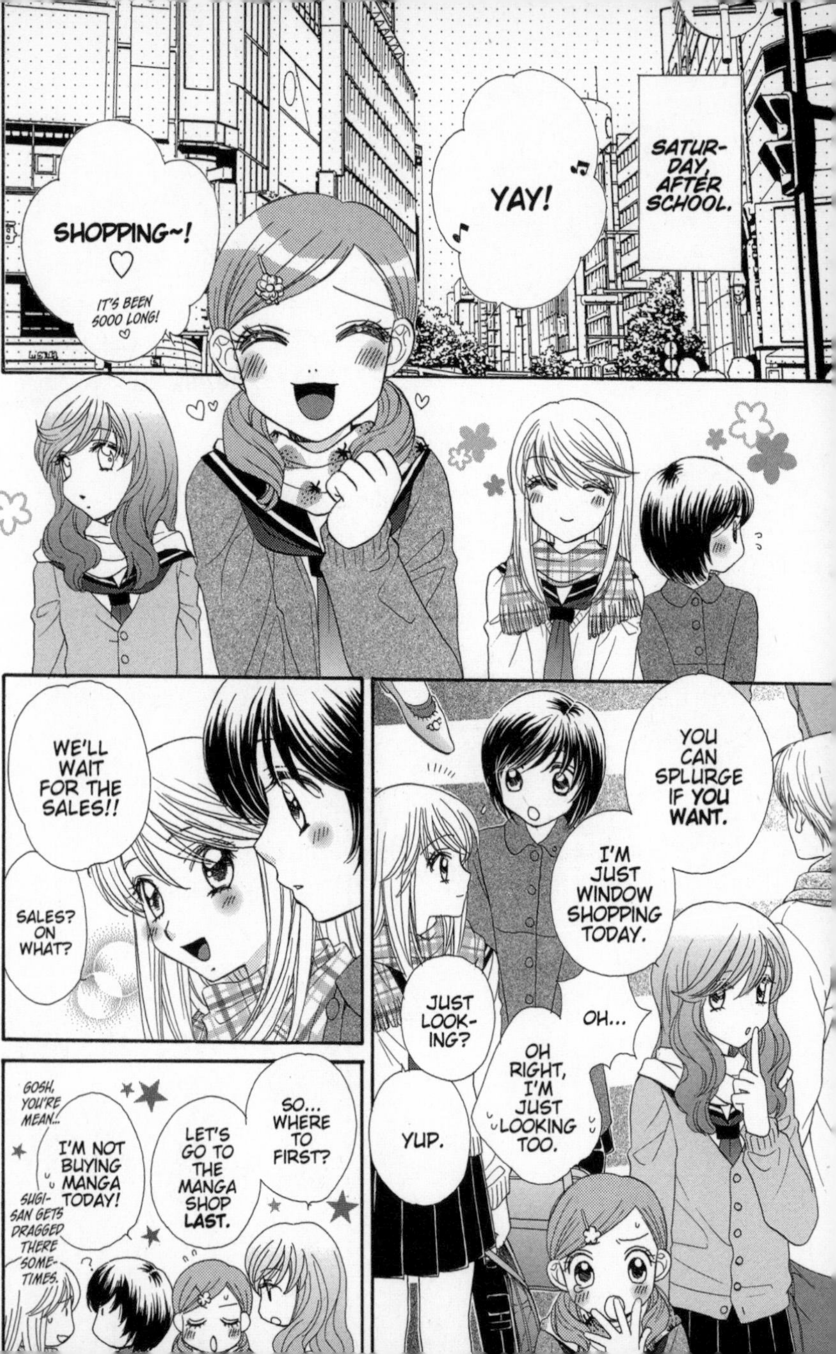
SATURDAY, AFTER SCHOOL.
YAY!
SHOPPING~! ♡
IT'S BEEN SOOO LONG! ♡
YOU CAN SPLURGE IF YOU WANT.
I'M JUST WINDOW SHOPPING TODAY.
OH...
JUST LOOKING?
OH RIGHT, I'M JUST LOOKING TOO.
YUP.
WE'LL WAIT FOR THE SALES!!
SALES? ON WHAT?
SO... WHERE TO FIRST?
LET'S GO TO THE MANGA SHOP LAST.
I'M NOT BUYING MANGA TODAY!
GOSH, YOU'RE MEAN...
SUGI-SAN GETS DRAGGED THERE SOMETIMES.

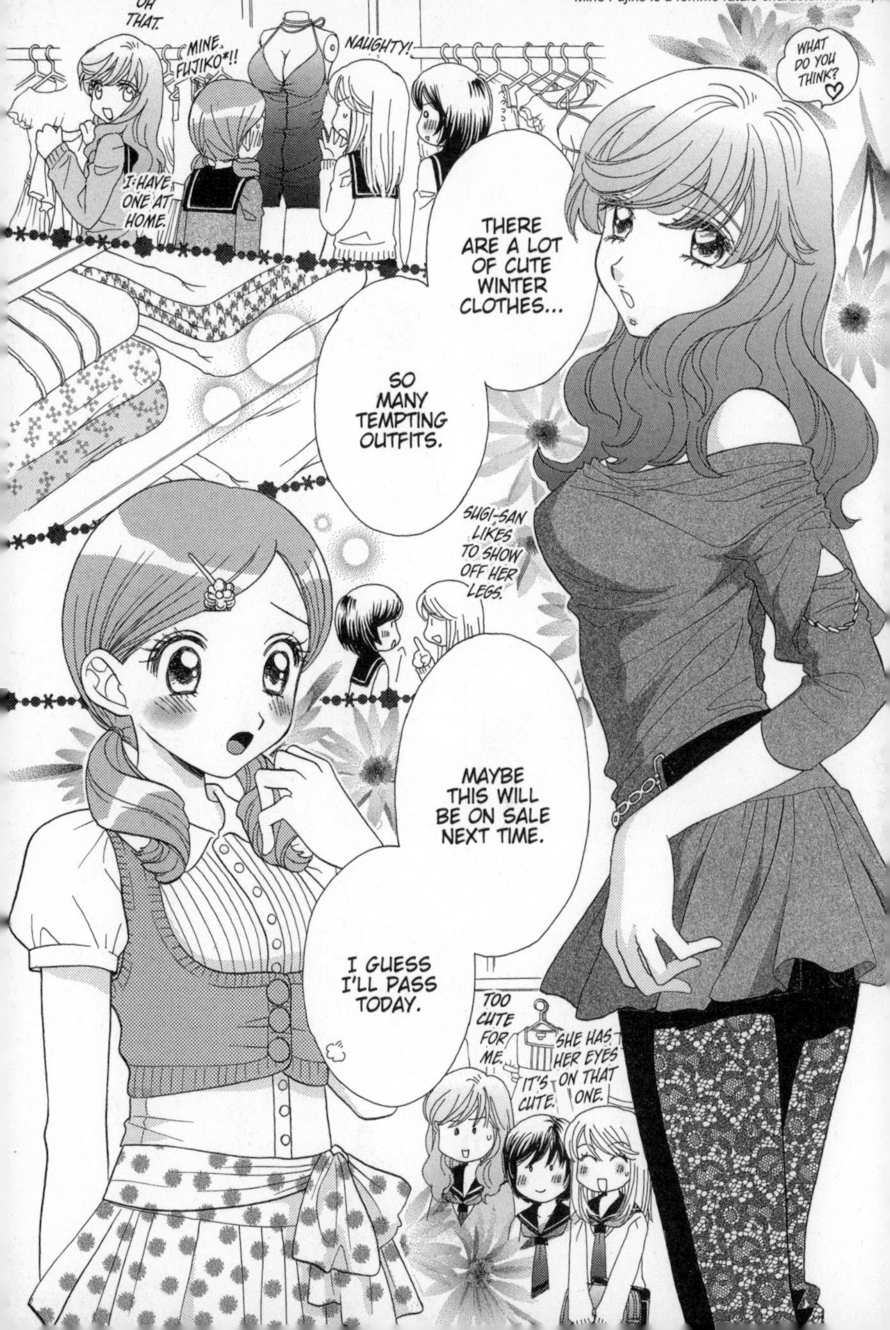
WHAT DO YOU THINK? ♡
THERE ARE A LOT OF CUTE WINTER CLOTHES...
SO MANY TEMPTING OUTFITS.
NAUGHTY!
MINE FUJIKO*!!
OH THAT.
I HAVE ONE AT HOME.
SUGI-SAN LIKES TO SHOW OFF HER LEGS.
MAYBE THIS WILL BE ON SALE NEXT TIME.
I GUESS I'LL PASS TODAY.
SHE HAS HER EYES ON THAT ONE.
IT'S CUTE.
TOO CUTE FOR ME.

*Mine Fujiko is a femme fatale character from Lupin

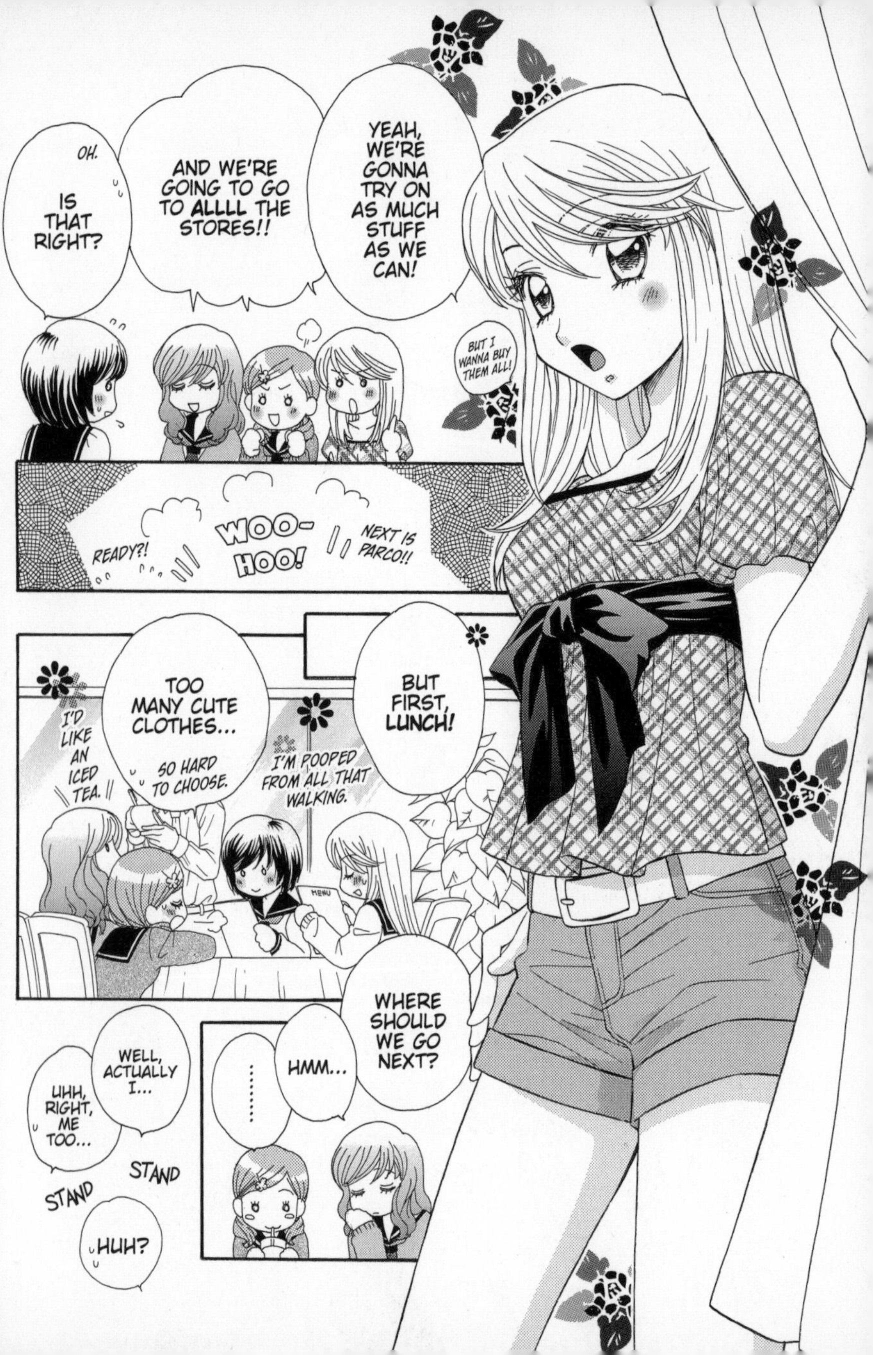
YEAH, WE'RE GONNA TRY ON AS MUCH STUFF AS WE CAN!
AND WE'RE GOING TO GO TO ALLLL THE STORES!!
OH. IS THAT RIGHT?
BUT I WANNA BUY THEM ALL!
NEXT IS PARCO!!
WOO-HOO!
READY?!
BUT FIRST, LUNCH!
TOO MANY CUTE CLOTHES...
I'M POOPED FROM ALL THAT WALKING.
SO HARD TO CHOOSE.
I'D LIKE AN ICED TEA.
WHERE SHOULD WE GO NEXT?
HMM...
......
WELL, ACTUALLY I...
UHH, RIGHT, ME TOO...
STAND
STAND
HUH?

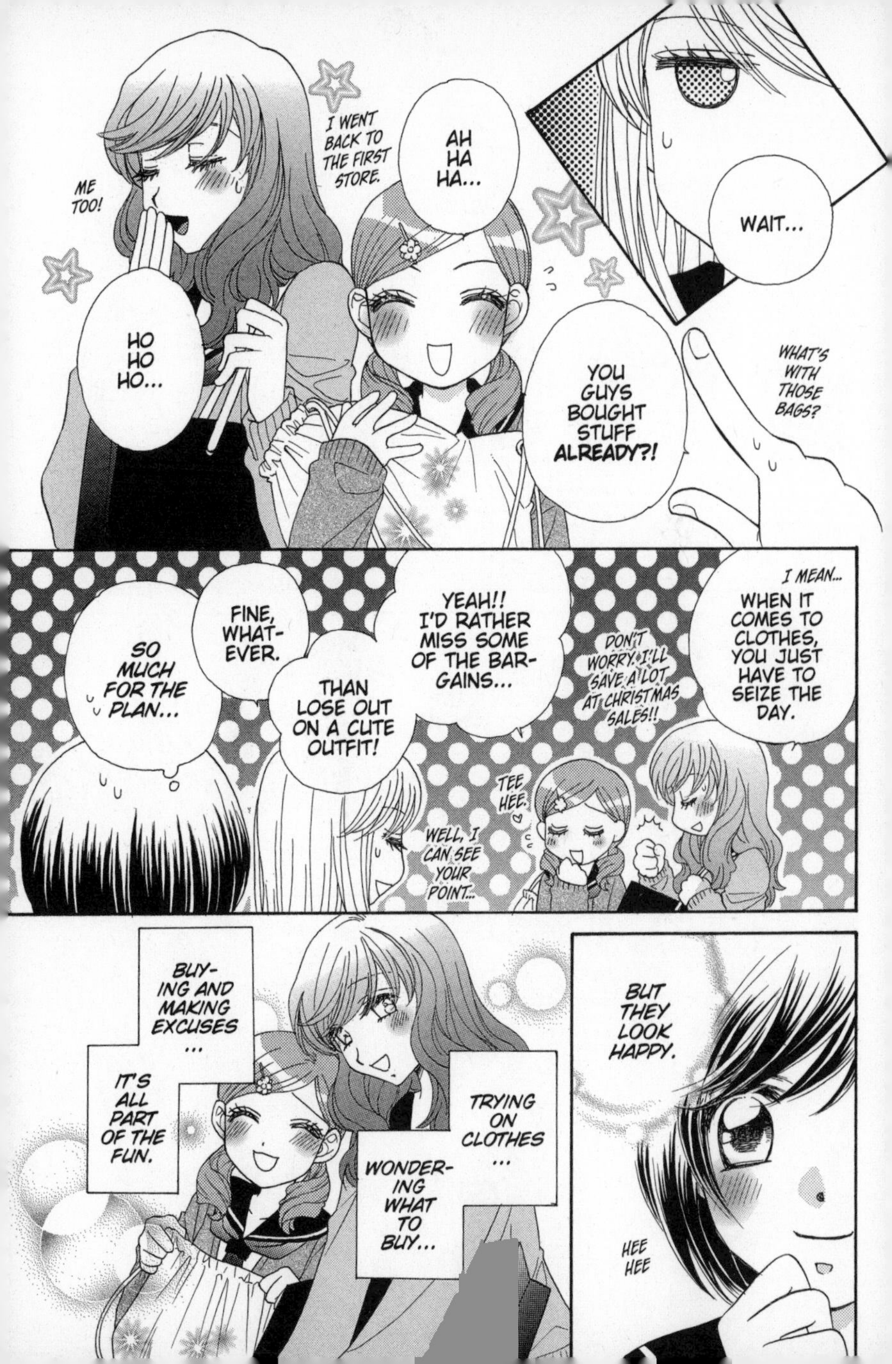
WAIT...
WHAT'S WITH THOSE BAGS?
YOU GUYS BOUGHT STUFF ALREADY?!
AH HA HA...
I WENT BACK TO THE FIRST STORE.
ME TOO!
HO HO HO...
I MEAN... WHEN IT COMES TO CLOTHES, YOU JUST HAVE TO SEIZE THE DAY.
DON'T WORRY. I'LL SAVE A LOT AT CHRISTMAS SALES!!
YEAH!! I'D RATHER MISS SOME OF THE BARGAINS...
THAN LOSE OUT ON A CUTE OUTFIT!
TEE HEE.
WELL, I CAN SEE YOUR POINT...
FINE, WHATEVER.
SO MUCH FOR THE PLAN...
BUT THEY LOOK HAPPY.
HEE HEE
TRYING ON CLOTHES...
WONDERING WHAT TO BUY...
BUYING AND MAKING EXCUSES...
IT'S ALL PART OF THE FUN.

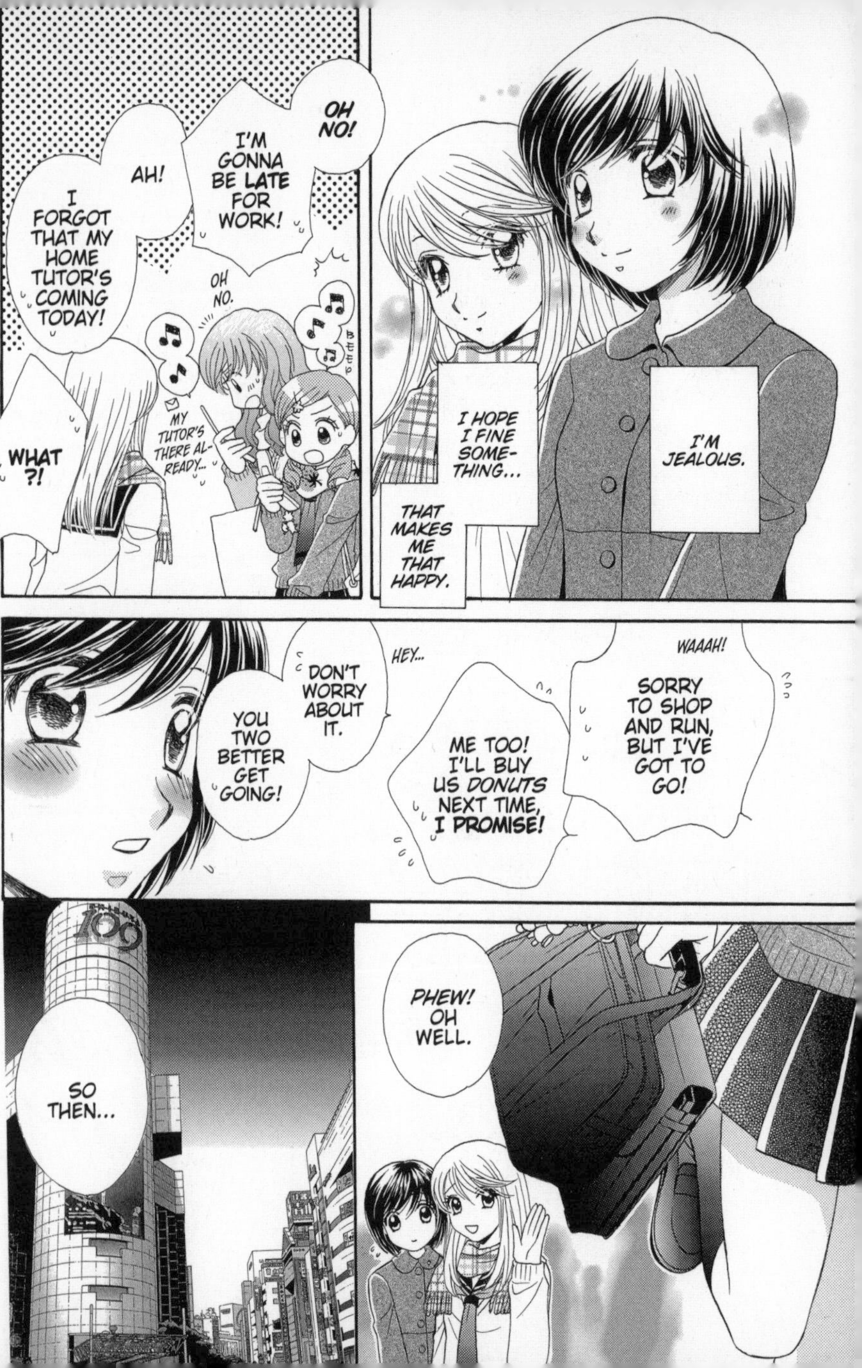
I'M JEALOUS.
I HOPE I FINE SOMETHING...
THAT MAKES ME THAT HAPPY.
OH NO!
I'M GONNA BE LATE FOR WORK!
AH!
I FORGOT THAT MY HOME TUTOR'S COMING TODAY!
OH NO.
MY TUTOR'S THERE ALREADY...
WHAT?!
WAAAH!
SORRY TO SHOP AND RUN, BUT I'VE GOT TO GO!
ME TOO! I'LL BUY US DONUTS NEXT TIME, I PROMISE!
HEY...
DON'T WORRY ABOUT IT.
YOU TWO BETTER GET GOING!
PHEW! OH WELL.
SO THEN...

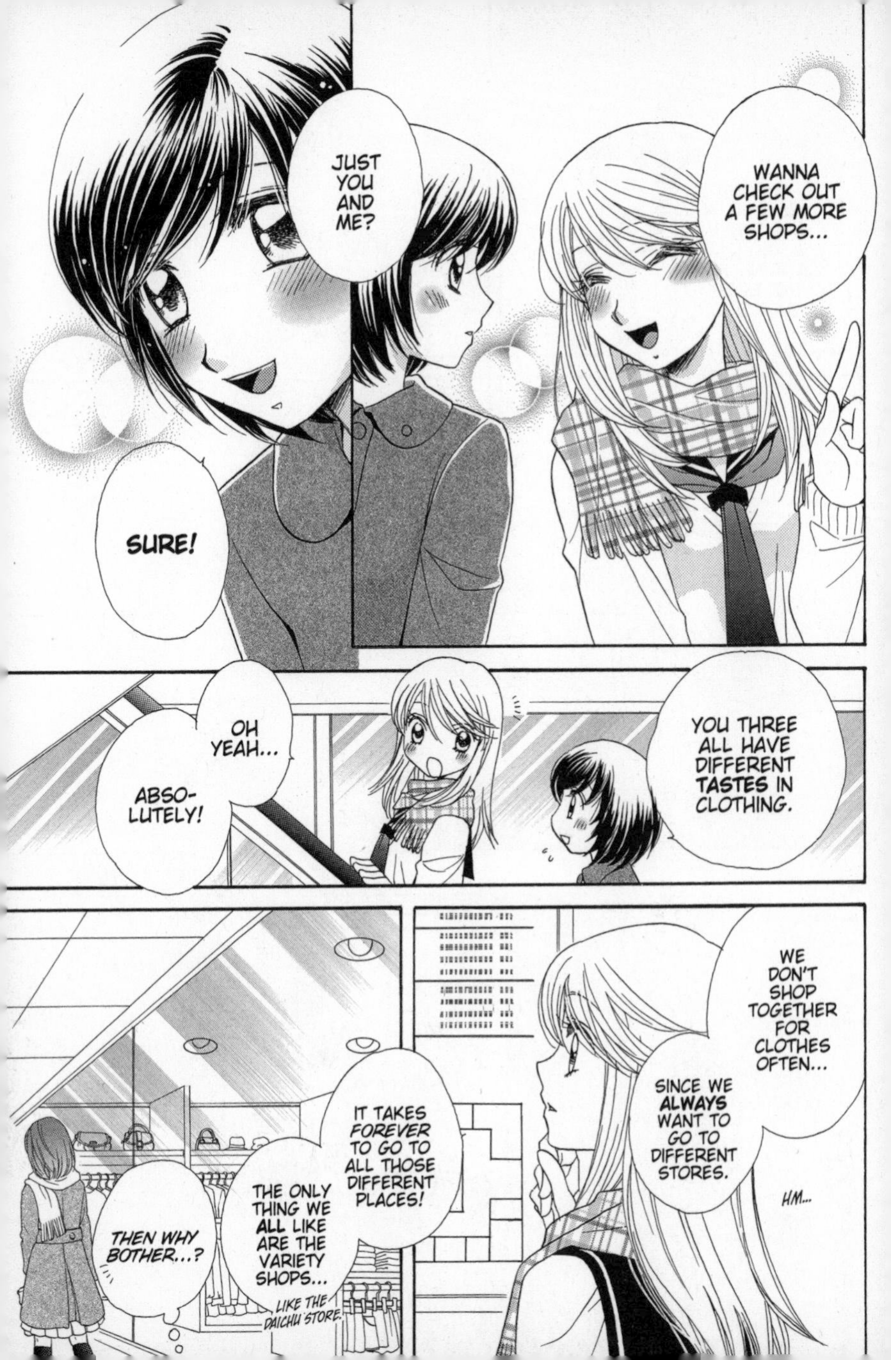
WANNA CHECK OUT A FEW MORE SHOPS...
JUST YOU AND ME?
SURE!
YOU THREE ALL HAVE DIFFERENT TASTES IN CLOTHING.
OH YEAH...
ABSO-LUTELY!
WE DON'T SHOP TOGETHER FOR CLOTHES OFTEN...
SINCE WE ALWAYS WANT TO GO TO DIFFERENT STORES.
HM...
IT TAKES FOREVER TO GO TO ALL THOSE DIFFERENT PLACES!
THE ONLY THING WE ALL LIKE ARE THE VARIETY SHOPS...
LIKE THE DAICHU STORE.
THEN WHY BOTHER...?

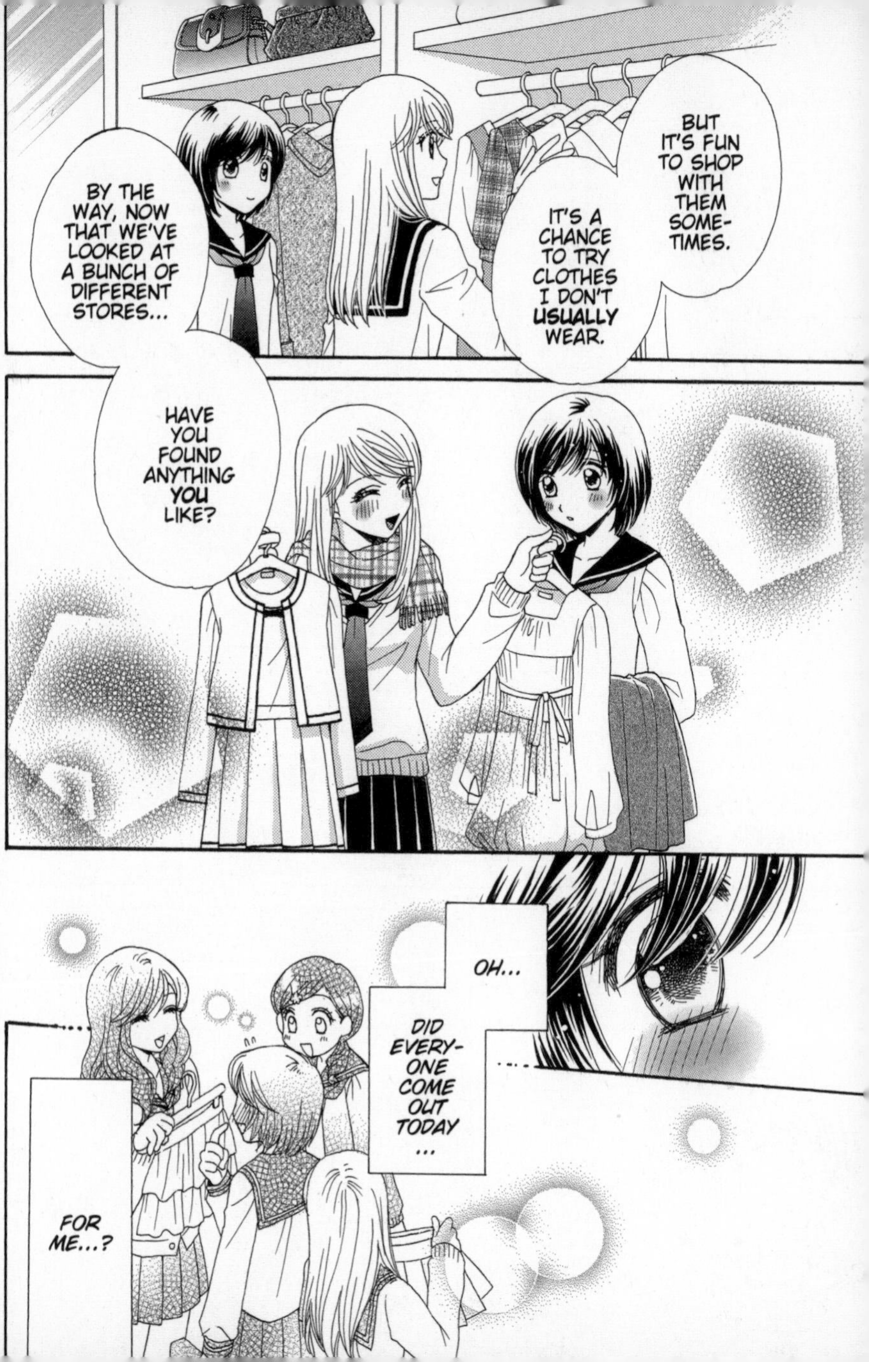
BUT IT'S FUN TO SHOP WITH THEM SOME-TIMES.
IT'S A CHANCE TO TRY CLOTHES I DON'T USUALLY WEAR.
BY THE WAY, NOW THAT WE'VE LOOKED AT A BUNCH OF DIFFERENT STORES...
HAVE YOU FOUND ANYTHING YOU LIKE?
OH...
DID EVERY-ONE COME OUT TODAY ...
FOR ME...?

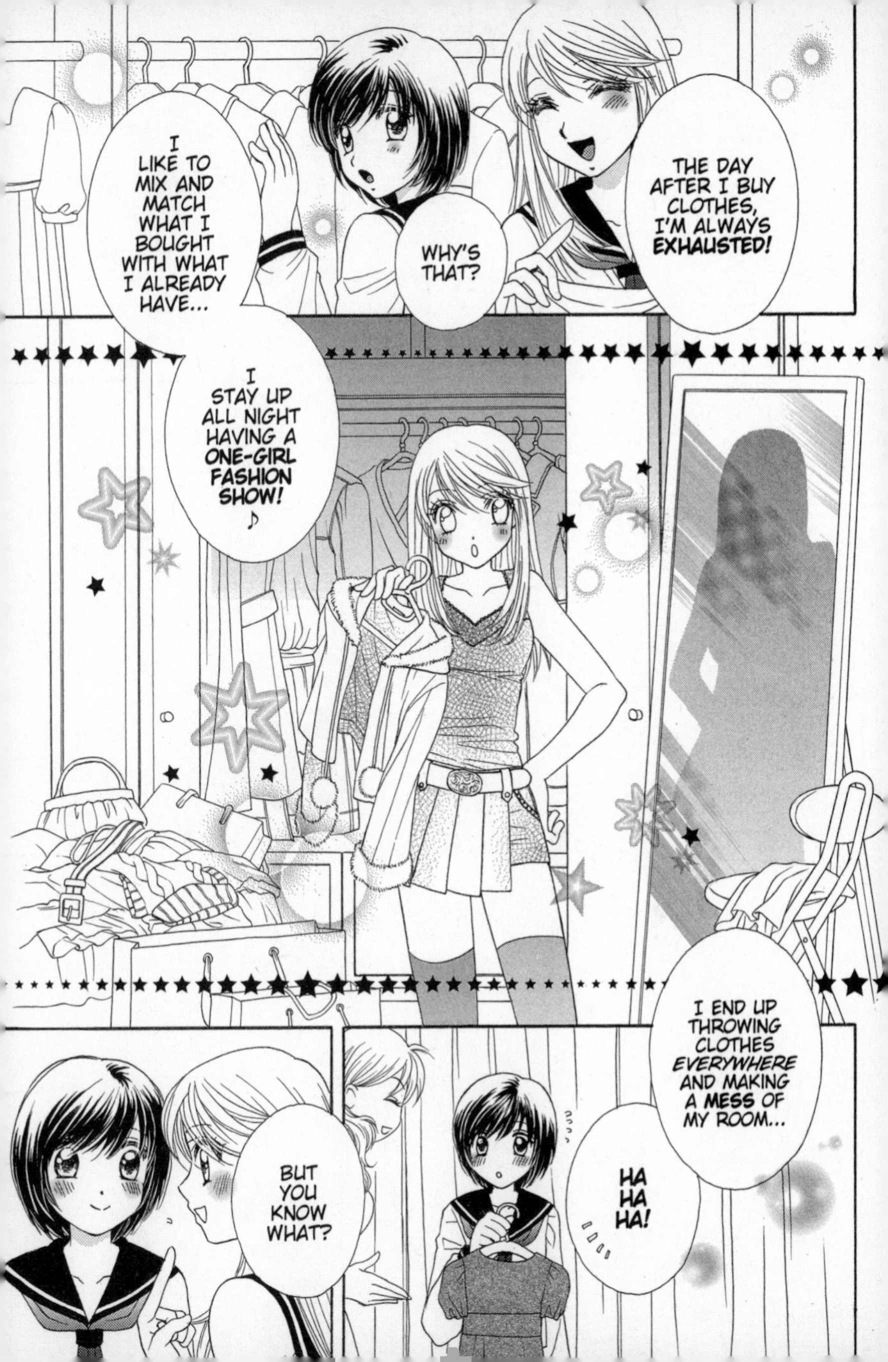
THE DAY AFTER I BUY CLOTHES, I'M ALWAYS **EXHAUSTED!**
WHY'S THAT?
I LIKE TO MIX AND MATCH WHAT I BOUGHT WITH WHAT I ALREADY HAVE...
I STAY UP ALL NIGHT HAVING A **ONE-GIRL FASHION SHOW!** ♪
I END UP THROWING CLOTHES *EVERYWHERE* AND MAKING A **MESS** OF MY ROOM...
HA HA HA!
BUT YOU KNOW WHAT?

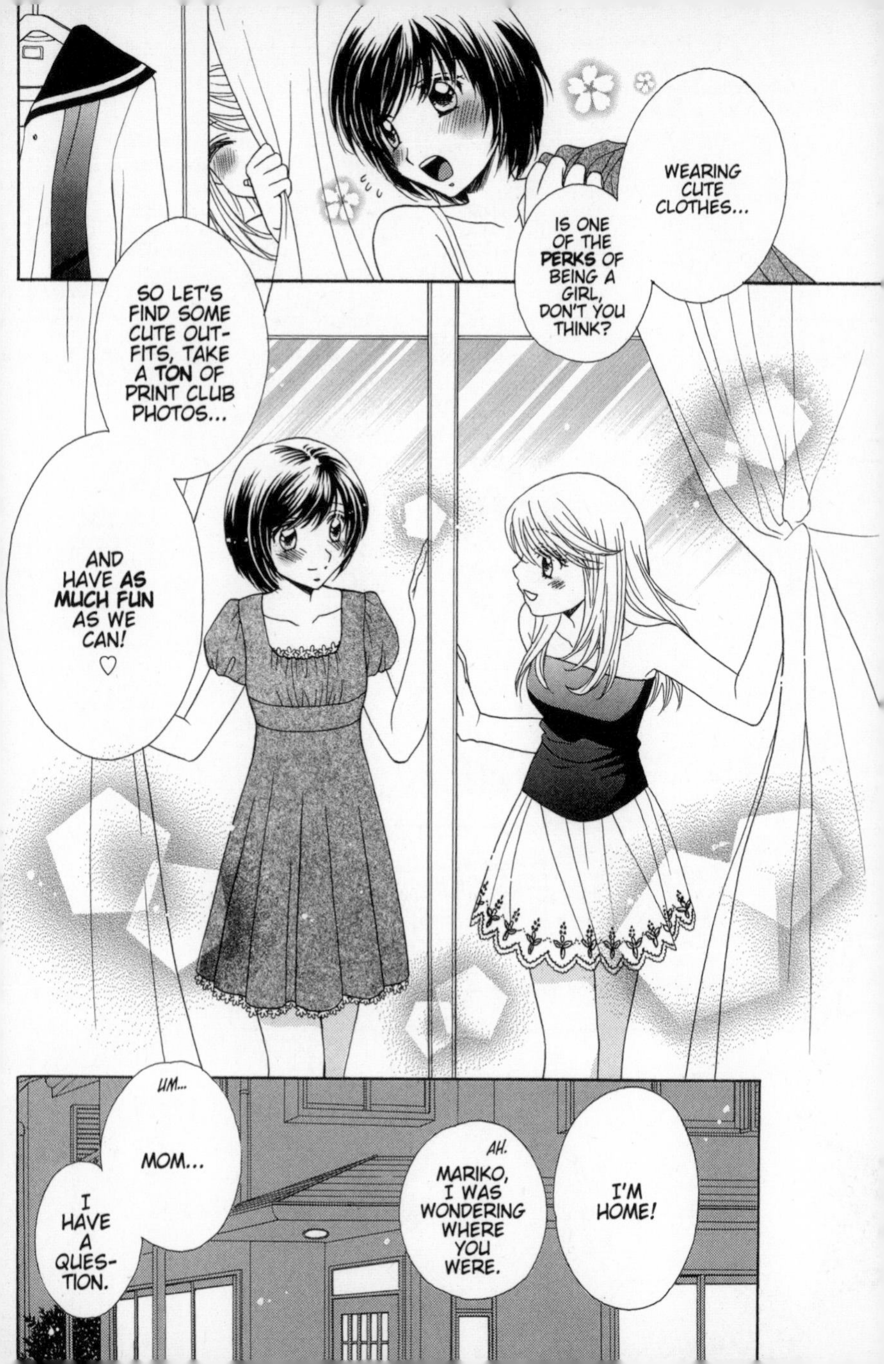
WEARING CUTE CLOTHES...
IS ONE OF THE **PERKS** OF BEING A GIRL, DON'T YOU THINK?
SO LET'S FIND SOME CUTE OUT-FITS, TAKE A **TON** OF PRINT CLUB PHOTOS...
AND HAVE **AS MUCH FUN** AS WE CAN! ♡
I'M HOME!
AH. MARIKO, I WAS WONDERING WHERE YOU WERE.
UM... MOM...
I HAVE A QUES-TION.

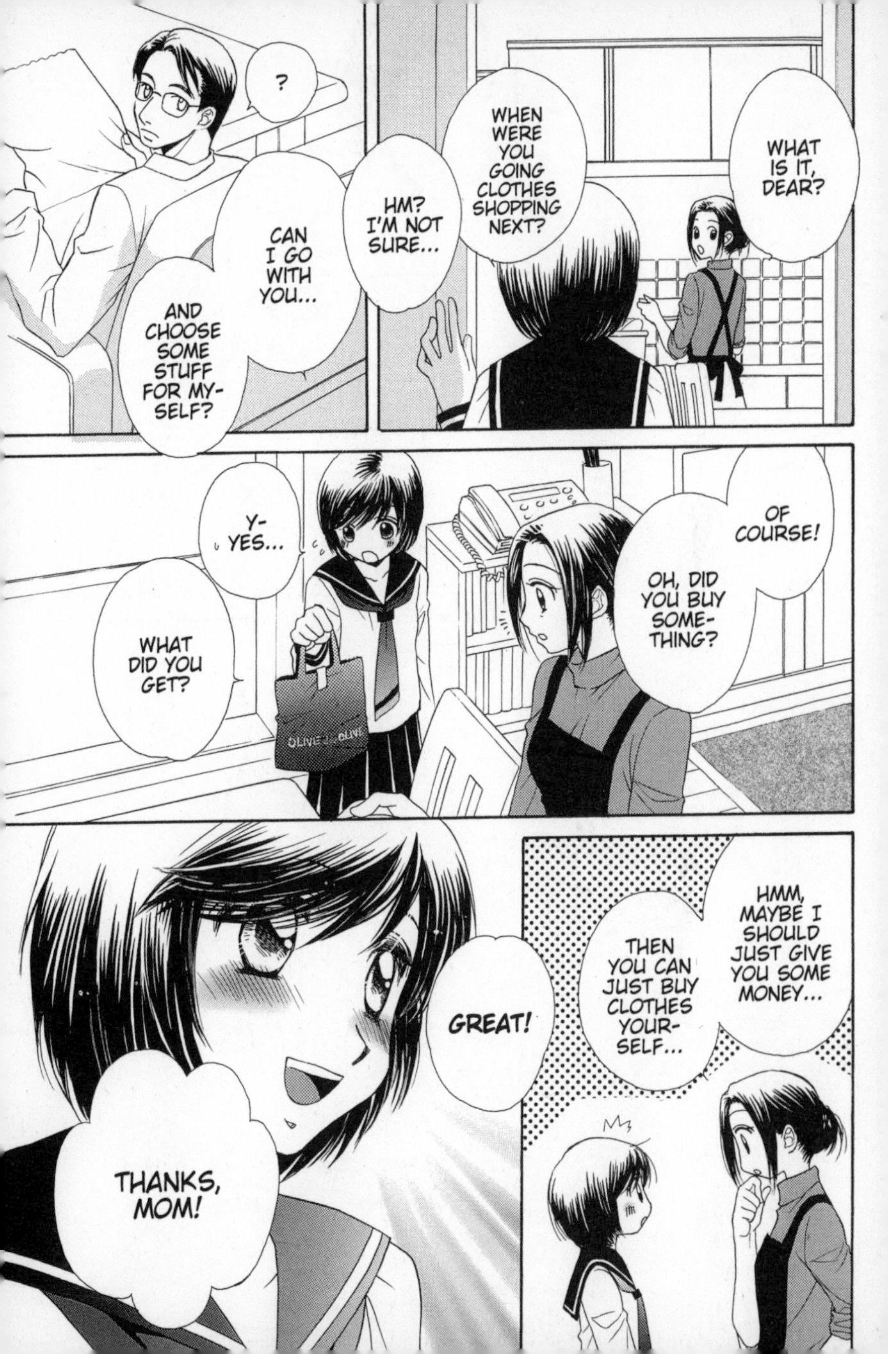
WHAT IS IT, DEAR?
WHEN WERE YOU GOING CLOTHES SHOPPING NEXT?
HM? I'M NOT SURE...
?
CAN I GO WITH YOU...
AND CHOOSE SOME STUFF FOR MY-SELF?
OF COURSE!
OH, DID YOU BUY SOME-THING?
Y-YES...
WHAT DID YOU GET?
HMM, MAYBE I SHOULD JUST GIVE YOU SOME MONEY...
THEN YOU CAN JUST BUY CLOTHES YOUR-SELF...
GREAT!
THANKS, MOM!

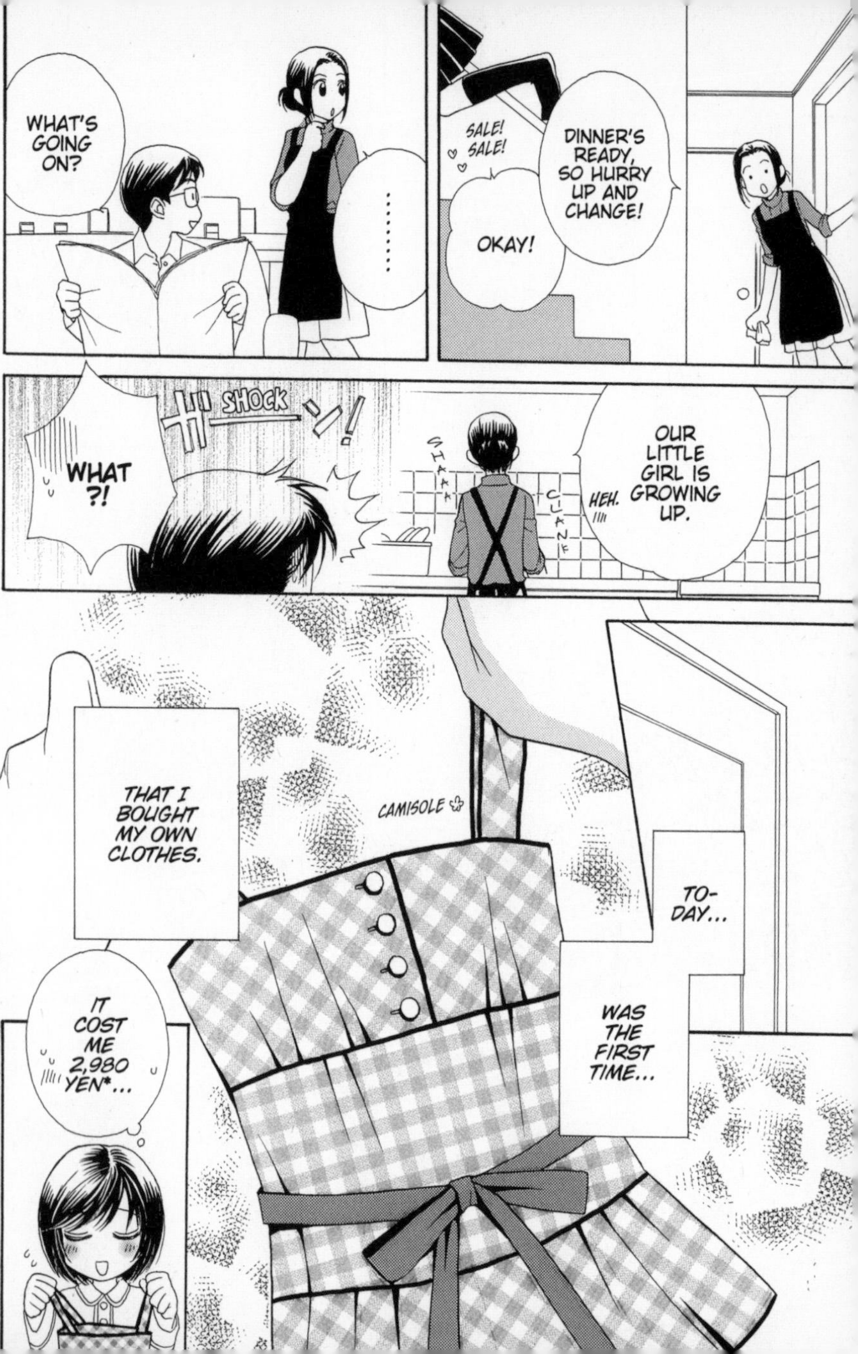
DINNER'S READY, SO HURRY UP AND CHANGE!
OKAY!
SALE! SALE!
......
WHAT'S GOING ON?
OUR LITTLE GIRL IS GROWING UP.
HEH.
CLANK
WHAT ?!
SHOCK
TO-DAY...
WAS THE FIRST TIME...
THAT I BOUGHT MY OWN CLOTHES.
CAMISOLE
IT COST ME 2,980 YEN*...

*About $35.

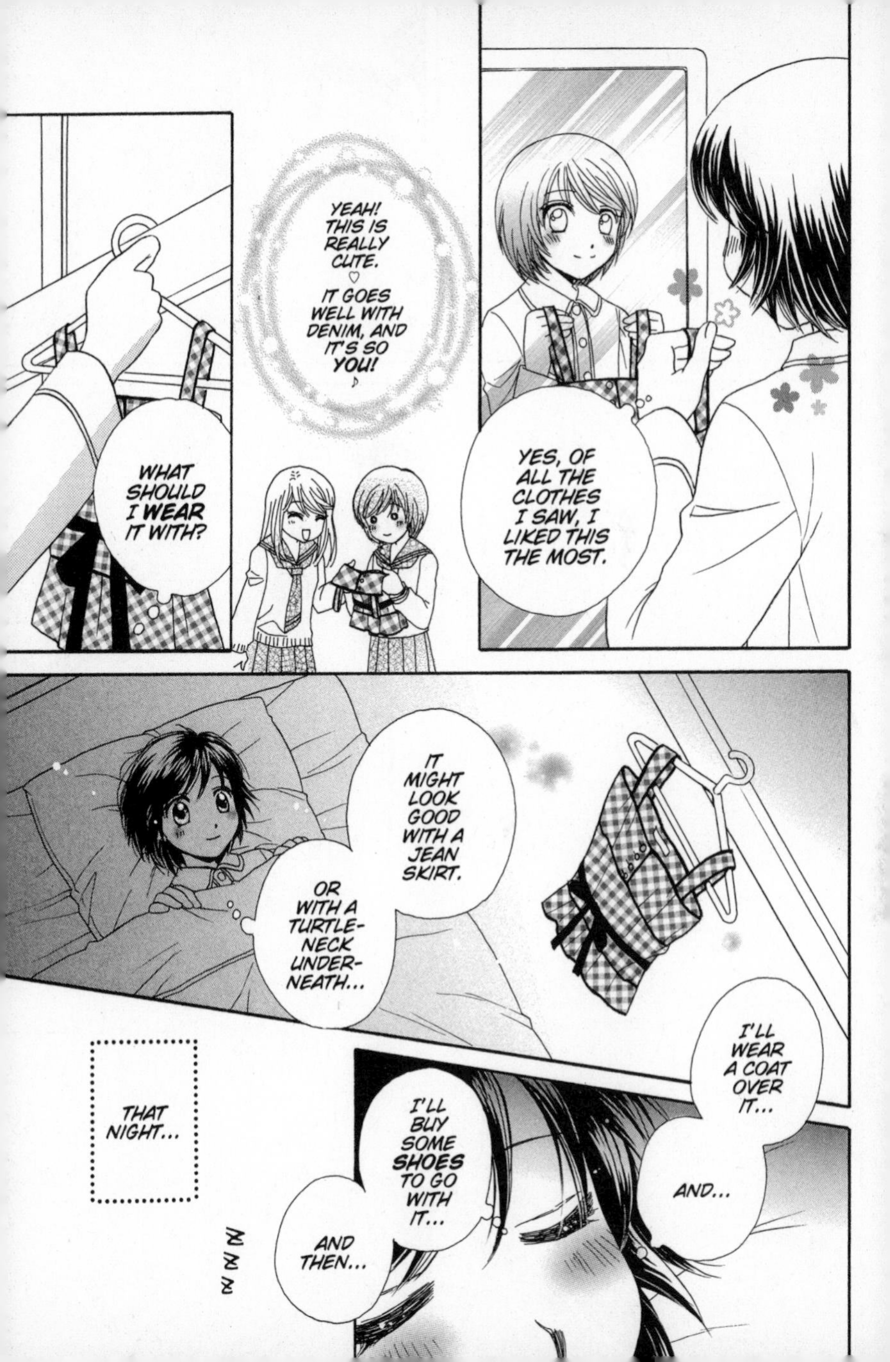
YES, OF ALL THE CLOTHES I SAW, I LIKED THIS THE MOST.
YEAH! THIS IS REALLY CUTE. ♡ IT GOES WELL WITH DENIM, AND IT'S SO YOU! ♪
WHAT SHOULD I WEAR IT WITH?
IT MIGHT LOOK GOOD WITH A JEAN SKIRT.
OR WITH A TURTLE-NECK UNDER-NEATH...
I'LL WEAR A COAT OVER IT...
AND...
I'LL BUY SOME SHOES TO GO WITH IT...
AND THEN...
THAT NIGHT...

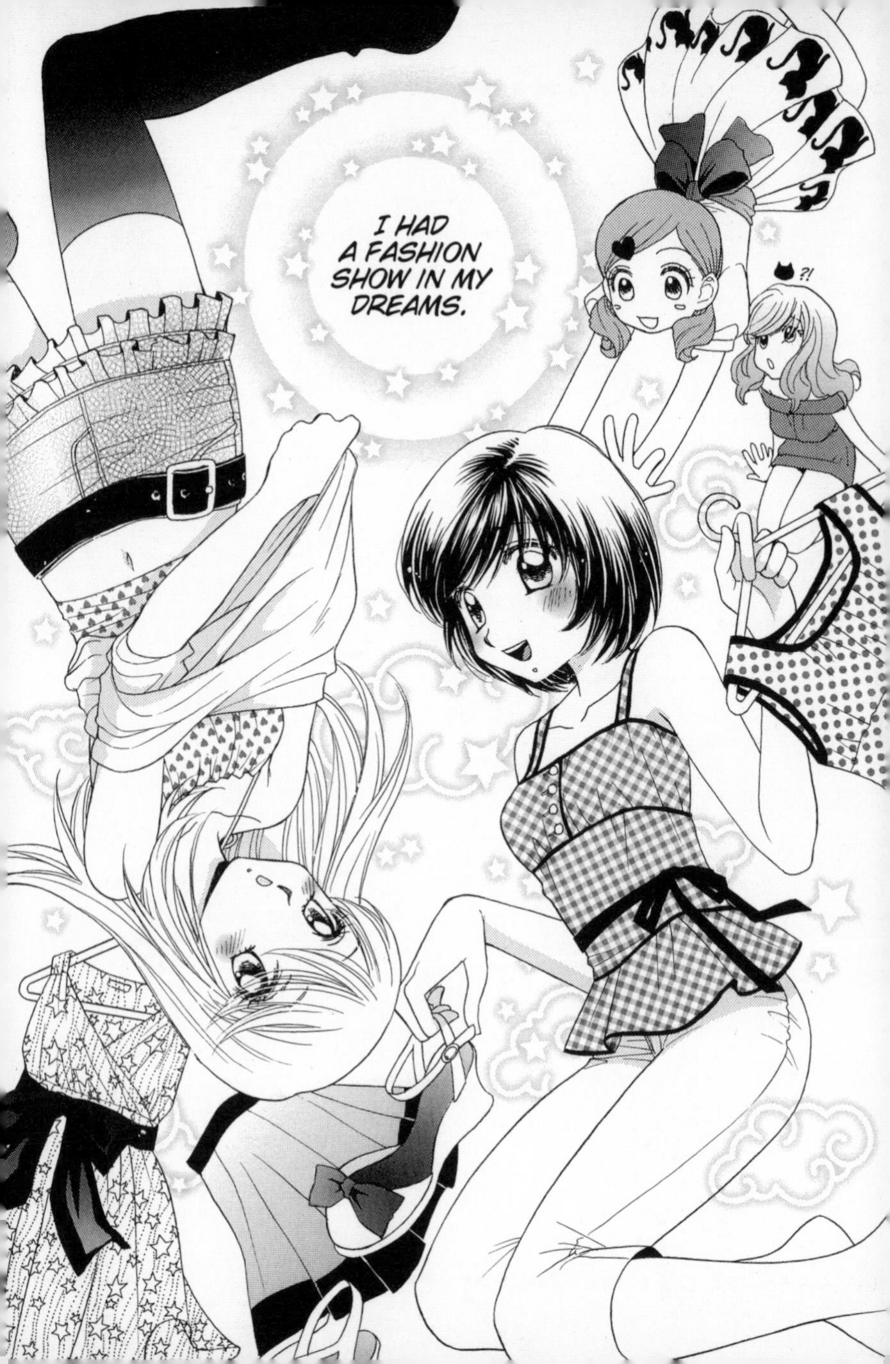
I HAD A FASHION SHOW IN MY DREAMS.
?!

WHEN I'M ON A TRAIN, IF THERE ARE ANY OPEN SEATS, I'LL SIT DOWN.

I READ NOVELS OR TEXTBOOKS. IT'S A GOOD TIME TO STUDY!

GIRL FRIENDS —ガールフレンズ—

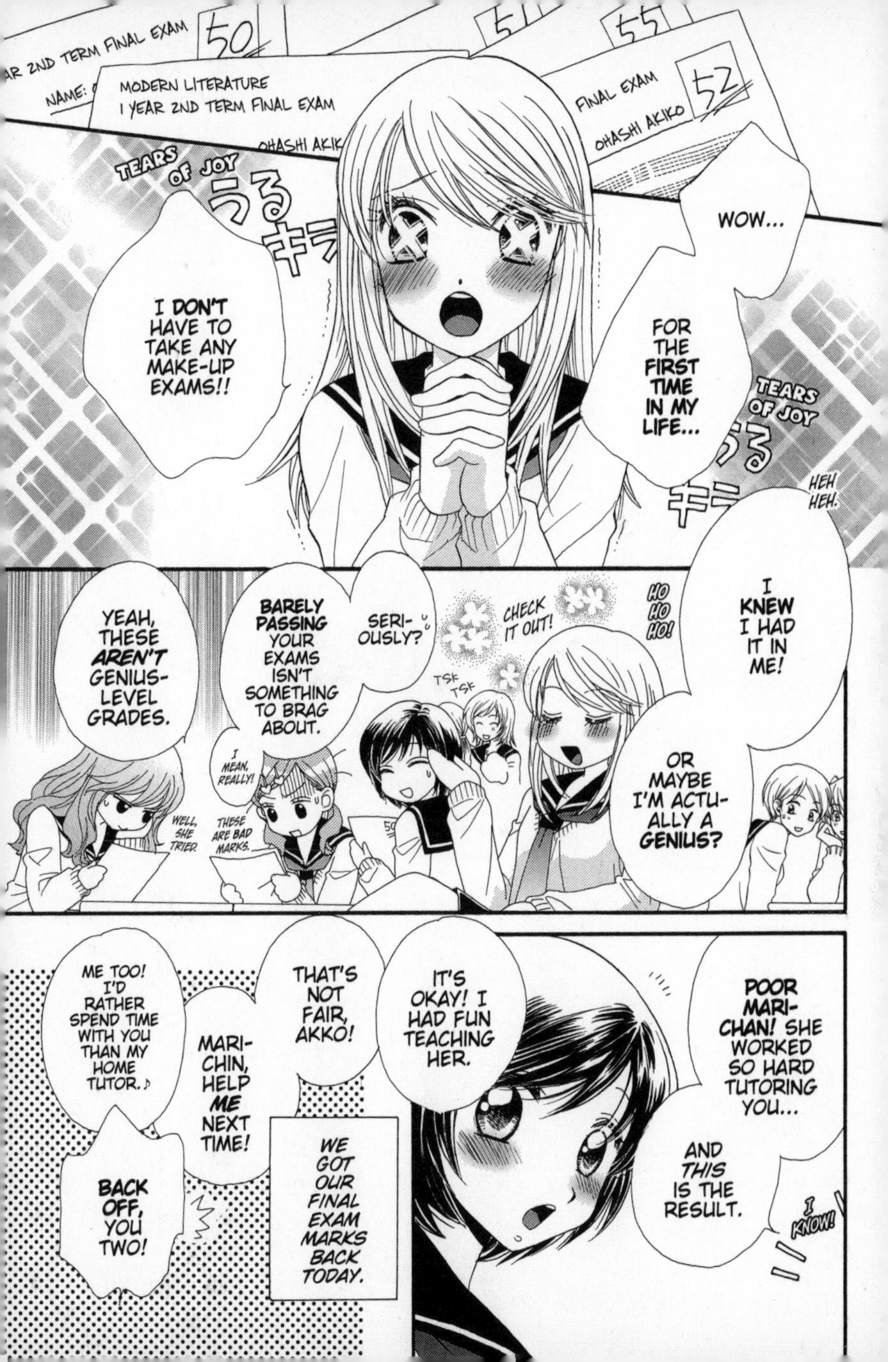
AR 2ND TERM FINAL EXAM
NAME:
MODERN LITERATURE
1 YEAR 2ND TERM FINAL EXAM
OHASHI AKIK
FINAL EXAM
OHASHI AKIKO
50
52
55
WOW...
FOR THE FIRST TIME IN MY LIFE...
TEARS OF JOY
I DON'T HAVE TO TAKE ANY MAKE-UP EXAMS!!
TEARS OF JOY
HEH HEH.
I KNEW I HAD IT IN ME!
OR MAYBE I'M ACTU-ALLY A GENIUS?
HO HO HO!
CHECK IT OUT!
TSK TSK
SERI-OUSLY?
BARELY PASSING YOUR EXAMS ISN'T SOMETHING TO BRAG ABOUT.
I MEAN, REALLY!
THESE ARE BAD MARKS.
YEAH, THESE AREN'T GENIUS-LEVEL GRADES.
WELL, SHE TRIED.
POOR MARI-CHAN! SHE WORKED SO HARD TUTORING YOU...
AND THIS IS THE RESULT.
I KNOW!
IT'S OKAY! I HAD FUN TEACHING HER.
THAT'S NOT FAIR, AKKO!
MARI-CHIN, HELP ME NEXT TIME!
WE GOT OUR FINAL EXAM MARKS BACK TODAY.
ME TOO! I'D RATHER SPEND TIME WITH YOU THAN MY HOME TUTOR.♪
BACK OFF, YOU TWO!

[CHAPTER 4]

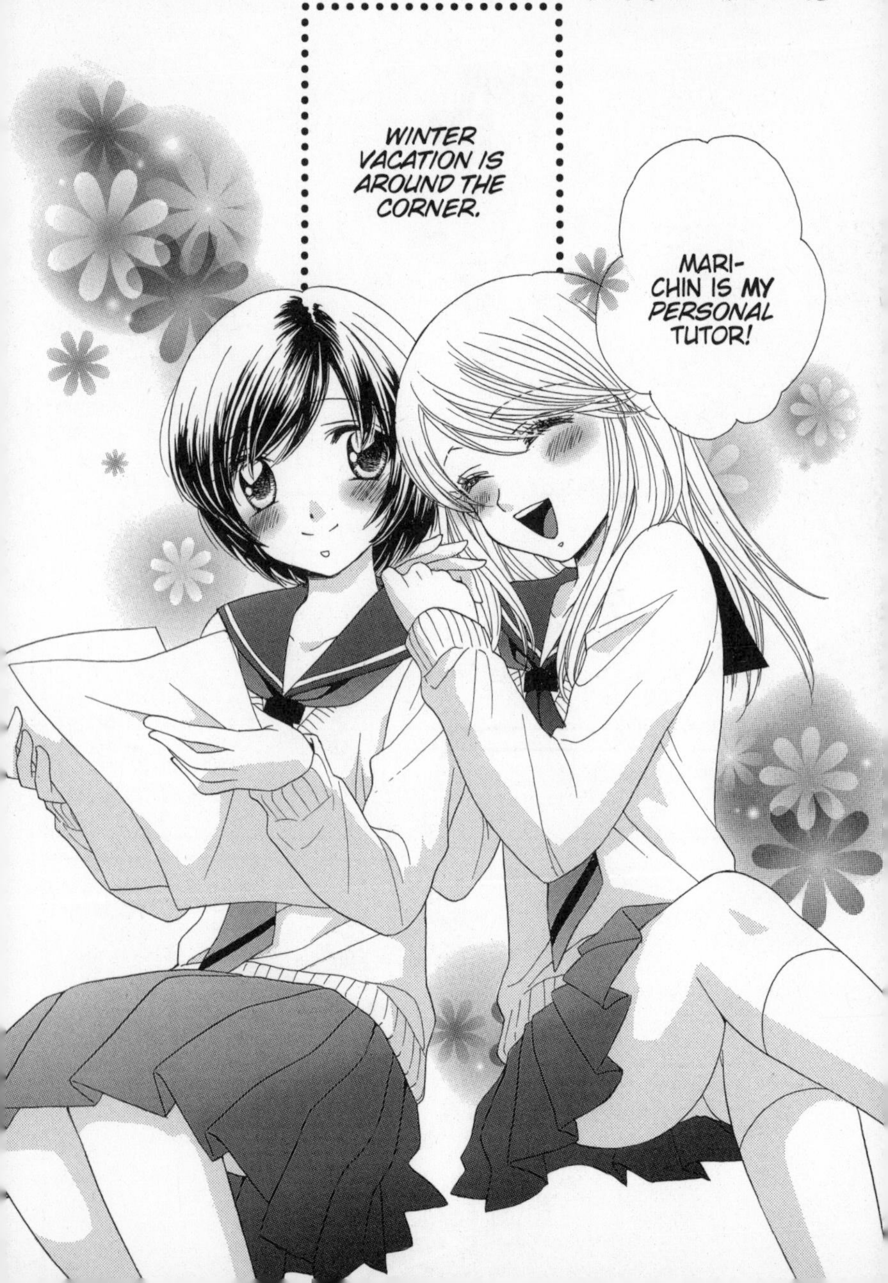
WINTER VACATION IS AROUND THE CORNER.
MARI-CHIN IS MY PERSONAL TUTOR!

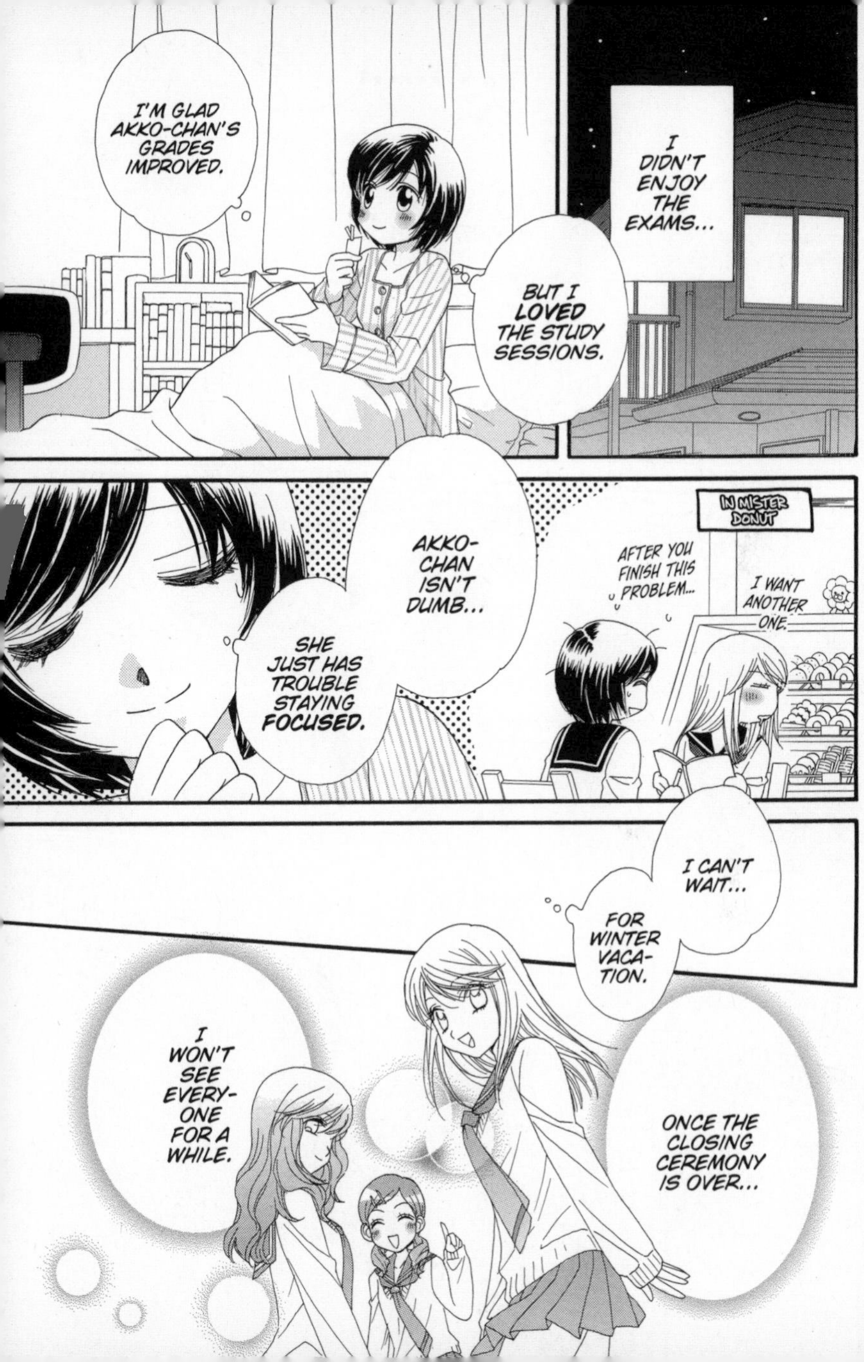
I DIDN'T ENJOY THE EXAMS...
BUT I **LOVED** THE STUDY SESSIONS.
I'M GLAD AKKO-CHAN'S GRADES IMPROVED.
IN MISTER DONUT
I WANT ANOTHER ONE.
AFTER YOU FINISH THIS PROBLEM...
AKKO-CHAN ISN'T DUMB...
SHE JUST HAS TROUBLE STAYING **FOCUSED.**
I CAN'T WAIT...
FOR WINTER VACATION.
ONCE THE CLOSING CEREMONY IS OVER...
I WON'T SEE EVERYONE FOR A WHILE.

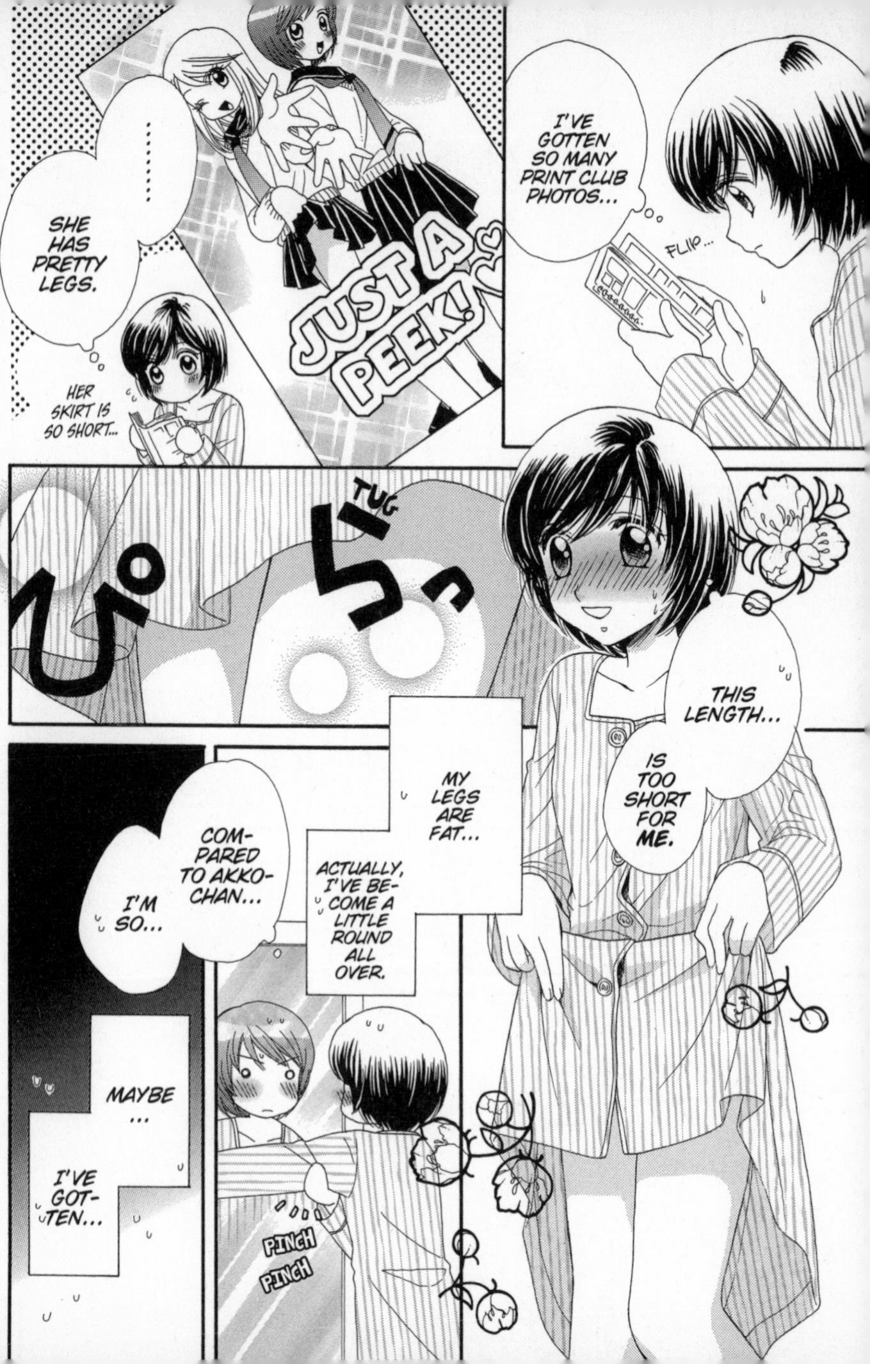
I'VE GOTTEN SO MANY PRINT CLUB PHOTOS...
FLIP...
JUST A PEEK!
......
SHE HAS PRETTY LEGS.
HER SKIRT IS SO SHORT...
THIS LENGTH...
IS TOO SHORT FOR ME.
TUG
MY LEGS ARE FAT...
ACTUALLY, I'VE BECOME A LITTLE ROUND ALL OVER.
COMPARED TO AKKO-CHAN...
I'M SO...
PINCH
PINCH
MAYBE...
I'VE GOTTEN...

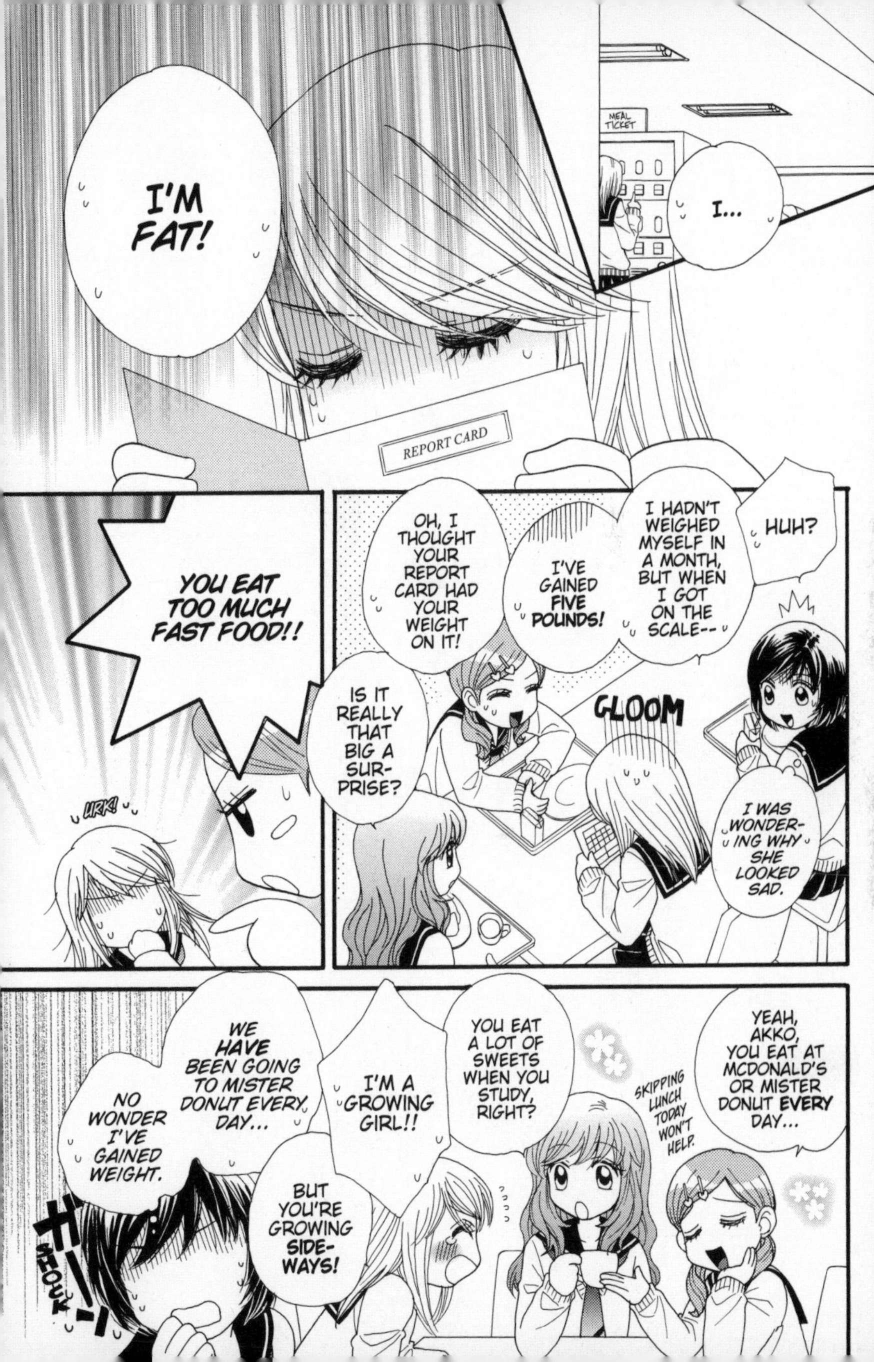

MEAL TICKET
I...
I'M FAT!
REPORT CARD
HUH?
I HADN'T WEIGHED MYSELF IN A MONTH, BUT WHEN I GOT ON THE SCALE--
I'VE GAINED FIVE POUNDS!
OH, I THOUGHT YOUR REPORT CARD HAD YOUR WEIGHT ON IT!
GLOOM
IS IT REALLY THAT BIG A SUR-PRISE?
I WAS WONDER-ING WHY SHE LOOKED SAD.
YOU EAT TOO MUCH FAST FOOD!!
URK!
YEAH, AKKO, YOU EAT AT MCDONALD'S OR MISTER DONUT EVERY DAY...
SKIPPING LUNCH TODAY WON'T HELP.
YOU EAT A LOT OF SWEETS WHEN YOU STUDY, RIGHT?
I'M A GROWING GIRL!!
WE HAVE BEEN GOING TO MISTER DONUT EVERY DAY...
NO WONDER I'VE GAINED WEIGHT.
BUT YOU'RE GROWING SIDE-WAYS!
SHOCK

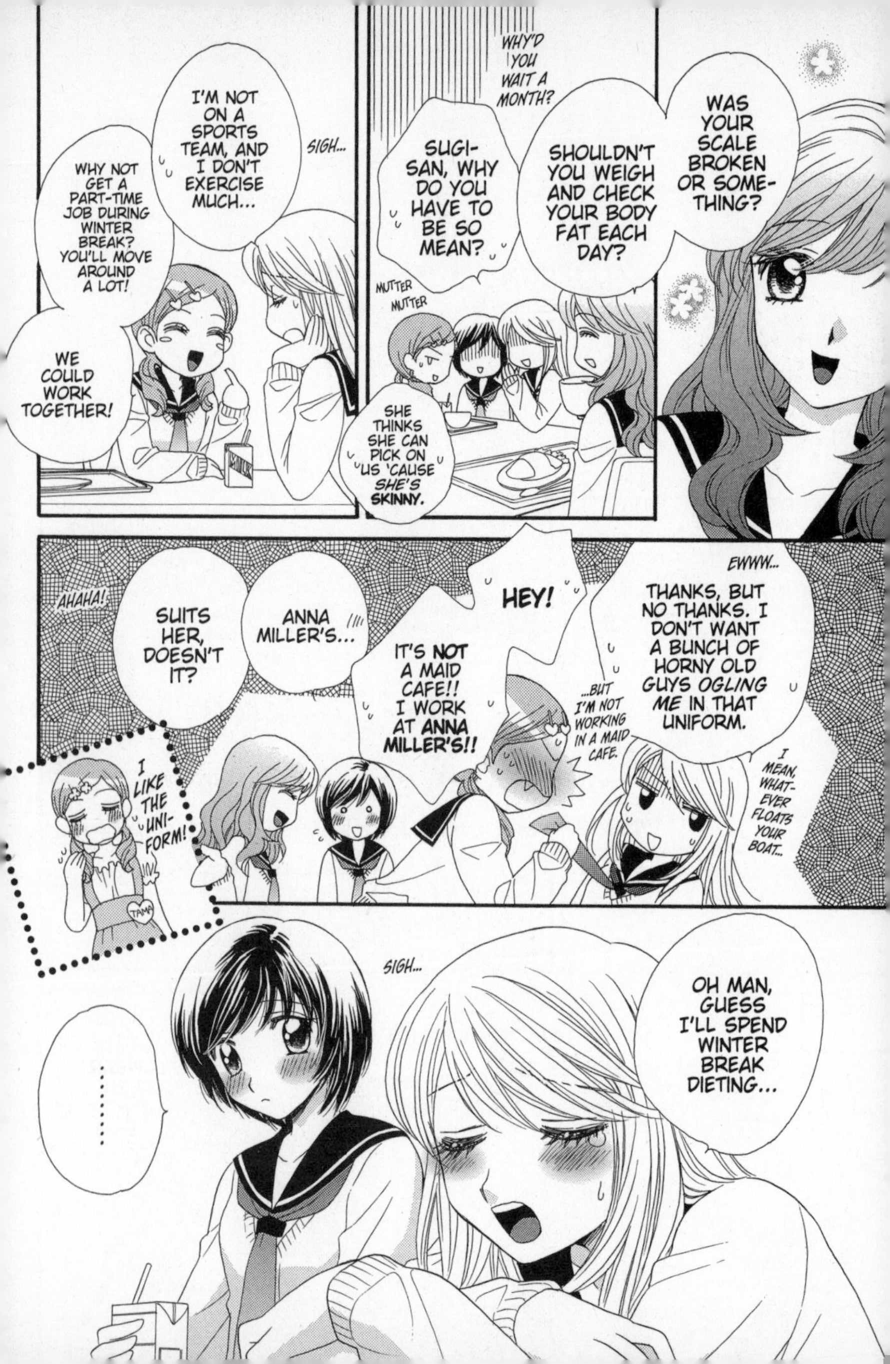

WAS YOUR SCALE BROKEN OR SOME-THING?
SHOULDN'T YOU WEIGH AND CHECK YOUR BODY FAT EACH DAY?
WHY'D YOU WAIT A MONTH?
SUGI-SAN, WHY DO YOU HAVE TO BE SO MEAN?
MUTTER MUTTER
SHE THINKS SHE CAN PICK ON US 'CAUSE SHE'S SKINNY.
SIGH...
I'M NOT ON A SPORTS TEAM, AND I DON'T EXERCISE MUCH...
WHY NOT GET A PART-TIME JOB DURING WINTER BREAK? YOU'LL MOVE AROUND A LOT!
WE COULD WORK TOGETHER!
EWWW...
THANKS, BUT NO THANKS. I DON'T WANT A BUNCH OF HORNY OLD GUYS OGLING ME IN THAT UNIFORM.
I MEAN, WHAT-EVER FLOATS YOUR BOAT...
HEY!
...BUT I'M NOT WORKING IN A MAID CAFE.
IT'S NOT A MAID CAFE!! I WORK AT ANNA MILLER'S!!
ANNA MILLER'S...
SUITS HER, DOESN'T IT?
AHAHA!
I LIKE THE UNI-FORM!
TAMA
OH MAN, GUESS I'LL SPEND WINTER BREAK DIETING...
SIGH...
......

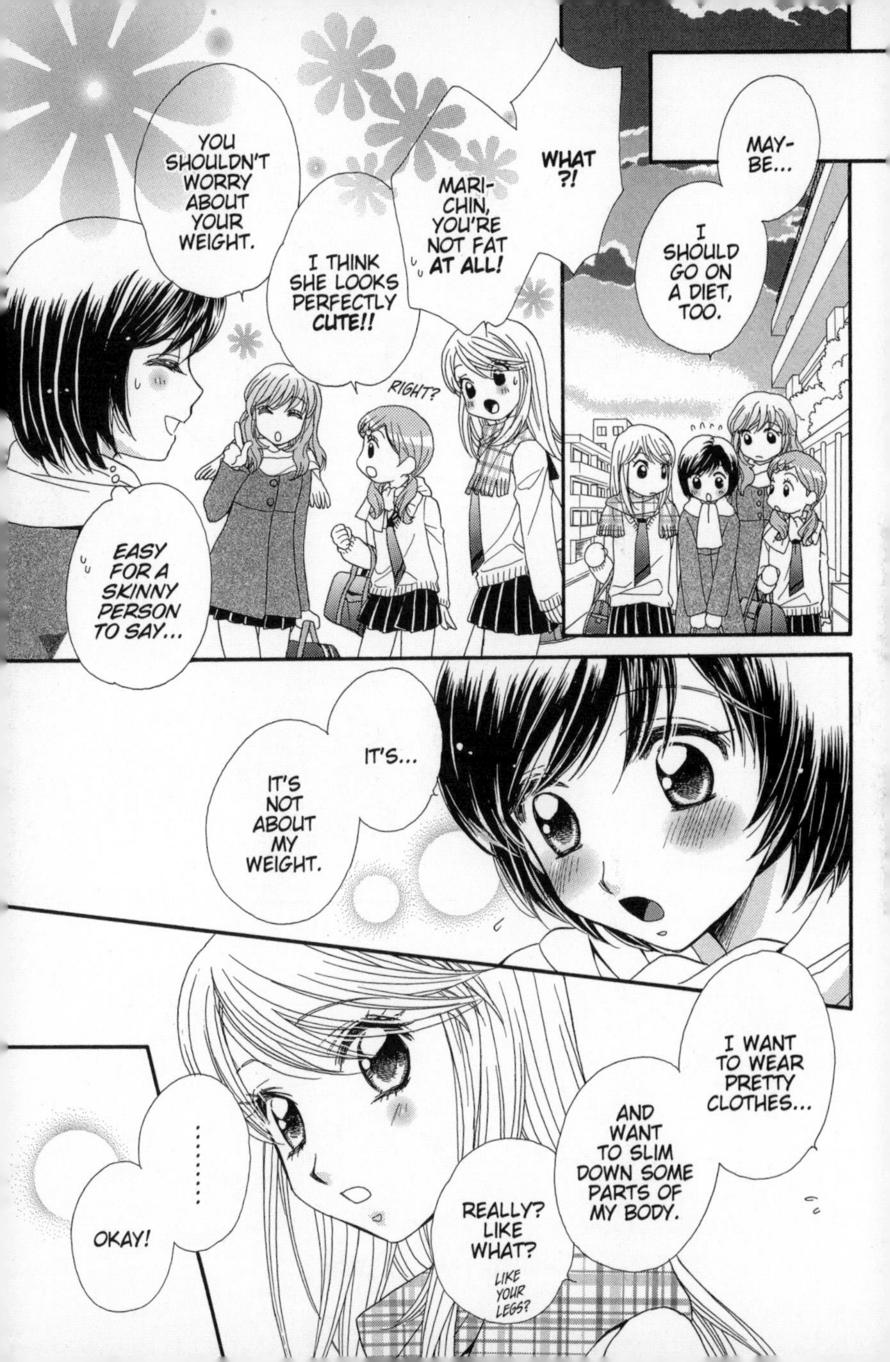
MAY-BE...
I SHOULD GO ON A DIET, TOO.
WHAT?!
MARI-CHIN, YOU'RE NOT FAT AT ALL!
I THINK SHE LOOKS PERFECTLY CUTE!!
RIGHT?
YOU SHOULDN'T WORRY ABOUT YOUR WEIGHT.
EASY FOR A SKINNY PERSON TO SAY...
IT'S...
IT'S NOT ABOUT MY WEIGHT.
I WANT TO WEAR PRETTY CLOTHES...
AND WANT TO SLIM DOWN SOME PARTS OF MY BODY.
REALLY? LIKE WHAT?
LIKE YOUR LEGS?
......
OKAY!

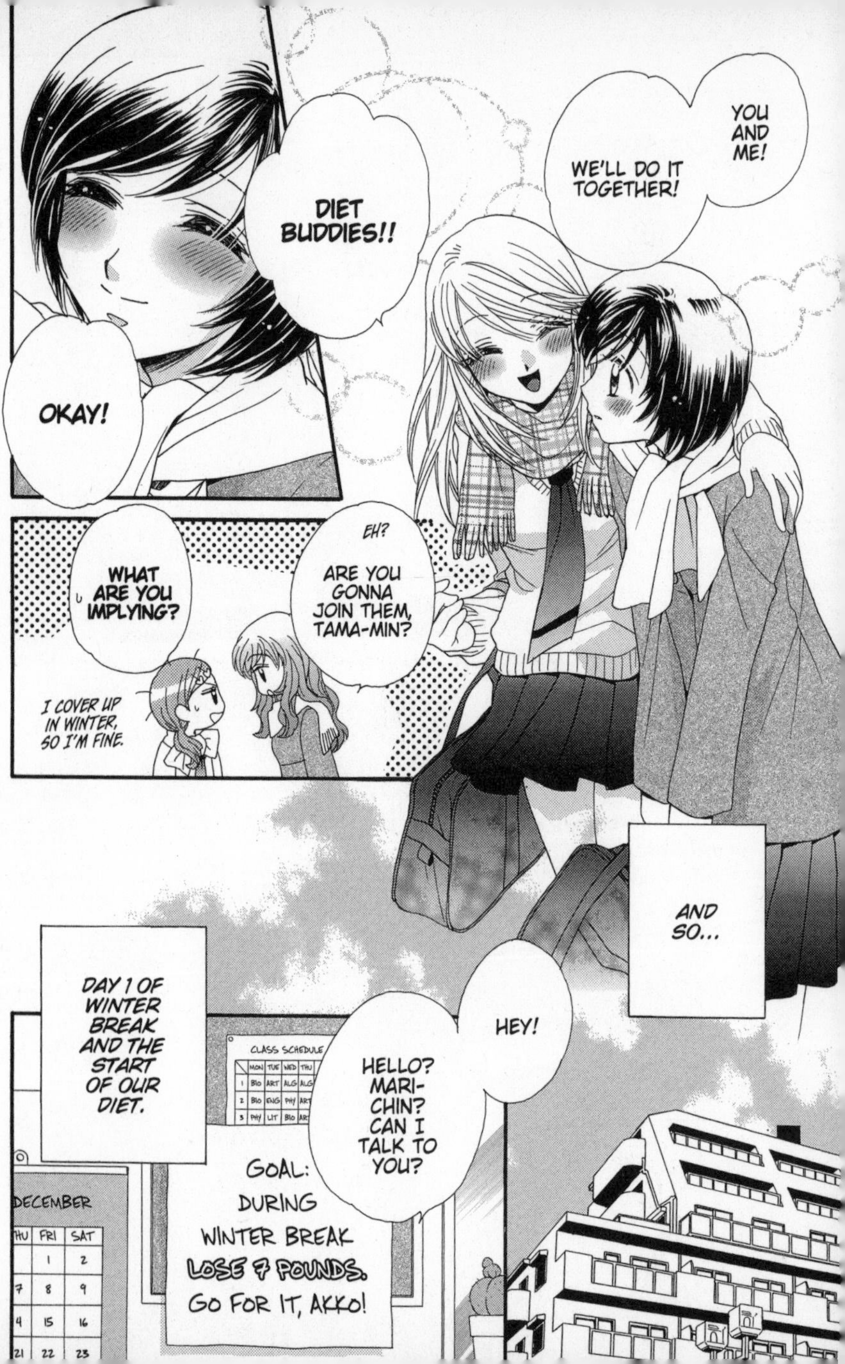
YOU AND ME!
WE'LL DO IT TOGETHER!
DIET BUDDIES!!
OKAY!
EH?
ARE YOU GONNA JOIN THEM, TAMA-MIN?
WHAT ARE YOU IMPLYING?
I COVER UP IN WINTER, SO I'M FINE.
AND SO...
HEY!
HELLO? MARI-CHIN? CAN I TALK TO YOU?
DAY 1 OF WINTER BREAK AND THE START OF OUR DIET.
CLASS SCHEDULE
MON TUE WED THU
1 BIO ART ALG ALG
2 BIO ENG PHY ART
3 PHY LIT BIO ART
GOAL: DURING WINTER BREAK LOSE 7 POUNDS. GO FOR IT, AKKO!
DECEMBER
THU FRI SAT
1 2
7 8 9
14 15 16
21 22 23

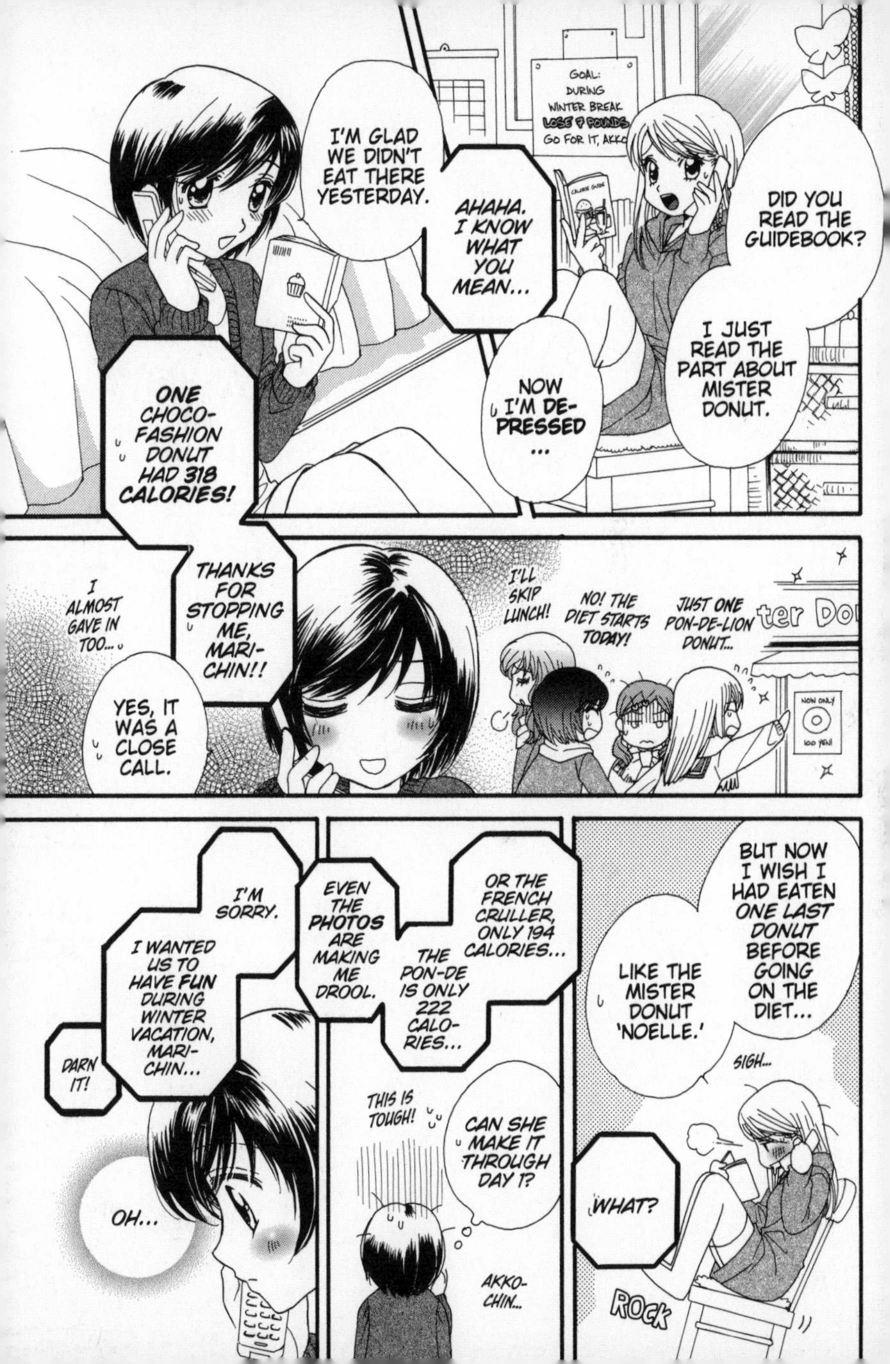
GOAL: DURING WINTER BREAK LOSE 7 POUNDS Go For It, Akko
CALORIE GUIDE
DID YOU READ THE GUIDEBOOK?
I JUST READ THE PART ABOUT MISTER DONUT.
NOW I'M DE-PRESSED...
AHAHA. I KNOW WHAT YOU MEAN...
I'M GLAD WE DIDN'T EAT THERE YESTERDAY.
ONE CHOCO-FASHION DONUT HAD 318 CALORIES!
ter Do
NOW ONLY 100 YEN!
JUST ONE PON-DE-LION DONUT...
NO! THE DIET STARTS TODAY!
I'LL SKIP LUNCH!
THANKS FOR STOPPING ME, MARI-CHIN!!
I ALMOST GAVE IN TOO...
YES, IT WAS A CLOSE CALL.
BUT NOW I WISH I HAD EATEN ONE LAST DONUT BEFORE GOING ON THE DIET...
LIKE THE MISTER DONUT 'NOELLE.'
SIGH...
WHAT?
ROCK
OR THE FRENCH CRULLER, ONLY 194 CALORIES...
THE PON-DE IS ONLY 222 CALO-RIES...
EVEN THE PHOTOS ARE MAKING ME DROOL.
CAN SHE MAKE IT THROUGH DAY 1?
THIS IS TOUGH!
AKKO-CHIN...
I'M SORRY.
I WANTED US TO HAVE FUN DURING WINTER VACATION, MARI-CHIN...
DARN IT!
OH...

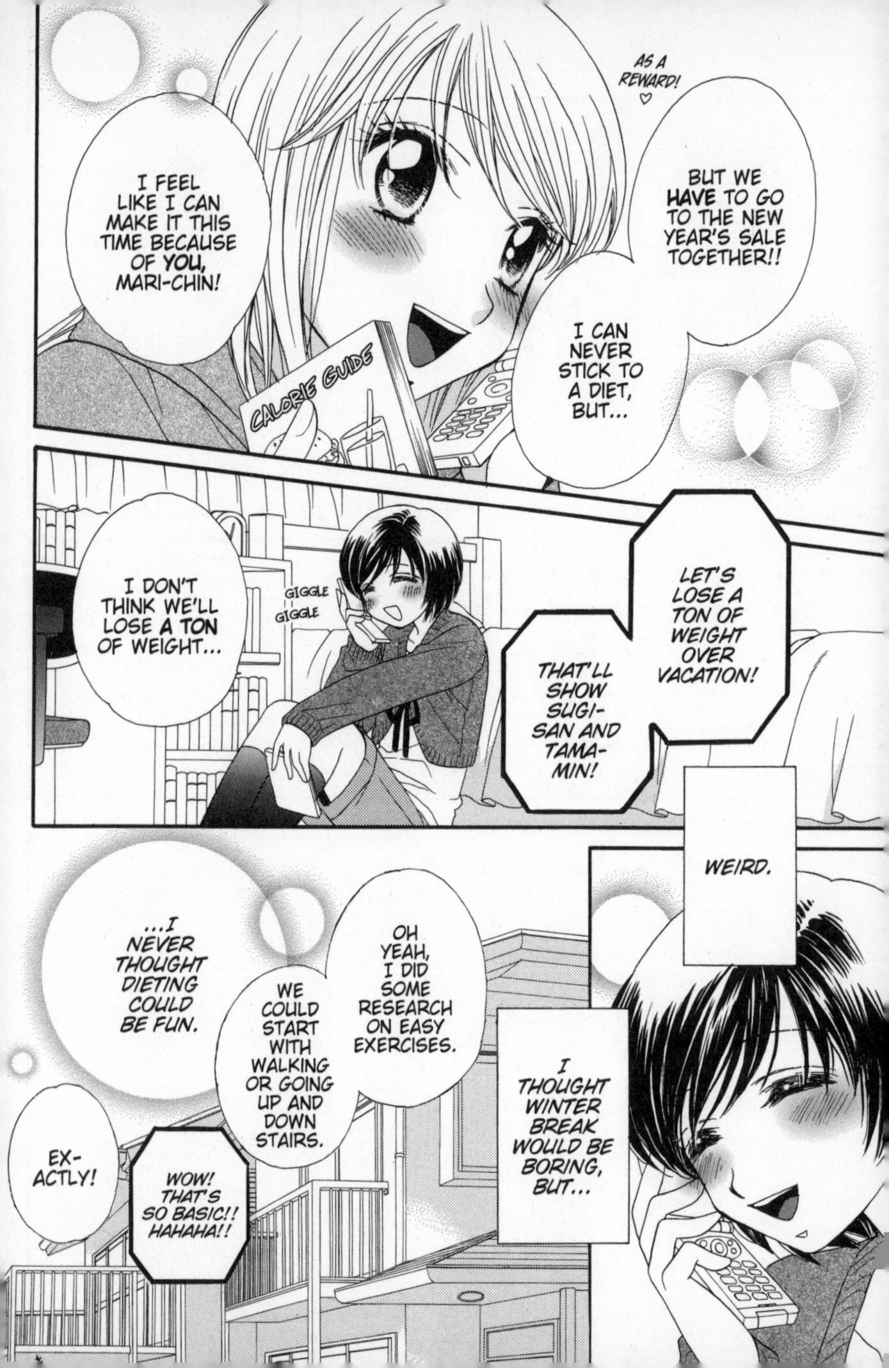
AS A REWARD! ♡
BUT WE HAVE TO GO TO THE NEW YEAR'S SALE TOGETHER!!
I CAN NEVER STICK TO A DIET, BUT...
I FEEL LIKE I CAN MAKE IT THIS TIME BECAUSE OF YOU, MARI-CHIN!
CALORIE GUIDE
LET'S LOSE A TON OF WEIGHT OVER VACATION!
THAT'LL SHOW SUGI-SAN AND TAMA-MIN!
GIGGLE GIGGLE
I DON'T THINK WE'LL LOSE A TON OF WEIGHT...
WEIRD.
I THOUGHT WINTER BREAK WOULD BE BORING, BUT...
OH YEAH, I DID SOME RESEARCH ON EASY EXERCISES.
WE COULD START WITH WALKING OR GOING UP AND DOWN STAIRS.
WOW! THAT'S SO BASIC!! HAHAHA!!
...I NEVER THOUGHT DIETING COULD BE FUN.
EX-ACTLY!

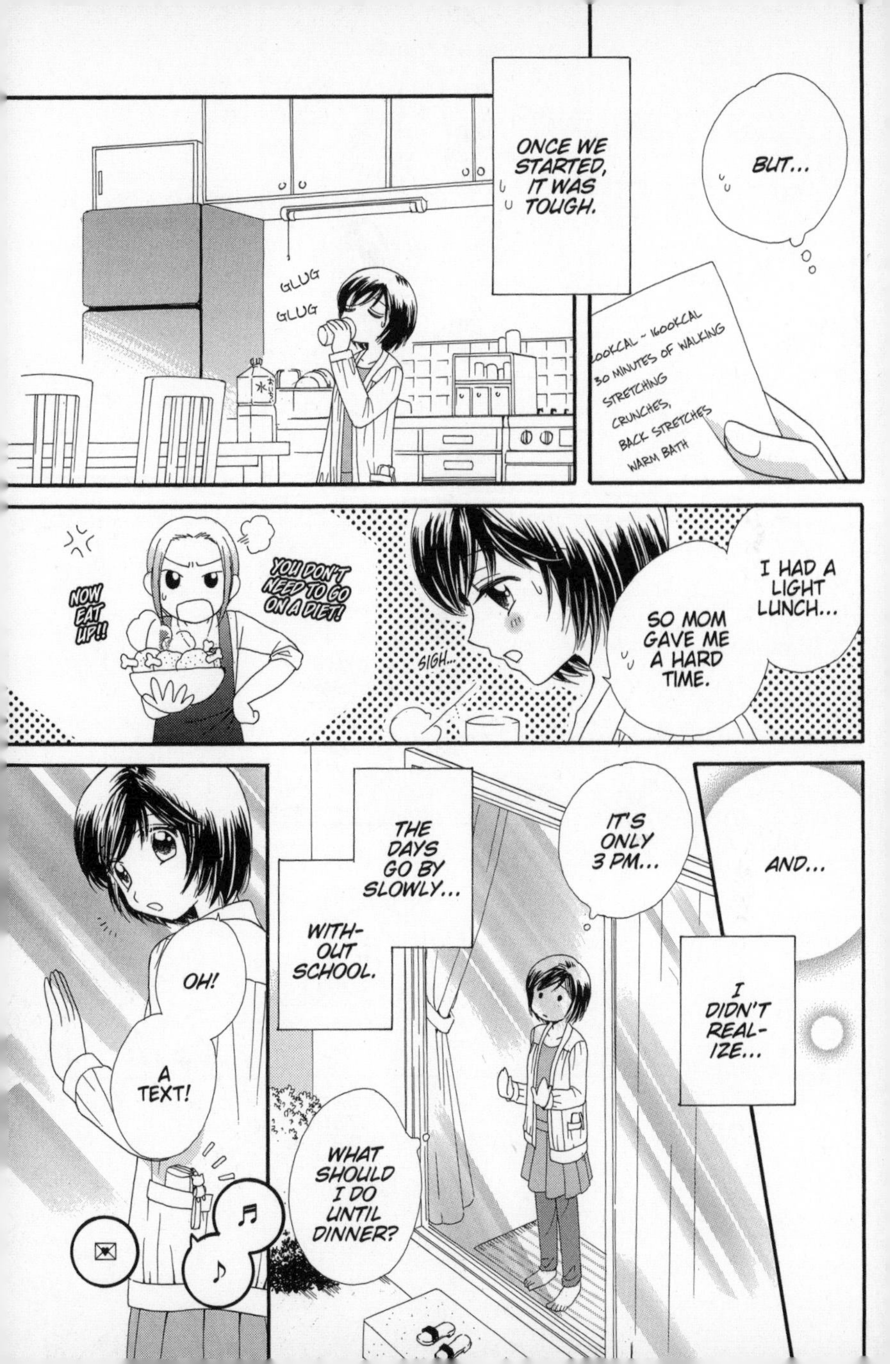

BUT...
OOKCAL ~ 1600KCAL
30 MINUTES OF WALKING
STRETCHING
CRUNCHES,
BACK STRETCHES
WARM BATH
ONCE WE STARTED, IT WAS TOUGH.
GLUG
GLUG
I HAD A LIGHT LUNCH...
SO MOM GAVE ME A HARD TIME.
SIGH...
YOU DON'T NEED TO GO ON A DIET!
NOW EAT UP!!
AND...
I DIDN'T REAL-IZE...
IT'S ONLY 3 PM...
THE DAYS GO BY SLOWLY...
WITH-OUT SCHOOL.
WHAT SHOULD I DO UNTIL DINNER?
OH!
A TEXT!

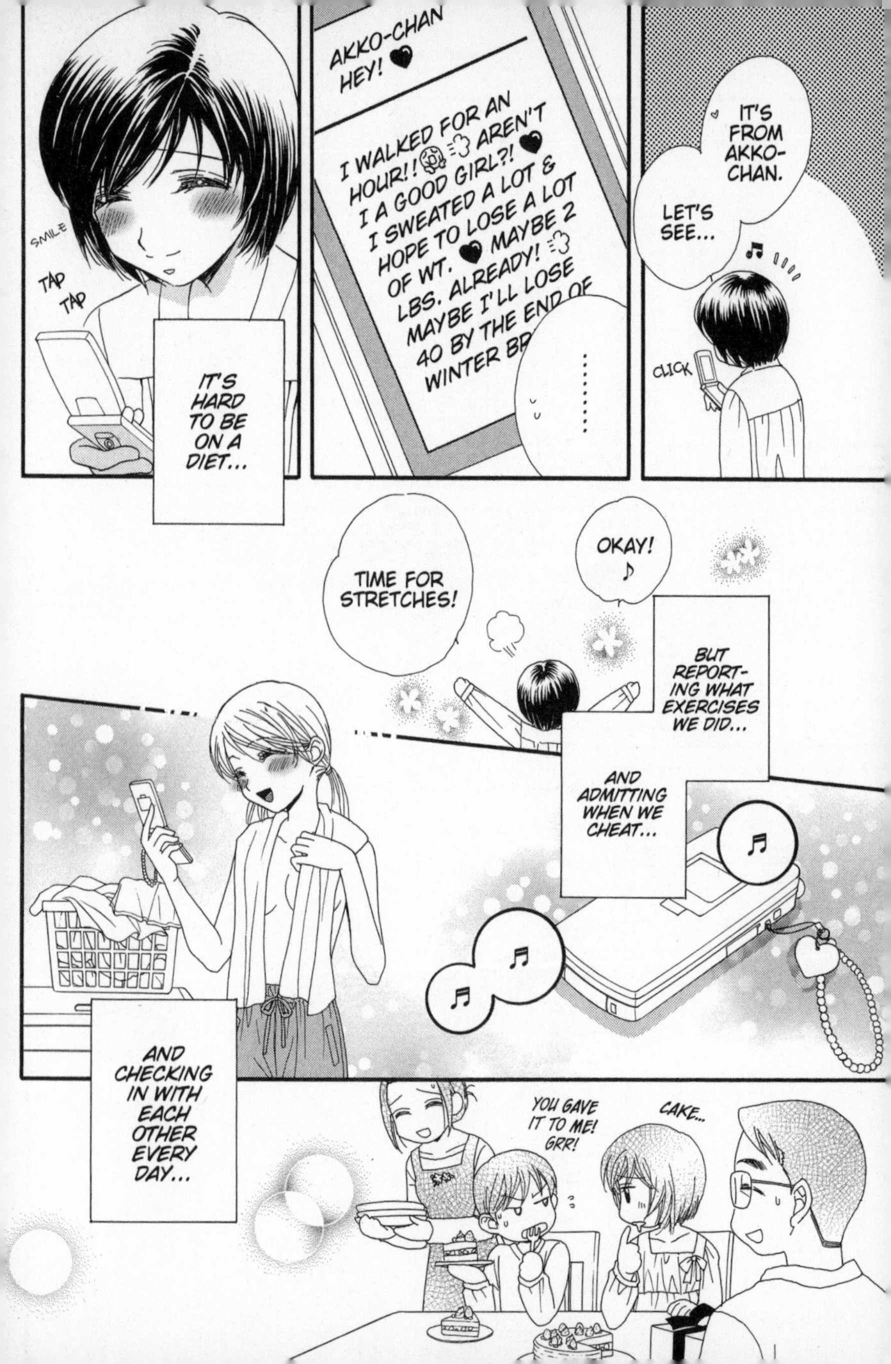
IT'S FROM AKKO-CHAN.
LET'S SEE...
♬
CLICK
AKKO-CHAN HEY!
I WALKED FOR AN HOUR!! AREN'T I A GOOD GIRL?! I SWEATED A LOT & HOPE TO LOSE A LOT OF WT. MAYBE 2 LBS. ALREADY! MAYBE I'LL LOSE 40 BY THE END OF WINTER BR
......
SMILE
TAP TAP
IT'S HARD TO BE ON A DIET...
OKAY! ♪
TIME FOR STRETCHES!
BUT REPORTING WHAT EXERCISES WE DID...
AND ADMITTING WHEN WE CHEAT...
♬
♬
♬
AND CHECKING IN WITH EACH OTHER EVERY DAY...
CAKE...
YOU GAVE IT TO ME! GRR!

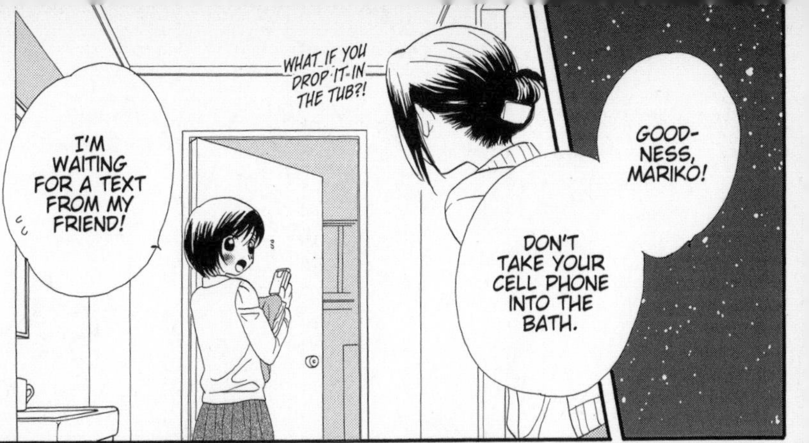
GOOD-NESS, MARIKO!
DON'T TAKE YOUR CELL PHONE INTO THE BATH.
WHAT IF YOU DROP IT IN THE TUB?!
I'M WAITING FOR A TEXT FROM MY FRIEND!

*Kohaku Uta Gassen is an annual New Year's Eve music program in Japan. **Otoshidama is money children receive on New Year's Day

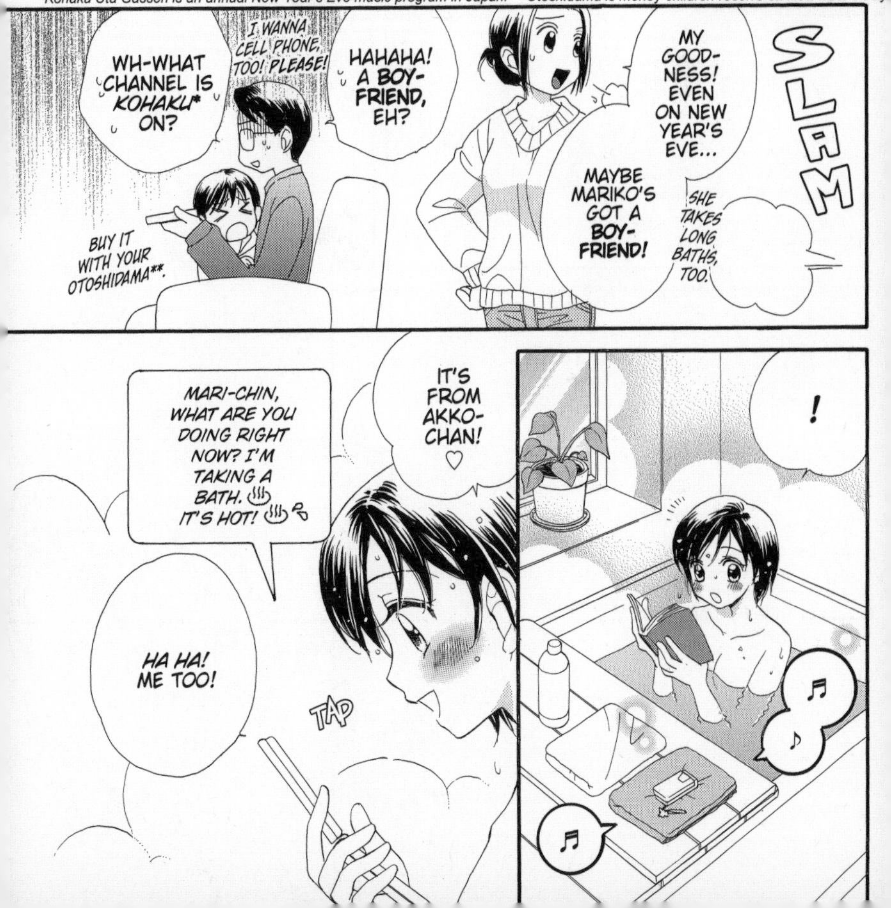
SLAM
MY GOOD-NESS! EVEN ON NEW YEAR'S EVE...
MAYBE MARIKO'S GOT A BOY-FRIEND!
SHE TAKES LONG BATHS, TOO.
HAHAHA! A BOY-FRIEND, EH?
I WANNA CELL PHONE, TOO! PLEASE!
WH-WHAT CHANNEL IS KOHAKU* ON?
BUY IT WITH YOUR OTOSHIDAMA**.
!
♪
♪
IT'S FROM AKKO-CHAN! ♡
MARI-CHIN, WHAT ARE YOU DOING RIGHT NOW? I'M TAKING A BATH. ♨ IT'S HOT! ♨
TAP
HA HA! ME TOO!

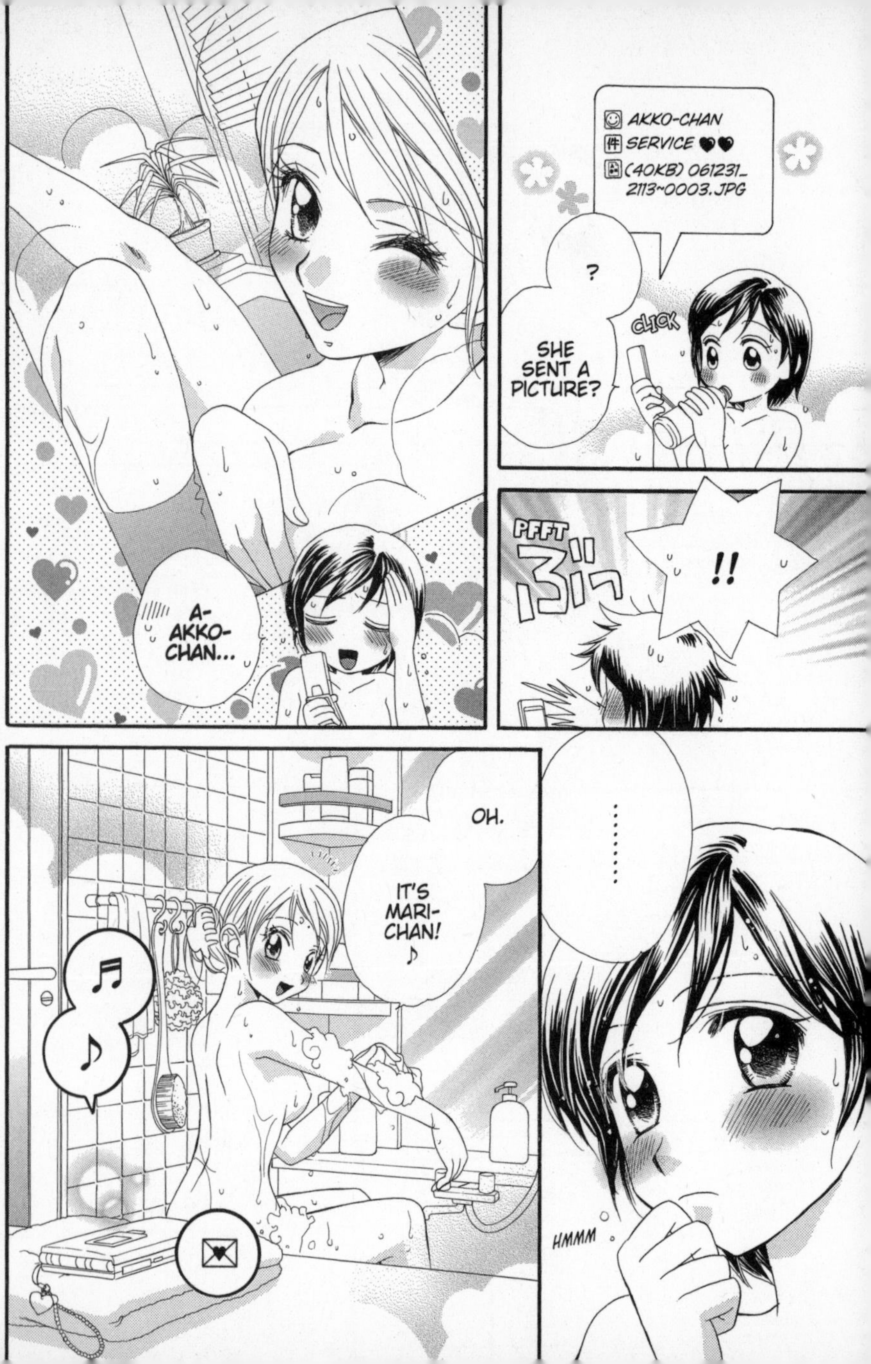
AKKO-CHAN
件 SERVICE ❤❤
(40KB) 061231_2113~0003.JPG
?
CLICK
SHE SENT A PICTURE?
!!
PFFT ぶっ
A-AKKO-CHAN...
......
HMMM
OH.
IT'S MARI-CHAN! ♪
♬ ♪

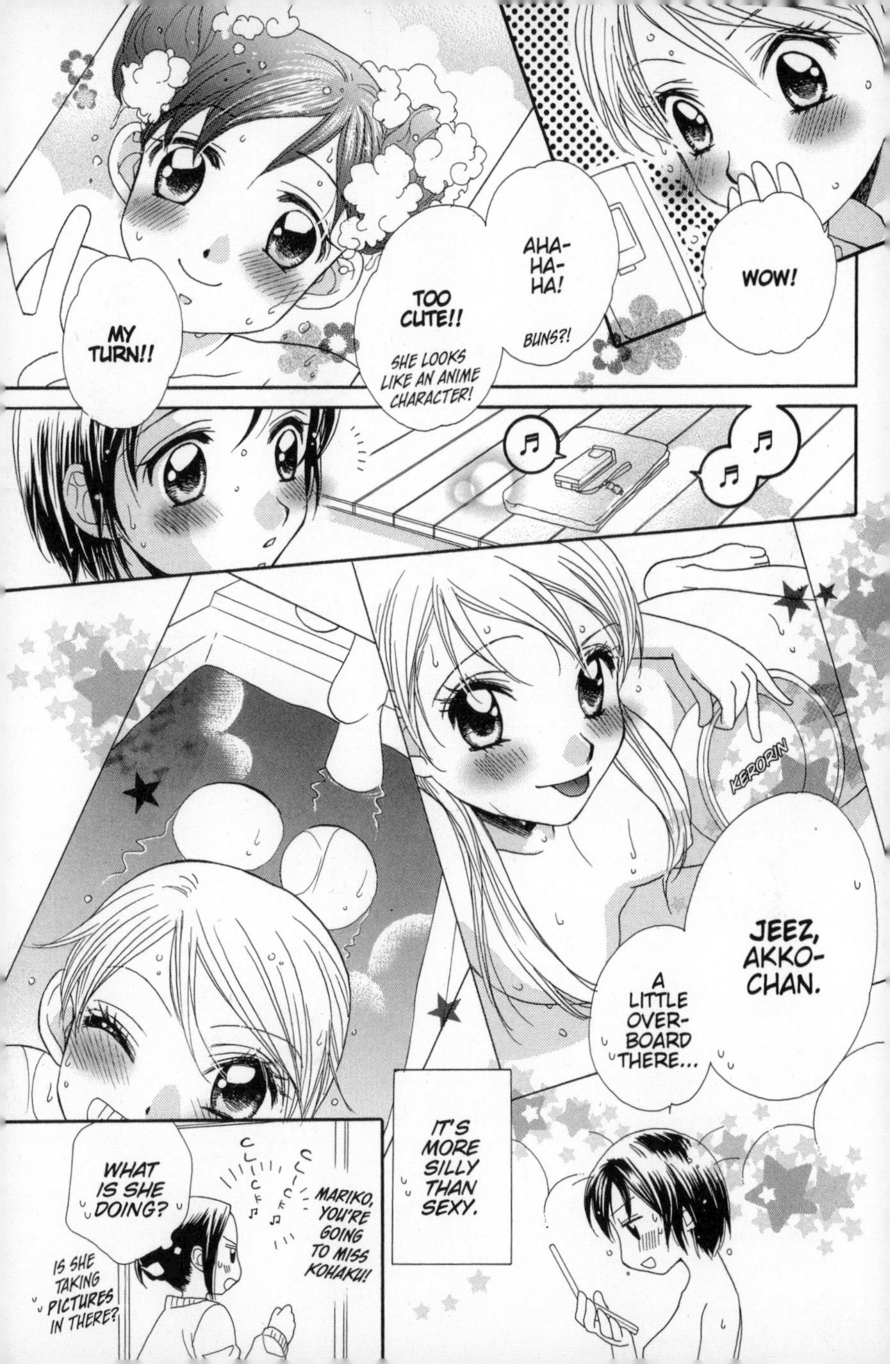
WOW!
AHA-HA-HA!
BUNS?!
TOO CUTE!!
SHE LOOKS LIKE AN ANIME CHARACTER!
MY TURN!!
KERORIN
JEEZ, AKKO-CHAN.
A LITTLE OVER-BOARD THERE...
IT'S MORE SILLY THAN SEXY.
MARIKO, YOU'RE GOING TO MISS KOHAKU!
CLICK CLICK
WHAT IS SHE DOING?
IS SHE TAKING PICTURES IN THERE?

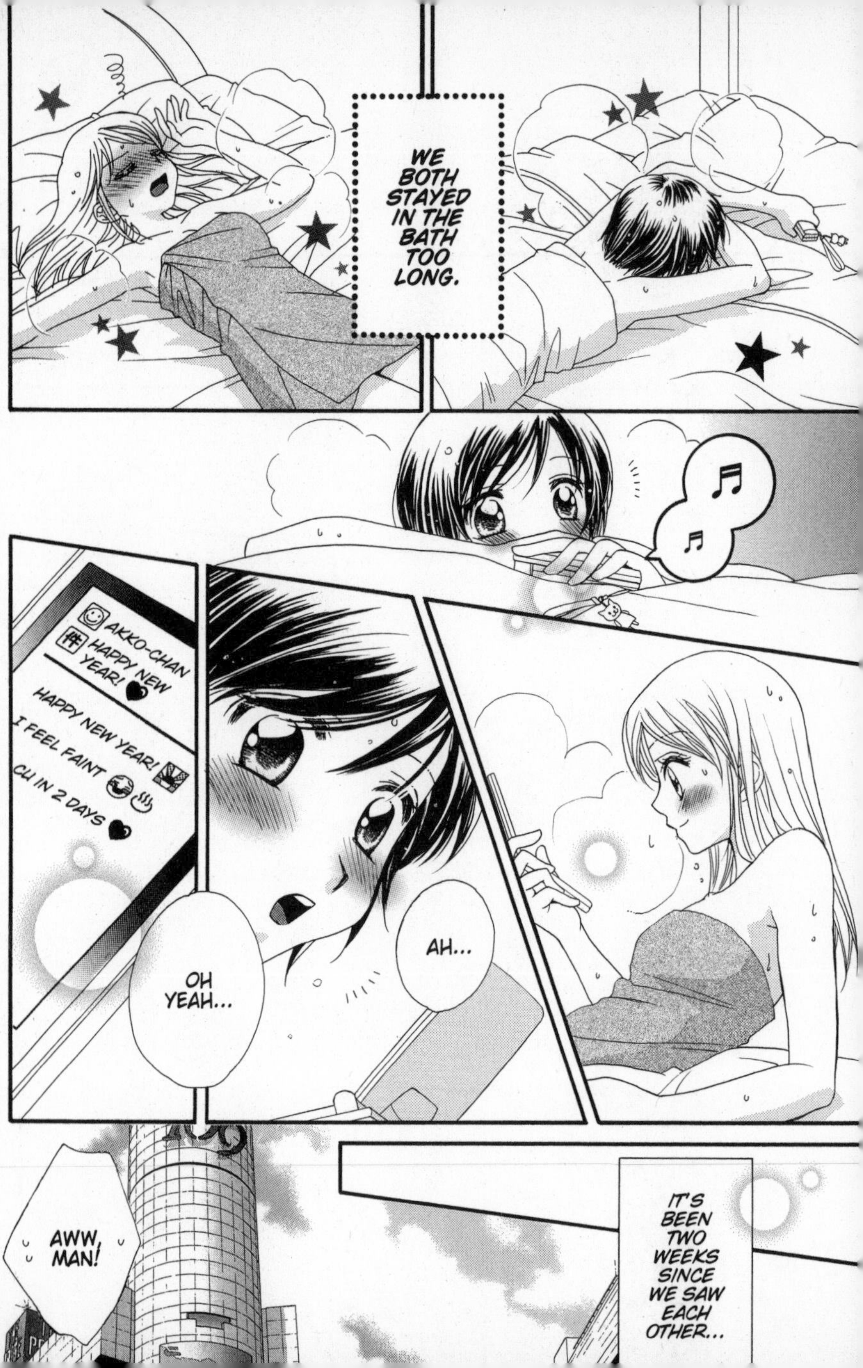
WE BOTH STAYED IN THE BATH TOO LONG.
♫ ♫
AH...
OH YEAH...
AKKO-CHAN
件 HAPPY NEW YEAR! ♥
HAPPY NEW YEAR!
I FEEL FAINT
CU IN 2 DAYS ♥
IT'S BEEN TWO WEEKS SINCE WE SAW EACH OTHER...
AWW, MAN!

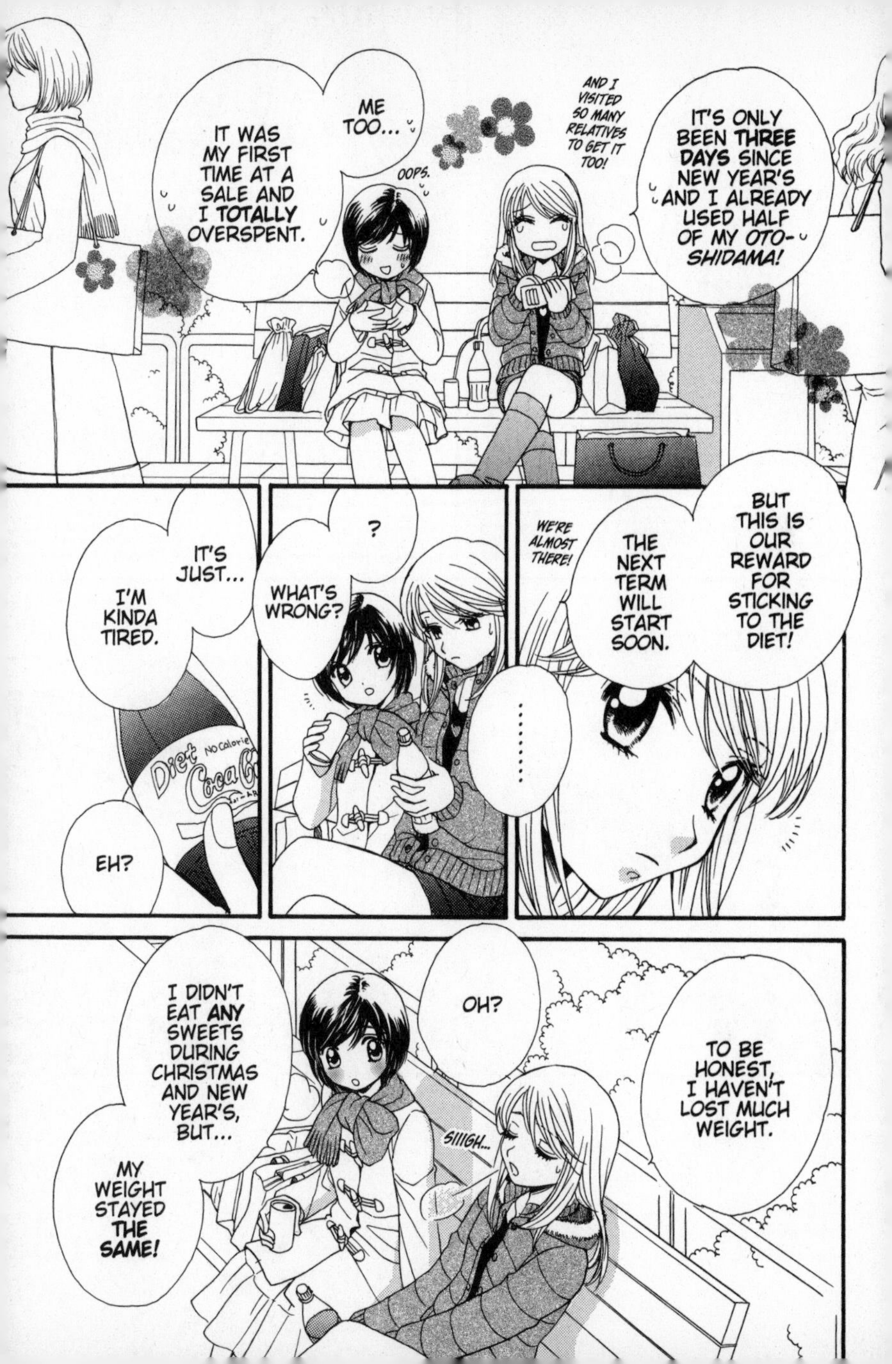
IT'S ONLY BEEN THREE DAYS SINCE NEW YEAR'S AND I ALREADY USED HALF OF MY OTO-SHIDAMA!
AND I VISITED SO MANY RELATIVES TO GET IT TOO!
ME TOO...
OOPS.
IT WAS MY FIRST TIME AT A SALE AND I TOTALLY OVERSPENT.
BUT THIS IS OUR REWARD FOR STICKING TO THE DIET!
THE NEXT TERM WILL START SOON.
WE'RE ALMOST THERE!
?
WHAT'S WRONG?
......
IT'S JUST...
I'M KINDA TIRED.
EH?
TO BE HONEST, I HAVEN'T LOST MUCH WEIGHT.
SIIIGH...
OH?
I DIDN'T EAT ANY SWEETS DURING CHRISTMAS AND NEW YEAR'S, BUT...
MY WEIGHT STAYED THE SAME!

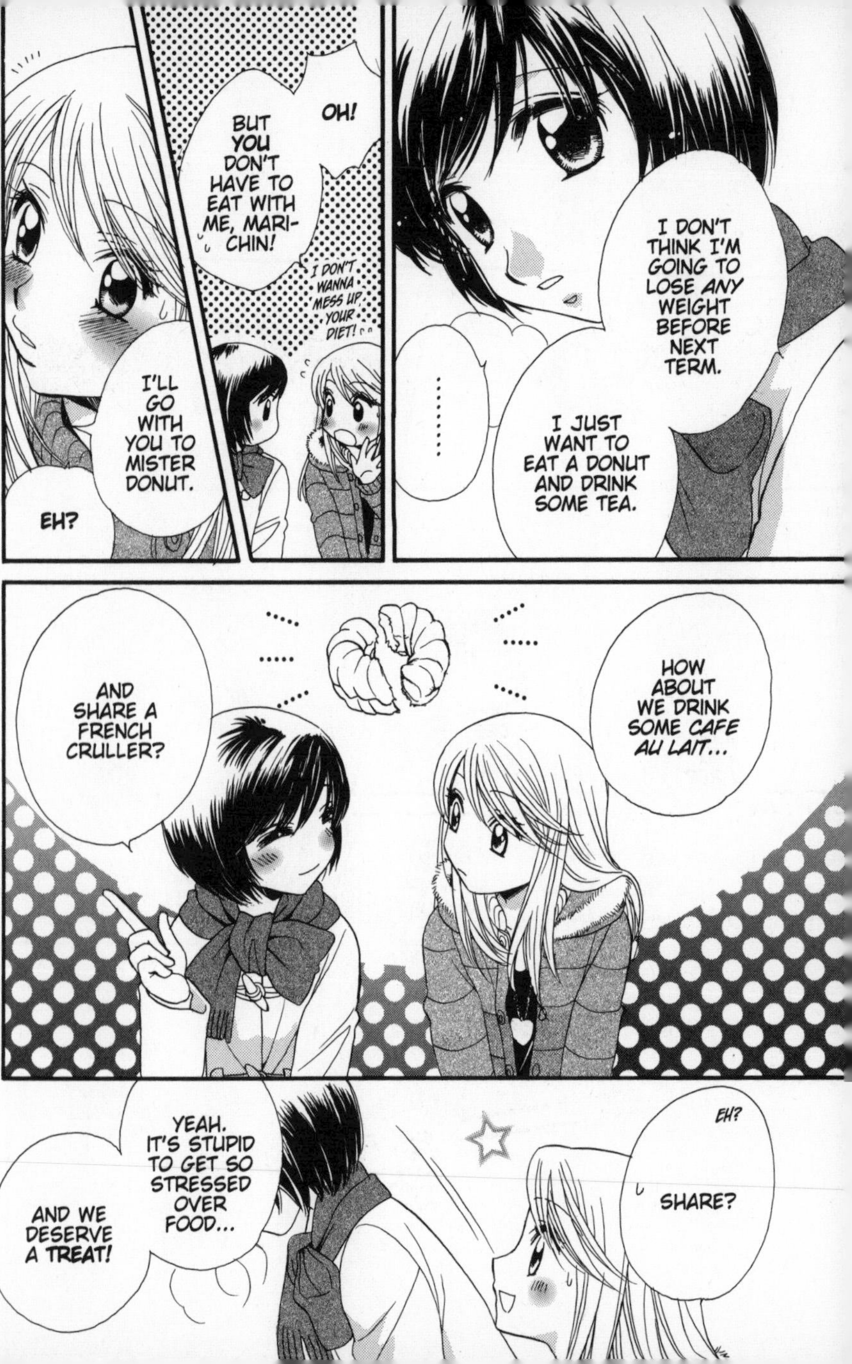
I DON'T THINK I'M GOING TO LOSE ANY WEIGHT BEFORE NEXT TERM.
I JUST WANT TO EAT A DONUT AND DRINK SOME TEA.
......
OH!
BUT YOU DON'T HAVE TO EAT WITH ME, MARI-CHIN!
I DON'T WANNA MESS UP YOUR DIET!
I'LL GO WITH YOU TO MISTER DONUT.
EH?
HOW ABOUT WE DRINK SOME CAFE AU LAIT...
AND SHARE A FRENCH CRULLER?
EH?
SHARE?
YEAH. IT'S STUPID TO GET SO STRESSED OVER FOOD...
AND WE DESERVE A TREAT!

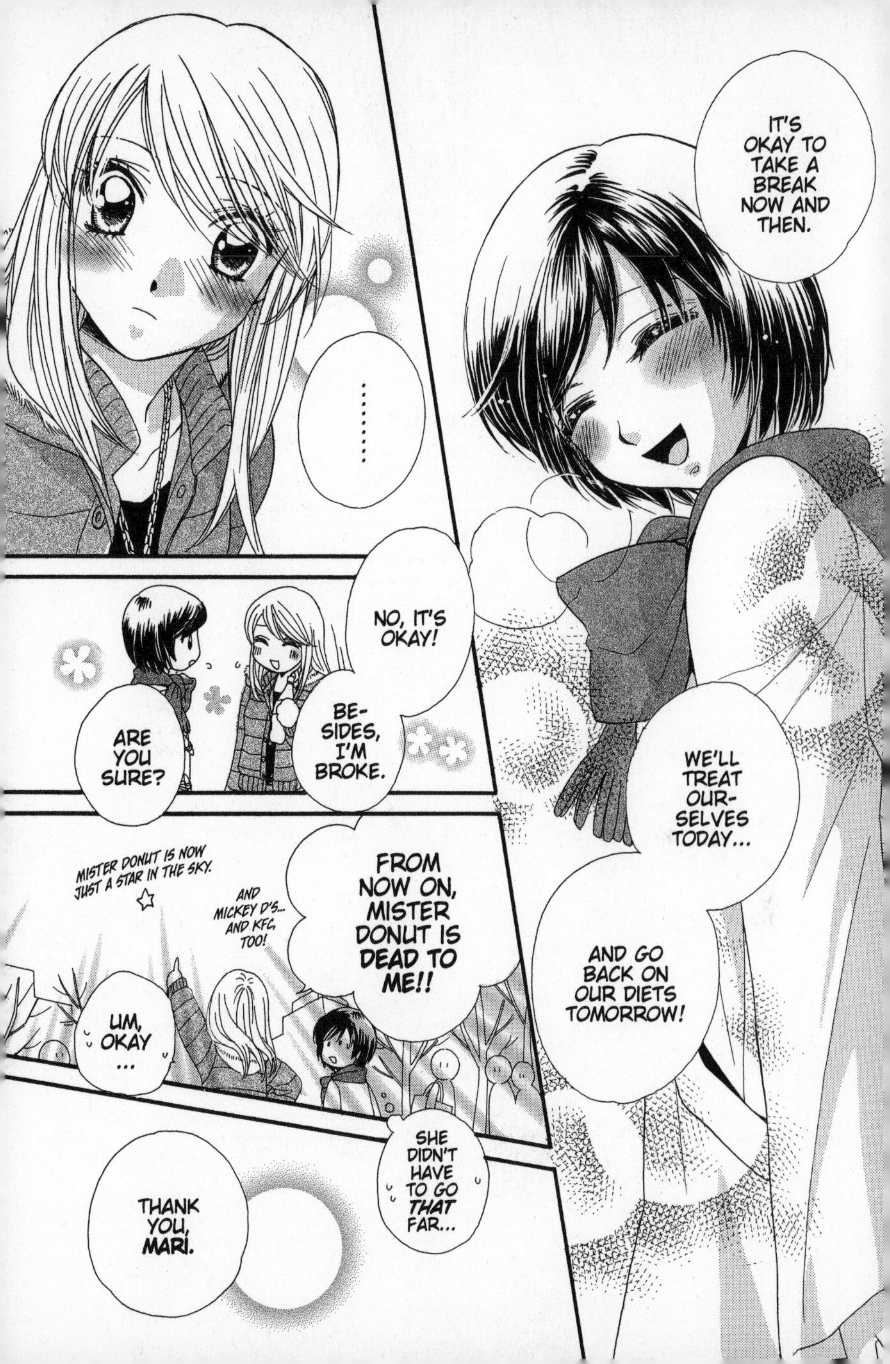
IT'S OKAY TO TAKE A BREAK NOW AND THEN.
WE'LL TREAT OUR-SELVES TODAY...
AND GO BACK ON OUR DIETS TOMORROW!
......
NO, IT'S OKAY!
BE-SIDES, I'M BROKE.
ARE YOU SURE?
FROM NOW ON, MISTER DONUT IS DEAD TO ME!!
AND MICKEY D'S... AND KFC, TOO!
MISTER DONUT IS NOW JUST A STAR IN THE SKY.
UM, OKAY ...
SHE DIDN'T HAVE TO GO *THAT* FAR...
THANK YOU, MARI.

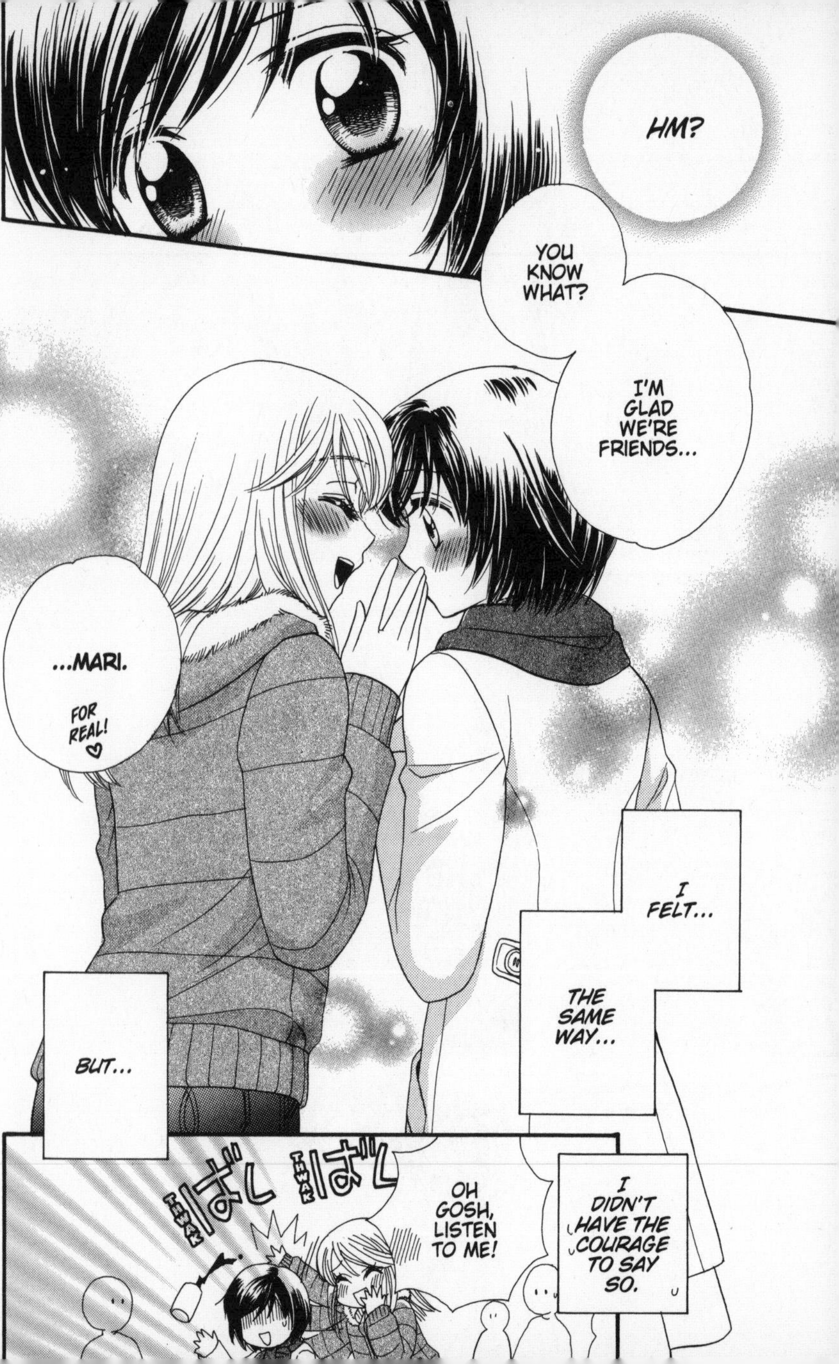
HM?
YOU KNOW WHAT?
I'M GLAD WE'RE FRIENDS...
...MARI.
FOR REAL! ♡
I FELT...
THE SAME WAY...
BUT...
I DIDN'T HAVE THE COURAGE TO SAY SO.
OH GOSH, LISTEN TO ME!
ばし THWAK
ばし THWAK

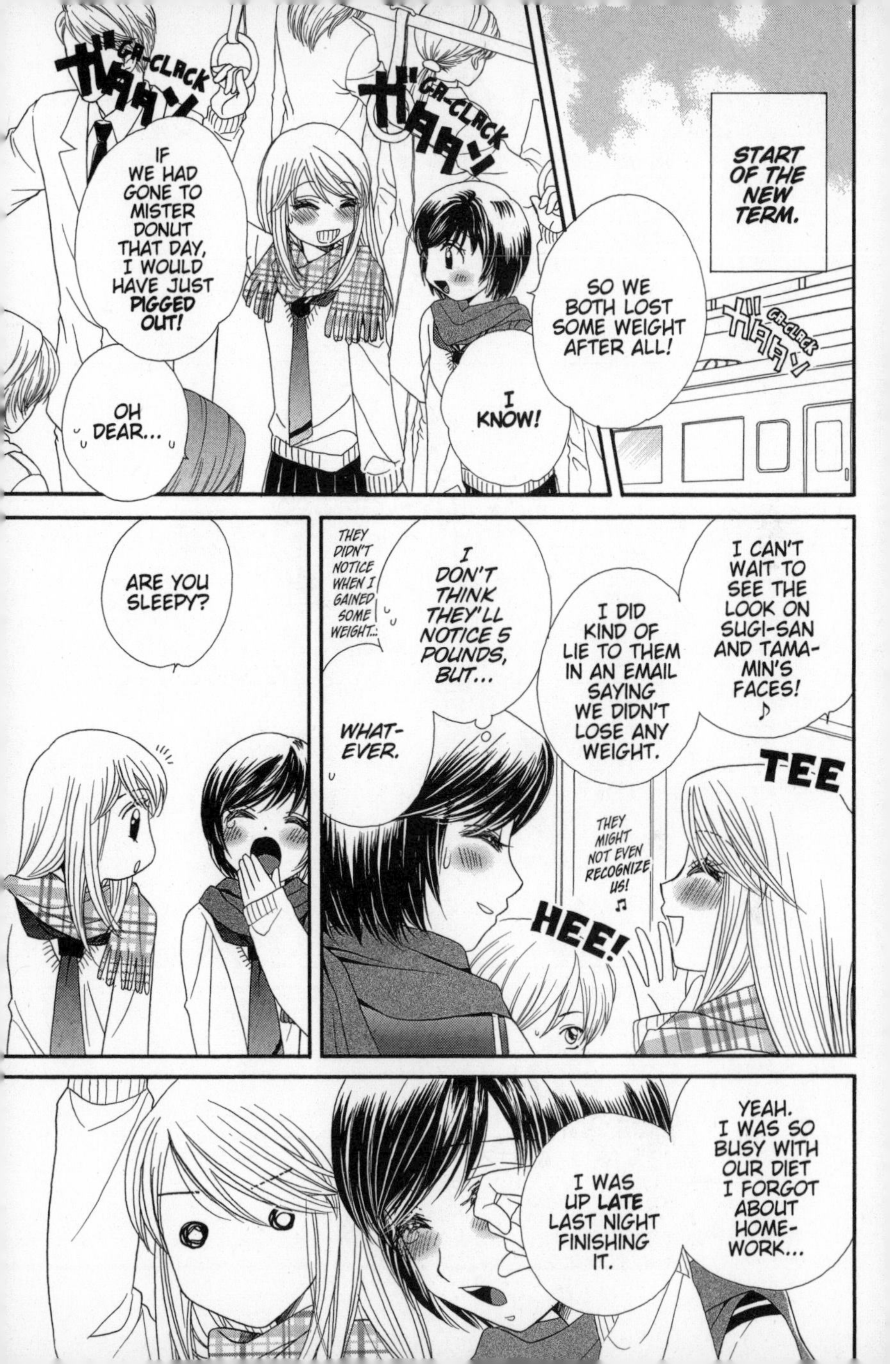
START OF THE NEW TERM.
GA-CLACK
SO WE BOTH LOST SOME WEIGHT AFTER ALL!
I KNOW!
GA-CLACK
IF WE HAD GONE TO MISTER DONUT THAT DAY, I WOULD HAVE JUST PIGGED OUT!
GA-CLACK
OH DEAR...
I CAN'T WAIT TO SEE THE LOOK ON SUGI-SAN AND TAMA-MIN'S FACES! ♪
I DID KIND OF LIE TO THEM IN AN EMAIL SAYING WE DIDN'T LOSE ANY WEIGHT.
TEE
I DON'T THINK THEY'LL NOTICE 5 POUNDS, BUT...
THEY DIDN'T NOTICE WHEN I GAINED SOME WEIGHT...
WHAT-EVER.
THEY MIGHT NOT EVEN RECOGNIZE US! ♫
HEE!
ARE YOU SLEEPY?
YEAH. I WAS SO BUSY WITH OUR DIET I FORGOT ABOUT HOME-WORK...
I WAS UP LATE LAST NIGHT FINISHING IT.

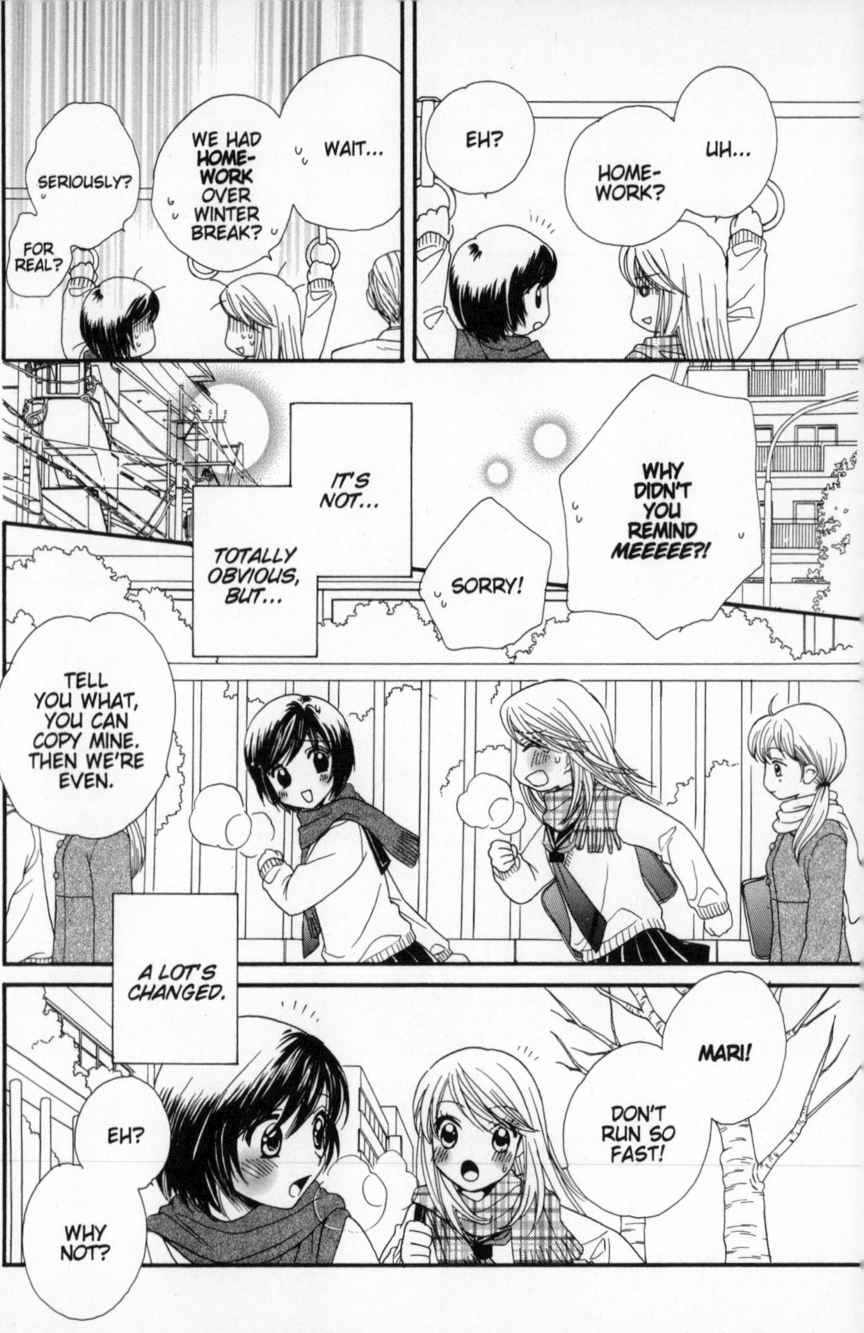
UH...
HOME-WORK?
EH?
WAIT...
WE HAD HOME-WORK OVER WINTER BREAK?
SERIOUSLY?
FOR REAL?
WHY DIDN'T YOU REMIND MEEEEE?!
SORRY!
IT'S NOT...
TOTALLY OBVIOUS, BUT...
TELL YOU WHAT, YOU CAN COPY MINE. THEN WE'RE EVEN.
A LOT'S CHANGED.
MARI!
DON'T RUN SO FAST!
EH?
WHY NOT?

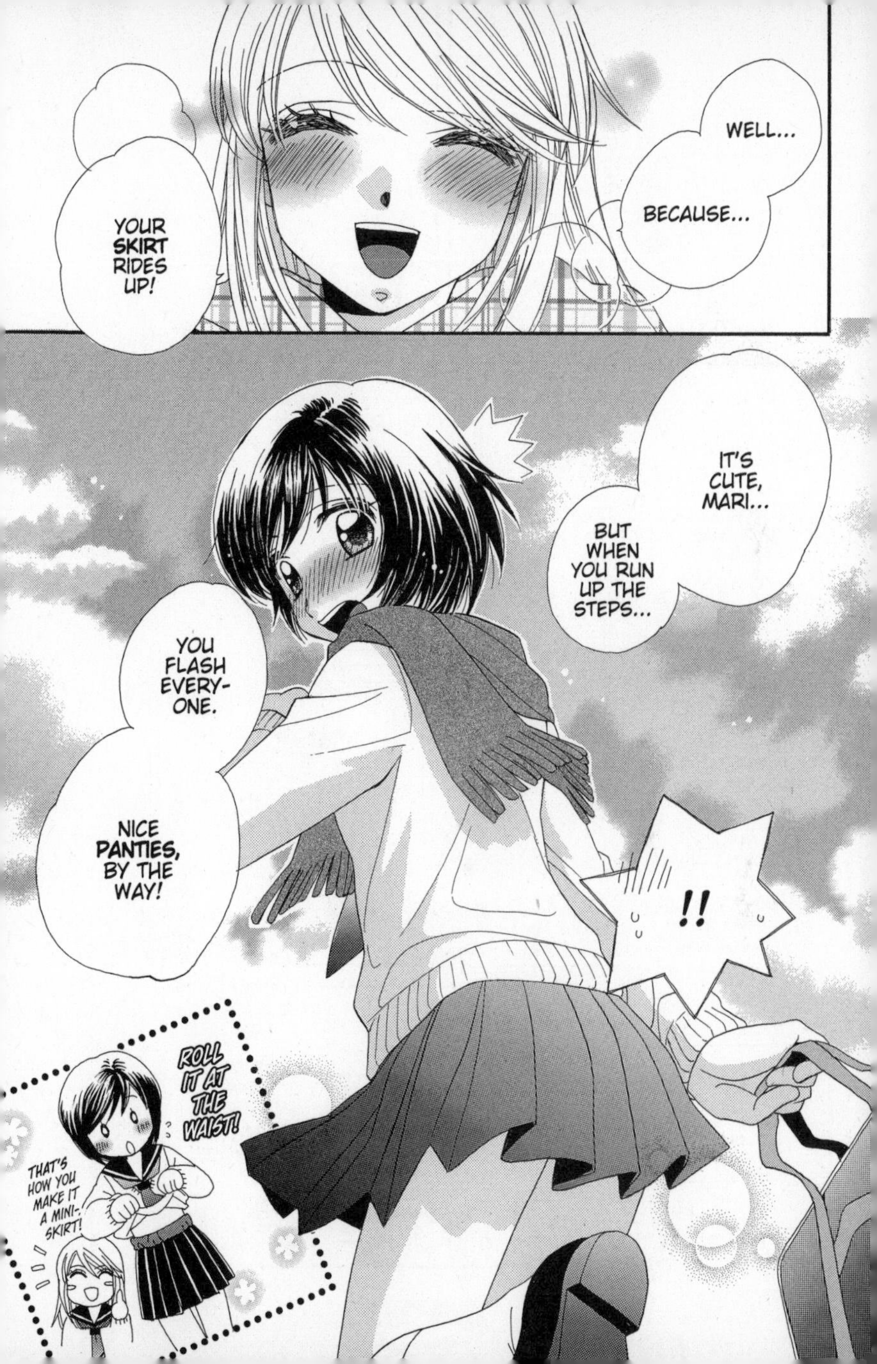
WELL...
BECAUSE...
YOUR SKIRT RIDES UP!
IT'S CUTE, MARI...
BUT WHEN YOU RUN UP THE STEPS...
YOU FLASH EVERY-ONE.
!!
NICE PANTIES, BY THE WAY!
ROLL IT AT THE WAIST!
THAT'S HOW YOU MAKE IT A MINI-SKIRT!

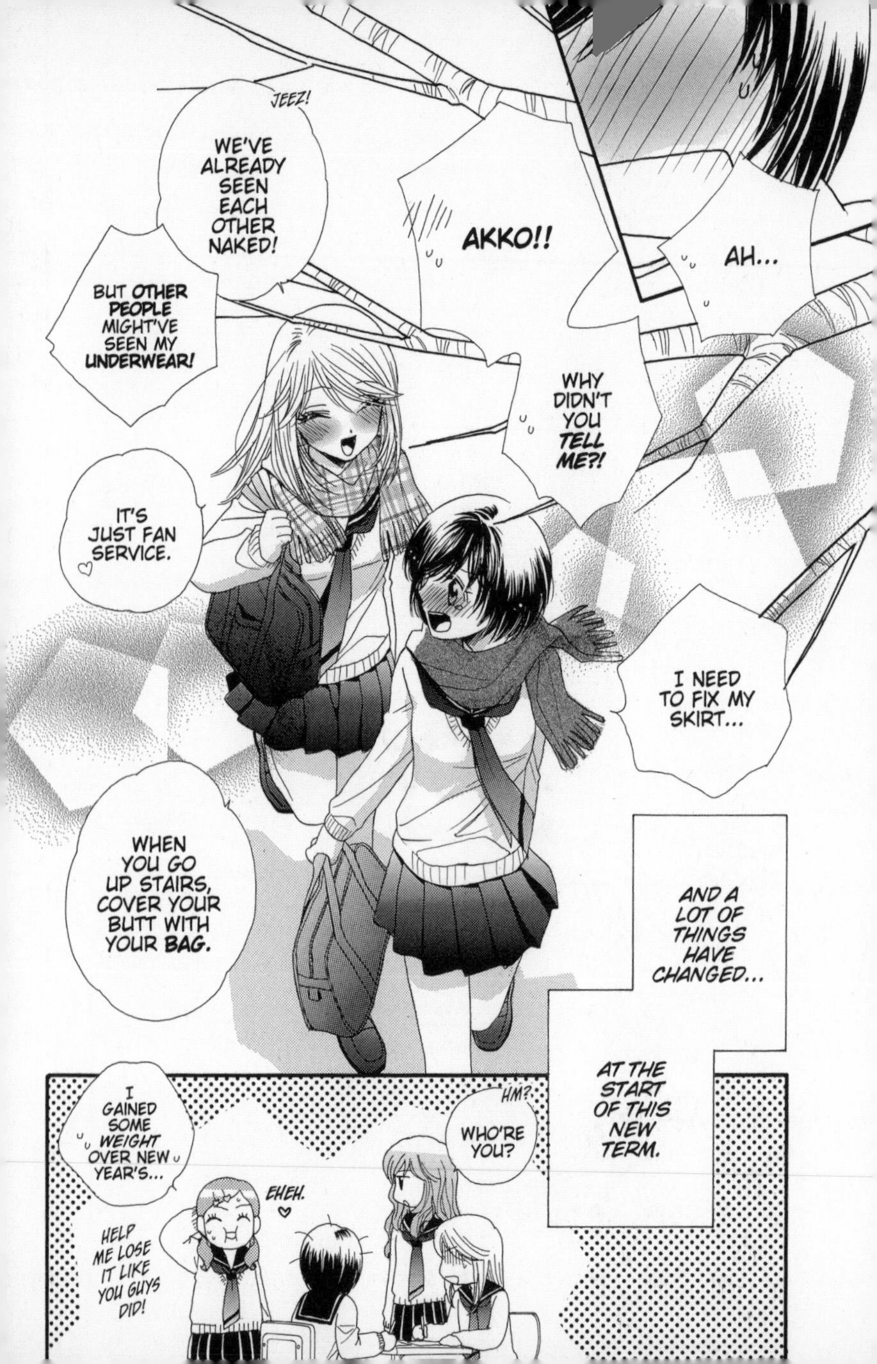
AH...
AKKO!!
WHY DIDN'T YOU TELL ME?!
JEEZ!
WE'VE ALREADY SEEN EACH OTHER NAKED!
BUT OTHER PEOPLE MIGHT'VE SEEN MY UNDERWEAR!
I NEED TO FIX MY SKIRT...
IT'S JUST FAN SERVICE. ♡
WHEN YOU GO UP STAIRS, COVER YOUR BUTT WITH YOUR BAG.
AND A LOT OF THINGS HAVE CHANGED...
AT THE START OF THIS NEW TERM.
HM?
WHO'RE YOU?
I GAINED SOME WEIGHT OVER NEW YEAR'S...
EHEH. ♡
HELP ME LOSE IT LIKE YOU GUYS DID!

YOU BURN MORE
CALORIES STANDING,
SO I NEVER SIT
ON THE TRAIN.

AND I CARRY MY BAG
AWAY FROM ME TO
WORK MY TRICEPS. ♡

GIRL FRIENDS ーガールフレンズー

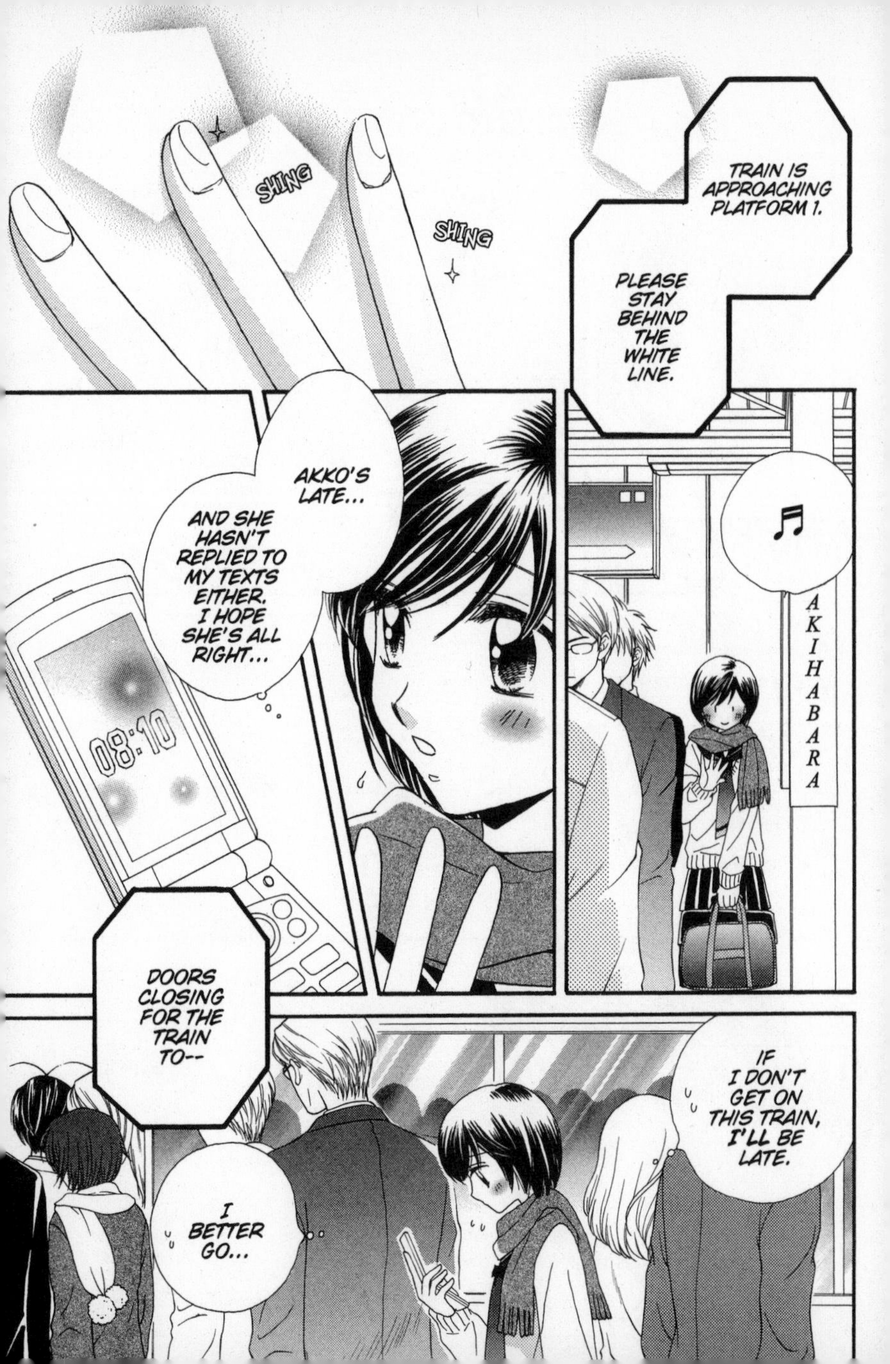
TRAIN IS APPROACHING PLATFORM 1.
PLEASE STAY BEHIND THE WHITE LINE.
SHING
SHING
♬
AKIHABARA
AKKO'S LATE...
AND SHE HASN'T REPLIED TO MY TEXTS EITHER. I HOPE SHE'S ALL RIGHT...
08:10
DOORS CLOSING FOR THE TRAIN TO--
IF I DON'T GET ON THIS TRAIN, I'LL BE LATE.
I BETTER GO...

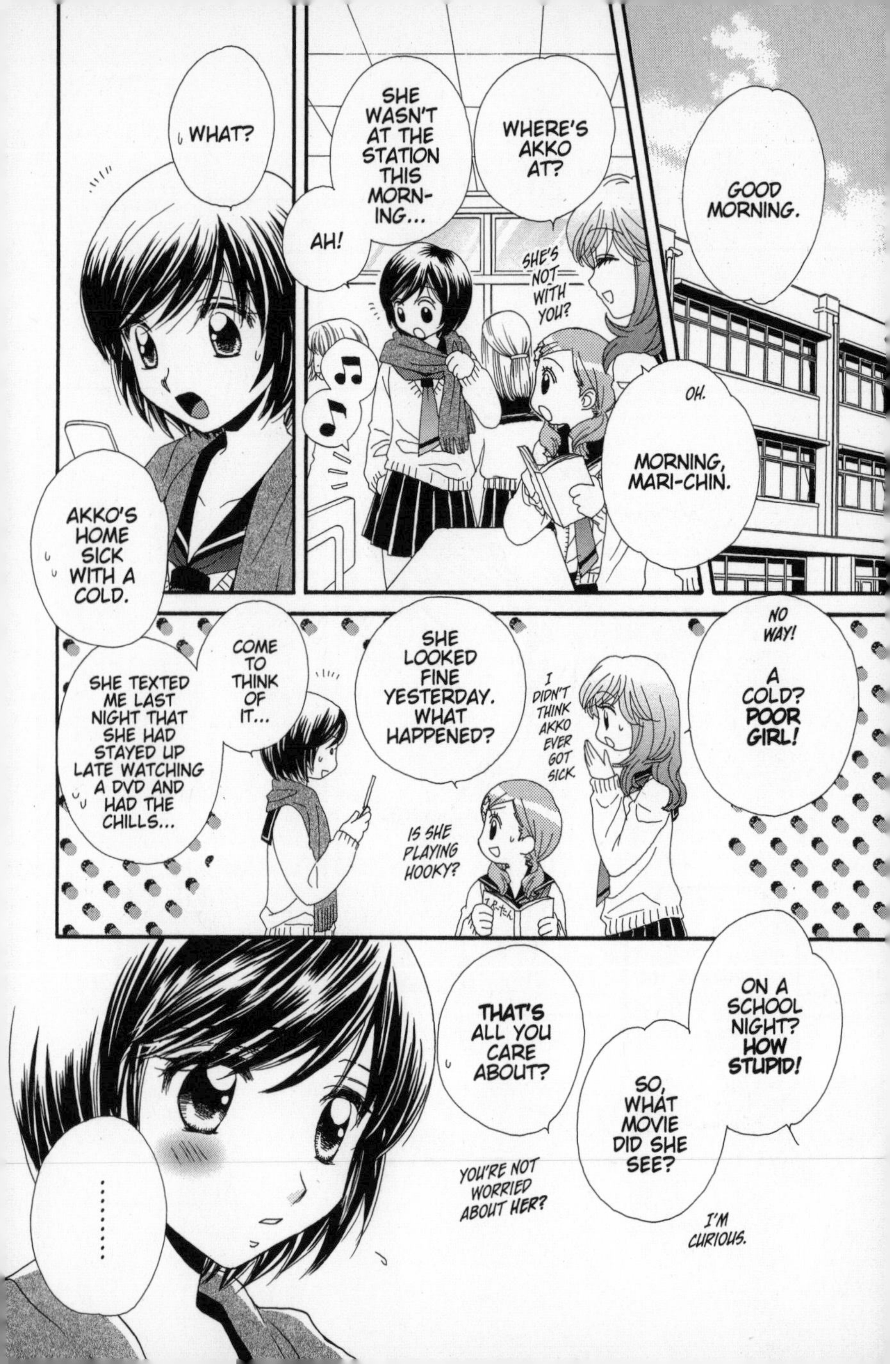
GOOD MORNING.
WHERE'S AKKO AT?
SHE'S NOT WITH YOU?
OH.
MORNING, MARI-CHIN.
SHE WASN'T AT THE STATION THIS MORNING...
AH!
WHAT?
AKKO'S HOME SICK WITH A COLD.
NO WAY! A COLD? POOR GIRL!
I DIDN'T THINK AKKO EVER GOT SICK.
SHE LOOKED FINE YESTERDAY. WHAT HAPPENED?
IS SHE PLAYING HOOKY?
COME TO THINK OF IT...
SHE TEXTED ME LAST NIGHT THAT SHE HAD STAYED UP LATE WATCHING A DVD AND HAD THE CHILLS...
ON A SCHOOL NIGHT? HOW STUPID!
SO, WHAT MOVIE DID SHE SEE?
I'M CURIOUS.
THAT'S ALL YOU CARE ABOUT?
YOU'RE NOT WORRIED ABOUT HER?
......

[CHAPTER 5]

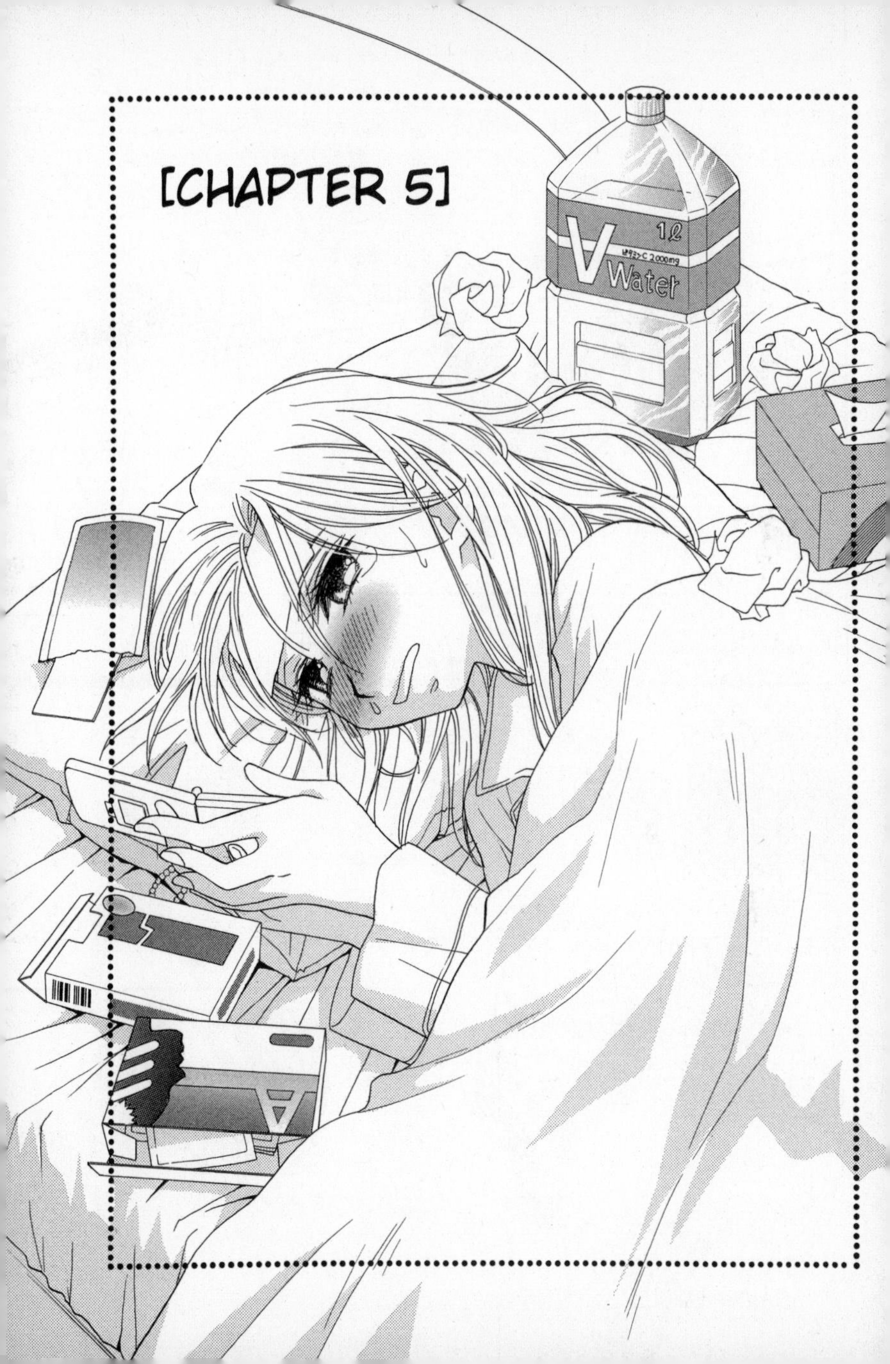
V
1ℓ
Water

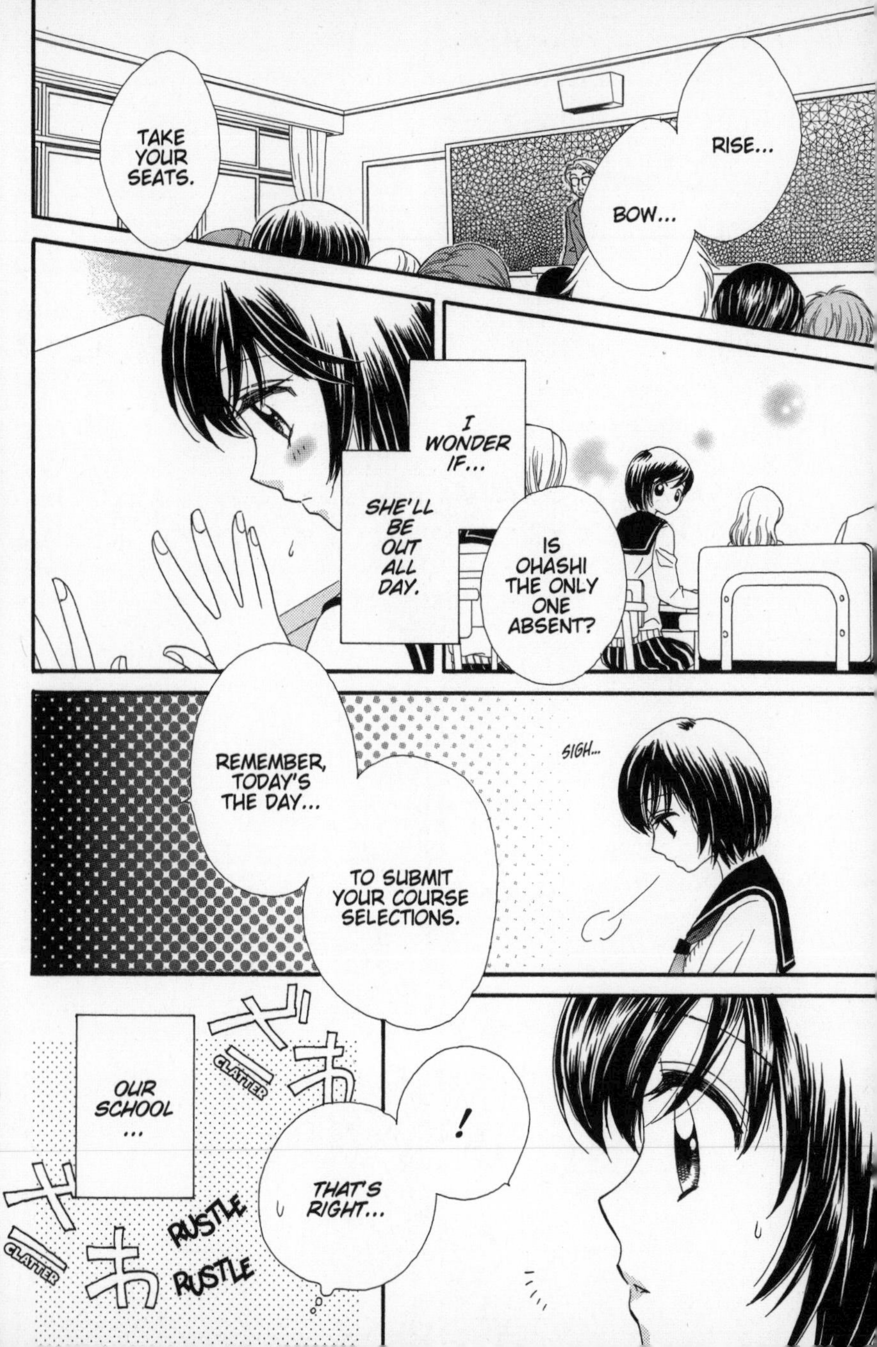
RISE...
BOW...
TAKE YOUR SEATS.
IS OHASHI THE ONLY ONE ABSENT?
I WONDER IF...
SHE'LL BE OUT ALL DAY.
SIGH...
REMEMBER, TODAY'S THE DAY...
TO SUBMIT YOUR COURSE SELECTIONS.
!
THAT'S RIGHT...
OUR SCHOOL ...
CLATTER
RUSTLE
CLATTER
RUSTLE

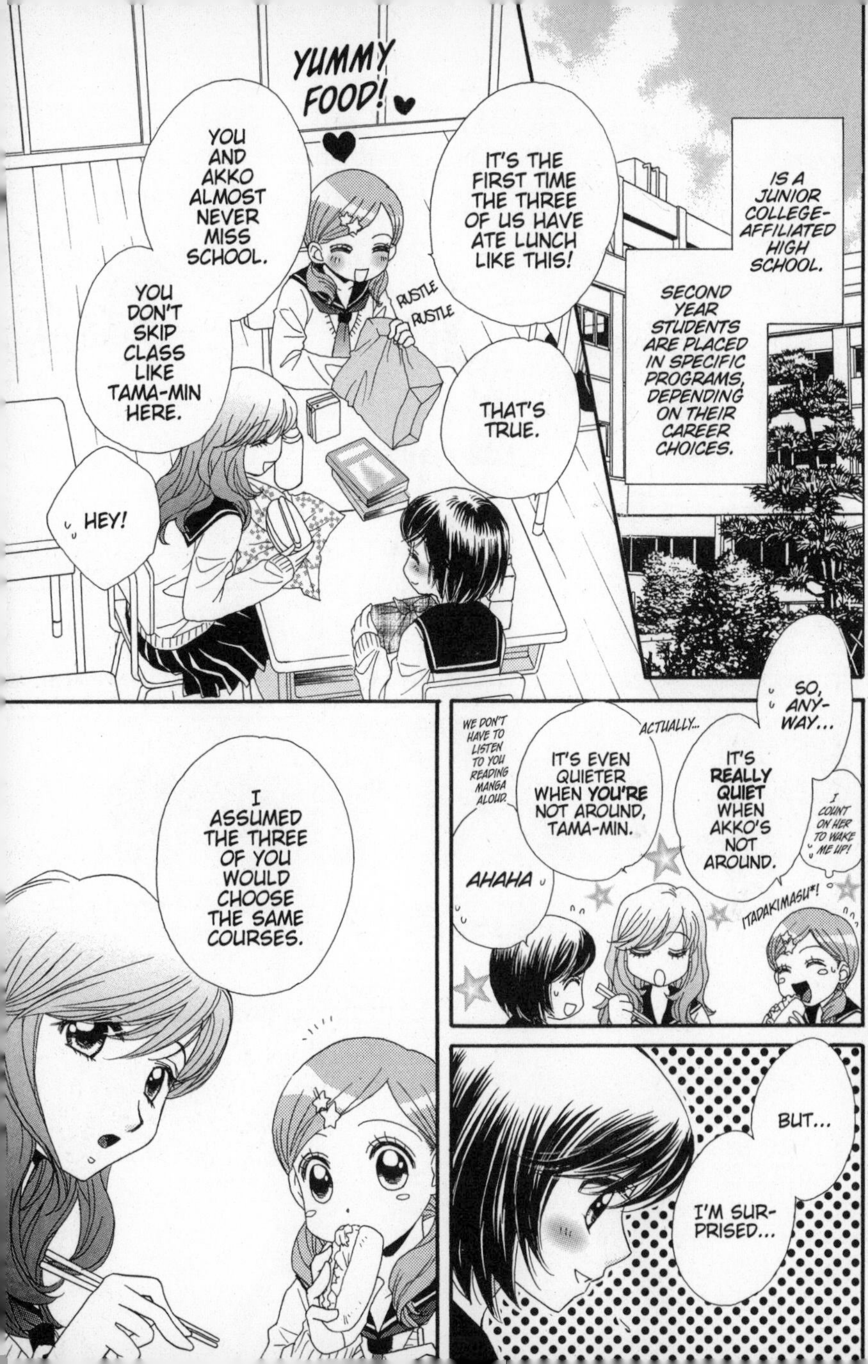
IS A JUNIOR COLLEGE-AFFILIATED HIGH SCHOOL.
SECOND YEAR STUDENTS ARE PLACED IN SPECIFIC PROGRAMS, DEPENDING ON THEIR CAREER CHOICES.
YUMMY FOOD!
IT'S THE FIRST TIME THE THREE OF US HAVE ATE LUNCH LIKE THIS!
YOU AND AKKO ALMOST NEVER MISS SCHOOL.
RUSTLE RUSTLE
THAT'S TRUE.
YOU DON'T SKIP CLASS LIKE TAMA-MIN HERE.
HEY!
SO, ANY-WAY...
IT'S REALLY QUIET WHEN AKKO'S NOT AROUND.
I COUNT ON HER TO WAKE ME UP!
ACTUALLY...
IT'S EVEN QUIETER WHEN YOU'RE NOT AROUND, TAMA-MIN.
WE DON'T HAVE TO LISTEN TO YOU READING MANGA ALOUD.
ITADAKIMASU*!
AHAHA
BUT...
I'M SUR-PRISED...
I ASSUMED THE THREE OF YOU WOULD CHOOSE THE SAME COURSES.

*Itadakimasu is a Japanese expression of gratitude said before meals meaning, "Thank you for this meal."

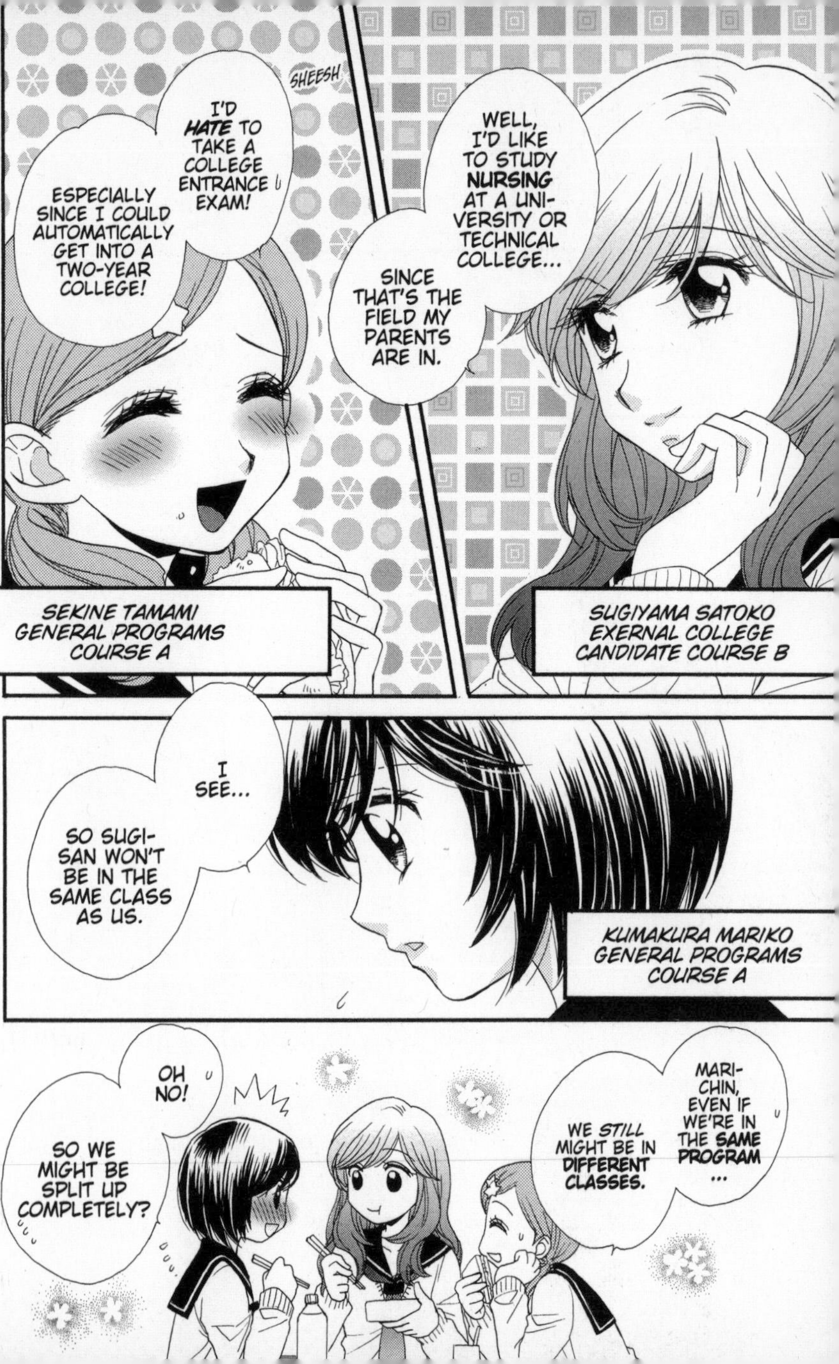
WELL, I'D LIKE TO STUDY NURSING AT A UNIVERSITY OR TECHNICAL COLLEGE...
SINCE THAT'S THE FIELD MY PARENTS ARE IN.
SUGIYAMA SATOKO EXERNAL COLLEGE CANDIDATE COURSE B
SHEESH
I'D HATE TO TAKE A COLLEGE ENTRANCE EXAM!
ESPECIALLY SINCE I COULD AUTOMATICALLY GET INTO A TWO-YEAR COLLEGE!
SEKINE TAMAMI GENERAL PROGRAMS COURSE A
I SEE...
SO SUGI-SAN WON'T BE IN THE SAME CLASS AS US.
KUMAKURA MARIKO GENERAL PROGRAMS COURSE A
MARI-CHIN, EVEN IF WE'RE IN THE SAME PROGRAM...
WE STILL MIGHT BE IN DIFFERENT CLASSES.
OH NO!
SO WE MIGHT BE SPLIT UP COMPLETELY?

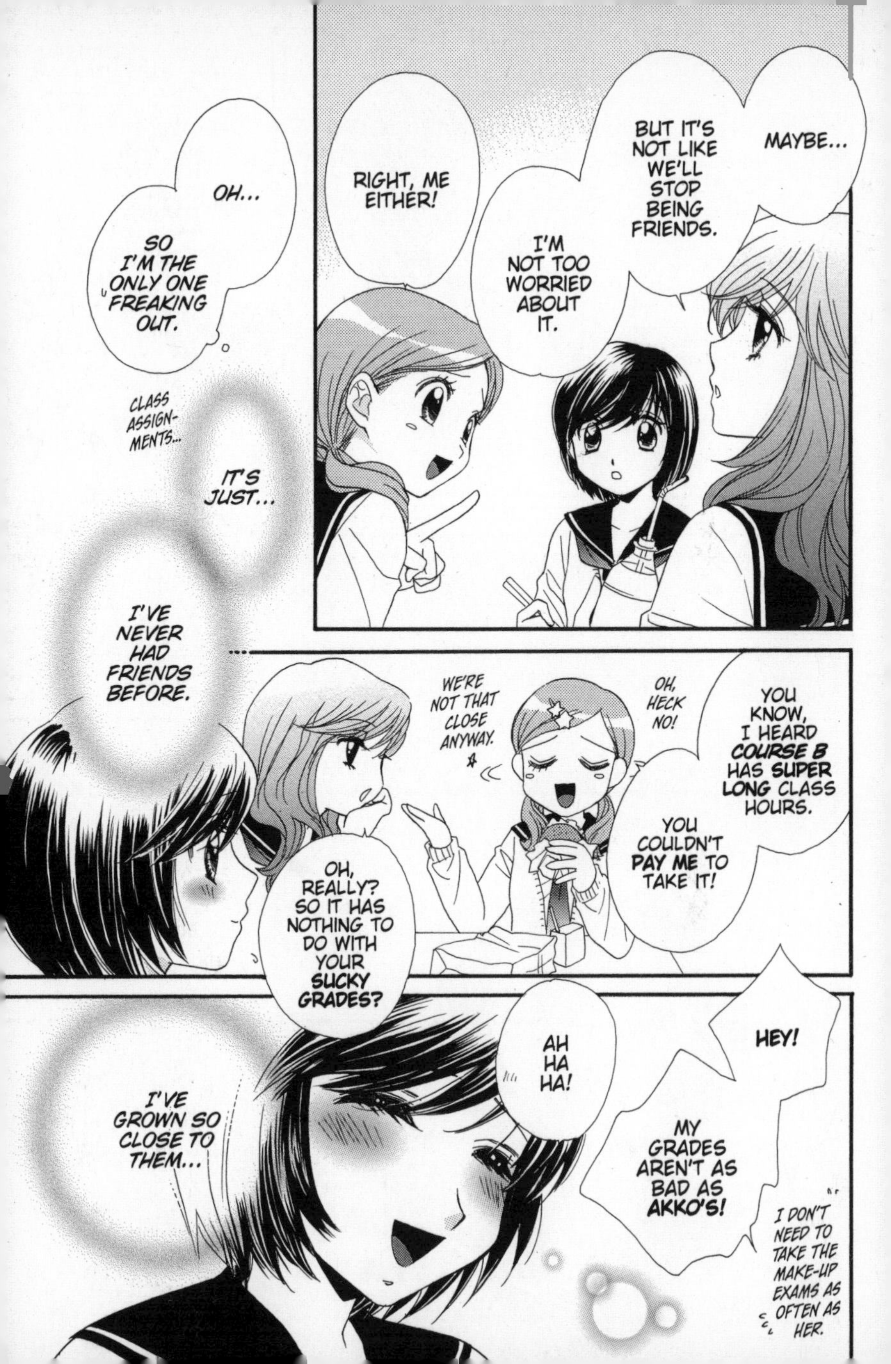
MAYBE...
BUT IT'S NOT LIKE WE'LL STOP BEING FRIENDS.
I'M NOT TOO WORRIED ABOUT IT.
RIGHT, ME EITHER!
OH...
SO I'M THE ONLY ONE FREAKING OUT.
CLASS ASSIGNMENTS...
IT'S JUST...
I'VE NEVER HAD FRIENDS BEFORE.
YOU KNOW, I HEARD COURSE B HAS SUPER LONG CLASS HOURS.
YOU COULDN'T PAY ME TO TAKE IT!
OH, HECK NO!
WE'RE NOT THAT CLOSE ANYWAY.
OH, REALLY? SO IT HAS NOTHING TO DO WITH YOUR SUCKY GRADES?
HEY!
MY GRADES AREN'T AS BAD AS AKKO'S!
I DON'T NEED TO TAKE THE MAKE-UP EXAMS AS OFTEN AS HER.
AH HA HA!
I'VE GROWN SO CLOSE TO THEM...

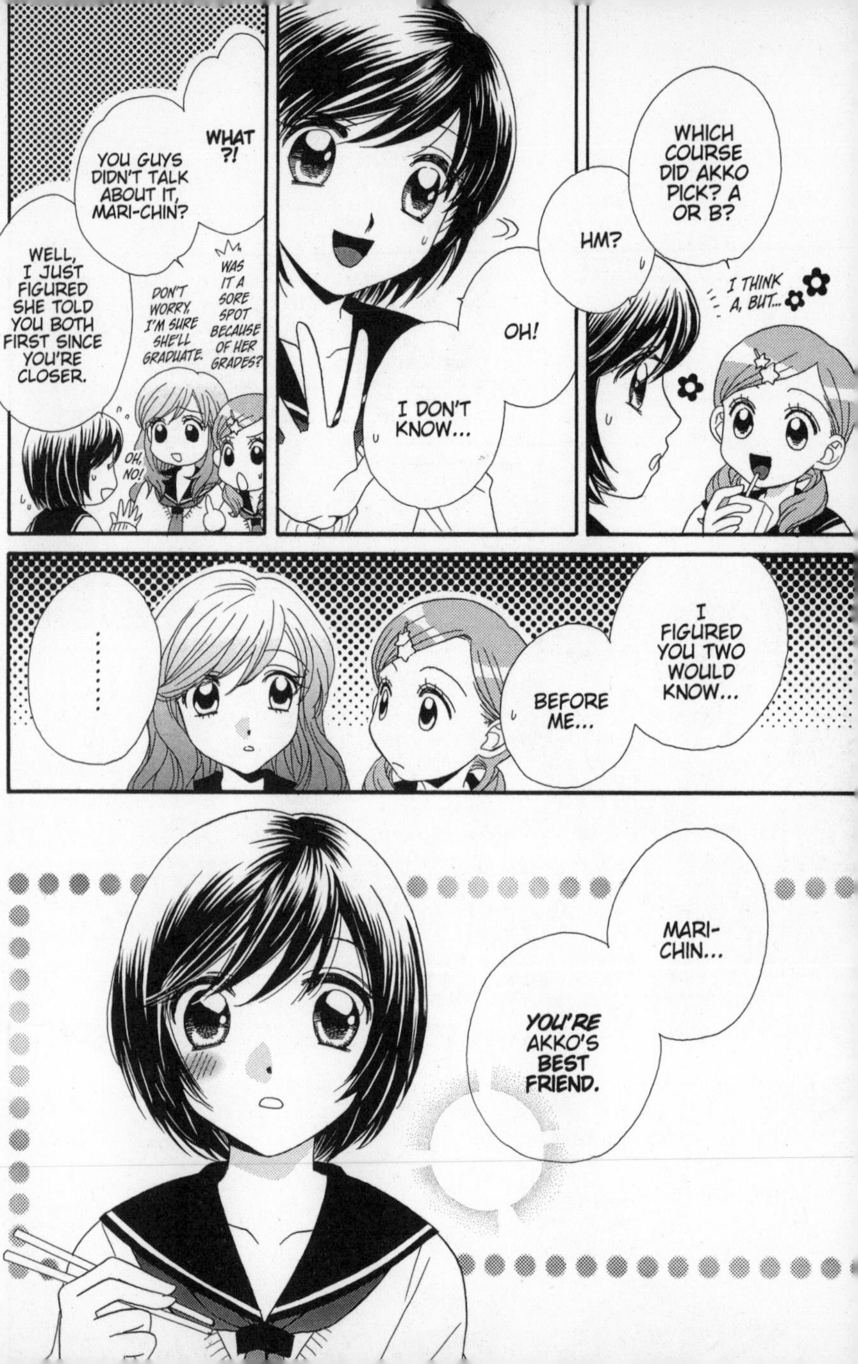
WHICH COURSE DID AKKO PICK? A OR B?
HM?
I THINK A, BUT...
OH!
I DON'T KNOW...
WHAT?!
YOU GUYS DIDN'T TALK ABOUT IT, MARI-CHIN?
WAS IT A SORE SPOT BECAUSE OF HER GRADES?
DON'T WORRY, I'M SURE SHE'LL GRADUATE.
WELL, I JUST FIGURED SHE TOLD YOU BOTH FIRST SINCE YOU'RE CLOSER.
OH, NO!
I FIGURED YOU TWO WOULD KNOW...
BEFORE ME...
......
MARI-CHIN...
YOU'RE AKKO'S BEST FRIEND.

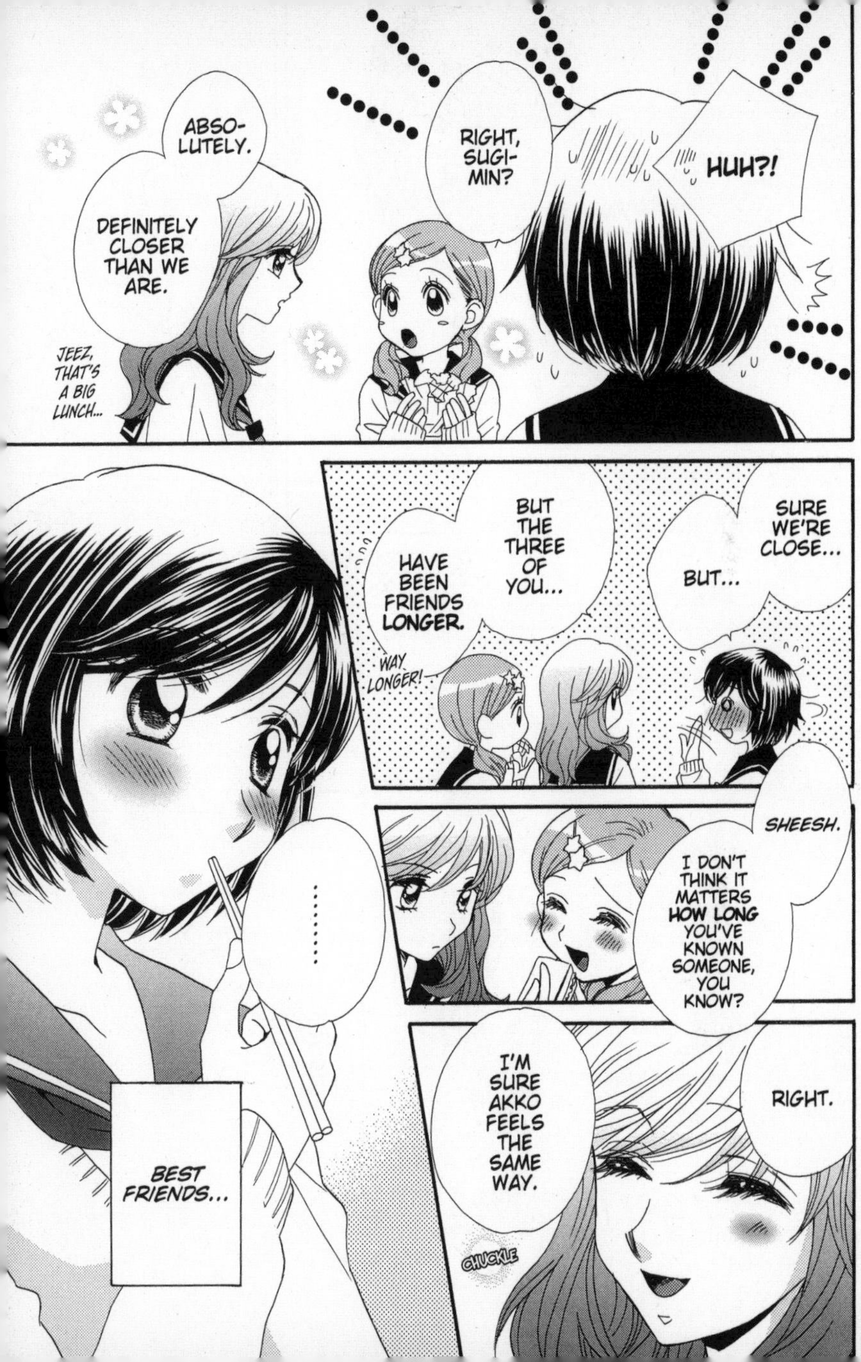
HUH?!
RIGHT, SUGIMIN?
ABSOLUTELY.
DEFINITELY CLOSER THAN WE ARE.
JEEZ, THAT'S A BIG LUNCH...
SURE WE'RE CLOSE... BUT...
BUT THE THREE OF YOU...
HAVE BEEN FRIENDS LONGER.
WAY LONGER!
SHEESH.
I DON'T THINK IT MATTERS HOW LONG YOU'VE KNOWN SOMEONE, YOU KNOW?
RIGHT.
I'M SURE AKKO FEELS THE SAME WAY.
CHUCKLE
......
BEST FRIENDS...

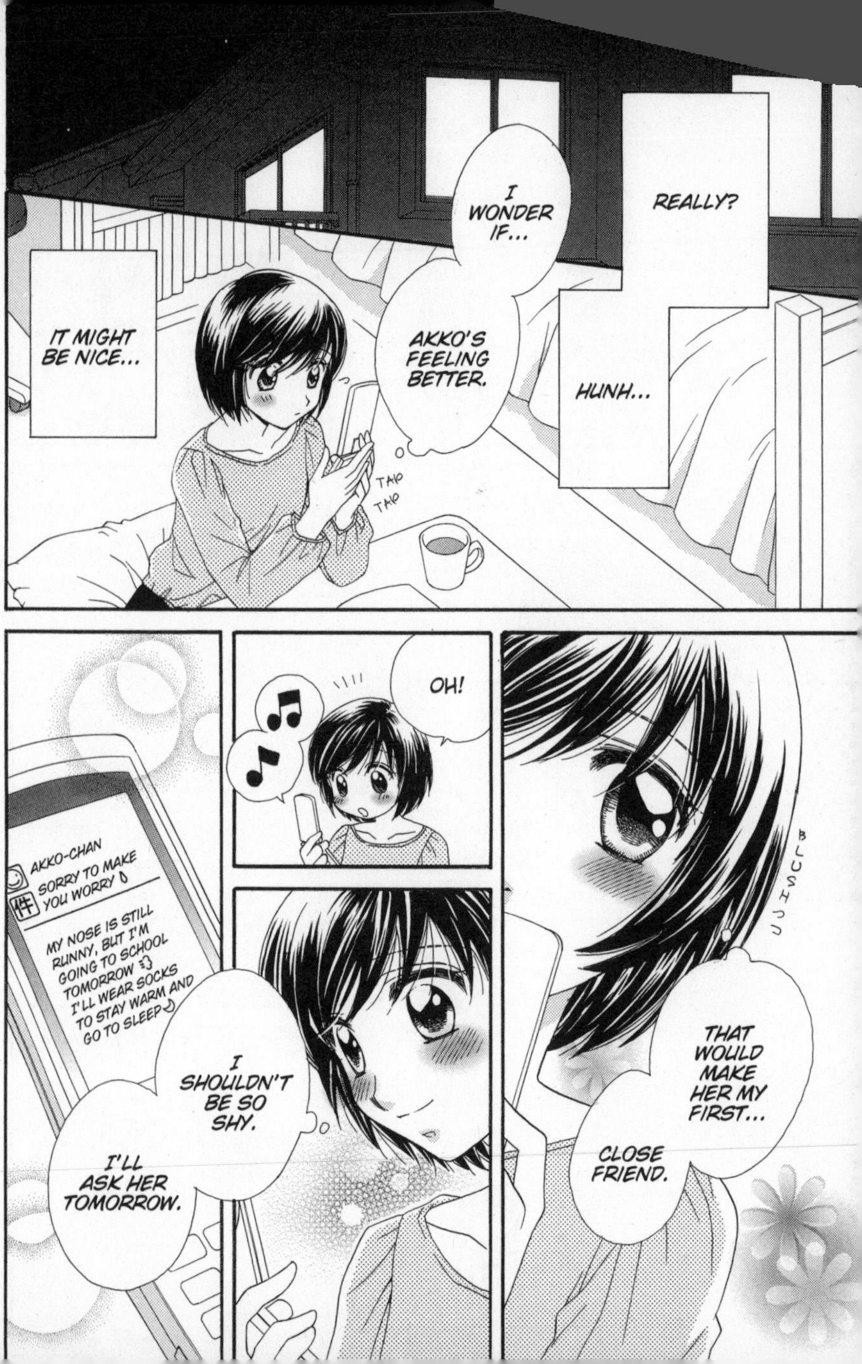
REALLY?
HUNH...
AKKO'S FEELING BETTER.
TAP TAP
I WONDER IF...
IT MIGHT BE NICE...
BLUSH
THAT WOULD MAKE HER MY FIRST...
CLOSE FRIEND.
OH!
I SHOULDN'T BE SO SHY.
I'LL ASK HER TOMORROW.
AKKO-CHAN
SORRY TO MAKE YOU WORRY
MY NOSE IS STILL RUNNY, BUT I'M GOING TO SCHOOL TOMORROW
I'LL WEAR SOCKS TO STAY WARM AND GO TO SLEEP

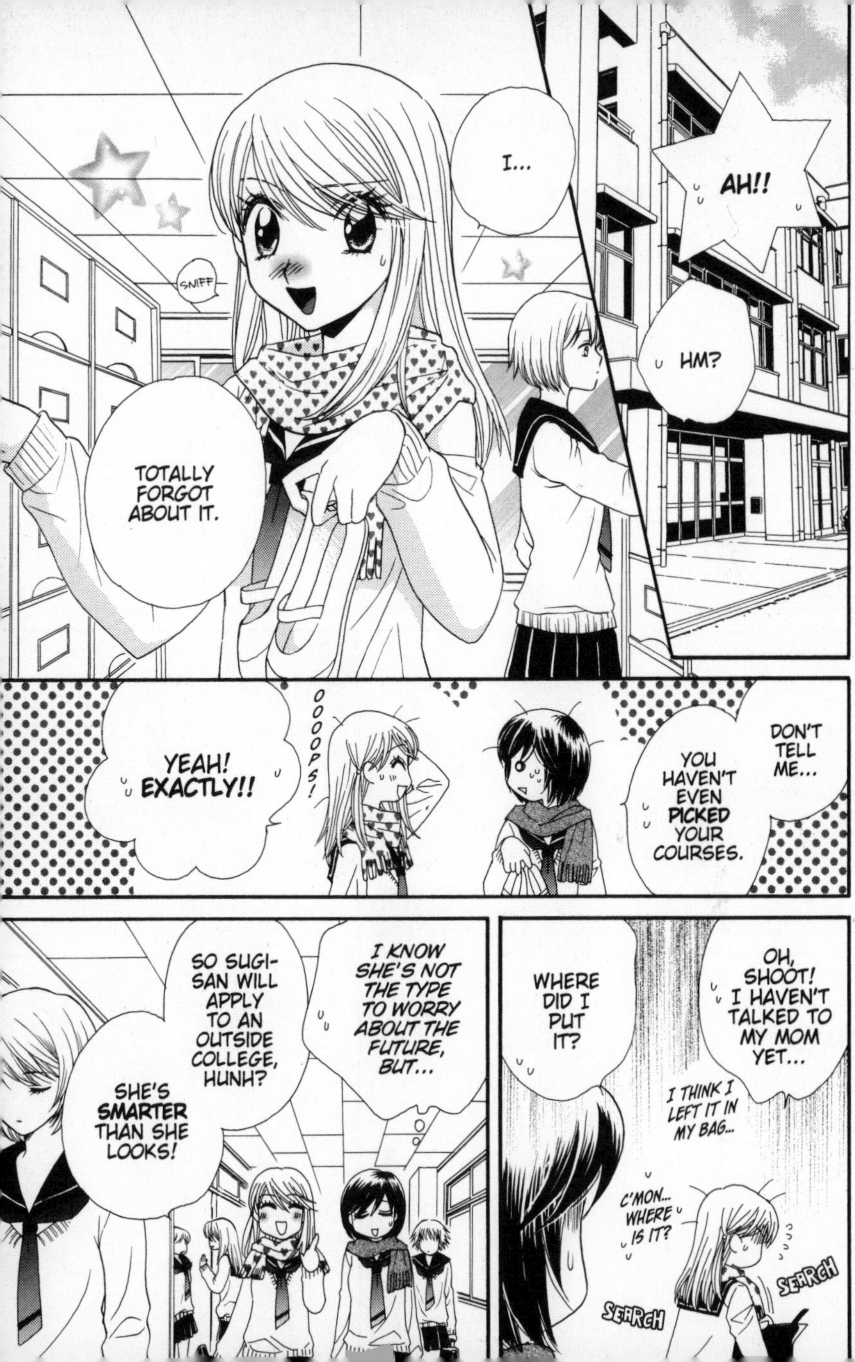
AH!!
HM?
I...
SNIFF
TOTALLY FORGOT ABOUT IT.
DON'T TELL ME...
YOU HAVEN'T EVEN **PICKED** YOUR COURSES.
OOOOOPS!
YEAH! **EXACTLY!!**
OH, SHOOT! I HAVEN'T TALKED TO MY MOM YET...
WHERE DID I PUT IT?
I THINK I LEFT IT IN MY BAG...
C'MON... WHERE IS IT?
SEARCH
SEARCH
I KNOW SHE'S NOT THE TYPE TO WORRY ABOUT THE FUTURE, BUT...
SO SUGI-SAN WILL APPLY TO AN OUTSIDE COLLEGE, HUNH?
SHE'S **SMARTER** THAN SHE LOOKS!

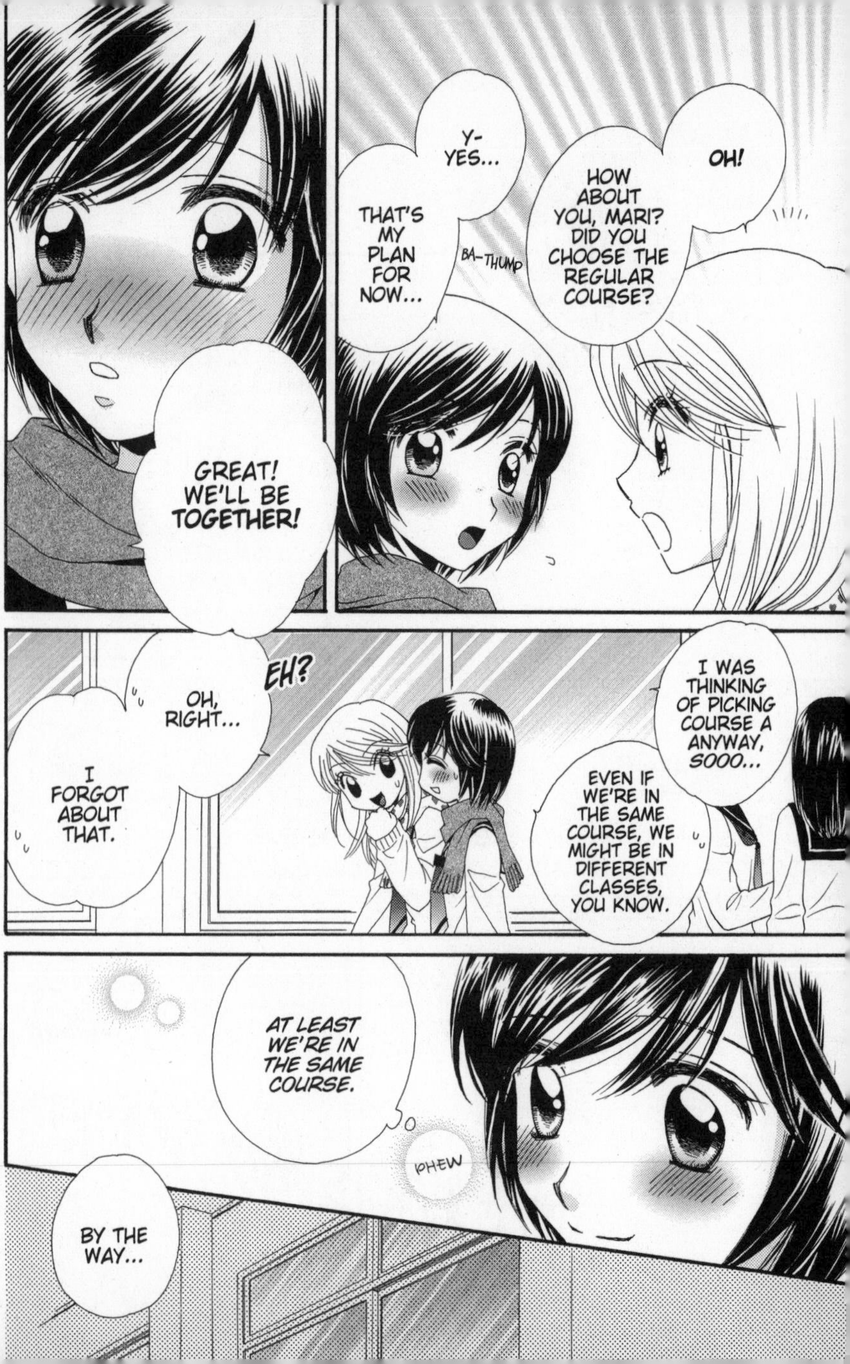
OH!
HOW ABOUT YOU, MARI? DID YOU CHOOSE THE REGULAR COURSE?
Y- YES...
BA-THUMP
THAT'S MY PLAN FOR NOW...
GREAT! WE'LL BE TOGETHER!
I WAS THINKING OF PICKING COURSE A ANYWAY, SOOO...
EVEN IF WE'RE IN THE SAME COURSE, WE MIGHT BE IN DIFFERENT CLASSES, YOU KNOW.
EH?
OH, RIGHT...
I FORGOT ABOUT THAT.
AT LEAST WE'RE IN THE SAME COURSE.
PHEW
BY THE WAY...

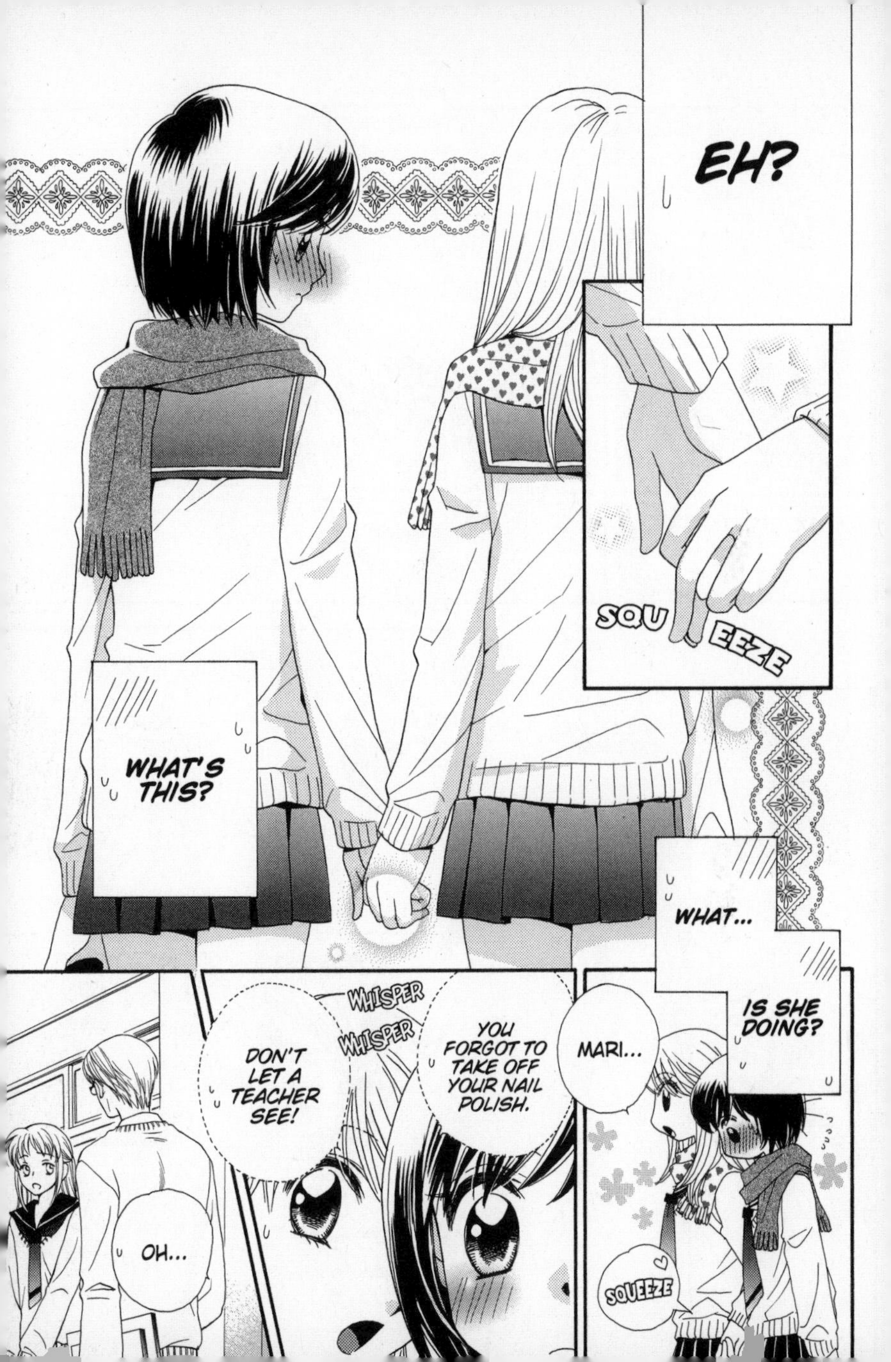
EH?
SQU EEZE
WHAT'S THIS?
WHAT...
IS SHE DOING?
MARI...
SQUEEZE
WHISPER
WHISPER
YOU FORGOT TO TAKE OFF YOUR NAIL POLISH.
DON'T LET A TEACHER SEE!
OH...

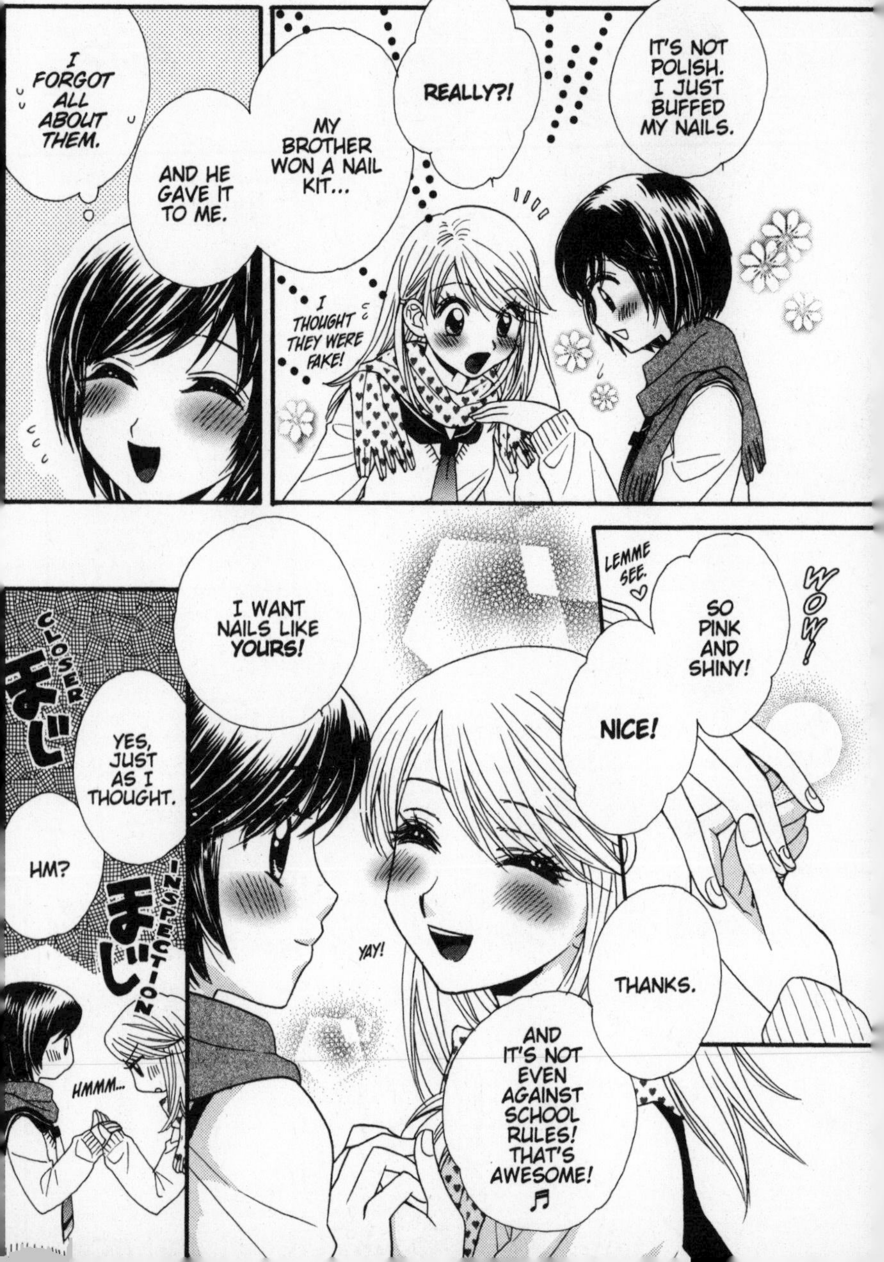
IT'S NOT POLISH. I JUST BUFFED MY NAILS.
REALLY?!
MY BROTHER WON A NAIL KIT...
I THOUGHT THEY WERE FAKE!
AND HE GAVE IT TO ME.
I FORGOT ALL ABOUT THEM.
WOW!
LEMME SEE. ♡
SO PINK AND SHINY!
NICE!
THANKS.
I WANT NAILS LIKE YOURS!
YAY!
AND IT'S NOT EVEN AGAINST SCHOOL RULES! THAT'S AWESOME! ♬
まじ
CLOSER
YES, JUST AS I THOUGHT.
HM?
まじ
INSPECTION
HMMM...

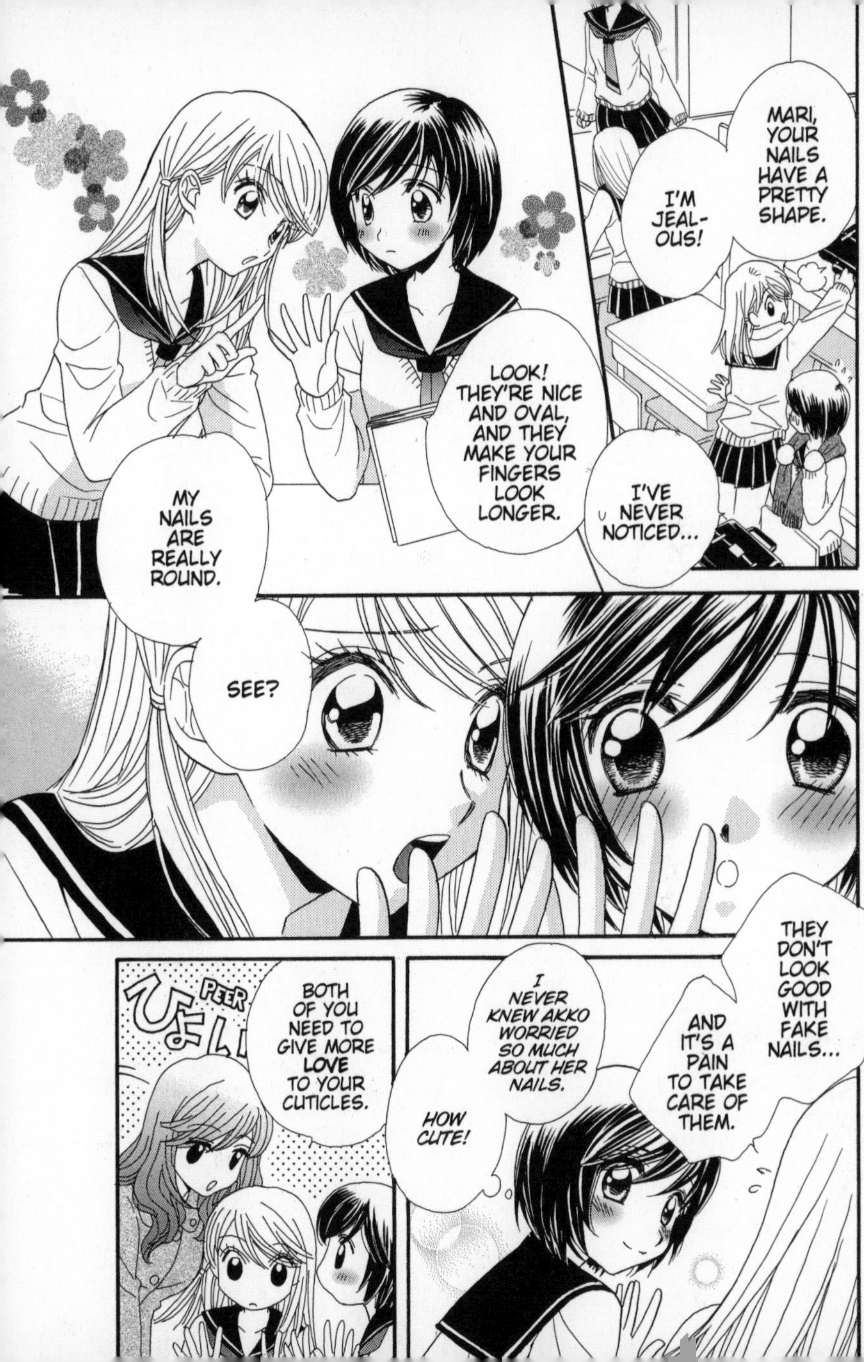
MARI, YOUR NAILS HAVE A PRETTY SHAPE.
I'M JEAL-OUS!
I'VE NEVER NOTICED...
LOOK! THEY'RE NICE AND OVAL, AND THEY MAKE YOUR FINGERS LOOK LONGER.
MY NAILS ARE REALLY ROUND.
SEE?
THEY DON'T LOOK GOOD WITH FAKE NAILS...
AND IT'S A PAIN TO TAKE CARE OF THEM.
I NEVER KNEW AKKO WORRIED SO MUCH ABOUT HER NAILS.
HOW CUTE!
PEER
BOTH OF YOU NEED TO GIVE MORE **LOVE** TO YOUR CUTICLES.

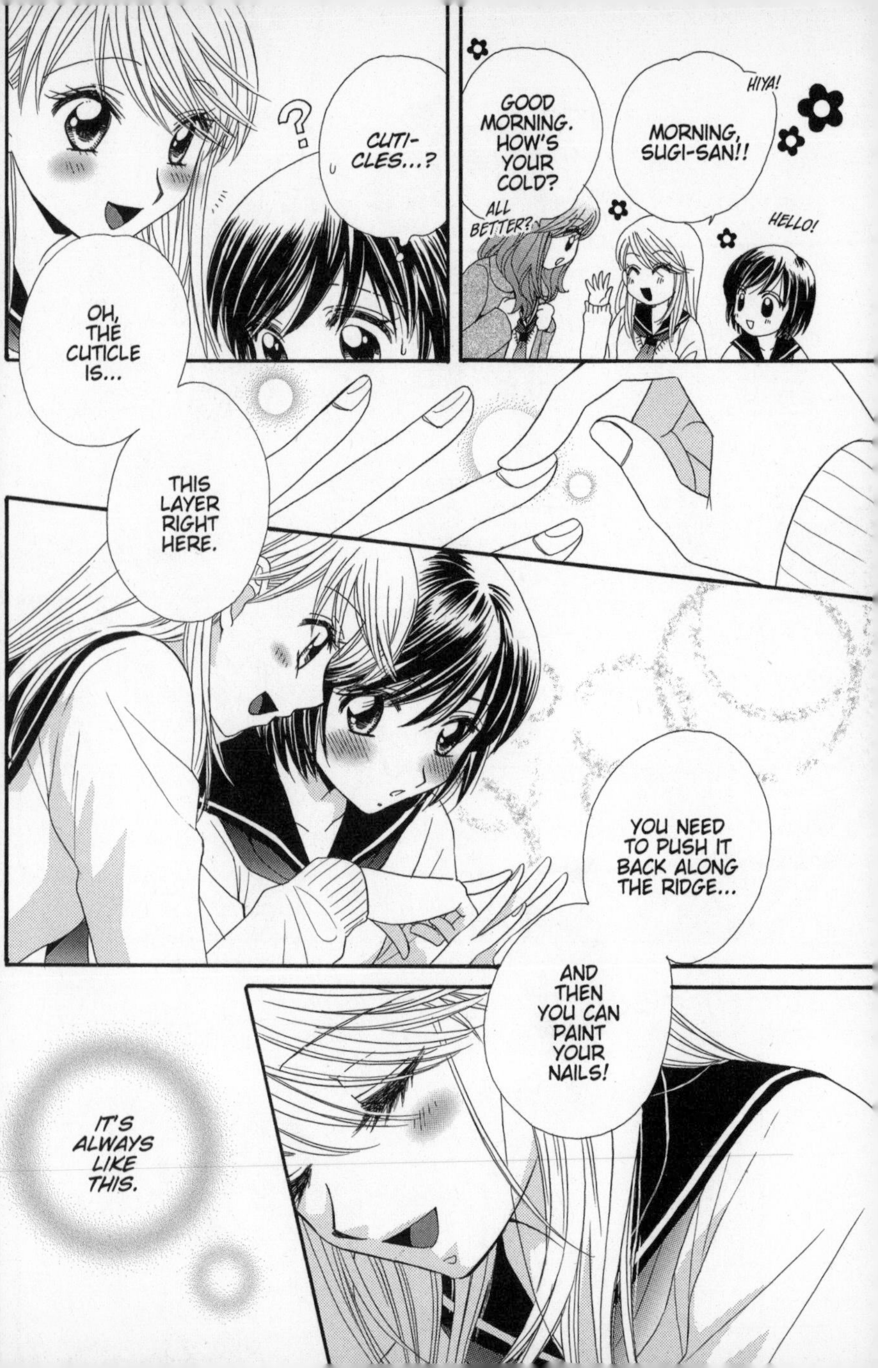
HIYA!
MORNING, SUGI-SAN!!
HELLO!
GOOD MORNING. HOW'S YOUR COLD?
ALL BETTER?
CUTI-CLES...?
OH, THE CUTICLE IS...
THIS LAYER RIGHT HERE.
YOU NEED TO PUSH IT BACK ALONG THE RIDGE...
AND THEN YOU CAN PAINT YOUR NAILS!
IT'S ALWAYS LIKE THIS.

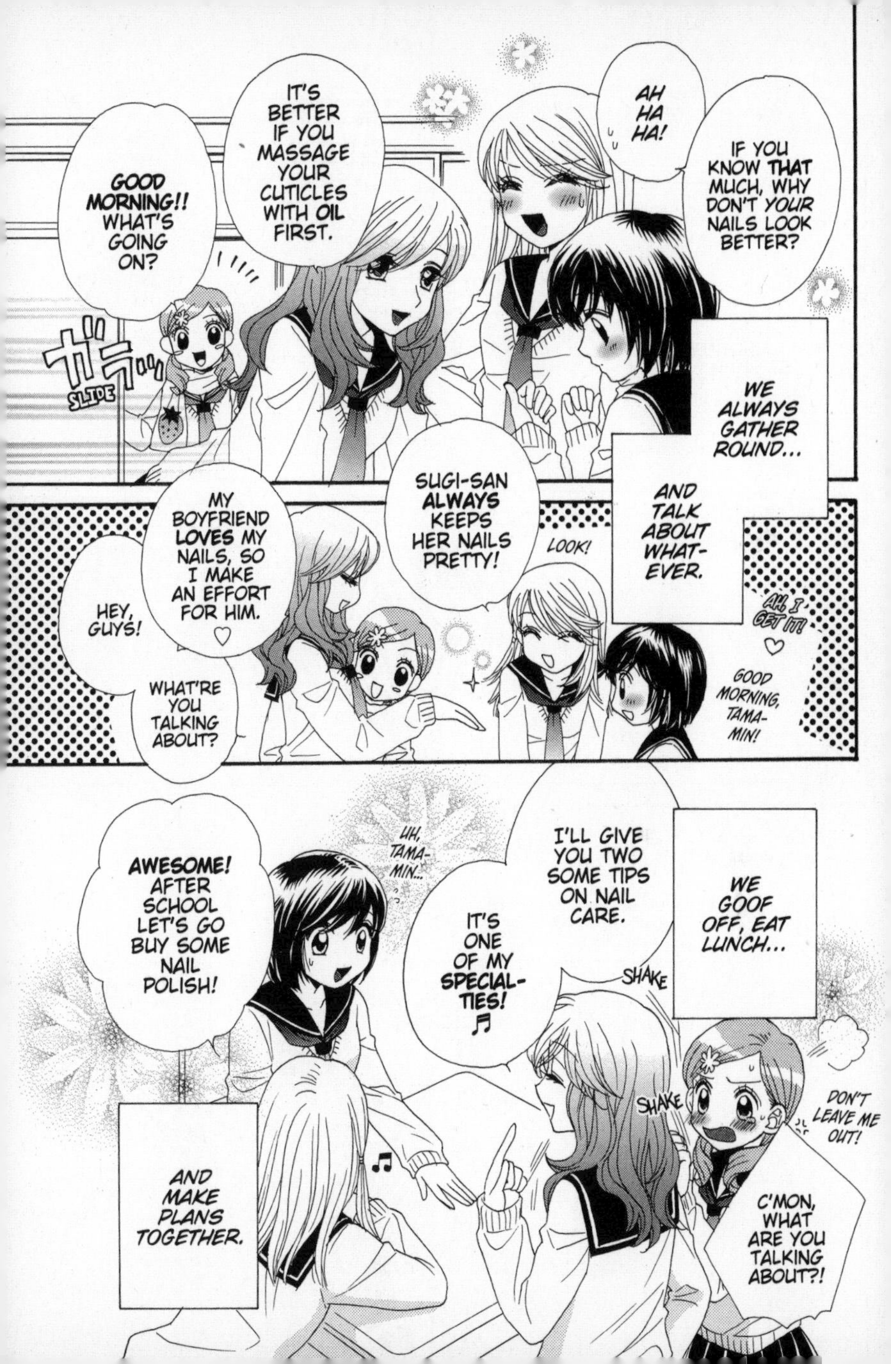
WE ALWAYS GATHER ROUND...
AH HA HA!
IF YOU KNOW THAT MUCH, WHY DON'T YOUR NAILS LOOK BETTER?
IT'S BETTER IF YOU MASSAGE YOUR CUTICLES WITH OIL FIRST.
GOOD MORNING!! WHAT'S GOING ON?
ガラ
SLIDE
AND TALK ABOUT WHAT-EVER.
AH, I GET IT! ♡
GOOD MORNING, TAMA-MIN!
SUGI-SAN ALWAYS KEEPS HER NAILS PRETTY!
LOOK!
MY BOYFRIEND LOVES MY NAILS, SO I MAKE AN EFFORT FOR HIM. ♡
HEY, GUYS!
WHAT'RE YOU TALKING ABOUT?
WE GOOF OFF, EAT LUNCH...
I'LL GIVE YOU TWO SOME TIPS ON NAIL CARE.
IT'S ONE OF MY SPECIAL-TIES! ♫
UH, TAMA-MIN...
AWESOME! AFTER SCHOOL LET'S GO BUY SOME NAIL POLISH!
SHAKE
SHAKE
DON'T LEAVE ME OUT!
C'MON, WHAT ARE YOU TALKING ABOUT?!
AND MAKE PLANS TOGETHER.

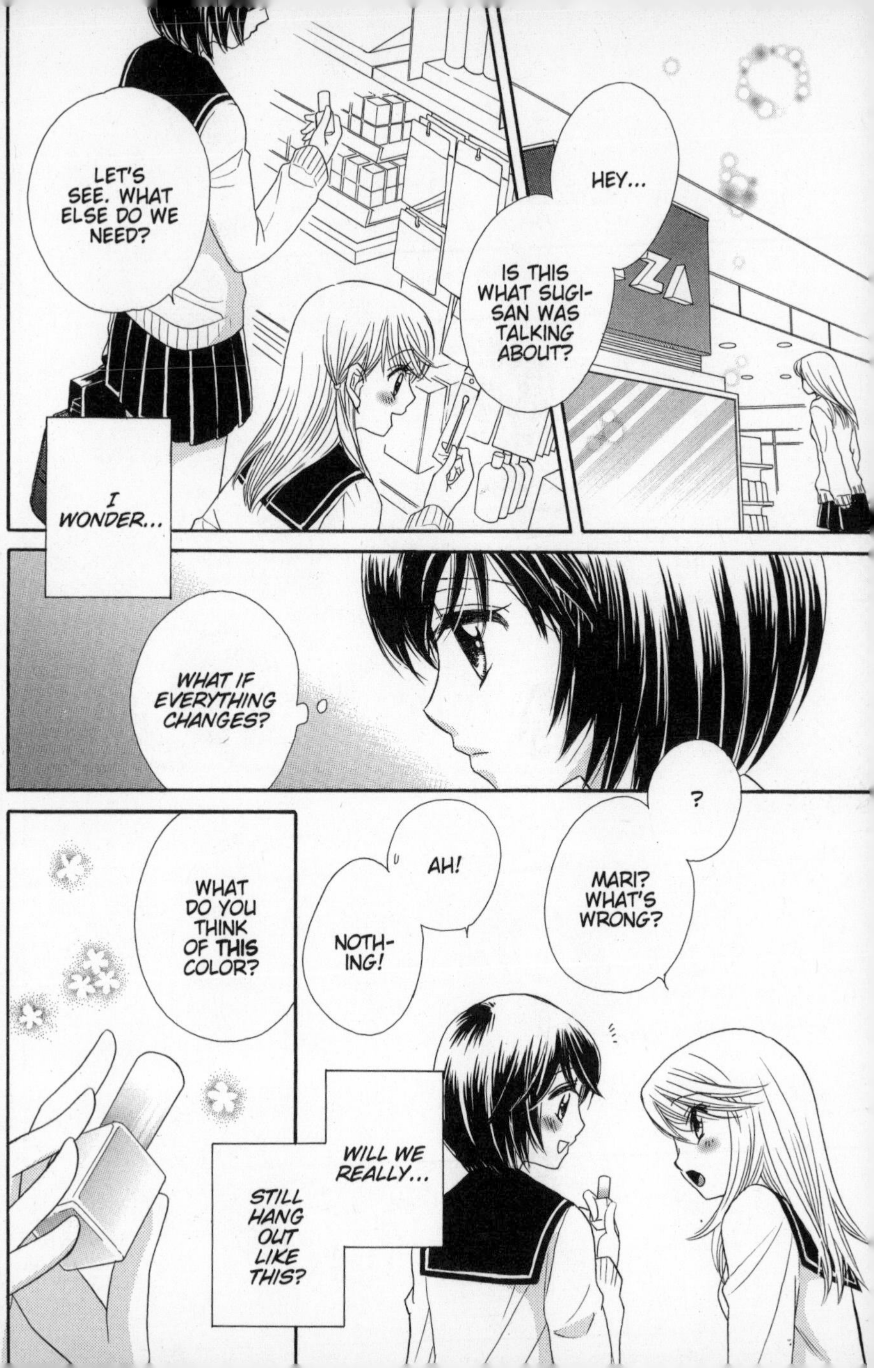
HEY...
IS THIS WHAT SUGI-SAN WAS TALKING ABOUT?
LET'S SEE. WHAT ELSE DO WE NEED?
I WONDER...
WHAT IF EVERYTHING CHANGES?
?
MARI? WHAT'S WRONG?
AH!
NOTH-ING!
WHAT DO YOU THINK OF THIS COLOR?
WILL WE REALLY...
STILL HANG OUT LIKE THIS?

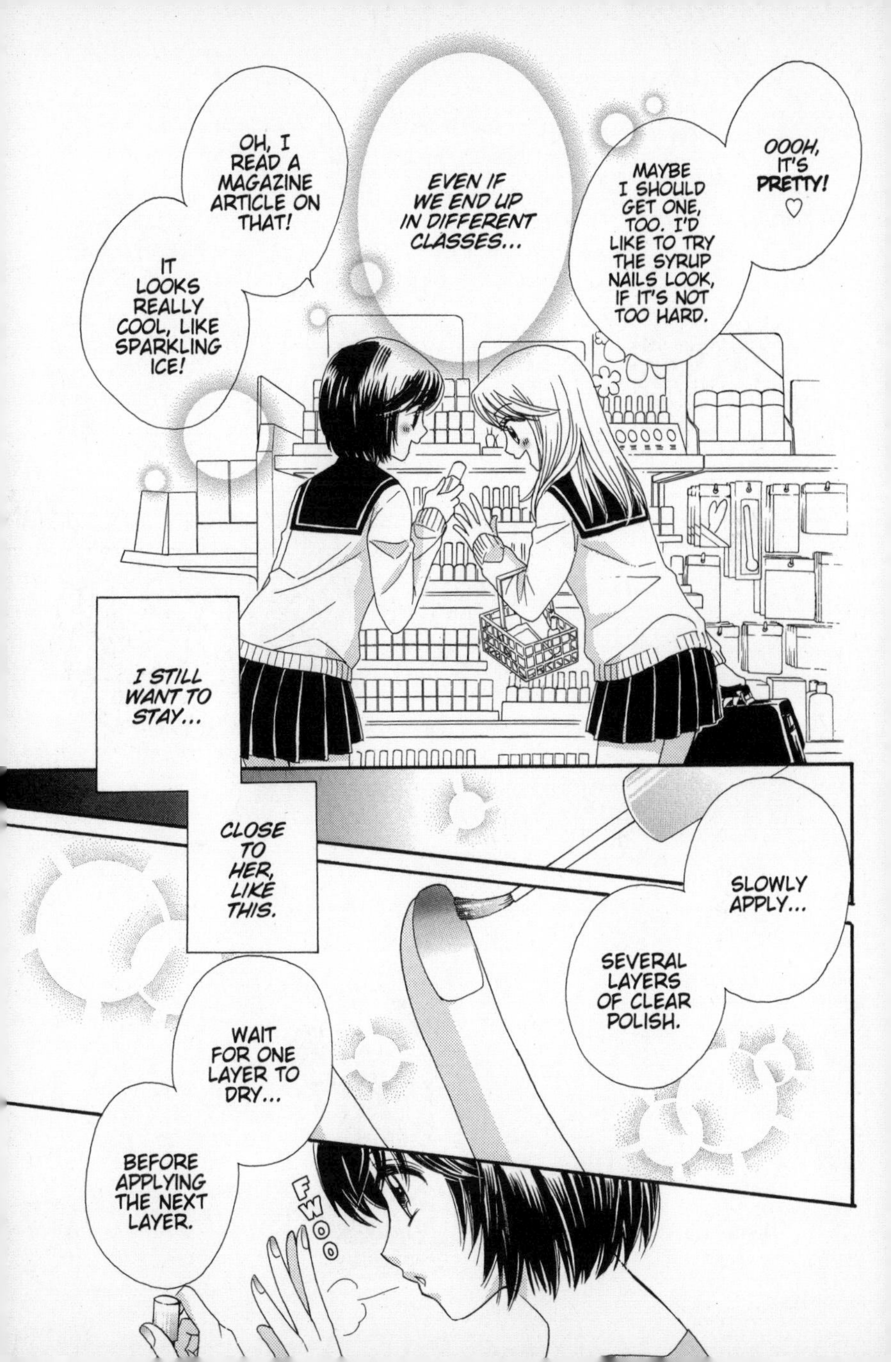
OOOH, IT'S PRETTY! ♡
MAYBE I SHOULD GET ONE, TOO. I'D LIKE TO TRY THE SYRUP NAILS LOOK, IF IT'S NOT TOO HARD.
EVEN IF WE END UP IN DIFFERENT CLASSES...
OH, I READ A MAGAZINE ARTICLE ON THAT!
IT LOOKS REALLY COOL, LIKE SPARKLING ICE!
I STILL WANT TO STAY...
CLOSE TO HER, LIKE THIS.
SLOWLY APPLY...
SEVERAL LAYERS OF CLEAR POLISH.
WAIT FOR ONE LAYER TO DRY...
BEFORE APPLYING THE NEXT LAYER.
FWOO

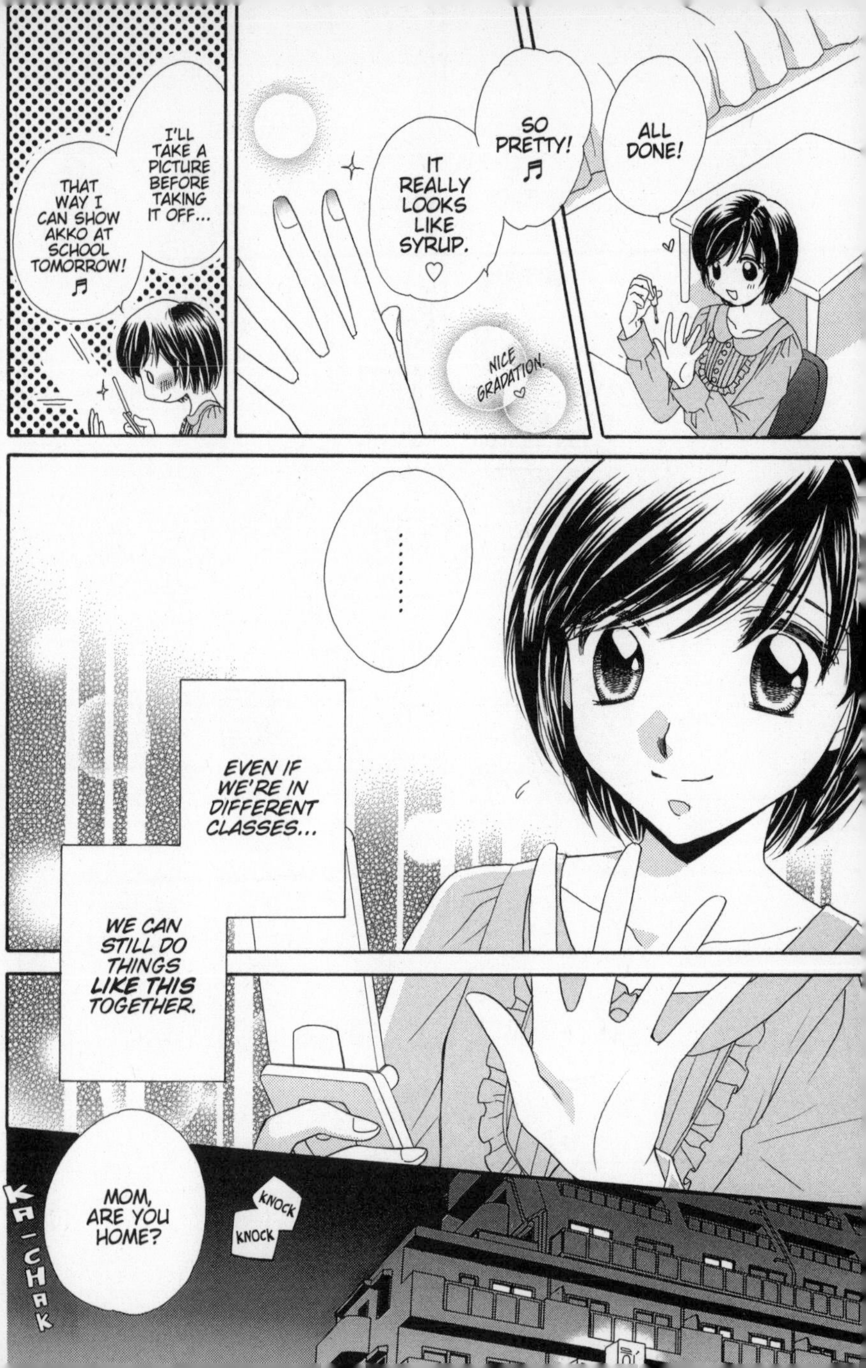
ALL DONE!
SO PRETTY! ♬
IT REALLY LOOKS LIKE SYRUP. ♡
NICE GRADATION. ♡
I'LL TAKE A PICTURE BEFORE TAKING IT OFF...
THAT WAY I CAN SHOW AKKO AT SCHOOL TOMORROW! ♬
......
EVEN IF WE'RE IN DIFFERENT CLASSES...
WE CAN STILL DO THINGS LIKE THIS TOGETHER.
KNOCK
KNOCK
MOM, ARE YOU HOME?
KA-CHAK

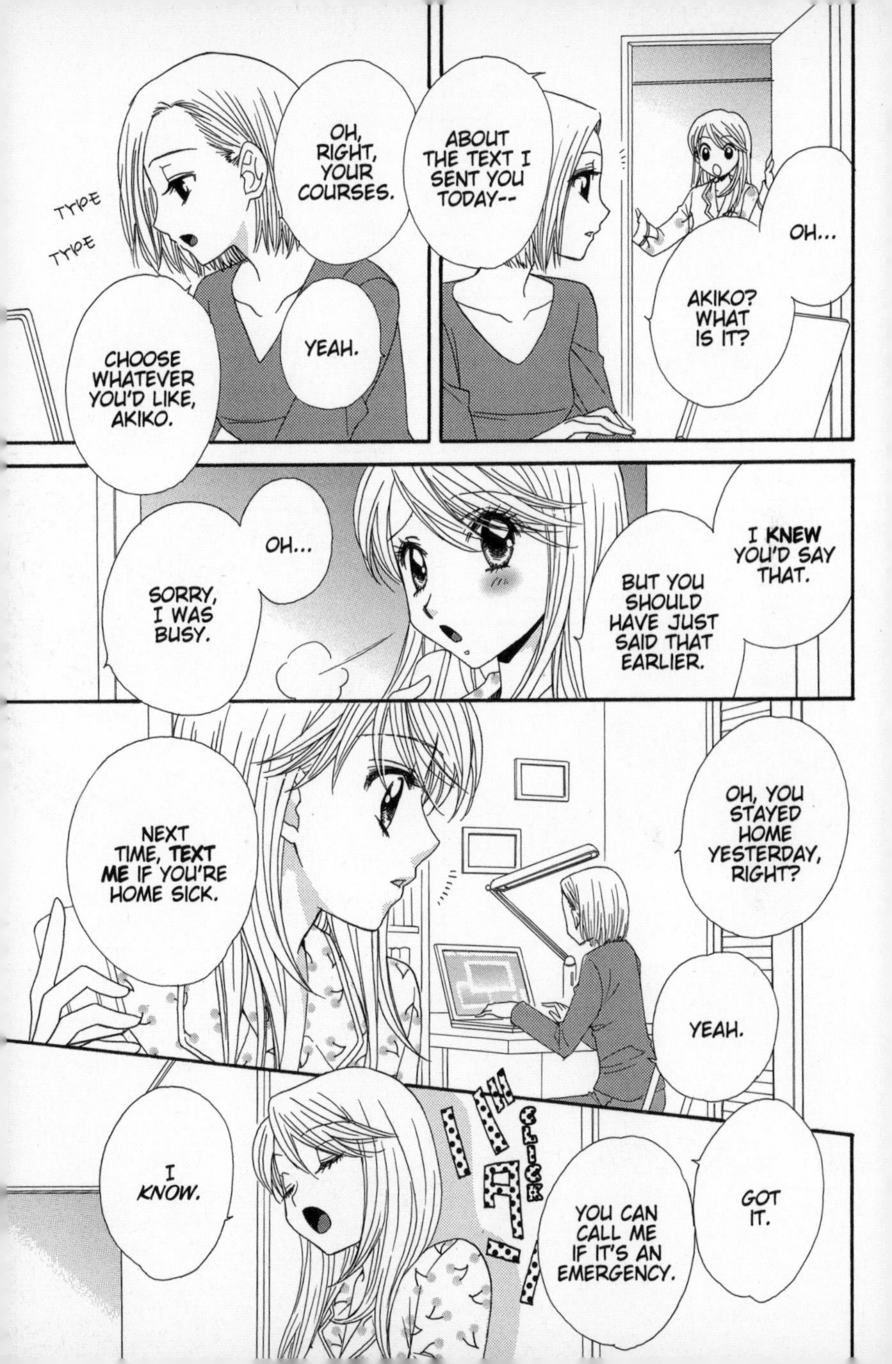
OH...
AKIKO? WHAT IS IT?
ABOUT THE TEXT I SENT YOU TODAY--
OH, RIGHT, YOUR COURSES.
YEAH.
TYPE TYPE
CHOOSE WHATEVER YOU'D LIKE, AKIKO.
I KNEW YOU'D SAY THAT.
BUT YOU SHOULD HAVE JUST SAID THAT EARLIER.
OH...
SORRY, I WAS BUSY.
OH, YOU STAYED HOME YESTERDAY, RIGHT?
YEAH.
NEXT TIME, TEXT ME IF YOU'RE HOME SICK.
GOT IT.
YOU CAN CALL ME IF IT'S AN EMERGENCY.
CLICK
I KNOW.

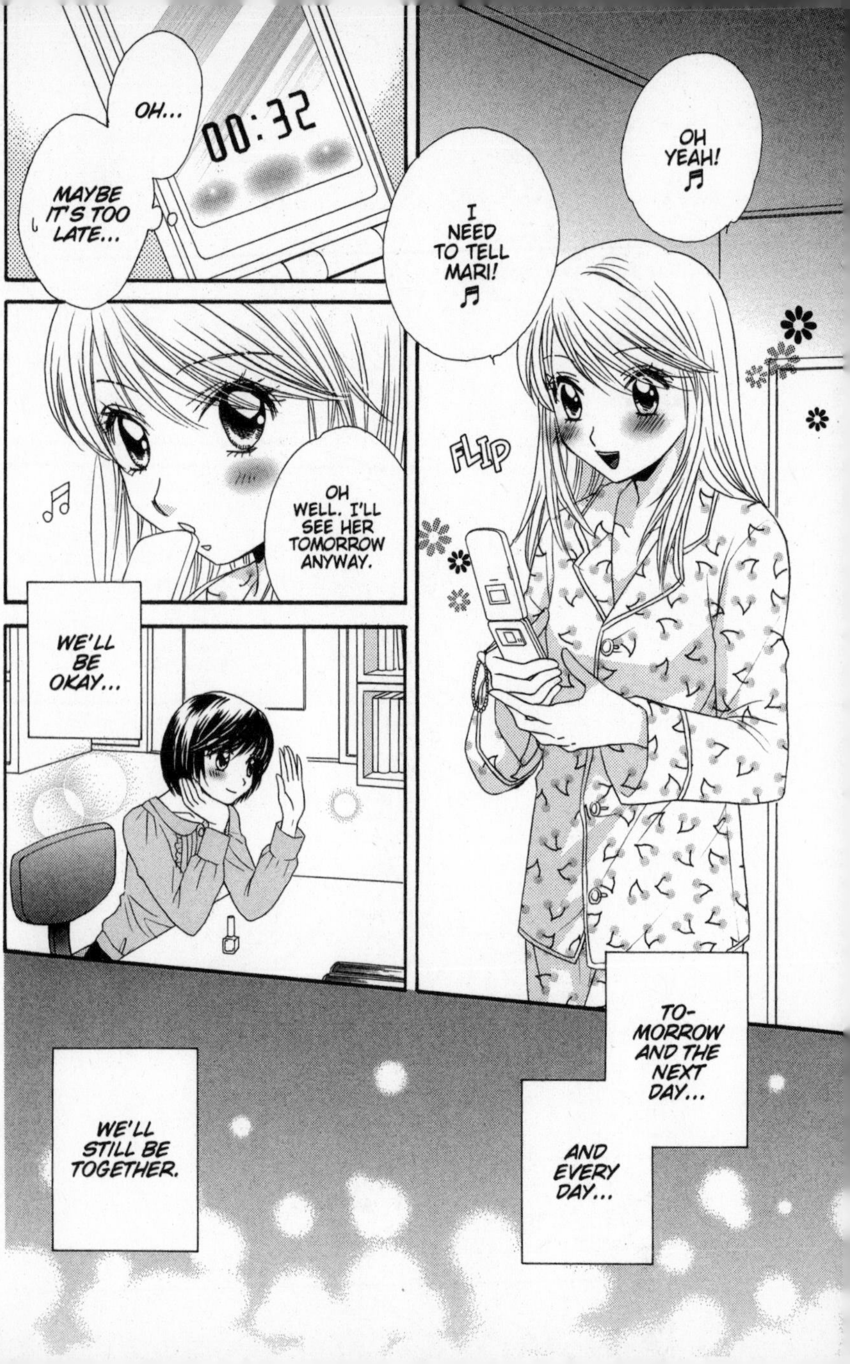
OH YEAH! ♬
I NEED TO TELL MARI! ♬
FLIP
00:32
OH...
MAYBE IT'S TOO LATE...
OH WELL. I'LL SEE HER TOMORROW ANYWAY.
WE'LL BE OKAY...
TO-MORROW AND THE NEXT DAY...
AND EVERY DAY...
WE'LL STILL BE TOGETHER.

DURING TRAIN RIDES, I READ MANGA.

I TRY REALLY HARD NOT TO LAUGH.

GIRL FRIENDS —ガールフレンズ—

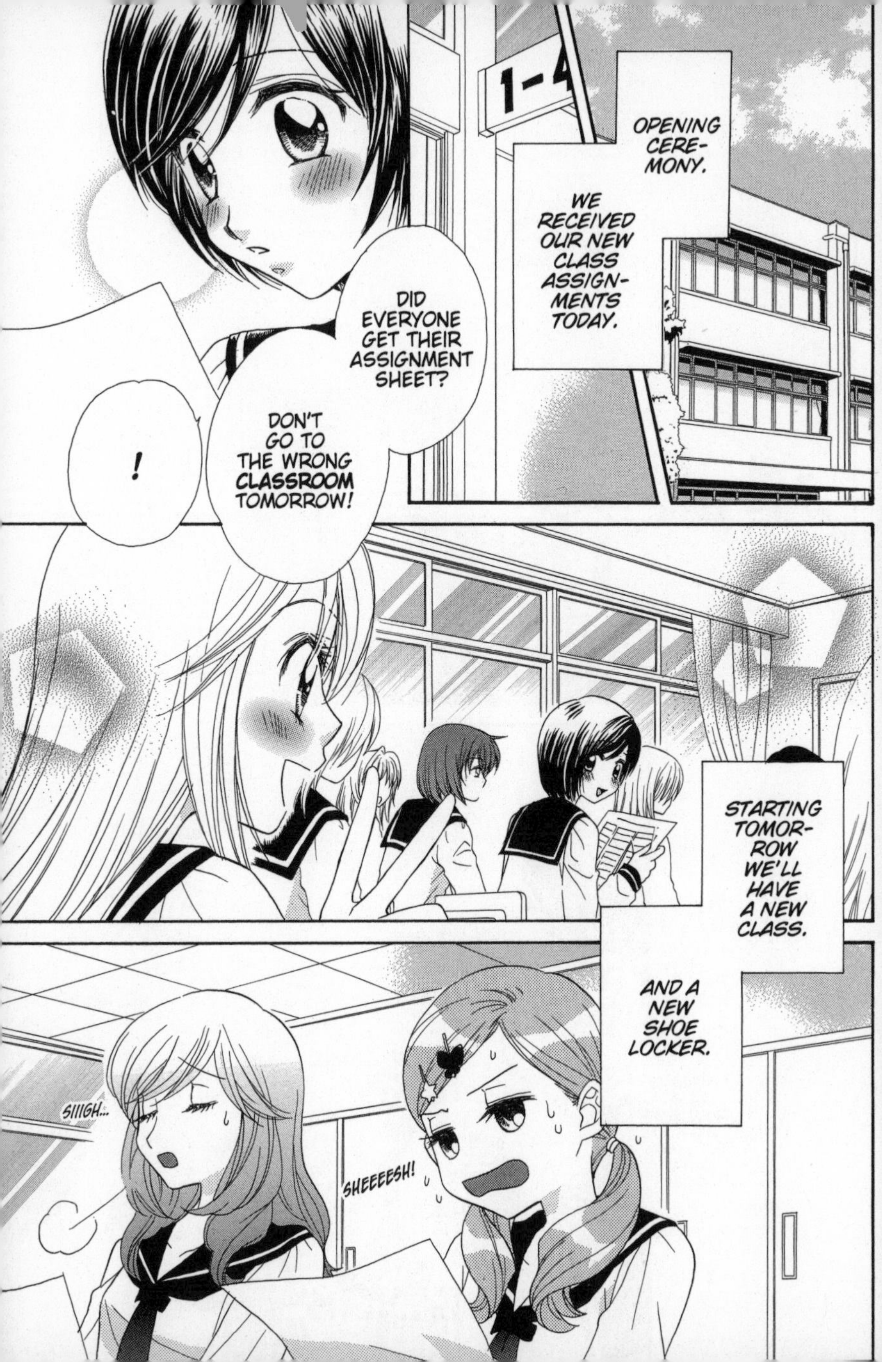
1-4
OPENING CERE-MONY.
WE RECEIVED OUR NEW CLASS ASSIGN-MENTS TODAY.
DID EVERYONE GET THEIR ASSIGNMENT SHEET?
DON'T GO TO THE WRONG CLASSROOM TOMORROW!
!
STARTING TOMOR-ROW WE'LL HAVE A NEW CLASS.
AND A NEW SHOE LOCKER.
SHEEEEESH!
SIIIGH...

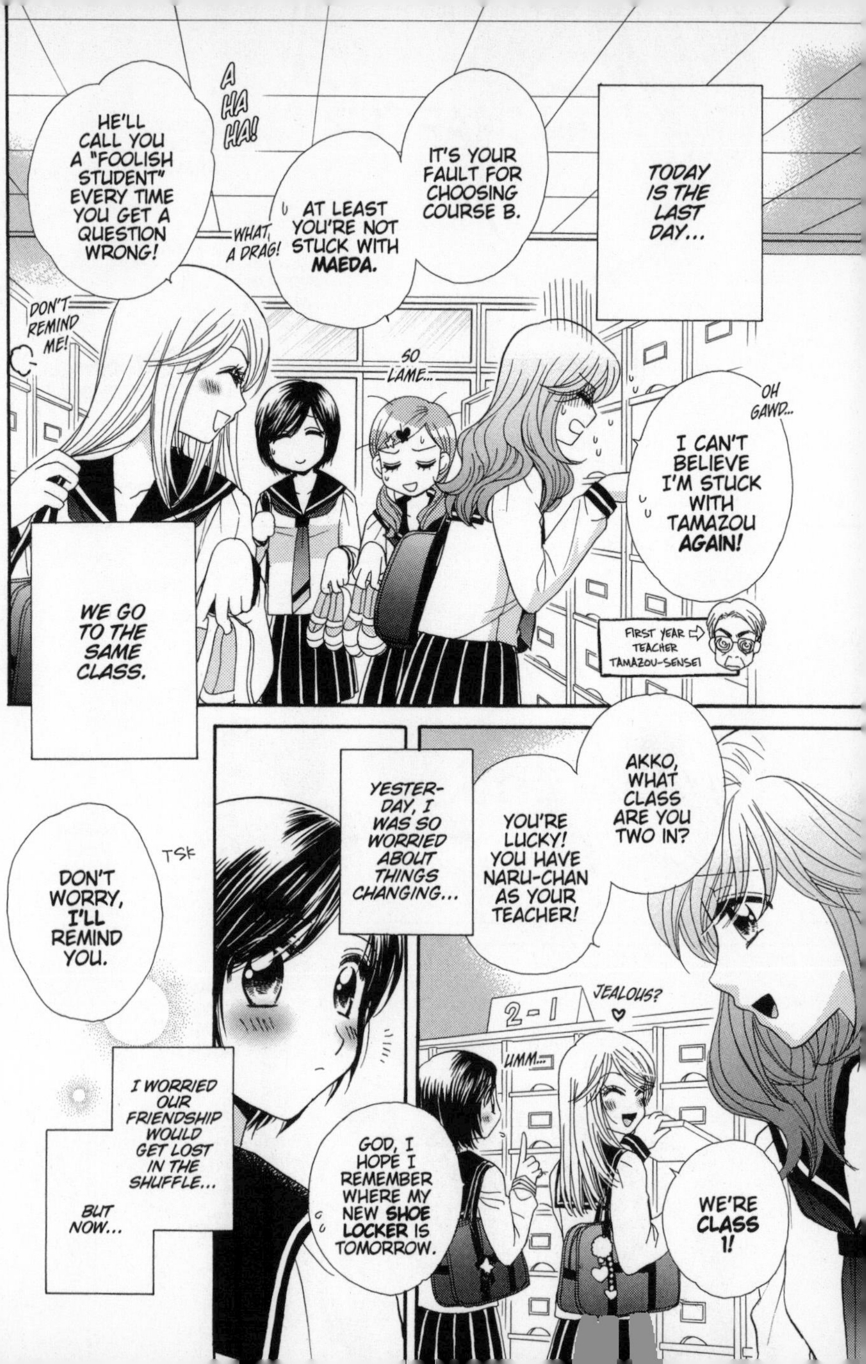
TODAY IS THE LAST DAY...
IT'S YOUR FAULT FOR CHOOSING COURSE B.
A HA HA!
HE'LL CALL YOU A "FOOLISH STUDENT" EVERY TIME YOU GET A QUESTION WRONG!
OH GAWD...
I CAN'T BELIEVE I'M STUCK WITH TAMAZOU AGAIN!
FIRST YEAR TEACHER TAMAZOU-SENSEI
SO LAME...
AT LEAST YOU'RE NOT STUCK WITH MAEDA.
WHAT A DRAG!
DON'T REMIND ME!
WE GO TO THE SAME CLASS.
AKKO, WHAT CLASS ARE YOU TWO IN?
YOU'RE LUCKY! YOU HAVE NARU-CHAN AS YOUR TEACHER!
JEALOUS?
2-1
UMM...
WE'RE CLASS 1!
GOD, I HOPE I REMEMBER WHERE MY NEW SHOE LOCKER IS TOMORROW.
YESTER-DAY, I WAS SO WORRIED ABOUT THINGS CHANGING...
TSK
DON'T WORRY, I'LL REMIND YOU.
I WORRIED OUR FRIENDSHIP WOULD GET LOST IN THE SHUFFLE...
BUT NOW...

[CHAPTER 6]

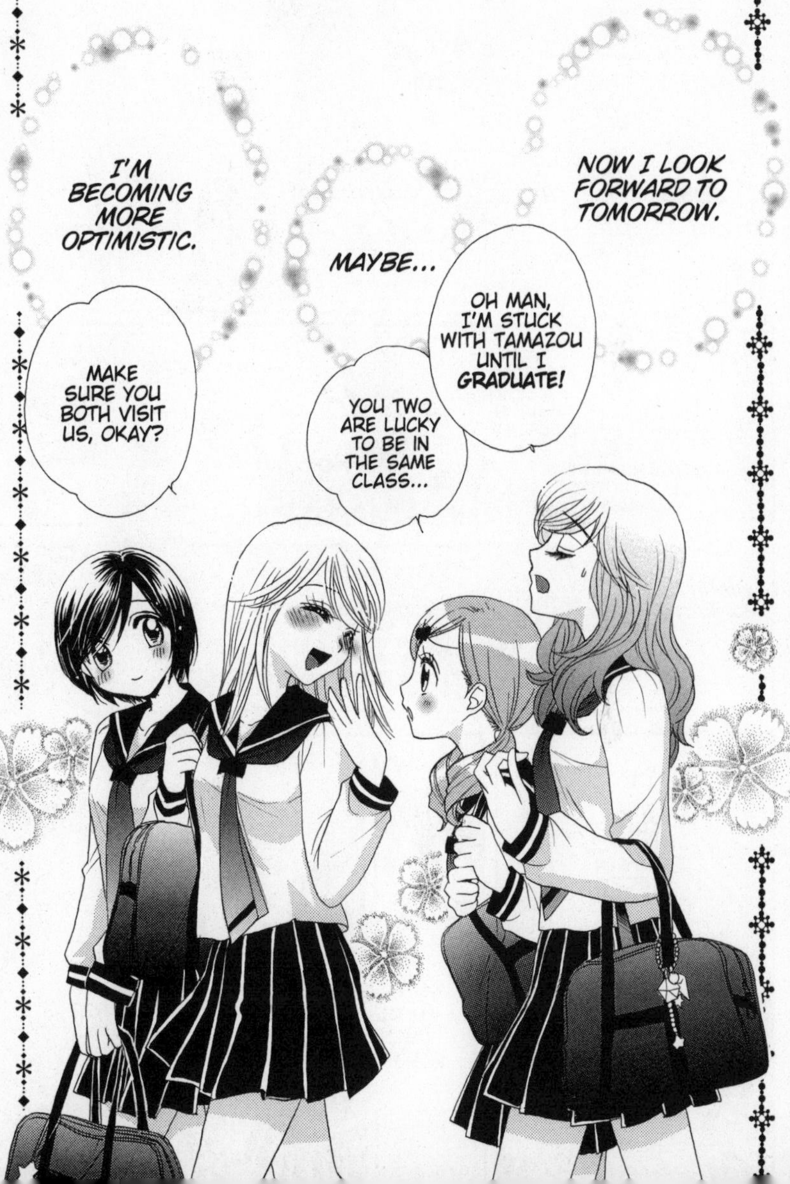

NOW I LOOK FORWARD TO TOMORROW.
MAYBE...
I'M BECOMING MORE OPTIMISTIC.
OH MAN, I'M STUCK WITH TAMAZOU UNTIL I **GRADUATE**!
YOU TWO ARE LUCKY TO BE IN THE SAME CLASS...
MAKE SURE YOU BOTH VISIT US, OKAY?

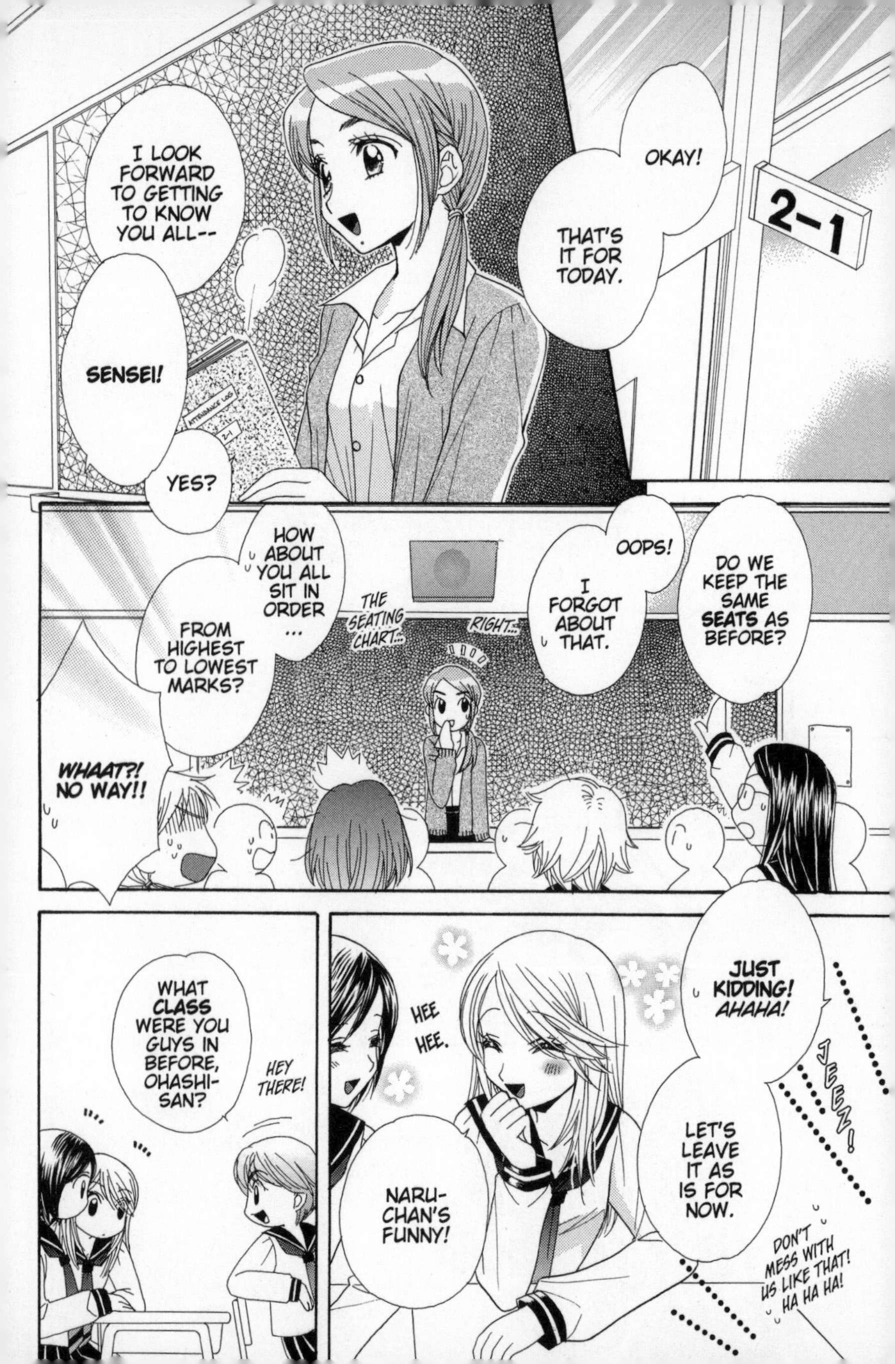
2-1
OKAY!
THAT'S IT FOR TODAY.
I LOOK FORWARD TO GETTING TO KNOW YOU ALL--
SENSEI!
YES?
DO WE KEEP THE SAME SEATS AS BEFORE?
OOPS!
I FORGOT ABOUT THAT.
RIGHT...
THE SEATING CHART...
HOW ABOUT YOU ALL SIT IN ORDER ...
FROM HIGHEST TO LOWEST MARKS?
WHAAT?! NO WAY!!
JUST KIDDING! AHAHA!
JEEZ!
LET'S LEAVE IT AS IS FOR NOW.
DON'T MESS WITH US LIKE THAT! HA HA HA!
HEE HEE.
NARU-CHAN'S FUNNY!
WHAT CLASS WERE YOU GUYS IN BEFORE, OHASHI-SAN?
HEY THERE!

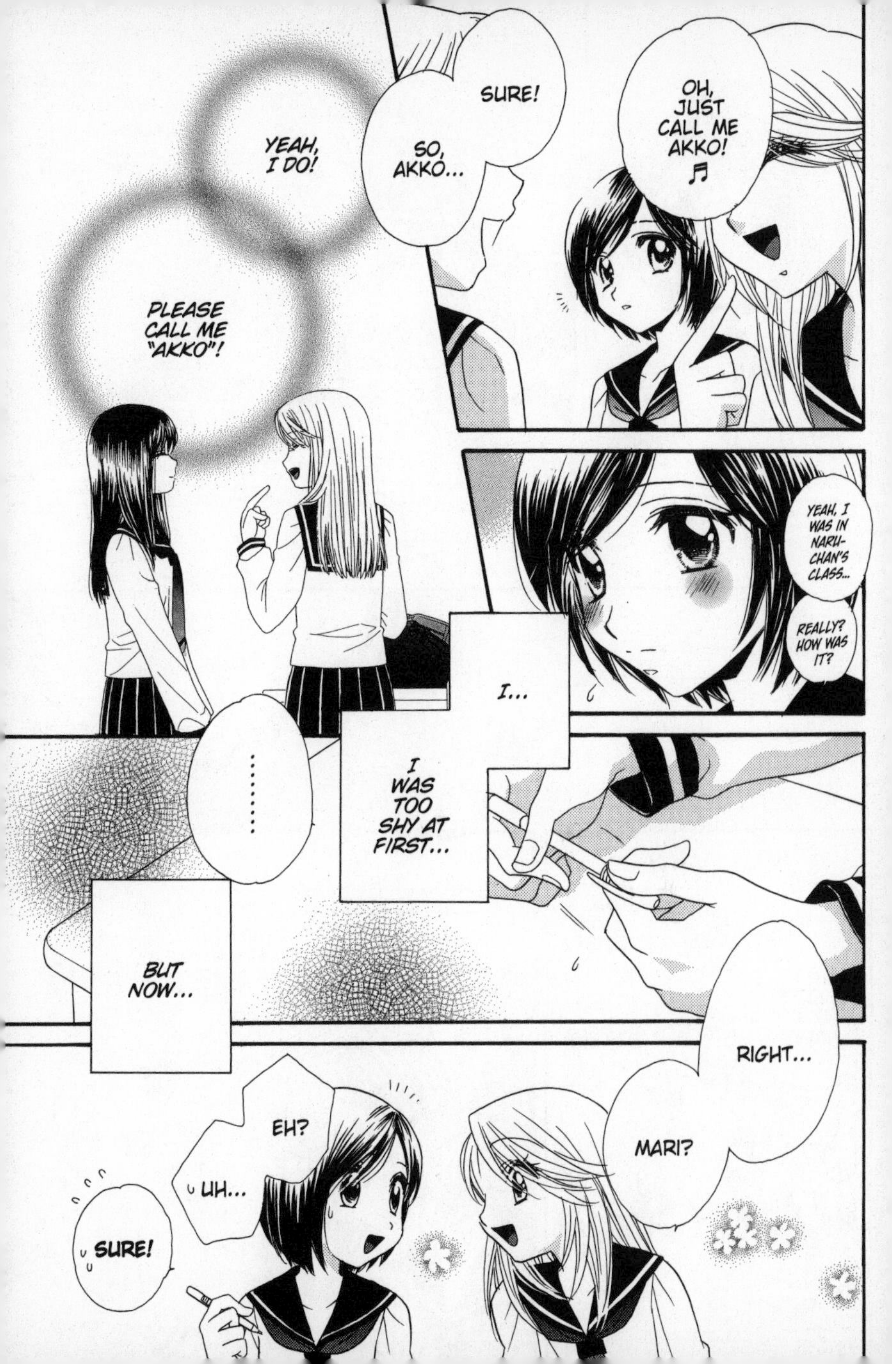
OH, JUST CALL ME AKKO! ♬
SURE!
SO, AKKO...
YEAH, I WAS IN NARU-CHAN'S CLASS...
REALLY? HOW WAS IT?
I...
YEAH, I DO!
PLEASE CALL ME "AKKO"!
I WAS TOO SHY AT FIRST...
......
BUT NOW...
RIGHT...
MARI?
EH?
UH...
SURE!

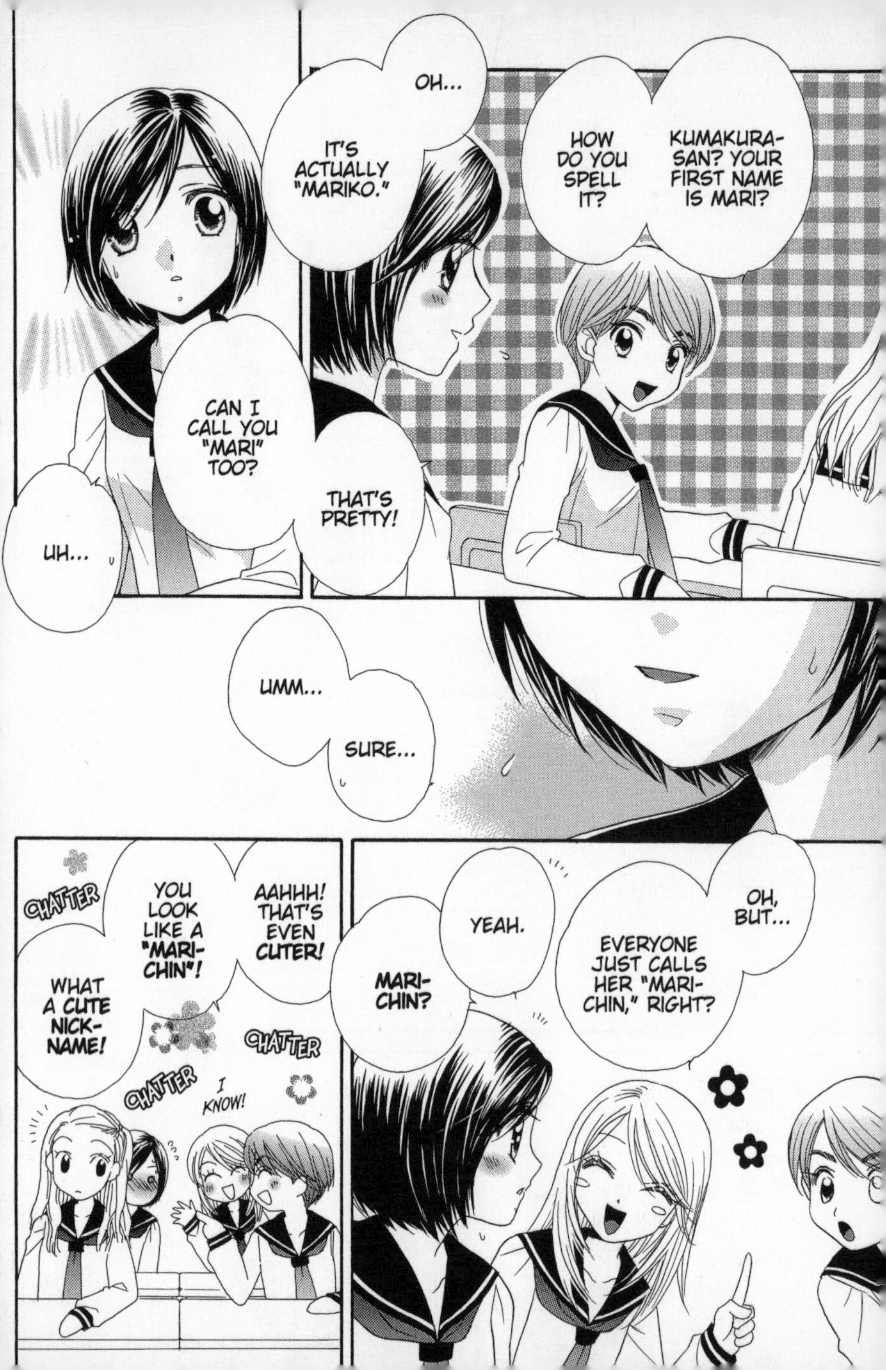
KUMAKURA-SAN? YOUR FIRST NAME IS MARI?
HOW DO YOU SPELL IT?
OH...
IT'S ACTUALLY "MARIKO."
THAT'S PRETTY!
CAN I CALL YOU "MARI" TOO?
UH...
UMM...
SURE...
OH, BUT...
EVERYONE JUST CALLS HER "MARI-CHIN," RIGHT?
YEAH.
MARI-CHIN?
AAHHH! THAT'S EVEN CUTER!
YOU LOOK LIKE A "MARI-CHIN"!
CHATTER
WHAT A CUTE NICK-NAME!
CHATTER
I KNOW!
CHATTER

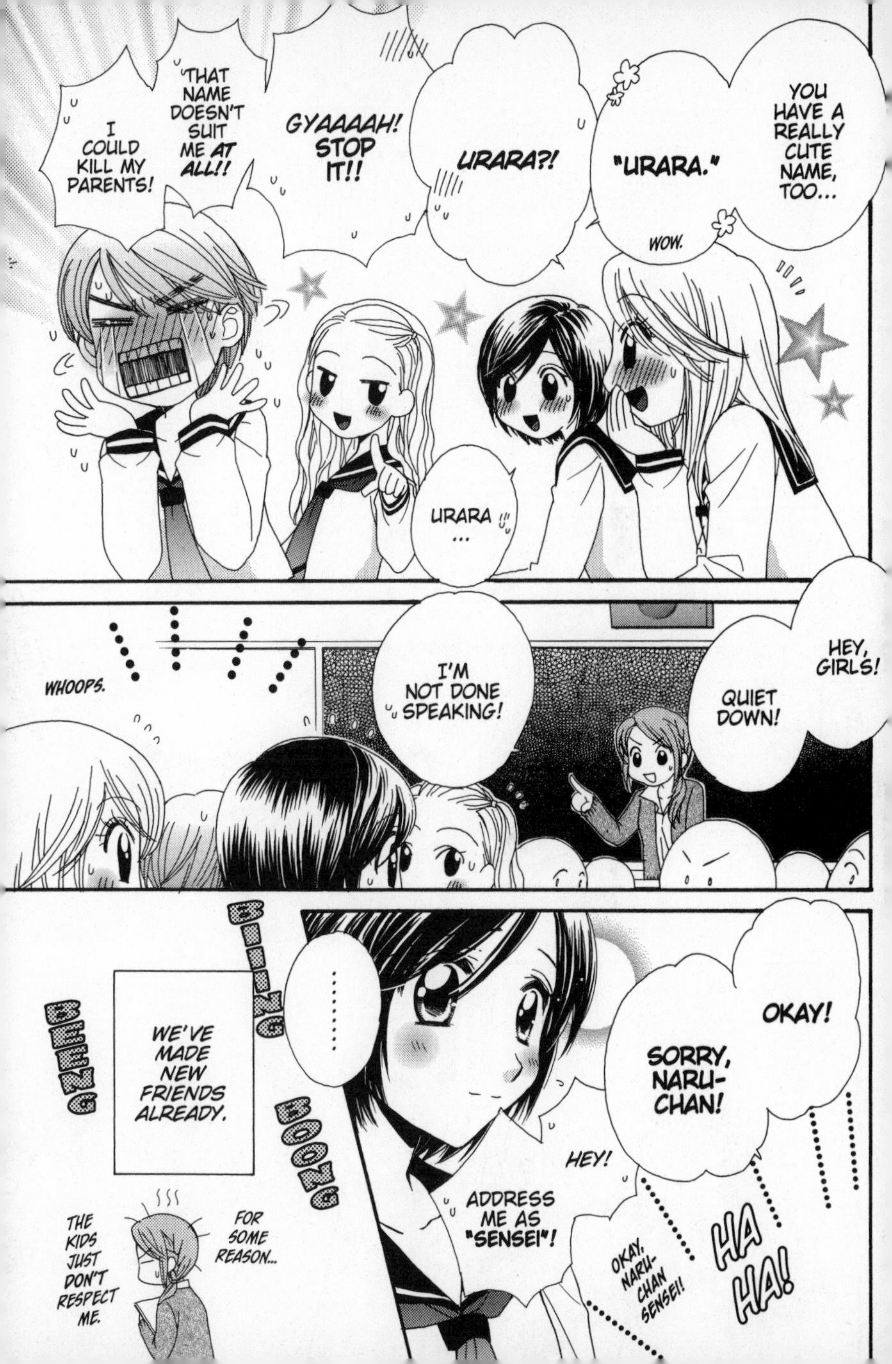
YOU HAVE A REALLY CUTE NAME, TOO...
WOW.
"URARA."
URARA?!
GYAAAAH! STOP IT!!
THAT NAME DOESN'T SUIT ME AT ALL!!
I COULD KILL MY PARENTS!
URARA ...
HEY, GIRLS!
QUIET DOWN!
I'M NOT DONE SPEAKING!
WHOOPS.
OKAY!
SORRY, NARU-CHAN!
HA HA!
HEY!
ADDRESS ME AS "SENSEI"!
OKAY, NARU-CHAN SENSEI!
......
BIIING
BOOONG
WE'VE MADE NEW FRIENDS ALREADY.
BEEENG
FOR SOME REASON...
THE KIDS JUST DON'T RESPECT ME.

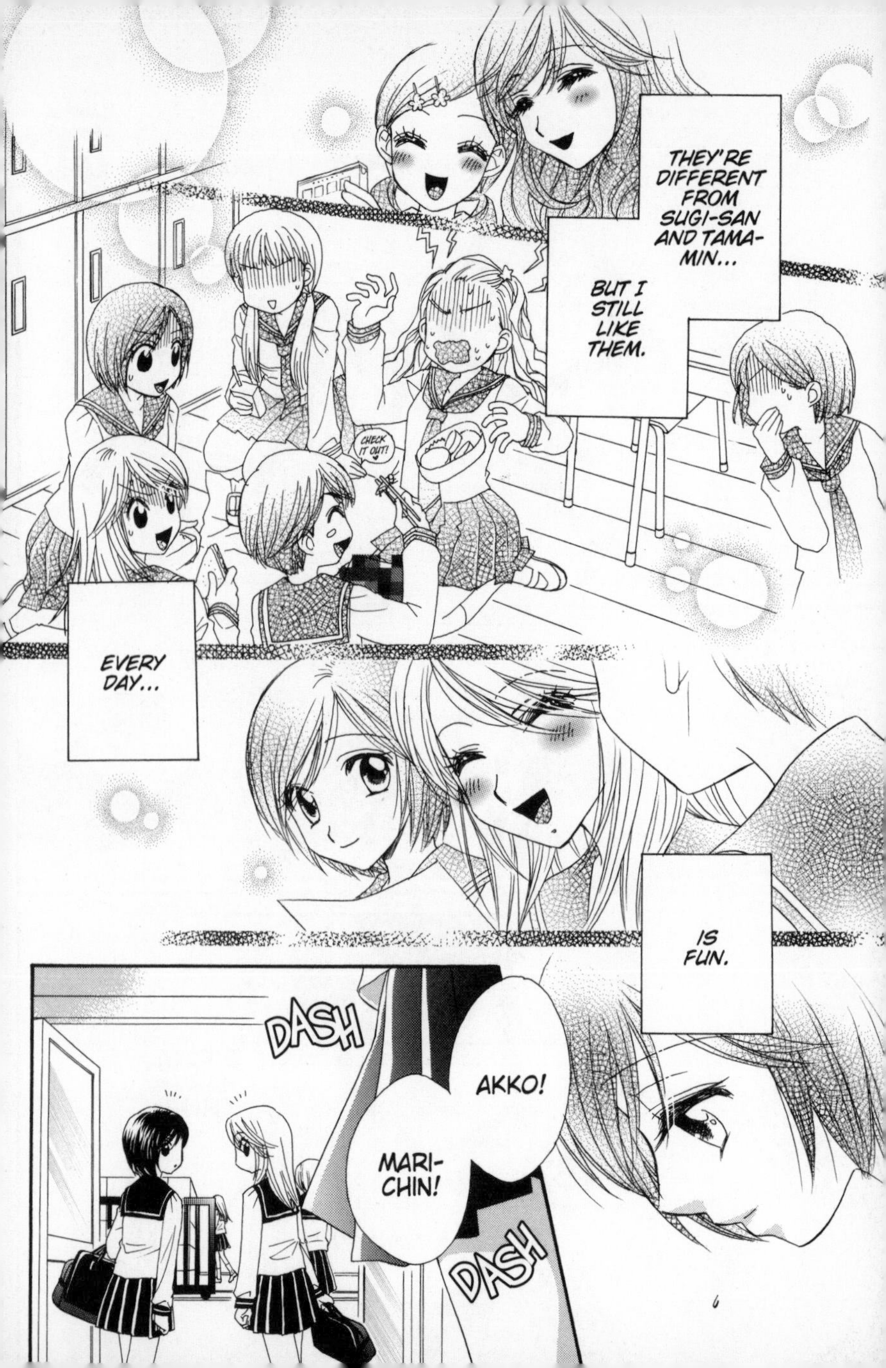
THEY'RE DIFFERENT FROM SUGI-SAN AND TAMA-MIN...
BUT I STILL LIKE THEM.
CHECK IT OUT!
EVERY DAY...
IS FUN.
DASH
AKKO!
MARI-CHIN!
DASH

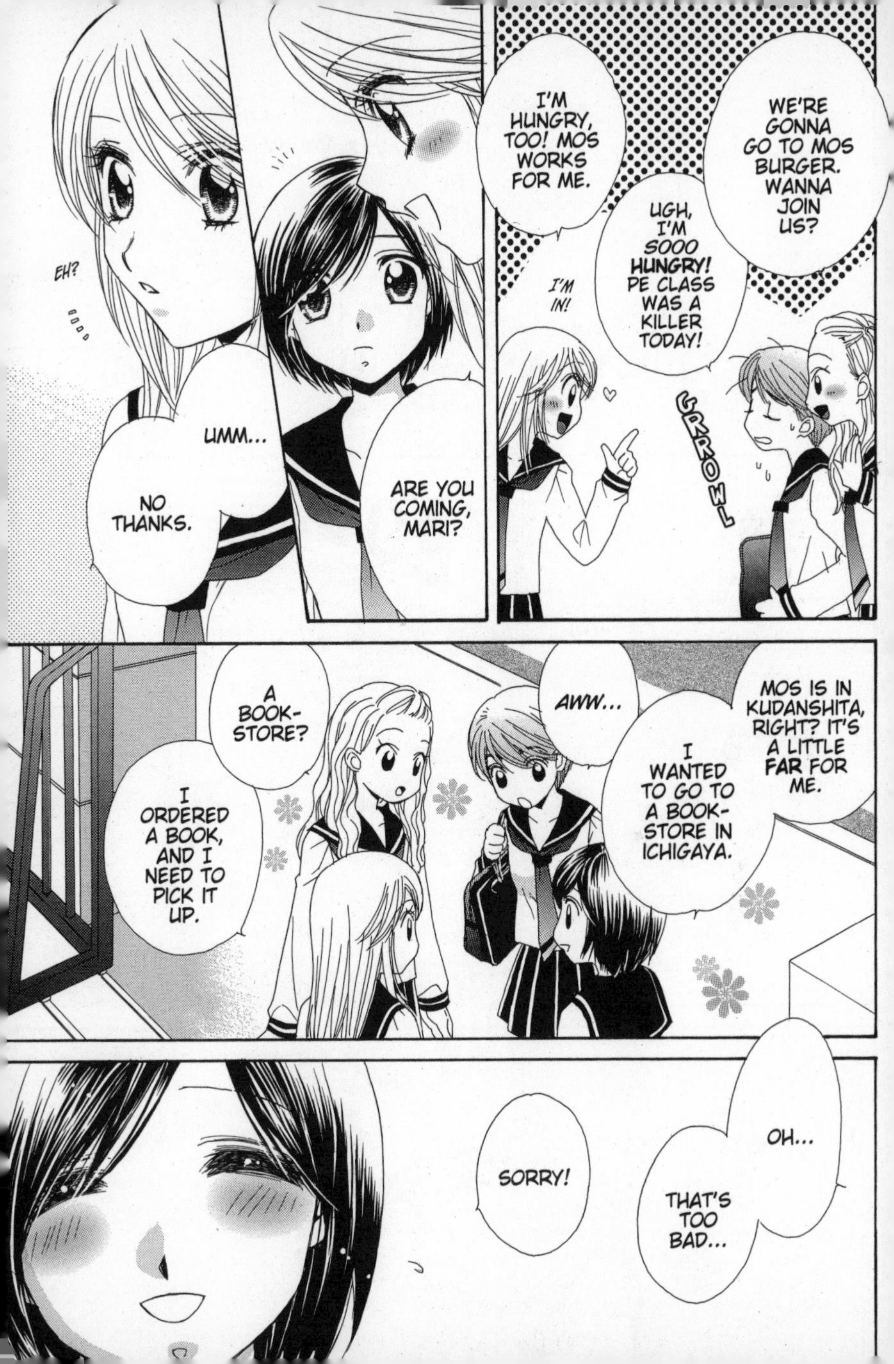
WE'RE GONNA GO TO MOS BURGER. WANNA JOIN US?
UGH, I'M SOOO HUNGRY! PE CLASS WAS A KILLER TODAY!
GRROWL
I'M HUNGRY, TOO! MOS WORKS FOR ME.
I'M IN!
ARE YOU COMING, MARI?
EH?
UMM...
NO THANKS.
MOS IS IN KUDANSHITA, RIGHT? IT'S A LITTLE FAR FOR ME.
I WANTED TO GO TO A BOOK-STORE IN ICHIGAYA.
AWW...
A BOOK-STORE?
I ORDERED A BOOK, AND I NEED TO PICK IT UP.
OH...
THAT'S TOO BAD...
SORRY!

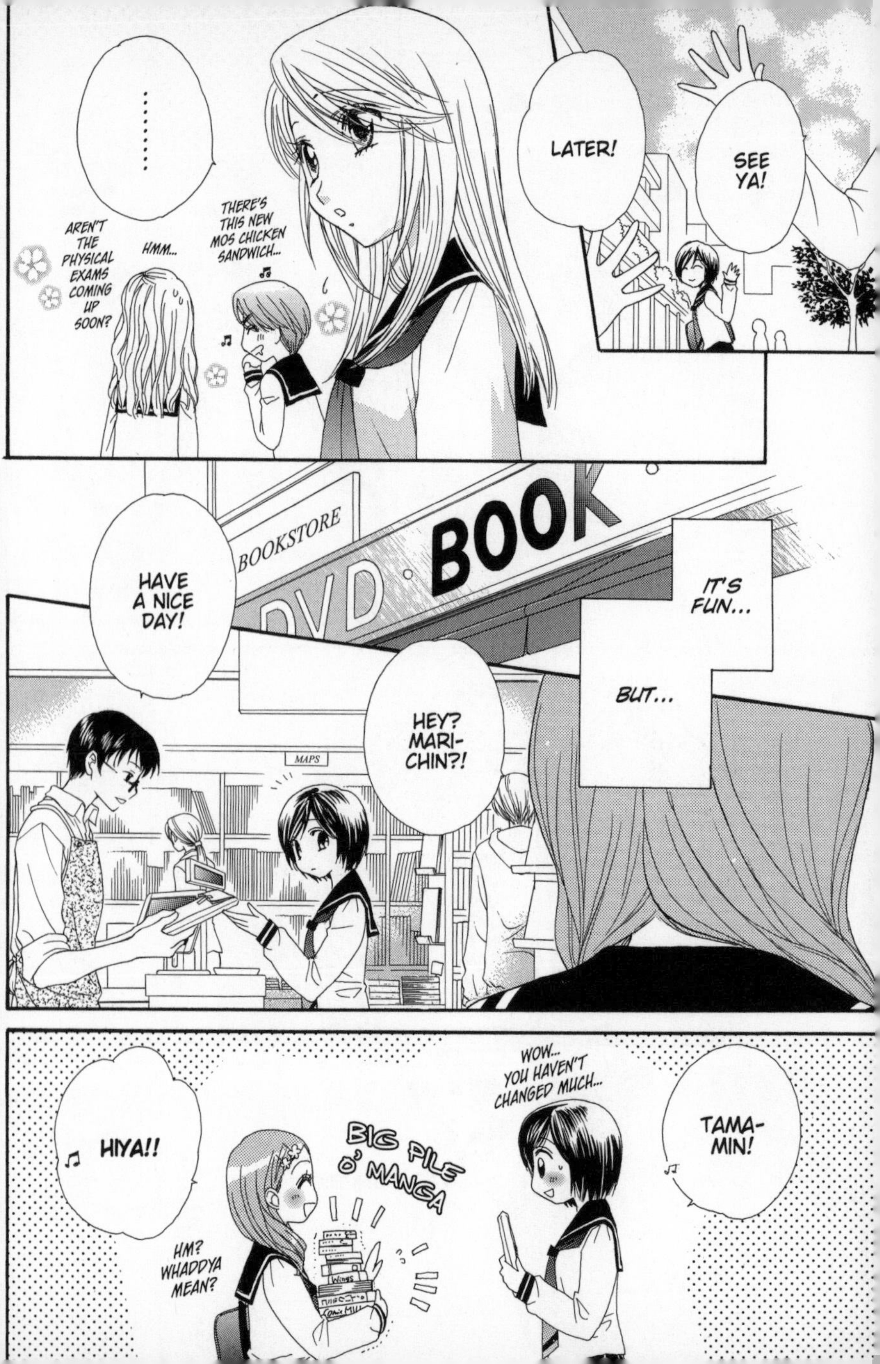
SEE YA!
LATER!
......
THERE'S THIS NEW MOS CHICKEN SANDWICH...
HMM...
AREN'T THE PHYSICAL EXAMS COMING UP SOON?
IT'S FUN...
BUT...
BOOK
DVD
BOOKSTORE
HAVE A NICE DAY!
HEY? MARI-CHIN?!
MAPS
TAMA-MIN!
WOW... YOU HAVEN'T CHANGED MUCH...
BIG PILE O' MANGA
HIYA!!
HM? WHADDYA MEAN?

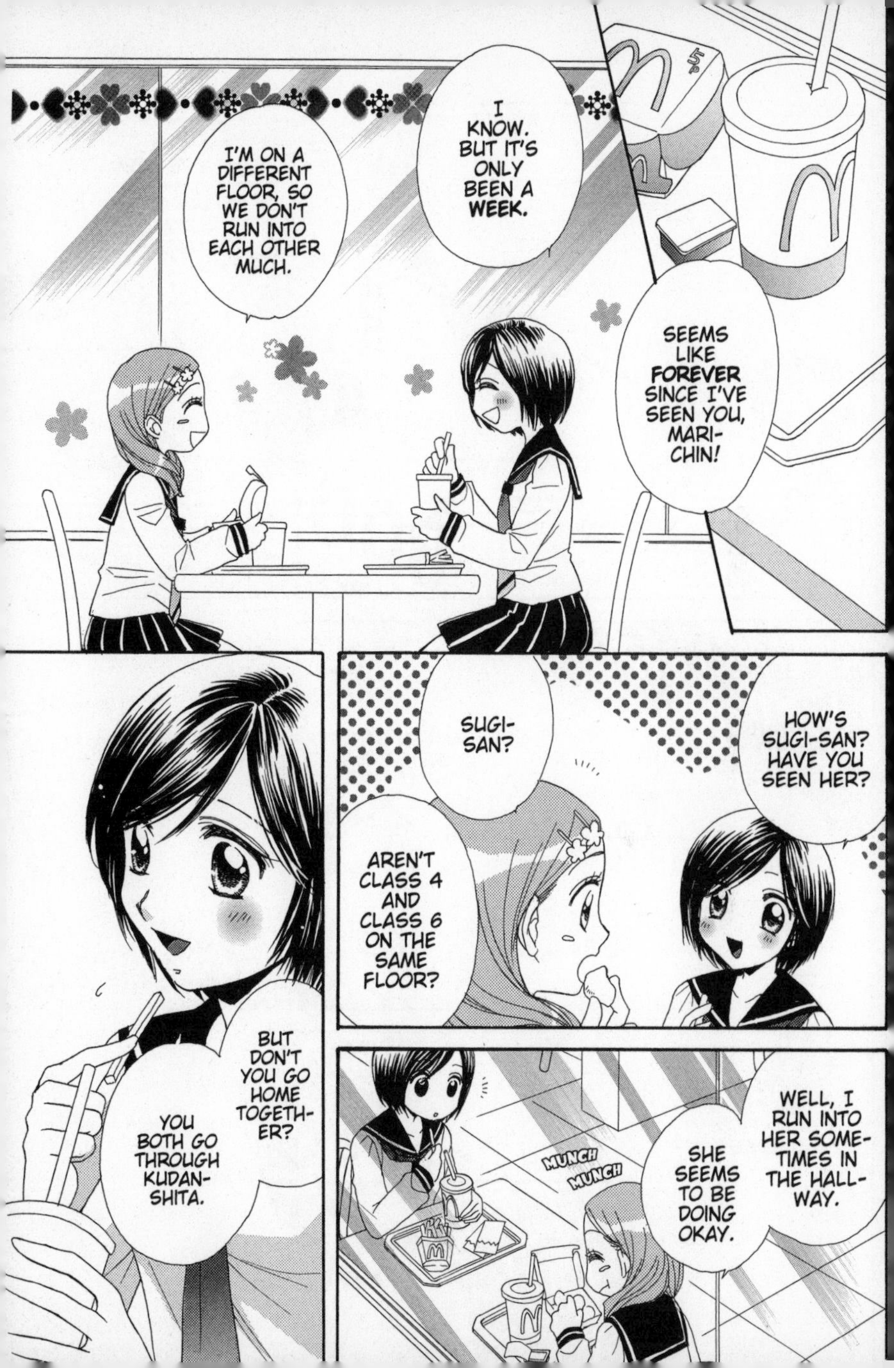
SEEMS LIKE FOREVER SINCE I'VE SEEN YOU, MARI-CHIN!
I KNOW. BUT IT'S ONLY BEEN A WEEK.
I'M ON A DIFFERENT FLOOR, SO WE DON'T RUN INTO EACH OTHER MUCH.
HOW'S SUGI-SAN? HAVE YOU SEEN HER?
SUGI-SAN?
AREN'T CLASS 4 AND CLASS 6 ON THE SAME FLOOR?
WELL, I RUN INTO HER SOME-TIMES IN THE HALL-WAY.
SHE SEEMS TO BE DOING OKAY.
MUNCH MUNCH
BUT DON'T YOU GO HOME TOGETH-ER?
YOU BOTH GO THROUGH KUDAN-SHITA.

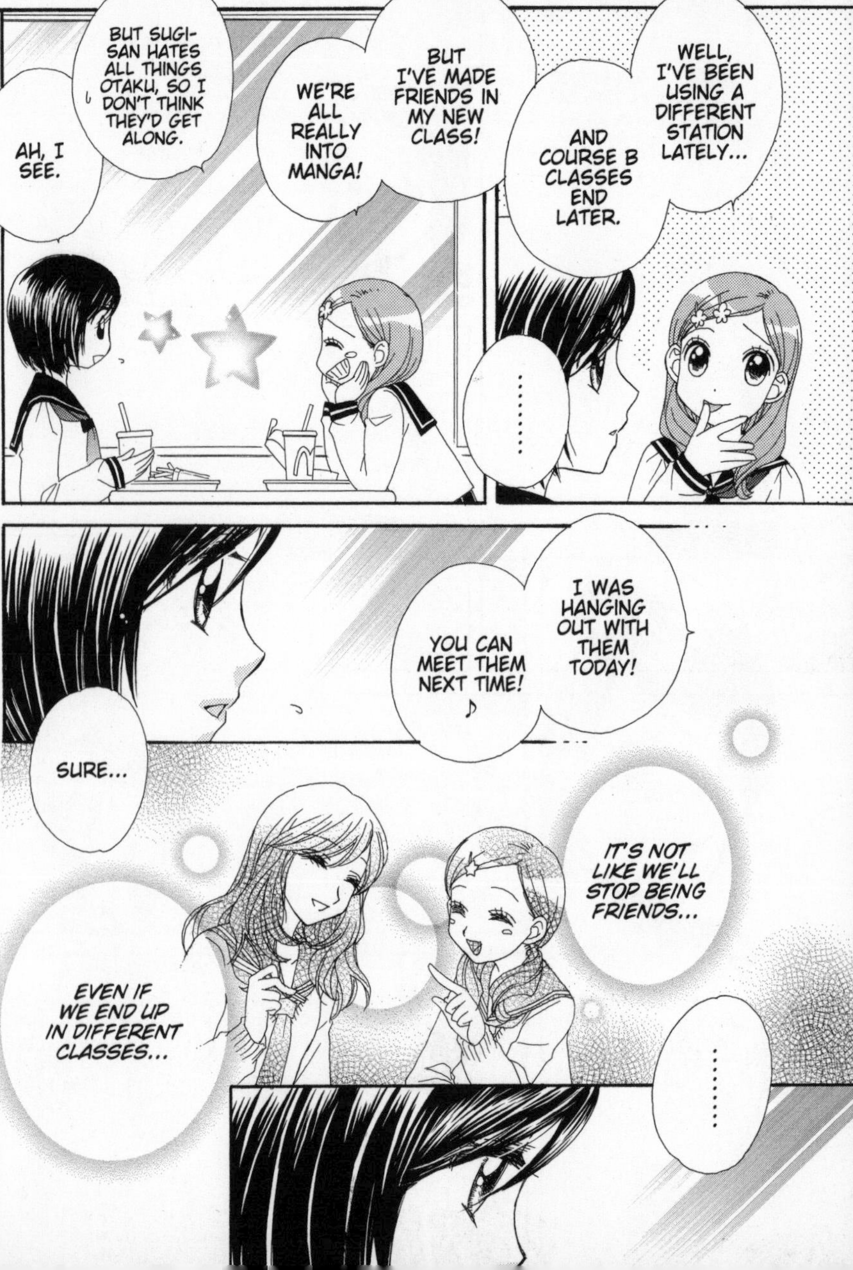
WELL, I'VE BEEN USING A DIFFERENT STATION LATELY...
AND COURSE B CLASSES END LATER.
......
BUT I'VE MADE FRIENDS IN MY NEW CLASS!
WE'RE ALL REALLY INTO MANGA!
BUT SUGI-SAN HATES ALL THINGS OTAKU, SO I DON'T THINK THEY'D GET ALONG.
AH, I SEE.
I WAS HANGING OUT WITH THEM TODAY!
YOU CAN MEET THEM NEXT TIME! ♪
SURE...
IT'S NOT LIKE WE'LL STOP BEING FRIENDS...
EVEN IF WE END UP IN DIFFERENT CLASSES...
......

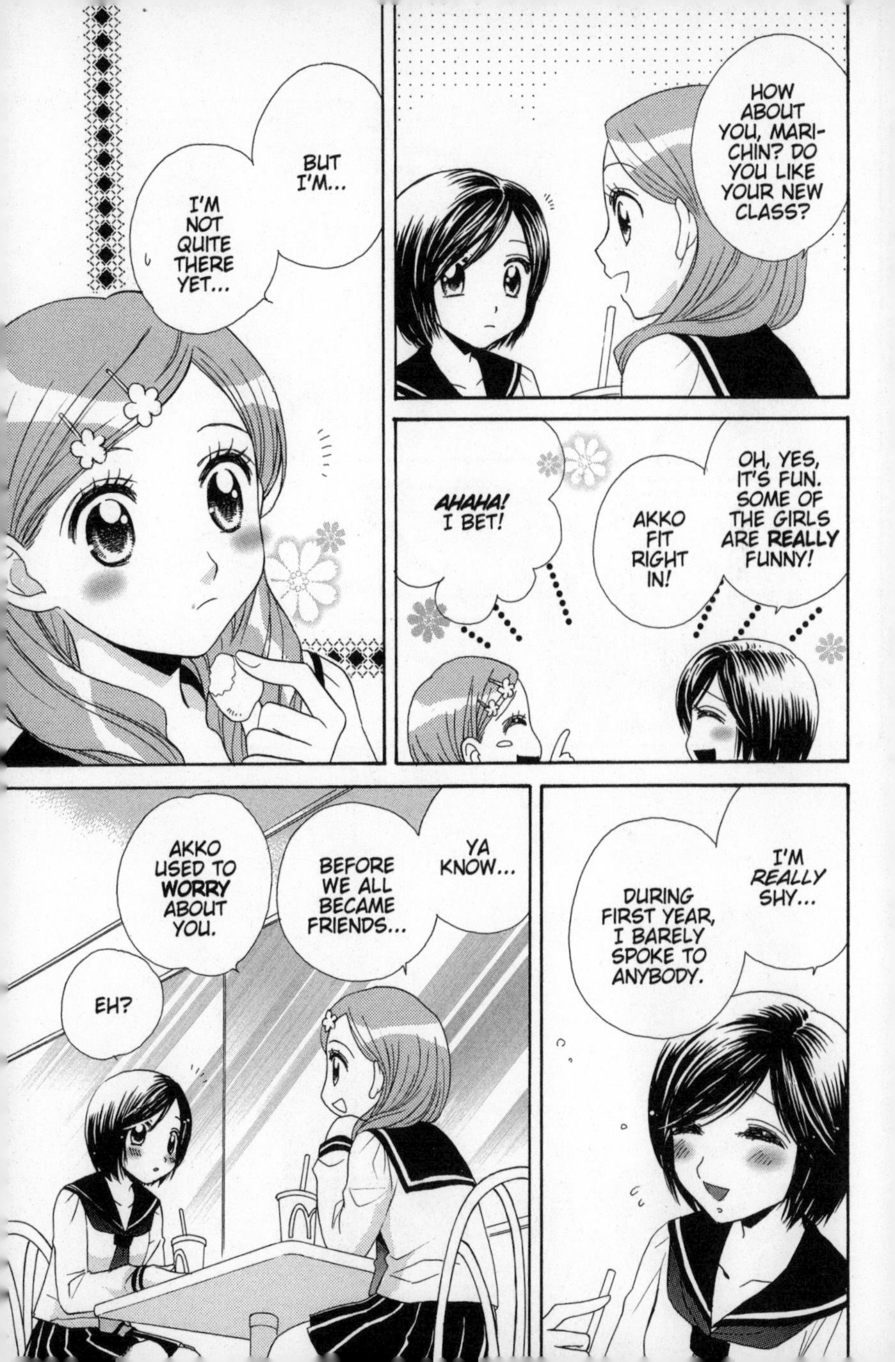
HOW ABOUT YOU, MARI-CHIN? DO YOU LIKE YOUR NEW CLASS?
OH, YES, IT'S FUN. SOME OF THE GIRLS ARE **REALLY** FUNNY!
AKKO FIT RIGHT IN!
AHAHA! I BET!
BUT I'M...
I'M NOT QUITE THERE YET...
I'M *REALLY* SHY...
DURING FIRST YEAR, I BARELY SPOKE TO ANYBODY.
YA KNOW...
BEFORE WE ALL BECAME FRIENDS...
AKKO USED TO **WORRY** ABOUT YOU.
EH?

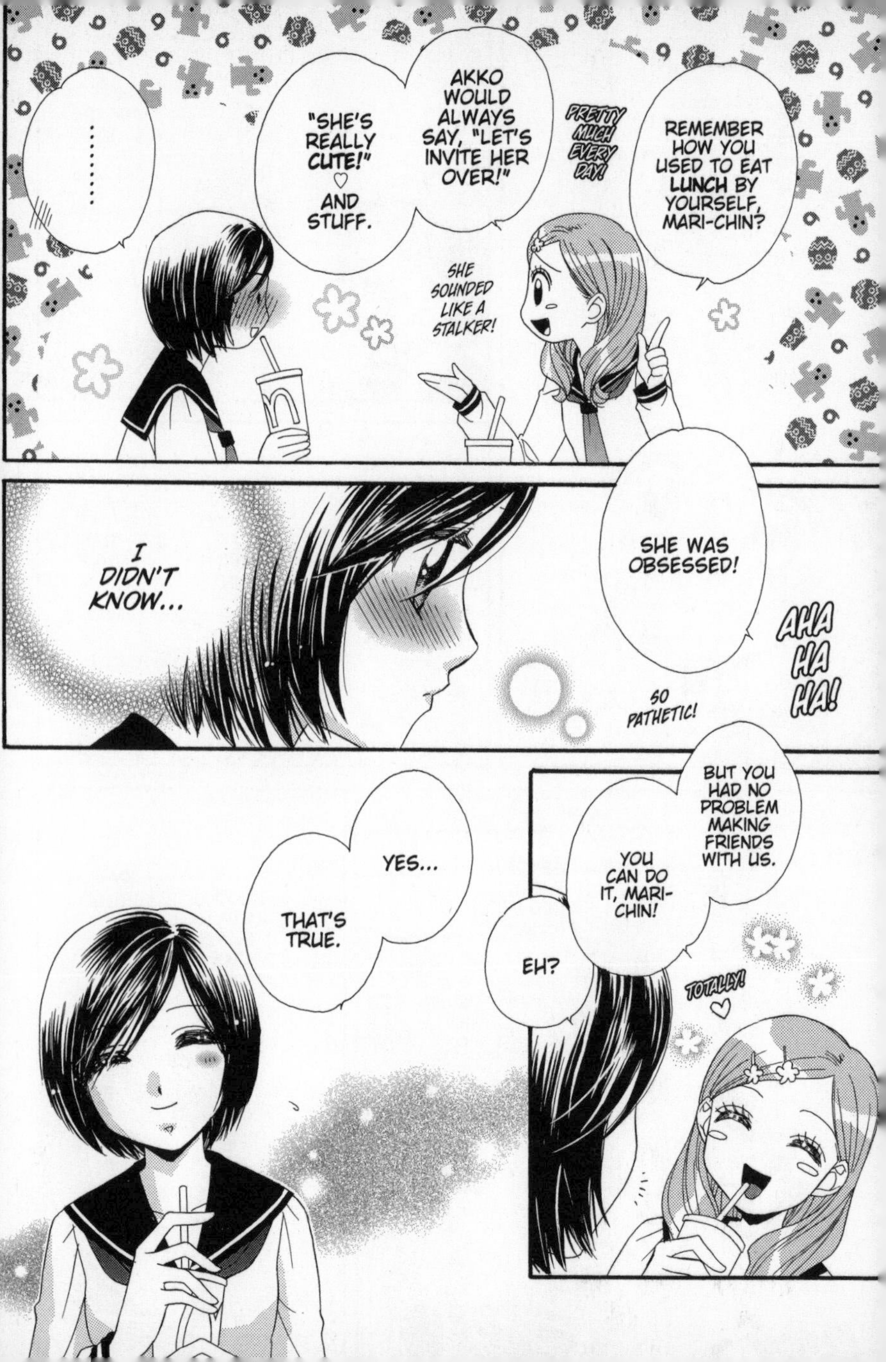
REMEMBER HOW YOU USED TO EAT LUNCH BY YOURSELF, MARI-CHIN?
PRETTY MUCH EVERY DAY!
SHE SOUNDED LIKE A STALKER!
AKKO WOULD ALWAYS SAY, "LET'S INVITE HER OVER!"
"SHE'S REALLY CUTE!" ♡ AND STUFF.
......
SHE WAS OBSESSED!
AHA HA HA!
SO PATHETIC!
I DIDN'T KNOW...
BUT YOU HAD NO PROBLEM MAKING FRIENDS WITH US.
YOU CAN DO IT, MARI-CHIN!
TOTALLY! ♡
EH?
YES...
THAT'S TRUE.

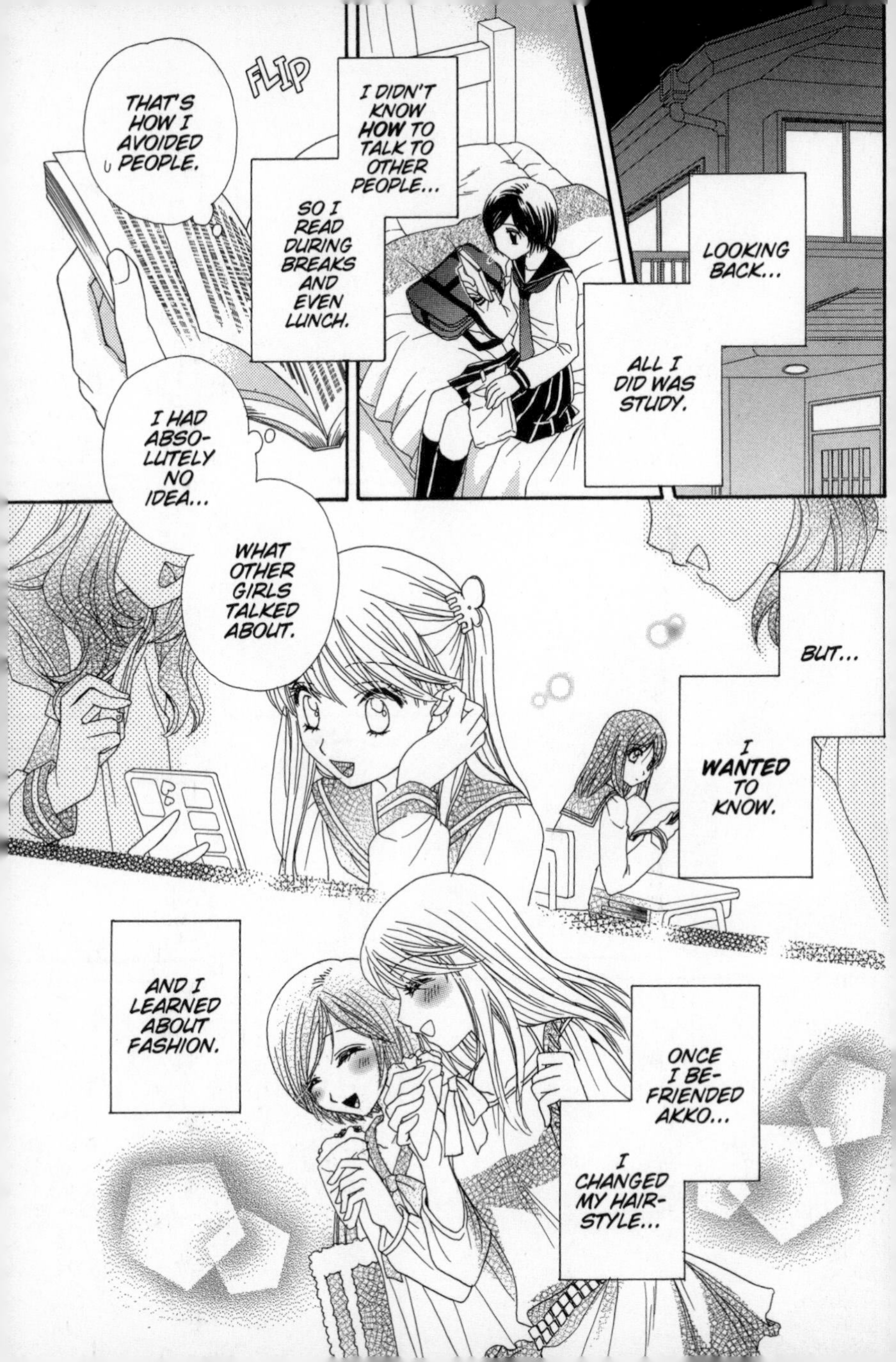
LOOKING BACK...
ALL I DID WAS STUDY.
I DIDN'T KNOW **HOW** TO TALK TO OTHER PEOPLE...
SO I READ DURING BREAKS AND EVEN LUNCH.
FLIP
THAT'S HOW I AVOIDED PEOPLE.
I HAD ABSOLUTELY NO IDEA...
WHAT OTHER GIRLS TALKED ABOUT.
BUT...
I **WANTED** TO KNOW.
ONCE I BEFRIENDED AKKO...
I CHANGED MY HAIRSTYLE...
AND I LEARNED ABOUT FASHION.

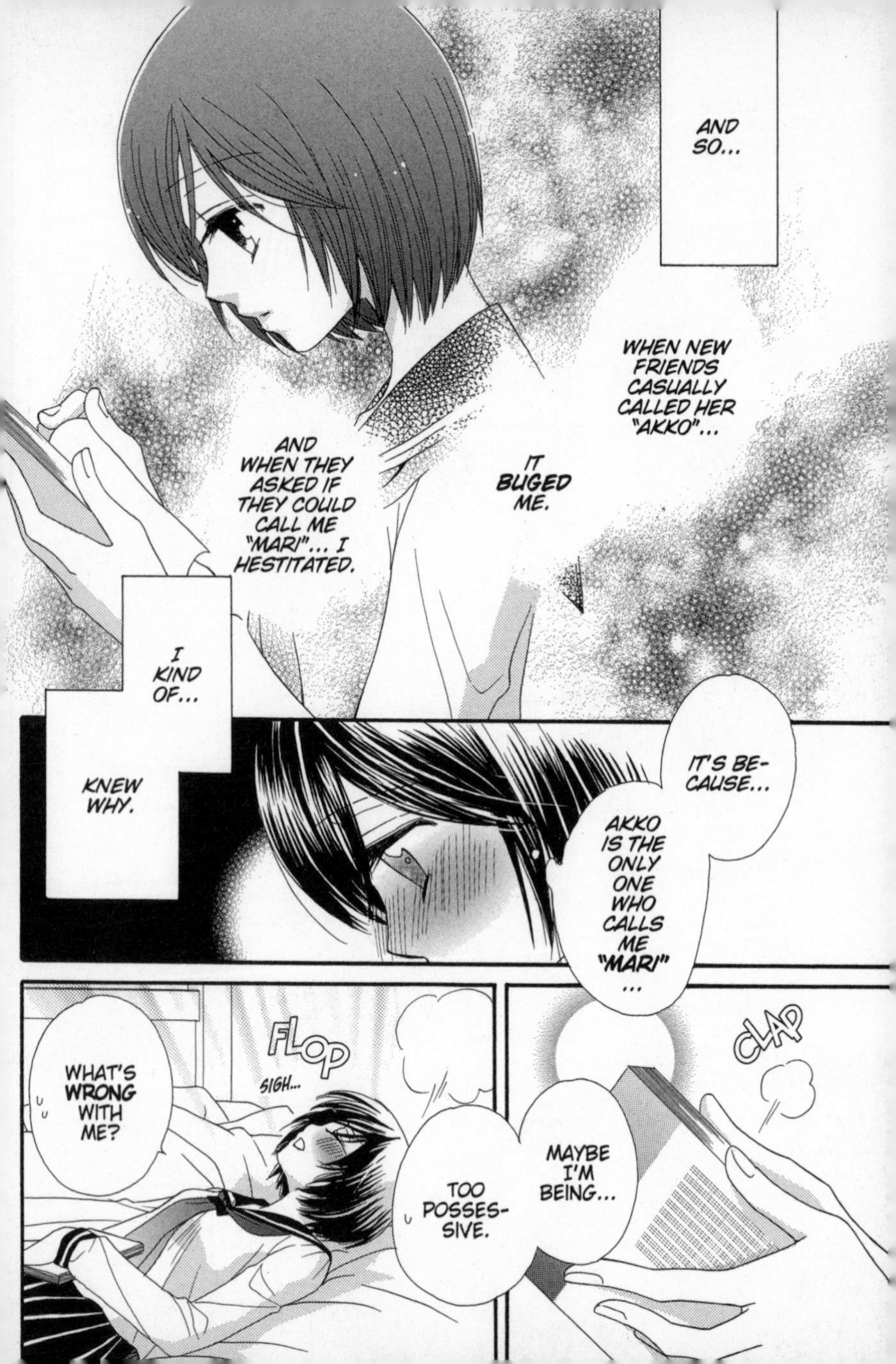
AND SO...
WHEN NEW FRIENDS CASUALLY CALLED HER "AKKO"...
IT BUGED ME.
AND WHEN THEY ASKED IF THEY COULD CALL ME "MARI"... I HESTITATED.
I KIND OF...
KNEW WHY.
IT'S BE-CAUSE...
AKKO IS THE ONLY ONE WHO CALLS ME "MARI"...
CLAP
MAYBE I'M BEING...
TOO POSSES-SIVE.
FLOP
SIGH...
WHAT'S WRONG WITH ME?

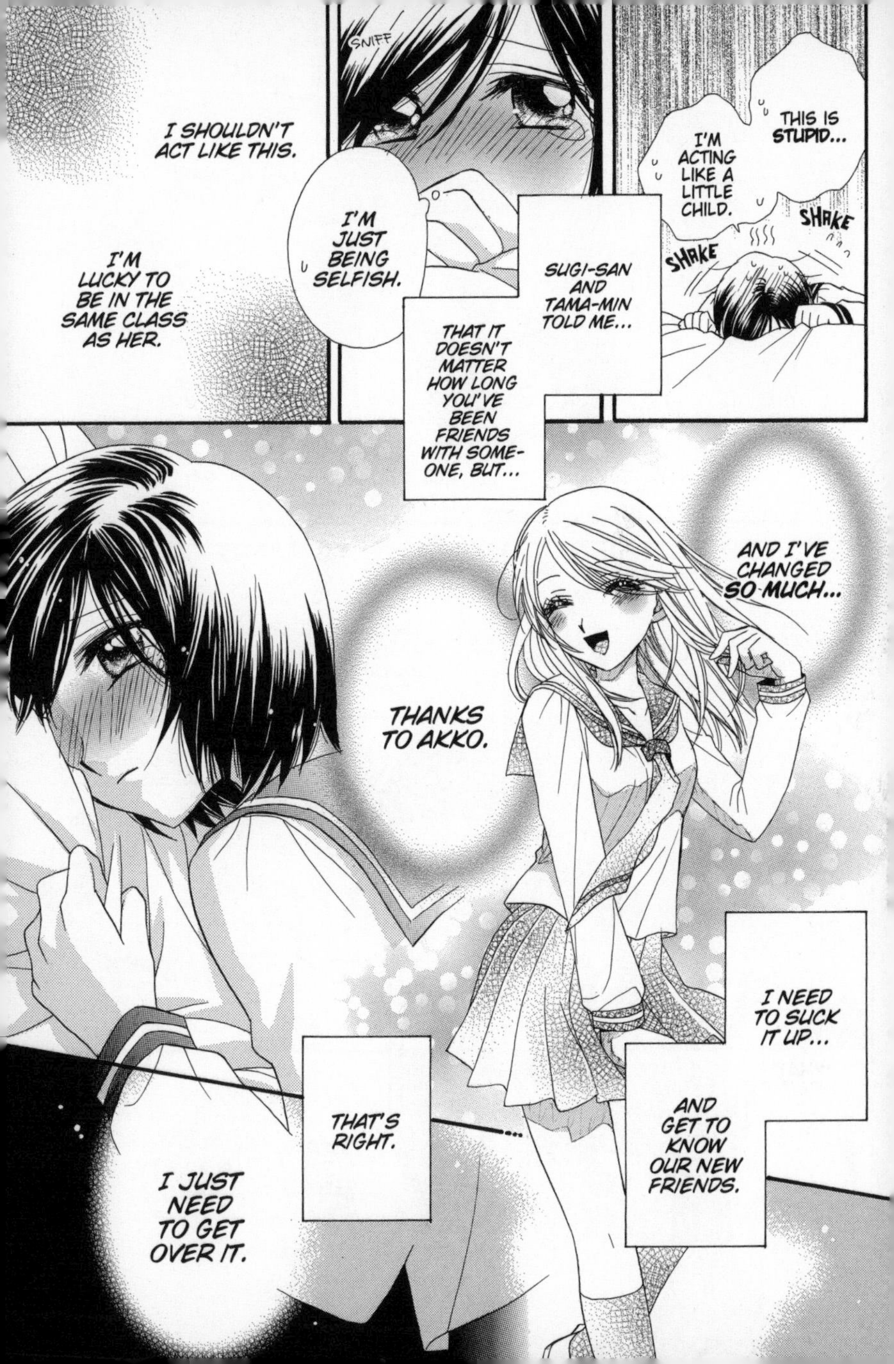
THIS IS STUPID...
I'M ACTING LIKE A LITTLE CHILD.
SHAKE
SHAKE
SNIFF
I'M JUST BEING SELFISH.
SUGI-SAN AND TAMA-MIN TOLD ME...
THAT IT DOESN'T MATTER HOW LONG YOU'VE BEEN FRIENDS WITH SOME-ONE, BUT...
I SHOULDN'T ACT LIKE THIS.
I'M LUCKY TO BE IN THE SAME CLASS AS HER.
AND I'VE CHANGED SO MUCH...
THANKS TO AKKO.
I NEED TO SUCK IT UP...
AND GET TO KNOW OUR NEW FRIENDS.
THAT'S RIGHT.
I JUST NEED TO GET OVER IT.

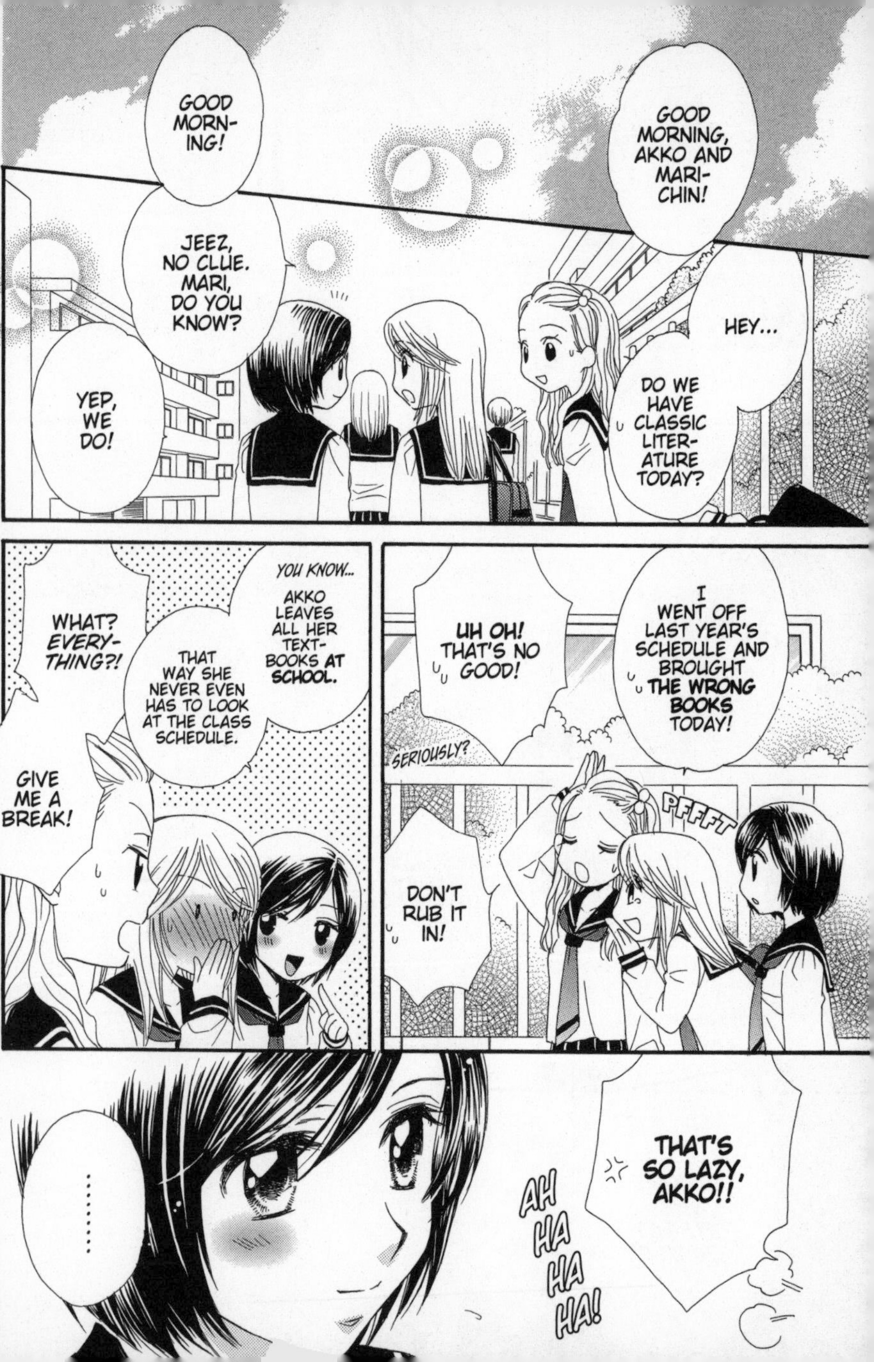

GOOD MORNING, AKKO AND MARI-CHIN!
GOOD MORNING!
HEY...
DO WE HAVE CLASSIC LITER-ATURE TODAY?
JEEZ, NO CLUE. MARI, DO YOU KNOW?
YEP, WE DO!
I WENT OFF LAST YEAR'S SCHEDULE AND BROUGHT THE WRONG BOOKS TODAY!
UH OH! THAT'S NO GOOD!
SERIOUSLY?
PFFFT
DON'T RUB IT IN!
YOU KNOW...
AKKO LEAVES ALL HER TEXT-BOOKS AT SCHOOL.
THAT WAY SHE NEVER EVEN HAS TO LOOK AT THE CLASS SCHEDULE.
WHAT? EVERY-THING?!
GIVE ME A BREAK!
THAT'S SO LAZY, AKKO!!
AH HA HA HA!
......

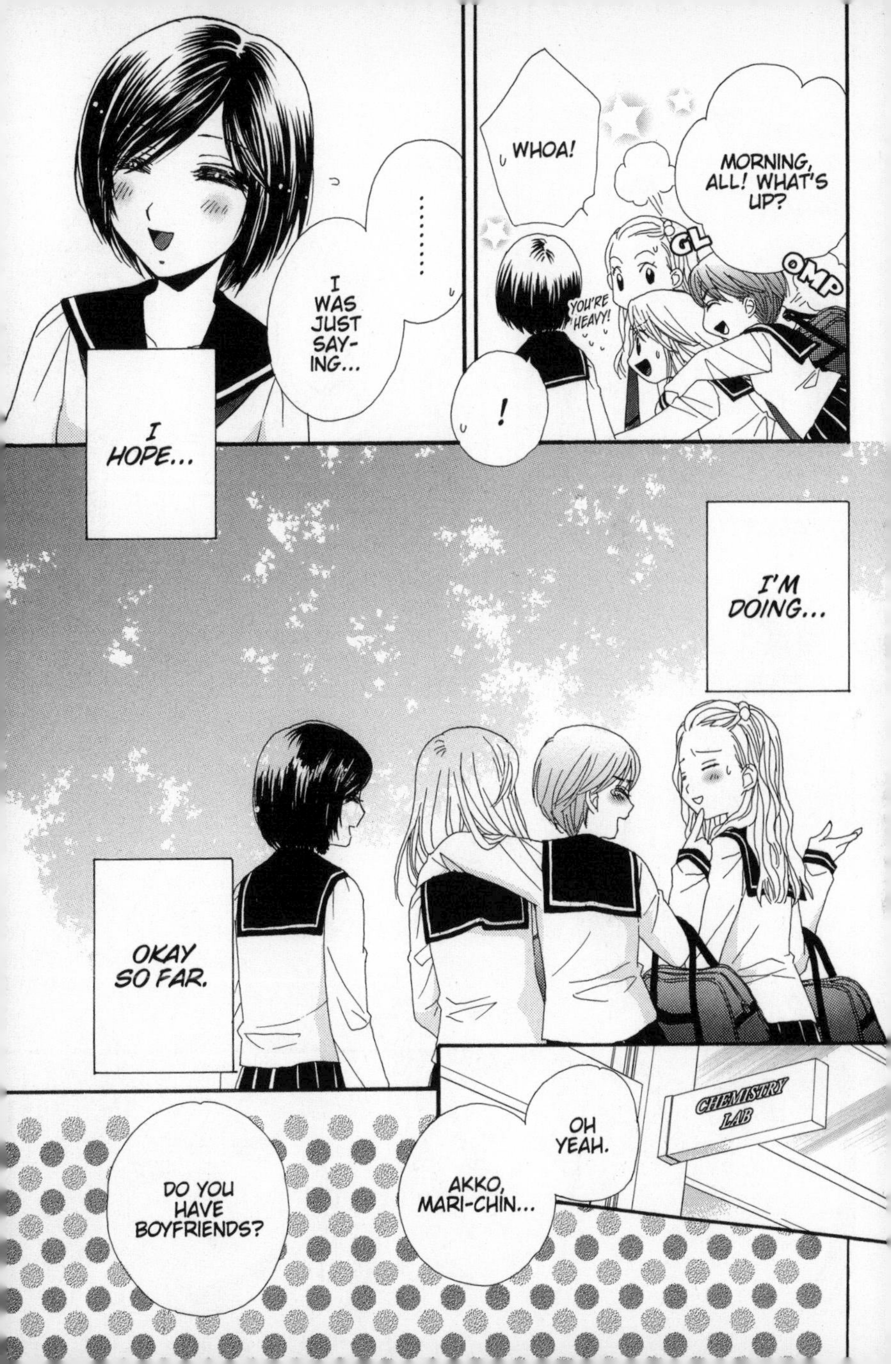
MORNING, ALL! WHAT'S UP?
GLOMP
YOU'RE HEAVY!
WHOA!
!
......
I WAS JUST SAYING...
I HOPE...
I'M DOING...
OKAY SO FAR.
CHEMISTRY LAB
OH YEAH.
AKKO, MARI-CHIN...
DO YOU HAVE BOYFRIENDS?

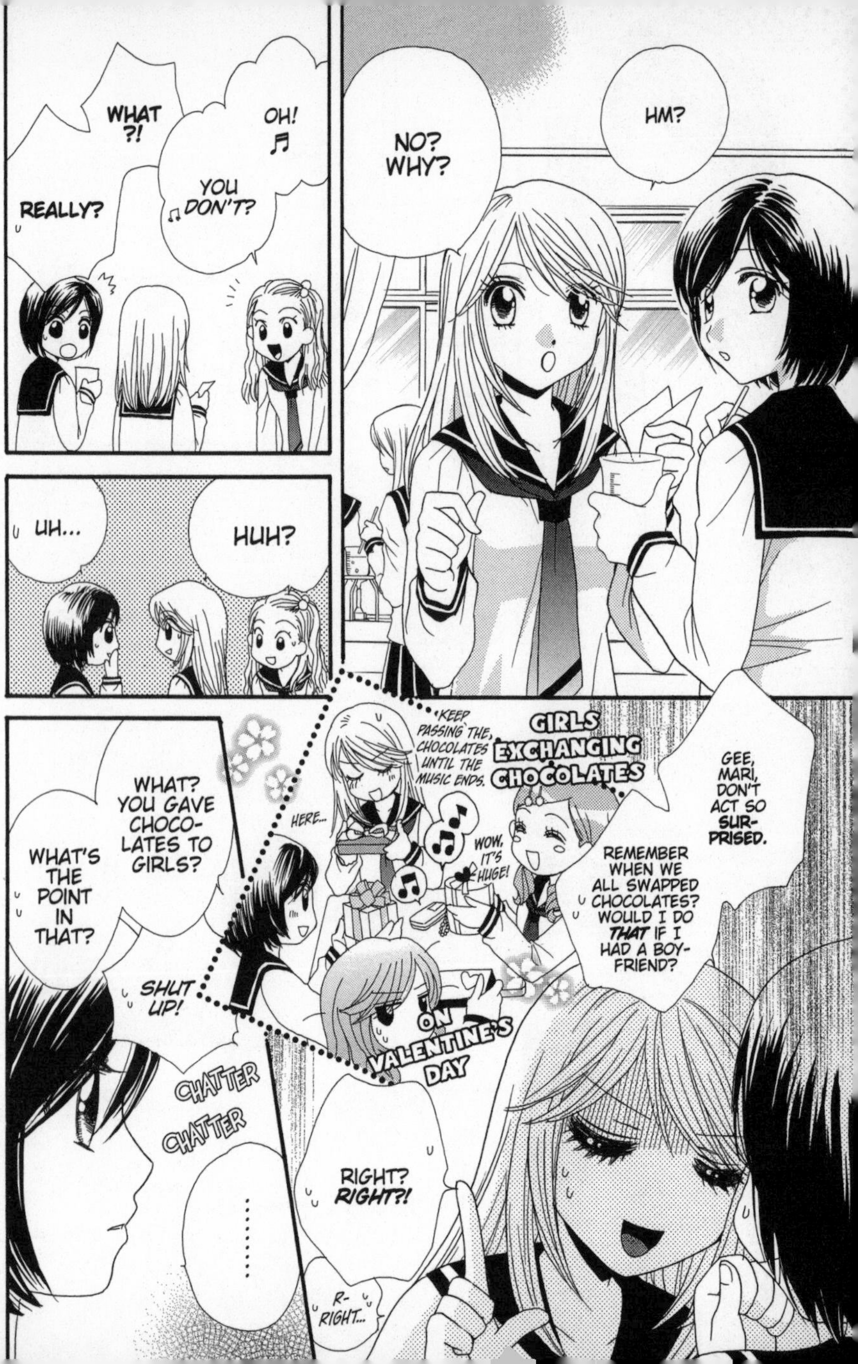
HM?
NO? WHY?
OH! ♬
YOU DON'T? ♫
WHAT?!
REALLY?
HUH?
UH...
GEE, MARI, DON'T ACT SO SUR-PRISED.
REMEMBER WHEN WE ALL SWAPPED CHOCOLATES? WOULD I DO THAT IF I HAD A BOY-FRIEND?
GIRLS EXCHANGING CHOCOLATES
ON VALENTINE'S DAY
KEEP PASSING THE CHOCOLATES UNTIL THE MUSIC ENDS.
WOW, IT'S HUGE!
HERE...
WHAT? YOU GAVE CHOCO-LATES TO GIRLS?
WHAT'S THE POINT IN THAT?
SHUT UP!
CHATTER
CHATTER
RIGHT? RIGHT?!
......
R-RIGHT...

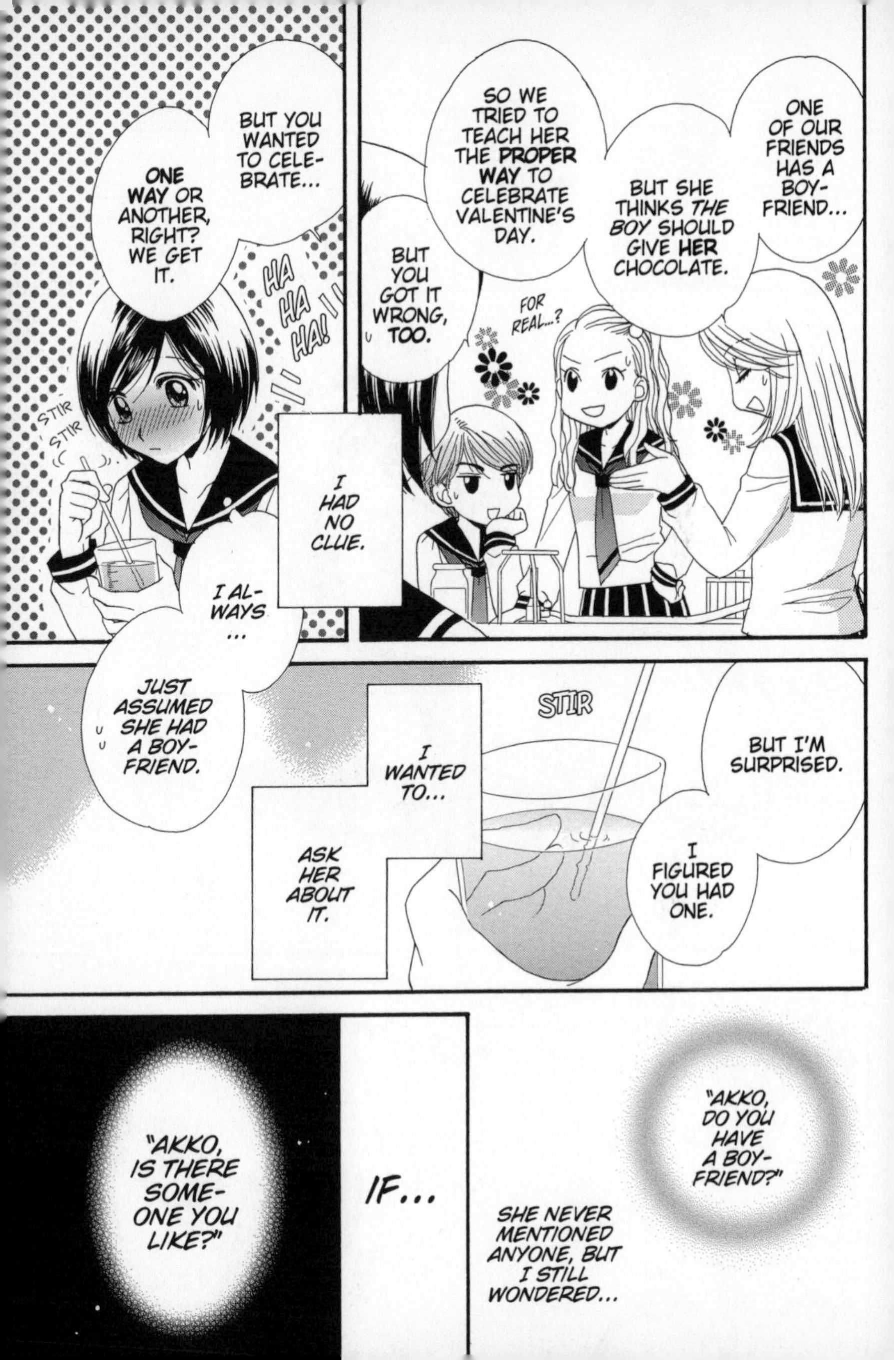
ONE OF OUR FRIENDS HAS A BOY-FRIEND...
BUT SHE THINKS THE BOY SHOULD GIVE HER CHOCOLATE.
SO WE TRIED TO TEACH HER THE PROPER WAY TO CELEBRATE VALENTINE'S DAY.
FOR REAL...?
BUT YOU GOT IT WRONG, TOO.
BUT YOU WANTED TO CELE-BRATE...
ONE WAY OR ANOTHER, RIGHT? WE GET IT.
HA HA HA!
STIR STIR
I HAD NO CLUE.
I AL-WAYS ...
JUST ASSUMED SHE HAD A BOY-FRIEND.
BUT I'M SURPRISED.
I FIGURED YOU HAD ONE.
STIR
I WANTED TO...
ASK HER ABOUT IT.
"AKKO, DO YOU HAVE A BOY-FRIEND?"
SHE NEVER MENTIONED ANYONE, BUT I STILL WONDERED...
IF...
"AKKO, IS THERE SOME-ONE YOU LIKE?"

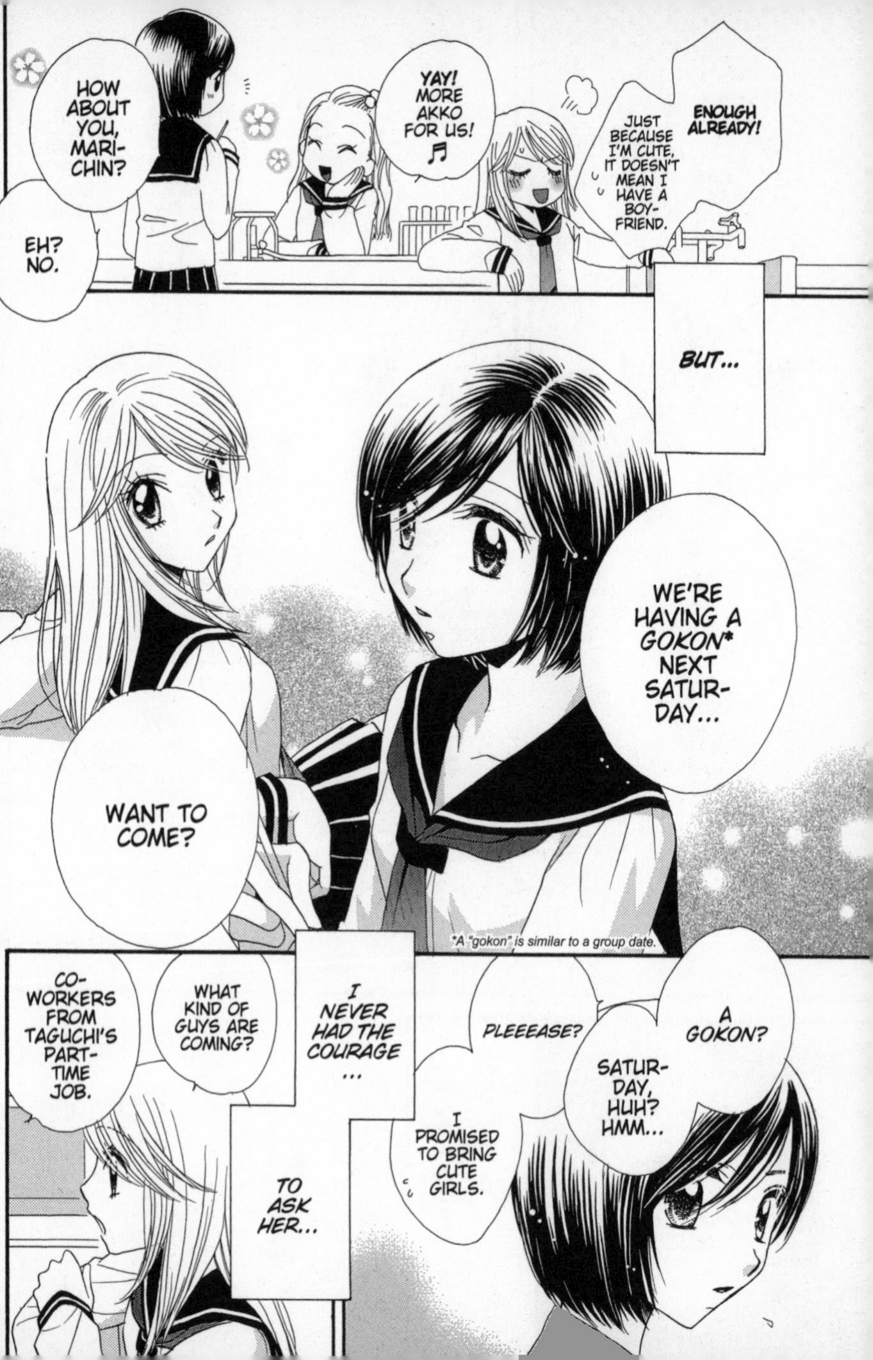
ENOUGH ALREADY!
JUST BECAUSE I'M CUTE, IT DOESN'T MEAN I HAVE A BOY-FRIEND.
YAY! MORE AKKO FOR US! ♫
HOW ABOUT YOU, MARI-CHIN?
EH? NO.
BUT...
WE'RE HAVING A GOKON* NEXT SATUR-DAY...
WANT TO COME?
A GOKON?
SATUR-DAY, HUH? HMM...
PLEEEASE?
I PROMISED TO BRING CUTE GIRLS.
I NEVER HAD THE COURAGE...
TO ASK HER...
WHAT KIND OF GUYS ARE COMING?
CO-WORKERS FROM TAGUCHI'S PART-TIME JOB.
*A "gokon" is similar to a group date.

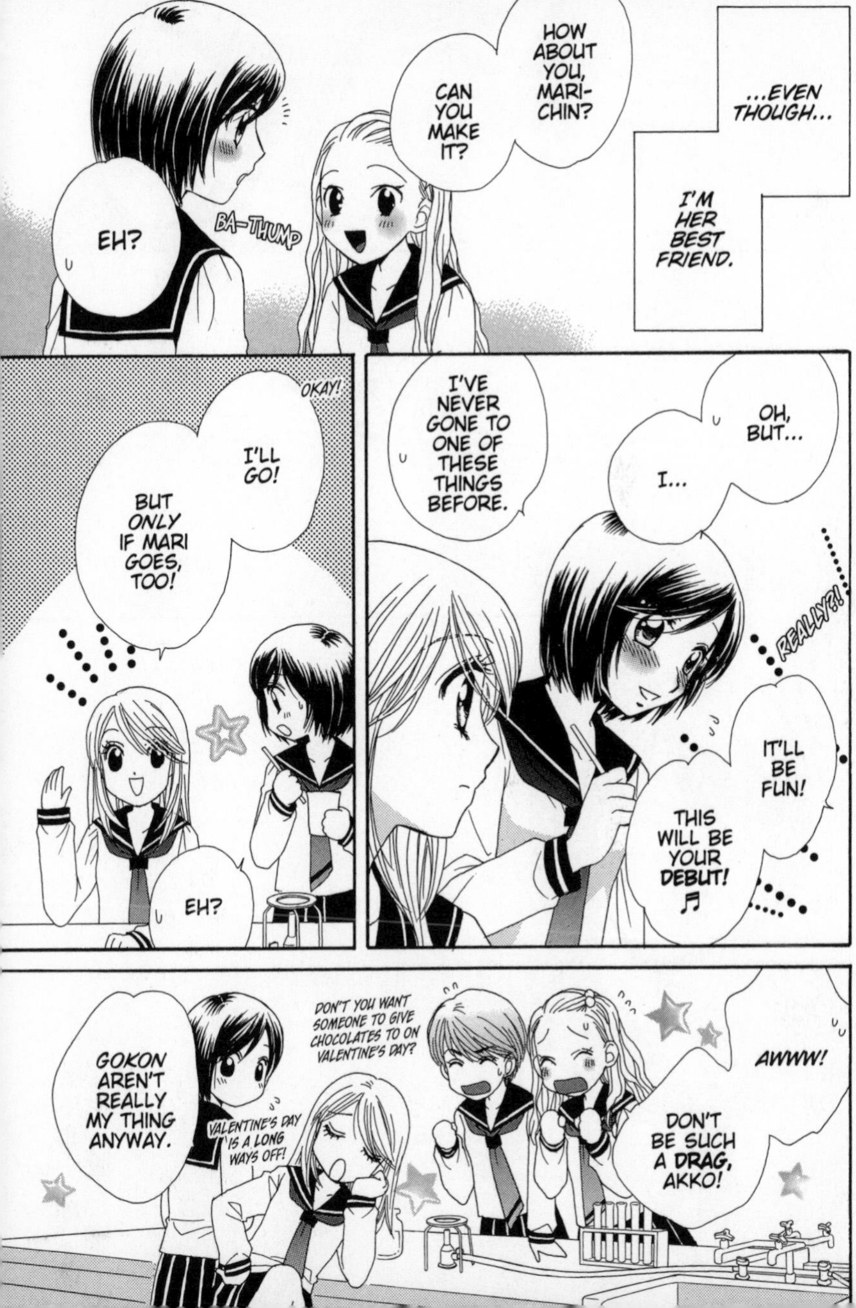
...EVEN THOUGH...
I'M HER BEST FRIEND.
HOW ABOUT YOU, MARI-CHIN?
CAN YOU MAKE IT?
BA-THUMP
EH?
OH, BUT...
I...
I'VE NEVER GONE TO ONE OF THESE THINGS BEFORE.
REALLY?!
IT'LL BE FUN!
THIS WILL BE YOUR DEBUT! ♬
OKAY!
I'LL GO!
BUT ONLY IF MARI GOES, TOO!
EH?
AWWW!
DON'T BE SUCH A DRAG, AKKO!
DON'T YOU WANT SOMEONE TO GIVE CHOCOLATES TO ON VALENTINE'S DAY?
VALENTINE'S DAY IS A LONG WAYS OFF!
GOKON AREN'T REALLY MY THING ANYWAY.

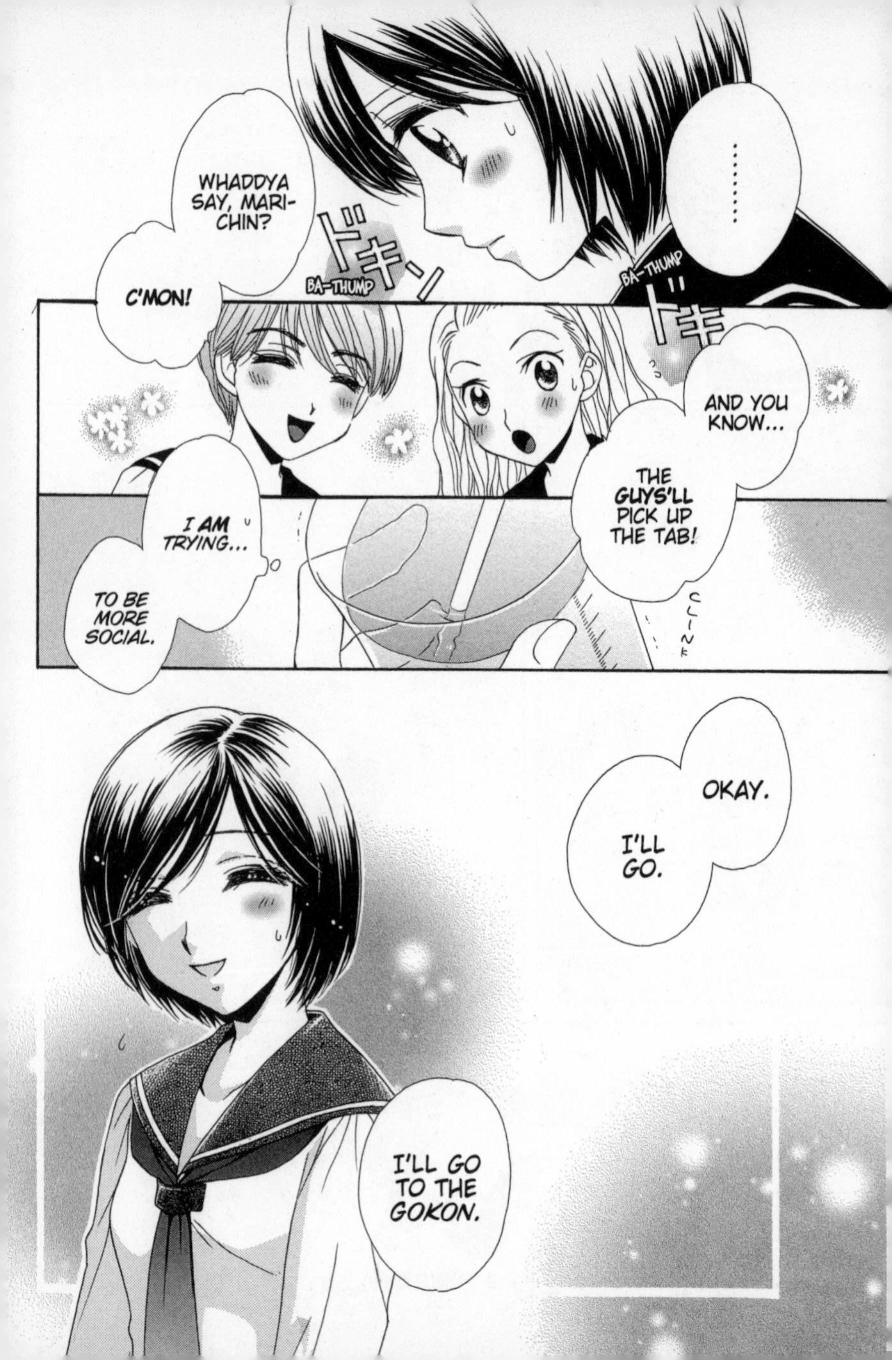
......
ドキ
BA-THUMP
WHADDYA SAY, MARI-CHIN?
ドキーン
BA-THUMP
C'MON!
AND YOU KNOW...
THE GUYS'LL PICK UP THE TAB!
I AM TRYING...
TO BE MORE SOCIAL.
CLINK
OKAY.
I'LL GO.
I'LL GO TO THE GOKON.

BEFORE WE KNOW IT...

WE'RE BOTH ASLEEP!

GIRL FRIENDS —ガールフレンズ—

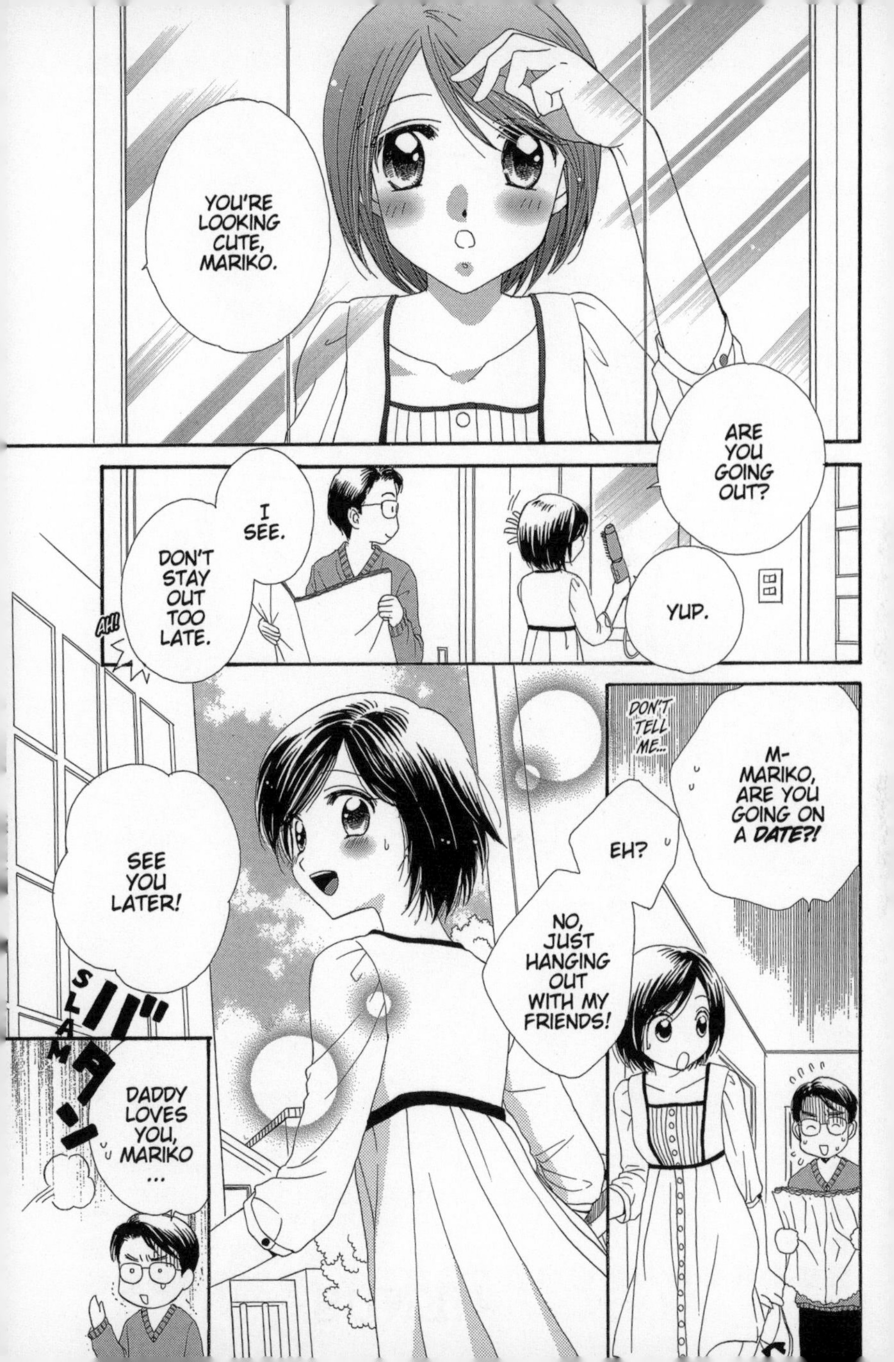
YOU'RE LOOKING CUTE, MARIKO.
ARE YOU GOING OUT?
YUP.
I SEE.
DON'T STAY OUT TOO LATE.
AH!
DON'T TELL ME...
M-MARIKO, ARE YOU GOING ON A *DATE?!*
EH?
NO, JUST HANGING OUT WITH MY FRIENDS!
SEE YOU LATER!
SLAM
DADDY LOVES YOU, MARIKO ...

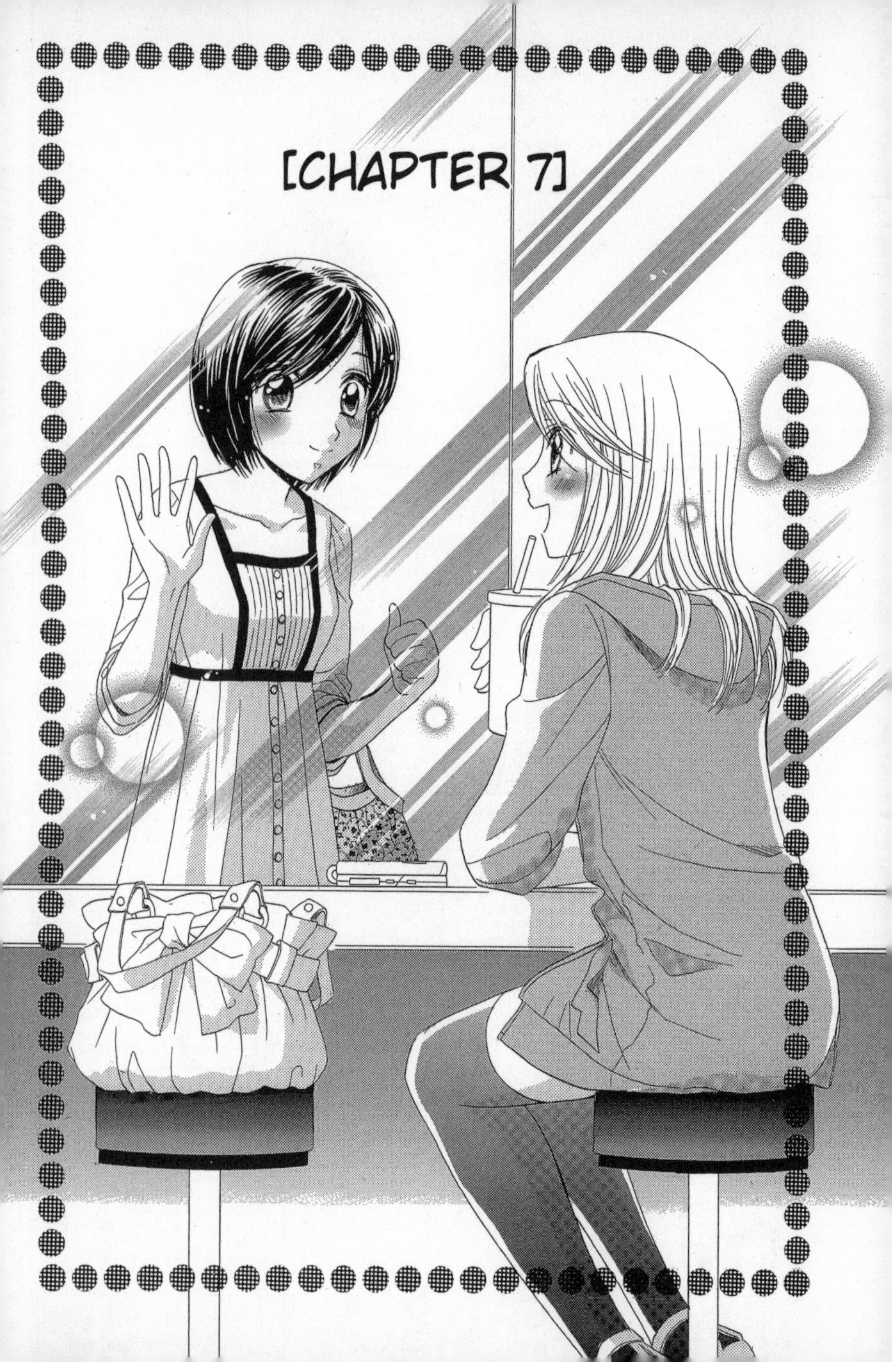
[CHAPTER 7]

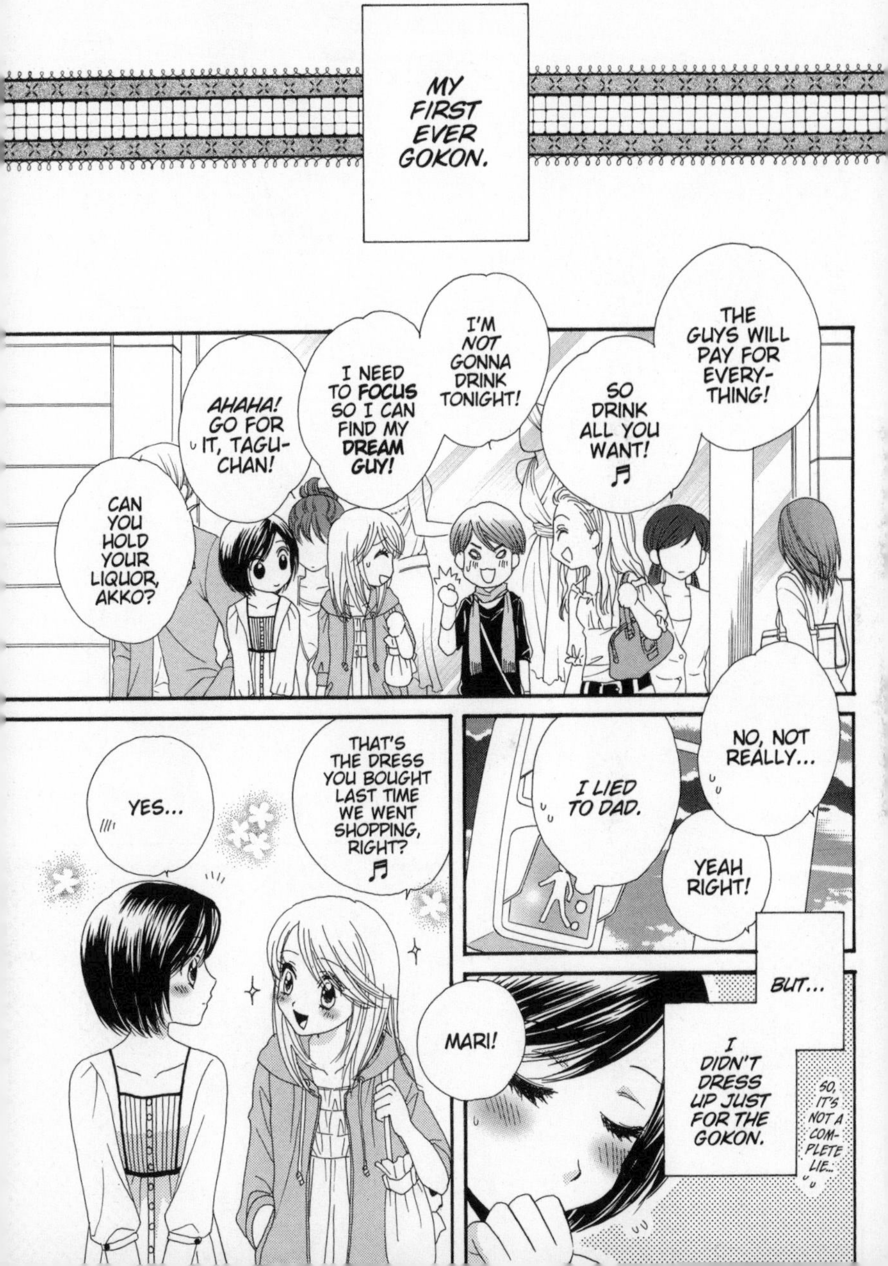
MY FIRST EVER GOKON.
THE GUYS WILL PAY FOR EVERY-THING!
SO DRINK ALL YOU WANT! ♬
I'M NOT GONNA DRINK TONIGHT!
I NEED TO FOCUS SO I CAN FIND MY DREAM GUY!
AHAHA! GO FOR IT, TAGU-CHAN!
CAN YOU HOLD YOUR LIQUOR, AKKO?
NO, NOT REALLY...
I LIED TO DAD.
YEAH RIGHT!
BUT...
I DIDN'T DRESS UP JUST FOR THE GOKON.
SO, IT'S NOT A COM-PLETE LIE...
THAT'S THE DRESS YOU BOUGHT LAST TIME WE WENT SHOPPING, RIGHT? ♬
YES...
MARI!

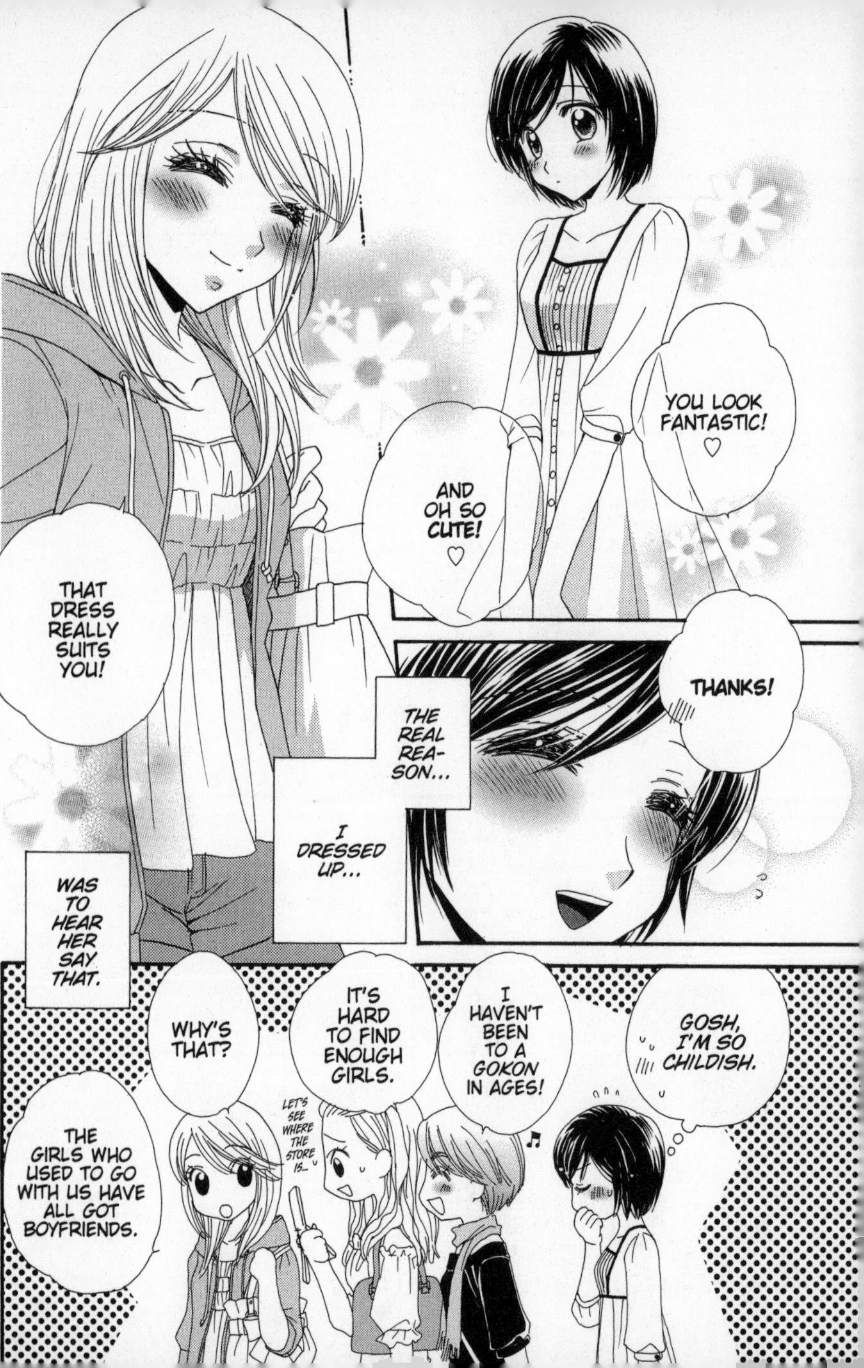
YOU LOOK FANTASTIC! ♡
AND OH SO CUTE! ♡
THAT DRESS REALLY SUITS YOU!
THANKS!
THE REAL REA-SON...
I DRESSED UP...
WAS TO HEAR HER SAY THAT.
GOSH, I'M SO CHILDISH.
I HAVEN'T BEEN TO A GOKON IN AGES!
IT'S HARD TO FIND ENOUGH GIRLS.
WHY'S THAT?
LET'S SEE WHERE THE STORE IS...
THE GIRLS WHO USED TO GO WITH US HAVE ALL GOT BOYFRIENDS.

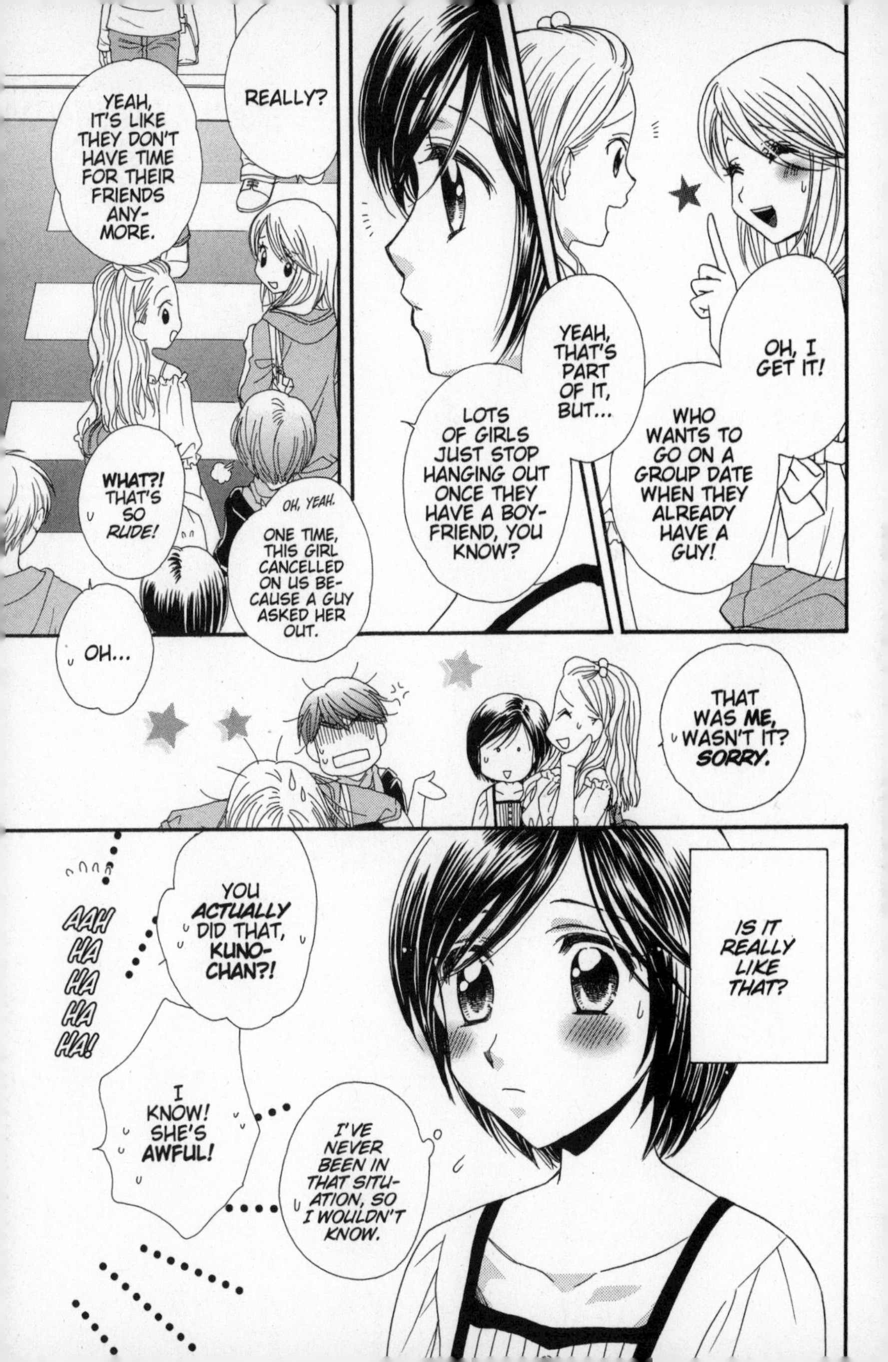

OH, I GET IT!
WHO WANTS TO GO ON A GROUP DATE WHEN THEY ALREADY HAVE A GUY!
YEAH, THAT'S PART OF IT, BUT...
LOTS OF GIRLS JUST STOP HANGING OUT ONCE THEY HAVE A BOY-FRIEND, YOU KNOW?
REALLY?
YEAH, IT'S LIKE THEY DON'T HAVE TIME FOR THEIR FRIENDS ANY-MORE.
OH, YEAH. ONE TIME, THIS GIRL CANCELLED ON US BE-CAUSE A GUY ASKED HER OUT.
WHAT?! THAT'S SO RUDE!
THAT WAS ME, WASN'T IT? SORRY.
OH...
IS IT REALLY LIKE THAT?
YOU ACTUALLY DID THAT, KUNO-CHAN?!
AAH HA HA HA HA!
I KNOW! SHE'S AWFUL!
I'VE NEVER BEEN IN THAT SITU-ATION, SO I WOULDN'T KNOW.

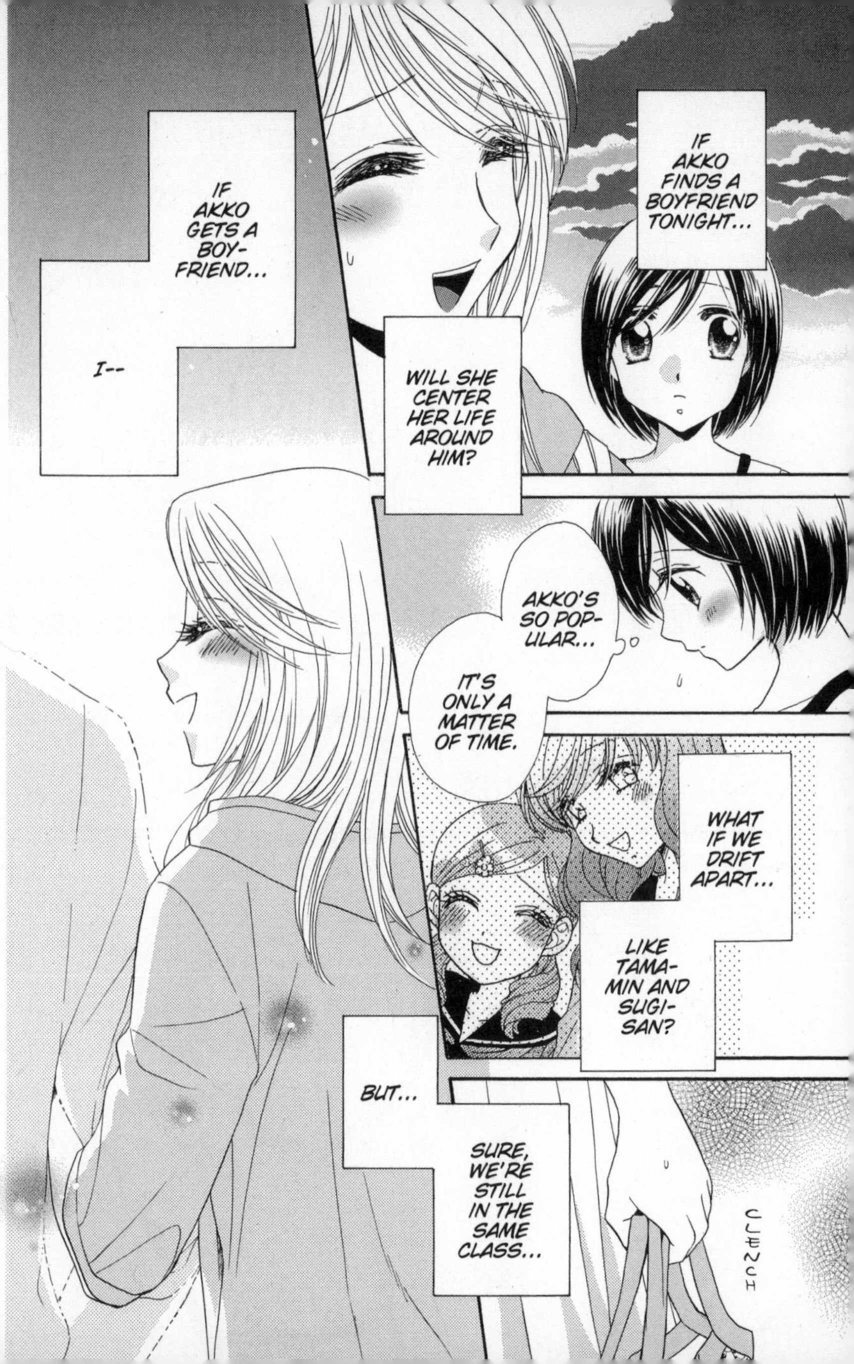
IF AKKO FINDS A BOYFRIEND TONIGHT...
WILL SHE CENTER HER LIFE AROUND HIM?
IF AKKO GETS A BOY-FRIEND...
I--
AKKO'S SO POP-ULAR...
IT'S ONLY A MATTER OF TIME.
WHAT IF WE DRIFT APART...
LIKE TAMA-MIN AND SUGI-SAN?
BUT...
SURE, WE'RE STILL IN THE SAME CLASS...
CLENCH

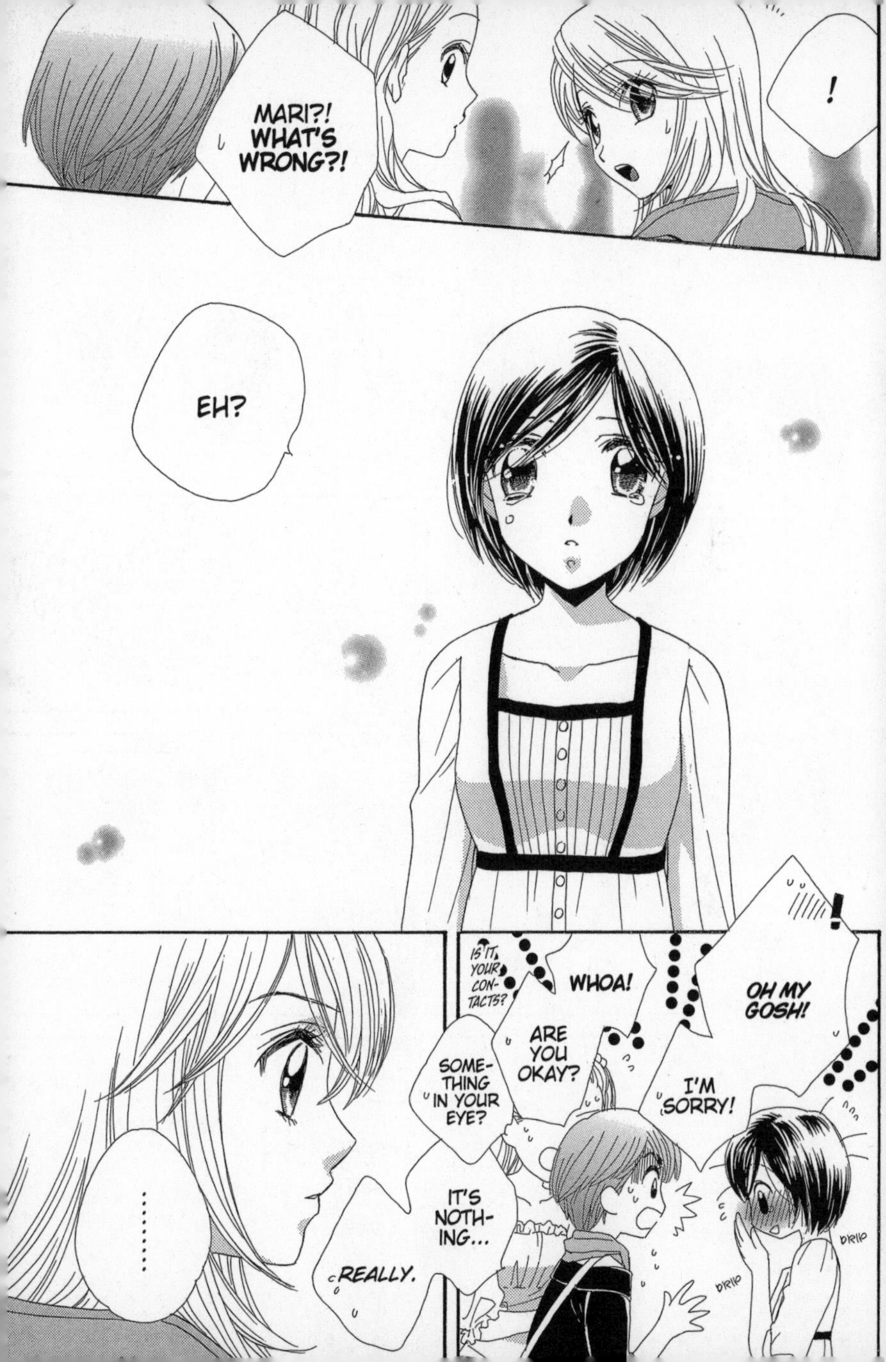

!
MARI?! WHAT'S WRONG?!
EH?
OH MY GOSH!
WHOA!
IS IT YOUR CONTACTS?
I'M SORRY!
ARE YOU OKAY?
SOMETHING IN YOUR EYE?
DRIP
DRIP
IT'S NOTHING...
REALLY.
....

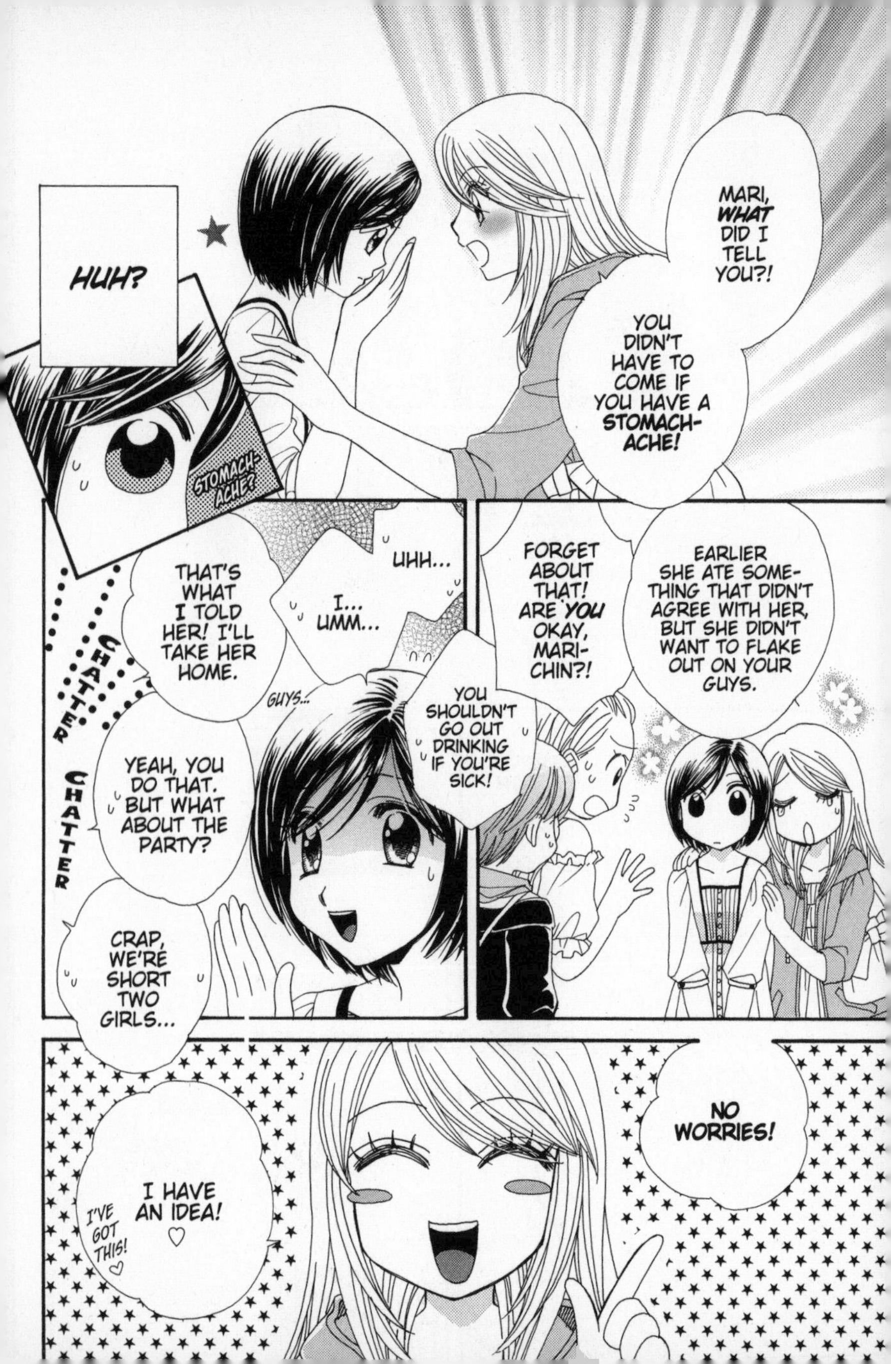
MARI, WHAT DID I TELL YOU?!
YOU DIDN'T HAVE TO COME IF YOU HAVE A STOMACH-ACHE!
STOMACH-ACHE?
HUH?
EARLIER SHE ATE SOME-THING THAT DIDN'T AGREE WITH HER, BUT SHE DIDN'T WANT TO FLAKE OUT ON YOUR GUYS.
FORGET ABOUT THAT! ARE YOU OKAY, MARI-CHIN?!
YOU SHOULDN'T GO OUT DRINKING IF YOU'RE SICK!
UHH...
I... UMM...
THAT'S WHAT I TOLD HER! I'LL TAKE HER HOME.
GUYS...
CHATTER CHATTER
YEAH, YOU DO THAT. BUT WHAT ABOUT THE PARTY?
CRAP, WE'RE SHORT TWO GIRLS...
NO WORRIES!
I HAVE AN IDEA!
I'VE GOT THIS!

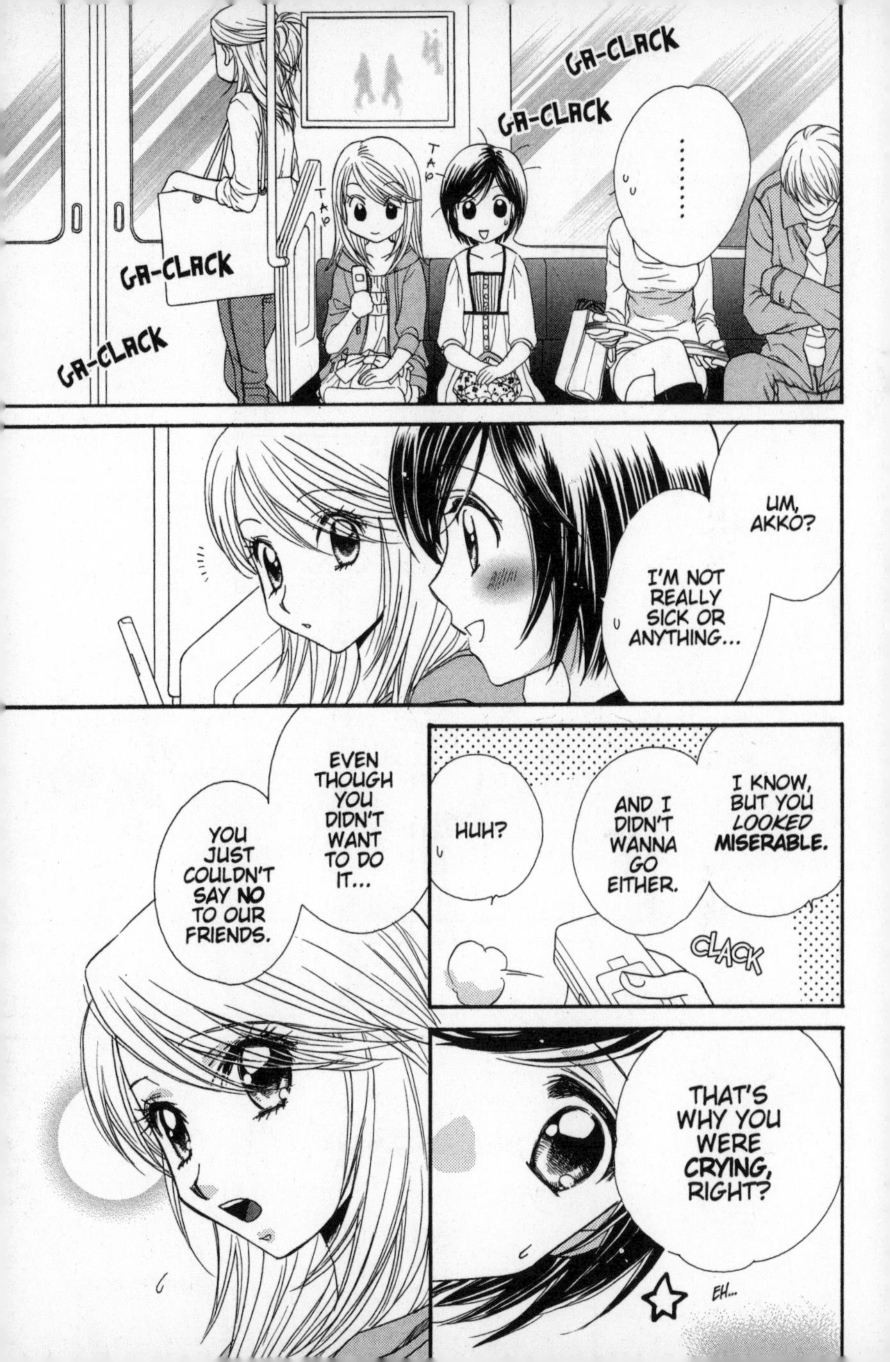
GA-CLACK
GA-CLACK
......
TAP TAP
GA-CLACK
GA-CLACK
UM, AKKO?
I'M NOT REALLY SICK OR ANYTHING...
I KNOW, BUT YOU *LOOKED* **MISERABLE.**
AND I DIDN'T WANNA GO EITHER.
HUH?
CLACK
EVEN THOUGH YOU DIDN'T WANT TO DO IT...
YOU JUST COULDN'T SAY NO TO OUR FRIENDS.
THAT'S WHY YOU WERE **CRYING,** RIGHT?
EH...

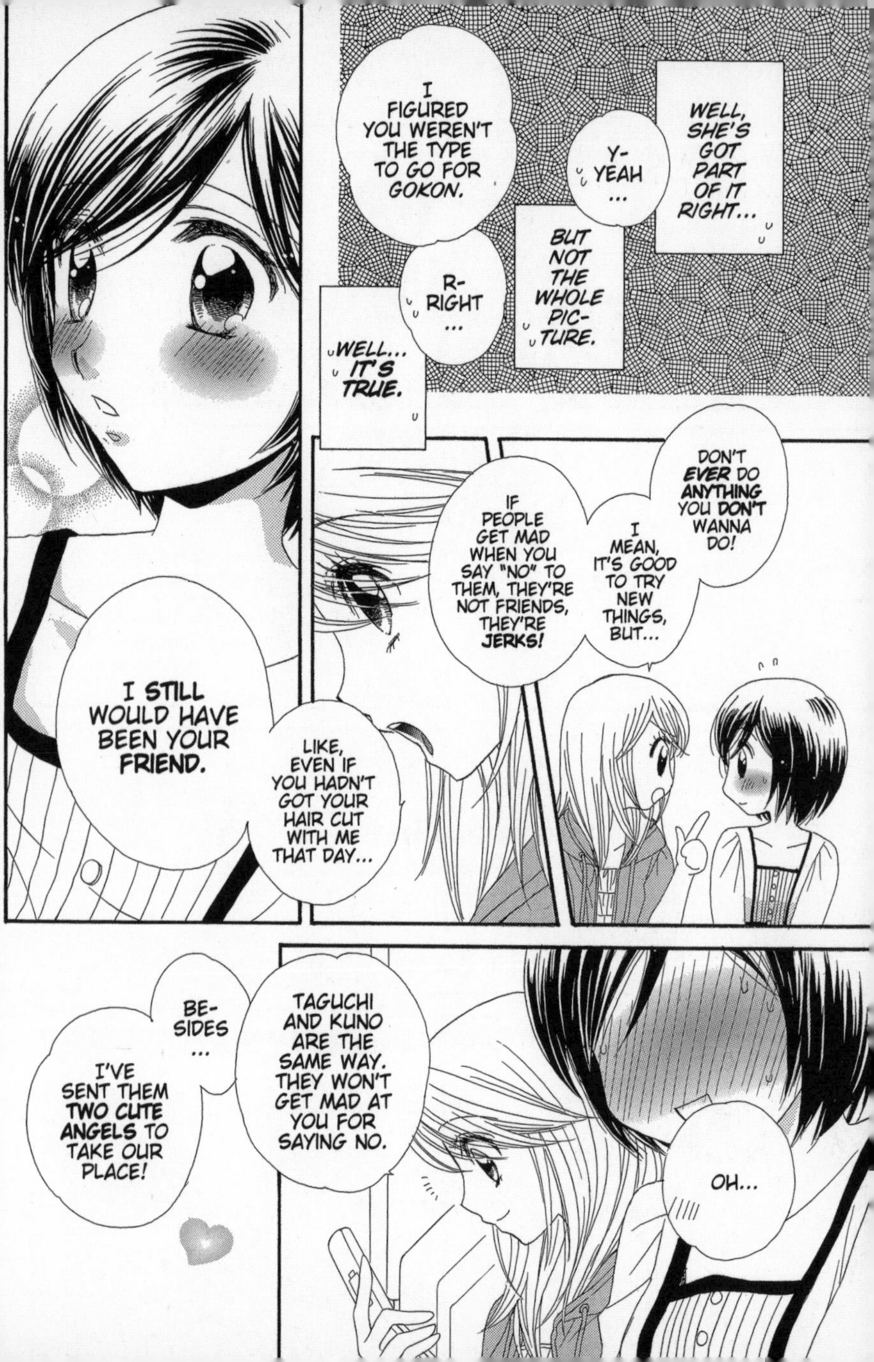

WELL, SHE'S GOT PART OF IT RIGHT...
Y-YEAH...
BUT NOT THE WHOLE PICTURE.
I FIGURED YOU WEREN'T THE TYPE TO GO FOR GOKON.
R-RIGHT...
WELL... IT'S TRUE.
DON'T EVER DO ANYTHING YOU DON'T WANNA DO!
I MEAN, IT'S GOOD TO TRY NEW THINGS, BUT...
IF PEOPLE GET MAD WHEN YOU SAY "NO" TO THEM, THEY'RE NOT FRIENDS, THEY'RE JERKS!
LIKE, EVEN IF YOU HADN'T GOT YOUR HAIR CUT WITH ME THAT DAY...
I STILL WOULD HAVE BEEN YOUR FRIEND.
OH...
TAGUCHI AND KUNO ARE THE SAME WAY. THEY WON'T GET MAD AT YOU FOR SAYING NO.
BE-SIDES...
I'VE SENT THEM TWO CUTE ANGELS TO TAKE OUR PLACE!

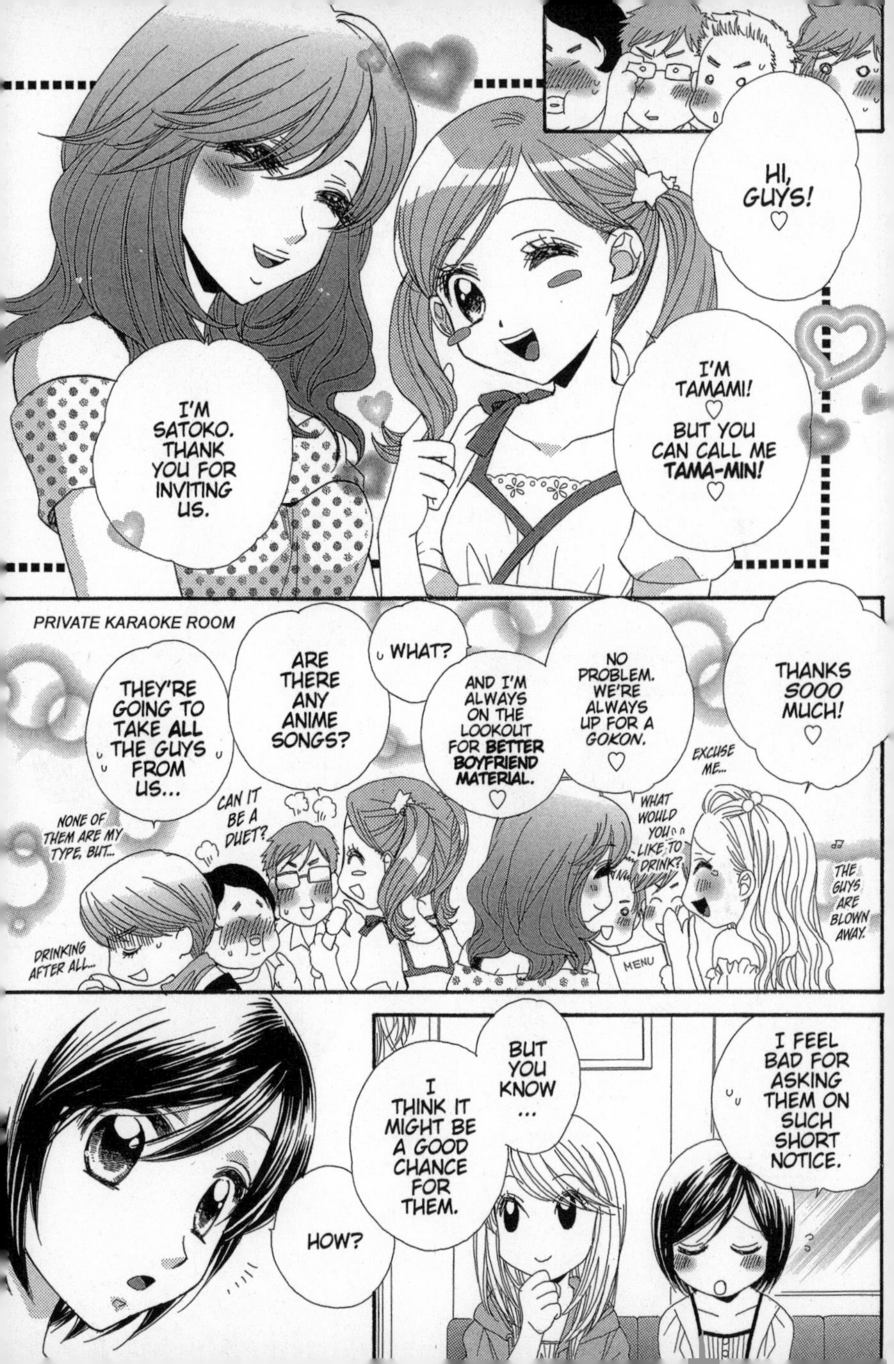
HI, GUYS! ♡
I'M TAMAMI! ♡ BUT YOU CAN CALL ME TAMA-MIN! ♡
I'M SATOKO. THANK YOU FOR INVITING US.
PRIVATE KARAOKE ROOM
THANKS SOOO MUCH! ♡
EXCUSE ME...
NO PROBLEM. WE'RE ALWAYS UP FOR A GOKON. ♡
AND I'M ALWAYS ON THE LOOKOUT FOR BETTER BOYFRIEND MATERIAL. ♡
WHAT?
ARE THERE ANY ANIME SONGS?
THEY'RE GOING TO TAKE ALL THE GUYS FROM US...
THE GUYS ARE BLOWN AWAY.
WHAT WOULD YOU LIKE TO DRINK?
MENU
CAN IT BE A DUET?
NONE OF THEM ARE MY TYPE, BUT...
DRINKING AFTER ALL...
I FEEL BAD FOR ASKING THEM ON SUCH SHORT NOTICE.
BUT YOU KNOW ...
I THINK IT MIGHT BE A GOOD CHANCE FOR THEM.
HOW?

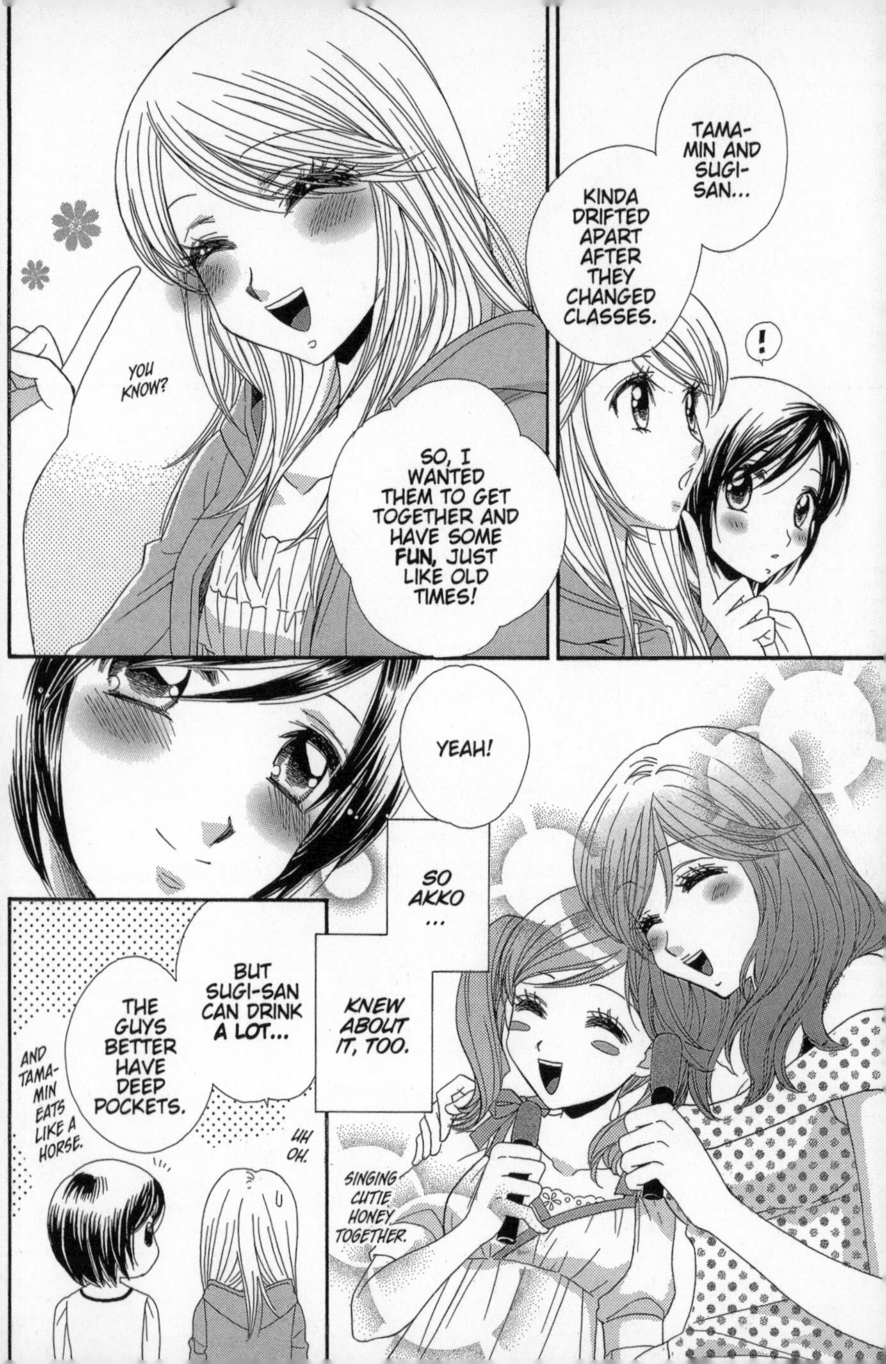
TAMA-MIN AND SUGI-SAN...
KINDA DRIFTED APART AFTER THEY CHANGED CLASSES.
!
YOU KNOW?
SO, I WANTED THEM TO GET TOGETHER AND HAVE SOME **FUN**, JUST LIKE OLD TIMES!
YEAH!
SO AKKO ...
KNEW ABOUT IT, TOO.
SINGING CUTIE HONEY TOGETHER.
BUT SUGI-SAN CAN DRINK **A LOT**...
THE GUYS BETTER HAVE DEEP POCKETS.
AND TAMA-MIN EATS LIKE A HORSE.
UH OH.

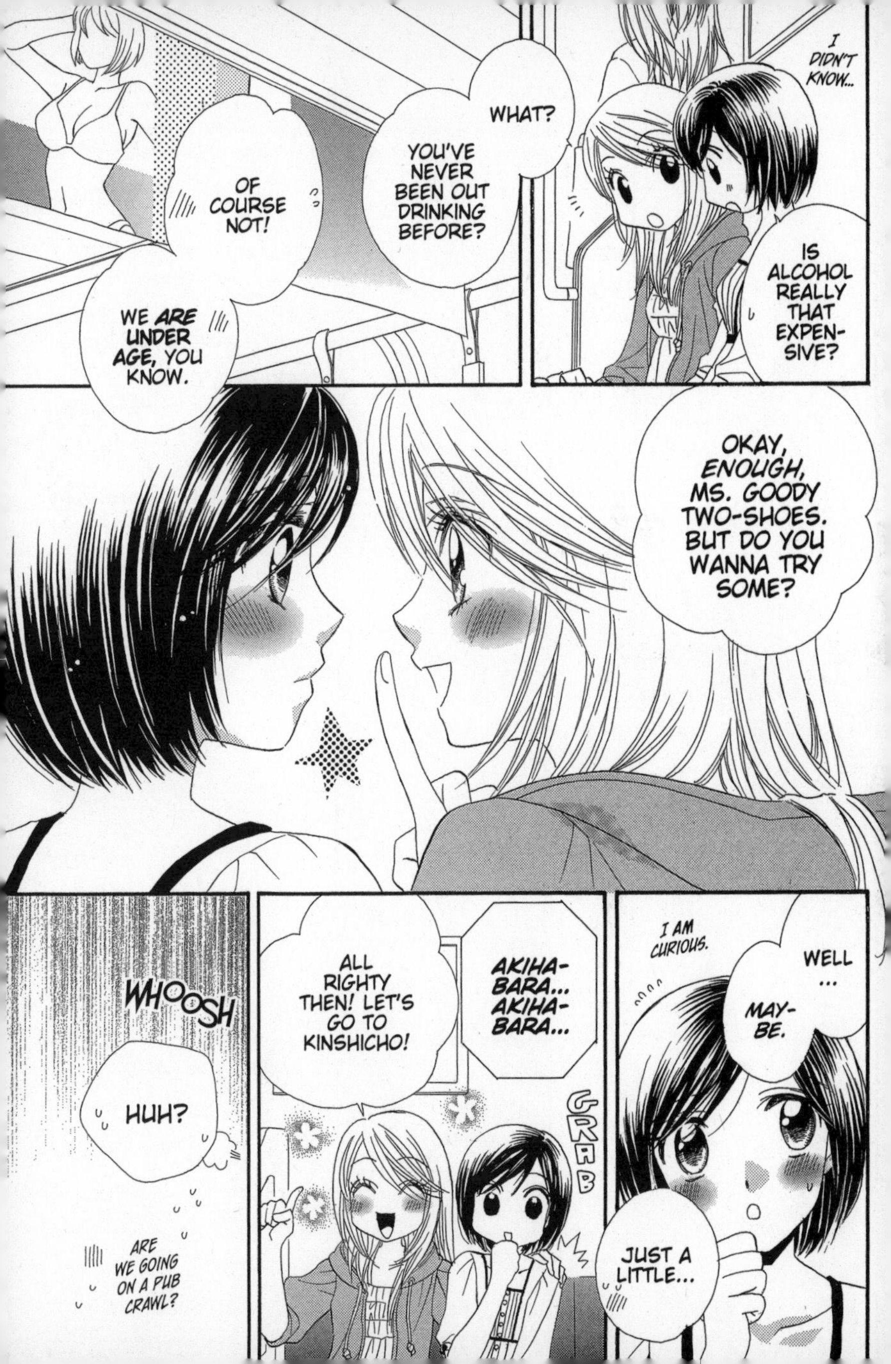
I DIDN'T KNOW...
IS ALCOHOL REALLY THAT EXPENSIVE?
WHAT?
YOU'VE NEVER BEEN OUT DRINKING BEFORE?
OF COURSE NOT!
WE *ARE* UNDER AGE, YOU KNOW.
OKAY, *ENOUGH*, MS. GOODY TWO-SHOES. BUT DO YOU WANNA TRY SOME?
I AM CURIOUS.
WELL ...
MAY-BE.
JUST A LITTLE...
AKIHA-BARA... AKIHA-BARA...
ALL RIGHTY THEN! LET'S GO TO KINSHICHO!
GRAB
WHOOSH
HUH?
ARE WE GOING ON A PUB CRAWL?

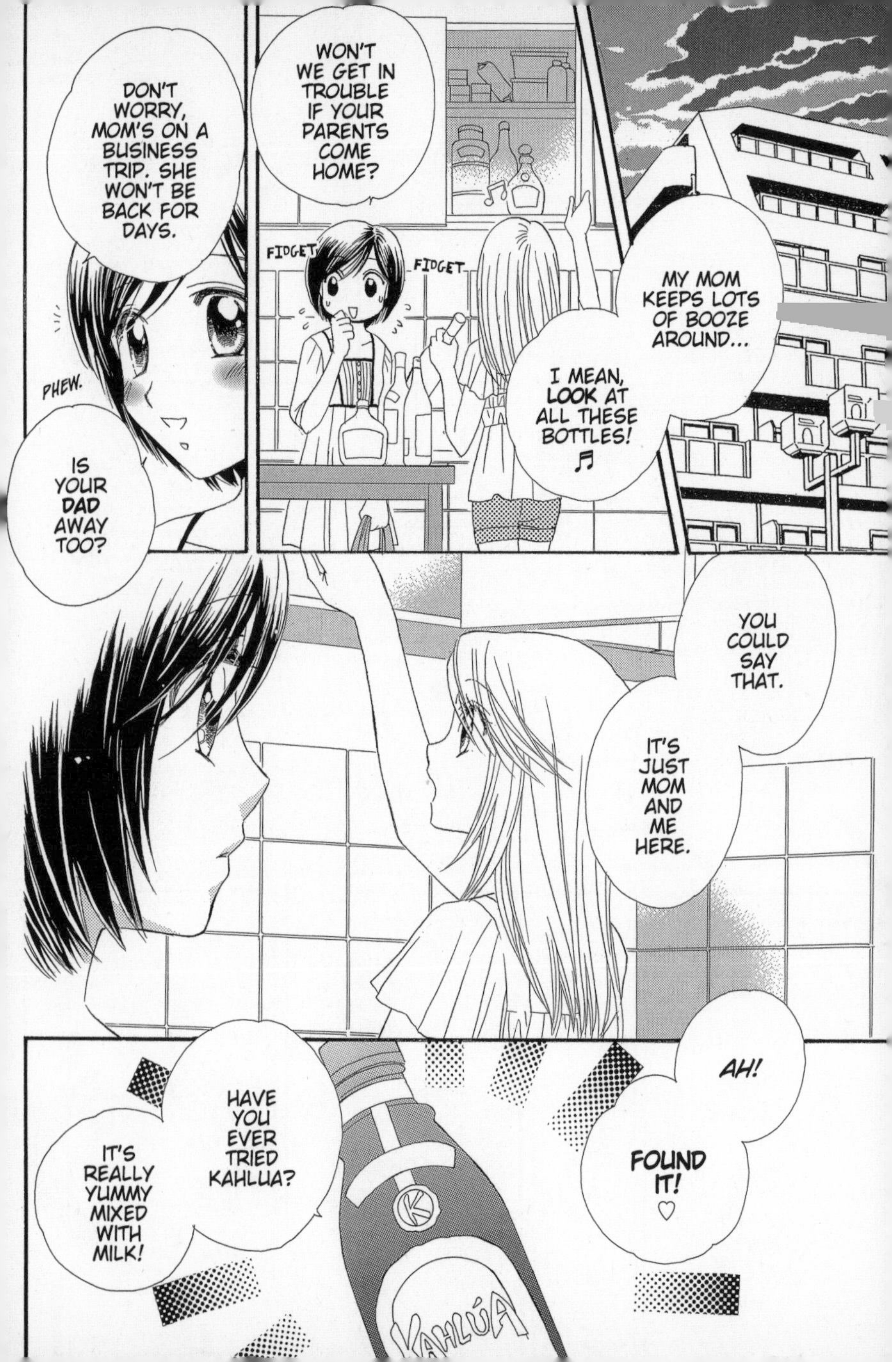

MY MOM KEEPS LOTS OF BOOZE AROUND...
I MEAN, LOOK AT ALL THESE BOTTLES! ♬
WON'T WE GET IN TROUBLE IF YOUR PARENTS COME HOME?
FIDGET
FIDGET
DON'T WORRY, MOM'S ON A BUSINESS TRIP. SHE WON'T BE BACK FOR DAYS.
PHEW.
IS YOUR DAD AWAY TOO?
YOU COULD SAY THAT.
IT'S JUST MOM AND ME HERE.
AH!
FOUND IT! ♡
HAVE YOU EVER TRIED KAHLUA?
IT'S REALLY YUMMY MIXED WITH MILK!
KAHLÚA

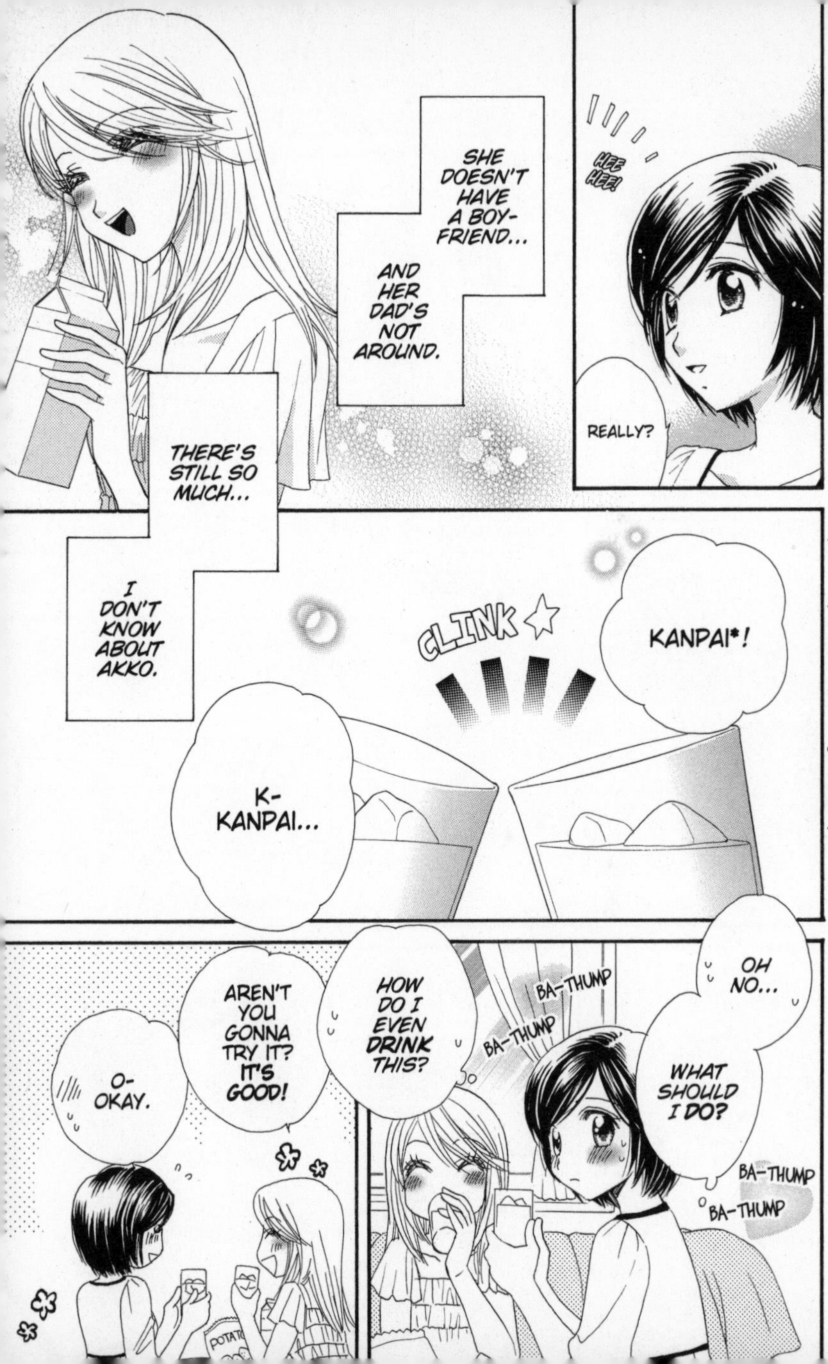
HEE HEE!
REALLY?
SHE DOESN'T HAVE A BOY-FRIEND...
AND HER DAD'S NOT AROUND.
THERE'S STILL SO MUCH...
I DON'T KNOW ABOUT AKKO.
KANPAI*!
CLINK
K-KANPAI...
OH NO...
WHAT SHOULD I DO?
BA-THUMP
BA-THUMP
BA-THUMP
BA-THUMP
HOW DO I EVEN DRINK THIS?
AREN'T YOU GONNA TRY IT? IT'S GOOD!
O-OKAY.
POTATO

*Kanpai is a Japanese toast, meaning "bottoms up/cheers."

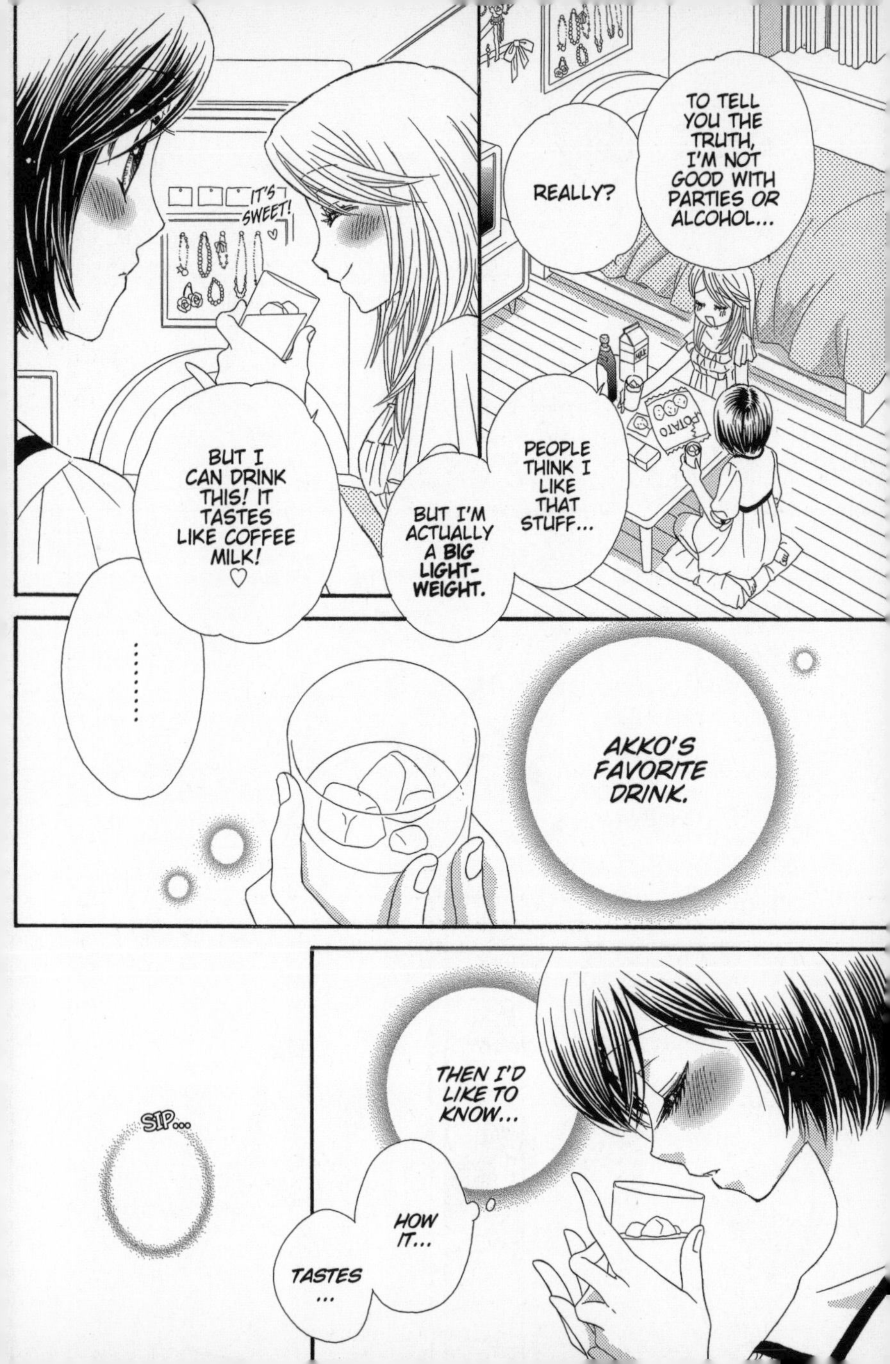
TO TELL YOU THE TRUTH, I'M NOT GOOD WITH PARTIES OR ALCOHOL...
REALLY?
PEOPLE THINK I LIKE THAT STUFF...
BUT I'M ACTUALLY A BIG LIGHT-WEIGHT.
IT'S SWEET! ♡
BUT I CAN DRINK THIS! IT TASTES LIKE COFFEE MILK! ♡
......
AKKO'S FAVORITE DRINK.
THEN I'D LIKE TO KNOW...
HOW IT...
TASTES ...
SIP...

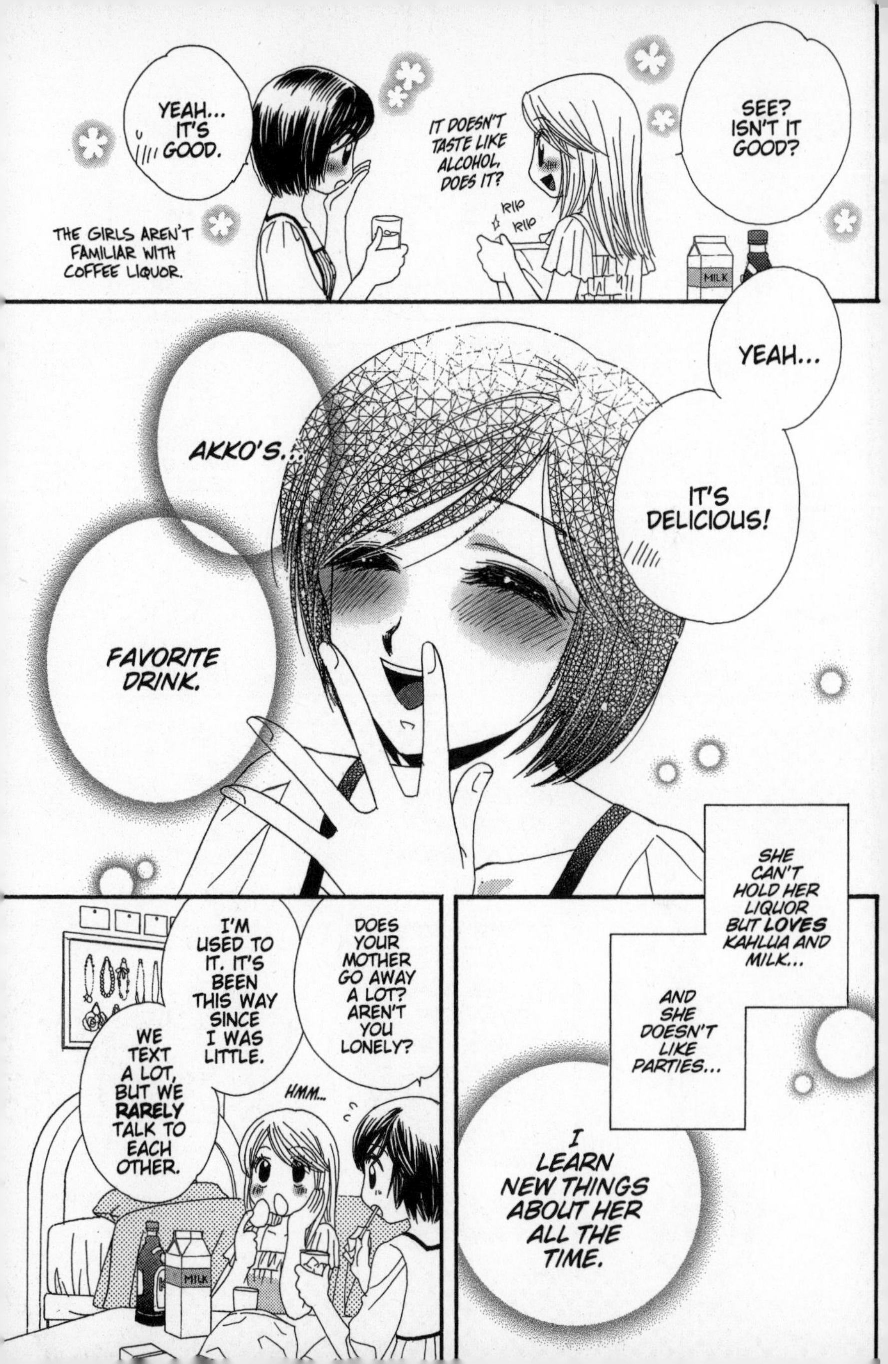
SEE? ISN'T IT GOOD?
IT DOESN'T TASTE LIKE ALCOHOL, DOES IT?
YEAH... IT'S GOOD.
THE GIRLS AREN'T FAMILIAR WITH COFFEE LIQUOR.
YEAH...
IT'S DELICIOUS!
AKKO'S...
FAVORITE DRINK.
SHE CAN'T HOLD HER LIQUOR BUT LOVES KAHLUA AND MILK...
AND SHE DOESN'T LIKE PARTIES...
I LEARN NEW THINGS ABOUT HER ALL THE TIME.
DOES YOUR MOTHER GO AWAY A LOT? AREN'T YOU LONELY?
I'M USED TO IT. IT'S BEEN THIS WAY SINCE I WAS LITTLE.
WE TEXT A LOT, BUT WE RARELY TALK TO EACH OTHER.
HMM...

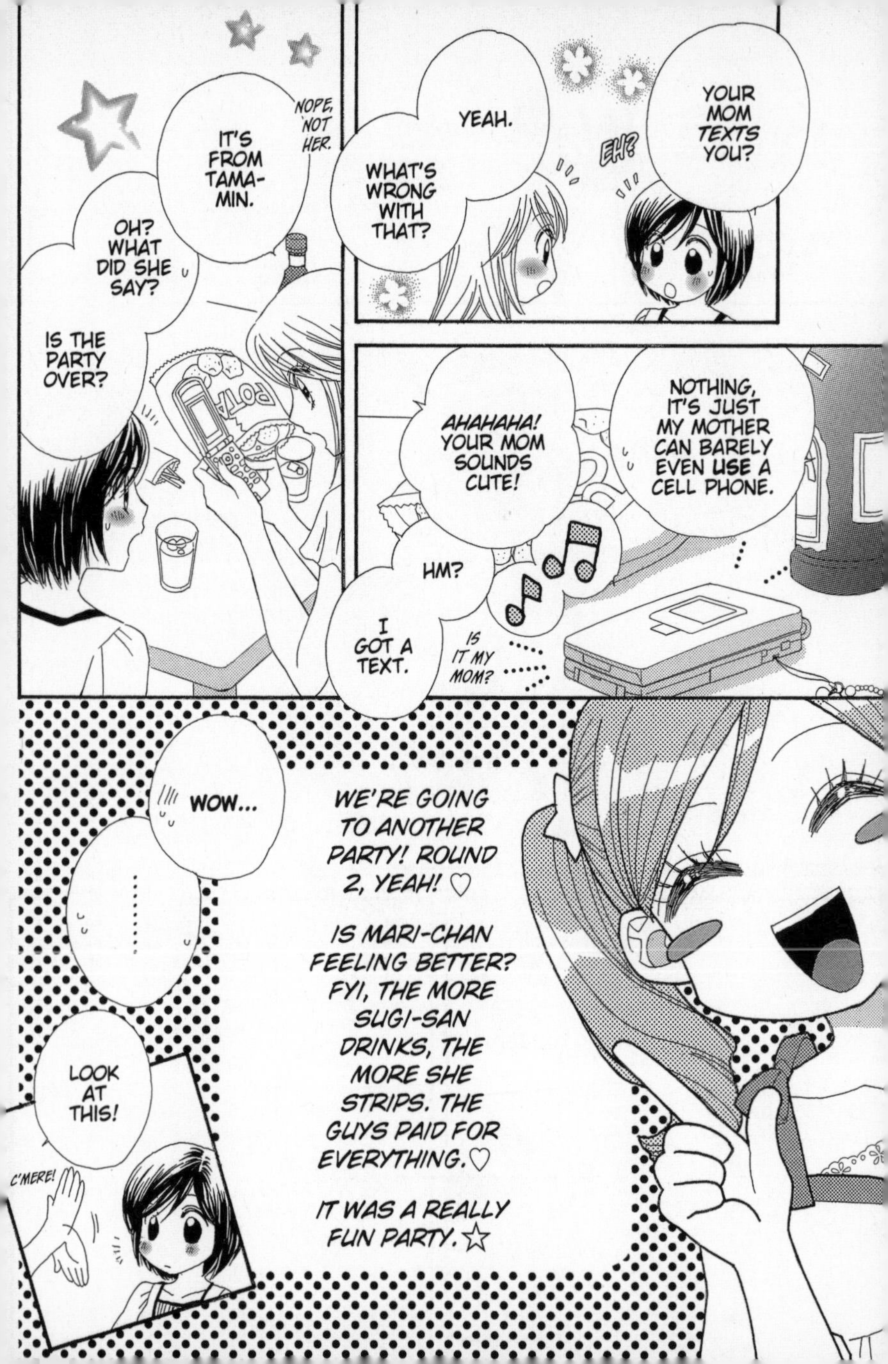

YOUR MOM TEXTS YOU?
EH?
YEAH.
WHAT'S WRONG WITH THAT?
NOTHING, IT'S JUST MY MOTHER CAN BARELY EVEN USE A CELL PHONE.
AHAHAHA! YOUR MOM SOUNDS CUTE!
HM?
I GOT A TEXT.
IS IT MY MOM?
NOPE, NOT HER.
IT'S FROM TAMA-MIN.
OH? WHAT DID SHE SAY?
IS THE PARTY OVER?
WE'RE GOING TO ANOTHER PARTY! ROUND 2, YEAH! ♡
IS MARI-CHAN FEELING BETTER? FYI, THE MORE SUGI-SAN DRINKS, THE MORE SHE STRIPS. THE GUYS PAID FOR EVERYTHING. ♡
IT WAS A REALLY FUN PARTY. ☆
WOW...
......
LOOK AT THIS!
C'MERE!

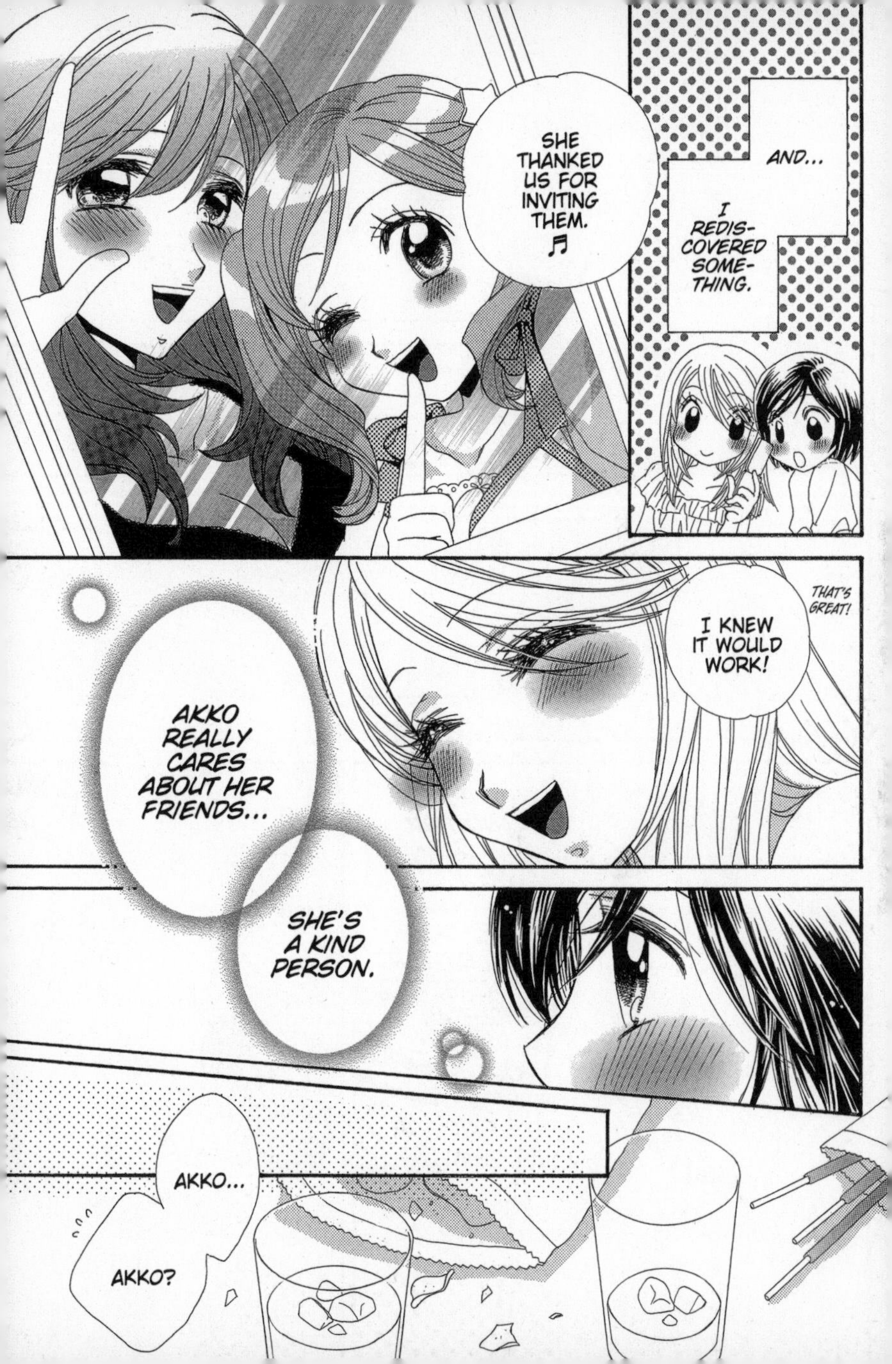
AND...
I REDISCOVERED SOMETHING.
SHE THANKED US FOR INVITING THEM. ♬
THAT'S GREAT!
I KNEW IT WOULD WORK!
AKKO REALLY CARES ABOUT HER FRIENDS...
SHE'S A KIND PERSON.
AKKO...
AKKO?

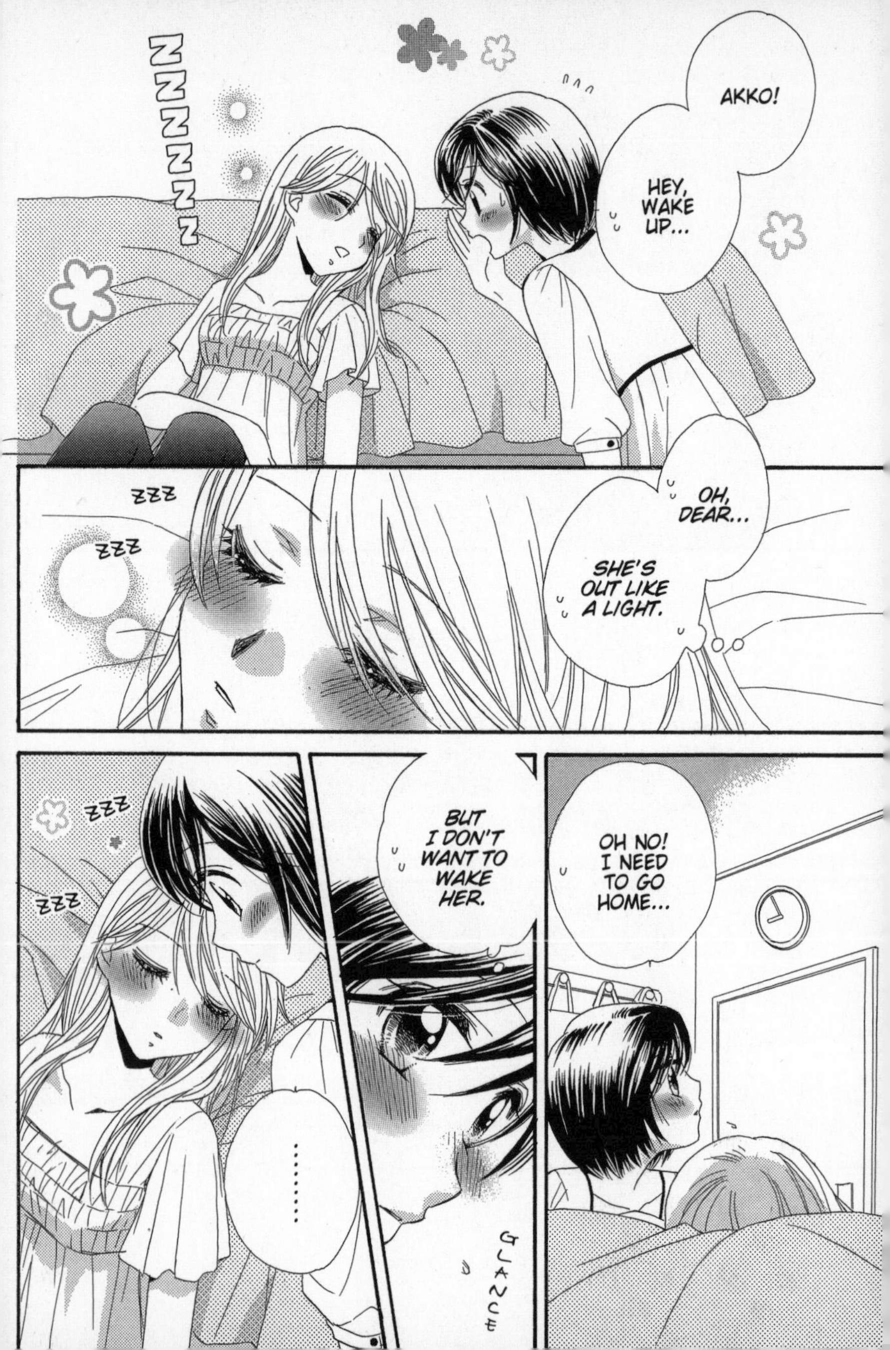
AKKO!
HEY, WAKE UP...
ZZZZZZZ
OH, DEAR...
SHE'S OUT LIKE A LIGHT.
ZZZ
ZZZ
OH NO! I NEED TO GO HOME...
BUT I DON'T WANT TO WAKE HER.
GLANCE
ZZZ
ZZZ
......

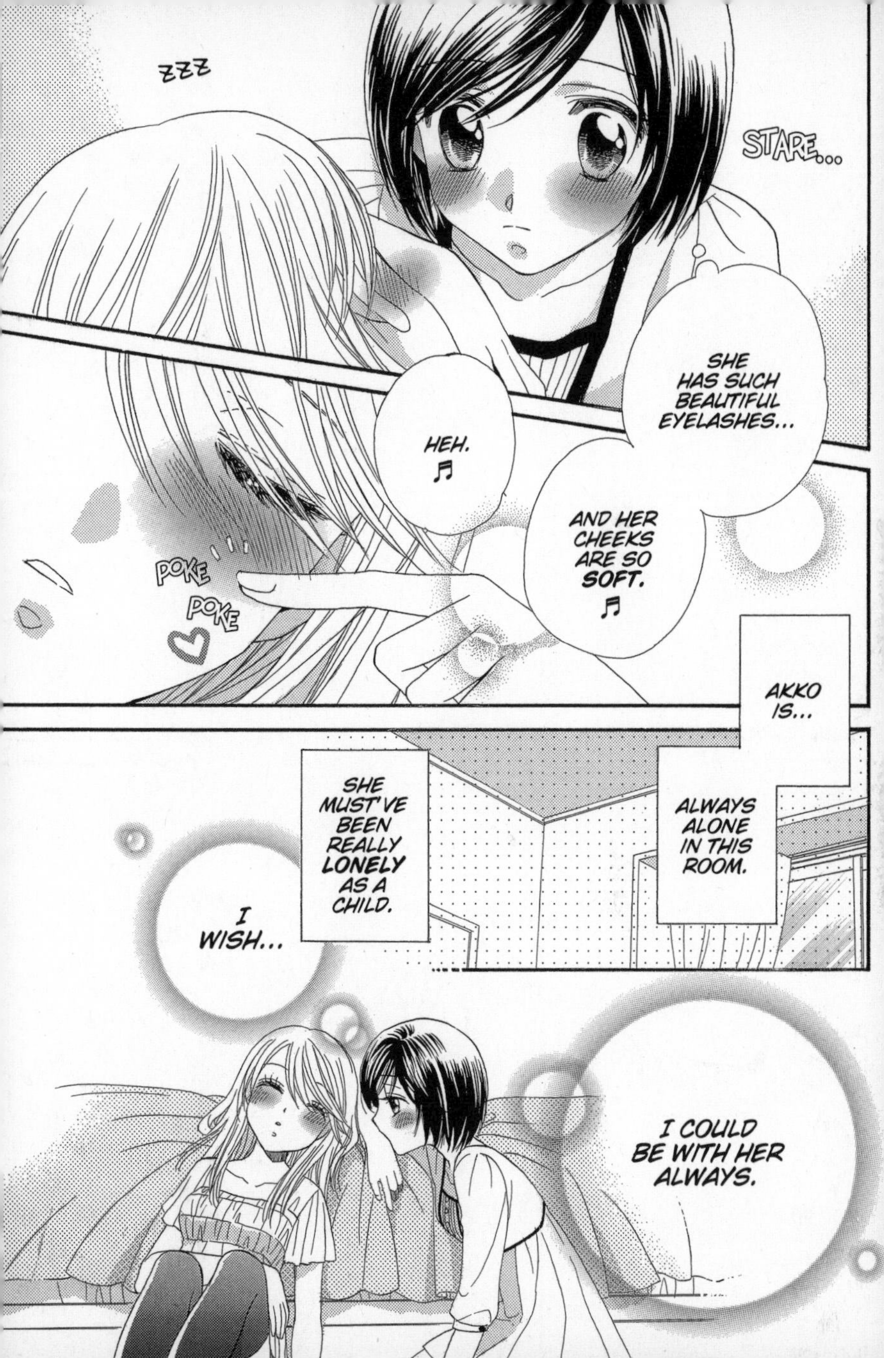
STARE...
ZZZ
SHE HAS SUCH BEAUTIFUL EYELASHES...
AND HER CHEEKS ARE SO SOFT. ♬
HEH. ♬
POKE
POKE
AKKO IS...
ALWAYS ALONE IN THIS ROOM.
SHE MUST'VE BEEN REALLY LONELY AS A CHILD.
I WISH...
I COULD BE WITH HER ALWAYS.

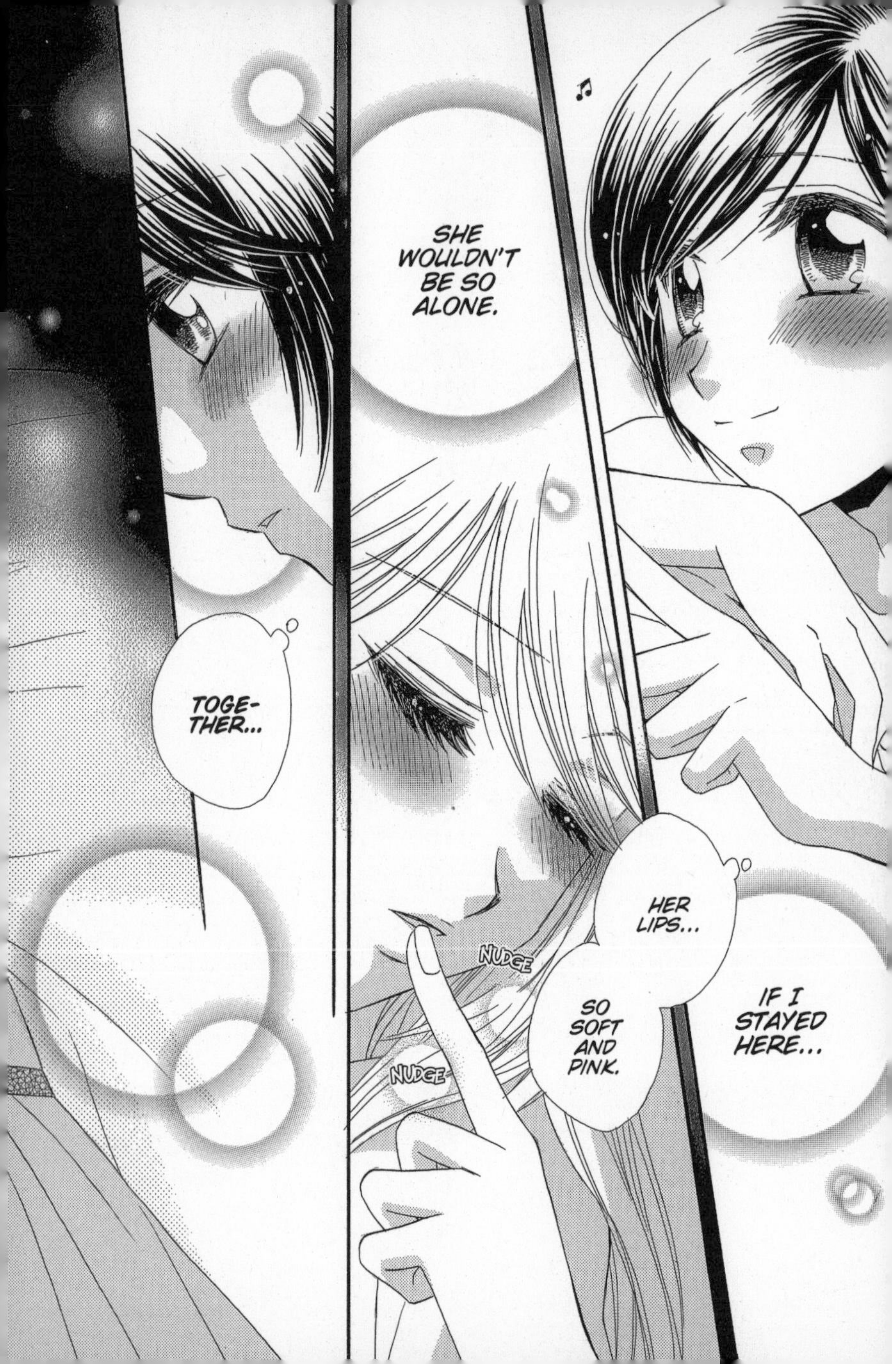
IF I STAYED HERE...
SHE WOULDN'T BE SO ALONE.
HER LIPS...
NUDGE
SO SOFT AND PINK.
NUDGE
TOGE-THER...

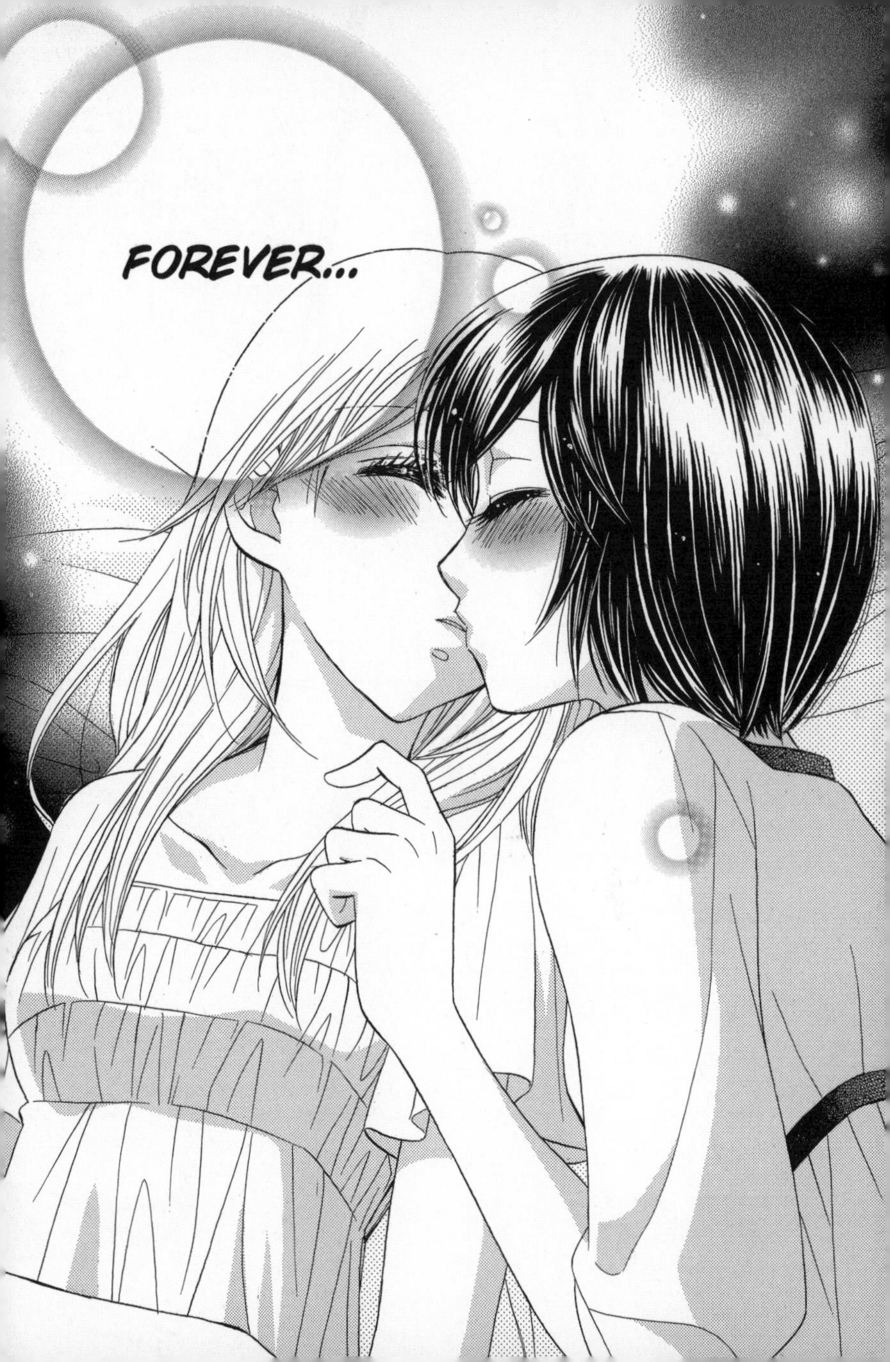
FOREVER...

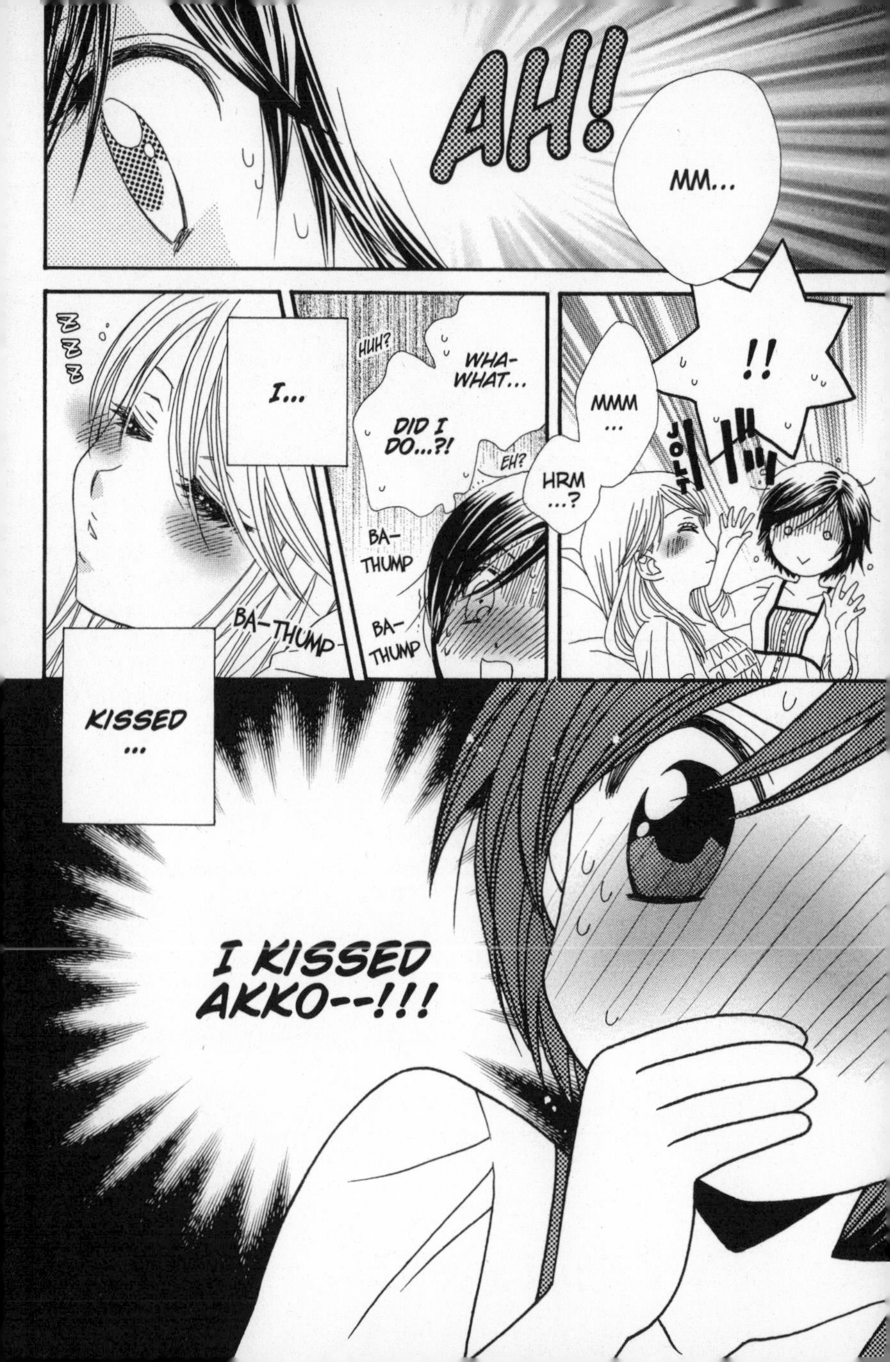

MM...
AH!
!!
MMM...
JOLT
HRM...?
WHA-WHAT...
HUH?
DID I DO...?!
EH?
BA-THUMP
BA-THUMP
I...
ZZZ
BA-THUMP
KISSED...
I KISSED AKKO--!!!

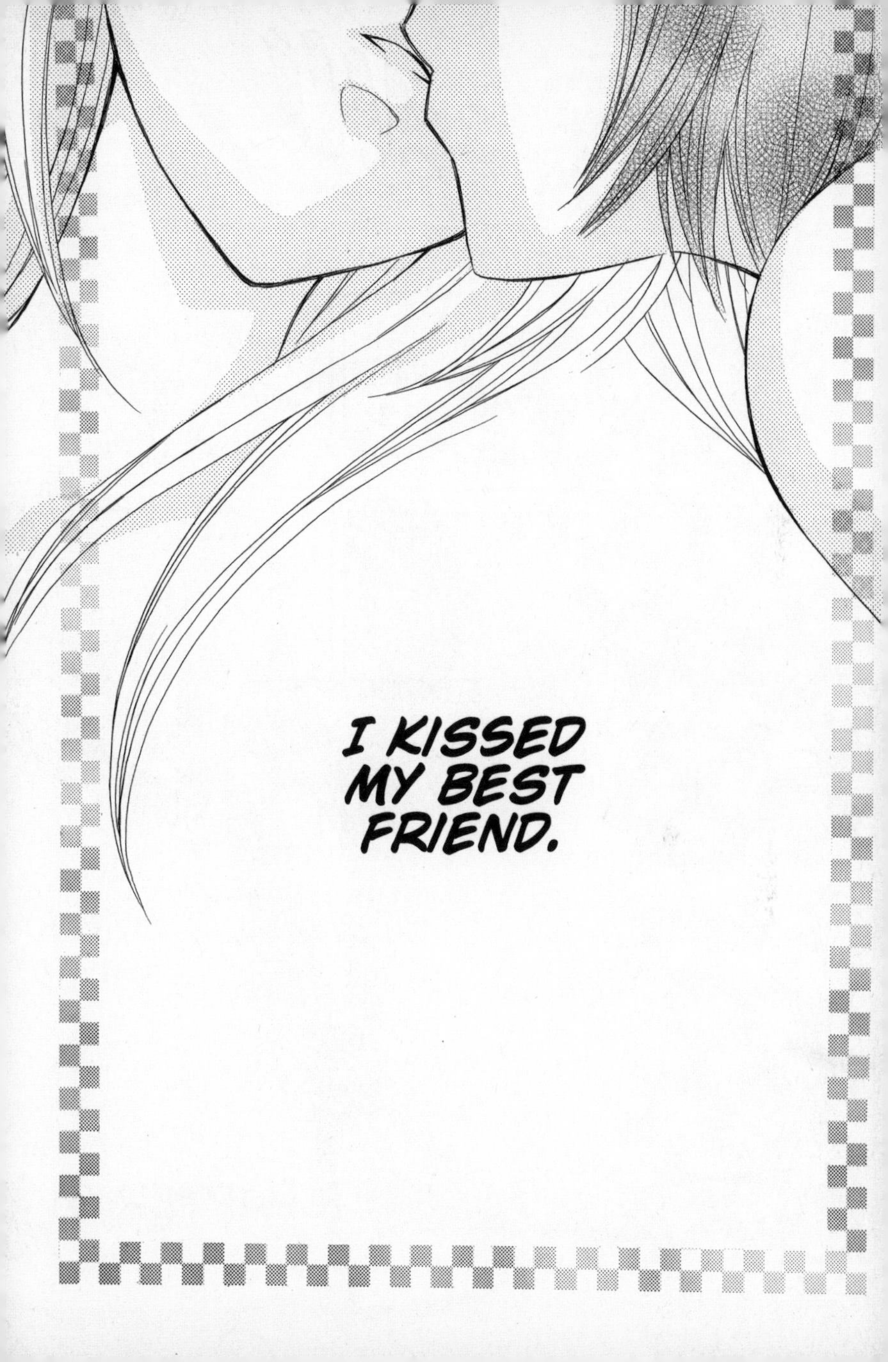
I KISSED MY BEST FRIEND.

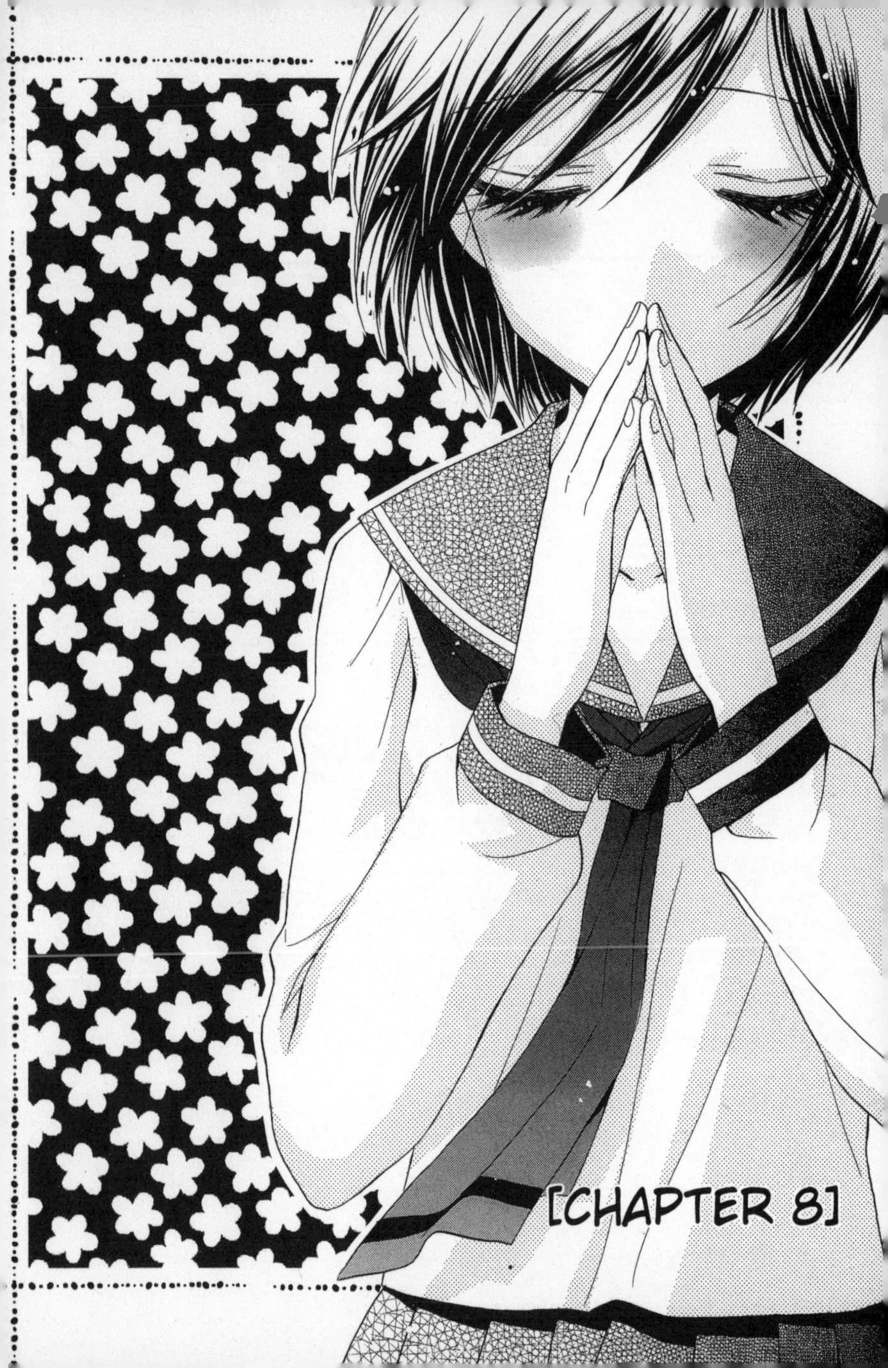
[CHAPTER 8]

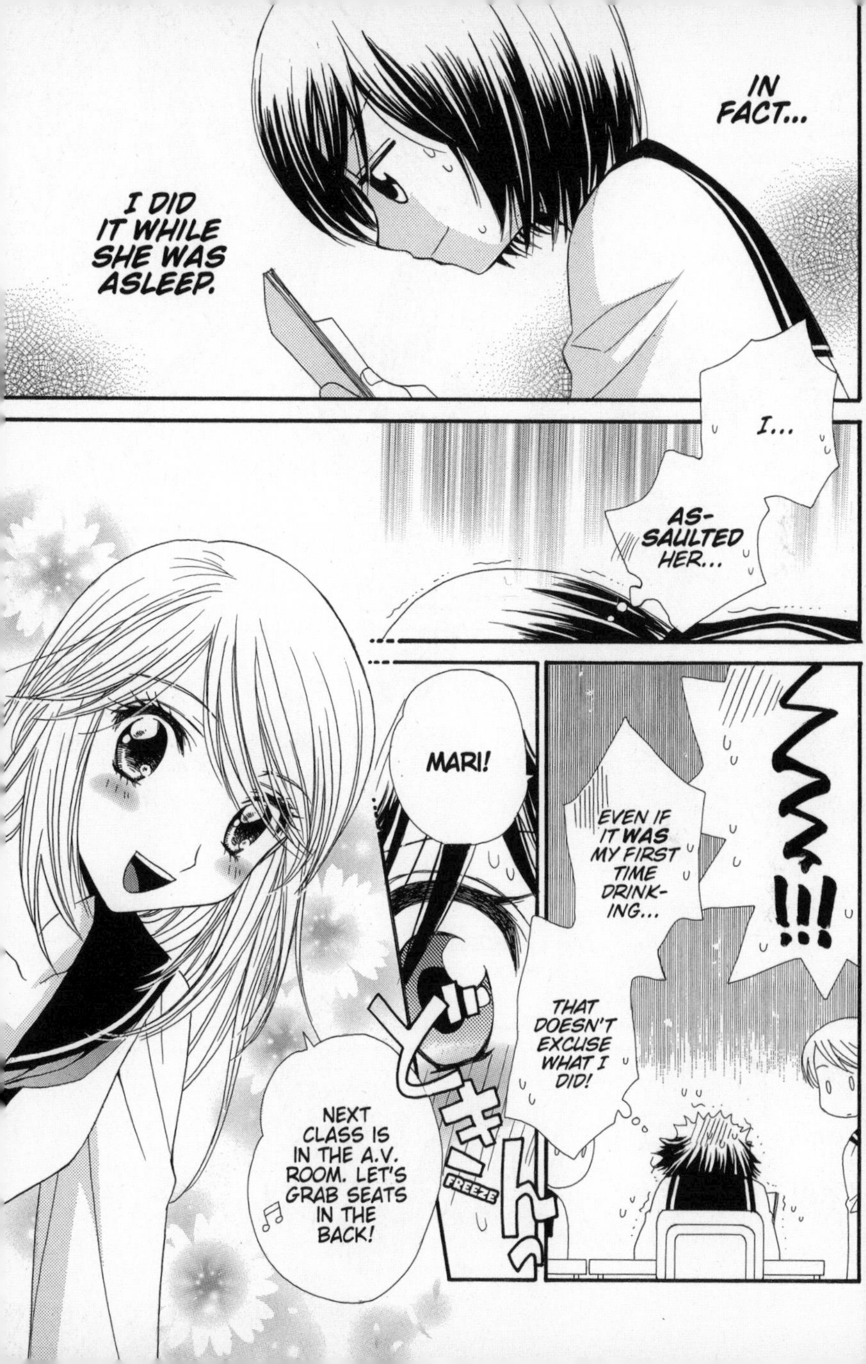
IN FACT...
I DID IT WHILE SHE WAS ASLEEP.
I...
AS-SAULTED HER...
!!!
EVEN IF IT WAS MY FIRST TIME DRINK-ING...
THAT DOESN'T EXCUSE WHAT I DID!
MARI!
FREEZE
NEXT CLASS IS IN THE A.V. ROOM. LET'S GRAB SEATS IN THE BACK!

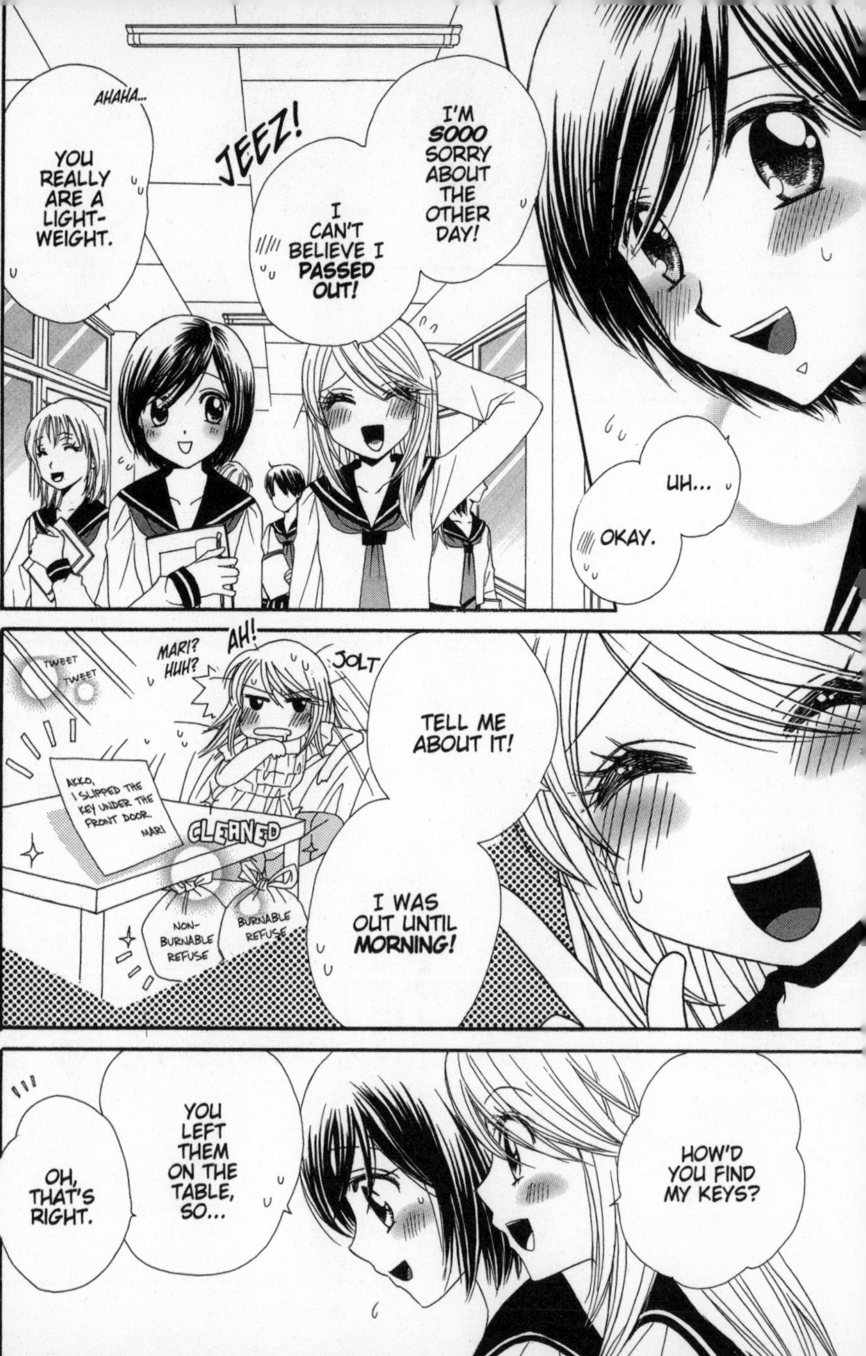
UH...
OKAY.
I'M SOOO SORRY ABOUT THE OTHER DAY!
JEEZ!
I CAN'T BELIEVE I PASSED OUT!
AHAHA...
YOU REALLY ARE A LIGHT-WEIGHT.
TELL ME ABOUT IT!
I WAS OUT UNTIL MORNING!
AH!
JOLT
MARI? HUH?
TWEET
TWEET
AKKO, I SLIPPED THE KEY UNDER THE FRONT DOOR. MARI
CLEANED
BURNABLE REFUSE
NON-BURNABLE REFUSE
HOW'D YOU FIND MY KEYS?
YOU LEFT THEM ON THE TABLE, SO...
OH, THAT'S RIGHT.

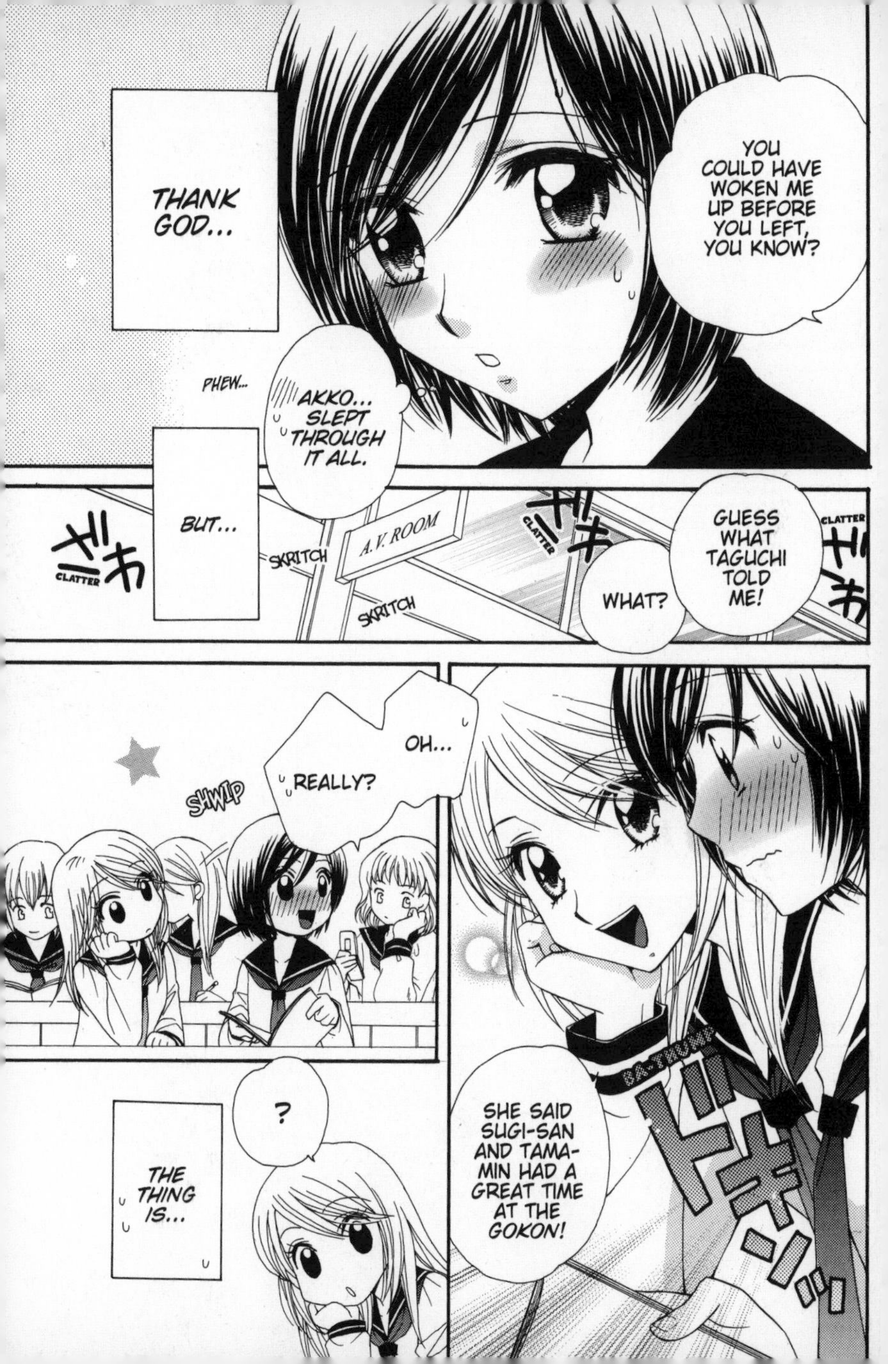
YOU COULD HAVE WOKEN ME UP BEFORE YOU LEFT, YOU KNOW?
AKKO... SLEPT THROUGH IT ALL.
THANK GOD...
PHEW...
CLATTER
GUESS WHAT TAGUCHI TOLD ME!
CLATTER
WHAT?
A.V. ROOM
SKRITCH
BUT...
SKRITCH
CLATTER
SHE SAID SUGI-SAN AND TAMA-MIN HAD A GREAT TIME AT THE GOKON!
BA-THUMP
OH... REALLY?
SHWIP
?
THE THING IS...

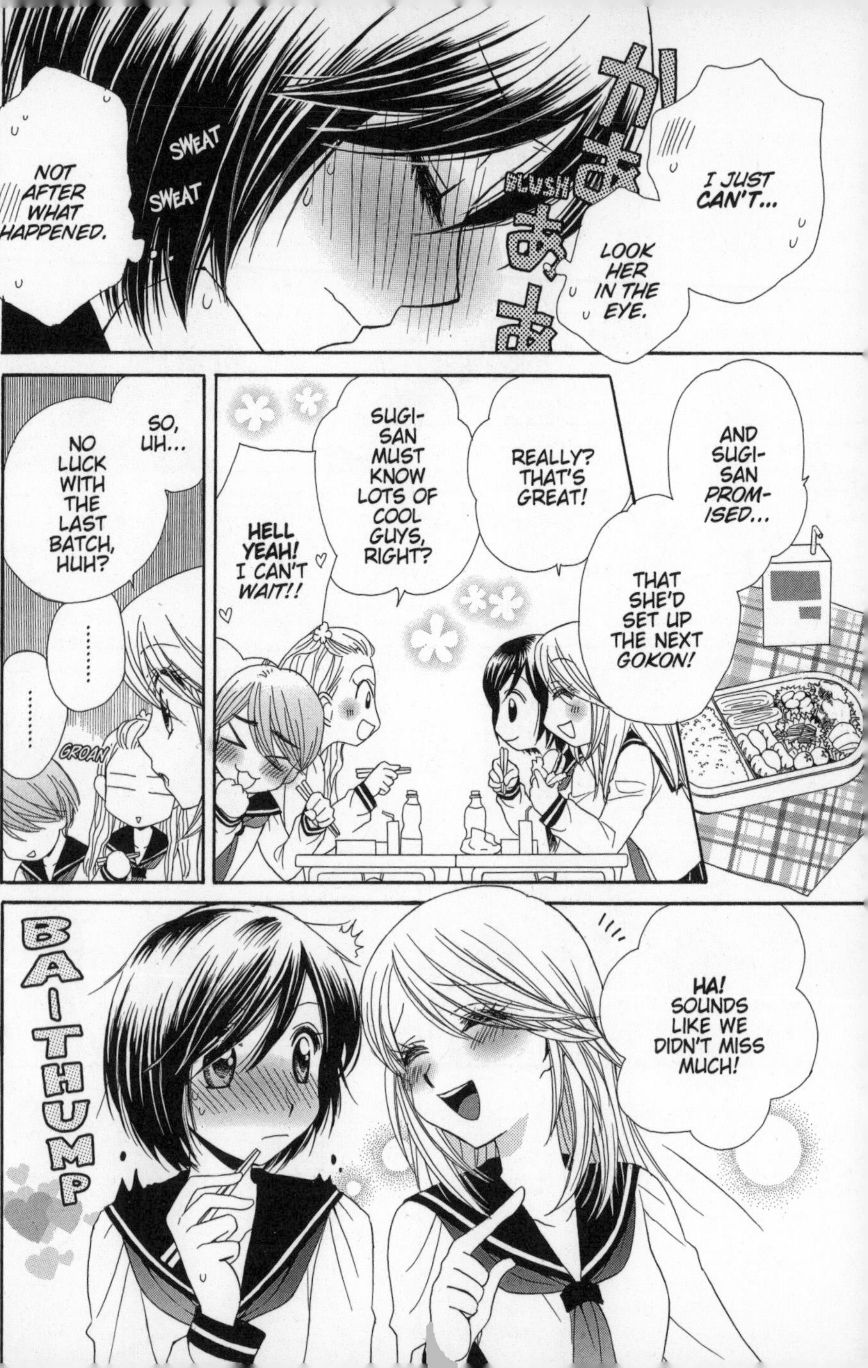
I JUST CAN'T...
LOOK HER IN THE EYE.
BLUSH
SWEAT
SWEAT
NOT AFTER WHAT HAPPENED.
AND SUGI-SAN PROMISED...
THAT SHE'D SET UP THE NEXT GOKON!
REALLY? THAT'S GREAT!
SUGI-SAN MUST KNOW LOTS OF COOL GUYS, RIGHT?
HELL YEAH! I CAN'T WAIT!!
SO, UH...
NO LUCK WITH THE LAST BATCH, HUH?
......
......
GROAN
HA! SOUNDS LIKE WE DIDN'T MISS MUCH!
BA-THUMP

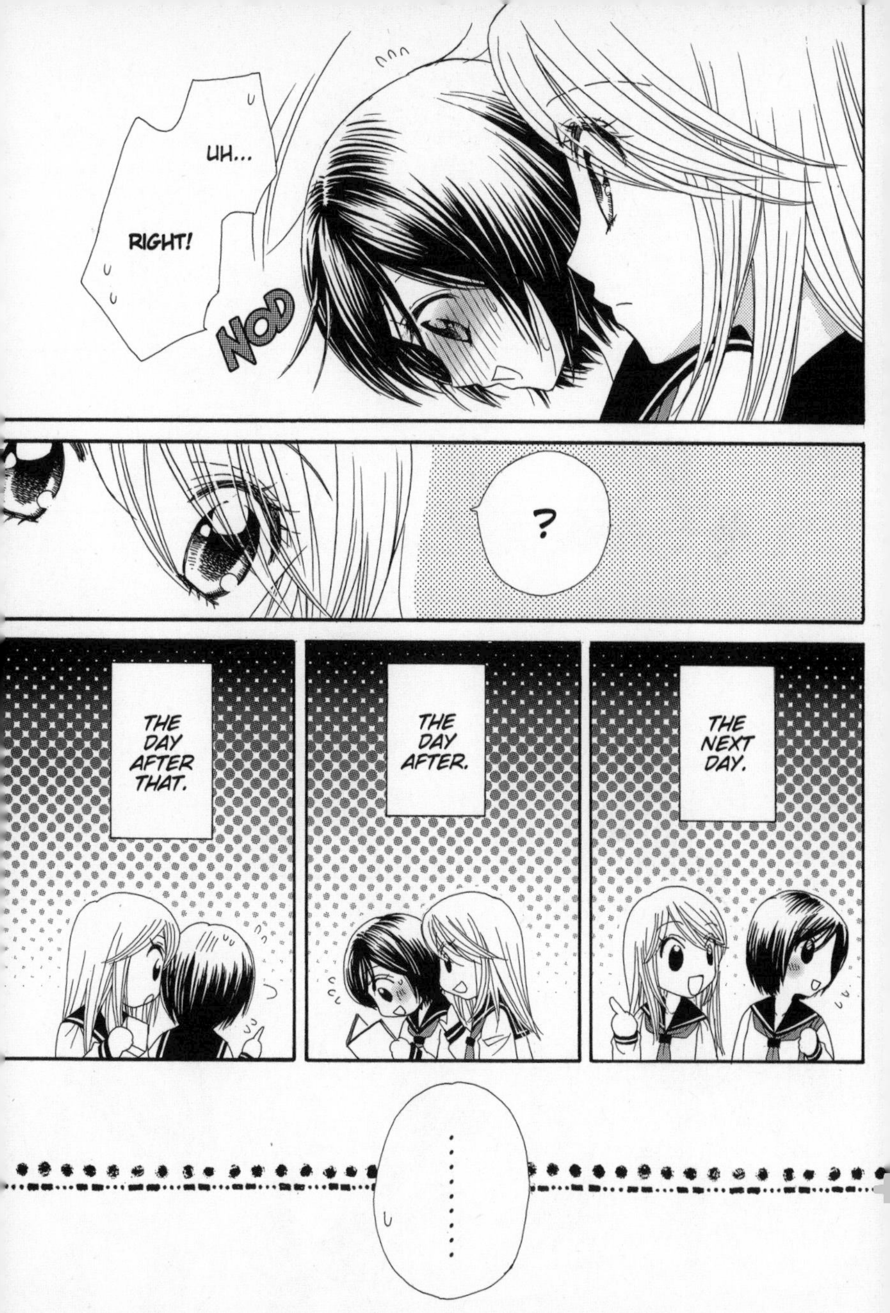
UH...
RIGHT!
NOD
?
THE NEXT DAY.
THE DAY AFTER.
THE DAY AFTER THAT.
......

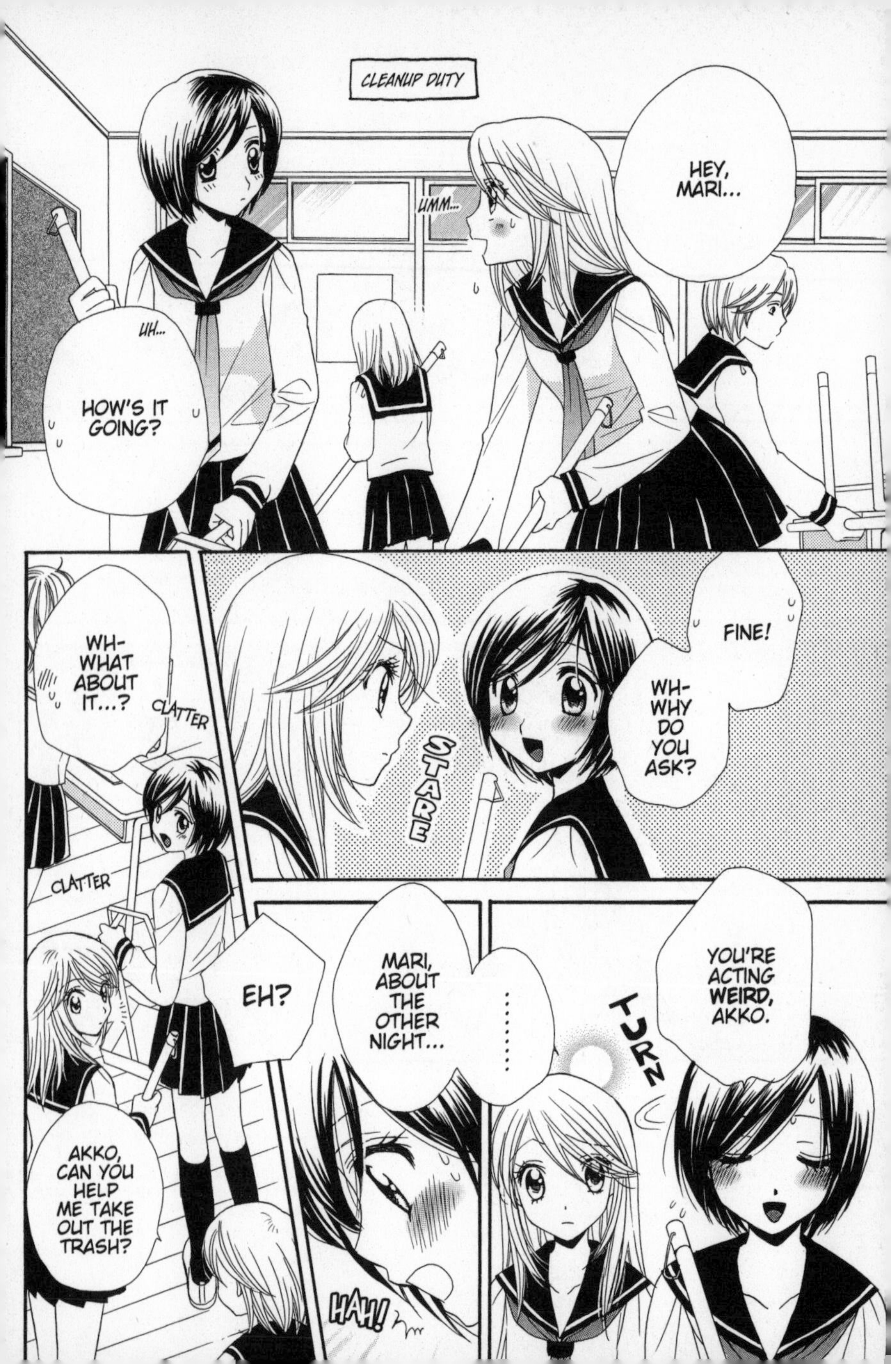
CLEANUP DUTY
HEY, MARI...
UMM...
UH...
HOW'S IT GOING?
FINE!
WH-WHY DO YOU ASK?
STARE
YOU'RE ACTING WEIRD, AKKO.
TURN
......
MARI, ABOUT THE OTHER NIGHT...
HAH!
WH-WHAT ABOUT IT...?
CLATTER
CLATTER
EH?
AKKO, CAN YOU HELP ME TAKE OUT THE TRASH?

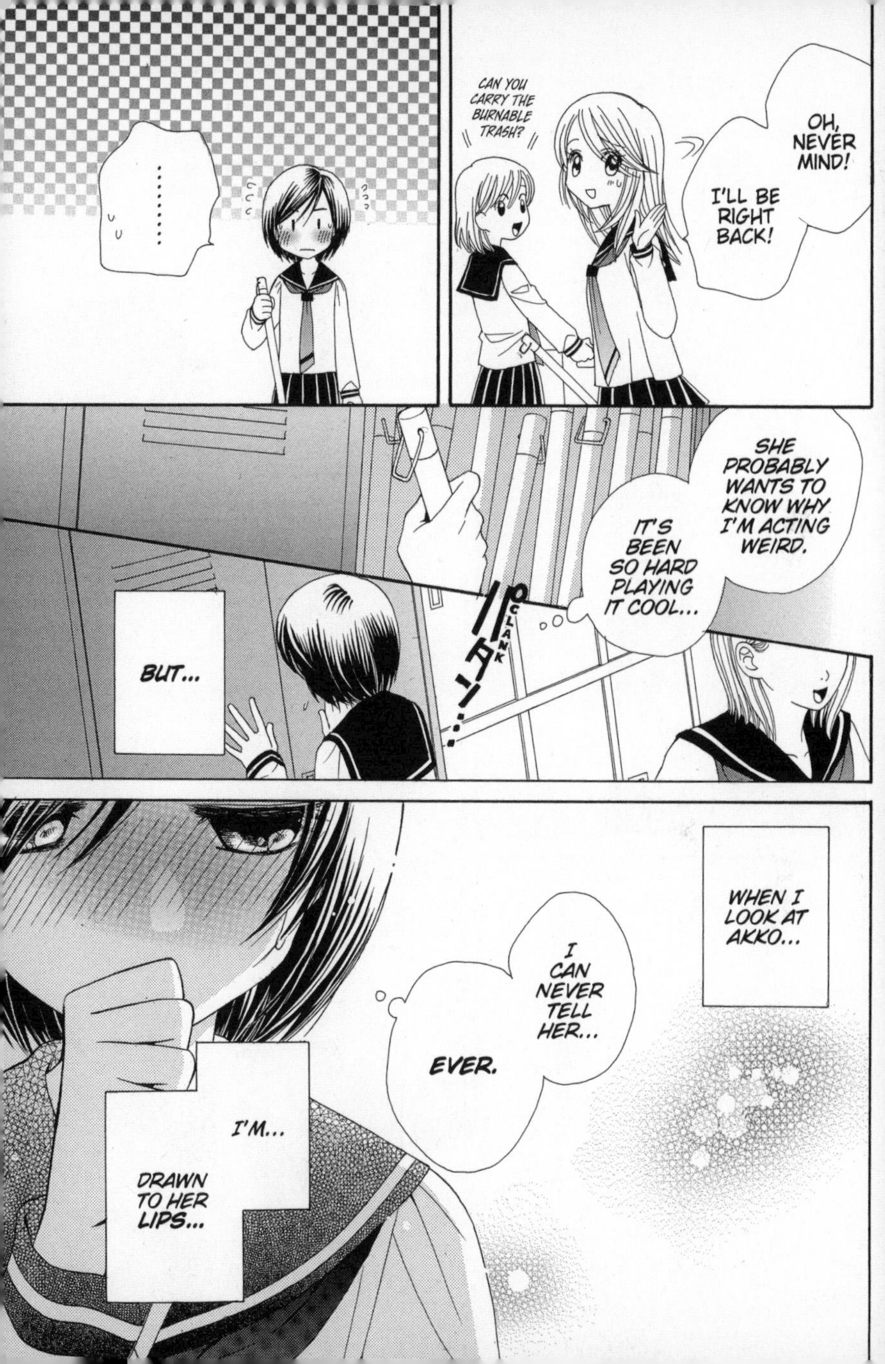
OH, NEVER MIND!
I'LL BE RIGHT BACK!
CAN YOU CARRY THE BURNABLE TRASH?
......
SHE PROBABLY WANTS TO KNOW WHY I'M ACTING WEIRD.
IT'S BEEN SO HARD PLAYING IT COOL...
CLANK
BUT...
WHEN I LOOK AT AKKO...
I CAN NEVER TELL HER...
EVER.
I'M...
DRAWN TO HER LIPS...

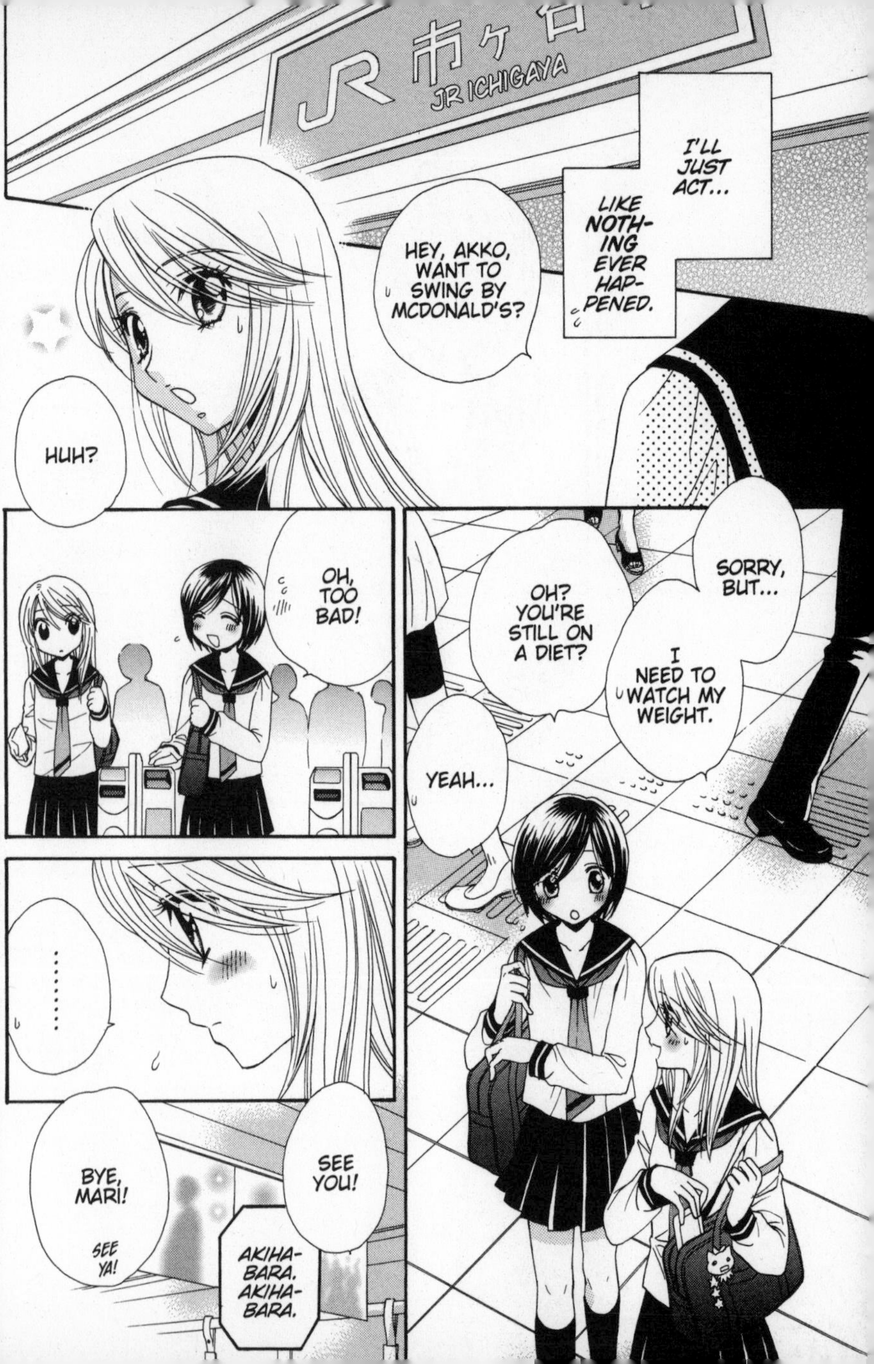
JR 市ヶ
JR ICHIGAYA
I'LL JUST ACT...
LIKE NOTHING EVER HAPPENED.
HEY, AKKO, WANT TO SWING BY MCDONALD'S?
HUH?
SORRY, BUT...
I NEED TO WATCH MY WEIGHT.
OH? YOU'RE STILL ON A DIET?
YEAH...
OH, TOO BAD!
......
SEE YOU!
BYE, MARI!
SEE YA!
AKIHABARA. AKIHABARA.

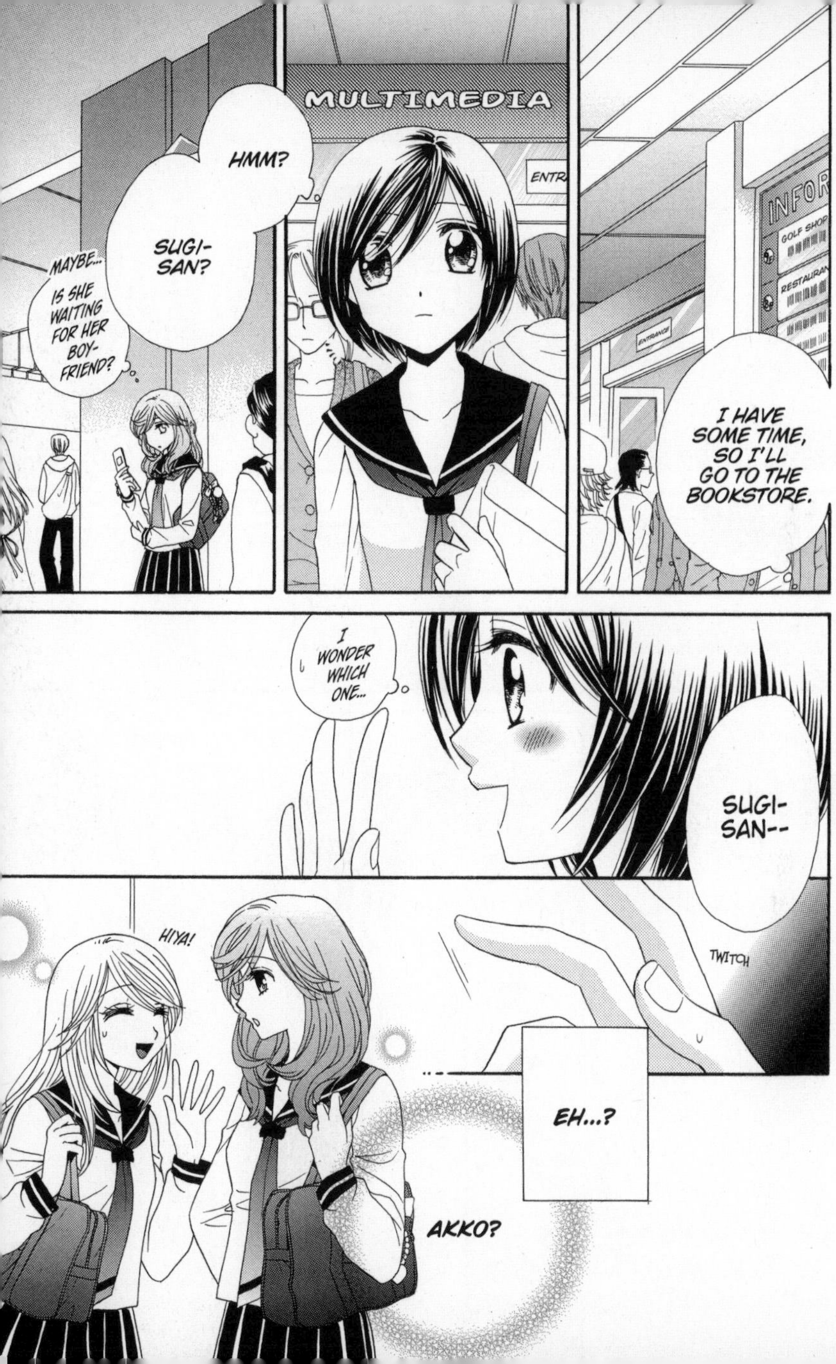
INFOR
GOLF SHOP
RESTAURAN
ENTRANCE
I HAVE SOME TIME, SO I'LL GO TO THE BOOKSTORE.
MULTIMEDIA
HMM?
SUGI-SAN?
MAYBE... IS SHE WAITING FOR HER BOY-FRIEND?
SUGI-SAN--
I WONDER WHICH ONE...
TWITCH
EH...?
AKKO?
HIYA!

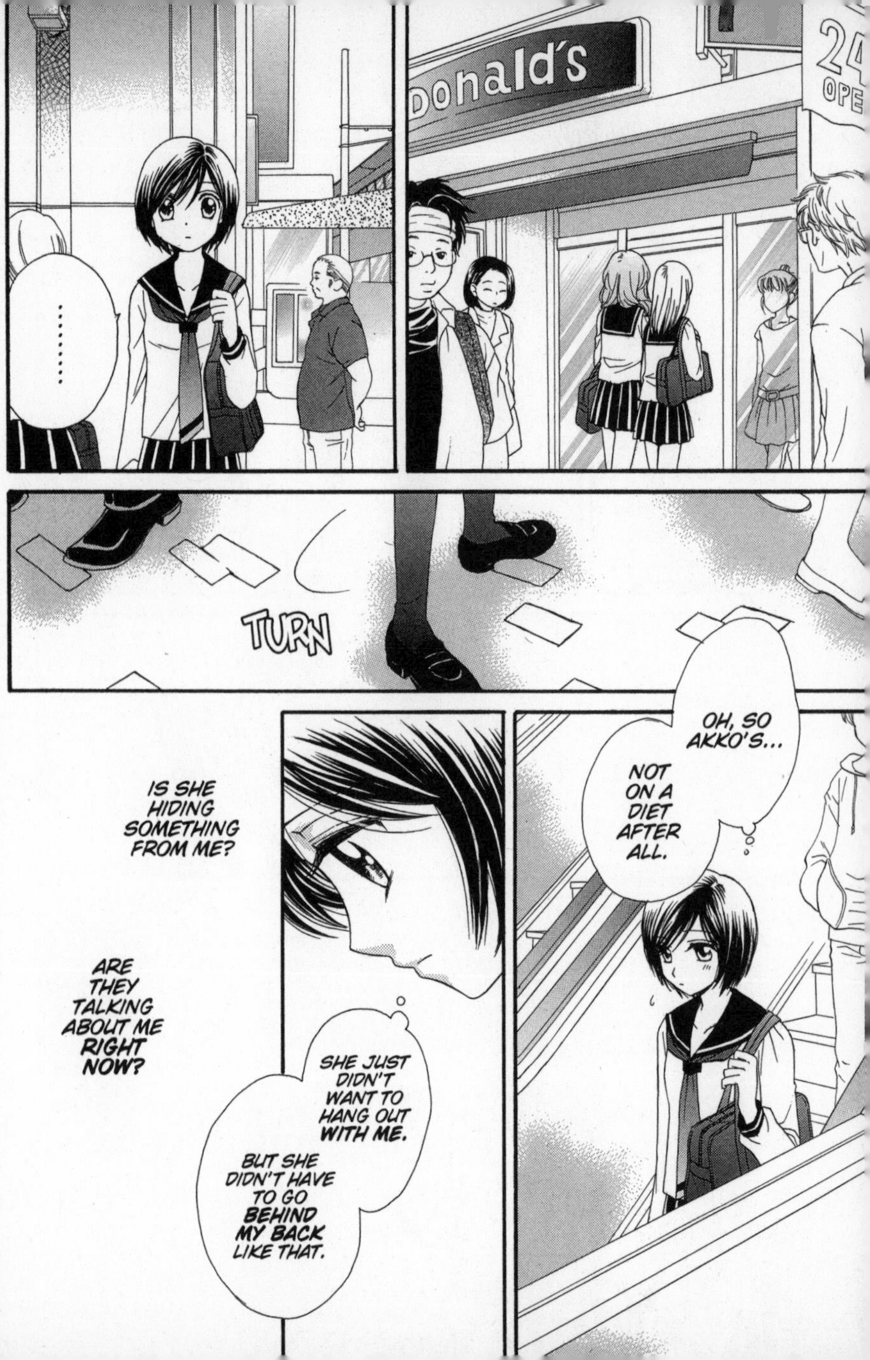

Donald's
24
OPE
......
TURN
OH, SO AKKO'S...
NOT ON A DIET AFTER ALL.
SHE JUST DIDN'T WANT TO HANG OUT WITH ME.
BUT SHE DIDN'T HAVE TO GO BEHIND MY BACK LIKE THAT.
IS SHE HIDING SOMETHING FROM ME?
ARE THEY TALKING ABOUT ME RIGHT NOW?

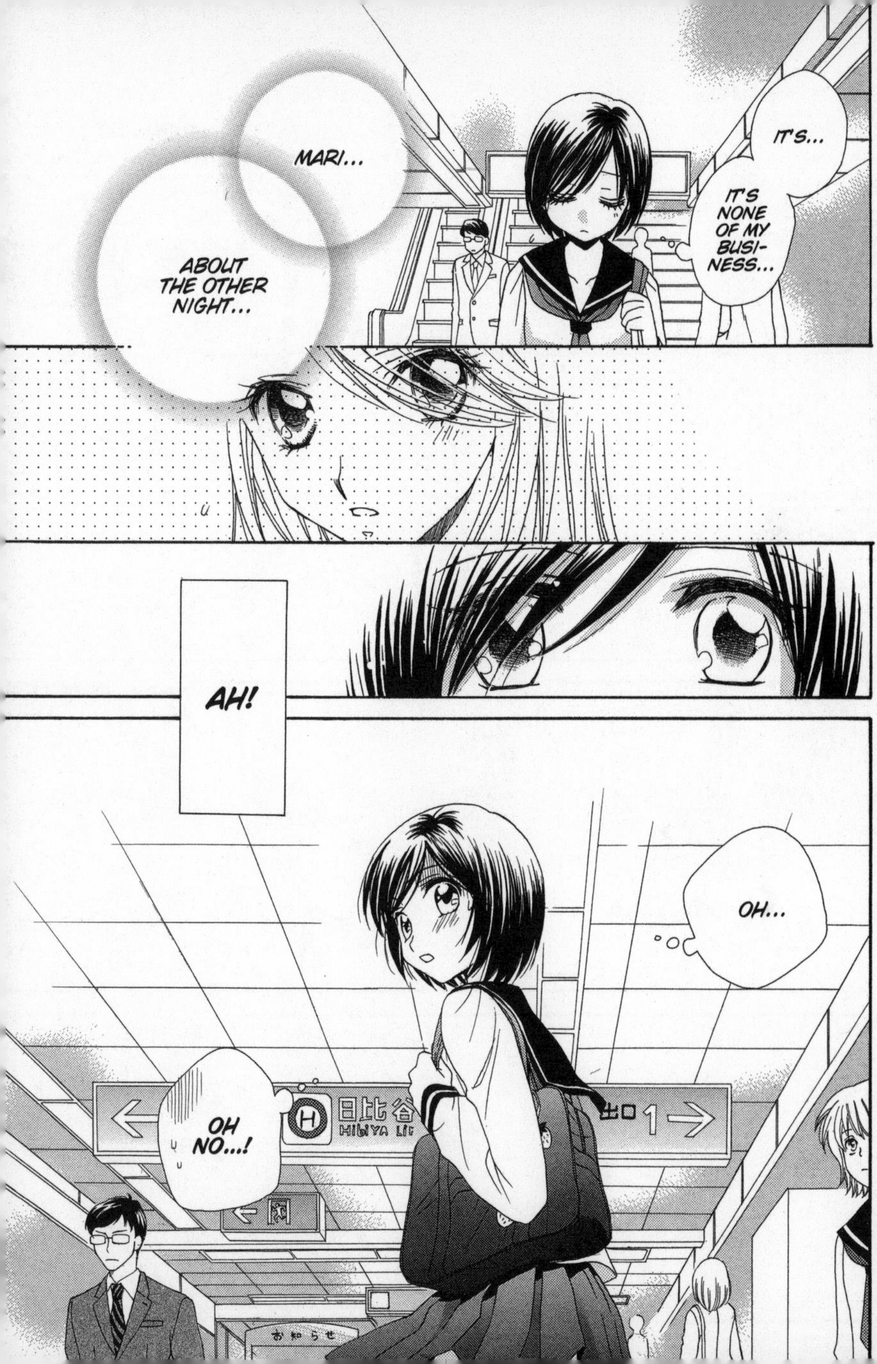
IT'S...
IT'S NONE OF MY BUSI-NESS...
MARI...
ABOUT THE OTHER NIGHT...
AH!
OH...
出口 1
日比谷
OH NO...!
お知らせ

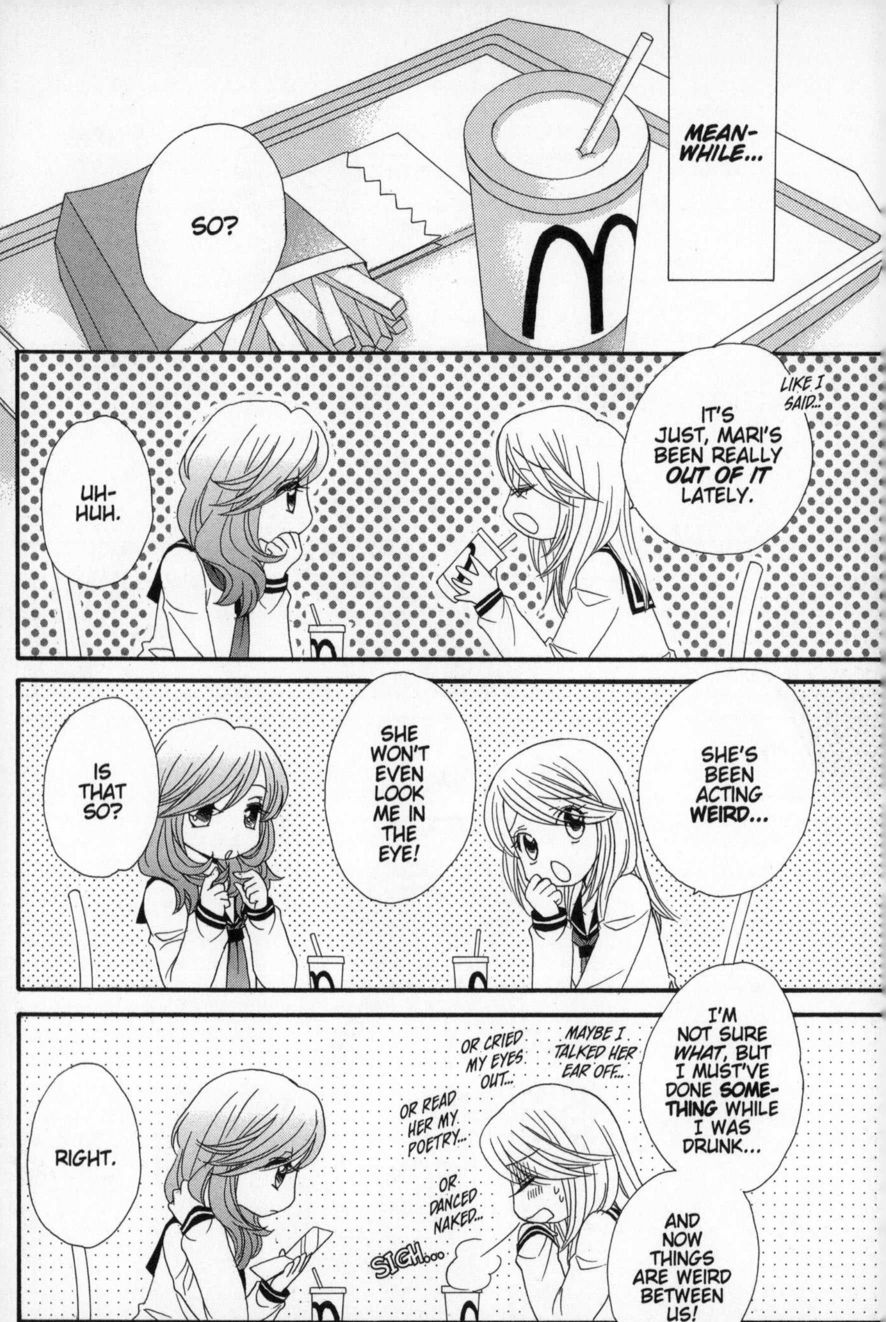
MEAN-WHILE...
SO?
LIKE I SAID...
IT'S JUST, MARI'S BEEN REALLY OUT OF IT LATELY.
UH-HUH.
SHE'S BEEN ACTING WEIRD...
SHE WON'T EVEN LOOK ME IN THE EYE!
IS THAT SO?
I'M NOT SURE WHAT, BUT I MUST'VE DONE SOMETHING WHILE I WAS DRUNK...
MAYBE I TALKED HER EAR OFF...
OR CRIED MY EYES OUT...
OR READ HER MY POETRY...
OR DANCED NAKED...
AND NOW THINGS ARE WEIRD BETWEEN US!
SIGH...
RIGHT.

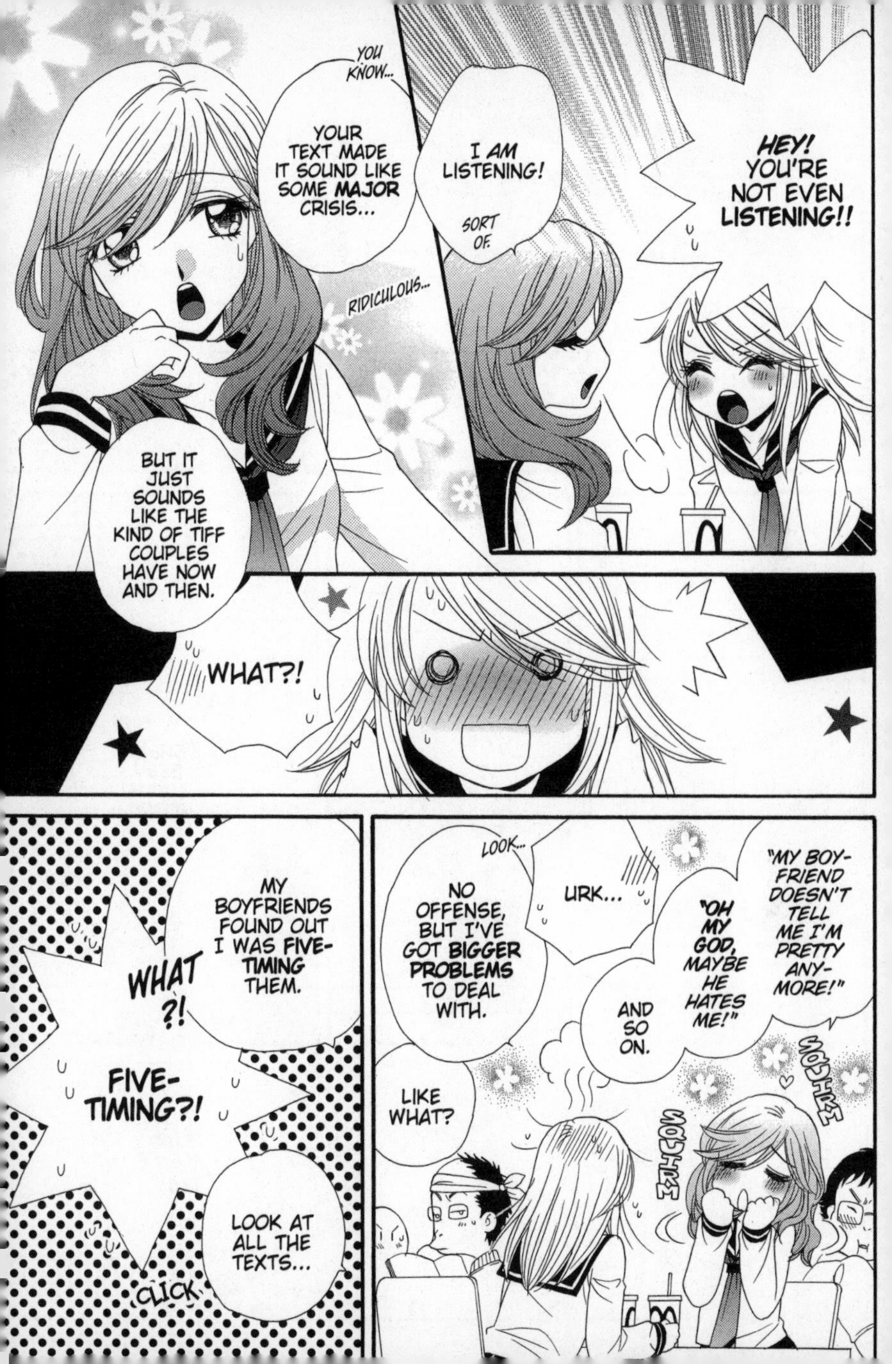

HEY! YOU'RE NOT EVEN LISTENING!!
I AM LISTENING!
SORT OF.
YOU KNOW...
YOUR TEXT MADE IT SOUND LIKE SOME MAJOR CRISIS...
RIDICULOUS...
BUT IT JUST SOUNDS LIKE THE KIND OF TIFF COUPLES HAVE NOW AND THEN.
WHAT?!
"MY BOY-FRIEND DOESN'T TELL ME I'M PRETTY ANY-MORE!"
"OH MY GOD, MAYBE HE HATES ME!"
AND SO ON.
URK...
LOOK...
NO OFFENSE, BUT I'VE GOT BIGGER PROBLEMS TO DEAL WITH.
LIKE WHAT?
LOOK AT ALL THE TEXTS...
CLICK
MY BOYFRIENDS FOUND OUT I WAS FIVE-TIMING THEM.
WHAT ?!
FIVE-TIMING?!

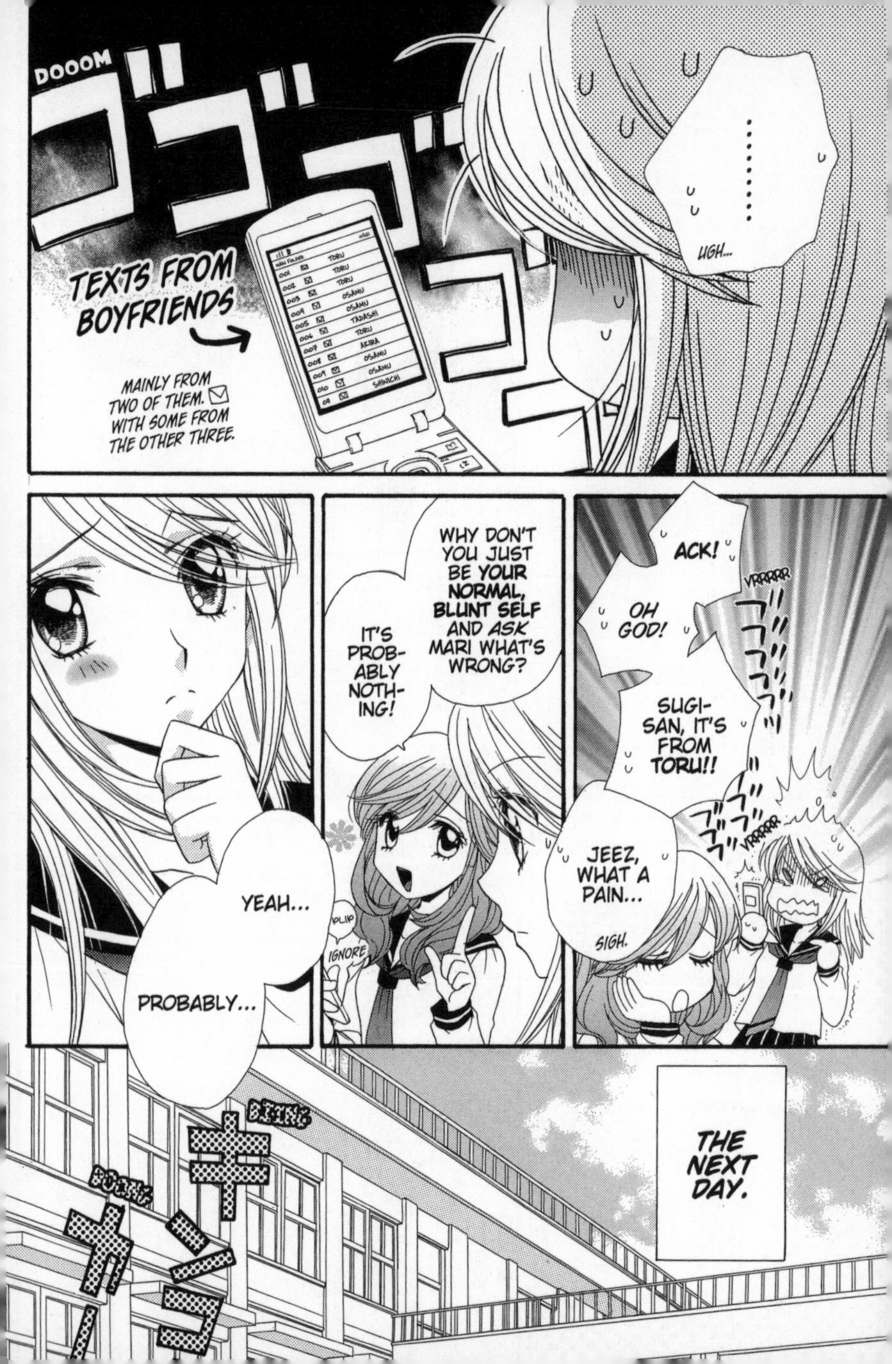

......
UGH...
DOOOM
TEXTS FROM BOYFRIENDS
MAINLY FROM TWO OF THEM. ✉ WITH SOME FROM THE OTHER THREE.
ACK!
OH GOD!
VRRRRRR
SUGI-SAN, IT'S FROM TORU!!
VRRRRRR
JEEZ, WHAT A PAIN...
SIGH.
WHY DON'T YOU JUST BE YOUR NORMAL, BLUNT SELF AND ASK MARI WHAT'S WRONG?
IT'S PROB-ABLY NOTH-ING!
FLIP
IGNORE
YEAH...
PROBABLY...
THE NEXT DAY.

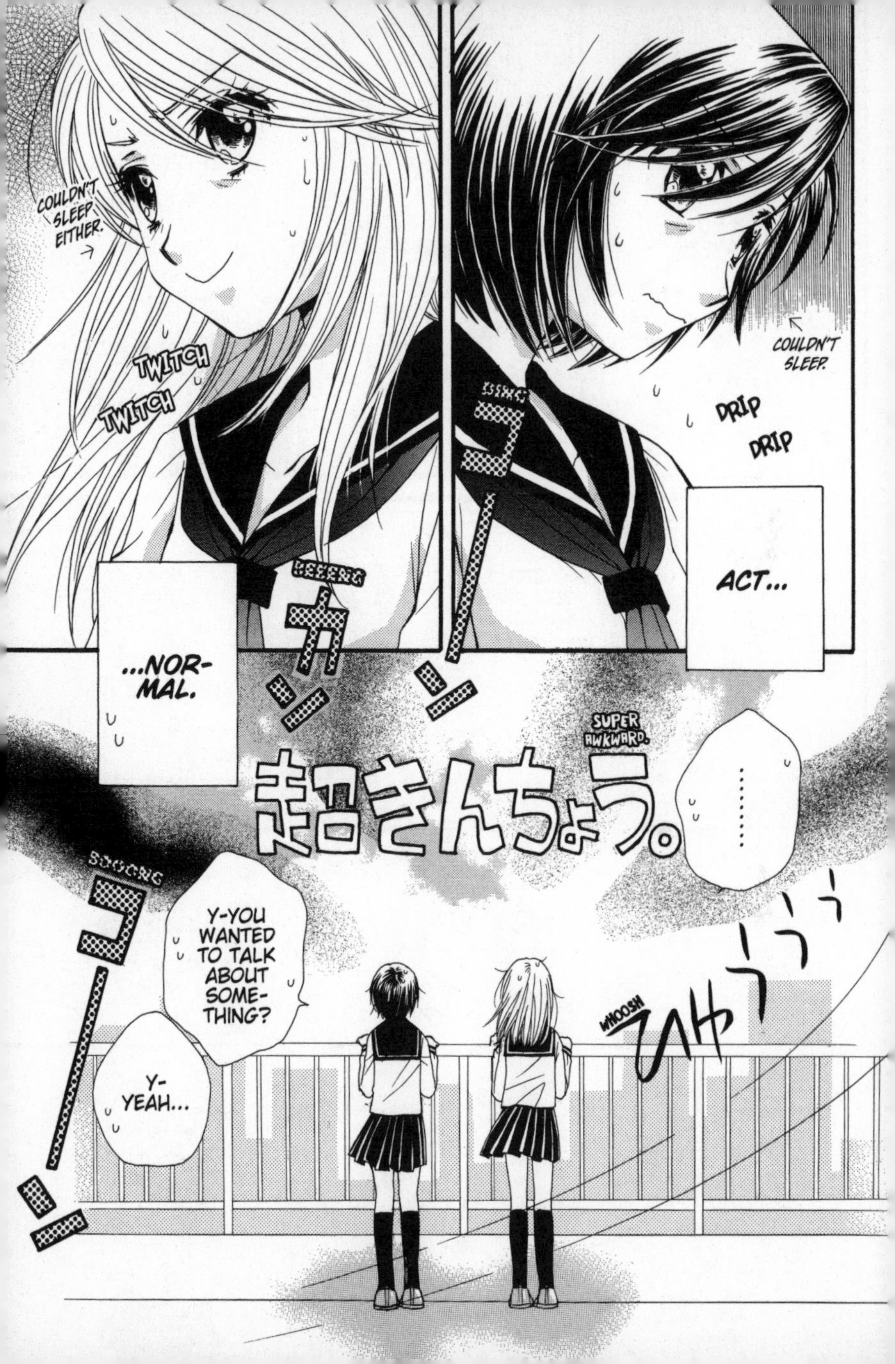
COULDN'T SLEEP.
DRIP
DRIP
ACT...
COULDN'T SLEEP EITHER.
TWITCH
TWITCH
...NOR-MAL.
SUPER AWKWARD.
超きんちょう。
......
Y-YOU WANTED TO TALK ABOUT SOME-THING?
Y-YEAH...
WHOOSH
ひゅう

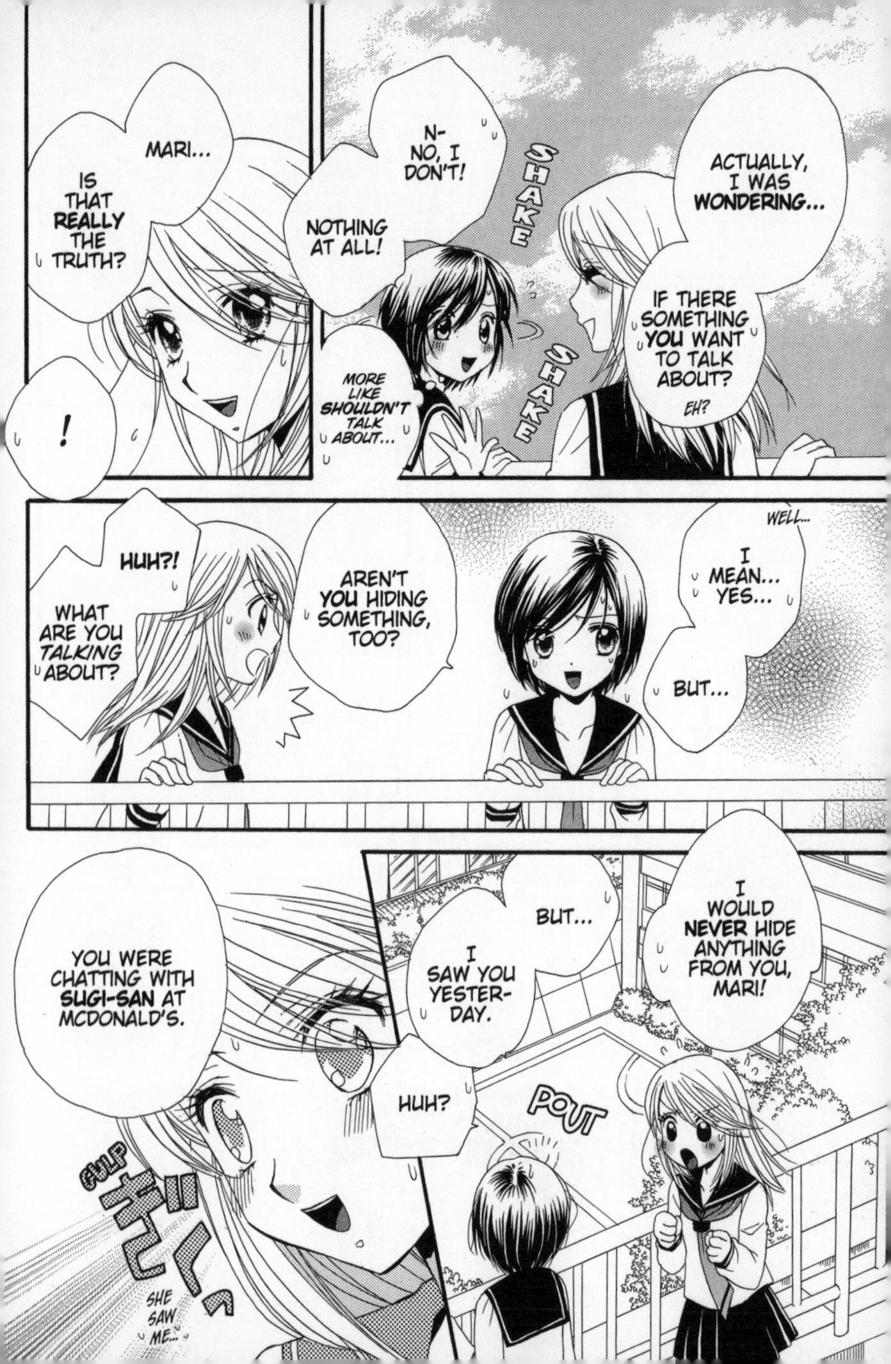
ACTUALLY, I WAS WONDERING...
IF THERE SOMETHING YOU WANT TO TALK ABOUT?
EH?
SHAKE
SHAKE
N- NO, I DON'T!
NOTHING AT ALL!
MORE LIKE SHOULDN'T TALK ABOUT...
MARI...
IS THAT REALLY THE TRUTH?
!
WELL...
I MEAN... YES...
BUT...
AREN'T YOU HIDING SOMETHING, TOO?
HUH?!
WHAT ARE YOU TALKING ABOUT?
I WOULD NEVER HIDE ANYTHING FROM YOU, MARI!
POUT
BUT...
I SAW YOU YESTER-DAY.
HUH?
YOU WERE CHATTING WITH SUGI-SAN AT MCDONALD'S.
GULP
SHE SAW ME...

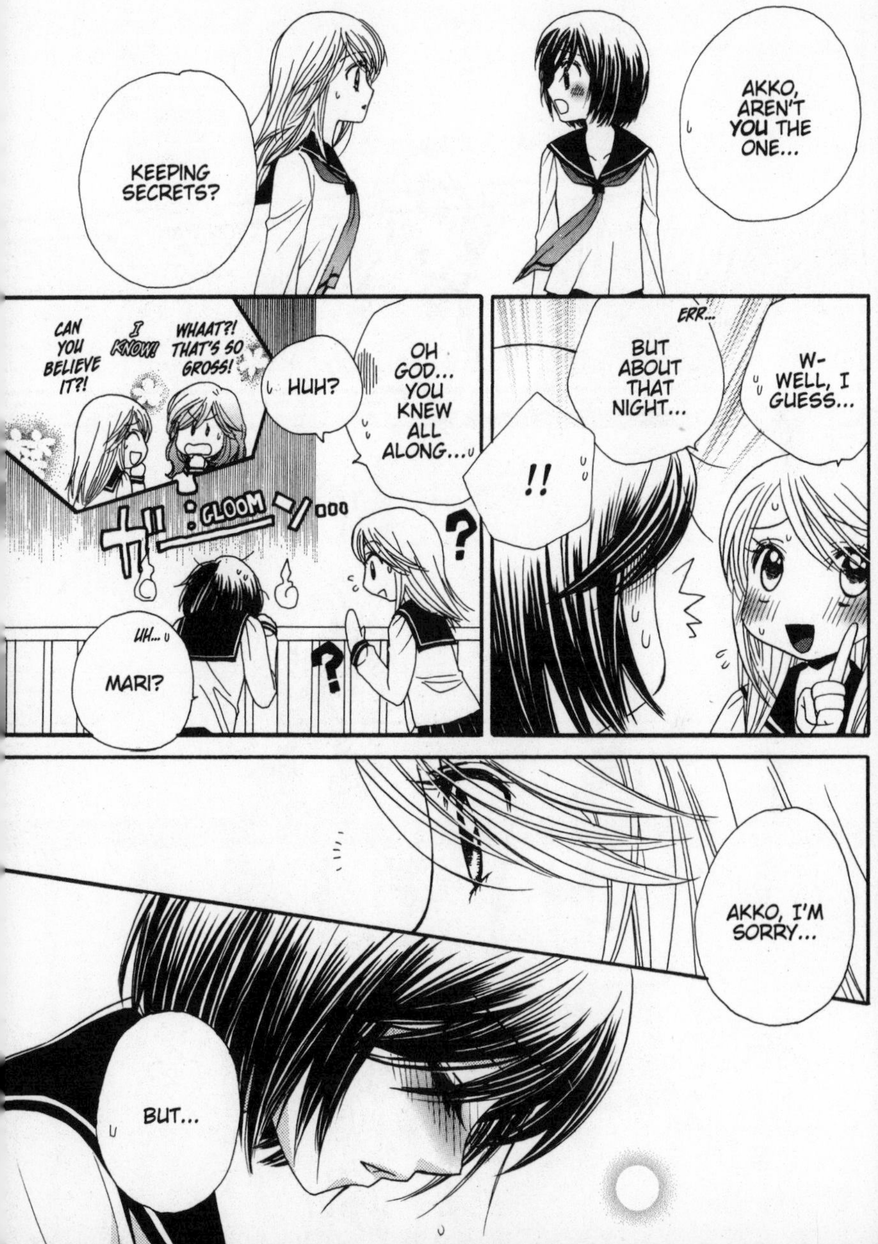
AKKO, AREN'T YOU THE ONE...
KEEPING SECRETS?
W-WELL, I GUESS...
ERR...
BUT ABOUT THAT NIGHT...
!!
OH GOD... YOU KNEW ALL ALONG...
HUH?
WHAAT?! THAT'S SO GROSS!
I KNOW!
CAN YOU BELIEVE IT?!
GLOOM
?
?
UH...
MARI?
AKKO, I'M SORRY...
BUT...

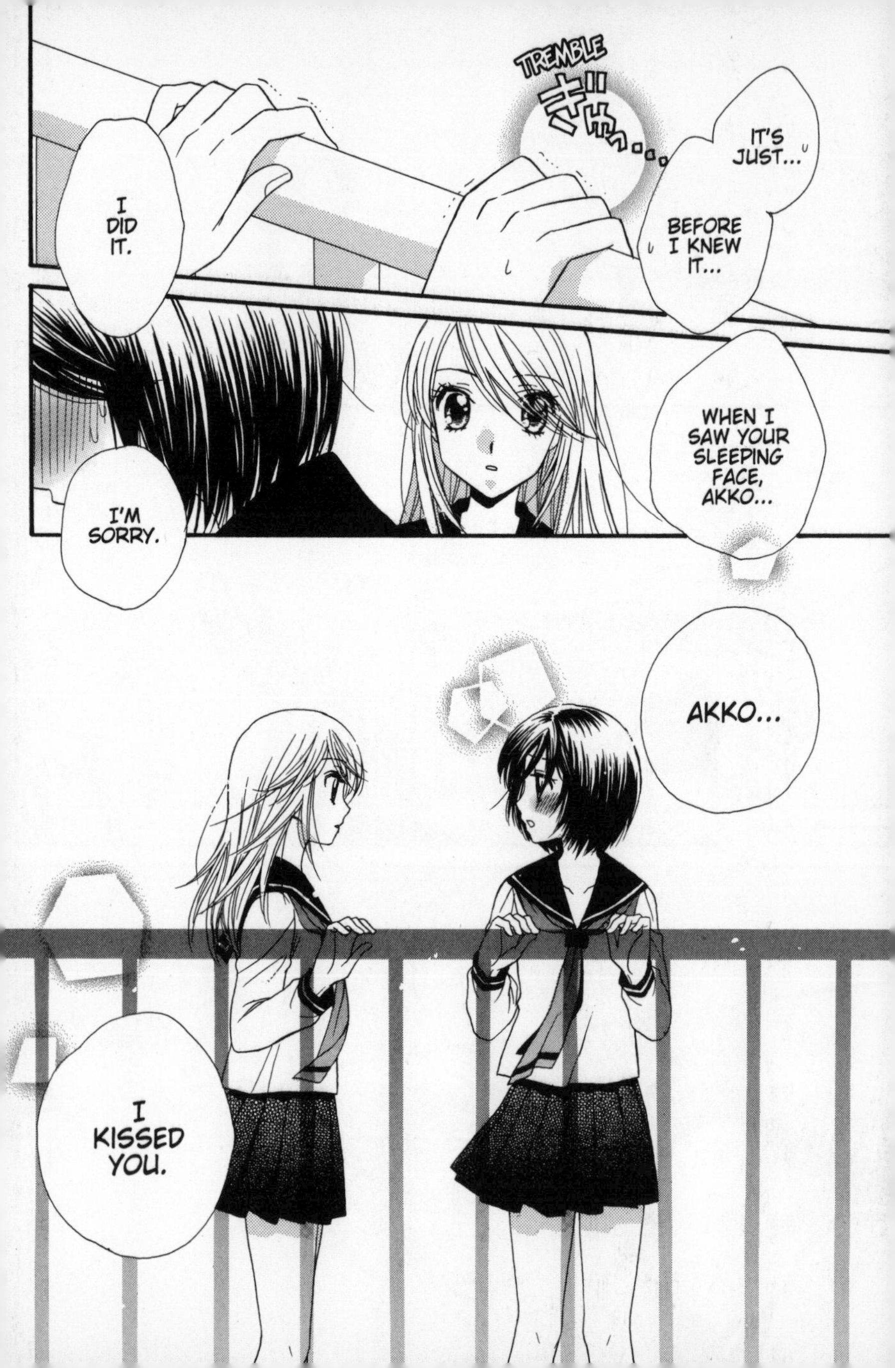

TREMBLE
ぎゅっ...
IT'S JUST...
BEFORE I KNEW IT...
I DID IT.
WHEN I SAW YOUR SLEEPING FACE, AKKO...
I'M SORRY.
AKKO...
I KISSED YOU.

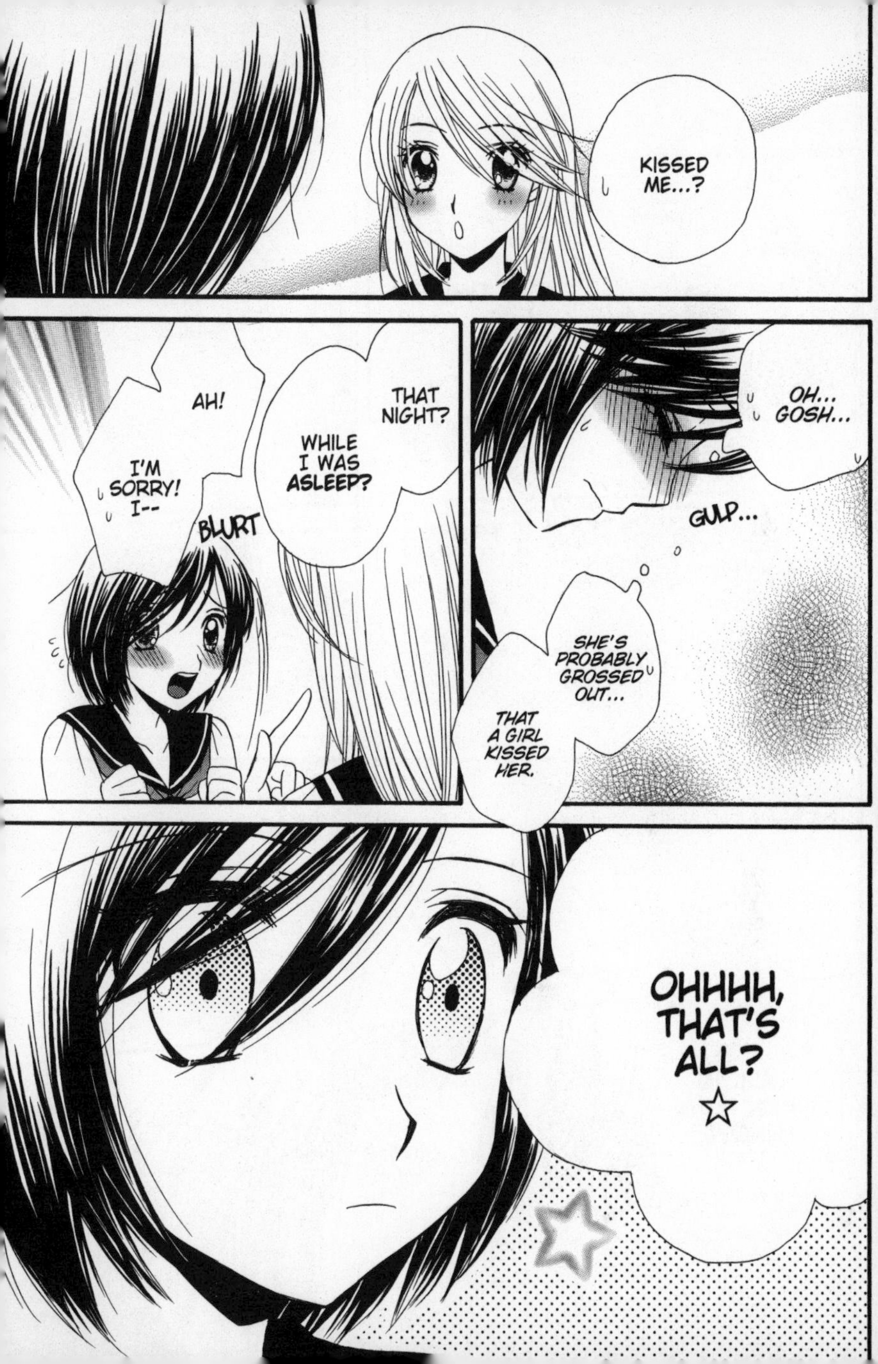
KISSED ME...?
OH... GOSH...
GULP...
SHE'S PROBABLY GROSSED OUT...
THAT A GIRL KISSED HER.
THAT NIGHT?
WHILE I WAS ASLEEP?
AH!
I'M SORRY! I--
BLURT
OHHHH, THAT'S ALL? ☆

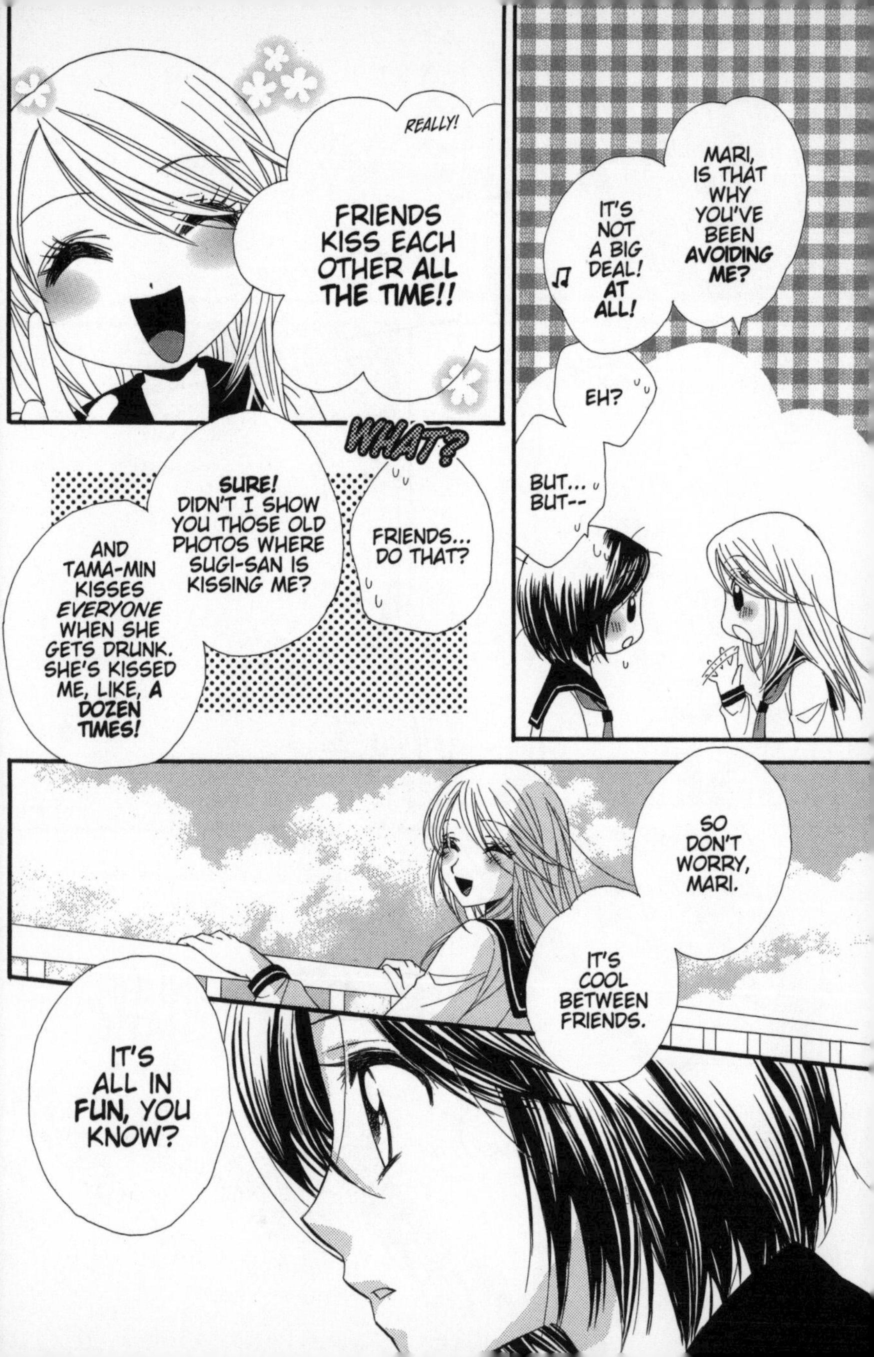

MARI, IS THAT WHY YOU'VE BEEN AVOIDING ME?
IT'S NOT A BIG DEAL! AT ALL! ♫
REALLY!
FRIENDS KISS EACH OTHER ALL THE TIME!!
EH?
BUT... BUT--
WHAT?
FRIENDS... DO THAT?
SURE! DIDN'T I SHOW YOU THOSE OLD PHOTOS WHERE SUGI-SAN IS KISSING ME?
AND TAMA-MIN KISSES EVERYONE WHEN SHE GETS DRUNK. SHE'S KISSED ME, LIKE, A DOZEN TIMES!
SO DON'T WORRY, MARI.
IT'S COOL BETWEEN FRIENDS.
IT'S ALL IN FUN, YOU KNOW?

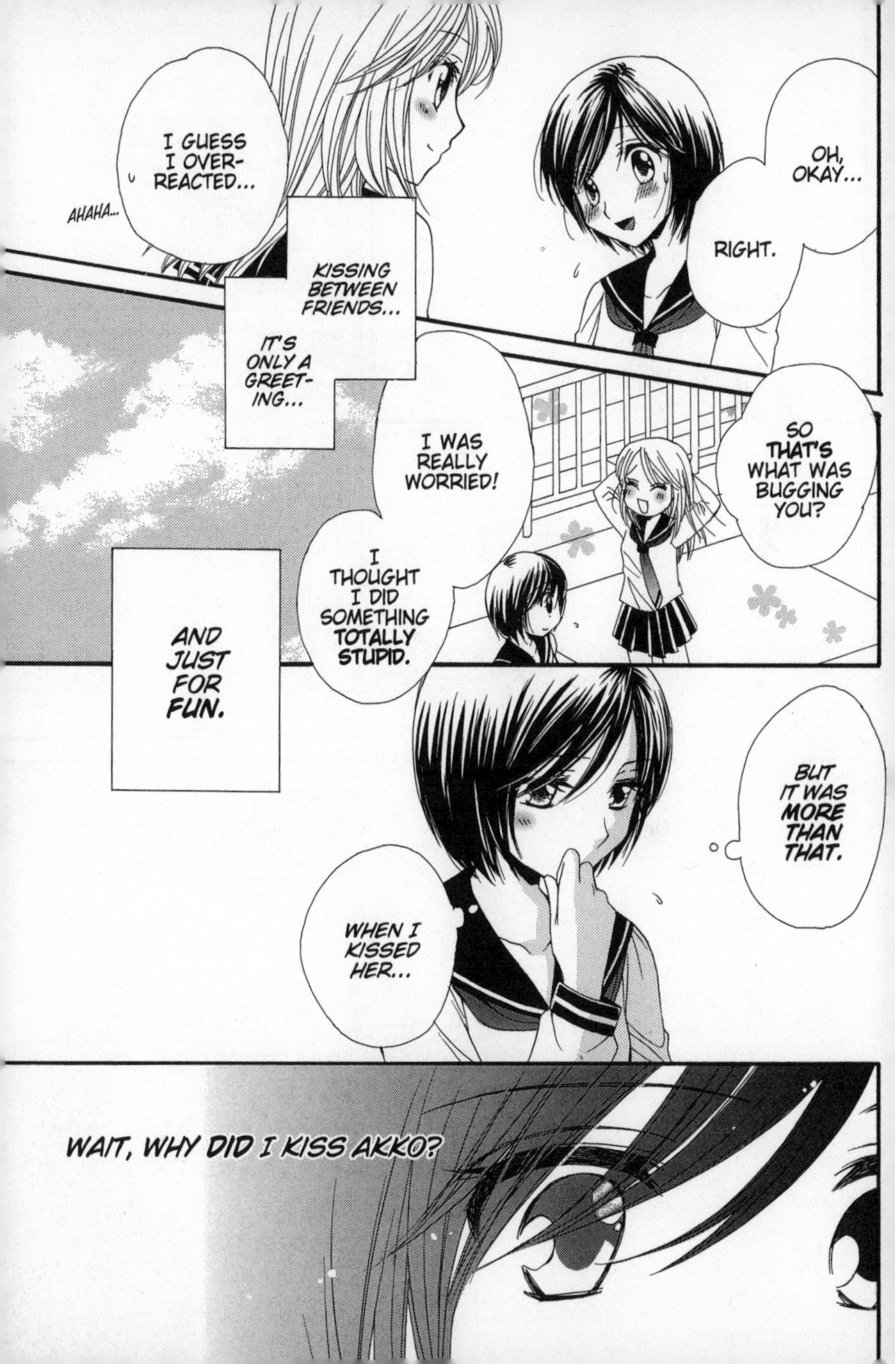
OH, OKAY...
RIGHT.
I GUESS I OVER-REACTED...
AHAHA...
KISSING BETWEEN FRIENDS...
IT'S ONLY A GREETING...
SO THAT'S WHAT WAS BUGGING YOU?
I WAS REALLY WORRIED!
I THOUGHT I DID SOMETHING TOTALLY STUPID.
AND JUST FOR FUN.
BUT IT WAS MORE THAN THAT.
WHEN I KISSED HER...
WAIT, WHY DID I KISS AKKO?

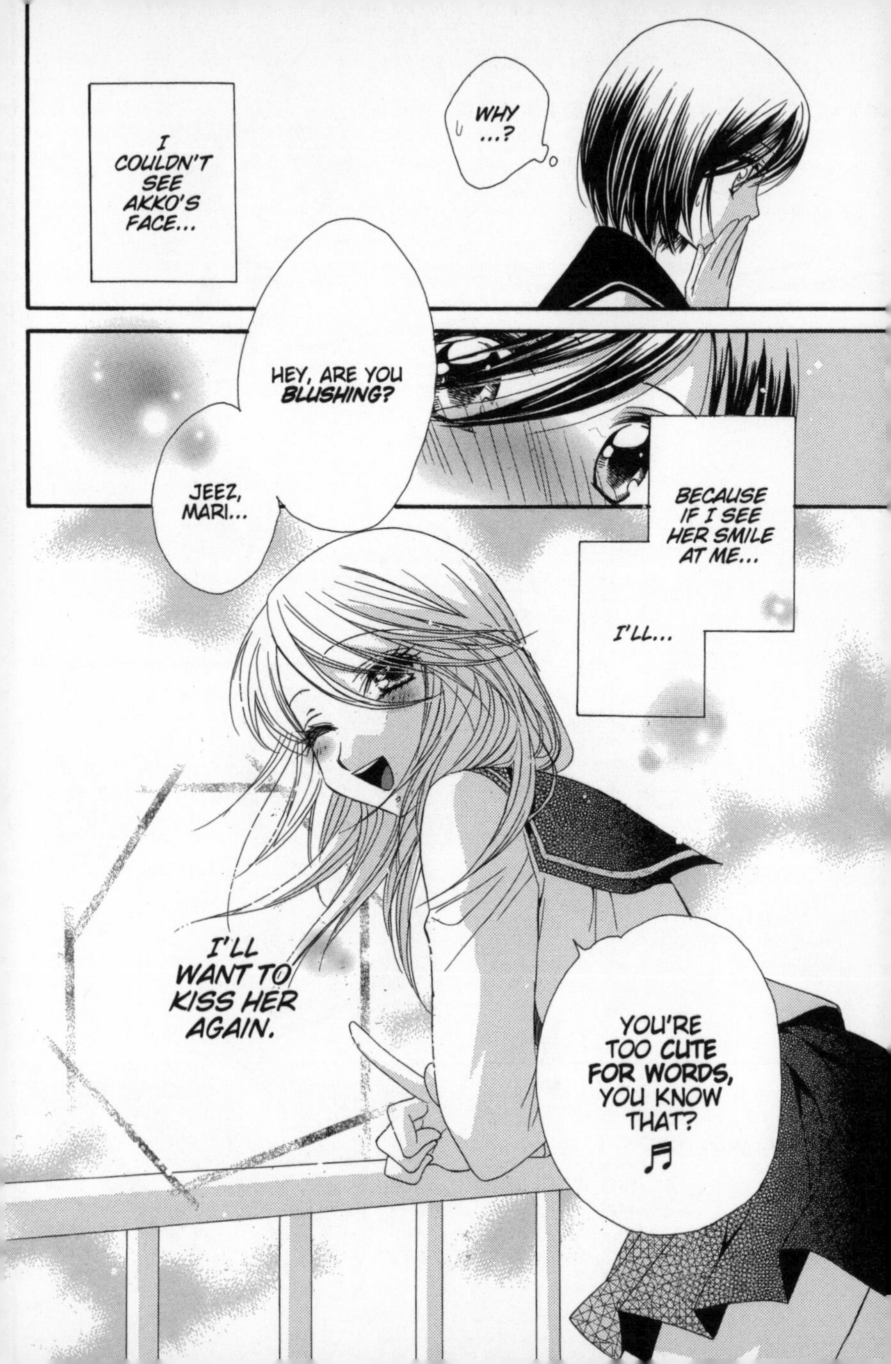
WHY ...?
I COULDN'T SEE AKKO'S FACE...
HEY, ARE YOU *BLUSHING?*
JEEZ, MARI...
BECAUSE IF I SEE HER SMILE AT ME...
I'LL...
YOU'RE TOO CUTE FOR WORDS, YOU KNOW THAT? ♬
I'LL WANT TO KISS HER AGAIN.

WINTER UNIFORM

THE UNIFORM
COLLECTION

GIRL FRIENDS －ガールフレンズ－

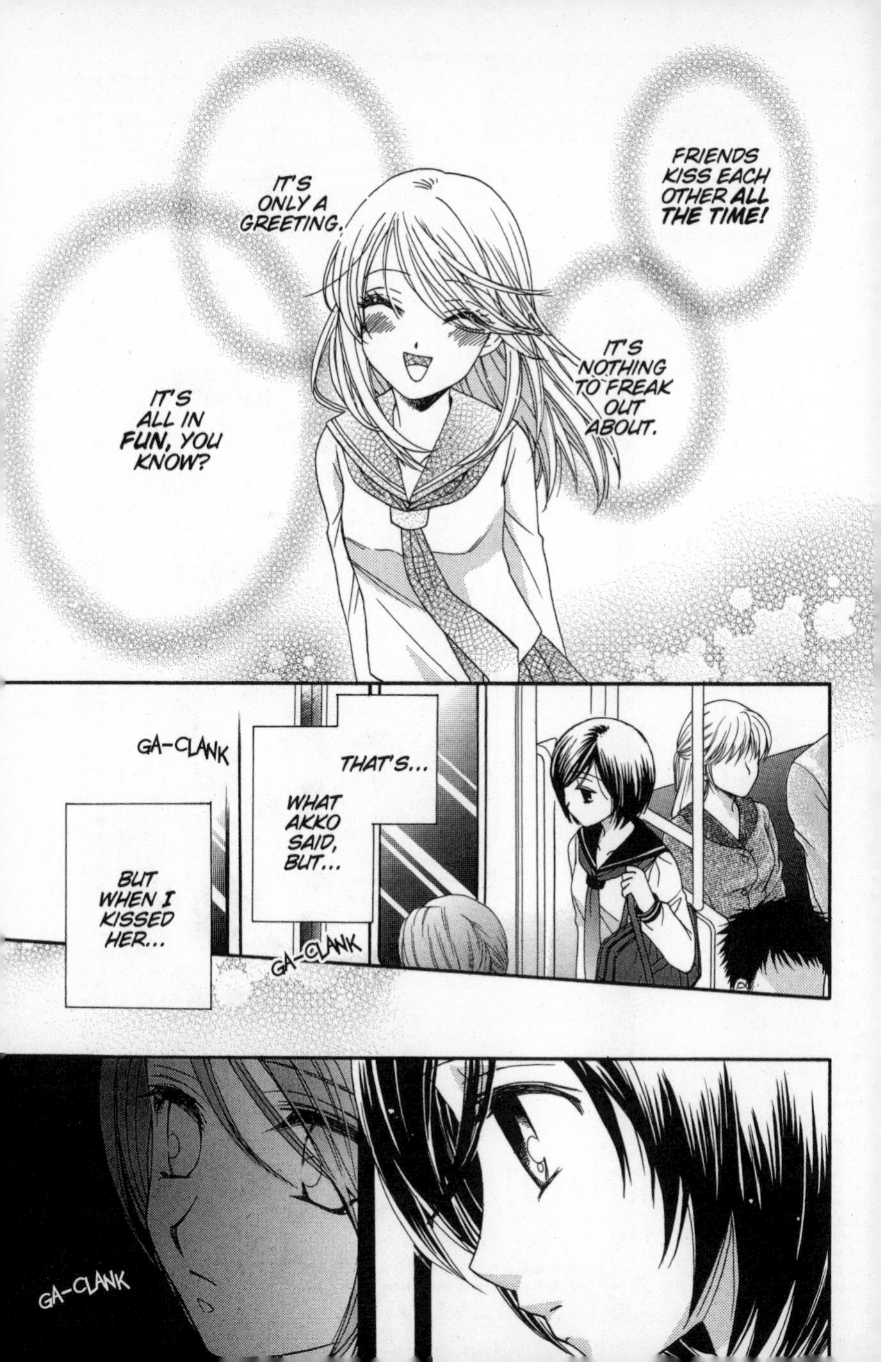
FRIENDS KISS EACH OTHER ALL THE TIME!
IT'S ONLY A GREETING.
IT'S NOTHING TO FREAK OUT ABOUT.
IT'S ALL IN FUN, YOU KNOW?
THAT'S...
WHAT AKKO SAID, BUT...
GA-CLANK
BUT WHEN I KISSED HER...
GA-CLANK
GA-CLANK

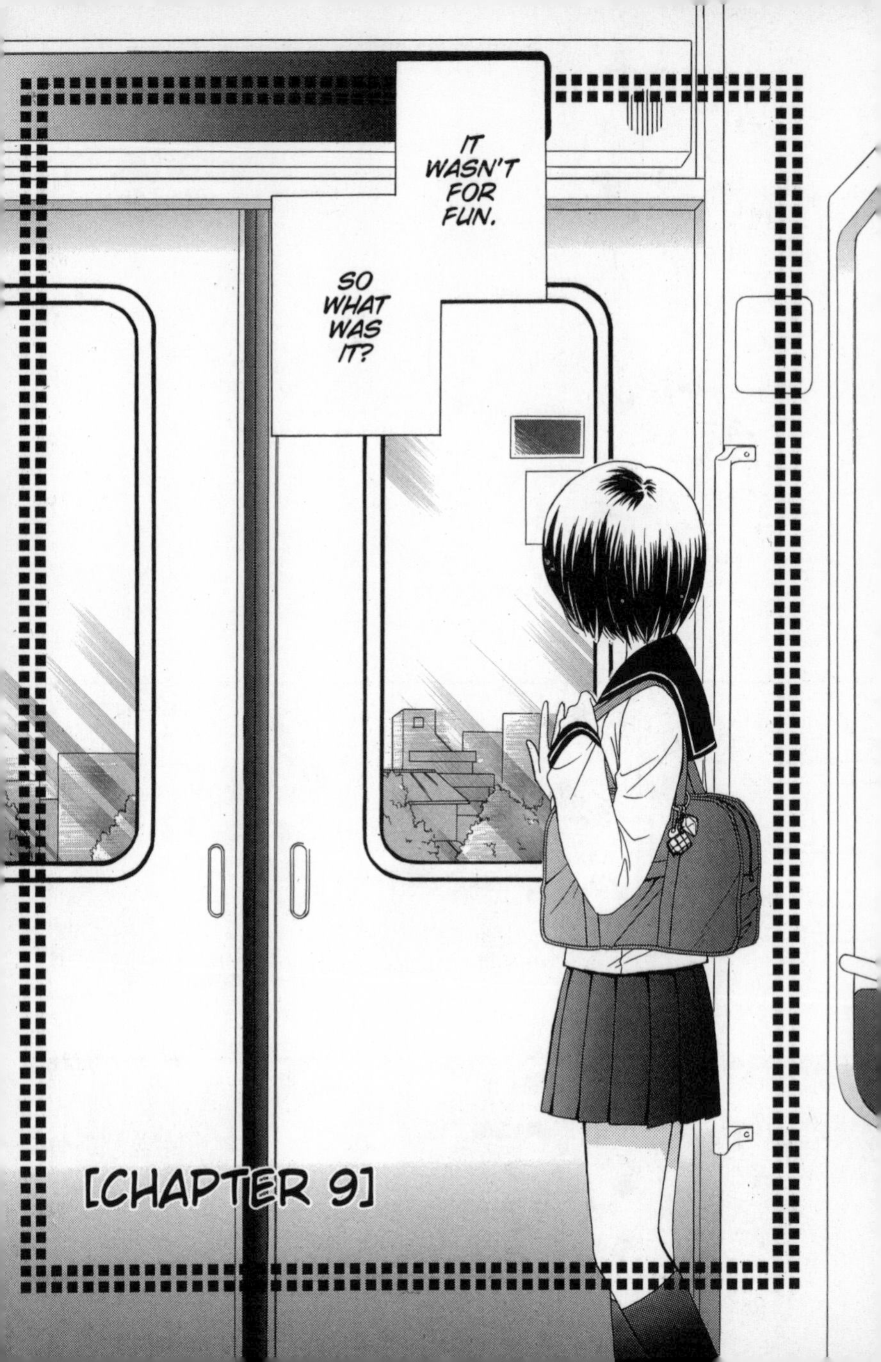
IT WASN'T FOR FUN.
SO WHAT WAS IT?
[CHAPTER 9]

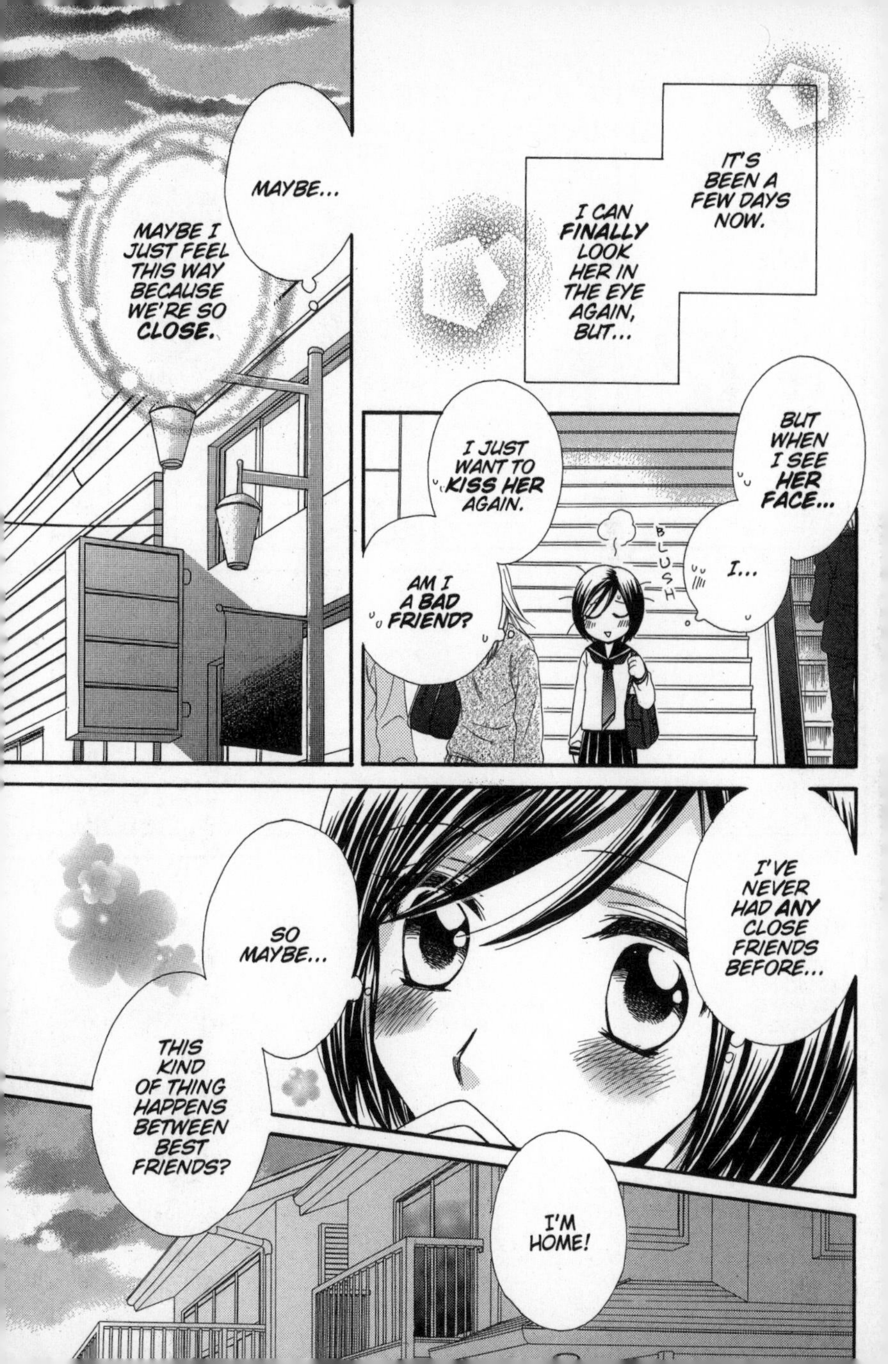
IT'S BEEN A FEW DAYS NOW.
I CAN FINALLY LOOK HER IN THE EYE AGAIN, BUT...
BUT WHEN I SEE HER FACE...
I...
BLUSH
I JUST WANT TO KISS HER AGAIN.
AM I A BAD FRIEND?
MAYBE...
MAYBE I JUST FEEL THIS WAY BECAUSE WE'RE SO CLOSE.
I'VE NEVER HAD ANY CLOSE FRIENDS BEFORE...
SO MAYBE...
THIS KIND OF THING HAPPENS BETWEEN BEST FRIENDS?
I'M HOME!

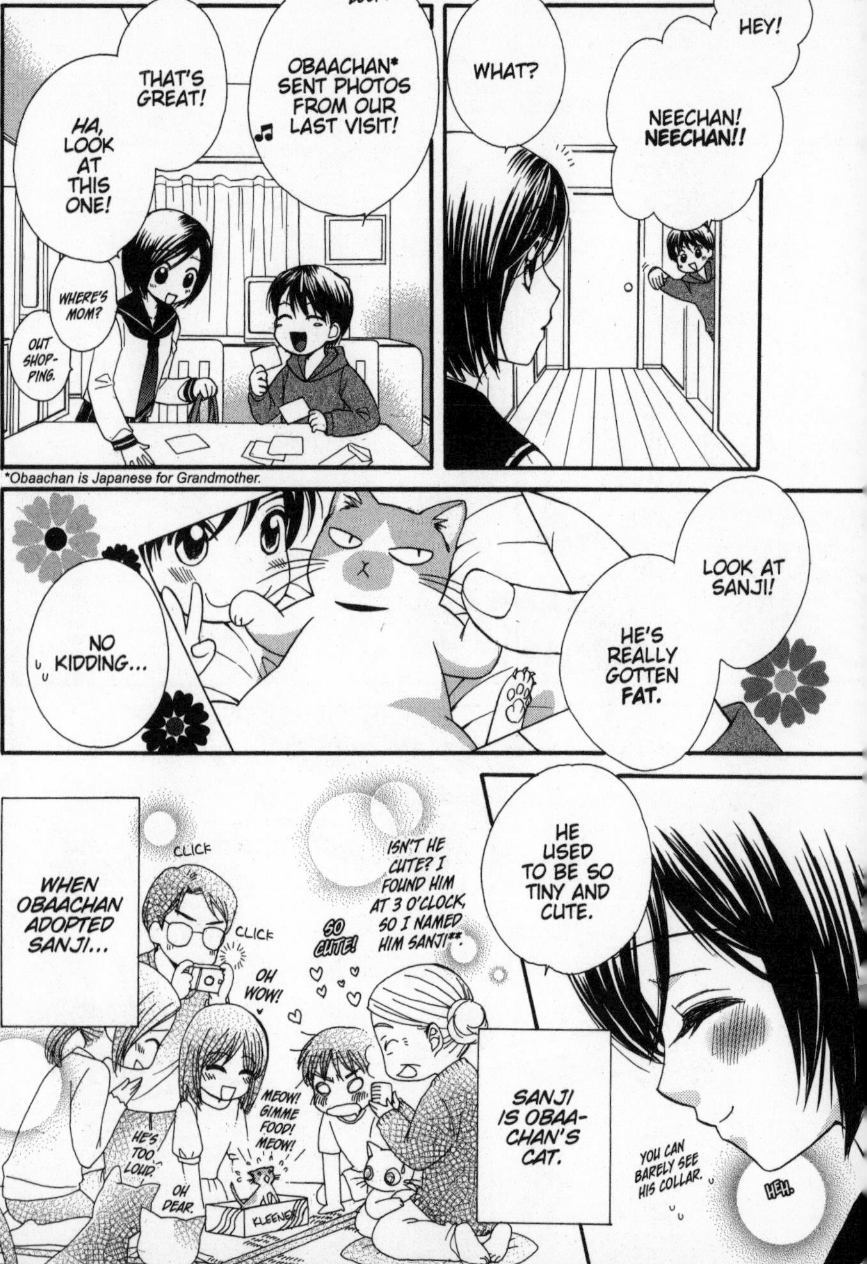

HEY!
NEECHAN! NEECHAN!!
WHAT?
LOOK!
OBAACHAN* SENT PHOTOS FROM OUR LAST VISIT! ♫
THAT'S GREAT!
HA, LOOK AT THIS ONE!
WHERE'S MOM?
OUT SHOP-PING.
LOOK AT SANJI!
HE'S REALLY GOTTEN FAT.
NO KIDDING...
HE USED TO BE SO TINY AND CUTE.
YOU CAN BARELY SEE HIS COLLAR.
HEH.
SANJI IS OBAA-CHAN'S CAT.
WHEN OBAACHAN ADOPTED SANJI...
ISN'T HE CUTE? I FOUND HIM AT 3 O'CLOCK, SO I NAMED HIM SANJI**.
CLICK
CLICK
SO CUTE!
OH WOW!
MEOW! GIMME FOOD! MEOW!
HE'S TOO LOUD.
OH DEAR.
KLEENEX

*Obaachan is Japanese for Grandmother.

**Sanji (サンジ) means 3 o'clock.

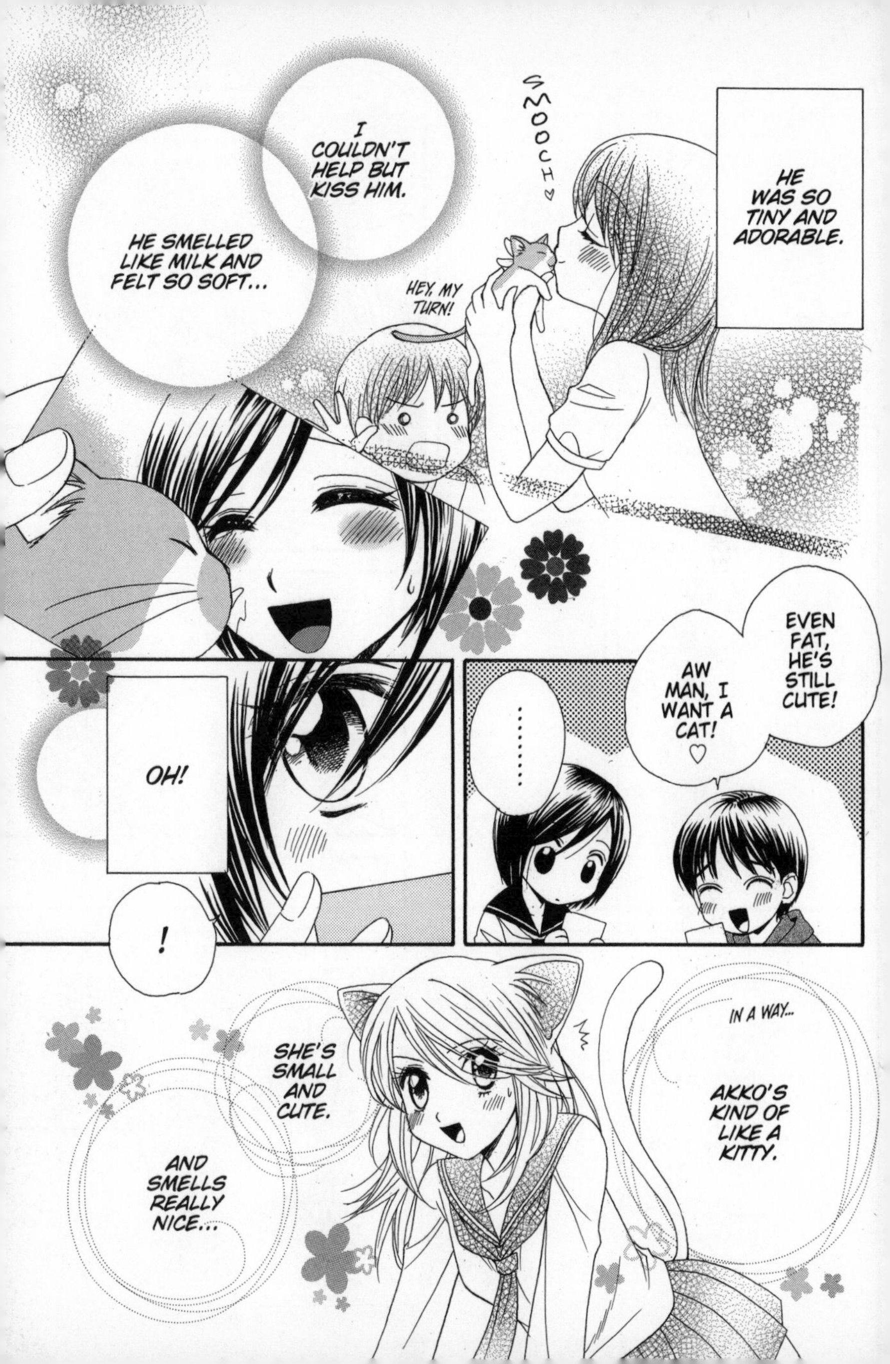
HE WAS SO TINY AND ADORABLE.
SMOOCH♡
HEY, MY TURN!
I COULDN'T HELP BUT KISS HIM.
HE SMELLED LIKE MILK AND FELT SO SOFT...
EVEN FAT, HE'S STILL CUTE!
AW MAN, I WANT A CAT! ♡
......
OH!
!
IN A WAY...
AKKO'S KIND OF LIKE A KITTY.
SHE'S SMALL AND CUTE.
AND SMELLS REALLY NICE...

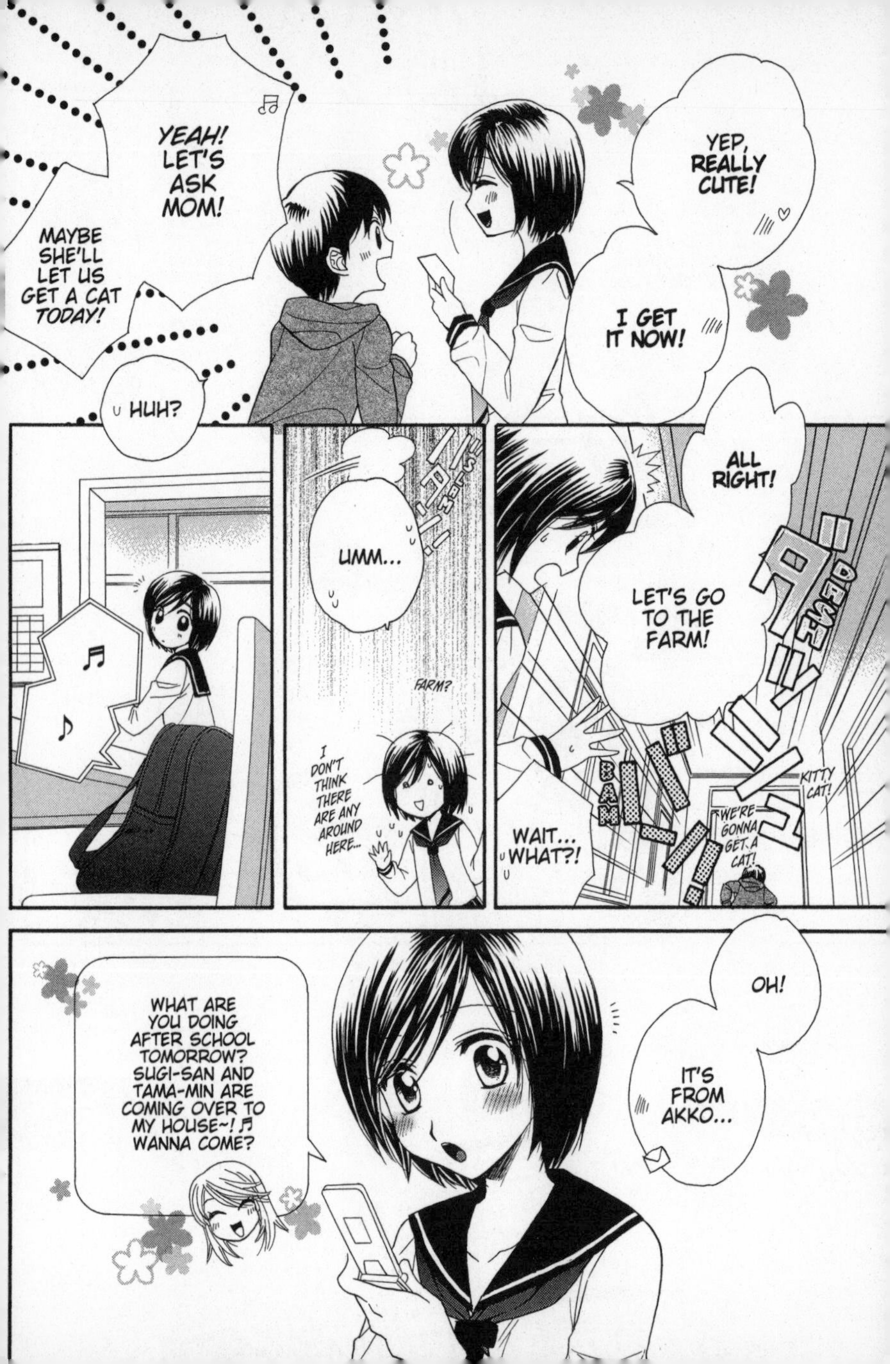
YEP, REALLY CUTE!
I GET IT NOW!
YEAH! LET'S ASK MOM!
MAYBE SHE'LL LET US GET A CAT TODAY!
HUH?
ALL RIGHT!
LET'S GO TO THE FARM!
DASH
BAM
KITTY CAT!
WE'RE GONNA GET A CAT!
WAIT... WHAT?!
SLAM
UMM...
FARM?
I DON'T THINK THERE ARE ANY AROUND HERE...
OH!
IT'S FROM AKKO...
WHAT ARE YOU DOING AFTER SCHOOL TOMORROW? SUGI-SAN AND TAMA-MIN ARE COMING OVER TO MY HOUSE~! ♬ WANNA COME?

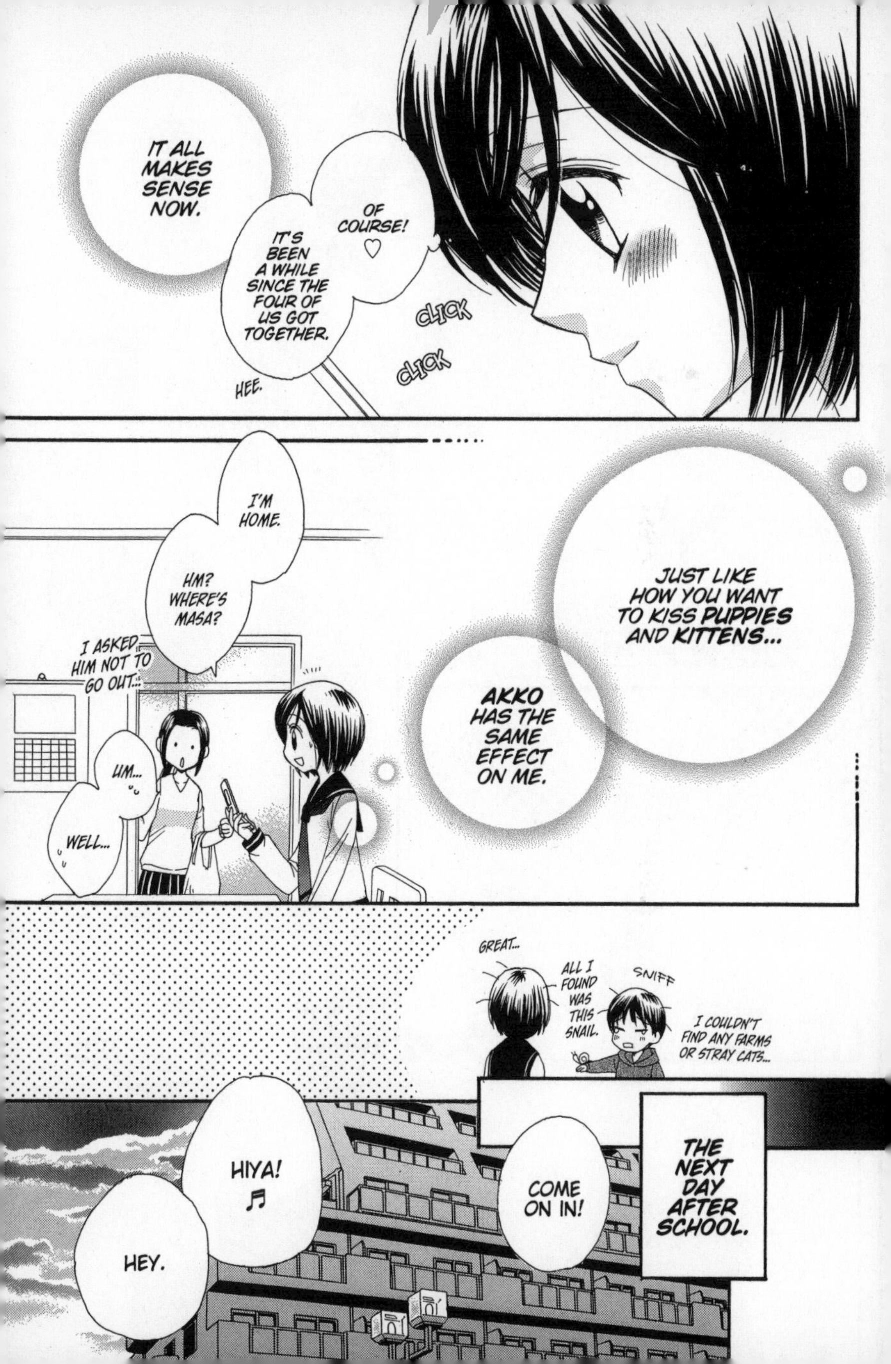
OF COURSE! ♡
IT'S BEEN A WHILE SINCE THE FOUR OF US GOT TOGETHER.
CLICK
CLICK
HEE.
IT ALL MAKES SENSE NOW.
JUST LIKE HOW YOU WANT TO KISS PUPPIES AND KITTENS...
AKKO HAS THE SAME EFFECT ON ME.
I'M HOME.
HM? WHERE'S MASA?
I ASKED HIM NOT TO GO OUT...
UM...
WELL...
SNIFF
I COULDN'T FIND ANY FARMS OR STRAY CATS...
GREAT...
ALL I FOUND WAS THIS SNAIL.
THE NEXT DAY AFTER SCHOOL.
COME ON IN!
HIYA! ♫
HEY.

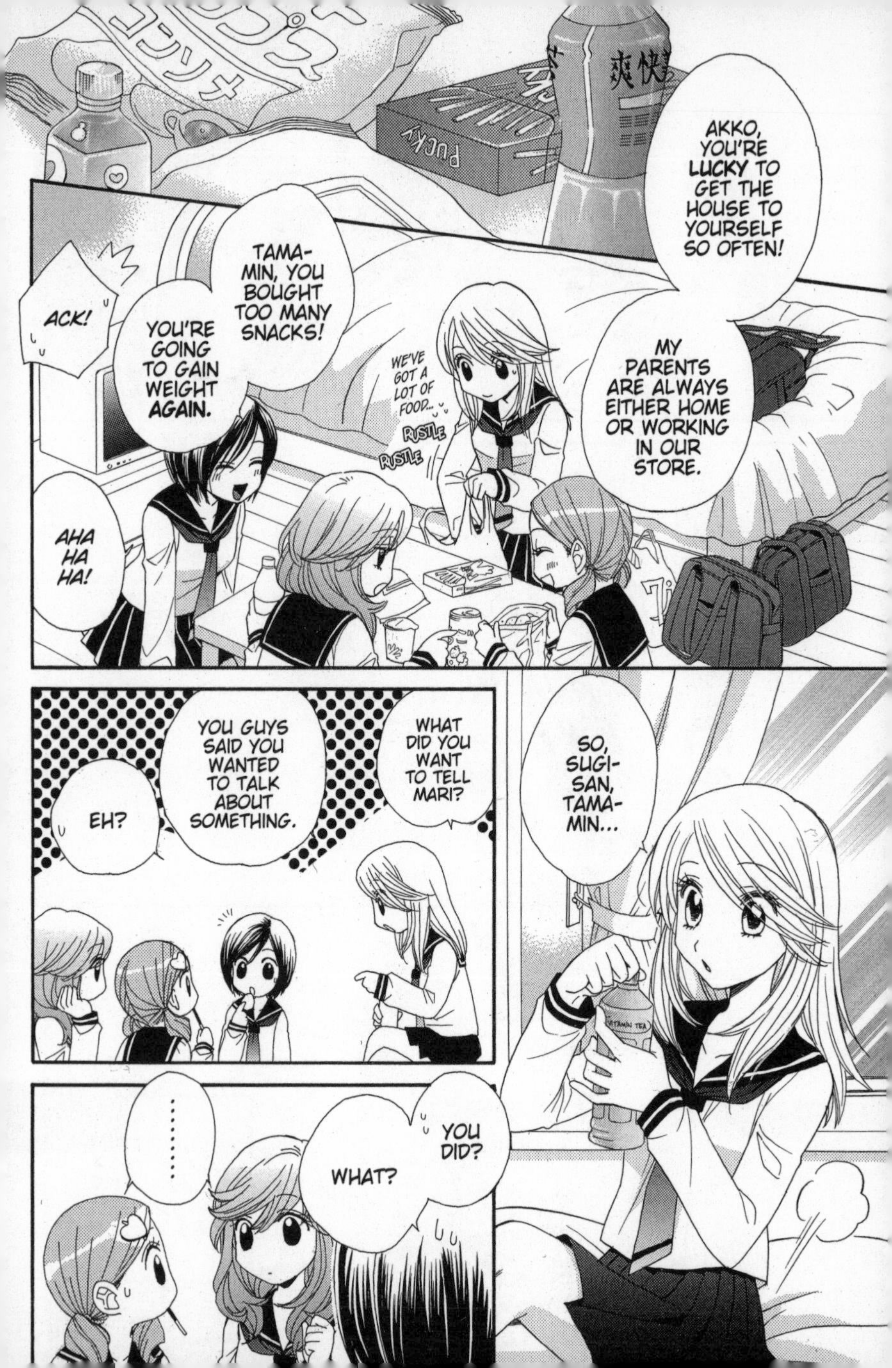
AKKO, YOU'RE LUCKY TO GET THE HOUSE TO YOURSELF SO OFTEN!
MY PARENTS ARE ALWAYS EITHER HOME OR WORKING IN OUR STORE.
WE'VE GOT A LOT OF FOOD...
RUSTLE
RUSTLE
TAMA-MIN, YOU BOUGHT TOO MANY SNACKS!
YOU'RE GOING TO GAIN WEIGHT AGAIN.
ACK!
AHA HA HA!
SO, SUGI-SAN, TAMA-MIN...
WHAT DID YOU WANT TO TELL MARI?
YOU GUYS SAID YOU WANTED TO TALK ABOUT SOMETHING.
EH?
YOU DID?
WHAT?
......

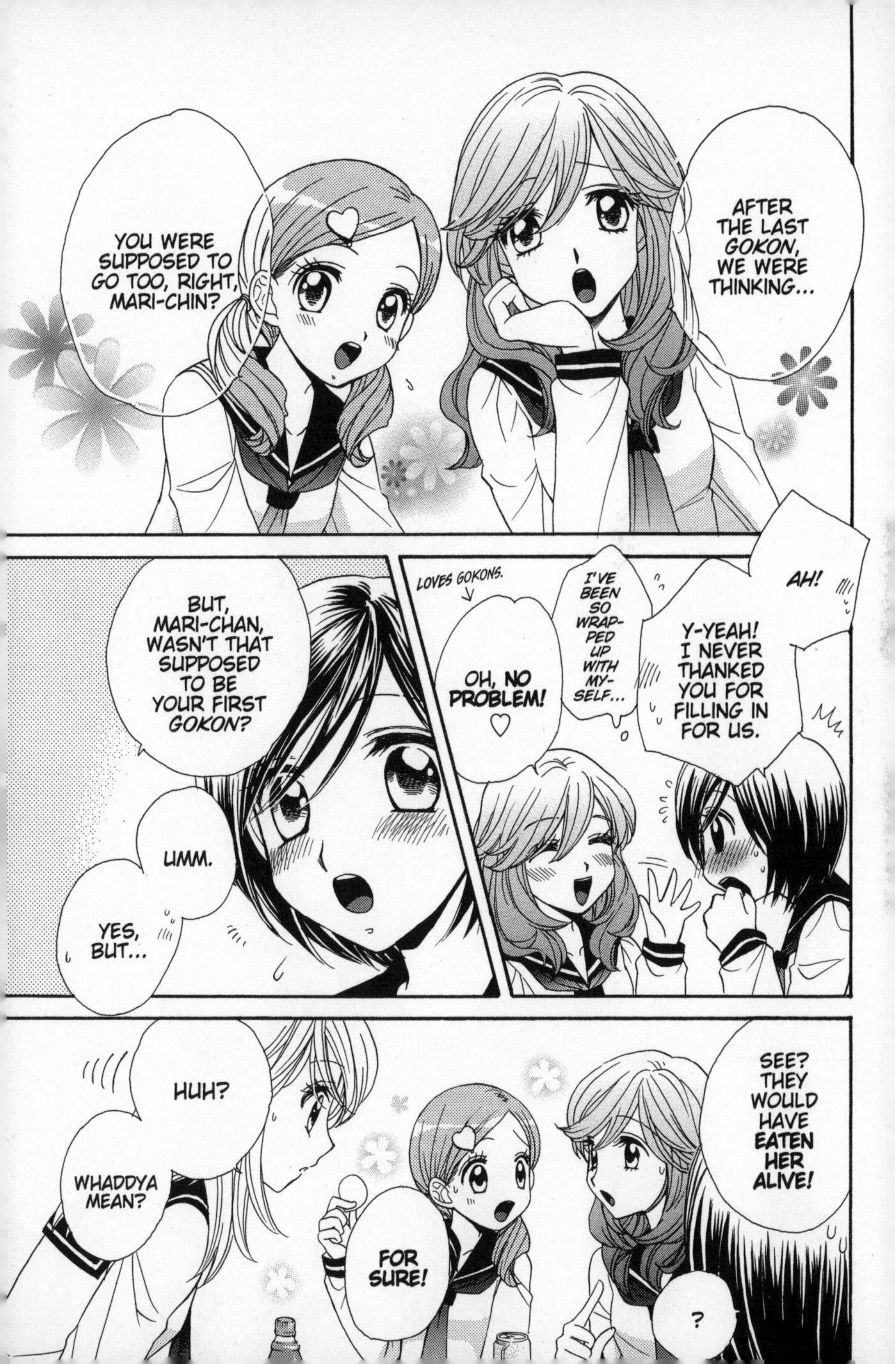
AFTER THE LAST GOKON, WE WERE THINKING...
YOU WERE SUPPOSED TO GO TOO, RIGHT, MARI-CHIN?
AH!
Y-YEAH! I NEVER THANKED YOU FOR FILLING IN FOR US.
I'VE BEEN SO WRAP-PED UP WITH MY-SELF...
LOVES GOKONS.
OH, NO PROBLEM! ♡
BUT, MARI-CHAN, WASN'T THAT SUPPOSED TO BE YOUR FIRST GOKON?
UMM.
YES, BUT...
SEE? THEY WOULD HAVE EATEN HER ALIVE!
?
FOR SURE!
HUH?
WHADDYA MEAN?

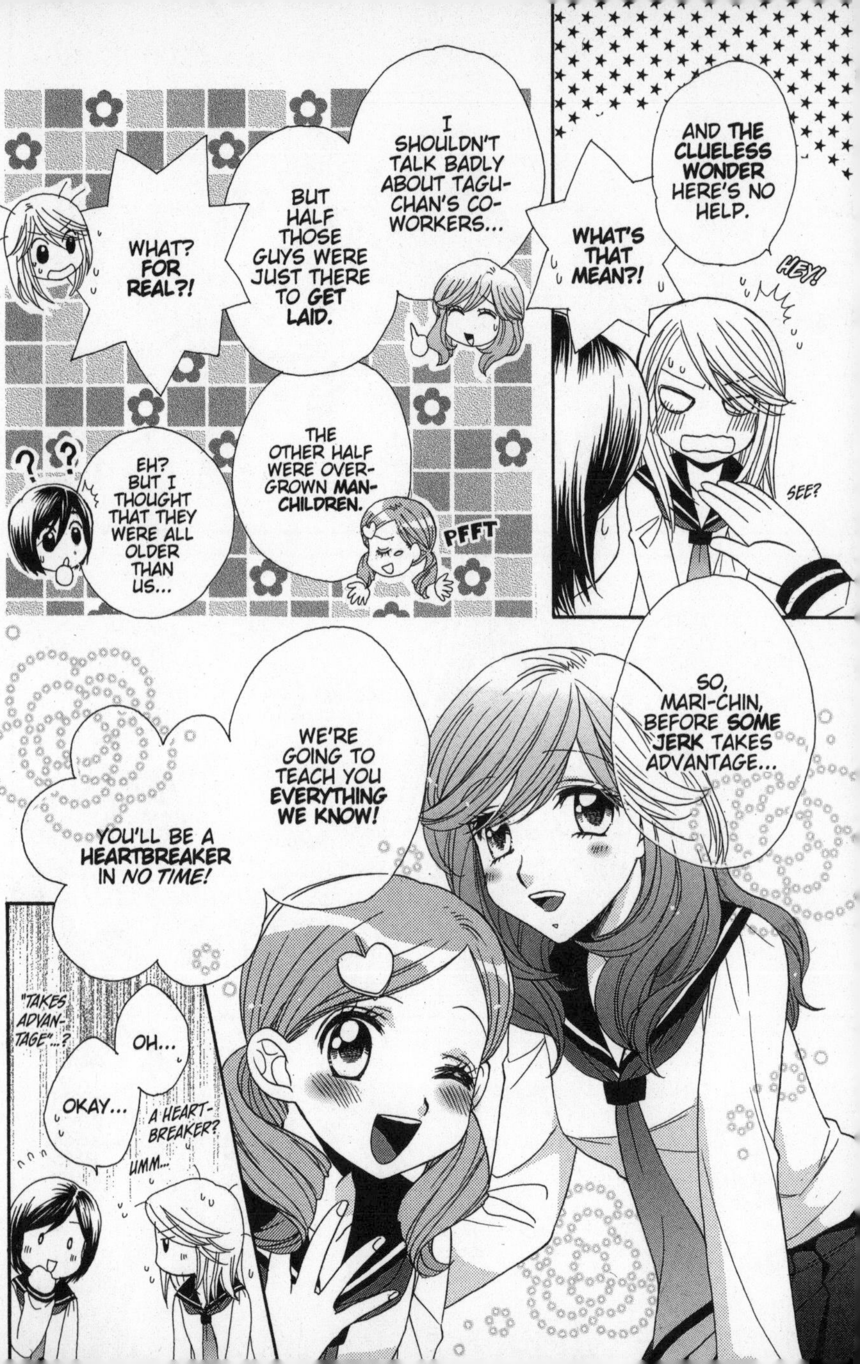
AND THE CLUELESS WONDER HERE'S NO HELP.
WHAT'S THAT MEAN?!
HEY!
SEE?
I SHOULDN'T TALK BADLY ABOUT TAGU-CHAN'S CO-WORKERS...
BUT HALF THOSE GUYS WERE JUST THERE TO GET LAID.
WHAT? FOR REAL?!
THE OTHER HALF WERE OVER-GROWN MAN-CHILDREN.
PFFT
EH? BUT I THOUGHT THAT THEY WERE ALL OLDER THAN US...
SO, MARI-CHIN, BEFORE SOME JERK TAKES ADVANTAGE...
WE'RE GOING TO TEACH YOU EVERYTHING WE KNOW!
YOU'LL BE A HEARTBREAKER IN NO TIME!
"TAKES ADVANTAGE"...?
OH...
OKAY...
A HEART-BREAKER?
UMM...

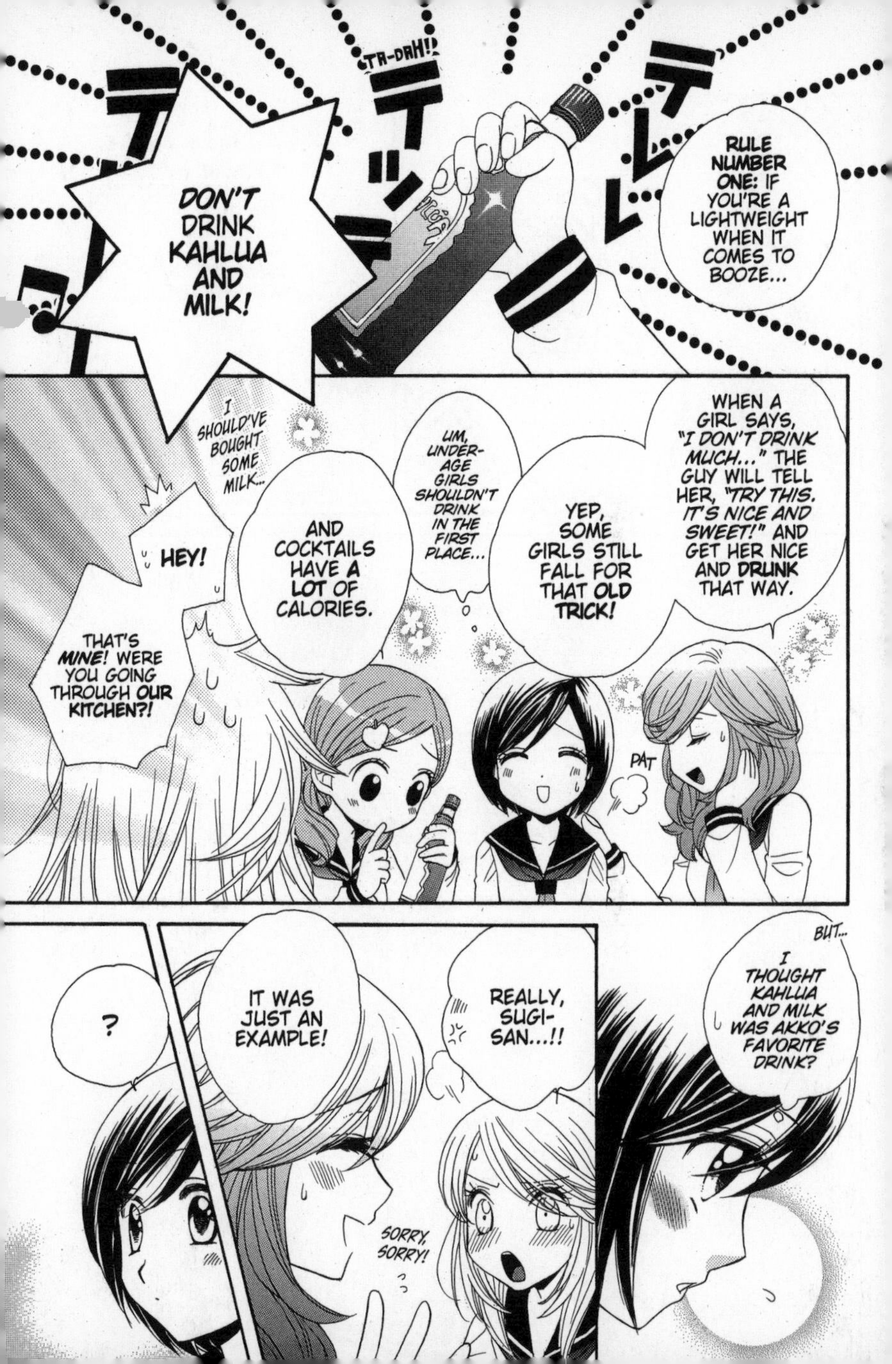
TA-DAH!!
RULE NUMBER ONE: IF YOU'RE A LIGHTWEIGHT WHEN IT COMES TO BOOZE...
DON'T DRINK KAHLUA AND MILK!
WHEN A GIRL SAYS, "I DON'T DRINK MUCH..." THE GUY WILL TELL HER, "TRY THIS. IT'S NICE AND SWEET!" AND GET HER NICE AND DRUNK THAT WAY.
PAT
YEP, SOME GIRLS STILL FALL FOR THAT OLD TRICK!
UM, UNDER-AGE GIRLS SHOULDN'T DRINK IN THE FIRST PLACE...
AND COCKTAILS HAVE A LOT OF CALORIES.
I SHOULD'VE BOUGHT SOME MILK...
HEY!
THAT'S MINE! WERE YOU GOING THROUGH OUR KITCHEN?!
BUT...
I THOUGHT KAHLUA AND MILK WAS AKKO'S FAVORITE DRINK?
REALLY, SUGI-SAN...!!
IT WAS JUST AN EXAMPLE!
SORRY, SORRY!
?

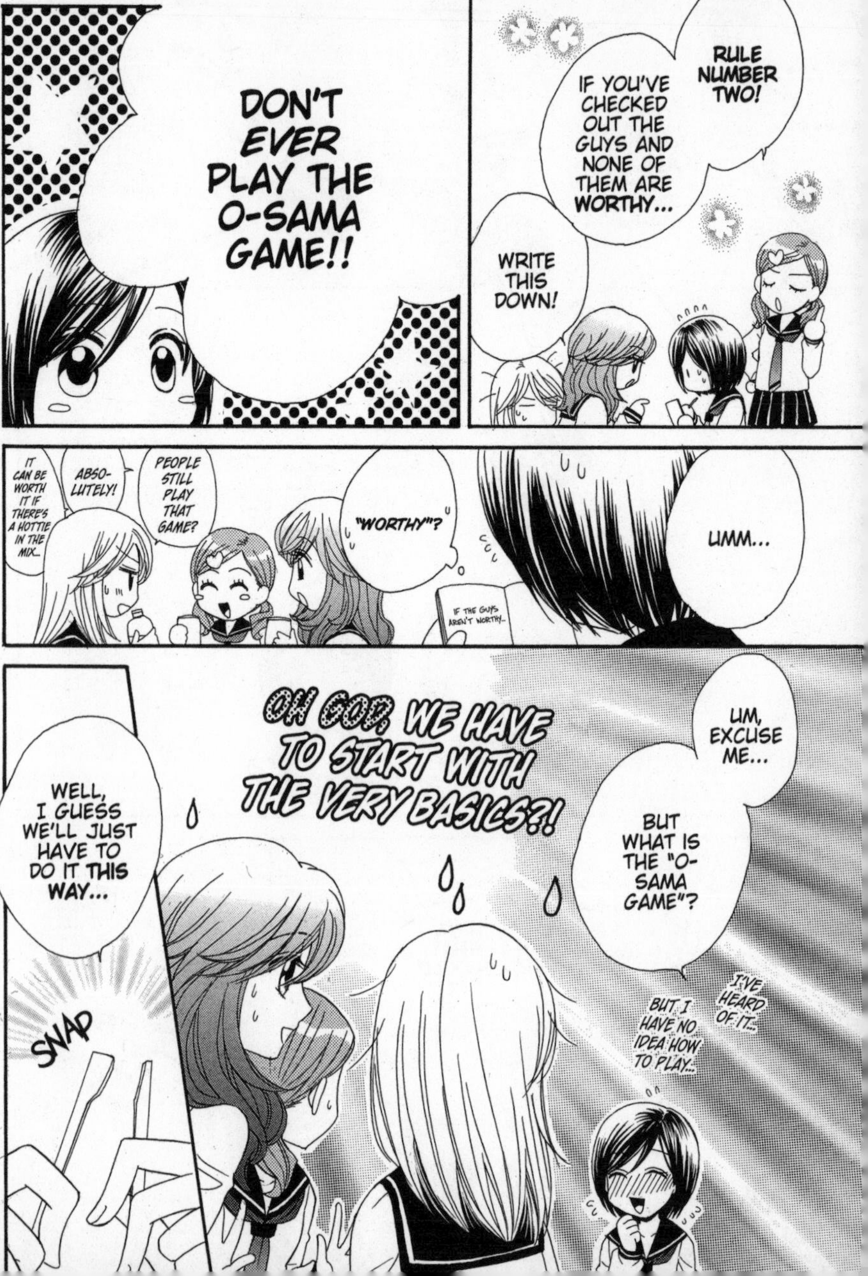
RULE NUMBER TWO!
IF YOU'VE CHECKED OUT THE GUYS AND NONE OF THEM ARE WORTHY...
WRITE THIS DOWN!
DON'T EVER PLAY THE O-SAMA GAME!!
UMM...
IF THE GUYS AREN'T WORTHY...
"WORTHY"?
PEOPLE STILL PLAY THAT GAME?
ABSO-LUTELY!
IT CAN BE WORTH IT IF THERE'S A HOTTIE IN THE MIX...
UM, EXCUSE ME...
BUT WHAT IS THE "O-SAMA GAME"?
I'VE HEARD OF IT...
BUT I HAVE NO IDEA HOW TO PLAY...
OH GOD, WE HAVE TO START WITH THE VERY BASICS?!
WELL, I GUESS WE'LL JUST HAVE TO DO IT THIS WAY...
SNAP

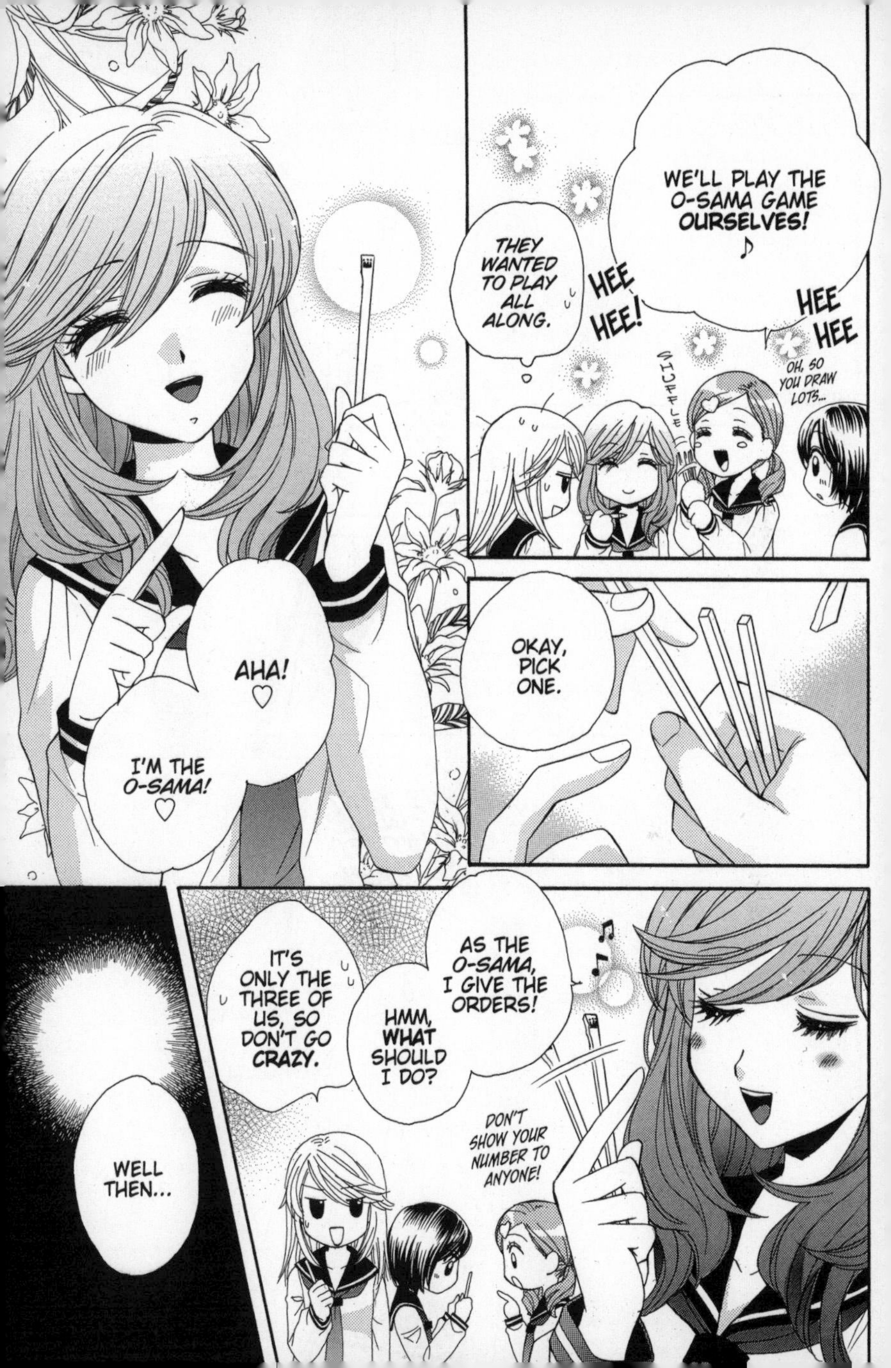
WE'LL PLAY THE O-SAMA GAME OURSELVES! ♪
HEE HEE
OH, SO YOU DRAW LOTS...
HEE HEE!
THEY WANTED TO PLAY ALL ALONG.
SHUFFLE
OKAY, PICK ONE.
AHA! ♡
I'M THE O-SAMA! ♡
AS THE O-SAMA, I GIVE THE ORDERS!
HMM, WHAT SHOULD I DO?
IT'S ONLY THE THREE OF US, SO DON'T GO CRAZY.
DON'T SHOW YOUR NUMBER TO ANYONE!
WELL THEN...

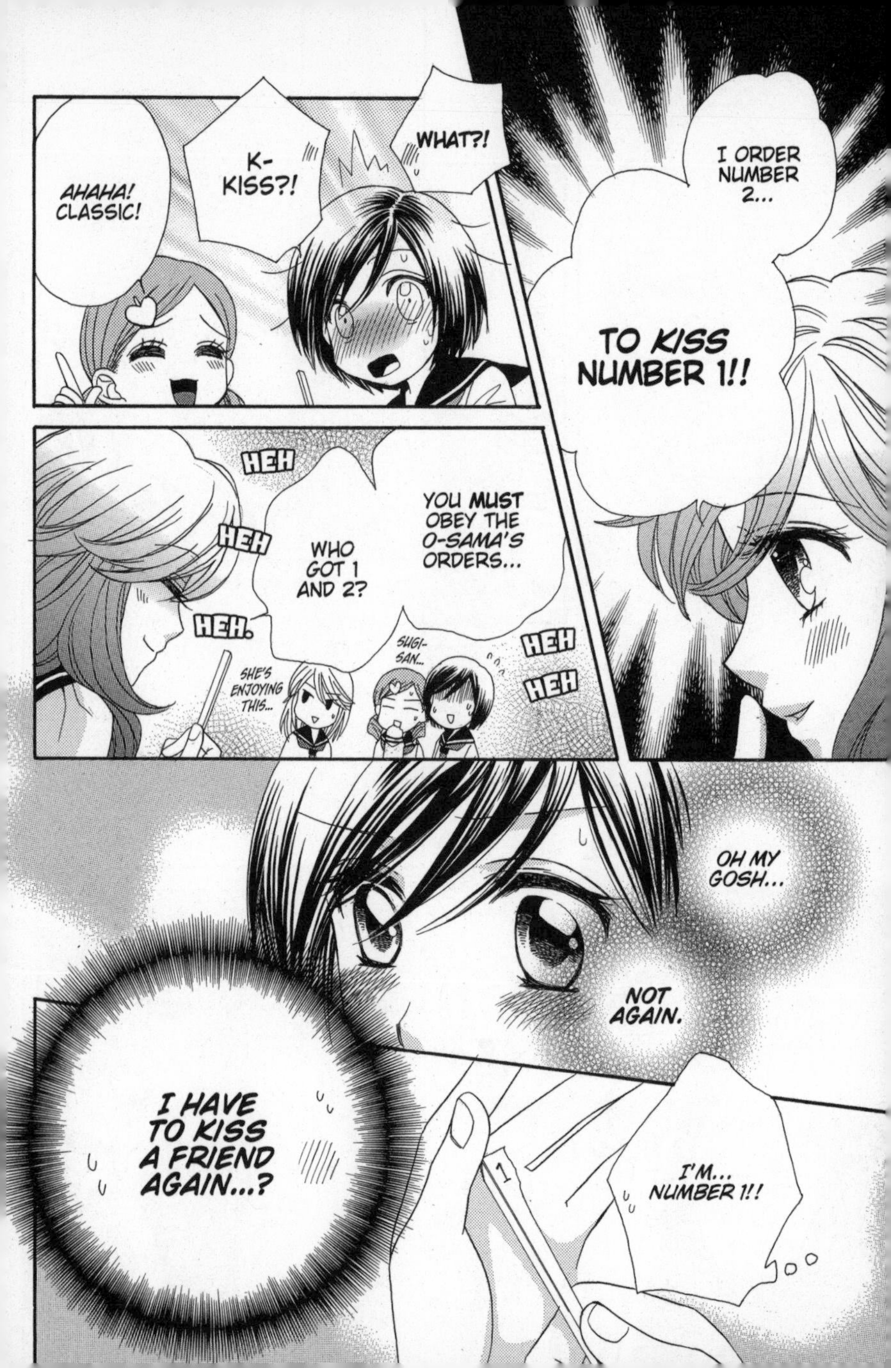
I ORDER NUMBER 2...
TO KISS NUMBER 1!!
WHAT?!
K-KISS?!
AHAHA! CLASSIC!
HEH HEH
YOU MUST OBEY THE O-SAMA'S ORDERS...
WHO GOT 1 AND 2?
HEH HEH
HEH HEH.
SUGI-SAN...
SHE'S ENJOYING THIS...
OH MY GOSH...
NOT AGAIN.
I'M... NUMBER 1!!
I HAVE TO KISS A FRIEND AGAIN...?

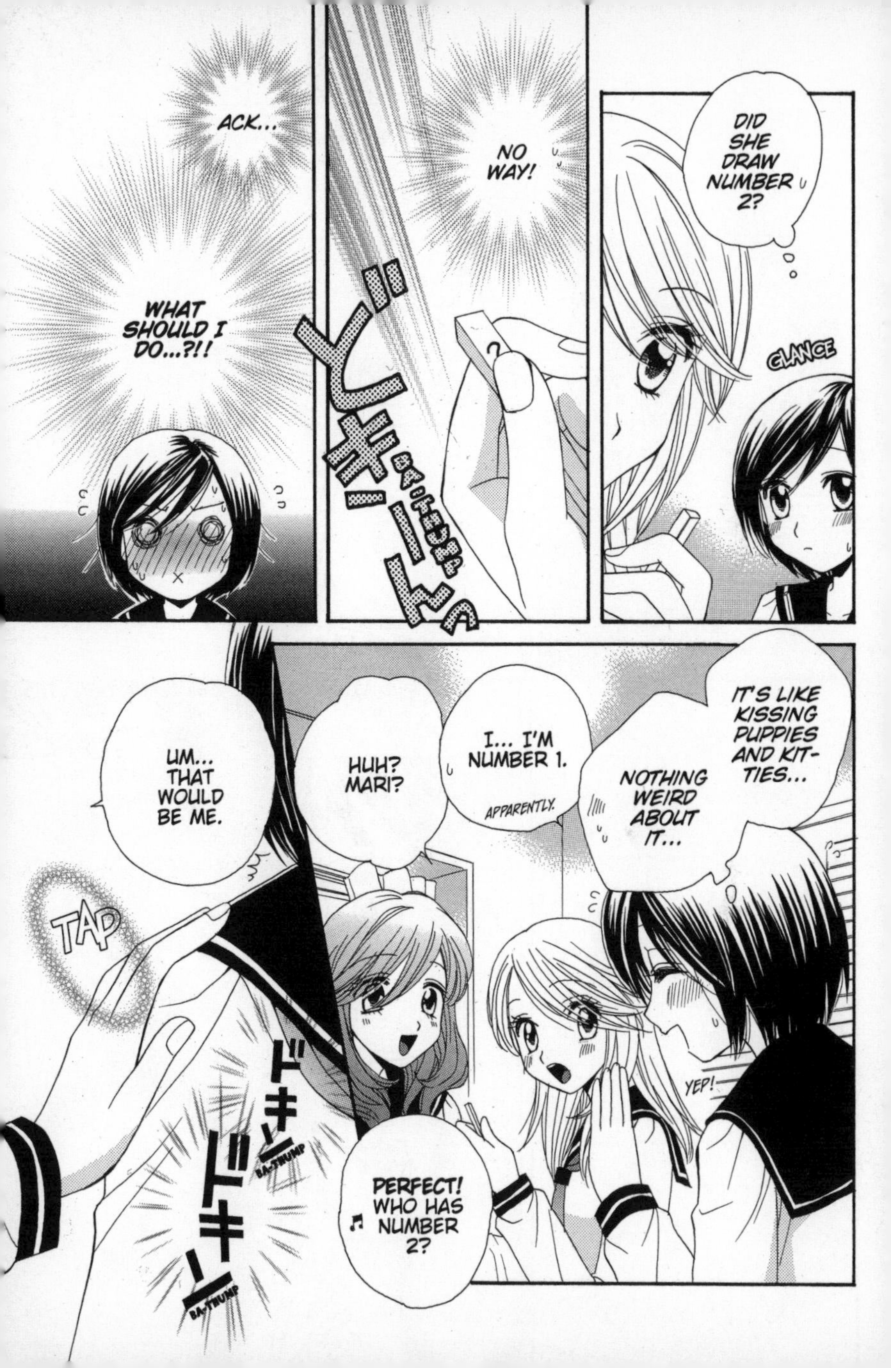
DID SHE DRAW NUMBER 2?
GLANCE
NO WAY!
ドギーん
BA-THUMP
ACK...
WHAT SHOULD I DO...?!!
IT'S LIKE KISSING PUPPIES AND KIT-TIES...
NOTHING WEIRD ABOUT IT...
YEP!
I... I'M NUMBER 1.
APPARENTLY.
HUH? MARI?
PERFECT! WHO HAS NUMBER 2? ♪
UM... THAT WOULD BE ME.
TAP
ドキ
BA-THUMP
ドキー
BA-THUMP

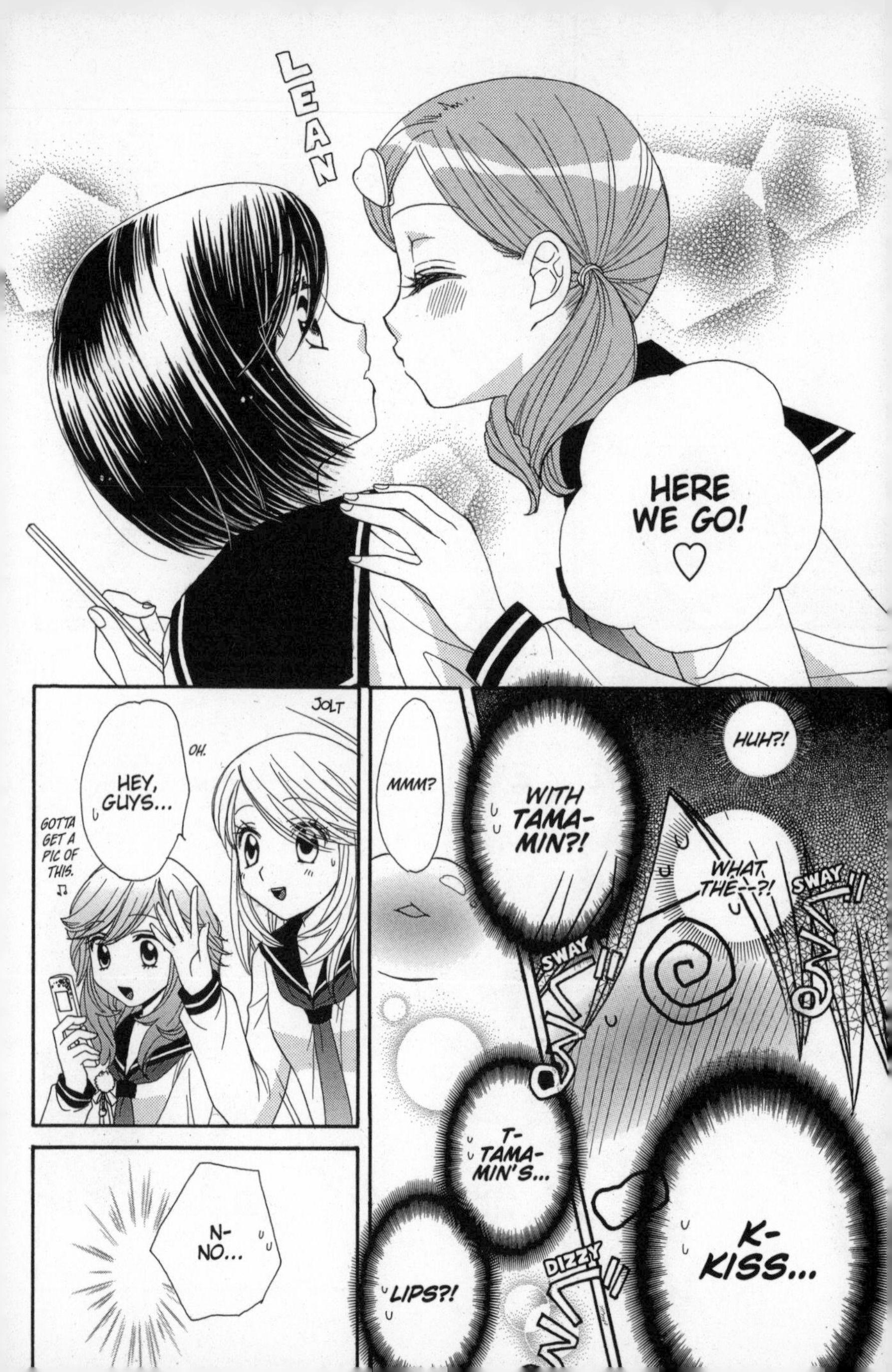
LEAN
HERE WE GO! ♡
HUH?!
WITH TAMA-MIN?!
WHAT THE--?!
SWAY
SWAY
T-TAMA-MIN'S...
K-KISS...
LIPS?!
DIZZY
MMM?
JOLT
OH.
HEY, GUYS...
GOTTA GET A PIC OF THIS. ♫
N-NO...

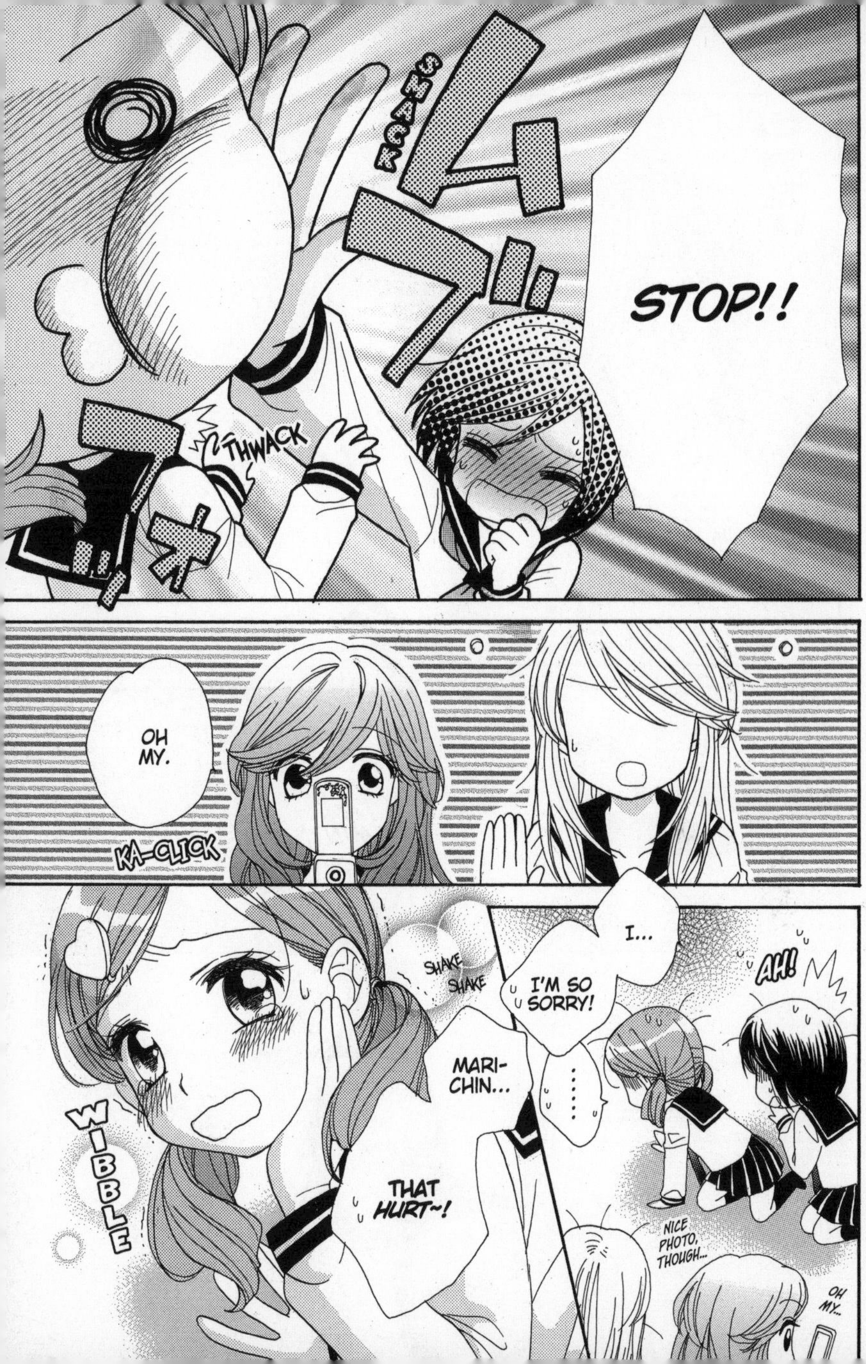

STOP!!
SMACK
THWACK
OH MY.
KA-CLICK
I...
I'M SO SORRY!
AH!
......
NICE PHOTO, THOUGH...
OH MY...
SHAKE SHAKE
MARI-CHIN...
THAT HURT~!
WIBBLE

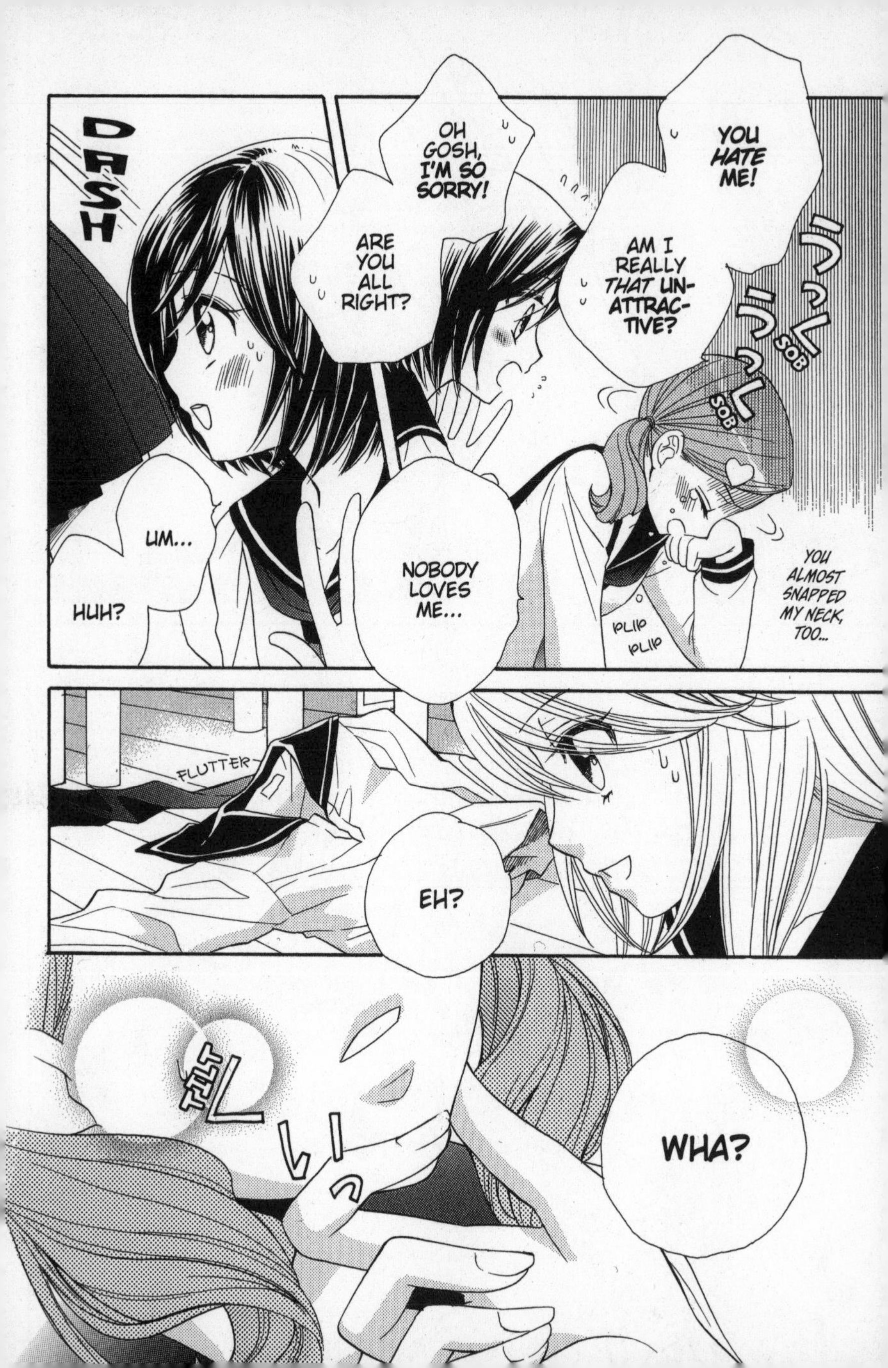
YOU HATE ME!
AM I REALLY THAT UN-ATTRACTIVE?
うっく
SOB
うっく
SOB
YOU ALMOST SNAPPED MY NECK, TOO...
OH GOSH, I'M SO SORRY!
ARE YOU ALL RIGHT?
NOBODY LOVES ME...
PLIP
PLIP
DASH
UM...
HUH?
FLUTTER
EH?
WHA?
TILT

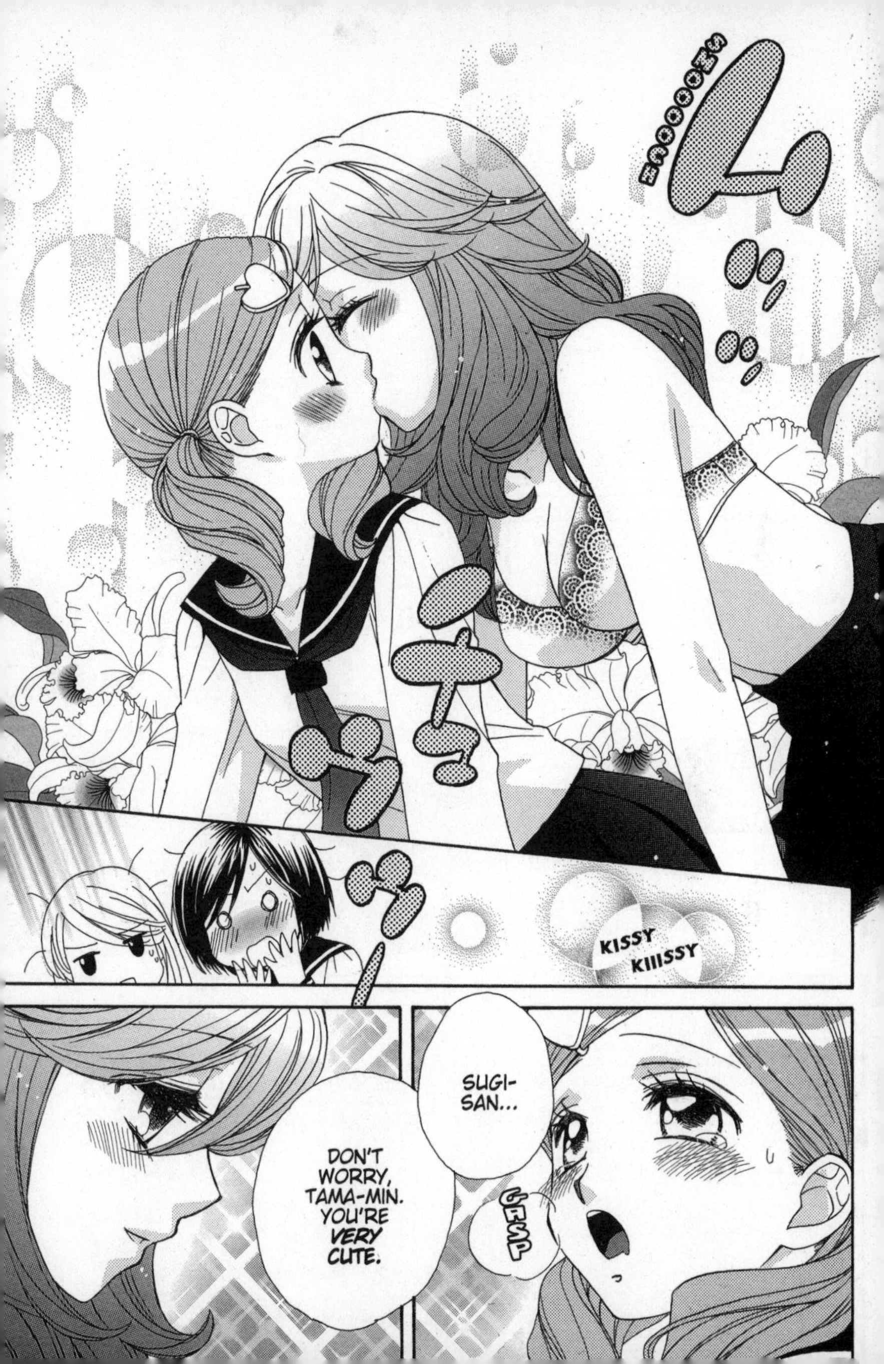
SMOOOOCH
KISSY
KIIISSY
SUGI-SAN...
DON'T WORRY, TAMA-MIN. YOU'RE VERY CUTE.
GASP

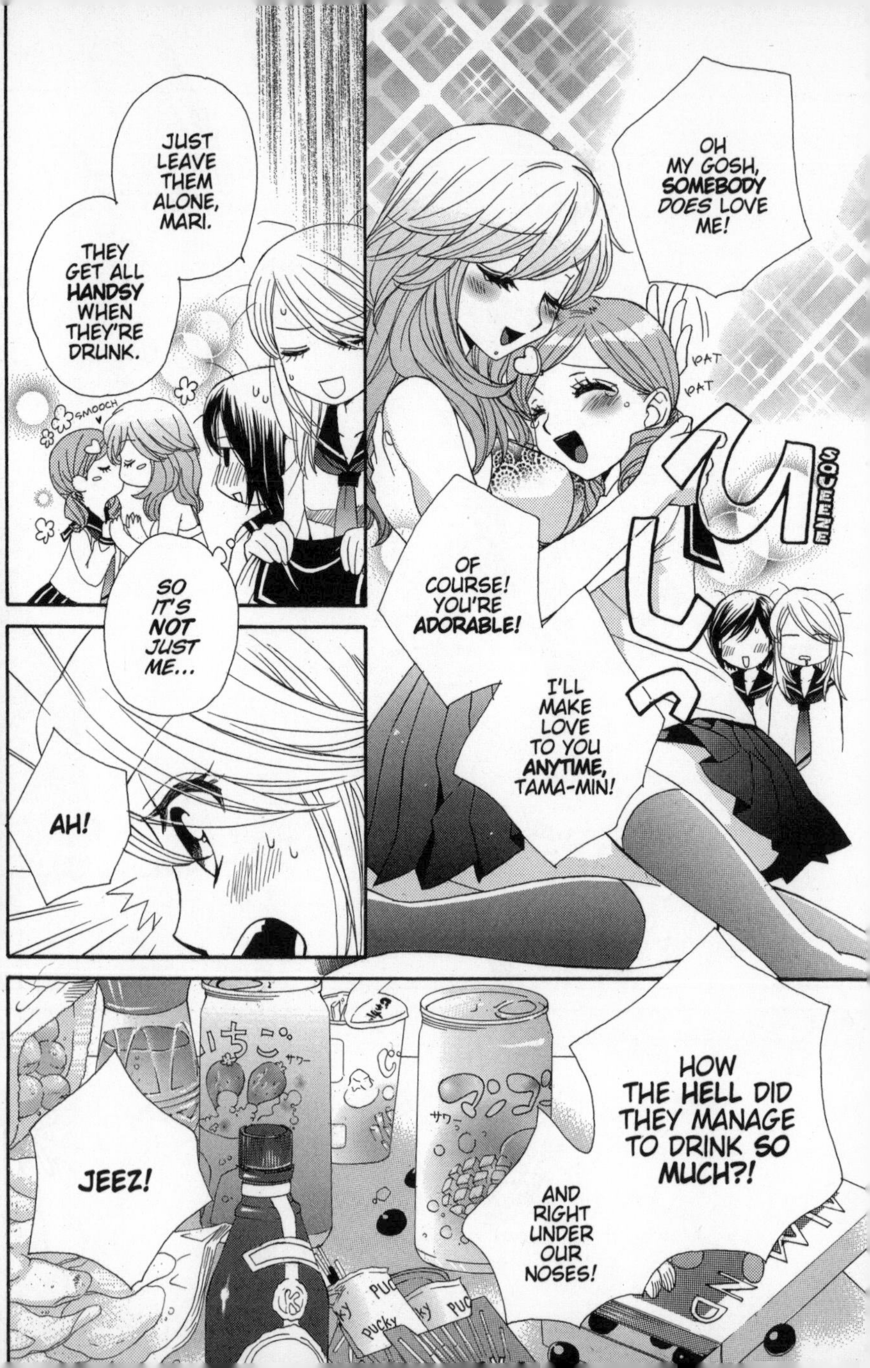
OH MY GOSH, SOMEBODY DOES LOVE ME!
PAT PAT
SQUEEZE
OF COURSE! YOU'RE ADORABLE!
I'LL MAKE LOVE TO YOU ANYTIME, TAMA-MIN!
JUST LEAVE THEM ALONE, MARI.
THEY GET ALL HANDSY WHEN THEY'RE DRUNK.
SMOOCH
SO IT'S NOT JUST ME...
AH!
HOW THE HELL DID THEY MANAGE TO DRINK SO MUCH?!
AND RIGHT UNDER OUR NOSES!
JEEZ!
いちご
サワー
PUCKY

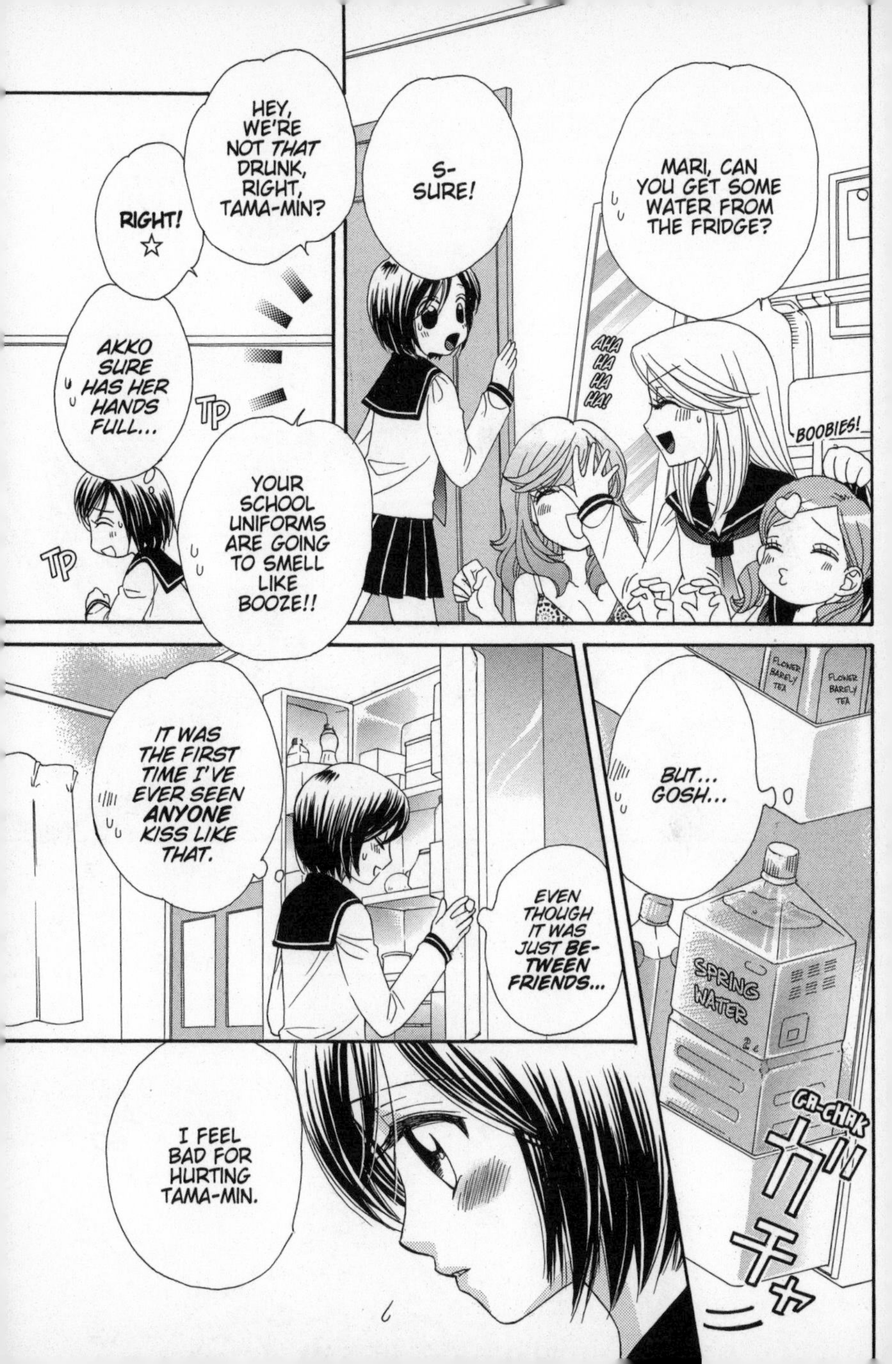
MARI, CAN YOU GET SOME WATER FROM THE FRIDGE?
AHA HA HA HA!
BOOBIES!
S-SURE!
HEY, WE'RE NOT THAT DRUNK, RIGHT, TAMA-MIN?
RIGHT! ☆
AKKO SURE HAS HER HANDS FULL...
TP
TP
YOUR SCHOOL UNIFORMS ARE GOING TO SMELL LIKE BOOZE!!
FLOWER BARELY TEA
FLOWER BARELY TEA
BUT... GOSH...
SPRING WATER
IT WAS THE FIRST TIME I'VE EVER SEEN ANYONE KISS LIKE THAT.
EVEN THOUGH IT WAS JUST BE-TWEEN FRIENDS...
CA-CHAK
I FEEL BAD FOR HURTING TAMA-MIN.

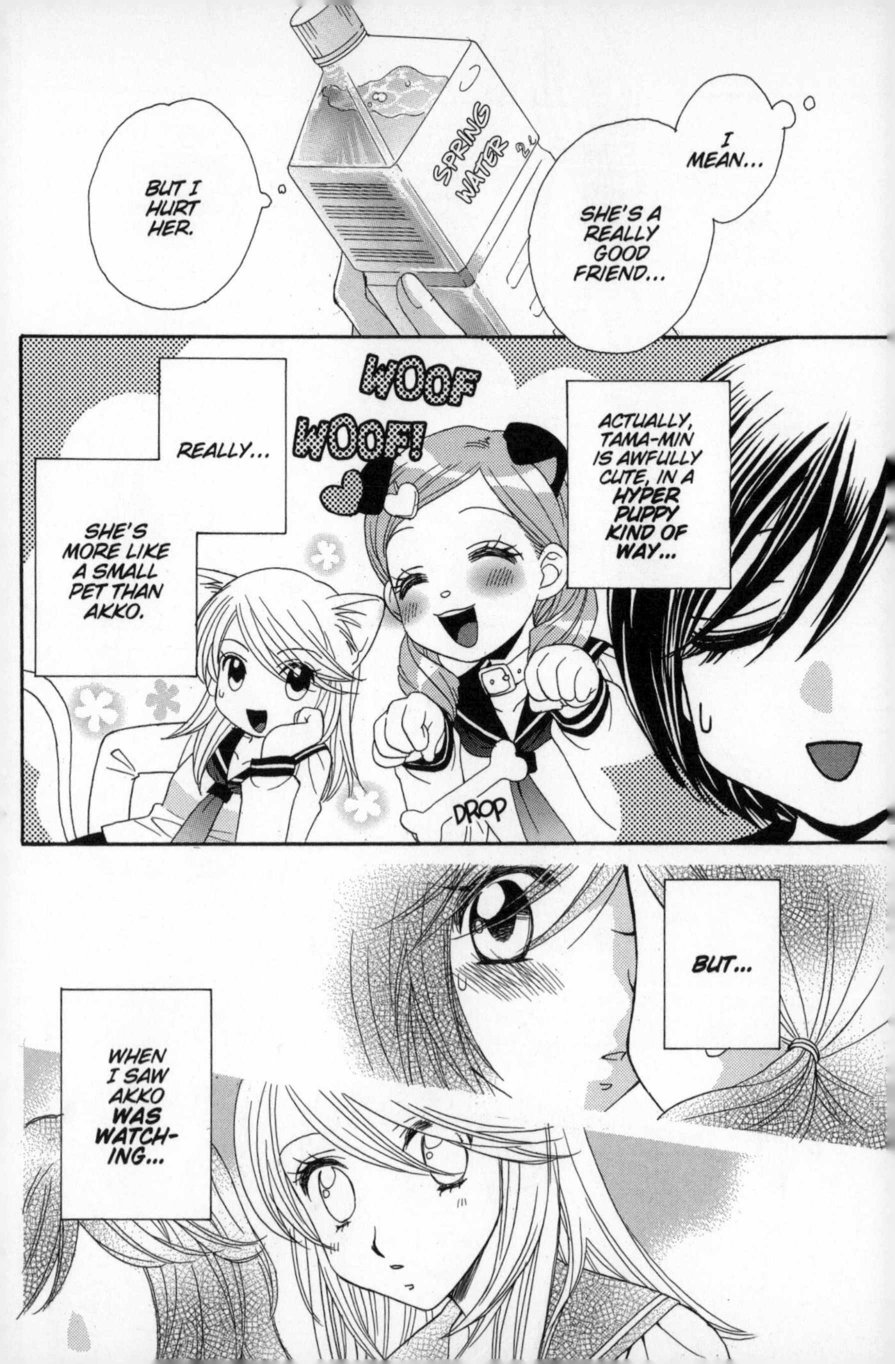
SPRING WATER
I MEAN...
SHE'S A REALLY GOOD FRIEND...
BUT I HURT HER.
ACTUALLY, TAMA-MIN IS AWFULLY CUTE, IN A HYPER PUPPY KIND OF WAY...
WOOF
WOOF!
DROP
REALLY...
SHE'S MORE LIKE A SMALL PET THAN AKKO.
BUT...
WHEN I SAW AKKO WAS WATCHING...

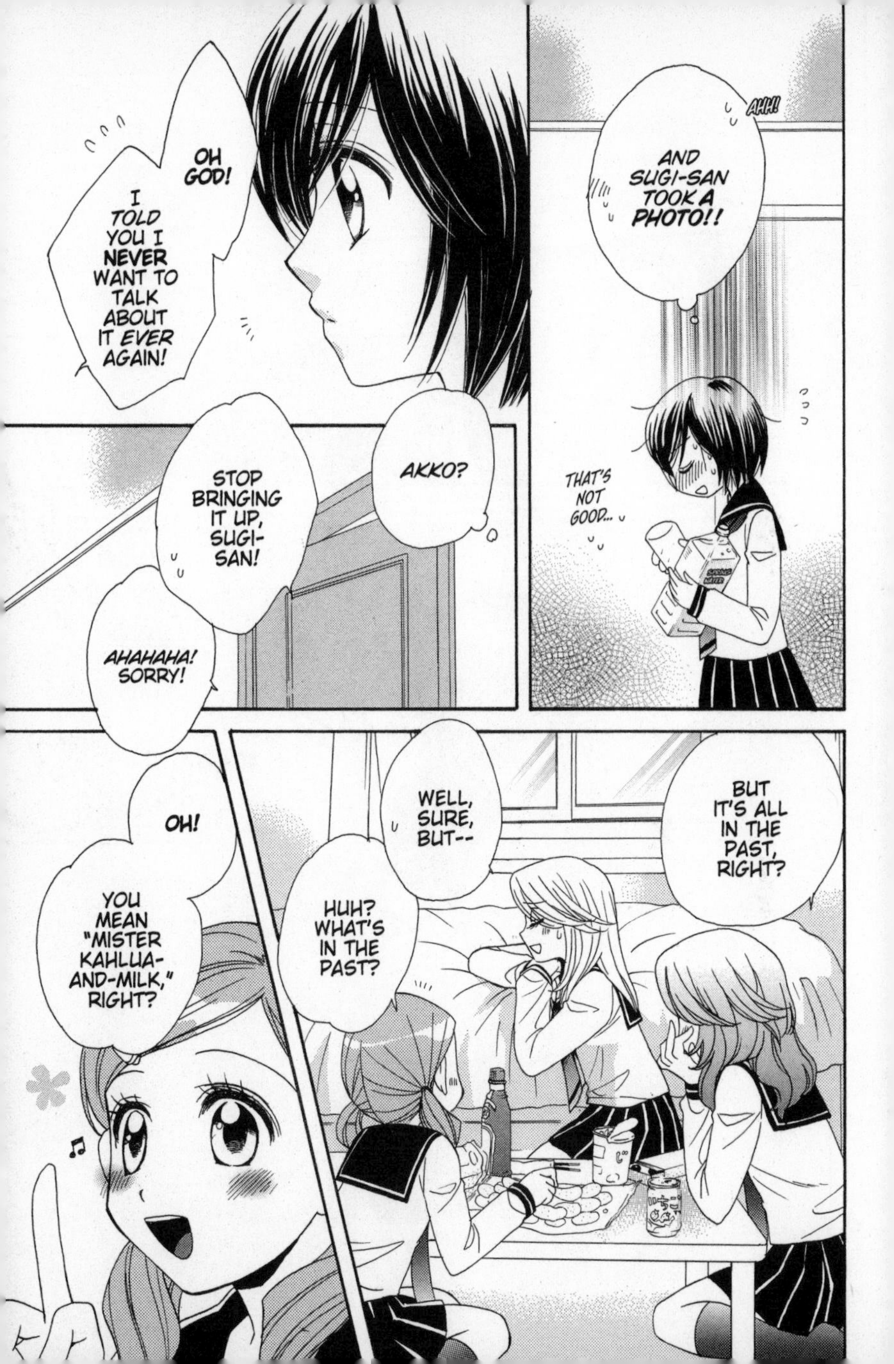
AHH!!
AND SUGI-SAN TOOK A PHOTO!!
THAT'S NOT GOOD...
OH GOD!
I TOLD YOU I NEVER WANT TO TALK ABOUT IT EVER AGAIN!
AKKO?
STOP BRINGING IT UP, SUGI-SAN!
AHAHAHA! SORRY!
BUT IT'S ALL IN THE PAST, RIGHT?
WELL, SURE, BUT--
HUH? WHAT'S IN THE PAST?
OH!
YOU MEAN "MISTER KAHLUA-AND-MILK," RIGHT?

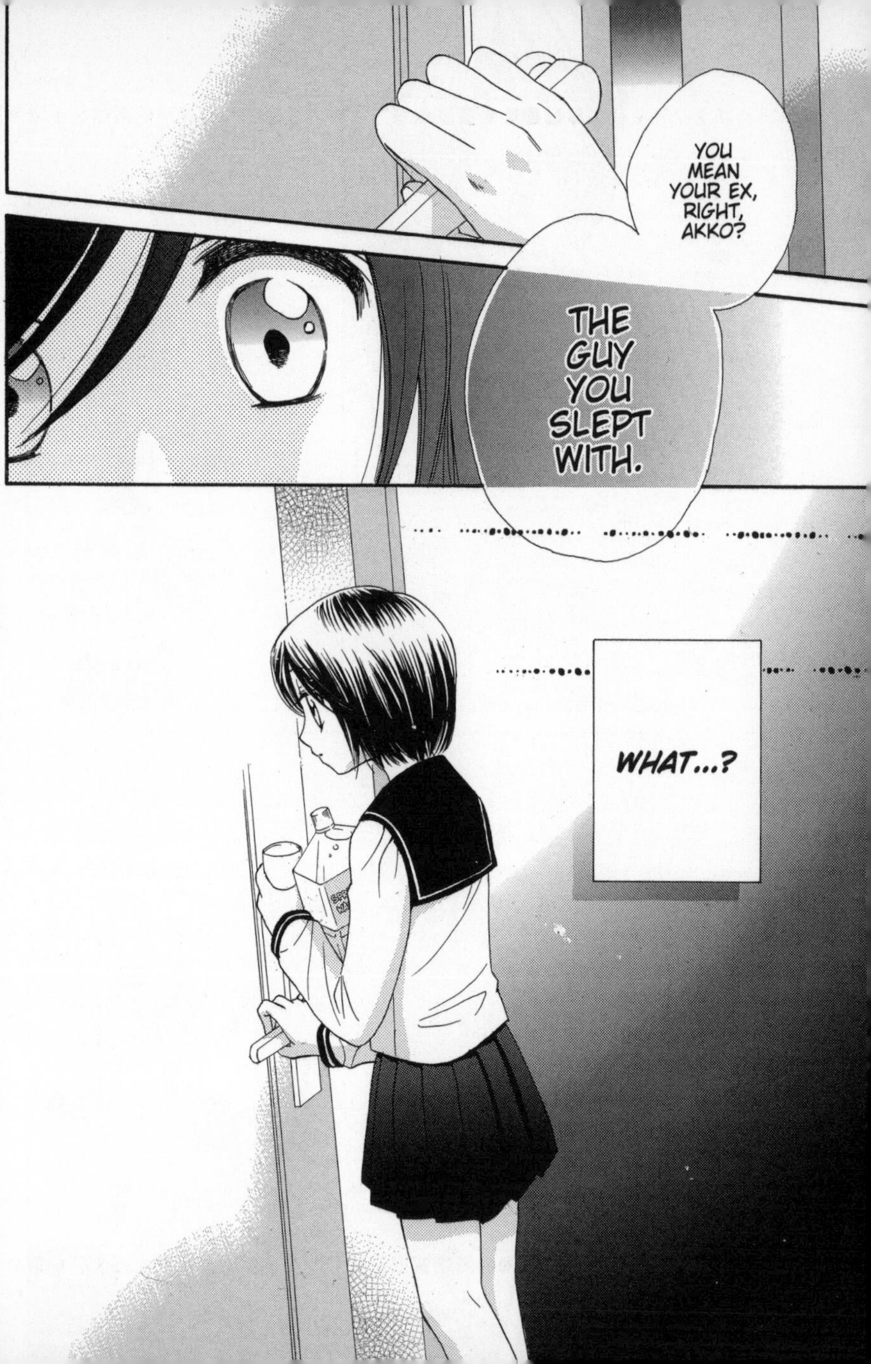
YOU MEAN YOUR EX, RIGHT, AKKO?
THE GUY YOU SLEPT WITH.
WHAT...?

WINTER
UNIFORM. &
SWEATER

GIRL FRIENDS −ガールフレンズ−

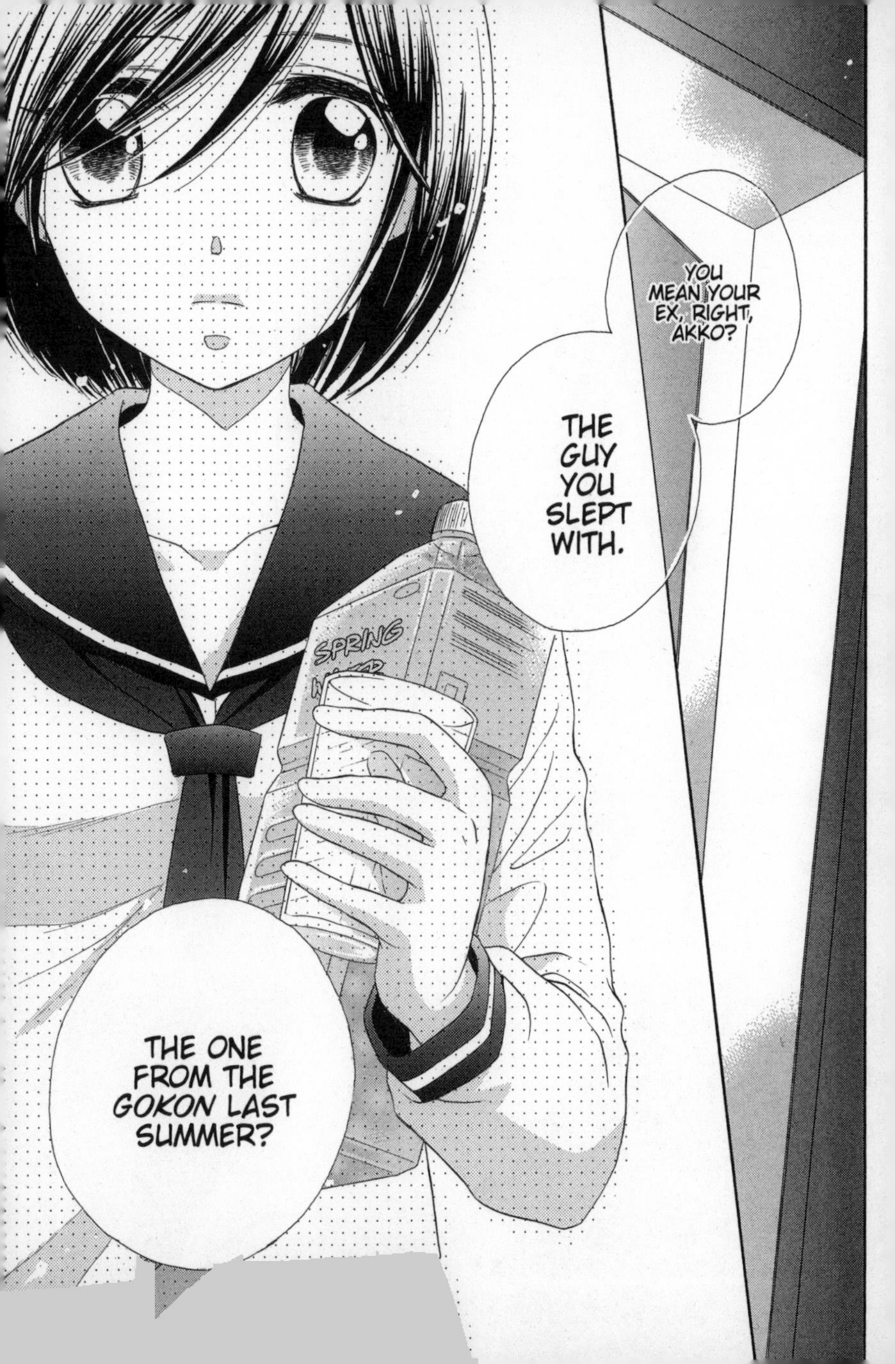
YOU MEAN YOUR EX, RIGHT, AKKO?
THE GUY YOU SLEPT WITH.
SPRING
THE ONE FROM THE GOKON LAST SUMMER?

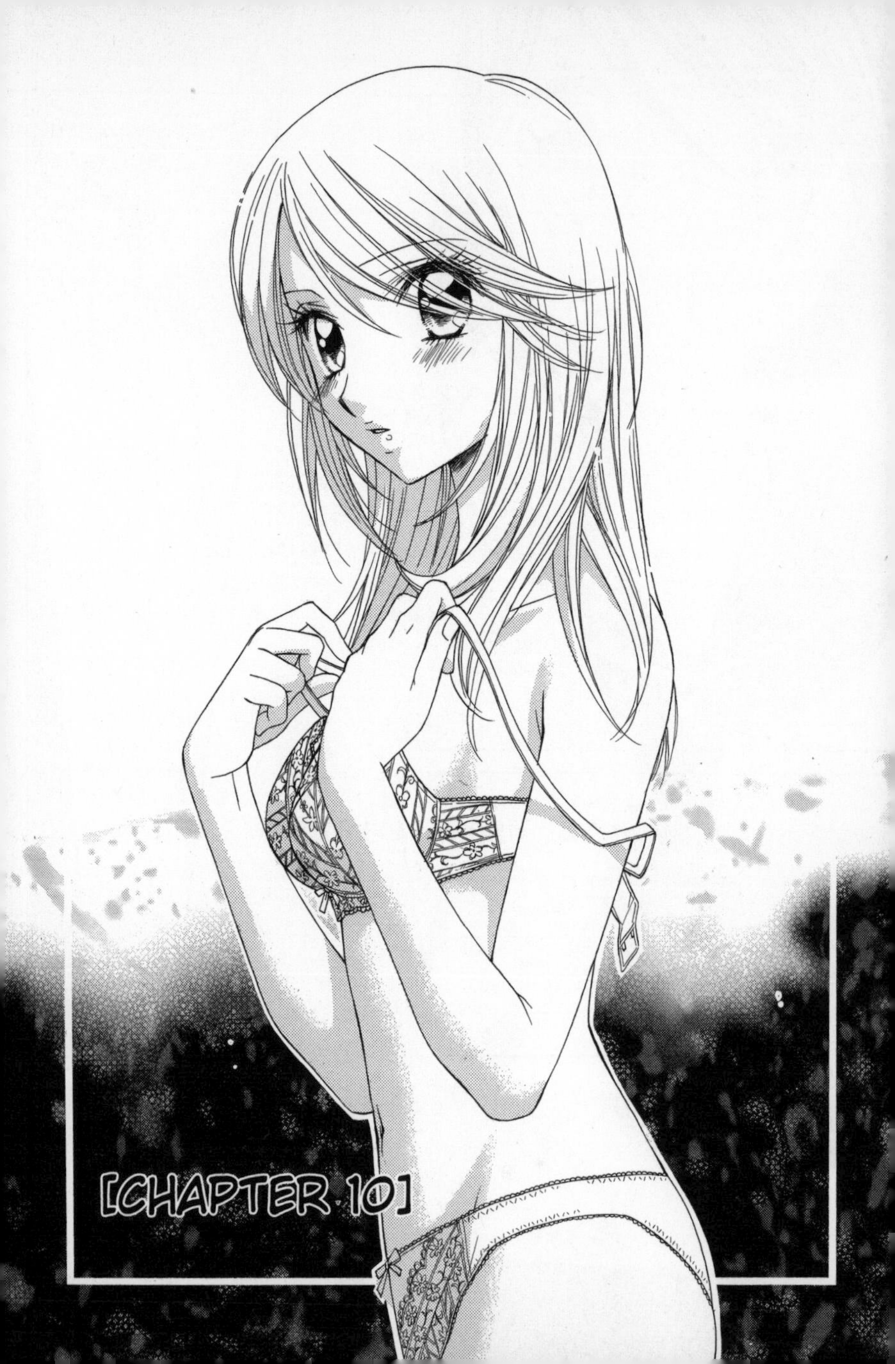
[CHAPTER 10]

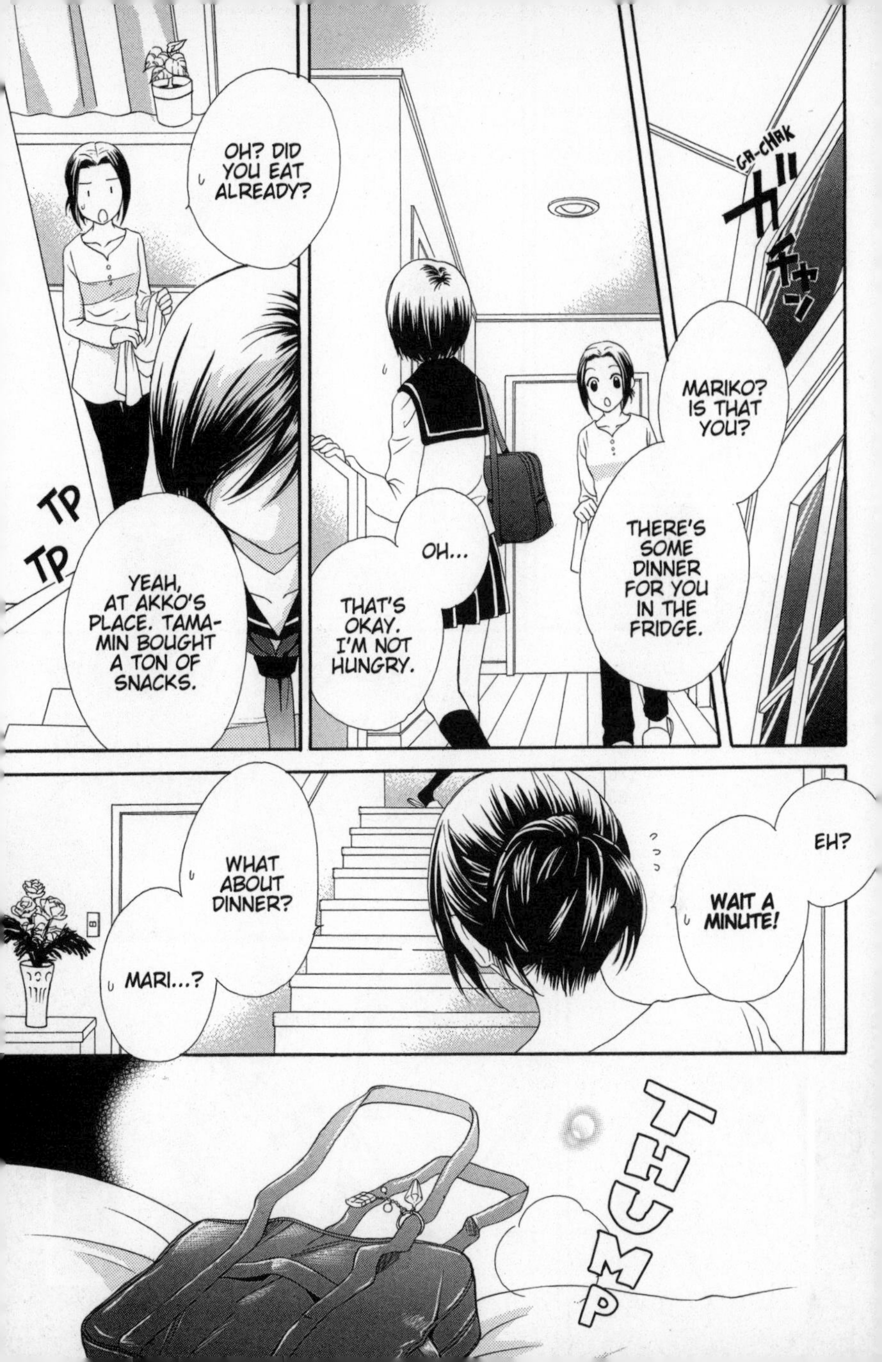
GA-CHAK
ガチャン
MARIKO? IS THAT YOU?
THERE'S SOME DINNER FOR YOU IN THE FRIDGE.
OH...
THAT'S OKAY. I'M NOT HUNGRY.
OH? DID YOU EAT ALREADY?
YEAH, AT AKKO'S PLACE. TAMA-MIN BOUGHT A TON OF SNACKS.
TP TP
EH?
WAIT A MINUTE!
WHAT ABOUT DINNER?
MARI...?
THUMP

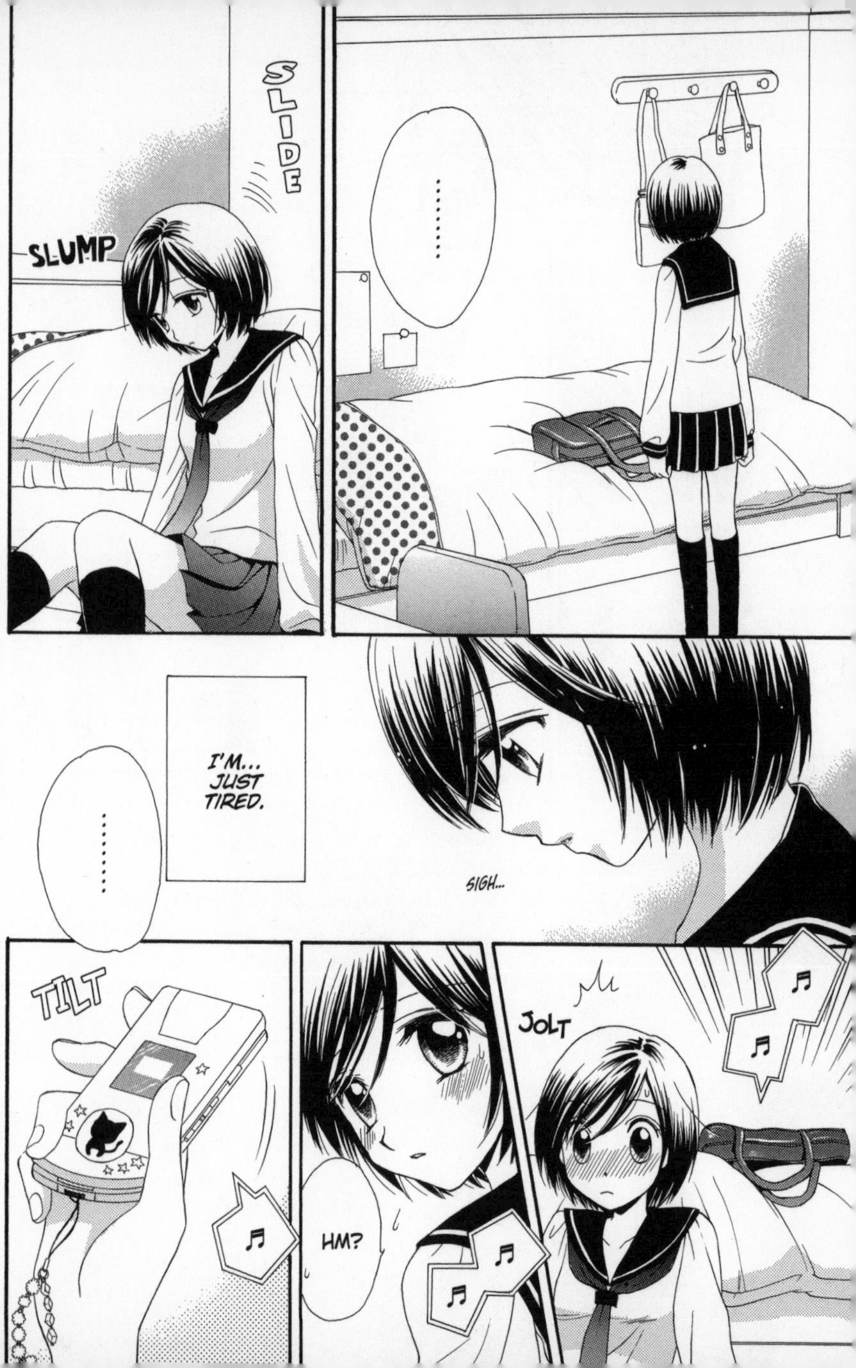
......
SLIDE
SLUMP
I'M... JUST TIRED.
......
SIGH...
JOLT
♪
♪
♪
♪
HM?
TILT
♪

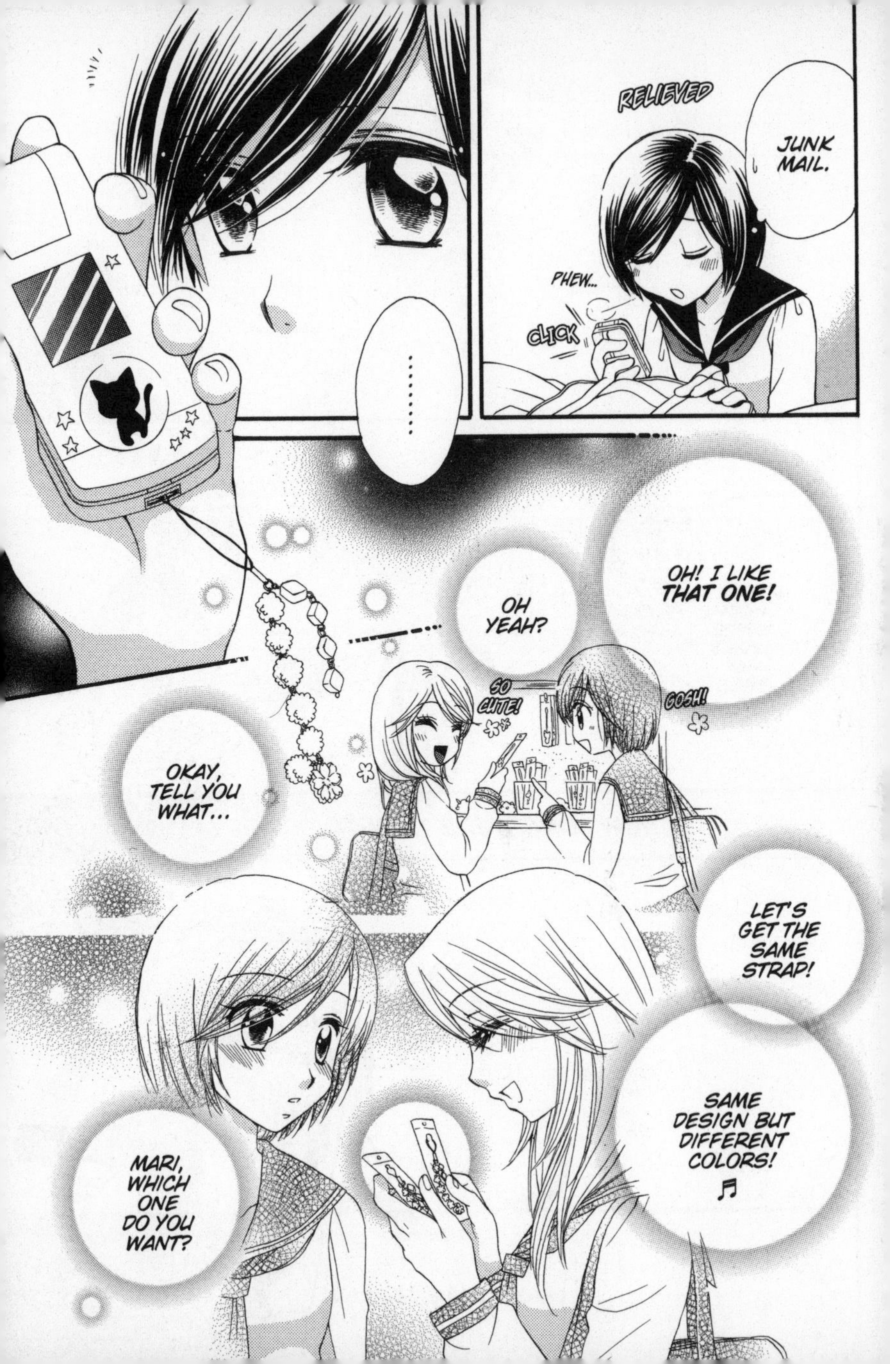
RELIEVED
JUNK MAIL.
PHEW...
CLICK
OH! I LIKE THAT ONE!
OH YEAH?
GOSH!
SO CUTE!
OKAY, TELL YOU WHAT...
LET'S GET THE SAME STRAP!
SAME DESIGN BUT DIFFERENT COLORS! ♬
MARI, WHICH ONE DO YOU WANT?

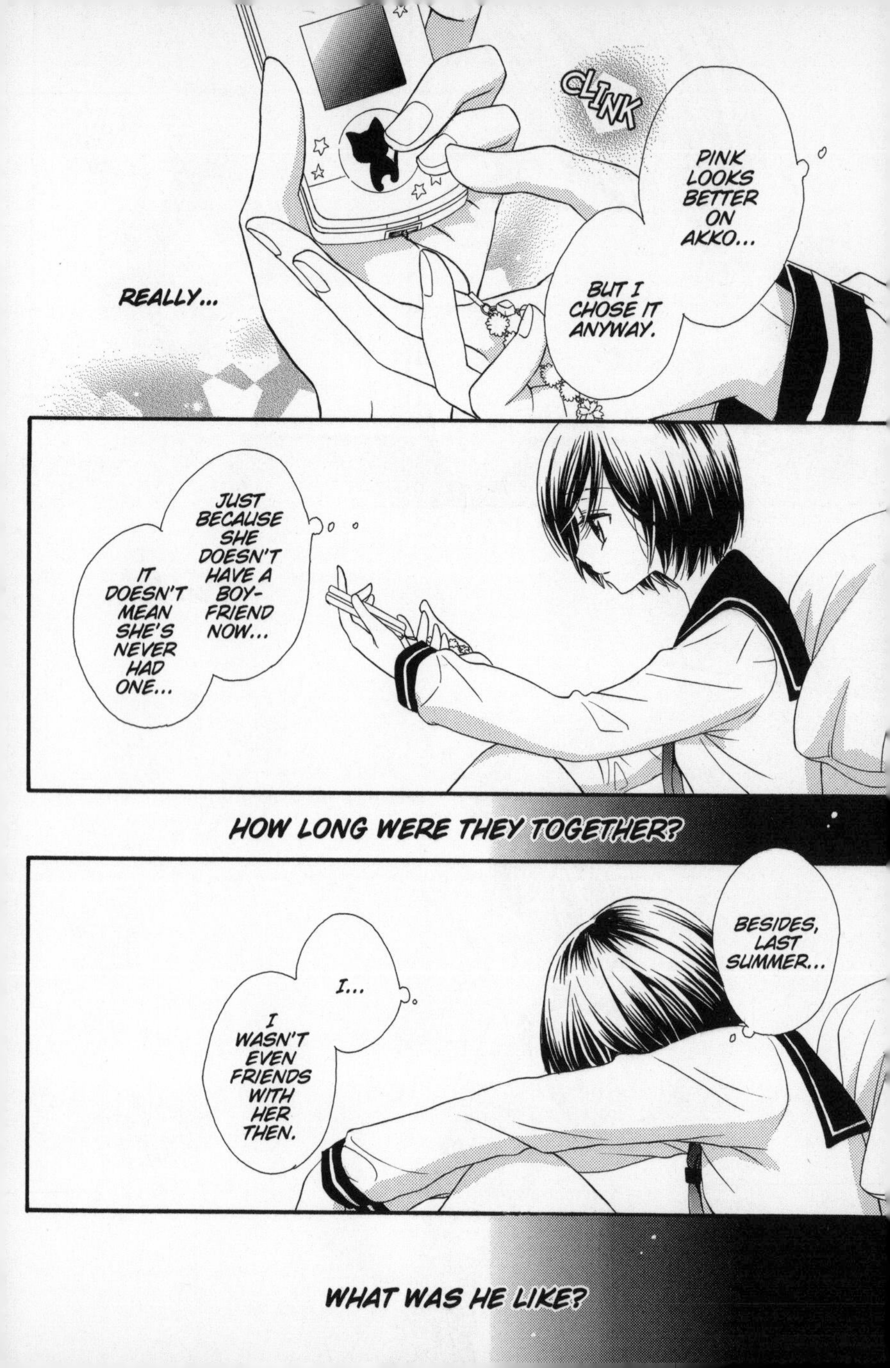
CLINK
PINK LOOKS BETTER ON AKKO...
BUT I CHOSE IT ANYWAY.
REALLY...
JUST BECAUSE SHE DOESN'T HAVE A BOY-FRIEND NOW...
IT DOESN'T MEAN SHE'S NEVER HAD ONE...
HOW LONG WERE THEY TOGETHER?
BESIDES, LAST SUMMER...
I...
I WASN'T EVEN FRIENDS WITH HER THEN.
WHAT WAS HE LIKE?

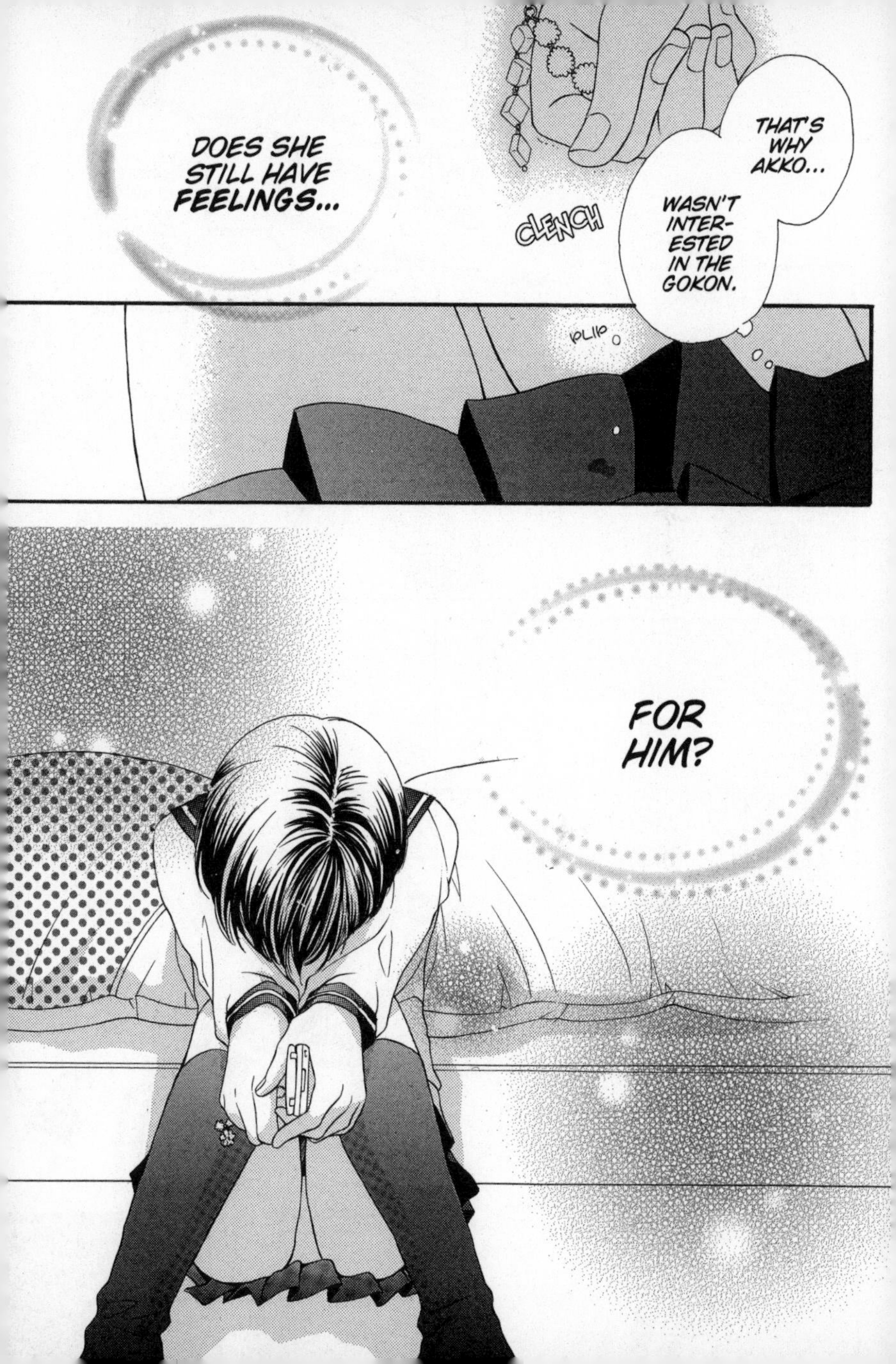
THAT'S WHY AKKO...
WASN'T INTER-ESTED IN THE GOKON.
CLENCH
DOES SHE STILL HAVE FEELINGS...
PLIP
FOR HIM?

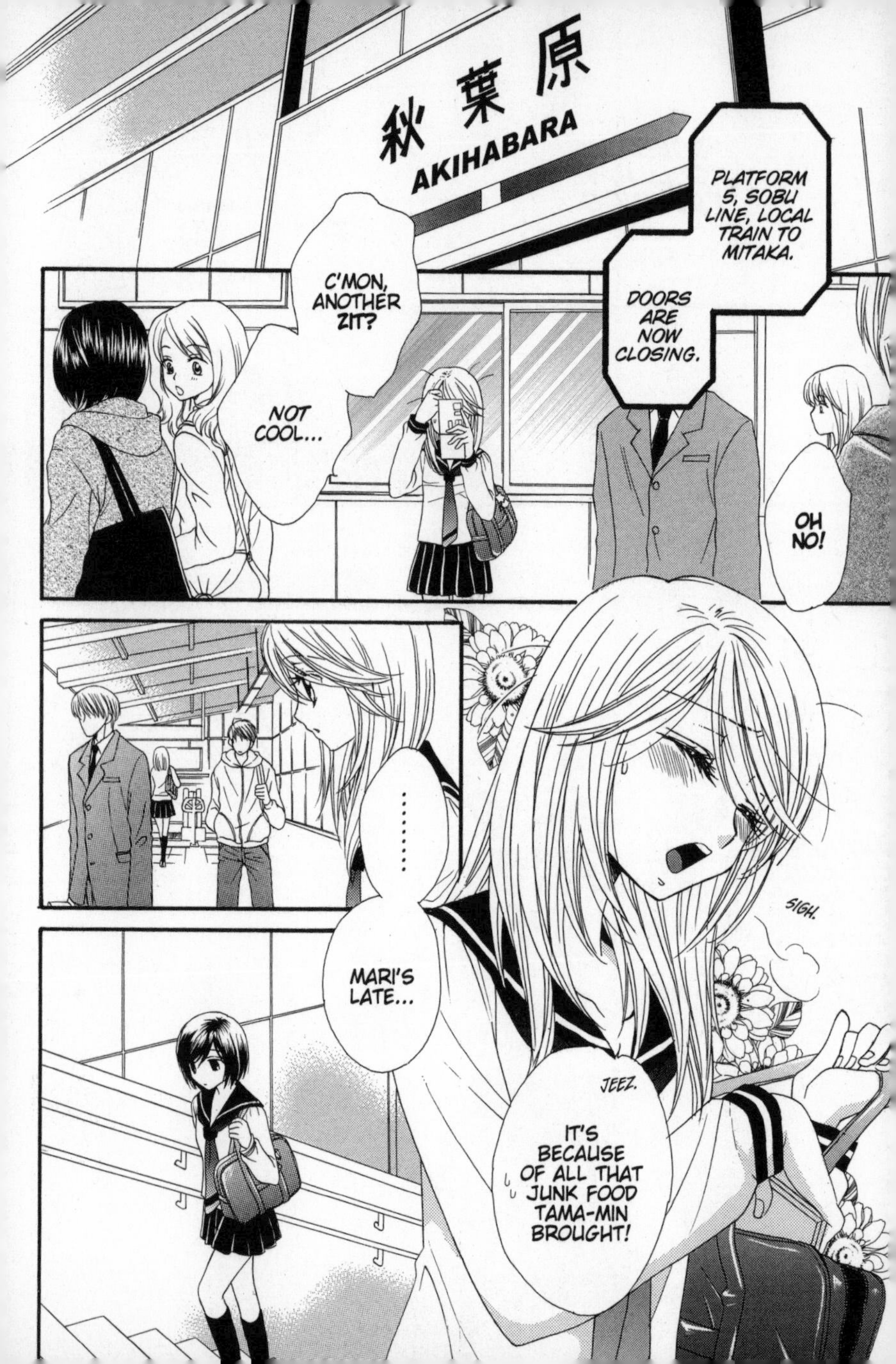
秋葉原
AKIHABARA
PLATFORM 5, SOBU LINE, LOCAL TRAIN TO MITAKA.
DOORS ARE NOW CLOSING.
OH NO!
C'MON, ANOTHER ZIT?
NOT COOL...
SIGH.
JEEZ.
IT'S BECAUSE OF ALL THAT JUNK FOOD TAMA-MIN BROUGHT!
......
MARI'S LATE...

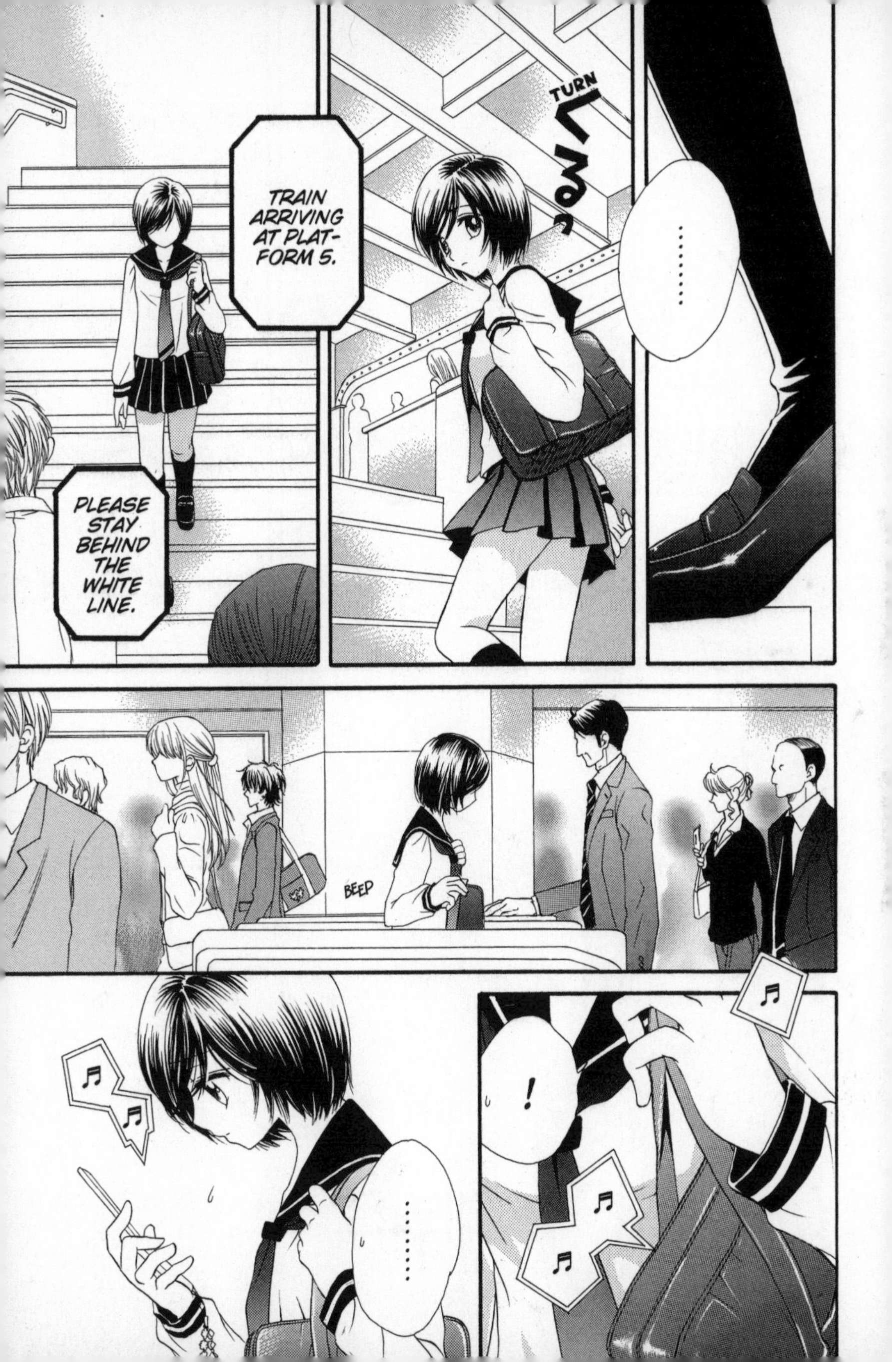
......
TURN
TRAIN ARRIVING AT PLATFORM 5.
PLEASE STAY BEHIND THE WHITE LINE.
BEEP
!
......

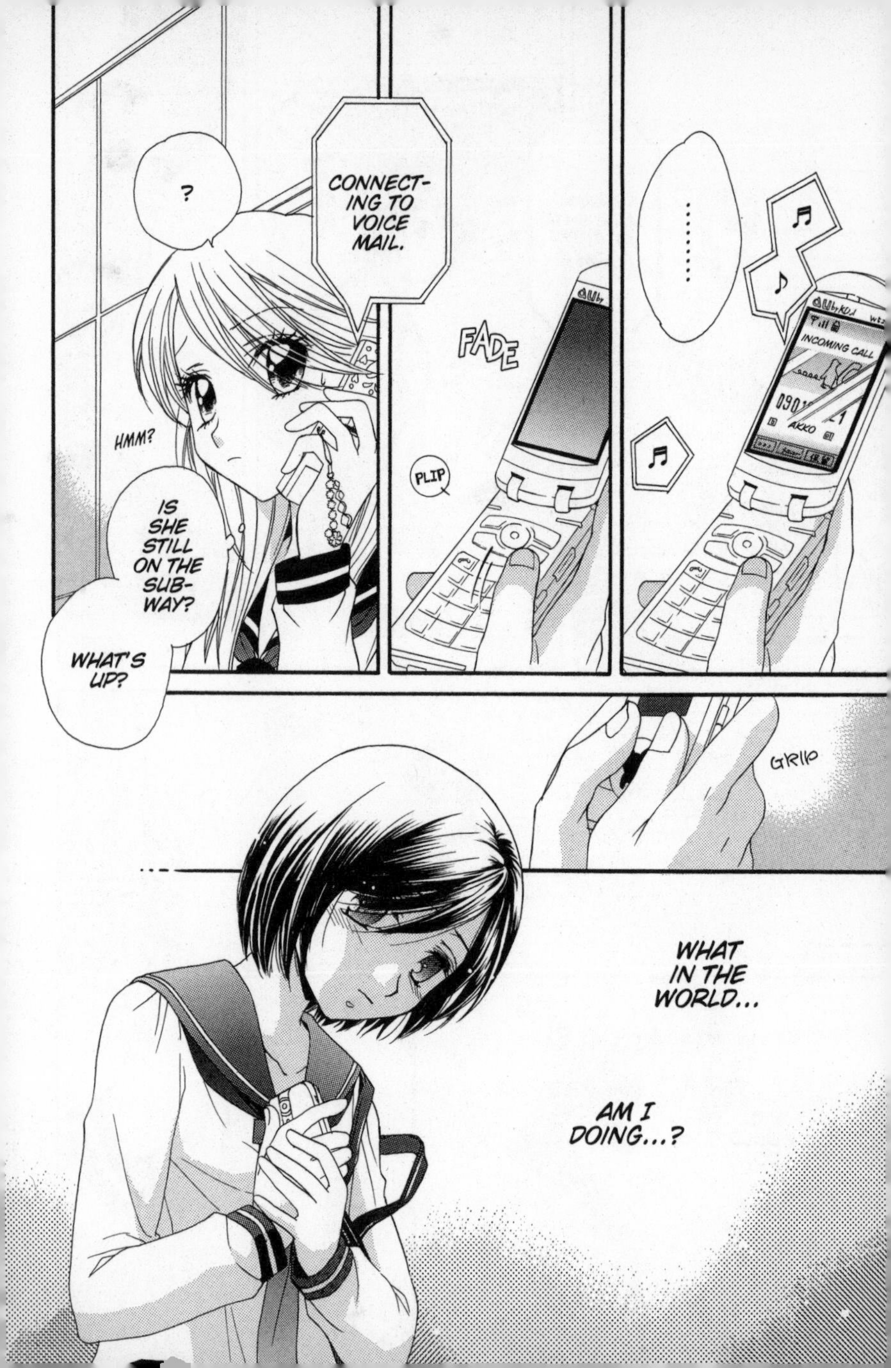
......
INCOMING CALL
AKKO
FADE
PLIP
?
CONNECTING TO VOICE MAIL.
HMM?
IS SHE STILL ON THE SUBWAY?
WHAT'S UP?
GRIP
...
WHAT IN THE WORLD...
AM I DOING...?

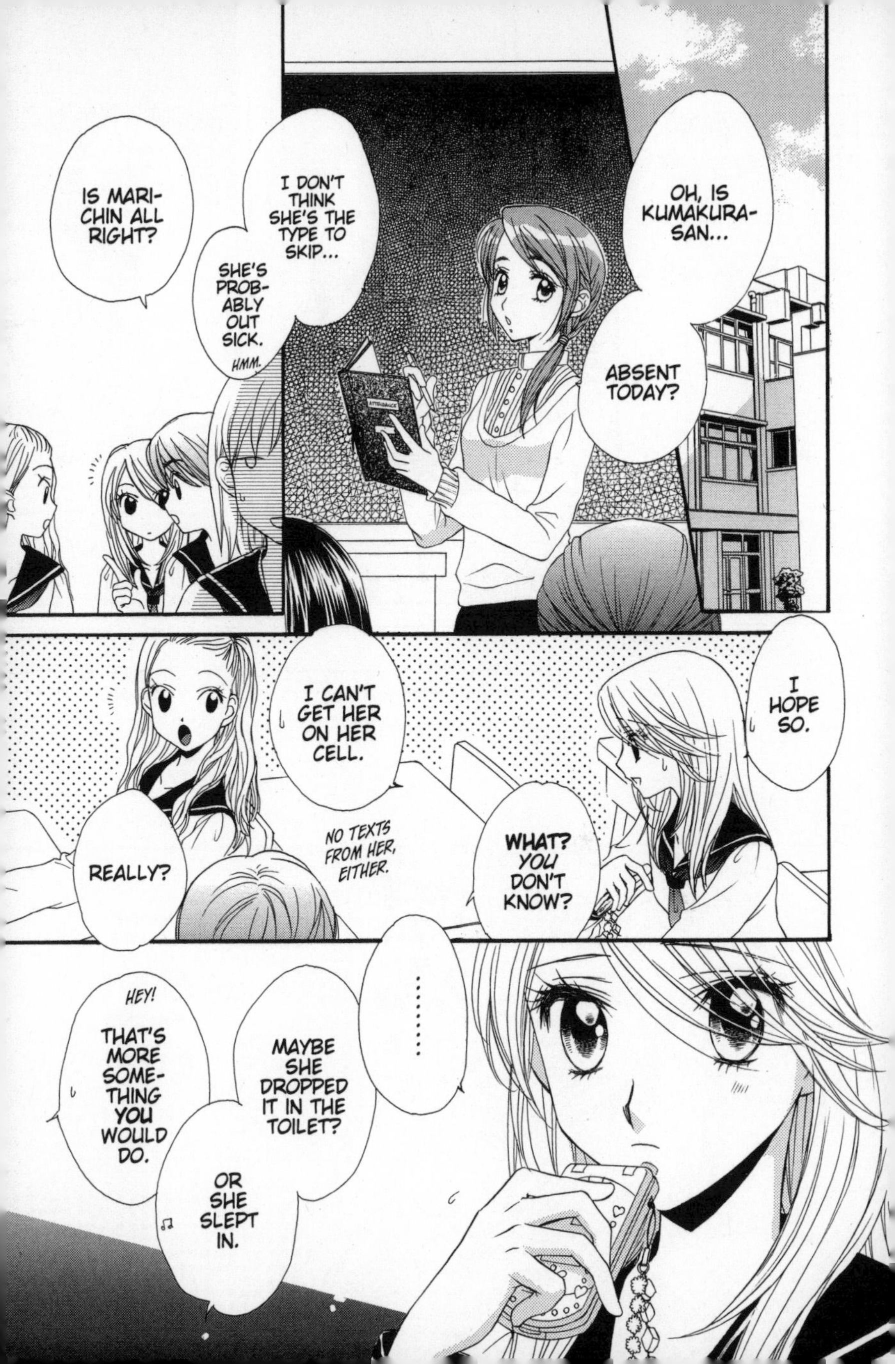
OH, IS KUMAKURA-SAN...
ABSENT TODAY?
I DON'T THINK SHE'S THE TYPE TO SKIP...
IS MARI-CHIN ALL RIGHT?
SHE'S PROBABLY OUT SICK.
HMM.
I HOPE SO.
I CAN'T GET HER ON HER CELL.
WHAT? YOU DON'T KNOW?
NO TEXTS FROM HER, EITHER.
REALLY?
......
MAYBE SHE DROPPED IT IN THE TOILET?
HEY!
THAT'S MORE SOMETHING YOU WOULD DO.
OR SHE SLEPT IN.

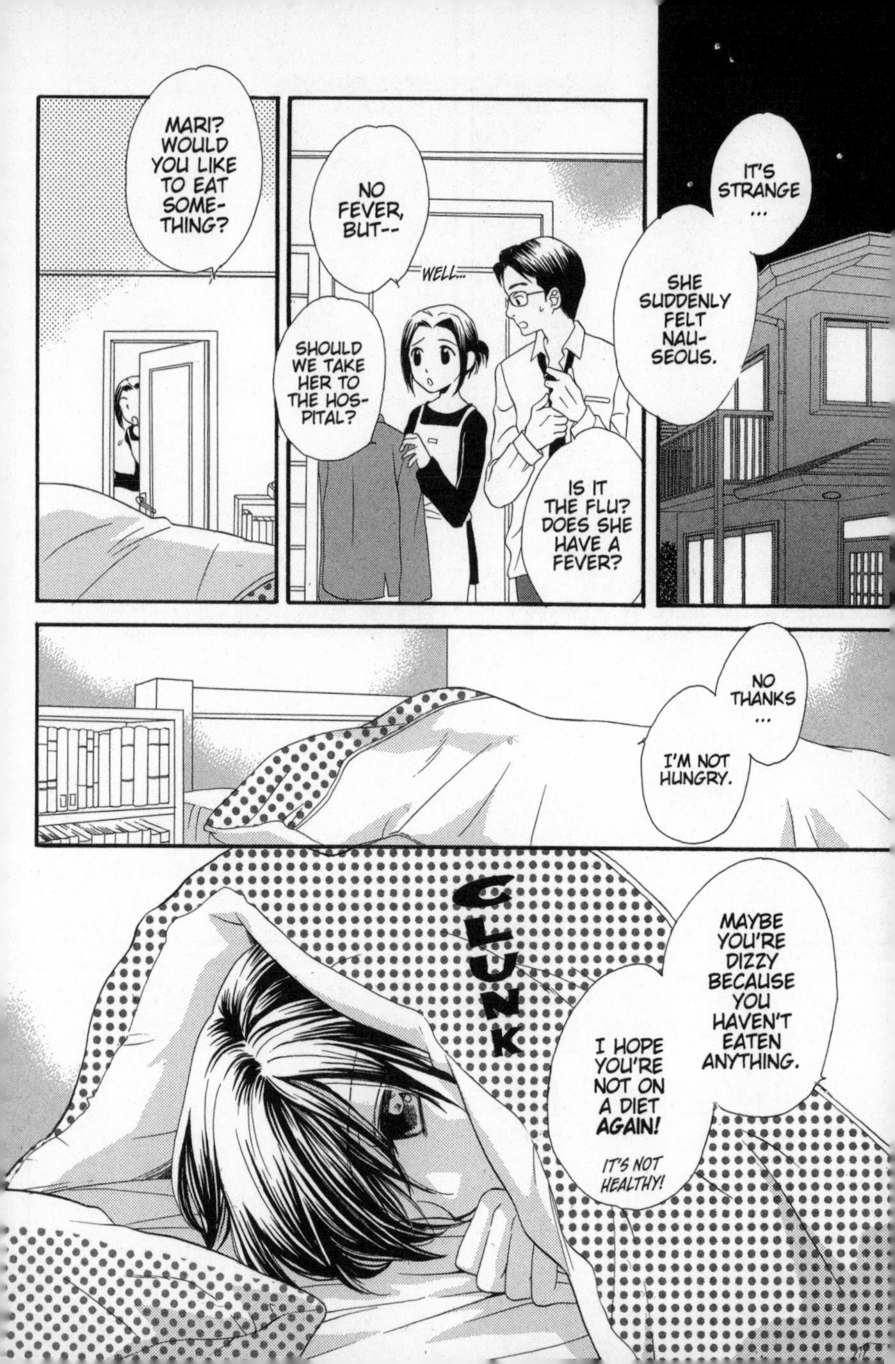

IT'S STRANGE...
SHE SUDDENLY FELT NAUSEOUS.
IS IT THE FLU? DOES SHE HAVE A FEVER?
NO FEVER, BUT--
WELL...
SHOULD WE TAKE HER TO THE HOSPITAL?
MARI? WOULD YOU LIKE TO EAT SOMETHING?
NO THANKS... I'M NOT HUNGRY.
CLUNK
MAYBE YOU'RE DIZZY BECAUSE YOU HAVEN'T EATEN ANYTHING.
I HOPE YOU'RE NOT ON A DIET AGAIN!
IT'S NOT HEALTHY!

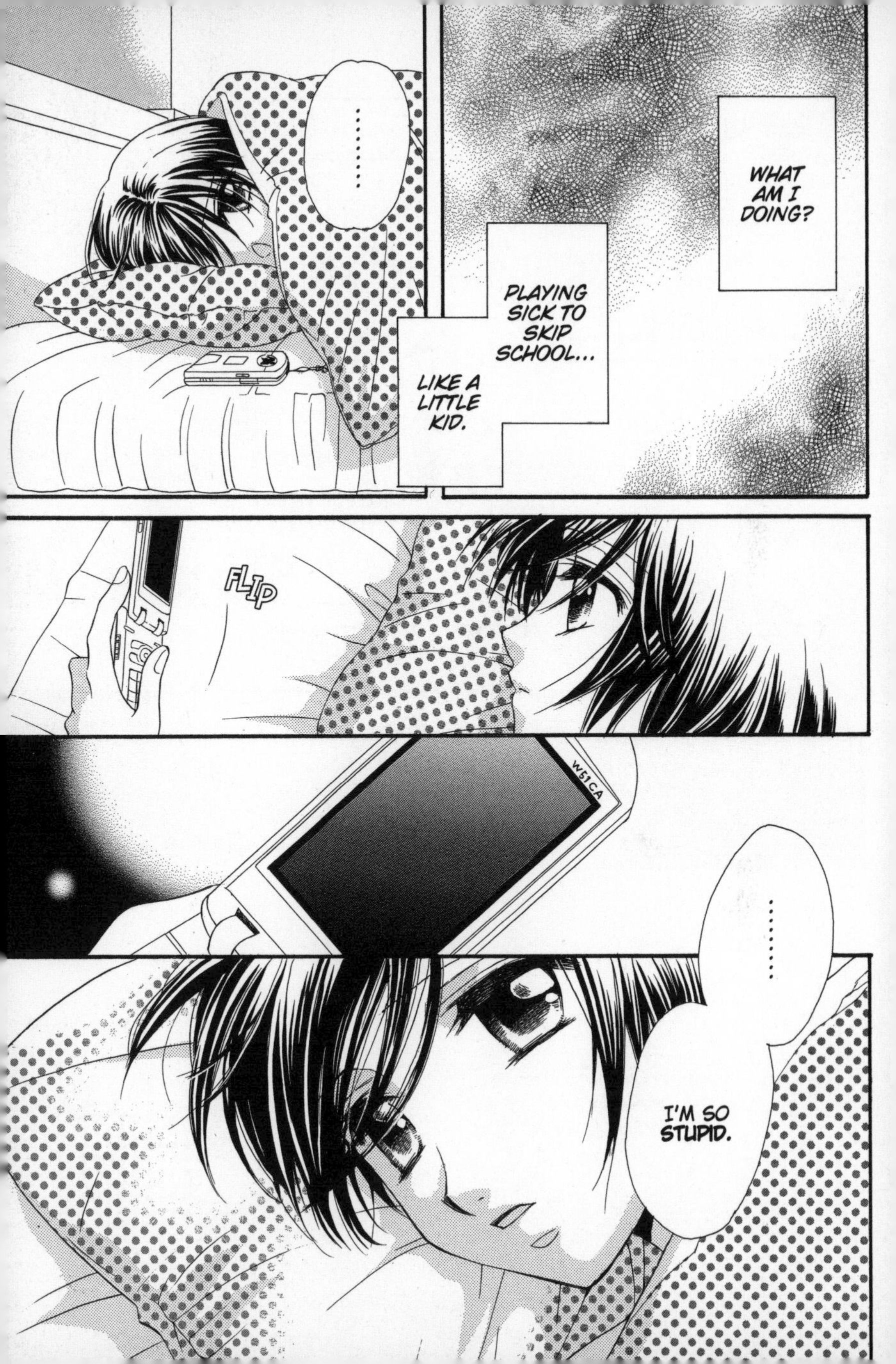

WHAT AM I DOING?
PLAYING SICK TO SKIP SCHOOL...
LIKE A LITTLE KID.
......
FLIP
W51CA
......
I'M SO STUPID.

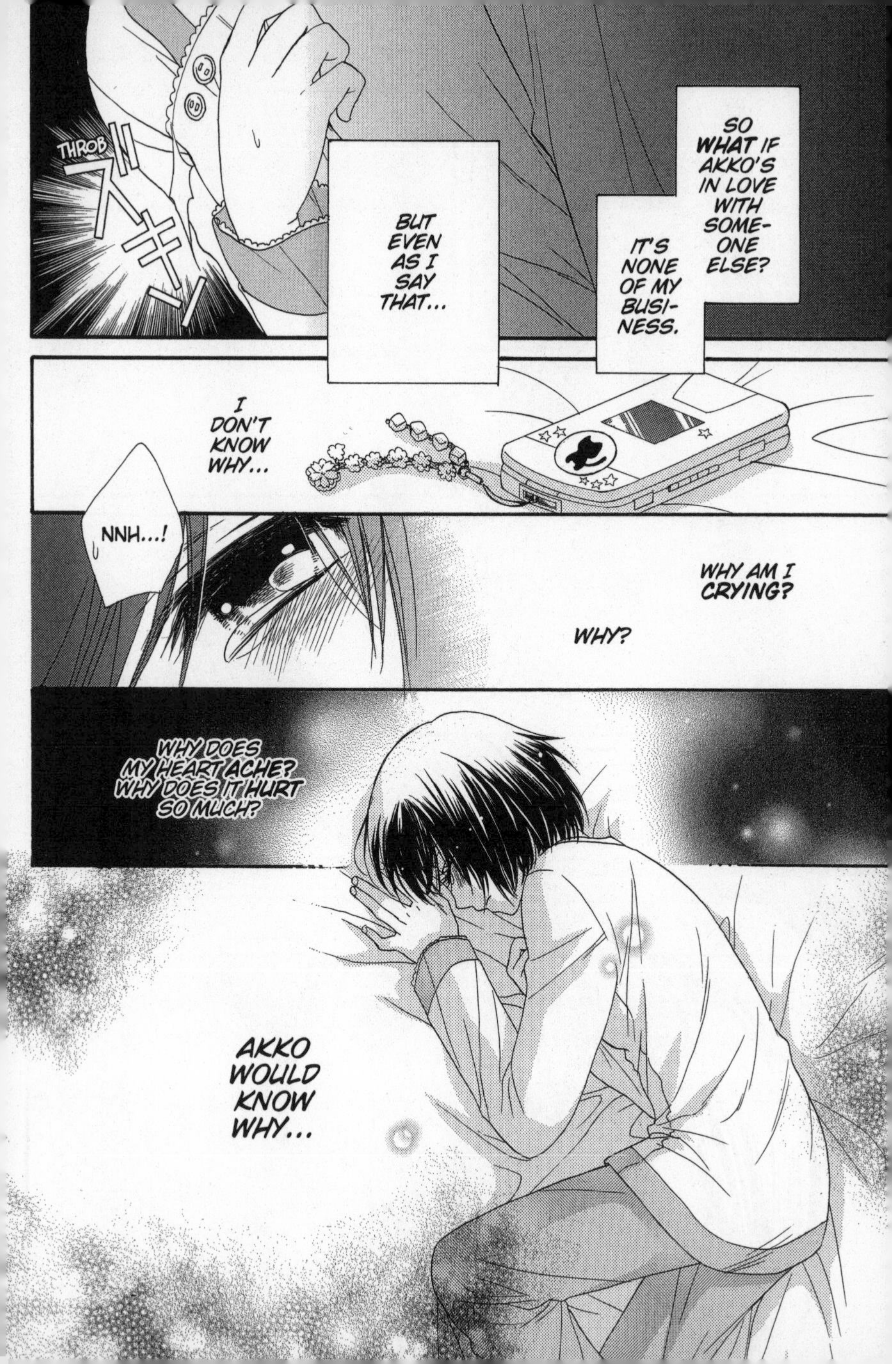

SO WHAT IF AKKO'S IN LOVE WITH SOME-ONE ELSE?
IT'S NONE OF MY BUSI-NESS.
BUT EVEN AS I SAY THAT...
THROB
I DON'T KNOW WHY...
WHY AM I CRYING?
WHY?
NNH...!
WHY DOES MY HEART ACHE? WHY DOES IT HURT SO MUCH?
AKKO WOULD KNOW WHY...

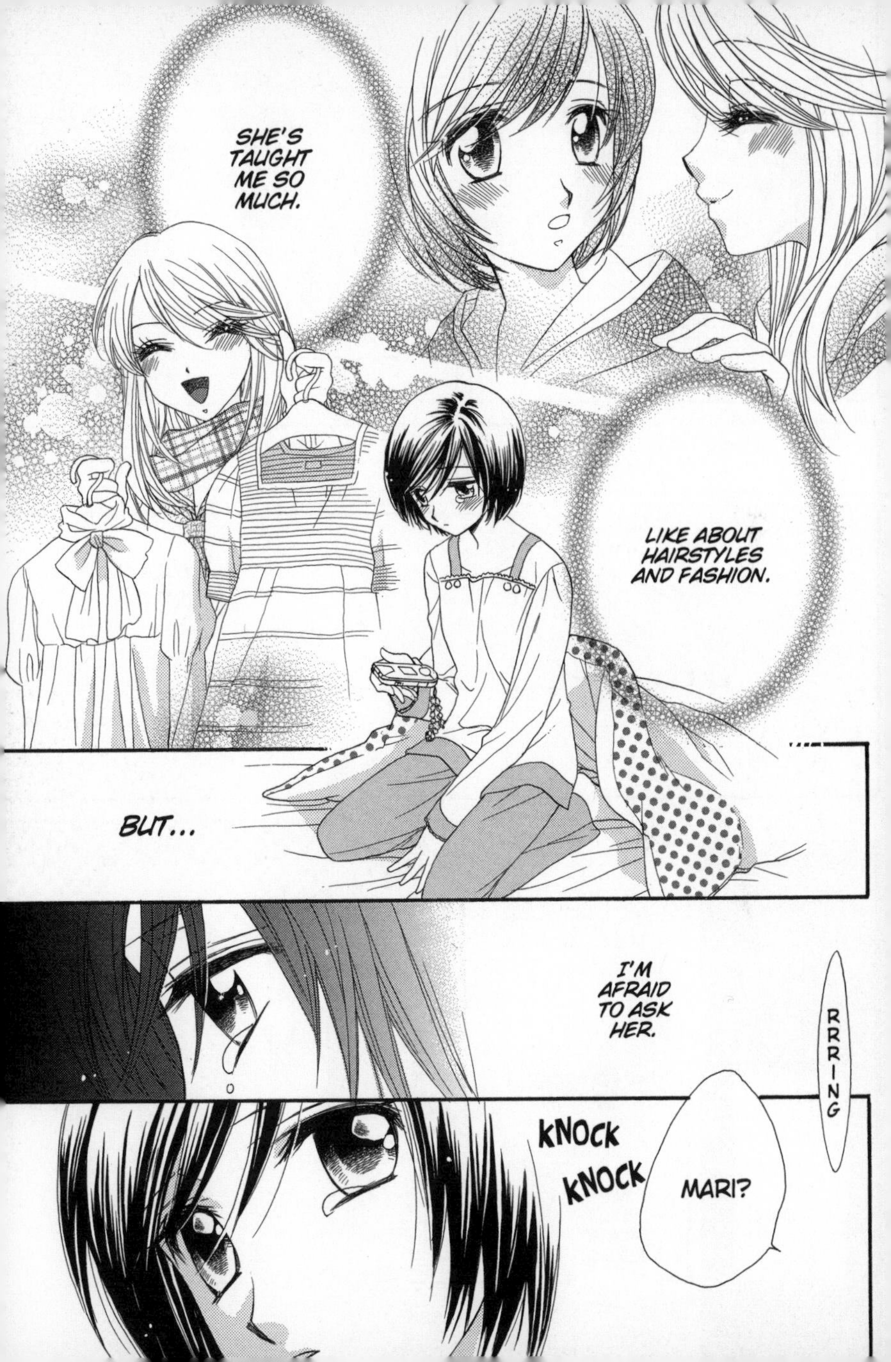
SHE'S TAUGHT ME SO MUCH.
LIKE ABOUT HAIRSTYLES AND FASHION.
BUT...
RRRING
I'M AFRAID TO ASK HER.
MARI?
KNOCK KNOCK

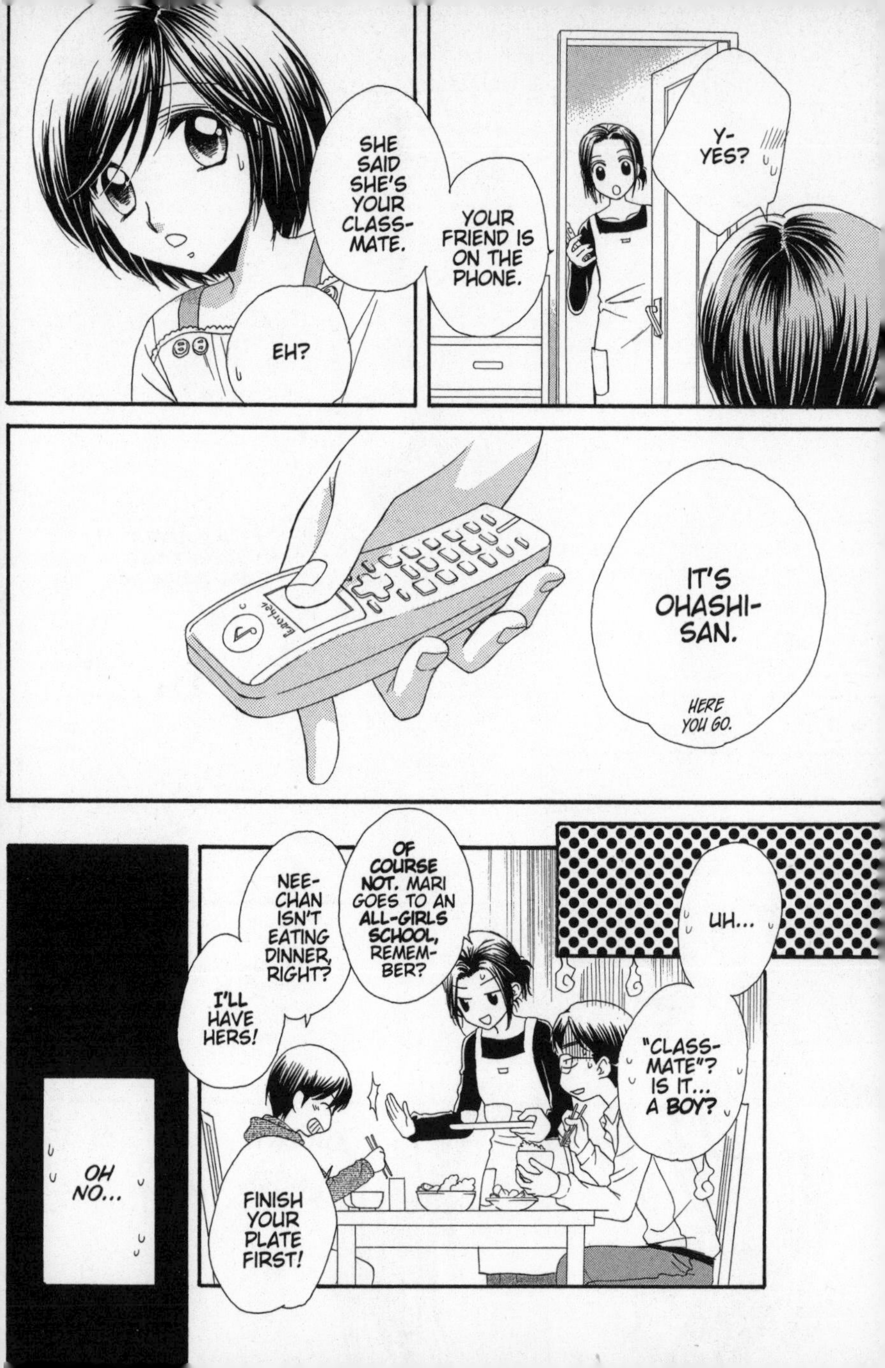
Y-YES?
YOUR FRIEND IS ON THE PHONE.
SHE SAID SHE'S YOUR CLASSMATE.
EH?
IT'S OHASHI-SAN.
HERE YOU GO.
UH...
"CLASSMATE"? IS IT... A BOY?
OF COURSE NOT. MARI GOES TO AN ALL-GIRLS SCHOOL, REMEMBER?
NEE-CHAN ISN'T EATING DINNER, RIGHT?
I'LL HAVE HERS!
FINISH YOUR PLATE FIRST!
OH NO...

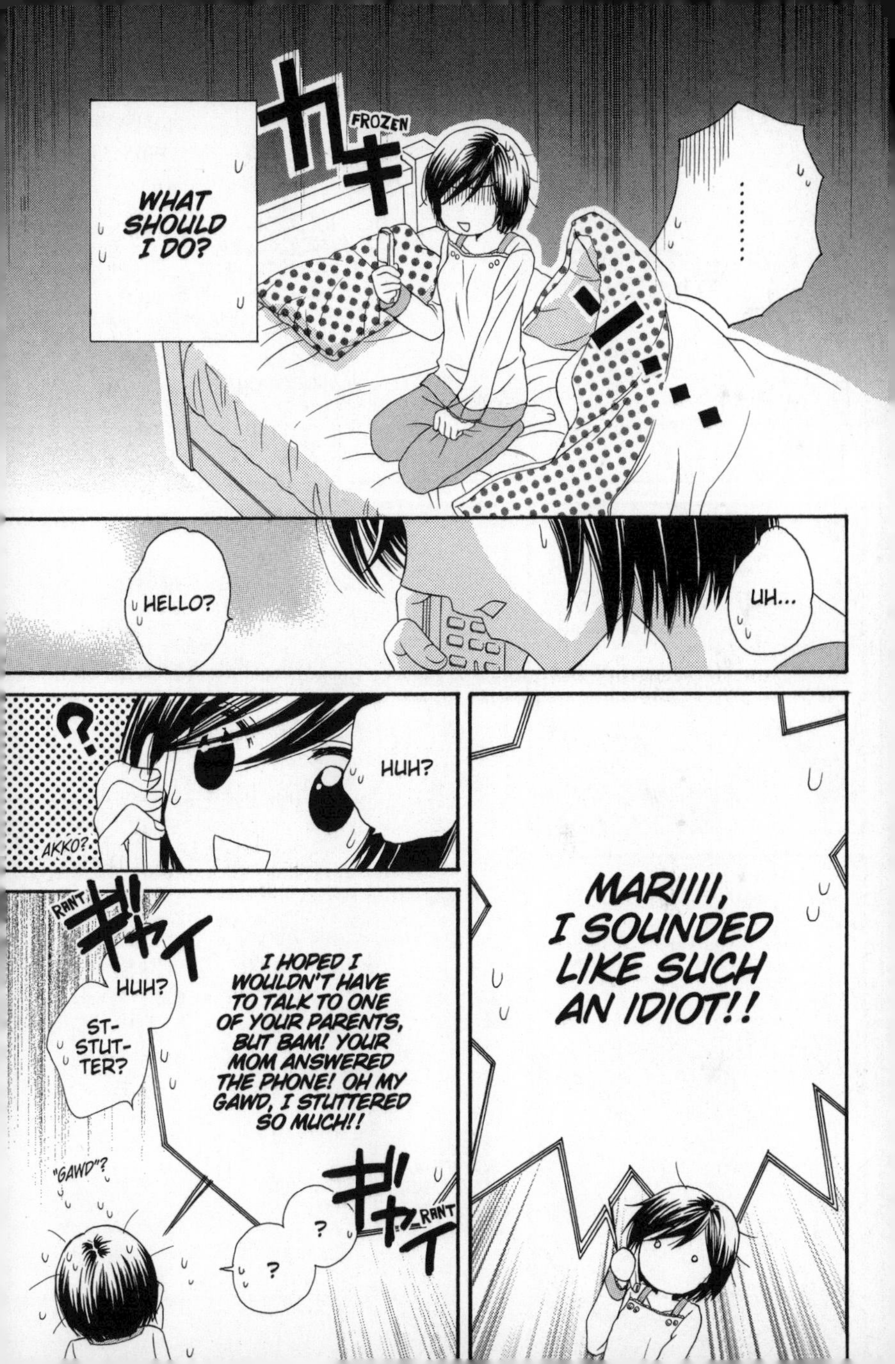
......
FROZEN
WHAT SHOULD I DO?
UH...
HELLO?
MARIIII, I SOUNDED LIKE SUCH AN IDIOT!!
HUH?
AKKO?
I HOPED I WOULDN'T HAVE TO TALK TO ONE OF YOUR PARENTS, BUT BAM! YOUR MOM ANSWERED THE PHONE! OH MY GAWD, I STUTTERED SO MUCH!!
RANT
HUH?
ST-STUT-TER?
RANT
?
?
"GAWD"?

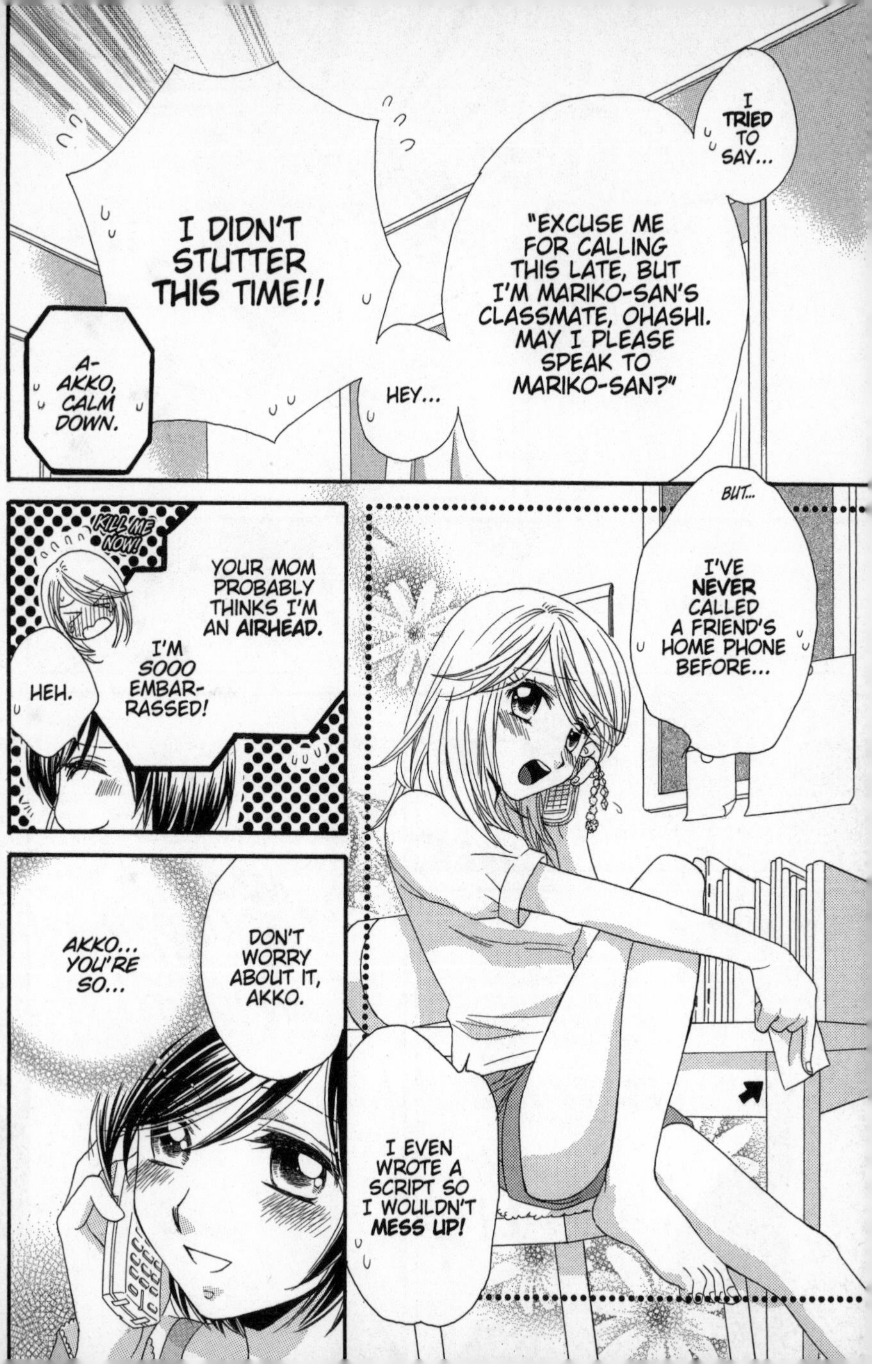
I TRIED TO SAY...
"EXCUSE ME FOR CALLING THIS LATE, BUT I'M MARIKO-SAN'S CLASSMATE, OHASHI. MAY I PLEASE SPEAK TO MARIKO-SAN?"
HEY...
I DIDN'T STUTTER THIS TIME!!
A-AKKO, CALM DOWN.
BUT...
I'VE NEVER CALLED A FRIEND'S HOME PHONE BEFORE...
I EVEN WROTE A SCRIPT SO I WOULDN'T MESS UP!
KILL ME NOW!
YOUR MOM PROBABLY THINKS I'M AN AIRHEAD.
I'M SOOO EMBARRASSED!
HEH.
DON'T WORRY ABOUT IT, AKKO.
AKKO... YOU'RE SO...

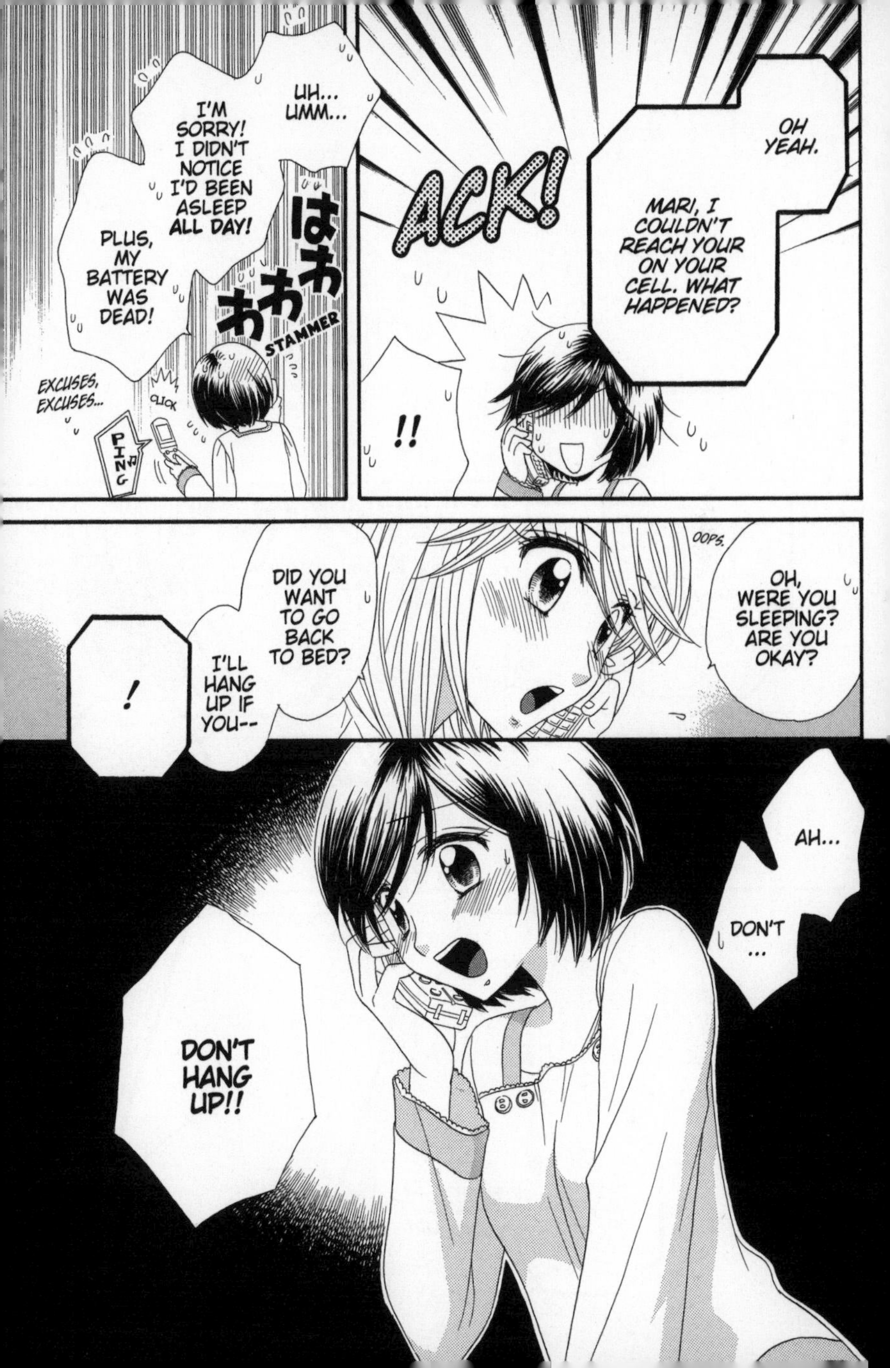
OH YEAH.
MARI, I COULDN'T REACH YOUR ON YOUR CELL. WHAT HAPPENED?
ACK!
!!
UH... UMM...
I'M SORRY! I DIDN'T NOTICE I'D BEEN ASLEEP ALL DAY!
PLUS, MY BATTERY WAS DEAD!
はわわわ
STAMMER
EXCUSES, EXCUSES...
CLICK
PING
OOPS.
OH, WERE YOU SLEEPING? ARE YOU OKAY?
DID YOU WANT TO GO BACK TO BED?
I'LL HANG UP IF YOU--
!
AH...
DON'T ...
DON'T HANG UP!!

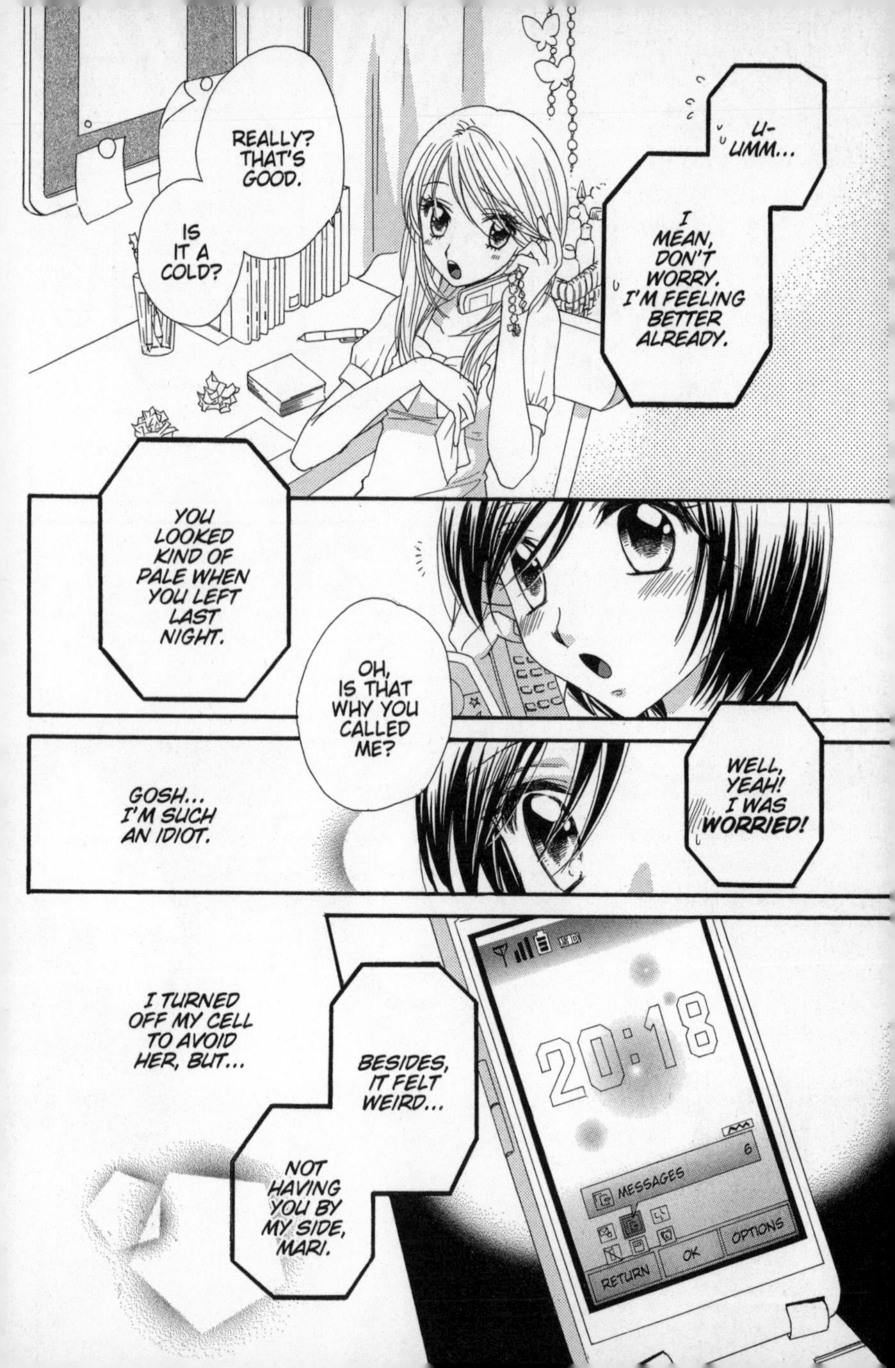
U-UMM...
I MEAN, DON'T WORRY. I'M FEELING BETTER ALREADY.
REALLY? THAT'S GOOD.
IS IT A COLD?
YOU LOOKED KIND OF PALE WHEN YOU LEFT LAST NIGHT.
OH, IS THAT WHY YOU CALLED ME?
WELL, YEAH! I WAS WORRIED!
GOSH... I'M SUCH AN IDIOT.
20:18
6
MESSAGES
OPTIONS
OK
RETURN
I TURNED OFF MY CELL TO AVOID HER, BUT...
BESIDES, IT FELT WEIRD...
NOT HAVING YOU BY MY SIDE, MARI.

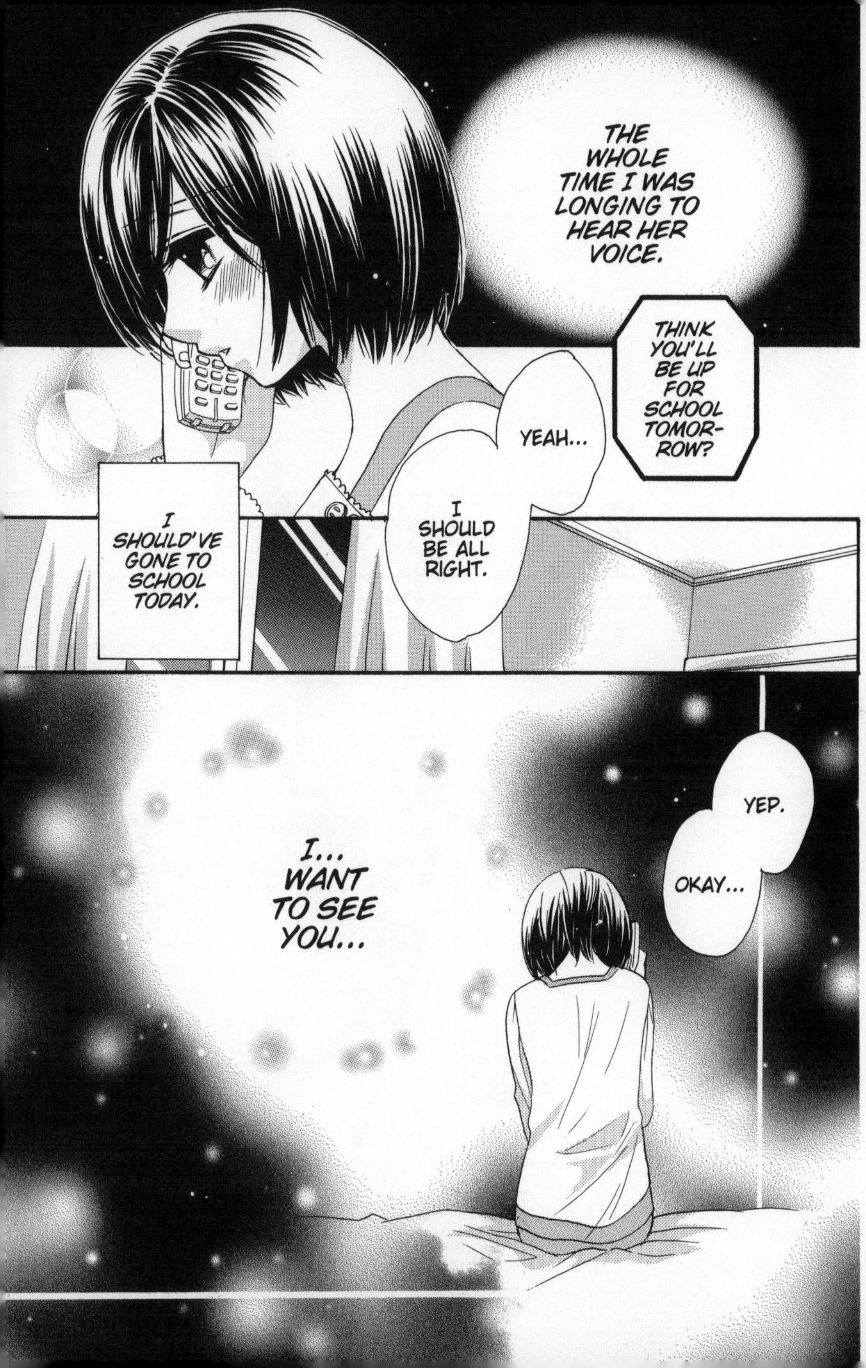
THE WHOLE TIME I WAS LONGING TO HEAR HER VOICE.
THINK YOU'LL BE UP FOR SCHOOL TOMOR-ROW?
YEAH...
I SHOULD BE ALL RIGHT.
I SHOULD'VE GONE TO SCHOOL TODAY.
YEP.
OKAY...
I... WANT TO SEE YOU...

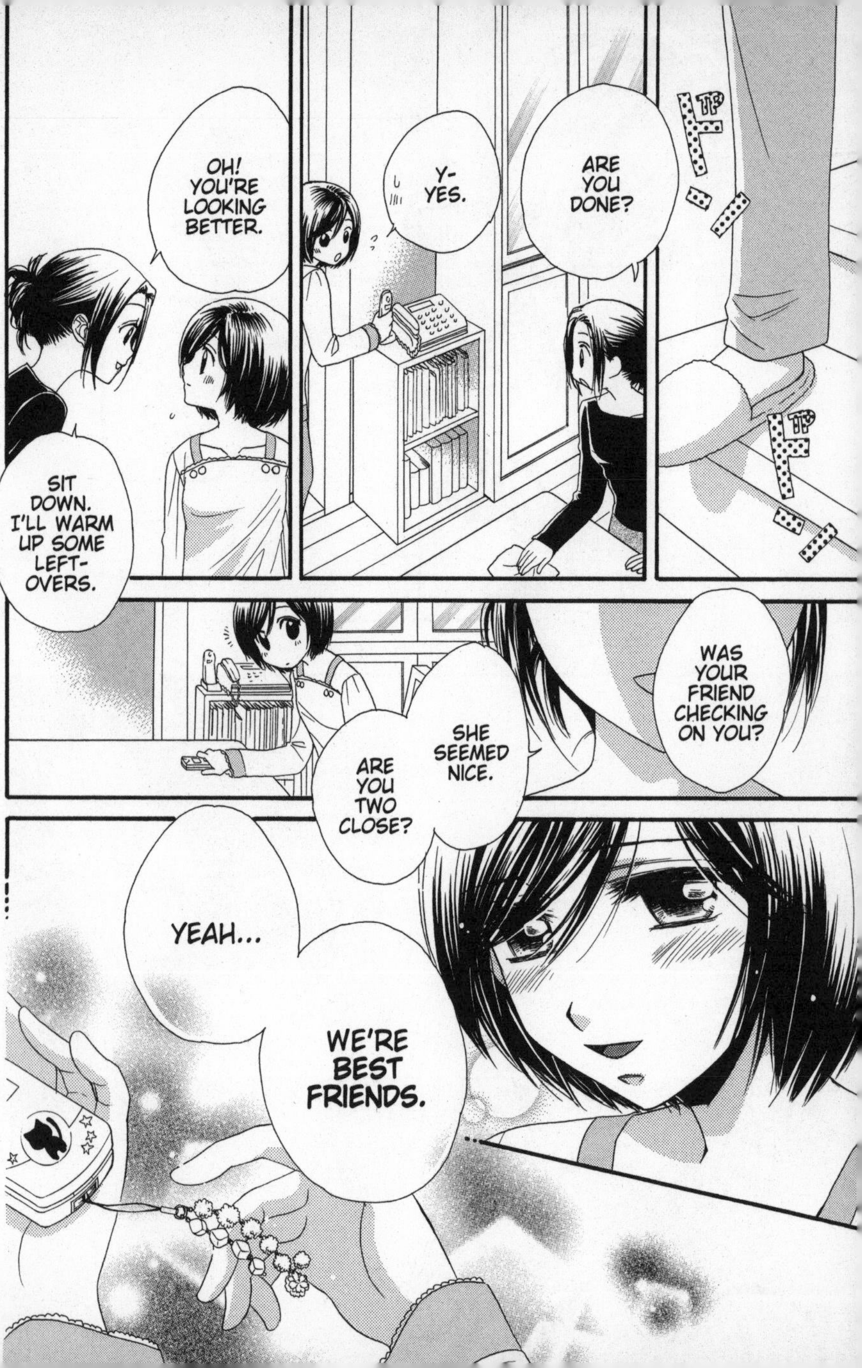
TP
TP
ARE YOU DONE?
Y- YES.
OH! YOU'RE LOOKING BETTER.
SIT DOWN. I'LL WARM UP SOME LEFT-OVERS.
WAS YOUR FRIEND CHECKING ON YOU?
SHE SEEMED NICE.
ARE YOU TWO CLOSE?
YEAH...
WE'RE BEST FRIENDS.

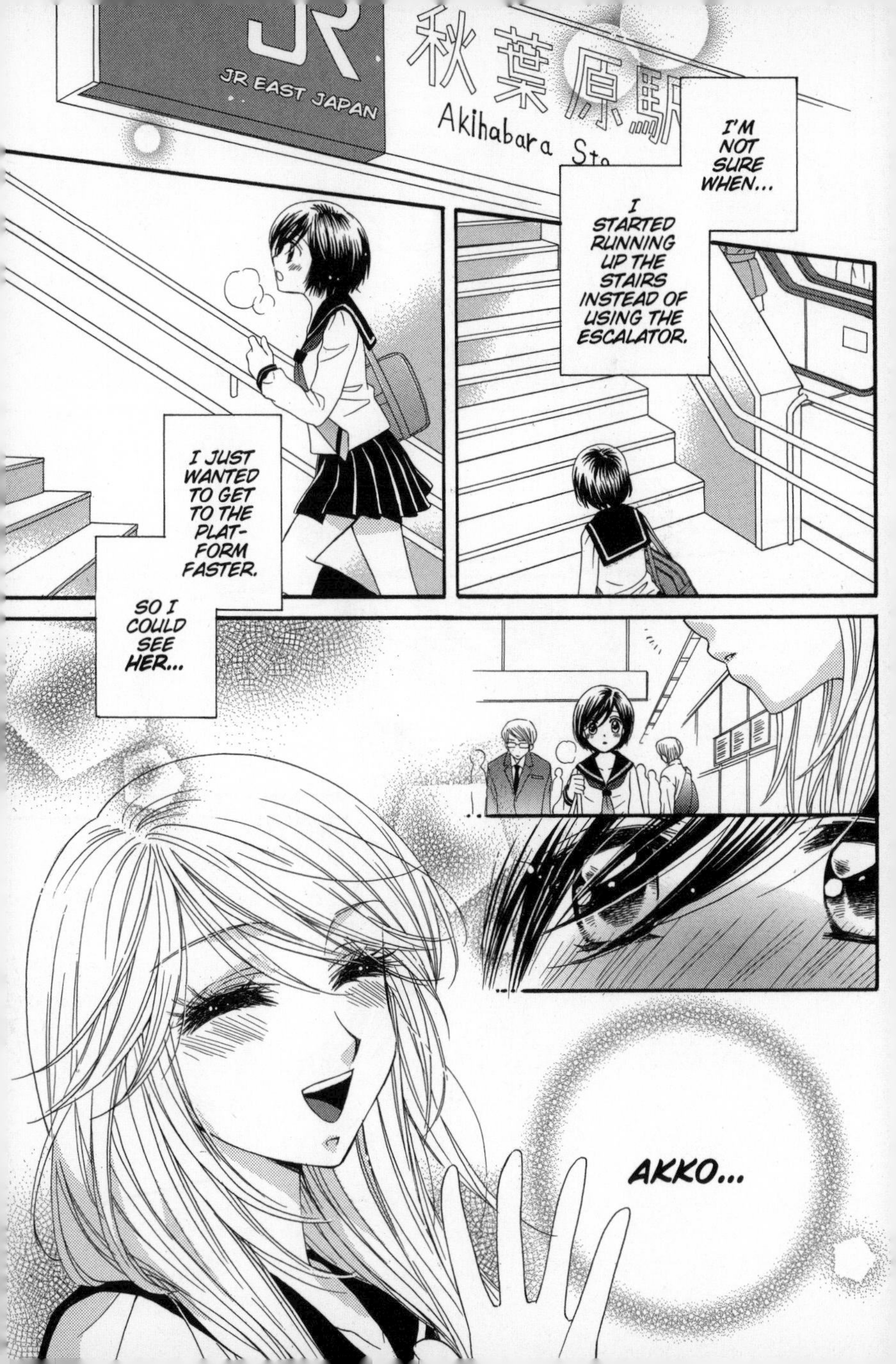
JR
JR EAST JAPAN
秋葉原駅
Akihabara Sta
I'M NOT SURE WHEN...
I STARTED RUNNING UP THE STAIRS INSTEAD OF USING THE ESCALATOR.
I JUST WANTED TO GET TO THE PLAT-FORM FASTER.
SO I COULD SEE HER...
AKKO...

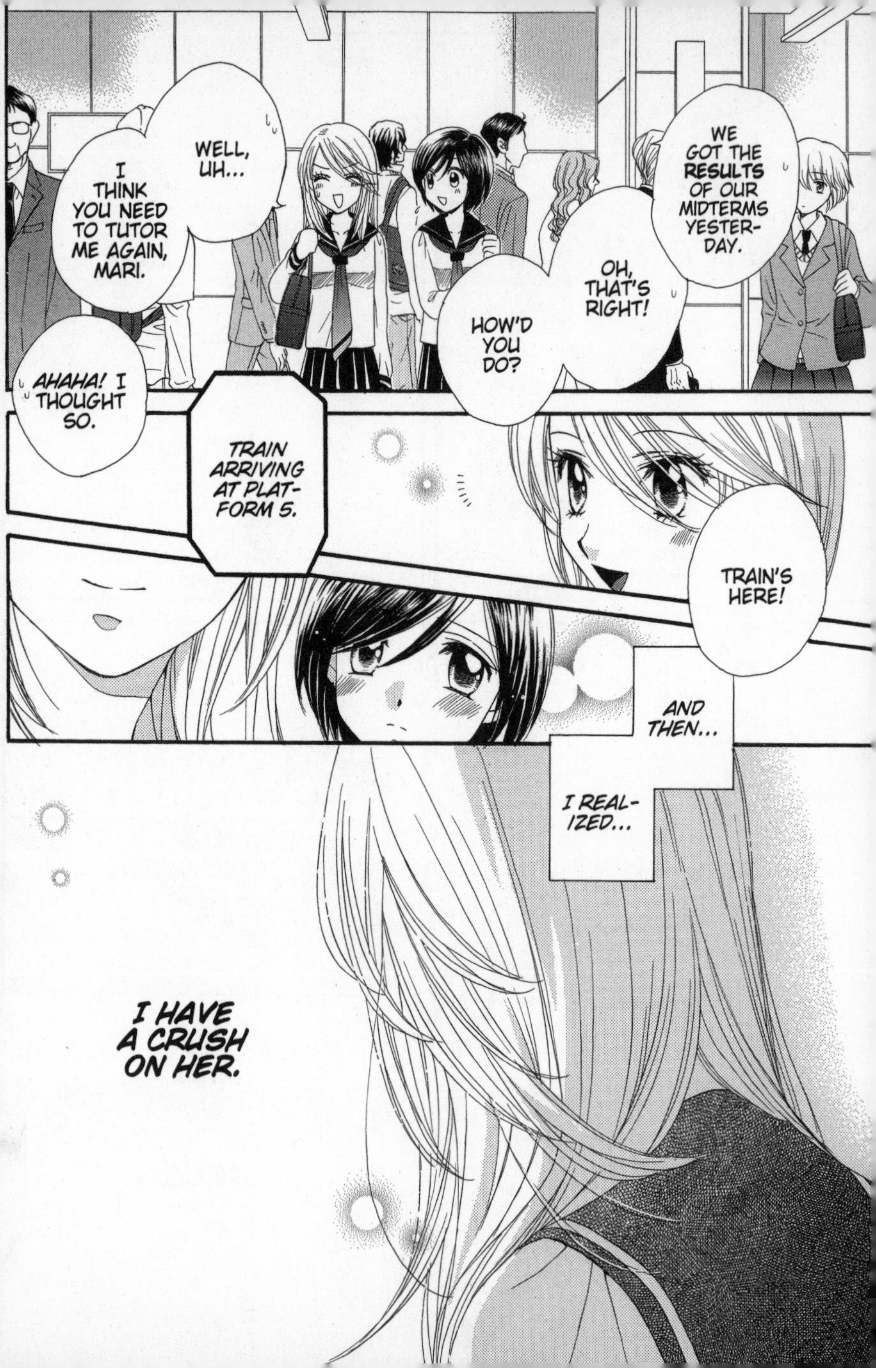
WE GOT THE RESULTS OF OUR MIDTERMS YESTER-DAY.
OH, THAT'S RIGHT!
HOW'D YOU DO?
WELL, UH...
I THINK YOU NEED TO TUTOR ME AGAIN, MARI.
AHAHA! I THOUGHT SO.
TRAIN'S HERE!
TRAIN ARRIVING AT PLAT-FORM 5.
AND THEN...
I REAL-IZED...
I HAVE A CRUSH ON HER.

P.E. UNIFORM

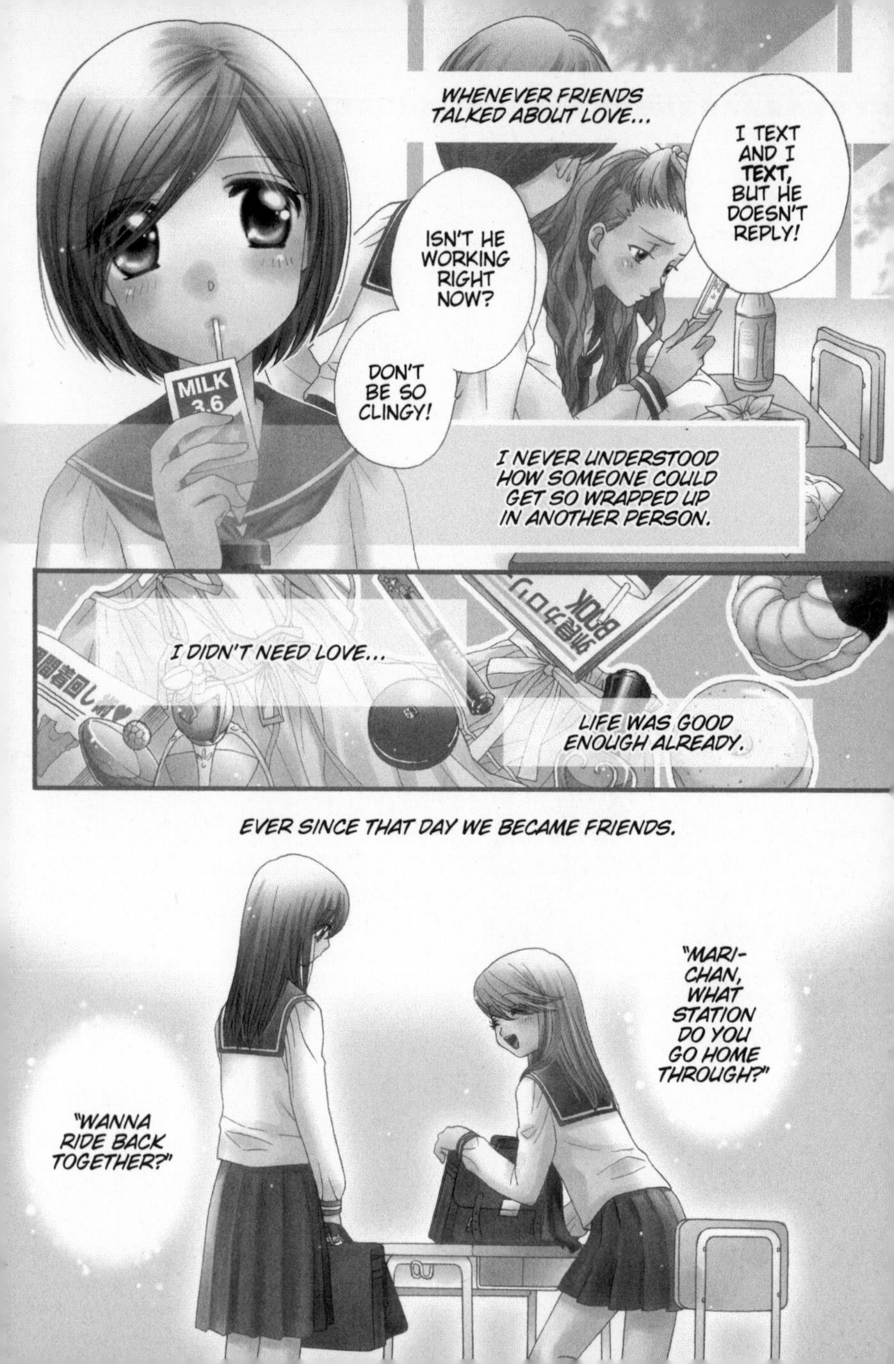
WHENEVER FRIENDS TALKED ABOUT LOVE...
I TEXT AND I TEXT, BUT HE DOESN'T REPLY!
ISN'T HE WORKING RIGHT NOW?
DON'T BE SO CLINGY!
MILK 3.6
I NEVER UNDERSTOOD HOW SOMEONE COULD GET SO WRAPPED UP IN ANOTHER PERSON.
I DIDN'T NEED LOVE...
LIFE WAS GOOD ENOUGH ALREADY.
BOOK
EVER SINCE THAT DAY WE BECAME FRIENDS.
"MARI-CHAN, WHAT STATION DO YOU GO HOME THROUGH?"
"WANNA RIDE BACK TOGETHER?"

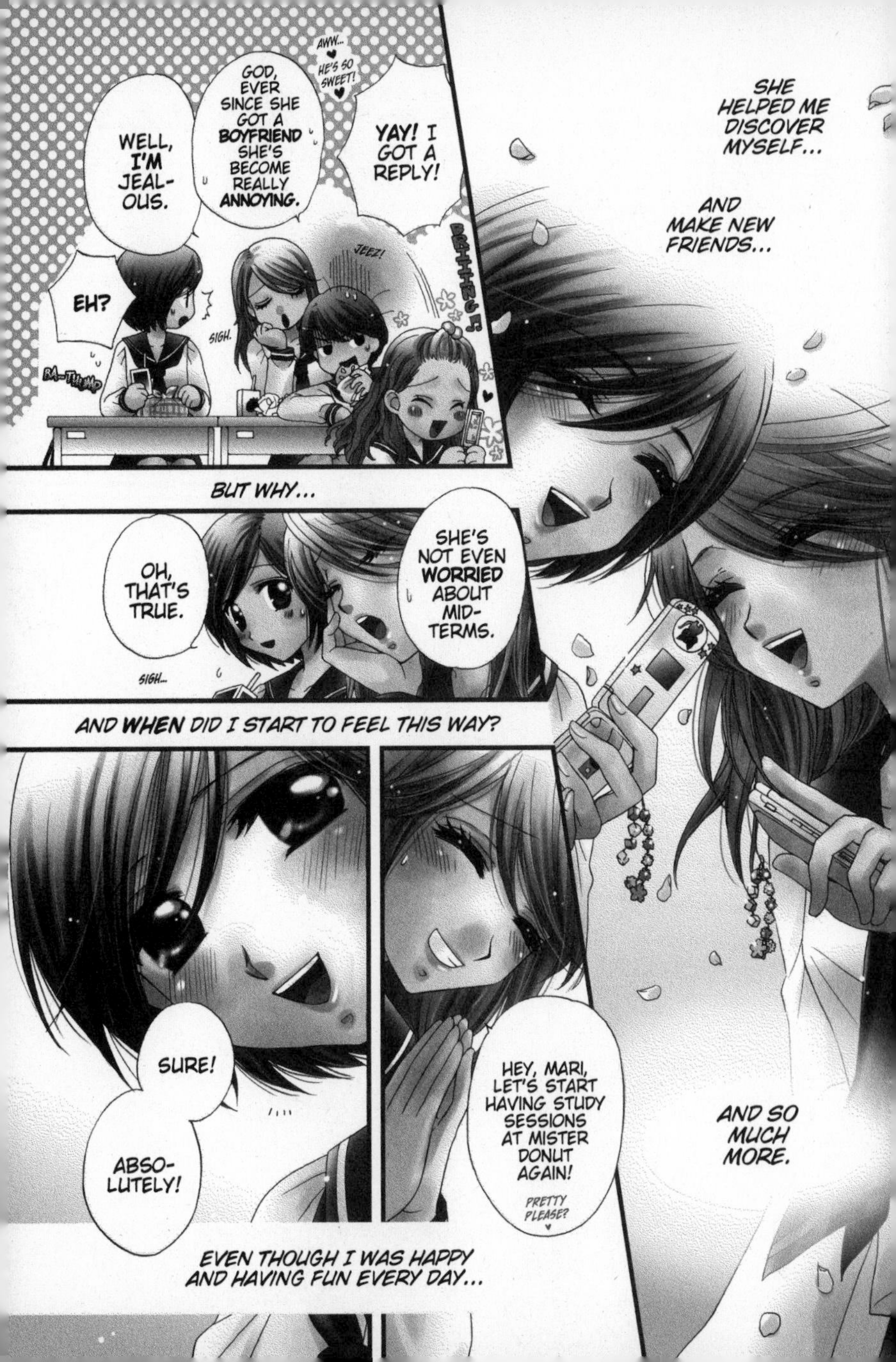
SHE HELPED ME DISCOVER MYSELF...
AND MAKE NEW FRIENDS...
AND SO MUCH MORE.
AWW... HE'S SO SWEET!
YAY! I GOT A REPLY!
BRRIIING♫
GOD, EVER SINCE SHE GOT A BOYFRIEND SHE'S BECOME REALLY ANNOYING.
JEEZ!
WELL, I'M JEAL-OUS.
EH?
SIGH.
BA-THUMP
BUT WHY...
SHE'S NOT EVEN WORRIED ABOUT MID-TERMS.
OH, THAT'S TRUE.
SIGH...
AND WHEN DID I START TO FEEL THIS WAY?
HEY, MARI, LET'S START HAVING STUDY SESSIONS AT MISTER DONUT AGAIN!
PRETTY PLEASE?
SURE!
ABSO-LUTELY!
EVEN THOUGH I WAS HAPPY AND HAVING FUN EVERY DAY...

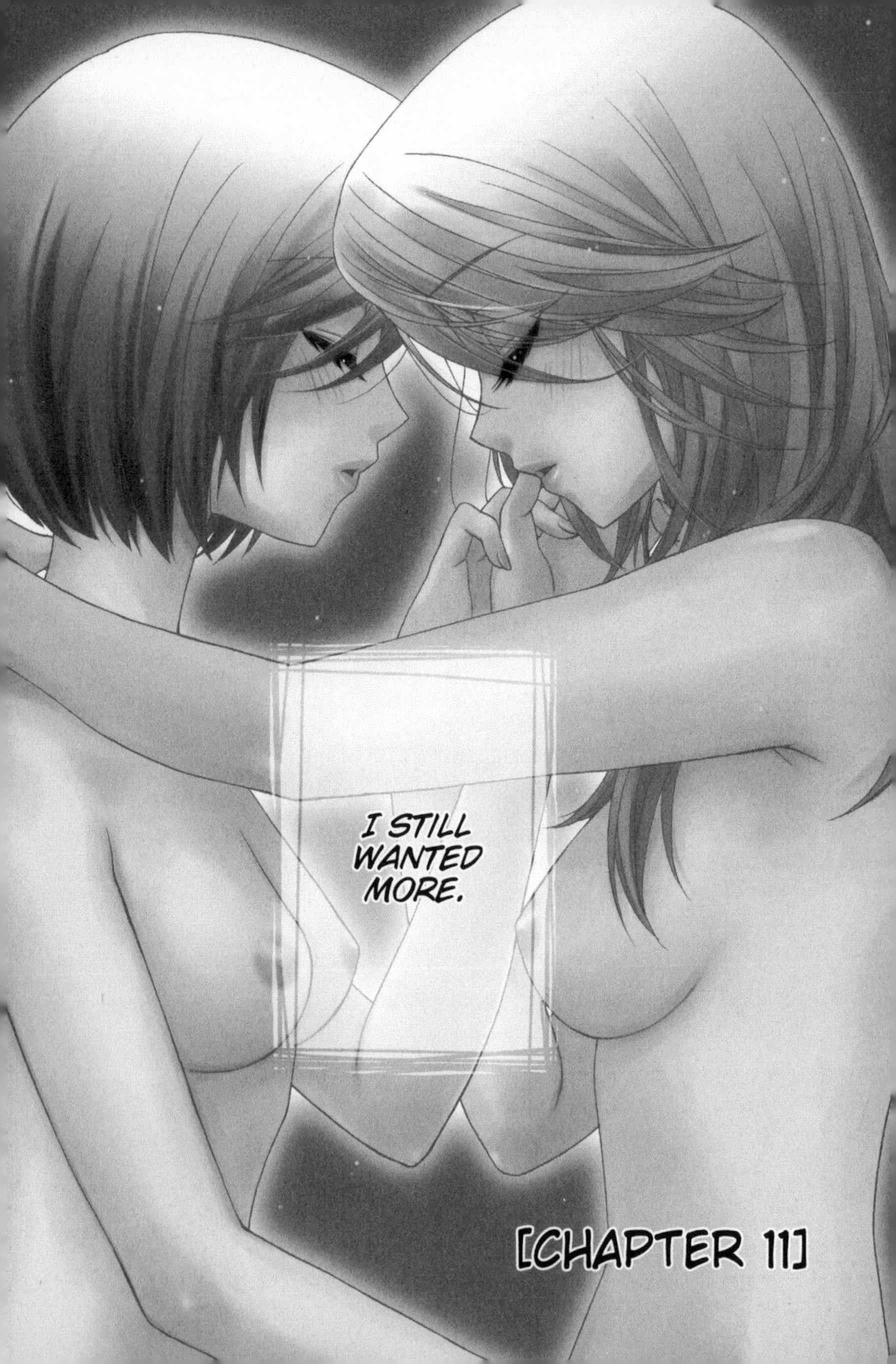
I STILL WANTED MORE.
[CHAPTER 11]

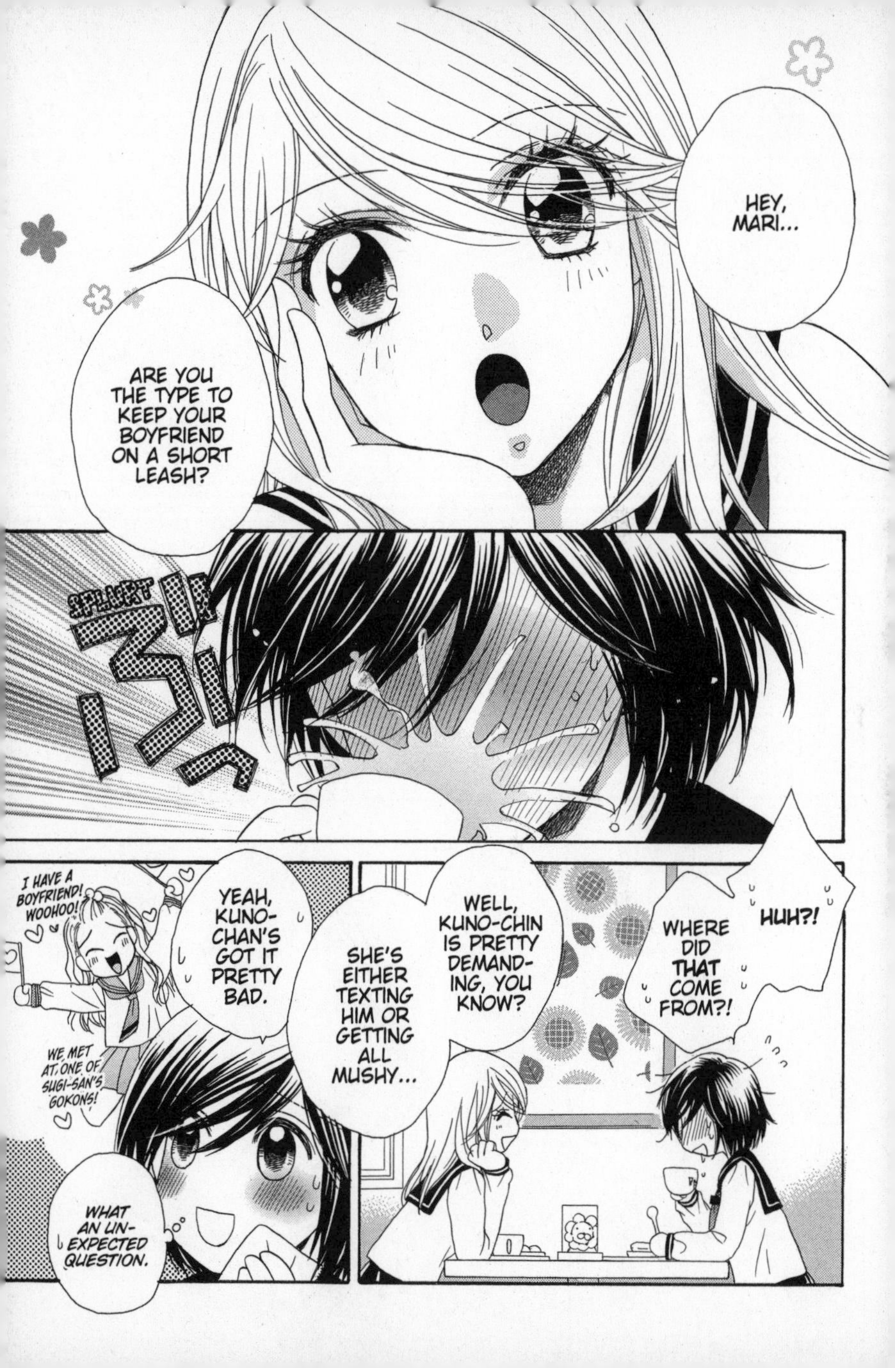

HEY, MARI...
ARE YOU THE TYPE TO KEEP YOUR BOYFRIEND ON A SHORT LEASH?
HUH?!
WHERE DID THAT COME FROM?!
WELL, KUNO-CHIN IS PRETTY DEMAND-ING, YOU KNOW?
SHE'S EITHER TEXTING HIM OR GETTING ALL MUSHY...
YEAH, KUNO-CHAN'S GOT IT PRETTY BAD.
I HAVE A BOYFRIEND! WOOHOO!
WE MET AT ONE OF SUGI-SAN'S GOKONS!
WHAT AN UN-EXPECTED QUESTION.

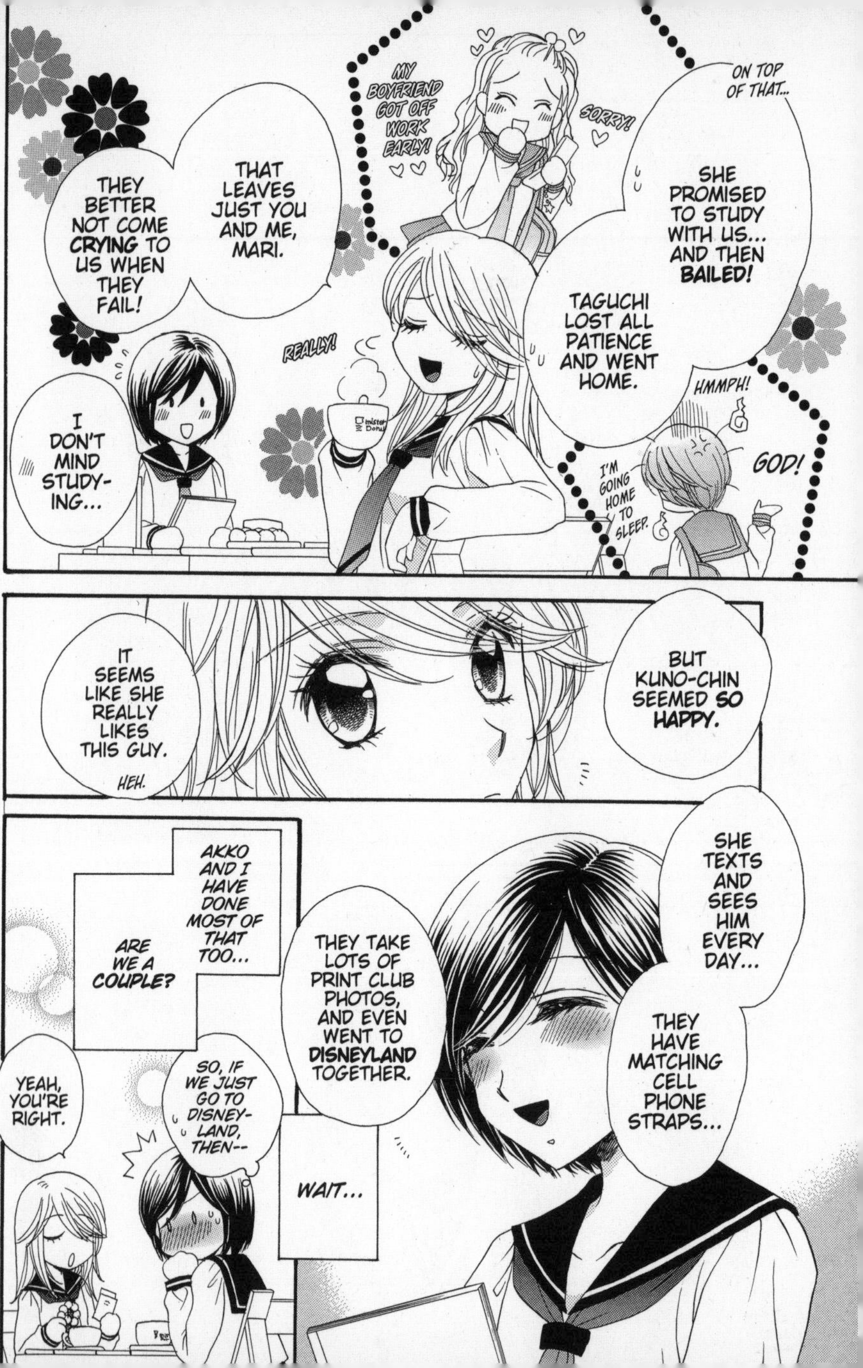

ON TOP OF THAT... SHE PROMISED TO STUDY WITH US... AND THEN BAILED!
SORRY!
MY BOYFRIEND GOT OFF WORK EARLY!
TAGUCHI LOST ALL PATIENCE AND WENT HOME.
HMMPH!
GOD!
I'M GOING HOME TO SLEEP.
THAT LEAVES JUST YOU AND ME, MARI.
THEY BETTER NOT COME CRYING TO US WHEN THEY FAIL!
REALLY!
I DON'T MIND STUDY-ING...
BUT KUNO-CHIN SEEMED SO HAPPY.
IT SEEMS LIKE SHE REALLY LIKES THIS GUY.
HEH.
SHE TEXTS AND SEES HIM EVERY DAY...
THEY HAVE MATCHING CELL PHONE STRAPS...
THEY TAKE LOTS OF PRINT CLUB PHOTOS, AND EVEN WENT TO DISNEYLAND TOGETHER.
AKKO AND I HAVE DONE MOST OF THAT TOO...
ARE WE A COUPLE?
WAIT...
SO, IF WE JUST GO TO DISNEY-LAND, THEN--
YEAH, YOU'RE RIGHT.

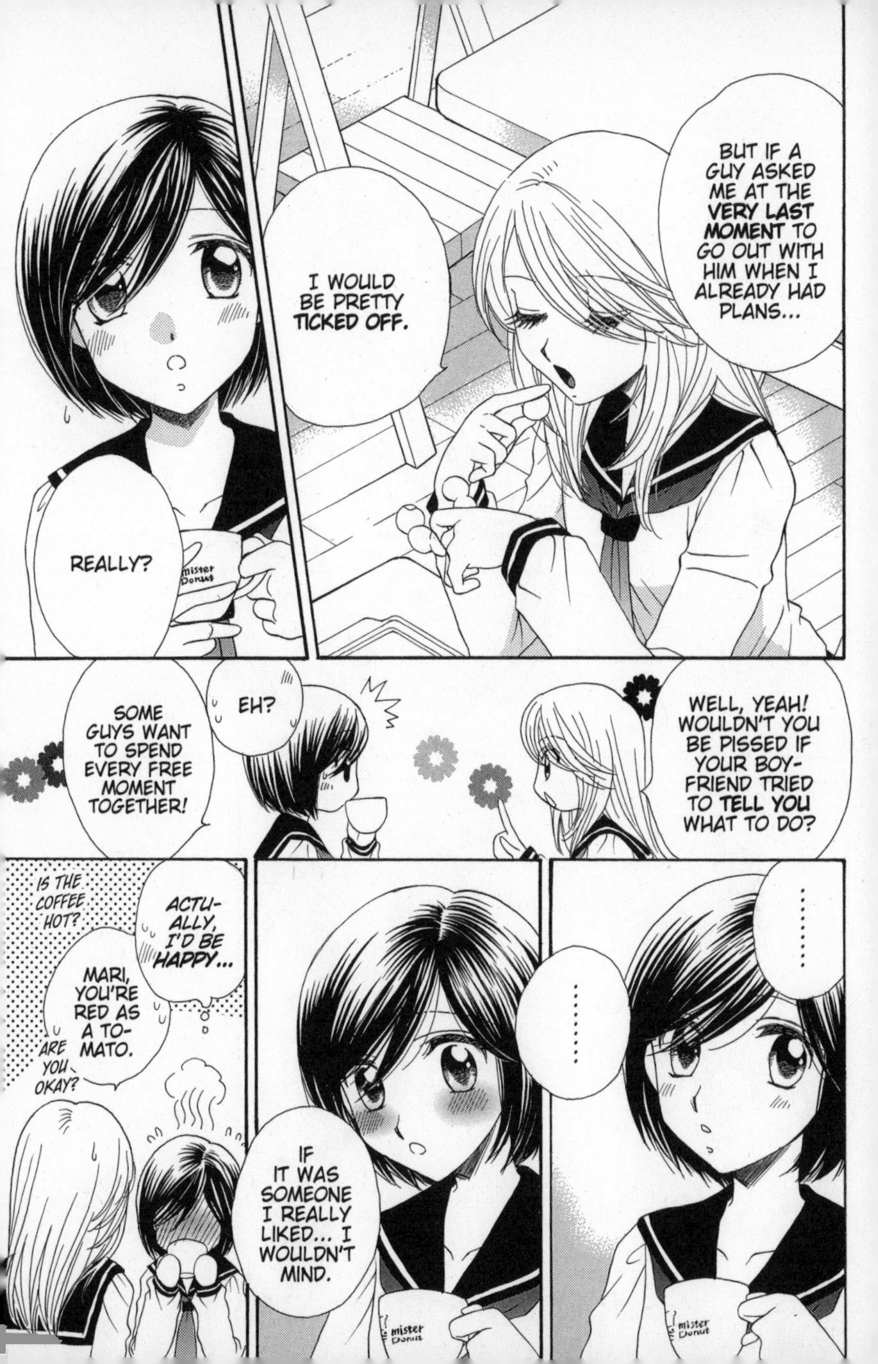

BUT IF A GUY ASKED ME AT THE VERY LAST MOMENT TO GO OUT WITH HIM WHEN I ALREADY HAD PLANS...
I WOULD BE PRETTY TICKED OFF.
REALLY?
WELL, YEAH! WOULDN'T YOU BE PISSED IF YOUR BOY-FRIEND TRIED TO TELL YOU WHAT TO DO?
EH?
SOME GUYS WANT TO SPEND EVERY FREE MOMENT TOGETHER!
......
......
IF IT WAS SOMEONE I REALLY LIKED... I WOULDN'T MIND.
ACTU-ALLY, I'D BE HAPPY...
IS THE COFFEE HOT?
MARI, YOU'RE RED AS A TO-MATO.
ARE YOU OKAY?

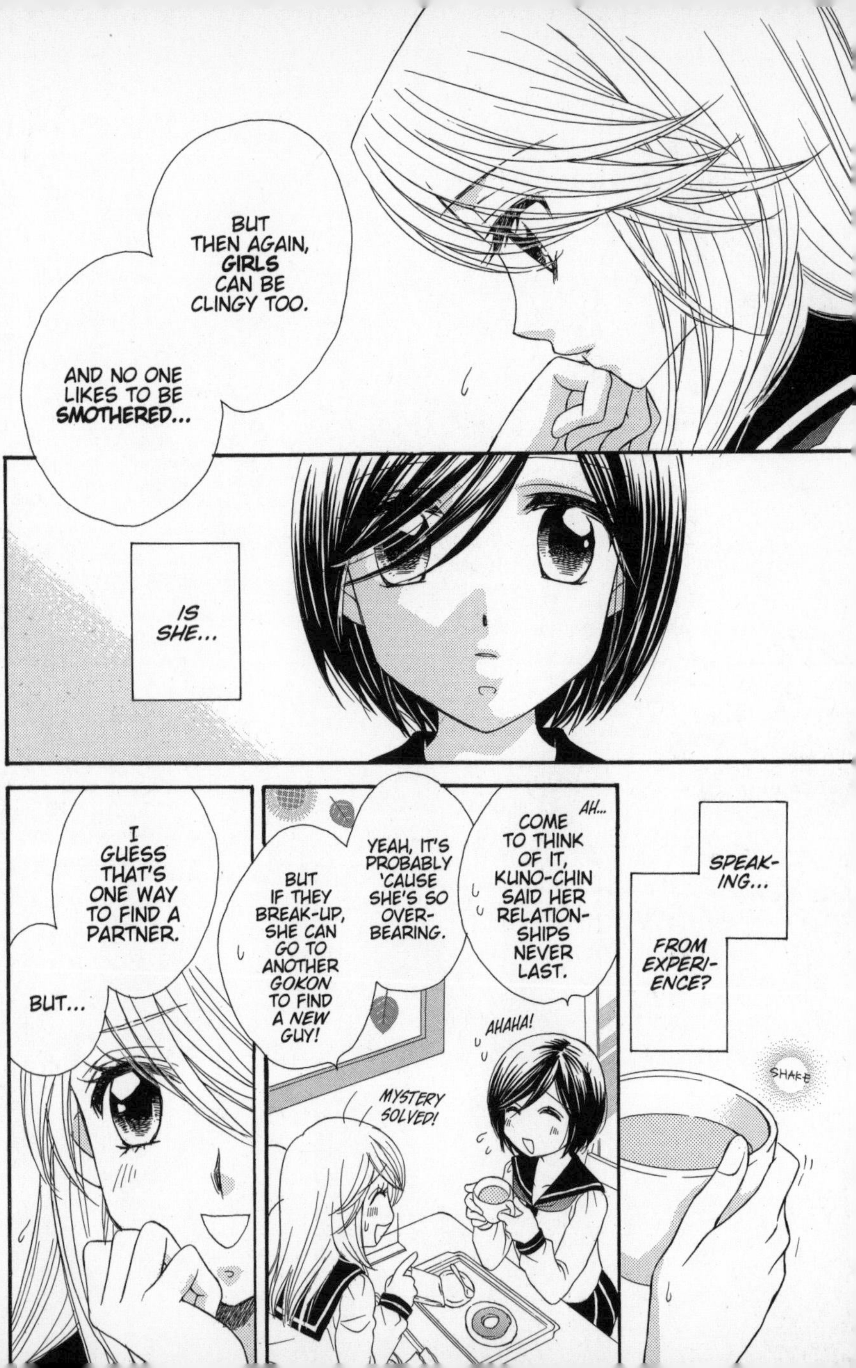
BUT THEN AGAIN, GIRLS CAN BE CLINGY TOO.
AND NO ONE LIKES TO BE SMOTHERED...
IS SHE...
SPEAKING...
FROM EXPERIENCE?
SHAKE
AH...
COME TO THINK OF IT, KUNO-CHIN SAID HER RELATIONSHIPS NEVER LAST.
YEAH, IT'S PROBABLY 'CAUSE SHE'S SO OVERBEARING.
BUT IF THEY BREAK-UP, SHE CAN GO TO ANOTHER GOKON TO FIND A NEW GUY!
AHAHA!
MYSTERY SOLVED!
I GUESS THAT'S ONE WAY TO FIND A PARTNER.
BUT...

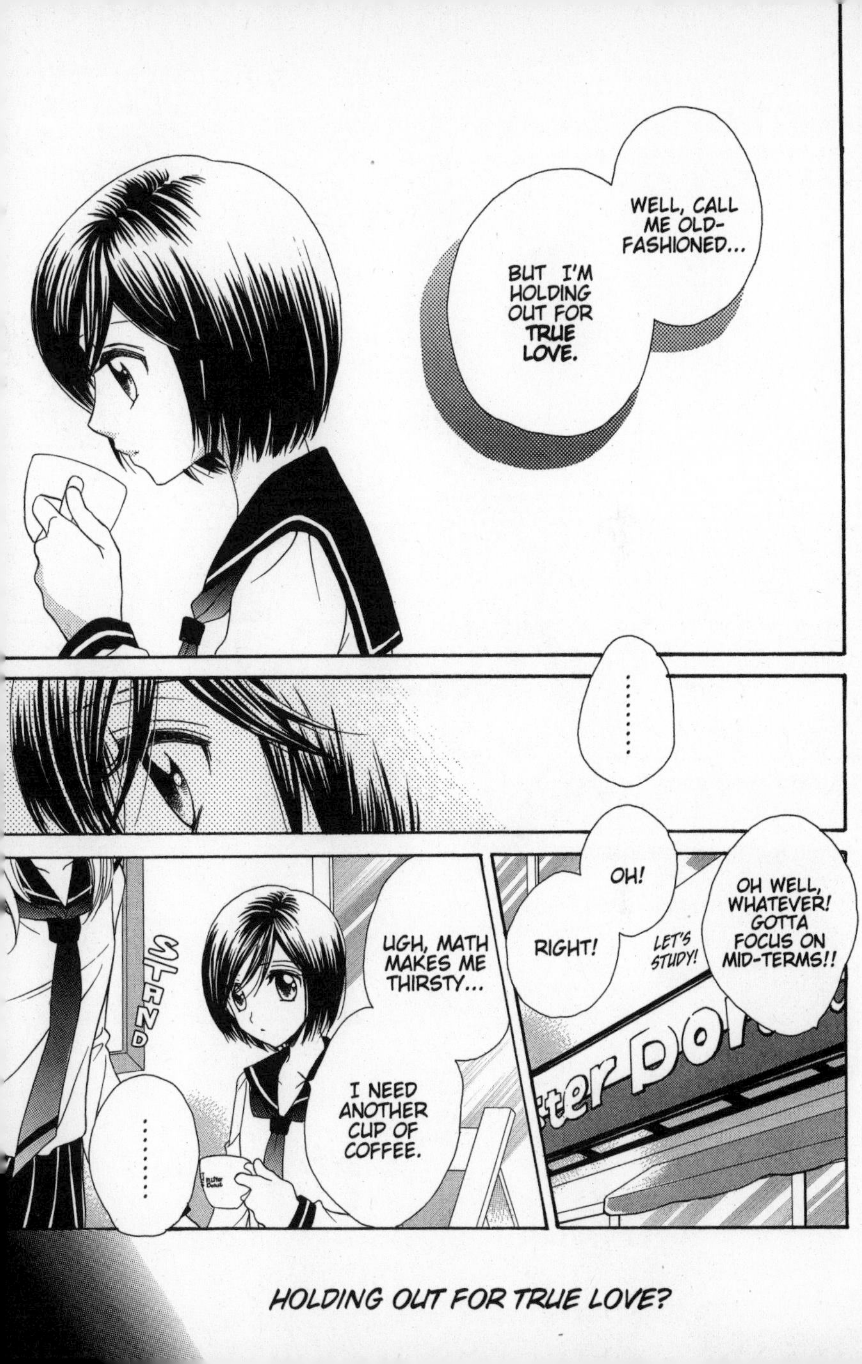
WELL, CALL ME OLD-FASHIONED...
BUT I'M HOLDING OUT FOR TRUE LOVE.
......
OH WELL, WHATEVER! GOTTA FOCUS ON MID-TERMS!!
OH!
LET'S STUDY!
RIGHT!
UGH, MATH MAKES ME THIRSTY...
STAND
I NEED ANOTHER CUP OF COFFEE.
......

HOLDING OUT FOR TRUE LOVE?

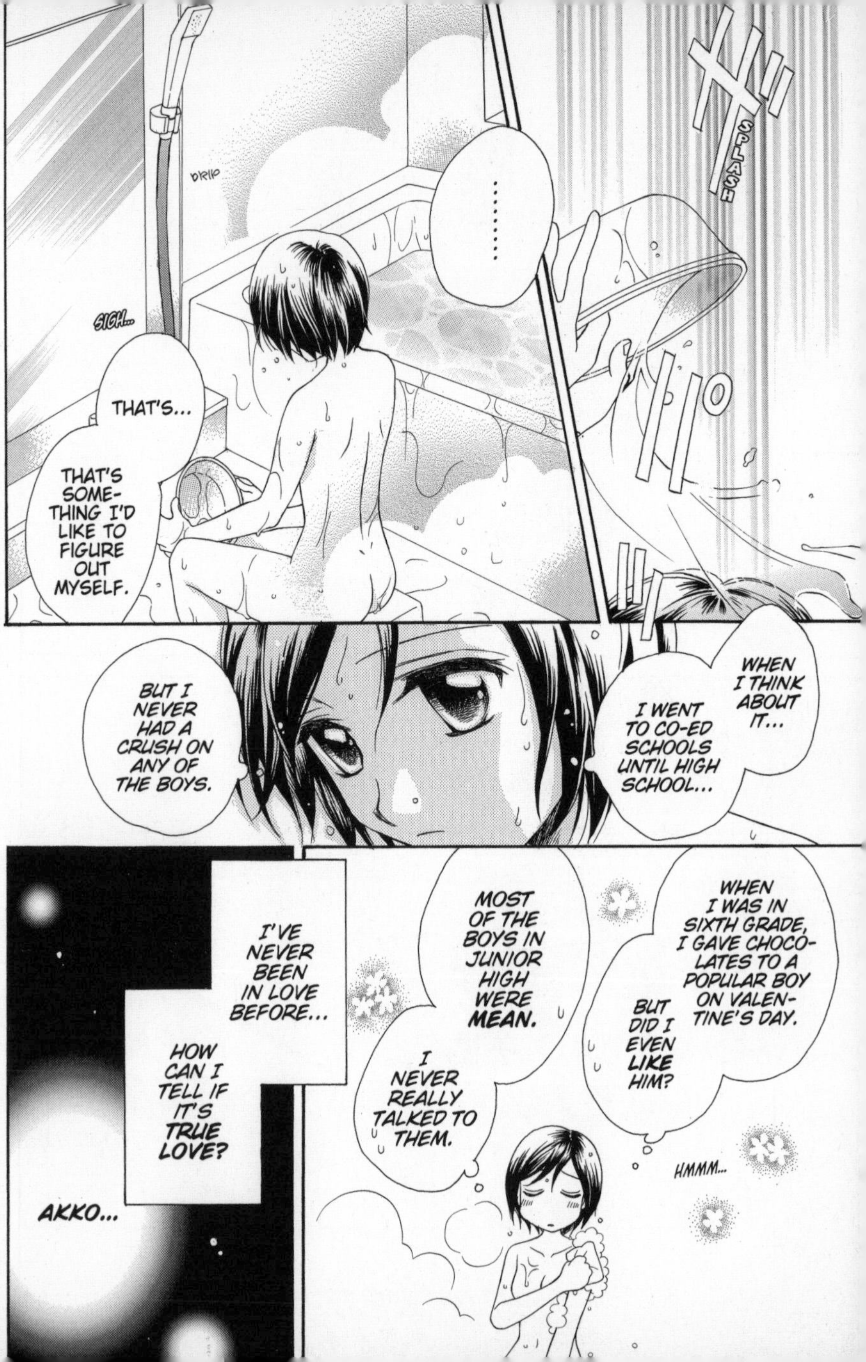
SPLASH
......
DRIP
SIGH...
THAT'S...
THAT'S SOMETHING I'D LIKE TO FIGURE OUT MYSELF.
WHEN I THINK ABOUT IT...
I WENT TO CO-ED SCHOOLS UNTIL HIGH SCHOOL...
BUT I NEVER HAD A CRUSH ON ANY OF THE BOYS.
WHEN I WAS IN SIXTH GRADE, I GAVE CHOCOLATES TO A POPULAR BOY ON VALENTINE'S DAY.
BUT DID I EVEN LIKE HIM?
MOST OF THE BOYS IN JUNIOR HIGH WERE MEAN.
I NEVER REALLY TALKED TO THEM.
HMMM...
I'VE NEVER BEEN IN LOVE BEFORE...
HOW CAN I TELL IF IT'S TRUE LOVE?
AKKO...

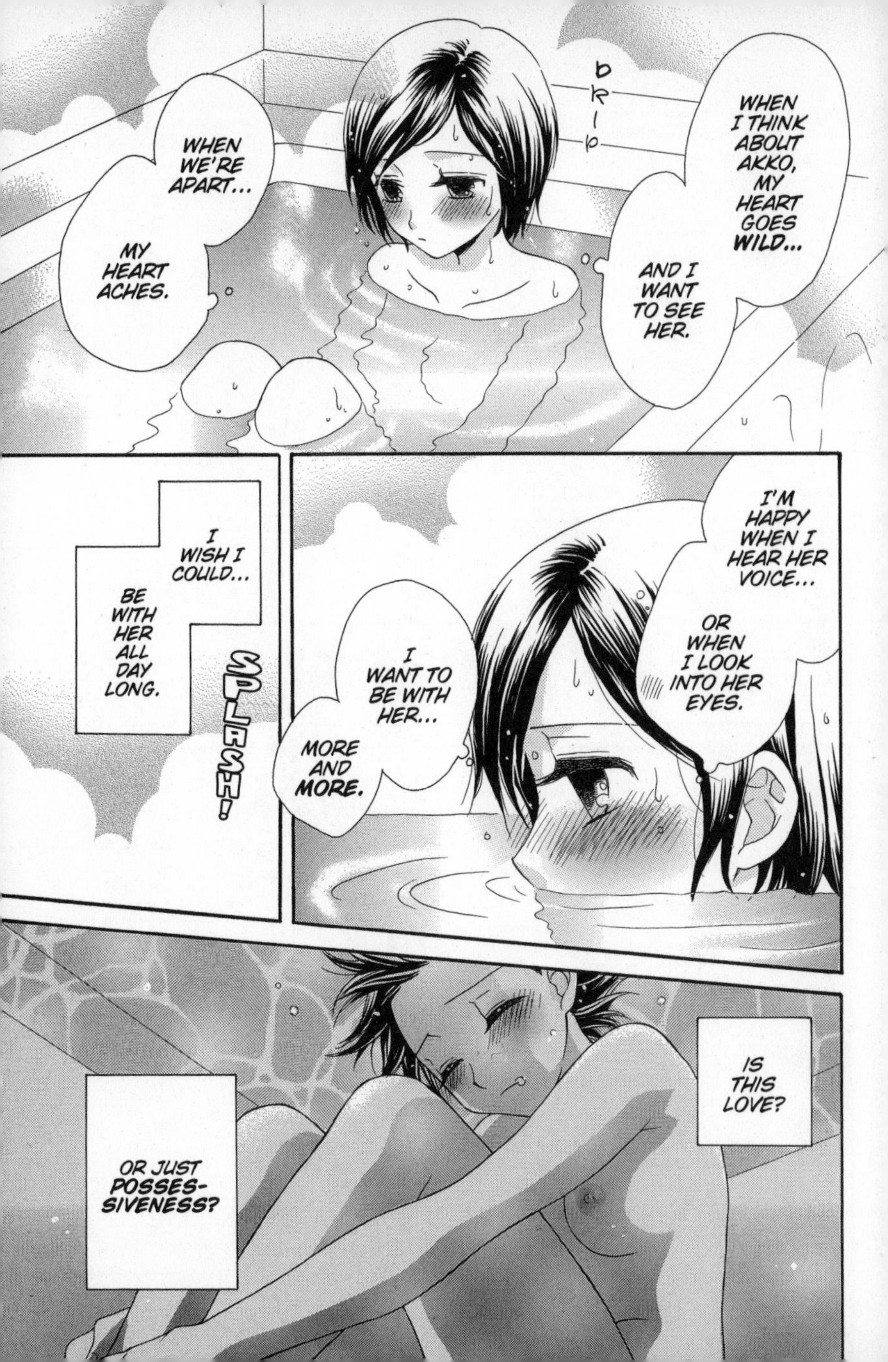
WHEN I THINK ABOUT AKKO, MY HEART GOES WILD...
AND I WANT TO SEE HER.
DRIP
WHEN WE'RE APART...
MY HEART ACHES.
I'M HAPPY WHEN I HEAR HER VOICE...
OR WHEN I LOOK INTO HER EYES.
I WANT TO BE WITH HER...
MORE AND MORE.
I WISH I COULD...
BE WITH HER ALL DAY LONG.
SPLASH!
IS THIS LOVE?
OR JUST POSSES-SIVENESS?

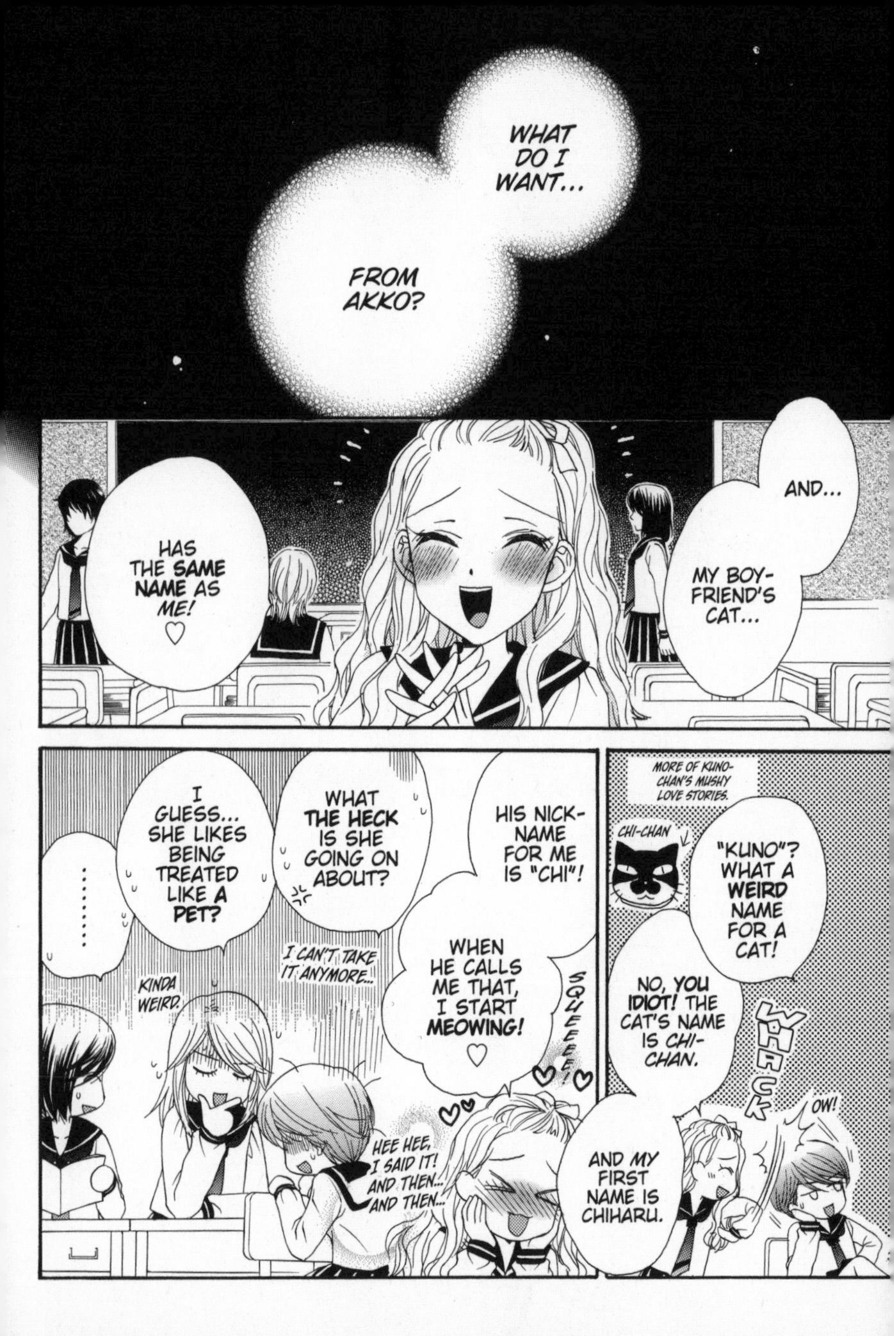
WHAT DO I WANT...
FROM AKKO?
AND...
MY BOY-FRIEND'S CAT...
HAS THE SAME NAME AS ME! ♡
MORE OF KUNO-CHAN'S MUSHY LOVE STORIES.
CHI-CHAN
"KUNO"? WHAT A WEIRD NAME FOR A CAT!
NO, YOU IDIOT! THE CAT'S NAME IS CHI-CHAN.
WHACK
OW!
AND MY FIRST NAME IS CHIHARU.
HIS NICK-NAME FOR ME IS "CHI"!
WHEN HE CALLS ME THAT, I START MEOWING! ♡
SQUEEEEE!
HEE HEE, I SAID IT! AND THEN... AND THEN...
WHAT THE HECK IS SHE GOING ON ABOUT?
I CAN'T TAKE IT ANYMORE...
I GUESS... SHE LIKES BEING TREATED LIKE A PET?
KINDA WEIRD.
......

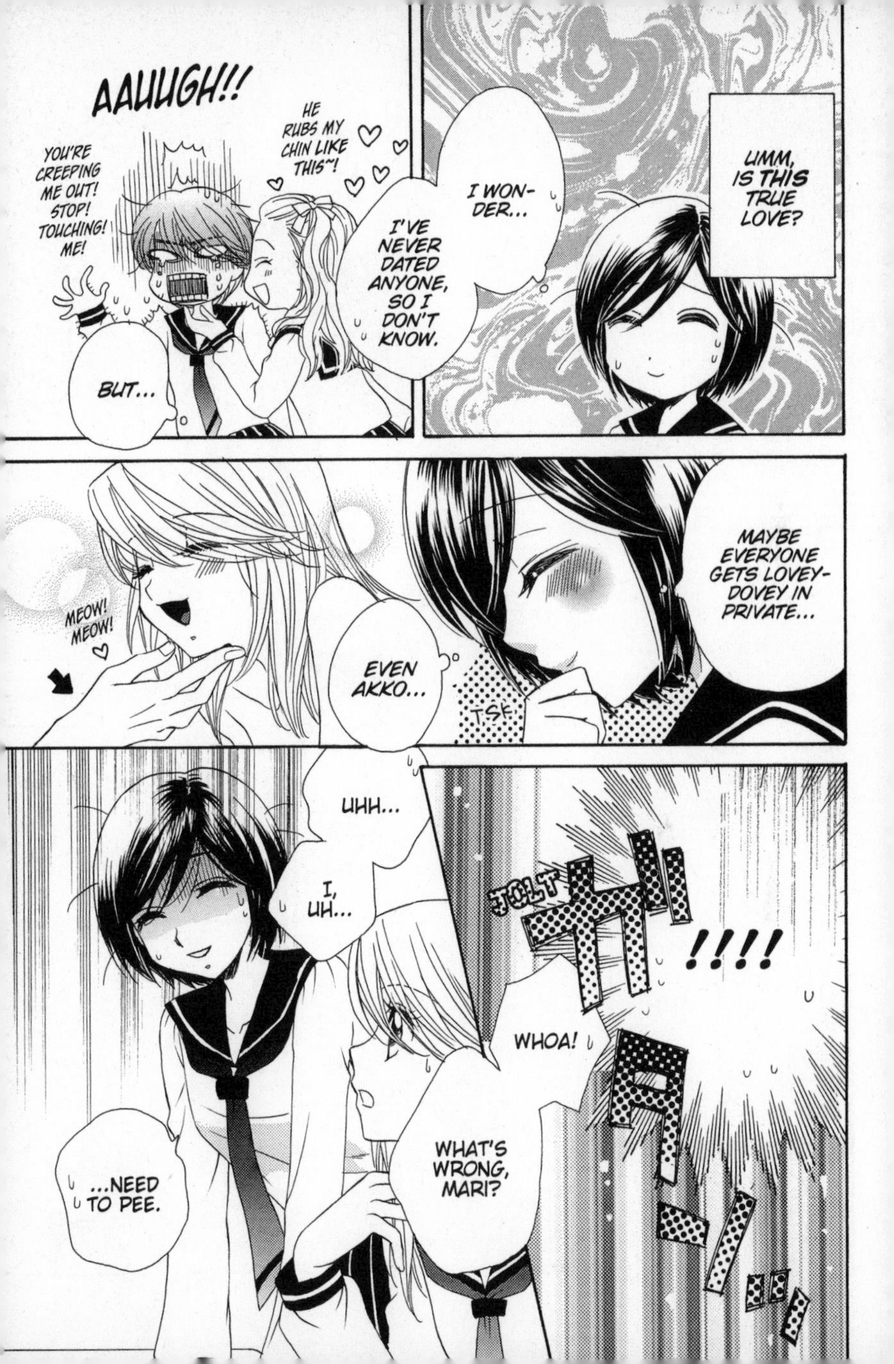
UMM, IS THIS TRUE LOVE?
I WON-DER...
I'VE NEVER DATED ANYONE, SO I DON'T KNOW.
AAUUGH!!!
HE RUBS MY CHIN LIKE THIS~!
YOU'RE CREEPING ME OUT! STOP! TOUCHING! ME!
BUT...
MAYBE EVERYONE GETS LOVEY-DOVEY IN PRIVATE...
TSK
EVEN AKKO...
MEOW! MEOW!
JOLT
!!!!
WHOA!
WHAT'S WRONG, MARI?
UHH...
I, UH...
...NEED TO PEE.

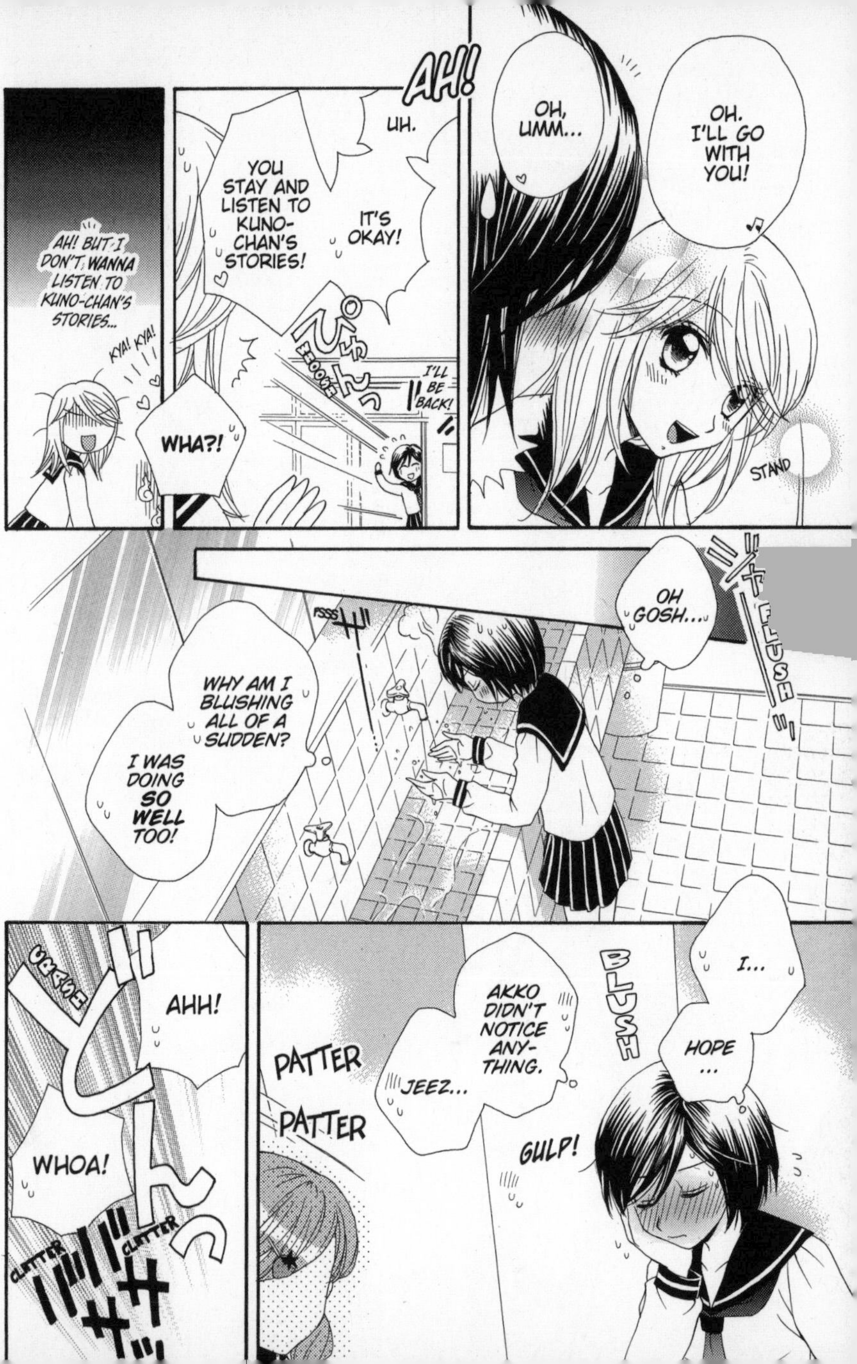

OH. I'LL GO WITH YOU!
OH, UMM...
AH!
STAND
UH.
IT'S OKAY!
YOU STAY AND LISTEN TO KUNO-CHAN'S STORIES!
WHOOSH
I'LL BE BACK!
WHA?!
AH! BUT I DON'T WANNA LISTEN TO KUNO-CHAN'S STORIES...
KYA! KYA!
BLUSH
OH GOSH...
FSSS
WHY AM I BLUSHING ALL OF A SUDDEN?
I WAS DOING SO WELL TOO!
I...
HOPE ...
BLUSH
AKKO DIDN'T NOTICE ANYTHING.
GULP!
JEEZ...
PATTER
PATTER
CRASH
AHH!
WHOA!
CLATTER
CLATTER

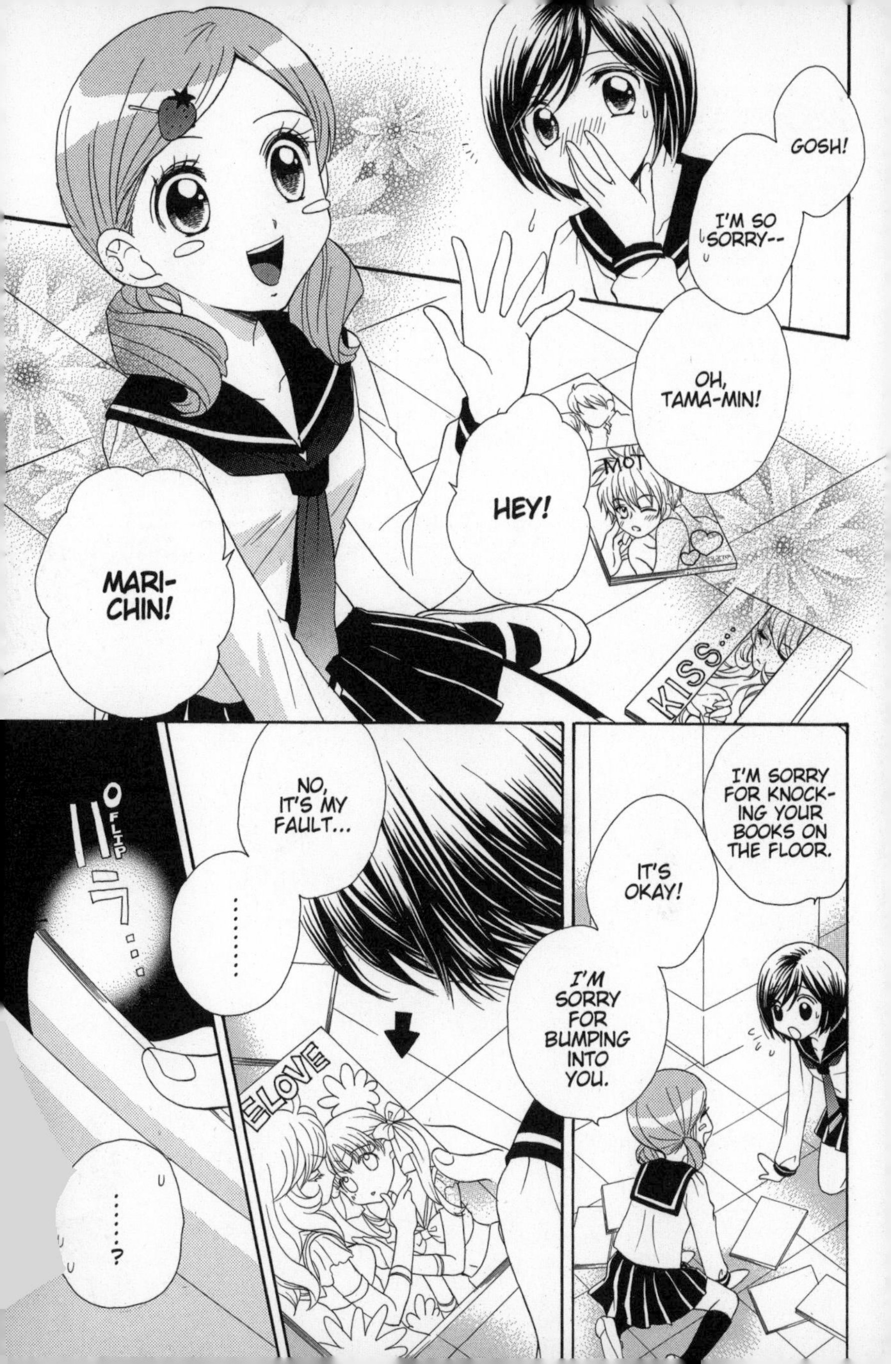
GOSH!
I'M SO SORRY--
OH, TAMA-MIN!
HEY!
MARI-CHIN!
KISS...
I'M SORRY FOR KNOCKING YOUR BOOKS ON THE FLOOR.
IT'S OKAY!
I'M SORRY FOR BUMPING INTO YOU.
NO, IT'S MY FAULT...
......
ELOVE
FLIP
.....?

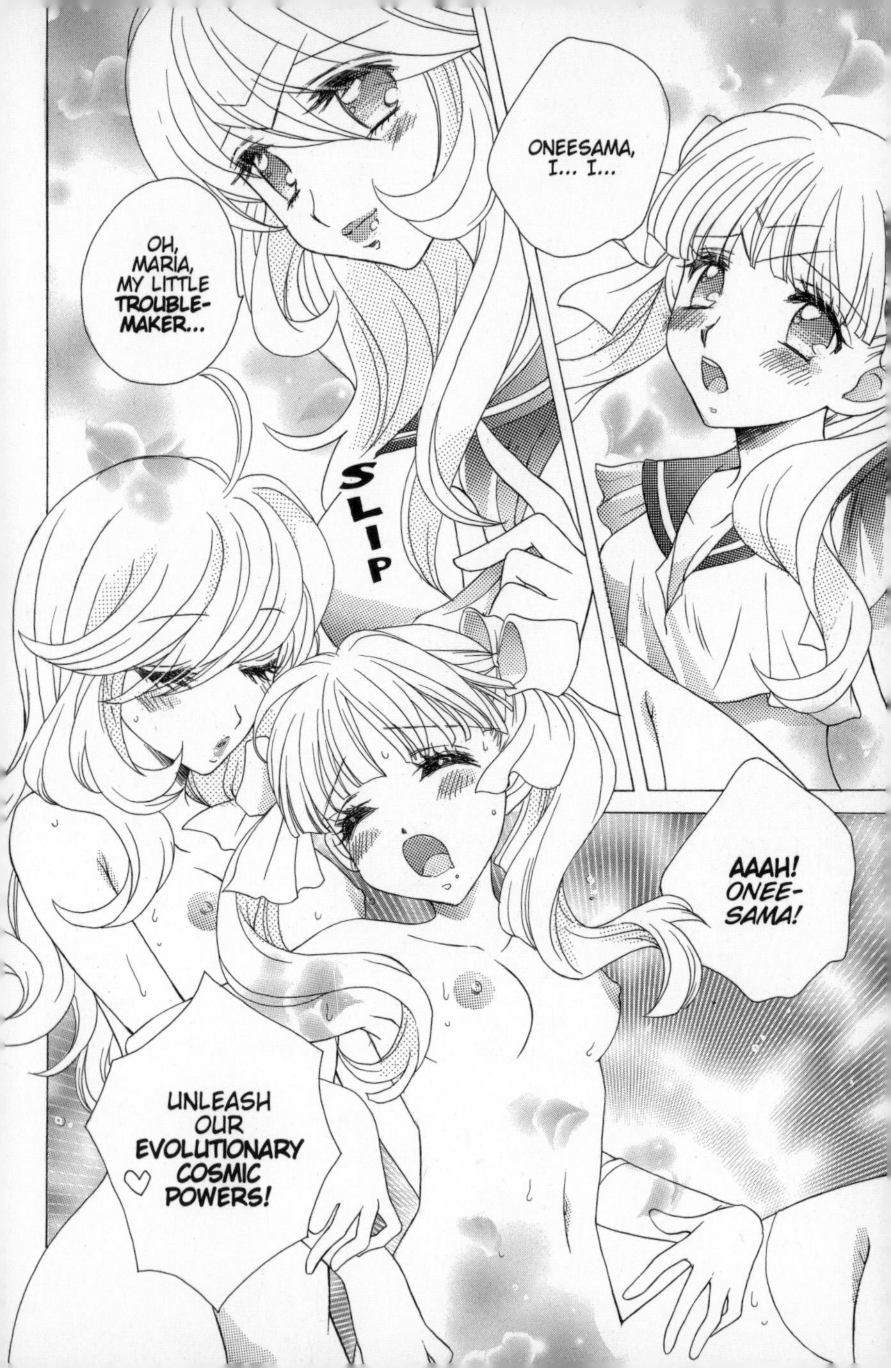
ONEESAMA, I... I...
OH, MARIA, MY LITTLE TROUBLE-MAKER...
SLIP
AAAH! ONEE-SAMA!
UNLEASH OUR EVOLUTIONARY COSMIC POWERS! ♡

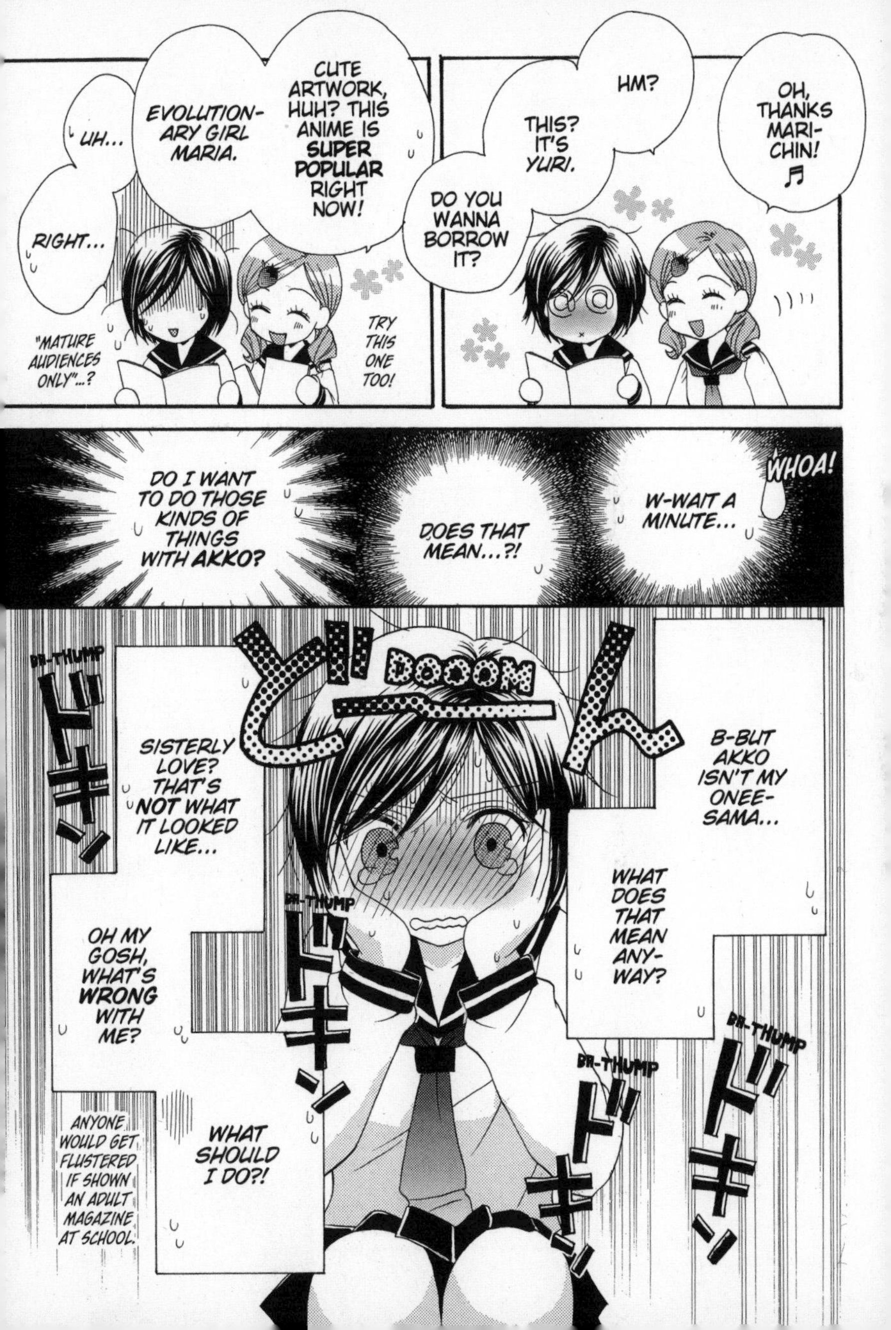
OH, THANKS MARI-CHIN! ♬
HM?
THIS? IT'S YURI.
DO YOU WANNA BORROW IT?
CUTE ARTWORK, HUH? THIS ANIME IS SUPER POPULAR RIGHT NOW!
EVOLUTIONARY GIRL MARIA.
UH...
RIGHT...
TRY THIS ONE TOO!
"MATURE AUDIENCES ONLY"...?
WHOA!
W-WAIT A MINUTE...
DOES THAT MEAN...?!
DO I WANT TO DO THOSE KINDS OF THINGS WITH AKKO?
DOOOM
B-BUT AKKO ISN'T MY ONEE-SAMA...
BR-THUMP
SISTERLY LOVE? THAT'S NOT WHAT IT LOOKED LIKE...
WHAT DOES THAT MEAN ANYWAY?
BR-THUMP
OH MY GOSH, WHAT'S WRONG WITH ME?
BR-THUMP
BR-THUMP
WHAT SHOULD I DO?!
ANYONE WOULD GET FLUSTERED IF SHOWN AN ADULT MAGAZINE AT SCHOOL.

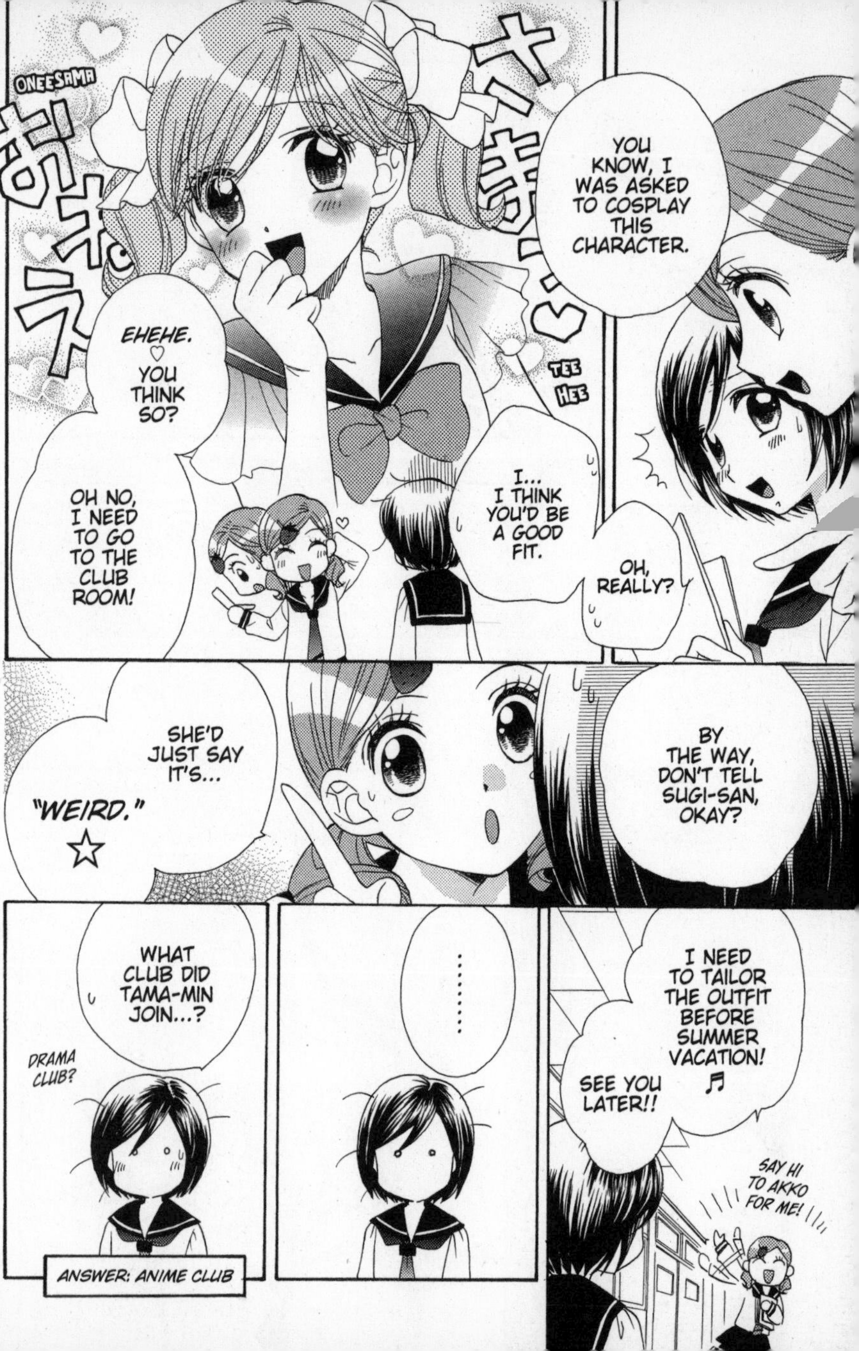
YOU KNOW, I WAS ASKED TO COSPLAY THIS CHARACTER.
OH, REALLY?
おねえさま♡
ONEESAMA
TEE HEE
EHEHE. ♡ YOU THINK SO?
I... I THINK YOU'D BE A GOOD FIT.
OH NO, I NEED TO GO TO THE CLUB ROOM!
BY THE WAY, DON'T TELL SUGI-SAN, OKAY?
SHE'D JUST SAY IT'S... "WEIRD." ☆
I NEED TO TAILOR THE OUTFIT BEFORE SUMMER VACATION! ♫
SEE YOU LATER!!
SAY HI TO AKKO FOR ME!
......
WHAT CLUB DID TAMA-MIN JOIN...?
DRAMA CLUB?
ANSWER: ANIME CLUB

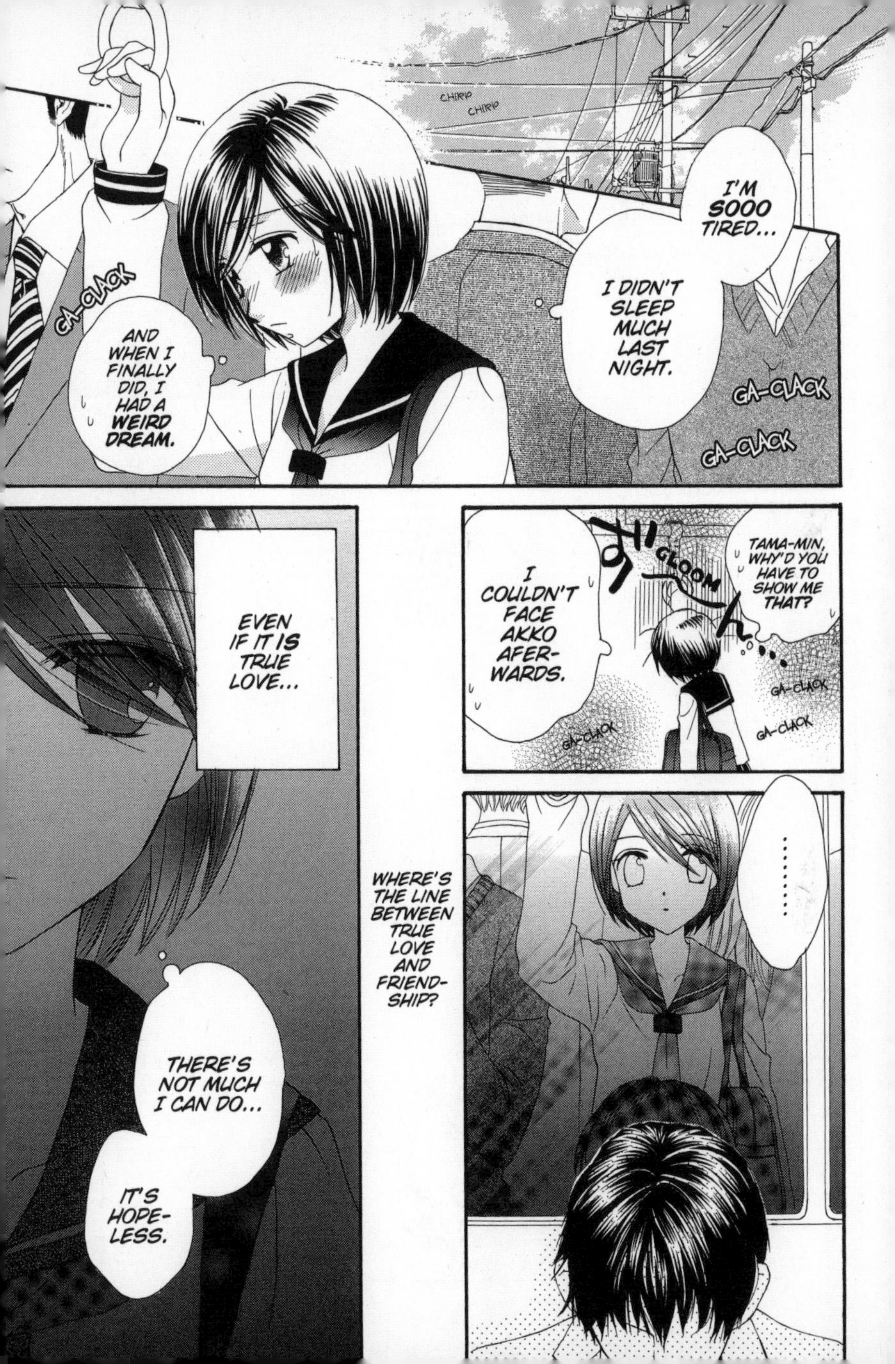

CHIRP
CHIRP
I'M **SOOO** TIRED...
I DIDN'T SLEEP MUCH LAST NIGHT.
GA-CLACK
GA-CLACK
GA-CLACK
AND WHEN I FINALLY DID, I HAD A **WEIRD DREAM.**
TAMA-MIN, WHY'D YOU HAVE TO SHOW ME THAT?
GLOOM
I COULDN'T FACE AKKO AFER-WARDS.
GA-CLACK
GA-CLACK
GA-CLACK
......
WHERE'S THE LINE BETWEEN TRUE LOVE AND FRIEND-SHIP?
EVEN IF IT **IS** TRUE LOVE...
THERE'S NOT MUCH I CAN DO...
IT'S HOPE-LESS.

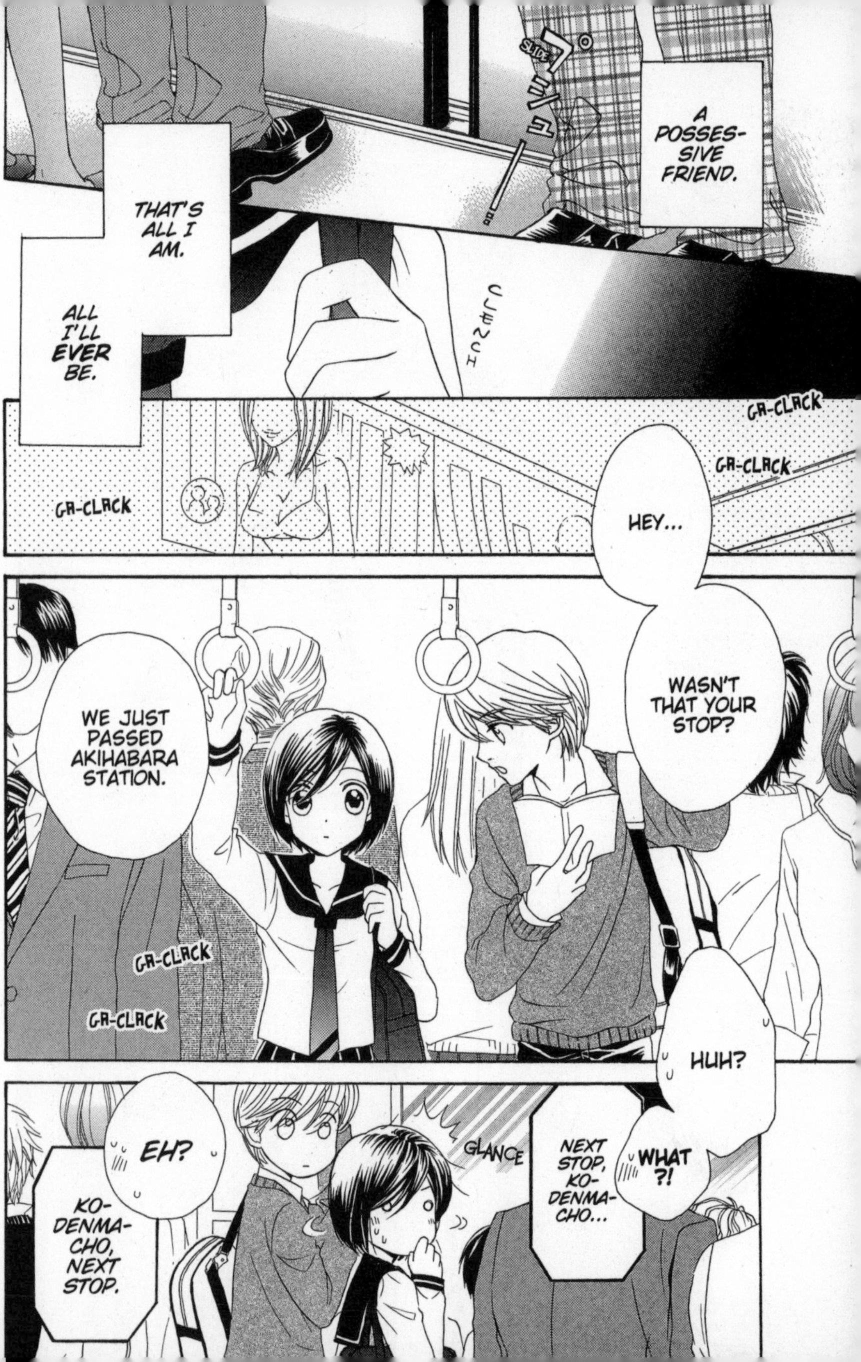

A POSSESSIVE FRIEND.
SLIDE
THAT'S ALL I AM.
ALL I'LL EVER BE.
CLENCH
GA-CLACK
GA-CLACK
HEY...
GA-CLACK
WASN'T THAT YOUR STOP?
WE JUST PASSED AKIHABARA STATION.
GA-CLACK
GA-CLACK
HUH?
WHAT?!
NEXT STOP, KODENMACHO...
GLANCE
EH?
KODENMACHO, NEXT STOP.

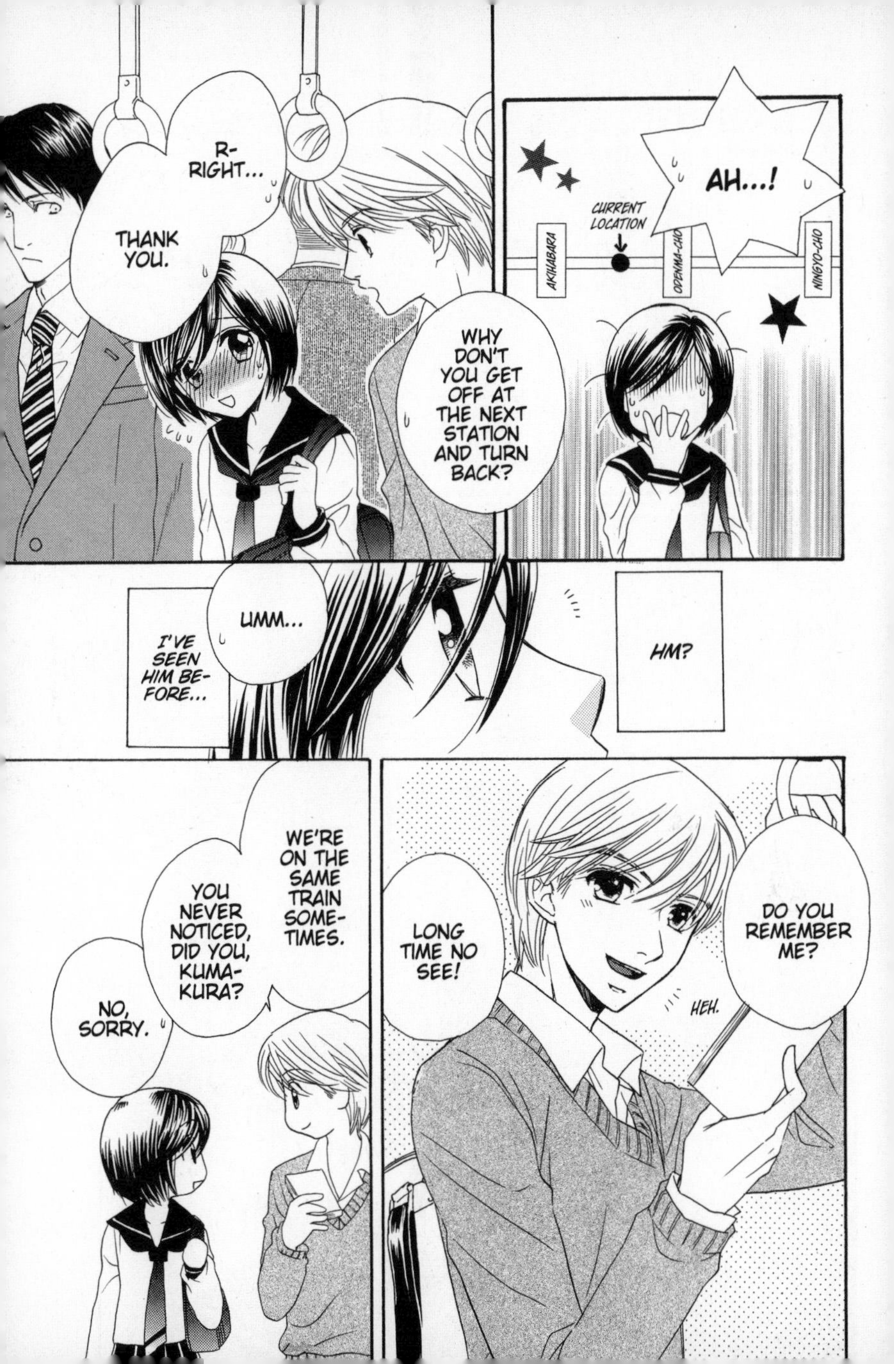
AH...!
CURRENT LOCATION
AKIHABARA
ODENMA-CHO
NINGYO-CHO
WHY DON'T YOU GET OFF AT THE NEXT STATION AND TURN BACK?
R-RIGHT...
THANK YOU.
HM?
UMM...
I'VE SEEN HIM BE-FORE...
DO YOU REMEMBER ME?
HEH.
LONG TIME NO SEE!
WE'RE ON THE SAME TRAIN SOME-TIMES.
YOU NEVER NOTICED, DID YOU, KUMA-KURA?
NO, SORRY.

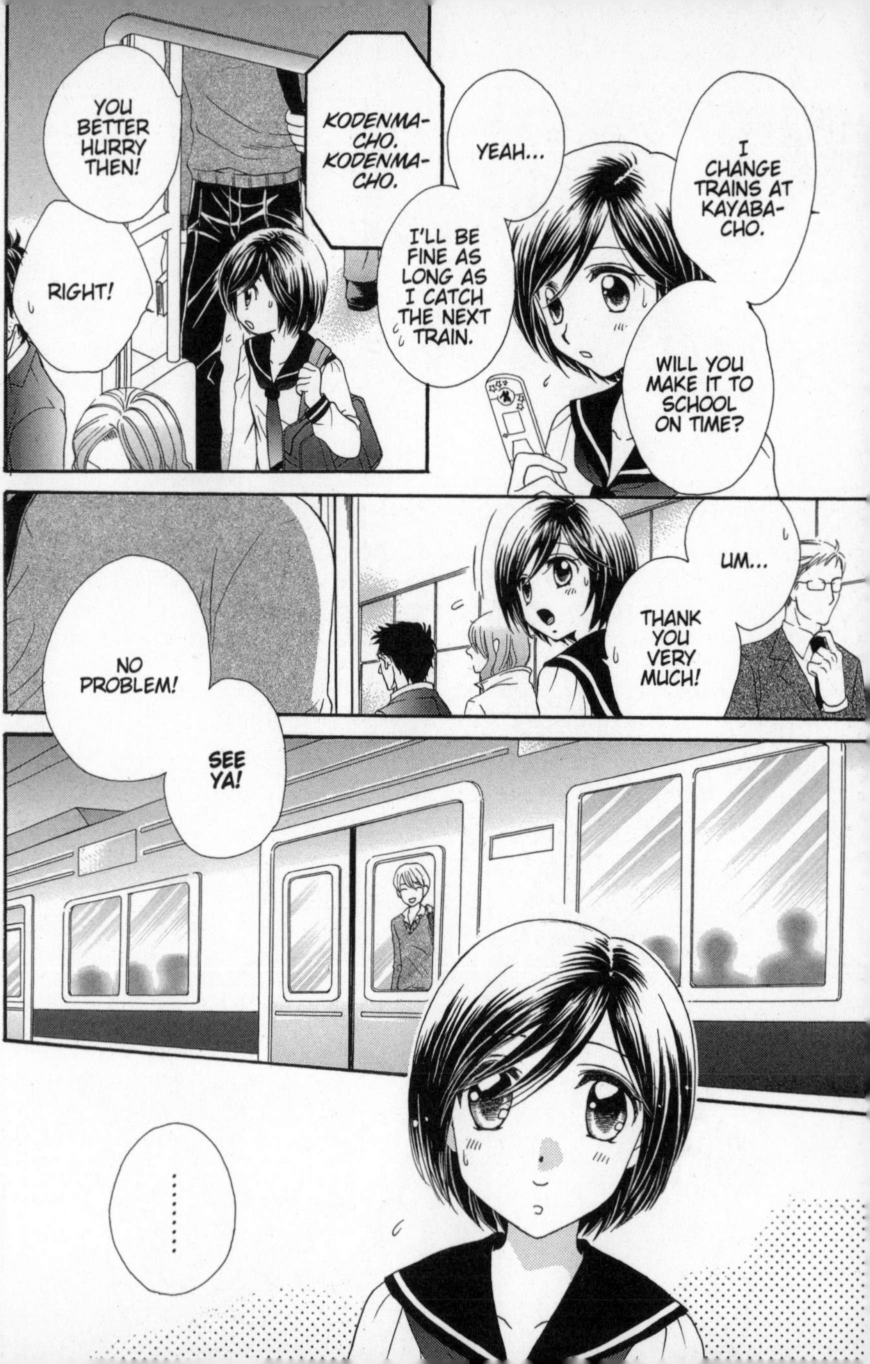
I CHANGE TRAINS AT KAYABA-CHO.
WILL YOU MAKE IT TO SCHOOL ON TIME?
YEAH...
I'LL BE FINE AS LONG AS I CATCH THE NEXT TRAIN.
KODENMA-CHO. KODENMA-CHO.
YOU BETTER HURRY THEN!
RIGHT!
UM...
THANK YOU VERY MUCH!
NO PROBLEM!
SEE YA!
......

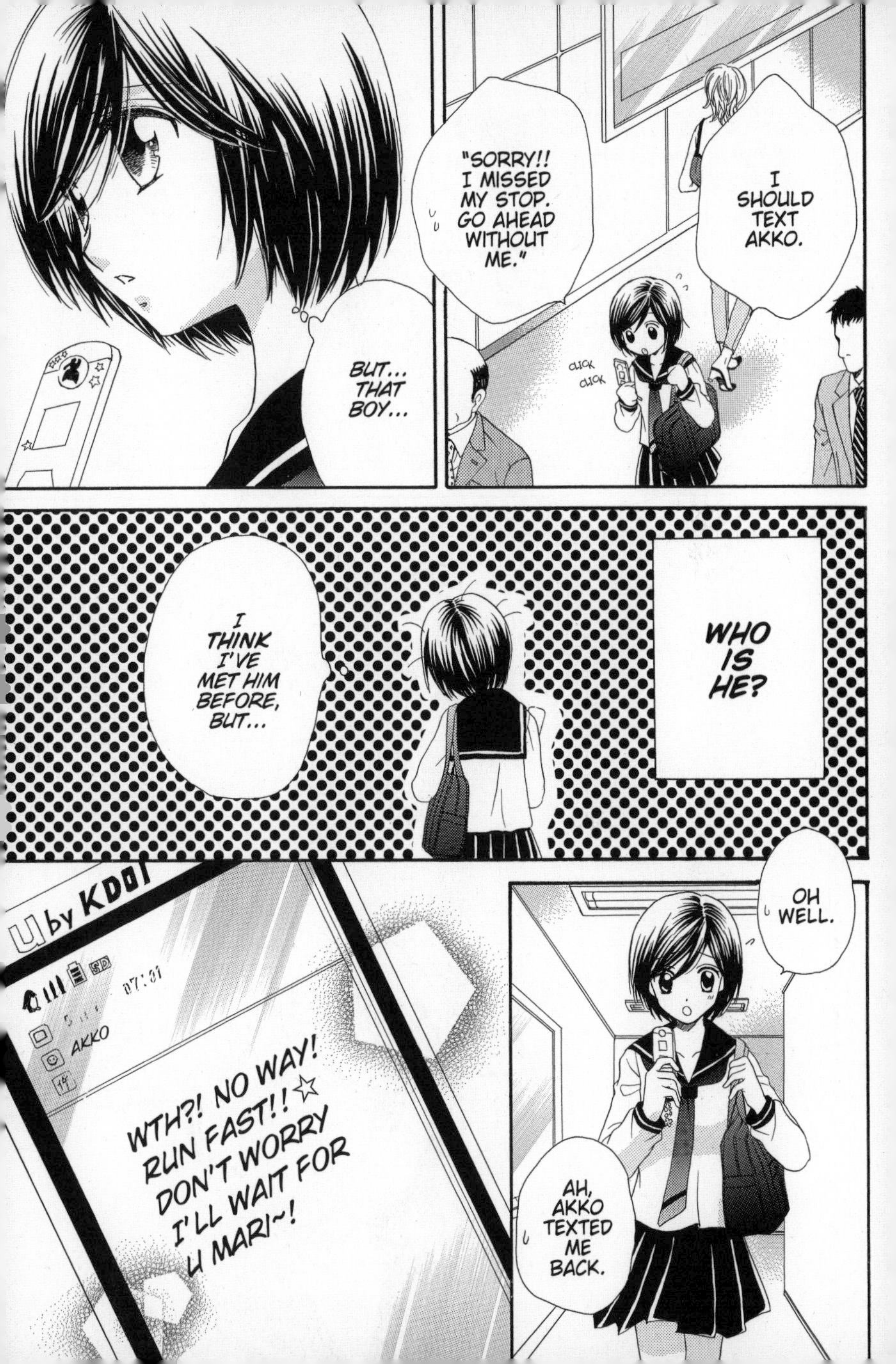
I SHOULD TEXT AKKO.
"SORRY!! I MISSED MY STOP. GO AHEAD WITHOUT ME."
CLICK
CLICK
BUT... THAT BOY...
WHO IS HE?
I THINK I'VE MET HIM BEFORE, BUT...
OH WELL.
AH, AKKO TEXTED ME BACK.
U by KDDI
07:01
AKKO
WTH?! NO WAY! RUN FAST!! ☆ DON'T WORRY I'LL WAIT FOR U MARI~!

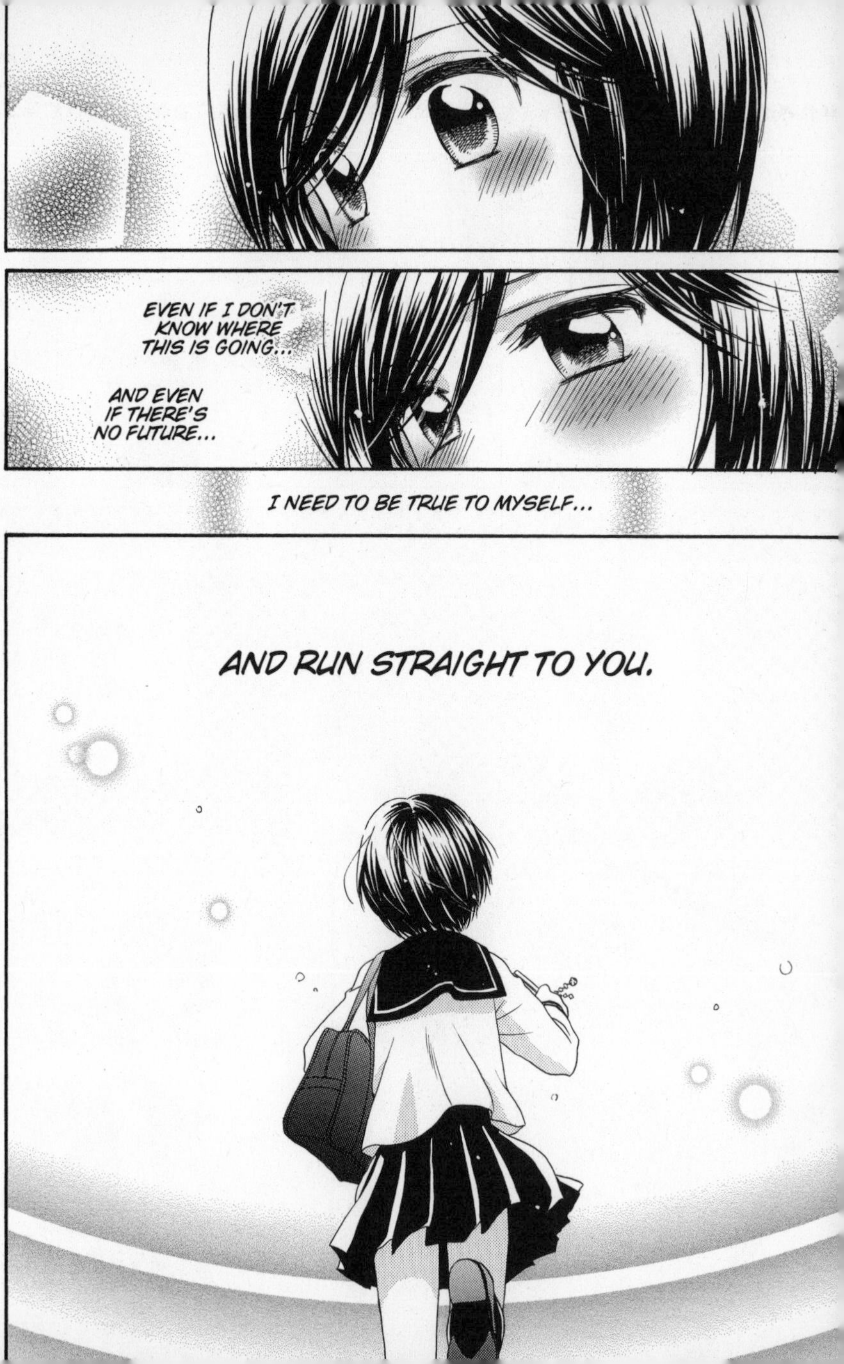
EVEN IF I DON'T KNOW WHERE THIS IS GOING...
AND EVEN IF THERE'S NO FUTURE...
I NEED TO BE TRUE TO MYSELF...
AND RUN STRAIGHT TO YOU.

DESIGNATED WINTER COAT.

GIRL FRIENDS －ガールフレンズ－

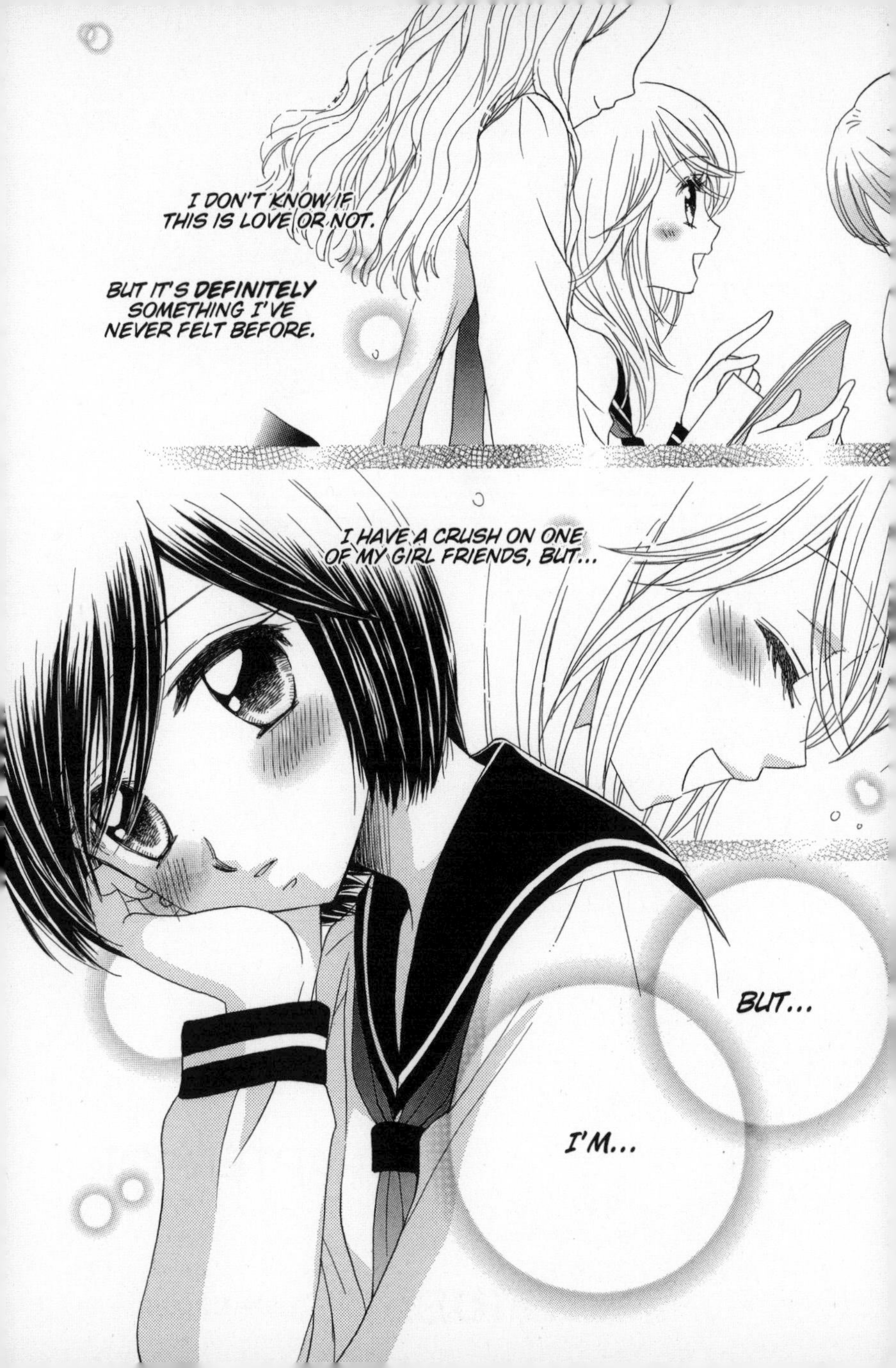
I DON'T KNOW IF THIS IS LOVE OR NOT.
BUT IT'S DEFINITELY SOMETHING I'VE NEVER FELT BEFORE.
I HAVE A CRUSH ON ONE OF MY GIRL FRIENDS, BUT...
BUT...
I'M...

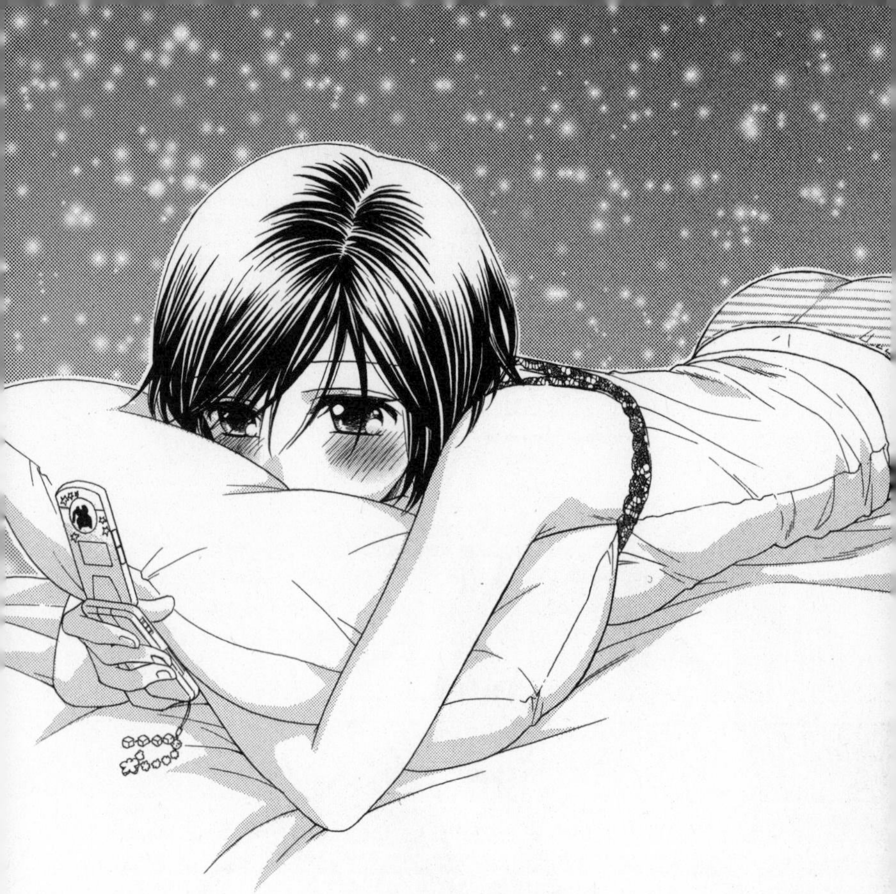

[CHAPTER 12]

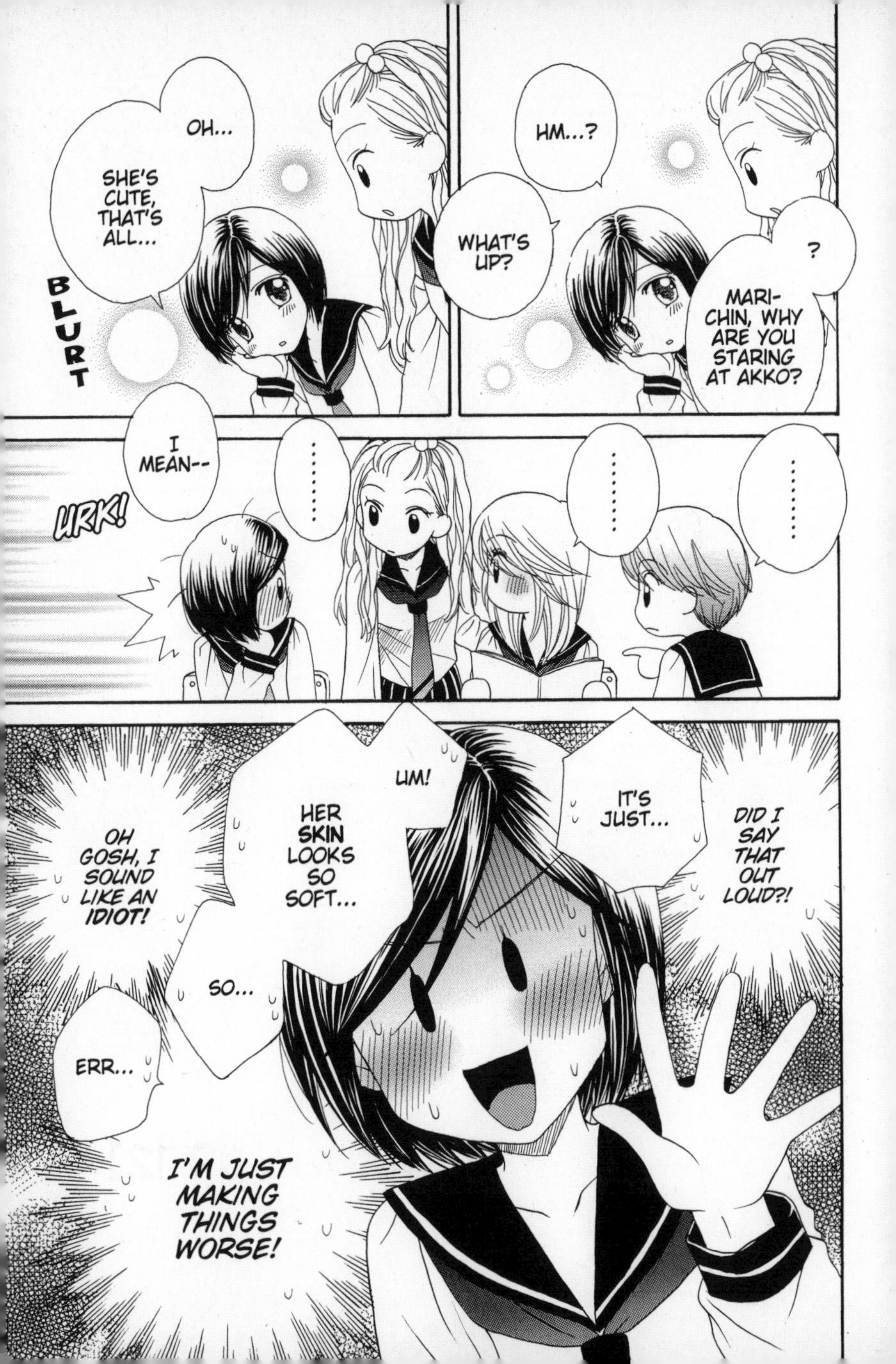
HM...?
WHAT'S UP?
?
MARI-CHIN, WHY ARE YOU STARING AT AKKO?
OH...
SHE'S CUTE, THAT'S ALL...
BLURT
......
......
......
I MEAN--
URK!
DID I SAY THAT OUT LOUD?!
UM!
IT'S JUST...
HER SKIN LOOKS SO SOFT...
OH GOSH, I SOUND LIKE AN IDIOT!
SO...
ERR...
I'M JUST MAKING THINGS WORSE!

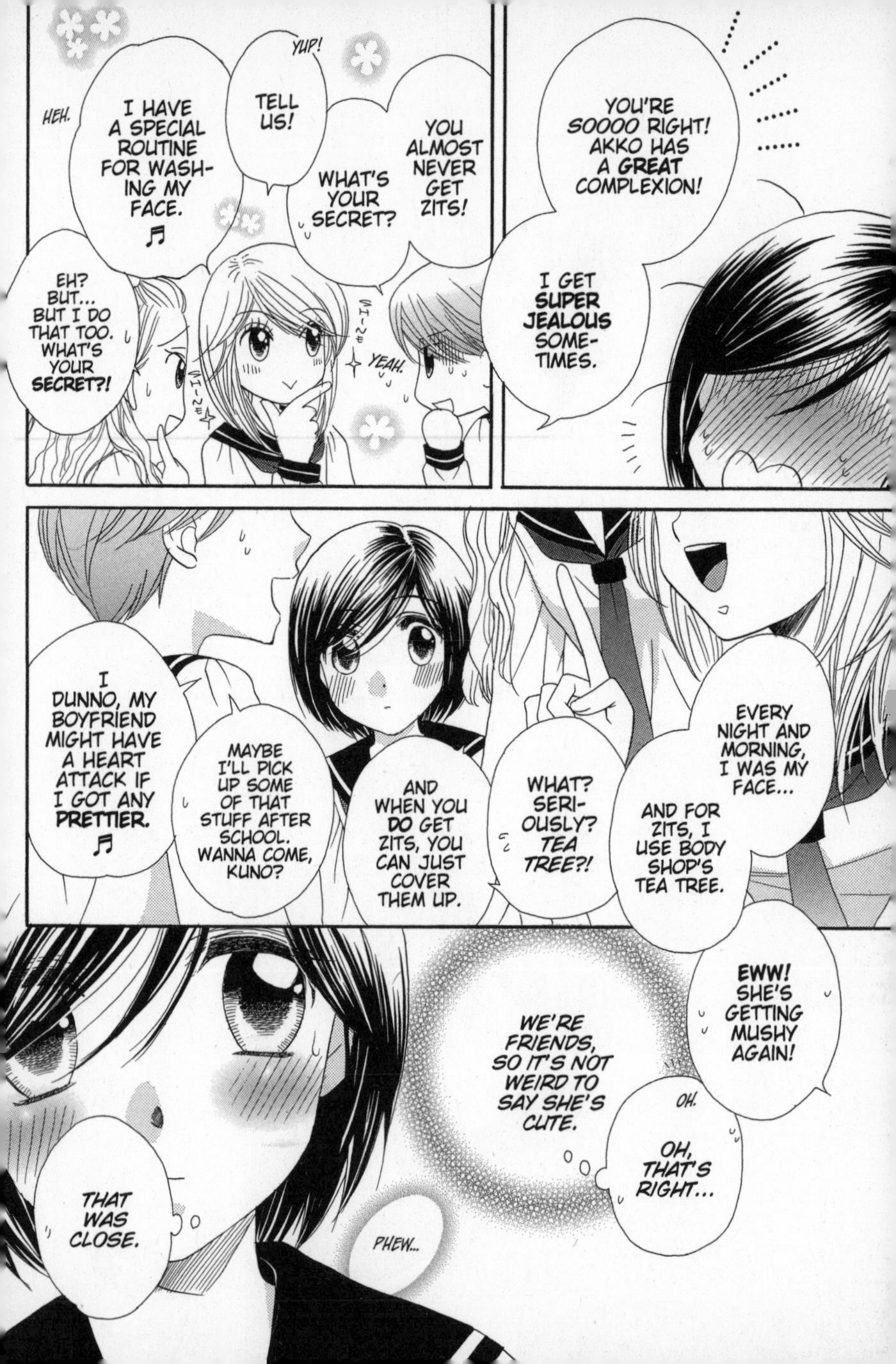
......
YOU'RE SOOOO RIGHT! AKKO HAS A GREAT COMPLEXION!
I GET SUPER JEALOUS SOMETIMES.
YOU ALMOST NEVER GET ZITS!
WHAT'S YOUR SECRET?
YUP!
TELL US!
I HAVE A SPECIAL ROUTINE FOR WASHING MY FACE. ♬
HEH.
SHINE
YEAH.
SHINE
EH? BUT... BUT I DO THAT TOO. WHAT'S YOUR SECRET?!
EVERY NIGHT AND MORNING, I WAS MY FACE...
AND FOR ZITS, I USE BODY SHOP'S TEA TREE.
WHAT? SERIOUSLY? TEA TREE?!
AND WHEN YOU DO GET ZITS, YOU CAN JUST COVER THEM UP.
MAYBE I'LL PICK UP SOME OF THAT STUFF AFTER SCHOOL. WANNA COME, KUNO?
I DUNNO, MY BOYFRIEND MIGHT HAVE A HEART ATTACK IF I GOT ANY PRETTIER. ♬
EWW! SHE'S GETTING MUSHY AGAIN!
OH.
OH, THAT'S RIGHT...
WE'RE FRIENDS, SO IT'S NOT WEIRD TO SAY SHE'S CUTE.
PHEW...
THAT WAS CLOSE.

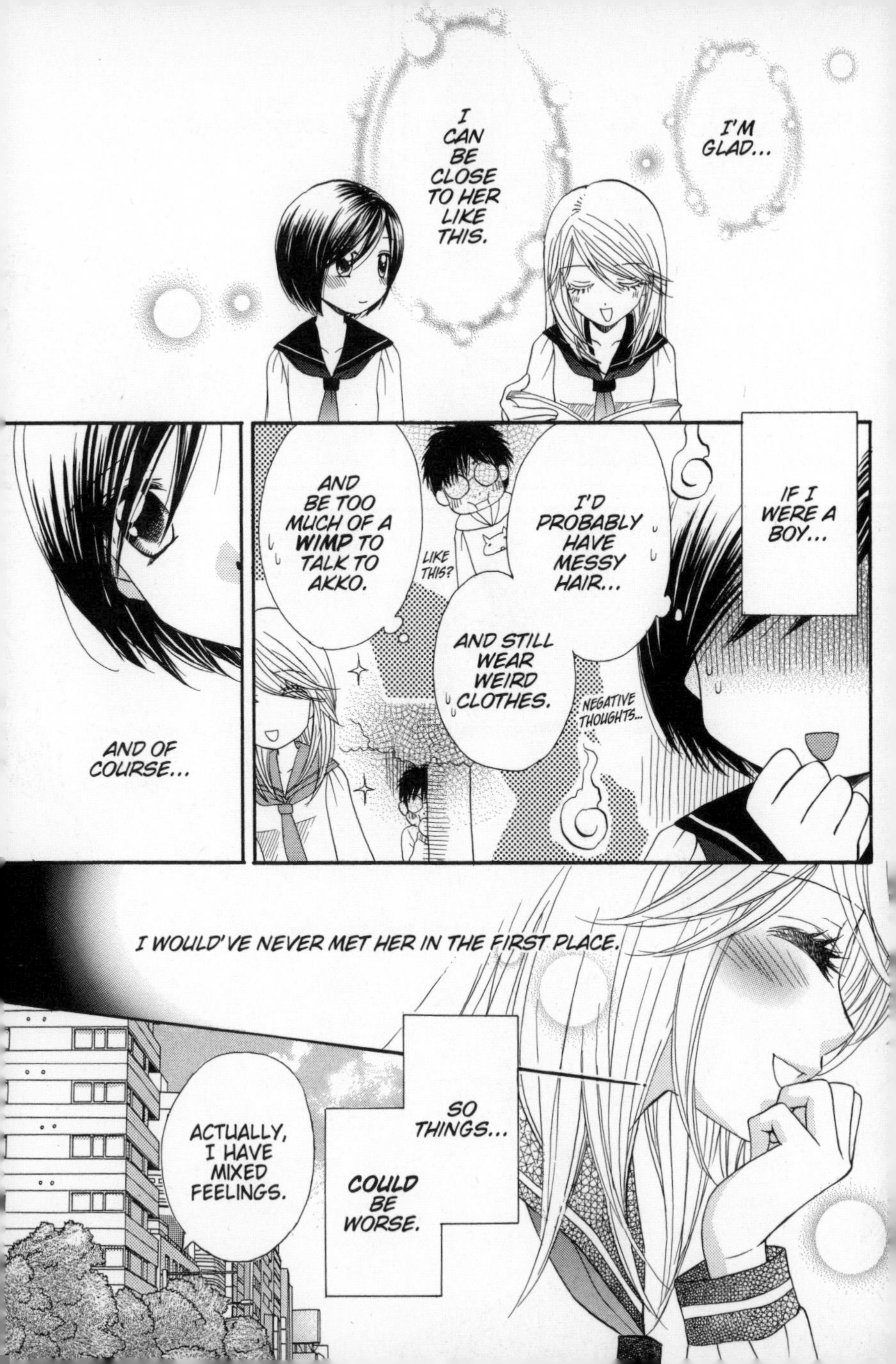
I'M GLAD...
I CAN BE CLOSE TO HER LIKE THIS.
IF I WERE A BOY...
I'D PROBABLY HAVE MESSY HAIR...
AND STILL WEAR WEIRD CLOTHES.
AND BE TOO MUCH OF A WIMP TO TALK TO AKKO.
LIKE THIS?
NEGATIVE THOUGHTS...
AND OF COURSE...
I WOULD'VE NEVER MET HER IN THE FIRST PLACE.
SO THINGS...
COULD BE WORSE.
ACTUALLY, I HAVE MIXED FEELINGS.

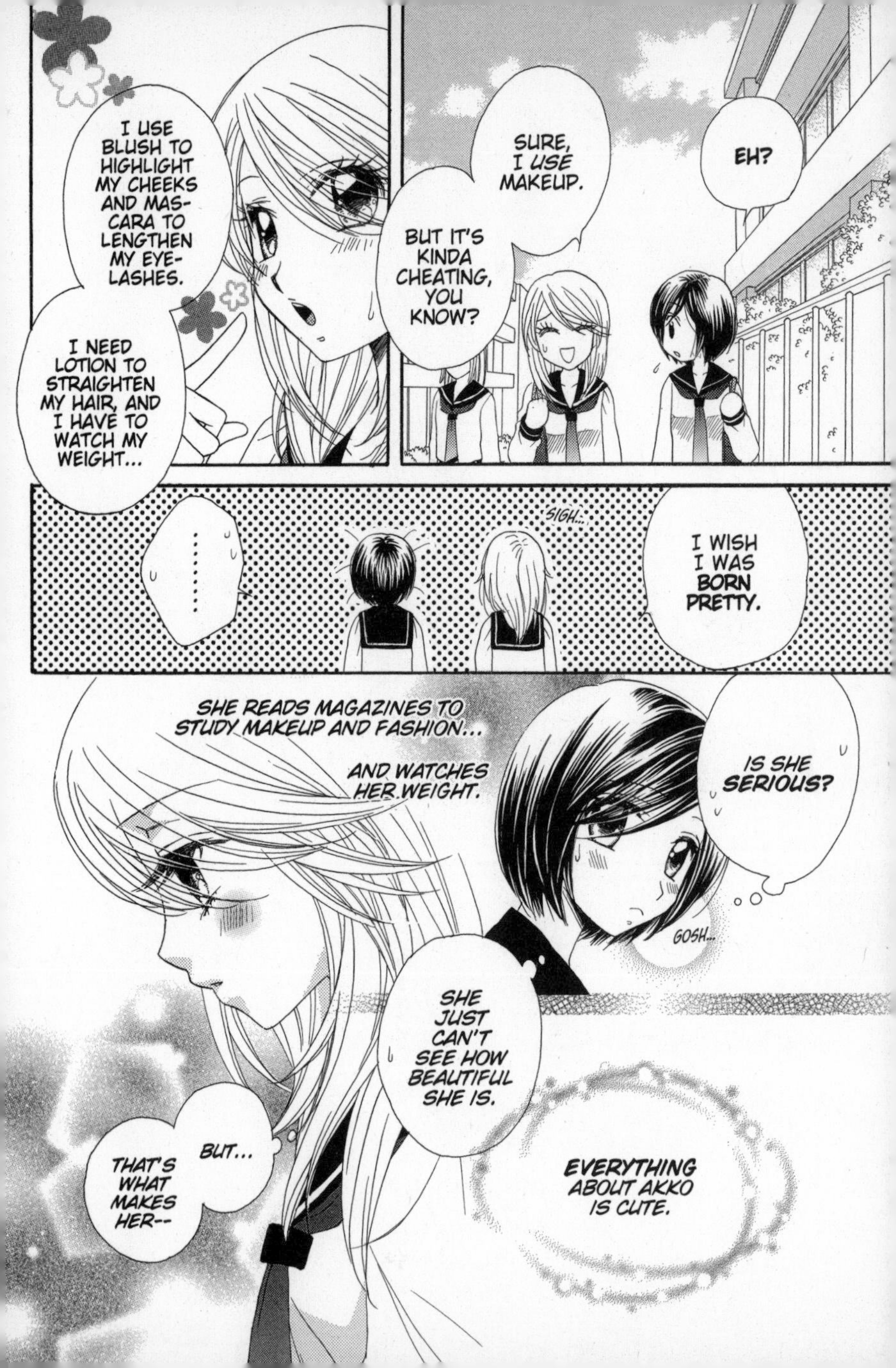
EH?
SURE, I USE MAKEUP.
BUT IT'S KINDA CHEATING, YOU KNOW?
I USE BLUSH TO HIGHLIGHT MY CHEEKS AND MAS-CARA TO LENGTHEN MY EYE-LASHES.
I NEED LOTION TO STRAIGHTEN MY HAIR, AND I HAVE TO WATCH MY WEIGHT...
I WISH I WAS BORN PRETTY.
SIGH...
......
IS SHE SERIOUS?
GOSH...
SHE READS MAGAZINES TO STUDY MAKEUP AND FASHION...
AND WATCHES HER WEIGHT.
SHE JUST CAN'T SEE HOW BEAUTIFUL SHE IS.
BUT...
THAT'S WHAT MAKES HER--
EVERYTHING ABOUT AKKO IS CUTE.

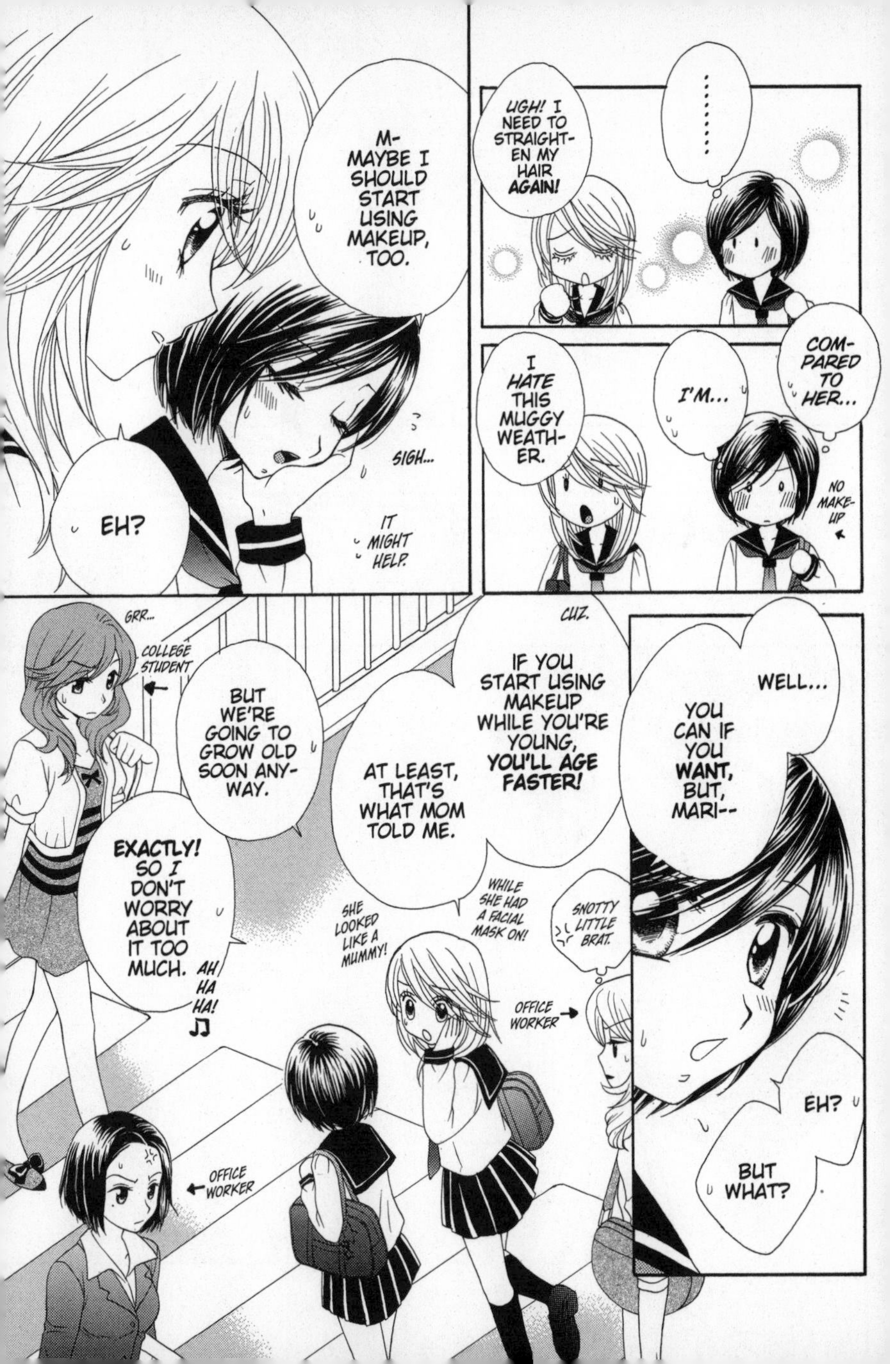
……
UGH! I NEED TO STRAIGHT-EN MY HAIR AGAIN!
COM-PARED TO HER...
I'M...
I HATE THIS MUGGY WEATH-ER.
NO MAKE-UP
M-MAYBE I SHOULD START USING MAKEUP, TOO.
SIGH...
IT MIGHT HELP.
EH?
WELL...
YOU CAN IF YOU WANT, BUT, MARI--
EH?
BUT WHAT?
CUZ.
IF YOU START USING MAKEUP WHILE YOU'RE YOUNG, YOU'LL AGE FASTER!
AT LEAST, THAT'S WHAT MOM TOLD ME.
WHILE SHE HAD A FACIAL MASK ON!
SNOTTY LITTLE BRAT.
SHE LOOKED LIKE A MUMMY!
OFFICE WORKER
BUT WE'RE GOING TO GROW OLD SOON ANY-WAY.
GRR...
COLLEGE STUDENT
EXACTLY! SO I DON'T WORRY ABOUT IT TOO MUCH.
AH HA HA! ♫
OFFICE WORKER

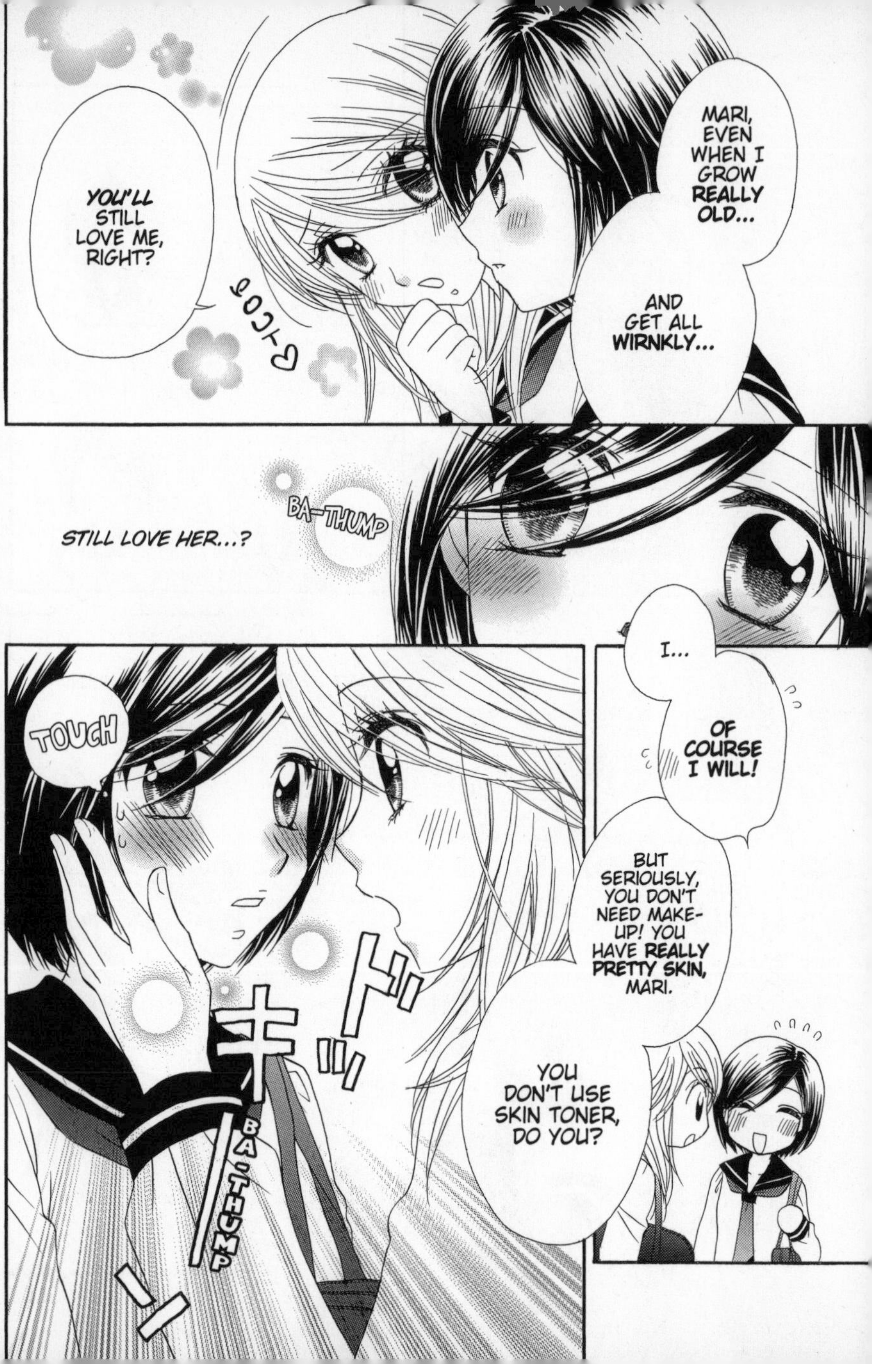

MARI, EVEN WHEN I GROW REALLY OLD...
AND GET ALL WIRNKLY...
YOU'LL STILL LOVE ME, RIGHT?
BA-THUMP
STILL LOVE HER...?
I...
OF COURSE I WILL!
BUT SERIOUSLY, YOU DON'T NEED MAKE-UP! YOU HAVE REALLY PRETTY SKIN, MARI.
YOU DON'T USE SKIN TONER, DO YOU?
TOUCH
ドキッ
BA-THUMP

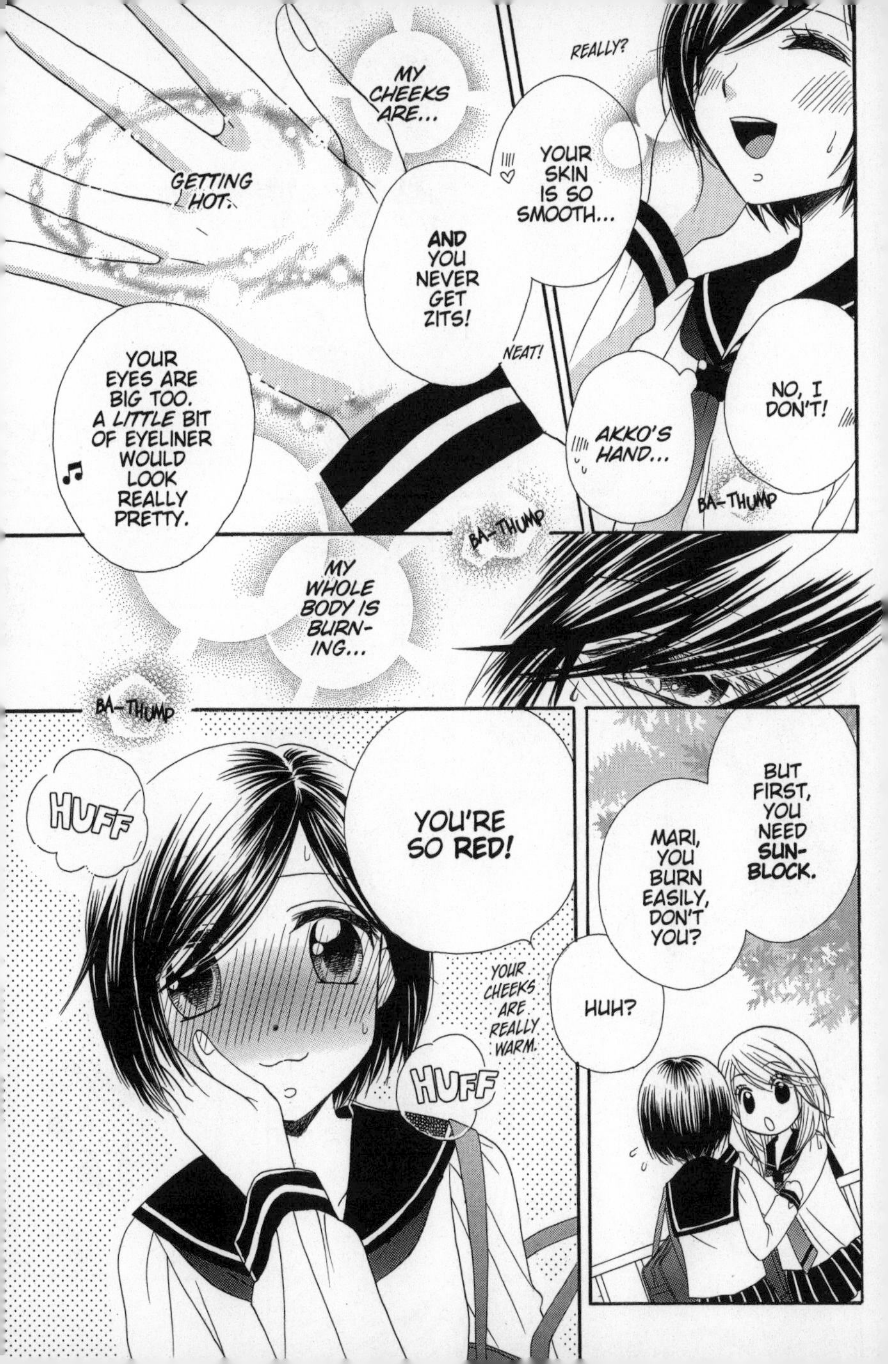
REALLY?
YOUR SKIN IS SO SMOOTH...
AND YOU NEVER GET ZITS!
NEAT!
NO, I DON'T!
AKKO'S HAND...
BA-THUMP
MY CHEEKS ARE...
GETTING HOT.
YOUR EYES ARE BIG TOO. A *LITTLE* BIT OF EYELINER WOULD LOOK REALLY PRETTY.
BA-THUMP
MY WHOLE BODY IS BURNING...
BA-THUMP
BUT FIRST, YOU NEED SUNBLOCK.
MARI, YOU BURN EASILY, DON'T YOU?
HUH?
YOU'RE SO RED!
YOUR CHEEKS ARE REALLY WARM.
HUFF
HUFF

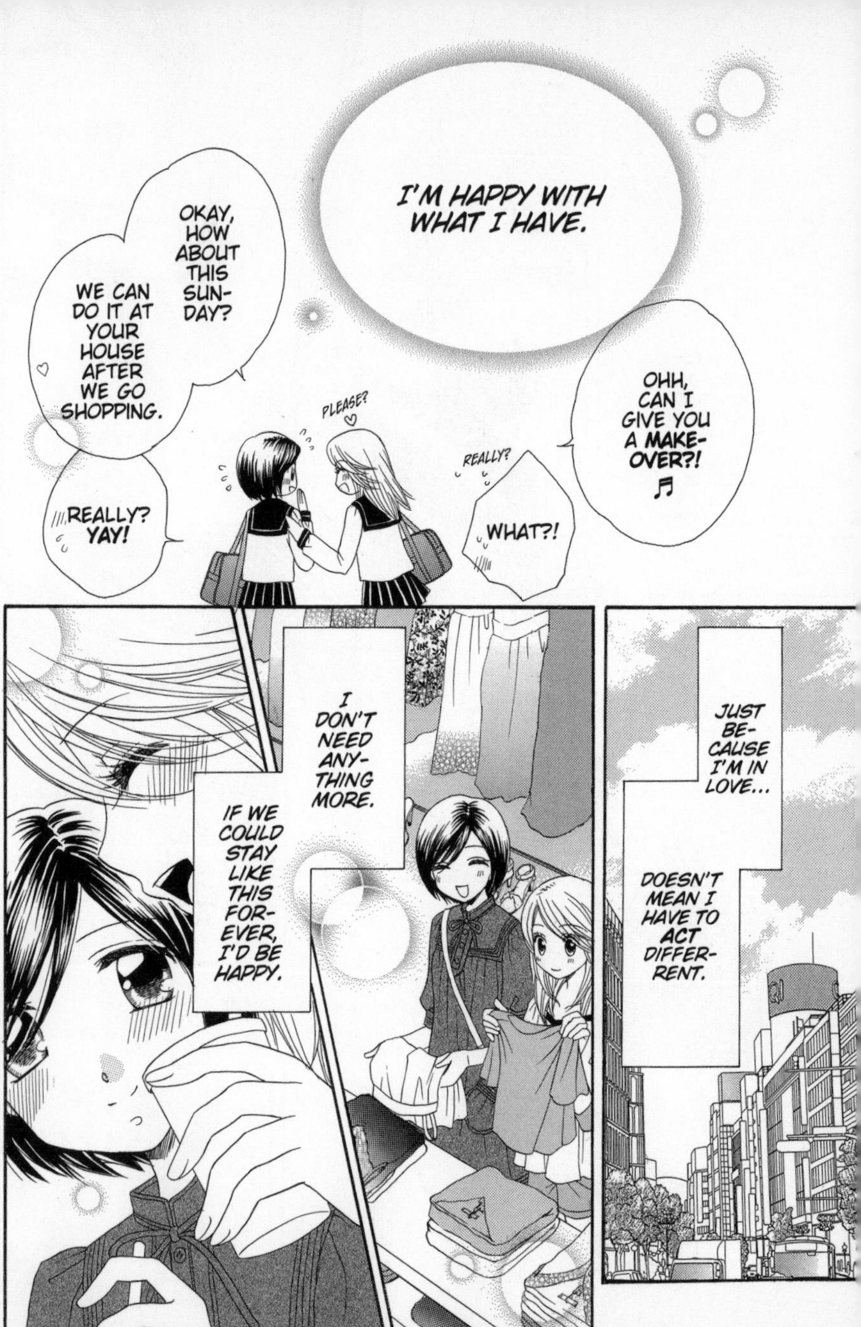
I'M HAPPY WITH WHAT I HAVE.
OHH, CAN I GIVE YOU A MAKE-OVER?! ♬
WHAT?!
REALLY?
OKAY, HOW ABOUT THIS SUNDAY?
PLEASE?
WE CAN DO IT AT YOUR HOUSE AFTER WE GO SHOPPING. ♡
REALLY? YAY!
JUST BECAUSE I'M IN LOVE...
DOESN'T MEAN I HAVE TO ACT DIFFERENT.
I DON'T NEED ANYTHING MORE.
IF WE COULD STAY LIKE THIS FOREVER, I'D BE HAPPY.

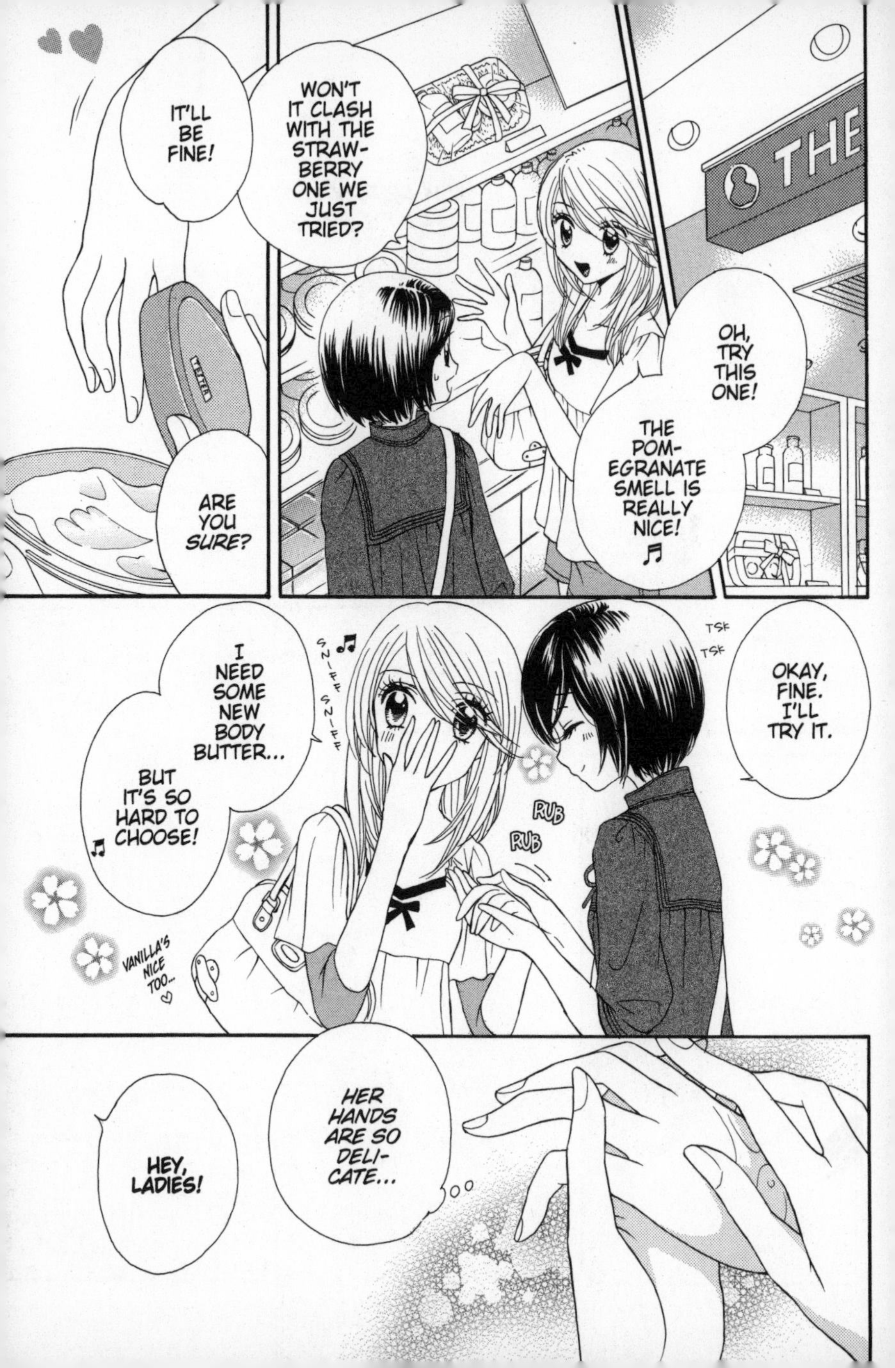
THE
OH, TRY THIS ONE!
THE POM-EGRANATE SMELL IS REALLY NICE! ♬
WON'T IT CLASH WITH THE STRAW-BERRY ONE WE JUST TRIED?
IT'LL BE FINE!
TESTER
ARE YOU SURE?
OKAY, FINE. I'LL TRY IT.
TSK TSK
RUB RUB
SNIFF SNIFF
I NEED SOME NEW BODY BUTTER...
BUT IT'S SO HARD TO CHOOSE! ♬
VANILLA'S NICE TOO... ♡
HER HANDS ARE SO DELI-CATE...
HEY, LADIES!

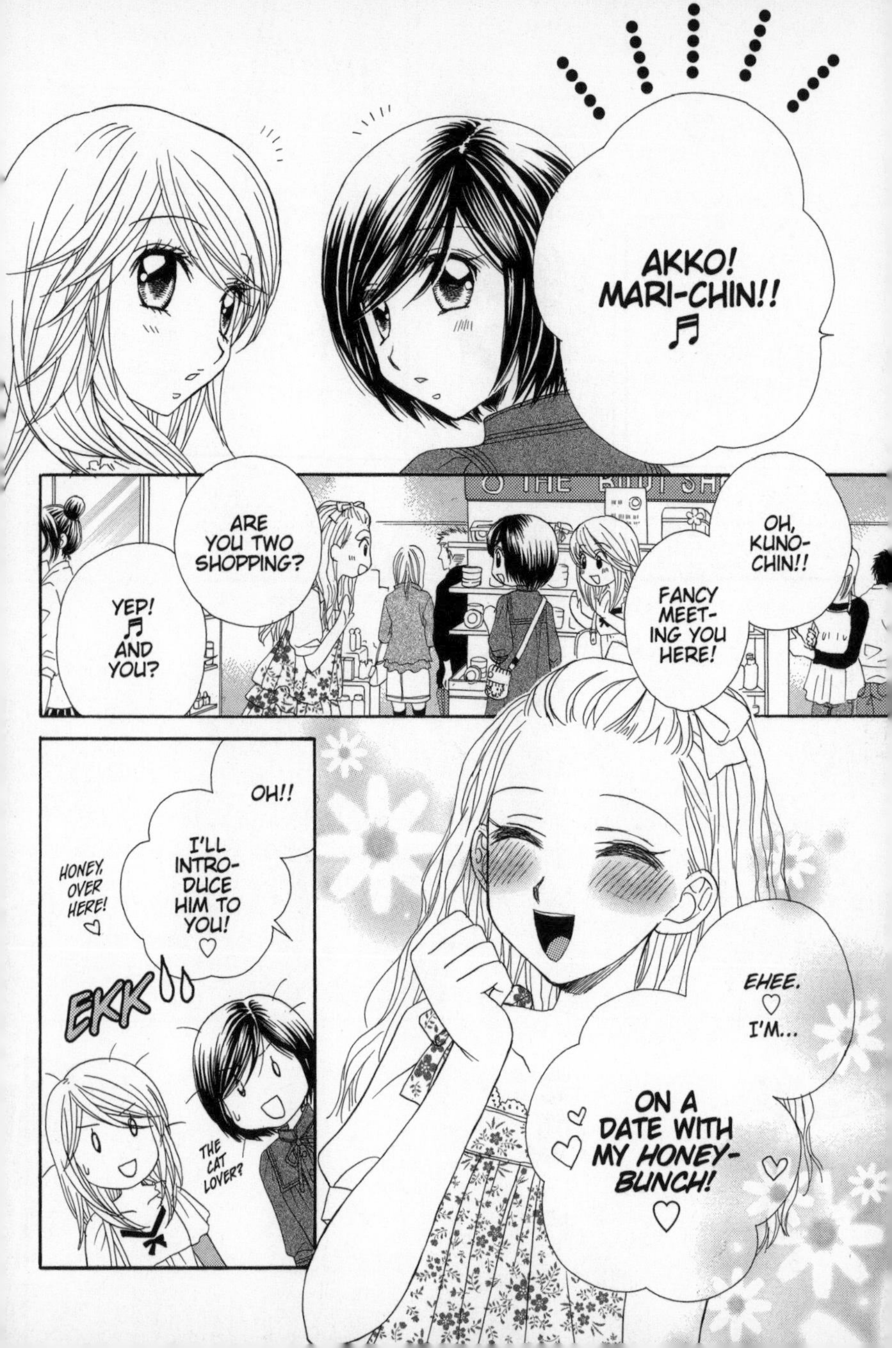
AKKO! MARI-CHIN!! ♬
OH, KUNO-CHIN!!
FANCY MEET-ING YOU HERE!
ARE YOU TWO SHOPPING?
YEP! ♬ AND YOU?
EHEE. ♡ I'M...
ON A DATE WITH MY HONEY-BUNCH! ♡
OH!!
I'LL INTRO-DUCE HIM TO YOU! ♡
HONEY, OVER HERE! ♡
EKK
THE CAT LOVER?

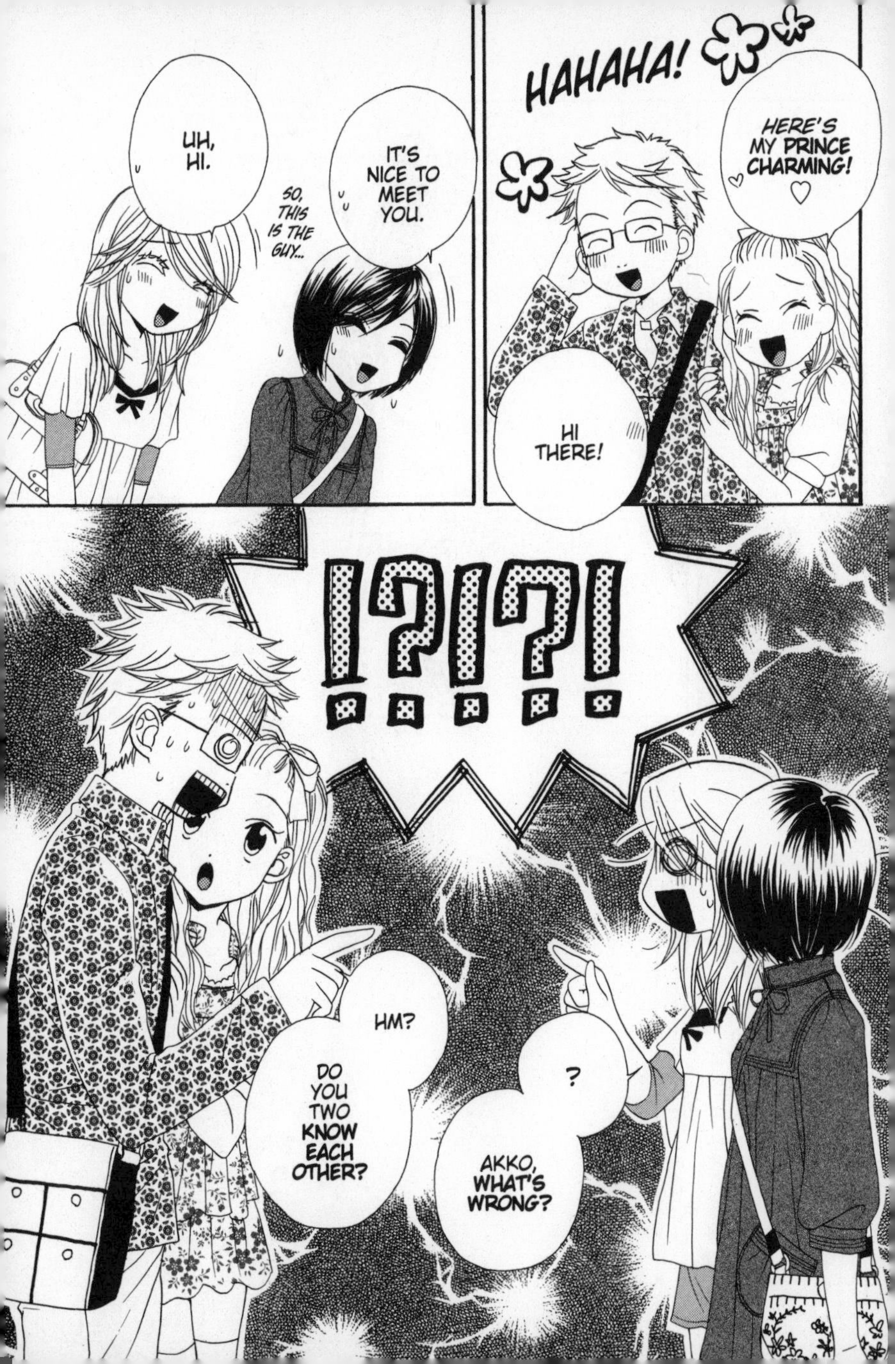
HAHAHA!
HERE'S MY PRINCE CHARMING!
HI THERE!
IT'S NICE TO MEET YOU.
SO, THIS IS THE GUY...
UH, HI.
!?!?!
?
AKKO, WHAT'S WRONG?
HM?
DO YOU TWO KNOW EACH OTHER?

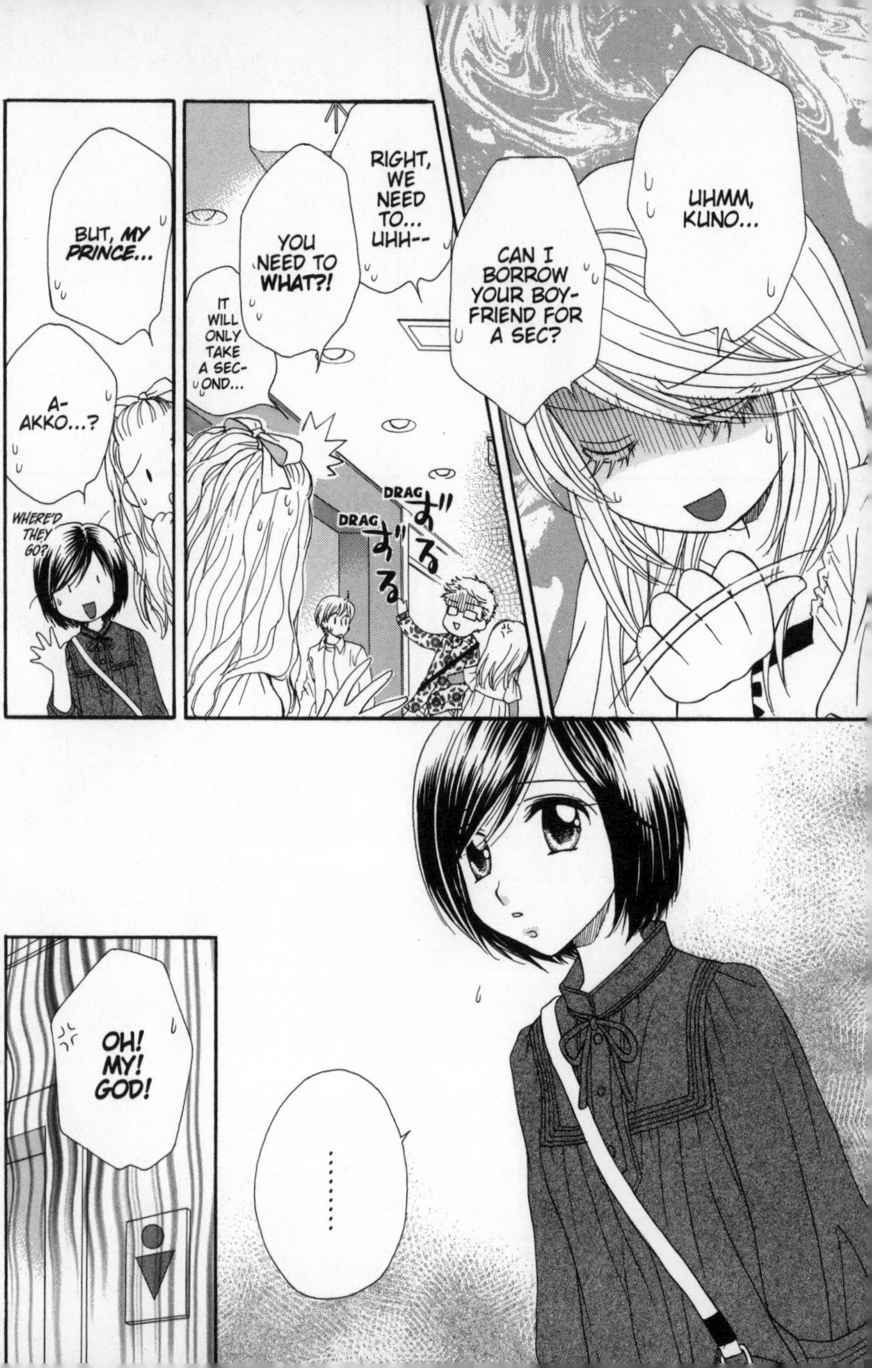
UHMM, KUNO...
CAN I BORROW YOUR BOY-FRIEND FOR A SEC?
RIGHT, WE NEED TO... UHH--
YOU NEED TO WHAT?!
IT WILL ONLY TAKE A SEC-OND...
DRAG ずる
DRAG ずる
BUT, MY PRINCE...
A-AKKO...?
WHERE'D THEY GO?
......
OH! MY! GOD!

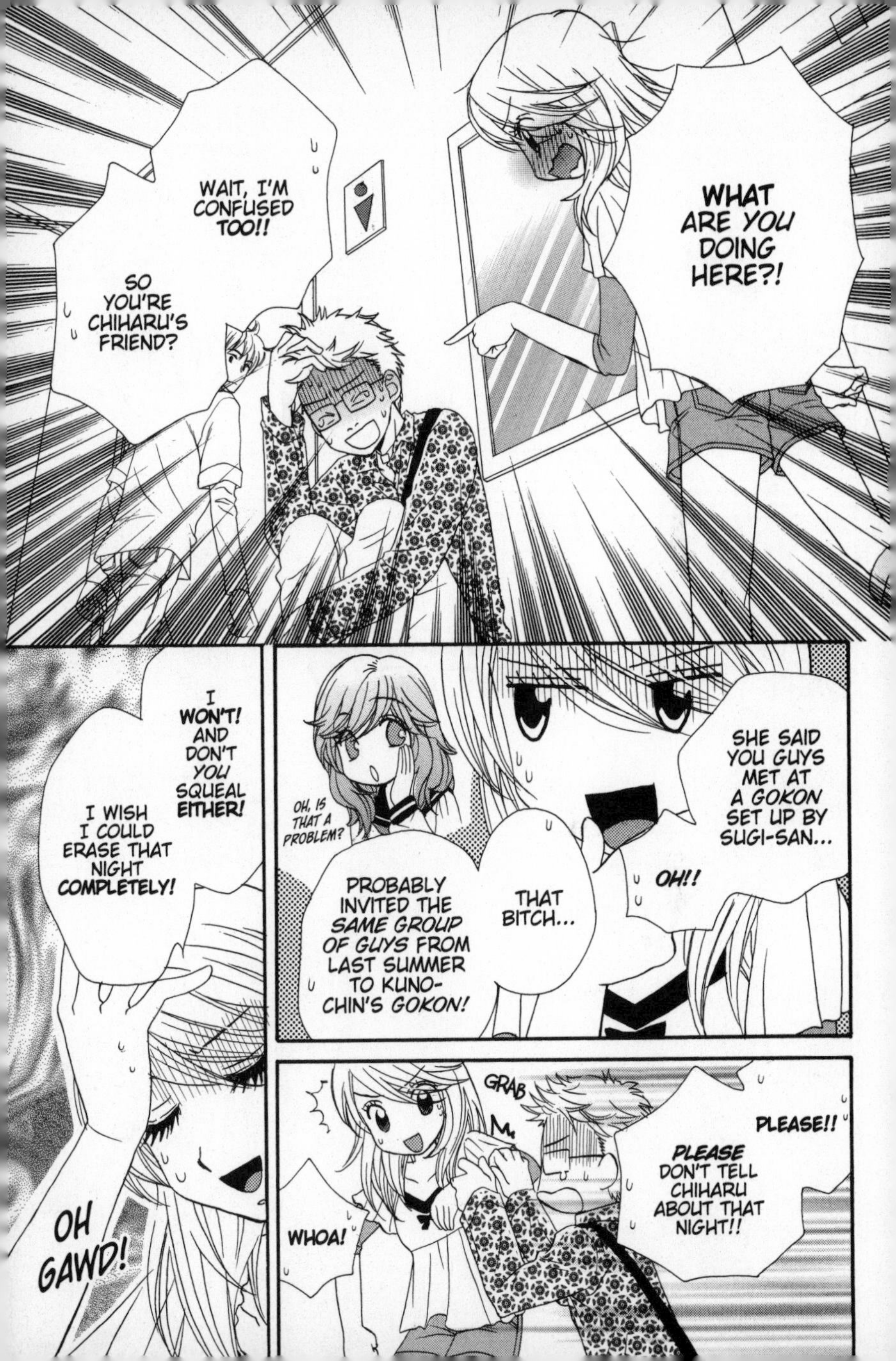

WHAT ARE YOU DOING HERE?!
WAIT, I'M CONFUSED TOO!!
SO YOU'RE CHIHARU'S FRIEND?
SHE SAID YOU GUYS MET AT A GOKON SET UP BY SUGI-SAN...
OH!!
THAT BITCH...
PROBABLY INVITED THE SAME GROUP OF GUYS FROM LAST SUMMER TO KUNO-CHIN'S GOKON!
OH, IS THAT A PROBLEM?
PLEASE!!
PLEASE DON'T TELL CHIHARU ABOUT THAT NIGHT!!
GRAB
WHOA!
I WON'T! AND DON'T YOU SQUEAL EITHER!
I WISH I COULD ERASE THAT NIGHT COMPLETELY!
OH GAWD!

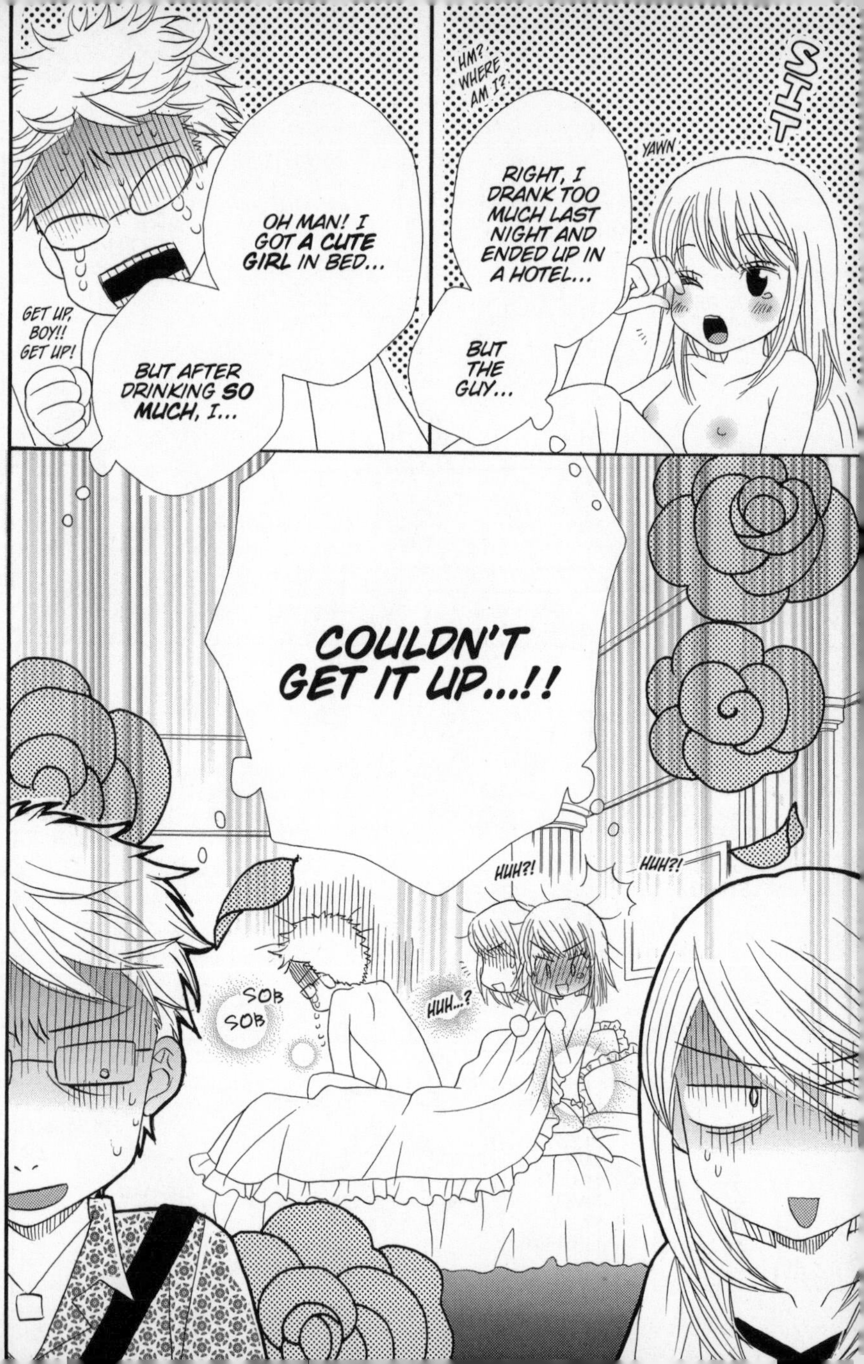
SHIT
HM? WHERE AM I?
YAWN
RIGHT, I DRANK TOO MUCH LAST NIGHT AND ENDED UP IN A HOTEL...
BUT THE GUY...
OH MAN! I GOT A CUTE GIRL IN BED...
GET UP, BOY!! GET UP!
BUT AFTER DRINKING SO MUCH, I...
COULDN'T GET IT UP...!!
HUH?!
HUH?!
HUH...?
SOB SOB

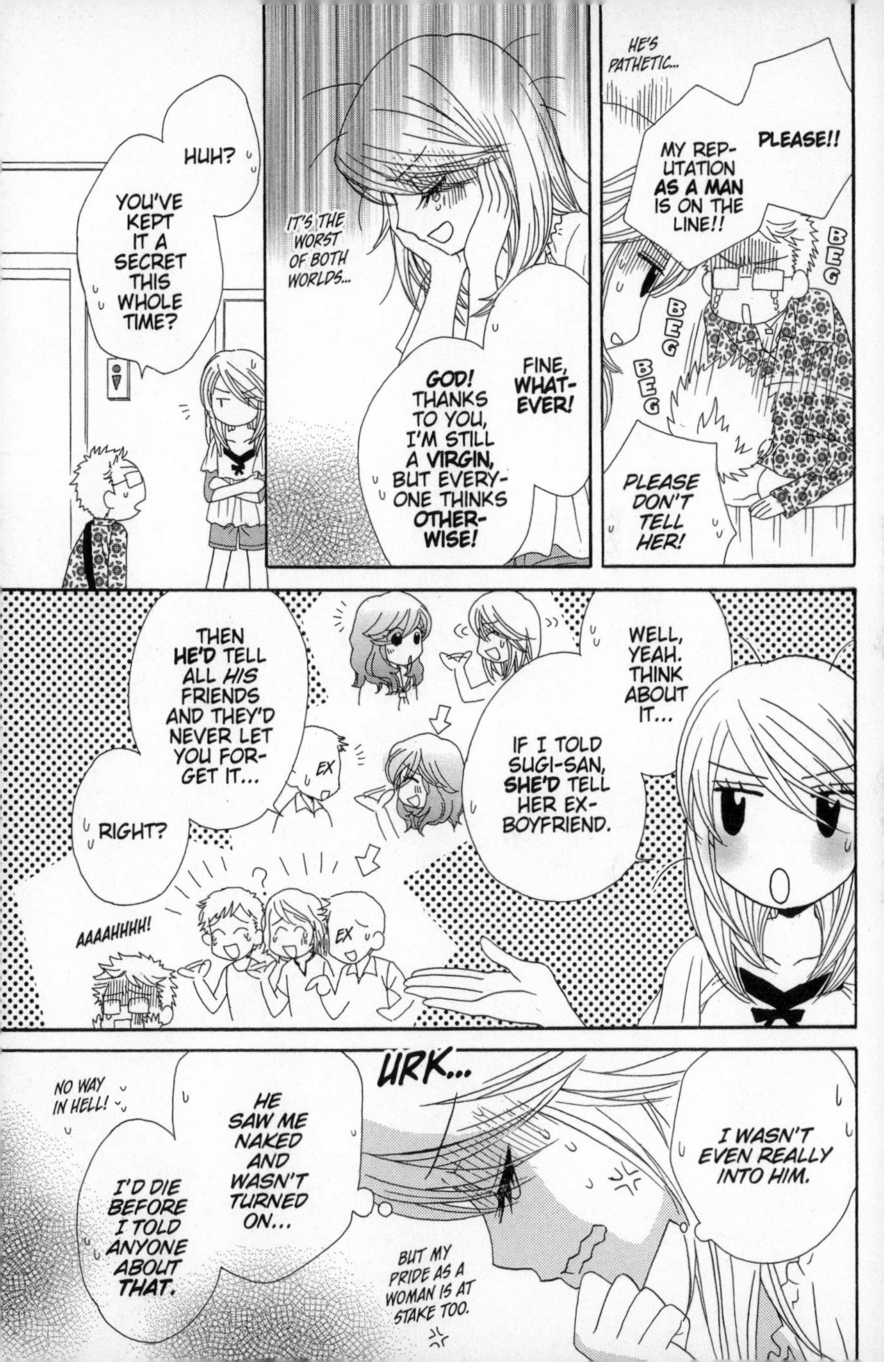
HE'S PATHETIC...
PLEASE!!
MY REPUTATION AS A MAN IS ON THE LINE!!
BEG BEG BEG BEG
PLEASE DON'T TELL HER!
IT'S THE WORST OF BOTH WORLDS...
FINE, WHATEVER!
GOD! THANKS TO YOU, I'M STILL A VIRGIN, BUT EVERYONE THINKS OTHERWISE!
HUH?
YOU'VE KEPT IT A SECRET THIS WHOLE TIME?
WELL, YEAH. THINK ABOUT IT...
IF I TOLD SUGI-SAN, SHE'D TELL HER EX-BOYFRIEND.
EX
THEN HE'D TELL ALL HIS FRIENDS AND THEY'D NEVER LET YOU FORGET IT...
RIGHT?
EX
AAAAHHHH!
I WASN'T EVEN REALLY INTO HIM.
URK...
BUT MY PRIDE AS A WOMAN IS AT STAKE TOO.
HE SAW ME NAKED AND WASN'T TURNED ON...
I'D DIE BEFORE I TOLD ANYONE ABOUT THAT.
NO WAY IN HELL!

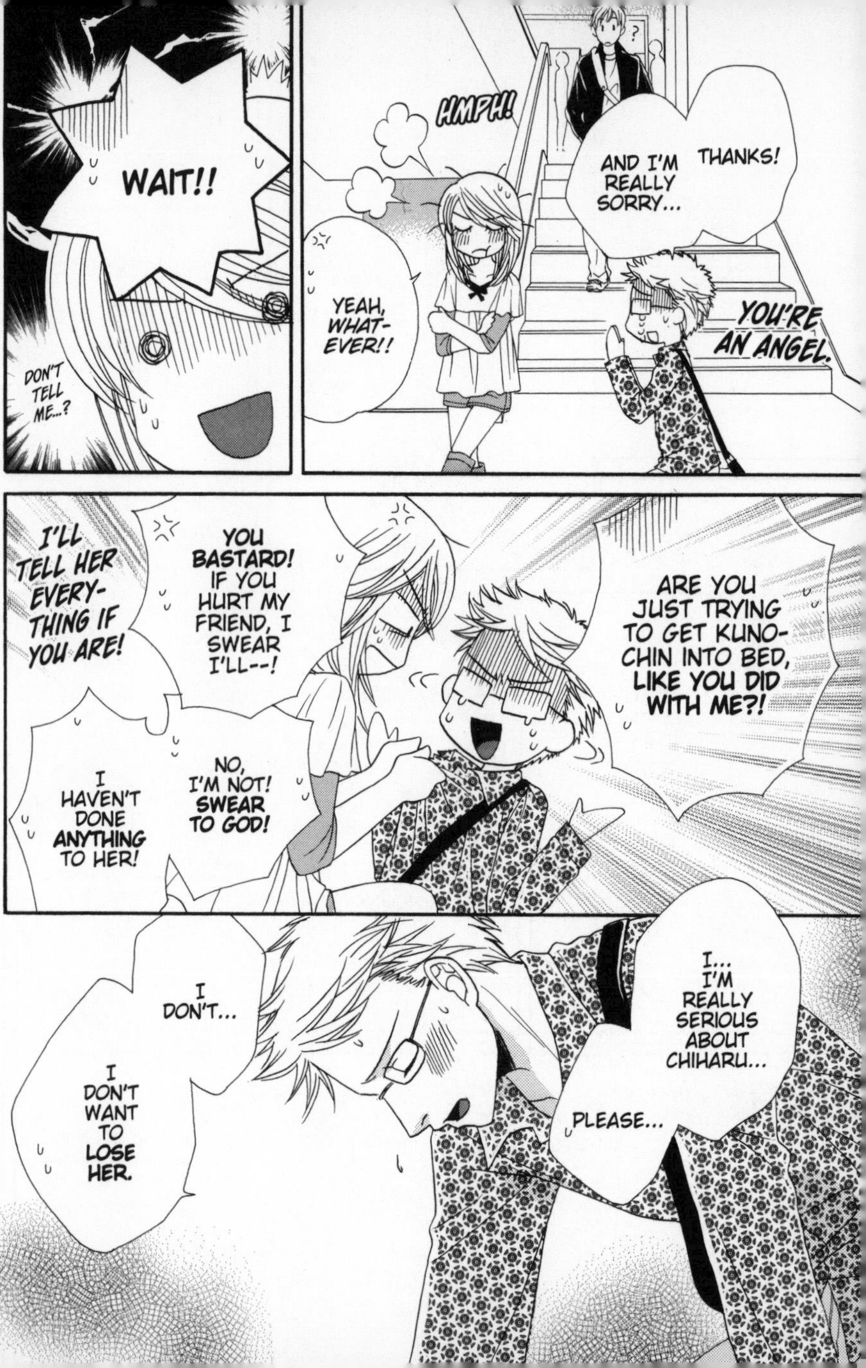
THANKS!
AND I'M REALLY SORRY...
YOU'RE AN ANGEL.
HMPH!
YEAH, WHATEVER!!
WAIT!!
DON'T TELL ME...?
ARE YOU JUST TRYING TO GET KUNO-CHIN INTO BED, LIKE YOU DID WITH ME?!
YOU BASTARD! IF YOU HURT MY FRIEND, I SWEAR I'LL--!
I'LL TELL HER EVERYTHING IF YOU ARE!
NO, I'M NOT! SWEAR TO GOD!
I HAVEN'T DONE ANYTHING TO HER!
I... I'M REALLY SERIOUS ABOUT CHIHARU...
PLEASE...
I DON'T...
I DON'T WANT TO LOSE HER.

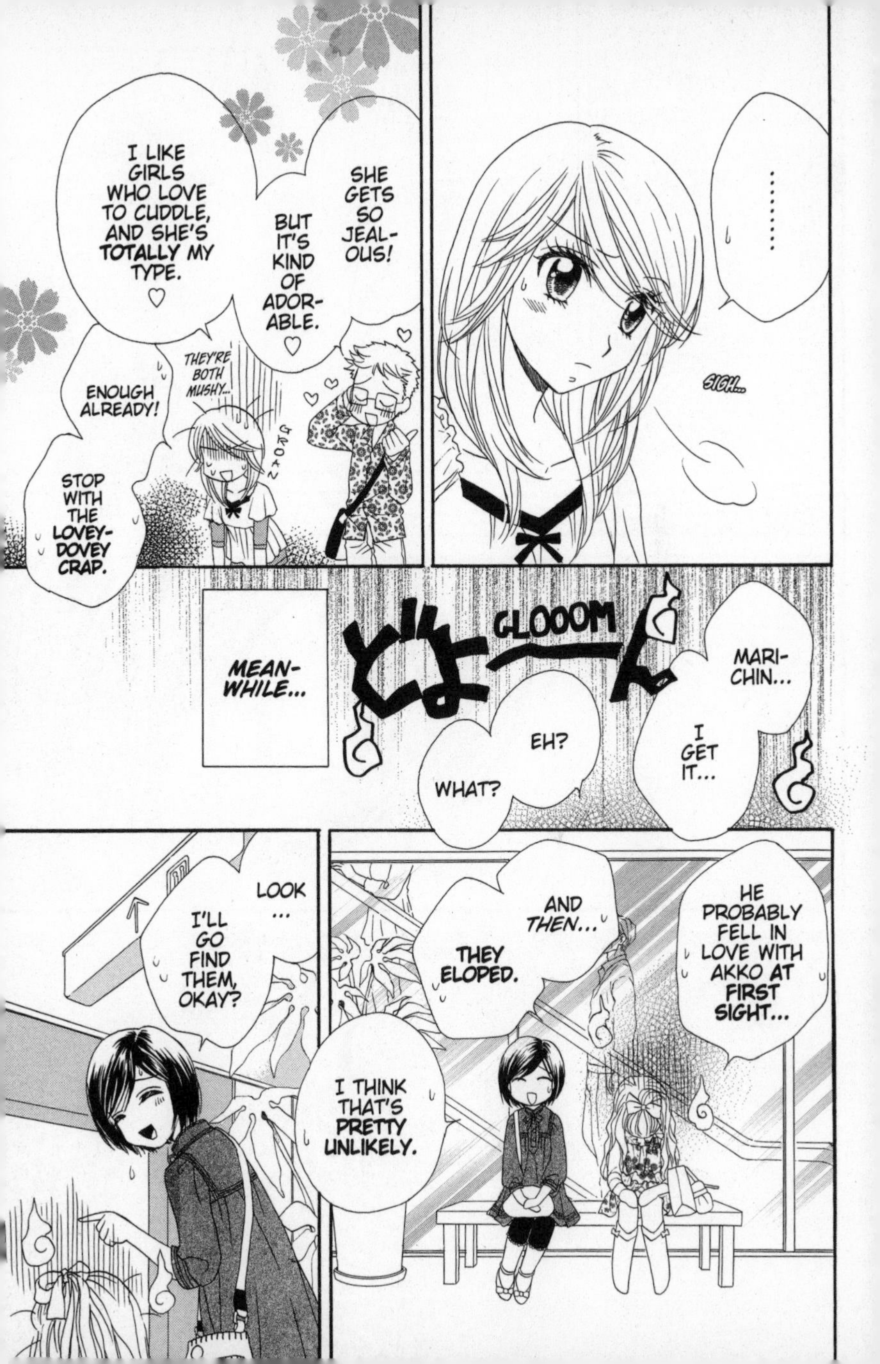
......
SIGH...
SHE GETS SO JEAL-OUS!
BUT IT'S KIND OF ADOR-ABLE. ♡
I LIKE GIRLS WHO LOVE TO CUDDLE, AND SHE'S TOTALLY MY TYPE. ♡
THEY'RE BOTH MUSHY...
GROAN
ENOUGH ALREADY!
STOP WITH THE LOVEY-DOVEY CRAP.
MARI-CHIN...
I GET IT...
EH?
WHAT?
GLOOOM
MEAN-WHILE...
HE PROBABLY FELL IN LOVE WITH AKKO AT FIRST SIGHT...
AND THEN...
THEY ELOPED.
I THINK THAT'S PRETTY UNLIKELY.
LOOK...
I'LL GO FIND THEM, OKAY?

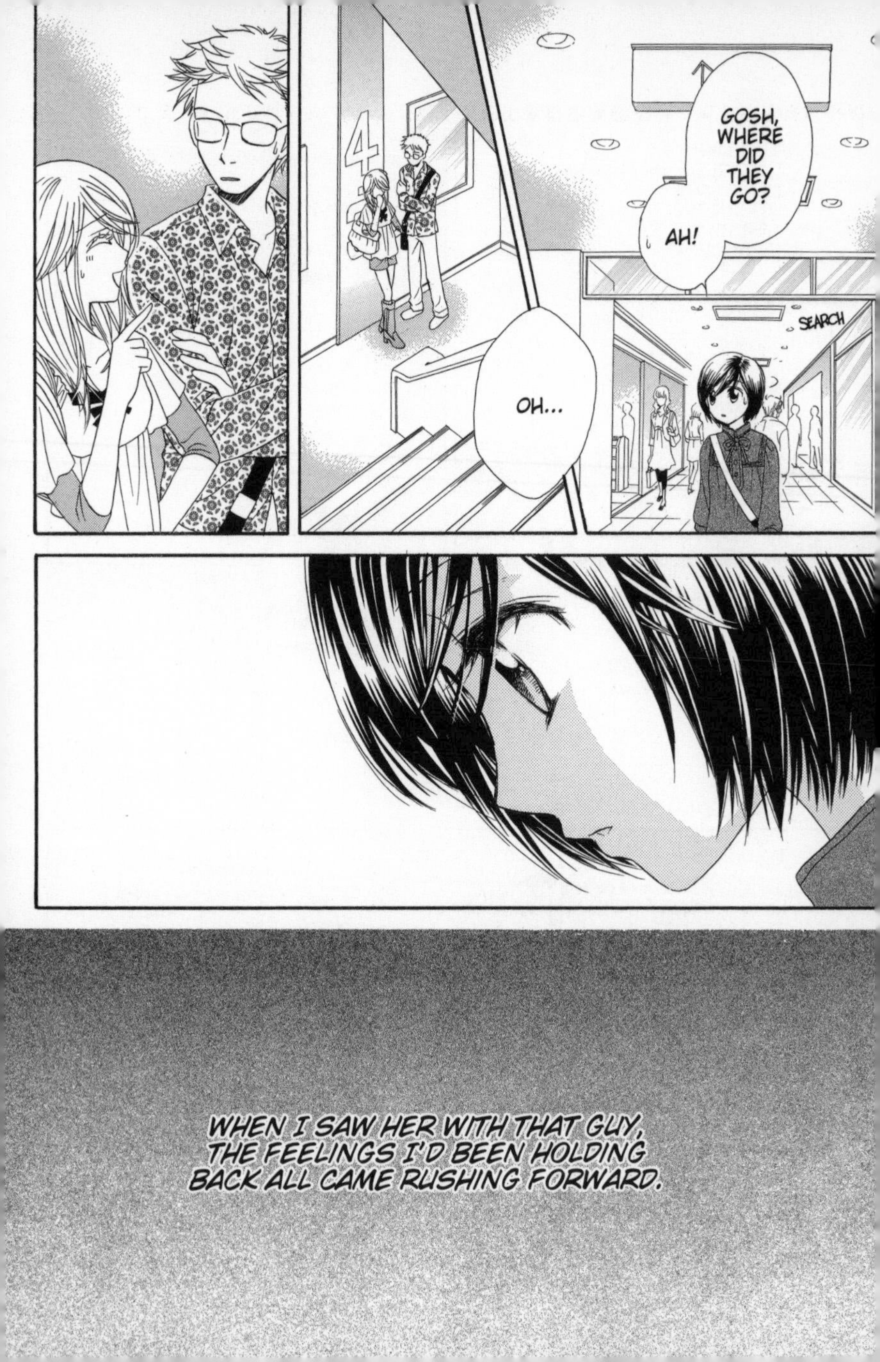
GOSH, WHERE DID THEY GO?
AH!
SEARCH
OH...
WHEN I SAW HER WITH THAT GUY, THE FEELINGS I'D BEEN HOLDING BACK ALL CAME RUSHING FORWARD.

SUMMER
UNIFORM

GIRL FRIENDS —ガールフレンズ—

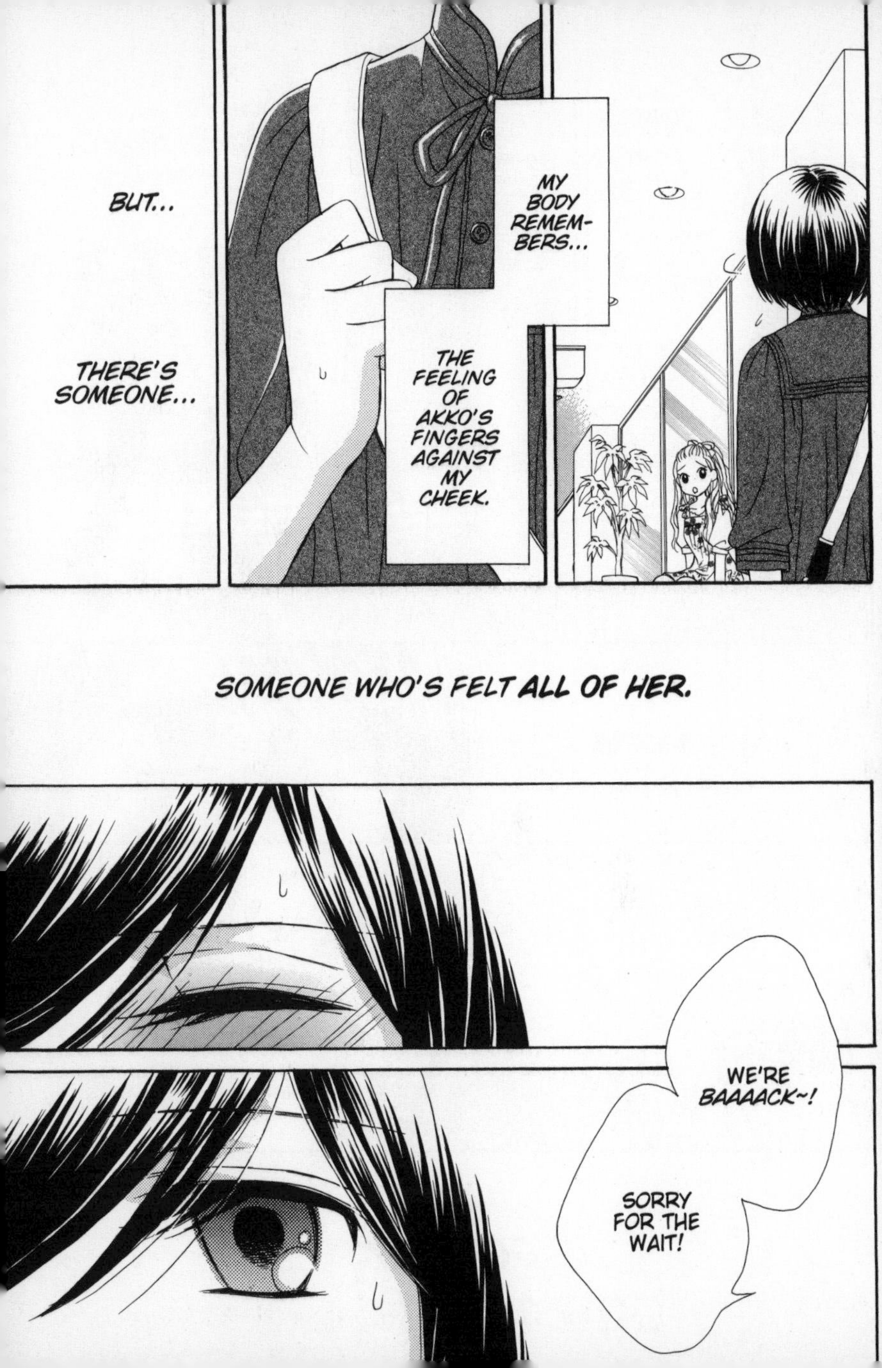
MY BODY REMEMBERS...
THE FEELING OF AKKO'S FINGERS AGAINST MY CHEEK.
BUT...
THERE'S SOMEONE...
SOMEONE WHO'S FELT ALL OF HER.
WE'RE BAAAACK~!
SORRY FOR THE WAIT!

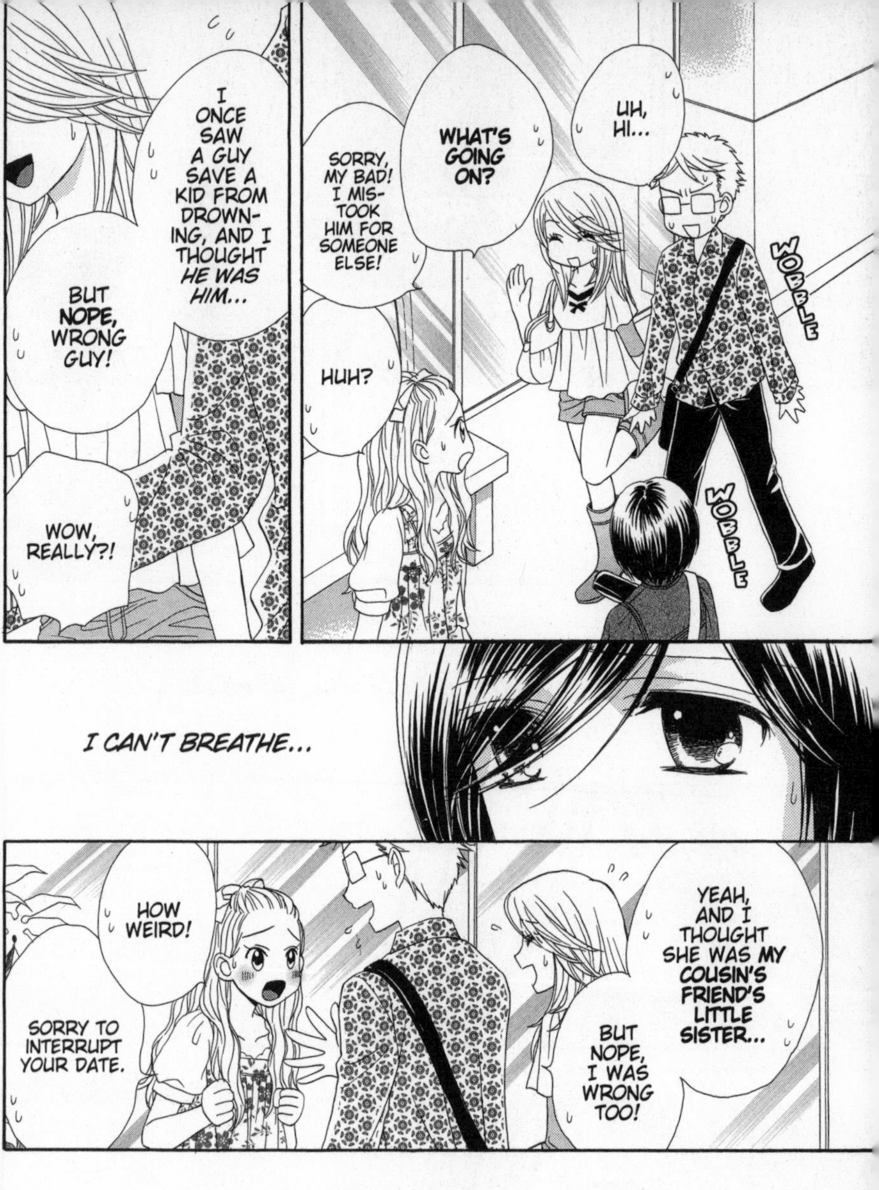
UH, HI...
WHAT'S GOING ON?
SORRY, MY BAD! I MISTOOK HIM FOR SOMEONE ELSE!
HUH?
WOBBLE
WOBBLE
I ONCE SAW A GUY SAVE A KID FROM DROWNING, AND I THOUGHT HE WAS HIM...
BUT NOPE, WRONG GUY!
WOW, REALLY?!
I CAN'T BREATHE...
YEAH, AND I THOUGHT SHE WAS MY COUSIN'S FRIEND'S LITTLE SISTER...
BUT NOPE, I WAS WRONG TOO!
HOW WEIRD!
SORRY TO INTERRUPT YOUR DATE.
GO AWAY.

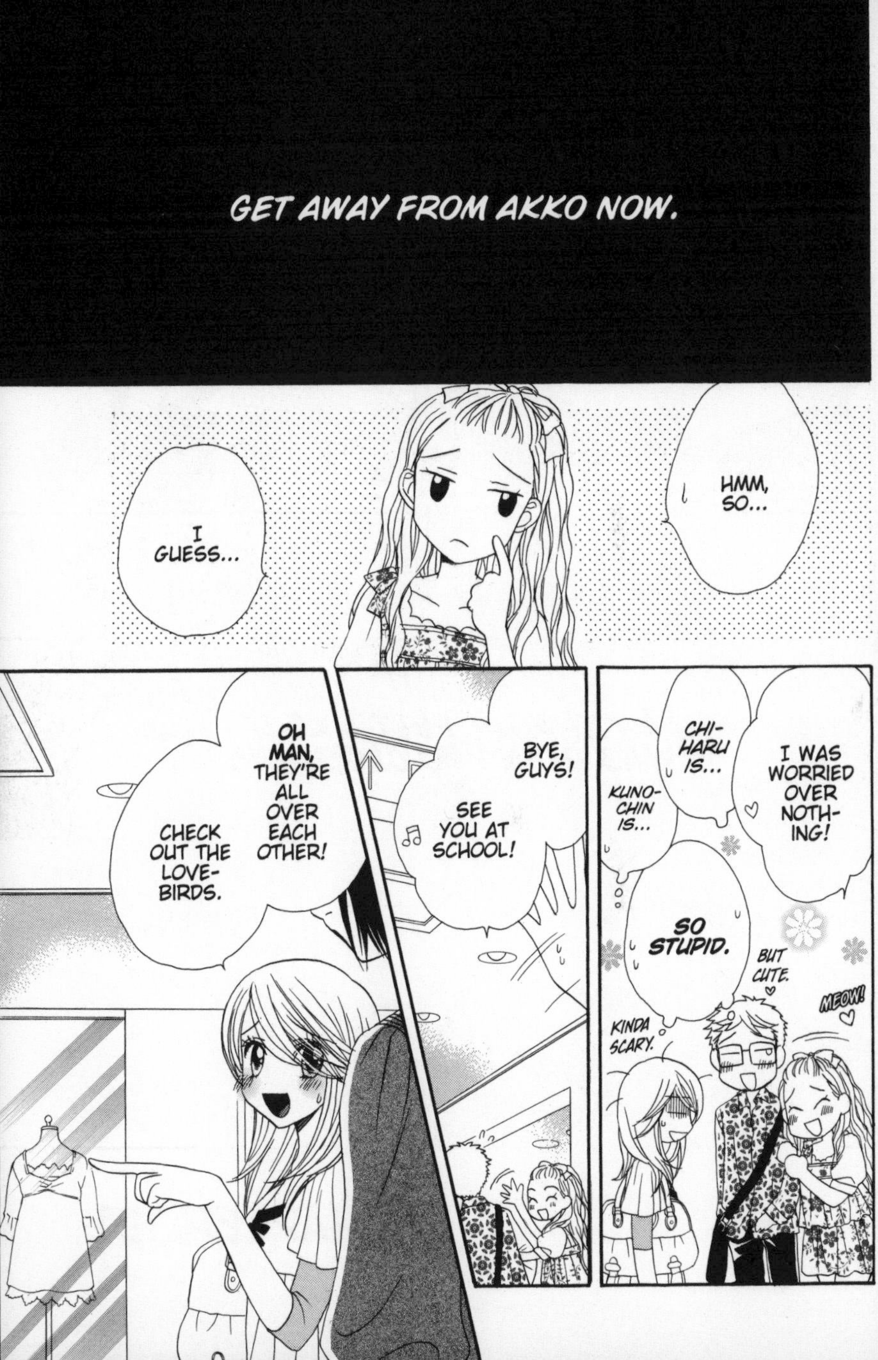
GET AWAY FROM AKKO NOW.
HMM, SO...
I GUESS...
I WAS WORRIED OVER NOTH-ING!
CHI-HARU IS...
KUNO-CHIN IS...
SO STUPID.
BUT CUTE.
MEOW!
KINDA SCARY.
BYE, GUYS!
SEE YOU AT SCHOOL!
OH MAN, THEY'RE ALL OVER EACH OTHER!
CHECK OUT THE LOVE-BIRDS.

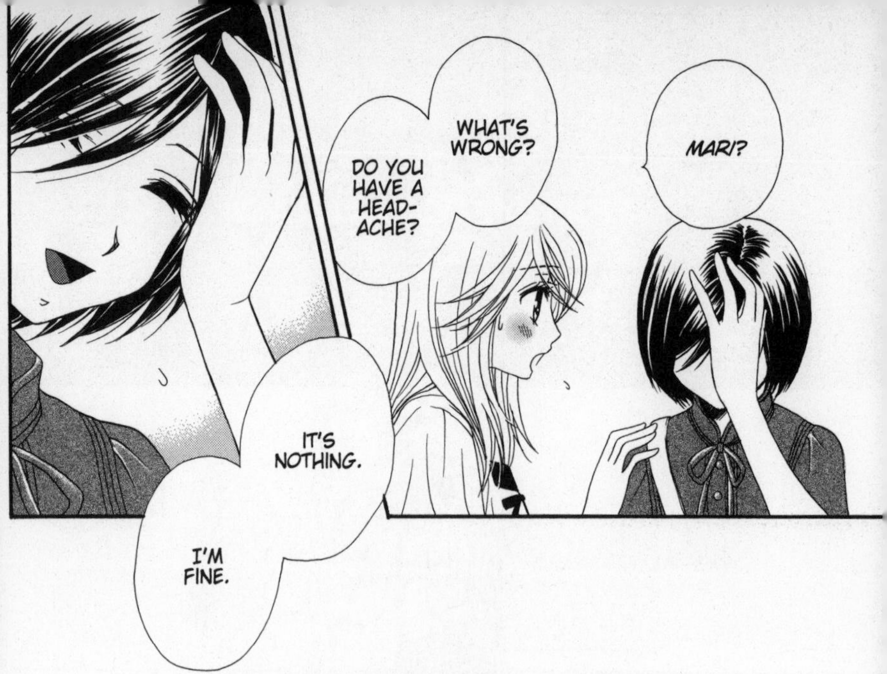
MARI?
WHAT'S WRONG?
DO YOU HAVE A HEAD-ACHE?
IT'S NOTHING.
I'M FINE.

MY THROAT FELT LIKE IT WAS GOING TO CLOSE UP.

[CHAPTER 13]

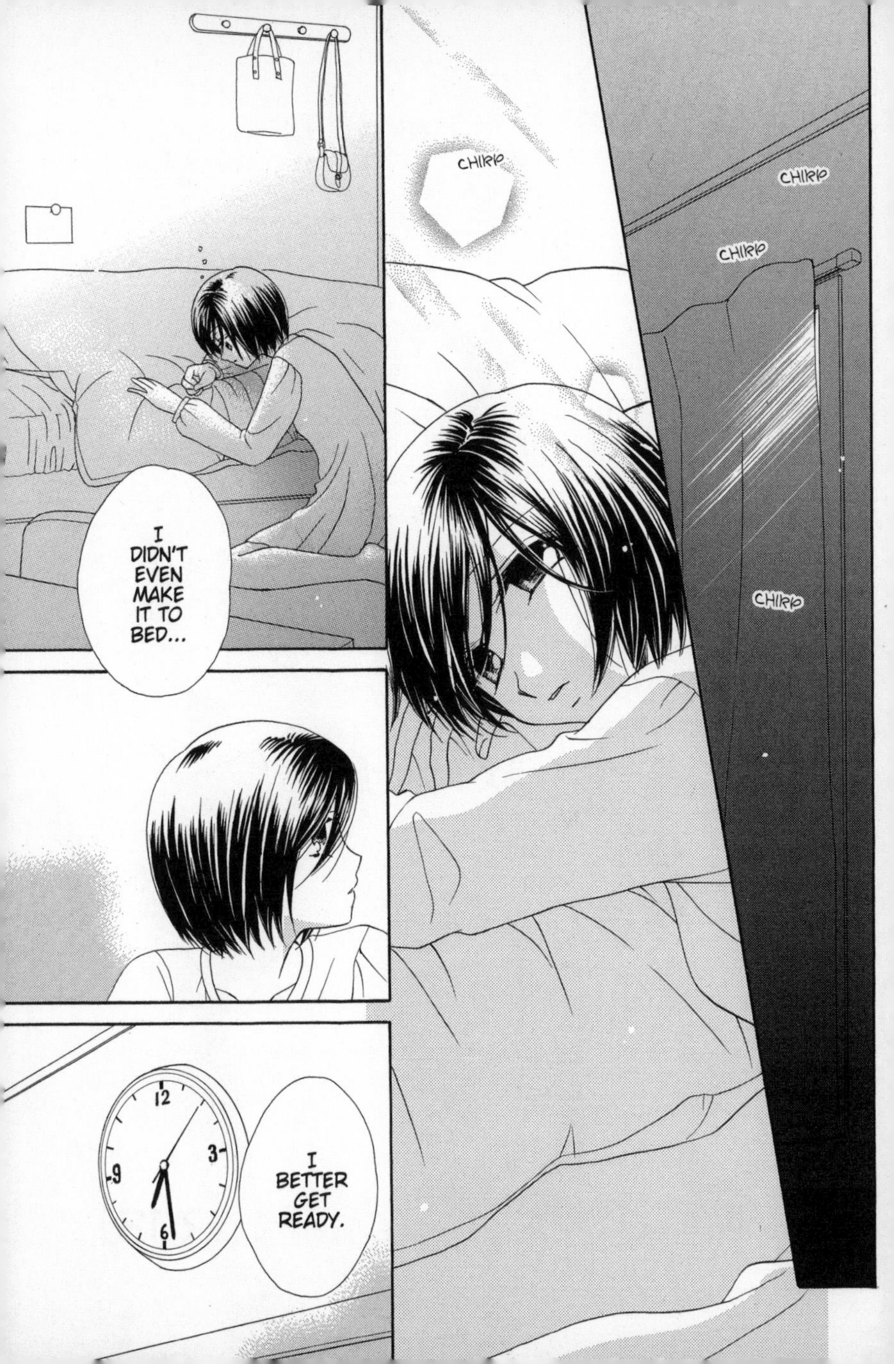
CHIRP
CHIRP
CHIRP
CHIRP
I DIDN'T EVEN MAKE IT TO BED...
I BETTER GET READY.

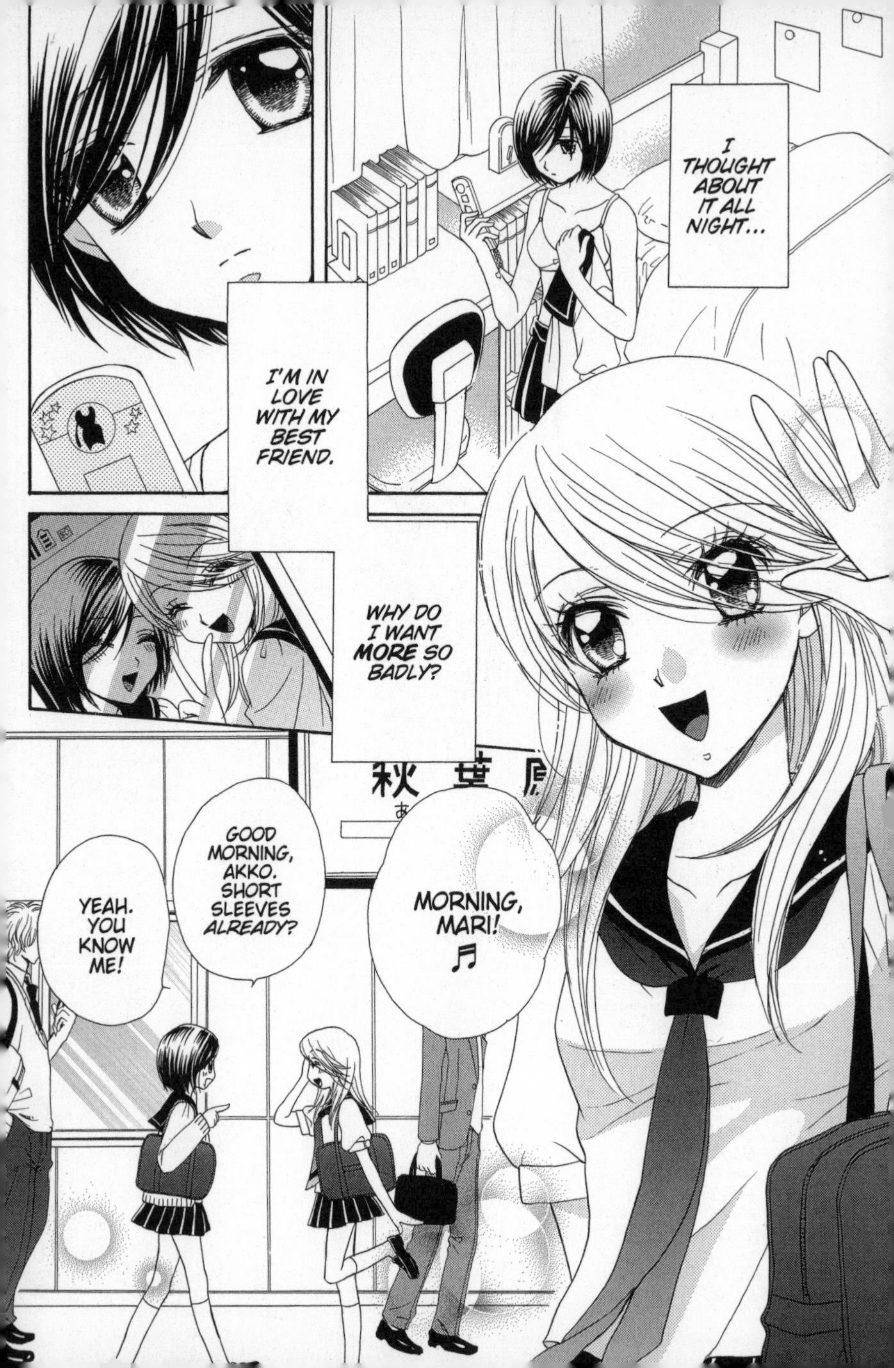
I THOUGHT ABOUT IT ALL NIGHT...
I'M IN LOVE WITH MY BEST FRIEND.
WHY DO I WANT MORE SO BADLY?
MORNING, MARI! ♬
GOOD MORNING, AKKO. SHORT SLEEVES ALREADY?
YEAH. YOU KNOW ME!

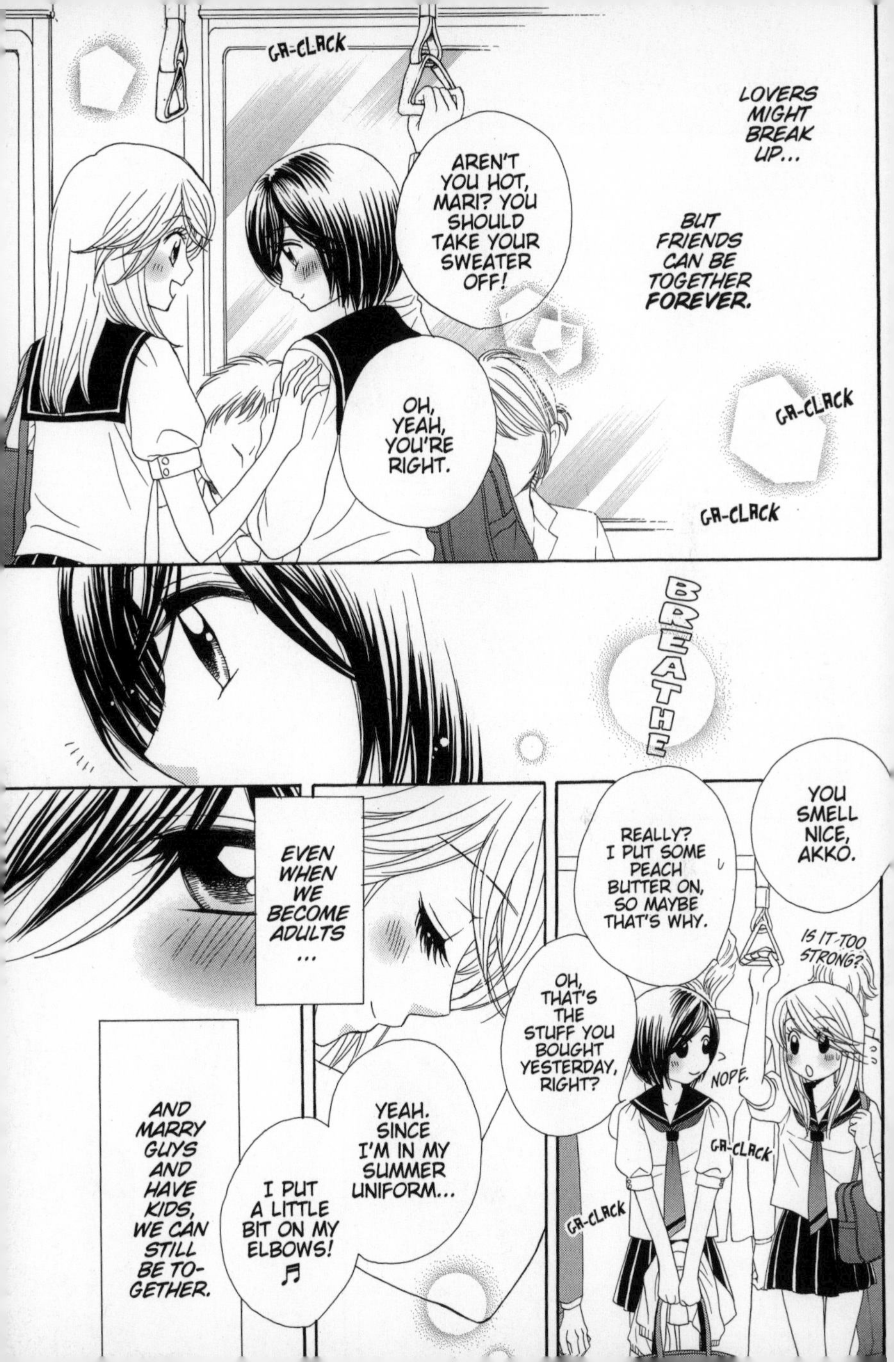
LOVERS MIGHT BREAK UP...
BUT FRIENDS CAN BE TOGETHER FOREVER.
GA-CLACK
GA-CLACK
AREN'T YOU HOT, MARI? YOU SHOULD TAKE YOUR SWEATER OFF!
OH, YEAH, YOU'RE RIGHT.
GA-CLACK
BREATHE
YOU SMELL NICE, AKKO.
REALLY? I PUT SOME PEACH BUTTER ON, SO MAYBE THAT'S WHY.
IS IT TOO STRONG?
NOPE.
OH, THAT'S THE STUFF YOU BOUGHT YESTERDAY, RIGHT?
GA-CLACK
GA-CLACK
EVEN WHEN WE BECOME ADULTS ...
YEAH. SINCE I'M IN MY SUMMER UNIFORM...
I PUT A LITTLE BIT ON MY ELBOWS! ♬
AND MARRY GUYS AND HAVE KIDS, WE CAN STILL BE TO-GETHER.

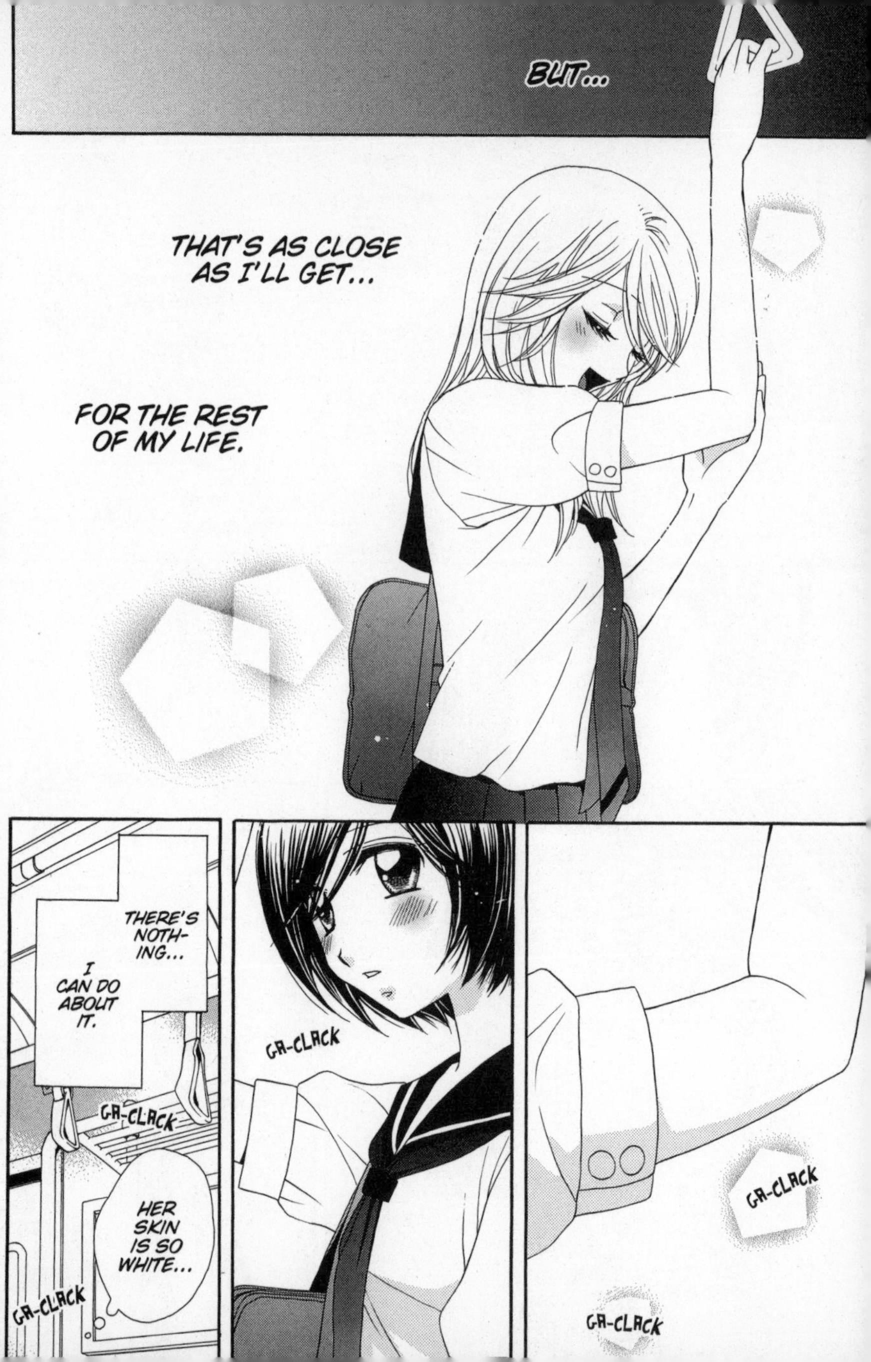
BUT...
THAT'S AS CLOSE AS I'LL GET...
FOR THE REST OF MY LIFE.
GA-CLACK
GA-CLACK
GA-CLACK
THERE'S NOTHING...
I CAN DO ABOUT IT.
GA-CLACK
HER SKIN IS SO WHITE...
GA-CLACK

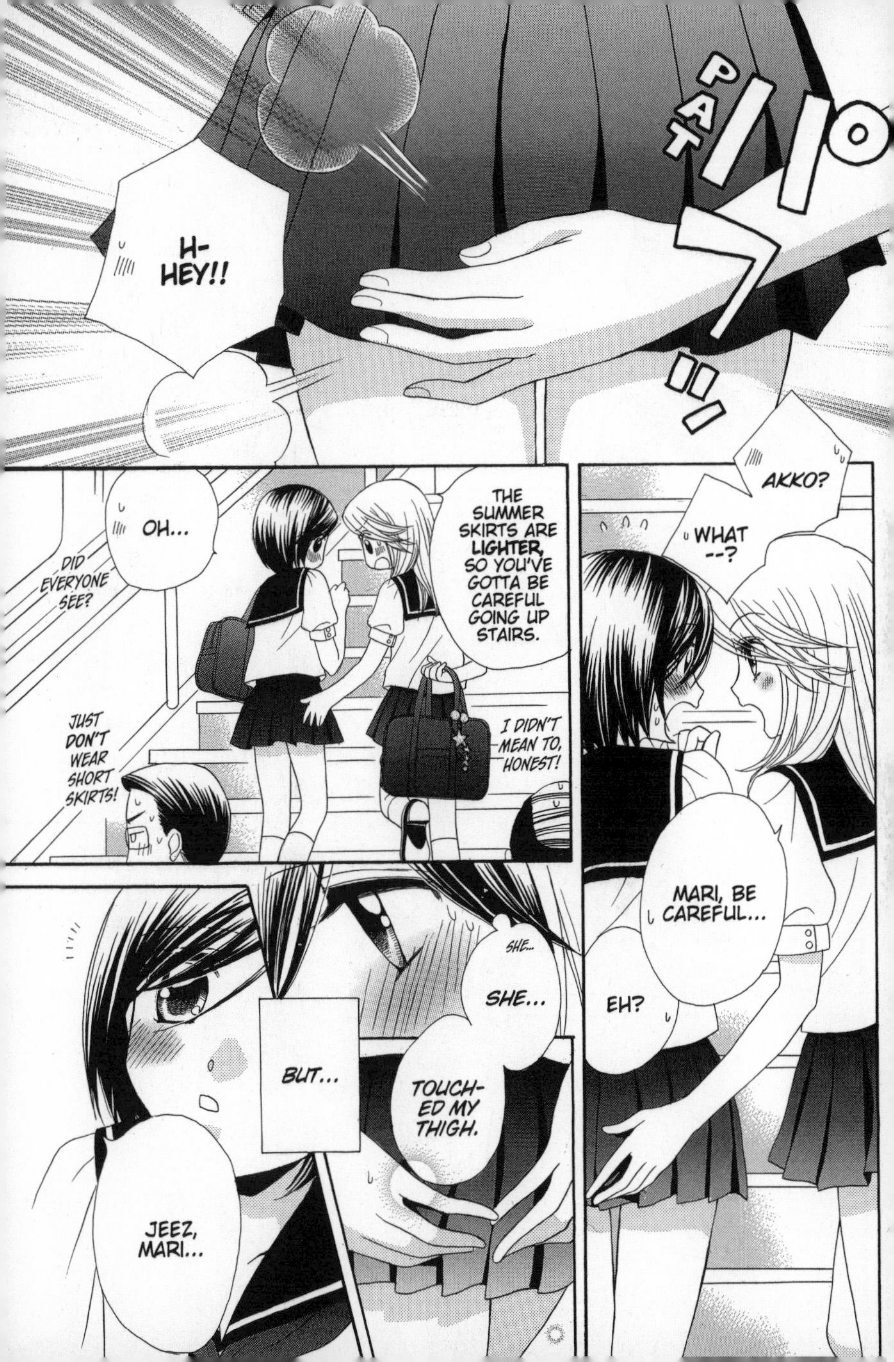
PAT
H-HEY!!
AKKO?
WHAT --?
MARI, BE CAREFUL...
EH?
THE SUMMER SKIRTS ARE LIGHTER, SO YOU'VE GOTTA BE CAREFUL GOING UP STAIRS.
OH...
DID EVERYONE SEE?
I DIDN'T MEAN TO, HONEST!
JUST DON'T WEAR SHORT SKIRTS!
SHE...
SHE...
TOUCHED MY THIGH.
BUT...
JEEZ, MARI...

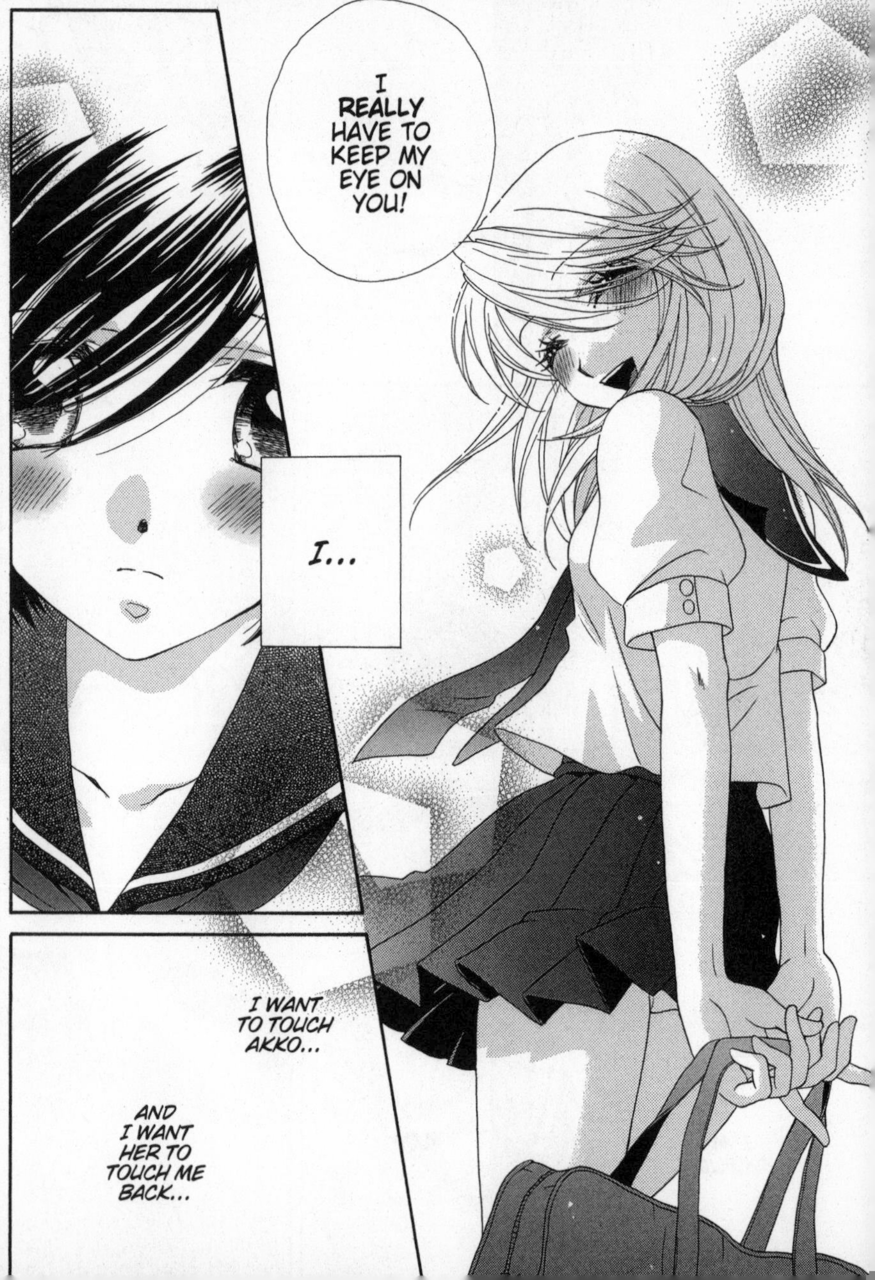
I REALLY HAVE TO KEEP MY EYE ON YOU!
I...
I WANT TO TOUCH AKKO...
AND I WANT HER TO TOUCH ME BACK...

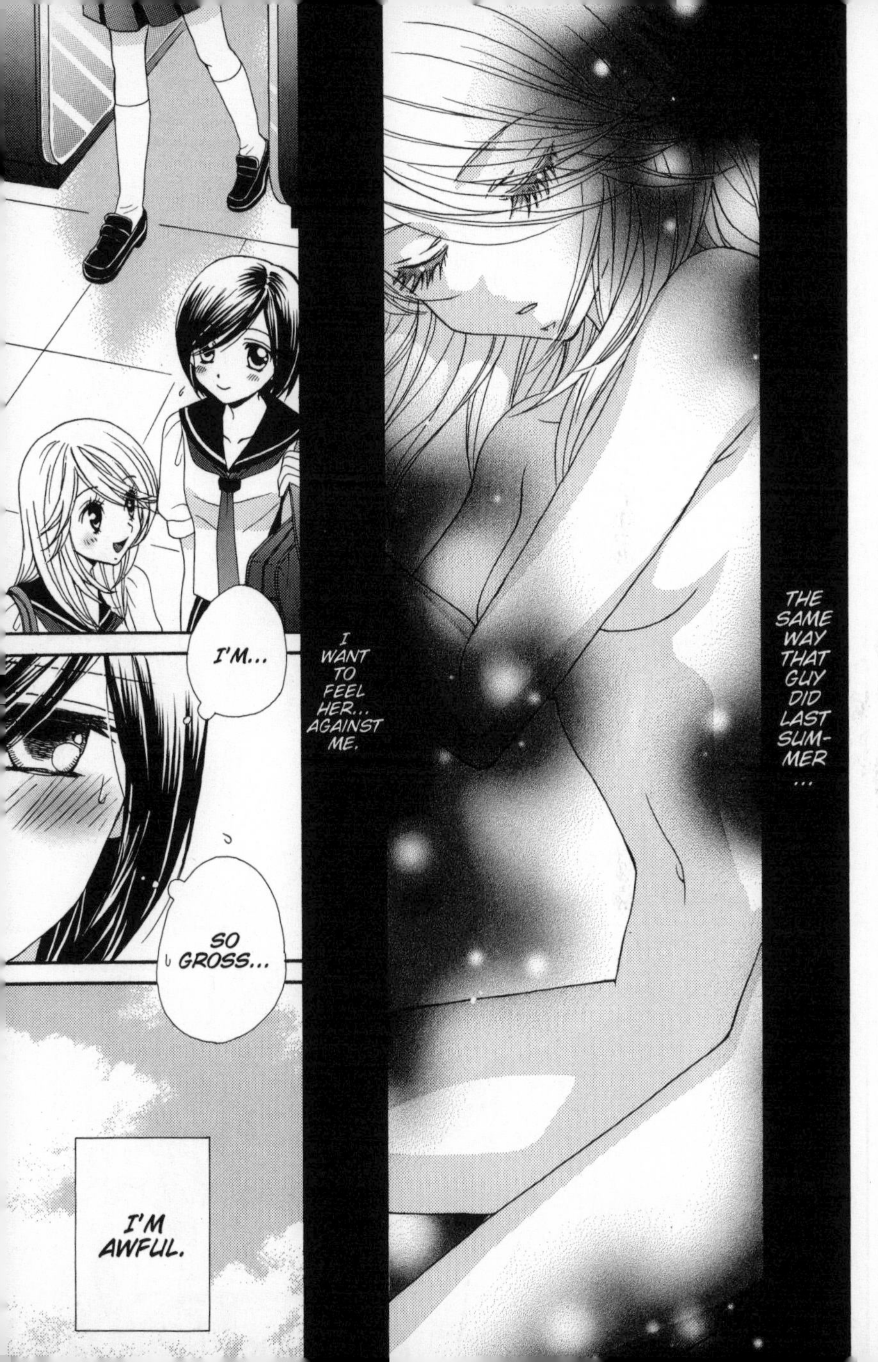
THE SAME WAY THAT GUY DID LAST SUMMER-MER...
I WANT TO FEEL HER... AGAINST ME.
I'M...
SO GROSS...
I'M AWFUL.

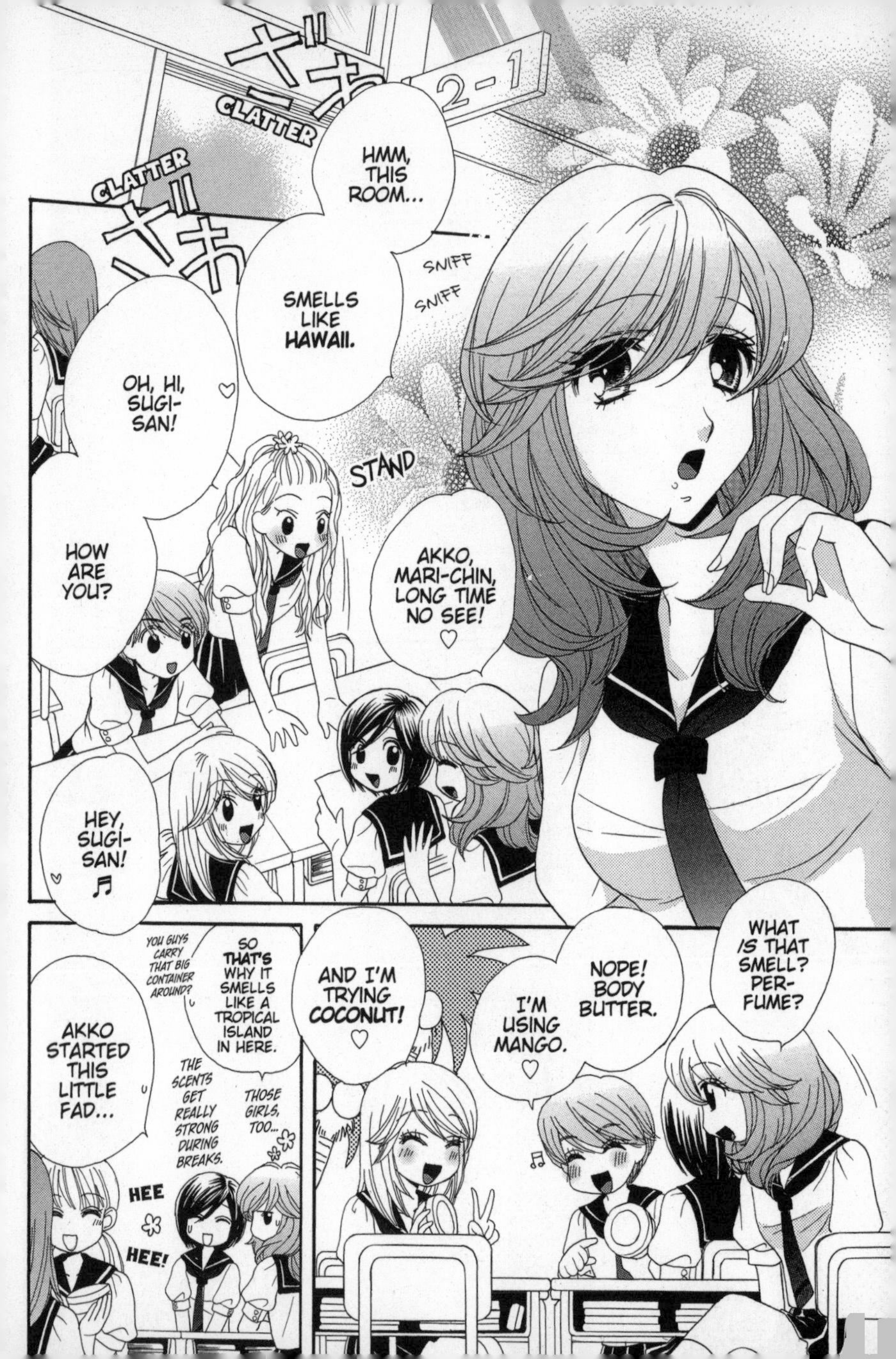
CLATTER
CLATTER
HMM, THIS ROOM...
SMELLS LIKE HAWAII.
SNIFF
SNIFF
STAND
AKKO, MARI-CHIN, LONG TIME NO SEE! ♡
OH, HI, SUGI-SAN! ♡
HOW ARE YOU?
HEY, SUGI-SAN! ♡ ♫
WHAT IS THAT SMELL? PER-FUME?
NOPE! BODY BUTTER.
I'M USING MANGO. ♡
AND I'M TRYING COCONUT! ♡
SO THAT'S WHY IT SMELLS LIKE A TROPICAL ISLAND IN HERE.
YOU GUYS CARRY THAT BIG CONTAINER AROUND?
THOSE GIRLS, TOO...
THE SCENTS GET REALLY STRONG DURING BREAKS.
AKKO STARTED THIS LITTLE FAD...
HEE
HEE!

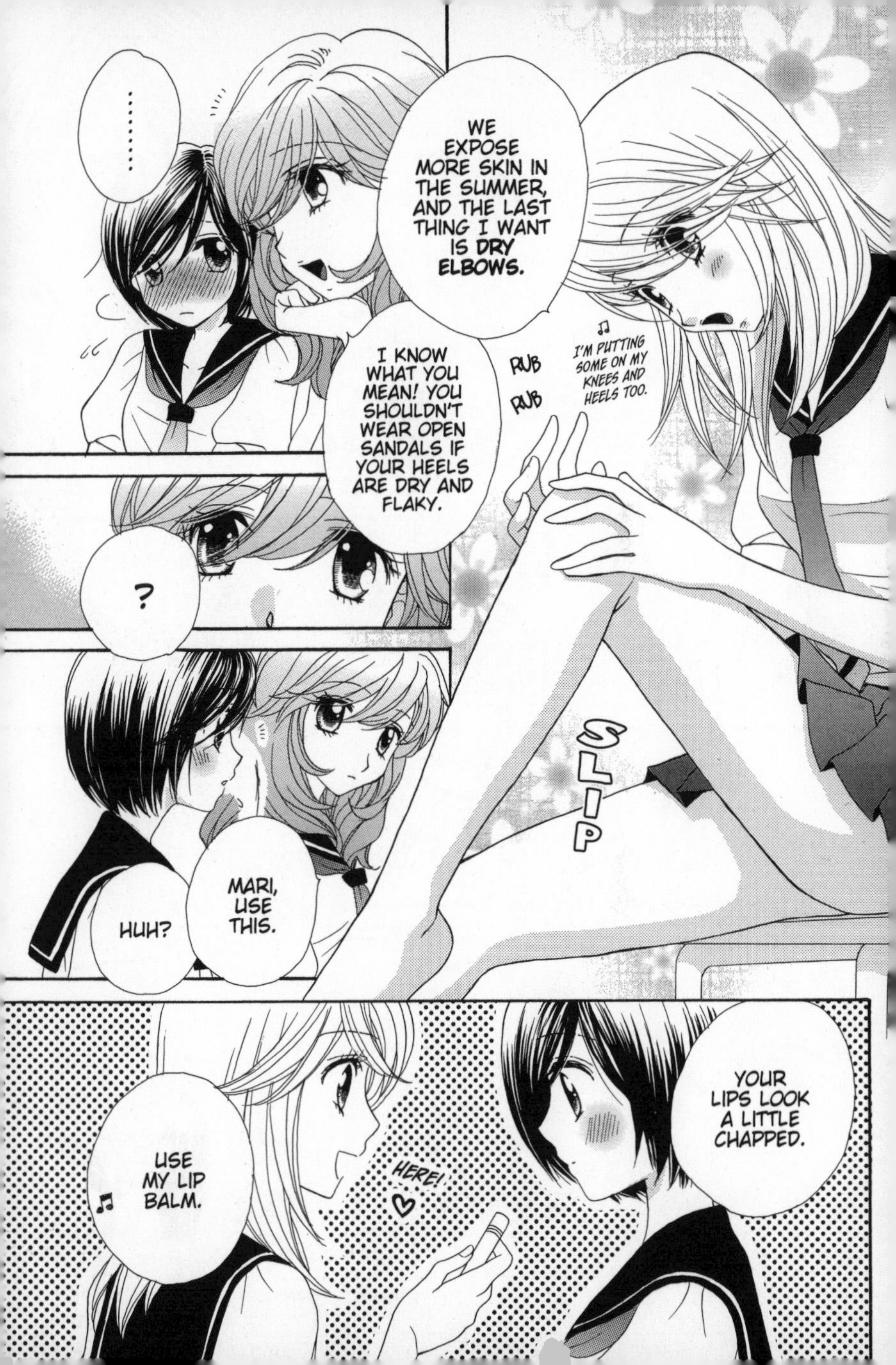
♫ I'M PUTTING SOME ON MY KNEES AND HEELS TOO.
RUB
RUB
SLIP
WE EXPOSE MORE SKIN IN THE SUMMER, AND THE LAST THING I WANT IS DRY ELBOWS.
......
I KNOW WHAT YOU MEAN! YOU SHOULDN'T WEAR OPEN SANDALS IF YOUR HEELS ARE DRY AND FLAKY.
?
MARI, USE THIS.
HUH?
YOUR LIPS LOOK A LITTLE CHAPPED.
HERE! ♡
USE MY LIP BALM. ♫

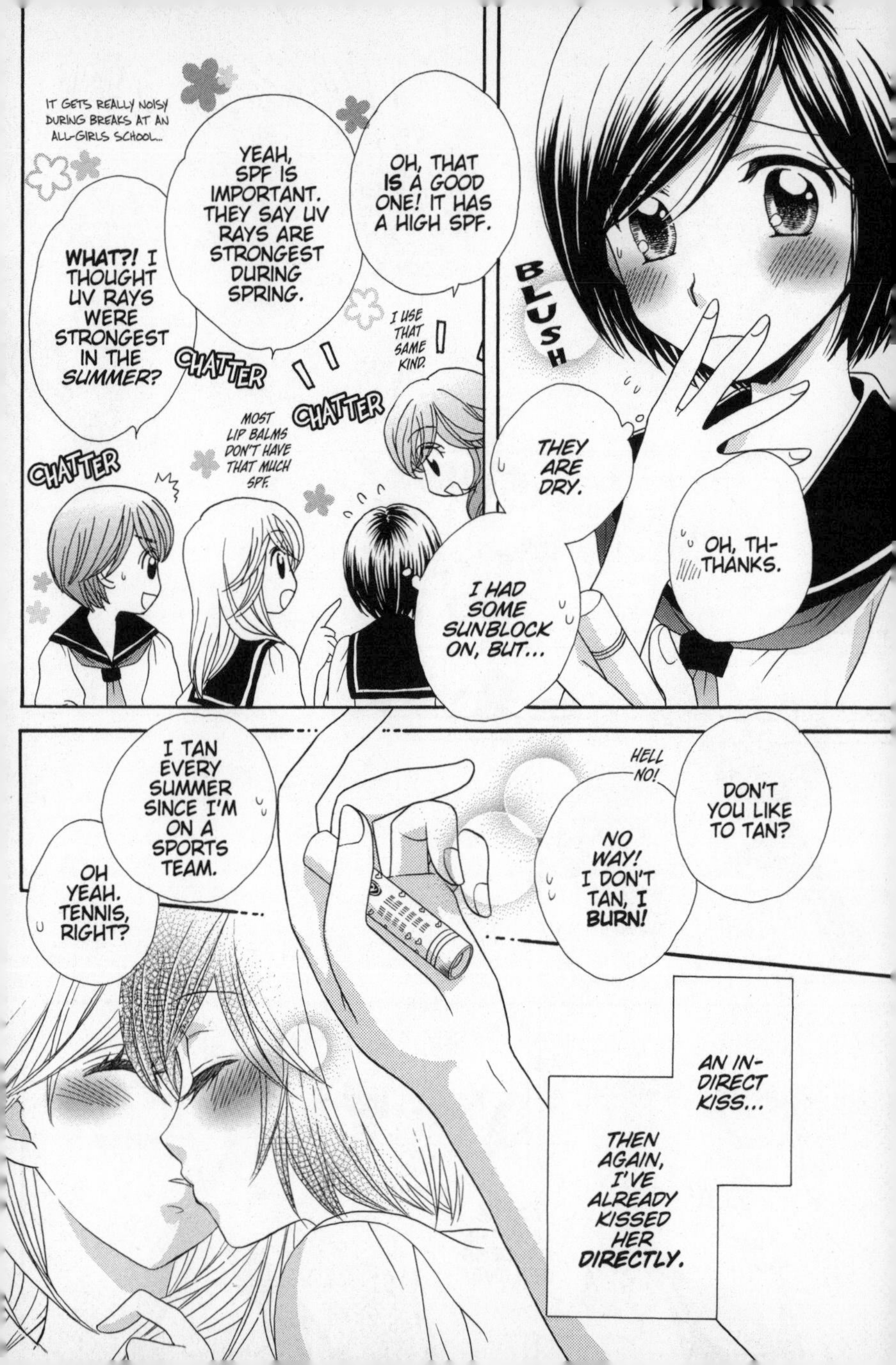
BLUSH
THEY ARE DRY.
OH, TH-THANKS.
I HAD SOME SUNBLOCK ON, BUT...
OH, THAT IS A GOOD ONE! IT HAS A HIGH SPF.
YEAH, SPF IS IMPORTANT. THEY SAY UV RAYS ARE STRONGEST DURING SPRING.
IT GETS REALLY NOISY DURING BREAKS AT AN ALL-GIRLS SCHOOL...
WHAT?! I THOUGHT UV RAYS WERE STRONGEST IN THE SUMMER?
I USE THAT SAME KIND.
CHATTER
CHATTER
MOST LIP BALMS DON'T HAVE THAT MUCH SPF.
CHATTER
DON'T YOU LIKE TO TAN?
HELL NO!
NO WAY! I DON'T TAN, I BURN!
I TAN EVERY SUMMER SINCE I'M ON A SPORTS TEAM.
OH YEAH. TENNIS, RIGHT?
AN IN-DIRECT KISS...
THEN AGAIN, I'VE ALREADY KISSED HER DIRECTLY.

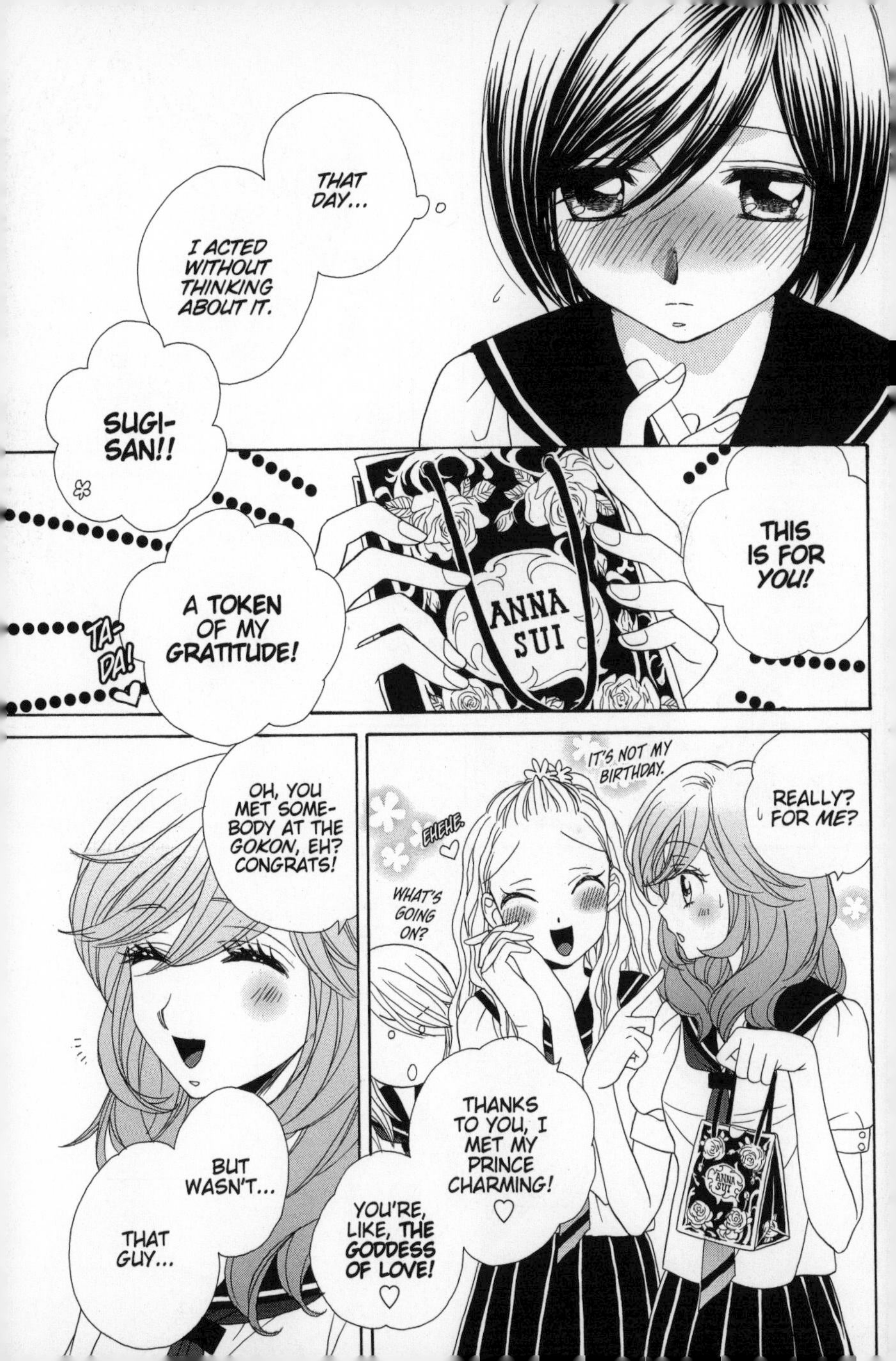
THAT DAY...
I ACTED WITHOUT THINKING ABOUT IT.
SUGI-SAN!!
THIS IS FOR YOU!
TA-DA!
A TOKEN OF MY GRATITUDE!
REALLY? FOR ME?
IT'S NOT MY BIRTHDAY.
EHEHE.
WHAT'S GOING ON?
THANKS TO YOU, I MET MY PRINCE CHARMING!
YOU'RE, LIKE, THE GODDESS OF LOVE!
OH, YOU MET SOME-BODY AT THE GOKON, EH? CONGRATS!
BUT WASN'T...
THAT GUY...

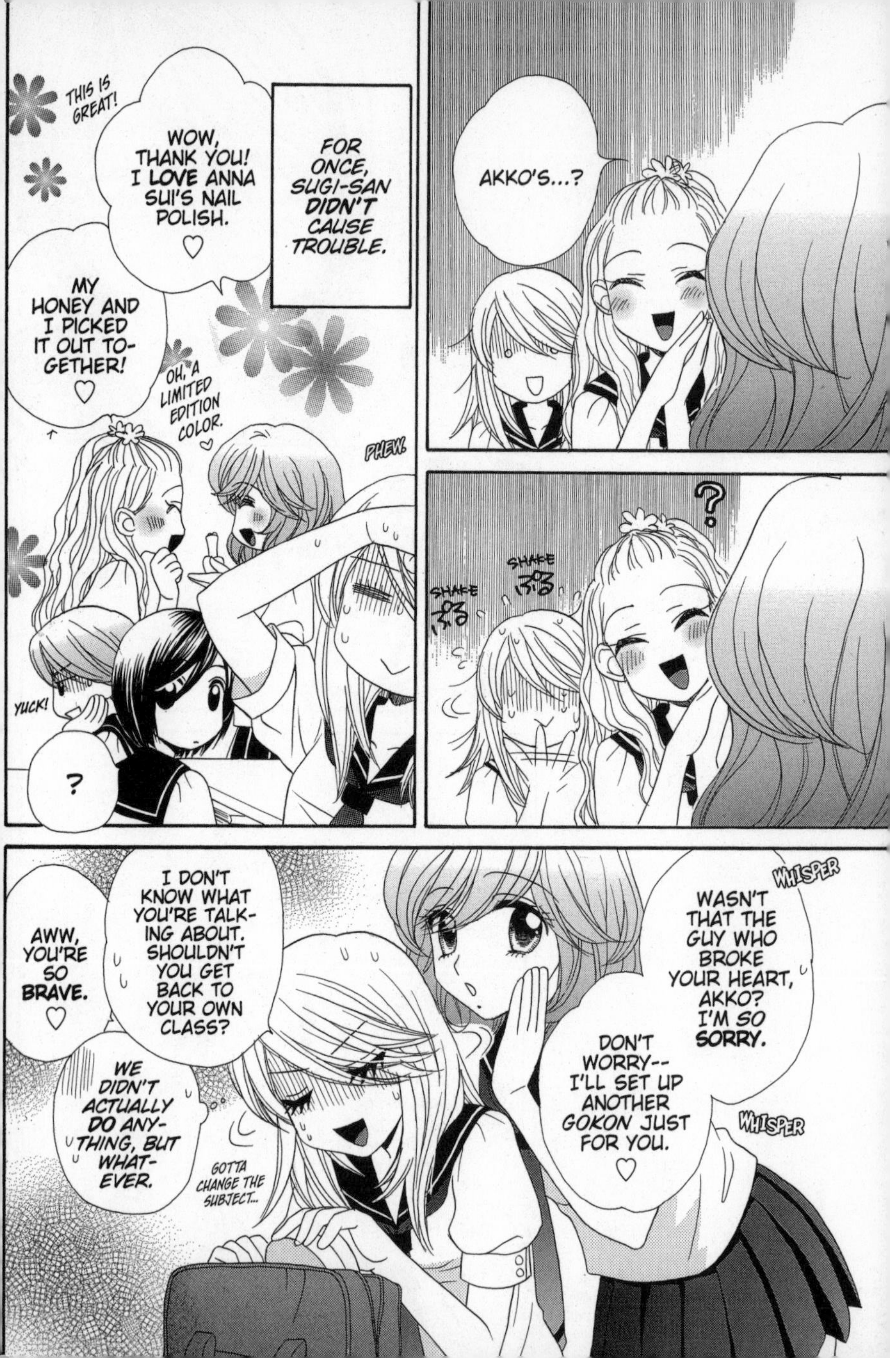
AKKO'S...?
?
SHAKE ぷる
SHAKE ぷる
FOR ONCE, SUGI-SAN DIDN'T CAUSE TROUBLE.
THIS IS GREAT!
WOW, THANK YOU! I LOVE ANNA SUI'S NAIL POLISH. ♡
MY HONEY AND I PICKED IT OUT TO-GETHER! ♡
OH, A LIMITED EDITION COLOR. ♡
PHEW.
YUCK!
?
WHISPER
WASN'T THAT THE GUY WHO BROKE YOUR HEART, AKKO? I'M SO SORRY.
WHISPER
DON'T WORRY-- I'LL SET UP ANOTHER GOKON JUST FOR YOU. ♡
I DON'T KNOW WHAT YOU'RE TALK-ING ABOUT. SHOULDN'T YOU GET BACK TO YOUR OWN CLASS?
AWW, YOU'RE SO BRAVE. ♡
WE DIDN'T ACTUALLY DO ANY-THING, BUT WHAT-EVER.
GOTTA CHANGE THE SUBJECT...

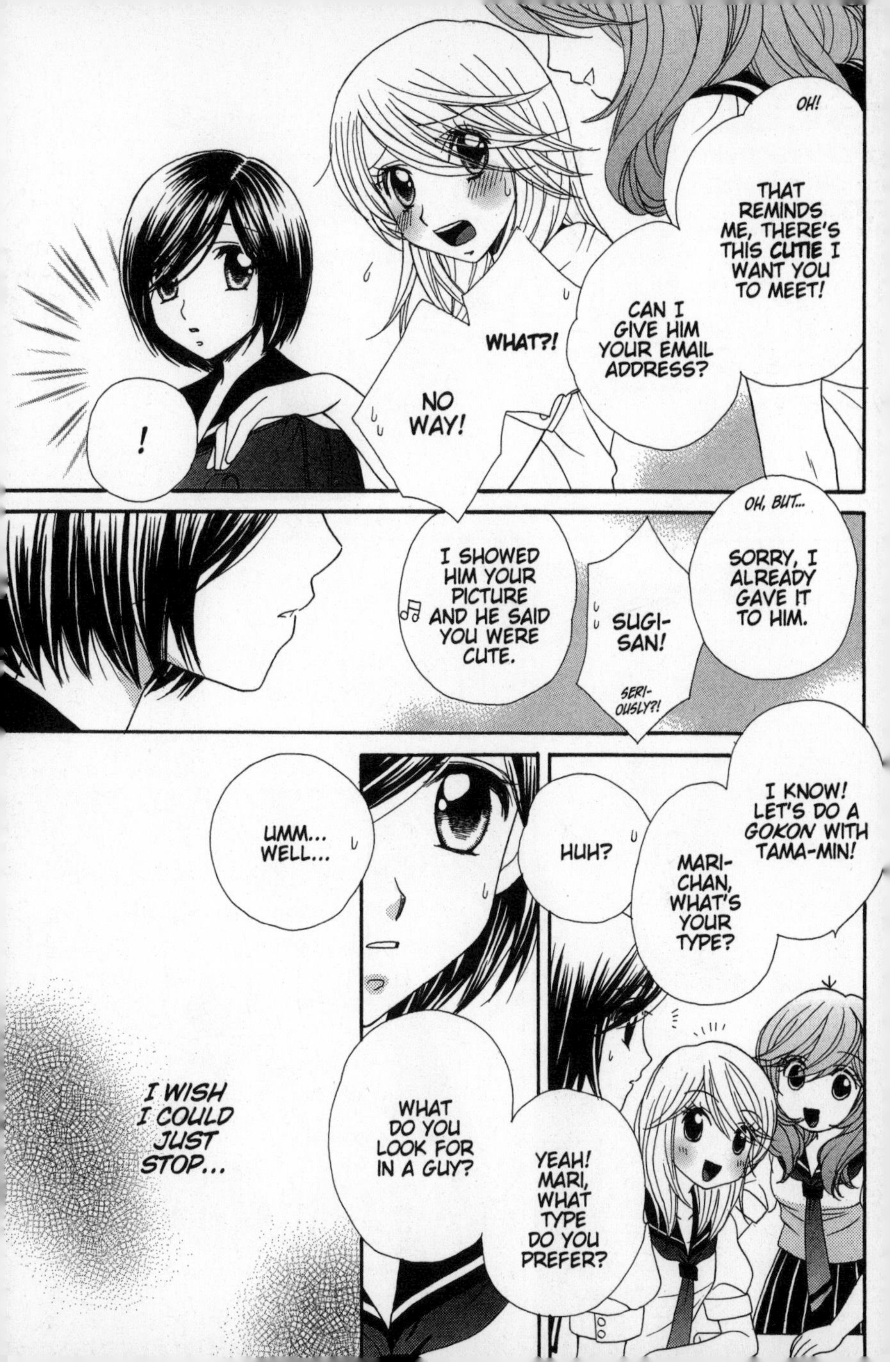
OH!
THAT REMINDS ME, THERE'S THIS CUTIE I WANT YOU TO MEET!
CAN I GIVE HIM YOUR EMAIL ADDRESS?
WHAT?!
NO WAY!
!
OH, BUT...
SORRY, I ALREADY GAVE IT TO HIM.
SUGI-SAN!
SERI-OUSLY?!
I SHOWED HIM YOUR PICTURE AND HE SAID YOU WERE CUTE.
I KNOW! LET'S DO A GOKON WITH TAMA-MIN!
MARI-CHAN, WHAT'S YOUR TYPE?
HUH?
YEAH! MARI, WHAT TYPE DO YOU PREFER?
WHAT DO YOU LOOK FOR IN A GUY?
UMM... WELL...
I WISH I COULD JUST STOP...

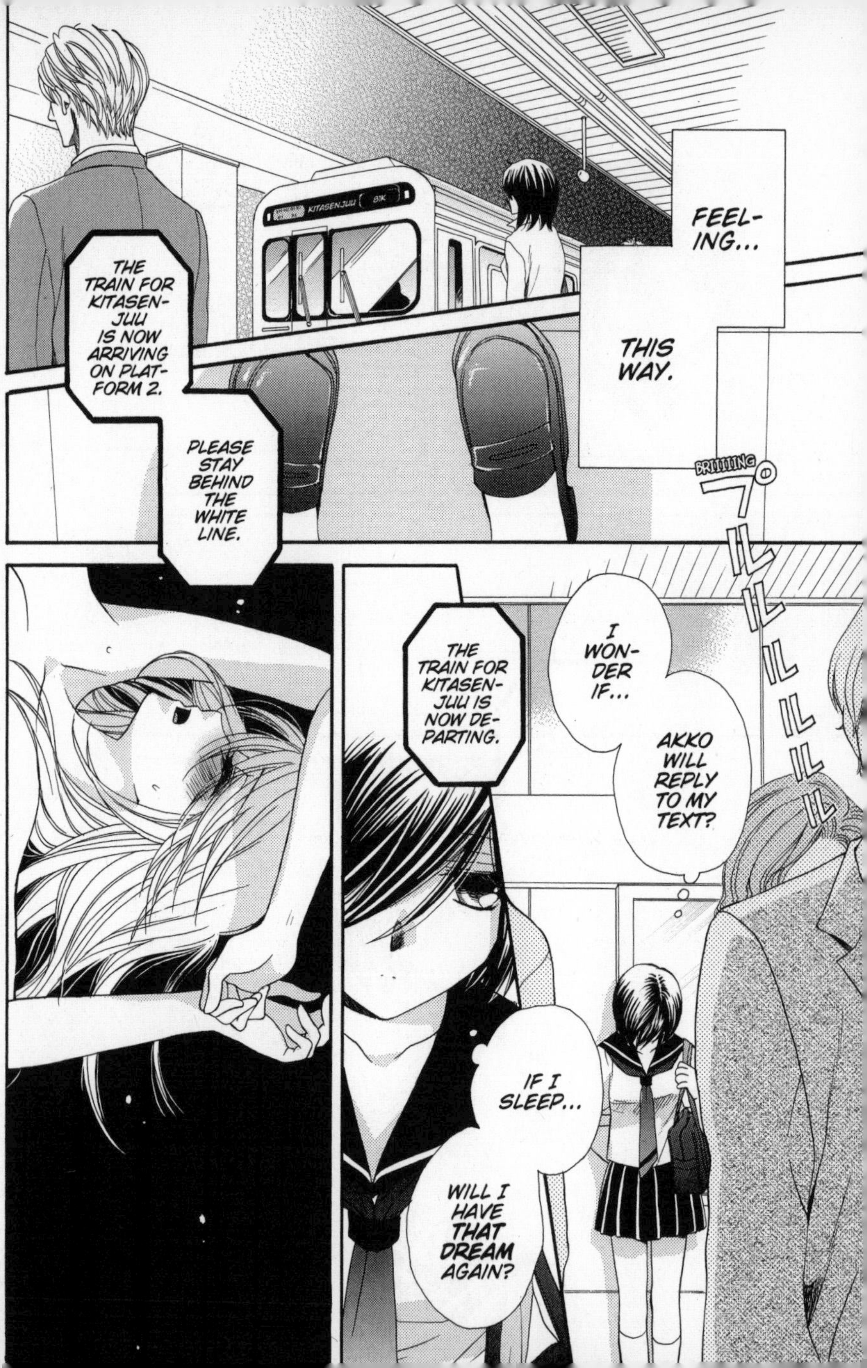
FEELING...
THIS WAY.
KITASENJUU 81K
THE TRAIN FOR KITASENJUU IS NOW ARRIVING ON PLATFORM 2.
PLEASE STAY BEHIND THE WHITE LINE.
BRIIIIING
I WONDER IF...
AKKO WILL REPLY TO MY TEXT?
THE TRAIN FOR KITASENJUU IS NOW DEPARTING.
IF I SLEEP...
WILL I HAVE THAT DREAM AGAIN?

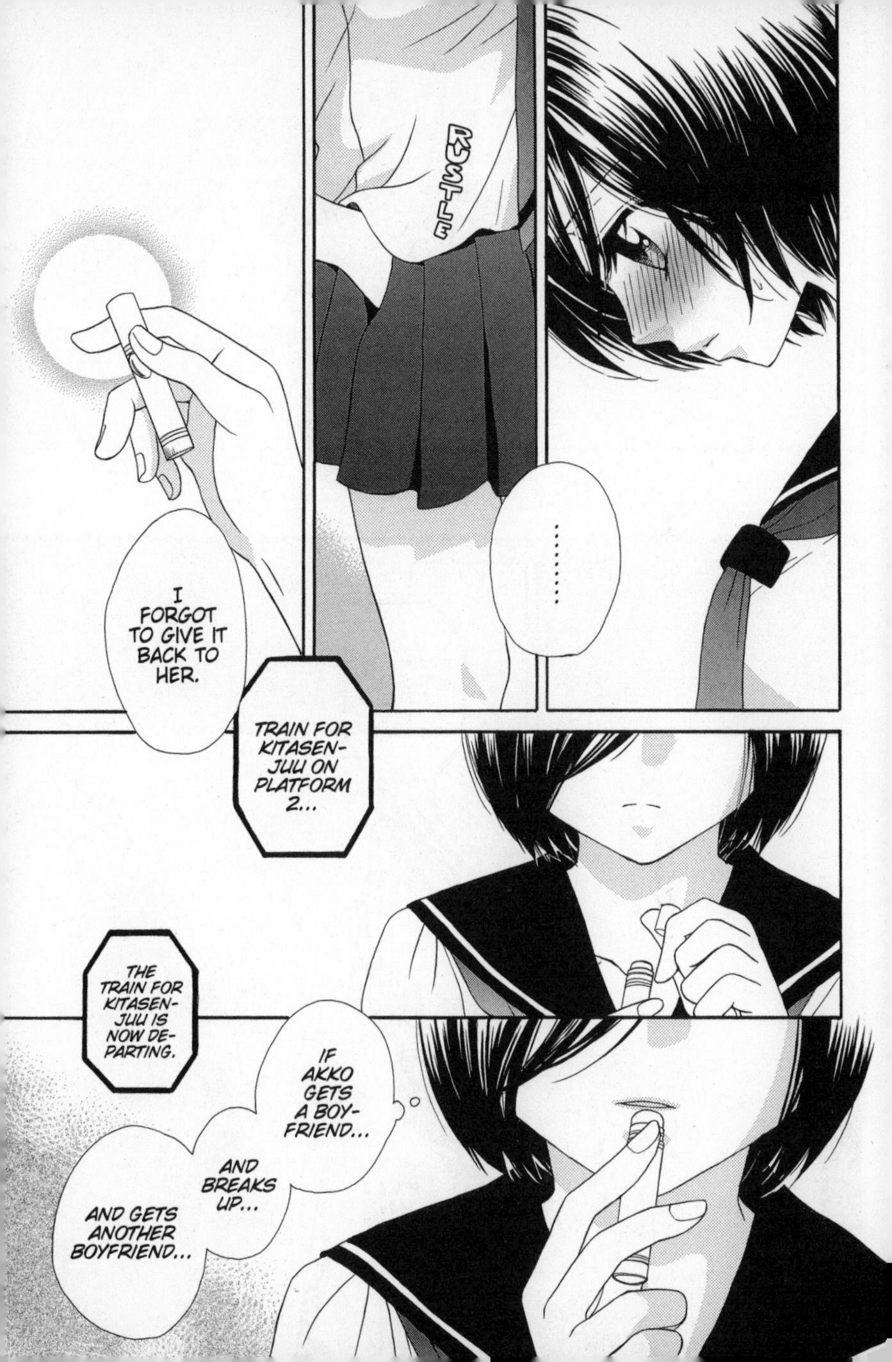
……
RUSTLE
I FORGOT TO GIVE IT BACK TO HER.
TRAIN FOR KITASEN-JUU ON PLATFORM 2…
THE TRAIN FOR KITASEN-JUU IS NOW DE-PARTING.
IF AKKO GETS A BOY-FRIEND…
AND BREAKS UP…
AND GETS ANOTHER BOYFRIEND…

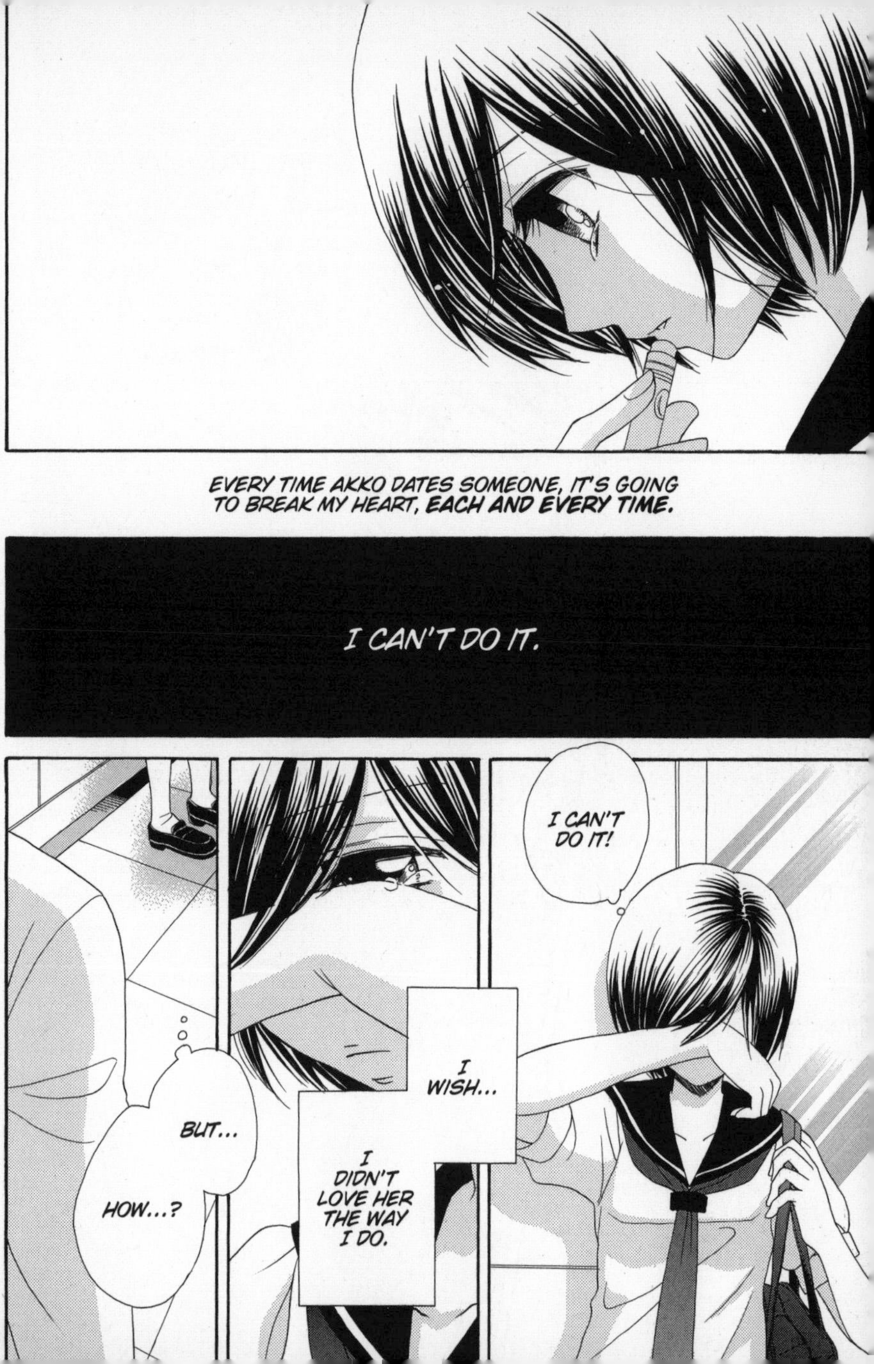
EVERY TIME AKKO DATES SOMEONE, IT'S GOING TO BREAK MY HEART, EACH AND EVERY TIME.
I CAN'T DO IT.
I CAN'T DO IT!
I WISH...
I DIDN'T LOVE HER THE WAY I DO.
BUT...
HOW...?

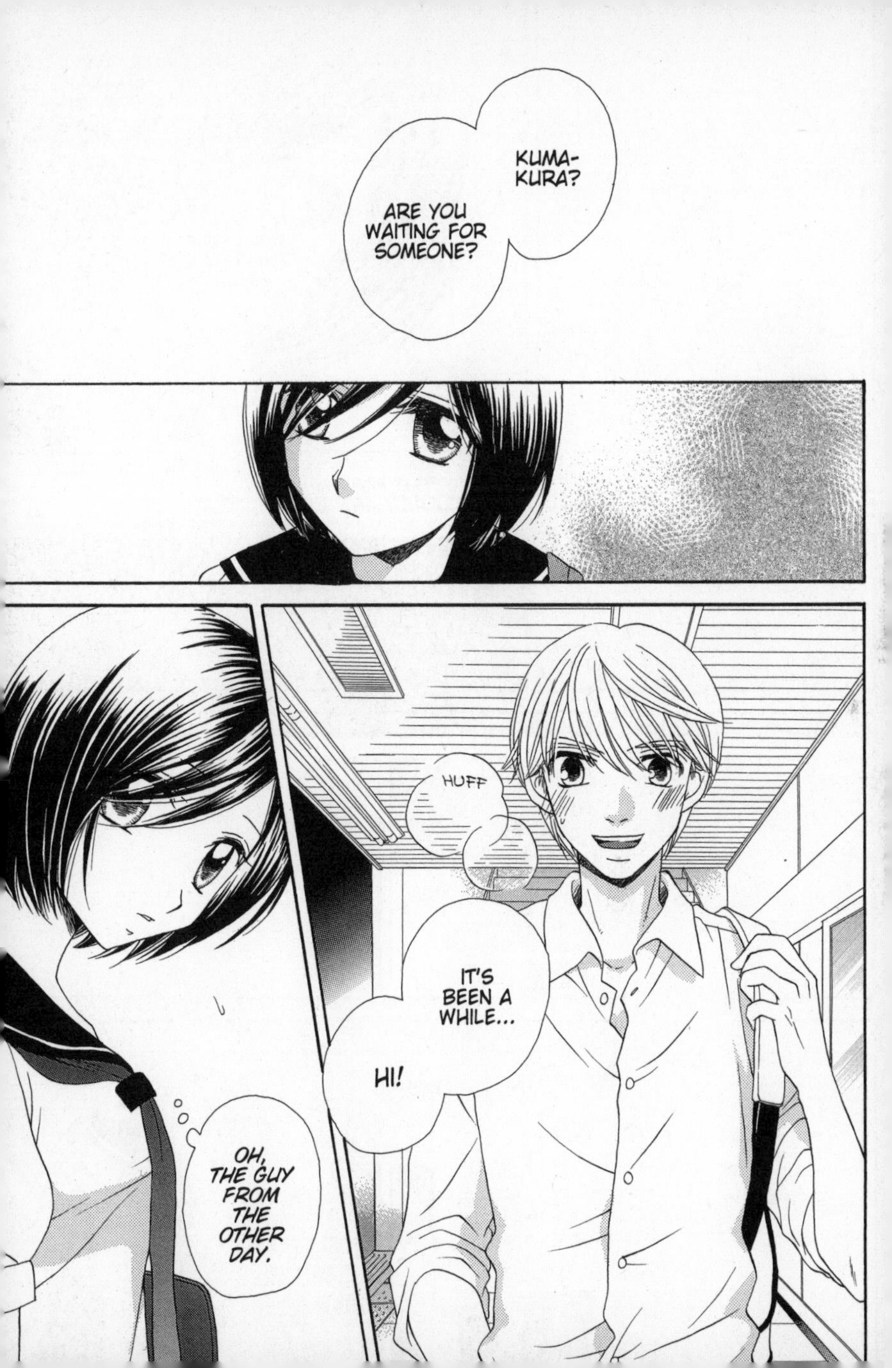
KUMA-KURA?
ARE YOU WAITING FOR SOMEONE?
HUFF
IT'S BEEN A WHILE...
HI!
OH, THE GUY FROM THE OTHER DAY.

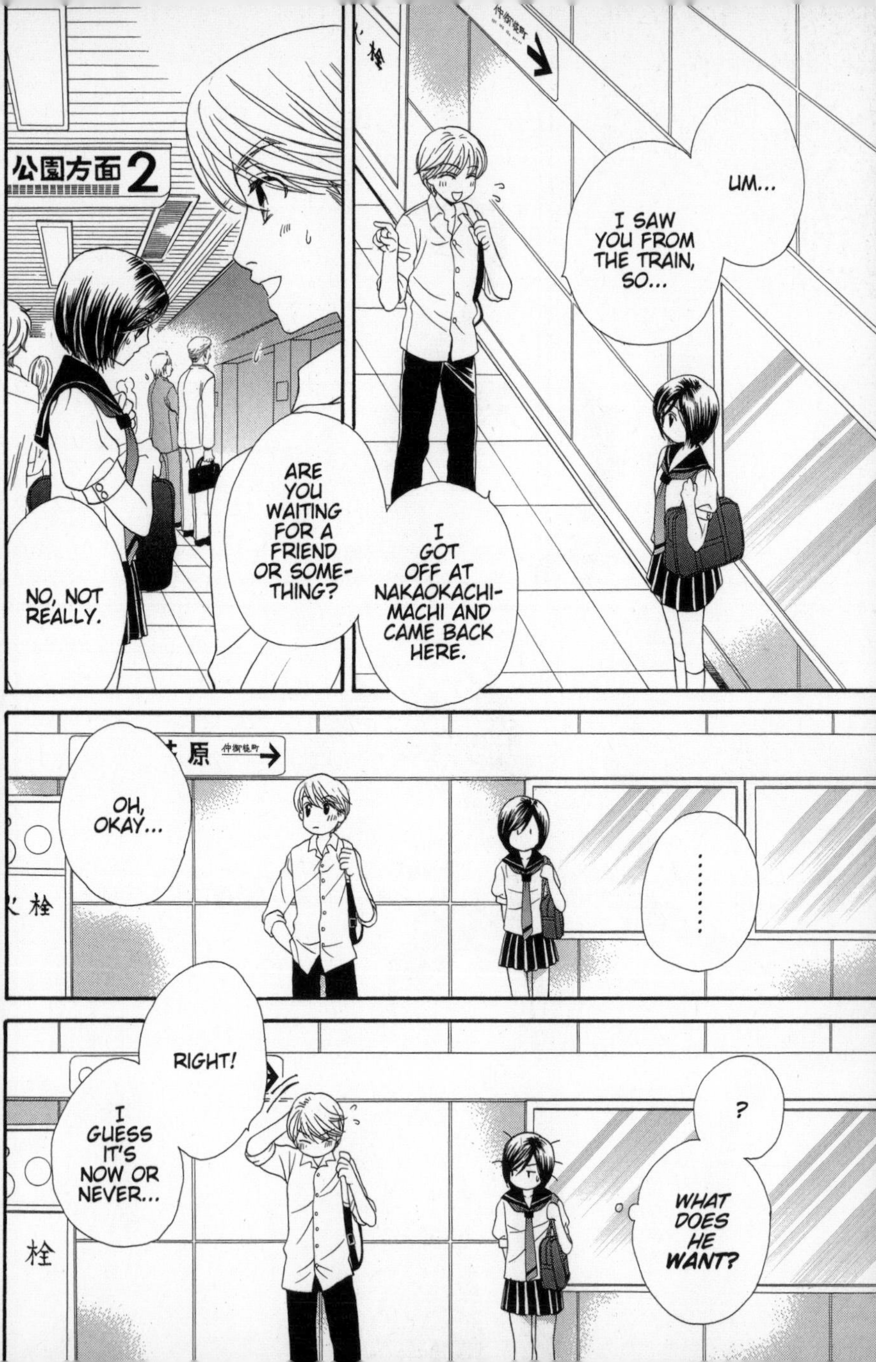
UM...
I SAW YOU FROM THE TRAIN, SO...
I GOT OFF AT NAKAOKACHI-MACHI AND CAME BACK HERE.
公園方面2
ARE YOU WAITING FOR A FRIEND OR SOME-THING?
NO, NOT REALLY.
......
OH, OKAY...
?
WHAT DOES HE WANT?
RIGHT!
I GUESS IT'S NOW OR NEVER...

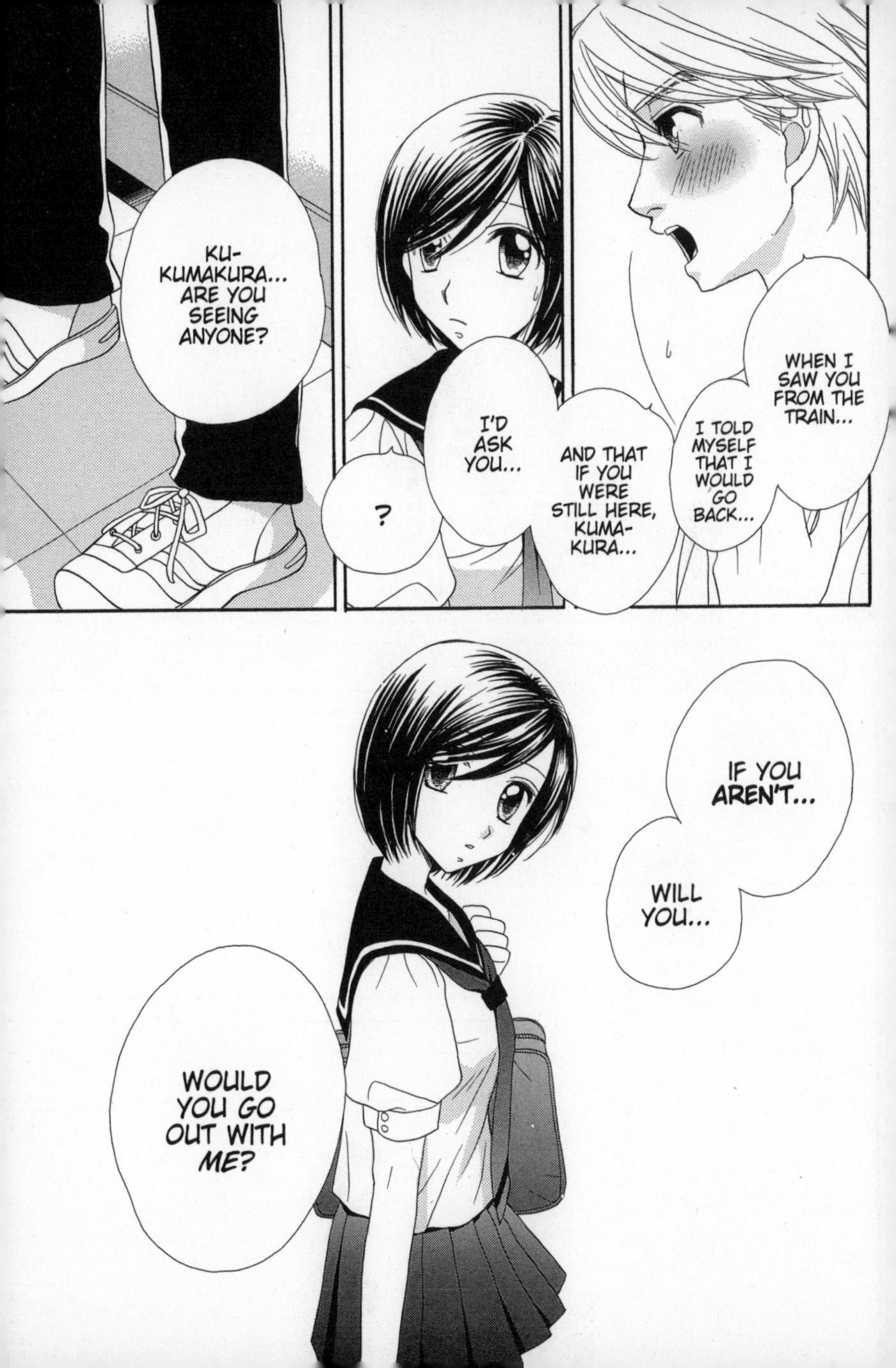
WHEN I SAW YOU FROM THE TRAIN...
I TOLD MYSELF THAT I WOULD GO BACK...
AND THAT IF YOU WERE STILL HERE, KUMA-KURA...
I'D ASK YOU...
?
KU-KUMAKURA... ARE YOU SEEING ANYONE?
IF YOU AREN'T...
WILL YOU...
WOULD YOU GO OUT WITH *ME?*

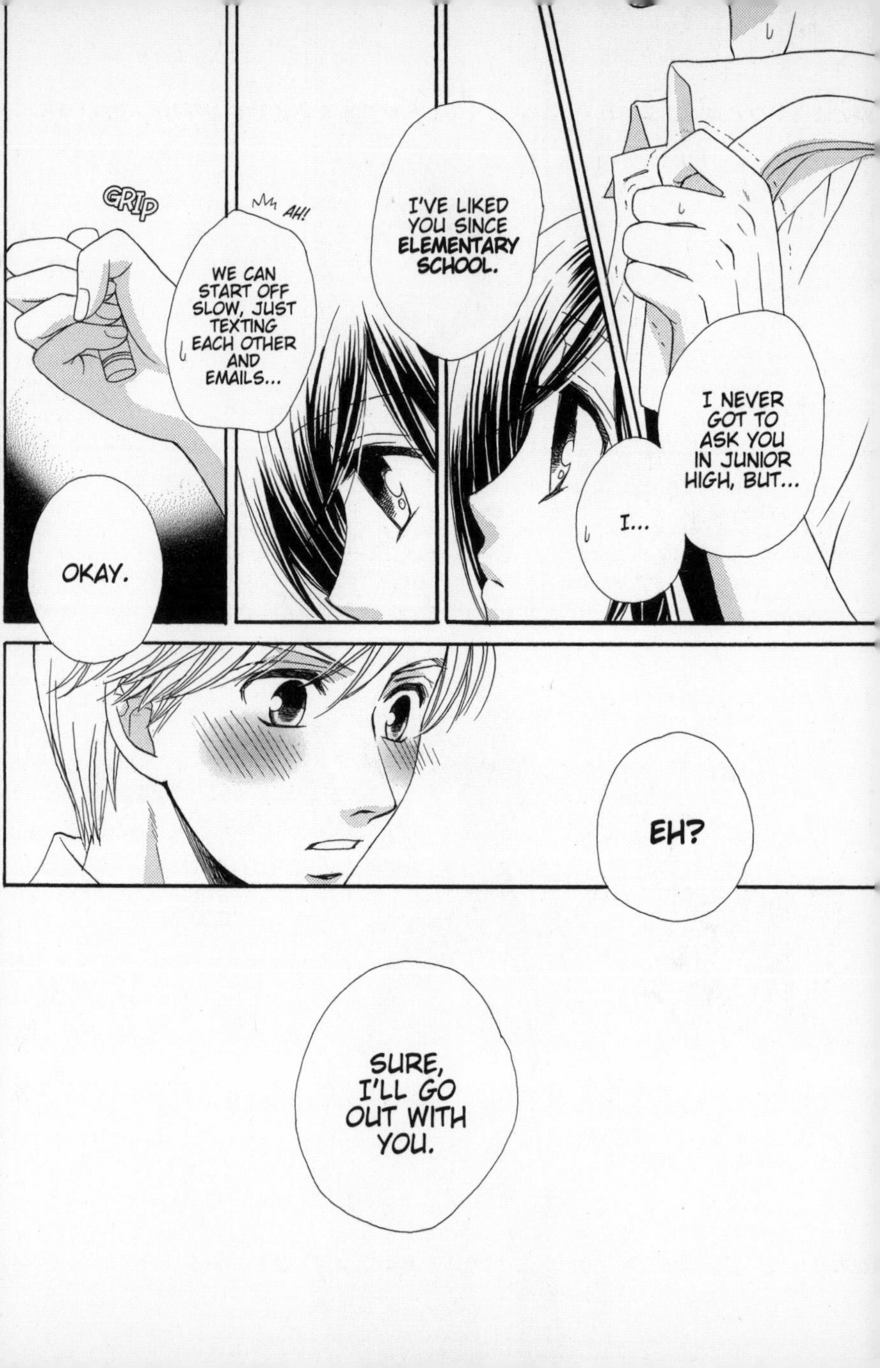
I NEVER GOT TO ASK YOU IN JUNIOR HIGH, BUT...
I...
I'VE LIKED YOU SINCE ELEMENTARY SCHOOL.
AH!
WE CAN START OFF SLOW, JUST TEXTING EACH OTHER AND EMAILS...
GRIP
OKAY.
EH?
SURE, I'LL GO OUT WITH YOU.

SUMMER UNIFORM & KNIT VEST

GIRL FRIENDS —ガールフレンズ—

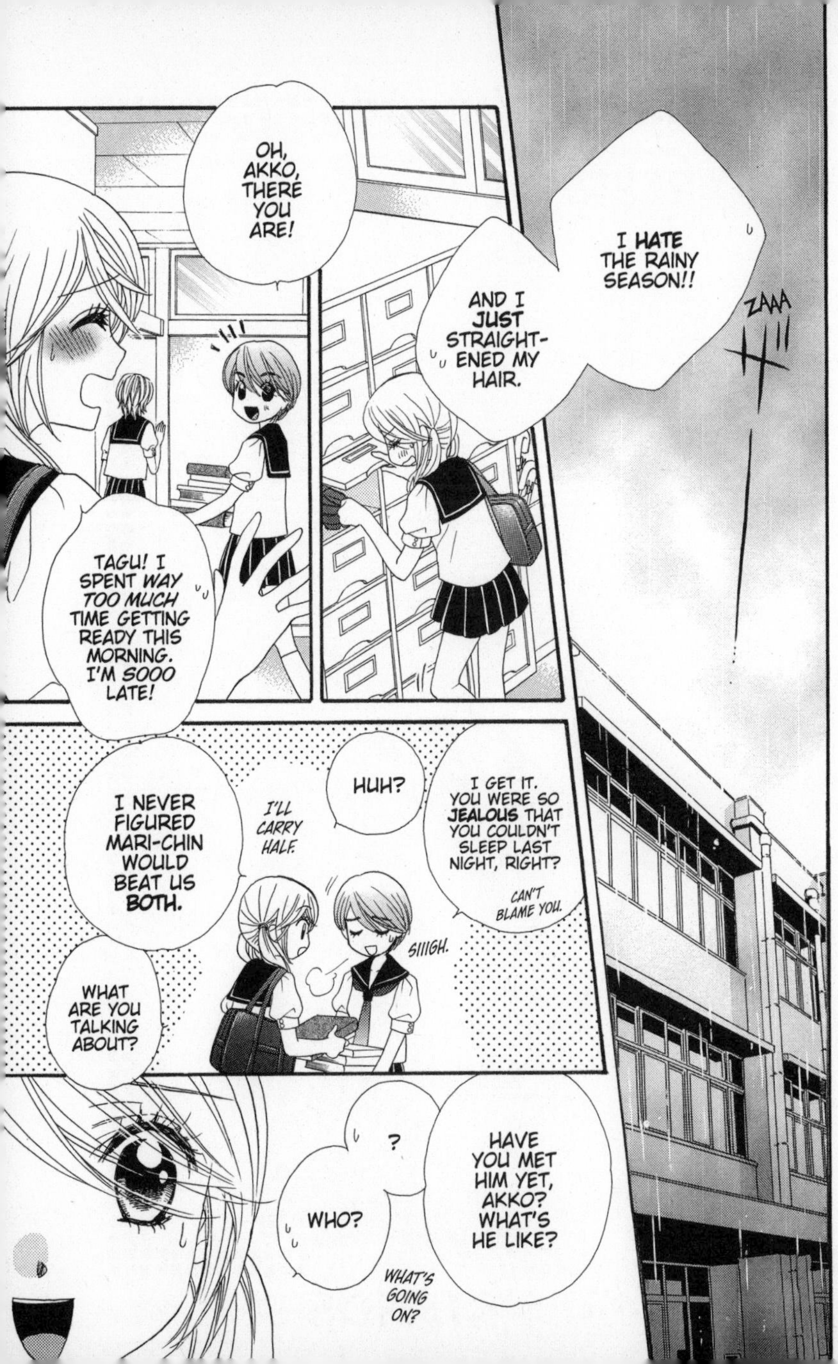
I HATE THE RAINY SEASON!!
ZAAA
AND I JUST STRAIGHT-ENED MY HAIR.
OH, AKKO, THERE YOU ARE!
TAGU! I SPENT WAY TOO MUCH TIME GETTING READY THIS MORNING. I'M SOOO LATE!
I GET IT. YOU WERE SO JEALOUS THAT YOU COULDN'T SLEEP LAST NIGHT, RIGHT?
CAN'T BLAME YOU.
HUH?
I'LL CARRY HALF.
SIIIGH.
I NEVER FIGURED MARI-CHIN WOULD BEAT US BOTH.
WHAT ARE YOU TALKING ABOUT?
HAVE YOU MET HIM YET, AKKO? WHAT'S HE LIKE?
?
WHO?
WHAT'S GOING ON?

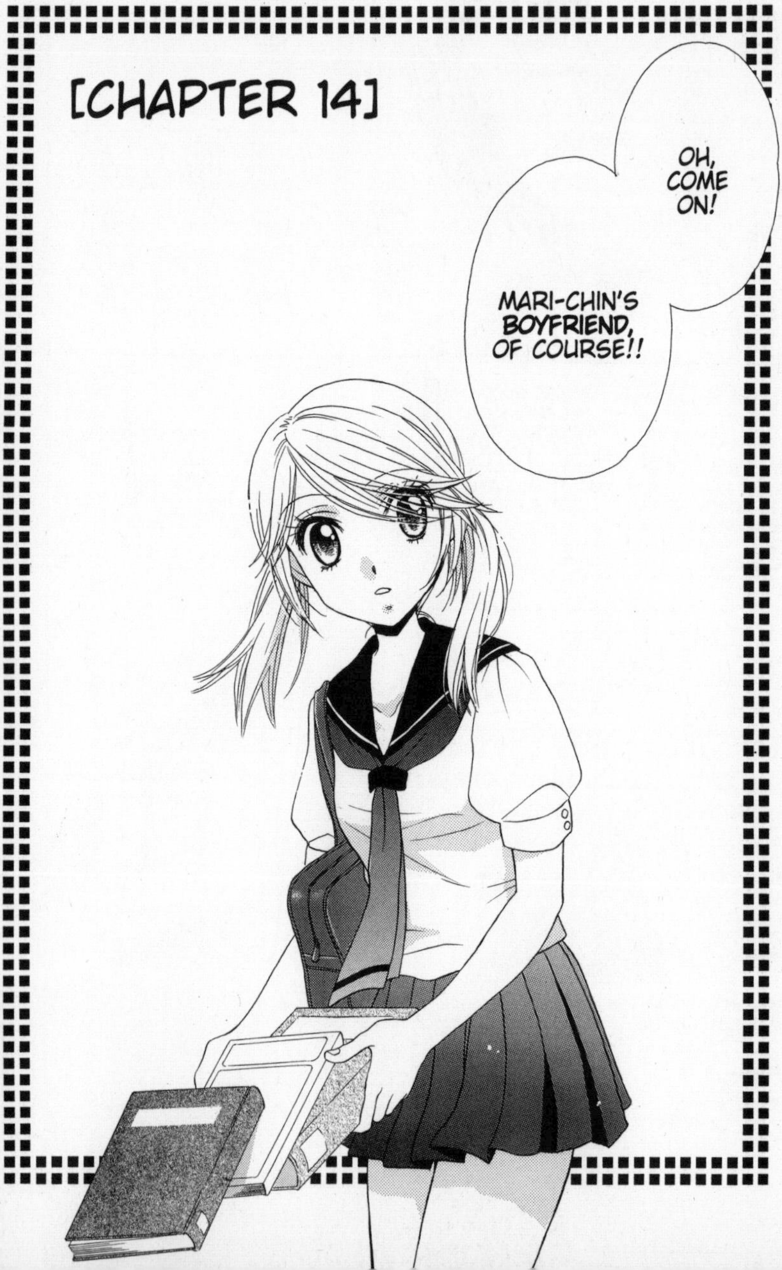
[CHAPTER 14]
OH, COME ON!
MARI-CHIN'S BOYFRIEND, OF COURSE!!

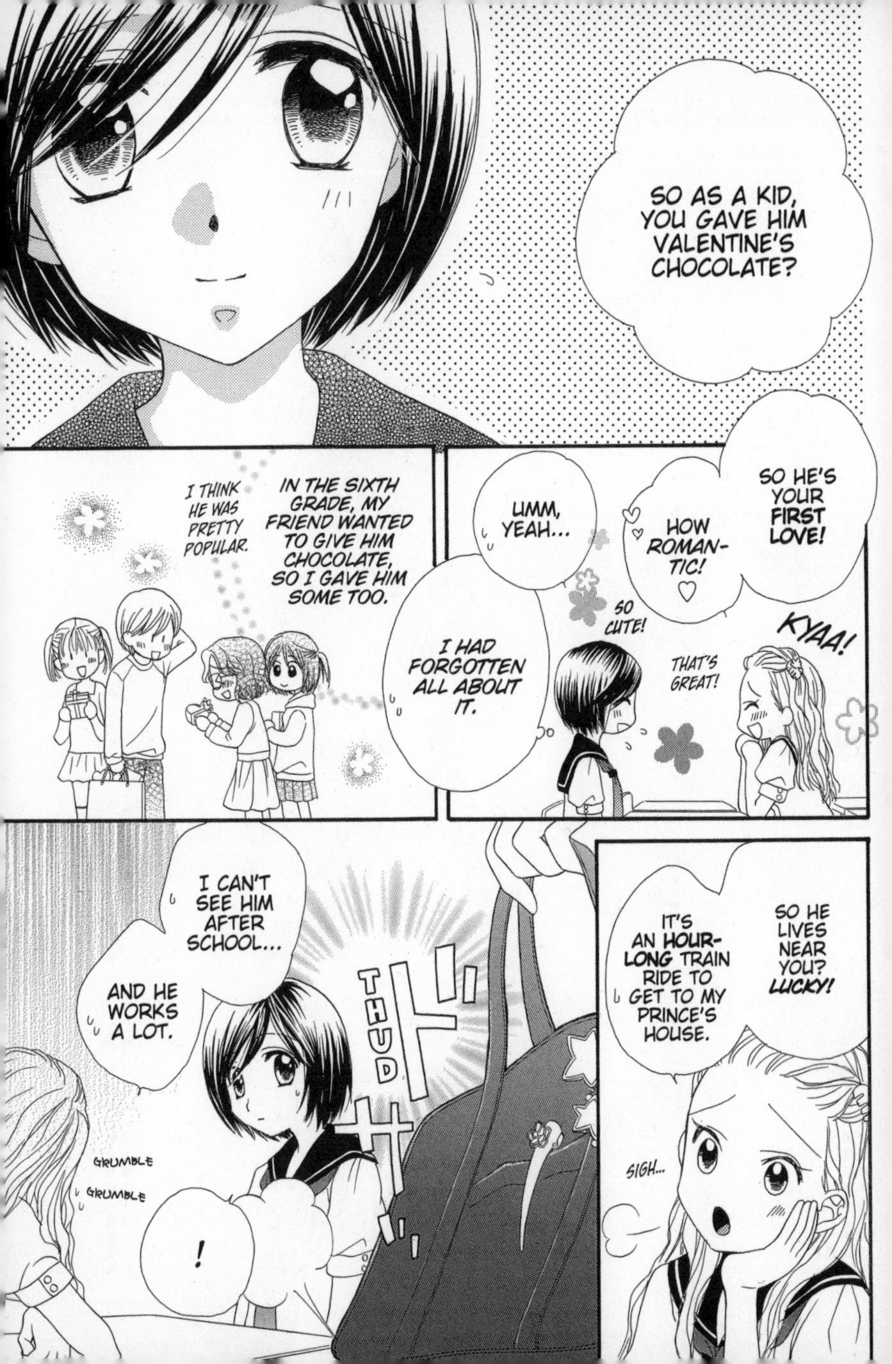
SO AS A KID, YOU GAVE HIM VALENTINE'S CHOCOLATE?
SO HE'S YOUR FIRST LOVE!
HOW ROMANTIC! ♡
KYAA!
SO CUTE!
THAT'S GREAT!
UMM, YEAH...
I HAD FORGOTTEN ALL ABOUT IT.
IN THE SIXTH GRADE, MY FRIEND WANTED TO GIVE HIM CHOCOLATE, SO I GAVE HIM SOME TOO.
I THINK HE WAS PRETTY POPULAR.
SO HE LIVES NEAR YOU? LUCKY!
IT'S AN HOUR-LONG TRAIN RIDE TO GET TO MY PRINCE'S HOUSE.
SIGH...
I CAN'T SEE HIM AFTER SCHOOL...
AND HE WORKS A LOT.
THUD
GRUMBLE
GRUMBLE
!

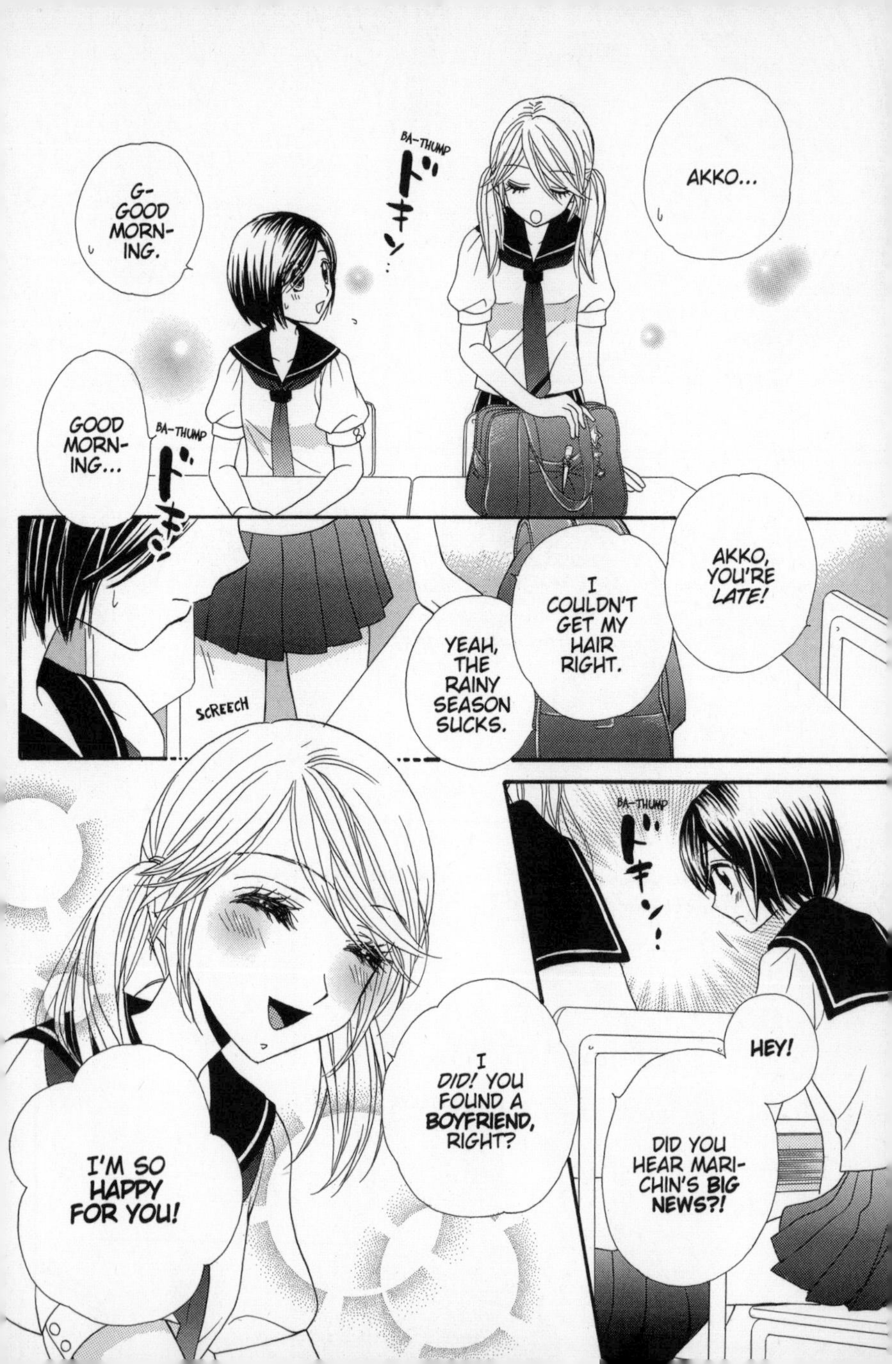
AKKO...
BA-THUMP
ドキン
G-GOOD MORNING.
GOOD MORNING...
BA-THUMP
ドキン
AKKO, YOU'RE LATE!
I COULDN'T GET MY HAIR RIGHT.
YEAH, THE RAINY SEASON SUCKS.
SCREECH
BA-THUMP
ドキン
HEY!
DID YOU HEAR MARI-CHIN'S BIG NEWS?!
I DID! YOU FOUND A BOYFRIEND, RIGHT?
I'M SO HAPPY FOR YOU!

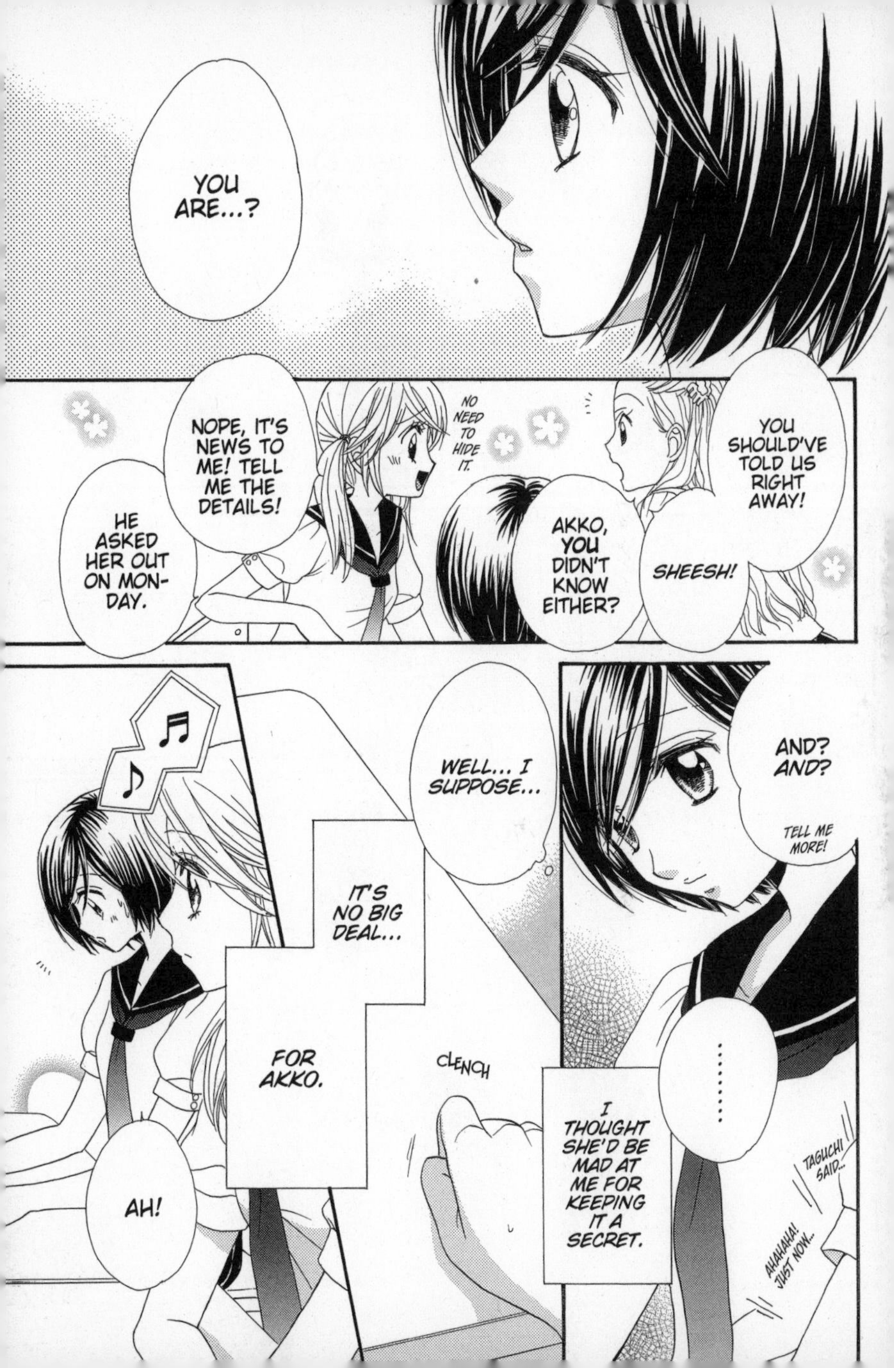
YOU ARE...?
YOU SHOULD'VE TOLD US RIGHT AWAY!
SHEESH!
AKKO, YOU DIDN'T KNOW EITHER?
NO NEED TO HIDE IT.
NOPE, IT'S NEWS TO ME! TELL ME THE DETAILS!
HE ASKED HER OUT ON MON-DAY.
AND? AND?
TELL ME MORE!
WELL... I SUPPOSE...
......
TAGUCHI SAID...
AHAHAHA! JUST NOW...
I THOUGHT SHE'D BE MAD AT ME FOR KEEPING IT A SECRET.
CLENCH
IT'S NO BIG DEAL...
FOR AKKO.
AH!

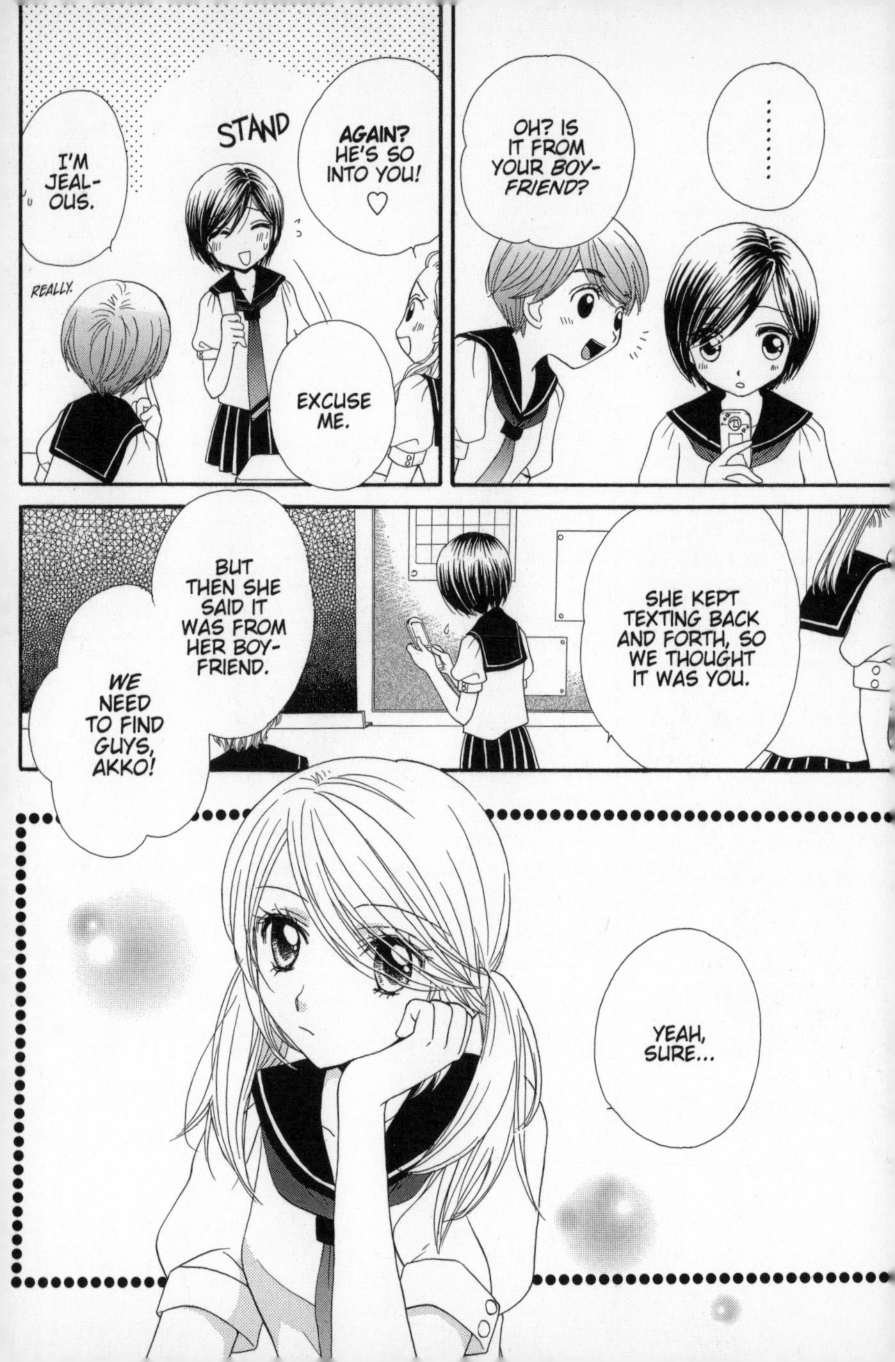
......
OH? IS IT FROM YOUR BOY-FRIEND?
AGAIN? HE'S SO INTO YOU! ♡
STAND
I'M JEAL-OUS.
REALLY.
EXCUSE ME.
SHE KEPT TEXTING BACK AND FORTH, SO WE THOUGHT IT WAS YOU.
BUT THEN SHE SAID IT WAS FROM HER BOY-FRIEND.
WE NEED TO FIND GUYS, AKKO!
YEAH, SURE...

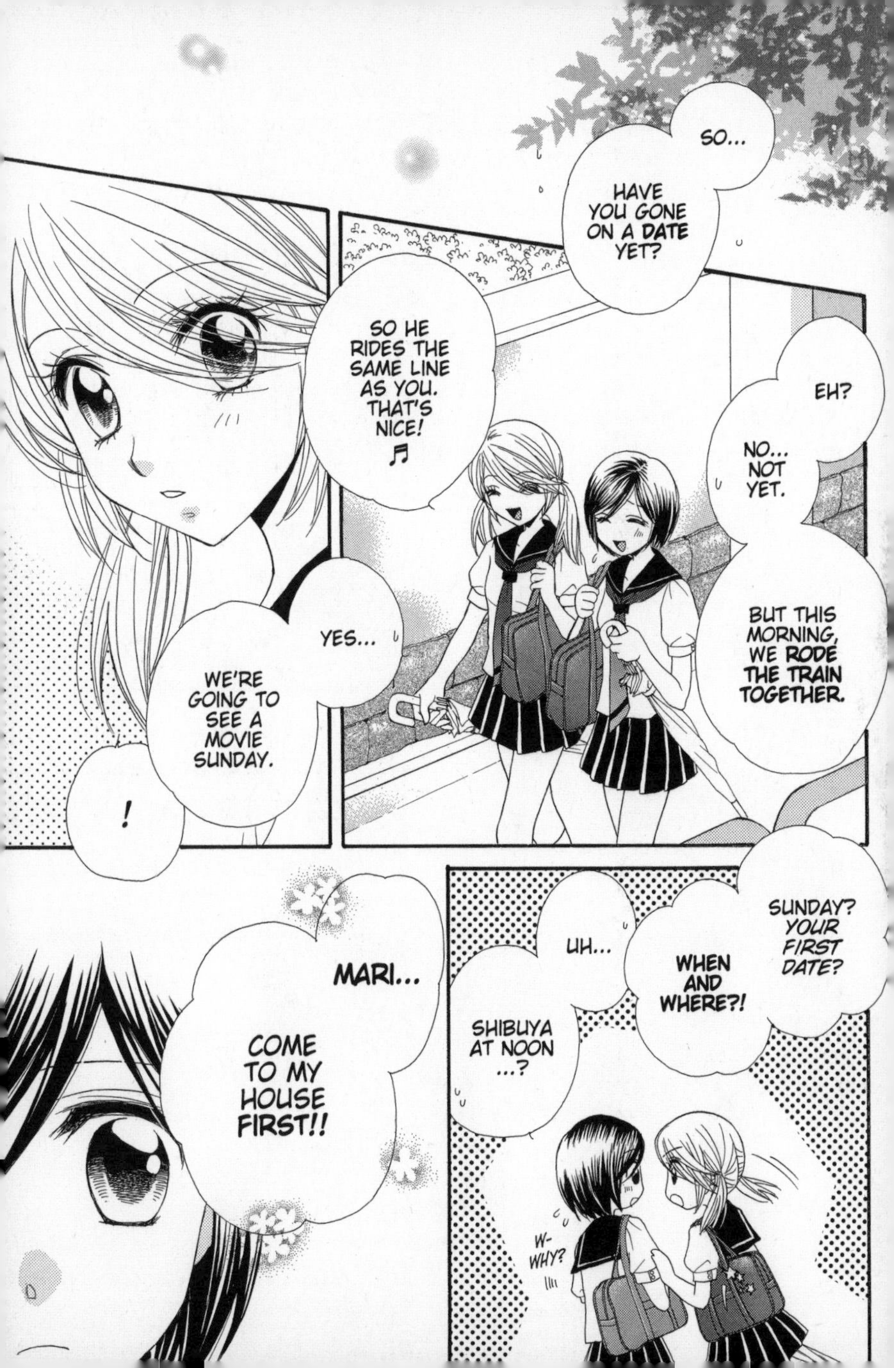

SO...
HAVE YOU GONE ON A DATE YET?
EH?
NO... NOT YET.
BUT THIS MORNING, WE RODE THE TRAIN TOGETHER.
SO HE RIDES THE SAME LINE AS YOU. THAT'S NICE! ♬
YES...
WE'RE GOING TO SEE A MOVIE SUNDAY.
!
SUNDAY? YOUR FIRST DATE?
WHEN AND WHERE?!
UH...
SHIBUYA AT NOON ...?
W-WHY?
MARI...
COME TO MY HOUSE FIRST!!

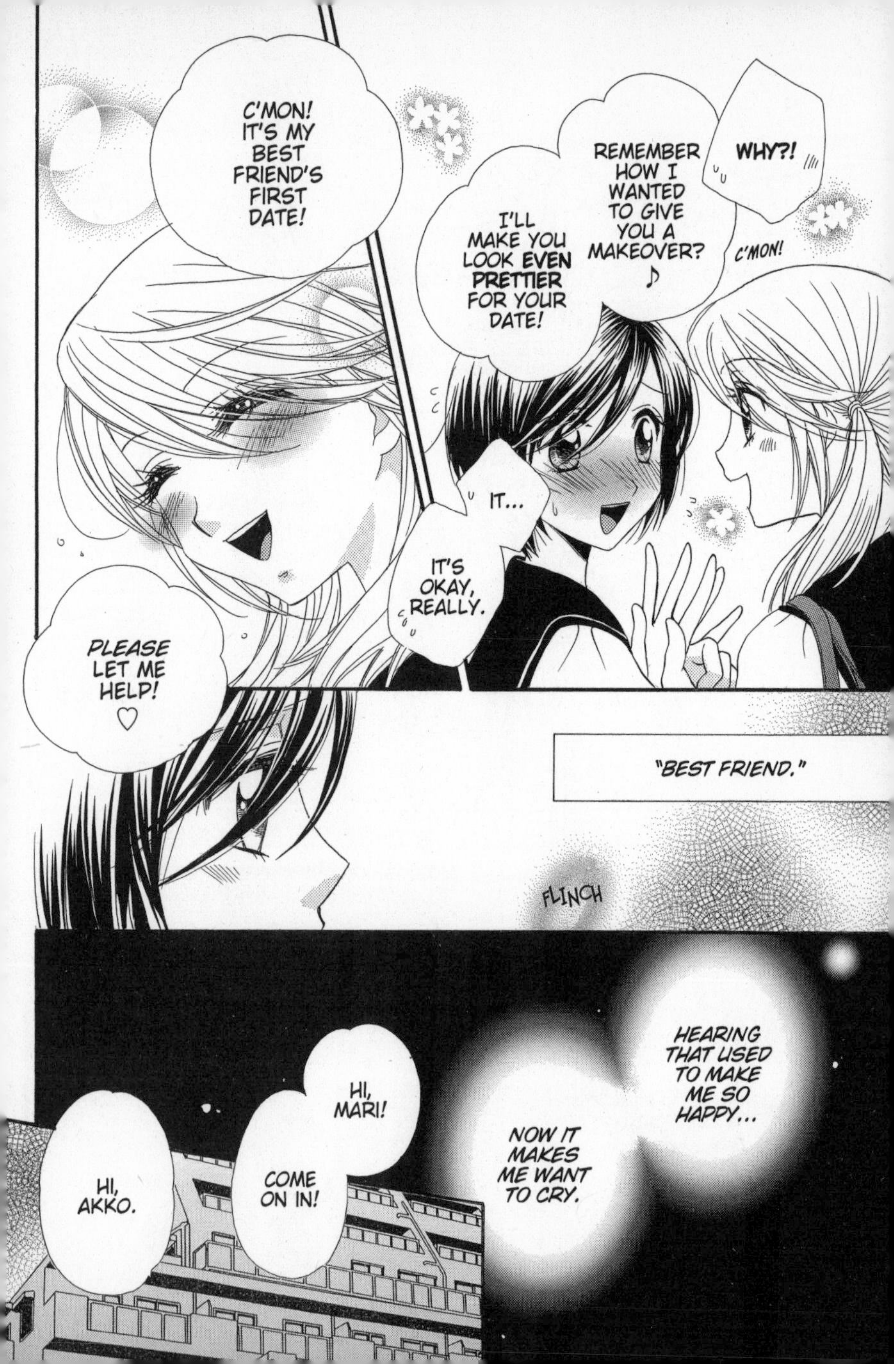
WHY?!
C'MON!
REMEMBER HOW I WANTED TO GIVE YOU A MAKEOVER? ♪
I'LL MAKE YOU LOOK EVEN PRETTIER FOR YOUR DATE!
IT...
IT'S OKAY, REALLY.
C'MON! IT'S MY BEST FRIEND'S FIRST DATE!
PLEASE LET ME HELP! ♡
"BEST FRIEND."
FLINCH
HEARING THAT USED TO MAKE ME SO HAPPY...
NOW IT MAKES ME WANT TO CRY.
HI, MARI!
COME ON IN!
HI, AKKO.

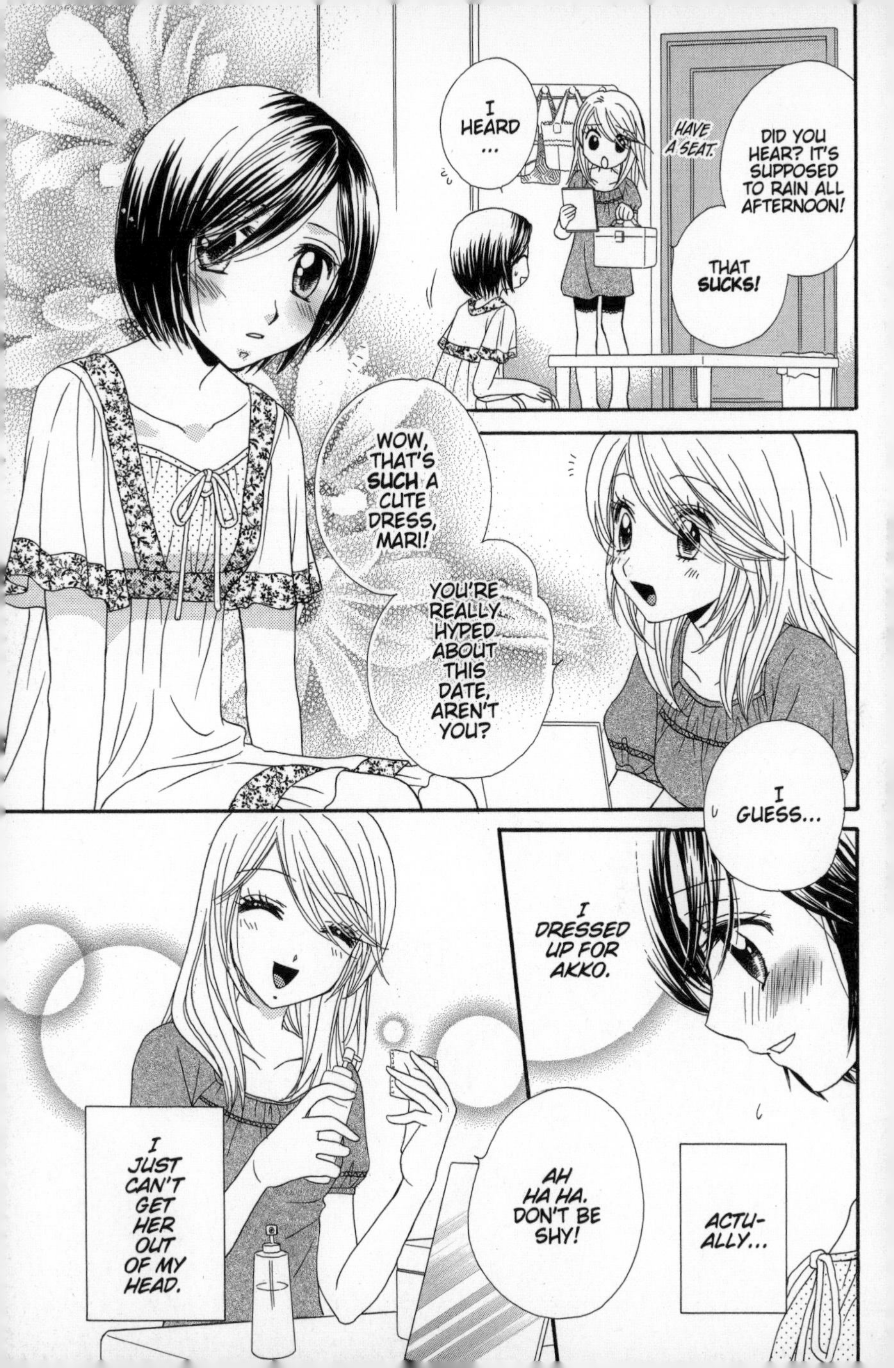
DID YOU HEAR? IT'S SUPPOSED TO RAIN ALL AFTERNOON!
THAT SUCKS!
HAVE A SEAT.
I HEARD ...
WOW, THAT'S SUCH A CUTE DRESS, MARI!
YOU'RE REALLY HYPED ABOUT THIS DATE, AREN'T YOU?
I GUESS...
ACTU-ALLY...
I DRESSED UP FOR AKKO.
AH HA HA. DON'T BE SHY!
I JUST CAN'T GET HER OUT OF MY HEAD.

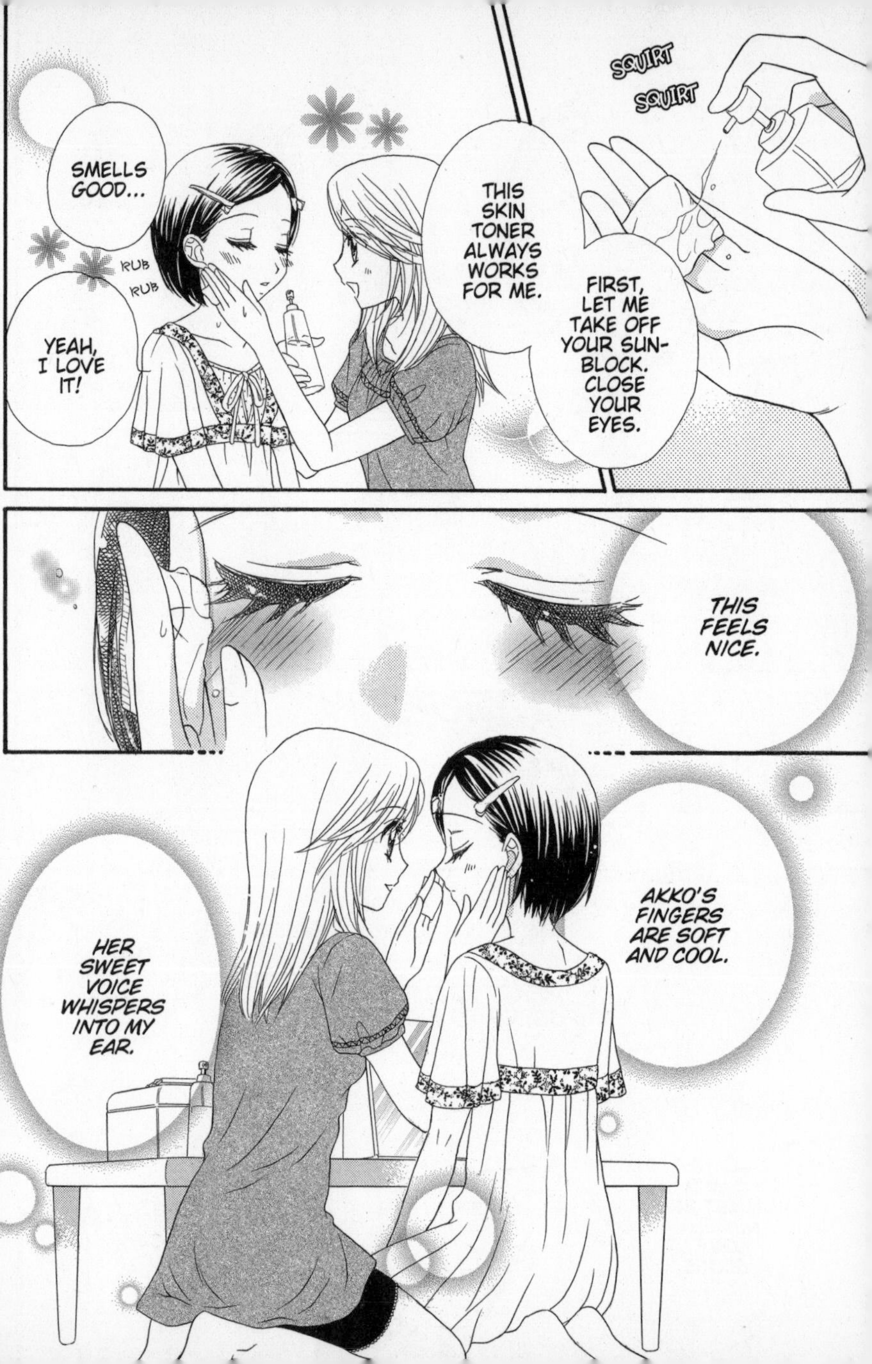
SQUIRT
SQUIRT
THIS SKIN TONER ALWAYS WORKS FOR ME.
FIRST, LET ME TAKE OFF YOUR SUN-BLOCK. CLOSE YOUR EYES.
SMELLS GOOD...
RUB RUB
YEAH, I LOVE IT!
THIS FEELS NICE.
AKKO'S FINGERS ARE SOFT AND COOL.
HER SWEET VOICE WHISPERS INTO MY EAR.

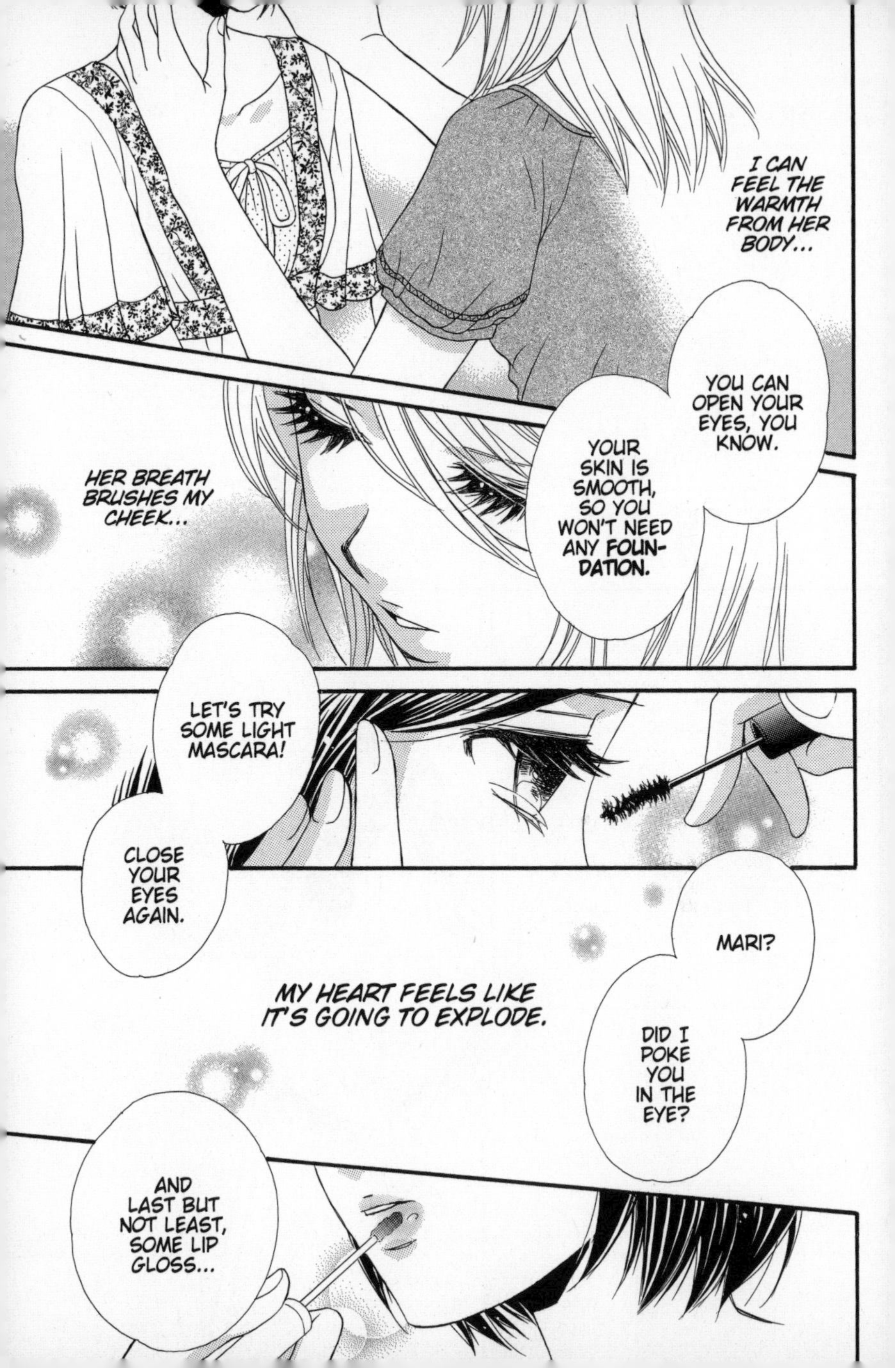
I CAN FEEL THE WARMTH FROM HER BODY...
YOU CAN OPEN YOUR EYES, YOU KNOW.
YOUR SKIN IS SMOOTH, SO YOU WON'T NEED ANY FOUNDATION.
HER BREATH BRUSHES MY CHEEK...
LET'S TRY SOME LIGHT MASCARA!
CLOSE YOUR EYES AGAIN.
MARI?
DID I POKE YOU IN THE EYE?
MY HEART FEELS LIKE IT'S GOING TO EXPLODE.
AND LAST BUT NOT LEAST, SOME LIP GLOSS...

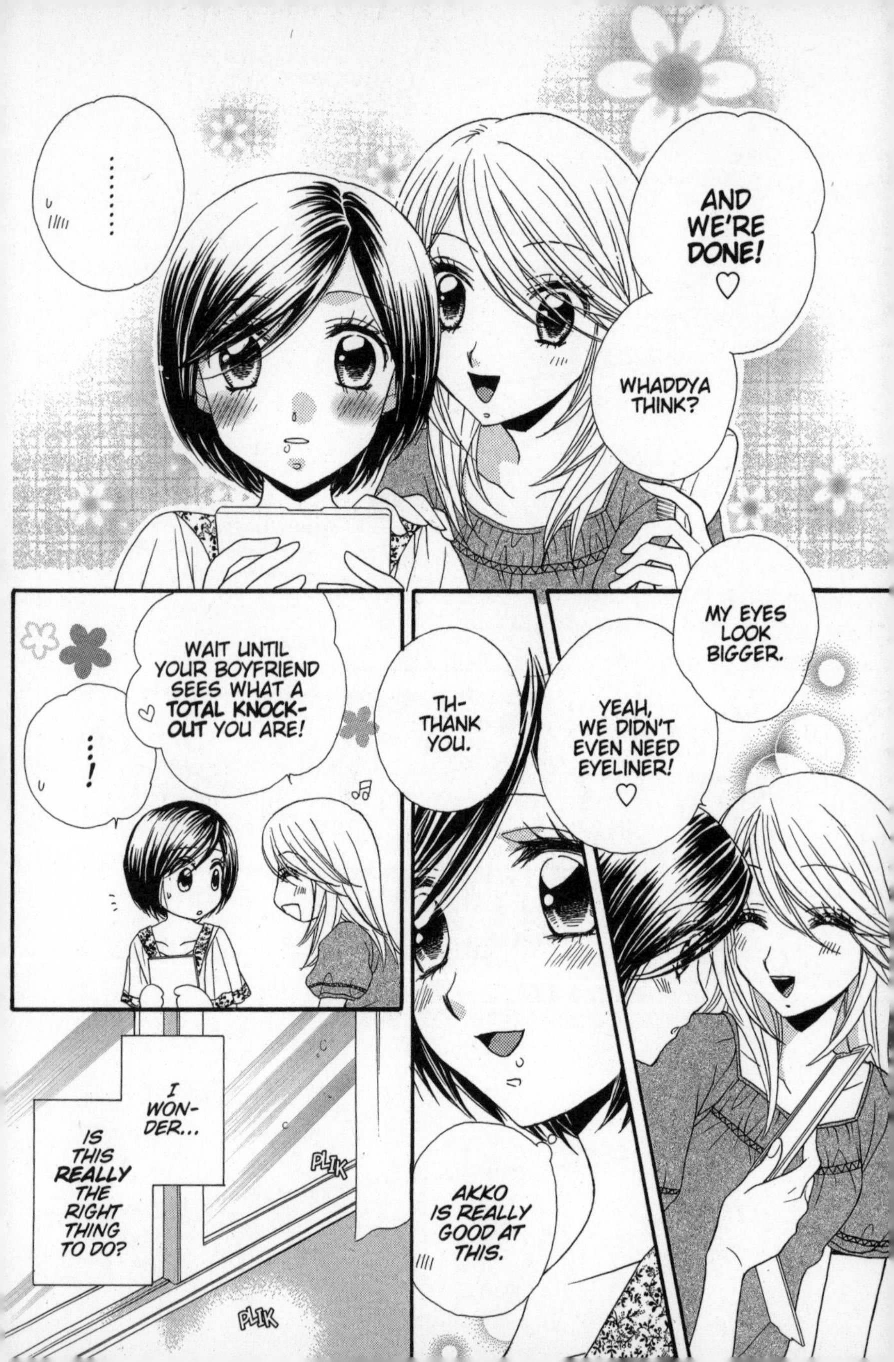
AND WE'RE DONE! ♡
WHADDYA THINK?
......
MY EYES LOOK BIGGER.
YEAH, WE DIDN'T EVEN NEED EYELINER! ♡
TH- THANK YOU.
AKKO IS REALLY GOOD AT THIS.
WAIT UNTIL YOUR BOYFRIEND SEES WHAT A TOTAL KNOCK-OUT YOU ARE! ♡
...!
I WONDER...
IS THIS REALLY THE RIGHT THING TO DO?
PLIK
PLIK

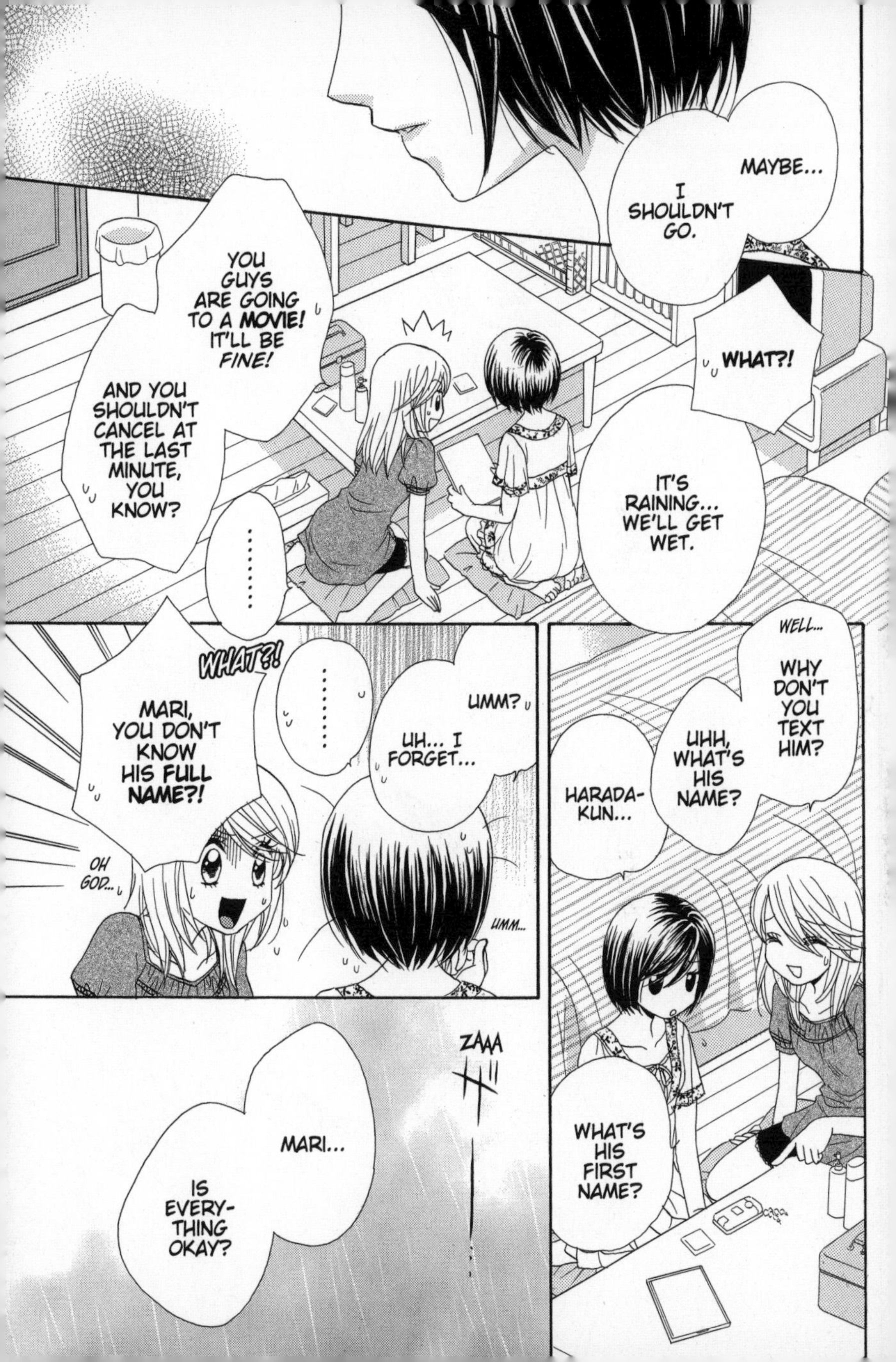
MAYBE... I SHOULDN'T GO.
WHAT?!
YOU GUYS ARE GOING TO A MOVIE! IT'LL BE FINE!
AND YOU SHOULDN'T CANCEL AT THE LAST MINUTE, YOU KNOW?
IT'S RAINING... WE'LL GET WET.
......
WELL...
WHY DON'T YOU TEXT HIM?
UHH, WHAT'S HIS NAME?
HARADA-KUN...
WHAT'S HIS FIRST NAME?
UMM?
UH... I FORGET...
......
UMM...
WHAT?!
MARI, YOU DON'T KNOW HIS FULL NAME?!
OH GOD...
ZAAA
MARI...
IS EVERY-THING OKAY?

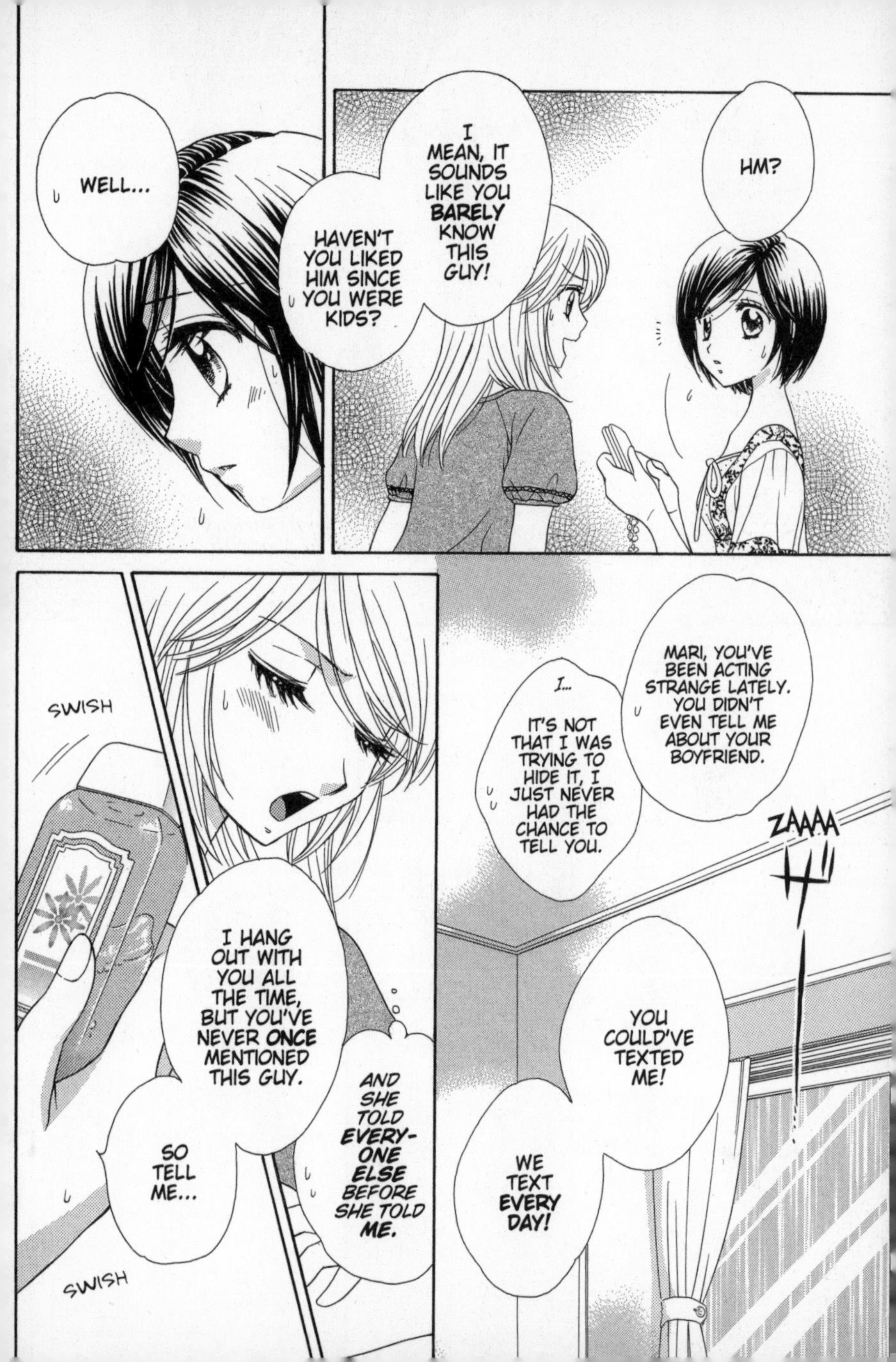
HM?
I MEAN, IT SOUNDS LIKE YOU BARELY KNOW THIS GUY!
HAVEN'T YOU LIKED HIM SINCE YOU WERE KIDS?
WELL...
MARI, YOU'VE BEEN ACTING STRANGE LATELY. YOU DIDN'T EVEN TELL ME ABOUT YOUR BOYFRIEND.
I...
IT'S NOT THAT I WAS TRYING TO HIDE IT, I JUST NEVER HAD THE CHANCE TO TELL YOU.
ZAAAAH
YOU COULD'VE TEXTED ME!
WE TEXT EVERY DAY!
SWISH
I HANG OUT WITH YOU ALL THE TIME, BUT YOU'VE NEVER ONCE MENTIONED THIS GUY.
AND SHE TOLD EVERY-ONE ELSE BEFORE SHE TOLD ME.
SO TELL ME...
SWISH

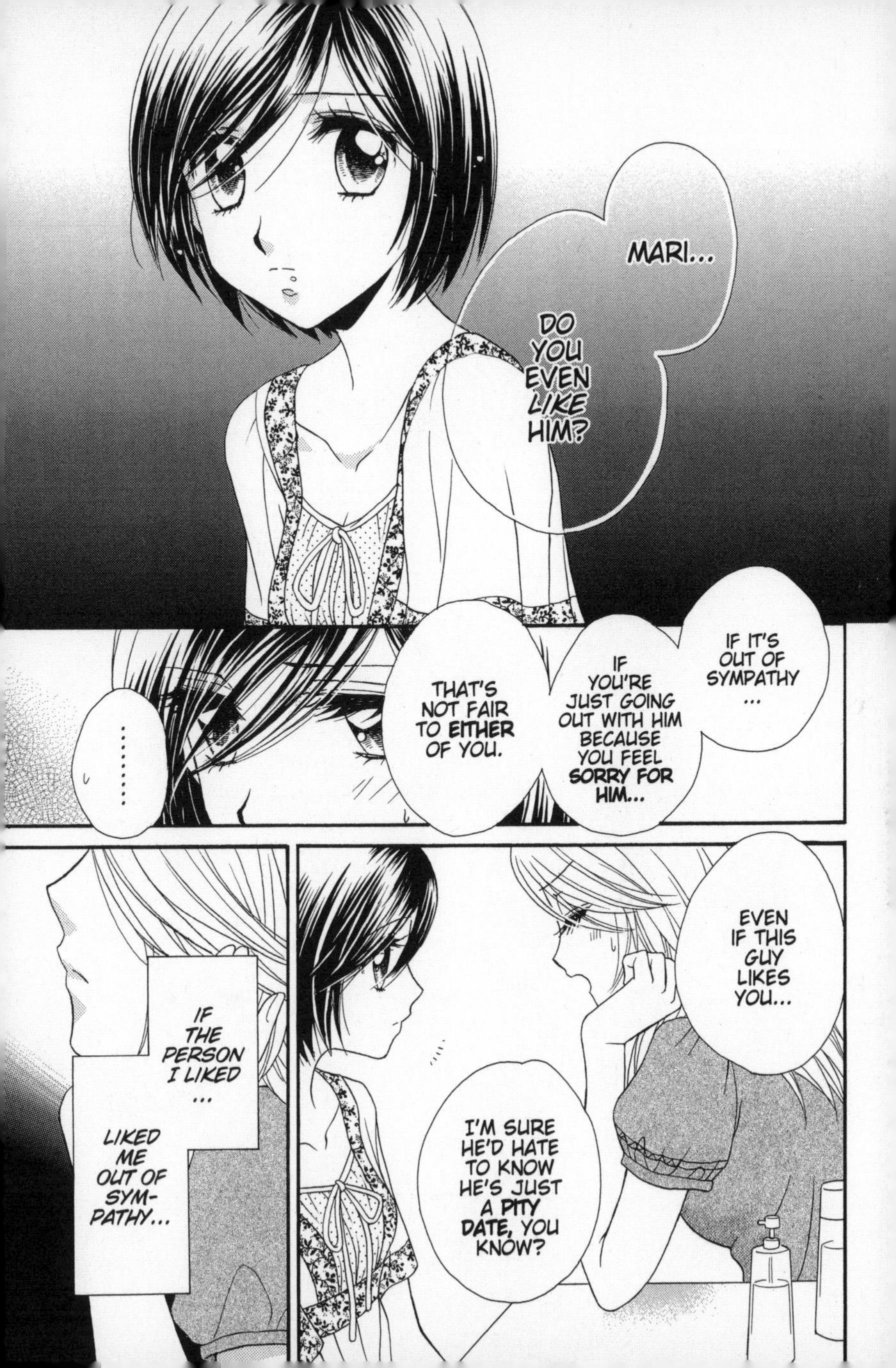
MARI...
DO YOU EVEN LIKE HIM?
IF IT'S OUT OF SYMPATHY ...
IF YOU'RE JUST GOING OUT WITH HIM BECAUSE YOU FEEL **SORRY FOR HIM...**
THAT'S NOT FAIR TO **EITHER** OF YOU.
......
EVEN IF THIS GUY LIKES YOU...
I'M SURE HE'D HATE TO KNOW HE'S JUST **A PITY DATE,** YOU KNOW?
IF THE PERSON I LIKED ...
LIKED ME OUT OF SYM-PATHY...

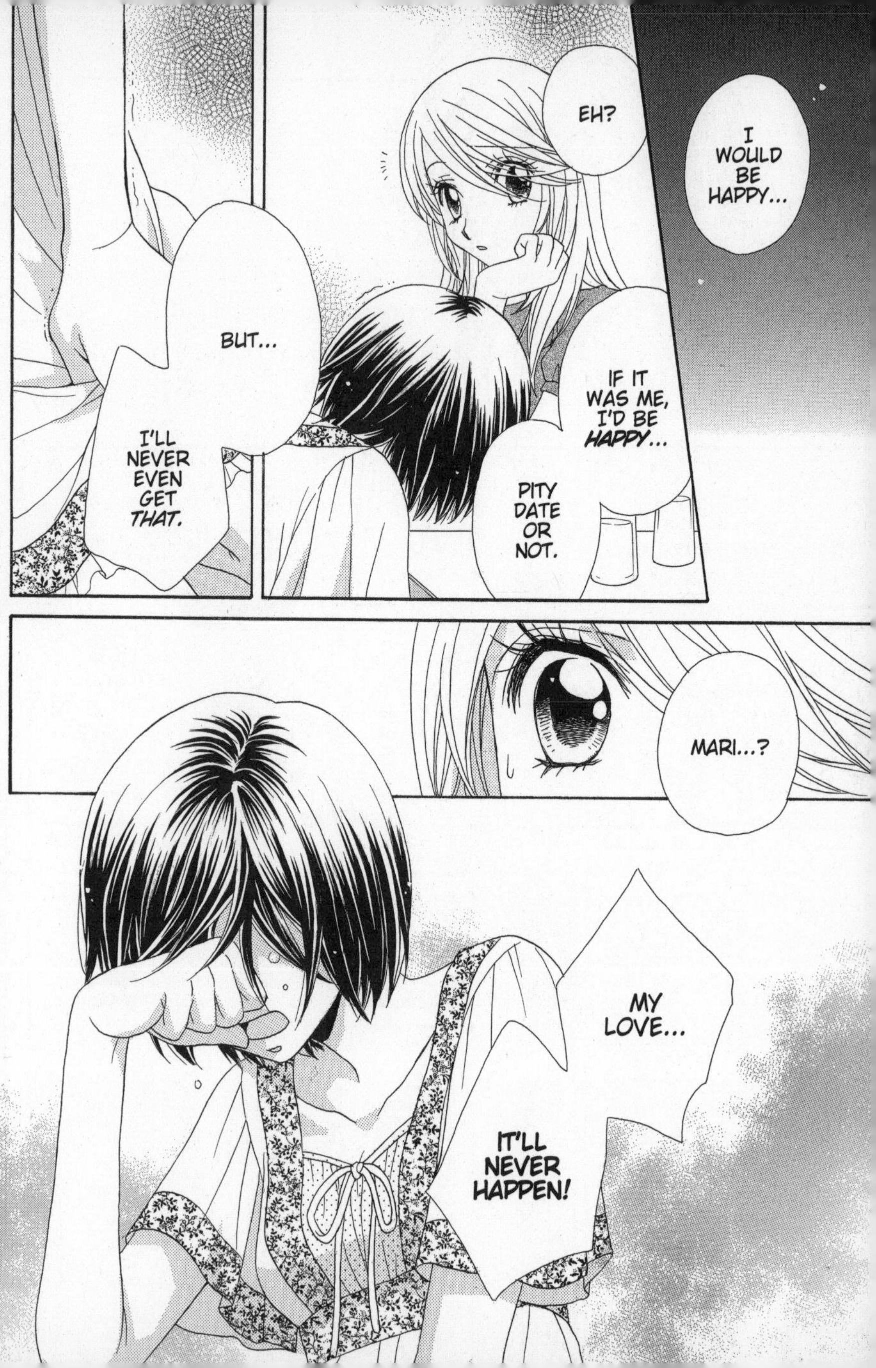
I WOULD BE HAPPY...
EH?
IF IT WAS ME, I'D BE *HAPPY*...
PITY DATE OR NOT.
BUT...
I'LL NEVER EVEN GET *THAT*.
MARI...?
MY LOVE...
IT'LL NEVER HAPPEN!

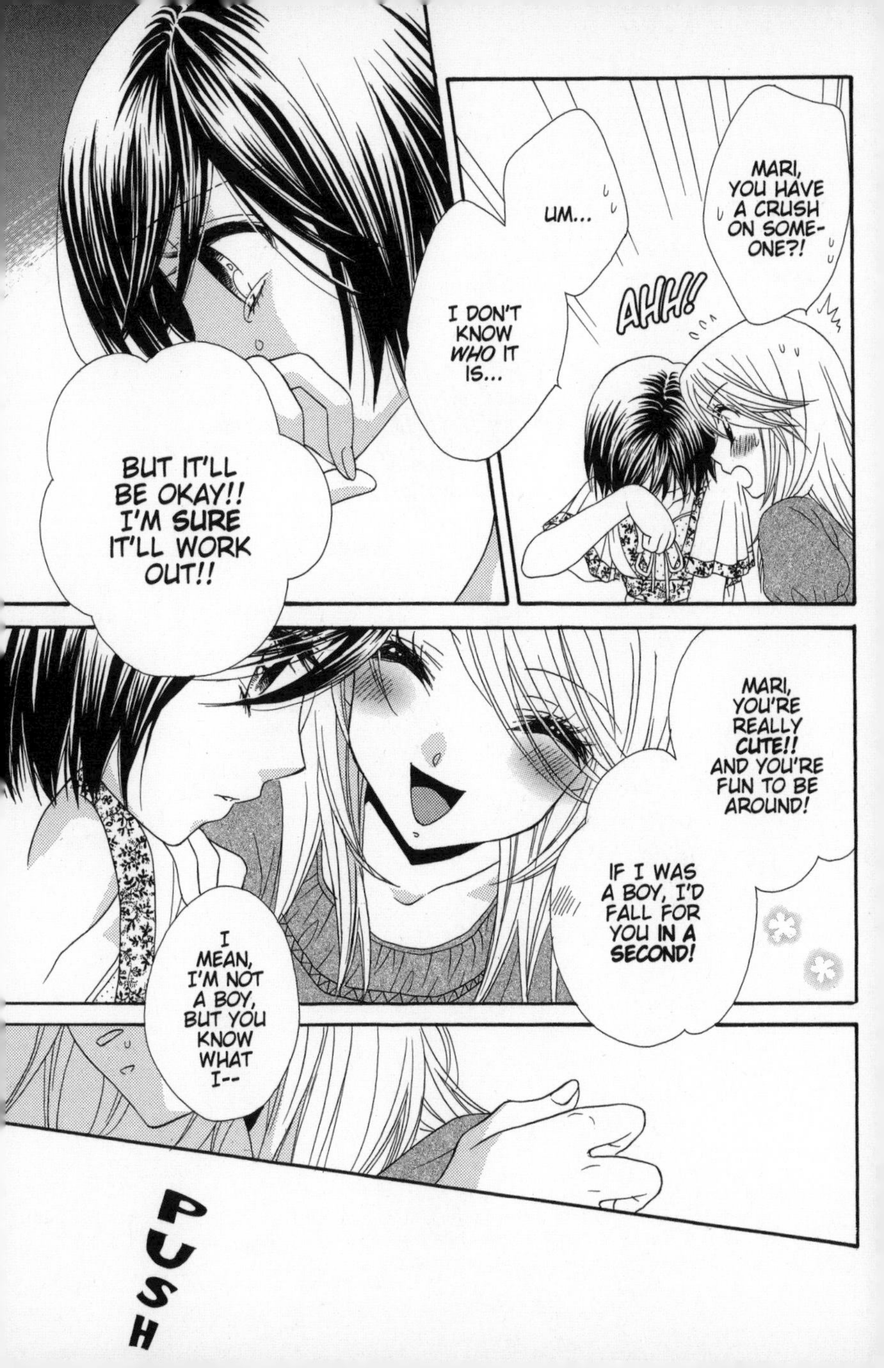
MARI, YOU HAVE A CRUSH ON SOME-ONE?!
UM...
AHH!!
I DON'T KNOW WHO IT IS...
BUT IT'LL BE OKAY!! I'M SURE IT'LL WORK OUT!!
MARI, YOU'RE REALLY CUTE!! AND YOU'RE FUN TO BE AROUND!
IF I WAS A BOY, I'D FALL FOR YOU IN A SECOND!
I MEAN, I'M NOT A BOY, BUT YOU KNOW WHAT I--
PUSH

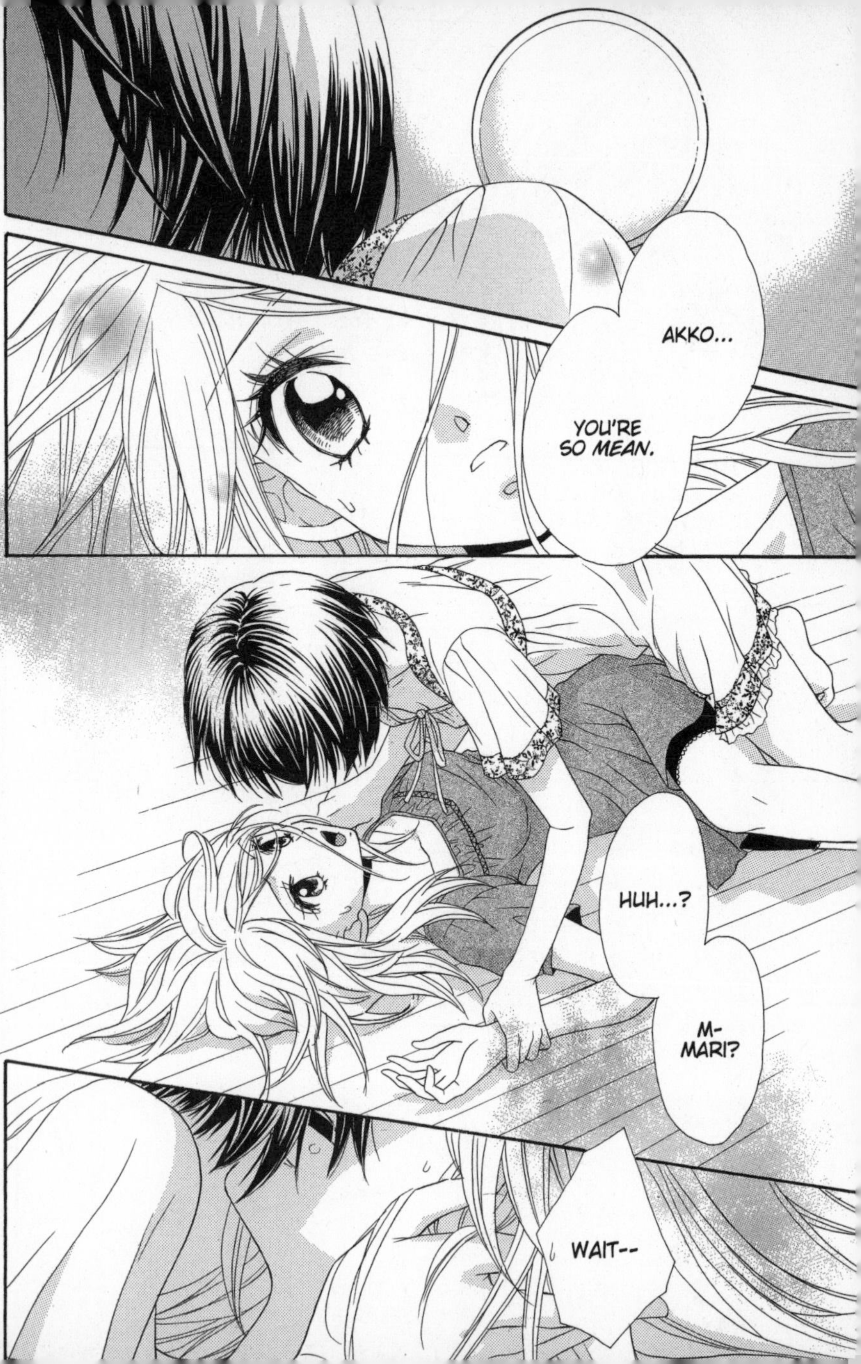
AKKO...
YOU'RE SO MEAN.
HUH...?
M-MARI?
WAIT--

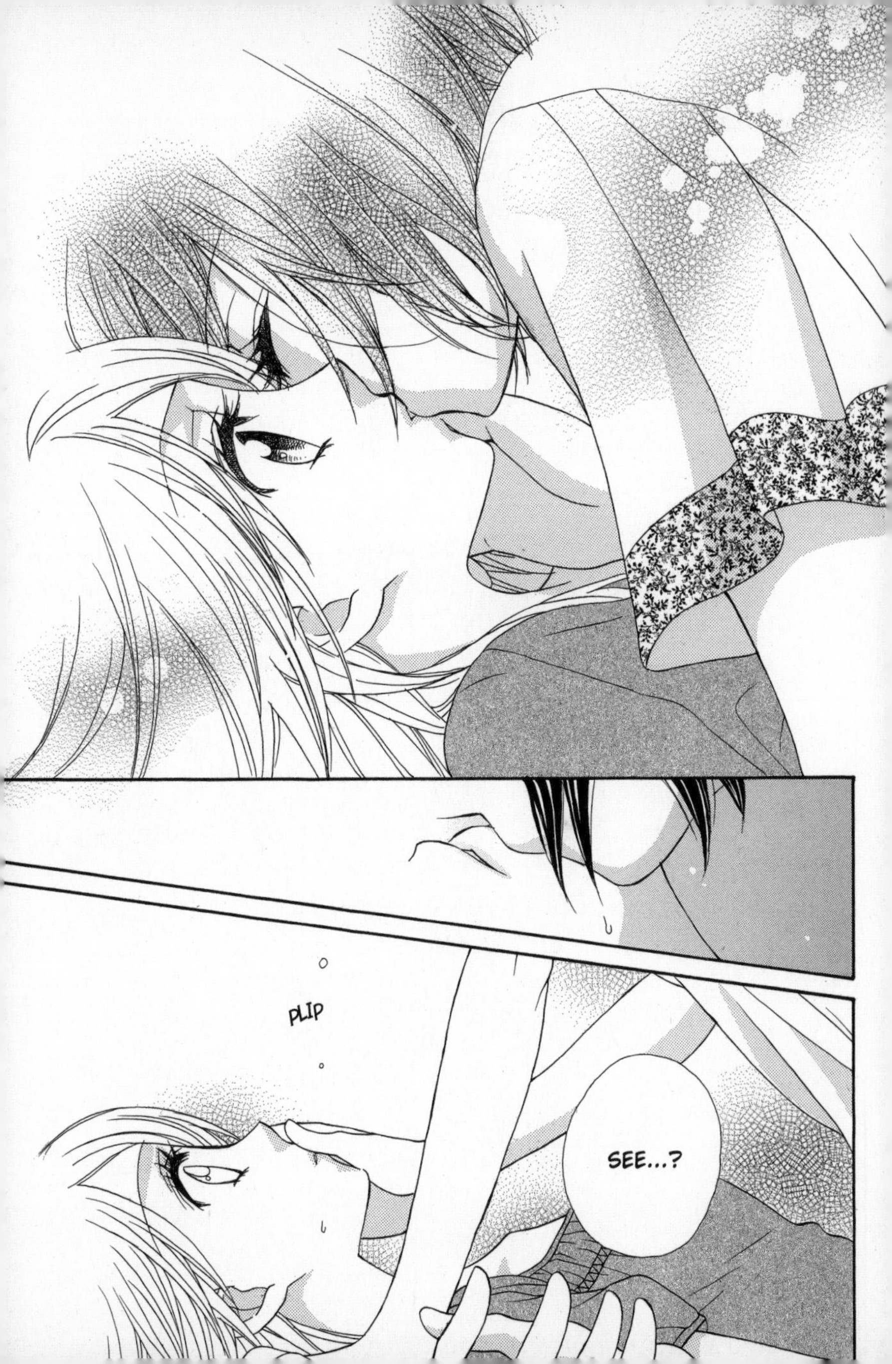
PLIP
SEE...?

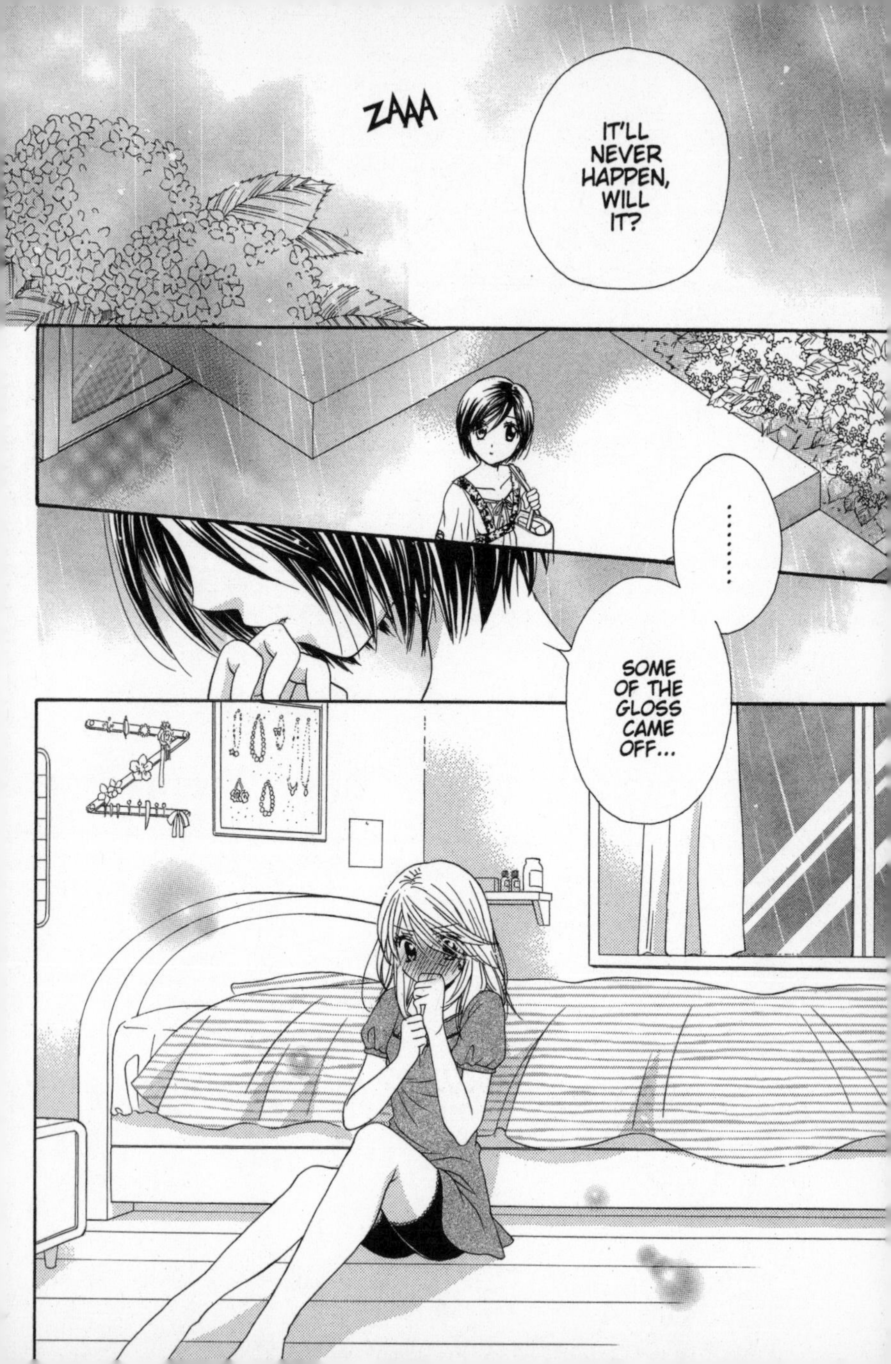
ZAAA
IT'LL NEVER HAPPEN, WILL IT?
......
SOME OF THE GLOSS CAME OFF...

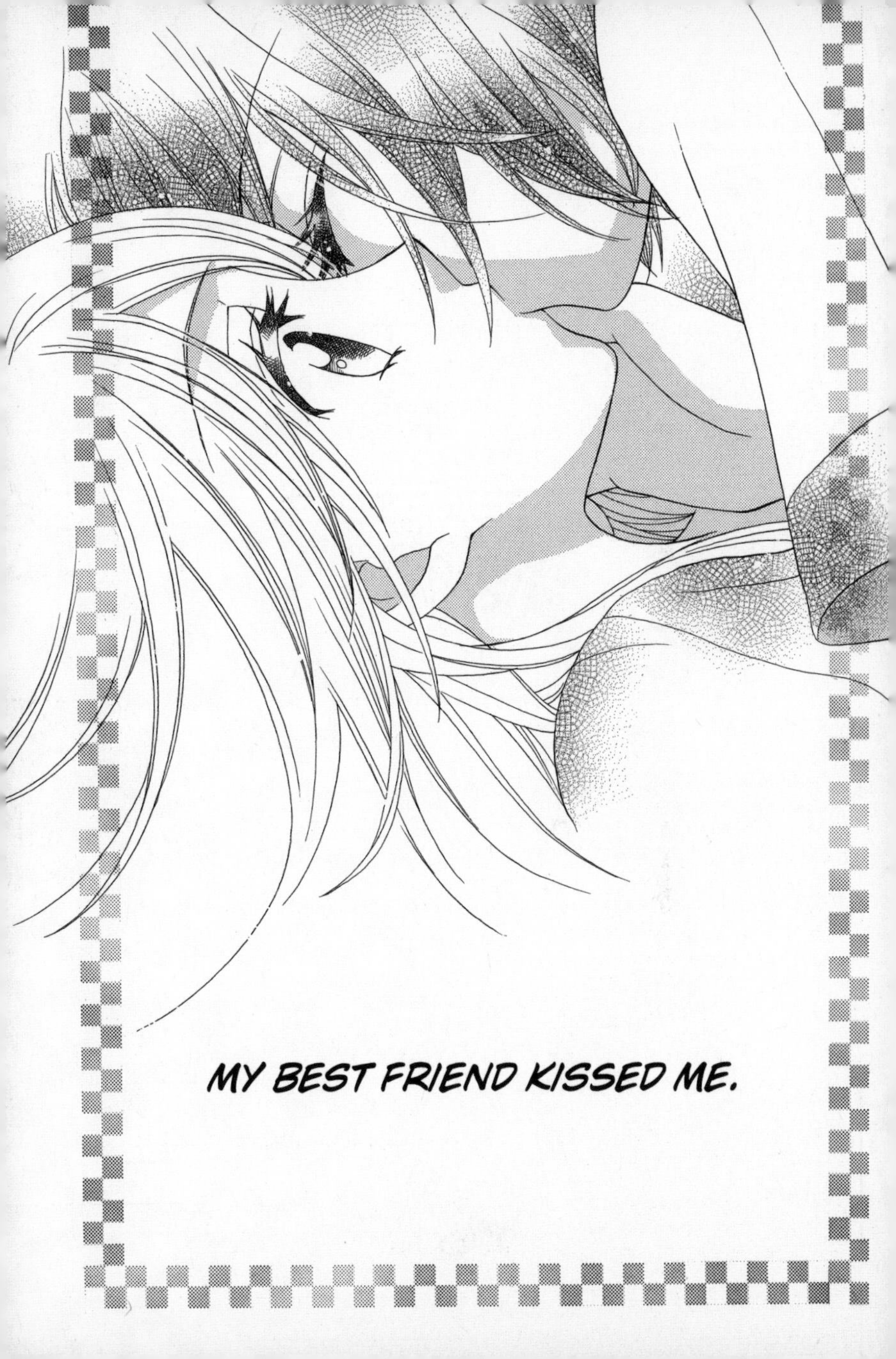
MY BEST FRIEND KISSED ME.

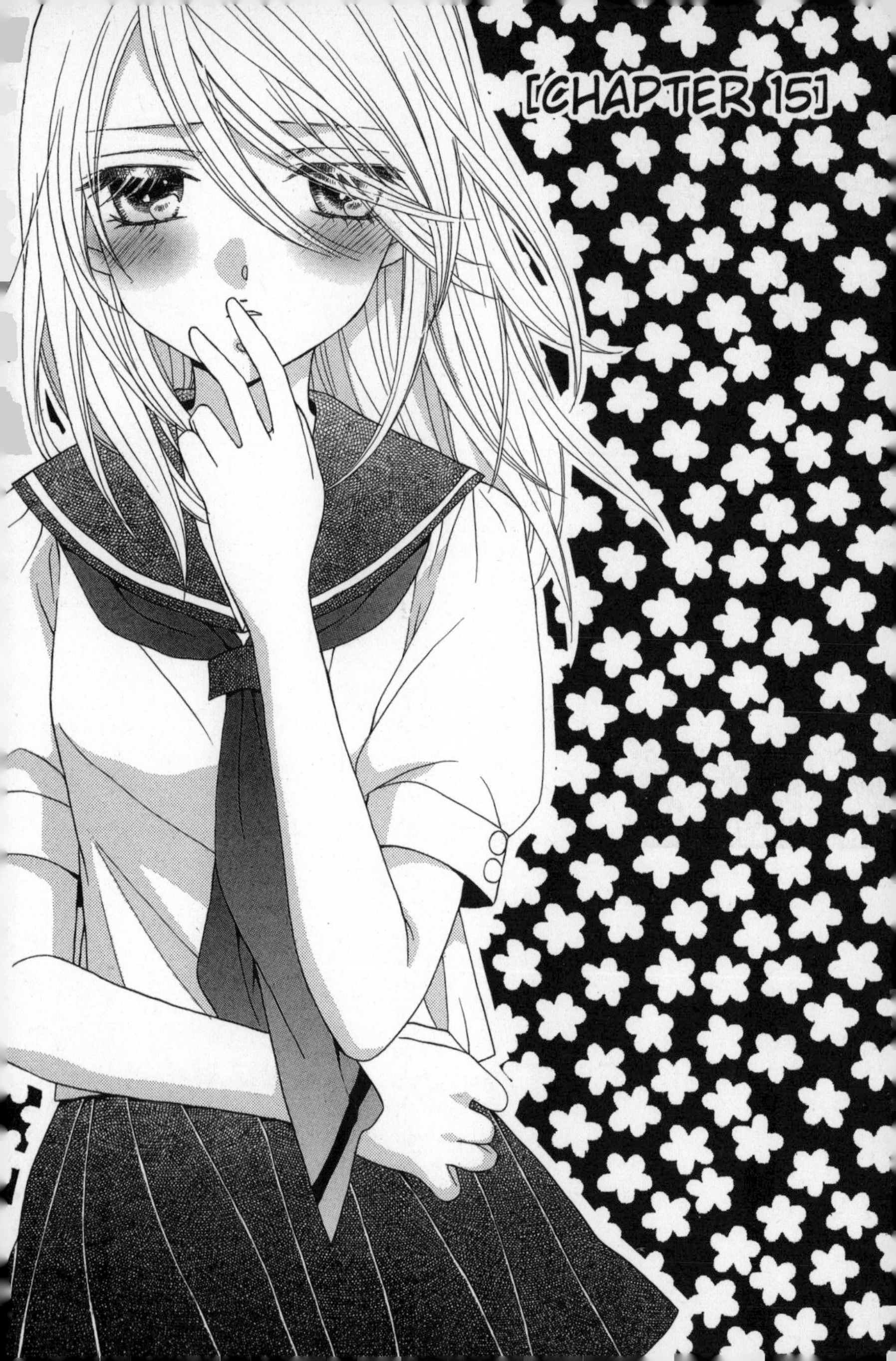
[CHAPTER 15]

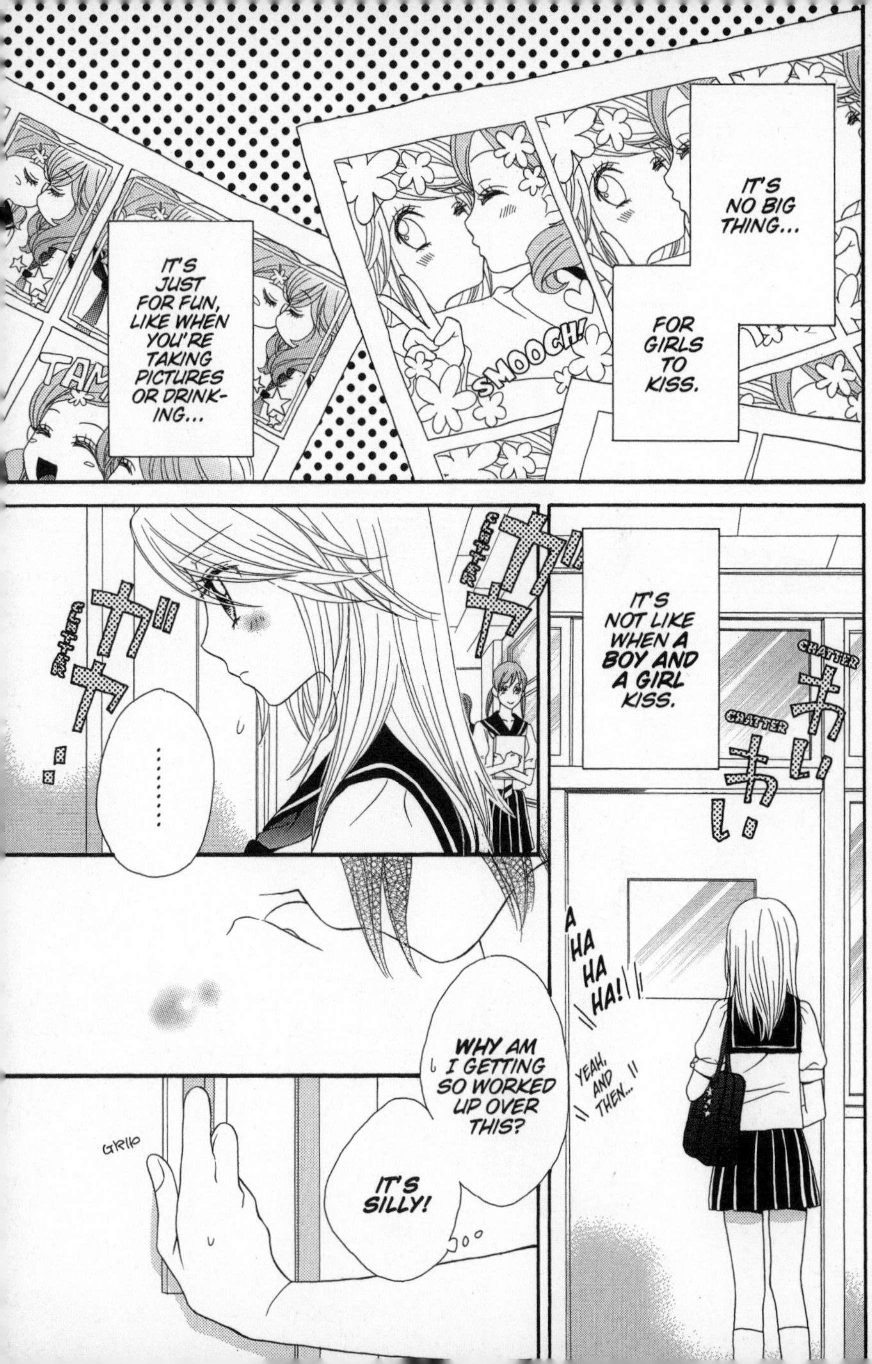
IT'S NO BIG THING...
FOR GIRLS TO KISS.
SMOOCH!
IT'S JUST FOR FUN, LIKE WHEN YOU'RE TAKING PICTURES OR DRINK-ING...
IT'S NOT LIKE WHEN A BOY AND A GIRL KISS.
CHATTER
CHATTER
......
A HA HA HA!
YEAH, AND THEN...
WHY AM I GETTING SO WORKED UP OVER THIS?
IT'S SILLY!
GRIP

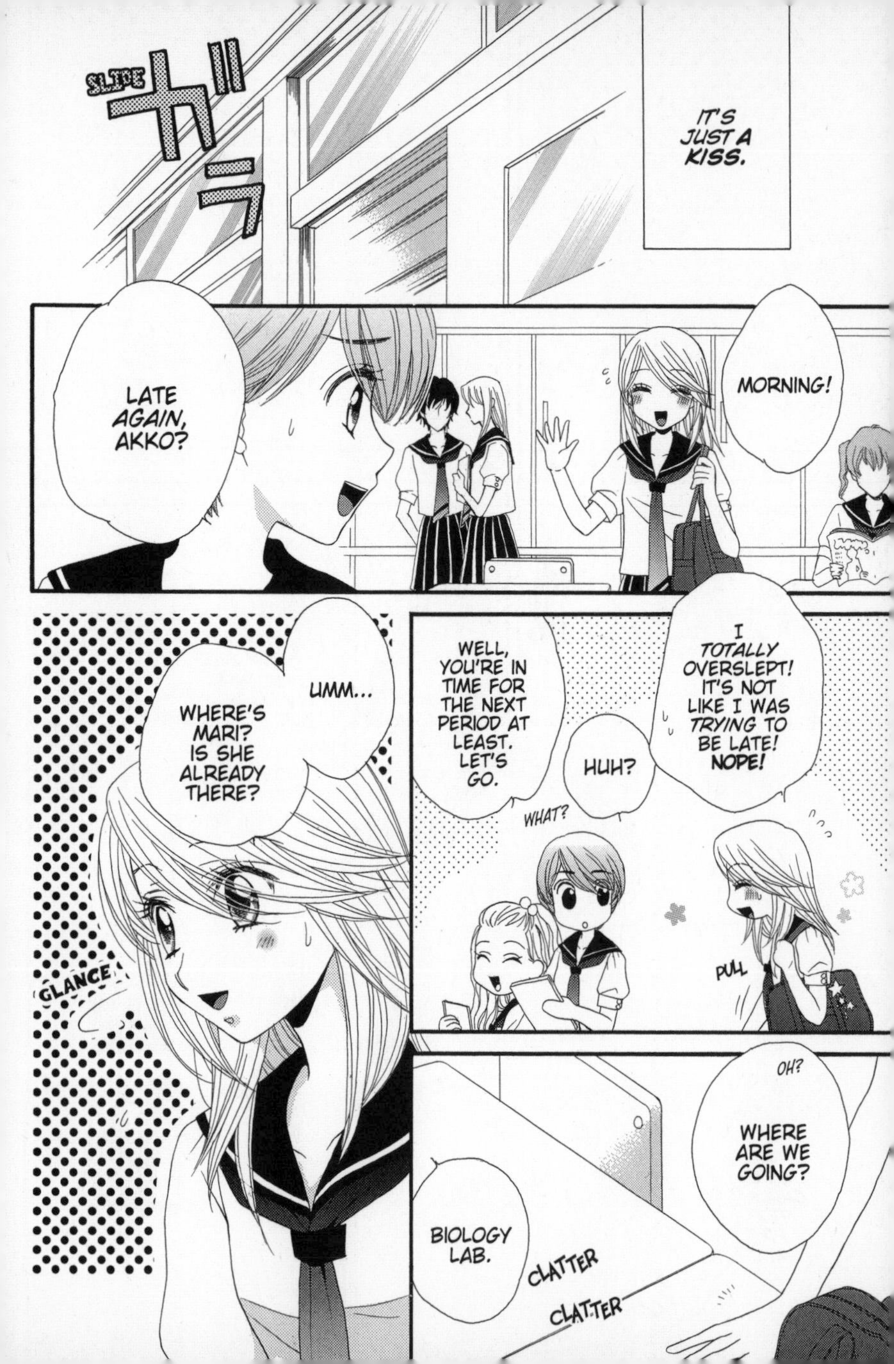
IT'S JUST A KISS.
SLIDE ガラ
MORNING!
LATE AGAIN, AKKO?
I TOTALLY OVERSLEPT! IT'S NOT LIKE I WAS TRYING TO BE LATE! NOPE!
HUH?
WELL, YOU'RE IN TIME FOR THE NEXT PERIOD AT LEAST. LET'S GO.
WHAT?
PULL
OH?
WHERE ARE WE GOING?
BIOLOGY LAB.
CLATTER
CLATTER
UMM...
WHERE'S MARI? IS SHE ALREADY THERE?
GLANCE

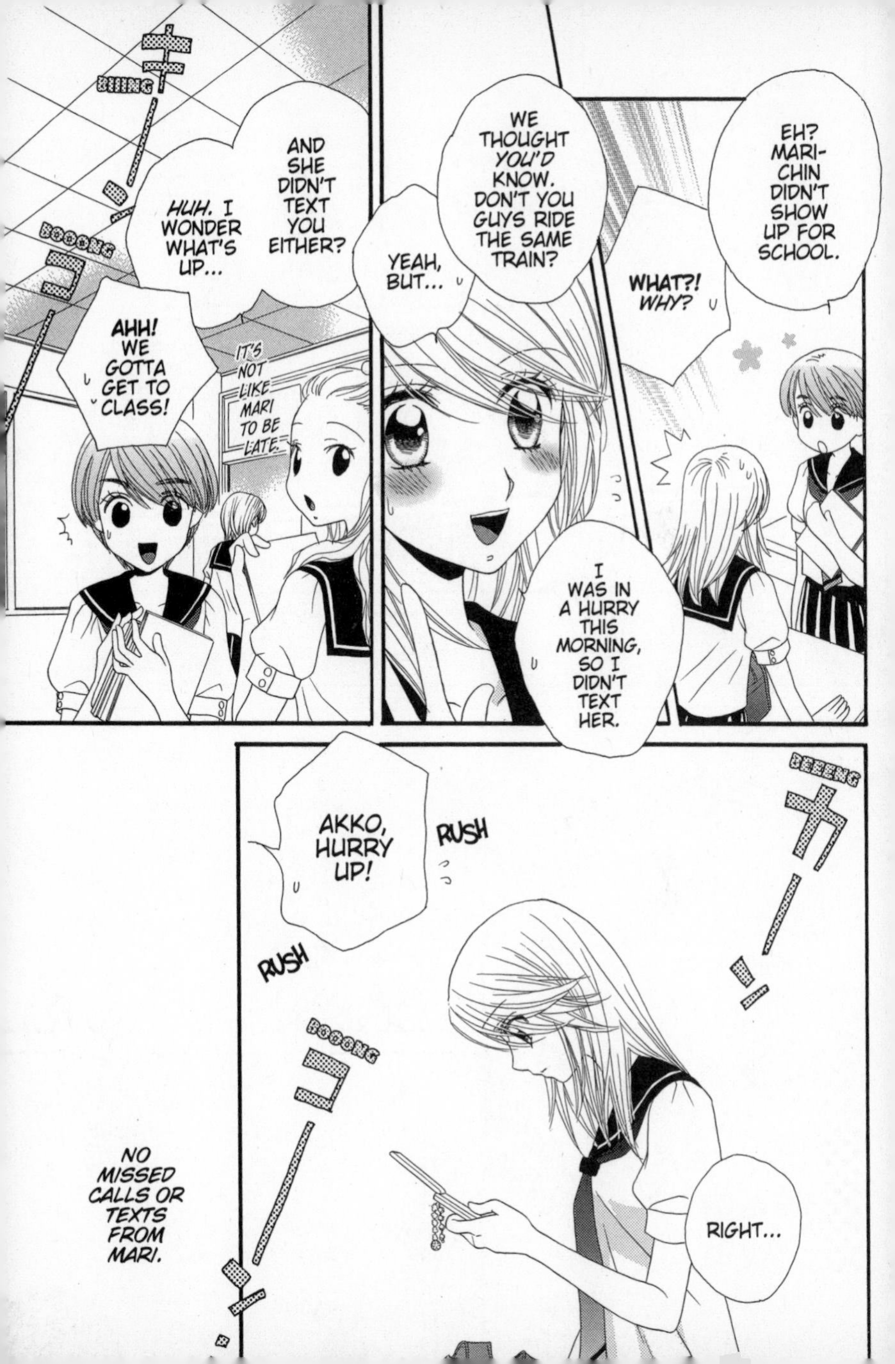
EH? MARI-CHIN DIDN'T SHOW UP FOR SCHOOL.
WHAT?! WHY?
WE THOUGHT YOU'D KNOW. DON'T YOU GUYS RIDE THE SAME TRAIN?
YEAH, BUT...
I WAS IN A HURRY THIS MORNING, SO I DIDN'T TEXT HER.
AND SHE DIDN'T TEXT YOU EITHER?
HUH. I WONDER WHAT'S UP...
BIIING
BOOONG
AHH! WE GOTTA GET TO CLASS!
IT'S NOT LIKE MARI TO BE LATE.
DEEENG
AKKO, HURRY UP!
RUSH
RUSH
BOOONG
RIGHT...
NO MISSED CALLS OR TEXTS FROM MARI.

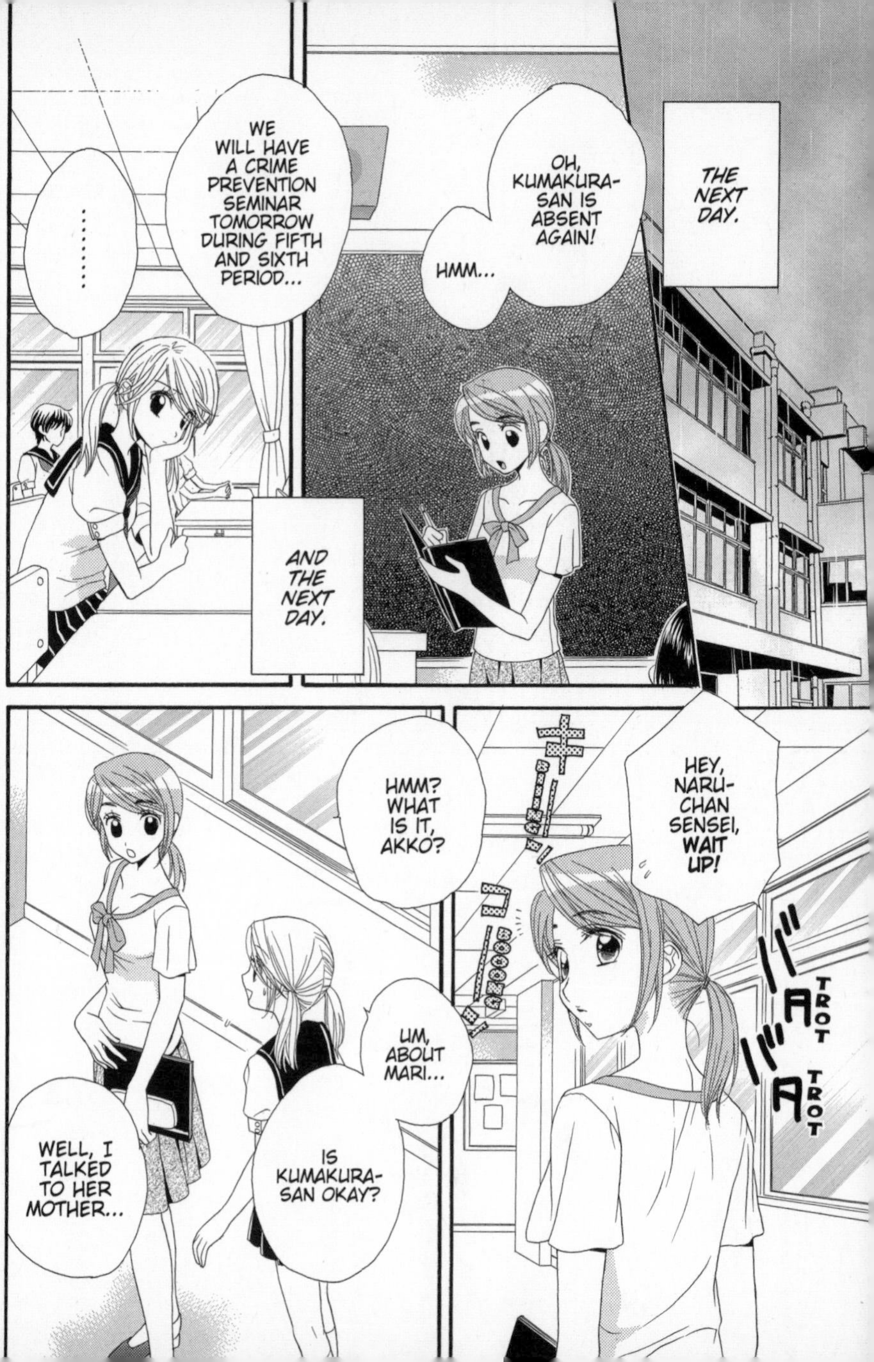
THE NEXT DAY.
OH, KUMAKURA-SAN IS ABSENT AGAIN!
HMM...
AND THE NEXT DAY.
WE WILL HAVE A CRIME PREVENTION SEMINAR TOMORROW DURING FIFTH AND SIXTH PERIOD...
......
HEY, NARU-CHAN SENSEI, WAIT UP!
TROT TROT
HMM? WHAT IS IT, AKKO?
UM, ABOUT MARI...
IS KUMAKURA-SAN OKAY?
WELL, I TALKED TO HER MOTHER...

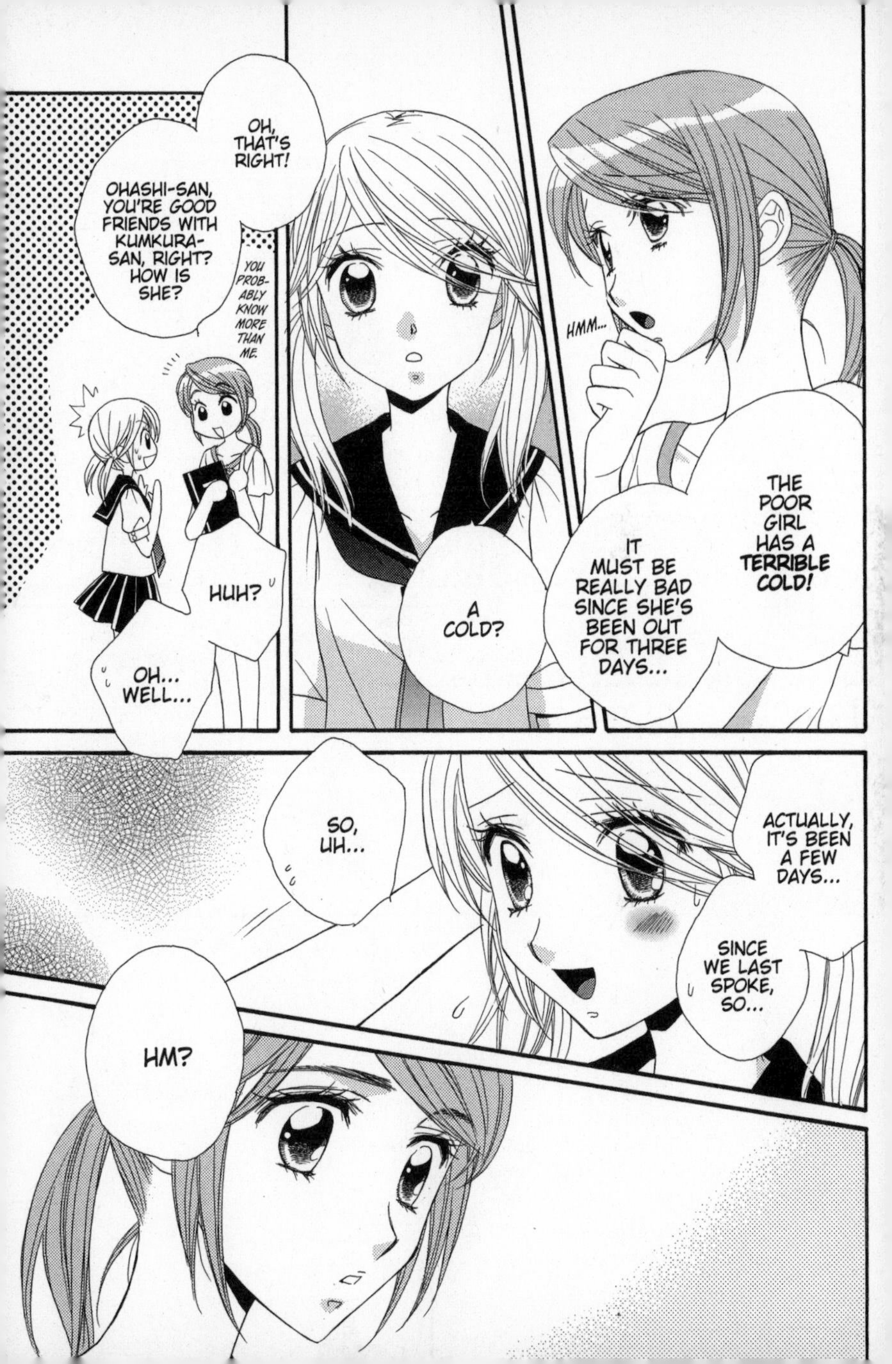

HMM...
THE POOR GIRL HAS A TERRIBLE COLD!
IT MUST BE REALLY BAD SINCE SHE'S BEEN OUT FOR THREE DAYS...
A COLD?
OH, THAT'S RIGHT!
OHASHI-SAN, YOU'RE GOOD FRIENDS WITH KUMKURA-SAN, RIGHT? HOW IS SHE?
YOU PROBABLY KNOW MORE THAN ME.
HUH?
OH... WELL...
SO, UH...
ACTUALLY, IT'S BEEN A FEW DAYS...
SINCE WE LAST SPOKE, SO...
HM?

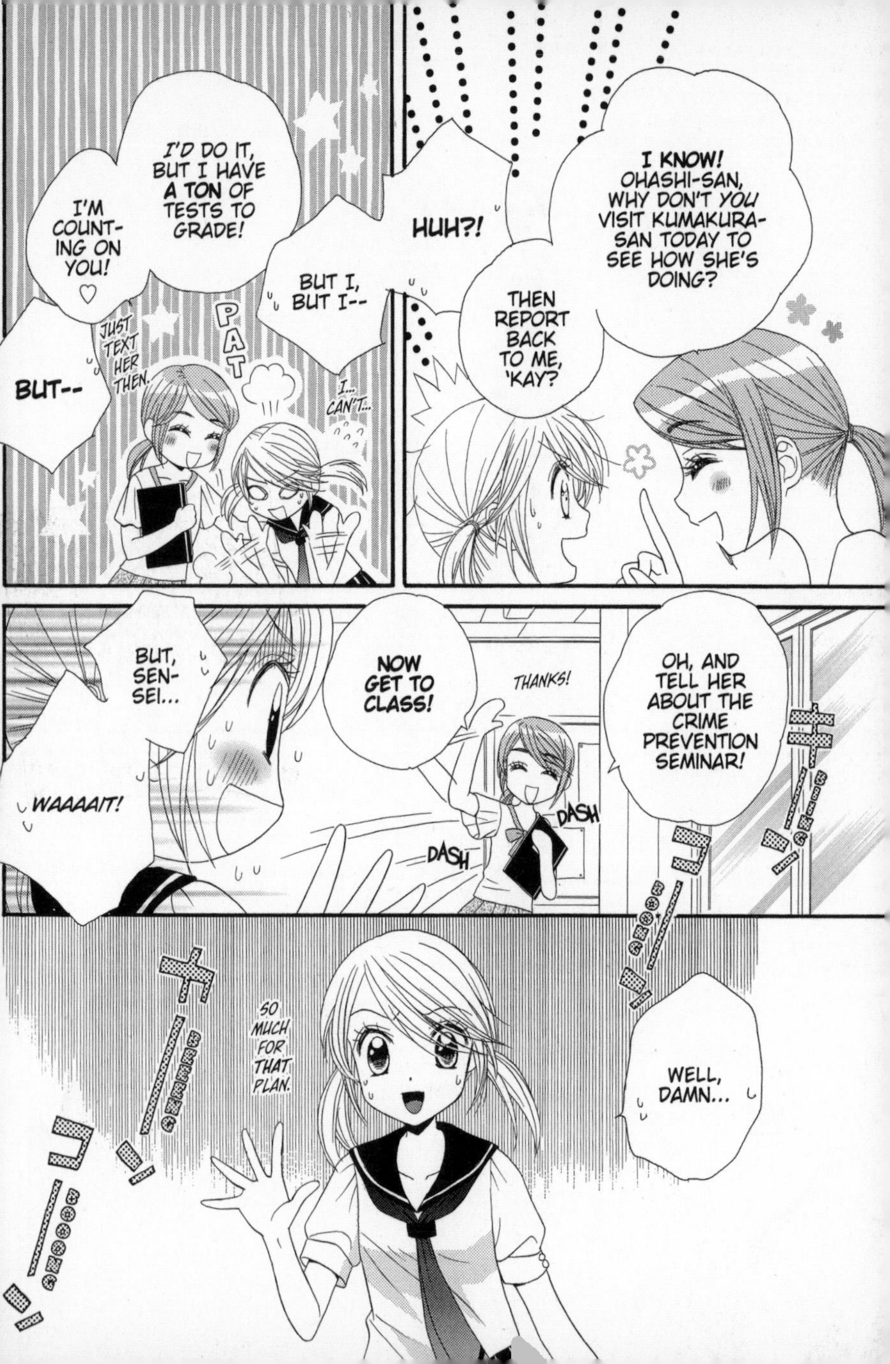
I KNOW! OHASHI-SAN, WHY DON'T YOU VISIT KUMAKURA-SAN TODAY TO SEE HOW SHE'S DOING?
THEN REPORT BACK TO ME, 'KAY?
HUH?!
BUT I, BUT I--
I'D DO IT, BUT I HAVE A TON OF TESTS TO GRADE!
I'M COUNTING ON YOU! ♡
PAT
I... CAN'T...
JUST TEXT HER THEN.
BUT--
OH, AND TELL HER ABOUT THE CRIME PREVENTION SEMINAR!
NOW GET TO CLASS!
THANKS!
DASH
DASH
BUT, SEN-SEI...
WAAAAIT!
WELL, DAMN...
SO MUCH FOR THAT PLAN.

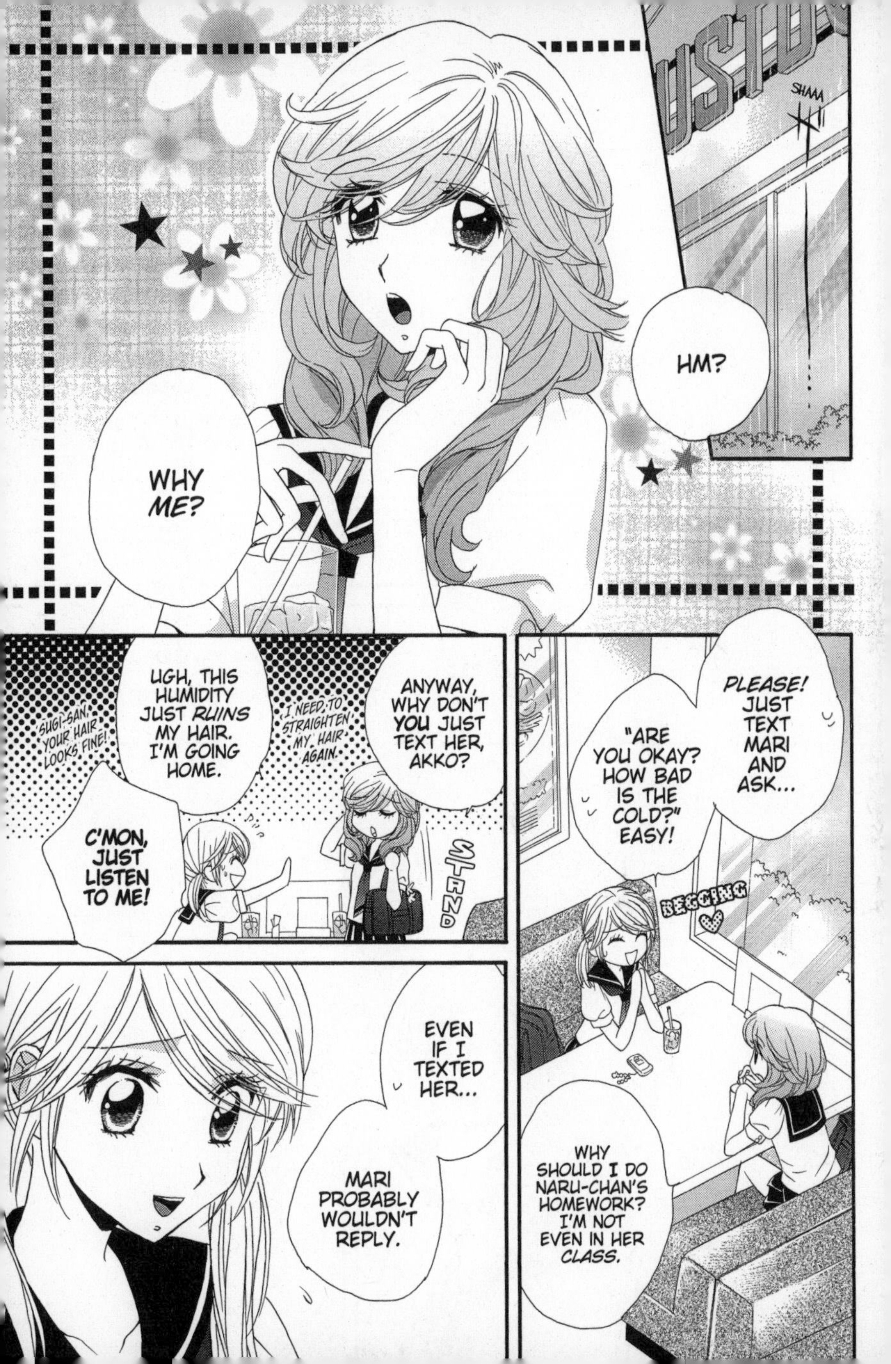
SHAAA
HM?
WHY ME?
PLEASE! JUST TEXT MARI AND ASK...
"ARE YOU OKAY? HOW BAD IS THE COLD?" EASY!
BEGGING
WHY SHOULD I DO NARU-CHAN'S HOMEWORK? I'M NOT EVEN IN HER CLASS.
ANYWAY, WHY DON'T YOU JUST TEXT HER, AKKO?
I NEED TO STRAIGHTEN MY HAIR AGAIN.
UGH, THIS HUMIDITY JUST RUINS MY HAIR. I'M GOING HOME.
SUGI-SAN, YOUR HAIR LOOKS FINE!
STAND
C'MON, JUST LISTEN TO ME!
EVEN IF I TEXTED HER...
MARI PROBABLY WOULDN'T REPLY.

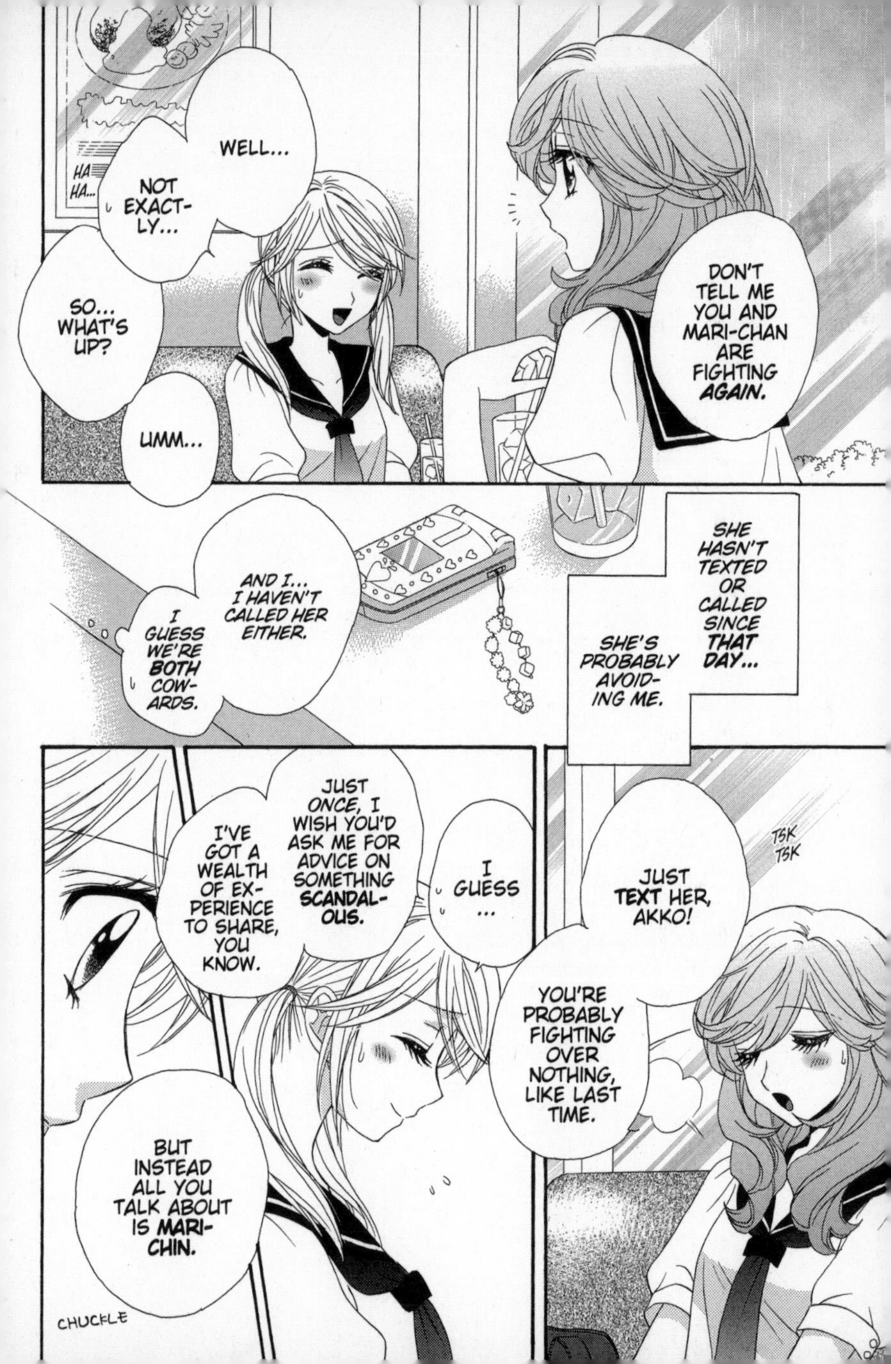
DON'T TELL ME YOU AND MARI-CHAN ARE FIGHTING AGAIN.
WELL...
NOT EXACTLY...
HA HA...
SO... WHAT'S UP?
UMM...
SHE HASN'T TEXTED OR CALLED SINCE THAT DAY...
SHE'S PROBABLY AVOIDING ME.
AND I... I HAVEN'T CALLED HER EITHER.
I GUESS WE'RE BOTH COWARDS.
TSK TSK
JUST TEXT HER, AKKO!
YOU'RE PROBABLY FIGHTING OVER NOTHING, LIKE LAST TIME.
I GUESS...
JUST ONCE, I WISH YOU'D ASK ME FOR ADVICE ON SOMETHING SCANDALOUS.
I'VE GOT A WEALTH OF EXPERIENCE TO SHARE, YOU KNOW.
BUT INSTEAD ALL YOU TALK ABOUT IS MARI-CHIN.
CHUCKLE

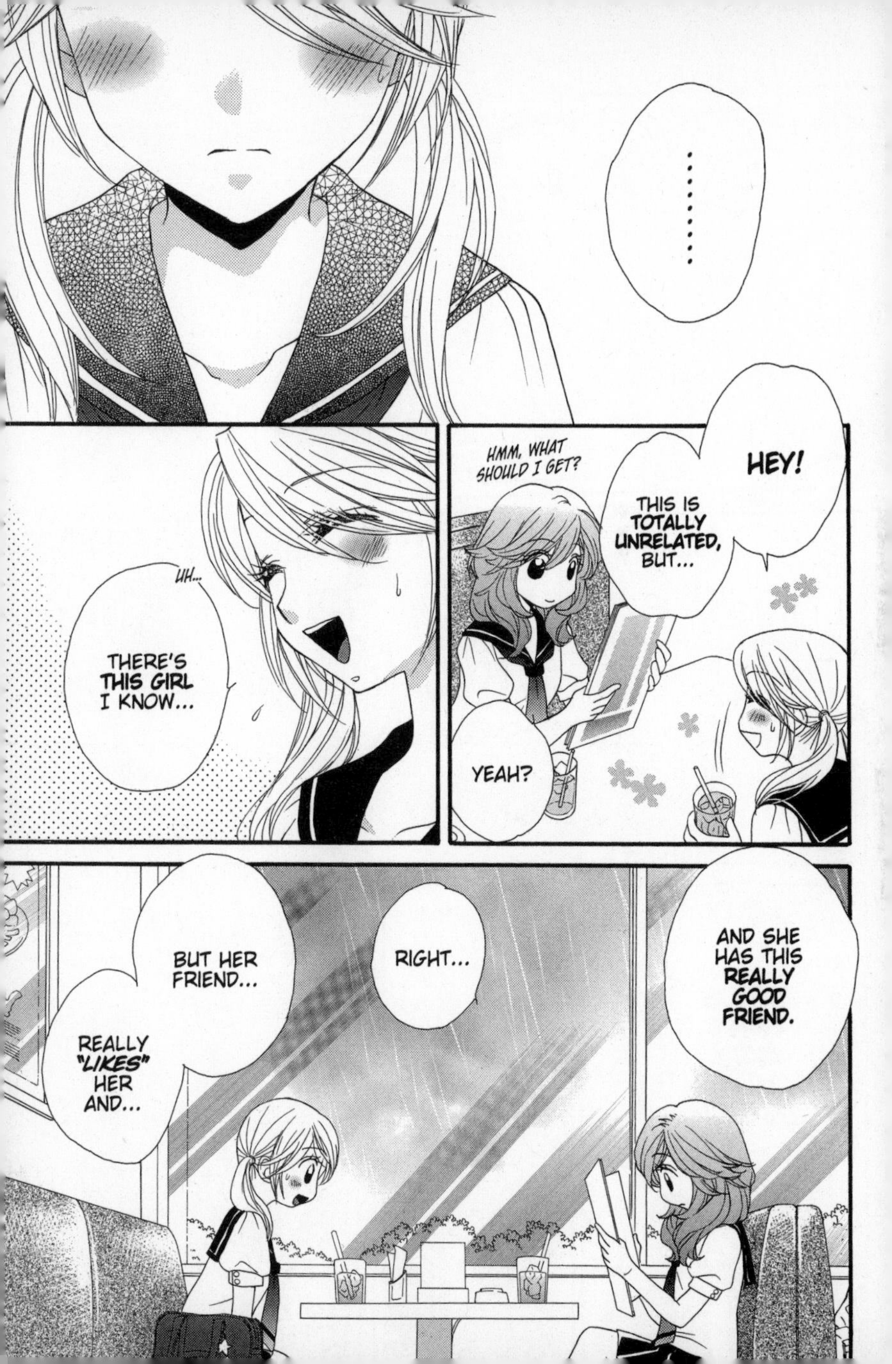
......
HEY!
THIS IS TOTALLY UNRELATED, BUT...
HMM, WHAT SHOULD I GET?
YEAH?
UH...
THERE'S THIS GIRL I KNOW...
AND SHE HAS THIS REALLY GOOD FRIEND.
RIGHT...
BUT HER FRIEND...
REALLY "LIKES" HER AND...

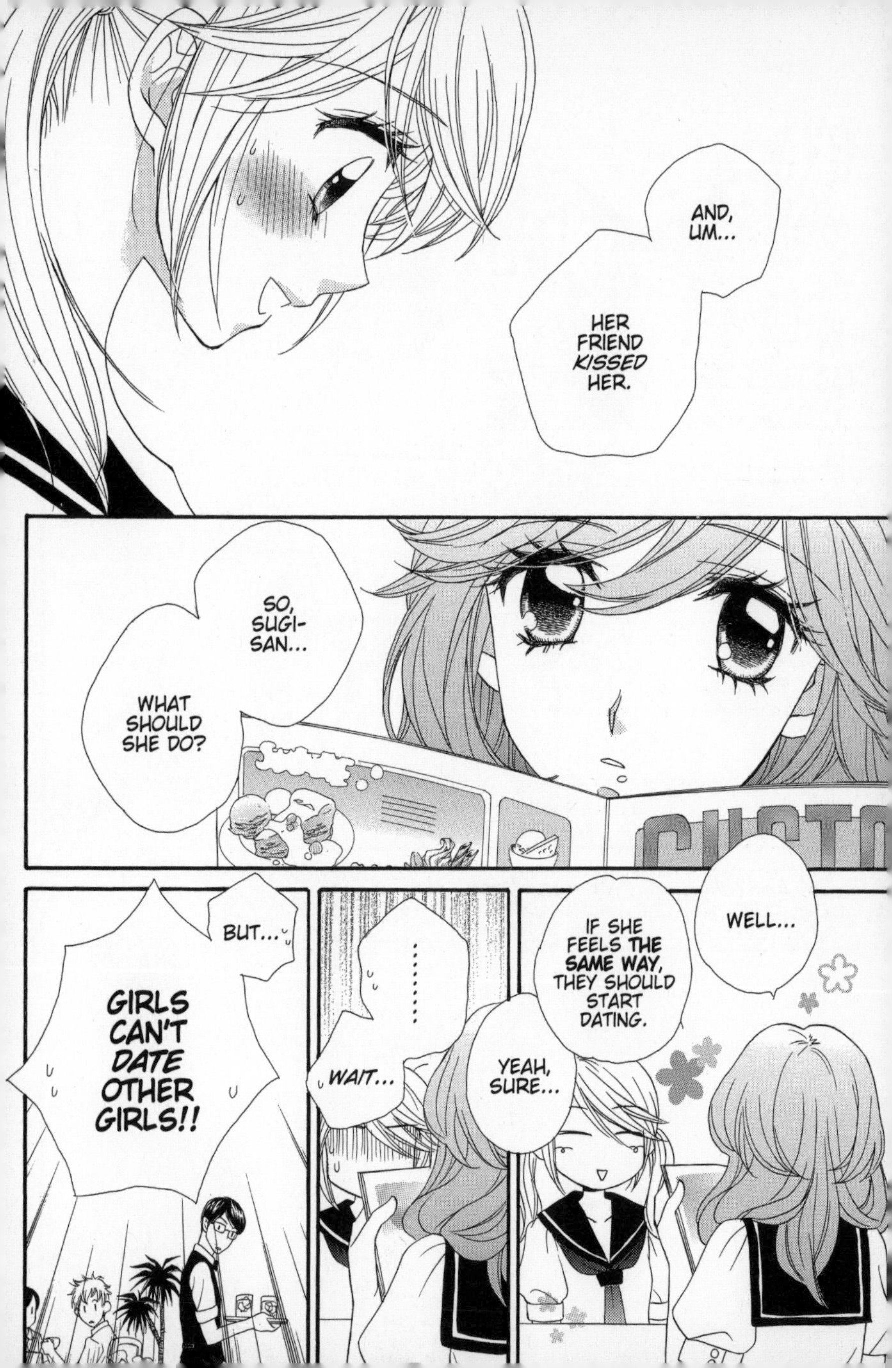
AND, UM...
HER FRIEND *KISSED* HER.
SO, SUGI-SAN...
WHAT SHOULD SHE DO?
WELL...
IF SHE FEELS THE SAME WAY, THEY SHOULD START DATING.
YEAH, SURE...
......
WAIT...
BUT...
GIRLS CAN'T *DATE* OTHER GIRLS!!

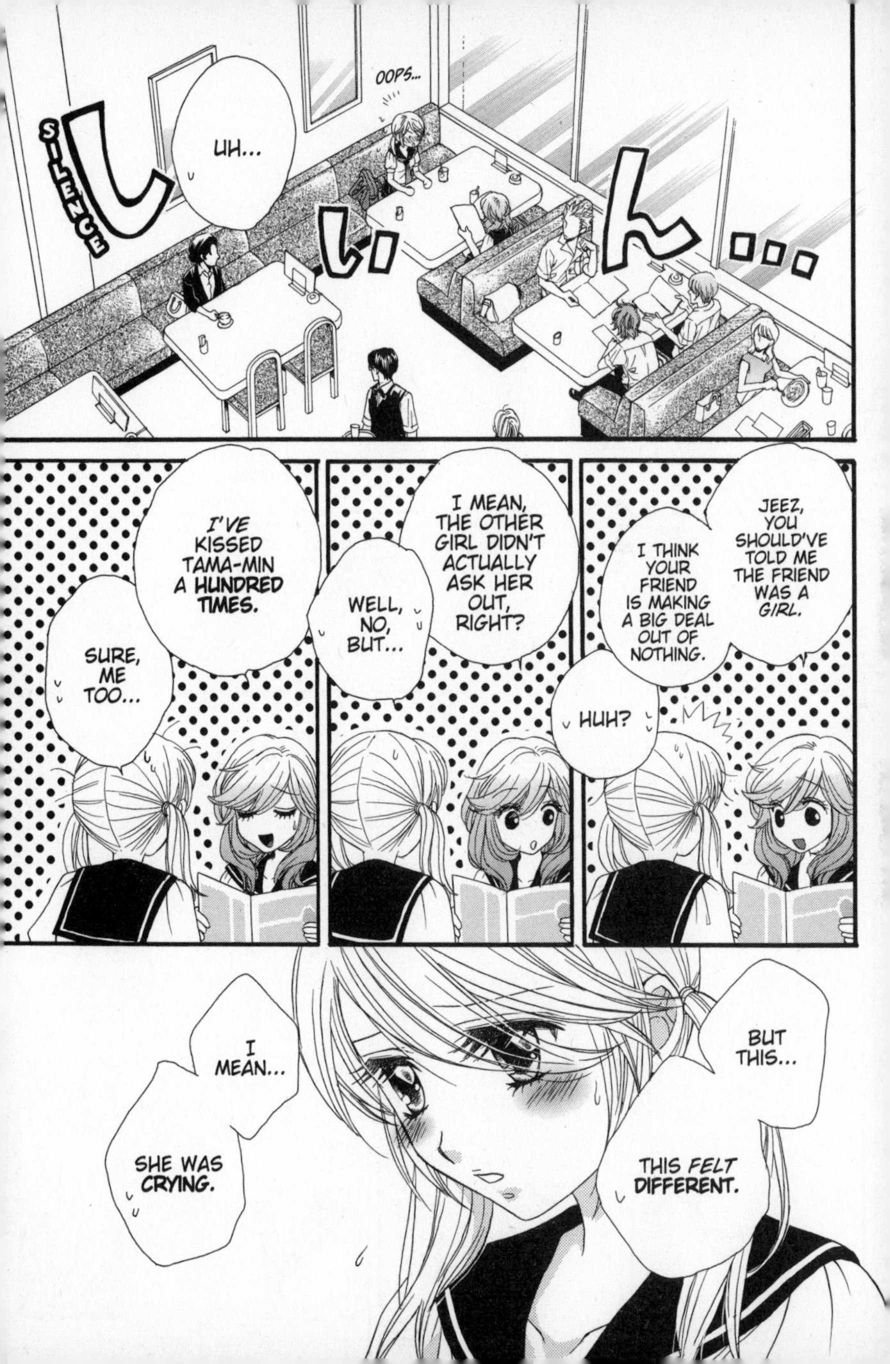
OOPS...
UH...
SILENCE
JEEZ, YOU SHOULD'VE TOLD ME THE FRIEND WAS A GIRL.
I THINK YOUR FRIEND IS MAKING A BIG DEAL OUT OF NOTHING.
HUH?
I MEAN, THE OTHER GIRL DIDN'T ACTUALLY ASK HER OUT, RIGHT?
WELL, NO, BUT...
I'VE KISSED TAMA-MIN A HUNDRED TIMES.
SURE, ME TOO...
BUT THIS...
THIS FELT DIFFERENT.
I MEAN...
SHE WAS CRYING.

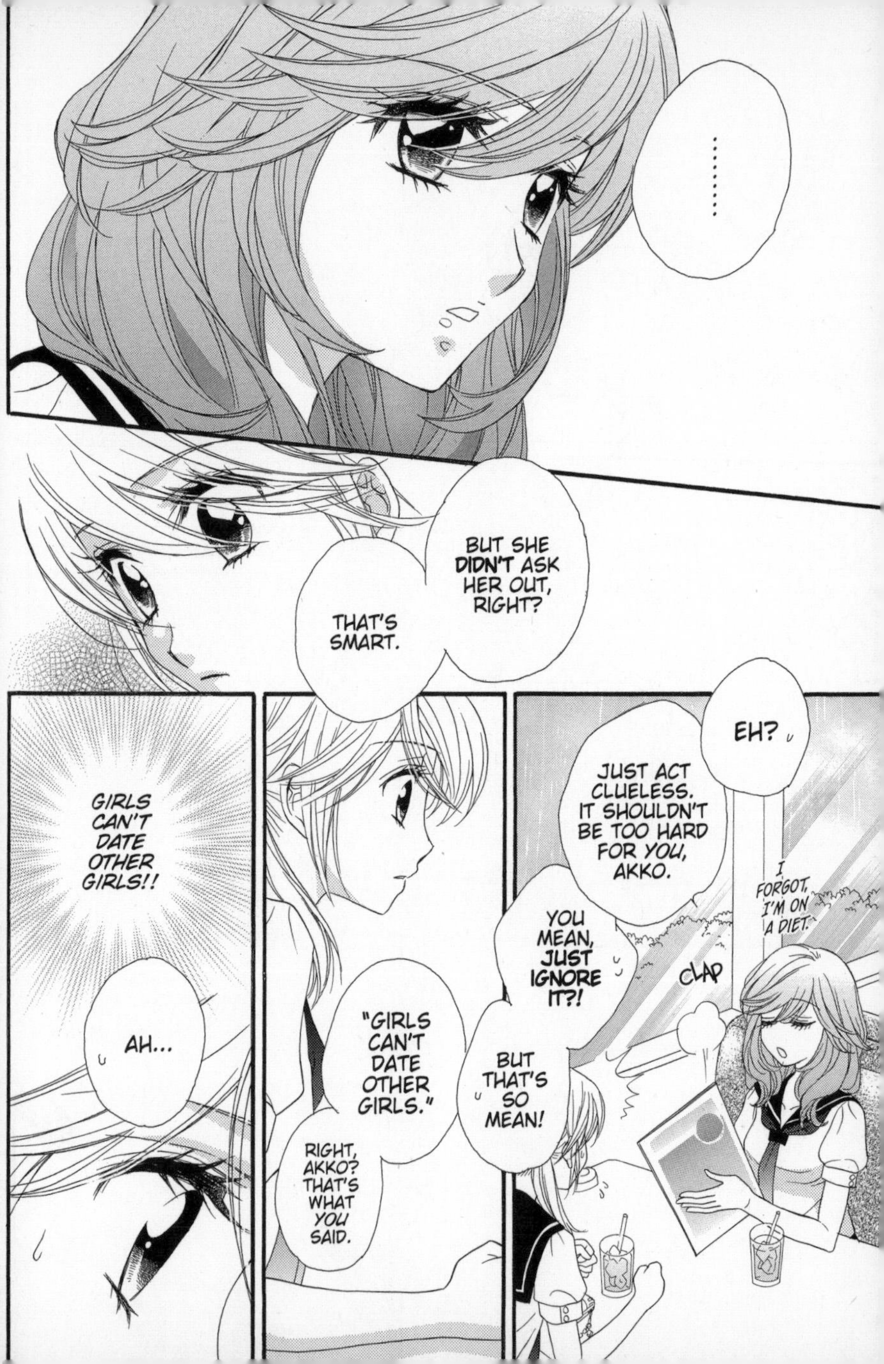
......
BUT SHE DIDN'T ASK HER OUT, RIGHT?
THAT'S SMART.
EH?
I FORGOT, I'M ON A DIET.
CLAP
JUST ACT CLUELESS. IT SHOULDN'T BE TOO HARD FOR YOU, AKKO.
YOU MEAN, JUST IGNORE IT?!
BUT THAT'S SO MEAN!
"GIRLS CAN'T DATE OTHER GIRLS."
RIGHT, AKKO? THAT'S WHAT YOU SAID.
GIRLS CAN'T DATE OTHER GIRLS!!
AH...

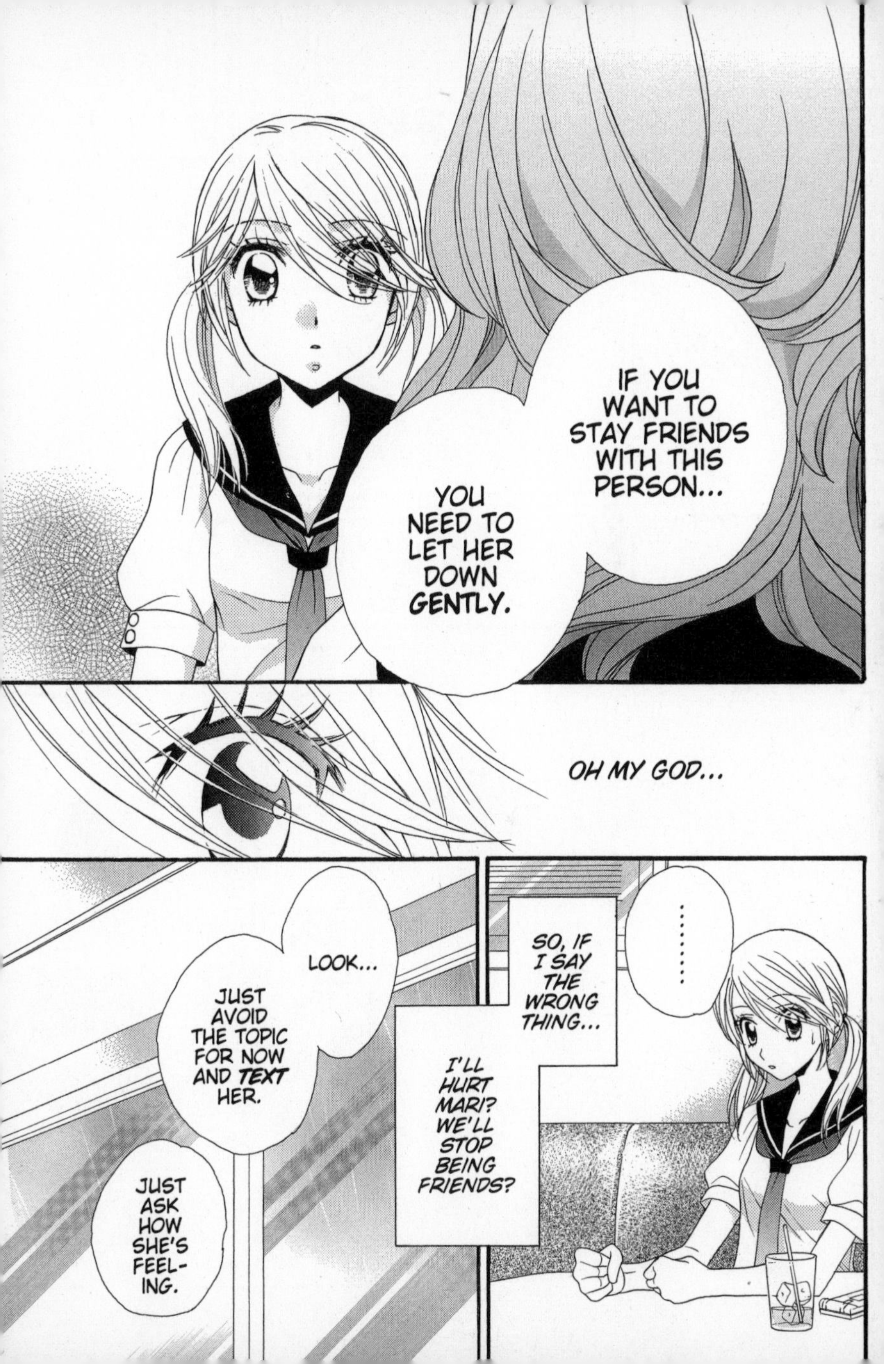
IF YOU WANT TO STAY FRIENDS WITH THIS PERSON...
YOU NEED TO LET HER DOWN GENTLY.
OH MY GOD...
......
SO, IF I SAY THE WRONG THING...
I'LL HURT MARI? WE'LL STOP BEING FRIENDS?
LOOK...
JUST AVOID THE TOPIC FOR NOW AND TEXT HER.
JUST ASK HOW SHE'S FEEL-ING.

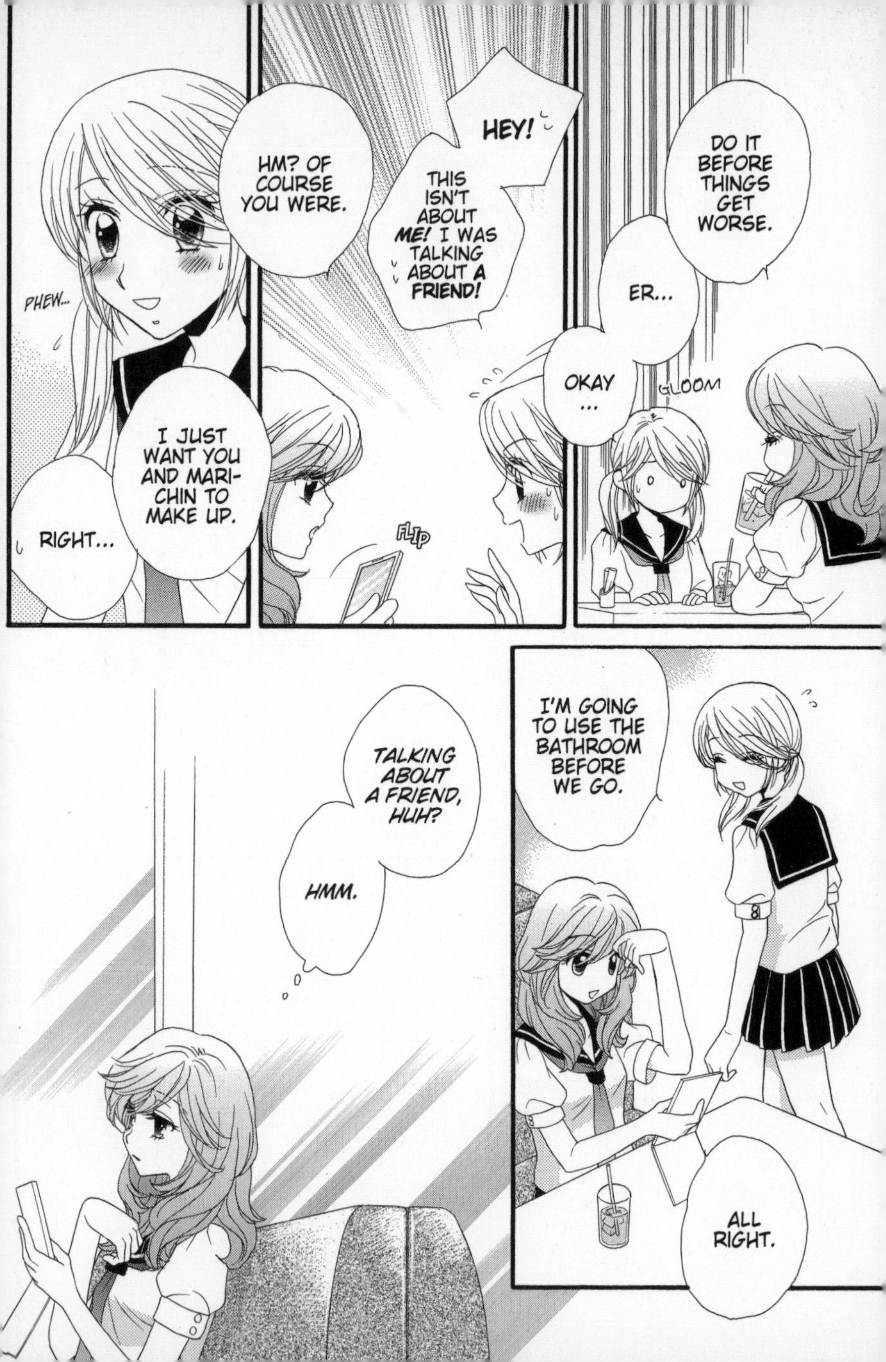
DO IT BEFORE THINGS GET WORSE.
ER...
OKAY ...
GLOOM
HEY!
THIS ISN'T ABOUT ME! I WAS TALKING ABOUT A FRIEND!
FLIP
HM? OF COURSE YOU WERE.
PHEW...
I JUST WANT YOU AND MARI-CHIN TO MAKE UP.
RIGHT...
I'M GOING TO USE THE BATHROOM BEFORE WE GO.
ALL RIGHT.
TALKING ABOUT A FRIEND, HUH?
HMM.

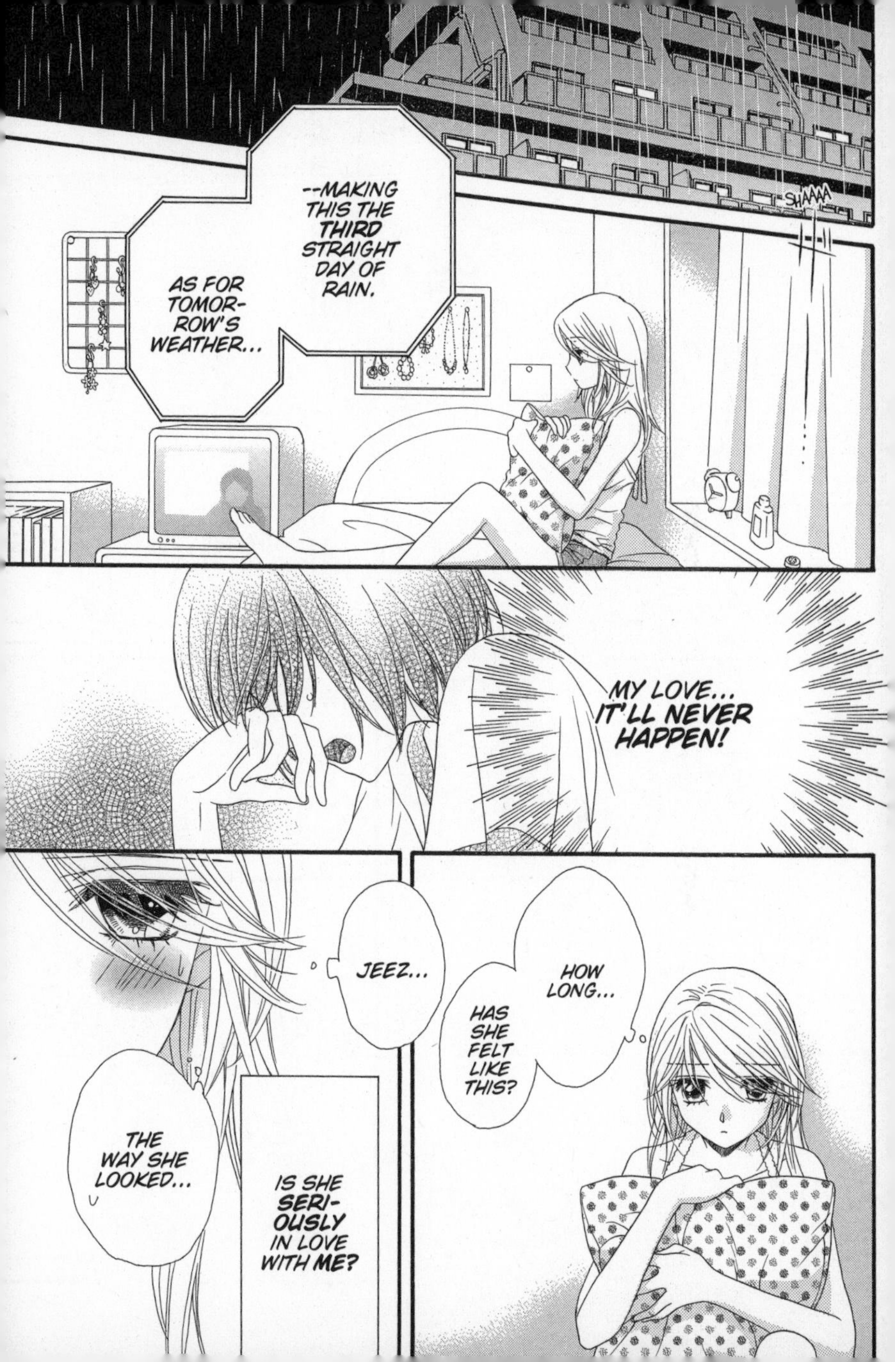
SHAAAA
--MAKING THIS THE THIRD STRAIGHT DAY OF RAIN.
AS FOR TOMORROW'S WEATHER...
MY LOVE... IT'LL NEVER HAPPEN!
HOW LONG...
HAS SHE FELT LIKE THIS?
JEEZ...
THE WAY SHE LOOKED...
IS SHE SERIOUSLY IN LOVE WITH ME?

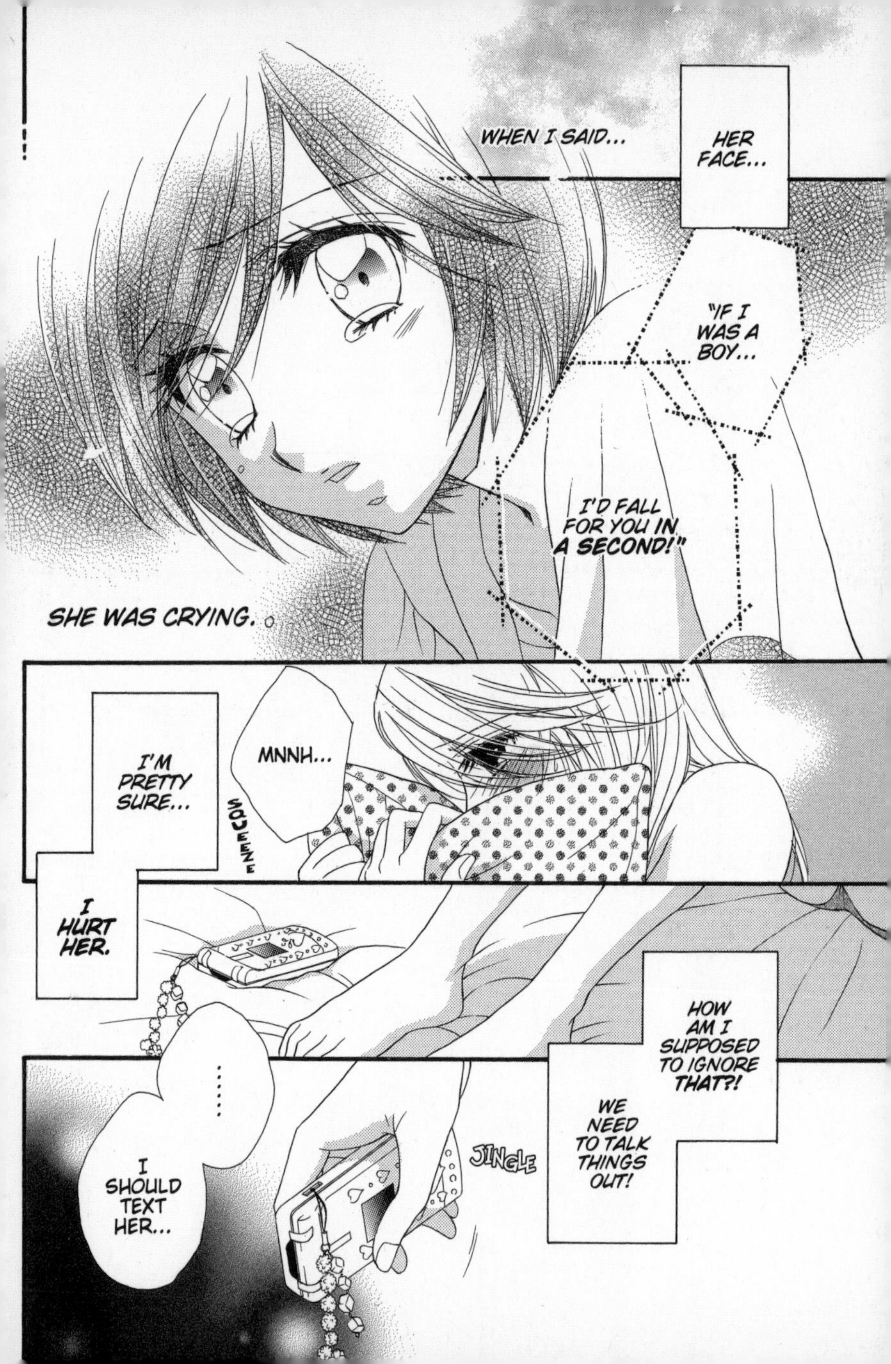
HER FACE...
WHEN I SAID...
"IF I WAS A BOY...
I'D FALL FOR YOU IN A SECOND!"
SHE WAS CRYING.
MNNH...
SQUEEZE
I'M PRETTY SURE...
I HURT HER.
HOW AM I SUPPOSED TO IGNORE THAT?!
WE NEED TO TALK THINGS OUT!
JINGLE
......
I SHOULD TEXT HER...

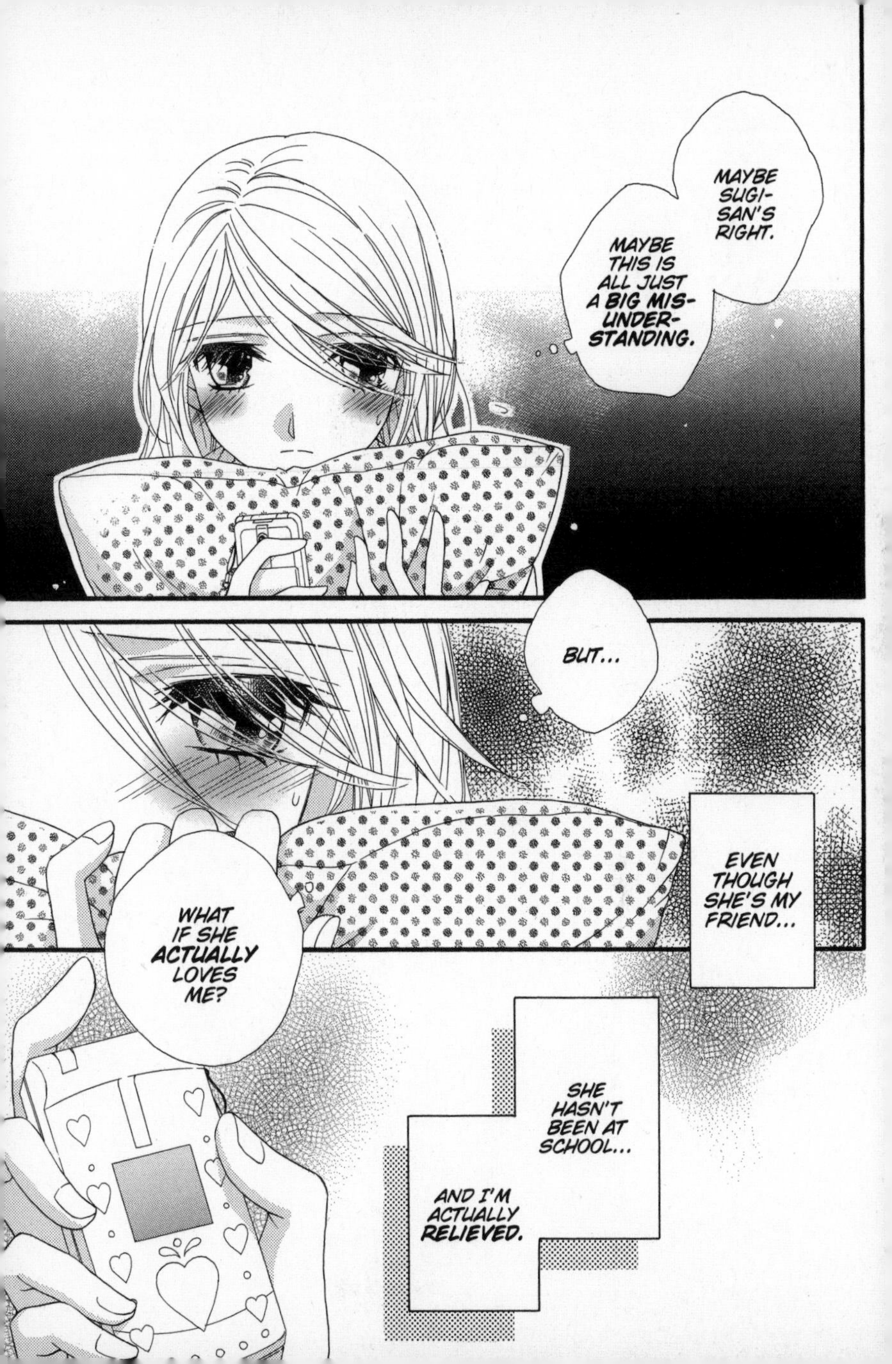
MAYBE SUGI-SAN'S RIGHT.
MAYBE THIS IS ALL JUST A BIG MIS-UNDER-STANDING.
BUT...
EVEN THOUGH SHE'S MY FRIEND...
WHAT IF SHE ACTUALLY LOVES ME?
SHE HASN'T BEEN AT SCHOOL...
AND I'M ACTUALLY RELIEVED.

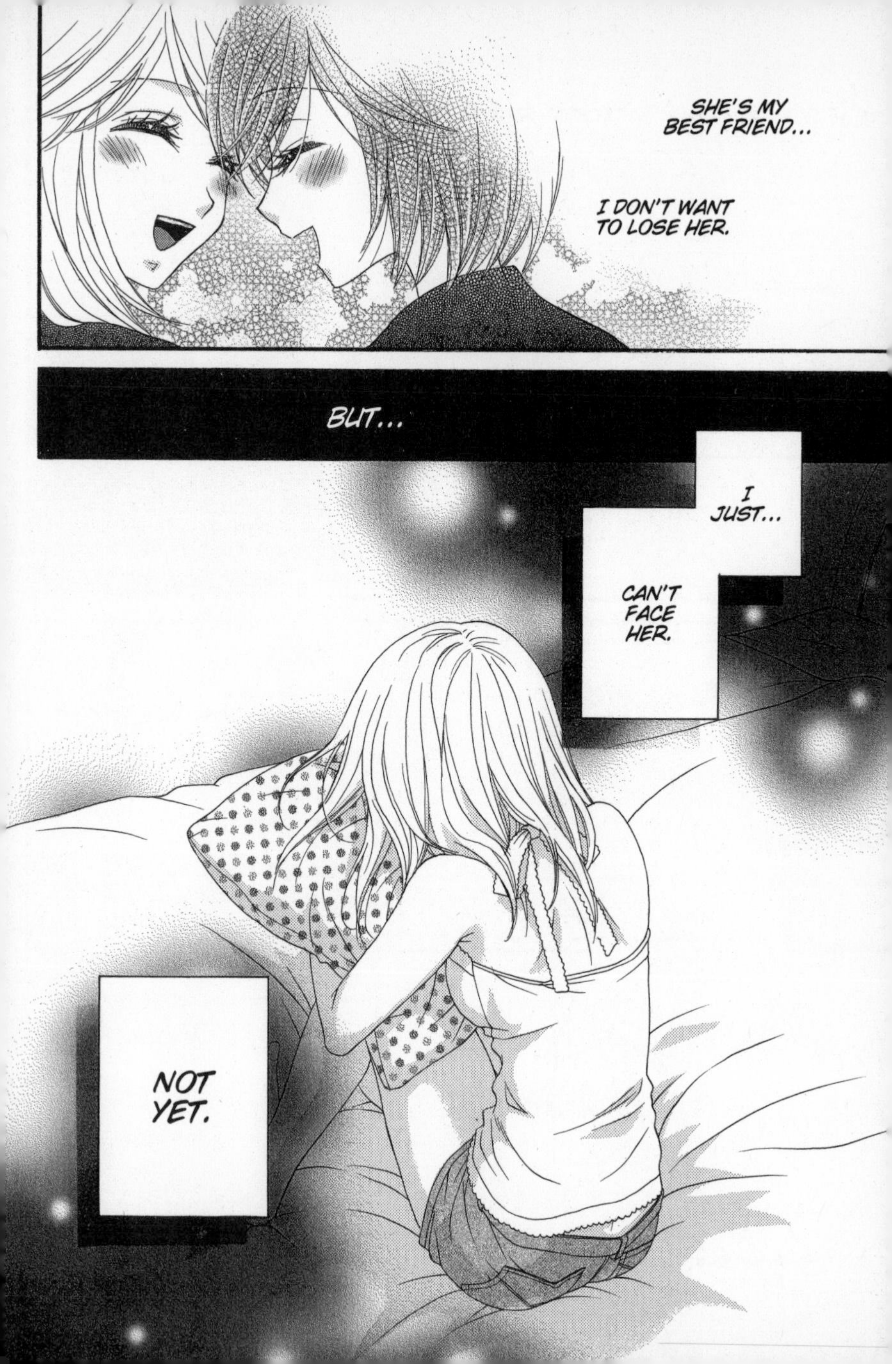
SHE'S MY BEST FRIEND...
I DON'T WANT TO LOSE HER.
BUT...
I JUST...
CAN'T FACE HER.
NOT YET.

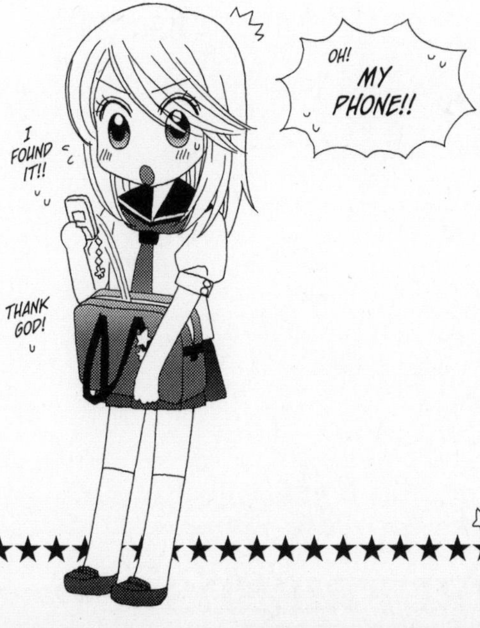
OH! MY PHONE!!
I FOUND IT!!
THANK GOD!

WHAT CAN'T YOU LIVE WITHOUT?

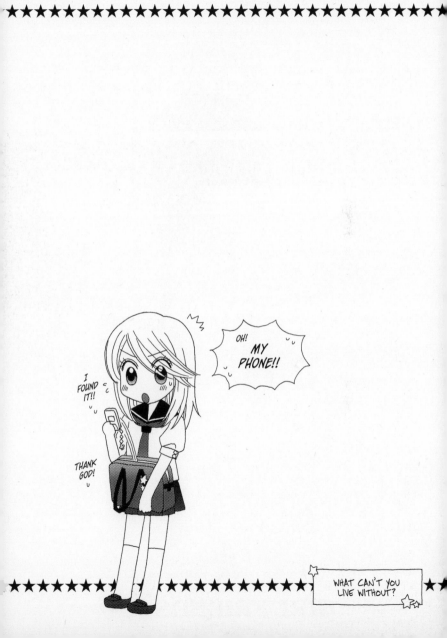

GIRL FRIENDS－ガールフレンズ－

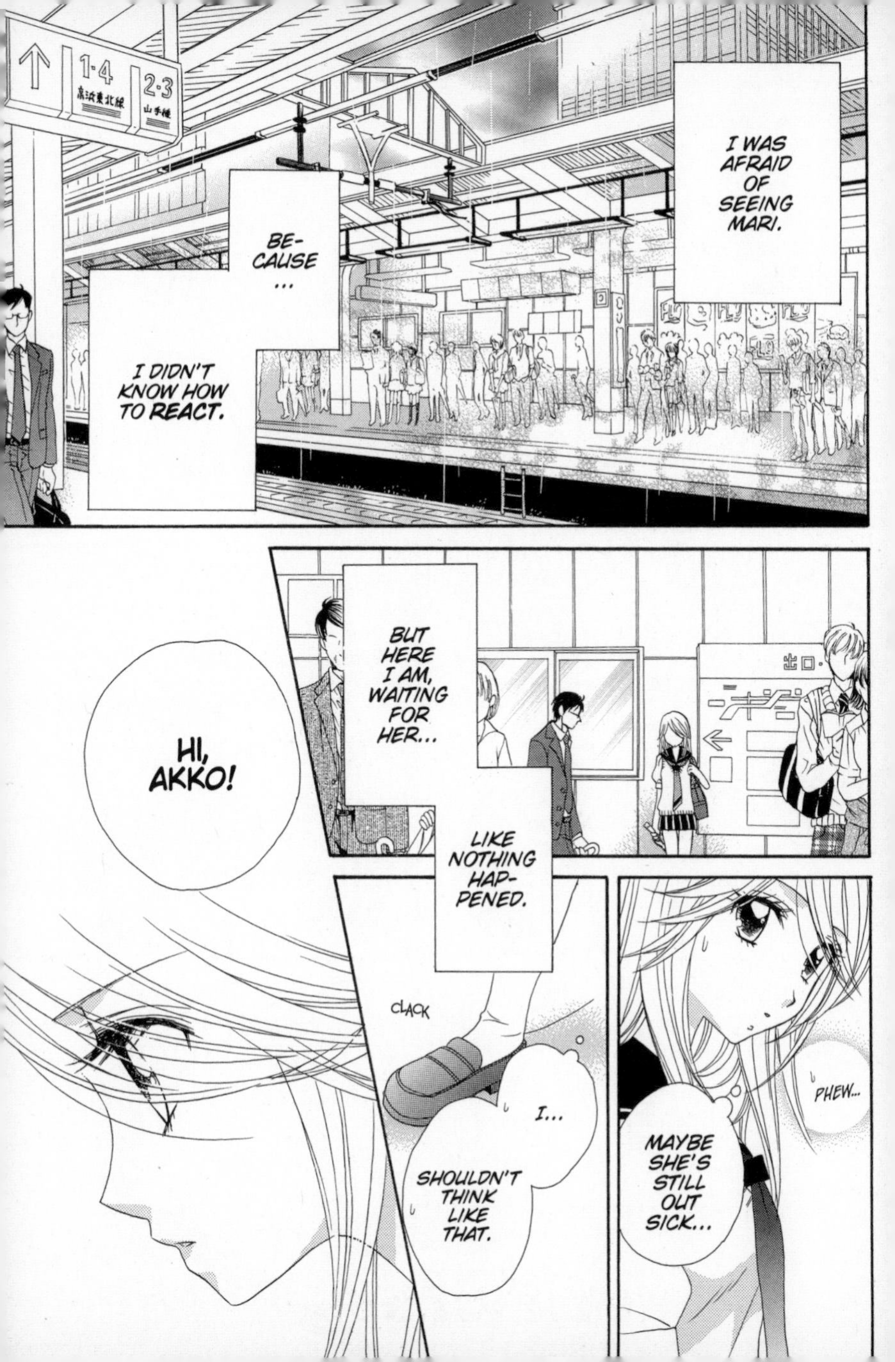
1·4
2·3
I WAS AFRAID OF SEEING MARI.
BE-CAUSE...
I DIDN'T KNOW HOW TO REACT.
BUT HERE I AM, WAITING FOR HER...
LIKE NOTHING HAP-PENED.
PHEW...
MAYBE SHE'S STILL OUT SICK...
I...
SHOULDN'T THINK LIKE THAT.
CLACK
HI, AKKO!

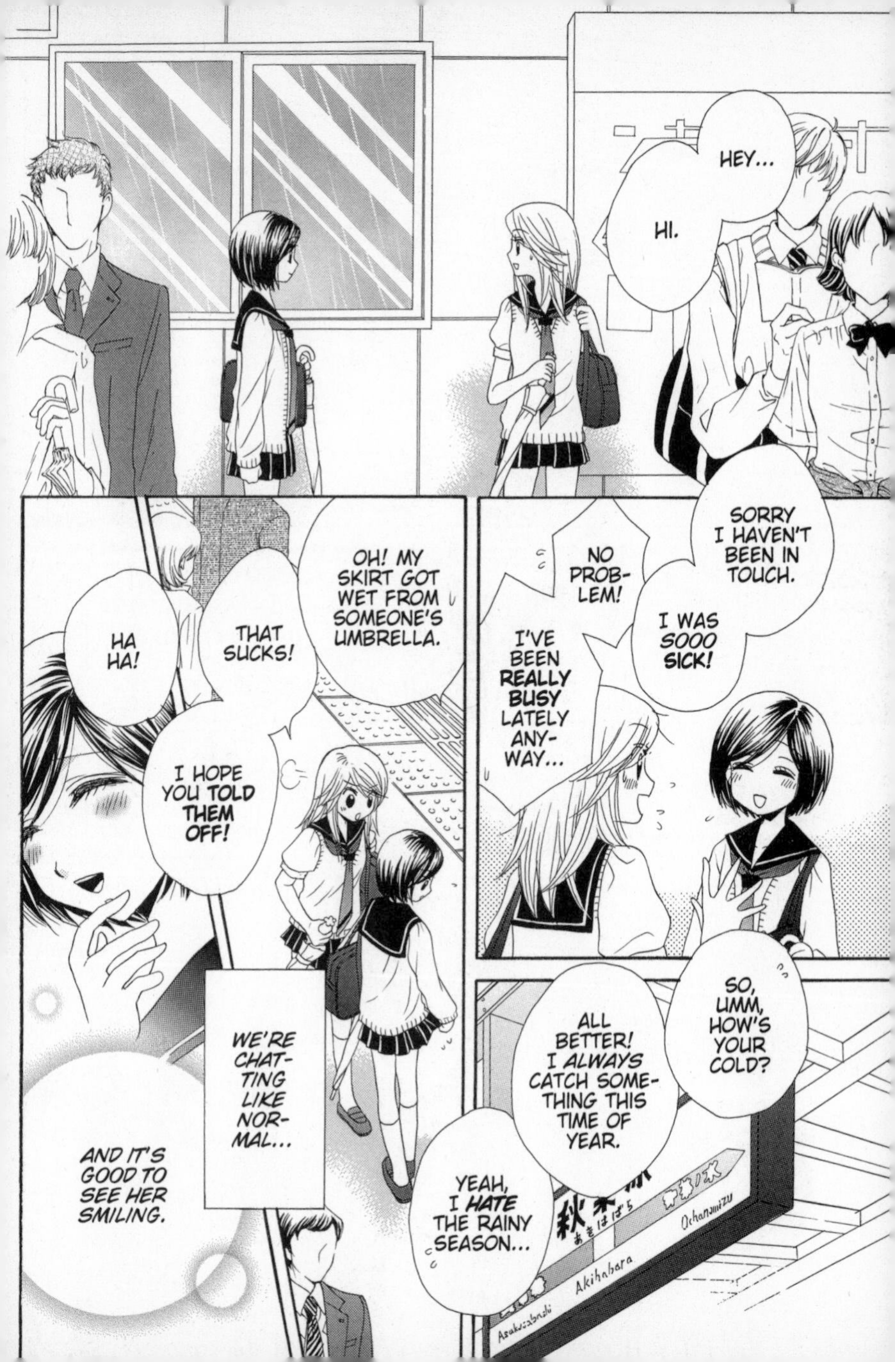
HEY...
HI.
SORRY I HAVEN'T BEEN IN TOUCH.
I WAS SOOO SICK!
NO PROB-LEM!
I'VE BEEN REALLY BUSY LATELY ANY-WAY...
SO, UMM, HOW'S YOUR COLD?
ALL BETTER! I ALWAYS CATCH SOME-THING THIS TIME OF YEAR.
YEAH, I HATE THE RAINY SEASON...
あきはばら
Akihabara
Asakusabashi
Ochanomizu
OH! MY SKIRT GOT WET FROM SOMEONE'S UMBRELLA.
THAT SUCKS!
HA HA!
I HOPE YOU TOLD THEM OFF!
WE'RE CHAT-TING LIKE NOR-MAL...
AND IT'S GOOD TO SEE HER SMILING.

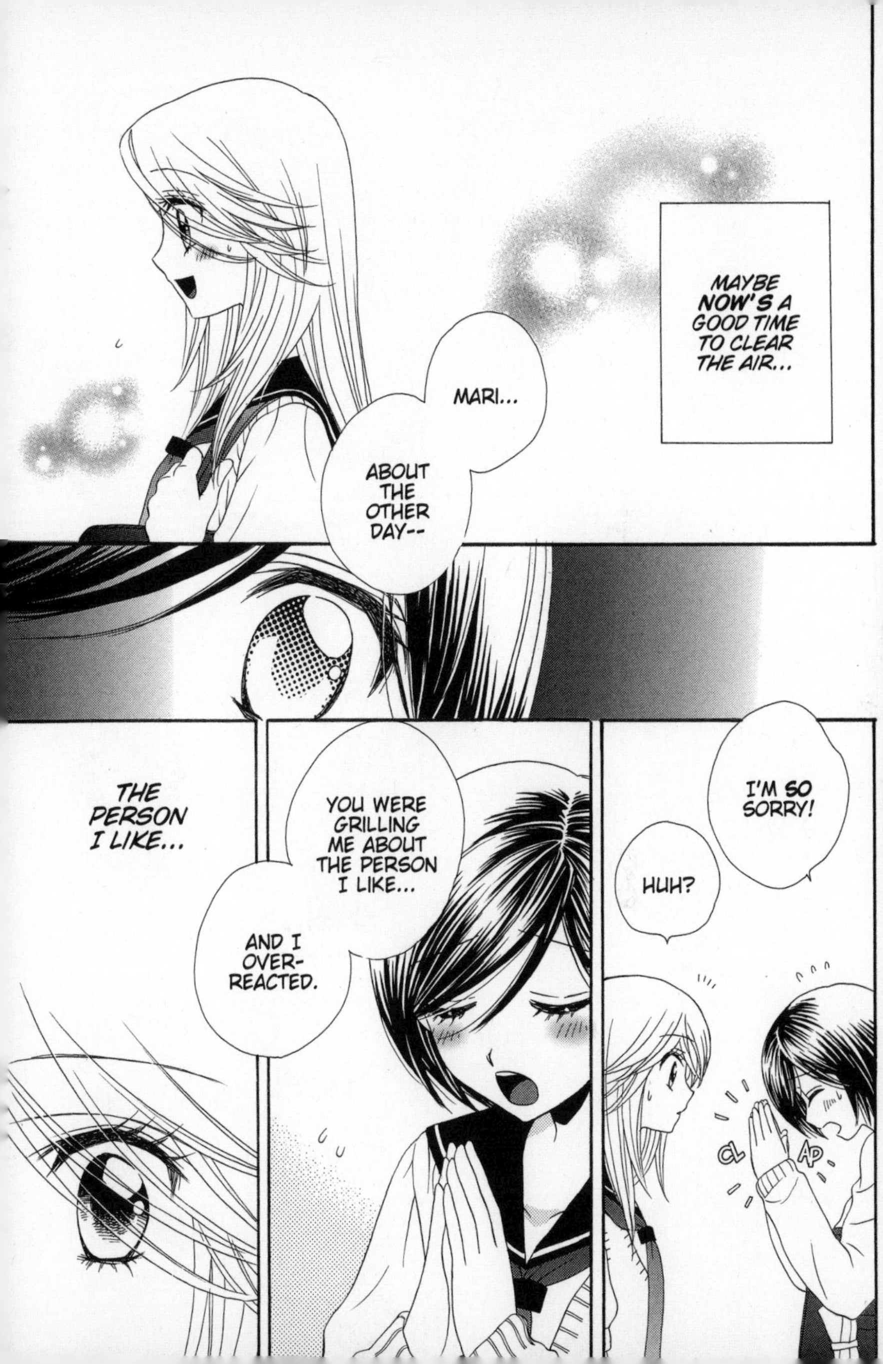
MAYBE NOW'S A GOOD TIME TO CLEAR THE AIR...
MARI...
ABOUT THE OTHER DAY--
I'M SO SORRY!
HUH?
CLAP
YOU WERE GRILLING ME ABOUT THE PERSON I LIKE...
AND I OVER-REACTED.
THE PERSON I LIKE...

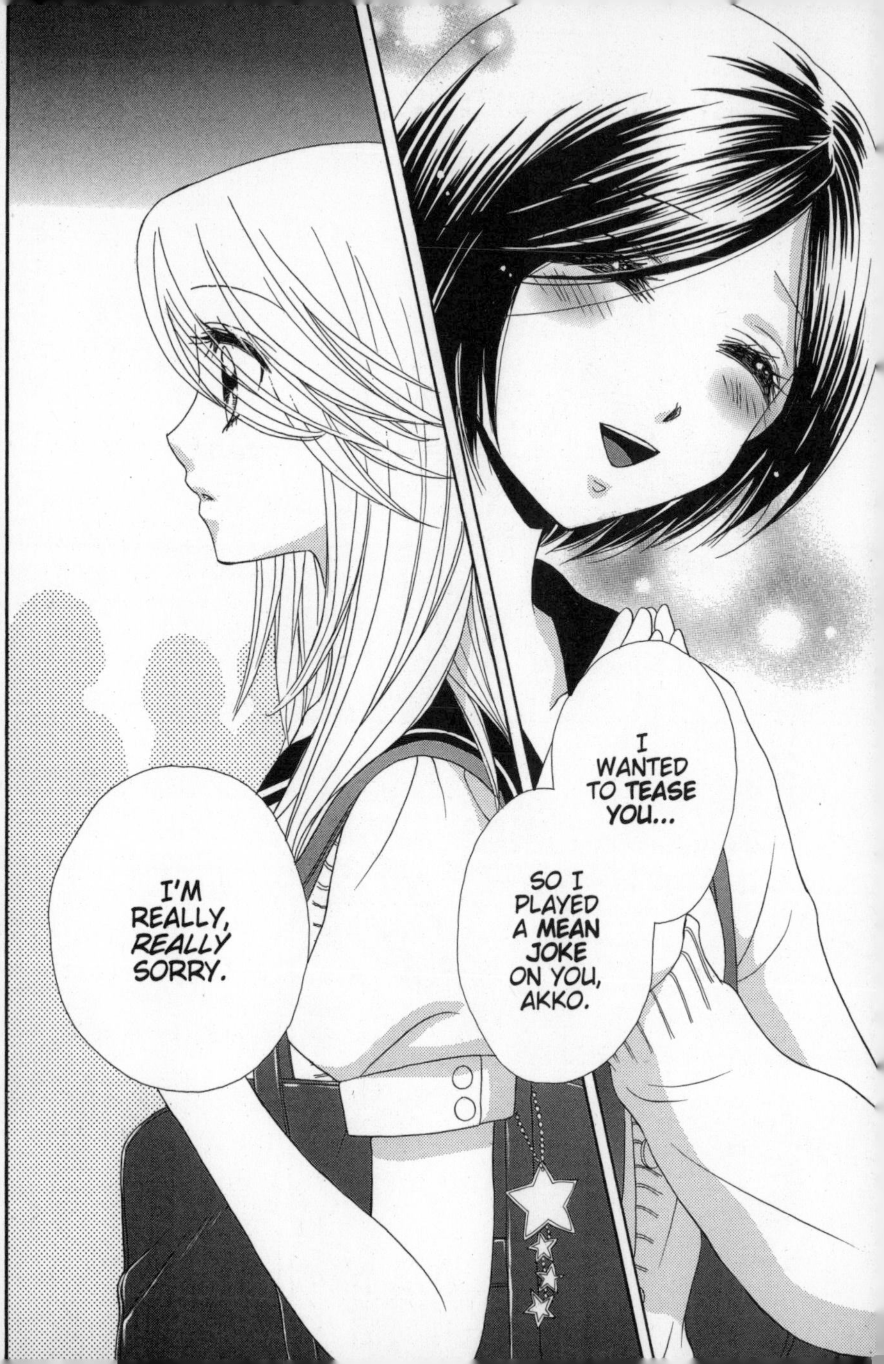
I WANTED TO TEASE YOU...
SO I PLAYED A MEAN JOKE ON YOU, AKKO.
I'M REALLY, *REALLY* SORRY.

[CHAPTER 16]

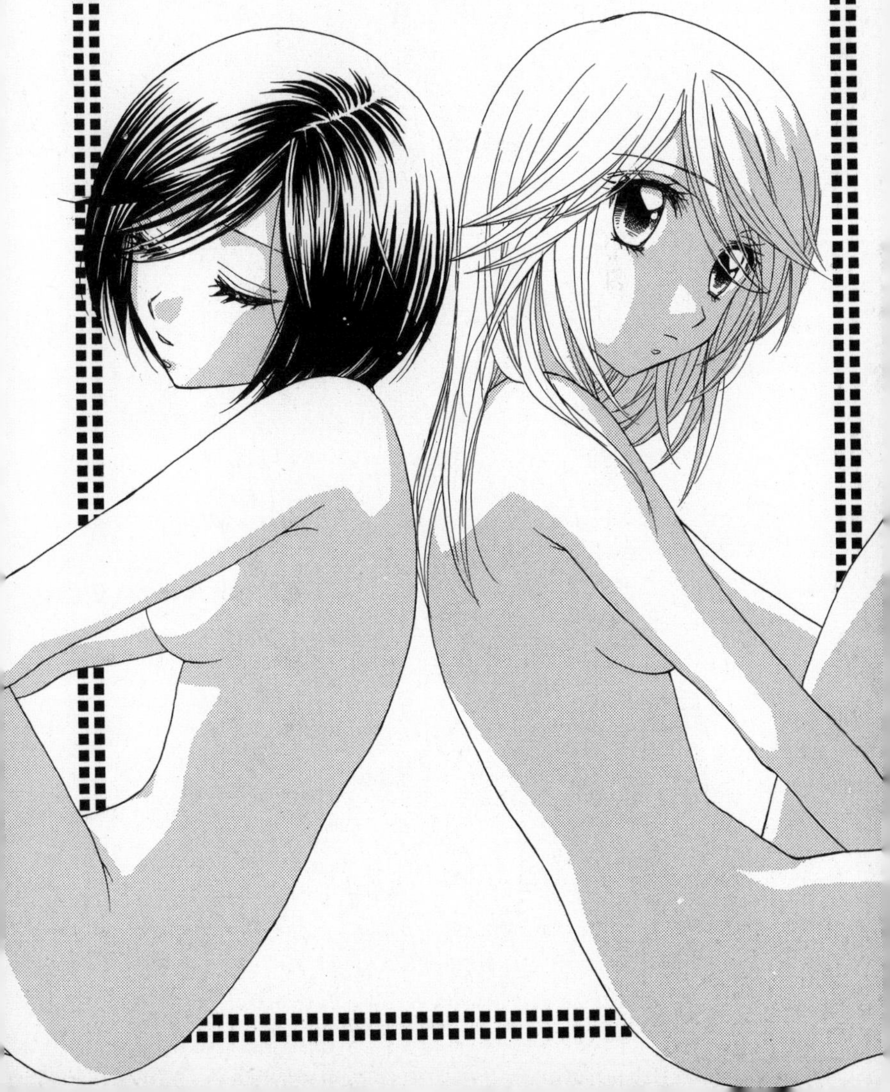

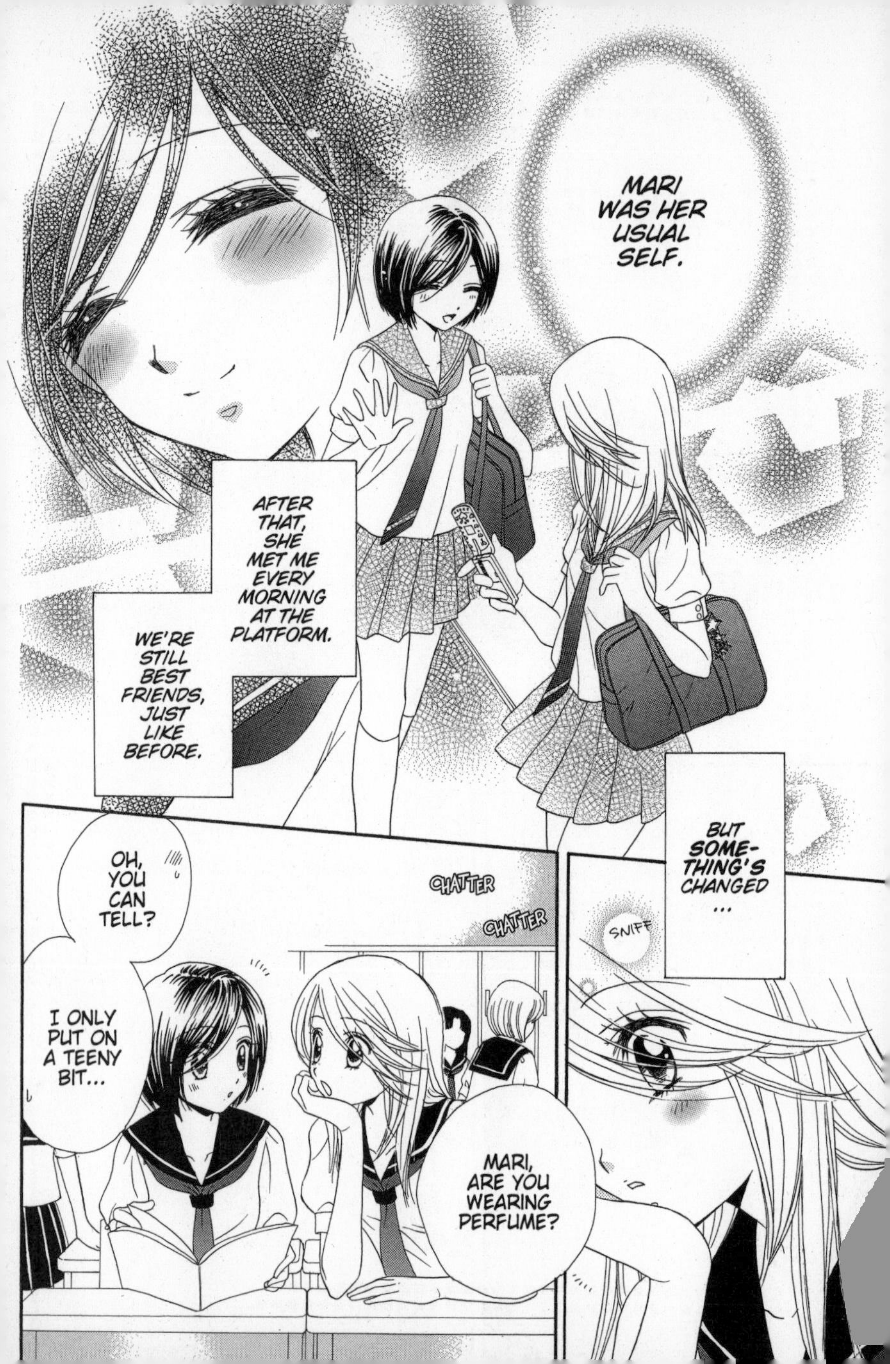
MARI WAS HER USUAL SELF.
AFTER THAT, SHE MET ME EVERY MORNING AT THE PLATFORM.
WE'RE STILL BEST FRIENDS, JUST LIKE BEFORE.
BUT SOMETHING'S CHANGED...
SNIFF
MARI, ARE YOU WEARING PERFUME?
CHATTER
CHATTER
OH, YOU CAN TELL?
I ONLY PUT ON A TEENY BIT...

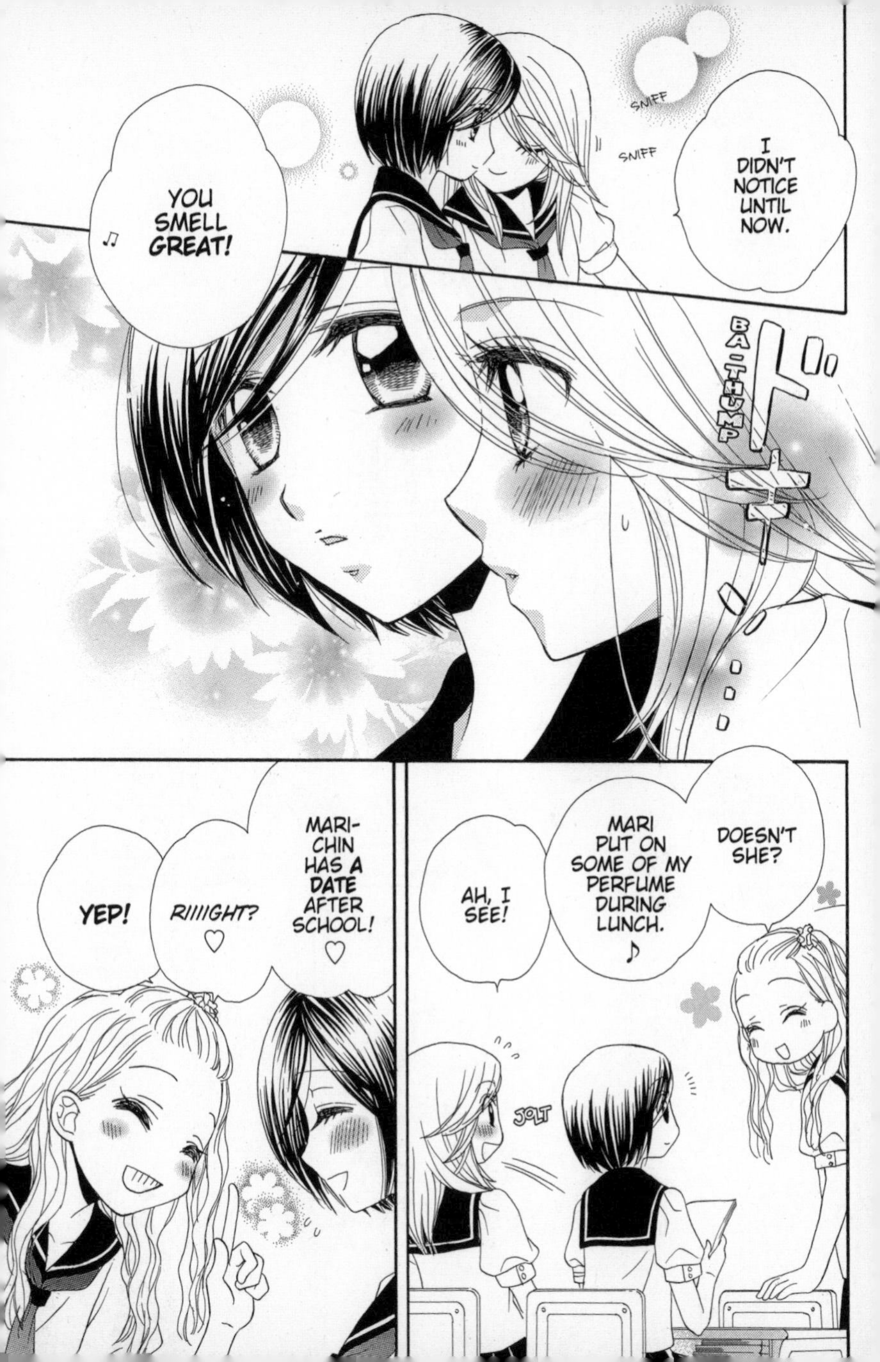
I DIDN'T NOTICE UNTIL NOW.
SNIFF
SNIFF
YOU SMELL GREAT! ♫
BA-THUMP
DOESN'T SHE?
MARI PUT ON SOME OF MY PERFUME DURING LUNCH. ♪
AH, I SEE!
JOLT
MARI-CHIN HAS A DATE AFTER SCHOOL! ♡
RIIIIGHT? ♡
YEP!

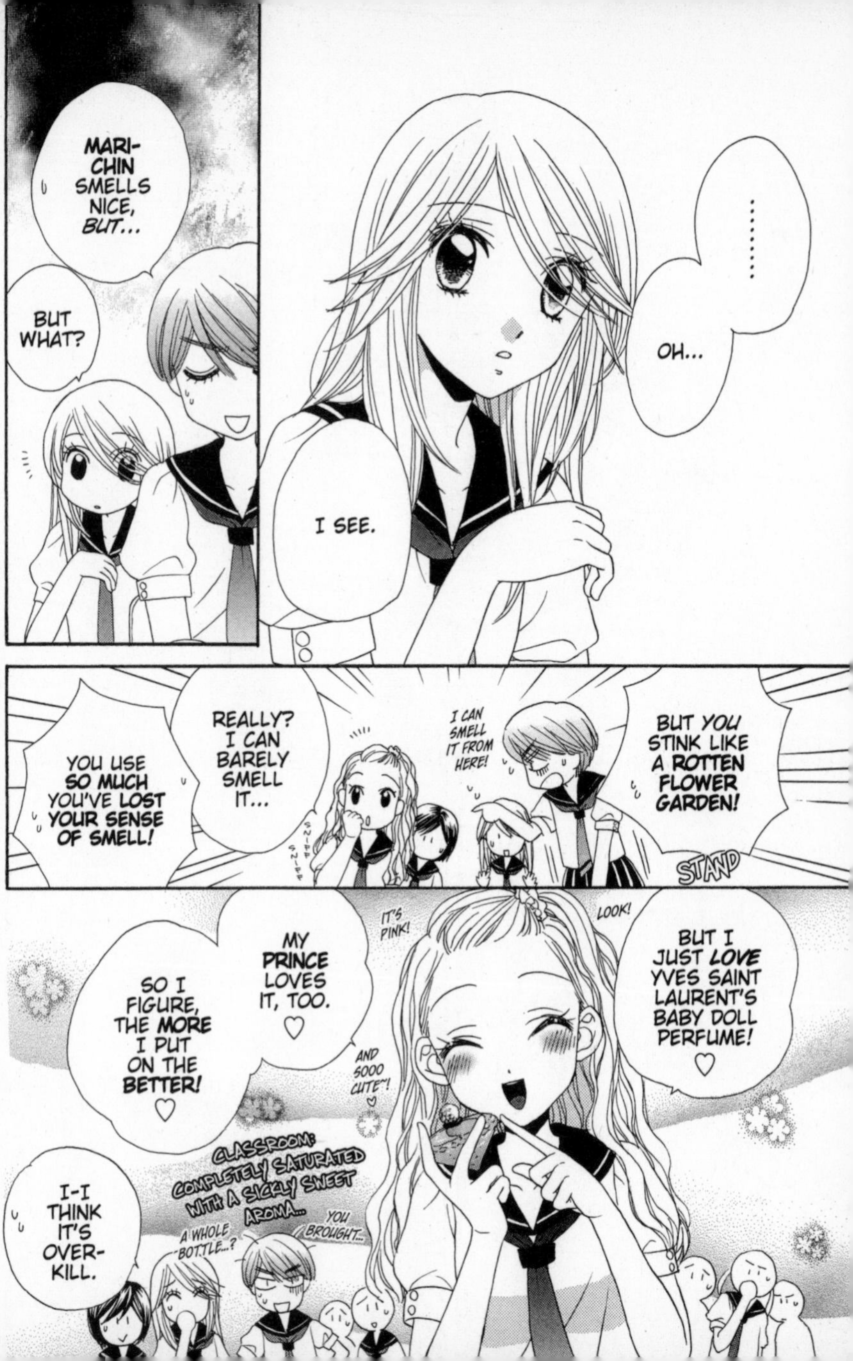
......
OH...
I SEE.
MARI-CHIN SMELLS NICE, BUT...
BUT WHAT?
BUT YOU STINK LIKE A ROTTEN FLOWER GARDEN!
STAND
I CAN SMELL IT FROM HERE!
REALLY? I CAN BARELY SMELL IT...
SNIFF SNIFF
YOU USE SO MUCH YOU'VE LOST YOUR SENSE OF SMELL!
LOOK!
BUT I JUST LOVE YVES SAINT LAURENT'S BABY DOLL PERFUME! ♡
IT'S PINK!
AND SOOO CUTE~!
MY PRINCE LOVES IT, TOO. ♡
SO I FIGURE, THE MORE I PUT ON THE BETTER! ♡
CLASSROOM: COMPLETELY SATURATED WITH A SICKLY SWEET AROMA...
YOU BROUGHT...
A WHOLE BOTTLE...?
I-I THINK IT'S OVER-KILL.

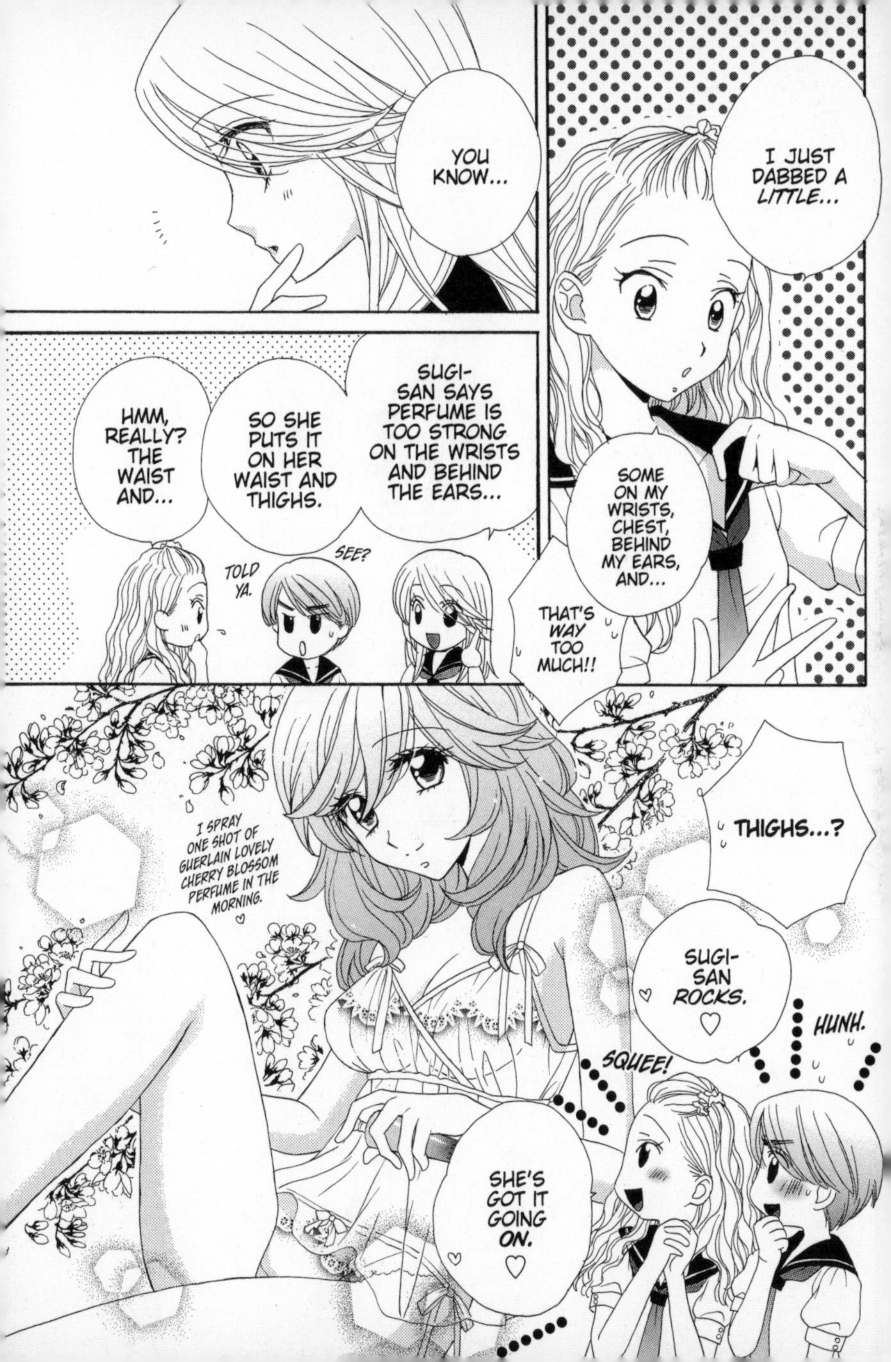
I JUST DABBED A *LITTLE...*
SOME ON MY WRISTS, CHEST, BEHIND MY EARS, AND...
THAT'S *WAY* TOO MUCH!!
YOU KNOW...
SUGI-SAN SAYS PERFUME IS TOO STRONG ON THE WRISTS AND BEHIND THE EARS...
SO SHE PUTS IT ON HER WAIST AND THIGHS.
HMM, REALLY? THE WAIST AND...
SEE?
TOLD YA.
THIGHS...?
I SPRAY ONE SHOT OF GUERLAIN LOVELY CHERRY BLOSSOM PERFUME IN THE MORNING. ♡
SUGI-SAN *ROCKS.* ♡
HUNH.
SQUEE!
SHE'S GOT IT GOING *ON.* ♡

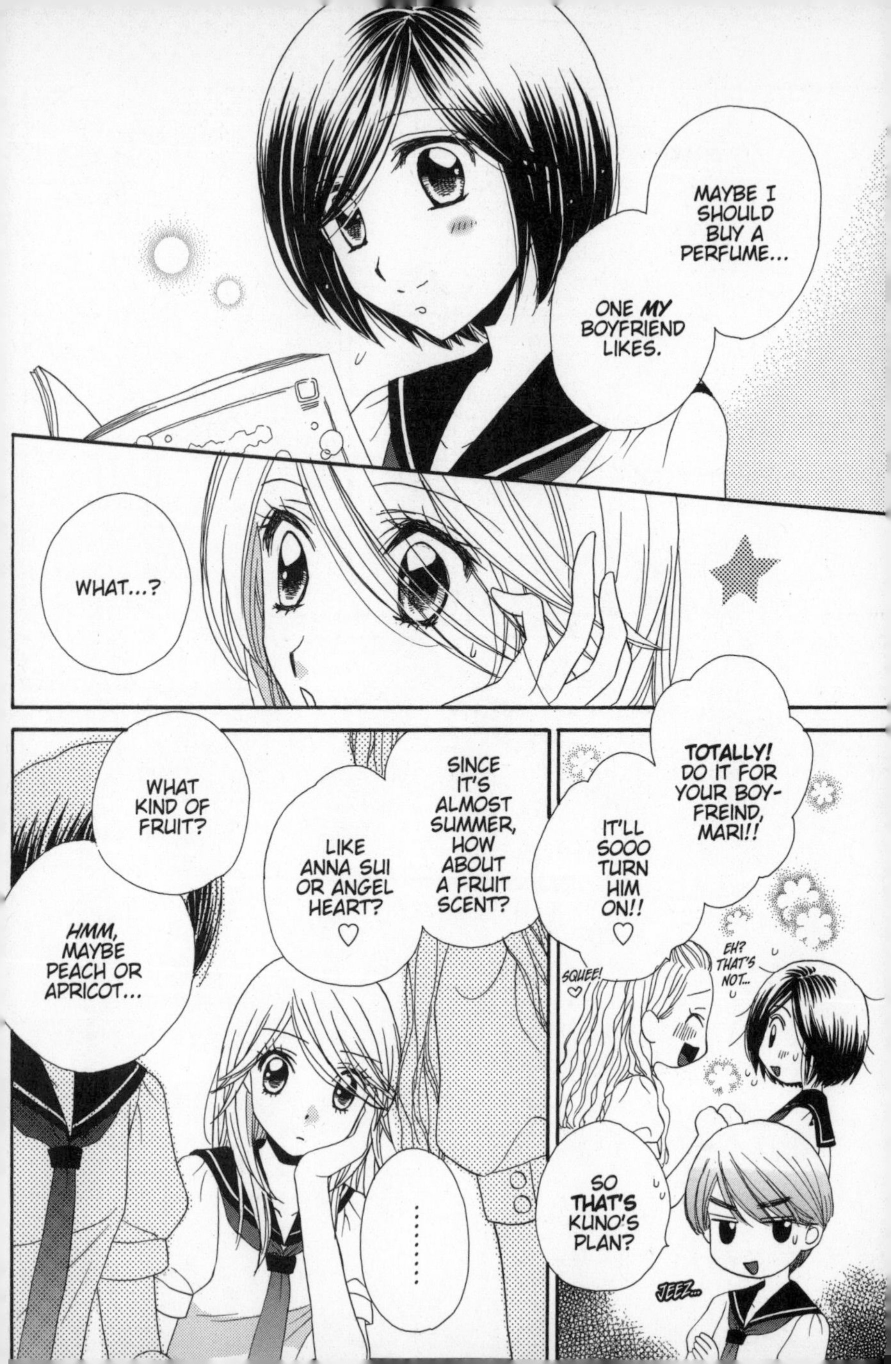
MAYBE I SHOULD BUY A PERFUME...
ONE *MY* BOYFRIEND LIKES.
WHAT...?
TOTALLY! DO IT FOR YOUR BOY-FREIND, MARI!!
IT'LL SOOO TURN HIM ON!! ♡
SQUEE! ♡
EH? THAT'S NOT...
SO THAT'S KUNO'S PLAN?
JEEZ...
SINCE IT'S ALMOST SUMMER, HOW ABOUT A FRUIT SCENT?
LIKE ANNA SUI OR ANGEL HEART? ♡
WHAT KIND OF FRUIT?
HMM, MAYBE PEACH OR APRICOT...
......

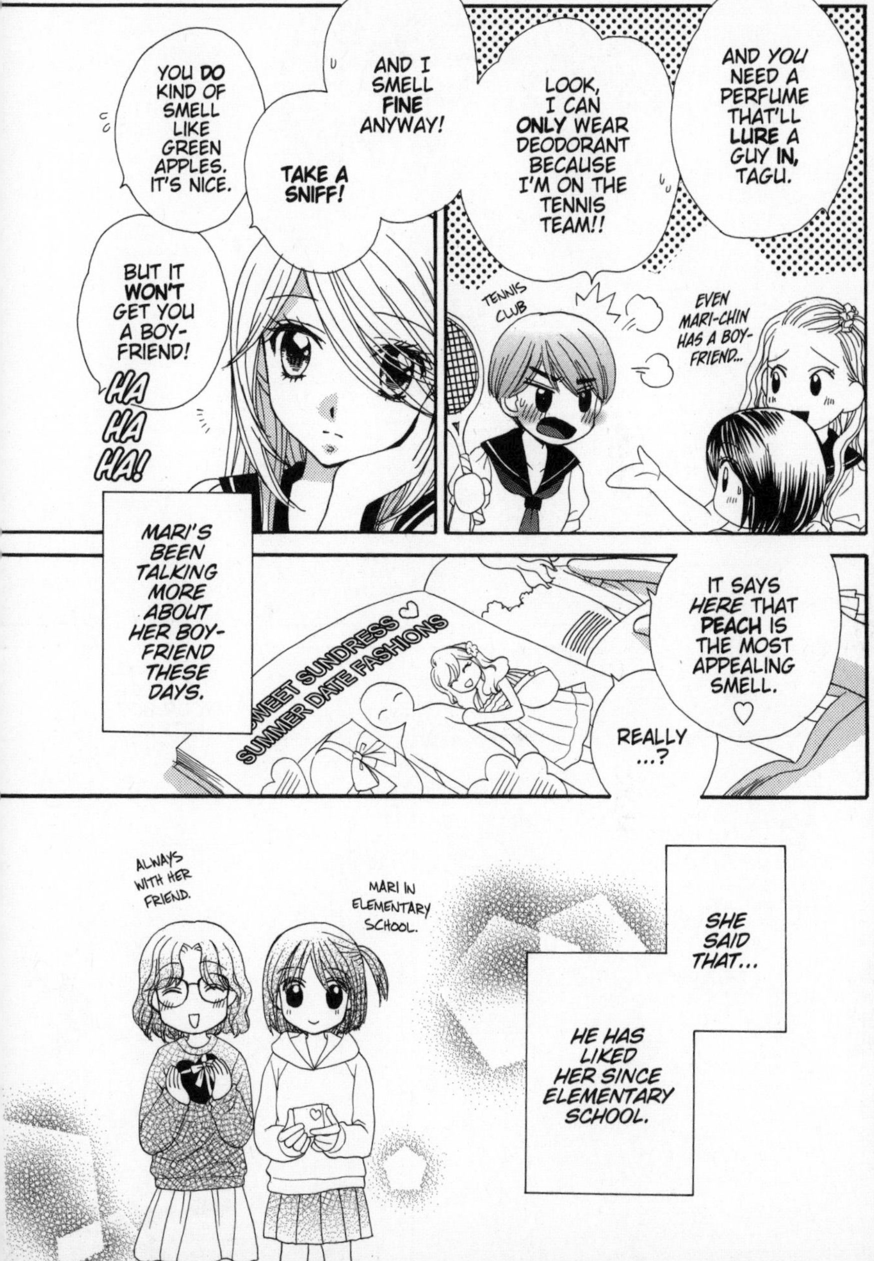
AND YOU NEED A PERFUME THAT'LL LURE A GUY IN, TAGU.
LOOK, I CAN ONLY WEAR DEODORANT BECAUSE I'M ON THE TENNIS TEAM!!
AND I SMELL FINE ANYWAY!
TAKE A SNIFF!
TENNIS CLUB
EVEN MARI-CHIN HAS A BOY-FRIEND...
YOU DO KIND OF SMELL LIKE GREEN APPLES. IT'S NICE.
BUT IT WON'T GET YOU A BOY-FRIEND!
HA HA HA!
IT SAYS HERE THAT PEACH IS THE MOST APPEALING SMELL. ♡
REALLY ...?
SWEET SUNDRESS ♡
SUMMER DATE FASHIONS
MARI'S BEEN TALKING MORE ABOUT HER BOY-FRIEND THESE DAYS.
SHE SAID THAT...
HE HAS LIKED HER SINCE ELEMENTARY SCHOOL.
MARI IN ELEMENTARY SCHOOL.
ALWAYS WITH HER FRIEND.

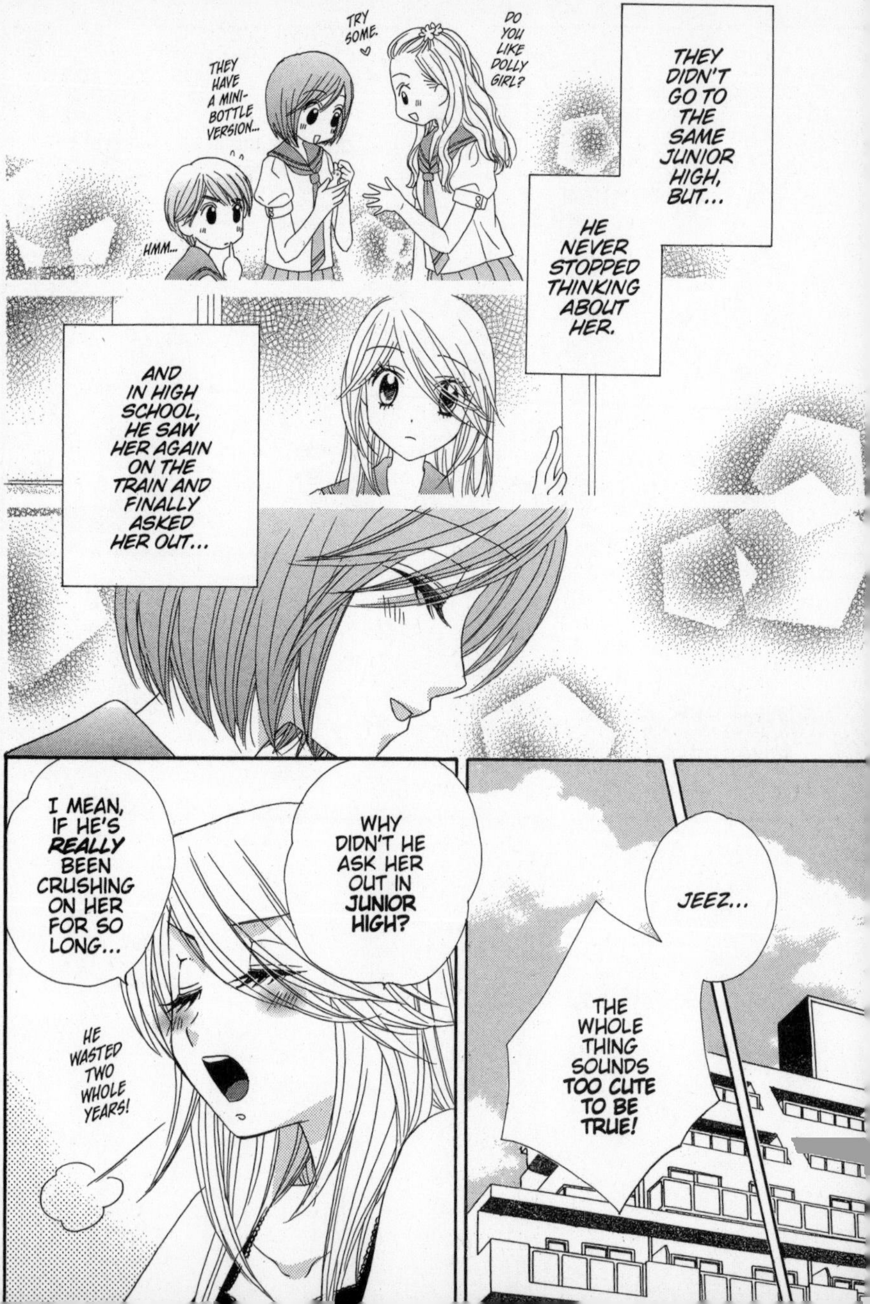

THEY DIDN'T GO TO THE SAME JUNIOR HIGH, BUT...
DO YOU LIKE DOLLY GIRL?
TRY SOME. ♡
THEY HAVE A MINI-BOTTLE VERSION...
HMM...
HE NEVER STOPPED THINKING ABOUT HER.
AND IN HIGH SCHOOL, HE SAW HER AGAIN ON THE TRAIN AND FINALLY ASKED HER OUT...
JEEZ...
THE WHOLE THING SOUNDS TOO CUTE TO BE TRUE!
WHY DIDN'T HE ASK HER OUT IN JUNIOR HIGH?
I MEAN, IF HE'S REALLY BEEN CRUSHING ON HER FOR SO LONG...
HE WASTED TWO WHOLE YEARS!

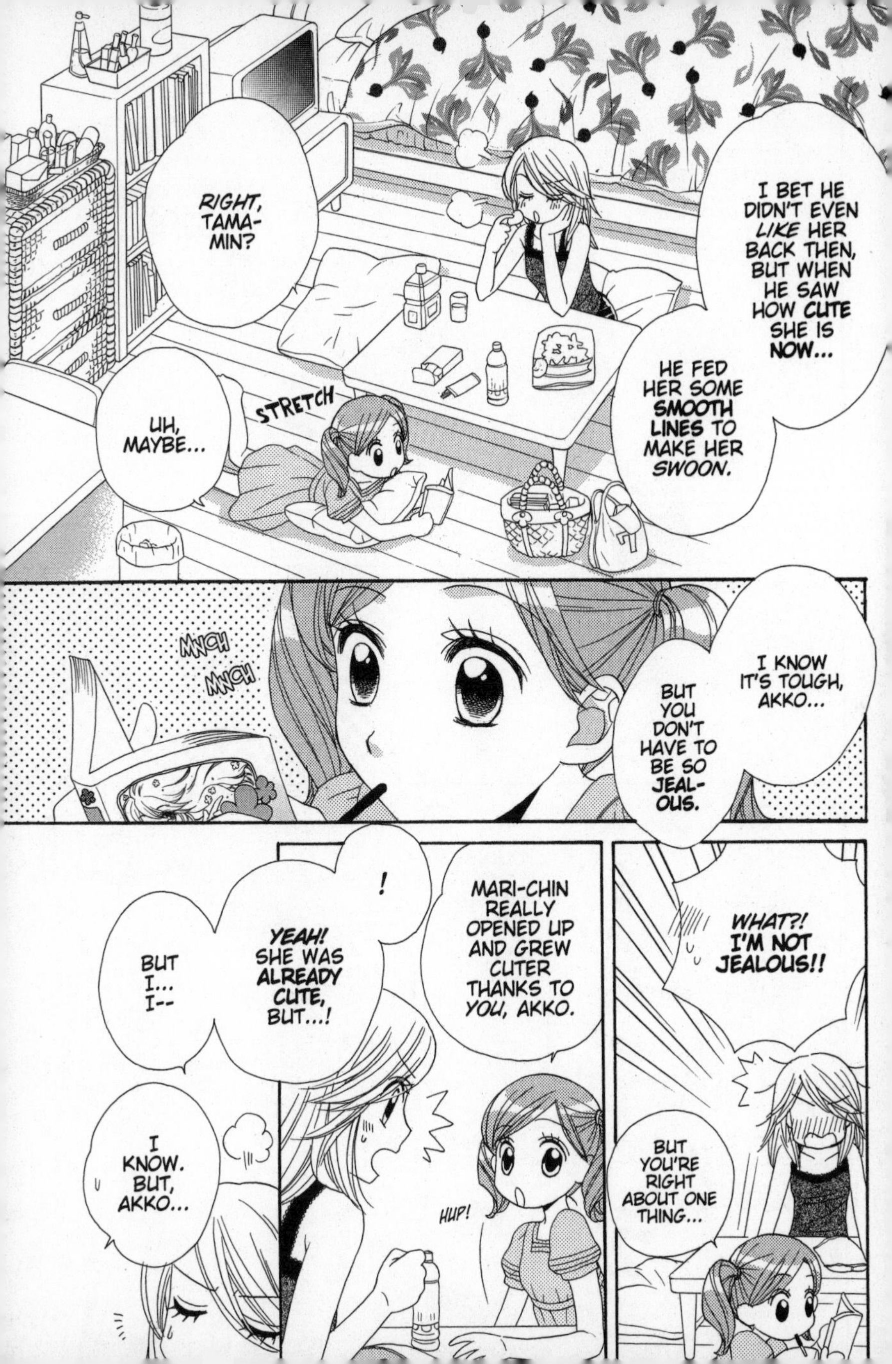
I BET HE DIDN'T EVEN *LIKE* HER BACK THEN, BUT WHEN HE SAW HOW **CUTE** SHE IS **NOW...**
HE FED HER SOME **SMOOTH LINES** TO MAKE HER *SWOON.*
RIGHT, TAMA-MIN?
STRETCH
UH, MAYBE...
I KNOW IT'S TOUGH, AKKO...
BUT YOU DON'T HAVE TO BE SO JEAL-OUS.
MNCH
MNCH
WHAT?! **I'M NOT JEALOUS!!**
BUT YOU'RE RIGHT ABOUT ONE THING...
MARI-CHIN REALLY OPENED UP AND GREW CUTER THANKS TO *YOU,* AKKO.
!
YEAH! SHE WAS **ALREADY CUTE,** BUT...!
HUP!
BUT I... I--
I KNOW. BUT, AKKO...

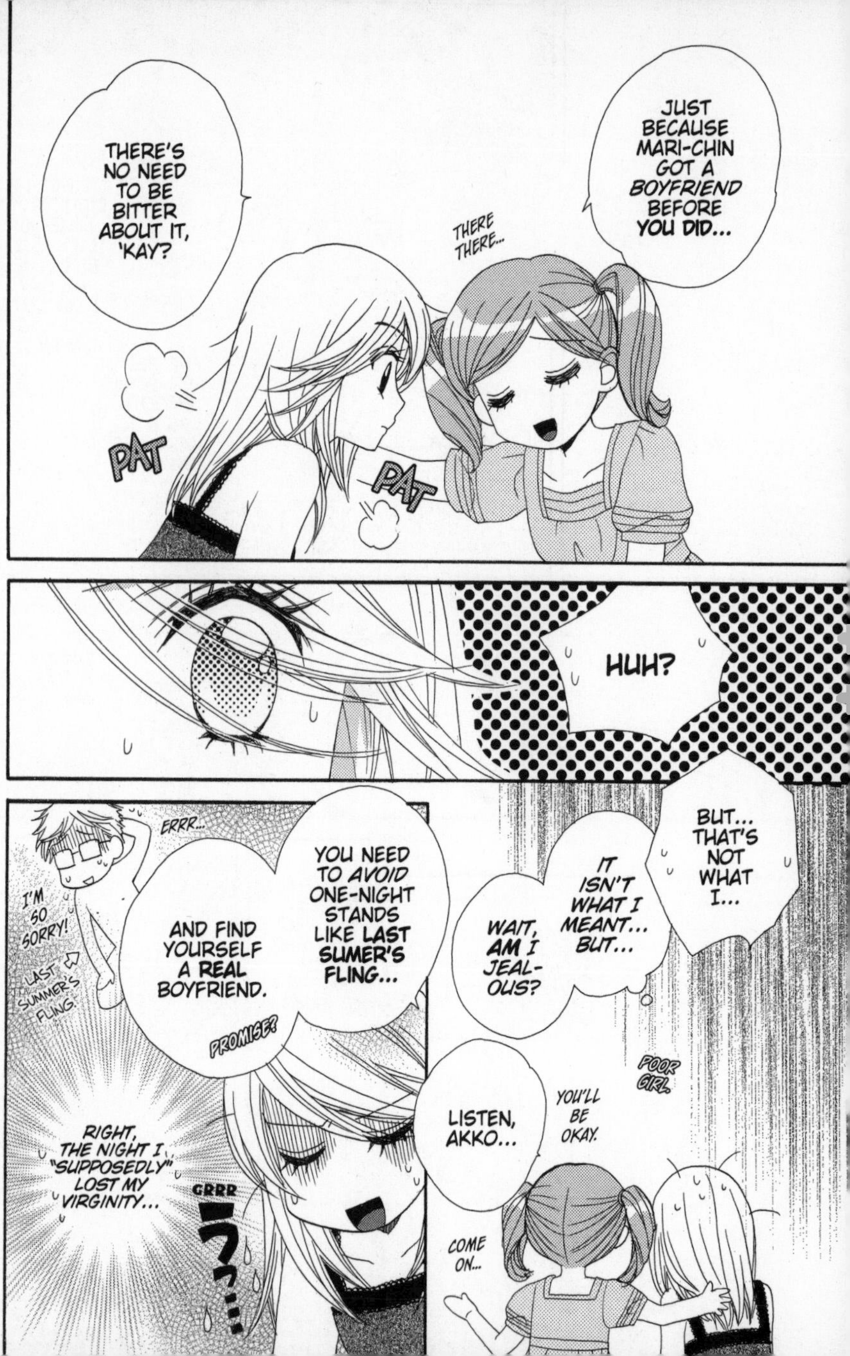
JUST BECAUSE MARI-CHIN GOT A BOYFRIEND BEFORE YOU DID...
THERE THERE...
THERE'S NO NEED TO BE BITTER ABOUT IT, 'KAY?
PAT
PAT
HUH?
BUT... THAT'S NOT WHAT I...
IT ISN'T WHAT I MEANT... BUT...
WAIT, AM I JEALOUS?
YOU NEED TO AVOID ONE-NIGHT STANDS LIKE LAST SUMER'S FLING...
AND FIND YOURSELF A REAL BOYFRIEND.
PROMISE?
POOR GIRL.
YOU'LL BE OKAY.
LISTEN, AKKO...
COME ON...
ERRR...
I'M SO SORRY!
LAST SUMMER'S FLING.
RIGHT, THE NIGHT I "SUPPOSEDLY" LOST MY VIRGINITY...
GRRR

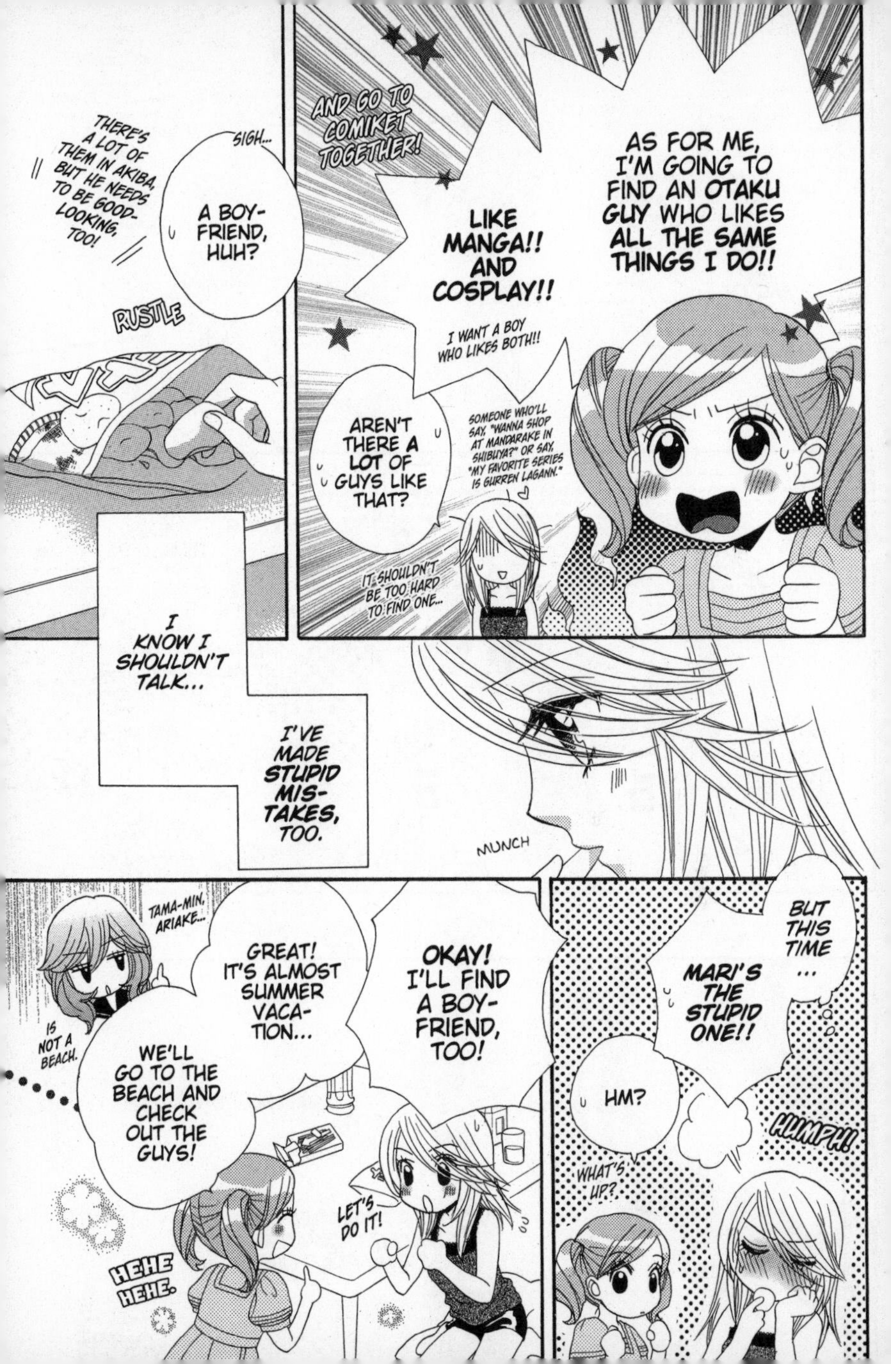
AS FOR ME, I'M GOING TO FIND AN OTAKU GUY WHO LIKES ALL THE SAME THINGS I DO!!
AND GO TO COMIKET TOGETHER!
LIKE MANGA!! AND COSPLAY!!
I WANT A BOY WHO LIKES BOTH!!
SOMEONE WHO'LL SAY, "WANNA SHOP AT MANDARAKE IN SHIBUYA?" OR SAY, "MY FAVORITE SERIES IS GURREN LAGANN."
AREN'T THERE A LOT OF GUYS LIKE THAT?
IT SHOULDN'T BE TOO HARD TO FIND ONE...
SIGH...
A BOY-FRIEND, HUH?
THERE'S A LOT OF THEM IN AKIBA, BUT HE NEEDS TO BE GOOD-LOOKING, TOO!
RUSTLE
I KNOW I SHOULDN'T TALK...
I'VE MADE STUPID MIS-TAKES, TOO.
MUNCH
BUT THIS TIME...
MARI'S THE STUPID ONE!!
HUMPH!!
HM?
WHAT'S UP?
OKAY! I'LL FIND A BOY-FRIEND, TOO!
GREAT! IT'S ALMOST SUMMER VACA-TION...
TAMA-MIN, ARIAKE...
IS NOT A BEACH.
WE'LL GO TO THE BEACH AND CHECK OUT THE GUYS!
LET'S DO IT!
HEHE HEHE.

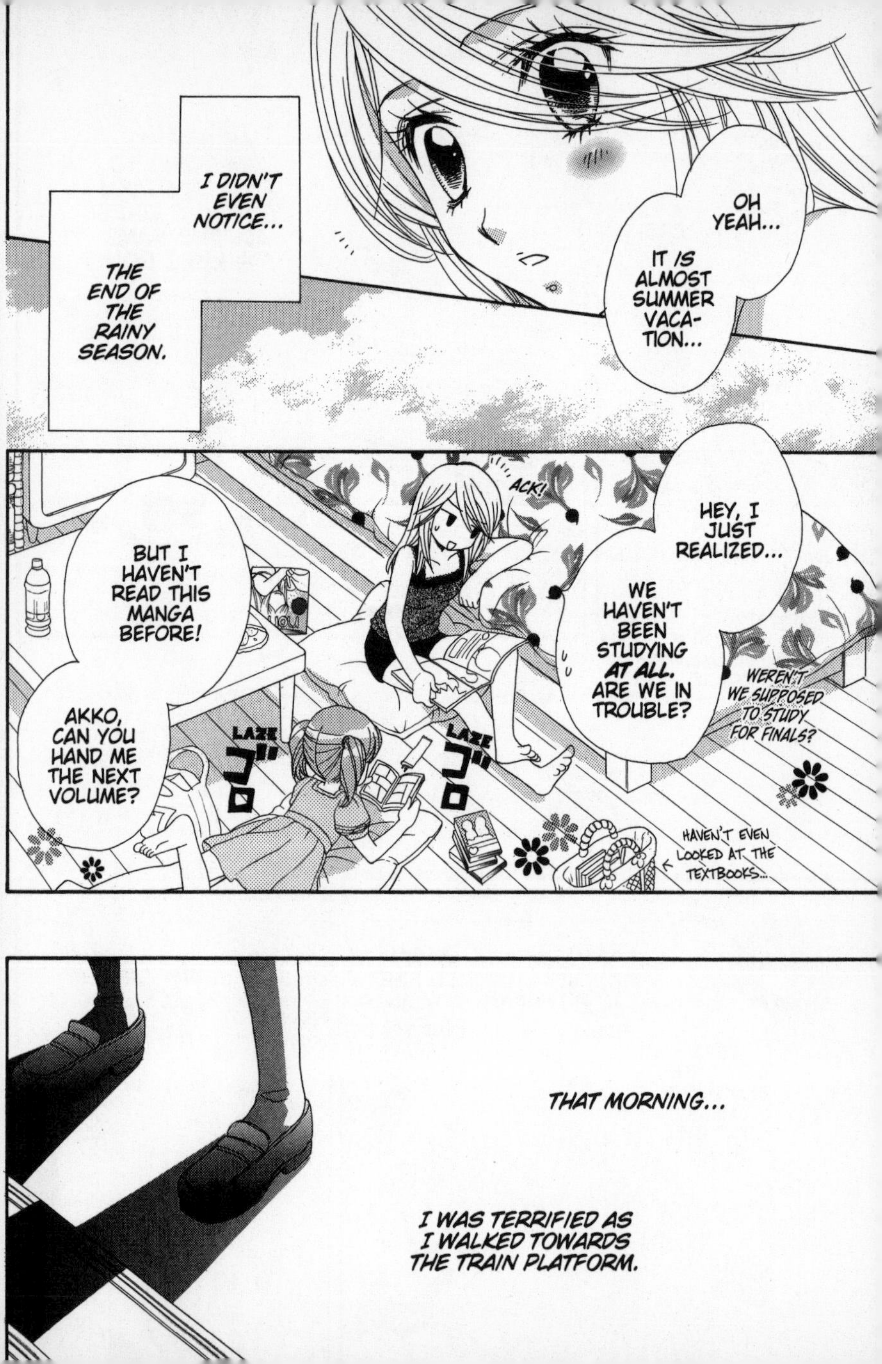
OH YEAH... IT IS ALMOST SUMMER VACATION...
I DIDN'T EVEN NOTICE... THE END OF THE RAINY SEASON.
HEY, I JUST REALIZED... WE HAVEN'T BEEN STUDYING AT ALL. ARE WE IN TROUBLE?
WEREN'T WE SUPPOSED TO STUDY FOR FINALS?
ACK!
HAVEN'T EVEN LOOKED AT THE TEXTBOOKS...
LAZE ゴロ
LAZE ゴロ
BUT I HAVEN'T READ THIS MANGA BEFORE!
AKKO, CAN YOU HAND ME THE NEXT VOLUME?
THAT MORNING...
I WAS TERRIFIED AS I WALKED TOWARDS THE TRAIN PLATFORM.

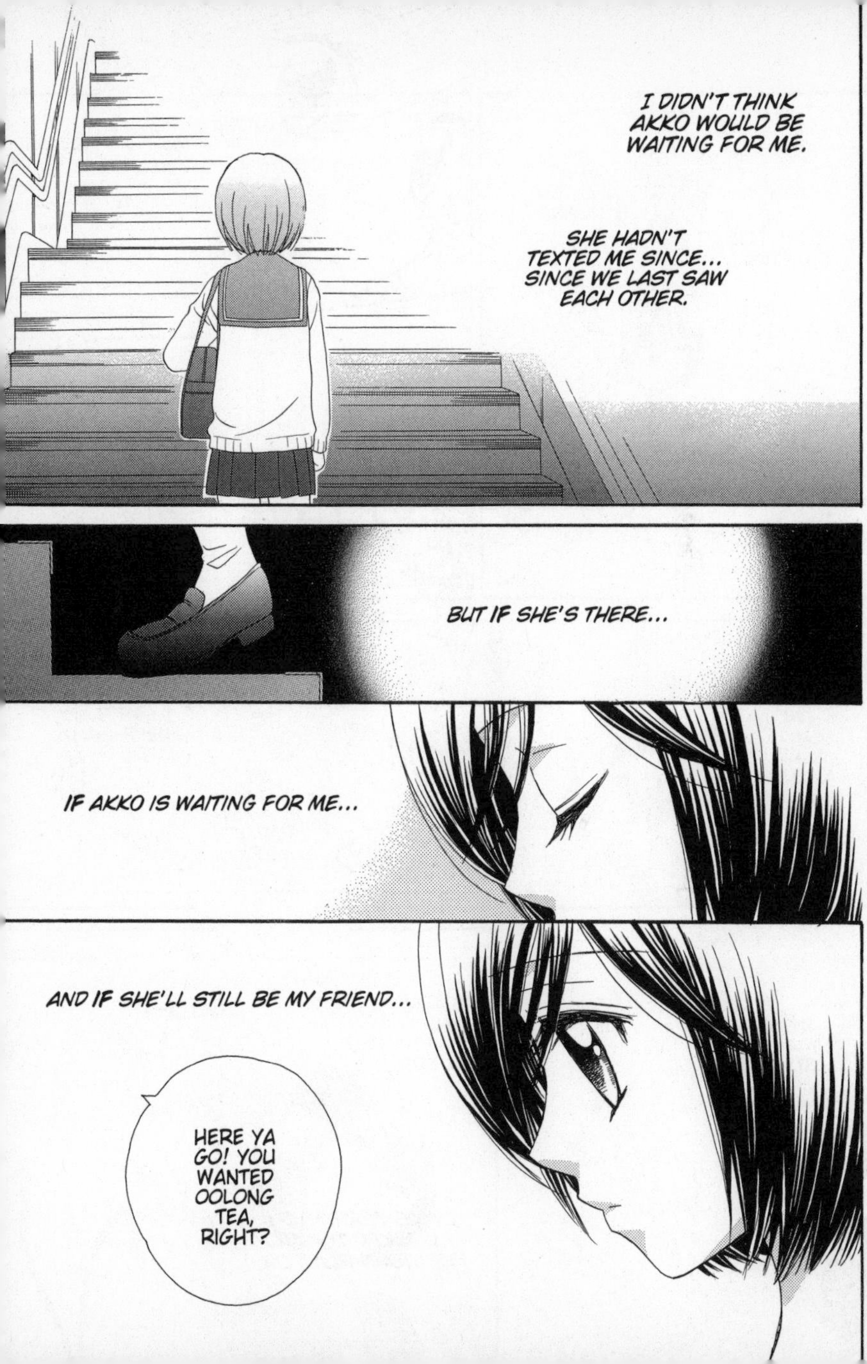
I DIDN'T THINK AKKO WOULD BE WAITING FOR ME.
SHE HADN'T TEXTED ME SINCE... SINCE WE LAST SAW EACH OTHER.
BUT IF SHE'S THERE...
IF AKKO IS WAITING FOR ME...
AND IF SHE'LL STILL BE MY FRIEND...
HERE YA GO! YOU WANTED OOLONG TEA, RIGHT?

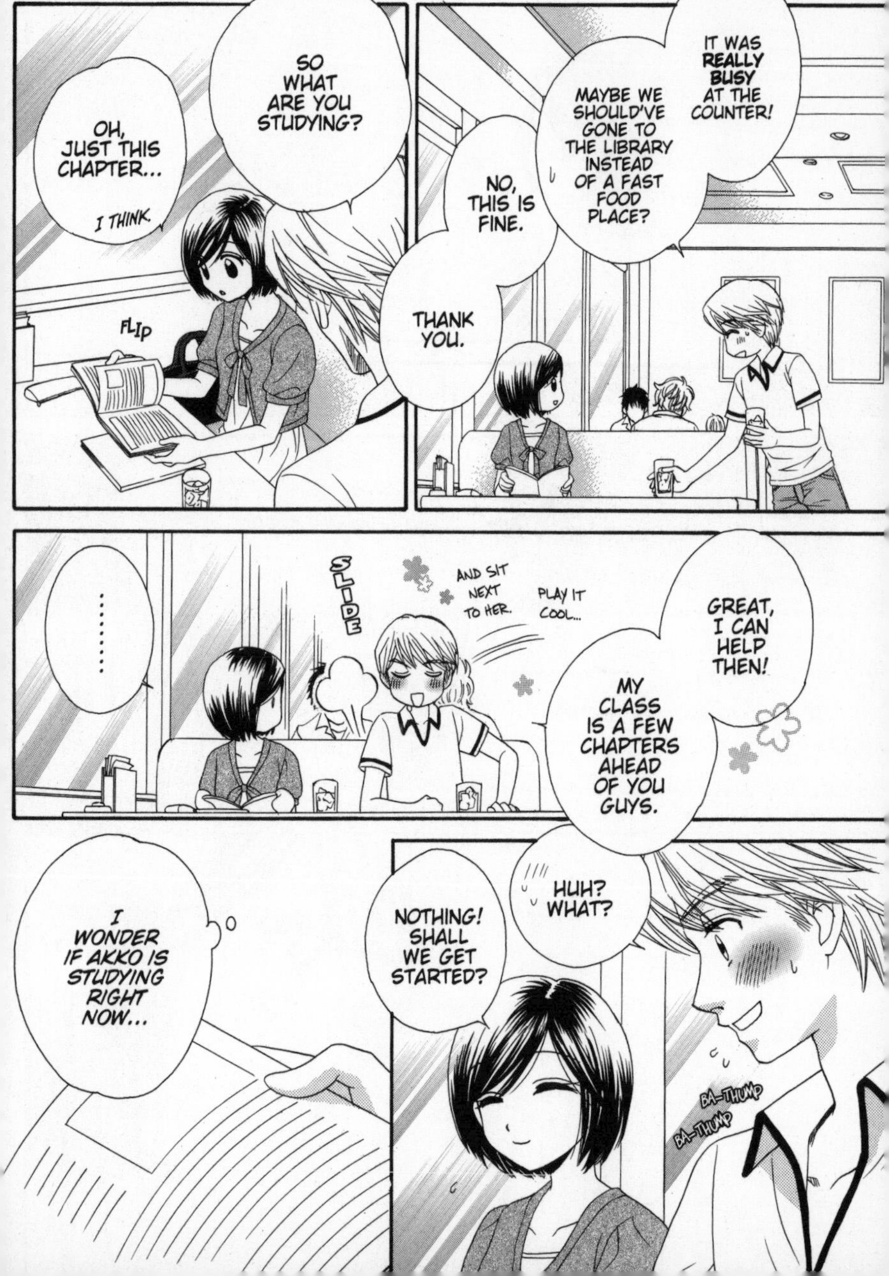
IT WAS REALLY BUSY AT THE COUNTER!
MAYBE WE SHOULD'VE GONE TO THE LIBRARY INSTEAD OF A FAST FOOD PLACE?
NO, THIS IS FINE.
THANK YOU.
SO WHAT ARE YOU STUDYING?
OH, JUST THIS CHAPTER...
I THINK.
FLIP
GREAT, I CAN HELP THEN!
MY CLASS IS A FEW CHAPTERS AHEAD OF YOU GUYS.
PLAY IT COOL...
AND SIT NEXT TO HER.
SLIDE
......
HUH? WHAT?
NOTHING! SHALL WE GET STARTED?
BA-THUMP
BA-THUMP
I WONDER IF AKKO IS STUDYING RIGHT NOW...

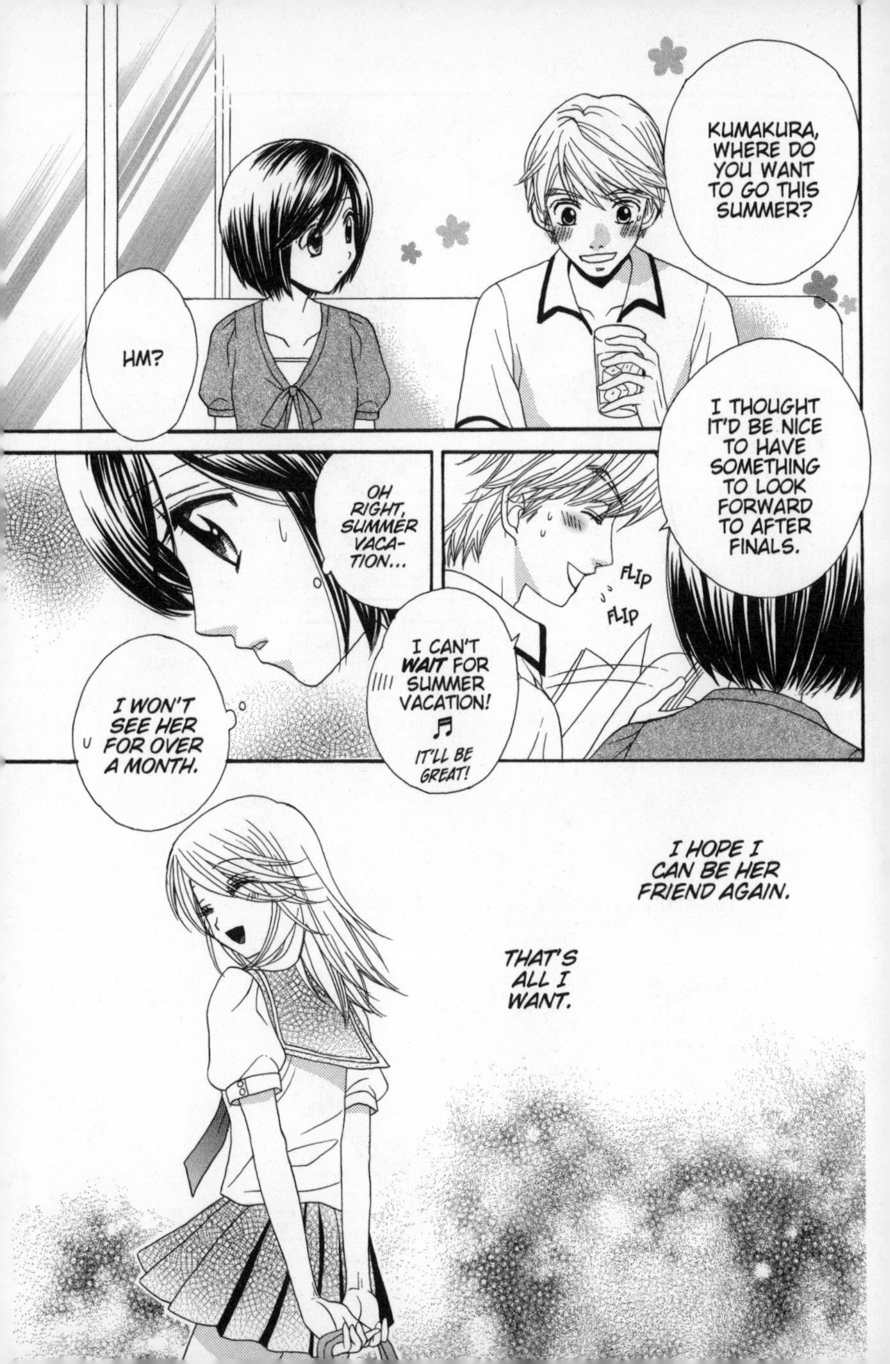
KUMAKURA, WHERE DO YOU WANT TO GO THIS SUMMER?
HM?
I THOUGHT IT'D BE NICE TO HAVE SOMETHING TO LOOK FORWARD TO AFTER FINALS.
FLIP
FLIP
I CAN'T *WAIT* FOR SUMMER VACATION! ♬
IT'LL BE GREAT!
OH RIGHT, SUMMER VACATION...
I WON'T SEE HER FOR OVER A MONTH.
I HOPE I CAN BE HER FRIEND AGAIN.
THAT'S ALL I WANT.

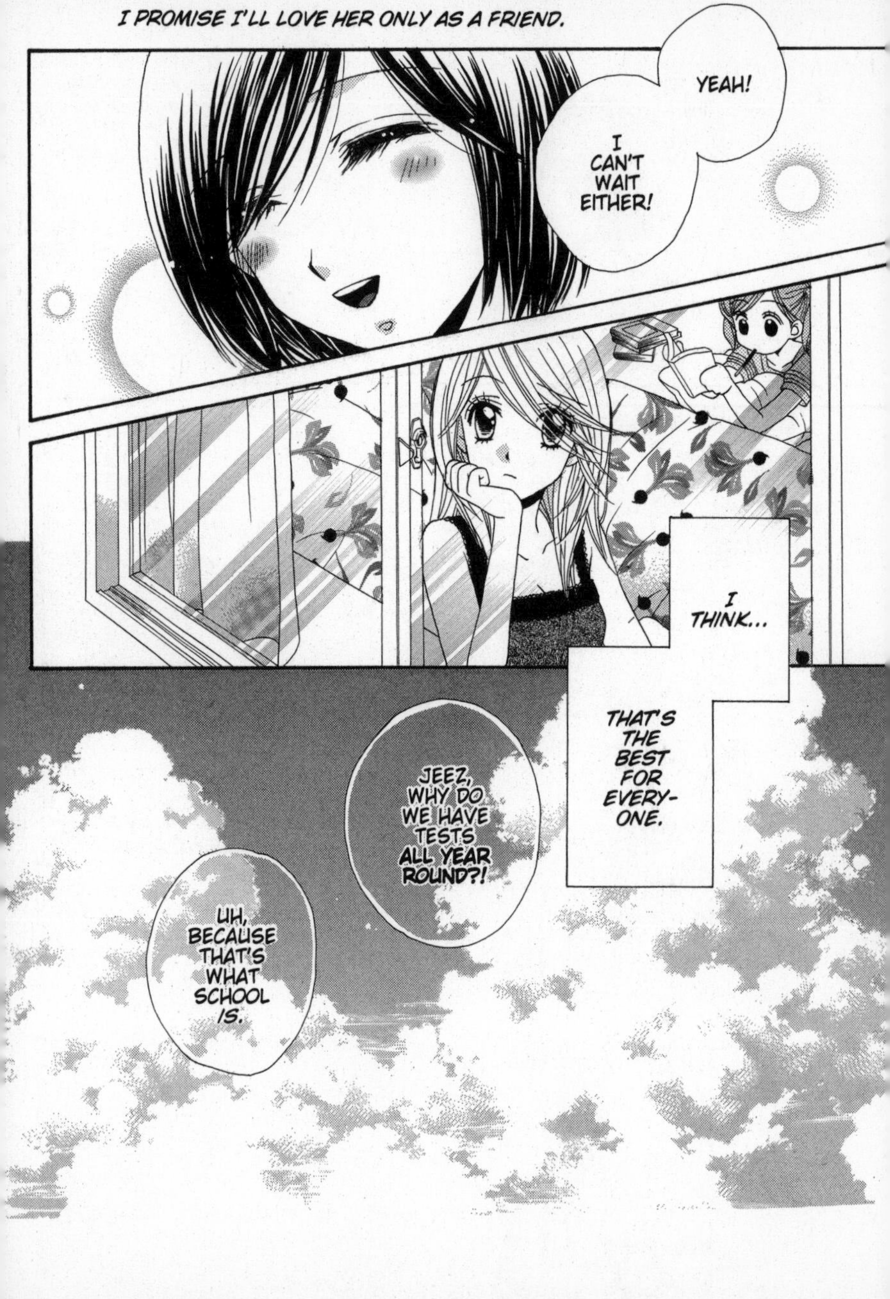
I PROMISE I'LL LOVE HER ONLY AS A FRIEND.
YEAH! I CAN'T WAIT EITHER!
I THINK...
THAT'S THE BEST FOR EVERYONE.
JEEZ, WHY DO WE HAVE TESTS ALL YEAR ROUND?!
UH, BECAUSE THAT'S WHAT SCHOOL IS.

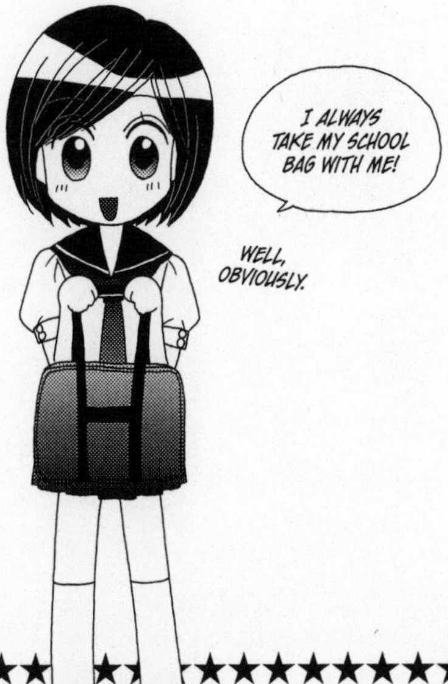
I ALWAYS TAKE MY SCHOOL BAG WITH ME!
WELL, OBVIOUSLY.

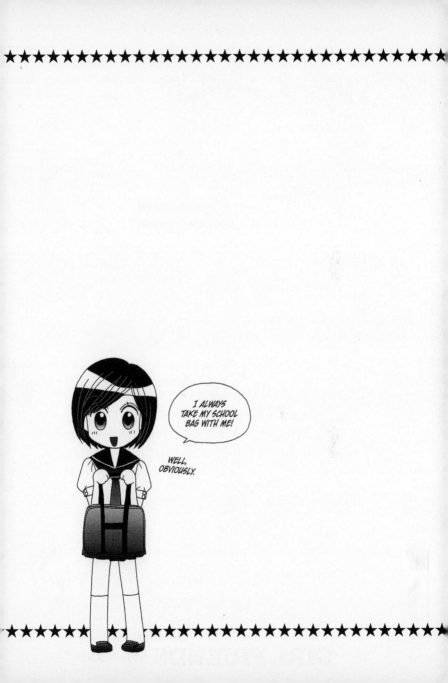

GIRL FRIENDS ーガールフレンズー

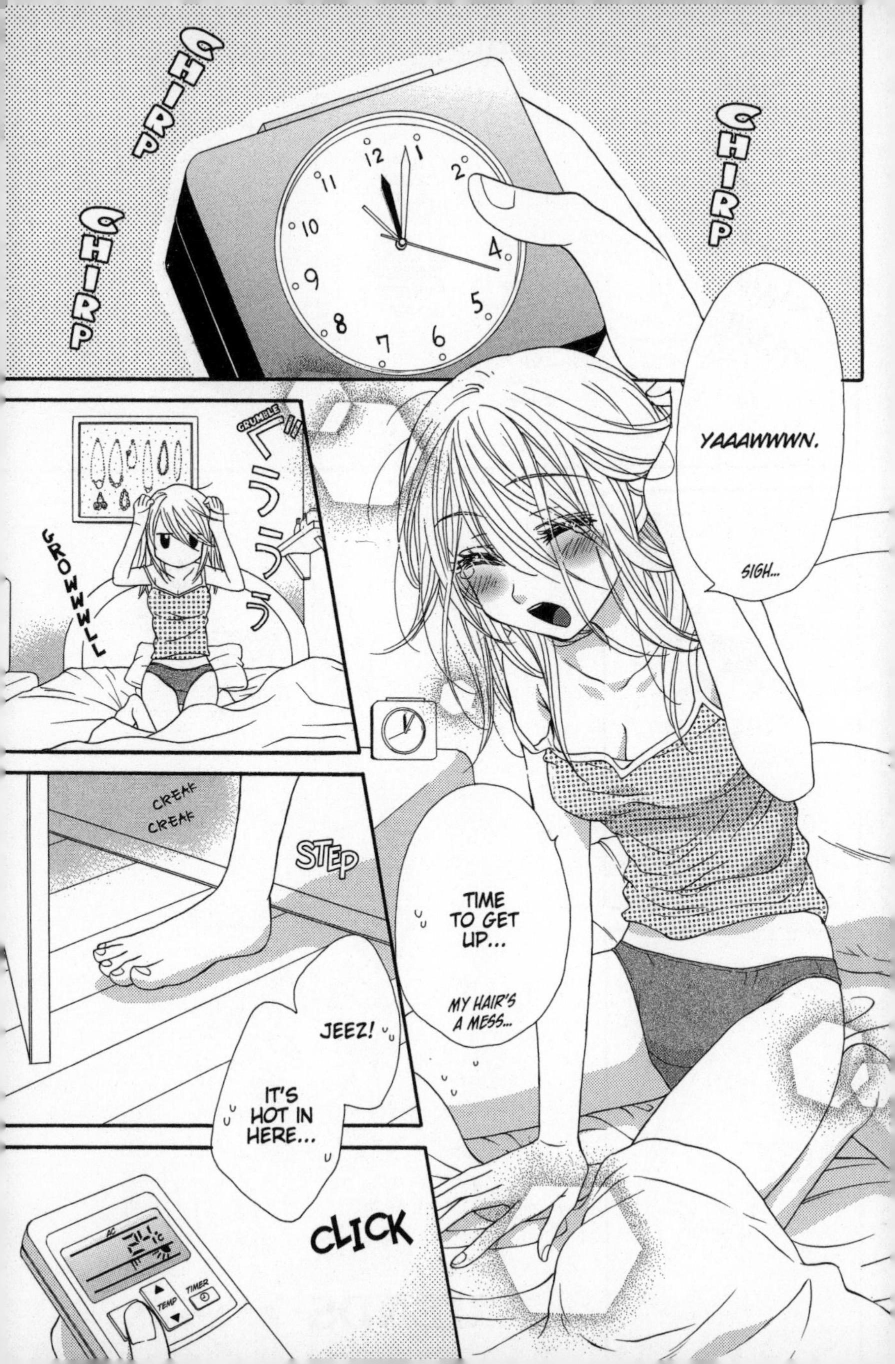
CHIRP
CHIRP
CHIRP
YAAAWWWN.
SIGH...
TIME TO GET UP...
MY HAIR'S A MESS...
GRUMBLE
ぐううう
GROWWWLLL
CREAK CREAK
STEP
JEEZ!
IT'S HOT IN HERE...
CLICK
AC
TEMP
TIMER

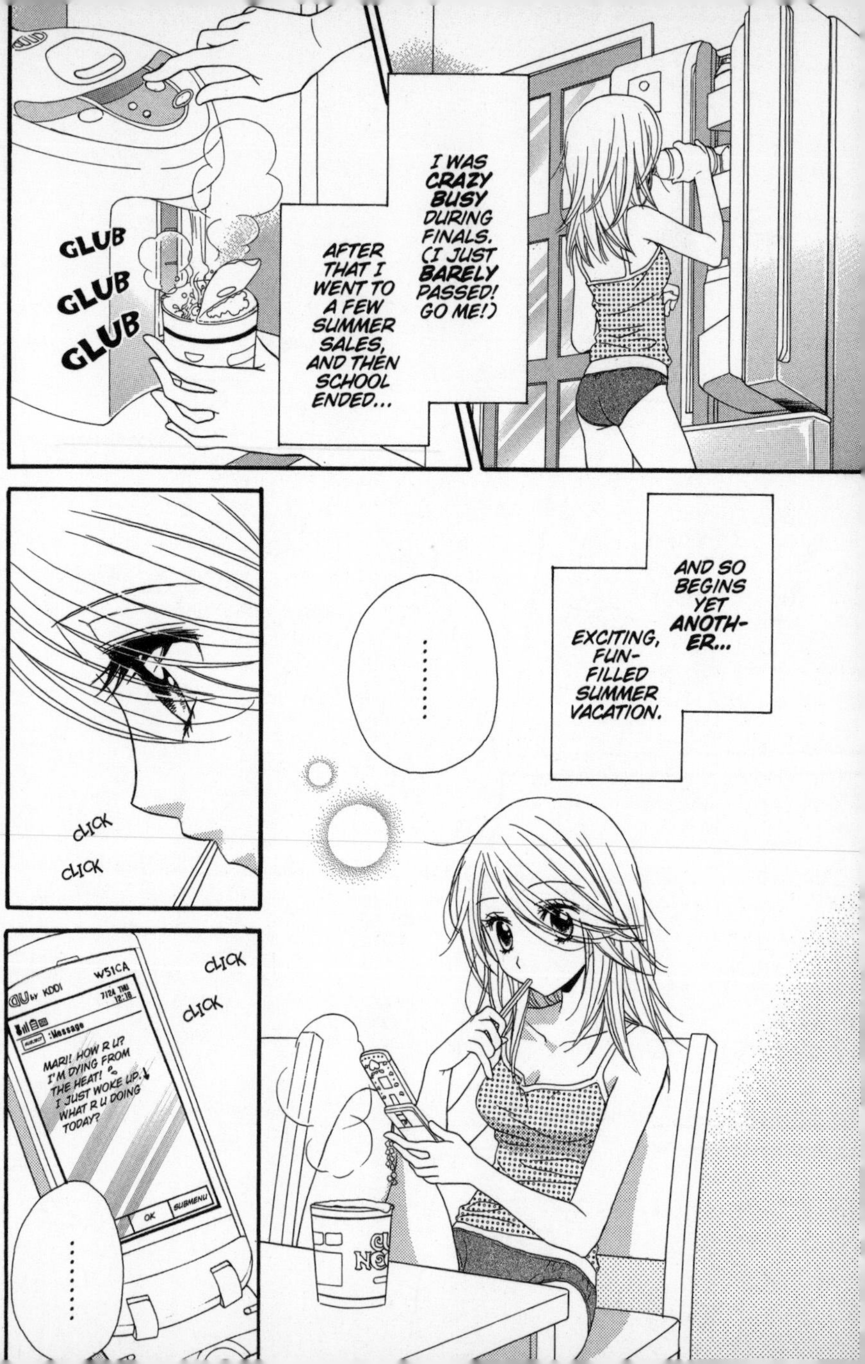
I WAS CRAZY BUSY DURING FINALS. (I JUST BARELY PASSED! GO ME!)
AFTER THAT I WENT TO A FEW SUMMER SALES, AND THEN SCHOOL ENDED...
GLUB
GLUB
GLUB
AND SO BEGINS YET ANOTHER...
EXCITING, FUN-FILLED SUMMER VACATION.
......
CLICK
CLICK
CLICK
CLICK
W51CA
7/24 THU 12:18
:Message
MARI! HOW R U? I'M DYING FROM THE HEAT! I JUST WOKE UP. WHAT R U DOING TODAY?
OK
SUBMENU
......

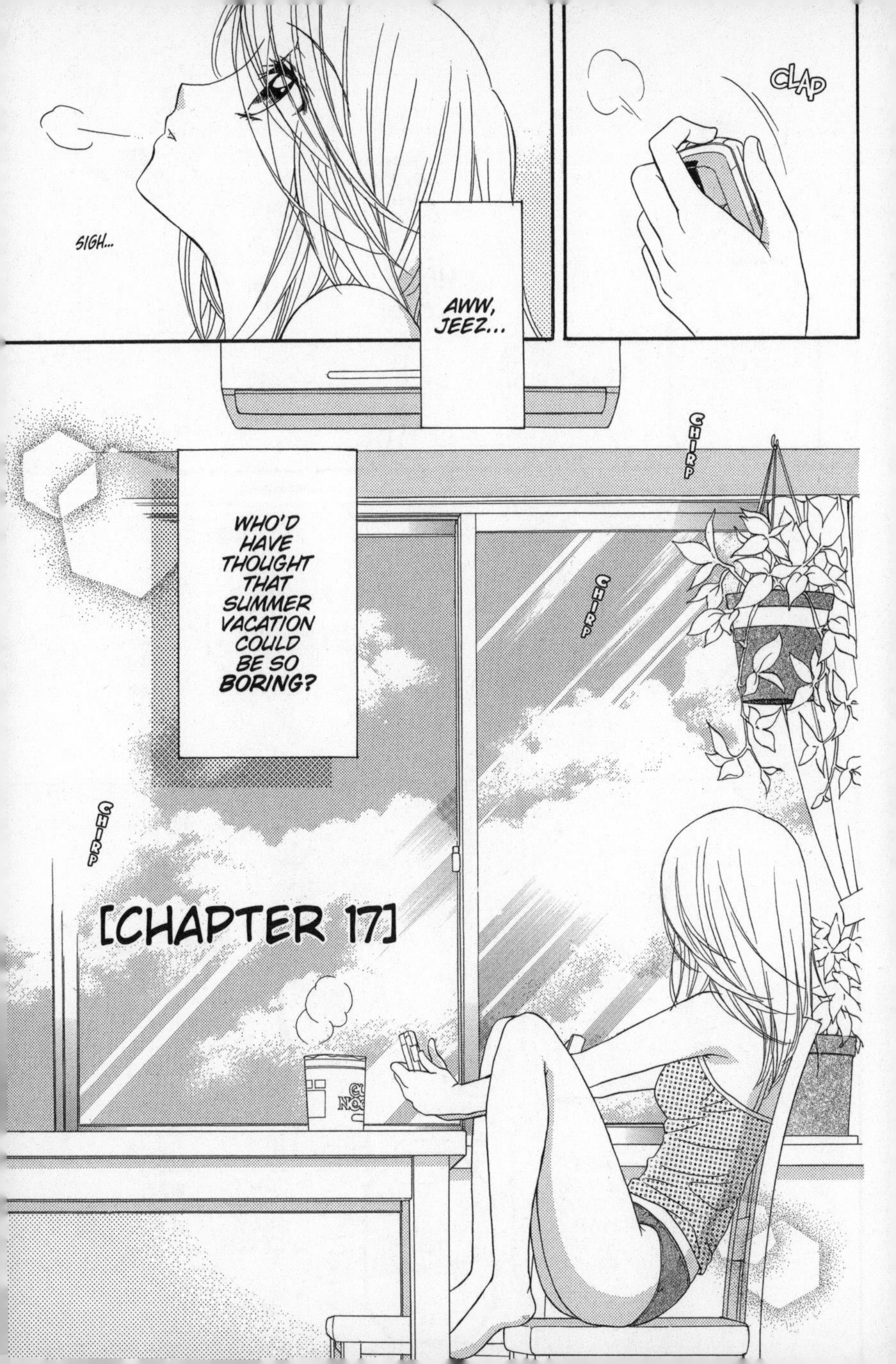
CLAP
AWW, JEEZ...
SIGH...
CHIRP
WHO'D HAVE THOUGHT THAT SUMMER VACATION COULD BE SO BORING?
CHIRP
CHIRP
[CHAPTER 17]

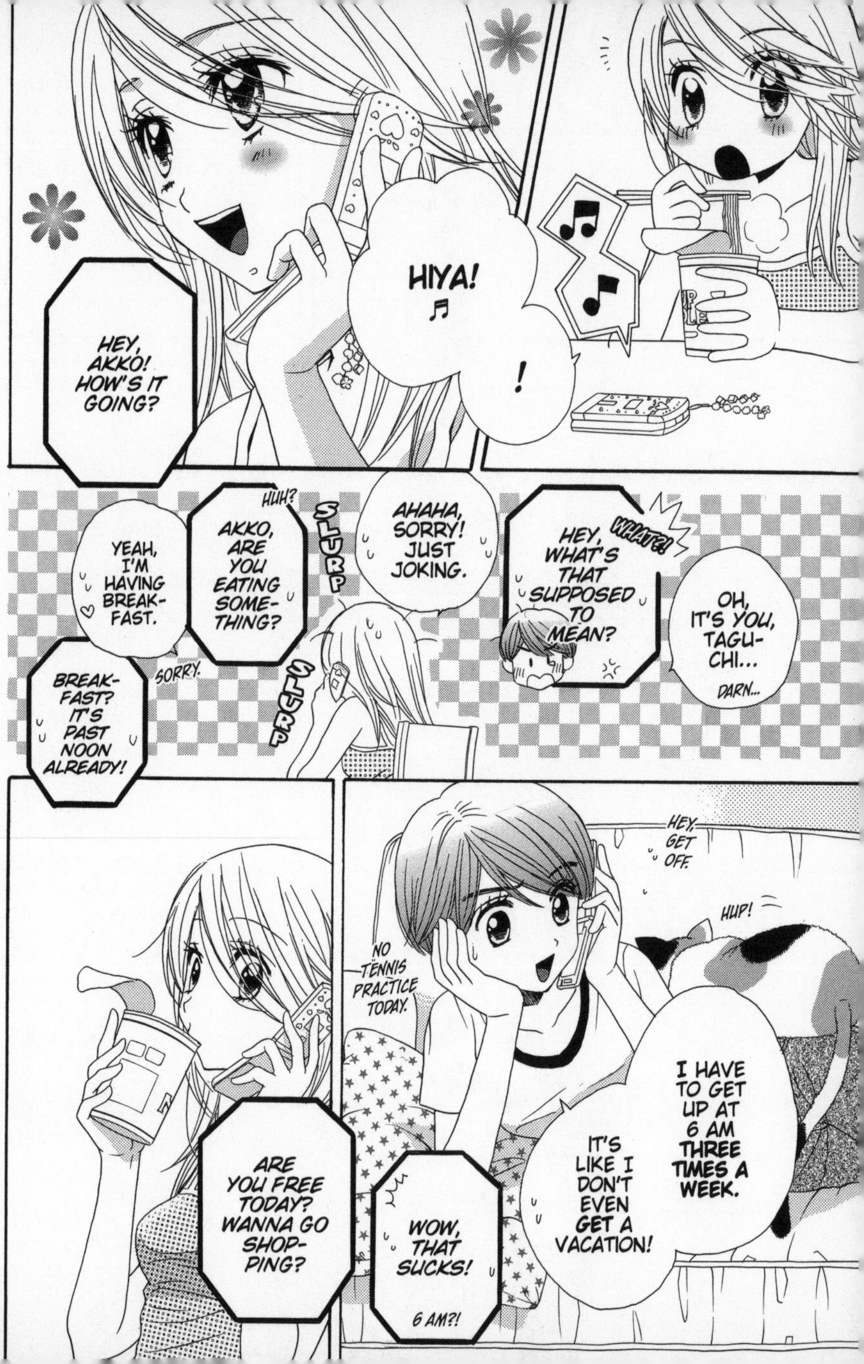
HIYA! ♬
!
HEY, AKKO! HOW'S IT GOING?
OH, IT'S YOU, TAGUCHI...
DARN...
WHAT?!
HEY, WHAT'S THAT SUPPOSED TO MEAN?
AHAHA, SORRY! JUST JOKING.
SLURP
HUH?
AKKO, ARE YOU EATING SOMETHING?
YEAH, I'M HAVING BREAKFAST.
SLURP
BREAKFAST? IT'S PAST NOON ALREADY!
SORRY.
HEY, GET OFF.
HUP!
I HAVE TO GET UP AT 6 AM THREE TIMES A WEEK.
IT'S LIKE I DON'T EVEN GET A VACATION!
NO TENNIS PRACTICE TODAY.
WOW, THAT SUCKS!
6 AM?!
ARE YOU FREE TODAY? WANNA GO SHOPPING?

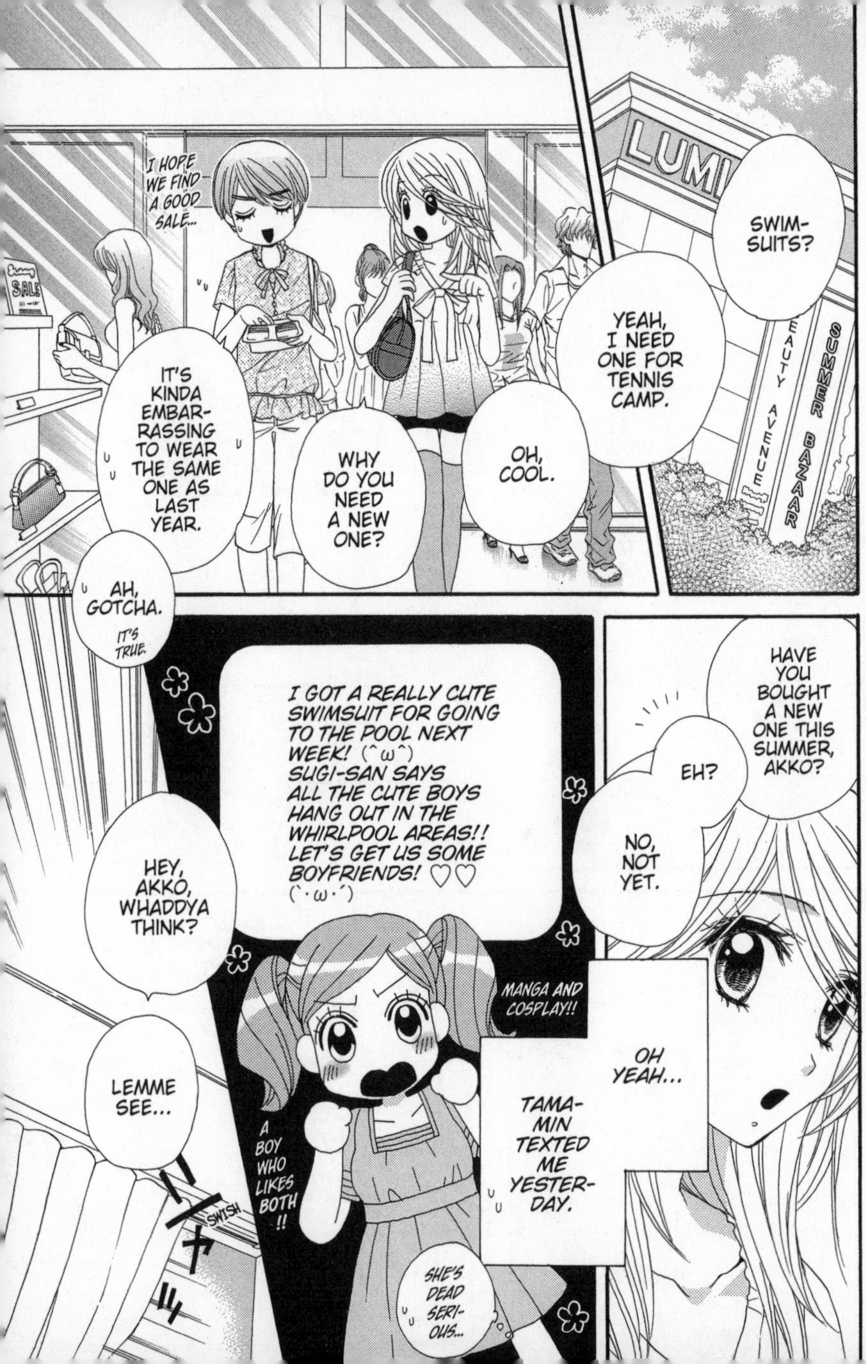

LUMI
SWIM-SUITS?
YEAH, I NEED ONE FOR TENNIS CAMP.
BEAUTY AVENUE
SUMMER BAZAAR
OH, COOL.
WHY DO YOU NEED A NEW ONE?
I HOPE WE FIND A GOOD SALE...
SALE
IT'S KINDA EMBARRASSING TO WEAR THE SAME ONE AS LAST YEAR.
AH, GOTCHA.
IT'S TRUE.
HAVE YOU BOUGHT A NEW ONE THIS SUMMER, AKKO?
EH?
NO, NOT YET.
OH YEAH... TAMA-MIN TEXTED ME YESTERDAY.
I GOT A REALLY CUTE SWIMSUIT FOR GOING TO THE POOL NEXT WEEK! (^ω^) SUGI-SAN SAYS ALL THE CUTE BOYS HANG OUT IN THE WHIRLPOOL AREAS!! LET'S GET US SOME BOYFRIENDS! ♡♡ (`･ω･´)
MANGA AND COSPLAY!!
A BOY WHO LIKES BOTH!!
SHE'S DEAD SERIOUS...
HEY, AKKO, WHADDYA THINK?
LEMME SEE...
SWISH

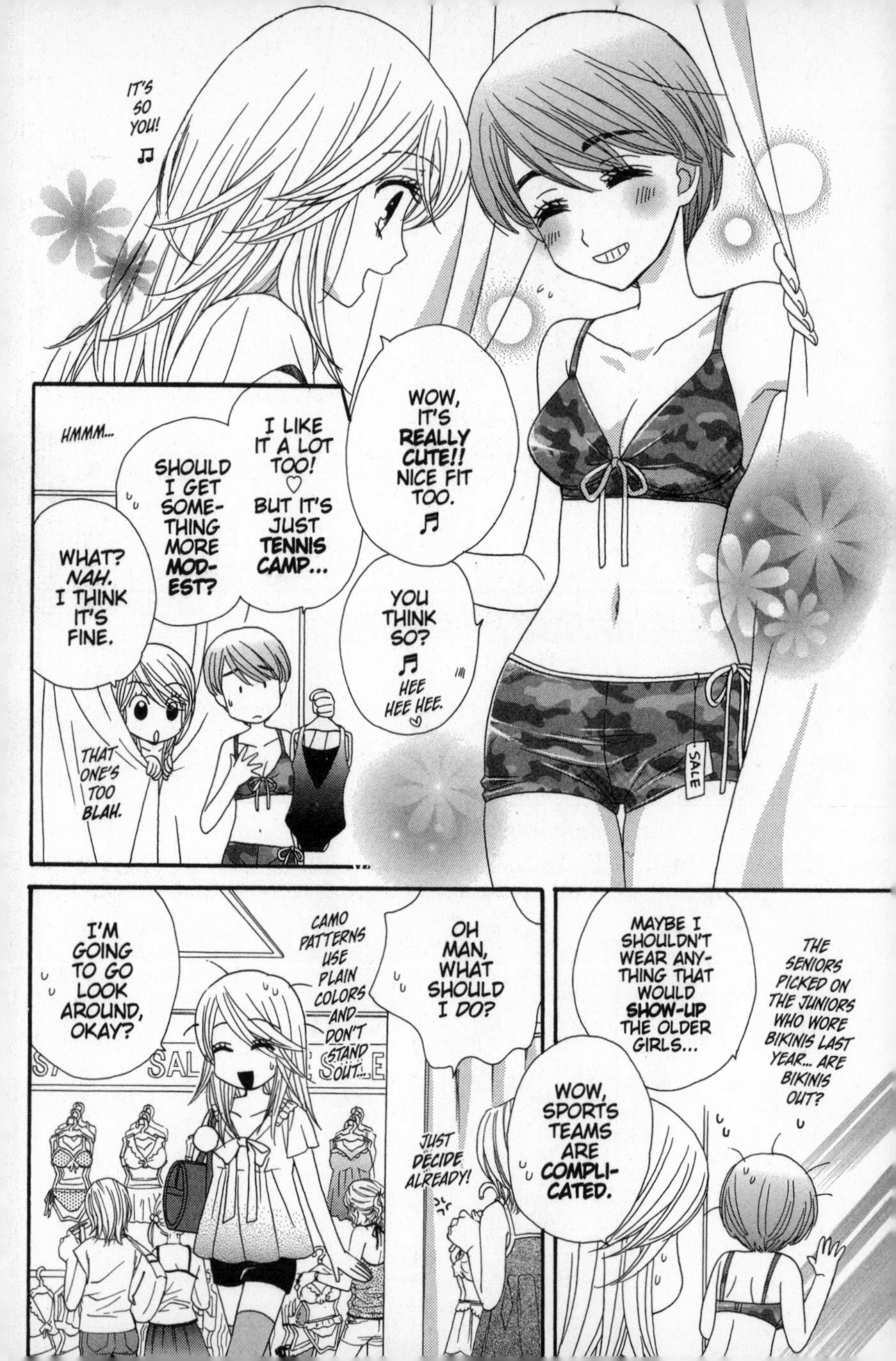
IT'S SO YOU! ♫
WOW, IT'S REALLY CUTE!! NICE FIT TOO. ♫
YOU THINK SO? ♫ HEE HEE HEE. ♡
I LIKE IT A LOT TOO! ♡ BUT IT'S JUST TENNIS CAMP...
SHOULD I GET SOME-THING MORE MOD-EST?
HMMM...
WHAT? NAH. I THINK IT'S FINE.
THAT ONE'S TOO BLAH.
SALE
THE SENIORS PICKED ON THE JUNIORS WHO WORE BIKINIS LAST YEAR... ARE BIKINIS OUT?
MAYBE I SHOULDN'T WEAR ANY-THING THAT WOULD SHOW-UP THE OLDER GIRLS...
WOW, SPORTS TEAMS ARE COMPLI-CATED.
OH MAN, WHAT SHOULD I DO?
CAMO PATTERNS USE PLAIN COLORS AND DON'T STAND OUT...
I'M GOING TO GO LOOK AROUND, OKAY?
JUST DECIDE ALREADY!

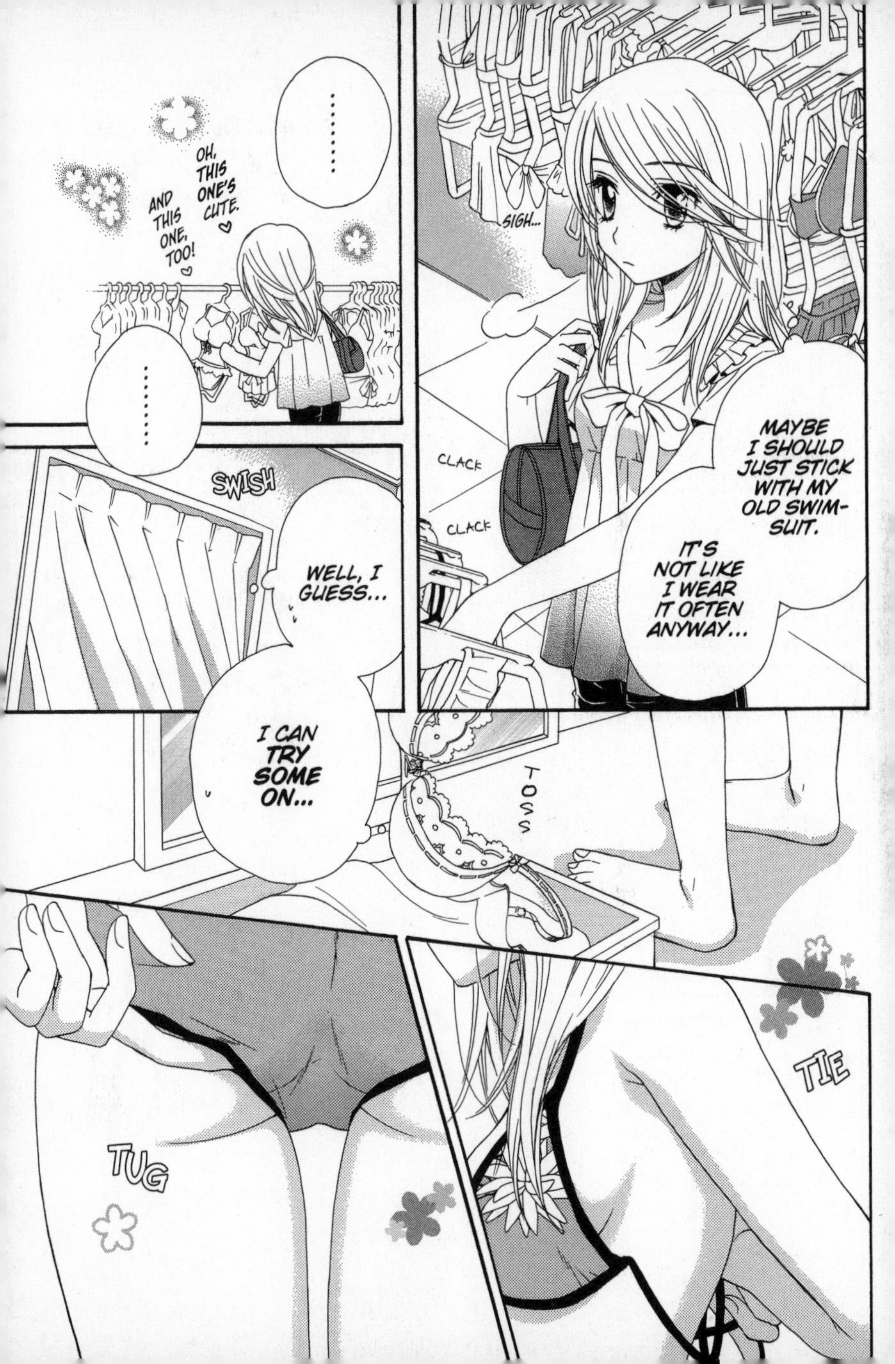
SIGH...
MAYBE I SHOULD JUST STICK WITH MY OLD SWIM-SUIT.
IT'S NOT LIKE I WEAR IT OFTEN ANYWAY...
CLACK
CLACK
......
OH, THIS ONE'S CUTE.
AND THIS ONE, TOO!
......
SWISH
WELL, I GUESS...
I CAN TRY SOME ON...
TOSS
TIE
TUG

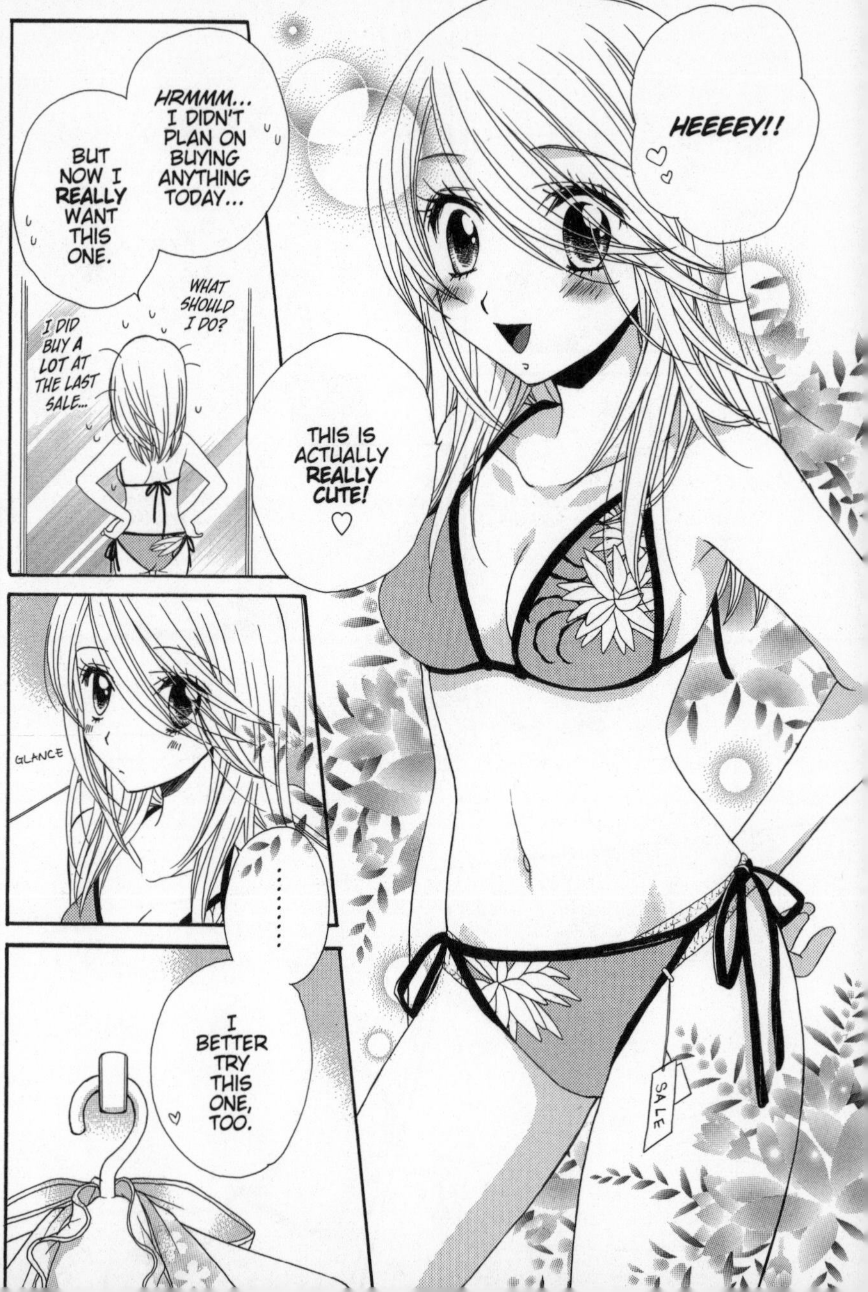
HEEEEY!! ♡ ♡
THIS IS ACTUALLY REALLY CUTE! ♡
SALE
HRMMM... I DIDN'T PLAN ON BUYING ANYTHING TODAY...
BUT NOW I REALLY WANT THIS ONE.
WHAT SHOULD I DO?
I DID BUY A LOT AT THE LAST SALE...
GLANCE
......
I BETTER TRY THIS ONE, TOO. ♡

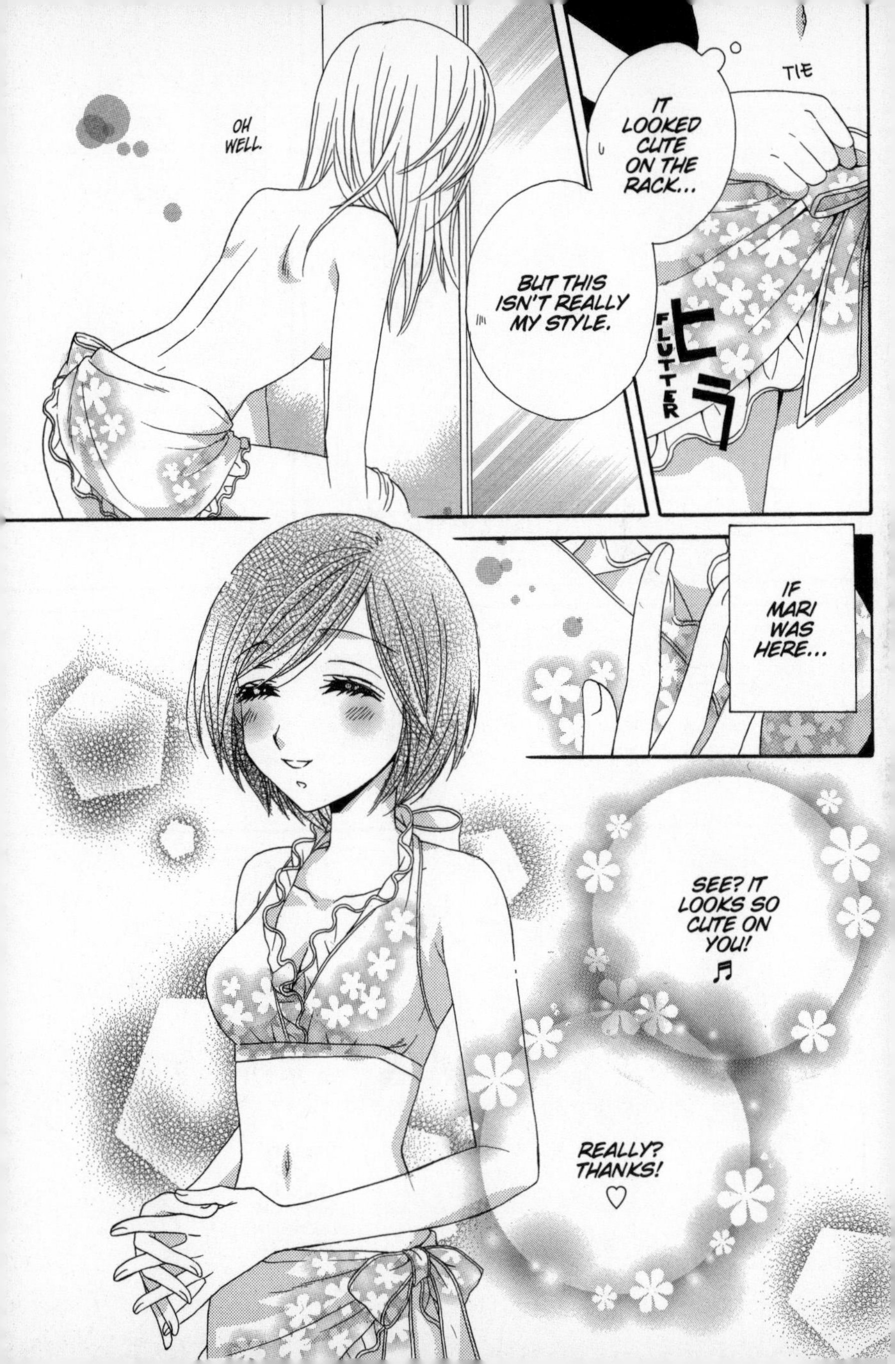
TIE
IT LOOKED CUTE ON THE RACK...
BUT THIS ISN'T REALLY MY STYLE.
ヒラ FLUTTER
OH WELL.
IF MARI WAS HERE...
SEE? IT LOOKS SO CUTE ON YOU! ♪
REALLY? THANKS! ♡

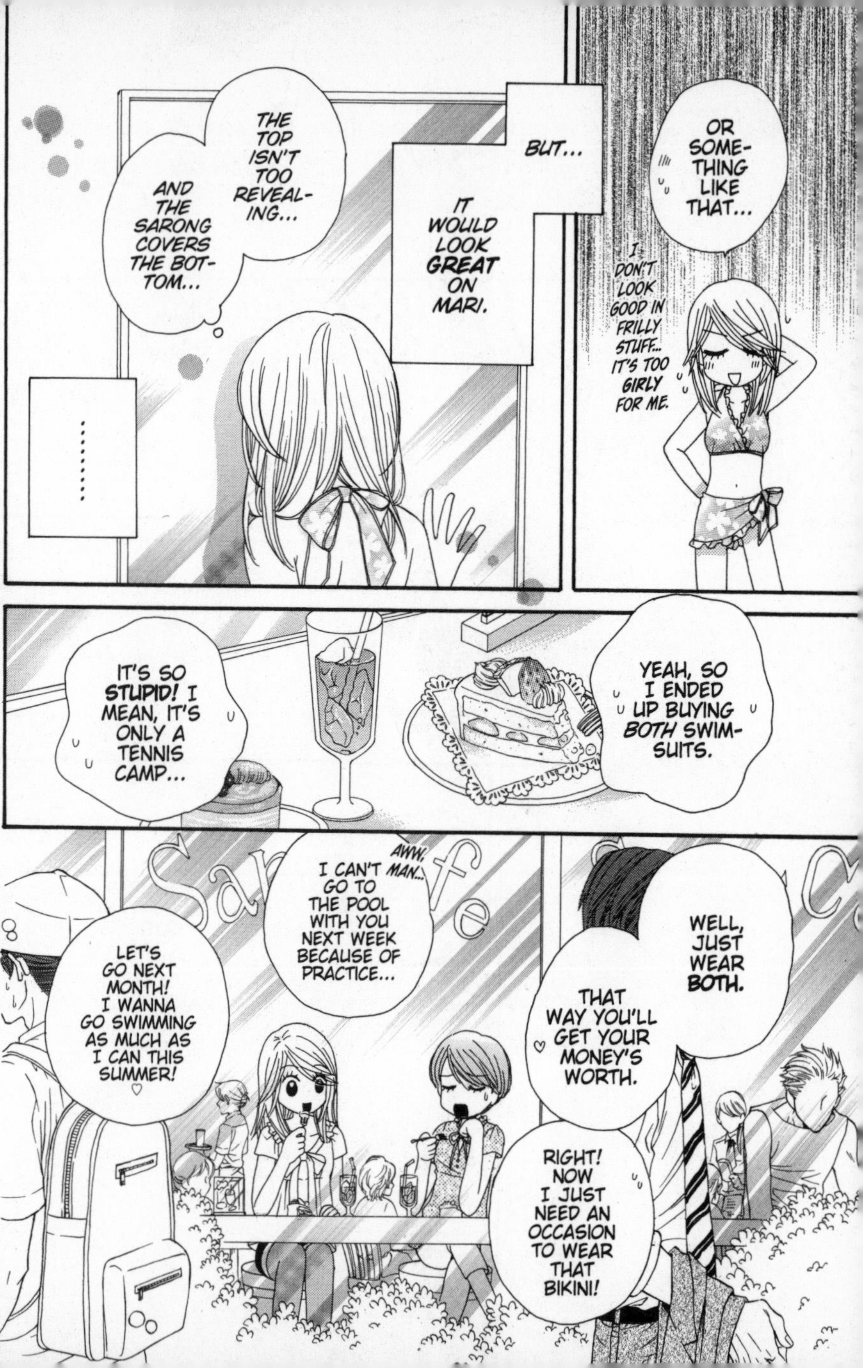
OR SOMETHING LIKE THAT...
I DON'T LOOK GOOD IN FRILLY STUFF... IT'S TOO GIRLY FOR ME.
BUT...
IT WOULD LOOK GREAT ON MARI.
THE TOP ISN'T TOO REVEALING...
AND THE SARONG COVERS THE BOTTOM...
......
YEAH, SO I ENDED UP BUYING BOTH SWIMSUITS.
IT'S SO STUPID! I MEAN, IT'S ONLY A TENNIS CAMP...
WELL, JUST WEAR BOTH.
THAT WAY YOU'LL GET YOUR MONEY'S WORTH.
RIGHT! NOW I JUST NEED AN OCCASION TO WEAR THAT BIKINI!
AWW, MAN...
I CAN'T GO TO THE POOL WITH YOU NEXT WEEK BECAUSE OF PRACTICE...
LET'S GO NEXT MONTH! I WANNA GO SWIMMING AS MUCH AS I CAN THIS SUMMER!

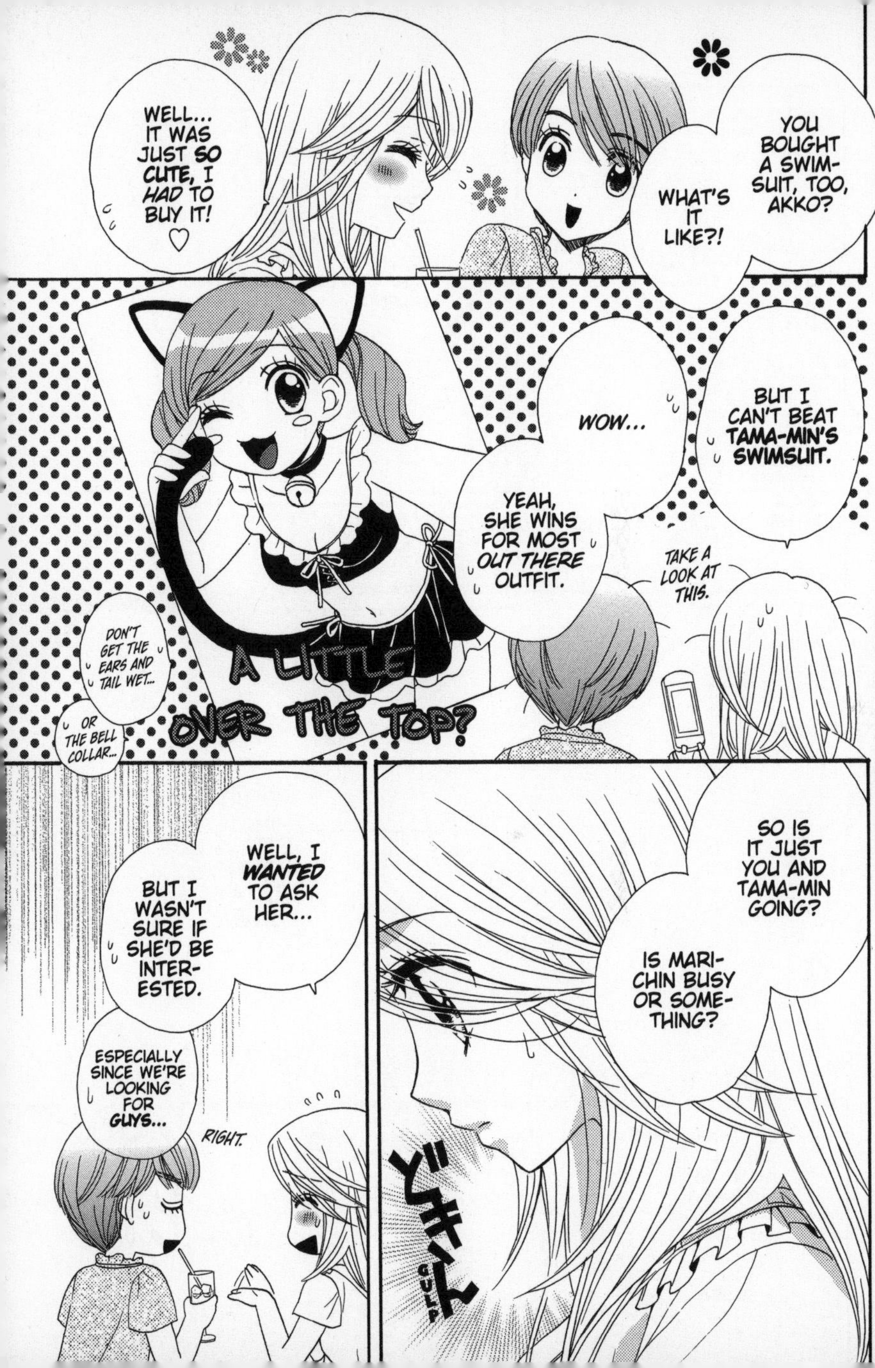
YOU BOUGHT A SWIM-SUIT, TOO, AKKO?
WHAT'S IT LIKE?!
WELL... IT WAS JUST SO CUTE, I HAD TO BUY IT! ♡
BUT I CAN'T BEAT TAMA-MIN'S SWIMSUIT.
WOW...
YEAH, SHE WINS FOR MOST OUT THERE OUTFIT.
TAKE A LOOK AT THIS.
A LITTLE OVER THE TOP?
DON'T GET THE EARS AND TAIL WET...
OR THE BELL COLLAR...
SO IS IT JUST YOU AND TAMA-MIN GOING?
IS MARI-CHIN BUSY OR SOME-THING?
GULP
WELL, I WANTED TO ASK HER...
BUT I WASN'T SURE IF SHE'D BE INTER-ESTED.
ESPECIALLY SINCE WE'RE LOOKING FOR GUYS...
RIGHT.

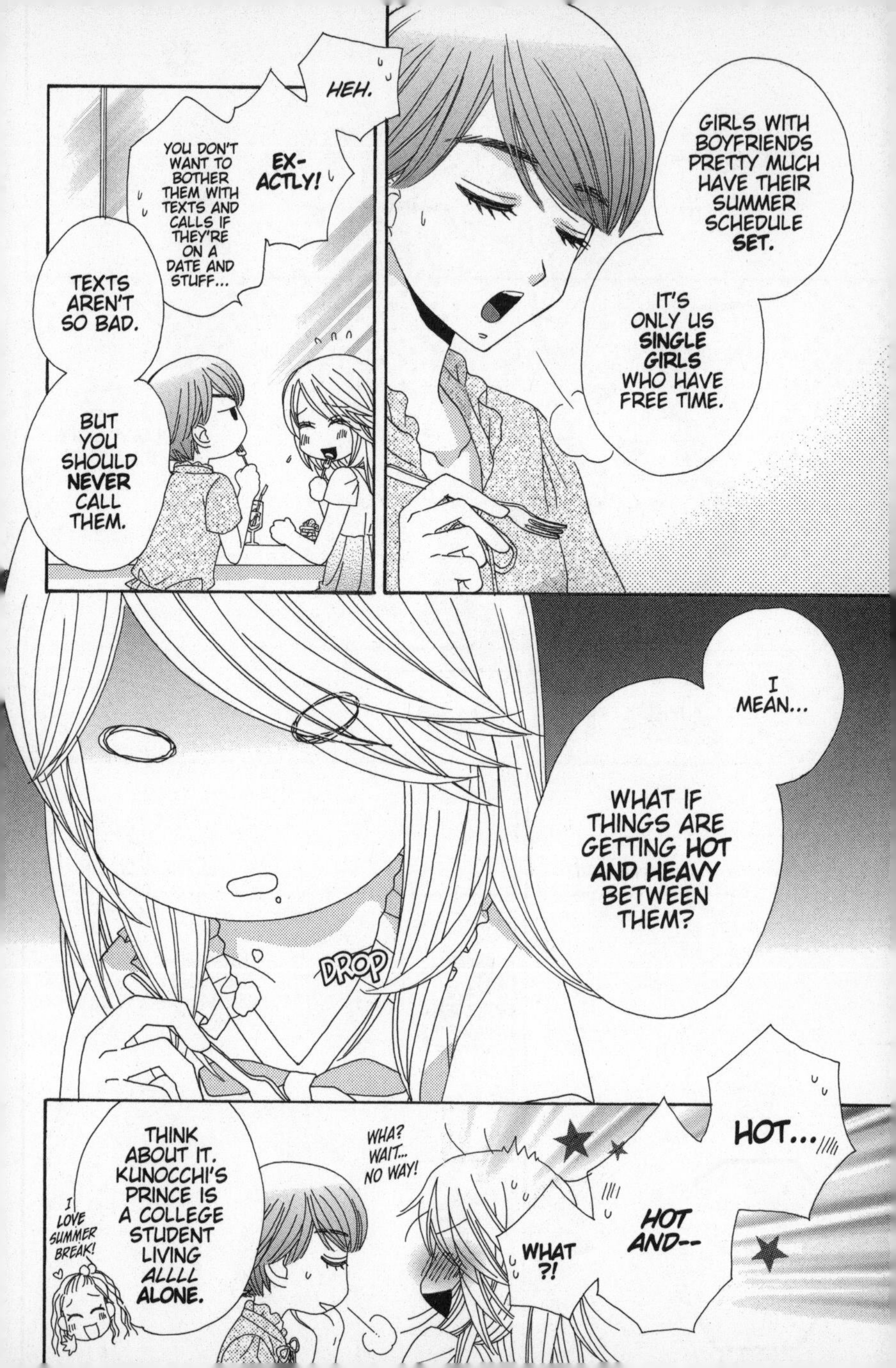
GIRLS WITH BOYFRIENDS PRETTY MUCH HAVE THEIR SUMMER SCHEDULE SET.
IT'S ONLY US SINGLE GIRLS WHO HAVE FREE TIME.
HEH.
EX-ACTLY!
YOU DON'T WANT TO BOTHER THEM WITH TEXTS AND CALLS IF THEY'RE ON A DATE AND STUFF...
TEXTS AREN'T SO BAD.
BUT YOU SHOULD NEVER CALL THEM.
I MEAN...
WHAT IF THINGS ARE GETTING HOT AND HEAVY BETWEEN THEM?
DROP
HOT...
HOT AND--
WHAT ?!
WHA? WAIT... NO WAY!
THINK ABOUT IT. KUNOCCHI'S PRINCE IS A COLLEGE STUDENT LIVING ALLLL ALONE.
I LOVE SUMMER BREAK!

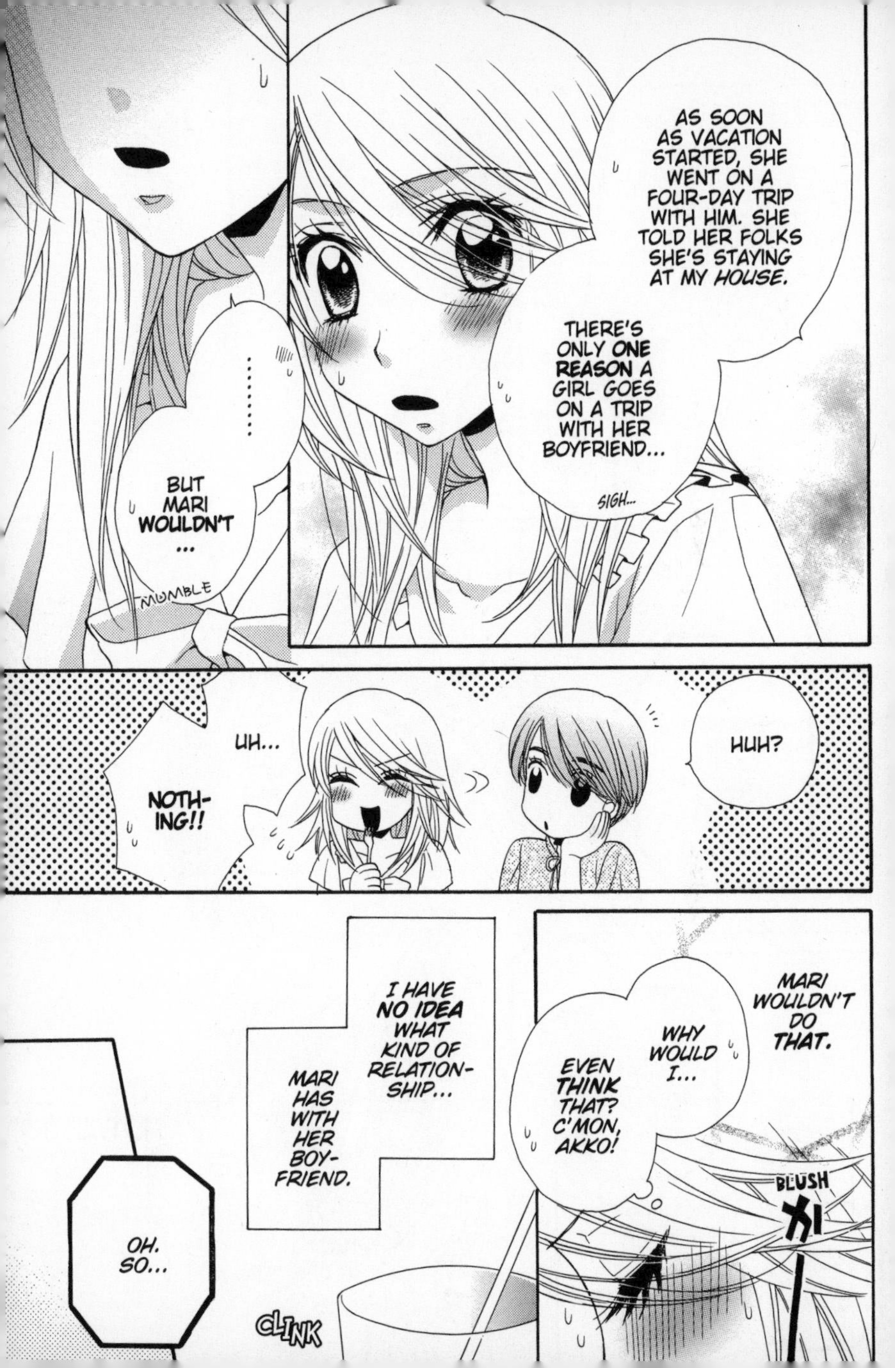
AS SOON AS VACATION STARTED, SHE WENT ON A FOUR-DAY TRIP WITH HIM. SHE TOLD HER FOLKS SHE'S STAYING AT MY *HOUSE*.
THERE'S ONLY **ONE REASON** A GIRL GOES ON A TRIP WITH HER BOYFRIEND...
SIGH...
......
BUT MARI **WOULDN'T** ...
MUMBLE
HUH?
UH...
NOTHING!!
MARI WOULDN'T DO **THAT.**
WHY WOULD I... EVEN **THINK** THAT? C'MON, AKKO!
BLUSH
カ
I HAVE **NO IDEA** WHAT KIND OF RELATIONSHIP...
MARI HAS WITH HER BOYFRIEND.
OH. SO...
CLINK

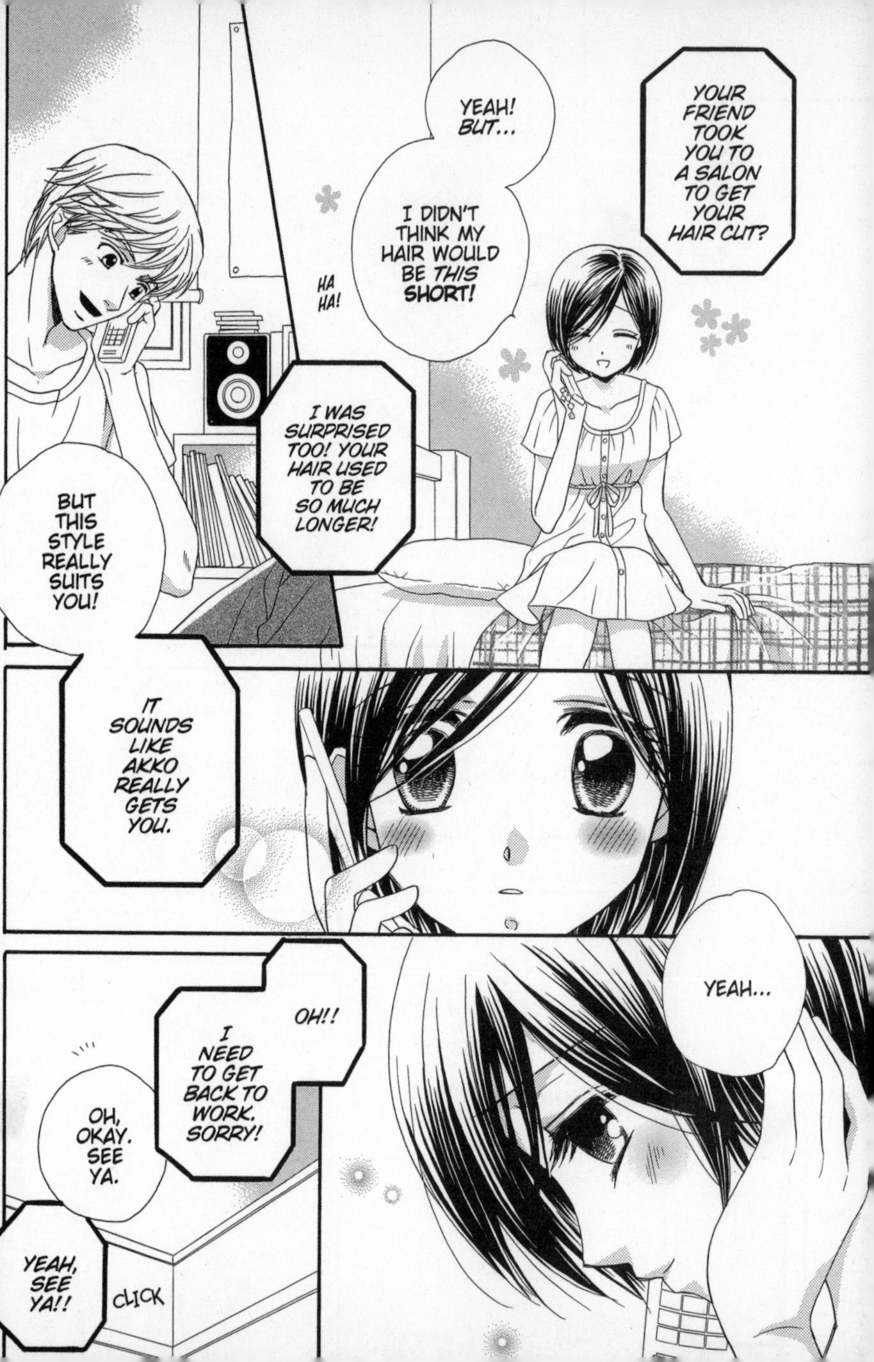
YOUR FRIEND TOOK YOU TO A SALON TO GET YOUR HAIR CUT?
YEAH! BUT...
I DIDN'T THINK MY HAIR WOULD BE *THIS* SHORT!
HA HA!
I WAS SURPRISED TOO! YOUR HAIR USED TO BE SO MUCH LONGER!
BUT THIS STYLE REALLY SUITS YOU!
IT SOUNDS LIKE AKKO REALLY GETS YOU.
YEAH...
OH!!
I NEED TO GET BACK TO WORK. SORRY!
OH, OKAY. SEE YA.
YEAH, SEE YA!!
CLICK

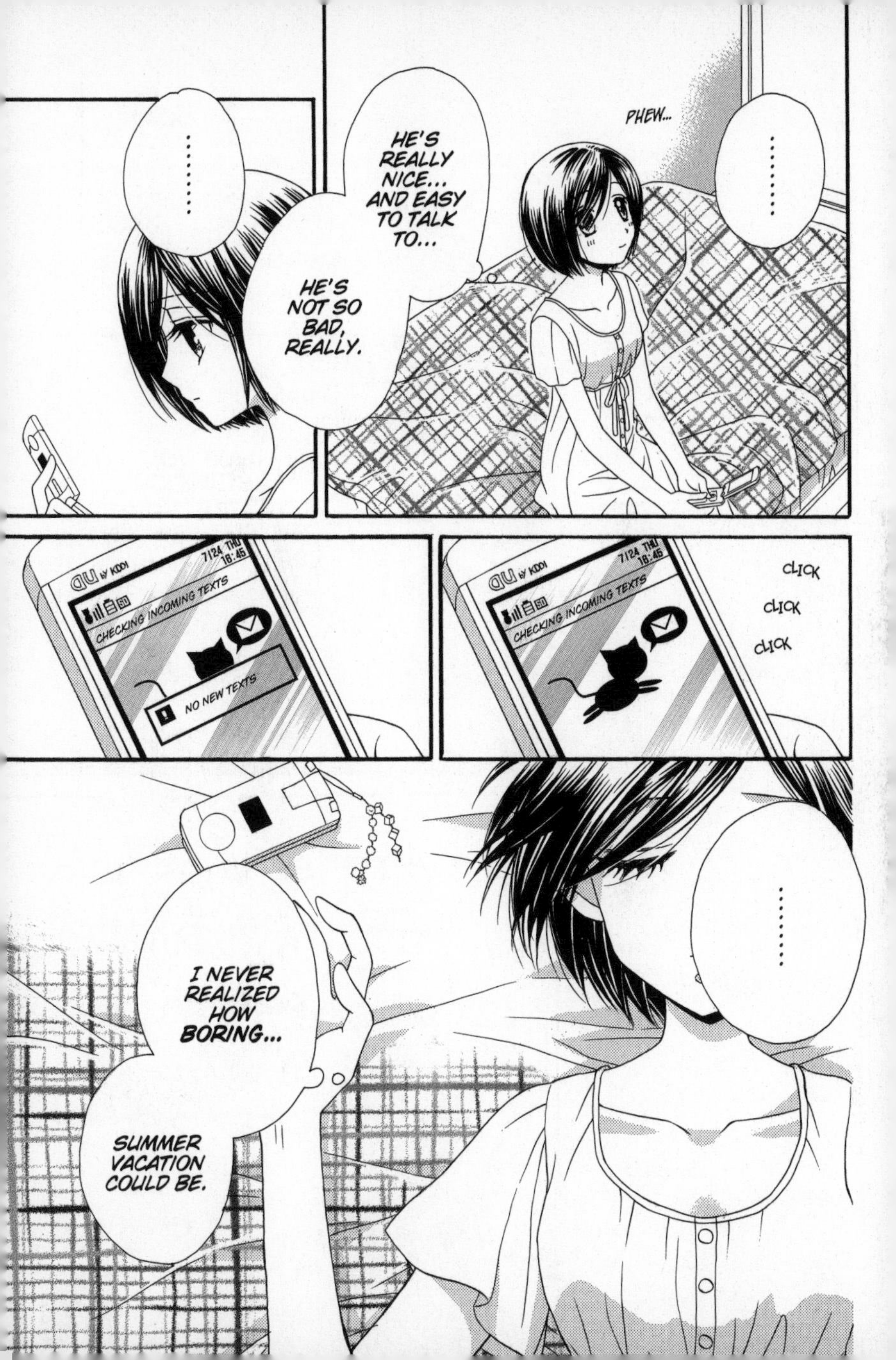
PHEW...
......
HE'S REALLY NICE... AND EASY TO TALK TO...
HE'S NOT SO BAD, REALLY.
......
CLICK
CLICK
CLICK
au by KDDI
7/24 THU 18:45
CHECKING INCOMING TEXTS
au by KDDI
7/24 THU 18:45
CHECKING INCOMING TEXTS
NO NEW TEXTS
......
I NEVER REALIZED HOW BORING...
SUMMER VACATION COULD BE.

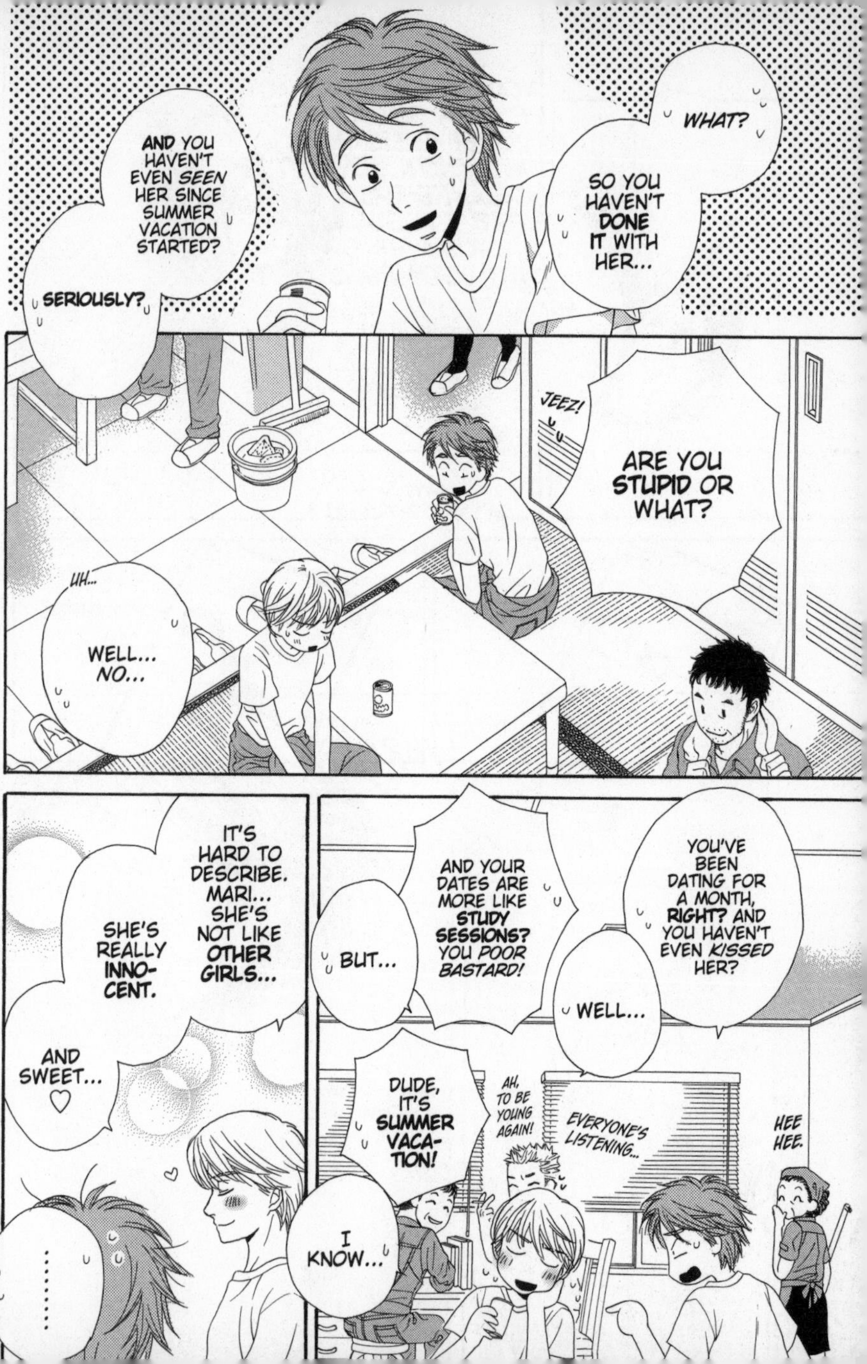
WHAT?
SO YOU HAVEN'T DONE IT WITH HER...
AND YOU HAVEN'T EVEN SEEN HER SINCE SUMMER VACATION STARTED?
SERIOUSLY?
JEEZ!
ARE YOU STUPID OR WHAT?
UH...
WELL... NO...
YOU'VE BEEN DATING FOR A MONTH, RIGHT? AND YOU HAVEN'T EVEN KISSED HER?
WELL...
AND YOUR DATES ARE MORE LIKE STUDY SESSIONS? YOU POOR BASTARD!
BUT...
HEE HEE.
EVERYONE'S LISTENING...
AH, TO BE YOUNG AGAIN!
DUDE, IT'S SUMMER VACATION!
I KNOW...
IT'S HARD TO DESCRIBE. MARI... SHE'S NOT LIKE OTHER GIRLS...
SHE'S REALLY INNOCENT.
AND SWEET... ♡
......

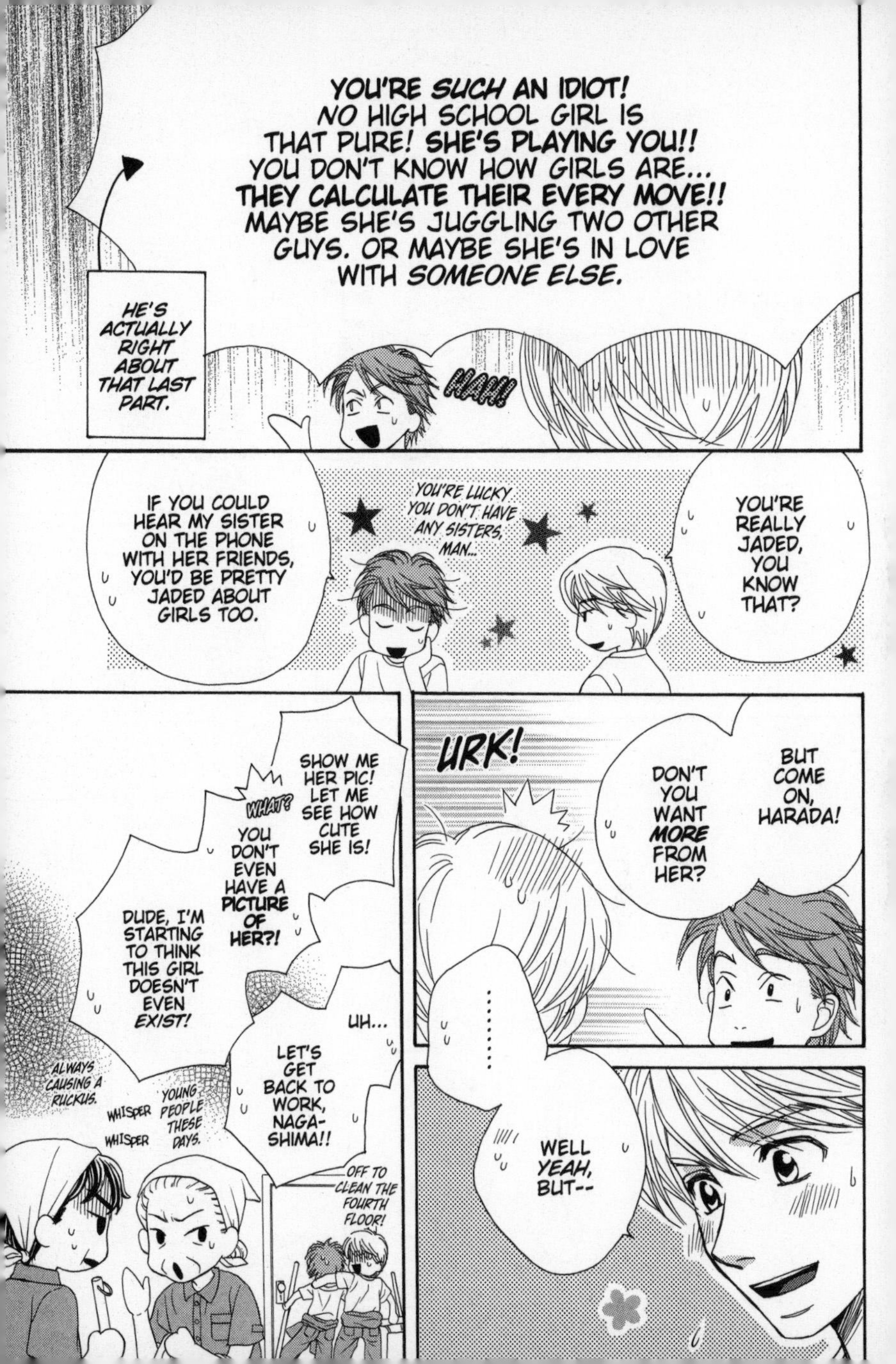
YOU'RE SUCH AN IDIOT! NO HIGH SCHOOL GIRL IS THAT PURE! SHE'S PLAYING YOU!! YOU DON'T KNOW HOW GIRLS ARE... THEY CALCULATE THEIR EVERY MOVE!! MAYBE SHE'S JUGGLING TWO OTHER GUYS. OR MAYBE SHE'S IN LOVE WITH SOMEONE ELSE.
HAH!
HE'S ACTUALLY RIGHT ABOUT THAT LAST PART.
YOU'RE REALLY JADED, YOU KNOW THAT?
YOU'RE LUCKY YOU DON'T HAVE ANY SISTERS, MAN...
IF YOU COULD HEAR MY SISTER ON THE PHONE WITH HER FRIENDS, YOU'D BE PRETTY JADED ABOUT GIRLS TOO.
BUT COME ON, HARADA!
DON'T YOU WANT MORE FROM HER?
URK!
......
WELL YEAH, BUT--
SHOW ME HER PIC! LET ME SEE HOW CUTE SHE IS!
WHAT?
YOU DON'T EVEN HAVE A PICTURE OF HER?!
DUDE, I'M STARTING TO THINK THIS GIRL DOESN'T EVEN EXIST!
UH...
LET'S GET BACK TO WORK, NAGA-SHIMA!!
OFF TO CLEAN THE FOURTH FLOOR!
YOUNG PEOPLE THESE DAYS.
WHISPER
WHISPER
ALWAYS CAUSING A RUCKUS.

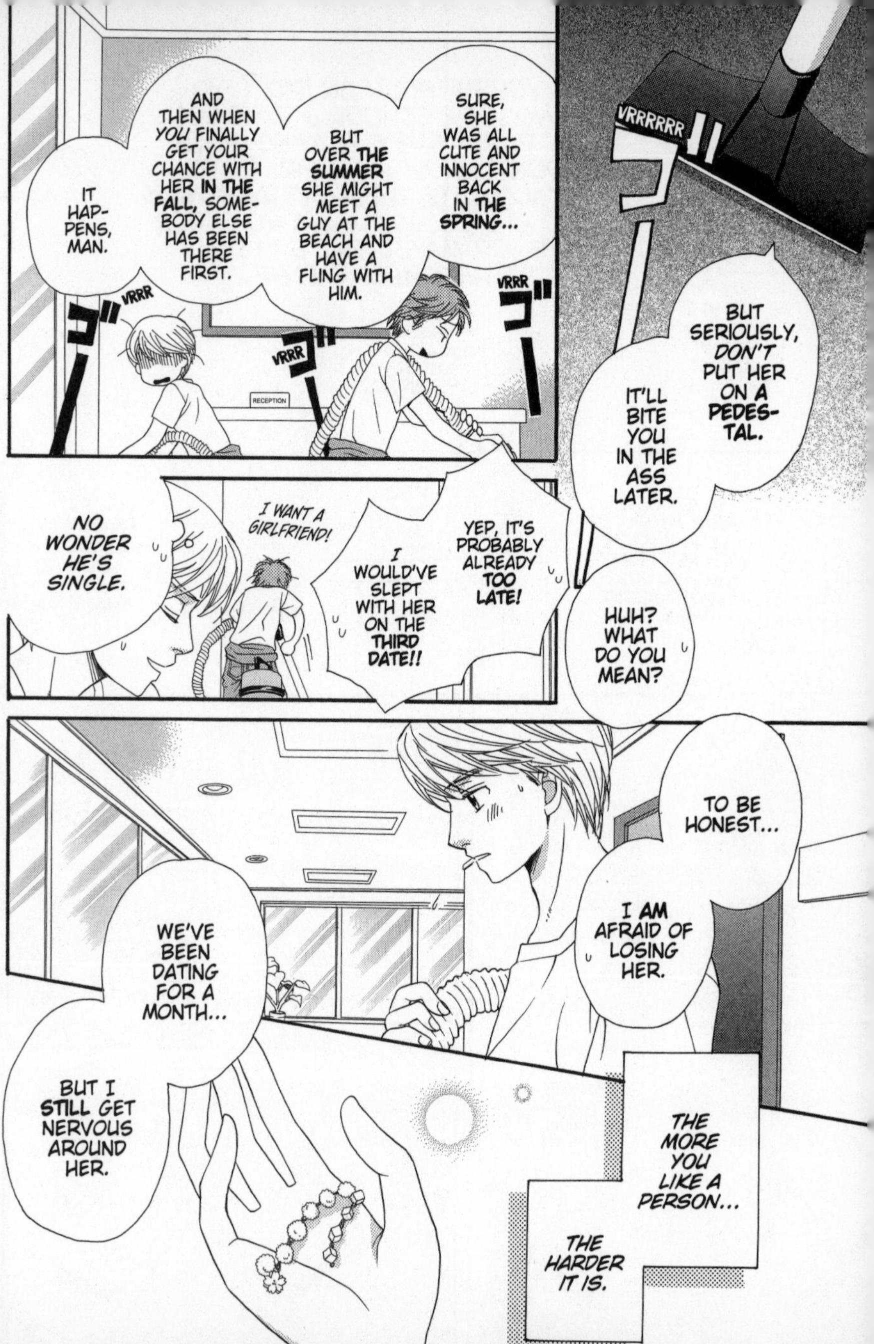
VRRRRRR
BUT SERIOUSLY, DON'T PUT HER ON A PEDESTAL.
IT'LL BITE YOU IN THE ASS LATER.
SURE, SHE WAS ALL CUTE AND INNOCENT BACK IN THE SPRING...
BUT OVER THE SUMMER SHE MIGHT MEET A GUY AT THE BEACH AND HAVE A FLING WITH HIM.
AND THEN WHEN YOU FINALLY GET YOUR CHANCE WITH HER IN THE FALL, SOMEBODY ELSE HAS BEEN THERE FIRST.
IT HAPPENS, MAN.
VRRR
VRRR
VRRR
RECEPTION
HUH? WHAT DO YOU MEAN?
YEP, IT'S PROBABLY ALREADY TOO LATE!
I WOULD'VE SLEPT WITH HER ON THE THIRD DATE!!
I WANT A GIRLFRIEND!
NO WONDER HE'S SINGLE.
TO BE HONEST...
I AM AFRAID OF LOSING HER.
WE'VE BEEN DATING FOR A MONTH...
BUT I STILL GET NERVOUS AROUND HER.
THE MORE YOU LIKE A PERSON...
THE HARDER IT IS.

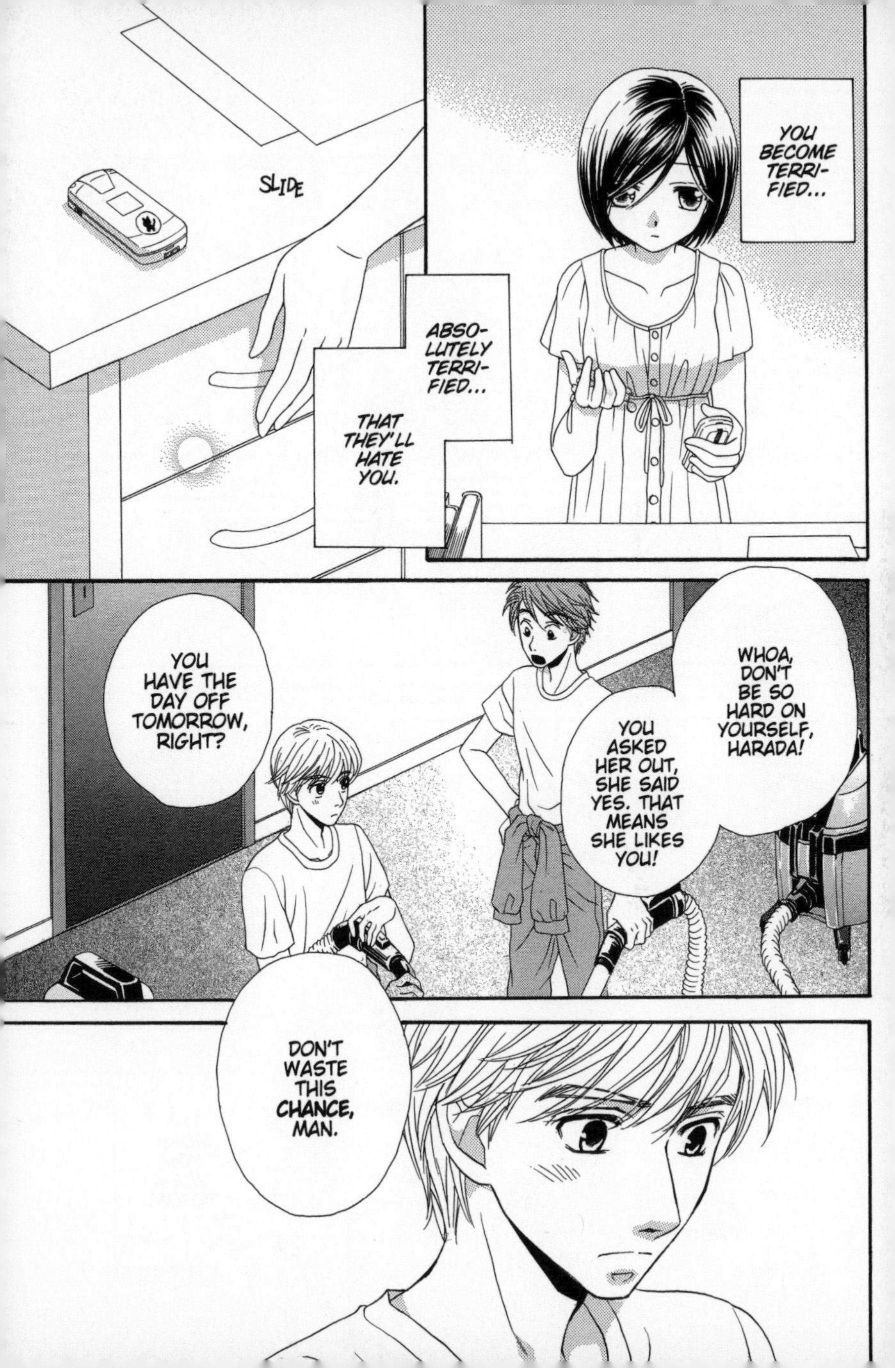
YOU BECOME TERRI-FIED...
ABSO-LUTELY TERRI-FIED...
THAT THEY'LL HATE YOU.
SLIDE
WHOA, DON'T BE SO HARD ON YOURSELF, HARADA!
YOU ASKED HER OUT, SHE SAID YES. THAT MEANS SHE LIKES YOU!
YOU HAVE THE DAY OFF TOMORROW, RIGHT?
DON'T WASTE THIS CHANCE, MAN.

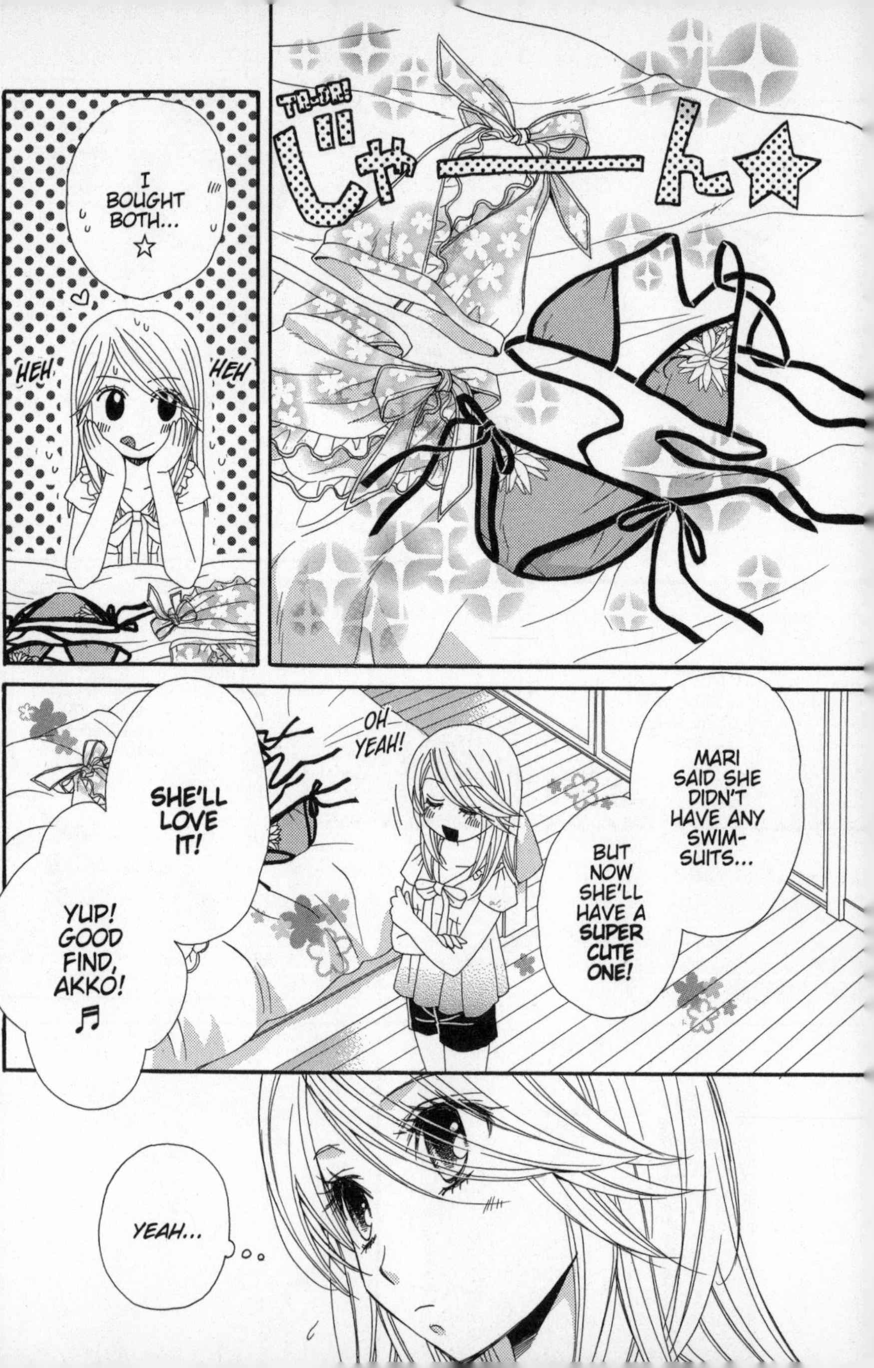
TA-DA!
じゃーん☆
I BOUGHT BOTH... ☆
HEH HEH
MARI SAID SHE DIDN'T HAVE ANY SWIM-SUITS...
BUT NOW SHE'LL HAVE A SUPER CUTE ONE!
OH YEAH!
SHE'LL LOVE IT!
YUP! GOOD FIND, AKKO! ♬
YEAH...

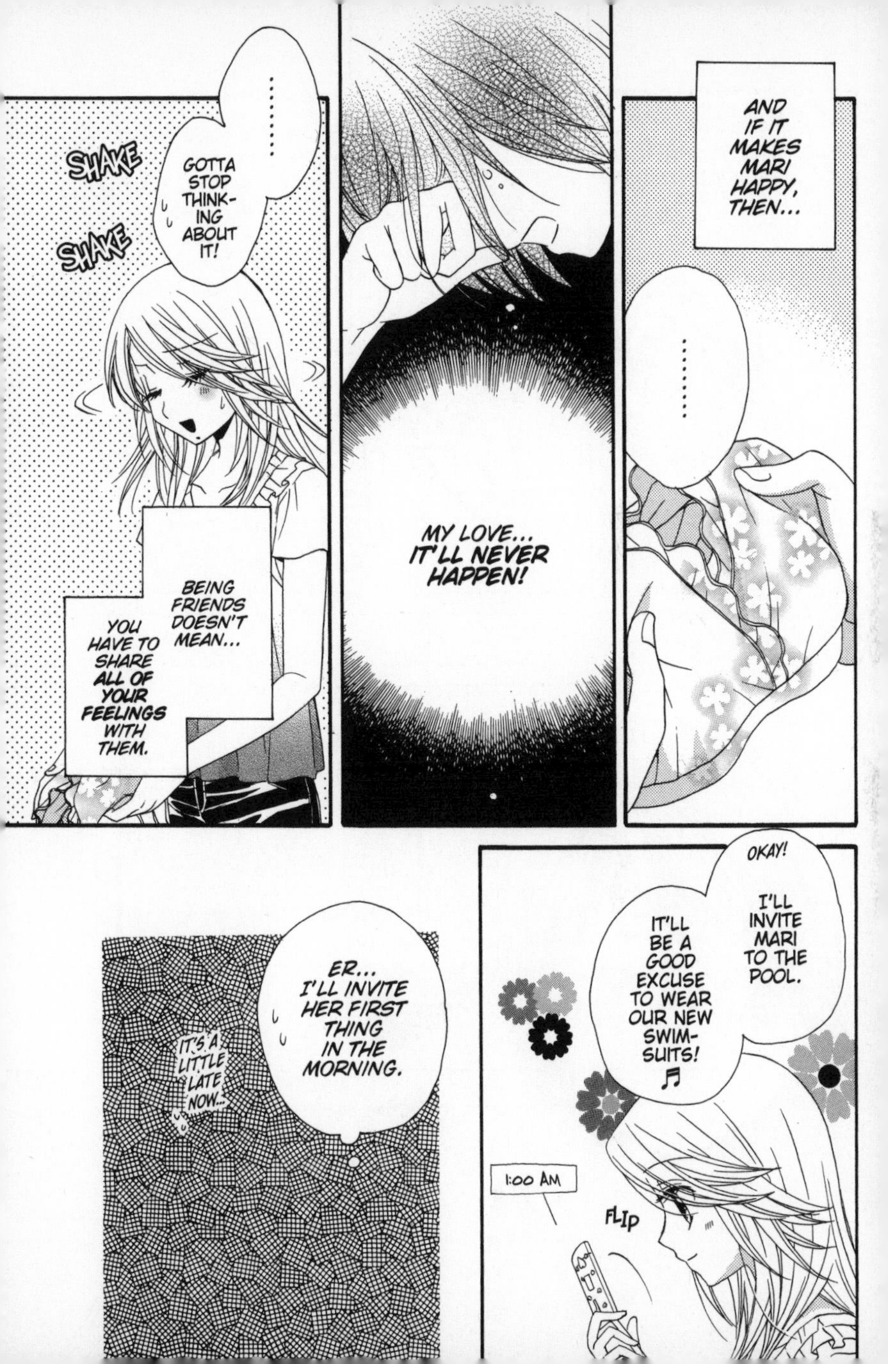
AND IF IT MAKES MARI HAPPY, THEN...
......
MY LOVE... IT'LL NEVER HAPPEN!
......
GOTTA STOP THINKING ABOUT IT!
SHAKE
SHAKE
BEING FRIENDS DOESN'T MEAN...
YOU HAVE TO SHARE ALL OF YOUR FEELINGS WITH THEM.
OKAY!
I'LL INVITE MARI TO THE POOL.
IT'LL BE A GOOD EXCUSE TO WEAR OUR NEW SWIM-SUITS! ♫
1:00 AM
FLIP
ER... I'LL INVITE HER FIRST THING IN THE MORNING.
IT'S A LITTLE LATE NOW...

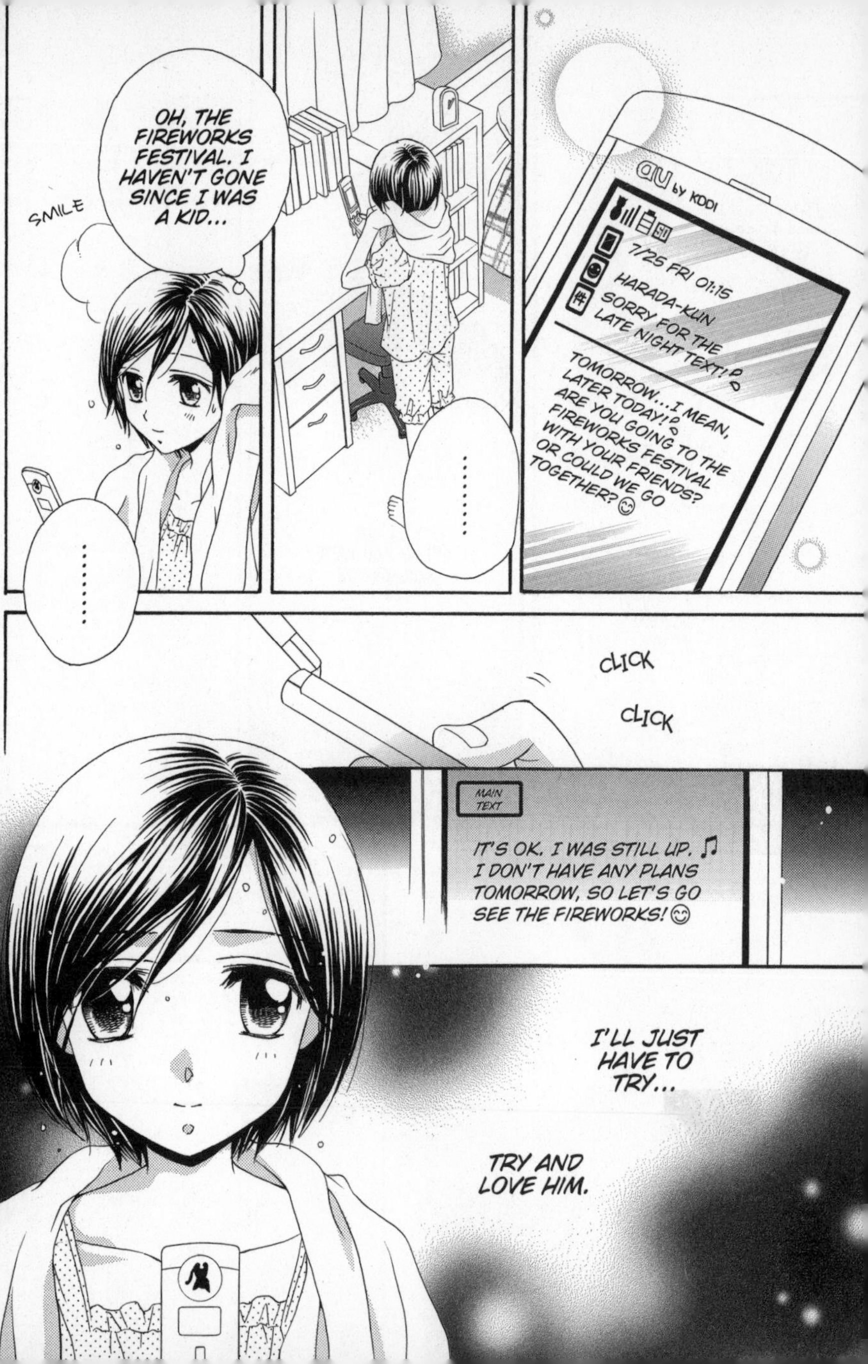
au by KDDI
7/25 FRI 01:15
HARADA-KUN
SORRY FOR THE LATE NIGHT TEXT!
TOMORROW...I MEAN, LATER TODAY! ARE YOU GOING TO THE FIREWORKS FESTIVAL WITH YOUR FRIENDS? OR COULD WE GO TOGETHER?
......
OH, THE FIREWORKS FESTIVAL. I HAVEN'T GONE SINCE I WAS A KID...
SMILE
......
CLICK
CLICK
MAIN TEXT
IT'S OK. I WAS STILL UP. ♫ I DON'T HAVE ANY PLANS TOMORROW, SO LET'S GO SEE THE FIREWORKS!
I'LL JUST HAVE TO TRY...
TRY AND LOVE HIM.

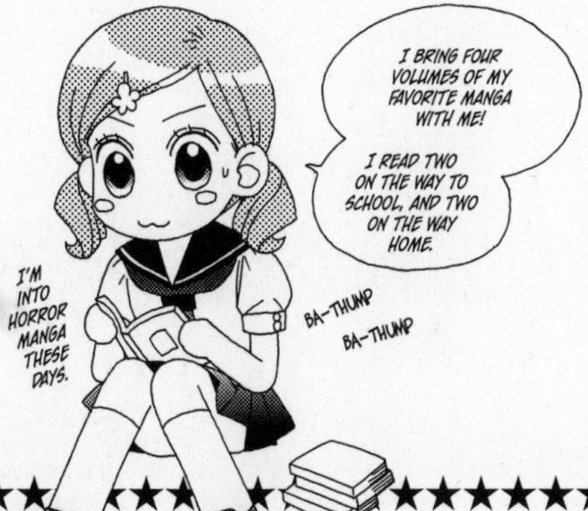
I BRING FOUR VOLUMES OF MY FAVORITE MANGA WITH ME!
I READ TWO ON THE WAY TO SCHOOL, AND TWO ON THE WAY HOME.
BA-THUMP
BA-THUMP
I'M INTO HORROR MANGA THESE DAYS.

GIRL FRIENDS－ガールフレンズ－

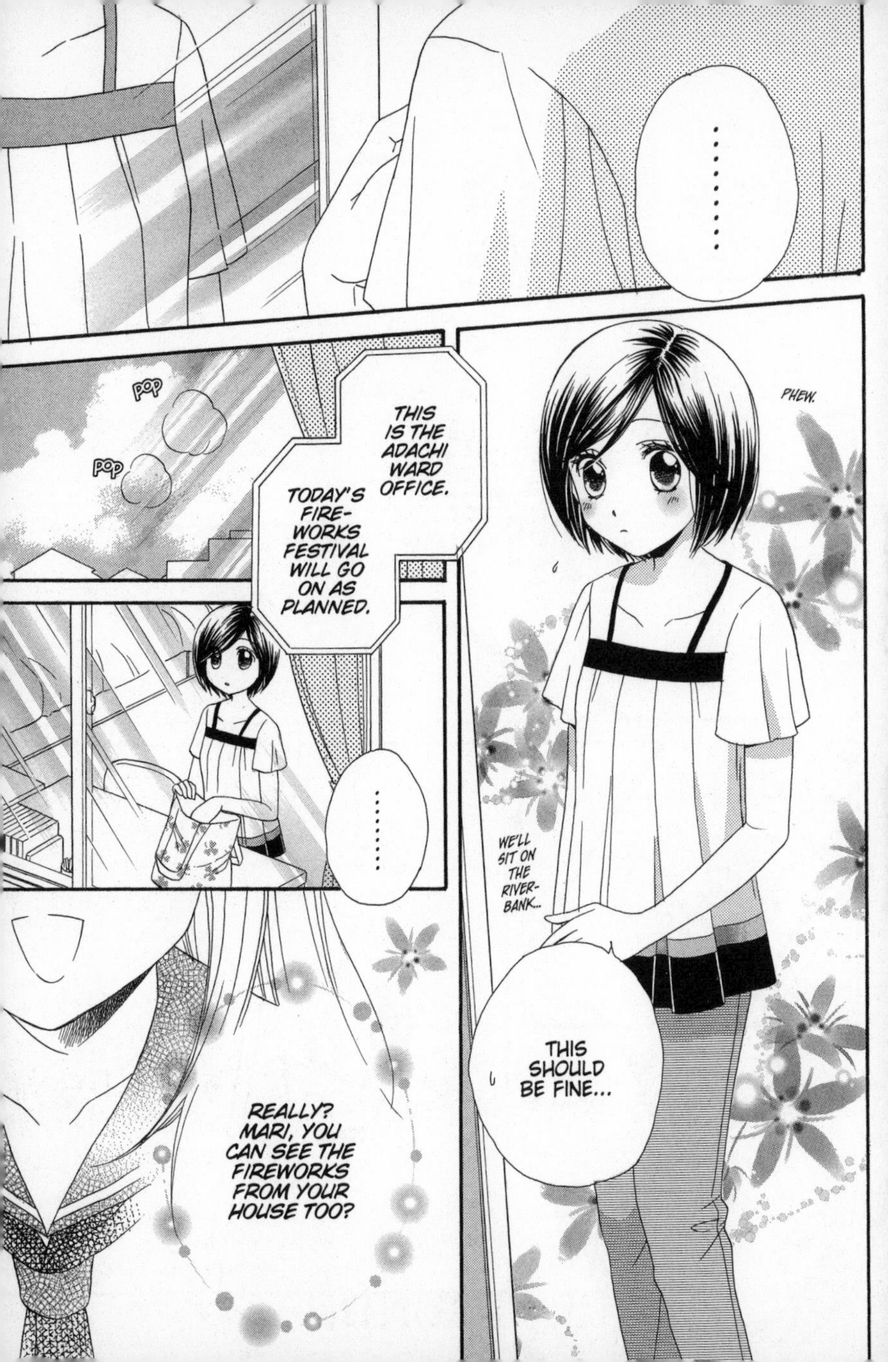

......
PHEW.
WE'LL SIT ON THE RIVER-BANK...
THIS SHOULD BE FINE...
POP
POP
THIS IS THE ADACHI WARD OFFICE.
TODAY'S FIRE-WORKS FESTIVAL WILL GO ON AS PLANNED.
......
REALLY? MARI, YOU CAN SEE THE FIREWORKS FROM YOUR HOUSE TOO?

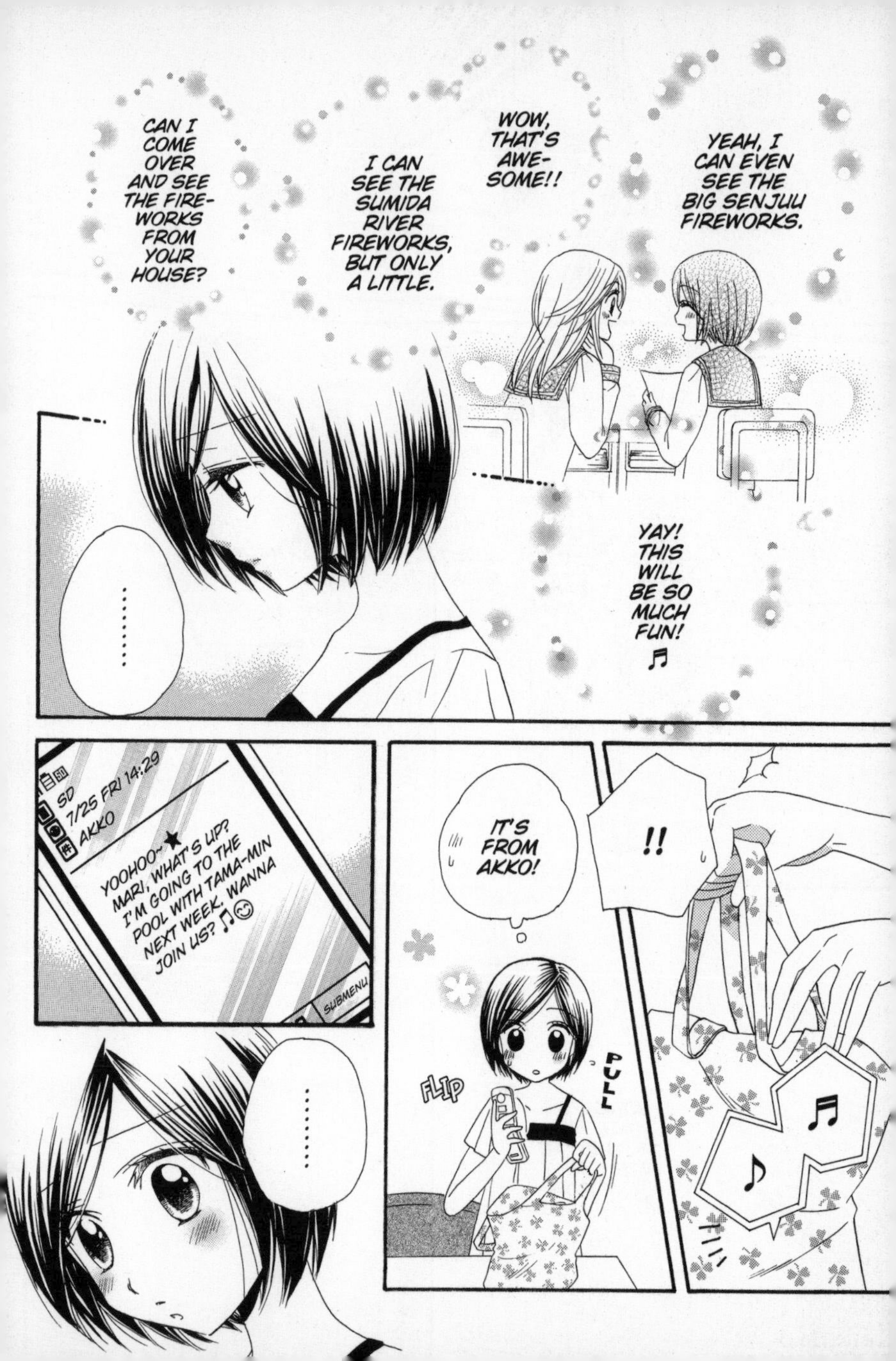

YEAH, I CAN EVEN SEE THE BIG SENJUU FIREWORKS.
WOW, THAT'S AWE-SOME!!
I CAN SEE THE SUMIDA RIVER FIREWORKS, BUT ONLY A LITTLE.
CAN I COME OVER AND SEE THE FIRE-WORKS FROM YOUR HOUSE?
...
YAY! THIS WILL BE SO MUCH FUN! ♬
......
!!
♬ ♪
IT'S FROM AKKO!
PULL
FLIP
SD
7/25 FRI 14:29
AKKO
YOOHOO~★ MARI, WHAT'S UP? I'M GOING TO THE POOL WITH TAMA-MIN NEXT WEEK. WANNA JOIN US? ♫☺
SUBMENU
......

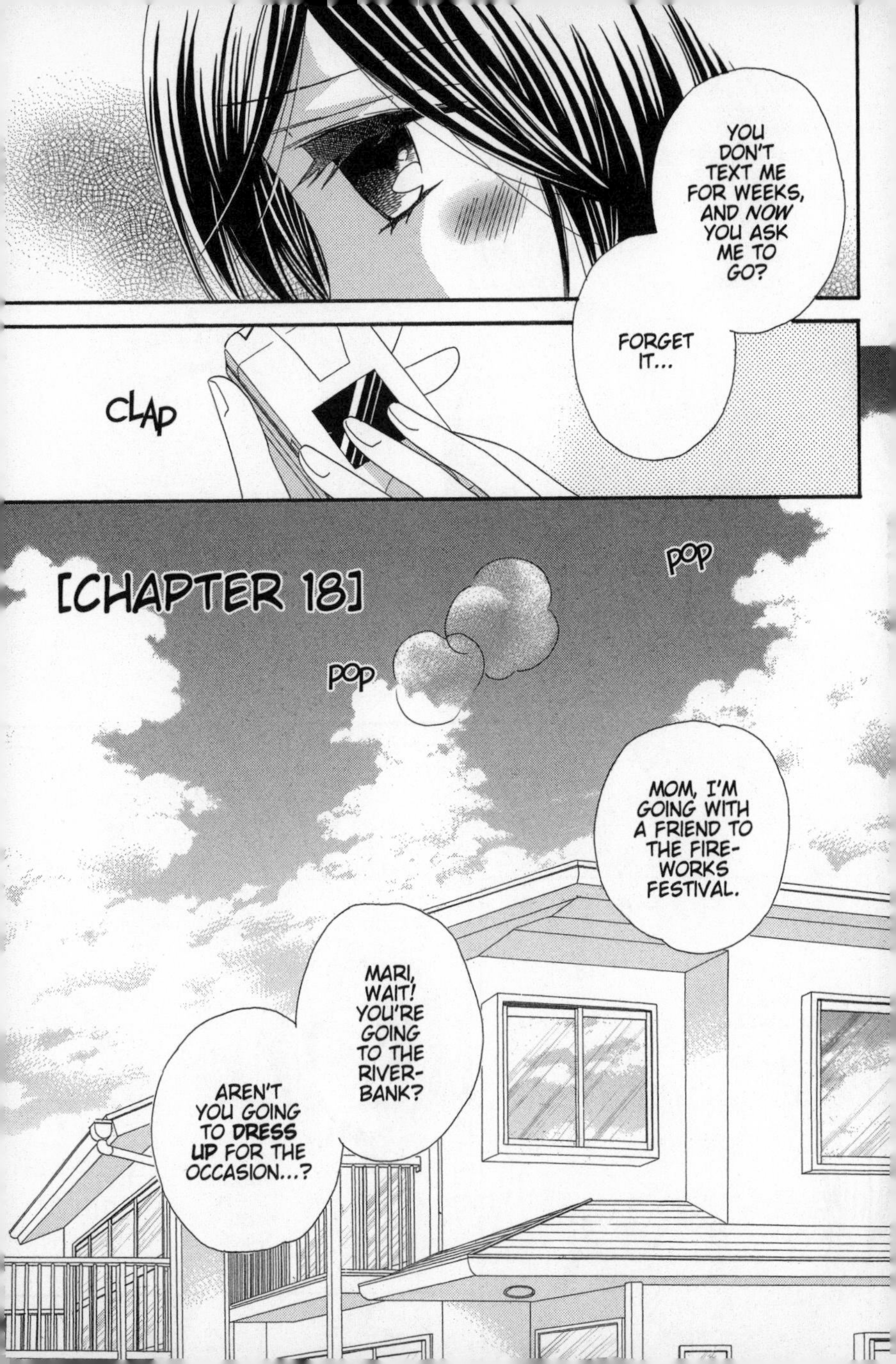

YOU DON'T TEXT ME FOR WEEKS, AND *NOW* YOU ASK ME TO GO?
FORGET IT...
CLAP
POP
[CHAPTER 18]
POP
MOM, I'M GOING WITH A FRIEND TO THE FIRE-WORKS FESTIVAL.
MARI, WAIT! YOU'RE GOING TO THE RIVER-BANK?
AREN'T YOU GOING TO **DRESS UP** FOR THE OCCASION...?

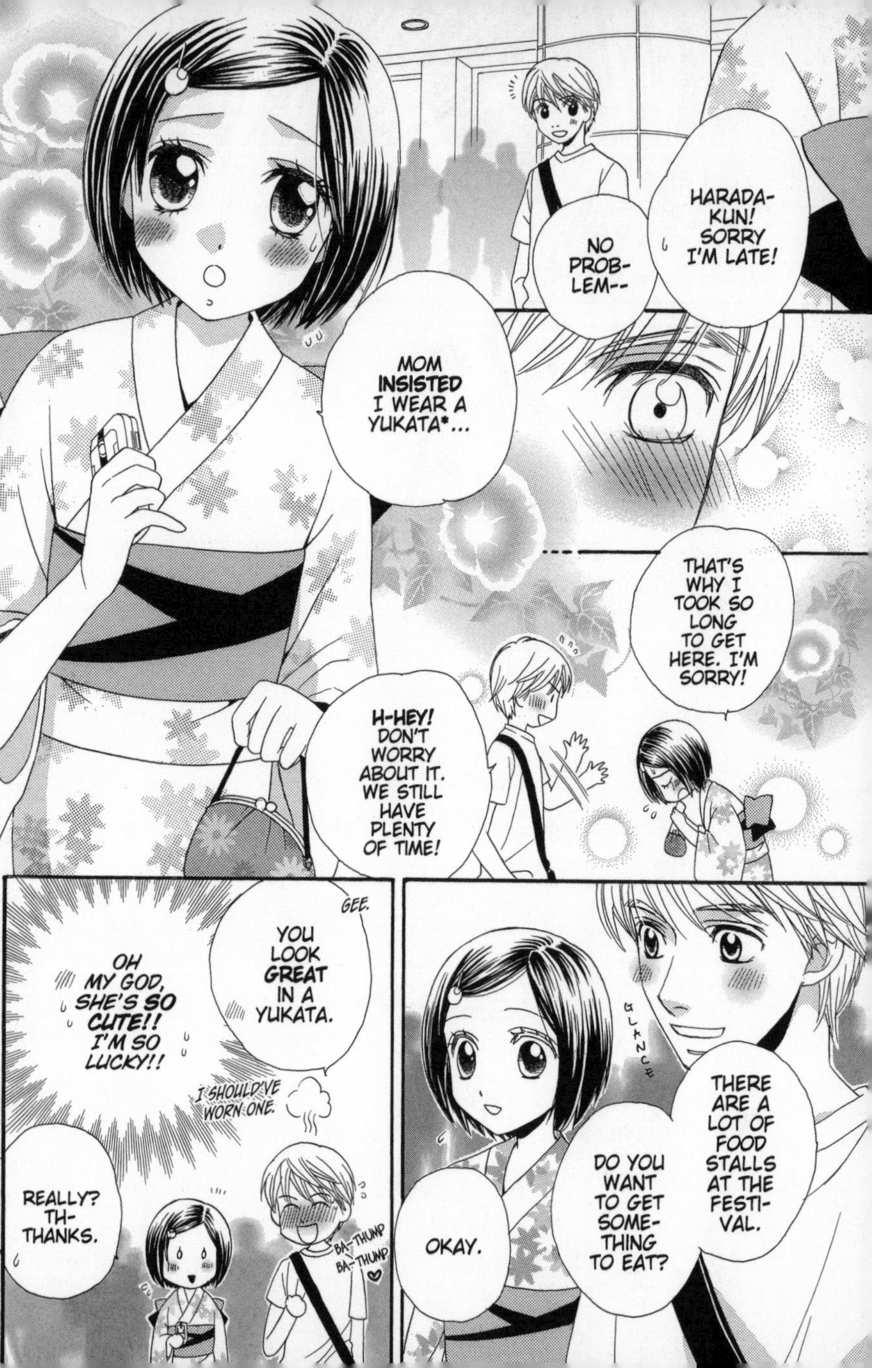
HARADA-KUN! SORRY I'M LATE!
NO PROB-LEM--
MOM INSISTED I WEAR A YUKATA*...
THAT'S WHY I TOOK SO LONG TO GET HERE. I'M SORRY!
H-HEY! DON'T WORRY ABOUT IT. WE STILL HAVE PLENTY OF TIME!
THERE ARE A LOT OF FOOD STALLS AT THE FESTI-VAL.
DO YOU WANT TO GET SOME-THING TO EAT?
GLANCE
OKAY.
GEE.
YOU LOOK GREAT IN A YUKATA.
OH MY GOD, SHE'S SO CUTE!! I'M SO LUCKY!!
I SHOULD'VE WORN ONE.
REALLY? TH-THANKS.
BA-THUMP BA-THUMP

*A yukata is a light kimono often worn during summer festivals.

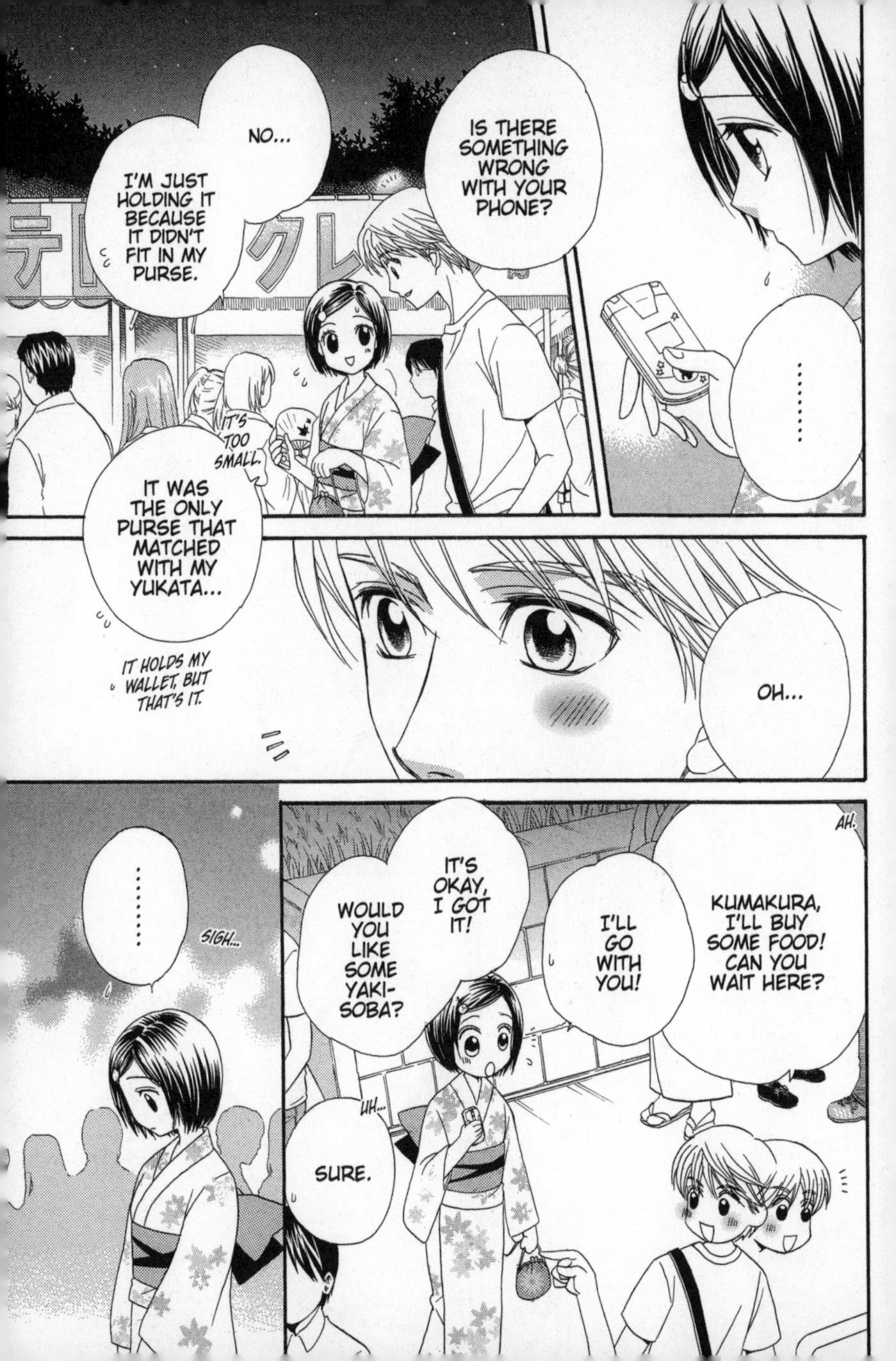
IS THERE SOMETHING WRONG WITH YOUR PHONE?
......
NO...
I'M JUST HOLDING IT BECAUSE IT DIDN'T FIT IN MY PURSE.
IT'S TOO SMALL.
IT WAS THE ONLY PURSE THAT MATCHED WITH MY YUKATA...
IT HOLDS MY WALLET, BUT THAT'S IT.
OH...
AH.
KUMAKURA, I'LL BUY SOME FOOD! CAN YOU WAIT HERE?
I'LL GO WITH YOU!
IT'S OKAY, I GOT IT!
WOULD YOU LIKE SOME YAKI-SOBA?
UH...
SURE.
......
SIGH...

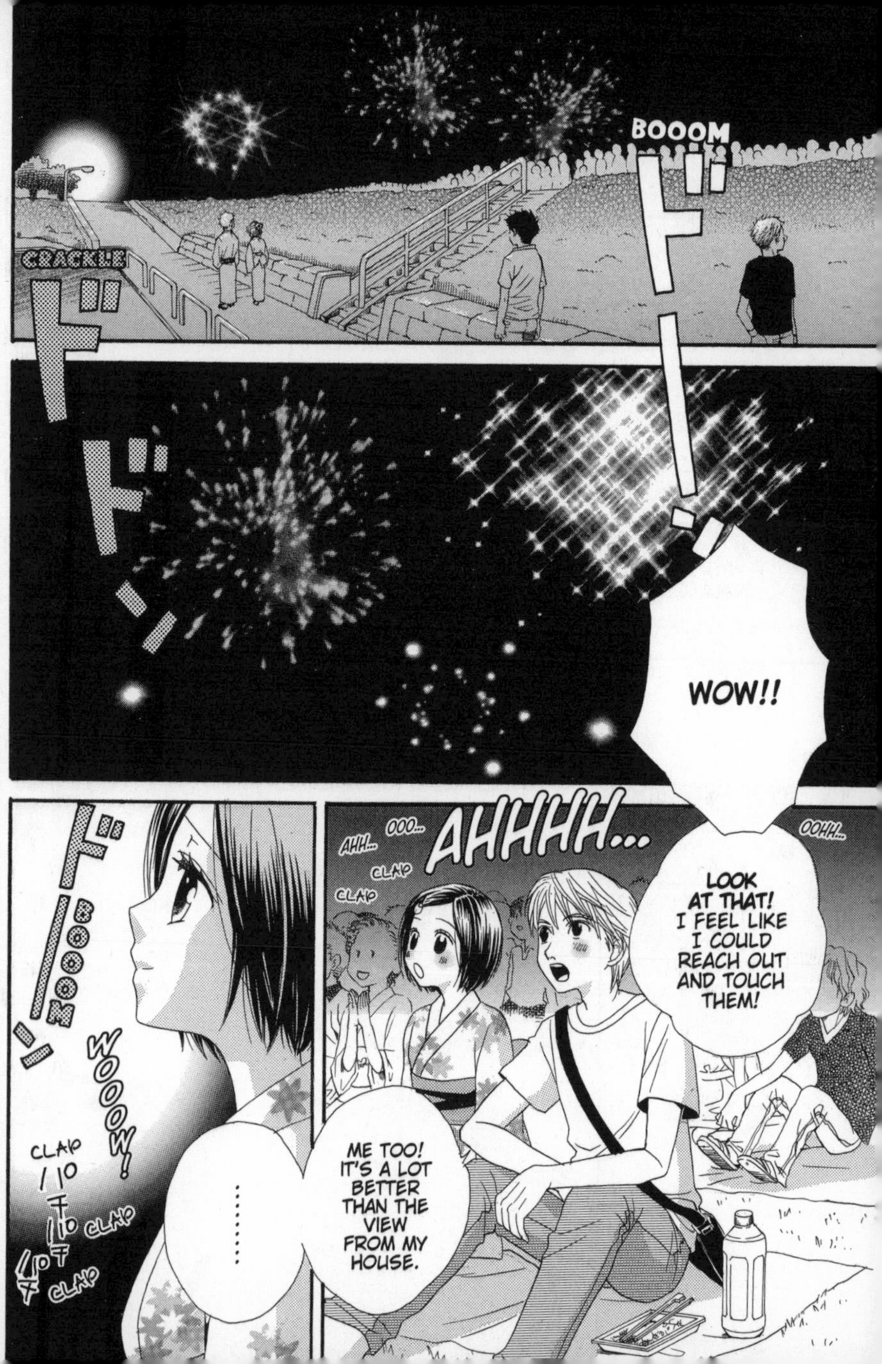
BOOOM
CRACKLE
WOW!!
OOHH...
AHHHH...
OOO...
AHH...
CLAP
CLAP
LOOK AT THAT! I FEEL LIKE I COULD REACH OUT AND TOUCH THEM!
ME TOO! IT'S A LOT BETTER THAN THE VIEW FROM MY HOUSE.
BOOOOOM
WOOOOW!
......
CLAP
CLAP
CLAP

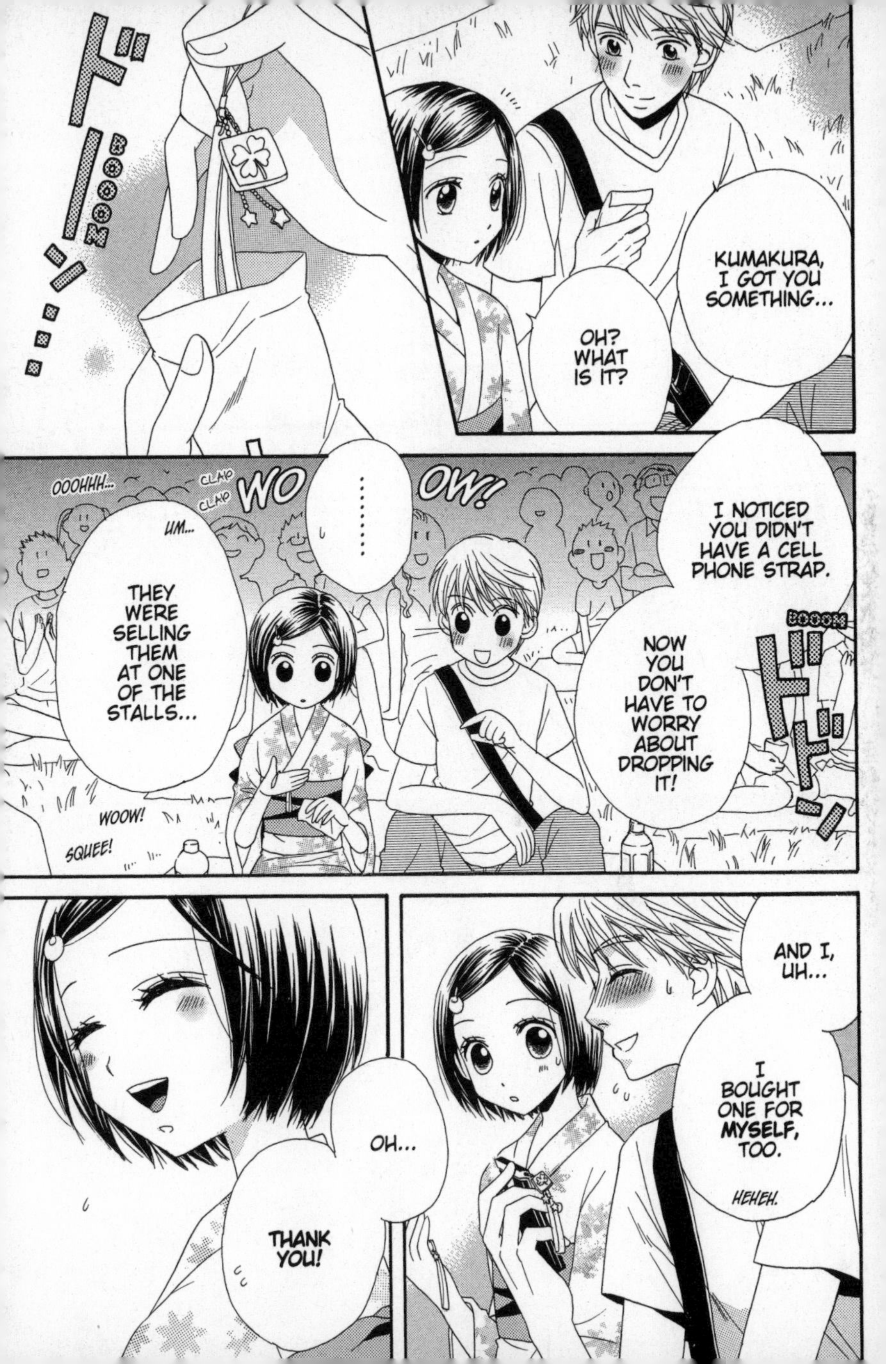
KUMAKURA, I GOT YOU SOMETHING...
OH? WHAT IS IT?
BOOOOM
I NOTICED YOU DIDN'T HAVE A CELL PHONE STRAP.
BOOOM
NOW YOU DON'T HAVE TO WORRY ABOUT DROPPING IT!
WO OW!
......
CLAP CLAP
UM...
OOOHHH...
THEY WERE SELLING THEM AT ONE OF THE STALLS...
WOOW!
SQUEE!
AND I, UH...
I BOUGHT ONE FOR MYSELF, TOO.
HEHEH.
OH...
THANK YOU!

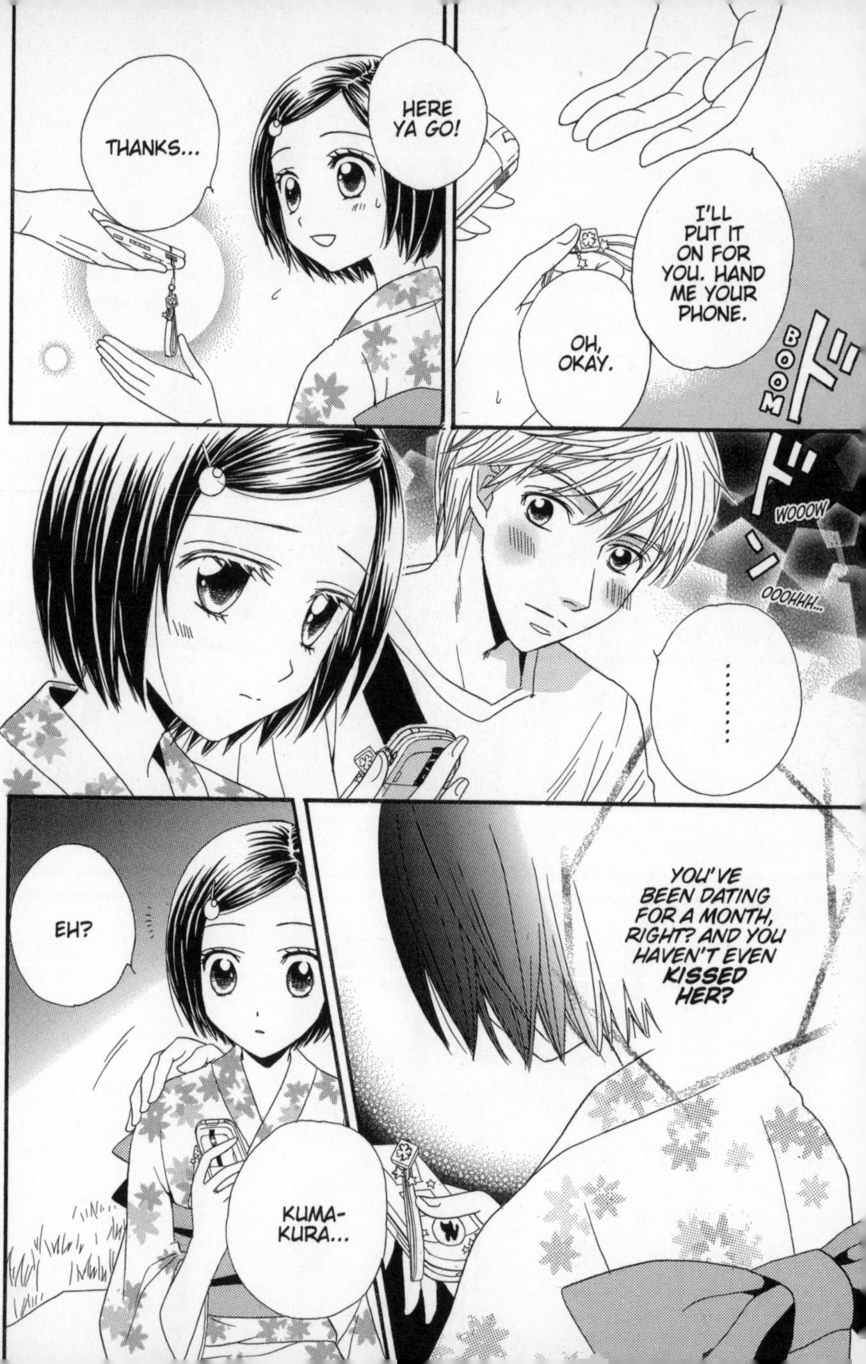
I'LL PUT IT ON FOR YOU. HAND ME YOUR PHONE.
BOOM
OH, OKAY.
HERE YA GO!
THANKS...
WOOOW
OOOHHH...
......
YOU'VE BEEN DATING FOR A MONTH, RIGHT? AND YOU HAVEN'T EVEN KISSED HER?
EH?
KUMA-KURA...

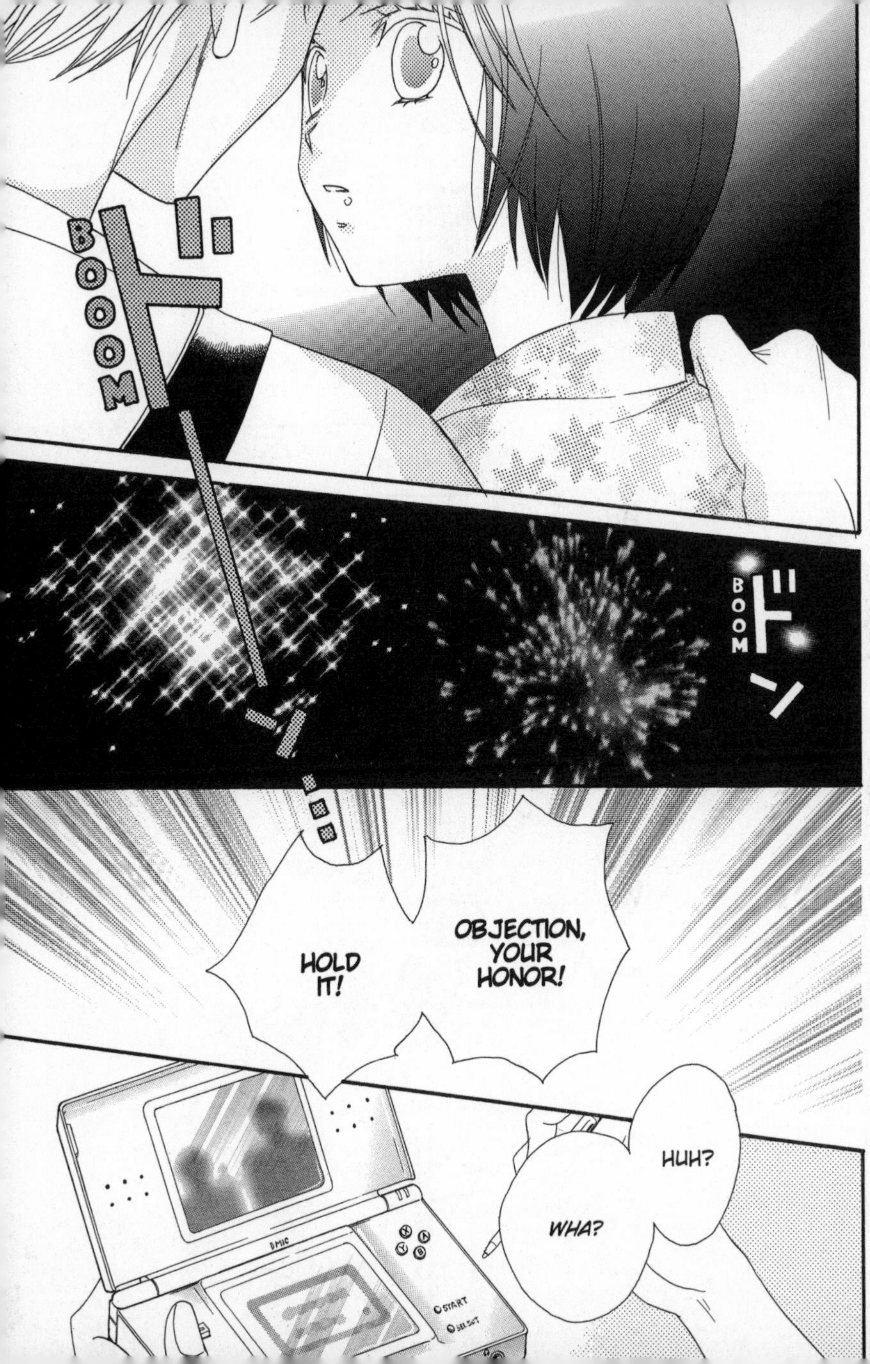
BOOOOM
BOOM
ドン
OBJECTION, YOUR HONOR!
HOLD IT!
HUH?
WHA?

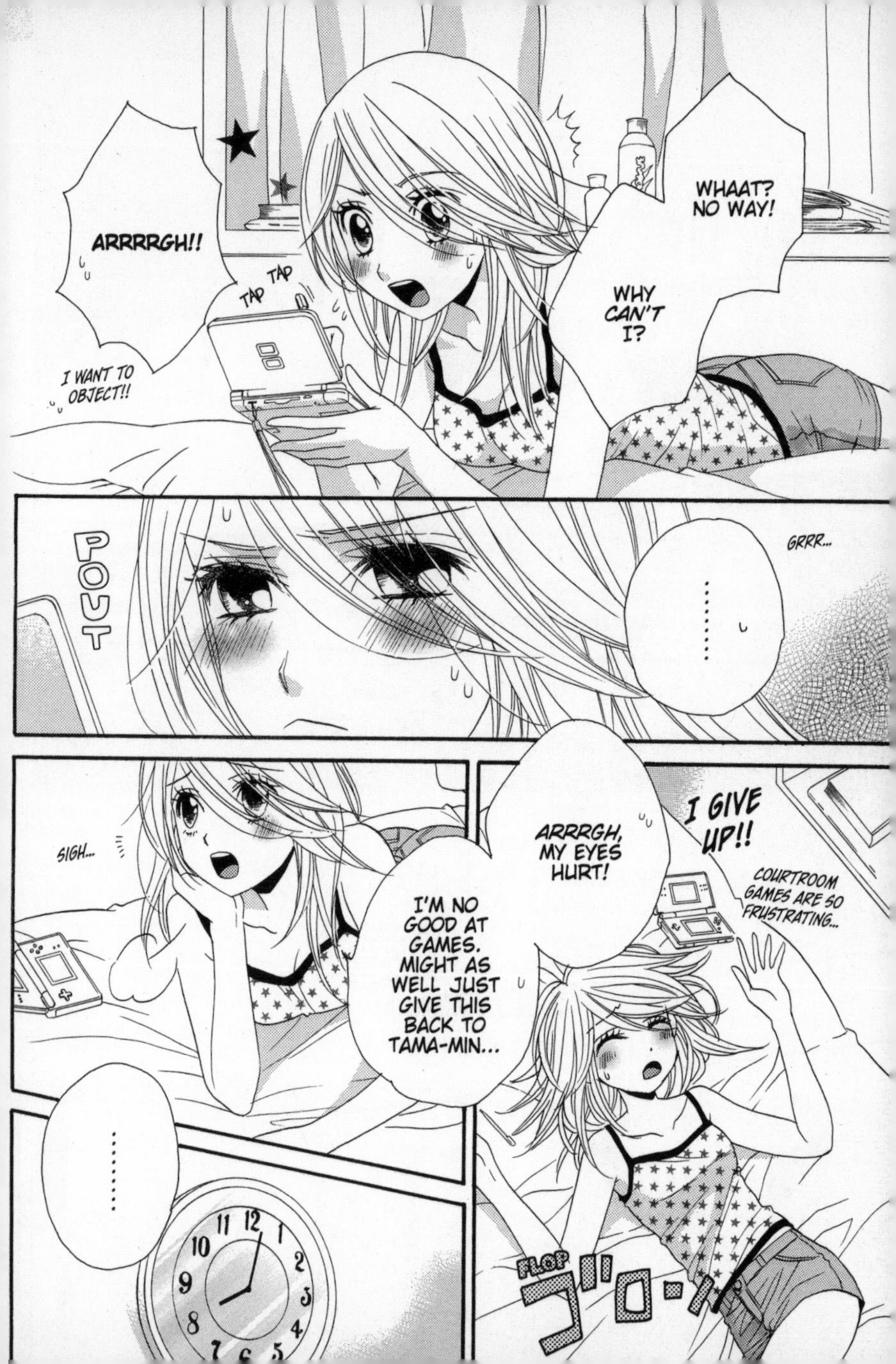
WHAAT? NO WAY!
WHY CAN'T I?
TAP TAP
ARRRRGH!!
I WANT TO OBJECT!!
GRRR...
......
POUT
I GIVE UP!!
COURTROOM GAMES ARE SO FRUSTRATING...
ARRRGH, MY EYES HURT!
FLOP
I'M NO GOOD AT GAMES. MIGHT AS WELL JUST GIVE THIS BACK TO TAMA-MIN...
SIGH...
......

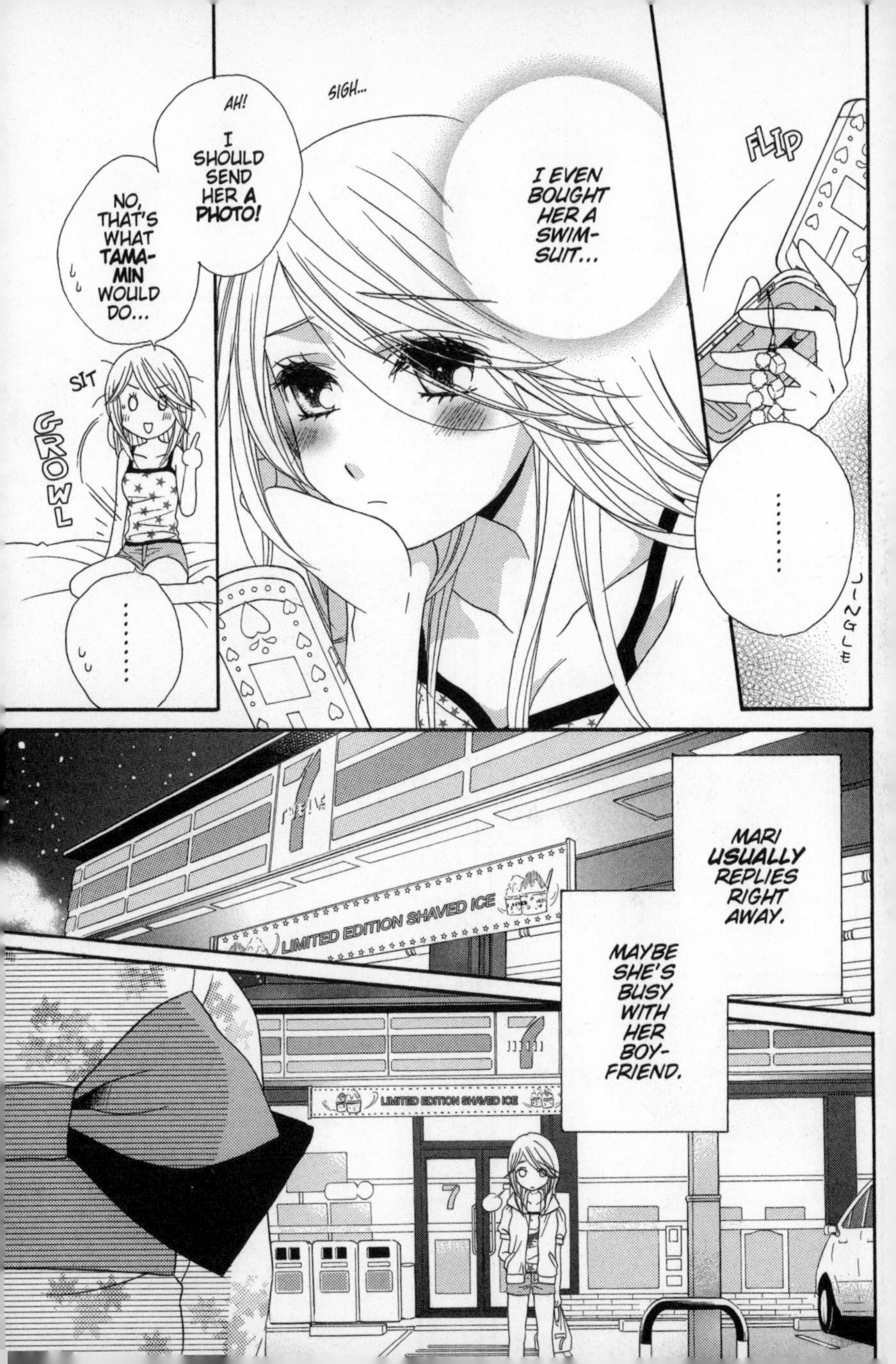
FLIP
......
JINGLE
SIGH...
I EVEN BOUGHT HER A SWIM-SUIT...
AH! I SHOULD SEND HER A PHOTO!
NO, THAT'S WHAT TAMA-MIN WOULD DO...
SIT
GROWL
......
MARI USUALLY REPLIES RIGHT AWAY.
MAYBE SHE'S BUSY WITH HER BOY-FRIEND.
LIMITED EDITION SHAVED ICE
LIMITED EDITION SHAVED ICE

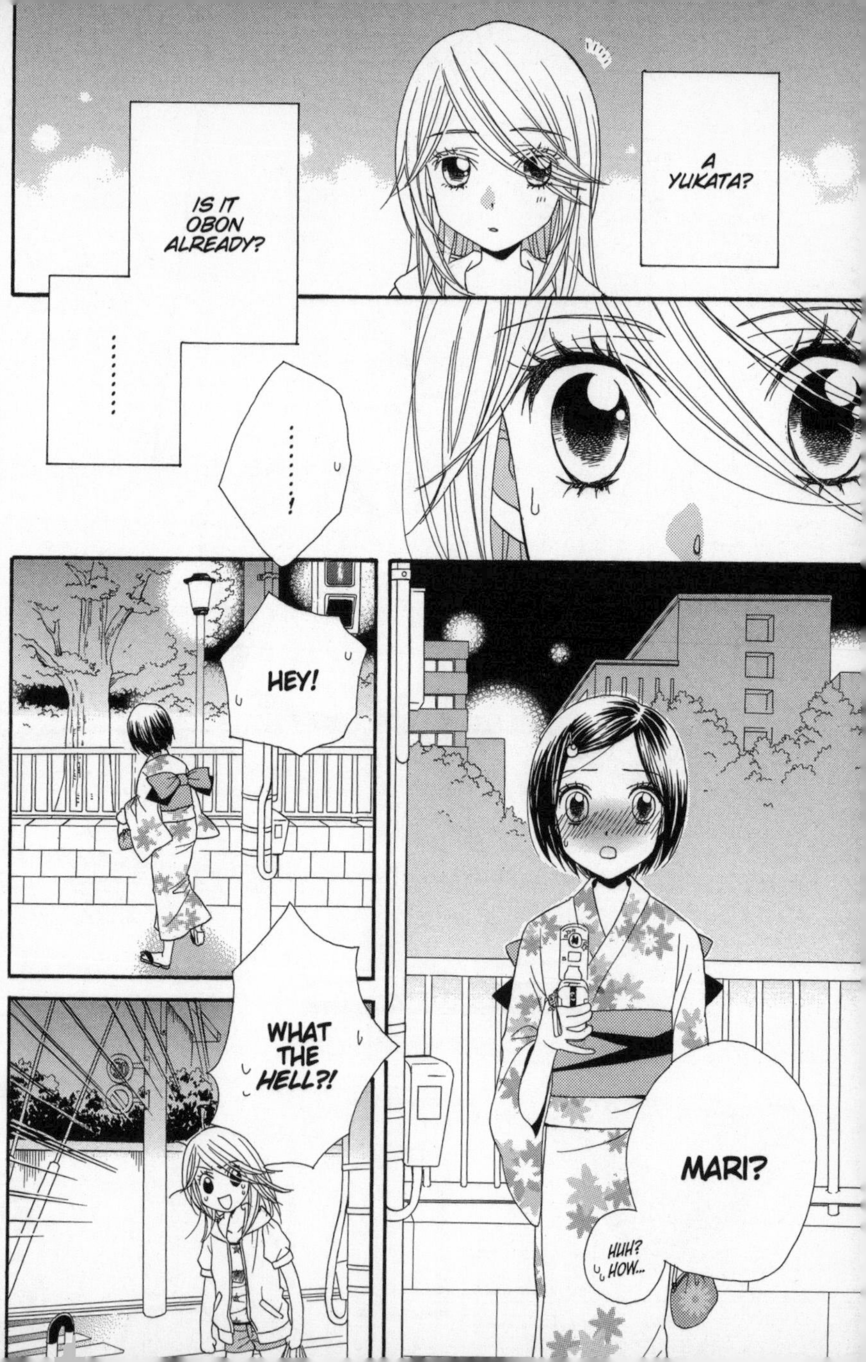
A YUKATA?
IS IT OBON ALREADY?
......
......!
MARI?
HUH? HOW...
HEY!
WHAT THE HELL?!

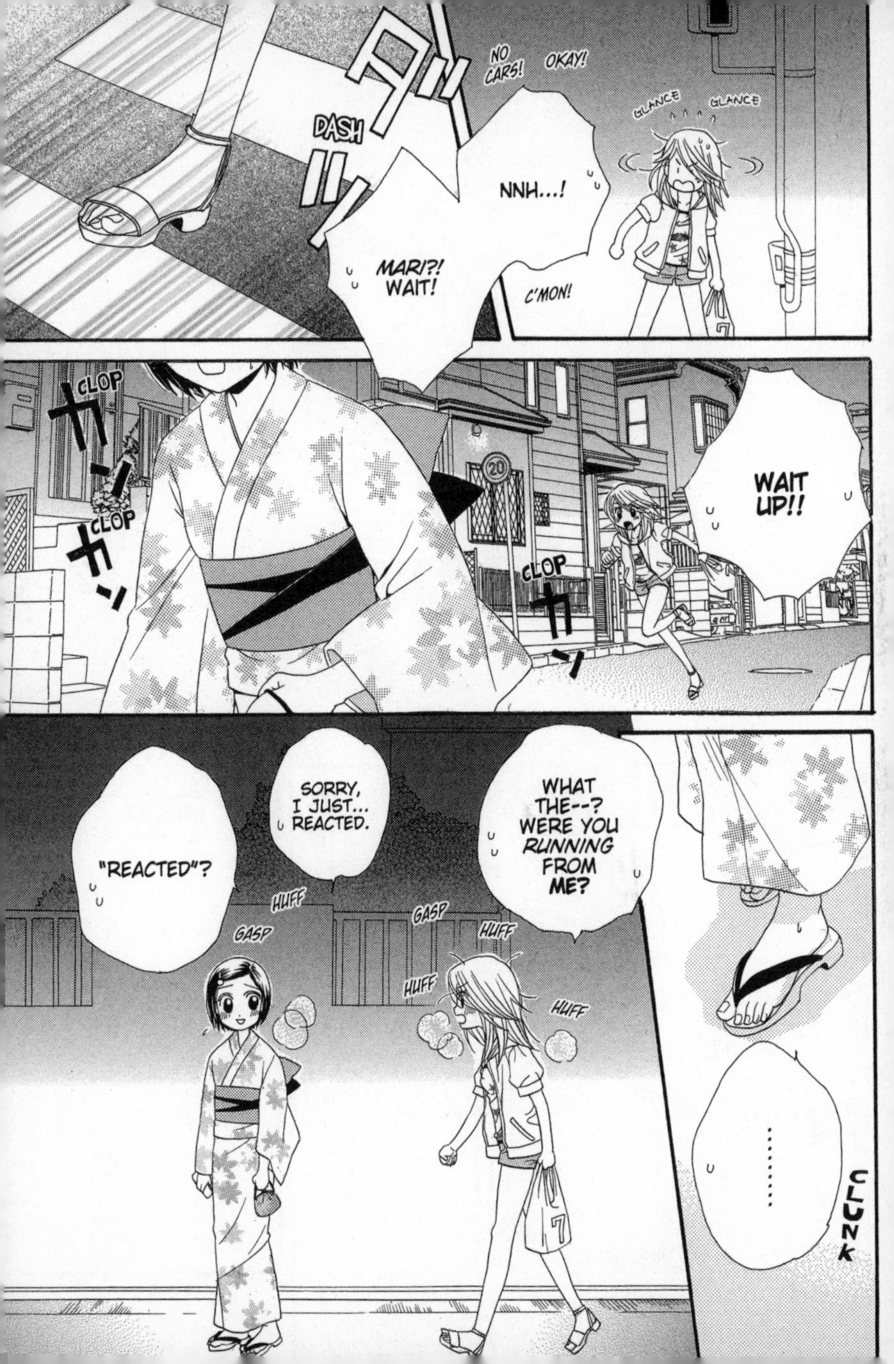
NO CARS!
OKAY!
GLANCE
GLANCE
NNH...!
C'MON!
DASH
MARI?! WAIT!
WAIT UP!!
CLOP
CLOP
CLOP
CLUNK
......
WHAT THE--? WERE YOU RUNNING FROM ME?
SORRY, I JUST... REACTED.
"REACTED"?
HUFF
GASP
HUFF
HUFF
GASP
HUFF

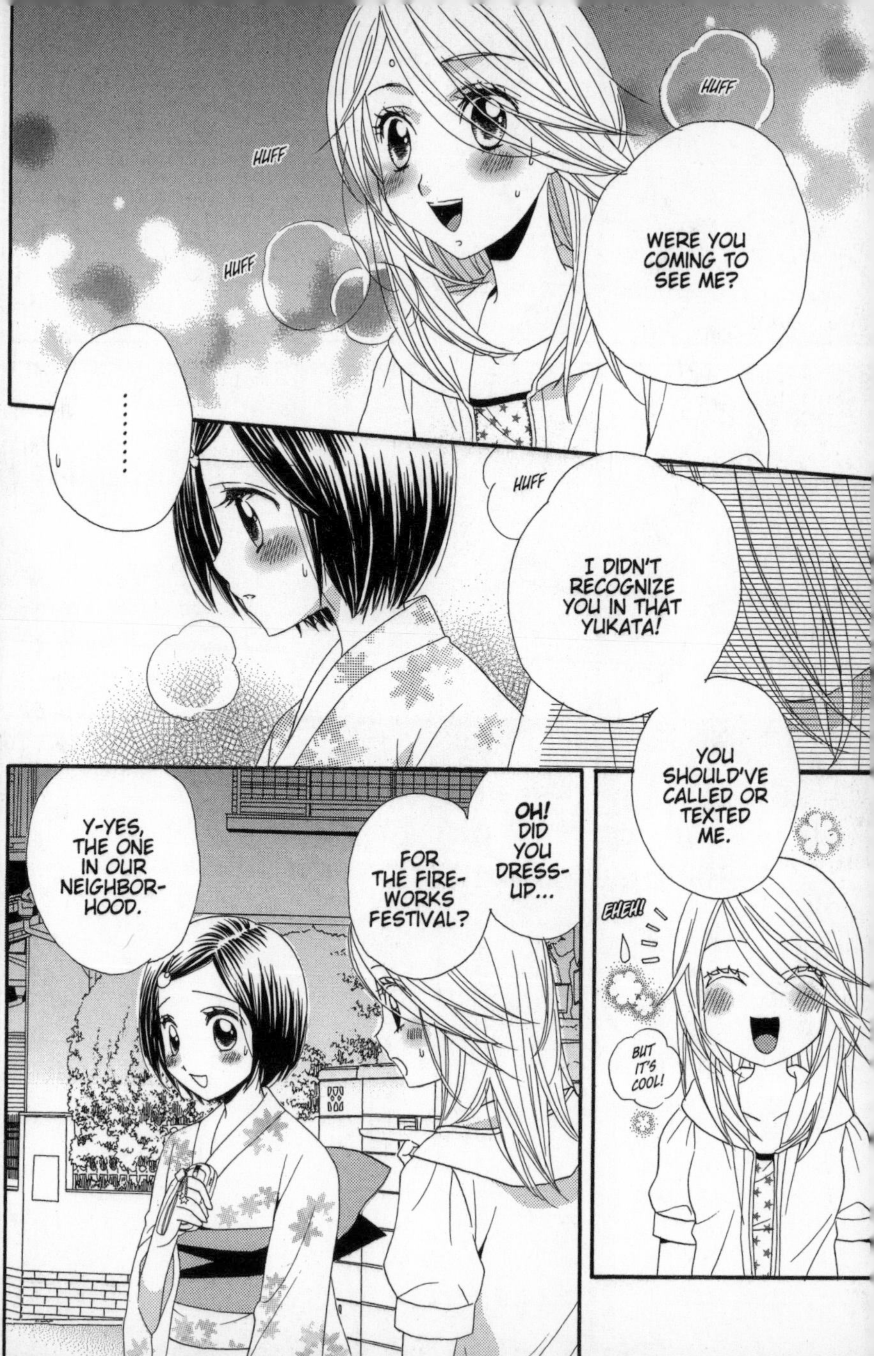
HUFF
WERE YOU COMING TO SEE ME?
HUFF
HUFF
......
HUFF
I DIDN'T RECOGNIZE YOU IN THAT YUKATA!
YOU SHOULD'VE CALLED OR TEXTED ME.
EHEH!
BUT IT'S COOL!
OH! DID YOU DRESS-UP...
FOR THE FIRE-WORKS FESTIVAL?
Y-YES, THE ONE IN OUR NEIGHBOR-HOOD.

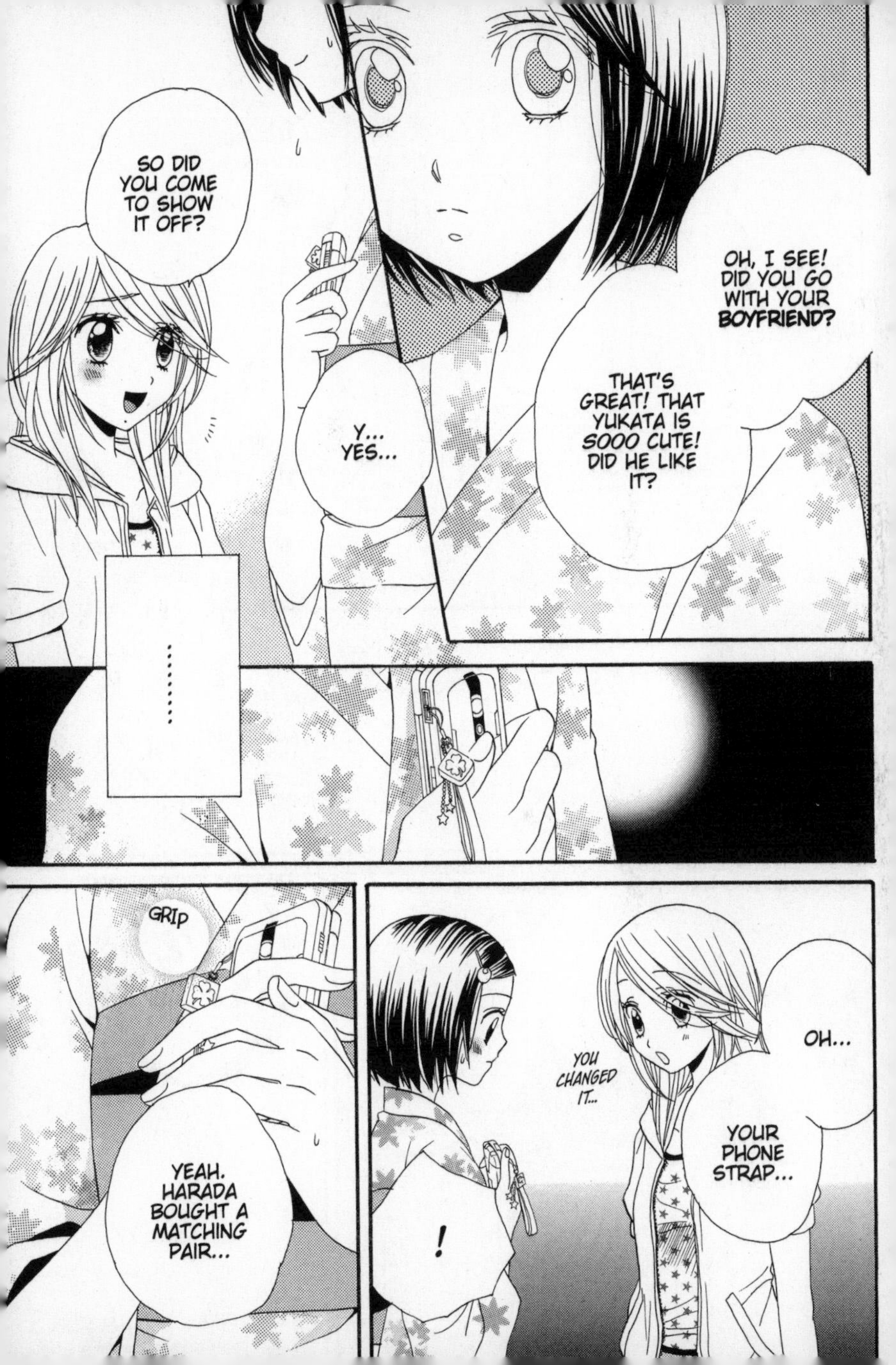
OH, I SEE! DID YOU GO WITH YOUR **BOYFRIEND?**
THAT'S GREAT! THAT YUKATA IS SOOO CUTE! DID HE LIKE IT?
Y... YES...
SO DID YOU COME TO SHOW IT OFF?
......
OH...
YOUR PHONE STRAP...
YOU CHANGED IT...
!
GRIP
YEAH. HARADA BOUGHT A MATCHING PAIR...

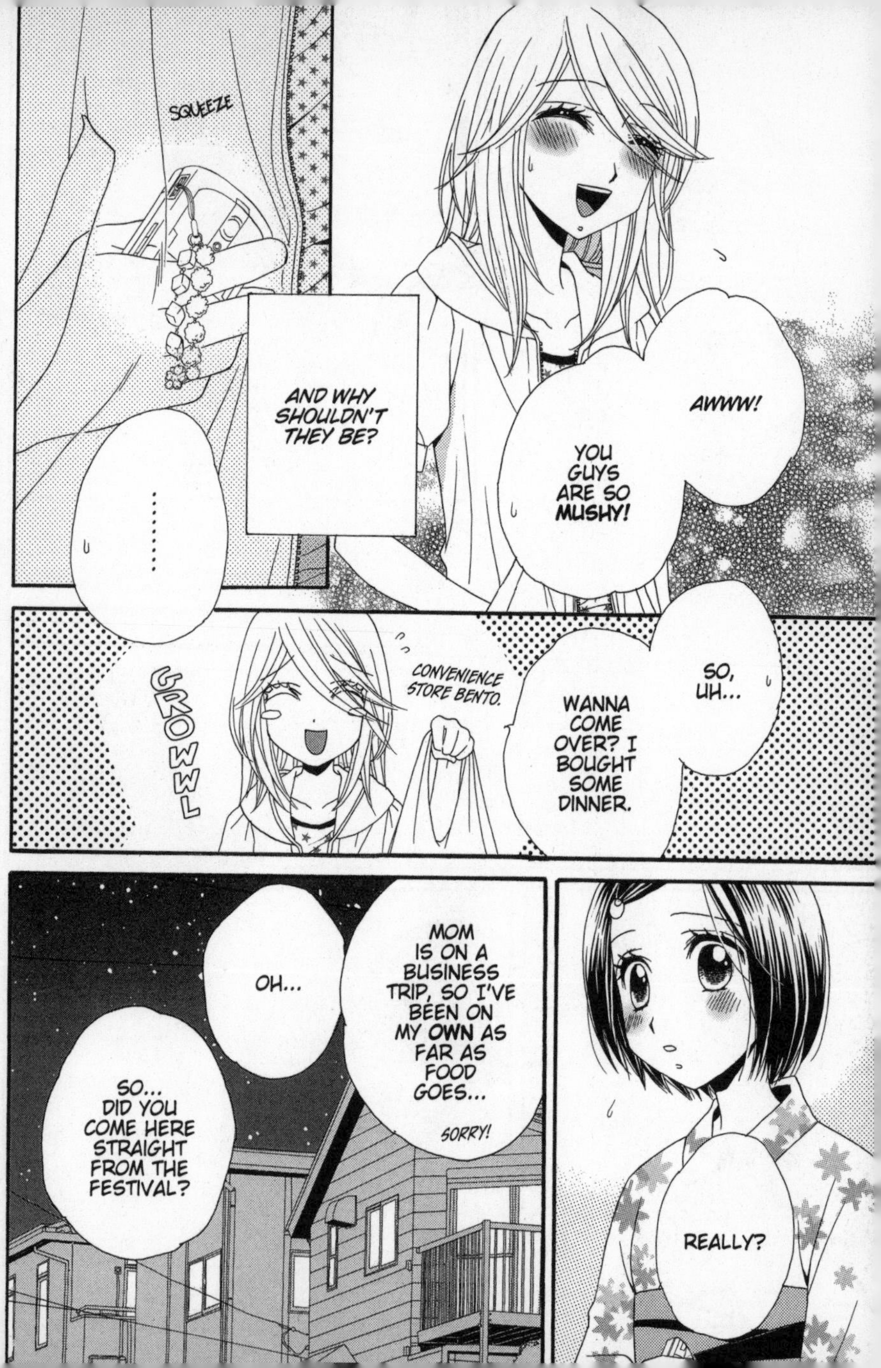
AWWW!
YOU GUYS ARE SO MUSHY!
AND WHY SHOULDN'T THEY BE?
SQUEEZE
......
SO, UH...
WANNA COME OVER? I BOUGHT SOME DINNER.
CONVENIENCE STORE BENTO.
GROWWL
REALLY?
MOM IS ON A BUSINESS TRIP, SO I'VE BEEN ON MY OWN AS FAR AS FOOD GOES...
SORRY!
OH...
SO... DID YOU COME HERE STRAIGHT FROM THE FESTIVAL?

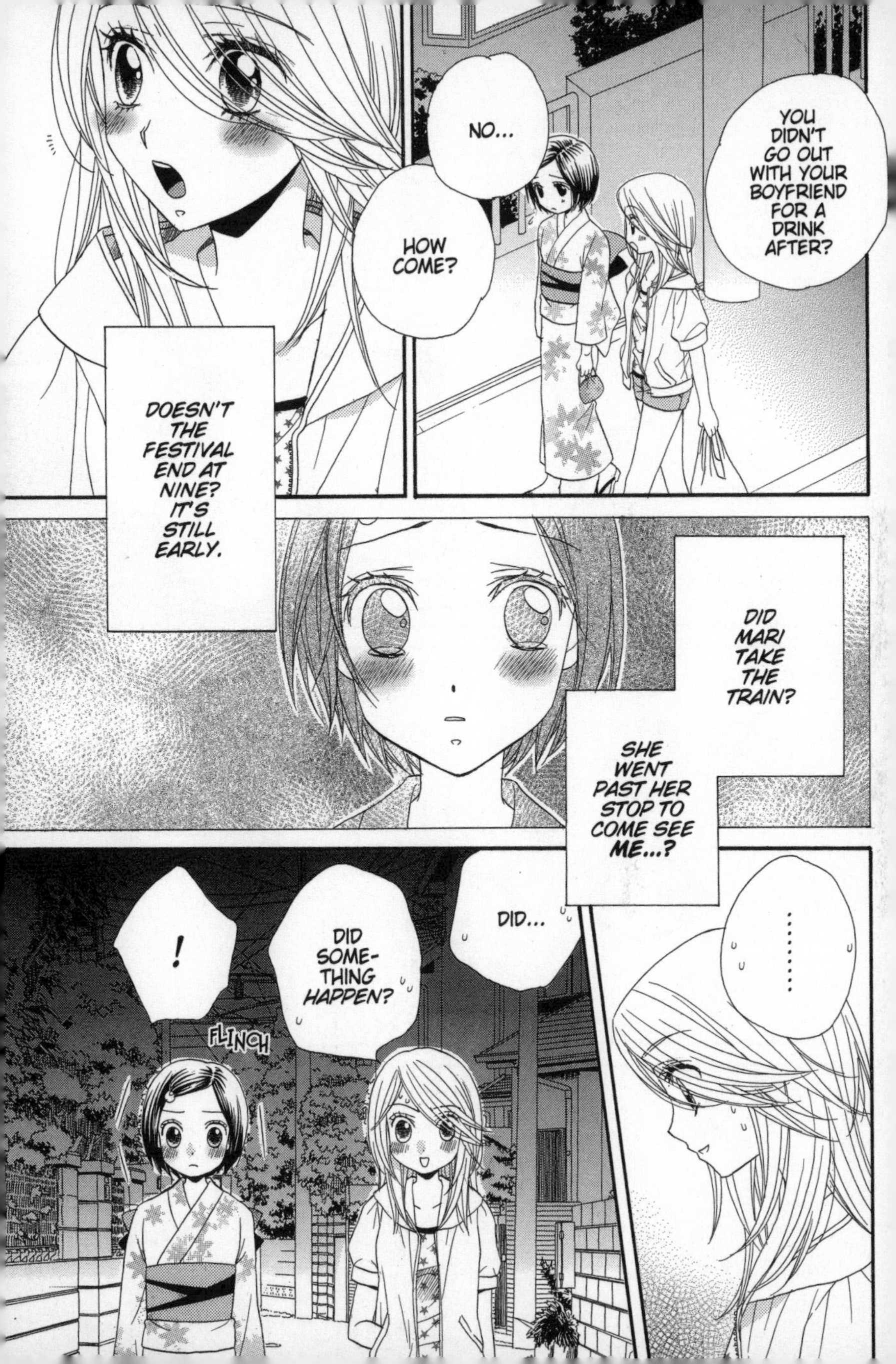
YOU DIDN'T GO OUT WITH YOUR BOYFRIEND FOR A DRINK AFTER?
NO...
HOW COME?
DOESN'T THE FESTIVAL END AT NINE? IT'S STILL EARLY.
DID MARI TAKE THE TRAIN?
SHE WENT PAST HER STOP TO COME SEE ME...?
......
DID...
DID SOME-THING HAPPEN?
!
FLINCH

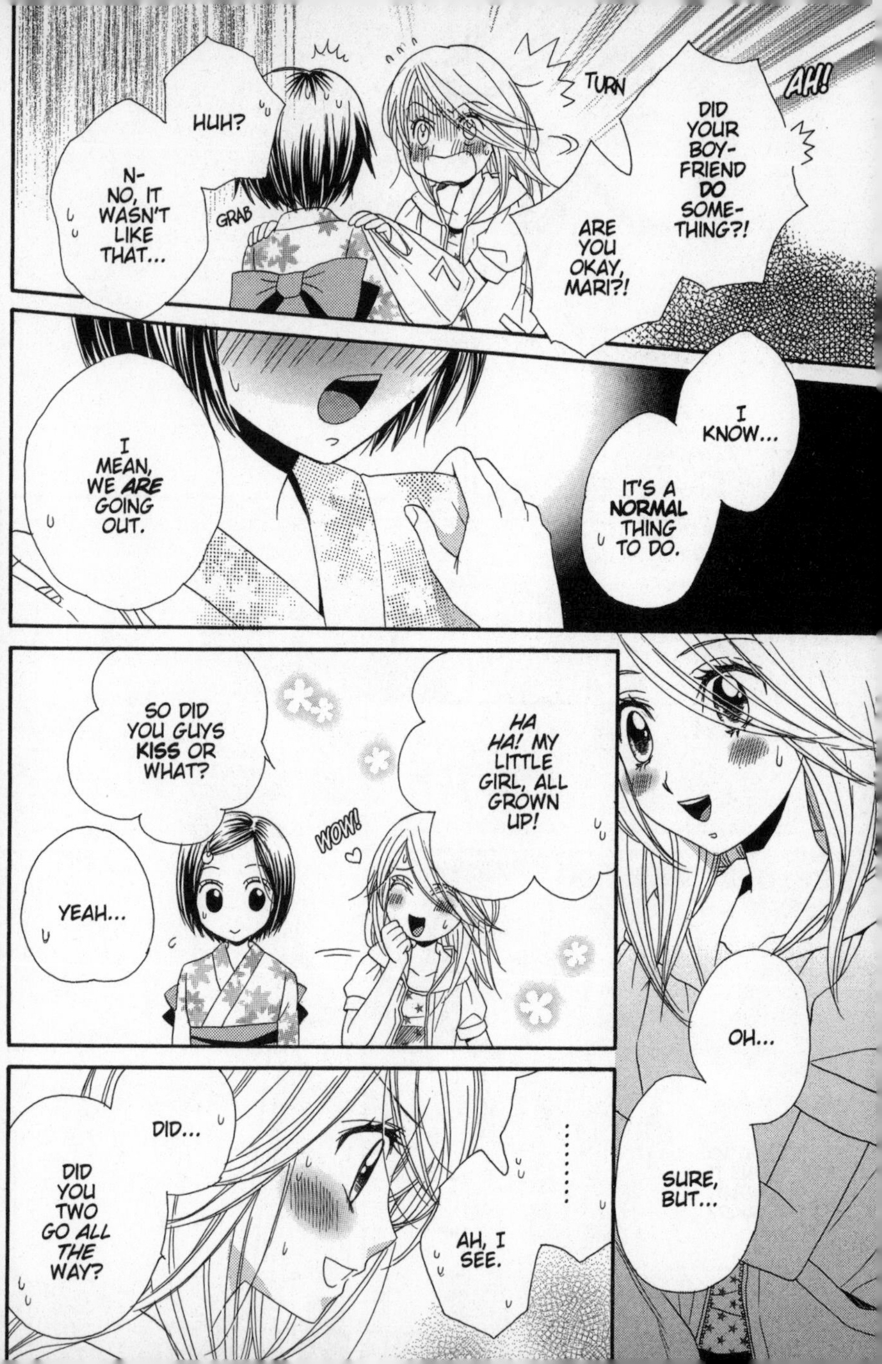

AH!
DID YOUR BOY-FRIEND DO SOME-THING?!
ARE YOU OKAY, MARI?!
TURN
HUH?
GRAB
N-NO, IT WASN'T LIKE THAT...
I KNOW...
IT'S A NORMAL THING TO DO.
I MEAN, WE ARE GOING OUT.
OH...
SURE, BUT...
HA HA! MY LITTLE GIRL, ALL GROWN UP!
SO DID YOU GUYS KISS OR WHAT?
WOW!
YEAH...
......
AH, I SEE.
DID...
DID YOU TWO GO ALL THE WAY?

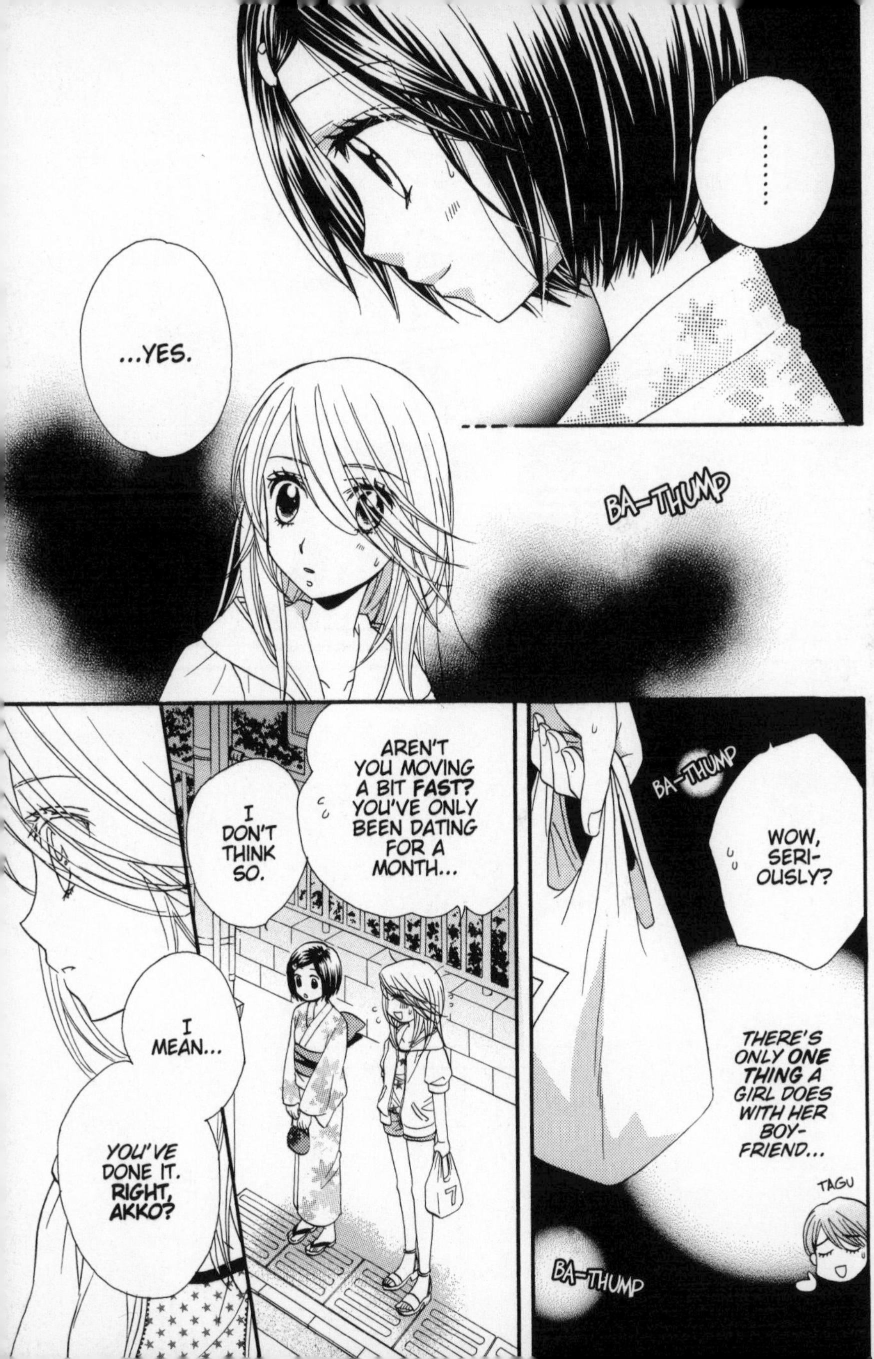
......
...YES.
BA-THUMP
BA-THUMP
WOW, SERIOUSLY?
THERE'S ONLY ONE THING A GIRL DOES WITH HER BOY-FRIEND...
TAGU
BA-THUMP
AREN'T YOU MOVING A BIT FAST? YOU'VE ONLY BEEN DATING FOR A MONTH...
I DON'T THINK SO.
I MEAN...
YOU'VE DONE IT. RIGHT, AKKO?

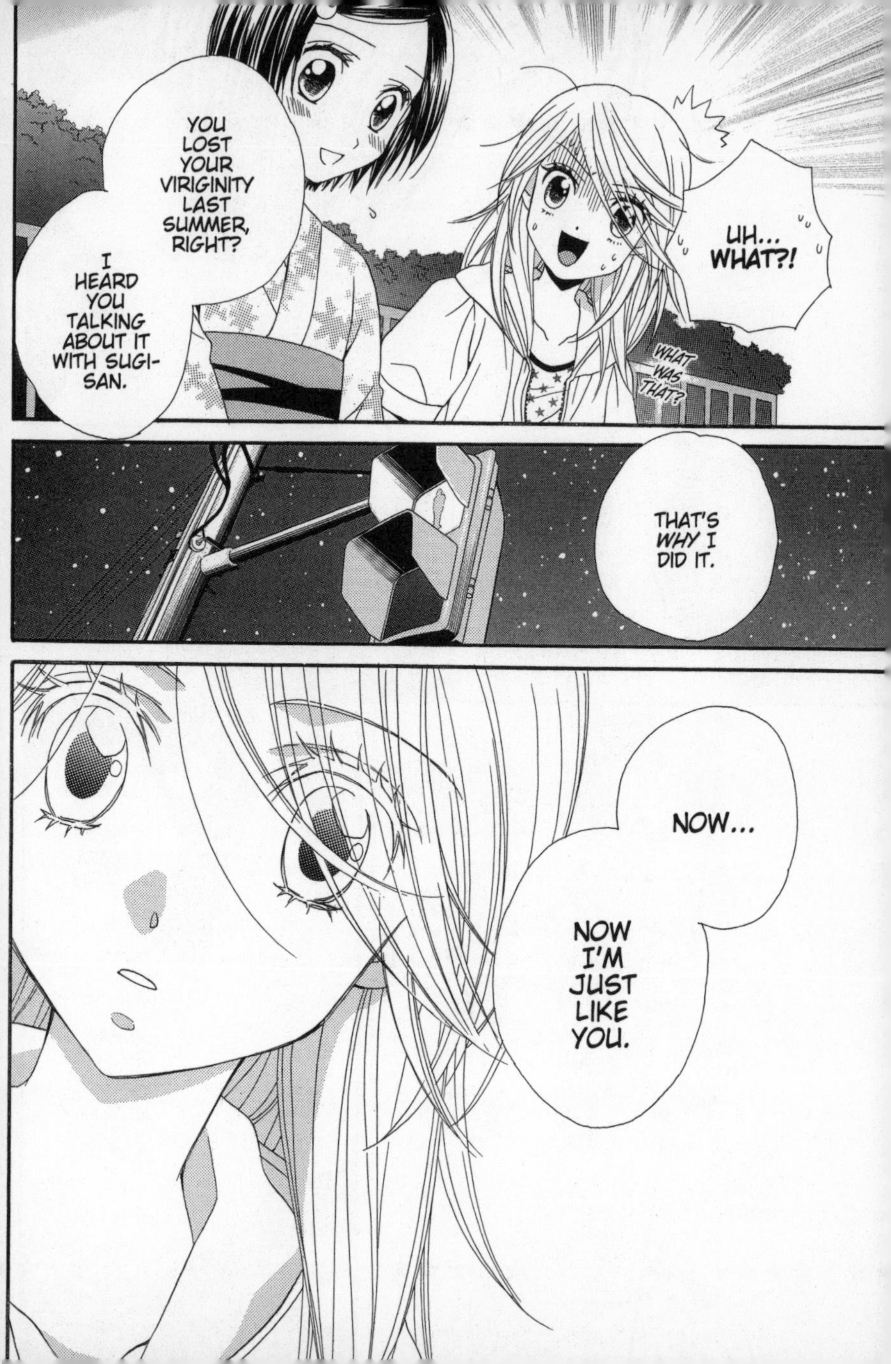
UH... WHAT?!
WHAT WAS THAT?
YOU LOST YOUR VIRIGINITY LAST SUMMER, RIGHT?
I HEARD YOU TALKING ABOUT IT WITH SUGI-SAN.
THAT'S *WHY* I DID IT.
NOW...
NOW I'M JUST LIKE YOU.

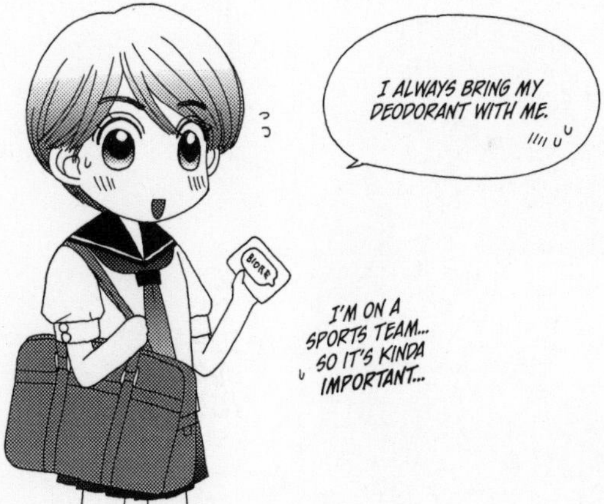
I ALWAYS BRING MY DEODORANT WITH ME.
I'M ON A SPORTS TEAM... SO IT'S KINDA IMPORTANT...

GIRL FRIENDS─ガールフレンズ─

EXTRAS

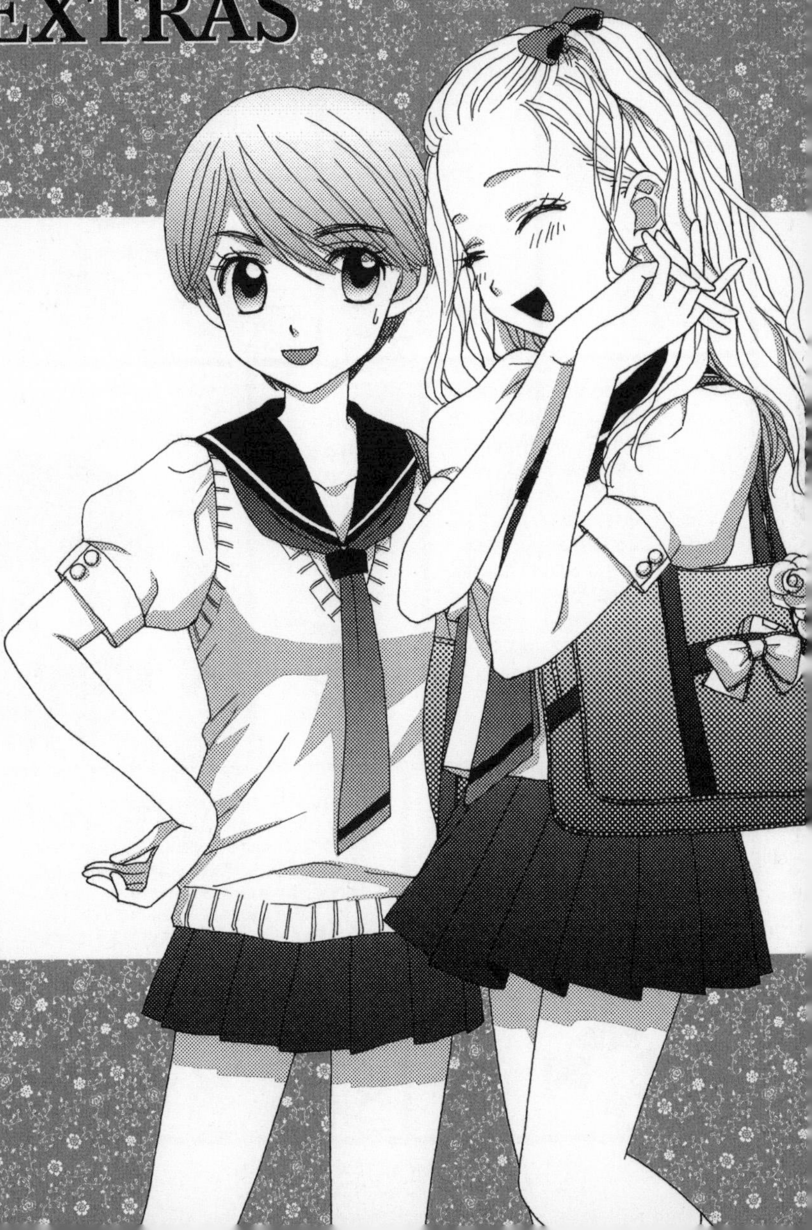

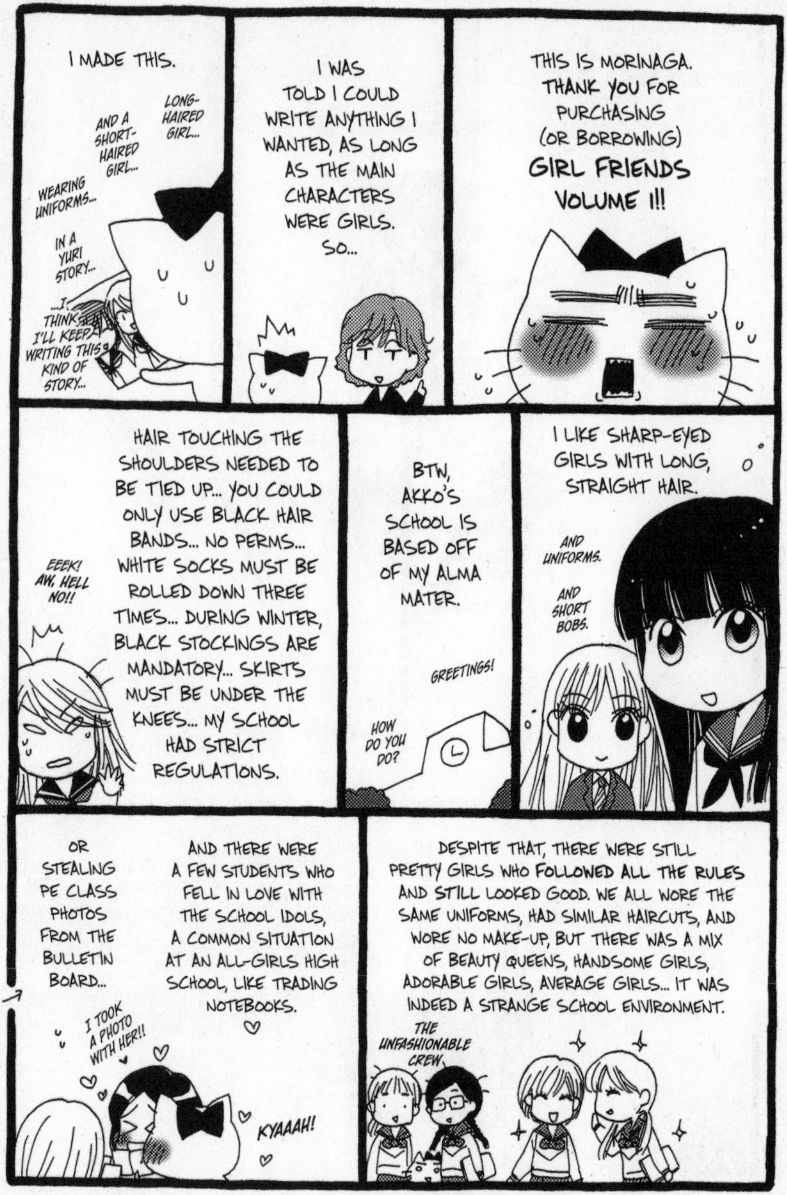
THIS IS MORINAGA. THANK YOU FOR PURCHASING (OR BORROWING) GIRL FRIENDS VOLUME 1!!!
I WAS TOLD I COULD WRITE ANYTHING I WANTED, AS LONG AS THE MAIN CHARACTERS WERE GIRLS. SO...
I MADE THIS.
LONG-HAIRED GIRL...
AND A SHORT-HAIRED GIRL...
WEARING UNIFORMS...
IN A YURI STORY...
...I THINK I'LL KEEP WRITING THIS KIND OF STORY...
I LIKE SHARP-EYED GIRLS WITH LONG, STRAIGHT HAIR.
AND UNIFORMS.
AND SHORT BOBS.
BTW, AKKO'S SCHOOL IS BASED OFF OF MY ALMA MATER.
GREETINGS!
HOW DO YOU DO?
HAIR TOUCHING THE SHOULDERS NEEDED TO BE TIED UP... YOU COULD ONLY USE BLACK HAIR BANDS... NO PERMS... WHITE SOCKS MUST BE ROLLED DOWN THREE TIMES... DURING WINTER, BLACK STOCKINGS ARE MANDATORY... SKIRTS MUST BE UNDER THE KNEES... MY SCHOOL HAD STRICT REGULATIONS.
EEEK! AW, HELL NO!!
DESPITE THAT, THERE WERE STILL PRETTY GIRLS WHO FOLLOWED ALL THE RULES AND STILL LOOKED GOOD. WE ALL WORE THE SAME UNIFORMS, HAD SIMILAR HAIRCUTS, AND WORE NO MAKE-UP, BUT THERE WAS A MIX OF BEAUTY QUEENS, HANDSOME GIRLS, ADORABLE GIRLS, AVERAGE GIRLS... IT WAS INDEED A STRANGE SCHOOL ENVIRONMENT.
THE UNFASHIONABLE CREW
AND THERE WERE A FEW STUDENTS WHO FELL IN LOVE WITH THE SCHOOL IDOLS, A COMMON SITUATION AT AN ALL-GIRLS HIGH SCHOOL, LIKE TRADING NOTEBOOKS.
OR STEALING PE CLASS PHOTOS FROM THE BULLETIN BOARD...
CAUSE YOU AN'T BUY HOTOS OF EOPLE N A FERENT RADE.
I TOOK A PHOTO WITH HER!!
KYAAAH!

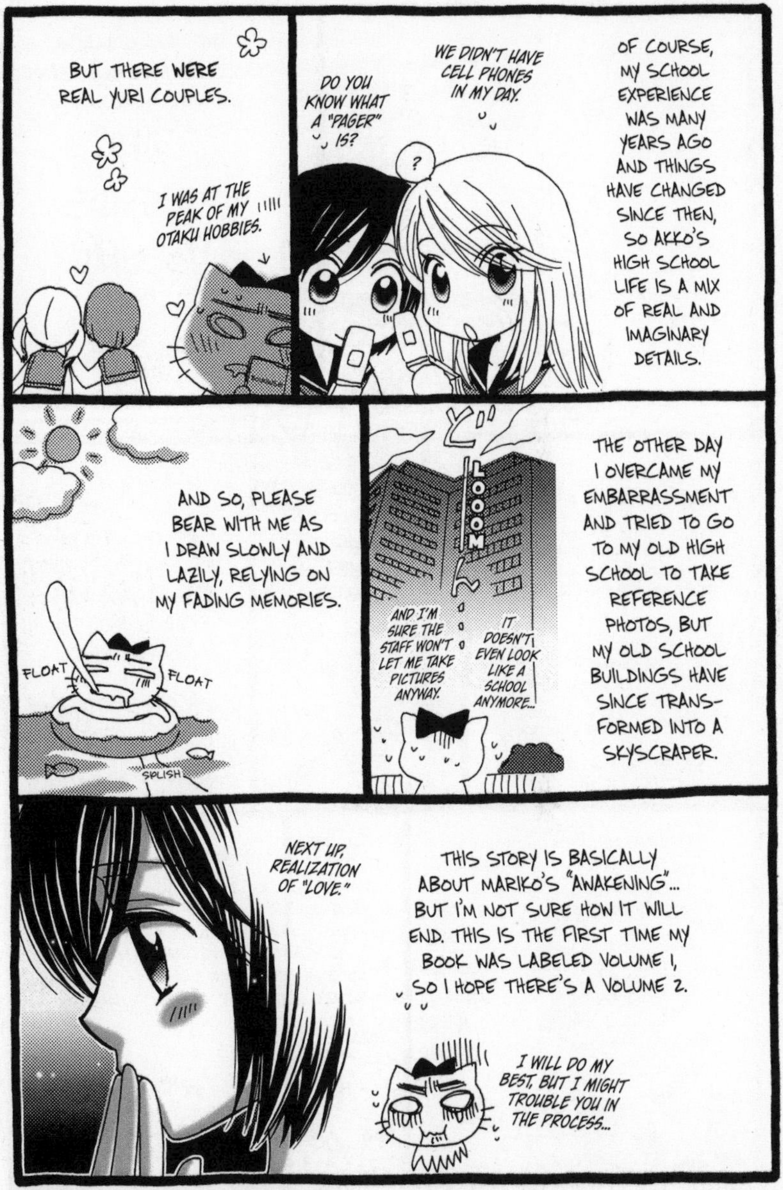
OF COURSE, MY SCHOOL EXPERIENCE WAS MANY YEARS AGO AND THINGS HAVE CHANGED SINCE THEN, SO AKKO'S HIGH SCHOOL LIFE IS A MIX OF REAL AND IMAGINARY DETAILS.
WE DIDN'T HAVE CELL PHONES IN MY DAY.
DO YOU KNOW WHAT A "PAGER" IS?
BUT THERE WERE REAL YURI COUPLES.
I WAS AT THE PEAK OF MY OTAKU HOBBIES.
THE OTHER DAY I OVERCAME MY EMBARRASSMENT AND TRIED TO GO TO MY OLD HIGH SCHOOL TO TAKE REFERENCE PHOTOS, BUT MY OLD SCHOOL BUILDINGS HAVE SINCE TRANS-FORMED INTO A SKYSCRAPER.
LOOOM
IT DOESN'T EVEN LOOK LIKE A SCHOOL ANYMORE...
AND I'M SURE THE STAFF WON'T LET ME TAKE PICTURES ANYWAY.
AND SO, PLEASE BEAR WITH ME AS I DRAW SLOWLY AND LAZILY, RELYING ON MY FADING MEMORIES.
FLOAT
FLOAT
SPLISH
THIS STORY IS BASICALLY ABOUT MARIKO'S "AWAKENING"... BUT I'M NOT SURE HOW IT WILL END. THIS IS THE FIRST TIME MY BOOK WAS LABELED VOLUME 1, SO I HOPE THERE'S A VOLUME 2.
NEXT UP, REALIZATION OF "LOVE."
I WILL DO MY BEST, BUT I MIGHT TROUBLE YOU IN THE PROCESS...

THANK YOU FOR HELPING ME ♥♥♥ MIMI-CHAN & ATSUYO-CHAN & MAYU-SAN & FUSHIGI-TAN.

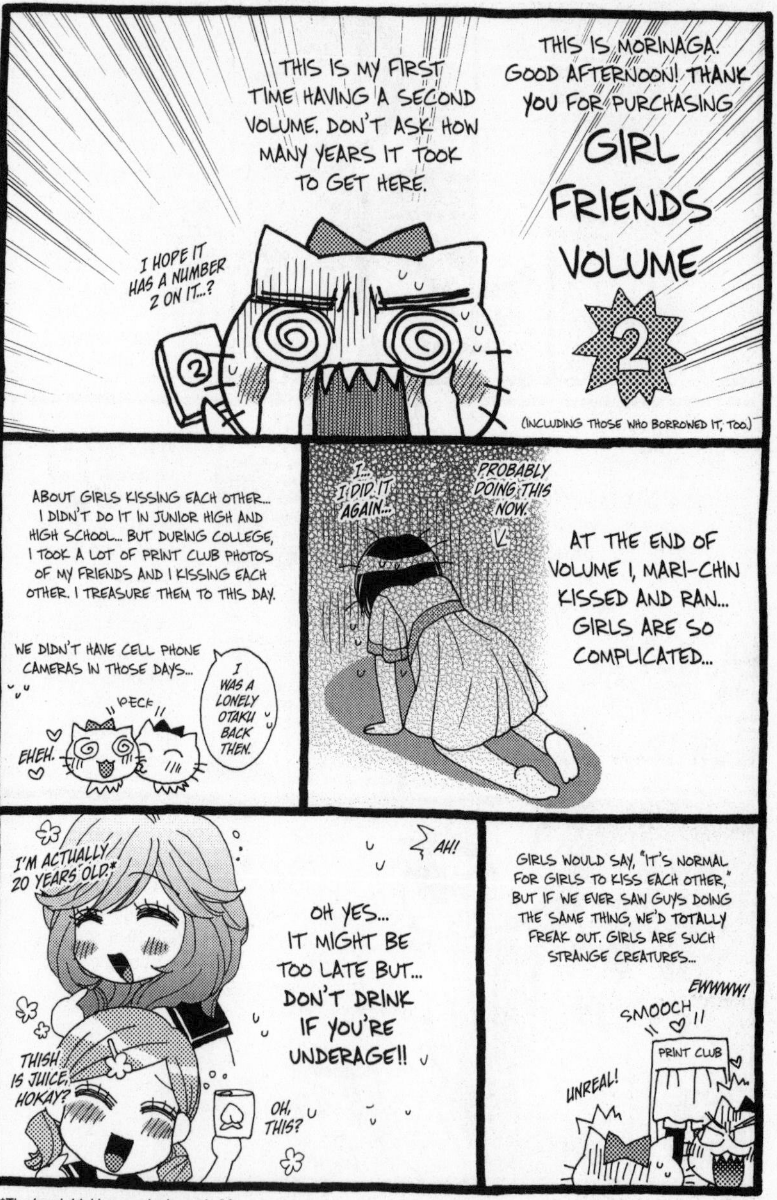

THIS IS MORINAGA. GOOD AFTERNOON! THANK YOU FOR PURCHASING GIRL FRIENDS VOLUME 2
THIS IS MY FIRST TIME HAVING A SECOND VOLUME. DON'T ASK HOW MANY YEARS IT TOOK TO GET HERE.
I HOPE IT HAS A NUMBER 2 ON IT...?
2
(INCLUDING THOSE WHO BORROWED IT, TOO.)
PROBABLY DOING THIS NOW.
I... I DID IT AGAIN...
AT THE END OF VOLUME 1, MARI-CHIN KISSED AND RAN... GIRLS ARE SO COMPLICATED...
ABOUT GIRLS KISSING EACH OTHER... I DIDN'T DO IT IN JUNIOR HIGH AND HIGH SCHOOL... BUT DURING COLLEGE, I TOOK A LOT OF PRINT CLUB PHOTOS OF MY FRIENDS AND I KISSING EACH OTHER. I TREASURE THEM TO THIS DAY.
WE DIDN'T HAVE CELL PHONE CAMERAS IN THOSE DAYS...
I WAS A LONELY OTAKU BACK THEN.
PECK
EHEH.
GIRLS WOULD SAY, "IT'S NORMAL FOR GIRLS TO KISS EACH OTHER," BUT IF WE EVER SAW GUYS DOING THE SAME THING, WE'D TOTALLY FREAK OUT. GIRLS ARE SUCH STRANGE CREATURES...
EWWWW!
SMOOCH
PRINT CLUB
UNREAL!
AH!
I'M ACTUALLY 20 YEARS OLD.*
OH YES... IT MIGHT BE TOO LATE BUT... DON'T DRINK IF YOU'RE UNDERAGE!!
THISH IS JUICE, HOKAY?
OH, THIS?

*The legal drinking age in Japan is 20.

*Look for all the "Extra Manga" episodes in the back of Girl Friends: The Complete Collection 2!

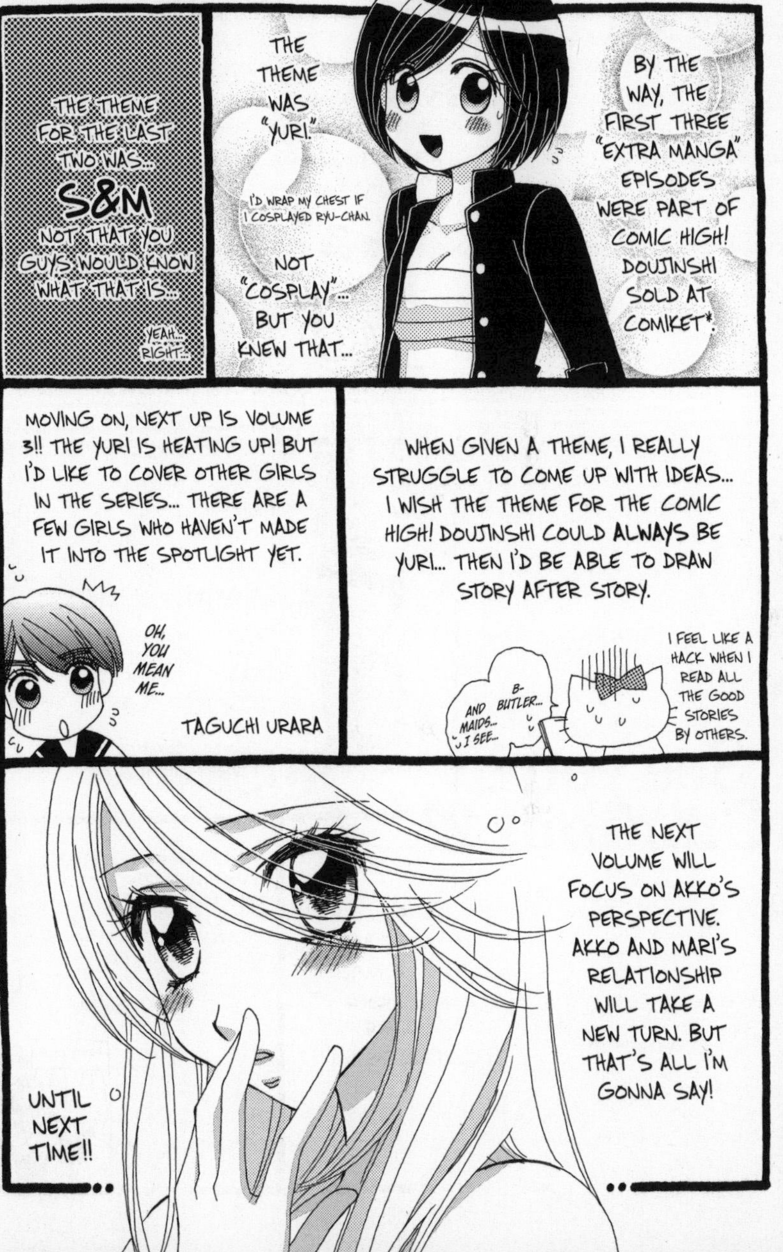
BY THE WAY, THE FIRST THREE "EXTRA MANGA" EPISODES WERE PART OF COMIC HIGH! DOUJINSHI SOLD AT COMIKET*.
THE THEME WAS "YURI."
I'D WRAP MY CHEST IF I COSPLAYED RYU-CHAN.
NOT "COSPLAY"... BUT YOU KNEW THAT...
THE THEME FOR THE LAST TWO WAS... S&M NOT THAT YOU GUYS WOULD KNOW WHAT THAT IS...
YEAH... RIGHT...
WHEN GIVEN A THEME, I REALLY STRUGGLE TO COME UP WITH IDEAS... I WISH THE THEME FOR THE COMIC HIGH! DOUJINSHI COULD ALWAYS BE YURI... THEN I'D BE ABLE TO DRAW STORY AFTER STORY.
I FEEL LIKE A HACK WHEN I READ ALL THE GOOD STORIES BY OTHERS.
B-BUTLER...
AND MAIDS... I SEE...
MOVING ON, NEXT UP IS VOLUME 3!! THE YURI IS HEATING UP! BUT I'D LIKE TO COVER OTHER GIRLS IN THE SERIES... THERE ARE A FEW GIRLS WHO HAVEN'T MADE IT INTO THE SPOTLIGHT YET.
OH, YOU MEAN ME...
TAGUCHI URARA
THE NEXT VOLUME WILL FOCUS ON AKKO'S PERSPECTIVE. AKKO AND MARI'S RELATIONSHIP WILL TAKE A NEW TURN. BUT THAT'S ALL I'M GONNA SAY!
UNTIL NEXT TIME!!

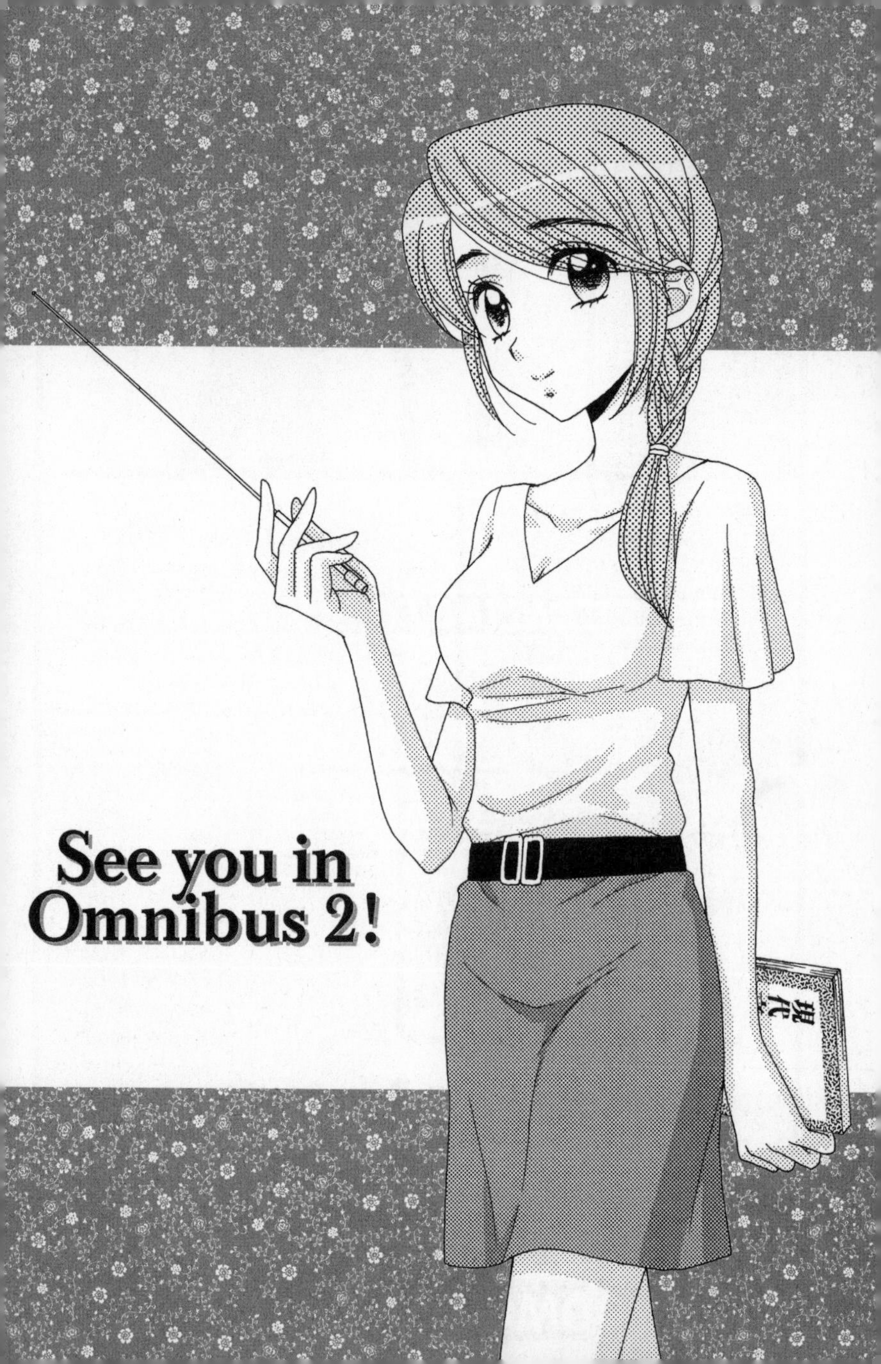
See you in
Omnibus 2!
現代